Contemporary
Literary Criticism

Guide to Gale Literary Criticism Series

For criticism on	Consult these Gale series
Authors now living or who died after December 31, 1959	*CONTEMPORARY LITERARY CRITICISM (CLC)*
Authors who died between 1900 and 1959	*TWENTIETH-CENTURY LITERARY CRITICISM (TCLC)*
Authors who died between 1800 and 1899	*NINETEENTH-CENTURY LITERATURE CRITICISM (NCLC)*
Authors who died between 1400 and 1799	*LITERATURE CRITICISM FROM 1400 TO 1800 (LC)* *SHAKESPEAREAN CRITICISM (SC)*
Authors who died before 1400	*CLASSICAL AND MEDIEVAL LITERATURE CRITICISM (CMLC)*
Black writers of the past two hundred years	*BLACK LITERATURE CRITICISM (BLC)*
Authors of books for children and young adults	*CHILDREN'S LITERATURE REVIEW (CLR)*
Dramatists	*DRAMA CRITICISM (DC)*
Hispanic writers of the late nineteenth and twentieth centuries	*HISPANIC LITERATURE CRITICISM (HLC)*
Native North American writers and orators of the eighteenth, nineteenth, and twentieth centuries	*NATIVE NORTH AMERICAN LITERATURE (NNAL)*
Poets	*POETRY CRITICISM (PC)*
Short story writers	*SHORT STORY CRITICISM (SSC)*
Major authors from the Renaissance to the present	*WORLD LITERATURE CRITICISM, 1500 TO THE PRESENT (WLC)*

ISSN 0091-3421

Volume 100

Contemporary Literary Criticism

Excerpts from Criticism of the Works
of Today's Novelists, Poets, Playwrights,
Short Story Writers, Scriptwriters, and
Other Creative Writers

Deborah A. Stanley
EDITOR

Jeff Chapman
Pamela S. Dear
Jeff Hunter
Daniel Jones
John D. Jorgenson
Jerry Moore
Polly A. Vedder
Thomas Wiloch
Kathleen Wilson
ASSOCIATE EDITORS

GALE

DETROIT • NEW YORK • TORONTO • LONDON

STAFF

Deborah A. Stanley, *Editor*

Jeff Chapman, Pamela S. Dear, Jeff Hunter, Daniel Jones, John D. Jorgenson, Jerry Moore,
Polly A. Vedder, Thomas Wiloch, and Kathleen Wilson, *Associate Editors*

Tracy Arnold-Chapman, John P. Daniel, Christopher Giroux, Joshua Lauer,
Linda Quigley, and Janet Witalec, *Contributing Editors*

Susan Trosky, *Permissions Manager*
Margaret A. Chamberlain, Maria Franklin, and Kimberly F. Smilay, *Permissions Specialists*
Sarah Chesney, Edna Hedblad, Michele Lonoconus, and Shalice Shah, *Permissions Associates*

Victoria B. Cariappa, *Research Manager*
Julia C. Daniel, Tamara C. Nott, Michele P. Pica, Tracie A. Richardson,
Norma Sawaya, and Cheryl L. Warnock, *Research Associates*
Laura C. Bissey, Alfred A. Gardner I, and Sean R. Smith, *Research Assistants*

Mary Beth Trimper, *Production Director*
Deborah L. Milliken, *Production Assistant*

Barbara J. Yarrow, *Graphic Services Manager*
Sherrell Hobbs, *Macintosh Artist*
Randy Bassett, *Image Database Supervisor*
Robert Duncan and Mikal Ansari, *Scanner Operators*
Pamela Reed, *Photography Coordinator*

Library of Congress Catalog Card Number 76-46132
ISBN 0-7876-1066-6
ISSN 0091-3421

Printed in the United States of America
10 9 8 7 6 5 4 3 2 1

Contents

Preface vii

Acknowledgments xi

Celebrating 100 Volumes of *CLC*

Since its inception in 1973, *CLC* has become the world's most respected, most comprehensive, and most widely consulted source of information on contemporary literature. Now in its one-hundredth volume, *CLC* offers coverage on over 4,000 authors and is a fixture in libraries across the globe. In total, the series presents criticism and commentary on over 80,000 individual works of literature and contains upwards of 38,000 critical essays.

Each of the Editors of *CLC* has brought to the series his or her unique perspective on how best to engage readers in the study of literature. Yet the series' objective has always been the same: to gather in one place the outstanding commentary on authors' lives and works. Over the years, *CLC* has evolved to meet readers' needs more effectively. Today, *CLC* seeks to document the cutting edge of literature while simultaneously building and maintaining a repository of information that covers the great—and near great—authors of the modern era.

Looking into the future, *CLC* will continue to adapt to meet readers' needs, whatever they may be. The Editors welcome comments and will continue to strive to satisfy each of our many enthusiasts who rely on us to help broaden and amplify their understanding of world literature.

The Editors of *Contemporary Literary Criticism*

Preface

A Comprehensive Information Source
on Contemporary Literature

Named "one of the twenty-five most distinguished reference titles published during the past twenty-five years" by *Reference Quarterly,* the *Contemporary Literary Criticism (CLC)* series provides readers with critical commentary and general information on more than 2,000 authors now living or who died after December 31, 1959. Previous to the publication of the first volume of *CLC* in 1973, there was no ongoing digest monitoring scholarly and popular sources of critical opinion and explication of modern literature. *CLC,* therefore, has fulfilled an essential need, particularly since the complexity and variety of contemporary literature makes the function of criticism especially important to today's reader.

Scope of the Series

CLC presents significant passages from published criticism of works by creative writers. Since many of the authors covered by *CLC* inspire continual critical commentary, writers are often represented in more than one volume. There is, of course, no duplication of reprinted criticism.

Authors are selected for inclusion for a variety of reasons, among them the publication or dramatic production of a critically acclaimed new work, the reception of a major literary award, revival of interest in past writings, or the adaptation of a literary work to film or television.

Attention is also given to several other groups of writers-authors of considerable public interest—about whose work criticism is often difficult to locate. These include mystery and science fiction writers, literary and social critics, foreign writers, and authors who represent particular ethnic groups within the United States.

Format of the Book

Each *CLC* volume contains about 500 individual excerpts taken from hundreds of book review periodicals, general magazines, scholarly journals, monographs, and books. Entries include critical evaluations spanning from the beginning of an author's career to the most current commentary. Interviews, feature articles, and other published writings that offer insight into the author's works are also presented. Students, teachers, librarians, and researchers will find that the generous excerpts and supplementary material in *CLC* provide them with vital information required to write a term paper, analyze a poem, or lead a book discussion group. In addition, complete bibliographical citations note the original source and all of the information necessary for a term paper footnote or bibliography.

Features

A *CLC* author entry consists of the following elements:

- The **Author Heading** cites the author's name in the form under which the author has most commonly published, followed by birth date, and death date when applicable. Uncertainty as to a birth or death date is indicated by a question mark.

- A **Portrait** of the author is included when available.

- A brief **Biographical and Critical Introduction** to the author and his or her work precedes the excerpted criticism. The first line of the introduction provides the author's full name, pseudonyms (if applicable), nationality, and a listing of genres in which the author has written. To provide users with easier access to information, the biographical and critical essay included in each author entry is divided into four categories: "Introduction," "Biographical Information," "Major Works," and "Critical Reception." The introductions to single-work entries—entries that focus on well known and frequently studied books, short stories, and poems—are similarly organized to quickly provide readers with information on the plot and major characters of the work being discussed, its major themes, and its critical reception. Previous volumes of *CLC* in which the author has been featured are also listed in the introduction.

- A list of **Principal Works** notes the most important writings by the author. When foreign-language works have been translated into English, the English-language version of the title follows in brackets.

- The **Excerpted Criticism** represents various kinds of critical writing, ranging in form from the brief review to the scholarly exegesis. Essays are selected by the editors to reflect the spectrum of opinion about a specific work or about an author's literary career in general. The excerpts are presented chronologically, adding a useful perspective to the entry. All titles by the author featured in the entry are printed in boldface type, which enables the reader to easily identify the works being discussed. Publication information (such as publisher names and book prices) and parenthetical numerical references (such as footnotes or page and line references to specific editions of a work) have been deleted at the editor's discretion to provide smoother reading of the text.

- Critical essays are prefaced by **Explanatory Notes** as an additional aid to readers. These notes may provide several types of valuable information, including: the reputation of the critic, the importance of the work of criticism, the commentator's approach to the author's work, the purpose of the criticism, and changes in critical trends regarding the author.

- A complete **Bibliographical Citation** designed to help the user find the original essay or book precedes each excerpt.

- Whenever possible, a recent, previously unpublished **Author Interview** accompanies each entry.

- A concise **Further Reading** section appears at the end of entries on authors for whom a significant amount of criticism exists in addition to the pieces reprinted in *CLC*. Each citation in this section is accompanied by a descriptive annotation describing the content of that article. Materials included in this section are grouped under various headings (e.g., Biography, Bibliography, Criticism, and Interviews) to aid users in their search for additional information. Cross-references to other useful sources published by Gale Research in which the author has appeared are also included: *Authors in the News, Black Writers, Children's Literature Review, Contemporary Authors, Dictionary of Literary Biography, DISCovering Authors, Drama Criticism, Hispanic Literature Criticism, Hispanic Writers, Native North American Literature, Poetry Criticism, Something about the Author, Short Story Criticism, Contemporary Authors Autobiography Series,* and *Something about the Author Autobiography Series.*

Other Features

CLC also includes the following features:

- An **Acknowledgments** section lists the copyright holders who have granted permission to reprint material in this volume of *CLC*. It does not, however, list every book or periodical reprinted or consulted during the preparation of the volume.

- Each new volume of *CLC* includes a **Cumulative Topic Index,** which lists all literary topics treated in *CLC, NCLC, TCLC,* and *LC 1400-1800.*

- A **Cumulative Author Index** lists all the authors who have appeared in the various literary criticism series published by Gale Research, with cross-references to Gale's biographical and autobiographical series. A full listing of the series referenced there appears on the first page of the indexes of this volume. Readers will welcome this cumulated author index as a useful tool for locating an author within the various series. The index, which lists birth and death dates when available, will be particularly valuable for those authors who are identified with a certain period but whose death dates cause them to be placed in another, or for those authors whose careers span two periods. For example, Ernest Hemingway is found in *CLC,* yet F. Scott Fitzgerald, a writer often associated with him, is found in *Twentieth-Century Literary Criticism.*

- A **Cumulative Nationality Index** alphabetically lists all authors featured in *CLC* by nationality, followed by numbers corresponding to the volumes in which the authors appear.

- An alphabetical **Title Index** accompanies each volume of *CLC.* Listings are followed by the author's name and the corresponding page numbers where the titles are discussed. English translations of foreign titles and variations of titles are cross-referenced to the title under which a work was originally published. Titles of novels, novellas, dramas, films, record albums, and poetry, short story, and essay collections are printed in italics, while all individual poems, short stories, essays, and songs are printed in roman type within quotation marks; when published separately (e.g., T. S. Eliot's poem *The Waste Land),* the titles of long poems are printed in italics.

- In response to numerous suggestions from librarians, Gale has also produced a **Special Paperbound Edition** of the *CLC* title index. This annual cumulation, which alphabetically lists all titles reviewed in the series, is available to all customers and is typically published with every fifth volume of *CLC.* Additional copies of the index are available upon request. Librarians and patrons will welcome this separate index: it saves shelf space, is easy to use, and is recyclable upon receipt of the next edition.

Citing *Contemporary Literary Criticism*

When writing papers, students who quote directly from any volume in the Literary Criticism Series may use the following general forms to footnote reprinted criticism. The first example pertains to material drawn from periodicals, the second to material reprinted in books:

[1]Alfred Cismaru, "Making the Best of It," *The New Republic,* 207, No. 24, (December 7, 1992), 30, 32; excerpted and reprinted in *Contemporary Literary Criticism,* Vol. 85, ed. Christopher Giroux (Detroit: Gale Research, 1995), pp. 73-4.

[2]Yvor Winters, *The Post-Symbolist Methods* (Allen Swallow, 1967); excerpted and reprinted in *Contemporary Literary Criticism,* Vol. 85, ed. Christopher Giroux (Detroit: Gale Research, 1995), pp. 223-26.

Suggestions Are Welcome

The editors hope that readers will find *CLC* a useful reference tool and welcome comments about the work. Send comments and suggestions to: Editors, *Contemporary Literary Criticism,* Gale Research, Penobscot Building, Detroit, MI 48226-4094.

Acknowledgments

The editors wish to thank the copyright holders of the excerpted criticism included in this volume and the permissions managers of many book and magazine publishing companies for assisting us in securing reproduction rights. We are also grateful to the staffs of the Detroit Public Library, the Library of Congress, the University of Detroit Mercy Library, Wayne State University Purdy/Kresge Library Complex, and the University of Michigan Libraries for making their resources available to us. Following is a list of the copyright holders who have granted us permission to reproduce material in this volume of *CLC*. Every effort has been made to trace copyright, but if omissions have been made, please let us know.

COPYRIGHTED EXCERPTS IN *CLC*, VOLUME 100, WERE REPRODUCED FROM THE FOLLOWING PERIODICALS:

America, v. 173, July 1, 1995; v. 175, August 3, 1996. © 1995, 1996. All rights reserved. All reprinted with permission of America Press, Inc., 106 West 56th Street, New York, NY 10019 and the authors.—*American Book Review,* v. 9, January-February, 1987. Both reproduced by permission.—*American Poetry Review,* v. 17, November/December, 1988; v. 18, September/October, 1989. Copyright © 1988, 1989 by World Poetry, Inc. Both reprinted by permission of the authors.—*The Armchair Detective,* v. 27, Summer, 1994. Copyright © 1994 by The Armchair Detective. Reprinted by permission of the publisher.—*The Atlantic Journal/Constitution,* January 21, 1996. Reproduced by permission of The Atlanta Journal and The Atlanta Constitution.—*The Atlantic Monthly,* v. 277, February, 1996. Reproduced by permission.—*Belles Lettres: A Review of Books by Women,* v. 8, Spring, 1993. Reproduced by permission.—*Book World--The Washington Post,* v. XI, September 6, 1981; v. XXII, May 10, 1992; v. XXII, May 31, 1992; November 29, 1992; v. XXV, April 30, 1995; January 7, 1996. © 1981, 1992, 1995, 1996, Washington Post Book World Service/Washington Post Writers Group. All reprinted with permission.—*Booklist,* v. 83, September 1, 1986; v. 91, July, 1995; September 15, 1995; v. 92, November 1, 1995; v. 92, February 1, 1996; v. 93, November 1, 1996. Reproduced by permission.—*Books,* November, 1987. Reproduced by permission.—*Boston Review,* January/February, 1993. Copyright © 1993 by the Boston Critic, Inc. Reprinted by permission of the author.—*British Book News,* November, 1984. Reproduced by permission.—*Chicago Tribune,* May 27, 1992; January 5, 1993; February 20, 1994; January 28, 1996. © Copyrighted Chicago Tribune Company. All rights reserved. All used with permission.—*Choice,* v. 24, December, 1986; v. 26, February, 1989. Copyright © 1986, 1989 by American Library Association. Both reprinted by permission of the publisher.—*College Literature,* v. 21, February, 1994. Copyright © 1994 by West Chester University. Reprinted by permission of the publisher.—*Commonweal,* v. XCIV, March 19, 1971; v. CII, October 24, 1975; v. CIX, July 16, 1982; v. CXIII, May 9, 1986; v. CXXII, May 19, 1995; v. CXXIII, February 9, 1996. Copyright © 1971, 1975, 1982, 1986, 1995, 1996 Commonweal Publishing Co., Inc. All reproduced by permission of Commonweal Foundation.—*Comparative Literature,* v. 36, Summer, 1984. Reproduced by permission of the author.—*Contemporary Review,* v. 245, November, 1984. Reproduced by permission.—*Dalhousie French Studies,* v. 33, Winter, 1995. Reprinted by permission.—*Interpretation: A Journal of Bible and Theology,* v. XL, July, 1986. Reproduced by permission.—*Journal of Religious Ethics,* v. 13, Fall, 1985. Reproduced by permission.—*Kirkus Reviews,* v. LIII, February 15, 1985; v. LX, September 15, 1992; v. LXIV, January 1, 1995; v. LXIV, January 15, 1996. Copyright © 1985, 1992, 1995, 1996 The Kirkus Service, Inc. All rights reserved. All reprinted by permission of the publisher, Kirkus Reviews and Kirkus Associates, LP.—*Library Journal,* v. 111, July, 1986; v. 119, December, 1994. Copyright © 1986, 1994 by Reed Publishing, USA, Division of Reed Holdings, Inc. Both reproduced from Library Journal, a Division of Reed Publishing, USA, by permission of the publisher and the author.—*Listener,* v. 105, February 26, 1981. Reproduced by permission of the publisher.—*London Review of Books,* v. 6, October 18-31, 1984 for "Arsenals" by Nicholas Spice; v. 14, September 24, 1992 for "Sydney's Inferno" by Jonathon Coe; v. 17, July 20, 1995 for "The Lady Vanishes" by Zoe Heller; v. 17, September 7, 1995 for "Shenanigans" by Michael Wood. All appear here by permission of the London Review of Books and the authors.—*Los Angeles Times,* August 16, 1987; February 26, 1990; February 19, 1996; April 10, 1996. Copyright, 1987, 1990, 1996, Los Angeles Times. All reproduced by permission.—*Los Angeles Times Book Review,* July 28, 1985; September 18, 1988; October 1,

COPYRIGHTED EXCERPTS IN *CLC,* VOLUME 100, WERE REPRODUCED FROM THE FOLLOWING BOOKS:

Budick, Emily Miller. From *Engendering Romance: Women Writers and the Hawthorne Tradition, 1850-1990.* Yale University Press, 1994. Reproduced by permission.—Carr, Virginia Spencer. From *Understanding Carson McCullers.* University of South Carolina Press, 1990. Reproduced by permission.—Jardine, Alice A. From an interview with Marguerite Duras, translated by Katherine Ann Jensen, in *Shifting Scenes: Interviews on Women, Writing, and Politics in Post-68 France.* Edited by Alice A. Jardine and Anne M. Menke. Columbia University Press, 1991. Copyright © 1991 Columbia University Press, New York. All rights reserved. Reprinted with the permission of the publisher.

PHOTOGRAPHS AND ILLUSTRATIONS APPEARING IN *CLC,* VOLUME 100, WERE RECEIVED FROM THE FOLLOWING SOURCES:

Blackwood, Caroline, photograph by Jerry Bauer. Reproduced by permission.—Brodsky, Joseph, photograph. Archive Photos. Reproduced by permission.—Brown, George Mackay, photograph. Reproduced by permission.—Condon, Richard, photograph. AP/Wide World Photos. Reproduced by permission.—Duras, Marguerite, photograph by Jerry Bauer. Reproduced by permission.—Elytis, Odysseus, photograph. AP/Wide World Photos. Reproduced by permission.—McCullers, Carson, photograph. AP/Wide World Photos. Reproduced by permission.—Miles, Jack, photograph by Jerry Bauer. Reproduced by permission.—Rushdie, Salman, photograph. Archive Photos. Reproduced by permission.—Stern, Gerald, photograph. AP/Wide World Photos. Reproduced by permission.

Caroline Blackwood
1931-1996

(Full name Lady Caroline Maureen Hamilton-Temple-Blackwood) Anglo-Irish novelist, short story writer, essayist, biographer, and nonfiction writer.

The following entry provides an overview of Blackwood's career. For further information on her life and works, see *CLC*, Volumes 6 and 9.

INTRODUCTION

An Anglo-Irish writer and journalist, Blackwood is best known for her short stories and novels, which offer gothic descriptions of modern relations told with sharp wit and black humor. She is known as well for her journalistic accounts of such controversial subjects as nuclear arms protesting and fox hunting.

Biographical Information

Blackwood was born in Northern Ireland on July 16, 1931, to aristocratic parents. Her mother Maureen was heir to the Guinness fortune and Blackwood's father Basil was a friend of Evelyn Waugh's and the grandson of Lord Dufferin, rumored to be the illegitimate son of Disraeli. Blackwood was educated in boarding schools and embarked on a career in journalism after completing her education. She published her first collection of short stories and essays, *For All That I Found There,* in 1973 and her first novel, *The Stepdaughter,* three years later. Blackwood was married three times: to the painter Lucian Freud, whom she divorced in 1956; to the American composer and pianist Israel Citkowitz with whom she had three daughters and divorced in 1972; and to late poet Robert Lowell with whom she had a son. Blackwood lived in Paris, London, and Northern Ireland before settling in the United States. She died of cancer in Manhattan in 1996.

Major Works

Blackwood published ten books, including three short story collections, three novels, three works of nonfiction, and a cookbook. In 1973 she published *For All That I Found There,* a collection of short stories and autobiographical accounts of her life in Ulster. She followed this with the epistolary novel *The Stepdaughter* in 1976 and a collection of short stories *Great Granny Webster* (1977). Both works focus on women and their struggles to deal with family members. She published a third short story collection *Good Night Sweet Ladies* in 1983; many of these stories also deal with family relations. Blackwood employed a similar narrative device in her two

novels *The Fate of Mary Rose* (1981) and *Corrigan* (1984). In each the narrator calls into question the events of the story, adding an element of suspense which is instrumental in establishing a dark, gothic mood. Blackwood also published three works of nonfiction: *On the Perimeter* (1984), which concerns a group of women protesting nuclear weapons at an American military base in England; *In the Pink* (1987), an anecdotal account of fox hunting in England; and *The Last of the Duchess* (1995), an account of the life of Wallis Simpson and Blackwood's efforts to interview the ailing Duchess. Blackwood employs a faux-naif style in her non-fiction, feigning naivete as a means of circumventing controversial opinions about her subject matters.

Critical Reception

Blackwood's first book, *For All That I Found There,* garnered much favorable attention. Critics admired her keen observations about her fellow humans and her biting wit. She received similar accolades for her novel *The Stepdaughter,* which some critics consider to be her best work. Commentators were particularly impressed with the novel's dark humor. Many critics did not believe that *Great Granny Webster* and *The Fate of Mary Rose* measured up to the standard Blackwood set in her earlier works. In particular, reviewers were critical of Blackwood's element of suspense in *The Fate of Mary Rose*. Critics have praised Blackwood's objectiveness in her first two nonfiction works. While some critics believe that *In the Pink* contributed little new knowledge about fox hunting, they praised the author for providing a balanced view of the sport. However, reviewers criticized Blackwood for inaccuracies and speculation in *In the Pink* and particularly in *The Last of the Duchess*. In her review of *The Last of the Duchess*, Zoë Heller claims that Blackwood's ". . . ill-advised response to her lack of hard facts, is to fill in the holes with speculation and gossip . . . as if her duty as a journalist did not extend beyond reproducing hearsay."

PRINCIPAL WORKS

For All That I Found There (short stories and essays) 1973
The Stepdaughter (novel) 1976
Great Granny Webster (novel) 1977
Darling, You Shouldn't Have Gone to So Much Trouble [with Anna Haycraft] (cookbook) 1980
The Fate of Mary Rose (novel) 1981
Goodnight Sweet Ladies (short stories) 1983
Corrigan (novel) 1984
On the Perimeter (nonfiction) 1984
In the Pink: Caroline Blackwood on Hunting (nonfiction) 1987
The Last of the Duchess (biography) 1995

CRITICISM

Peter Kemp (review date 26 February 1981)

SOURCE: "Wounded Children," in *Listener,* Vol. 105, No. 2707, February 26, 1981, p. 288.

[*Below, Kemp reviews* The Fate of Mary Rose *and discusses Blackwood's style of detached writing about very emotional subjects, particularly wounded children.*]

Wounds appall and fascinate Caroline Blackwood: her imagination can hardly tear itself away from them. Confronted with life's damage, she seems like the woman in one of her stories who—after a bungled operation—cannot close her eyes and is afraid to weep in case of dangerous inflammation. With unsparing lucidity, her books pore over maimings, physical and psychological. An early essay, **'Burns Unit'**, itemises hideous injuries—breasts like 'giant vermilion blisters', bodies 'the colour of blackened bacon'—then goes on to assess reactions to these horrors. The useless anguish of the patients'

relatives is set against the emotionless efficiency of the medical staff. To the latter, precision is 'incomparably superior to compassion'; 'even the coldest and most impersonal curative action' is 'less inhuman than sentimental and empathising inaction'. It is just such valuably unfeeling responses that Caroline Blackwood imitates as a writer. Swabbing her emotions with the antiseptics of logic, she opts for the precise and impersonally curative. Detachment is worn like a surgical mask. Though her novels all argue for compassion and involvement, they operate through unflinching probings into physical and emotional damage.

Like the cameras monitoring danger-list cases in **'Burns Unit'**, Caroline Blackwood's fictions regularly focus on wounded children. In her novels, they are always under threat, frighteningly vulnerable to the ravages of time, accident and other human beings. Bitterly smarting from the hurt of a broken relationship, the woman who narrates *The Stepdaughter* is shamingly made to see how her partner's neglected child has been far more badly mauled by life. Exploring the fusty recesses of an Ulster Protestant family, *Great Granny Webster* brings to light spectacular instances of warping by early influence. Like *The Stepdaughter,* too, it seethes with emotional disturbance. Under the taut prose—pegged down by sharp factual detail—lunacy, neurosis and suicidal melancholia strain furiously. Despite this nervous intensity, both books—controlled accounts of hysteria—are often hysterically funny.

Her new novel, *The Fate of Mary Rose,* is very much in this tradition, though adding some ingredients her previous fiction has been short on—a good plot and fast narrative pace. At its centre is an ugly murder: six-year-old Maureen Sutton is abducted, sexually assaulted, killed. This extreme instance of a child's vulnerability is used to set in motion a more complex demonstration of the same idea. What the book aims to show is that there are more ways of destroying a child than homicidal assault. Like the Alsatians hunting for the killer, nemesis is finally unleashed at smug parental irresponsibility.

The book makes much use of adroit counterpoint. Its febrile story is narrated by a man who is emotionally tepid. A self-centred historian, he is taught—hilariously and harrowingly—the importance of other people's pasts. When the story opens, Rowan—early thirties, elegant, single-mindedly careerist—is complacently ensconced in a double life. In London, there is Gloria, whom he doesn't want to marry, but enjoys spending time with; in Beckham, there is Cressida, whom he doesn't enjoy spending time with, but has married—because she was pregnant with his child, Mary Rose, now six years old like the murdered girl. Beckham is a show-piece village: bees drone reassuringly in the wistaria; the tock of cricket balls sounds across the green. Reputable folk with decent incomes prosper decorously behind the period façades. Under her oak beams, dotingly maternal Cressida launders Mary Rose's clothes by hand, plies her with health food and wholesome sentiments.

Maureen's murder bespatters this idyll. Everywhere, niceness is shattered as—magnet-like—the presence of the sexual maniac draws psychosis, disturbance, hysteria to the surface. Horror-comic happenings, escalating frantically, propel the book through weird turnings to a grim ending.

Picking over perverse attitudes to childhood, the novel nods sarcastically towards James Barrie. Beckham is a 'never-never land'; an injured child resembles Wendy shot down by the Lost Boys. Mary Rose is linked ironically with her fictional namesake—not carried off from the real world by fairies, but taken over by the demons of psychiatric breakdown. Images from necromancy keep materialising in this book: appropriately, since it deals with the way people can be hag-ridden by childhood trauma.

Cressida, for instance, boiling cauldrons of black dye, becomes more and more witch-like. She also becomes—as her behaviour skids increasingly out of control—more and more appallingly funny. As her black obsessions swell up to crescendo so does the book's comedy. The novel's final sections are almost unbearably hilarious: again, because of counterpoint. In a last desperate effort to keep uninvolved, Rowan dispatches his secretary, beige-clad, temperate Fay Wisherton, to stay with the now feverishly funereal Cressida, unstoppably voluble, behind her black veil, on the subject of sexual atrocity. At times, as you laugh, you reflect a little uneasily on one of the book's lines, a reference to 'the beautiful finesse that mitigates the cruelty of the bullfighter'. But this is never just sadistic entertainment. The aghast guffaws the book provokes are safety-valve laughs relieving a remorselessly built-up pressure. Ferociously moral behind its harsh jokes, *The Fate of Mary Rose* gives new life to the cliché, 'agonisingly funny'.

Edith Milton (review date 26 July 1981)

SOURCE: "Fathers and Daughters," in *The New York Times Book Review,* July 26, 1981, pp. 8-9.

[*In the following excerpt, Milton argues that Blackwood successfully develops conflict between the characters in* The Fate of Mary Rose *but deviates from her initial concerns and fails to conclude the "who-dunnit" satisfactorily.*]

Both Julian Gloag's contemplative new novel, *Lost and Found,* and Caroline Blackwood's horror tale, *The Fate of Mary Rose,* are set in rural villages invaded by contemporary ugliness, but the more telling similarity is that they are also

both about fathers and fatherhood and that each touches upon the rape of a little girl. In Mr. Gloag's book, rape is only the worst of many outrages, and springs from the brutish, stultifying impact of rustic life. In Miss Blackwood's book, rape is central, an emanation of insanity spawned in urban chaos. Both novels suggest that men cannot accept the fact that violation is a serious threat in their daughters' lives, and that, failing to recognize it, they become in a sense accessories to violation. In its own way each novel offers some poignant insights with considerable skill, and in its own way each novel fails. . . .

The ingredients of *The Fate of Mary Rose* should also combine into a more satisfying book than in fact they do Like Caroline Blackwood's quite perfect earlier novella *The Stepdaughter,* which made palpable its protagonist's eerie self-imprisonment in the glass-walled tower of a New York penthouse, *The Fate of Mary Rose* appears to focus on the destruction of a young girl, while in fact it explores obliquely the insane compulsions that destroy the adults responsible for her.

The novel moves between the male narrator's London apartment and the tiny, tidy village of Beckham, where his wife, Cressida, lives a life of housewifely sacrifice, devoted to the moral and dental hygiene of their 6-year-old daughter, Mary Rose. Through the narrator's eyes, we soon see enough to suspect that behind the jars of homemade preserves and beneath the hand-washed sheets, Cressida nurtures a monstrous obsession. The narrator tells us that his fatherhood, like his marriage, is purely technical; that he is having a quite ordinarily chaotic love affair with a bright young model, and that his life operates, not very comfortably, on a sort of stubborn apathy. But it becomes apparent that he, too, is playing host to an obsessive illusion. While Cressida tries to nourish her sad little life by acting the part of the perfect mother, the narrator hides himself behind an equally false mask of callow masculinity. Beyond his role in conception, he tries to tell himself, fatherhood demands only that he pay the bills and make a ritual monthly appearance for form's sake.

His careful posture of unconcern is the mirror image of Cressida's mad fiction of loving care; the two fantasies, feeding each other, destroy every relationship they touch, and when an unknown attacker rapes and murders a little girl who lives in the public housing near Cressida's cozy cottage, the pair are themselves exploded to reveal the truth beyond their facades. Simple terror lies under Cressida's maternal charade and a hysterical need to indoctrinate her small daughter with her own fear of men and of life. Behind his own mask of indifference, the narrator, who in fact feels a growing concern for his child, also hides fear—fear not merely of women, but of himself and the violence he may do to them.

"She was really the child of the media," the narrator says of the murdered child. "She emerged from the glass of the television set in my livingroom." And her violation and death, like the Council Estate where she lived, are an intrusion of modern hideousness into the artfully preserved myth of rural beauty and bucolic harmony. But like the dovetailing fantasies of the narrator and his wife, the village's violent crime and its delusion of peace almost define and explain each other, like opposite sides of a false equation.

Miss Blackwood portrays the antagonism between her characters with sometimes brilliant irony; in particular, the conflict between the narrator and his wife, which is exaggerated to seem insane and archetypal at the same time, is presented as both a deviation from what society sees as normal behavior between the sexes and also its prototype.

But having set the stage for an intricate and ambiguous drama, Miss Blackwood fails to develop it. In the last third of the novel, her concern with the narrator's murky morality is suddenly overwhelmed by a suspense plot and Beckham's allegorical landscape becomes the backdrop of a rather ordinary thriller. Rather ordinary, I should add, except that instead of providing the final revelation of who did what, why and how, in the usual way of thrillers, the novel veers again and returns for a few last inconclusive pages to the psychological concerns of its beginning.

Disappointed, with an appetite whetted by possibilities that are not fulfilled in *The Fate of Mary Rose,* one has no recourse but to hope for satisfaction in Miss Blackwood's next novel.

Grace Ingoldby (review date 16 September 1983)

SOURCE: "Ogres," in *New Statesman,* Vol. 106, No. 2739, September 16, 1983, p. 23.

[*In the excerpt below, Ingoldby describes the characters from* Good Night Sweet Ladies *as well-developed and the story as funny, but suggests that Blackwood does not develop conflict within the stories sufficiently.*]

Caroline Blackwood's characters are a neatly observed group of humans, vain, selfish and self-deluding, who peep at the truth about themselves and then quietly, quickly, close the door. They are great betrayers of themselves, their animals and each other, and stylish inventors of strategies which just enable them to circumnavigate the truth. Taft, the social worker, protects himself from intimacy ('as a lover he merely obliged') by the invention of the tragic loss of his wife, which always gets him out of a hole; Mrs Burton can persuade herself that a dinner appointment is more important than a dying dog. Such strategies invite prodigious guilt which in several

instances is quite enough to put the characters off their food. Mrs Burton cannot even face her soup, which appears as a dangerous lake into which she must dive to save her croutons. She doesn't dive but watches hopelessly as the last sinking square of bread appears first as her mother (waving?) and then as her dying dog. *Good Night Sweet Ladies* is very funny and the writing, as always, is stylish and close to the bone, but there is a sense in this collection that perhaps this time she might have gone just a little further than she has. Her vision is, one suspects, blacker than she is yet prepared to admit—almost as if Saul, having seen the light on the road to Damascus, decided, disappointingly, to keep it to himself.

Malise Ruthven (review date 21 September 1984)

SOURCE: "Cassandras at Camp," in *The Times Literary Supplement,* No. 4251, September 21, 1984, p. 1048.

[*Below, Ruthven reviews* On the Perimeter, *a nonfiction account of women campaigning against an American cruise missile base in England.*]

Caroline Blackwood first visited the Cruise missile protest camps at Greenham Common in March this year. Her curiosity had been aroused by the "loathsome and frightening" adjectives applied to the women peace campaigners in the newspapers. Auberon Waugh had said the women smelt of "fish paste and bad oysters". Other less gifted polemicists had described them as "screaming destructive witches", "sex-starved harpies" or just a "bunch of lesbians". They were accused of being in the pay of Moscow, or of being red spies who lived like dogs and smeared the town of Newbury with excrement.

In her partisan, but far from one-sided, account of the Greenham camps [*On the Perimeter*], Blackwood relates what she found out through talking both to the women and to their opponents. Nightmarish terrors of nuclear war or accident had driven the protestors to exchange home and family for the cold, the mud, the damp and squalor of the "benders", the home-made tents made from branches and sheets of polythene which are the only dwellings available to the women because tents and caravans have been forbidden by the local council. Here they withstand the harassment of policemen and bailiffs and the sexual taunting of the soldiers, as well as the sheer tedium of maintaining a round-the-clock vigil at the entrance to the base, because "they found it impossible to have faith in the untested theory that deterrents give humanity endless safety". The only relief in this monotonous existence is the occasional visit to the courtroom in Newbury or a spell in Holloway Prison which many regard as a rest camp.

As Blackwood sees it, the protest is a matter of feeling rather than politics. The women's attitude may appear simplistic, but they have a "common sense approach" which stems directly from their daily experience. "It was the protest of all women who have ever looked after children. It gave a black warning that came direct from personal experience. 'If you let children play with dangerous instruments, it won't be very long before there is a hideous accident.'"

In contrast with this down-to-earth view of nuclear matters, Blackwood's account of the childishness of the people defending the base arouses deep misgivings. The soldiers behind the wire keep the women awake at night by shouting obscenities. Once, on leaving the base in a military coach, they bared their bottoms in a gesture that had clearly been rehearsed with parade-ground precision. Even the American children living in the base appear to have been trained to make the "Fuck You" sign as they pass by in the school bus.

Not all of this silliness is on the anti-protestor side. The ideological lesbians cloud the issue by ostentatiously hugging and kissing in the courtroom or at the approach of the TV crews. But, according to Blackwood, all the women arouse a degree of hostility far in excess of any inconvenience they may cause to soldiers, policemen or residents living near the base. Shopkeepers and publicans refuse to serve them; hooligans unexpectedly join forces with the establishment and actualize the verbal insults by smearing the benders with excrement and pig's blood. A huntsman goes berserk in one of the camps, flaying the women with his whip while abandoning his hounds to the oncoming traffic. One of the leaders of RACE—Ratepayers Against Greenham Encampments—leans out of her top-floor window and actually cheers one of the missiles as it leaves the base.

The anti-protestors seem to lose all sense of proportion. For them it is the women's encampments, rather than the base itself that has become an eyesore. It is not the nine miles of fence and barbed wire, the acres of concrete, the hideous hangers and screaming jet aircraft that have desecrated this English common, once the haunt of the Pied Fly-Catcher and Little Ringed Plover, but the handful of sodden and bedraggled women, with their frumpy clothes, their pots of tea and their benders.

Why have these women aroused such irrational furies? Partly, no doubt, it is due to the same mythopoeic power that has made them saints and martyrs for peace groups all over the world. The hysterical response to the women, both by government and local establishments may really be due to underlying fears about nuclear war and the effectiveness of deterrence as a policy. Cassandras, as Blackwood points out, have never been popular. But there also appear to be deeper levels at which the rage of the anti-protestors is aroused. This spontaneous and voluntary association of females, without formal leadership or hierarchy, seems to threaten the soldiers,

the local gentry, the bourgeoisie of Newbury and even its hooligans far more than the missiles, although the latter would be a prime target in the event of nuclear war. Can it be that the women are really right in seeing the Bomb and its phallic projectiles as the linch-pin of a system of patriarchal dominance? Caroline Blackwood does not ask such questions, but her absorbing, witty and compassionate narrative leads one to search for answers in this direction.

Nicholas Spice (review date 18-31 October 1984)

SOURCE: "Arsenals," in *London Review of Books,* Vol. 6, No. 19, October 18-31, 1984, pp. 16-17.

[*In the following excerpt, Spice compares Blackwood's views on women, as presented in* On the Perimeter, *to those presented in John Updike's* The Witches of Eastwick.]

It can't be doubted that **On the Perimeter** and *The Witches of Eastwick* are quite different kinds of book. They were destined to be sold, reviewed and read separately. They have fallen together here by chance and a certain editorial logic, and though at first they appear strange bedfellows, they turn out to breed fruitfully with one another. They should be bought and read together, for they are both in their different ways texts for (and perhaps of) the end of time, books of the Apocalypse. Between them they raise many important issues about the nature of men and women and the nature of nature: **On the Perimeter** by virtue of a chilling subject-matter fixed with a steady eye, *The Witches of Eastwick* through the potency of John Updike's imaginative release.

On the Perimeter records what Caroline Blackwood found at Greenham Common and in the town of Newbury, when she visited the nuclear protest encampments there in March this year, shortly before the town council attempted to evict the women for good. One of the incidents Blackwood describes involved a coachload of soldiers from the base. As the bus emerged from the main gate and passed the women camped outside, the soldiers took down their trousers and exposed their backsides:

> The military buttocks loomed at us from the windows of the bus. They looked like huge white one-eyed sea monsters in a tank. The nasty ink black eyes of the anuses stared at us. They were very malevolent and they seemed to be surrounded by murky perimeters that varied in their shades of darkness.

Place beside this an episode from *The Witches of Eastwick.* Darryl Van Horne has been playing tennis on his indoor court one winter afternoon, with Sukie Rougemont, a witch. After the game he asks Sukie a favour:

'Kiss my ass,' he said huskily. He offered it to her over the net. It was hairy, or downy, depending on how you felt about men. Left, right . . .

'And in the middle.' he demanded.

The smell seemed to be a message he must deliver, a word brought from afar, not entirely unsweet, a whiff of camel essence coming through the flaps of the silken tents of the Dragon Throne's encampment in the Gobi Desert.

Caroline Blackwood and the women at the Greenham Common main gate have no difficulty interpreting the message the soldiers feel compelled to deliver *them*. It shouts at them coarsely from very near—of contempt, hatred, aggression and fear. To the women, the incident is just another example of the sadistic male behaviour they have had to put up with from the military ever since the start of their peace vigil, two and a half years ago. It is a form of assault, on a continuum with rape. Like the victims of rape, they are afraid to appeal to the law for redress, because the law, being male, secretly sides with the men who abuse them, and is liable to tell them they asked for what they got.

Reading the second passage one could be forgiven for coming away with the impression that in John Updike's imagination there are women who do not mind having a man's bottom shoved into their faces. But, unlike *On the Perimeter,* which is written in a style halfway between documentary and polemic, designed to leave the reader in no doubt about how what it describes is to be understood, *The Witches of Eastwick* is a hyperbolical fiction which floats us into a constant state of interpretative uncertainty. If Sukie doesn't want to kiss Darryl's ass, she can, we know, transform it at the murmur of an abracadabra into a pancake or a huge marshmallow or a backgammon board. So what are we to make of her compliance? Is she degrading herself, or are we to regard such practices as quite ordinary? Is Darryl trying to humiliate her? Or is he just a great big baby wanting his bottom kissed by a surrogate mummy? Is John Updike trying to humiliate Sukie? Does she really think Darryl smells like a Chinese camel? Or is it John Updike who thinks that's what Darryl would smell like? What, in any case, is the camel doing inside the tent? And does John Updike really intend to propel the whole episode through metaphorical hyperbole to the edges of the hilarious and the absurd?

The equivocal character of Updike's vision in *The Witches of Eastwick* has provided widely divergent accounts of the book in the American press. By some it has been cast as a comedy of manners, a charming period divertissement on life in middle-class America during the Vietnam era. Others have seen it as a diseased farce, a bilious Thersitical outpouring, soured by a deep-seated misogyny. I think it is both these

things and more, all at the same time, which is why reading it is such a queasy experience, like eating an over-ripe mango, at once richly appetising and prone to make one gag. . . .

In its portrayal of the feminine, *The Witches of Eastwick* is something of a *tour de force*. There are four major female characters in the book, each given distinct life. Moreover, Updike gets inside the skins of his women and tells us what it feels like. Yet the plot moves contrary to this sympathy for the female, tugging us in the direction of a virulent misogyny. It is as though Updike created his characters out of love, setting them in motion only to punish them. He makes them strong but deprives them of the will to use their strength constructively. He grants them independence, then causes them to squander it and finally takes it away from them again altogether. Having endowed them with creativity, he reveals what they do with it to be mediocre. He forbids them to love their children or keep their houses clean. Worst of all, he refuses them morality and fathers upon them a deed (the hexing of Jenny Gabriel) as evil as anything in the history of Western literature.

> **Caroline Blackwood's chief stylistic resource is simplicity. She writes as though she were an immensely clever and articulate child or an *enfant sauvage* launched upon the world for the first time in adulthood.**
>
> **—*Nicholas Spice***

To leave the Eastwick succubae soaking in Darryl Van Horne's eight-foot oak tub, pleasantly stoned and drinking Margaritas, and to move to the half-starved peace women at Greenham Common huddled in their makeshift polythene tents with little to eat, no means to stay dry and no water to wash with, is to cross a fair portion of the entire spectrum of what contemporary Western society currently has to offer in the way of images of women. Nor at Greenham Common is there any ambivalence about the significance of the feminine. The symbolism the protest proclaims—of women as the guardians of peace, men the wagers of war—is a traditional one, and one that most people, even those who revile the Greenham women most bitterly, accept, just as they accept that Mrs Thatcher, in becoming a tough and warlike leader, had perforce, like Lady Macbeth, to unsex herself, an assumption fatuously confirmed by President Reagan some years ago when he called Mrs Thatcher 'the best man amongst us'. Though Caroline Blackwood finds the militant lesbianism of a few of the Greenham women regrettable because it blurs the real issues at stake, she tends to obscure matters herself by reinforcing the interpretation of events near

Newbury as a confrontation between female and male. Her description of the busful of bums, for example, amplifies the incident beyond a point where we can view it dispassionately. By conflating the image of a male posterior with the missile base (a *terminus ad quem* for the species) she turns the incident to splendid rhetorical advantage. But rhetoric only excites us and we need above all to keep clam. There may be more sinister and complex forces at work in the nuclear arms race than the need for the male to assert itself.

The soldiers' bottoms might more provokingly remind us of the part played by anality in the build-up of nuclear arsenals. 'Cleaning up' and 'mopping up' and similar expressions are standard jargon in military operations. If it wasn't for the mess they create afterwards, nuclear weapons would provide the species with an unprecedented means to cleanse itself. Hence the frisson of fascinated horror that met the invention of the neutron bomb—the ultimately 'clean' weapon. It is especially interesting how frequently the local residents interviewed by Caroline Blackwood complain about the Greenham women on the grounds of their dirtiness, smell, disorderliness and mess. One of the reasons given by the council for evicting the women was that the camps constituted 'an environmental health hazard'. The nuclear missile base is at least neat and clean.

One of the most disturbing moments in *The Witches of Eastwick* occurs when Alexandra, who has been resisting the plan to cast a spell on Jenny, finally gives in: 'She said, "Oh hell. Let's do it." It seemed simplest, a way of cleaning up another tiny pocket of the world's endless dirt.' Of all the witches Alexandra is the closest to nature. Natural forces are said to flow through her. But nature in Updike's universe is no less ambiguous in her purposes than woman. Rapturous descriptions fill this book, setting up a natural world of breathtaking gorgeousness and delicacy, while the characters are obsessed with nature's cruelty, her ruthless and obscene flux. 'Nature kills constantly, and we call her beautiful,' muses Alexandra. She sees signs of cancer everywhere. In the Unitarian church Van Horne gives a sermon entitled 'This is a terrible creation'. The subject is parasites. As Brenda Parsley coughs up bees and butterflies while trying to give a sermon on evil, Jenny Gabriel, who is dying, wonders who can be responsible for this new outburst of magic. She reflects: 'Perhaps none of the three was willing this, it was something they had loosed on the air, like those nuclear scientists cooking up the atomic bomb to beat Hitler and Tojo and now so remorseful, like Eisenhower refusing to sign the truce with Ho Chi Minh that would have ended all the trouble, like the late-summer wildflowers, goldenrod and Queen Anne's lace, now loosed from dormant seeds upon the shaggy fallow fields where once black slaves had opened the gates for galloping squires in swallowtail coats and top hats of beaver and felt.' On Greenham Common a very different view of nature pre-

vails. The Greenham women are also Green women. Feeling themselves to live in the shadow of imminent annihilation, they cling to a belief in nature as wholly benign, having recourse to the thought of the Common before the base was built, as a fortifying symbol of all they are fighting for. The idea that the Cruise missile might be in some way consonant with nature's purposes would appal them. I hope they are right to be appalled.

Caroline Blackwood's chief stylistic resource is simplicity. She writes as though she were an immensely clever and articulate child or an *enfant sauvage* launched upon the world for the first time in adulthood. In her approach to life on and around Greenham Common she affects a total lack of preconception, which leads her to express more than usual surprise at the things she finds. When people speak, she takes it for granted they mean what they say, and goes on to wonder why they said it. When something happens, she takes it at face value, deducing its significance from an ingenuous scrutiny of surface characteristics. This allows her to give the impression (often, in fact, sly) of letting things speak for themselves, and it helps her to tie down to particulars what could so easily have drifted into pontificating and prejudice. *Corrigan*, her latest novel, has the same simplicity and clarity of exposition as **On the Perimeter**, making it read a little like a children's book, with that overaccentuation also typical of people talking to foreigners or to the slightly deaf.

Corrigan tells the story of how an elderly widow, Devina Blunt, is conned by a sham Irish cripple called Corrigan. Arriving in her genteel Wiltshire drawing-room out of the blue, Corrigan sets to work milking Mrs Blunt of large sums of money by persuading her that she is helping support a home for the handicapped called St Crispin's. Corrigan is not in fact a cripple and St Crispin's is a pancake house behind Paddington Station, but the business of providing for it, and the enjoyment of looking after him, give Mrs Blunt a new sense of purpose and a reason to go on living, both of which she had lost after the death of her dear husband, 'the Colonel'. By the time Mrs Blunt dies of a heart attack while drinking champagne with Corrigan, she has, it seems, rumbled his game. But rather than expose his deceit, she has preferred to humour it, because of the meaning and pleasure it gives her. The other character to be deeply affected by the arrival of Corrigan is Mrs Blunt's daughter, Nadine, a sadly constrained young lady, whose life has dried out completely in the stifling atmosphere of marriage to an arrogant shit. In the process of coming to terms with the changes in her mother's behaviour brought about by Corrigan, Nadine discovers she too has unused potential, and she at last summons the strength to break out of her ghastly marriage. *Corrigan* argues for the wisdom of ingenuousness, the importance of the immediate, the superiority of means over ends. The virtues, in fact, of the Greenham Common peace protest.

Frank Longford (review date November 1984)

SOURCE: "The Greenham Peace Women," in *Contemporary Review,* Vol. 245, No. 1426, November, 1984, pp. 273-74.

[*In the following review, Longford favorably reviews* On the Perimeter, *arguing that Blackwood raises questions about many larger issues.*]

It is impossible to imagine a more vivid account of the Greenham Peace Women than that supplied [in *On the Perimeter*] by Lady Caroline Blackwood after intensive study on the spot. The women had been described to her in advance as 'belligerent harpies,' 'a bunch of smelly lesbians,' as 'rag-tag and bobtail,' but from the moment she arrived on the scene she was disarmed and one part of her critical faculties suspended. Her compassion was overwhelmingly aroused. 'I found that nothing had prepared me for the desolation of the camps the women inhabited. At first sight, the camps of the Greenham women looked like derelict piles of refuse that had been allowed to collect on the side of the road. The "benders" they inhabited were like crazy little igloos made of polythene.' As tents and caravans had been forbidden by the local council, 'they had erected these small and eccentric dwellings by draping a sheet of plastic over bending boughs which they had pegged into the mud.' Some of the benders were not more than two feet off the ground and had to be entered on all-fours. 'It was astonishing to see a grey-haired woman going into her bender with the scuttling movements of a rabbit vanishing into its burrow.' From then on, the story is one of unrelieved discomfort and extreme self-sacrifice. None of this one need question for a moment.

When I myself visited one of the camps it was moderately warm and fairly dry. It did not take much imagination to guess what conditions would be like when the weather was really nasty. Lady Caroline abstains from passing explicit value judgements. Her sympathies, however, whatever they may have been before her visits, are unrestrainedly in favour of the women and their anti-nuclear cause. She recognises the possibility that the 'great Powers' might defeat the protest, but she adds the defiant afterthought: 'The glorious victory could only be pyrrhic.' The women, with one exception, are presented as noble characters. The exception is provided by the lesbians, about whom Lady Caroline is unexpectedly sharp. She considers that they have done the anti-nuclear cause no good at all by their provocative gestures and parade, in season and out, of their personal tendencies.

The other characters in Lady Caroline's story are presented in a most unattractive light. The soldiers who, on one occasion, drove past with bare bottoms, show their contempt for the women, the police, the Americans, and the local inhabitants. In one or two cases, the latter revealed a sneaking sympathy but, on the whole, they and everyone other than the women, appear as ludicrous, at best. Frequently, as coarse and unfeeling. She quotes a British ex-magistrate who 'looked at all the hordes of police with a shudder.' She has been described as being sent to gaol many times since she had become a Greenham woman. 'I wonder,' she said, 'if this country can continue to have nuclear weapons without turning into a police state. More people ought to ask that. Who cares whether it's wrong to be lesbian and all that trivial, frivolous nonsense? All that's always only used to camouflage the issues that really matter.'

This must be the same lady who escorted me round, who afterwards had lunch with me and whom I later visited when she was once again in prison. She is a deeply impressive person, a former nurse, happily married, with five grown-up children and an admirable family life. A strong Catholic. But neither from her then nor from any of the other women did I extract any reasoned argument for the course they were pursuing. I am not suggesting that this lady or some of the others would have been incapable of sustaining such an argument, but it is part of the peculiar strength of the Greenham camps that they do not have any 'leaders.' There is an extraordinary solidarity, even more feminist than that of the Ulster Peace Women, with whom I could not help comparing them in my mind. Whether deliberately or otherwise, a united front is preserved by not emitting statements that could prove divisive. The problem of arguing with them becomes, therefore, almost impossible.

I am sure that anyone inclined to sympathise with the Greenham women will be drawn further in that direction by Caroline Blackwood's eloquent portrayal. Those who feel no such sympathy will be fortified in the belief that it is a purely emotional demonstration. But the sacrifice is real enough. Caroline Blackwood does well to give us such a telling glimpse of what it signifies.

Madeleine Simms (review date November 1984)

SOURCE: A review of *On the Perimeter,* in *British Book News,* November, 1984, p. 665.

[*Below, Simms provides a favorable review of* On the Perimeter.]

In March 1984, novelist Caroline Blackwood visited the Greenham Common women's peace camps for the first time. She was appalled by the conditions in which these women lived, and impressed by their courage and commitment. She decided to examine the impact of these camps, not on the international peace movement nor on the women's movement, but on their immediate neighbours in and around the country town of Newbury where the camps are sited. She talked not only to the women themselves, but also to local residents, shopkeepers, members of local pressure groups, including RAGE (Ratepayers Against Greenham Encampments), and sat in the local magistrates' courts when some of the women were arrested.

She was astonished to find that ratepayers who objected to peace camps on both political and amenity grounds appeared to have no objection to the miles of concrete and tangled barbed wire that the missile bases had brought to their common. She also witnessed systematic abuse of the women by members of the armed forces stationed at Greenham, who were never restrained or disciplined by their officers into civilized behaviour. [*On the Perimeter*] must make even those who disagree with the Greenham women's political views pause to consider what kind of civilization it is that we are defending by these means. It should certainly be read and its implications considered by all who profess to have strong views about Cruise missiles, whatever side they are on.

Kirkus Reviews (review date 15 February 1985)

SOURCE: A review of *Corrigan*, in *Kirkus Reviews*, Vol. LIII, No. 4, February 15, 1985, p. 145.

[*In the following review, the critic states that although Blackwood's plot in* Corrigan *is predictable, her dialogue and observations are well-written.*]

The life-enhancing, restorative con-man—generous despite his fakery, a giver of much-needed love and confidence—is a familiar figure in Anglo-American storytelling, from Dickens to Twain to *The Music Man*. And here [in *Corrigan*], though Blackwood (*The Stepdaughter, Great Granny Webster*) stylishly fleshes out the basic tale with ironic charm and some shrewd psychology, she eventually returns to the usual formula—complete with an O. Henry-ish windup of sentimental revelations. Devina Blunt, still grieving over the death of her beloved colonel-husband, has sunk into a life of gloomy idleness and near-invalidism in her lovely little country house. Her daughter Nadine, a very rare visitor and the unhappy wife of a selfish London journalist, has felt "totally defeated and frustrated by her inability to alleviate her mother's suffering." (She also feels long-standing anger and jealousy about her parents' all-consuming mutual devotion.) But then timid Mrs. Blunt gets a visit from handsome, articulate, passionate Corrigan—an Irishman in a wheelchair who delivers an eloquent fundraising pitch for St. Crispin's, an under-equipped London hospital for the disabled. Corrigan makes Mrs. Blunt feel ashamed of her defeatist sloth; he urges her to become a pen-pal for a depressed St. Crispin's inmate; soon she's reawakening to life—learning to drive, turning

her overgrown garden into a vegetable-farm, singing songs and reciting poetry with Corrigan . . . who has by now taken up disabled residence on Mrs. Blunt's renovated ground floor. But daughter Nadine, of course, is horrified by her mother's new domestic setup, by charismatic Corrigan's possessive power over Mrs. Blunt. So, after the now-happy widow dies of a heart attack, Nadine goes looking for the vanished Corrigan—discovering that he and St. Crispin's are utter frauds, that her mother knew the truth all along . . . and that she herself might benefit from some of Corrigan's liberating influence. (Says Nadine's model-friend Sabrina, another Corrigan convert: "What he gave her was priceless. Does it really matter that he never had a hospital, just as long as she got such great pleasure from working for it?") Most readers will catch on to Corrigan's scam from the start; many will find blatant implausibilities in its elaborate details. But, though creaky as suspense and predictably syrupy at the fadeout, this scenario gives Blackwood the opportunity to dish up more than a few fine scenes of gentle-humored dialogue, edgy domestic confrontation, and wryly detached observation in the British manner.

Carolyn Gaiser (review date 14 July 1985)

SOURCE: "Victim or Victor?," in *The New York Times Book Review*, July 14, 1985, p. 19.

[*In the following review, Gaiser examines Blackwood's depiction in* Corrigan *of victimization and malice.*]

In *Corrigan*, her fourth novel, the Irish writer Caroline Blackwood continues to expose the menace lurking beneath the seemingly benign surface of everyday life. Domesticity, for Miss Blackwood, has never been cozy; she listens for the ticking of the time bomb in the teapot. Her brilliantly executed thriller *The Fate of Mary Rose* offered a devastating portrait of a marriage of convenience in which a child and her father become the victims of a crazed mother's obsession.

The nature of victimization—and by implication of good and evil—is a recurring theme in Miss Blackwood's work. In *Corrigan* she has written a delightfully ingenious variation on a familiar story—the aging widow preyed on by a charming confidence man.

Devina Blunt has withdrawn completely from life since her beloved husband, the Colonel, died three years earlier. She rarely leaves "her pretty little period house" in the English village of Coombe Abbot; "sometimes it frightened her that she now lived so much in the past." She even welcomes the sound of Mrs. Murphy (her "astonishingly noisy" cleaning woman) "crashing about downstairs in the kitchen," for it gives her "the illusion that her house was still the centre of some kind of important activity."

Like Sleeping Beauty, Mrs. Blunt is awakened from her grieving sleep by a handsome stranger—a prince disguised in a wheelchair. The ebullient Corrigan comes to her cottage to ask for contributions to St. Crispins, a nursing home where he says he was once a patient. "They helped me so much there," he confides. "At the beginning, just after I had my accident, all I really craved were the poppies of oblivion. But they made me realise that I shouldn't see myself as ashes where I'd once been fire."

Miss Blackwood's sly wit and her affection for her characters bring a glow to these pages [in *Corrigan,*] a sunniness that manages to be believable without ever becoming sentimental.

—Carolyn Gaiser

Admiring his gallantry and happy-go-lucky attitude, Mrs. Blunt begins to "feel ashamed of her own aimless life. Corrigan, despite his handicap, was doing something worthwhile." Estranged from her only child, the unhappily married Nadine (who lives in London), Mrs. Blunt warms to his overtures.

Though Mrs. Murphy remains loudly skeptical about the Irishman's intentions, Mrs. Blunt sets about remaking her life under Corrigan's tutelage. She starts a correspondence with Rupert Sinclair, a patient at St. Crispins, and decides to "overhaul" her garden, extend the property, plant fruit and vegetables for the hospital patients. Conquering her timidity, she even learns to drive in order to help Corrigan with fund raising. She also learns to share his passion for poetry and his enjoyment of good champagne. On two issues, however, she remains intractable—her visits to her husband's grave and loyalty to Mrs. Murphy.

Among Mrs. Blunt's "unsuspected, untapped talents," Corrigan discovers a fluency in French and a flair for drawing; he urges her to read Pascal, then persuades her to take up painting. Through a London art gallery, her pictures of flowers find actual buyers. What began menacingly takes flight and becomes an enchanted fable about the transforming power of love.

When Nadine receives an ecstatic letter from her mother describing her new life and declaring her intention "to throw myself into charitable works," she dispatches her best friend, the successful fashion model Sabrina, to investigate: Sabrina's

report that the flirtatious, "very good-looking" Corrigan is now living with Mrs. Blunt (who has renovated her house to accommodate his disabilities) both frightens and enrages Nadine. Nor is she soothed by Sabrina's insistence that their relationship is completely platonic.

"It's as if Corrigan feels she belongs to him," Sabrina explains. "It's as if he thinks like Pygmalion, he has somehow created her." And so completely has Sabrina fallen under his spell that she has decided to give up modeling and return to school.

What Nadine discovers about the mysterious Corrigan and his complex relationship with her mother at the end of her life provides a denouement filled with surprises and irony. The returns on Mrs. Blunt's investments are beyond price, for "like someone in the Bible, her eyes had been opened by Corrigan."

The apparent victim emerges as the true victor, while the presumed villain turns out to have a heart, if not golden, at least touchingly human. The time bomb in the teapot is not only defused, it puts forth green shoots and blossoms into a rose.

Miss Blackwood's sly wit and her affection for her characters bring a glow to these pages, a sunniness that manages to be believable without ever becoming sentimental. She has written a charming tour de force.

Elaine Kendall (review date 28 July 1985)

SOURCE: A review of *Corrigan,* in *Los Angeles Times Book Review,* July 28, 1985, pp. 3, 5.

[*In the review below, Kendall explains the transformation of Devina Blunt from a depressed widow to a lively, caring woman.*]

Gentle, compliant and accomplished at all the wifely graces, Devina Blunt [the protagonist of ***Corrigan***] never had the slightest ambition to be anything but the Colonel's Lady, a role she fulfilled to perfection. Widowed now for three years, she still half expects to hear her husband's footsteps in the hall. His tweeds hang in the wardrobe; his shoes gleam in their rack; his shirts fill the drawers. These days, her only excursion is a stroll to the village churchyard to place flowers on his grave. Devina has never learned to drive, and, until the Colonel's death, had never even written a check. He had always managed their lives as if marriage were a colony and he were the viceroy. Like many Englishwomen of her generation, Devina would have regarded a more equitable arrangement unnatural. Although her daughter, Nadine, is impatient with her, Nadine's life is hardly less dependent.

The only difference is that Nadine's consciousness has been raised, making her miserable in the roles that her mother enjoyed.

Since the Colonel's death, Devina has been looked after by Mrs. Murphy, whose crude good humor hasn't shaken her employer's apathy. Wan and depressed, Devina daydreams her life away, recalling the dinner parties, jumble sales and flower shows that enlivened the tranquil routine of her marriage. She's in her nightgown when Mrs. Murphy shouts: "There's a crippled gentleman at the door. And he wants to see you." For a moment, Devina imagines the visitor is her beloved Colonel, disabled but alive. Forcing the absurd thought out of her mind, she finds an intense and vital Irishman installed in her living room, a box of paper flags in his lap. In an ingratiating lilt, he explains that he's canvassing the countryside on behalf of St. Crispin's Hospital, the private institution where his interest in life had been rekindled after his frightful accident. Corrigan is his name, and it's immediately clear that the cruel fates had left him the gift of gab and charm to spare.

In no time flat, Devina is offering Corrigan the Colonel's best claret and trying desperately to remember lines from the Irish poets. At the mention of her widowhood, Corrigan confides his anguish at the death of his mother, mutual grief creating an instant bond. Refusing her offer of a donation, he suggests that she contribute by corresponding with an inmate of St. Crispin's, a gift even more meaningful than cash. Obviously, Corrigan is not only a person of unusual sensitivity, but quite unaware of Mrs. Blunt's comfortable circumstances. Corrigan leaves with only that promise, briskly wheeling himself down the lane to finish his rounds.

Weeks go by before Devina's letter to the unfortunate Rupert Sinclair is answered, making the reply all the more welcome when it arrives. Sinclair is another kindred spirit: grateful, articulate and plainly a gentleman. "It's a pity all these men are crippled," Mrs. Murphy says, observing her employer's excitement and pleasure. Within two days, Corrigan himself is back, apologizing for the lapse between visits by explaining that he'd skidded off the road on one of his errands of mercy and barely escaped with his life. He's using a borrowed chair; his own was wrecked in the fall. After hearing the dramatic story over champagne and pate, Mrs. Blunt arranges to buy Corrigan a magnificent new chair, handling the matter anonymously through her solicitor to avoid embarrassing her guest. The delicate relationship escalates—long intimate letters back and forth to Rupert Sinclair; increasingly frequent and agreeable afternoons with Corrigan, who apparently finds the little country village of Coombe Abbot amazingly generous.

With a regular visitor to entertain, Devina's domestic talents revive. When Nadine drives down on one of her rare visits, she finds her mother and Corrigan cozily ensconced in front of the fire, sharing champagne and quoting Irish ballads to each other, a sight that profoundly disconcerts her. Nadine's subsequent visits are even more unsettling. A steel wheelchair ramp has been installed over the front steps; Devina has bought up several neighboring farms and is planting exotic fruit and vegetables for the hospital dining room. Most suggestive of all, carpenters are busily constructing an invalid's specially equipped bedroom and bath on the ground floor of the historic cottage. Corrigan is to be a permanent house guest. Devina has been bidding like a sheik at all the local estate sales, planning to resell her acquisitions for the benefit of St. Crispin's. Devina is a new person, her life transformed far more radically than Nadine ever could have wished.

And then abruptly and incredibly, Devina is found dead in her Victorian bedroom; Corrigan is nowhere to be found. With only the most rudimentary deductive skills, Nadine is left to discover who has been victim and who is the beneficiary in this ironic and artful psychological drama.

Marilynne Robinson (review date 1 December 1985)

SOURCE: "A Long and Wretched Vigil," in *The New York Times Book Review,* December 1, 1985, pp. 11-12.

[*In the following review, Robinson argues that Blackwood ignores such larger political issues as Britain's military commitments and instead focuses on the violence and sexuality associated with the women protestors.*]

Caroline Blackwood's **On the Perimeter**, though it is perfectly dreadful considered as prose and as journalism, merits attention all the same for the strange emotional charge it carries. The surreal warping of syntax, the dotty preoccupation with mud and sex and rude odors, are the testament to an anxiety so intense as to have lost a clear sense of its occasion.

Miss Blackwood's subject is a long and famous vigil by a band of women at Greenham Common, an American military base near Newbury, England, at which cruise missiles are deployed. Four years ago, in protest against their coming, a group of women and children walked 400 miles, from Wales, to establish a camp outside the base. Women are camped there still, maintaining a vigil notable for the extreme wretchedness of the conditions in which they live. Local authorities try to drive them away with bulldozers, midnight raids and confiscations. Local thugs set the surrounding bushes on fire. Still, women continue to live outside the gates of the base, in "benders," tiny shelters made of branches and plastic, in defiance of hostility, tedium, cold and mud, sustained by the gifts of well-wishers—of whom there are a great many—and by the fact that their protest has become a sort of pilgrimage site for like-minded people from the ends of the earth.

You would never know, reading this little book, how the world order creaked with stress as cruise missiles were planted through the west of Europe. You will not learn here that these protesters had hoped to prevent the nuclear missiles from arriving at all and that the machinations of the British Government in deploying them caused a notable uproar and ended in the trial and imprisonment of a young female bureaucrat who slipped information about the missiles to the press. You would never learn that there is an outside world at all, did its emissaries not arrive at Greenham Common with dogs and truncheons, or with brown bread and soup and £10 notes.

Nor does Miss Blackwood, who is a novelist and the widow of Robert Lowell, tell us much about Greenham Common itself. Who are these women? "Women often hardly knew each other's names on the camps. . . . They were just 'women' and they shared a terror of 'nukes' and that was all they had to unify them." Miss Blackwood makes the acquaintance of a nurse named Pat. When, later, she inquires after her, someone asks, "Do you mean older Pat?" She muses, "I imagined that I did, but they probably had many Pats on the base." There were as well a "mongol" (a person with Down's syndrome) and a girl who seemed mentally ill, punks with shaved heads and lesbians who, in Miss Blackwood's happy phrase, "seemed determined to overegg the sexual pudding." They kissed in public.

Never seeming to know it, Miss Blackwood describes a world in which things have fallen into rather lurid decay. Here is how she begins: "I was very curious to meet the Greenham women, for the press had decorated them with such loathsome and frightening adjectives, they had been made to sound almost mythical in their horror. They'd been described as 'belligerent harpies,' 'a bunch of smelly lesbians,' as 'ragtag and bobtall,' and 'the screaming destructive witches of Greenham.' . . . They were also described as being in the pay of the Soviet Union. . . . I found the charge that the Greenham women lived like dogs and that they were smearing Newbury with their excrement almost the most chilling one, although it had less grave political connotations."

Can this be true? Can the press really have charged the Greenham women with "smearing Newbury with their excrement"? Miss Blackwood is not very clear about the sources of these charges. For example, although the phrase "a bunch of smelly lesbians" appears to be quoted from somewhere, no newspaper is named. So perhaps she is merely creating phantom adversaries to add drama to her tale—reprehensible as technique, but not in itself alarming.

Then at the top of the next page, we find the English writer Auberon Waugh credited with the claim that "the Greenham women smelt of 'fish paste and bad oysters,'" which remark, Miss Blackwood says, "also haunted me for it had such distressing sexual associations." I must take her word for that. As to the health of political dialogue in which it is considered telling and appropriate to speak of one's adversaries in such terms, I have my own views. Miss Blackwood takes the stance of one entirely prepared to believe these reports. On approaching a gray-haired woman, she says: "If she was a Greenham witch, I hated the idea that she might get up and scream at me. If she was as destructive as I'd been told, she might give me a vicious stab with her knitting needles. But above all, I dreaded that she might suddenly behave like a dog and defecate."

Miss Blackwood spends vastly more time on the issue of whether or not the Greenham women truly do have an evil smell than she does on issues of seemingly greater moment. She pauses later in the book to ascribe the war fears of the women to a statement by Nikita Khrushchev disavowing overkill ("Once is quite enough. What good does it do to annihilate a country twice?"); and remarks by the Rev. Jerry Falwell to the effect that born-again Christians need not fear nuclear war or Armageddon. Of the citizens of Newbury, she says: "No one ever said that they found it frightening that Jerry Falwell claimed Ronald Reagan was a 'Born Again Christian.' They expressed no anxiety that an American president who felt he was going to be automatically 'raptured' might view nuclear war with a certain nonchalance." It is much, in our uncertain world, to ask anyone to share anxieties as attenuated as these are. After all, Khrushchev is long gone. And if President Reagan views death with nonchalance, he is still as willing as anyone else to take a rain check. I find little evidence that Miss Blackwood has inquired deeply into the concerns of politically minded people.

The real preoccupations of ***On the Perimeter*** are violence, sexuality and filth in various forms. In telling the story of "peace women" camped near a country town, Miss Blackwood has continual recourse to words like "loathing," "hatred," "terror," "repulsion." The two British paratroopers who watch her arrive are "like ferocious animals as they glared at the benders with an expression of venomous hatred." Their "nasty yellow-eyed expression" makes her speculate that "they saw the peace campers as leprous and felt that anyone who had any contact with them might spread the contagion throughout the community, and for this reason would be better exterminated." Nor are these yellow-eyed soldiers the worst of their troubles. "The hooligan youths from Newbury came down in the night and poured pigs' blood and maggots and excrement all over them"—enough, surely, to dispel the odor of sanctity. Of the soldiers' "bellowing their horrible obscenities," she says, "They seemed besplattered with their own oaths and soiled by their own sordid fantasies." She reports that "the brutal youths from Newbury . . . drove past the camps screaming maniacal abuse at the women," who, for their part, "loathed and feared" weapons and force as "manifestations of masculinity."

Take the book simply as artifact. Does it attempt to give a true image of reality? Are we really to believe that soldiers stand around with their faces twisted in hatred, day after day? Miss Blackwood describes them elsewhere as grumbling to the women about food on the base, even bringing them tea. We are told that the bailiffs who wreck the benders during working hours help to rebuild them on their own time. Details like these square better with ordinary life than do the Expressionist images of rage and hatred by which the book is dominated. Why do these palliative gestures not soften the anger with which these people are regarded? There is a cruelty in Miss Blackwood's own vision that she projects effortlessly onto others, as when she says, "On one of the camps I'd seen a mongol girl and I couldn't imagine what she was doing there. I wondered if she'd soon be spotted by a hostile photographer and presented as a typical Greenham woman." Yet the book was well received in Britain, so it must not seem grossly out of line to those in a better position to judge.

To understand the anxiety with which this book is so strongly charged, it is probably useful to consider what it does not acknowledge. For example, the idea that Britain is a potential target of Soviet missiles because American missiles are stationed there ignores the fact that Britain maintains nuclear missiles of its own, which it will not make subject to any arms control negotiation—to the Soviet Union's dismay, since they must be assumed to be intended for use against Russia in the worst case. Britain is therefore a target in its own right, and of its own choice.

Worse, Britain is a major producer of bomb-grade plutonium. During the period described in this book, the press was full of the news that the west coast of Britain had been, over 35 years, extensively contaminated with wastes from Sellafield, a nuclear fuel reprocessing plant. Miss Blackwood's references to plutonium and leukemia reflect, I suppose, the widely reported discovery that children in the villages near the reprocessing plant have one chance in 60 of developing leukemia by the age of 15. If the superpowers were to vanish tomorrow, Britain's troubles would still be very great. These women claim to look the harsh truth full in the face, yet they deny by ignoring it the responsibility of their own Government—and, if Britain is a democracy, their responsibility too—for the continuing contamination of their coast, the sea and the Irish coast.

Miss Blackwood says the women "believed that by their presence on Greenham Common they were acting as symbolic candles that represented the conscience of humanity." Let me refine her simile. Greenham Common is a candlelight vigil kept in a burning house.

Robert Jones (essay date 9 May 1986)

SOURCE: "The Illusion of Refuge," in *Commonweal,* Vol. CXIII, No. 9, May 9, 1986, pp. 279-82.

[*In the essay below, Jones examines themes common to five of Blackwood's works and argues that Blackwood writes in a Gothic tradition in which doom is inherent and life has no greater meaning.*]

Of the many lies our parents tell us, the myth of the happy life is the one we seem least willing to relinquish. If we no longer have much faith in historical progress, some still hope for the individual to beat the odds and live exempt from the injustices which afflict and define the past. Despite the detours and setbacks tripping everyone around us, we want to be optimistic for ourselves and believe that life has forward motion, that where we end will be some place further away and better from where we began.

Although we pay lip service to the genius of our most depressed artists, in our hearts most of us remain failed pessimists. Hope has many manifestations, of course, and the desire to live happily ever after can be seen at its most rudimentary level as the pursuit of affluence, and at its most transcendent as belief in God. But in a certain sense, both attest to the indefatigable belief in the second chance, in our hope that somewhere lies the miracle cure, the last-minute rescue. Often there is, but often there is not. We ignore too easily the possibility of the sneak attack in the dark, the accident waiting to happen. In even the most mundane murder mystery, the family member is often the killer.

At the end of Caroline Blackwood's novel, *The Fate of Mary Rose,* a father kidnaps his daughter to save her from becoming paralyzed by her mother's terror of violence. But the child has learned to fear even her father and so flings herself from the car to escape him. As he sees the tiny body sprawled on the pavement, he thinks:

> And if the child were to survive . . . I wondered if she would ever manage to escape the demon-infested murky world of her mother, if for Mary Rose the plunge towards the tarmac would not always seem safer than life.

Our own lives are supposed to be a haven. But the refuge of the personal may be our most enduring illusion. The energy of human desire naturally seeks to protect us from the calamity, disillusion, and fear we have learned from experience. The curse is that trying to live happily, we are in constant flight from life itself.

This threat of the world outside has been the subject of Caroline Blackwood's previous novels. From the highrise apartment of *The Stepdaughter* to the Irish country house of *Great Granny Webster* to the middle-class bungalows of *The Fate of Mary Rose,* she cheerfully evokes the small terrors of the everyday and the more unwieldly evils stumbling anyone who ventures from their door. If she takes as her subject particular domestic dramas, and if her characters make bunkers out of their houses and rarely leave their rooms, it is only to demonstrate how the larger world is always with us. Lived history is not an abstraction functioning independently of the individual, but the narrative line which brings together the muddle of personal crises, feuds, and betrayals that are our heritage.

In describing Dunmartin Hall, the ancestral hall in *Great Granny Webster,* Blackwood writes:

> Dunmartin Hall always had an aura of impermanence. The house had both the melancholy and the magic of something inherently doomed by the height of its own, ancient, colonial aspirations. It was like a grey and decaying palace fortress beleaguered by invasions of hostile, natural forces.

If experience can be said to have a core, or if our place in the world has a character which defines it, we see it perpetually in the permanence of human folly. To understand the past clearly is to see that human beings are afterthoughts to creation, anxious visitors forever trying to bring reason to a universe that finds its power in chaos. The creations we force upon the world, from art and architecture to imperialist fantasies and philosophical ideas, are nothing more than tombstones which mark our passage through an inherently hostile, natural world.

Blackwood's novels unsettle us because she gives us the world as we suspect it exists in our most secret moments. She removes our usual recourse to consolation and security by quietly suggesting that there is nothing beyond the life into which we are born.

—*Robert Jones*

This apprehension of the fragility of the human form encircled and conquered by nature is the center of the Gothic imagination. Caroline Blackwood comes from the tradition of other Irish masters of this vision, like Sheridan LeFanu and Bram Stoker, in her acceptance of evil as the foundation of the universe and primal fright in human souls as the energy at the beginning of all experience. The terror in the Gothic vision emerges from the awareness of our irrevocable separation from nature and helplessness as its victims. It is to this fact

that experience continually returns and which exists as our natural, worldly inheritance.

In this almost primitive understanding of the mysteries of dread and the menace invading every moment of our lives, Blackwood is unnervingly anti-modern. Blackwood is rare among contemporary writers in that there are no elegies to loss in her work. If there is no indication of the betrayals common to the modern age's fall from grace, it is because the focus of her sight exists outside the history and locates the sinister in the world itself. And if her work is often chillingly comic and free of the beleaguered anguish we are used to hearing from our darkest writers, it is because nihilists are slow learners who have come late to the point. Their despair is always after-the-fact, the result of having once had hope and found it abolished by the capriciousness and malevolence of reality. The Gothic imagination continues to haunt us because it accepts doom and recognizes the world as it is and has always been. There is no exile from paradise in this vision, but an ever present horror into which each of us must awaken.

In the unrelenting integrity of her vision, Blackwood is most like Samuel Beckett. But there is a passivity in the face of nothingness in Beckett's work that is absent in her novels. To Blackwood seeing the nothing that is there is not the culmination of a vision, as with Beckett, but the originating word that has echoed since prehistory and which undercuts all human behavior. It is also, for her, the moment by which we come to consciousness.

In a letter from his cell in Reading Gaol, Oscar Wilde wrote of the perspective of the world seen from the bars of his window:

> Prison life makes one see people and life as they are, that is why it turns one to stone. It is the people outside who are deceived by the illusion of life in constant motion. They revolve with life and contribute to its unreality. We who are immobile both see and know.

The houses in Caroline Blackwood's fiction have a truth similar to Wilde's prison. Always the danger lies in stopping, in seeing existence freed of the vibrancy and distractions which hold us to our usual course. It is these revelations of immobility which reveal the self's movement as a paralysis of spirit and the reality outside it as a hallucination. The mystery is how we reintegrate ourselves into the casual order of life after these moments of doubt which strike the mind with the power of the truest enlightenment. For this is the impasse which holds most ordinary lives in suspension and in fear. But within this scope, within the delusions we mistake as reality and the bad faith we mistake as love, Caroline Blackwood's novels examine the possibilities of movement left to us, and whether it is conceivable to move one step forward without setting off another bomb.

In Blackwood's new novel, *Corrigan,* Devina Blunt has lived as a recluse all the years since her husband's death. Mrs. Blunt is like Blackwood's character in her short story, **"Angelica,"** who haunts the graveyard where her husband is buried and imagines that "all around her, the dead were lying there in the mud, waiting to be alive again." In Devina Blunt and Angelica, Blackwood captures the sense of the mind's conquering of time, of how the limbo of grief reduces the present to a vigil over the past. So the life of memory becomes ongoing existence.

Her daughter rails against Devina's passivity and refusal to reenter society. But Devina refuses to yield to the present until it becomes more compelling than the past. So until she first hears the sounds of Corrigan's wheelchair rattling up the stones of her drive, she is content to wander about her property talking to her dead husband, as she waits for something miraculous to happen. Corrigan, with his crippled legs, silken compassion, and repertoire of dreadful metaphors, is the miracle who returns Devina Blunt to the world.

When Corrigan arrives to sell a lapful of little white flags to raise money for St. Crispins, the hospital that saved his life, Devina is overwhelmed by Corrigan's apparent selflessness and desire to do good in the world. He speaks to her of the loneliness of the infirm and his dream to raise money to build a library to repay St. Crispins's kindness. "At the beginning, just after my accident," Corrigan tells her, "all I really craved were the poppies of oblivion. But they made me realize that I shouldn't see myself as ashes where once I had been fire."

Corrigan speaks throughout with the emotionalism of an inferior poet who believes fervently in his own genius and weeps at the depths of his feelings. But it is just the kind of exuberant sentimentality that can intimidate those with more subdued passions. Corrigan's tireless optimism convinces Devina of the aimlessness of her life. She comes to believe that if she succumbs to Corrigan's dream she, too, might save her soul from ruin.

Corrigan possesses the confidence of all little-league gurus who know how to strike most directly at the isolated heart. And his manipulation of Devina flourishes beyond his most extravagant hopes. She develops the singlemindedness of the convert who discovers a cause greater than the self. Devina decides to put her acreage to work to produce fruits and vegetables for the patients of St. Crispins. And as the farm project expands, Devina rebuilds her drawing room into sleeping quarters for Corrigan and disfigures her entranceway with a ramp for his chair. But just as Corrigan appears to have infiltrated every aspect of her life and diminished her ties to her family, Devina is found dead in her room.

If the novel followed the predictable course of stories of this kind, Corrigan would be held responsible for Devina's death. And indeed, as Mrs. Blunt's daughter investigates Corrigan's past to prove his guilt, she discovers what the reader has suspected from the beginning: that St. Crispins is a seedy pancake house, not a hospital, and that Corrigan's paralysis is as fraudulent as his dreams. She also learns that none of this would have been news to her mother. The mystery of *Corrigan* is not how Devina Blunt dies, but why she transformed her life to accommodate someone she knew was a fake.

After he had become part of the household, Corrigan spoke with his customary pretentiousness of Pascal:

> "Maybe I identify with him because he, too, had an unenviable physique. When he wrote '*Notre nature est dans le mouvement,*' it is proof that he transcended his afflictions. Finish the sentence for me, Devina."
>
> "'*Le repos entier est la mort,*'" Mrs. Blunt recited bashfully.

In Devina's return to vitality, Blackwood inverts Pascal's understanding of human nature existing within movement, and questions what it means to move about the world when it has no purpose. In so doing, she reveals a truth on the other side of hope: one which affirms the emptiness of life without thereby surrendering to that inertia which is death to the spirit. The issue central to *Corrigan* is how, then, do we act in the face of such hopelessness.

But Blackwood does not mean hopeless in the sense with which we are most familiar. It is not synonymous with the paralysis of despair. To be without hope in her sense is to discover in oneself the immobility Wilde speaks of in his letter from prison, a way of being or seeing that reveals our place in the world with the truest calm. It is absolutely opposed to the passivity that cripples the unloved Renata in *The Stepdaughter* or the weakling Mary Rose. Their helplessness allows them to be trampled and conquered, easy victims waiting for the "undesirable accident" that forever alters their lives.

Blackwood's novels unsettle us because she gives us the world as we suspect it exists in our most secret moments. She removes our usual recourse to consolation and security by quietly suggesting that there is nothing beyond the life into which we are born. In this isolation, we see ourselves like the people abandoned outside Wilde's prison, scrambling to find antidotes to the frailty and treachery that are the character of human experience.

To say that no resolution exists should come as no surprise, but even now we resist such matter-of-fact statements of our ill-fated purpose. It is a natural, protective response to dismiss such a view as pessimistic, but to do so evades the complexity of the issues Blackwood raises. There is a modesty in her acceptance of the insignificance of the human form that goes beyond any simplistic ideas of negativity. She makes us aware again of how dangerous the world is and of the impossible value we place on experience. In this light, our efforts to translate the ambiguity we know into the certainty we desire seem desperate in their intention.

Through Devina's knowing nod to Corrigan's paralysis, Blackwood implies that all transcendence is false transcendence. But we sustain the illusion of flight, even if it amounts to little in the end. In spite of himself, Corrigan leads Devina to the simple wisdom to say, "I have been fooled by none of this," and to go forward anyway until she decides she's had enough.

As he looked to the past before his death, Kafka wrote in his journal: "When considering the hopes I had formed for life, the one which appeared the most important was the desire to acquire a way of seeing . . . in which life would keep its heavy moments of rise and fall, but would at the same time be recognized, and with no less admirable clarity, as a nothing, a dream, a drifting state." The mobility that Blackwood imagines is just such a truce with existence: to find the elusive balance between the dazzle of nothing and the misbelief that our lives measurably touch the world.

Roger Longrigg (review date 25 September 1987)

SOURCE: "The Unreliable in Pursuit. . .," in *The Times Literary Supplement,* No. 4408, September 25, 1987, pp. 105-07.

[*In the review below, Lonrigg offers an unfavorable assessment of* In the Pink, *charging that the book is inaccurate and lacks purpose.*]

In the Pink reads as though Caroline Blackwood wrote a series of loosely connected articles about foxhunting for a glossy magazine, had them rejected, and then decided to bind them together in hard covers. It is difficult to guess why else this book should have been written; it is too unreliable in detail to be informative, and maintains too strict a moral neutrality to have the interest of a tract. It can be recommended neither to those who know about hunting nor to those who want to know about it. The sort of information we are given is that Victorian women "galloped alongside the bewhiskered men casting seductive glances from under their provocative hunting veils".

There are extended interviews with "antis" and others—apparently chosen because they are unrepresentative of those who follow the sport. There is no account of the physical act of chasing foxes on horseback—there are accounts of two days spent in cars attempting to follow the hunt, but apparently no hounds or horses were sighted after the meet. Literary quotations appear for no reason and in no historical context; there is no evidence of broad reading or serious research.

Someone going hunting is described by Blackwood as a "hunter" or "huntsman"; in Britain the former is a horse (in America a sportsman with a firearm) and the latter a person in charge of a pack of hounds in the field. William Somerville, most eminent of early Georgian hare-hunters, is described as a Regency fox-hunter, and "Nimrod" (uniquely influential as a hunting writer in the 1820s) and even Peter Beckford are thought to have been Victorians. A "drafted" hound means one transferred to another kennel, not condemned to death. In the season a hound today does not "walk about thirty miles to the meet several times a week". There was no hunting tailor called Mr Pink. "The Earl of Spencer" would be surprised by that partitive.

Max Hastings (review date 14 October 1987)

SOURCE: "Fox Trot," in *Punch,* Vol. 293, October 14, 1987, p. 72.

[*In the following excerpt, Hastings charges that* In the Pink *is not on par with Balckwood's earlier works and fails to capture the romance of fox hunting.*]

Caroline Blackwood . . . is a rich, somewhat fey lady who writes excellent magazine profiles and is the author of five novels. Her own family is seated in Northern Ireland, though she says that never since she was a child has she hunted, and then only after hares rather than foxes. But she became fascinated by the fact that more people in Britain today are following hounds than at any time in history, and installed herself in a large house in Leicestershire to write a book about the phenomenon.

The outcome [*In the Pink*] is a series of essays, some absurdly brief, about aspects of fox-hunting—hounds, quarry, devotees, and (not least) fanatical opponents. She was unimpressed by the "antis", whom she concluded, like others before her, are driven more by hatred of fox-hunters than enthusiasm for animal welfare.

But when she turns to hunting, she never comes close to gaining the feel for it that, say, Molly Keane possesses. First, although she writes with wonderment of its risks and the frightful serried ranks of wheelchairs that it promotes in the House of Lords, she did not try it herself.

This is a serious flaw, because one cannot write with conviction about fox-hunting without having experienced, even briefly, its terror and exhilaration. There is no intellectual case for field sports; only a very powerful romantic and emotional one, based upon the propriety of maintaining man's historic role as a hunter. It is almost impossible to argue about field sports with an opponent who has never tried them.

A day out hunting or shooting may well fail to convince the novice. But at least he can then perceive the basis of the argument and the experience, the priceless sense of intimacy with the countryside, that it inspires. Caroline Blackwood has tried to understand the fox-hunters, but has plainly never come close enough to them to do so. She has merely marvelled from a social distance, so to speak. Her book is full of little mistakes, irritating even to a non-fox-hunter like me: followers may join hounds at Second Horses, but never at Second Horse as she suggests. Colonel Derek Hignet, to whom she devotes a chapter, is a distinguished former Master of the Fernie, not the Pytchley; and so on.

Lady Caroline does not seriously discuss—or perhaps never identified—the central irony of fox-hunting today: that it is the principal force for the preservation of foxes. The fox-hunters will never admit this, for to do so would be to undercut all the traditional arguments about their social utility as fox controllers.

In reality, foxes are preserved in hunting countries with a fanaticism that commands derision in such areas as Hampshire, where they are shot, trapped and gassed whenever they show their faces. Here, the "antis", too, find themselves in hopelessly muddy waters. They cannot admit the role of hunts as fox protectors, because that would destroy the justification for all their agreeable little Saturday morning riots on winter days when *Socialist Worker* is not holding a seminar.

Caroline Blackwood limply concludes that it will be a sad day for England when fox-hunters can no longer etc, etc. But her uncertain meander across the hunting scene is put to shame by the cracking pace that Molly Keane and her peers sustain without faltering to the end.

Peter Parker (review date November 1987)

SOURCE: "The Thrill of the Chase," in *Books,* No. 8, November, 1987, pp. 19-20.

[*In the review below, Parker praises* In the Pink *as a well-written and impartial account of fox hunting in England.*]

As someone who was taken hunting as a child, I have always considered blood-sports more deserving of the attentions of the NSPCC than of the RSPCA. Not that my mother bullied me into it, but I was the hunting equivalent of the coward who would rather go to war than declare pacifism. I confess I had no *moral* objection to the hunt; I did not even think about our quarry. But if I had I would have reflected that Reynard epitomises by tooth and claw the true colour of nature. Anyone who has seen what a fox can do to a run of chickens, or indeed an enfeebled sheep, must waver in his wholehearted sympathy for the bushy-tailed gentleman whose picturesque qualities belie a character quite as bloodthirsty as any huntsman. And yet the human, unlike the animal, is blessed (or cursed) with moral choice. I would not hunt now; but equally would not attempt to prevent others from doing so.

I am as impartial, then, as Caroline Blackwood, whose engrossing study of fox-hunting demonstrates how little there is to choose between those who hunt and those who would stop them, between the late Duke of Beaufort and those who planned to send his severed head to Princess Anne. Like Noel Coward (in this respect only, one hastens to add), the Duke was known as 'Master' by everyone from the Queen to the local peasantry ('of Foxhounds' was understood). This gives some idea of the arrogance characteristic of the typical MFH, who tends to combine foul temper with what he considers to be immaculate manners: he has no qualms about being unforgivably rude to those he considers his inferiors in status and age (often almost everyone), but always raises his hat to ladies. An officer at the *League Against Cruel Sports* admits that most of the members were bullied at school and thus feel empathy for the fox. One imagines that their persecutors must have resembled the Quorn in full pursuit. Unfortunately for the 'antis', few of their number have the moral authority and intelligence of a Brigid Brophy or a Bernard Shaw. Indeed, many of them appear to be moral idiots, who have not thought out their objections at all. The vengeful vegan who doesn't 'see anything wrong with killing a huntsman', and whose uninformed meddling with wild creatures makes the average MFH look like an animal welfare officer, is as self-deceived and dangerous as the hunt supporter who talks of 'the sporting fox', yet digs it out of its earth if it manages to escape the hounds.

Blackwood has a sneaking, if appalled, admiration for the stoicism of the hunting fanatic who, to the accompaniment of spattering mud and splintering tibias, thunders across the English (and Irish) countryside. As during the advance upon the Somme, the true huntsman does not stop to assist the injured, and Lord Longford ascribes the high proportion of wheelchairs in the House of Lords to this Sport of Kings and Dukes and Earls. And Queens, Duchesses and Countesses, of course, for if anything Our Hunting Mothers are even tougher than Our Hunting Fathers. The most admired figure on the hunting-field of the 1920s was the mother-to-be who hunted until the last possible moment, paused briefly and impatiently for the *accouchement,* and was 'pulling on the hunting boots and the riding breeches the moment the umbilical cord had been severed'. Her greatest disgrace was that the baby should turn out to be one of those 'pale, uncourageous children', described by Molly Keane in *The Rising Tide,* who take no pleasure in galloping alongside irascible and often out-of-control adult riders or in receiving the caste-mark of being 'blooded' on the face by a hacked-off fox's brush. *In the Pink* is a marvellous book, evocative, humane, balanced, sometimes distressing but often very funny.

Kirkus Reviews (review date 1 January 1995)

SOURCE: A review of *The Last of the Duchess,* in *Kirkus Reviews,* Vol. LXIV, No. 1, January 1, 1995, p. 36.

[*In the following review, the critic describes Blackwood's account of Wallis Simpson's later life as a "dark fairy tale."*]

[*The Last of the Duchess* is] the chronicle of dogged journalist/novelistBlackwood'squest to discover the fate of Wallis Simpson—for whom King Edward VIII gave up the throne and settled for the title duke of Windsor—after the death of her husband.

Blackwood's obsession began with an impossible assignment—reporting on Lord Snowdon, who had been commissioned by the London *Sunday Times* to photograph the duchess—a celluloid encounter that was never to take place because her formidable keeper, the female French lawyer Maître Blum, never permitted it. But in trying to sway the terrifying octogenarian lawyer ("If you do not write a favorable article about the Duchess—I will not sue you . . . I will kill you"), who kept the duchess in her French home with no visitors for a decade, Blackwood became determined to comprehend "Master" Blum and her victim, the once "dreadful Mrs. Simpson." Blum, an accomplished lawyer whose clients included Charlie Chaplin and Walt Disney, was given the duchess's power of attorney soon after the duke's death. After a few fruitless interviews with Blum herself, in which the Windsors are exalted as a sober, cultured couple that no one knew them to be, Blackwood tracks down surviving Windsor pals. A parade of wistful, wizened aristocratic women—such as Lady Diana Mosley—tell tales about the duchess's love affair with Woolworth heir and profligate Jimmy Donahue and her public humiliations of the besotted duke. From other sources Blackwood hears that, in Blum's care, the duchess, once heralded for her sense of style and shunned as sex incarnate, has shriveled to half her size, turned black, and is fed through pipes in her nose. By weaving semi-sordid speculation with famous factual tidbits, Blackwood spins a very "dark fairy tale" indeed.

A terrifying look at how far the mighty can fall when infirmity and poor judgment put them into nefarious hands.

Michiko Kakutani (review date 3 March 1995)

SOURCE: "The Sad Later Years of the Woman He Loved," in *The New York Times,* March 3, 1995, p. C27.

[*In the review below, Kakutani argues that Blackwood does not stick to the facts in* The Last of the Duchess *and therefore destroys her credibility.*]

This fascinating but ultimately disingenuous new book about the Duchess of Windsor is part detective story, part biography, part hatchet job and part comedy of manners. It features characters who seem like exiles from *Les Liaisons Dangereuses,* a social backdrop reminiscent of Evelyn Waugh and a plot that might have been worthy of Henry James.

The Last of the Duchess begins with an assignment that the journalist and novelist Caroline Blackwood received from The Sunday Times of London in 1980: to write an article about the legendary Duchess of Windsor, the American divorcee Wallis Simpson who won the heart of Edward VIII and cost him the British throne.

Like A. J. A. Symon's classic study of Baron Corvo (*The Quest for Corvo*) and Ian Hamilton's much-contested 1988 "biography" of J. D. Salinger (*In Search of J. D. Salinger*), *The Last of the Duchess* is less a conventional biography, than an account of the author's efforts to come to terms with an elusive subject. Indeed, this book ends up revealing a good bit more about Ms. Blackwood and the Duchess's late lawyer, Maître Suzanne Blum (who apparently tried to thwart Ms. Blackwood's efforts), than it does about the Duchess herself.

In the book's opening pages, Ms. Blackwood tells us about her own childhood in Ulster and the uproar the Duchess created there in the late 1930's: "To an embattled Protestant community whose very identity depended on their loyalty to the British crown, Mrs. Simpson was a figure who was regarded with horror. She was a threat to the church and the monarchy. She symbolized sex and evil." By the end of her investigations into the Duchess's life, however, Ms. Blackwood has arrived at a very different conclusion: she says she has come to see the Duchess as "a figure of tragedy": a naive victim of her conniving lawyer, and eventually a pathetic prisoner in her own huge house in Paris.

Combining her own meditations with assorted interviews and material taken from other books (including *The Windsor Story,* by J. Bryan 3d and Charles J. V. Murphy; the Duchess's own memoir, *The Heart Has Its Reasons*, and the Duke of Windsor's autobiography, *A King's Story*), Ms. Blackwood gives the reader, a sharply observed (and sometimes very funny) portrait of the frivolous world of wealth and luxury inhabited by the Windsors.

As depicted in these pages, it's a world that's perilously close to parody, a world of willful superficiality and wretched excess. "The Duchess never became a Queen but she had done her best to live like a Queen," Ms. Blackwood writes. "She and the Duke had once traveled with insouciance through a war-torn Europe taking with them no less than 222 suitcases, and that was not counting all her extra hat and jewel boxes. Their entourage was enormous, it resembled an unaffliated army, it included so many maids carrying lapdogs that belonged to the Duchess."

Ms. Blackwood tells us that the Duchess was known for her "cunning use of mirrors," her fetish for shoes (she once bought 56 pairs at a single go), her 22-karat-gold bathtub, her quirky dinner-party edicts: no candles at eye level, platinum (not gold) jewelry at night. She quotes one friend who fondly recalls how the Duchess's butler "used to love kneeling in front of the Duchess and putting on her slippers" and another who describes the Duchess's folly-filled affair with a "seriously cruel and common" millionaire when she was married to the Duke.

If the Duchess comes off as a vain, hopelessly selfish woman in this volume, the Duke emerges as a dangerously naive, Nazi-loving twit who was easily taken in by demagogues and easily manipulated by his wife. Ms. Blackwood's greatest scorn, however, is reserved for the lawyer, Maître Blum, who is variously described as "necrophiliac," "ruthless" and "demented"—"a Narcissus," "a terrifying clown," a "malignant old spider."

"She kept glaring at me with the utmost hostility," Ms. Blackwood writes of an interview with Maître Blum. "She answered my questions with ill-mannered abruptness. Her slanting, unblinking eyes had a snakelike malevolence. She was perverse."

In the course of the book, Ms. Blackwood's wariness of Maître Blum escalates into out-and-out hatred. She suggests that the lawyer is deliberately—and painfully—prolonging the moribund Duchess's life for her own selfish ends, that she has cut off the Duchess from her dearest friends, and that she has blatantly lied about the Duchess, reinventing her fun-loving client in her own sour image. Much of Ms. Blackwood's writing about Maître Blum veers into the realm of pure speculation: there is little effort to verify the most outrageous rumors about the lawyer, and lots of hypothesizing about the old woman's obsessive, possibly erotic attachment to the Duchess.

Were *The Last of the Duchess* a novel, this vitriolic portrait of Maître Blum might make entertaining reading; it might even illuminate something about the dynamics of power and dependency and the creation of myths. As journalism, however, it is deeply and seriously flawed. Indeed, Ms. Blackwood completely undercuts her own credibility when she notes that she once wrote a profile of Maître Blum for *The Sunday Times* "that was bland and praising to the point of sycophancy."

"I said that Maître Blum was a marvelous old figure noted for her loyalty and devotion to the Duchess of Windsor," Ms. Blackwood says, "and as I wrote this, I realized that Maître Blum always managed to get her way."

Having spent the better part of this book railing against Maître Blum, it seems the very height of hypocrisy and deceit to have written and published such an article. It can only make the reader distrust the author of this book.

Jill Gerston (review date 19 March 1995)

SOURCE: A review of *The Last of the Duchess*, in *The New York Times Book Review*, March 19, 1995, p. 38.

[*In the review below, Gerston argues that* The Last of the Duchess *ultimately fails because Blackwood relies too much on speculation.*]

Caroline Blackwood's investigation into the last years of the bedridden octogenarian Duchess of Windsor—whose fragile existence was fiercely controlled by Suzanne Blum, her belligerent octogenarian lawyer—is a tale as bizarre as it is poignant. Asked in 1980 by *The Sunday Times* of London to write an article about the divorced American woman for whom Edward VIII renounced the throne in 1936, Miss Blackwood interviewed several dowagers—Lady Diana Cooper and Lady Diana Mosley, among others—who had hobnobbed with the Duchess. Their gossipy reminiscences about "poor Wallis," including some titillating anecdotes about Jimmy Donahue, the Woolworth heir with whom the Duchess was infatuated, are colorful and amusing. Miss Blackwood's biographical account of the Duchess's pre-Windsor years is also absorbing. However, *The Last of the Duchess* sorely disappoints by never answering the cardinal question: How did the Duchess of Windsor spend her final years, before her death in 1986 at the age of 89? The book is heavy on speculation and hearsay but weak on facts. Central to the story is Blum, whom the author portrays as a vengeful, paranoid battle-ax with an obsessional attachment to her client. Although Miss Blackwood, whose novels include *The Stepdaughter* and *Great Granny Webster*, suspects her of having exploited the enfeebled Duchess, she nevertheless wrote a fawning profile of Blum for The Sunday Times. (Miss Blackwood postponed the publication of her book until the notoriously litigious lawyer died last year.) The author finally inveigles her way into the Duchess's Bois de Boulogne mansion, but is stopped by the butler at the doorway. One needs a more seasoned reporter to break through the labyrinth.

The Last of the Duchess sorely disappoints by never answering the cardinal question: How did the Duchess of Windsor spend her final years, before her death in 1986 at the age of 89? The book is heavy on speculation and hearsay but weak on facts.

—Jill Gerston

Jonathan Yardley (review date 22 March 1995)

SOURCE: "The Duchess and Her Keeper," in *Washington Post,* March 22, 1995, p. C2.

[*In the review below, Yardley describes* The Last of the Duchess *as an odd, dark story that is both witty and perceptive.*]

This peculiar but beguiling book is the account of how its author, a British journalist and novelist who now lives in the United States, tried to obtain an interview with the Duchess of Windsor in the last years of that controversial woman's long life. She failed, but she managed to hook up with a woman even odder—if one can imagine such—than the duchess herself.

That woman was Suzanne Blum, universally known as Maître Blum, the octogenarian French attorney who seized control of the duchess's life after the death in 1972 of the duke—the onetime King of England, Edward VIII. By 1980 she had the duchess locked away in the Paris house that the French government had given to the exiled Windsors and permitted no one to visit her. It was variously rumored that the duchess had shrunk to the size of a baby, that her skin had turned black, that she was in fact dead.

Whatever the case, it developed that Lord Snowdon wanted to photograph her in whatever state she might have attained. This was proposed to the *Sunday Times* of London, which in turn proposed that Caroline Blackwood, herself well connected in the circles that surround the British crown, write an accompanying article. This would entail an interview, which in turn would entail approaching the formidable Maître Blum,

the "bellicose old eminence grise who was lurking behind the stricken Duchess."

Thus Blackwood set off on her mission. She wrote this account of it at the time but withheld it from publication, "for obvious reasons," until after Maître Blum's death, which took place a year ago. *The Last of the Duchess* is a chronicle with no real narrative line and no particular surprises, either. One reads it because Blackwood is witty, understated and perceptive, and because the fascination that the duchess exerted in life has not entirely evaporated even now, nearly a decade after her death, even at a time when the British crown has been sullied far more than it ever was by Wallis Warfield Simpson and her little duke.

Much of the fascination of this particular book lies in the unfathomable mystery at its center. How did the duchess allow herself to be sequestered—imprisoned, really—in isolation, and how did Suzanne Blum achieve such total mastery over her? We know that the duchess was incompetent at financial matters and thus would have welcomed so self-confident and celebrated an adviser as Maître Blum, but it is one thing to turn over one's books to an outsider and quite another to relinquish one's entire existence.

"If the Duchess sometimes regained consciousness," Blackwood speculates, "she must [have felt] that few people were as abandoned as she was, few people had been left so completely alone in the dark." What emerges as Blackwood makes her inquiries and draws conclusions from them is a "very symbiotic relationship" in which the duchess and her attorney "were totally dependent on each other." She writes: "Wallis Windsor owed her life to Maître Blum, and Maître Blum had fused her identity with the Duchess to such an intense degree that she seemed to feel that her own life had little emotional validity apart from her role as the sole custodian and adorer of Wallis Windsor."

Blackwood implies but does not directly claim that Maître Blum may have nursed sexual as well as emotional feelings about the duchess, feelings presumably both unrequited and unfulfilled. Whatever the case, Maître Blum went beyond mere adoration to self-aggrandizement of a sort, selling off the duchess's baubles and treasures for reasons that remain mysterious, given the duchess's considerable wealth. To Blackwood it "seemed unfair that at the end of the Duchess's life, Maître Blum should zoom in and appropriate all the Duchess's gains without having lived through any of the vicissitudes by which they had been acquired," a telling and important point.

But if Blackwood's tale has its undeniable dark side, it is also a comedy. After all, as one of the innumerable British grand dames to whom she talked put it, "There's something so comic about . . . the idea of that horrible old lady being locked up by another horrible old lady." When it comes to Maître Blum, "horrible" is pure understatement. As portrayed herein she is a monster of the first rank, a gnomish Rasputin in spoken of by all "with an awe that was curiously akin to pure terror." The descriptions of Maître Blum in her dreary mausoleum of a house, a sniveling protege in attendance, are immensely amusing, though Blackwood lets the humor speak for itself.

Blackwood sees the story of the duchess and Maître Blum, she says in her preface, as "a lesson for those who are vulnerable to being overprotected" as well as "a real study in the fatal effects of myth." Perhaps so. But it's also, as told herein, simply a very good if very odd story, and it will be welcomed by all connoisseurs of the outre.

Gabriele Annan (review date 23 March 1995)

SOURCE: "Through the Looking Glass," in *The New York Review of Books,* Vol. XLII, No. 5, March 23, 1995, pp. 18-20.

[*In the following review, Annan argues that although Blackwood does not present any new revelations in* The Last of the Duchess, *her sharp perception and witty style make for enjoyable reading.*]

The Last of the Duchess is detective thriller, Gothic horror story, and society gossip column all in one: a publisher's dream. It is also a grisly anatomy of old age.

The duchess in question is the Duchess of Windsor. In 1980, eight years after the Duke's death, the London *Sunday Times* decided to ask Lord Snowdon to go to Paris and photograph her. She had not been seen in public for some years, and lurid rumors were circulating about her fate. Caroline Blackwood was to write the accompanying copy. She thought "it might be interesting for someone to take a photograph of Lord Snowdon caught in the act of photographing the Duchess. One royal divorcée taking a snap of another. Surely this would have a certain historic value and be a record of an event that had an Alice in Wonderland unreality."

But it was not to be. The Duchess's lawyer, Maître Suzanne Blum, vetoed the whole enterprise. She had power of attorney. At first she refused to see Blackwood, and when she finally received her in her hideous and forbidding flat, she bullied and insulted her, threatening to sue (she was famous for suing) and even to kill her if she wrote unfavorably about the Duchess—a threat which Blackwood, not quite convincingly, pretends to believe. "There was something ruthless and demented in her glinting, paranoid eyes." Maître Blum and her client were both eighty-four years old, but whereas the lawyer rushed around acting on behalf of rich old women (in

the Fifties she had specialized in Hollywood personalities like Rita Hayworth, Douglas Fairbanks, Jack Warner, Walt Disney, and Merle Oberon), the Duchess was assumed to be terminally ill or gaga or both. Blackwood heard that she never left her house in Neuilly, that Maître Blum called every day and forbade the door to everyone except the three nurses in attendance. The butler (rumored to be armed) had orders to turn away all callers. Blackwood surmises that the Duchess's periodic spells in the American Hospital were necessitated not so much by crises in her health as by the butler's holidays.

She had planned to interview as many of the Duchess's acquaintances as she could: a string of pearls with the Duchess's portrait in the central medallion. Things did not turn out as planned: there was to be no portrait, but the pearls are real pearls all right: vivid evocations—cruel, comical, and sometimes heartbreaking—of ancient survivors from an extinct culture. The Windsors' closest friends after the war were the British fascist leader Sir Oswald Mosley and his wife, who was still so beautiful that Blackwood was reluctantly beguiled. Both couples had flirted with Hitler. The Mosleys were locked up during the war, but the Windsors, according to Blackwood, kept in touch with Mosley even after the Duke was appointed governor of the Bahamas. After the war all four of them settled in exile outside Paris and dined in each other's impeccably decorated houses. When Blackwood telephoned Lady Mosley, "she said she had become stone deaf. I then realized that if I hoped to talk to people who had once surrounded the Duchess, I must expect to encounter the hurdle of various physical disabilities." This demure statement should be taken as a coded health warning for sensitive readers.

Lady Mosley was about to publish a life of the Duchess. Not having heard exactly what Blackwood said, she imagined that she wanted to review it, and invited her to lunch. Sir Oswald made up to the visitor, but kept losing the thread of his disquisitions.

> "The trouble with England now . . ." Sir Oswald said to me. All his statements were delivered with such self-importance they sounded like pronunciamentos. "The trouble with England now . . ." he repeated. He never stopped trying to be hypnotic. I braced myself waiting for some abrasive opinion. But the trouble with England now was that it no longer had any hostesses. "Where are the great hostesses?" Sir Oswald asked with rhetorical melancholy. "Tell me where are the great hostesses of the ilk of Sibyl Colefax and Emerald Cunard?

After the Duke of Windsor's death, his cousin, Lord Mountbatten, proposed to the Duchess that she should set up a charitable trust in the Duke's name. The Duchess was said to be delighted, but Maître Blum scotched the plan and was thought to have sold off many valuable items which might have been included. Lord Mountbatten was now dead, and when Blackwood telephoned his daughter,

> Countess Mountbatten became so agitated she sounded close to tears. "Oh, it's the most ghastly business! Daddy minded about it all so much. The lawyer has got all those lovely things. I can't tell you how many she's got. You'd never believe what beautiful things the Duke and Duchess used to have. And all of them royal. . . ."

> "I believe that Maître Blum also has some of the royal swords?"

> Countess Mountbatten gave a heavy, upper-class sigh. "Oh, my dear, I'm afraid it's very much worse than that," she whispered mournfully. "That frightful old woman's got the royal insignia and the regimental drums."

Blackwood is a dangerous interviewer. You can hear her subjects' intonations. And sometimes you can hear her own—for instance when she talks about the Duchess's former sister-in-law, Mrs. Maud Kerr-Smiley, "who considered that Ernest [Simpson] had married beneath him." Every time Blackwood mentions Mrs. Maud Kerr-Smiley a hiss of ridicule goes whistling through the syllables. True, the name is a gift—perhaps from P. G. Wodehouse in the Great Beyond. There are Wodehouse touches in Blackwood's book anyway, and it is all the better for them. Both writers have a fine sense of upper-class absurdity.

Sir Walter Monckton was the Duke of Windsor's legal adviser and friend: he helped him write his abdication speech and accompanied him across the Channel afterward. Blackwood went to see his widow in the "home" where she lived. It was a beautiful country house with golden pheasants parading on the lawns.

> Fires had been lit in the fireplaces and above them were ancient portraits of somebody's ancestors to give a feeling of continuity. Only a faint smell of antiseptic and the terrible state of the inmates ruined the imposing atmosphere. Having lost all their faculties, they sat motionless in their various chairs. Some of them looked at television with their eyes closed.

Lady Monckton was thrilled by Blackwood's visit, though she thought she was Lady Mountbatten (not the one who grieved so for the regimental drums, but her dead mother).

Yet when the old lady spoke of the past she was lucid. She told Blackwood that while the Duke had always been "madly in love" with his wife, the Duchess was never in love: she just wanted to be Queen. This was not news: it was the accepted opinion. It doesn't matter. The interview with Lady Monckton is a little masterpiece. The old lady's charm revives and she begins to sparkle at the thought of what fun life used to be in the Duchess's entourage. Eventually a nurse asks Blackwood to leave. Lady Monckton will be exhausted. "I couldn't see any real reason why Lady Monckton shouldn't be allowed to become overtired if she was enjoying herself for one moment . . . I wished . . . she could get on a jet and fly to Paris to join the young Duchess and her dead husband. I wished she could have a glamorous dinner with the Duchess, that all the flowers on the table could be sprayed with Diorissimo"—which is what used to happen for the Windsors' parties.

Lady Diana Cooper was a famous wit and beauty and the widow of Britain's first postwar ambassador to France. "I hear she makes no sense," she said when Blackwood told her about Lady Monckton. "She's much luckier than me. I make perfect sense and I am absolutely miserable. I loathe being old. I hate every second of my life. My eyes, my ears, are going. Everything is going. All I enjoy now is driving my car. And I suppose I won't be able to do that much longer. I can't walk a step without it hurting. But let's have a drink." She envied even the incarcerated Duchess, artificially kept alive and tortured by expensive doctors, because she had heard that the Duchess was unconscious. And she envied her friend the playwright Enid Bagnold: "Enid is now ninety-two and she is as mad as a coot. She's become totally gaga. She hardly makes a grain of sense when I go to see her. But Enid claims that old age has been the happiest time of her life." Blackwood checked this out with a friend of Bagnold's: "It was nonsense. Enid Bagnold was not at all happy. She was in a desperate state of ill health and she minded it as much as anyone else. She liked to pretend to Lady Diana Cooper that she was ecstatically happy." Blackwood concludes from this: "Old ladies had their own form of one-upmanship."

The Marchesa Casa Maury (formerly Mrs. Dudley Ward) became the Duke's mistress in 1919. He dropped her when he met Mrs. Simpson, and never spoke to her again. He told the palace switchboard to refuse her calls. When Blackwood went to see her, she was confined to a chair. She had broken her hip and just come out of hospital. "'We never stopped dancing,' she said. 'The Duke was mad about dancing. In a way that was all we did—well, not quite.' She gave another little laugh.

> "I doted on the Duke," she said.

Her husband didn't mind. "If it's the Prince of Wales—no husbands ever mind." The Marchesa was willing to admit the Duke was "very sexy" (qualified a moment later to "quite sexy"), and also "a pretty miserable fellow . . . He was always crying. He was always in floods of tears. It was usually because he'd had some row with his father. The Duke hated his father. The King was horrible to him. His mother was horrible to him too . . ."

Blackwood fell for this "gallant, old, humorous lady of eighty-six." The Marchesa displayed a liberal and generous nature. She blamed herself for being conventional, "I would never have dreamt of doing anything to upset the monarchy. That's why I knew our romance would never last. In that way I was never fair to him. My attitudes were just as bad as those of the Palace . . . When I heard he had abdicated to marry the Duchess—I really admired him. It was very brave of him." She wouldn't talk about the Duchess except to say she had made the duke "very nasty. He never used to be nasty. But now I hear all these stories that he has become so mean with money—that he never tips his servants. He didn't used to be like that. She must have made him like that." Blackwood "wondered if she had taken in that the Duke was dead."

The only person in England sufficiently concerned about the Duchess to plan to go and see her was the Duchess of Marlborough. "Then at the very last moment she canceled her flight. She told me that she had a cold and she had to restring her pearls." And the only person who thought the Duchess was probably quite all right was cheery Lady Tomkins, the wife of another former British ambassador to France. "Suzanne Blum is rather a splendid old girl," she said, after describing her as "not the sort of woman one could have as a friend." She thought that if it hadn't been for Maître Blum, after the Duke's death the other royals would have pounced on the treasures he had given his wife. Especially Lord Mountbatten.

And this is the big question, the crux of the book, the mystery waiting to be unraveled by the detective. Was Maître Blum exploiting the Duchess or was she protecting her? Blackwood dismisses both these obvious possibilities and decides instead that "the necrophiliac lawyer" was in love with her client and wanted to keep her alive at any cost, even when it would be kinder to let her die. If she was selling off the Duchess's valuable possessions, it was to pay the doctors. Maître Blum was ecstatic about the Duchess's appearance: she "still had the most fantastic body. You ought to see it. The skin on her body is perfect. It doesn't have a line. She has the lovely, soft body of a young girl." This clearly wasn't true any more than Blum's assertion that the Duchess had always been exceptionally kind, charitable, cultured, and dignified, that she did not sleep with the Duke until they were married, after which they led a secluded life, reading good books, shunning nightclubs, and only occasionally taking a minuscule drink when politeness demanded it.

Some Spanish paparazzi managed to photograph the Duch-

ess with a longrange lens when she was being lifted by a nurse: her body was shrunken and her face "looked a little like a Chinese mandarin, but more like a dead monkey." A friend who had threatened his way through Maître Blum's barriers a few years before reported, "The Duchess had shrunk to half her original size and she seemed to be unconscious. She was lying in bed looking like a tiny prune. She had turned completely black." Blackwood stood outside the Duchess's house. The gold-spiked gates were locked, the windows shuttered all except one. "It was disquieting to picture Maître Blum . . . creeping up the stairs to the Duchess's bedroom, and pulling down the poor woman's sheets in order to gaze at her." Maybe it is as a small token revenge on behalf of the poor woman that Blackwood constantly refers to the "brown flowers" of age on her lawyer's hands and arms.

Like all respectable witches, Maître Blum has a familiar. Hers is not an owl or a cat, but a young Ulsterman called Michael Bloch who wrote to her when he was doing research for a book on Sibyl Colefax. He became her law pupil and moved in with her and her second husband—a retired general who dies during the period of Blackwood's interviews. His widow arranges a spectacular funeral, but otherwise his death does not seem to affect her, except that her wardrobe changes from *comme il faut* beige to deepest *comme il faut* black. Michael Bloch, on the other hand, habitually wears a red-and-white-striped cricket blazer with flowers in the buttonhole. She bawls him out and he fawns on her; he calls her "mon Maître" and—absurdly—"My Master," when speaking English with Blackwood. He appears terrified of his Master, but once he is indiscreet enough to let slip that her relationship with the Duchess is "very special . . . of a romantic nature . . ."

Naturally Lord Snowdon was not permitted to photograph the prune Duchess, nor was Blackwood allowed to interview her. So she decided to write a profile of Maître Blum instead. Maître Blum refused, abusively, as usual. *The Sunday Times* tried bribery: they offered her a photo session of her very own with Lord Snowdon. She was beside herself with excitement and joy. Her snobbery, especially about royalty, had always been out of control; in Blackwood's opinion it was the fount of her passion for the Duchess. She chose to regard her own interview as a sacrifice made for the sake of her idol, but of course she censored it. The *Sunday Times* profile was bland compared to this book, which could not be published until after Maître Blum's death last year.

Two years after her interview, Maître Blum announced in the press that the Duchess had made a miraculous recovery and it was now a problem how to amuse her. Maître Blum said that the Duchess was "sitting up and was listening to Cole Porter." There were rumors that the Duke's collection of Sèvres snuffboxes had been offered for sale. A detective told Blackwood that the Neuilly house was so well protected that only a helicopter raid could establish what was going on there, and "that would be against the law and therefore very expensive." He wondered whether the Duchess might not be dead. Suppressing deaths was also illegal, but it was sometimes done, just the same: "Usually it was because there were trusts involved." A doctor from the American Hospital said that when the Duchess had been admitted eight months before "her condition had been so pitiable it had upset the nurses."

When Blackwood was next in Paris, she rang the bell by the spiked gate. The butler turned her away on the intercom. At her second attempt he let her in because she was able to say that she was the niece of one of the Duchess's friends and was bringing flowers from her. The garden was neglected, the house pitch dark, the silence unearthly. It was impossible to believe that nurses or anyone could be in it.

That is the spine-chilling, and at the same time affecting, end to both the Gothic tale and the detective story. They are interspersed with ruminative passages; what would Maître Blum have felt if she had been invited to accompany the Duchess to the Duke's funeral at Frogmore? Not a very rewarding speculation, but an opportunity for a riveting step-by-step account of the event, at which the Duchess was already showing pathetic signs of senility. There is an attempt to see parallels in the lots of the Duchess and her lawyer. Both were brought up in genteel poverty and taught to regard marriage as the only way out. Suzanne Blum fought her way to a career. Wallis Warfield didn't. So what? An opportunity for a mildly feminist lament on the fate of women in their generation. But being déclassée in Baltimore and marrying a king, and being the child of an Alsatian Jewish grocer in Niort and becoming a lawyer are not really comparable destinies. Blackwood sees a symbiotic relationship between the Duchess and her lawyer which made them both look Oriental. But since she tells us they both had face-lifts, that idea doesn't really work either.

More to the point are biographies of the Duke and Duchess that fill in the background. They have never been told with more wit and deadpan wickedness, and if there are no new revelations about major facts, there are previously unpublished and unpublishable horror stories about the behavior of the ducal couple and their friends. They make one "gasp and stretch one's eyes" in pleasurable disapproval and dismay.

Michael Kimmelman (essay date 2 April 1995)

SOURCE: "Titled Bohemian: Caroline Blackwood," in *The New York Times Magazine,* April 2, 1995, pp. 32, 34-5.

[*In the following essay, Kimmelman surveys Blackwood's life and literary career.*]

When Lady Caroline Blackwood, the Irish writer and Guinness heiress, was living in Paris in the early 1950's, she and her first husband, the painter Lucian Freud, were invited to visit Picasso.

"Picasso got one of his followers to ask Lucian if he would like to see Picasso's paintings," Blackwood says. "Of course, Lucian said yes. Meanwhile Picasso asked me if I wanted to see his doves: he had this spiral iron staircase leading to the roof, and off we go, winding round and round to the top, until we reached these doves in cages and all around us was the best view of Paris, the best. Whereupon immediately, standing on this tiny, tiny space, way above the city, Picasso does a complete plunge at me. All I felt was fear. I kept saying, 'Go down the stairs, go down.' He said, 'No, no, we are together above the roofs of Paris.' It was so absurd, and to me Picasso was just as old as the hills, an old letch, genius or no.

"I wonder," Blackwood pauses to ask, "what we were supposed to have done if I accepted? There was no space to make love with all those doves. And think how many other people he had up there. Did they go through with it? And technically, *how* did they go through with it? And with the husband downstairs?"

She then adds a coda: "Lucian got a call out of nowhere from a mistress of Picasso's who asked him if he could come round and paint her. She wanted to make Picasso jealous. Lucian very politely said maybe he could paint her portrait later, but not now because he happened to be in the midst of doing his wife's portrait."

That picture, Blackwood says, turned out to be Freud's "Girl in Bed." Years later, in 1977, it played a curious part in the death of the poet Robert Lowell, another of Lady Caroline's husbands. Their marriage was in tatters when, as the story goes, he left her in Ireland and returned to the United States. After Lowell's taxi arrived at his apartment on West 67th Street, the driver found him slumped over. A doorman summoned Elizabeth Hardwick, the writer and editor whom Lowell had left to marry Blackwood; she happened to live in the same building. Hardwick opened the taxi door—only to be confronted with her ex-husband's corpse. He was holding "Girl in Bed."

With its macabre humor, the Lowell story is one Blackwood might have written if she hadn't lived through it. "I think it's partly Irish," Blackwood says over lunch at Coco Pazzo, an elegant restaurant on the East Side of Manhattan. "Irish people are very funny but have this tragic sense.

"As Cal wrote," she continues, referring to Lowell, "if there's light at the end of the tunnel, it's the light of the oncoming train. He was a humorous poet, you know, though people don't ever say that about him. He also wrote that in the end, every hypochondriac is his own prophet, which is very funny, don't you think?"

Blackwood is a delicate woman of 63, slightly stooped yet graceful, with a husky, smoker's voice. She is dressed in a loose-fitting black pants suit, the sort of unbourgeois outfit that pegs her immediately as an upperclass bohemian. Her extraordinary eyes—big opalescent pools, which Freud made into giant spheres in his hypnotic portraits—are the principal signs of the beauty she was in her youth. Her looks are striking but weatherbeaten.

It's not just that Blackwood likes to drink. She has also endured a series of Job-like catastrophes over the years: the death of her second husband, the American composer and pianist Israel Citkowitz; Lowell's crippling manic depression and early death; the death from AIDS of her brother, Sheridan, to whom she was very close; the death of her eldest daughter, Natalya, after a drug overdose, and her own bout with cervical cancer, for which she had an operation that left her in constant pain.

Though on one level she thrives on tragedy—is even defined by it—Blackwood can't abide maudlin sentiments; bringing up these episodes with her elicits an awkward silence. At first during lunch she gives only clipped responses to questions or just nods in agreement. She orders one vodka after another, tonic on the side. She is more comfortable discussing her new book, *The Last of the Duchess*. But still she's cautious.

She also greets with silence a question about her flamboyant socialite mother, Maureen, the Marchioness of Dufferin and Ava. When Maureen was young she reportedly once gave Sir Oswald Mosley, the English fascist, a black eye after he made a pass at her in Antibes. In recent years, though vastly rich, she has complained that her children haven't helped support her and the several houses she lives in. The Picasso biographer John Richardson recalls that Maureen's son, Sheridan, used to bemoan having to help pay for her villa in Sardinia, which he nicknamed the Villa Costalota. Lately, Blackwood, her sister and sister-in-law have wrangled with Maureen over the disposition of $24 million in Guinness inheritance money. The dispute, ultimately settled in Maureen's favor, underscores the nearly nonexistent relationship between Caroline and her mother, a topic Caroline prefers not to discuss.

Gradually, though, as she relaxes, Blackwood emerges as a strangely dramatic woman: intense and vulnerable, with quirky affections like abbreviating words (Champagne becoming "champ"), a dark, razorsharp sense of humor and an offbeat sensibility.

Geordie Greig the New York correspondent for The Sunday Times of London and a family friend, gives an apt description of her: "When she calls on the phone she'll say 'Hiiii,

it's Carrr-oline,' and there's always that enigmatic, Eartha Kitt-like purr. But in conversation she's unpredictable. Caroline's physical demeanor is so unforceful that the force of her words, which can be lethally accurate, is made doubly strong. She has an artist's sensibility to shift through any social niceties and get straight to the point. Even with her house on Long Island nothing follows the rules. Lunch might be a huge feast of lobsters and champagne, or her fridge may be completely out of food."

Over the years, Blackwood has moved easily among several worlds: from the insular, horsy Anglo-Irish upper classes to the hard-drinking smart set of postwar England, to the liberal intelligentsia of New York City in the 1960's and 70's. She has lived in the United States for much of the last 35 years. Nowadays, she's often with her children, who also live here. Her son, Sheridan Lowell, 23, works for a small publishing firm in Manhattan. Her youngest daughter, Ivana Lowell (she has taken her stepfather's name) is 28; she works for the publishing arm of the media company Miramax and has become a lively presence in New York society since moving from London a few years ago. Another daughter, Evgenia Citkowitz, 30, is a screenwriter in Los Angeles married to the English actor Julian Sands.

Blackwood spends many mornings in her kitchen writing longhand. A broken back she suffered when she was young has made it impossible for her to type. She has published nine books that have been richly admired in Britain, where she is best known. They include collections of short stories and essays of stringent, sly, entirely anticonformist social criticism. Her novels are stylish, remorseless, frightening and wickedly funny. They can sometimes remind you a little of Beckett, except that Blackwood's nihilistic sensibility is more gothic than his: it's Beckett crossed with Bram Stoker.

The Last of the Duchess is her mesmeric account of a vain attempt to visit the ailing Duchess of Windsor in 1980 and of Blackwood's encounters with the Duchess's ruthless and highly powerful octogenarian lawyer, Maître Suzanne Blum, a woman obsessed with her client to the point of erotic fantasy. Blum was the Cerberus at the Duchess's door, blocking even old friends from contacting her, according to Blackwood. Was the sick Duchess tortured by being kept alive, Blackwood wondered, or might she even be dead? Was Blum only saying she was alive so that she could sell the royal jewels and claim the money as her legal fee?

How much of the book is Irish blarney? After all, the story of Blum, like so many of the stories Blackwood tells, is so bizarre it sounds like fiction. In a sense, though, that's Blackwood's point. She writes as she speaks, with a dramatic flair that can seduce you even as you wonder how precise she is. (Freud, for instance, recalls the Picasso incident very differently.) "You can't really get the truth about anybody from an interview," Blackwood says. "It's all fiction in a way."

She portrays herself in her books as a wide-eyed innocent, astonished by the horrors around her. In person, though, she has a disconcerting habit of staring at you, coolly sizing you up while she picks demurely at her meal. You can see how she could drive Maître Blum mad.

"If it's berserk behavior I like it as a subject," Blackwood says. "If you write about bland people there's no story, is there? I hated Blum and was really scared of her," Blackwood recalls, "but she thought I was a complete idiot because I acted the dumb journalist with her a bit. She wouldn't even have seen me if I didn't have a title. On the other hand she wouldn't have been so rude if I were a crowned head."

Her full name is Lady Caroline Hamilton Temple Blackwood: she's a descendant on her father's side of the great 18th-century dramatist and wit Richard Brinsley Sheridan. She is a Guinness on her mother's side. (She says she finds stout undrinkable.)

"Brewers or bankers, aristocrats or plutocrats, the Guinnesses are apt to be a law unto themselves," John Richardson says. "This Anglo-Irish dynasty is famously cultivated, brilliant, profligate, witty and beguiling. Caution and abstemiousness are not their forte. Caroline upholds her family's reputation for courage, eccentricity and subversive humor. She most certainly does not hold with the ultraconservative views of some of her cousins."

She grew up in the ancestral stone mansion called Clandeboye in County Down in Northern Ireland. "My great-grandfather built a wing every time he had another child," Blackwood says. "You didn't build a room then, you built a wing. It was terribly rundown when I was a child, the typical joke Irish house with all the pails to catch dripping water all over the place."

Her great-grandfather, Lord Dufferin, was an eminent Victorian, rumored to have been Disraeli's illegitimate son. "I think he was," says Blackwood, mischievously. "Why would a Scottish landowner have a son who looked like Disraeli? He once got up in the House of Lords and denied that he was Disraeli's son, because it was terrible for his mother's honor, but that sort of implies that he was, doesn't it?"

Queen Victoria made him Victory of India, where he used to sit on his throne, fanned by peacock feathers, while processions of rajahs paid him homage. At Clandeboye he built a stone shrine to his mother, an immense architectural folly called Helen's Tower that inspired poems by Browning, Kipling and Tennyson. "Kipling loved my great-grandfather

and wrote lots of very bad poems to him," Blackwood says. "He had a fatal effect on poets. I mean, the Tennyson poem is a jingle that goes on and on." She discovered not long ago that Helen's Tower inspired a World War I memorial in France to Irish soldiers. "I mean, Helen's Tower is really odd, isn't it? Victorians thought it was fine someone building a tower to his mother while she was alive, but can you imagine doing it now, in post-Freudian times?"

Blackwood's father, Basil, the Marquess of Dufferin and Ava, was a close friend of Evelyn Waugh and part of the glittering circle he recalled in *Brideshead Revisited*. When the Marquess was killed in 1943 by the Japanese in the jungle in Burma, he was 35. Blackwood was 12 at the time and has only dim memories of her father.

Like other women of her class she skipped college; instead she went to work for Claud Cockburn, an influential left-wing journalist who wrote for, among others, *The Times Literary Supplement*. "Claud was a reviewer for *TLS* and I read books for him, because in those days the reviews were unsigned," Blackwood says. "It was really corrupt but I was extremely diligent."

She recalls meeting Freud around then, at a party memorable for the fact that the painter Francis Bacon caused a row when he hooted down Princess Margaret, who had just started singing "Let's Do It." Blackwood becomes testy when asked if a reference to her in a recent book as Margaret's lady-in-waiting is true. "That's a lie and I'll sue you if you say it," she says, only half kidding and appalled that anyone could imagine her in such a role.

She changes the subject. "Lucian was fantastic, very brilliant, incredibly beautiful, though not in a movie-star way," she says. "I remember he was very mannered, he wore these long side whiskers, which nobody else had then. And he wore funny trousers, deliberately. He wanted to stand out in a crowd, and he did."

When Freud and Blackwood returned to London from Paris, they settled into the circle that included Bacon, Cyril Connolly and the other artists and writers who gathered nightly at the fabled Gargoyle and Colony Clubs. "As a concept the Gargoyle was brilliant," Blackwood states. "O.K., everyone there would be a bit drunk. But you could wander in any night and find the cleverest people in England. After the war it was completely normal for intellectuals to knock each other down if someone had written a bad review or taken someone's girl. Then they always sent flowers the next day."

Gradually her marriage to Freud crumbled. When she left him, he was devastated. Blackwood says only that "Lucian and I couldn't be married, not endlessly. We were both too restless."

She fled to Los Angeles, installed herself at the Chateau Marmont and got a tiny part in the television series "Have Gun Will Travel." But she hated the city. The best thing to come out of it was that Stephen Spender asked her to do an article for *Encounter* magazine about California beatniks. It turned out to be a sendup that launched her writing career. Beatnik culture, she wrote, "has all the trappings of the subversive, the meeting in the darkened cellar, the conspiratorial whisper behind the candle in the Chianti bottle, the nihilistic mutter, without the mildest element of subversion."

Not long after Blackwood moved from Los Angeles to New York she met Israel Citkowitz, a former student of Aaron Copland, some 20 years her senior. They married. Today Blackwood speaks warmly but vaguely about Citkowitz. She describes him as "gorgeous and brilliant, which wasn't a bad combination." But they separated after a few years and she became involved with Robert Silvers, the founding editor of *The New York Review of Books*. Through Silvers she met Lowell.

Citkowitz and she remained friendly until he died, and he sometimes lived in the London house she shared with Lowell in the 1970's, helping her to care for the children during Lowell's bouts of madness. Lowell would write a poem to Citkowitz, lines of which Blackwood used as an epitaph on Citkowitz's grave. Her three daughters were born while she was still married to him. She had a son, Sheridan, by Lowell in 1971.

In 1972 she and Lowell flew to Santo Domingo for a joint divorce-marriage. "Nobody could understand the service because it was all in Spanish," she remembers. "It was in a hut, with chickens coming in and out. You'd move to one hut and they'd say you're divorced. Then to another hut where they'd say you're married. All the time there was lots of loud typing. So romantic."

It pains Blackwood that her marriage with Lowell is often described solely in terms of his breakup with Hardwick and illness. She recalls periods at Milgate, their house in Kent, as idyllic. But she acknowledges that Lowell's episodes of manic depression became increasingly unmanageable.

"I wanted Israel to be in the house because I couldn't deal with it alone," she explains. "Not that Cal would have hurt the children, he wasn't murderous. But I had to watch him all day and all night because a manic never sleeps." One day she found him hacking holes in the wall with a carving knife. He told her he was looking for Etruscan treasures. "It was a horrible affliction to not know when your mind was suddenly going to go—particularly when you had got this huge mind."

Then Lowell died; then Natalya. Through it all, Blackwood managed to turn out a remarkable string of books. One of them, *On the Perimeter*, was a report about the women who had camped for years in the mud at Greenham Common in England to protest the American nuclear missile base there. *The Stepdaughter* was a short epistolary novel about an abusive woman abandoned by her husband and left with his hideous daughter. Another novel, *The Fate of Mary Rose*, is a chilling tale about an increasingly deranged mother's fatal obsession with her daughter's safety.

Blackwood even wrote a lighthearted cookbook with her friend the English novelist Anna Haycraft (who wrote under the name of Alice Thomas Ellis) that featured celebrity recipes. Blackwood asked Francis Bacon for a recipe. "I doubt anybody had ever asked him for one before. But he was a fantastic cook, and he had this very smart recipe for mayonnaise. Then it turned out that he was such a perfectionist that he kept holding up the publication to make revisions. Eventually Anna called in a panic, saying she'd forgotten to put in Francis's very last revision before the book went to press. 'It had less to do with salt and more to do with vinegar,' she said. Francis brought 100 copies of the book anyway."

In 1980, Blackwood began work on *The Last of the Duchess*. "It was pathetic Blum being so old and in love with the Duchess," Blackwood muses. "What a stupid thing to do. But of course the Duchess was ridiculous, too. A more noble figure than she wouldn't have let this lawyer take over her life." The paradox, as Blackwood implies in the book, is that the socialite Duchess spent her last days in solitary confinement, and—considering the Windsors' connection to Hitler—that her jailer was a Jew.

Writing kept Blackwood going through one calamity after another—until the cancer a few years ago. "I really don't like talking about it," she says, after a long pause. "I just kept on trying to do what I do, no matter what life did to me. But after the cancer I became so used to the idea that I would be dead that I had reconciled myself to the idea of not writing anymore. Once you've accepted you're dead, why write?

"It took me a long time to get back to writing. For a while I didn't have any ideas, none." She smiles. "But now I try and write all morning. It may be so awful that I put my pencil through the whole thing and start over the next day. But at least I've got plenty of ideas."

Laurie Stone (review date 25 June 1995)

SOURCE: "Gothic Arch," in *Village Voice*, Vol. 30, June 25, 1995, p. 47.

[*Below, Stone criticizes Blackwood's plot and character development in* Corrigan.]

Caroline Blackwood tends to see human relationships as sick jokes. Her novels are variations on *The Defiant Ones,* full of contrary types unhappily shackled together: a philandering rogue and his pathologically passive wife; a secretly raging woman and her belligerent, obese stepdaughter; a watchful 14-year-old and her rich, miserly great-grandmother, a gargoyle who flourishes the best silver for a dinner of canned spaghetti. Along with a number of other British writers—Beryl Bainbridge, Bernice Rubens, and Emma Tennant come to mind—Blackwood reaps startling insights by telling gothic stories (about murders, closeted skeletons, false identities) using a psychologically probing voice.

The technique is in place in **Corrigan**, her latest novel. Devina Blunt, the Colonel's widow, is wasting to a frizzle of grief in a remote Wiltshire village. Every day, she walks to the cemetery and places expensive bouquets from a Salisbury florist on her husband's grave. In the past, Devina grew her own flowers and whipped things up to eat; now she subsists on air. She's never been able to stomach the cooking of her housekeeper, Mrs. Murphy, a woman who considers pan grease sauce for any dish. Into this forlorn life, Corrigan hurtles his handsome, wheelchair-bound 35-year-old body. He's collecting contributions for a hospital, he says, in his high-flown, hysterical style, and within minutes, Devina is offering him the Colonel's best claret. Within weeks, he's ensconced in her pretty period house, and the two are sharing afternoon champagne and goose liver pâté. Within months, Devina has bought the surrounding farmland, started trucking produce to the hospital, purchased warehouses full of antique furniture, begun to paint, had a London gallery show, and sold all her work.

Meanwhile, Devina's daughter, Nadine, discovers that she loathes her journalist husband, madly envies her mother, and finds savage ill will toward Corrigan. All is wittily confessed to best-friend Sabrina, a luminous model with a predilection for fragile men. "If you can't bear to speak to someone on the telephone . . . I don't really see that you can start asking them for money," Nadine says, explaining why she can't solicit aid from Devina. Contemplating her smug husband, she wonders whether his tallness is the cause of his "lack of normal human response." She suspects he doesn't have "a sufficient supply of blood in his long body for the necessary amount to reach his brain." Sabrina's current companion is Coco, an Algerian homosexual who claims to be Italian. Visiting him in the hospital after one of his suicide attempts, she finds him woefully transformed: "His whole sexuality seemed to have been dried out along with the drugs to which he'd been addicted. . . . She felt that he had all the limpness of the despondent-looking ducks that she'd seen hanging upside-down in the windows of cheap Chinese restaurants."

Alas, such stylish observations are in far shorter supply here than in Blackwood's previous books. For all the outlandish-ness of the Wiltshire ménage and the rueful satire of London neurotics, this novel registers as a dutifully completed exercise. Most of the chapters are devoted to Devina, Corrigan, and Mrs. Murphy—Dickensian types composed entirely of quirks and pet phrases. They soon become tiresome; Devina's change is described rather than dramatized, and the plot isn't surprising either. The intended "mystery" of Corrigan is solvable in the first pages. Blackwood devised these cartoons, it seems, only to lose interest in them for having no inner lives.

Ambivalent Nadine is the most realized character, but the book feels lopsided with her as the emotional center, because she's relatively peripheral. There's another problem too: Nadine is one of Blackwood's inert, seething doormats, a creature she's limned many times. The author tries to evoke our sympathy by making Nadine's husband and twin sons selfish monsters, but the tactic backfires—Nadine seems responsible for choosing and raising despicable males. She pities herself with too much pleasure for us to care about her fate. Sabrina, alone, is both sufficiently knowing and knowable to arouse interest—but she's an even more marginal character than Nadine. This is a sign, if ever there was one, of a writer's fatigue with her creation—an exhaustion, I hope, which means that Blackwood is gathering energy for a book that will pique her imagination.

Zoë Heller (review date 20 July 1995)

SOURCE: "The Lady Vanishes," in *London Review of Books,* Vol. 17, No. 14, July 20, 1995, p. 18.

[*In the following review, Heller contends that Blackwood's account of Simpson's life in* The Last of the Duchess *relies too heavily on speculation and contributes little to her subject's story.*]

'As a siren Wallis Windsor had been a figure who had changed historical events more drastically than any other woman in human history.' If one could only believe that the Duchess of Windsor *had* changed historical events more drastically than Mary Queen of Scots, or Joan of Arc, or even Margaret Thatcher, then perhaps Caroline Blackwood's recycled revelations about the Duchess—her expertise at fellatio, her 22 carat gold bath-tub at Cap d'Antibes, the amusing tricks that her homosexual lover, the Woolworth heir Jimmy Donahue, liked to perform with his penis at dinner parties—might seem quite, you know, *important.* The disappointing alternative is that **The Last of the Duchess** is just what it appears: a book of snobby royal tittle-tattle on which Blackwood is attempting, rather late in the day, to confer some gravitas. British newspapers do much the same thing, when they affect concern about the 'constitutional implications' of the Prince of Wales's desire to be a tampon.

In 1980, Caroline Blackwood was approached by Francis Wyndham, one of the editors of the *Sunday Times* magazine, to accompany Lord Snowden on a trip to photograph the 84-year-old Duchess of Windsor, now an invalid recluse, holed up in a house in Paris. Snowden would take pictures and Blackwood would record the historic encounter between the two royal divorcees. As it turned out, Snowden's request for an audience was refused by the Duchess's French lawyer, another 84-year-old woman named Maître Blum. So Wyndham proposed that Blackwood interview the lawyer instead.

For several years, Blum had not only held the Duchess's power of attorney but had acted as her chief spokesperson and protector. Blackwood ended up going three times to see Blum in Paris and these awkward, frightening encounters form the basis of her book. Blum, who appears to have worshipped her client, insisted on upholding a variety of manifest untruths about the Duchess: that she and the Duke had not had sex before they were married, that she rarely drank alcohol, that she was a dedicated intellectual, and so on. Blum also promised to kill Blackwood if she did not reproduce these lies in her article. 'I suddenly remembered that Maître Blum had tangled with Lord Mountbatten,' Blackwood writes. 'With a chill, I remembered what had happened to him. She finally had compounded all the other injuries she had inflicted upon me by making a terrorist threat on my life.'

Interviews are a very specific and bizarre form of interaction. Any temporary discomfort that an interview subject may occasion by being ill-mannered, belligerent—or, as in this case, authentically tonto—tends to be cancelled out for the interviewer by the felicitous prospect of 'good copy'. In fact, behaviour that would be embarrassing or disastrous in any other form of human encounter is usually a source of secret elation to the journalist. (Blackwood doesn't own up to this sort of professional delight in Blum's awfulness, but we get a strong sense of it, in the relish with which she recounts the old lady's 'terrorist threat'.) Still, there is a limit to the amusement value of even the most dramatic battiness, and the fact remains that Blum, as Blackwood's star witness, is next to useless as a source of reliable information. Blackwood responds to this problem in two ways. After her second interview, she decides that in order to write 'any form of sane article on the Duchess of Windsor', she will have to seek out more of the Duchess's contemporaries, to obtain reliable estimations of the Duchess's personality. Her trawl through the nursing homes and sick-beds of various, ancient, aristocratic ladies yields some fascinating fragments of oral history and some wonderfully sad vignettes of old age.

Her other, more ill-advised response to her lack of hard facts, is to fill in the holes with speculation and gossip. She 'hears' that the Duchess is said to have turned black as a prune. It was always 'said' that the Duchess picked up her most excit-ing sexual skills while travelling in the Orient. These snippets she blithely records as if her duty as journalist did not extend beyond reproducing hearsay. About Maître Blum, her surmise grows even wilder. She entertains an extended reverie on how Blum might have felt if she had attended the Duke of Windsor's funeral. (She didn't.) She indulges an elaborate flight of fancy about what funeral arrangements Blum might be planning for the Duchess. (She never actually enquires.) She imagines Blum physically attacking her. 'She was seething with such rage that there seemed a danger she suddenly might be unable to control it, that she might spring at me like an uncontrollable beast and claw me with her yellow nails.' (She didn't.) Curious as to how the lawyer fills her days, Blackwood considers the possibility that one of her daily duties is to pick out nightdresses for the invalid Duchess. 'She must know all about the Duchess's old passion for exquisite lingerie and would therefore take this duty very seriously. It was not inconceivable that she bought her client some new and perfect nightdress nearly every other day.' (Well not inconceivable, but pretty unlikely all the same.) 'If she took hours choosing the Duchess's bedtime attire,' she continues, 'and her brown-speckled hands lovingly, but critically, fingered hundreds of silk and satin and broderie anglaise items of nightwear, this activity would eat into her working day.' We have entered into an uncomfortable place, here. It is not inconceivable that Blum practises satanic rituals at the Duchess's bedside, but it seems a little unfair to elaborate on the fantasy without any supporting evidence.

One of Blackwood's justifications for all this supposing and conceiving is how 'terrified' and 'passive' the old lawyer makes her feel. 'There were questions to be asked,' she writes of her first encounter with Blum, 'but she had made me too tired to ask them. And because she had worn me down and sapped my courage, I retaliated by allowing my mind to wander off into realms of purest speculation where Maître Blum could neither bring lawsuits nor injunctions for all my queries remained unvoiced.' This is rather like a coal-miner complaining that he doesn't like working in confined, dark spaces. If Blackwood is so cowed and exhausted by hostile interviews, the reader may be forgiven for asking why she doesn't find herself another job.

On two separate occasions, Blackwood mentions the 'ominous' way that Blum pronounces 'hate' without an 'h'. Her references to the brown freckles of old age on Blum's hands and arms are countless. All this is done with the apparent intention of making us share her vehement dislike of Blum, but the exuberant animosity has the perverse effect of encouraging rather protective feelings towards the beleaguered old lady. The Freudian irony at the heart of this book is that Blackwood commits exactly those crimes of which she accuses her subject—recklessly projecting the lurid stuff of her own fantasies, and showing herself, time and again, indifferent to the evidence of a more mundane reality. Before

Blackwood meets Blum, she phones her to make an appointment and Blum picks up the phone herself. 'I was appalled,' Blackwood writes. 'When Stalin in his last years was sealed away, dangerous and brooding in the Kremlin, no stranger could have put through a call and reached him personally. It therefore shocked me that the fierce and despotic Maître Blum, whom I'd begun to see as equally unapproachable, should turn out to be so unbecomingly accessible.' It may strike the reader that Blackwood has got a lot of mileage out of a negative here. Her first contact with Blum suggests that she is *not,* after all, like the dangerous and brooding Stalin, but Blackwood, having grown attached to her imagining, contrives to make the melodramatic point anyway.

One of Blackwood's primary contentions is that Blum's passionate possessiveness of the Duchess is born of some sinister, erotic attachment. She bases this belief on the fact that at one point, Blum tells her she has a relationship 'de chaleur' with the Duchess (Blackwood translates the phrase literally, as a relationship 'of heat') and that on another occasion, Blum's assistant, a young Anglo-Irishman called Michael Bloch, describes the connection between the two women as being 'of a romantic nature'. Blum is married to an ailing old French general, but Blackwood is not convinced of her heterosexual credentials. 'It was impossible to visualise her lying throbbing with unabashed passion and pleasure in the arms of her husband, the general. Her whole personality was too essentially unyielding. It seemed almost obscene to try to picture her in the nude let alone in some subjugated erotic position . . . it was always feasible that she . . . had insisted on maintaining a nun-like sexual abstinence in all the years that had followed her own marriage to General Spillman . . . It was conceivable that the pains of his constant frustration had slowly sapped all his *joie de vivre* and been instrumental in his current decline.' At this juncture, a reader may also consider it possible/feasible/conceivable that Blackwood's vulgar speculations about the sexual proclivities of 84-year-old Blum denote a quite irrational enmity.

Rather late on in the book, we come across this: 'The Duchess created by Maître Blum was a Jewish Duchess in the sense that, despite her unenviable current condition, she'd been made the very embodiment of her lawyer's superego. It was unlikely there had ever been a Duchess like her.' I don't wish to sound paranoid here, so let me just say, these strike me as a puzzling couple of sentences. Blackwood makes explicit reference to Maître Blum's Jewishness on only one other occasion, when she mentions how 'ironic' it is that Diana Mosley, who 'bravely' endured war-time imprisonment for her Nazi sympathies, should, in old age, be so intimidated by an old Jewish lawyer. Blum's Jewishness clearly has a significance for Blackwood, but the manners or qualities that it is supposed to stand for are never explained. One longs to know what aspects of Blum's projected superego are recognisably semitic and how a Jewish Duchess is so vividly

and amusingly unlike any other Duchess. Does she exclaim 'Oy vey!' when agitated? Are there gefilte fish stains on her twin-set? We receive a clue, a little later on, when Blackwood describes Blum ransoming off the rights to a photograph of the Duchess for £400. 'The style with which the Duchess of Windsor had lived her strange life might not have always been commendable,' Blackwood writes, 'but at least it always had largesse . . . Now at the end of her life it seemed humiliating for the helpless Duchess that Maître Blum with her petit bourgeois greed should be trying to extort piddling little sums like £400 on her behalf.'

In other words, though Wallis Windsor may have had humble, American origins, though she may have been ugly and whoreish and had a rather prole tendency to show off her wealth—parading through war-ravaged Europe with 222 suitcases was not nice—at least, damn it, she had style. European royalty has had a long tradition of absorbing courtesans and colonials and all sorts of ambitious riff-raff into the regal mix, but that flexibility stops short of tolerating petit bourgeois Jews. Looking through Maître Blum's scrapbook, Blackwood comes across a newspaper photograph of the jumped-up lawyer standing next to Queen Elizabeth at a public function. She can hardly contain her outrage and repulsion. 'Maître Blum must have tenaciously elbowed through hundreds of guests at the soirée in order to get as close to the Queen of England as she had managed. She had got herself so close that she had made herself almost invisible for her body had blended into the Queen's fur. And Queen Elizabeth seemed totally unaware that Maître Blum was so near to her, that the Duchess of Windsor's lawyer was gazing up at her with slobbering love and wonder.'

Blackwood, who, lest we forget, has her own title—she is Lady Caroline Blackwood—does not need to creep and elbow to gain access to the monarch. When she wants to put a word in to Queenie—warning her, like the good, loyal subject that she is, that Blum is selling off the royal Sèvres snuff-boxes—she simply telephones Lord Mountbatten's daughter with whom she is on chummy terms, and the message is passed on. Meanwhile, the article that she ends up writing for the *Sunday Times* contains none of the nastiness that she will later spill out in this book, once Blum is safely dead. By her own admission, the piece she composes about the Duchess and her lawyer in 1980 is 'bland and praising to the point of sycophancy'. Petty minds may wish to think of this as cowardice, or even bad journalism, but Blackwood seems to know better: judicious grovelling is, after all, a Lady's prerogative.

Michael Kimmelman (obituary date 15 February 1996)

SOURCE: "Lady Caroline Blackwood, Wry Novelist, Is Dead at 64," in *The New York Times,* February 15, 1996, p. B16.

[In the obituary below, Kimmelman provides an overview of Blackwood's life and career.]

Lady Caroline Blackwood, a writer of wry, macabre novels and essays, and a beguiling Anglo-Irish aristocrat who married the painter Lucian Freud and the poet Robert Lowell, died yesterday in the Mayfair Hotel in Manhattan, where she stayed the last few weeks while she was ill. She was 64.

The cause was cancer, said her daughter Ivana Lowell.

She published nine books and was best known and much admired in Britain. Among her works was **The Stepdaughter**, a short epistolary novel about an abusive woman abandoned by her husband and left with his hideous daughter. Another novel, **The Fate of Mary Rose**, was about an increasingly deranged mother's fatal obsession with her daughter's safety.

Her most recent book, **The Last of the Duchess**, was an eccentric, Kafkaesque account of her vain attempt to visit the ailing Duchess of Windsor. It revolved mostly around the Duchess's powerful lawyer, Suzanne Blum, portrayed in the book as obsessed with her client to the point of erotic fantasy.

British critics noted the "brilliant irony" and "rather brilliant bitchiness" of her writing, comparing it with the work of Muriel Spark and Iris Murdoch, among others. In her prose and in person, she exhibited a razor-sharp wit and offbeat sensibility. A dramatic woman, delicately built, intense and vulnerable, she was a famous beauty in her youth, and in later years remained striking for her extraordinary eyes, which Mr. Freud made into giant spheres in his hypnotic portraits.

One portrait played a curious role in her life, as she related in an interview last year. During the 1950's, when she and Mr. Freud were living in Paris, "Lucian got a call out of nowhere from a mistress of Picasso's who asked him if he could come round and paint her," she said. "The woman wanted to make Picasso jealous. Lucian very politely said maybe he could paint her portrait later, but not now because he happened to be in the midst of doing his wife's portrait."

That picture, she said, was "Girl in Bed," a work that years later also figured in the death of Robert Lowell, her third husband. Their marriage was in tatters when, the story goes, Lowell left her in Ireland and flew to New York City. When his taxi arrived at his apartment on West 67th Street, the driver found Lowell slumped over. A doorman summoned Elizabeth Hardwick, the writer and editor, whom Lowell had left to marry Lady Caroline; she happened to live in the same apartment house. Ms. Hardwick opened the taxi door to be confronted with her former husband's corpse. He was clutching "Girl in Bed."

Lady Caroline moved among several worlds: from the insular Anglo-Irish upper classes, which she largely rejected for the smart set of postwar England and then for the liberal intelligentsia of New York City in the 1960's and 70's. During much of the last 35 years, she lived in the United States, splitting her time in recent years between an apartment in Manhattan and a house in Sag Harbor, L.I., that once belonged to President Chester A. Arthur.

Lady Caroline Hamilton Temple Blackwood was born in London on July 16, 1931. She was descended on her father's side from the great 18th-century dramatist Richard Brinsley Sheridan and was a Guinness on her mother's side. (She liked to joke that she found stout undrinkable.) She grew up in the ancestral stone mansion, Clandeboye, in County Down in Northern Ireland.

Her great-grandfather, Lord Dufferin, was an eminent Victorian rumored to have been Disraeli's illegitimate son. Queen Victoria made him Viceroy of India, where he used to sit on his throne, fanned by peacock feathers. "Kipling loved my great-grandfather and wrote lots of very bad poems to him," Lady Caroline said. "He had a fatal effect on poets."

Her mother, Maureen, the Marchioness of Dufferin and Ava, is a flamboyant figure in London who, according to one newspaper account, gave a black eye to Sir Oswald Mosley, the English Fascist, after he made a pass at her in Antibes. Her father, Basil, the Marquess, was a friend of Evelyn Waugh and part of the circle described in *Brideshead Revisited*. He was killed in Burma during World War II, when Caroline was 12.

> **British critics noted the "brilliant irony" and "rather brilliant bitchiness" of [Blackwood's] writing, comparing it with the work of Muriel Spark and Iris Murdoch, among others. In her prose and in person, she exhibited a razor-sharp wit and offbeat sensibility.**
>
> **—Michael Kimmelman**

Like other women of her class, she skipped college; she moved to London and worked for Claud Cockburn, the influential left-wing journalist. She recalled meeting Mr. Freud at that time at a party memorable because the painter Francis Bacon caused a row when he hooted down Princess Margaret, who had just started singing "Let's Do it." She and Mr. Freud then became part of the group that included Bacon, Cyril Connolly and the other artists and writers who gathered nightly to drink at the Gargoyle and Colony Clubs.

When her marriage to Mr. Freud ended in 1956, she installed herself at the Chateau Marmont in Los Angeles. She got a tiny part in the television series "Have Gun Will Travel." Stephen Spender asked her to write an article for *Encounter* magazine about California beatniks, and it was a sendup that launched her writing career.

She next moved to New York and married Israel Citkowitz, an American composer and pianist, and a student of Aaron Copland, 20 years her senior. They were divorced in 1972, when she married Lowell, but they remained close.

During the next years she endured a series of Job-like catastrophes: the death of Citkowitz; Lowell's crippling manic depression and early death; the death from AIDS of her brother, Sheridan, to whom she was very close; the death of her eldest daughter, Natalya, after a drug overdose, and her own bout with cervical cancer, for which she had an operation that left her in constant pain.

Throughout, she maintained her dark humor and creatively transformed her experiences into her novels and essays. "I think it's partly Irish," she once explained. "Irish people are very funny but have this tragic sense.

"As Cal wrote," she added, referring to Lowell, "if there's light at the end of the tunnel, it's the light of the oncoming train."

In addition to her daughter Ivana, of Manhattan, she is survived by her mother, of London; a sister, Lady Perdita Blackwood, of Ulster; another daughter, Evgenia Citkowitz of Los Angeles, and a son, Sheridan Lowell of Manhattan.

FURTHER READING

Criticism

Ableman, Paul. "Unthrilling." *Spectator* 246, No. 7965 (7 March 1981): 24.
> Describes the characters in *The Fate of Mary Rose* as believable, if not sufficiently developed, but argues that the novel's conclusion fails to resolve the issues Blackwood raises.

Andrew, Nigel. "A Deal of Nastiness." *Listener* 118, No. 3032 (8 October 1987): 25.
> Praises *In the Pink* as well-written, enjoyable, and balanced.

Barrow, Andrew. "The Sleeping Booty." *Spectator* 274, No. 8699 (1 April 1995): 32-3.
> Argues that *The Last of the Duchess* is a "deceptively simple" story told with unusual wit and black humour.

Carr, Raymond. "Up the Airy Mountain, Down the Rushy Glen. . . ." *Spectator* 259, No. 8308 (10 October 1987): 34-5.
> Commends Blackwood's treatment of fox hunting in *In the Pink* as fair and balanced despite some inaccuracies.

Craig, Patricia. "Domestic Evils." *Times Literary Supplement,* No. 4065 (27 February 1981): 220.
> Praises *The Fate of Mary Rose* as an improvement on Blackwood's previous novels.

Kemp, Peter. "Wounded Children." *Listener* 105, No. 2707 (28 February 1981): 288.
> Discusses Blackwood's style of detached writing about very emotional subjects, particularly wounded children, in *The Fate of Mary Rose.*

Mellors, John. "Ex-leg and Toeprints." *Listener* 111, No. 2841 (19 January 1984): 26.
> Remarks on *Good Night Sweet Ladies* and states that the most memorable of the stories is the least macabre.

Mellors, John. "Ladies' Knights." *Listener* 112, No. 2883 (8 November 1984): 28.
> Argues that Blackwood's character development in *Corrigan* is uneven.

A review of *On the Perimeter,* by Caroline Blackwood. *Publishers Weekly* 228, No. 10 (6 September 1985): 65.
> Comments favorably on *On the Perimeter.*

Vaill, Amanda. "Windsor Knot." *Chicago Tribune* (2 April 1995): 3.
> Argues that the interviews are the best part of *The Last of the Duchess* while Blackwood's overview of Simpson's life is the weakest.]

Waugh, Harriet. "Pitiless." *Spectator* 251, No. 8101 (15 October 1983): 23-4.
> Describes the stories in *Good Night Sweet Ladies* as too sad and bleak, and argues that although Blackwood employs imagery successfully, she evinces no sympathy for her characters.

Additional coverage of Blackwood's life and career is contained in the following sources published by Gale Research: *Contemporary Authors*, Vols. 85-88, 151; *Contemporary Authors New Revision Series*, Vol. 32; *Dictionary of Literary Biography*, Vol. 14; and *Major Twentieth Century Writers.*

Joseph Brodsky
1940-1996

(Full name Joseph Alexandrovich Brodsky; also transliterated as Iosif, Josif, Yosif, or Josip; also Alexander or Aleksandrovich; also Brodski, Brodskii, or Brodskij)

Russian-born American poet, essayist, and translator.

The following entry provides an overview of Brodsky's career through 1996. For further information on his life and works, see *CLC,* Volumes 4, 6, 13, 36, and 50.

INTRODUCTION

Often called the best Russian poet of his generation, Brodsky was born and raised in the former Soviet Union and became an American citizen in 1977. He was known for poetry in which he used complex rhythm and meter and extensive word play to address such themes as exile, loss, and death. He also frequently incorporated classical Western mythology and philosophy as well as Judeo-Christian theology into his works. Brodsky is best known for his poetry collections originally written in Russian, *Chast' rechi* (1977; *A Part of Speech*) and *Uraniia* (1984; *To Urania*), and his essay collections written in English, *Less Than One* (1986) and *On Grief and Reason* (1995). In 1987, Brodsky was awarded the Nobel Prize in Literature. The Swedish Academy, the bestowing body of the award, cited Brodsky's "all-embracing authorship imbued with clarity of thought and poetic intensity" and described his writing as "rich and intensely vital." Brodsky was also appointed poet laureate of the United States in 1991. During his one-year tenure, he extolled American poetry, calling it "this country's greatest patrimony," and worked to have it published much more widely.

Biographical Information

Brodsky was born in Leningrad to Jewish parents. Disenchanted with formal education, he left school at the age of fifteen to study independently. He taught himself English and Polish, purportedly so he could translate the works of English poet John Donne and Polish poet Czeslaw Milosz. As he developed a reputation among other Russian writers as a young poet with exceptional promise, he garnered the disfavor of Soviet authorities who arrested him in 1964 on charges of "social parasitism" under a controversial law meant to punish citizens who refused gainful employment. Although Brodsky argued that his activities as a poet and translator constituted legitimate work, the judge at the trial reacted scornfully to his defense. "Who has recognized you as a poet? Who has given you a place among the poets?" she demanded of

Brodsky, to which he retorted, "No one. And who included me among the ranks of the human race?" Brodsky was sentenced to five years of hard labor on a state farm near the Arctic Circle. Due in part to a petition signed by numerous prominent persons in the Soviet Union, Europe, and North America, including the Russian poet Anna Akhmatova, Brodsky was released after serving less than two years of his sentence. However, he was still regarded as an undesirable element in Soviet society, and in 1972 officials forced him to leave the country despite his protests. Befriended by American poet W. H. Auden, Brodsky settled in the United States, where he worked as an instructor of literature and creative writing at several universities, including the University of Michigan, Queens College, and Mount Holyoke College. Brodsky had open-heart surgery in 1979 and later had two heart bypass operations. He died of a heart attack in New York City on January 28, 1996 and was buried in Venice, Italy.

Major Works

Brodsky's early works are mostly brief, simple lyrics written in free verse, while those written in the late 1960s and beyond exhibit his command of longer, increasingly complex poetic forms. His early poems are also considered more personal than his later works, which treat more universal subject matter. *A Part of Speech* contains thirty-six poems, many of which originally appeared in Russian in such volumes as *Ostanovka v pustyne* (1970) and *Konets prekrasnoi epokhi* (1977). Although many of the poems address Brodsky's life in his homeland and chronicle his feelings of loss and loneliness after leaving Russia, other works in the collection incorporate American themes and describe American landscapes. *Less Than One,* which won the National Book Critics Circle Award in 1986, contains eighteen essays and focuses on twentieth century poetry in Russian and English. In addition to works on such writers as Russian Fyodor Dostoevsky and West Indian poet Derek Walcott, *Less Than One* contains two memoirs of Brodsky's childhood in Leningrad. Brodsky's second essay collection, *On Grief and Reason,* is comprised of twenty-one essays, all but one of which was written after 1986. This collection contains analyses of individual poems by English writer Thomas Hardy, American poet Robert Frost, and German writer Ranier Maria Rilke as well as essays about Roman ruler Marcus Aurelius and Roman poet Horace. Brodsky also published a book-length essay, *Watermark,* in 1992. Focusing on his experiences in Venice, Italy, where Brodsky spent many of his winters, this work has been described as a metaphorical, witty, and unconventional treatment of the Italian city. At the time of his death, Brodsky was in the process of completing the poetry collection *So Forth,* which was published later in 1996.

Critical Reception

During his life, Brodsky earned recognition from both critics and his peers as an extraordinarily gifted writer. He was lauded for imbuing classical themes with contemporary significance and for writing in both English and Russian. A few commentators have disputed the opinion that he is among the most influential Russian poets of the second half of the twentieth century, suggesting that sympathy for the oppression Brodsky suffered in the former Soviet Union led some to overrate his talents. Some critics have also faulted his poetry for what they consider its sexism, didacticism, and lack of clarity and emotional intimacy. Nevertheless, Brodsky was widely praised for his commitment to poetry, his vast knowledge of Western poetic traditions, and his mastery of numerous verse forms. Regarding Brodsky's influence on contemporary literature, Seamus Heaney observed that he was "regarded as the figure of the representative poet, sounding prophetic even though he might demur at the notion of the prophetic role, and impressing the academics by the depth of his knowledge of the poetic tradition from classical times up through the Renaissance and in modern European languages, including English." Heaney has also commented on Brodsky's belief that poetry has the power to transform individual consciousness and transcend political and social constraints: "[Brodsky

had] total conviction about the trustworthiness of poetry as a force for good—not so much 'for the good of society' as for the health of the individual mind and soul." Brodsky himself emphasized his views on the role of the poet in his Nobel lecture: "The poet . . . is language's means for existence. I who write these lines will cease to be; so will you who read them. But the language in which they are written and in which you read them will remain, not merely because language is a more lasting thing than man, but because it is more capable of mutation."

PRINCIPAL WORKS

Stikhotvoreniia i poemy (poetry) 1965
Collines et autres poemes (poetry) 1966
Ausgewahlte Gedichte (poetry) 1966
Elegy to John Donne and Other Poems (poetry) 1967
Velka elegie (poetry) 1968
Ostanovka v pustyne (poetry) 1970
Poems by Joseph Brodsky (poetry) 1972
Selected Poems, Joseph Brodsky (poetry) 1973
Modern Russian Poets on Poetry: Blok, Mandelstam, Pasternak, Mayakovsky, Gumilev, Tsvetaeva [editor with Carl Proffer] (nonfiction) 1976
Chast' rechi: Stikhotvoreniia, 1972-1976 [*A Part of Speech*] (poetry) 1977
Konets prekrasnoi epokhi: Stikhotvoreniia, 1964-1971 (poetry) 1977
V Anglii (poetry) 1977
Verses on the Winter Campaign 1980 (poetry) 1981
Rimskie elegii (poetry) 1982
Novye stansy k Avguste: Stikhi k M. B., 1962-1982 (poetry) 1983
Mramor [*Marbles: A Play in Three Acts*] (drama) 1984
Uraniia: Novaia kniga stikhov [*To Urania: Selected Poems, 1965-1985*] (poetry) 1984
Less Than One: Selected Essays (essays) 1986
Watermark (essay) 1992
On Grief and Reason (essays) 1995
So Forth (poetry) 1996

CRITICISM

Karen De Witt (essay date 10 December 1991)

SOURCE: "Poet Laureate on Mission to Supermarket's Masses," in *The New York Times,* December 10, 1991, p. B15.

[*In the following essay, De Witt discusses Brodsky's appointment to U.S. poet laureate, focusing in particular on Brodsky's belief that poetry should be published much more widely.*]

Small and balding, wisps of light hair straggling across his scalp, Joseph Brodsky hunkered down on a balcony step outside the poetry office in the attic of the Library of Congress. Absent-mindedly he gazed through his cigarette's smoke and the balcony's balustrade at the Capitol where a group of gay activists were protesting.

"Look," he recently commanded a visitor, standing up and peering south at the horizon. "Too late. There was a plane, the sun shining on it like a rocket."

Mr. Brodsky is the first foreign-born poet laureate of the United States, but if one expected probings into the capital's consciousness or weighty epiphanies on the evanescence of power from him, forget it. Poets, like the rich, are different. They find the motion of light on a jet far more intriguing than political demonstrations.

"I'm not here to keep an eye on the place." said Mr. Brodsky. "But my eyes are open."

And if Mr. Brodsky's past impressions of the city are any indication, any poems that come out of a sojourn in the city will probably be discomforting.

Here, from his poem **"Near Alexandria,"** for example, is the Washington Monument:

> The concrete needle is shooting its
> heroin into cumulous wintry muscle.

Here the Capitol dome:

> as the train creeps knowingly, like
> a snake.
> to the capital's only nipple.

Of course, Mr. Brodsky, the fifth poet laureate of the United States, doesn't have to write one line about the place. Unlike the British laureate, who is appointed for life, the American laureate has a job that lasts one year and carries no expectations that the poet will chronicle national events.

The poet, who receives a stipend, gives a public poetry reading and a public lecture, advises the Library of Congress on its literary program and recommends new poetry for the Library's Archive of Recorded Poetry and Literature. The post can be renewed once.

Yet there is considerable public interest in Mr. Brodsky's tenure. In making the appointment last May, the Librarian of Congress James H. Billington said Mr. Brodsky, who replaced Mark Strand as laureate, would bring to the post the "pen-etrating observations of the outsider while exploring with increasing versatility his own and poetry's Americaness."

Shortly after his arrival, Mr. Brodsky was being trailed by a television crew from "Nightline." For this Russian, exiled because he wrote poetry, and despite American citizenship and nearly 20 years in this country, might have interesting things to say about the unravelings of the Soviet Union. Here, too, was a laureate who had announced plans to wrest the masses of Americans away from Monday night sports and the cable shopping channels and thrust them into the joys of poetry.

"My idea is simply, is very simple, is that the books of poetry should be published in far greater volume and be distributed in far greater volume, in far more substantial manner," he said. "You can sell in supermarkets very cheaply. In paperbacks. You can sell in drugstores."

When he speaks of poetry for the masses, Mr. Brodsky talks in sudden bursts of sentences, punctuated, rat-a-tat-tat, with "yeahs," "you sees" and asides rolling over one another as if someone has disputed what he said, in this case about the moral consequences of not having poetry available in checkout lines. "This assumption that the blue collar crowd is not supposed to read it," he concludes, "or a farmer in his overalls is not to read poetry, seems to be dangerous, if not tragic."

When he gets warmed up, Mr. Brodsky can be prodded into breaking his pledge not to discuss American politics.

The confrontation between Judge Clarence Thomas and Anita F. Hill before the Senate Judiciary Committee struck him as "two kinds of baloney in the supermarket: neither was a delicacy."

But of the two, he found Judge Thomas' testimony "less appealing."

"His wasn't a terribly imaginative performance: He simply stonewalled," Mr. Brodsky concluded, displaying his poet's sense of human fallibility. "I've done that myself."

Despite the raucousness of American political campaigns, though, Mr. Brodsky said that American democracy was the best political system in the world.

"It has its ills and evils but they appear to be organic in nature, not ideological evils," he said. "And sometimes people chance upon something that works and to my eye, to say the least, this system here works. It doesn't make everyone happy, but there is no blueprint for happiness."

For Mr. Brodsky, writing poetry has brought both joy and tragedy. Born in 1940 in Leningrad, he worked as a laborer, mill worker and merchant seaman while writing poetry. He taught himself English by translating metaphysical poetry word by word. Though his work became popular with underground Soviet literary circles, Soviet authorities considered his work "social parasitism." As a result he was sentenced to hard labor at a work camp in the Arctic near Archangel.

After serving 18 months of a five-year sentence, he was exiled from the Soviet Union in 1972, and moved to the United States, eventually becoming a citizen. One of his earliest supporters was the poet W. H. Auden, who introduced him to a wider audience.

Poet-in-residence at the University of Michigan in 1972-73, Mr. Brodsky was one of the first recipients of a MacArthur Award in 1981. His collection of essays, **Less Than One,** won the National Book Award for criticism in 1986, and he won the Nobel Prize in Literature in 1987. This year, France awarded him membership in the Legion of Honor.

Mr. Brodsky's own poems are formal structures with intricate patterns of stanza, meter and rhyme. He writes in English and Russian. He likes Robert Frost, a poet whose work he considers full of terror. And as poet laureate, Mr. Brodsky can, through the poets he introduces at Library of Congress readings, influence the current canon of poetry by his of stamp of approval.

Mr. Brodsky said he is quite proud to have been appointed poet laureate, and sees the position as "a job in the spirit of public service." The job, he observes, offers more opportunity for promoting poetry than improving his own work.

My idea is simply, is very simple, is that the books of poetry should be published in far greater volume and be distributed in far greater volume, in far more substantial manner. You can sell in supermarkets very cheaply. In paperbacks. You can sell in drugstores.

—Joseph Brodsky

"As a poet, it doesn't encourage me," he said. "But I'm paid by the government and so for the moment, I'm a government worker as it were. So my concern here is not so much the well-being of poets themselves, my concern is with the well-being of the audience, the size of the audience. This year looks like and next year looks more like reading and chatting than scribbling.

"For a year I can do it," he added. "For me it's in many ways to pay back what I've been given by the country, if you will."

Mr. Brodsky has been described by some as arrogant, but during a luncheon at the Library of Congress he came across as shy and diffident, his tie askew, a button open on his shirt exposing his belly. When asked whether it made a difference whether the poet operates in a democracy or a repressive regime, Mr. Brodsky provides a hard answer for those who would use their circumstances to explain their silences: not at all. Poets make poems wherever they are.

His friend and translator, Anthony Hecht, a former Library of Congress poetry consultant, said that those who think Mr. Brodsky arrogant may be confusing the man with the intellect.

"But like many Europeans who are at all interested in literature, Joseph has a very ample command of what amounts to a Continental tradition of poetry and philosophy so he has easily at his fingertips great traditions in a number of languages," said Dr. Hecht. "So consequently a lot of them think of him as a show-off."

Arrogant or not, Mr. Brodsky is a very private man who will make no comment on his personal life beyond the simple biographical data and listing of writings, appointments and honors in his vita. He has one grown son. And a year ago, he married a young Italian-Russian woman who is finishing a degree at the University of Milan.

Despite three heart attacks, two heart operations, depravation and exile, he said that he does not think he has changed in all his life.

"I remember myself, age five, sitting on a porch overlooking a very muddy road." he said. "The day was rainy. I was wearing rubber boots, yellow, no, not yellow, green, and for all I know I'm still there."

Anthony Thwaite (review date 10 May 1992)

SOURCE: "Picture Postcards from Venice," in *Book World—The Washington Post,* Vol. XXII, No. 19, May 10, 1992, p. 7.

[*In the following review of* Watermark, *Thwaite discusses Brodsky's descriptions of Venice.*]

Over the years, Venice hasn't lacked its literary memorialists and scene-setters, some of them almost as familiar as Canaletto's paintings. From Ruskin to Mary McCarthy, from Byron to Ian McEwan, from both Brownings to Thomas Mann and beyond, the city has been described, analyzed, apostrophized, employed as backdrop, symbol, analogue and template. It has probably inspired more postcard-from poems than any other city in the world. Indeed, Mary McCarthy called it "a folding picture-postcard of itself."

Joseph Brodsky has already used it in his two sets of **"Venetian Stanzas"** (1962):

> I am writing these lines sitting outdoors,
> in winter,
> on a white iron chair, in my shirtsleeves,
> a little drunk;
> the lips move slowly enough to hinder
> the vowels of the mother tongue,
> and the coffee grows cold. And the blind-
> ing lagoon is lapping
> at the shore as the dim human pupil's
> bright penalty
> for its wish to arrest a landscape quite
> happy here without me.
> —**"Venetian Stanzas II,"** stanza VIII

This winter setting is made plain in **Watermark,** a brief but also extended bravura performance in prose: Winter is the season when Brodsky likes to visit, and stay in, Venice, reminding him as it does of his own native St. Petersburg. Meditating on and playing with his memories, Brodsky tells one nothing substantial about his life there, or even his reactions to it. It's an exercise in style, full of the "curlicue, siroccoperused scribblings" of the canals' surface, busy with twirls, diversions and arabesques.

Each of *Watermark*'s 48 short sections is a capricious flight into disconnected connections, personal impersonalities, adding up to a fragmented kaleidoscope that, shaken, reflects Brodsky's own insouciant, untethered later life as much as it does the evanescence of Venice.

—*Anthony Thwaite*

He is taken, for example, to visit a vast and almost totally unfurnished *palazzo*, owned by the last of a long line of admirals, "no navy man; he was a bit of a playwright, and a bit of a painter," who guides Brodsky through its occluded emptiness; "It felt like an underwater journey—we were like a school of fish passing through a sunken galleon loaded with treasure, but not opening our mouths, since water would rush in." The book has many such playful whimsies, teasing bits

of atmospherics in which human beings play only a small part. It is a collection of whatever fancies pass through Brodsky's own largely unpeopled imagination.

Towards the end, Brodsky asserts that "should dreams ever be designated a genre, their main stylistic device would doubtless be the non-sequitur. That at least could be a justification for what has transpired thus far in these pages." Each of **Watermark**'s 48 short sections is a capricious flight into disconnected connections, personal impersonalities ("It is a virtue, I came to believe long ago, not to make a meal of one's emotional life"), adding up to a fragmented kaleidoscope that, shaken, reflects Brodsky's own insouciant, untethered later life as much as it does the evanescence of Venice—though the fragments sometimes hint at his earlier trials.

Only once, describing a visit with Susan Sontag to Ezra Pound's longtime companion Olga Rudge, who unstoppably plays a familiar tune, "her master's voice," does Brodsky allow any acid to leak into his watery reflections. "I think I'd never met a Fascist—young or old; I'd dealt with a considerable number of old Communists, and that's what it felt like in the house of Olga Rudge, with that bust of Ezra sitting on the floor." It's a sharp moment, deeply etched, and it throws into relief the delicate marine and submarine ripples that surround it.

Brodsky's solutions to the problems of Venice (the pollution, the sagging Atlantis) are as whimsical as the rest. Among other things, he suggests "one could try dumping blocks of ice into the canals or, failing that, routinely void the natives' freezers of ice cubes, since whiskey is not very much in vogue here, not even in winter." It's a characteristically frivolous aside in a book which is wintry only in its setting, never in its moods.

David Streitfield (essay date 31 May 1992)

SOURCE: "Poet Laureate Lambastes Library," in *Book World—The Washington Post*, Vol. XXII, No. 22, May 31, 1992, p. 15.

[*In the essay below, Streitfield discusses Brodsky's term as U.S. poet laureate, focusing in particular on the poet's disgruntlement with the lack of support for the position.*]

Joseph Brodsky's term as poet laureate, which officially concluded with a reading of his work to an overflow crowd of several hundred at the Library of Congress May 14, was stormier and more colorful than those of his four predecessors put together, and not coincidentally probably did more to boost the profile of this obscure post.

It wasn't raised nearly enough to satisfy Brodsky, however. In his favorite Capitol Hill cafe the morning after his final appearance, the poet waffled about whether he regretted taking the job, but made his feelings clear: "I could have happily lived without it. The job was ill-paid, ill-defined and ultimately ill-executed . . . I'm glad it's behind me."

In spite of the attention he has drawn to poetry since September, Brodsky had hoped and expected to do much more, and blames the library and its bureaucracy for his failure. "I experienced more hindrance than support," he said. "The library's chief interest is in sustaining things the way they are," and his tiny staff was "fairly inept."

His pet project, an anthology of American verse that would be as plentiful and as widely available as a telephone directory, isn't moving as fast as he wished; a plan for a major, freewheeling conference here on the state of American poetry at the end of the century is, at best, delayed.

The office of poet laureate, created by Congress in 1985 but not given much of a mandate, is, Brodsky said, "nothing but a feather in the library's cap—or rather, given the cloudiness of its mental operations, in its turban. (A turban looks like a cloud, yeah?) It should be a bully pulpit from which to address the entire nation."

At about this point, the Russian exile will be criticized for being at best unrealistic, at worst naive. American-born poets, no matter how serious about their work, tend to be resigned to spending their lives without ever running into anyone out in the real world who can quote the title of a poem, much less a line or two. Yet Mark Strand, the previous laureate, echoed many of Brodsky's complaints in a phone interview from his home in Salt Lake City.

"If the position were taken more seriously, and there was a greater commitment to poetry, perhaps there would be more people at poetry readings," Strand said. "The whole poetry program and the laureateship has to be rethought. It's a tremendous mess."

Strand also said, somewhat contradictorily, that "it's not the library's fault. It's an institution, and like all institutions it works slowly." At readings he organized during his stint here, 30 to 50 people came. "That's disgraceful." Brodsky averaged more, but then he chose better-known poets.

Even though Strand's expectations weren't enormous, he was disappointed. "In Salt Lake City, you'd expect most people to be reading The Book of Mormon, which in fact is what most people do read. In Washington, with a highly educated professional population, you'd expect a greater literacy or greater interest in literature. But there's this great silence, and no sign that they ever read anything."

He traces it all the way to the top. "Here's a president whose supposed to be the education president, and I have not heard tell of one book he's supposed to have read while in office. Wouldn't it be wonderful if Bush could say, `Boy, I really liked that last novel of Updike's'?"

Among Strand's off-the-cuff recommendations for improving things: "They have to say poetry is important, they have to do twice as much advertising, they have to take it off the ugly brown paper they do the announcements on and have to revise the mailing list. They have to say, `Let's do something.' Start a poetry bookstore in the library. Take out a big ad in the paper and let people know what the schedule is through the year, so people can put it on the refrigerator. Do something that's better and different."

To these comments, Prosser Gifford, the library's director of scholarly programs, responds that the poetry position is indeed underfunded. "We certainly do have a commitment to poetry and literature but we could do more if we had more funds, and we'll soon develop a procedure for doing so."

To his knowledge, Gifford said, there haven't been any major new gifts since the original establishment of the poetry endowment in 1954. As for other complaints by Brodsky, he said a bit cryptically: "Each poet laureate is his or her own personality."

Brodsky certainly has a flamboyant one. Anyone who's been sentenced to five years at hard labor simply for declaring himself a poet—as Brodsky was in the Soviet Union in 1964—might naturally tend to have feelings about the form that are larger than life.

His last library reading was a remarkable performance simply as theater: The poet insisting on beginning with two works of Robert Frost, then moving onto his own work, alternating in Russian and English, doing much of it from memory. His favorite poem written here, he said, was also the shortest:

> I sit at my desk
> My life's grotesque.

It was, in truth, often difficult to make out the roughly accented words, but no one seemed to feel that really mattered: This was more akin to a musical performance. Through much of it Brodsky's final pre-performance cigarette, dumped hastily into a plant on the podium, continued to billow forth. For a smoker so devout that he should be doing advertisements for Marlboro, it was particularly appropriate.

The poet's trouble at the library was compounded by the fact that he is not what one would call a natural administrator. His staff would tell callers they never knew when or if he'd show up. Inviting a poet to come and read was often a last-minute decision. Brodsky said it was "psychologically impossible" to do things any other way. In his office in the library's dusty, cluttered attic, I once saw the start of a letter that could be his slogan: *I apologize for not responding promptly* . . . There is, in short, probably enough blame to go around.

When Brodsky was announced as laureate last year, there was some grumbling over the fact that he wasn't American-born. Yet he quickly won most over with his ardent partisanship of the native verse. And he is increasingly an American poet: He continues to write in Russian, but now translates himself. His passion for English is one of the more dramatic things about him, although his words often seem to come out of a private time warp. "He still believes he's the cat's pajamas," he says of one exile. Or to a friend on the phone: "Call me Monday morning when the rooster sings."

American poetry is even better, Brodsky is fond of saying, than the country's two most famous cultural creations: jazz and cinema. An American citizen for 15 years, this guy's been in love with our verse since he taught himself the language three decades ago, and he doesn't see why everyone else shouldn't feel the same way. Just give them a chance.

Merely as a statement of ambition, this is wildly different from Brodsky's four predecessors. Robert Penn Warren, Richard Wilbur and Howard Nemerov, for various reasons including age and health, didn't move to Washington for their stints. Strand did but could only do so because he had a MacArthur fellowship to supplement the $35,000 the library pays.

Brodsky—even commuting from New York two or three days a week—assumed a much higher profile than any of them. "You want to be self-effacing in poetry," he said during a lecture at the library last year, "you might as well take the next step and shut up."

Before there was a poet laureate, the library had a consultant in poetry who performed some of the same roles. As the Library of Congress is still at the service of the legislators it was originally set up to serve, so too was the consultant (as is the laureate).

"Nobody ever consulted me on anything," Brodsky remembered. Then he brightened: One member of Congress actually did call, Sen. Larry Pressler (R-S.D.). "He said he would like to upgrade his sense of American poetry." The other 534 members were presumably busy confirming Mark Strand's vision of Washington as a place where the elite are uncultured. Brodsky's own verdict on the city: "Lively, but on the whole it wasn't called Ground Zero for nothing."

Yet there were a few encouraging signs of movement. A minor one that could stand for the whole: Two mid-level executives of the Pathmark supermarket chain, responding to the poet's plea, sent him a letter saying: "If you want an 'in' to getting poetry to the supermarket checkout line (Think you can beat 'Baby born with map of solar system on his back'?), we'd be willing to do everything within our limited authority. Just for the hell of it."

Poetry isn't in supermarkets, or drugstores. Almost everywhere, the status quo is that verse goes unrecognized. Poets, too. The guy behind the counter of the cafe the morning Brodsky was being interviewed, apparently with no idea who he was even after his many visits there, motioned for him to put out his cigarette. "Hey, this is a cafe!" the poet yelled back. And defiantly continued to smoke.

Tony Whedon (essay date Winter 1993)

SOURCE: "A Ramble on Joseph Brodsky," in *Salmagundi*, No. 97, Winter, 1993, pp. 152-68.

[*In the essay below, Whedon contrasts Brodsky's poetry and essays, finding his verse obscure and emotionally distant in comparison to his essays, in which he finds "a sensitivity and introspection, a humaneness."*]

I stop at a little diner outside the college where I teach and watch Joseph Brodsky lunch on a sausage sandwich and a beer. The Russian poet is convivial, and grows suddenly animated when we chat about C. P. Cavafy, the subject of Brodsky's essay, **"The Pendulum's Swing."** He complains of the poor English and French translations of the Greek poet. Brodsky is at work on a Russian translation of Cavafy who, like Brodsky, was most at home in an alien culture (Cavafy lived in Alexandria, Egypt all his life, writing poems that celebrate as much as they mourn his permanent exile). Like Brodsky, Cavafy was as fluent in English as he was in his mother tongue; but despite his beautifully written English, Brodsky's pronunciation is somewhat indistinct, and I have trouble following what he is saying. He appears to me headstrong, eccentric. I feel an impatience in him, a disturbing lack of focus, and I wonder about his odd, even old-fashioned stuffiness.

Brodsky quit school at the age of sixteen and seems to carry with him a sense that he isn't fully educated; he is—in the most complete sense—an auto-didact. In my class at Johnson State College that afternoon, a woman student in her mid-thirties announces proudly that she, too, is a high school drop out, to which the Russian poet responds, rather unkindly I think, "And look where it's gotten you." He distributes to my class photocopies of three Hardy poems and proceeds with a brilliant analysis of Hardy's irascible style, his gloomy world view, surprising everyone by declaring that poetry is a masculine art, that it should be written with a kind of male vigour. The students are fascinated by Brodsky, the traditionalist. He tells us that at Mount Holyoke College, where he teaches each spring, he expects students to learn by rote thousands of lines from the classics and the great moderns in the same way that students came to understand literature a hundred years ago. He punctuates his talk with brief questions to the students, and rapidly answers them himself. When the subject of his own work comes up, Brodsky is clearly uncomfortable. He has come to talk about literature, not to speak about his life's work, his past. And for this reason, we're not impatient to ask Brodsky about himself. Again—reluctantly—he admits he is probably the greatest living Russian poet—which to his mind isn't very great. What about Wallace Stevens and John Ashbery? He hesitates, calls Ashbery talented, but misguided; Stevens has a few good poems, a few good poems. . . .

The hour-long class comes to an end, but Brodsky doesn't want to stop, he has other matters to discuss and rides along on gusts of his own volubility. He has angered and mystified my students by playing the role of genius, by revealing his disdain for them. But—in spite of this—he is redeemed for us by his love of poetry, his unremitting honesty. Later, at the college reception, he is irritated that his reading will follow a brief reception and dinner; he'd rather read and carry on partying—European fashion—late into the night. Once he plows into his reading—after a dinner where he's quizzed by students on perestroika and the Black Mountain poets—he can't be stopped. He alternates at the podium with his translator, Jane Miller, who gives the poems a quiet, spooky ring that contrasts with Brodsky's loud declamatory Russian style; he doesn't read his poems so much as fire them off in a language that is at times explosive, at times soporific; he smokes when Miller takes the podium, hardly acknowledging the crowd, storing energy for his next outburst. Finally, after two hours of Brodsky, I bring the reading to a close—to which the Russian poet raises his hands in the gesture of a child tugged away from a cherished amusement.

On my ride home that night I find it difficult to reconcile Brodsky the public speaker and poet with Brodsky the essayist. His essays have a sensitivity and introspection, a humaneness, that I find absent from the poetry. But both poetry and essays have a gallows humor, an abiding cynicism and hardened irony that few—save Steven Dobyns and C. K. Williams, both of whom are as prosey as Brodsky is poetic—share with him. Having first come to Brodsky through his essays, I'd been prepared for a poetry with a softer edge, whose historical sense could be less oblique and allusive than what I found. Brodsky is obsessed by history; one might say that much of his recent volume, *To Urania,* concerns itself with the various speakers' attempts to escape or circumvent history. As a result of this ambivalence toward his subject, much of Brodsky's work struggles to attain a desperate clarity in spite of the turbulence of history. There are several voices in

the collection, all of which, to one degree or another, reflect the cynically disengaged viewpoint of the emigre with time on his hands, the expatriate poet who's been permanently marked by politics. All of these poems are partially reflective of their translators' talents and biases; but I am happiest with Brodsky's own translations of his work, which seem more artfully rhymed, less hammered out, than translations by others.

Although Brodsky is a poet of the concrete, he's at his best when he also plays with abstraction. As much as he professes to dislike the willful obscurity of John Ashbery, there's an Ashberian tone to the last section of his **"Polonaise: A Variation"** which attempts an off-handed quirkiness, especially in its last stanza, where the blurring of pronouns and the use of abstractions provide a welcome relief from the relentless piling up of details in the poem's first section.

"Polonaise: A Variation"

To Z. K.

I

Autumn in your hemisphere whoops cranes and owls.
A lean nation's frontier slips off like a loosened harness.
And though windows aren't sealed yet, your camisole's
cleavage adds to the shadows the parlor harvests.
As the lamp flares up, one may well denounce
one's own curves as jarring the jigsaw puzzle
of the rooms whose air savors every ounce
perked by Frederyk's keyboard-bedeviled nozzle.
In the full moon, the stubble gets lavished with
nobody's silver by sloughy waters.
Roll on your side, and the dreams will blitz
out of the wall like those fabled warriors
heading east, through your yard, to dislodge the siege
of tall hemp. Still, their hauberks won't hide their tatters.
Yet, since they look alike, you, by getting hitched
only once, let an army across your mattress.

II

Reddish tiles of the homestead, and the yellow shade
of its stuccoed dwellings, beset with shingles.
Either cartwheels are carving an oval shape
or the mare's hoof, hitting the cow-moon, shimmies,
and slumped haystacks flash by. Alders, nothing-clad,
in their basket carry away the river.
And the leaden plow in the furrowed clouds

bodes no good to gray winter crops racked with
fever.
To your woolen stockings and linen hem
burdocks cling like nobody's child that loses
in the end its grip. And space is stitched firm
with the threadbare rain, and Copernicus turns out
useless.
Still the iris gleams, and the milky tint,
with those scattered birthmarks, your dress effaces.
Long a silhouette to yourself, you won't
fall into anyone's fond embraces.

                              III

I admit one's love should be greater, more
pure. That one could, like the son of Cronus,
size up the darkness, perfect its lore,
and drop, unnoticed, within your contours.
That one could reconstruct, pore by pore, your true
looks, with idle atoms and mental power;
or just peer at the mirror and state that you
are me: for whom do we love but ourselves? Yet chalk one up for Fate: your watch
may be running behind, for in our future
already that bomb has exploded which
leaves intact only the furniture.
Does it really matter who's run away from whom?
Neither time nor space is matchmaking for us
who took full advantage of sampling some
of those ages to come, and whatever follows.

It's clear that in other poems—especially in *To Urania*—
Brodsky chooses through veiled allegory to distance himself
from the troubling specifics of his time. And yet in his best
moments and without the least mention of the political events
in Poland in 1980-1981 that prompted **"Polonaise,"** we feel
the Russian poet's anguish at them. The expanding of man's
consciousness through the theories of Polish astronomer
Copernicus—who through his radical opposition to the Ptolemaic medieval cosmology dethroned man as the Lord of Creation—"turns out useless": so Brodsky says that Cronus, who
like Copernicus dethroned his father as ruler of the world,
was in turn dethroned by Zeus; he is also depicted in Roman
mythology, in the form of Saturn, as a devourer of his own
children. Zeus, the central authority and administrative intelligence that holds states together, becomes for Brodsky a symbol of the Copernican revolution, all revolutions, in fact, that
lead to the final scientific revolution epitomized for the poem's
speaker in "that bomb [which] has exploded [and] leaves /
intact only the furniture . . ."

Brodsky's very recognizable language, characterized by syntactical inversions, enjambments, and a kind of heightened
rhetoric, works best for him in the lines in the last stanza that
are lightened by a thematic playfulness coupled with a surprising shift in diction and tone. His **"Polonaise"** also has in
common with Chopin's composition a sad jauntiness, a bit-

tersweet tone that mourns the land's lost fecundity—"and the
leaden plow in the furrowed clouds / bodes no good to gray
winter crops racked with fever . . . "—just as it laments the
continual invasions that have wracked Poland's history: ". . .
dreams will blitz out the wall like those fabled warriors heading east, through your yard, to dislodge the siege of tall hemp
. . ."

Though Brodsky is writing about Poland here, he shares with
Chopin—writing in Mallorca about his homeland, like
Brodsky writing so often with a barely controlled irony about
the USSR—a deeply alienated sensibility. Brodsky's empathy reaches out to embrace not only Poland's present, but, as
the last stanza implies, the future. The rather puzzling lines
midway down the last stanza underscore the underplayed historical parallel suggested throughout the poem—". . .just peer
at the mirror and state that you / are me: for whom do we love
but our- / selves? . . ."—while they reinforce the sense of
narcissism that prevents people from seeing themselves as
they are. In the end, Brodsky appears to say, we're left only
with our own reflections.

If the last stanza of **"Polonaise"** moves us, it's partly because of the way he's prepared us texturally and thematically
in the previous two. I'm struck, especially, by the lines midway down the second stanza,

> To your woolen stockings and linen hem
> burdocks cling like nobody's child that loses
> in the end its grip. . . .

lines that carry a sadness, a resignation that leads to the hopeless cry of Brodsky's final lines:

> Does it really matter who's running from whom?
> Neither time nor space is matchmaking for us
> who took full advantage of sampling some
> of those ages to come, and whatever follows.

Brodsky's poems are as different from one-another—the nature poems, historical poems, comic poems, lyrics and narratives—as they are different from the essays. I'm torn between
liking the wrought texture of his poems, and feeling put off
by his calculated obliquities, his almost deliberate obscurity.
Oddly, it's poems like **"Polonaise"** and **"To Urania"**—discussed later in this essay—that I'm most enthusiastic about.
In these, a strong voice—a voice of control, of wit and intelligence—both distances his material and clarifies it for us.
When—stylistically and thematically—Brodsky assumes a
hieratic cloak, when the self is most completely dissolved
into a universal other, his work—not unlike that of Yeats in
his last years—asserts its power. More often than not, though,
Brodsky uses his hieratic voice to distance material which
deserves a more intimate tone, a warmer, more confiding
voice.

In my European novel class next day my students want only to talk about Brodsky. They're puzzled and put off by him, impressed by his analysis of the Hardy poems, a little dismayed by Brodsky's poetry, so rich and dense, allusive and awkwardly alliterative, that an oral presentation can't do it justice. We remark on Brodsky's comment in his prize-winning essay **"Less Than One"** that the past is of little inspiration to him, and observe there's a hidden self in his poems, that their elaborate structures and textures belie an enormous ego at work. I'm glad he came and proud of my students' honest, unsentimental, tolerant response to him. Though they're irritated by his lecturing and posturing they're fascinated—as anyone would be—by this glimpse into the literary world, and sympathize with Brodsky's rebelliousness—a rebelliousness that looks to the past for its inspiration. In class we discuss Brodsky's gorgeous **"Cape Cod"** poem, translated by the finest of contemporary formalists, Anthony Hecht. The students are fascinated by the poem's hexametrics, its rich allusive style. Brodsky had told us Hecht lengthened **"Cape Cod"** by some seventy lines, and we wonder how much it is faithful to the original version.

. . . . .

In his essay on Cavafy Brodsky notes that Cavafy benefits from translation, that the Greek poet's vision is intensified—paradoxically—by the distance afforded us through the process of translation. Included in Brodsky's new selection of poems are several versions of collaborative efforts between poet and translator. Brodsky's reverential admiration of Cavafy puzzles me, since Brodsky's prosody is as overtly "male" as Cavafy's voice is limpidly "female." I more easily understand Brodsky's affinity for Thomas Hardy's gnarled syntax than I can make sense of the enthusiasm Brodsky feels for Cavafy's long open lines. In any case, what principally attracts Brodsky to Cavafy and Hardy is the fact that both inhabit exclusively male worlds, that there is a willful exclusion of any "significant other" from Hardy and Cavafy's poetic consciousnesses (even in Cavafy's love poems, the lovers are most often unnamed casual partners). Brodsky seems drawn to poets who have shorn up their defenses against the world, whose strategies—be they the pliant syntactical strategies of Cavafy, the sure-footed iambics of Frost, or the explosive spondaics of Hardy—permit few vulnerabilities to enter the poetry. In subject matter, Brodsky is equally fortified against the intrusion of the feminine. There's almost no sense of personal memory in Brodsky's work: The past is remembered as an historical event, rather than something that's happened to him, a process which represents to me a psychic distancing occurring in much of his nature writing, especially in poems like **"Eclogue IV: Winter"** and **"The Hawk's Cry in Autumn,"** both of which lack the intimate personal contact characteristic of American nature poetry. Indeed, much of Brodsky's poetry finds as its subject a world that's nominally American, though the consciousness addressing it is late Nineteenth Century European in its use of personification and apostrophe, its naive approach to nature.

In the **"Hawk's Cry in Autumn"** the speaker makes a romantic identification with a hawk gliding high above the Connecticut Valley:

> . . . casting a downward gaze
> he sees the horizon growing dim,
> he sees, as it were, the features
> of the first thirteen colonies whose
>
> chimneys all puff out smoke. Yet it's their total
> within his sight
> that tells the bird of his elevation,
> of what altitude he's reached this trip.
> What am I doing at such a height?

An ambivalence about point of view in this poem, a not entirely willing suspension of disbelief, distances the hawk from us; the verbs—"he sees," "he senses"—appropriate the hawk's vision, anthropomorphize it; and by asking the question "What am I doing at such a height?" the speaker signals he's inside the hawk's consciousness. But we aren't persuaded of Brodsky's act of poetic faith because of the intercession, throughout, of abstract language, such as, ". . . it's their total within his sight / that tells the bird of his elevation," two lifeless lines that contrast with a lovely sonority in later stanzas where the hawk cannot descend and is forced by air currents higher than it wants to go:

> He! Whose innards are still so warm!
> Still higher! Into some blasted ionosphere!
> That astronomically objective hell
> of birds that lack oxygen, and where the
>   milling stars
> play millet served from a plate or a crescent.

Brodsky undercuts his pain/pleasure vision—his ironic Icarus vision—by attempting, as he does in so many poems, to explain, to rationalize. This dullness, this dearth of imagination—for what else could it be?—has to do with an excessive verbal busy-ness:

> What, for the bipeds, has always meant
> height, for the feathered is the reverse.
> Not with his puny brain, but with shriveled air sacs
> he guesses the truth of it: it's the end.
>
> And at this point he screams. From the hooklike
> beak
> there tears free from him and flies *ad luminem*

the sound Erinyes make to rend
souls; a mechanical, intolerable shriek,
the shriek of steel that devours aluminum;
"mechanical," for it's meant

for nobody, no living ears;
not for man's, not yelping foxes',
not squirrels' hurrying to the ground
from branches; not for tiny field mice whose tears
can't be avenged this way, which forces
them into their burrows. And only hounds

lift their muzzles (. . . .)

The first stanza might have been omitted here: it extrapolates the obvious, that the hawk inhabits an inverted world where up is hell and down a kind of heaven. Rather than underscore the hawk's pain, the poet imposes on us a strained interpretation of the way a hawk might feel from a human point of view. His animal catalogue in the next two stanzas is Disney-like in its sentimentality, in its anthropomorphizing of the "tiny mice whose tears / can't be avenged . . ." As the poem proceeds, I'm increasingly aware of the flimsiness, the underlying moral thinness of the vision, and I suspect—from his poems' complex surfaces—Brodsky also understands that beneath his dense language there's an unredeemed superficiality.

In his **"Eclogue IV: In Winter,"** Brodsky pursues the obvious with the same persistence; but, translated by the author with a more surefooted feel to it, the poem achieves a consistency missing from the previous one. Brodsky uses classical conventions, adapts them to his Baltic sensibility; the title of the poem signals he's addressing his subject from a noble Virgillian distance. In many respects **"In Winter"** reminds me of Auden's great "In Praise of Limestone," though Auden handles his subject with more grace and humor than I find anywhere in Brodsky. Both poems attempt to show how human characteristics can be causally linked to geography; but Auden's approach is exploratory, carries with it a sense of whimsicality: there's a stronger counterpoint in Auden's poem of the human against the natural world than in Brodsky's forced and sometimes strident eclogue. The fault, as in **"The Hawk's Cry in Autumn,"** lies in Brodsky's programmatic approach, his attempt to make winter—an abstraction representing the extremes of human experience—a precise correlative for a state of mind. Brodsky's heavy-handed prosody in this poem resembles that of the Eighteenth Century eclogue—with its hills, dales, shepherds and shepherdesses—though it has none of the wit of its most winning pastoralists.

Cold values space. Baring no rattling sabers,
it takes hill and dale, townships and hamlets
(the populace cedes without trying

tricks), mostly cities whose great ensembles,
whose arches and colonnades, in hundreds,
stand like prophets of cold's white triumph.

At best Brodsky achieves a charming synesthesia in this poem—"Cold is gliding / from the sky on parachute . . ."—but his knack for metaphor, more often than not, is undercut by forced attempts at punning and wordplay:

. . . Each and every column
looks like a fifth, desires an overthrow.

In successive lines, Brodsky nervously, compulsively, thrashes about for closure.

For Brodsky, memory is a painful weight. He embraces the rhetorical devices of classicism, believes intensely in traditional forms while he's opposed in his work to a personal reading of the past, as it limits the poet's perspective.

—*Tony Whedon*

One would expect he'd fare better when addressing a more civilized, more genteel subject, like Venice. However, **"Venetian Stanzas"** I and II suffer more from Brodsky's gassiness than do his eclogues. His Venetian poems meditate on the opulence of the Adriatic city without providing a narrative focus to drive the poems on. I try hard to find some undertow in the poems' subtexts, some emotional raison d'etre; but as in so much of his work, what I see is what I get. Brodsky hasn't let his guard down, and there is little to discover beneath their wrought surfaces. Both poems suffer terribly from an imitative fallacy: in attempting to communicate the stifling richness of Venice, the Russian poet bores us with his own excess. **"Venetian Stanzas"** have a pizza parlour prettiness—his art suffers from a surfeit of technique that jumbles perspective, calls attention to itself. The poems seem pale imitations of Anthony Hecht's "Venetian Vespers," a masterful sixty-page memory narrative on the decay of modern Venice, a poem which Brodsky surely pays homage to here. But unlike Hecht, Brodsky provides no synthesizing consciousness, no sense of who the narrator is until he announces himself at the close of **"Venetian Stanzas II,"** in lines that are the clearest, most straightforward in a poem otherwise muscle-bound by its own language:

I am writing these lines sitting outdoors, in winter,
on a white iron chair, in my shirtsleeves, a little
drunk;

the lips move slowly enough to hinder
the vowels of the mother tongue,
and the coffee grows cold and the blinding lagoon
is lapping
at the shore as the dim human pupil's bright
penalty
for its wish to arrest a landscape quite happy
here without me.

I can only speculate on how **"Venetian Stanzas"** might have
evolved had he chosen this last stanza as his first and located
the narrator in a more central position in the poem. Lacking
narrative focus and a coherent point of view, the poems feel
like overtures to unwritten stanzas—they're tourists' views
of Venice, and quite conventional views at that. As in much
of the poet's work, his eye for landscape is overwhelmed by
an obsession for extended metaphor:

A curly-maned cloud pack rushes to catch and
strangle
the radiant thief with its blazing hair—
a nor-easter is coming. The town is a crystal jumble
replete with smashed chinaware.

Brodsky is rarely content with things as they are; instead, he
personifies, endows the inanimate with human intent. The
following catalogue might have had a life of its own, but falls
victim to Brodsky's obsession with metaphoric control over
his material:

Motorboats, rowboats, gondolas, dinghies,
barges—
like odd scattered shoes, unmatched, God-size—
zealously trample pilasters, sharp spires, bridges'
arcs, the look in one's eyes.

Brodsky's statement that poetry is a masculine art is illustrated quite well in any of the passages I've quoted here—
assuming that Brodsky means by "masculine" an art that
strives for control, for a kind of verbal dominance, strives to
present and define the world hierarchically through generalization rather than through concrete description: though
Brodsky seems to relish descriptive writing, it's hard to find
a passage whose particulars are convincing. The masculine
control the poet tries for is also evident in the way he presents
the past—or, more correctly, the way he consciously excludes
from his poetry, except through veiled allusions, any sense
of a personal past. Hence, the notable lack in almost all his
poems of an observer-narrator; even in his dedicatory poems, there is little sense of dialogue with the person to whom
the poem is addressed. And when the narrator makes contact
with someone, as in his relatively early (1974) **"Lithuanian
Nocturne,"** dedicated to Thomas Venclova, the language is

torqued to the point at which meaning collapses, implodes
through the weight of language, as the opening stanza to the
poem illustrates:

Having roughed up the waters,
wind explodes like loud curses from fist-ravaged
lips
in the cold superpower's
innards, squeezing trite wobbles
of the do-re-mi from sooted trumpets that lisp.
Non-princesses and porous
nonfrogs hug the terrain,
and a star shines its mite clouds that don't bother to
tamper
with. A semblance of face
blots the dark windowpane
like the slap of a downpour.

. . . . .

In a number of essays Brodsky tells us that his past is of no
interest to him, that he's fortified himself with language to
protect himself from the suffering he's experienced as a displaced person. He expresses no remorse or nostalgia at leaving his homeland, considers himself not so much an exile
from the USSR as an immigrant to the US. In this sense, he
resembles his mentor, W. H. Auden. Auden's assumption of
US citizenship, his aesthetic that combines a dry classicism
with a pessimistic modernism, and, more importantly,
Auden's impersonal mask that serves to distance the narrator's
presence in much of his poetry, are models for Brodsky's
own life and work. Clearly for Brodsky the past represents a
threat not only to his shakey sense of well being, but to the
foundations of his poetry. There are no direct attempts in his
work to recall his two years at hard labor in a Siberian work
camp, or his painful childhood in Leningrad. On the one hand,
his refuge in language is a kind of salvation, filling a void
that otherwise might have been occupied by memory. On the
other, Brodsky's Herculean attempt to construct a Babylonian
tower of words represents the last refuge of the poet who's
equally ill-at-ease in his new home and his motherland. This
rootlessness results in a cultural anomie that finds expression
in a deep cynicism, the likes of which has been expressed by
many exiles. Like most of these writers, Brodsky embraces
an innately conservative politics; and like Nabokov and
Conrad, Brodsky spins around himself a baroque language
that shields both writer and reader from naked apprehension
of the past.

Brodsky's attitude toward the past is best illustrated in the
title poem to his recent volume:

"To Urania"

Everything has its limits, including sorrow.
A windowpane stalls a stare. Nor does a grill
abandon
a leaf. One may rattle the keys, gurgle down a
swallow.
Loneliness cubes a man at random.
A camel sniffs at the rail with a resentful nostril;
a perspective cuts emptiness deep and even.
And what is space any way if not the
body's absence at every given
point? That's why Urania's older than sister Clio!
In daylight or with the soot-rich lantern
you see the globe's pate free of any bio,
you see she hides nothing, unlike the latter.
There they are, blueberry-laden forests,
rivers where the folk with bare hands catch
sturgeon
or the town in whose soggy phone books
you are starring no longer; farther eastward surge
on
brown mountain ranges; wild mares carousing
in tall sedge; the cheekbones get yellower
as they turn numerous. And still farther east, steam
 dreadnoughts or cruisers,
and the expanse grows blue like lace underwear.

Here the contrasts between the pure spirit of poetry and that of narrative art are expressed in a manner uncharacteristic of most of Brodsky's work, which depends on a form of exposition. **"To Urania"** is a lyric statement that pits Clio, the muse of historical narrative, against Urania, the muse of astronomy in Greek mythology, usually represented pointing at a celestial globe with a staff. Milton, in "Paradise Lost," makes her the spirit of the loftiest poetry and calls her "the heavenly must" (the name means "heavenly one," "spirit of wisdom"). Clio is represented in this poem as a negative force, one which locks the speaker into his sorrow, prevents him from the divine flights of imagination associated with Urania, a more spiritual force. Contrasting Urania with Clio, the speaker says, "You see the globe's pate free from any bio, / you see she hides nothing, unlike the latter."

Clio, for Brodsky, clouds, obscures the poet's pure vision. Implicitly she also represents the darker forces of history, those "dreadnoughts / or cruisers" in the poem's final lines which the speaker confronts after his flight across the continent past "blueberry-laden forests" and "wild mares carousing in tall sedge." Brodsky has reached the antipodes of his geographical and poetic worlds at the close of his poem, bringing it full circle as he completes the piece with a return to his first few lines that begin: "Everything has its limits, including sorrow. . . ."

Very few of Brodsky's poems develop a thesis as economically, as succinctly, as does **"To Urania."** Present here are

his concerns about the limits imposed on the imagination by the state, and the accompanying depression that's a result of man's living in history. The poem suggests that even though with Urania's help we're provided a provisional freedom, after the voyage out, after we've contemplated nature and man from Urania's heavenly vista, we're obliged to return to Clio's historical-political perspective, which cuts "deep and even." Clio, the muse of historical poetry, the ally of the past, represents for Brodsky a painful limitation, an inevitability. But without her, his flights of imagination—so often identified in Brodsky's other work with a directionless thatch of language—seem to lack definition, focus. Although the poem is controlled by thematic opposites, it's also surprisingly open in its execution. I'm struck by the enjambments in **"To Urania"**:

And what is space anyway if not the
body's absence at any given
point. . . .

The lines combine a startling conceptual openness with two unexpected line-breaks that strongly emphasize the speaker's alienated singularity. The final lines of the poem,

. . . farther eastward surge on
brown mountain ranges; wild mares carousing
in tall sedge. . . .

use feminine endings—unlike those masculine end-stopped lines he's so fond of—and provide a needed hesitation, a downshifting, that anticipates the abrupt smack-in-the face closure of the poem.

It's appropriate that Brodsky chose **"To Urania"** as the title piece to his volume, as it not only helps to explain his poetics, but clarifies his unwillingness to face the past. The knotted spondaic strophes, the unabated lash of allusion and veiled reference are curtailed in **"To Urania,"** and the poem achieves a purity of form as it executes its dialectic, propelled forward toward its illusion-shattering ending. One paradox of the poem, however, is that Clio—whom the speaker scorns—provides a kind of detailed clarity lacking in the cosmic view. Equally paradoxical is the fact that Brodsky benefits from economy in a poem that, in itself, only briefly contemplates the possibility of limitlessness, of Urania's cosmic perspective. For Brodsky, memory—embodied in mythic form by Clio, the muse of history—is a painful weight, as we have seen. He embraces the rhetorical devices of classicism, believes intensely in traditional forms while he's opposed in his work to a personal reading of the past, as it limits the poet's perspective. Though **"To Urania"** is a surprisingly open poem, most of the other work in the volume has a peculiar density; one can't help feel the poet compelled to fill up spaces with qualifiers that don't quite qualify, with language that seems almost Victorian in its ornateness. But Brodsky can't escape history. While he is a weary fin de sieclist in his emotional indirection, like the speaker of **"To Urania,"** he is intent on leap-frogging into the poetic cosmos, on escaping the confines of current literary tradition and of the past. And like the current crop of American formalists—not the generation of which Hecht, Wilbur and Merrill are a part—Brodsky's obsession with form more often than not feels obfuscatory, marks off an attempt to dress up emotionally shallow material. His rejection of experimentalism in Russian poetry— oddly, he's enthusiastic about Soviet modernist fiction—is in keeping with his attitude toward western modernism: both traditions are too fragmented, too open, too emotionally unguarded for him. The flip side of Brodsky's poetic pugnacity, his tough-guy stance toward free-verse mushiness—as we have seen in my examination of **"A Hawk's Cry in Winter"**—is cloying sentimentalism. This too is another aspect of Brodsky's unwillingness to face the challenge of inventing new forms, of finding fresh ways to express direct feeling, and of coming to terms with a past that, if confronted with a degree of personal vulnerability, would create poetry more worthy of Brodsky's gifts and ambitions.

Malcolm Bowie (review date 30 April 1993)

SOURCE: "In the Mobile Labyrinth," in *The Times Literary Supplement,* No. 4700, April 30, 1993, pp. 12-13.

[*In the following excerpt from a comparative review of Brodsky's* Watermark, *Tony Tanner's* Venice Desired, *and Christopher Prendergast's* Paris and the Nineteenth Century, *Bowie praises Brodsky's unconventional depiction of Venice.*]

[Joseph Brodsky's ***Watermark***] . . . , which is not only an autobiographical essay but at moments a novella and a collection of epigrams, is cast as an irreverent riposte to the Venetian outpourings of the writers studied by Tony Tanner [in his *Venice Desired*]. How sumptuous and over-ripe Brodsky's spare notations make them all seem in their anxious quests for meaning. Even their negative epiphanies are impossibly fulsome when set against the street-corner incidents or failures of incident by which the nomadic poet measures out his Venetian winters. Speaking of his first arrival in Venice, he dissociates himself from the swollen ambitions of his predecessors: "If that night portended anything at all, it was that I'd never possess this city; but then I never had any such aspiration". Where others speak of honeymoons, or of the marriage between Venice and the sea, Brodsky thinks of Venice as a wonderful place in which to get divorced. When others mention Browning, they have in mind the author of *Sordello* and "A Toccata of

Galuppi's", but Brodsky dreams of the firearm with which a lost poet might end it all.

Yet the overall manoeuvre of this witty and graceful book is to establish a superior international community of poets, beyond the reach of the familiar Venice lobbyists. Venice has to be de-Ruskinized and un-Prousted if it is to make a new kind of sense to the professional writer. This does not involve ignoring or seeking to discredit the optical delights of the place, but it does mean being cautious about its insistent summons to representation. "Depict, depict!" the city cries to the artist and the camera-bearing tourist alike, but Brodsky pauses and with no trace of petulance asks "Why should I, yet?" Beyond the dissolving outlines and melting vistas of the city perhaps a tougher vision of hope and futurity is to be found, one that brings the wandering poet back from his solitude into the company of Dante, Akhmatova and the Montale of "The Eel".

It is in his handling of the Venetian waters themselves that Brodsky brings off his boldest reversal of the commonplace view. Art is one method among others, he says, by which the human organism compensates for its lack of retentiveness, and it is perhaps in this supremely watery and dissipated place that the artist can best join forces with a still greater work of retention: "if we are indeed partly synonymous with water, which is fully synonymous with time, then one's sentiment towards this place improves the future, contributes to that Adriatic or Atlantic of time which stores our reflections for when we are long gone". And at the very end: "By rubbing water, this city improves time's looks, beautifies the future". The finest tribute we pay to Venice lies in the tears we shed there, and only after that, and only if we happen to be writers, is it appropriate to shed sentences too.

Brodsky cheats with his Venice, of course, and manages to have it both ways: he drains the city of its conventional meanings, makes good jokes at its expense, pretends that it's just anywhere at all, yet uses it as a talisman and constantly calls upon its reserves of expressive energy. But this short book is a delight from start to finish, and in its moments of lagoonside anomie and depletion adds something quite new to the literary mythology of the city.

David Patterson (essay date Summer 1993)

SOURCE: "From Exile to Affirmation: The Poetry of Joseph Brodsky," in *Studies in Twentieth Century Literature,* Vol. 17, No. 2, Summer, 1993, pp. 365-83.

[*In the following essay, Patterson examines the theme of exile in Brodsky's works, stating that "Brodsky regards his exile not as a political condition but as an existential condition, one that is characteristic of his condition as a human being."*]

Joseph Brodsky is a poet whose concern with language is a concern for the sacred. In an interview with Nataliya Gorbanevskaya he says, "If I were to begin to create some form of theology, I think it would be a theology of language. In this sense, the word is really something sacred for me." The sacred, however, manifests itself only as something lost. The poet engages in his effort to join word and meaning not in the midst of the sacred but in a movement *toward* the sacred. The poet *in* exile thus becomes the poet *of* exile by undertaking this movement of return. He is the one who, in his homelessness, announces the homelessness of the human condition as it is defined by its distance from the sacred.

One understands, then, why [Valentina Polukhina asserts in her *Joseph Brodsky: A Poet for Our Times,* 1989] that "poetry itself is its own kind of alienation, for it is the exteriorization of one's own 'I,' the objectification of the poet's emotions and thoughts. In this sense any work of art, once finished, is alienated from the creator." Operating in a state of exile, the poet of exile finds that the completion of the poem precedes the condition it addresses. Thus the poet of exile is continually struggling in a time that is too late and a place that is elsewhere. "Perhaps exile is the natural condition of the poet," Brodsky comments in an interview with Giovanni Buttafava. "I feel a kind of great privilege in the coincidence of my existential condition and my occupation." One will notice that Brodsky regards his exile not as a political condition but as an existential condition, one that is characteristic of his condition as a human being; it is a general condition that invades anything he writes in the capacity of poet, regardless of the particular theme addressed in a given poem. Further, the occupation he undertakes is not simply a livelihood but a means by which he may occupy or endure the condition of exile and thus establish a place for himself within that condition. Yet Brodsky's occupation with his existential condition is not so much an occupation or even a preoccupation as it is a *post*-occupation. Again, the I becomes visible to itself in its exteriorization, in its self-alienation; the man becomes a poet after the fact. What George Kline says of Brodsky [in *Brodsky's Poetics and Aesthetics,* 1990] is true: "Few poets have expressed the sense of loss, separation, and estrangement more powerfully than Brodsky." And since what we find in Brodsky is indeed an *expression* of separation, the separation is sensed precisely in its expression; that is, the expression is itself a separation. It is the separation of word from meaning, of the I from the self, of the exile from his home. Meaning lies in the word yet to be uttered. And home is the place to which we have yet to return.

Much of his poetry, as Efim Etkind points out [in *Protsess Iosefa Brodskogo,* 1988], deals with a humanity "wandering about the planet without any goal or meaning, realizing that nothing changes anywhere and that all the notions of an earthly paradise are merely illusions." It must be noted that the primary threat to the poet in his own humanity—the chief danger of exile—lies not in illusion but in the indifference that may arise in the collision with changelessness. For here arises the temptation to slip into the deadly sleep of "it's all the same" and thus be swallowed up by the law of identity that [Pavel Florensky describes in *Stolp i utverzhdenie istiny,* 1970] as "the spirit of death, emptiness, and nothingness." In the process of undoing the illusion the poet not only posits a difference between reality and illusion or truth and lie; through the utterance of the poem he also transforms that difference into a non-indifference. This transformation makes a poetry of exile into a poetry of return. One example that may demonstrate this point can be found in just a few lines from Brodsky's **"Kolybel'naya treskovogo mysa" ("Lullaby of Cape Cod"):**

> In genuine tragedy
> it's not the fine hero that finally dies, it seems,
> but, from constant wear and tear, night after night,
> the old stage set itself, giving way at the seams.
>
> [*A Part of Speech*]

Here we see that the undoing of an illusion is the collapse of a ground: the wandering that distinguishes the state of exile is a condition of groundlessness, a distance from the ground or the soil itself. To be sure, the Russian word "bespochvennost" 'groundlessness,' literally means without "pochva" 'being without the soil.' That the breakdown of the illusion implies a need for return is more clearly seen in the original Russian verse. There the word translated as "stage" is "kulisa," which may be used in the singular to mean a flat scenery that projects out from the side. Once the scenery is exposed as flat, the homeland loses its dimensions of depth, a loss that parallels the word gone flat, drained of its meaning and its sanctity.

When the word shows itself as something drained of meaning, it posits a future—and a silence—in which the poet seeks to restore its meaning. Through the word that he holds sacred Brodsky becomes the messenger of the word forever yet to be uttered, the bearer of the silence of the yet-to-be. "The radiations of the future," Andre Neher observes in *The Exile of the Word,* "are totally silent. Indeed, of the three dimensions of time—present, past, and future—the future alone is completely identified with silence, in its plenitude but also in its remarkable ambivalence." As the messenger of silence the poet bears the memory of the future. In this condition of exile Brodsky affirms the dearness of a home that is forever elsewhere. Thus, as we shall see, the sacred, the silent, and the elsewhere are the terms that shape the notion of exile in Brodsky's poetry. Let us turn now to that poetry in an effort to hear the voice that issues from the core of this rupture—and perhaps to hear the cry of our own souls.

One task of the poet in his endeavor to make felt the dearness of what is lost is to make visible the sanctity of what is unseen. This ability is just what distinguishes Brodsky as a poet. W. H. Auden expresses it in his introduction to Brodsky's *Selected Poems* by noting the poet's unusual "capacity to envision material objects as sacramental signs, messengers from the unseen." This envisioning, of course, is a mode of hearing. Through the said we behold the unseen; through the seen we hear the unheard. A good illustration of Auden's statement appears in an untitled verse from the *Selected Poems:*

> In villages God does not live only
> in icon corners, as the scoffers claim,
> but plainly, everywhere. He sanctifies
> each roof and pan, divides each double door.
> In villages God acts abundantly—
> cooks lentils in iron pots on Saturdays,
> dances a lazy jig in flickering flames,
> and winks at me, witness to all of this.

Where God sanctifies, man dwells. The sacramental sign is the site of human dwelling, where each fixture has its place— roof, pan, and door—and each action has its time: on Saturdays. The illusion here unveiled as a lie is the illusion of the scoffers, who are deaf and blind to the sign and therefore to the holiness of the preparation of "lentils in iron pots." Like the word itself—like the word *pots*—such pots are the vessels of the sacred, preparing, as they do, the foodstuff that joins creature to creation and thus to the Creator. The dance underscores the harmony in this joining of word and thing, of the human and the divine. And the truth of this harmony, the truth *as* harmony, issues from the light of the flickering flame, calling to mind the light brought forth upon the first utterance of the Creator in His act of creation. Calling forth a world, the poet himself imitates the Creator in his response to creation. He looks on, and God looks back, ever so subtly, with a wink from between the lines, and thus transforms the man into a witness. A witness to what? To the dwelling in villages that occurs upon the hidden but abundant action of God.

From outside the poet looks on to become a link between the villagers and those of us who, like himself, live on the outside. The villagers dwell in the village, while his consciousness, or the inscription of that consciousness, places the poet *before* the village. And as he who thus reads the sacramental signs makes us into readers of the signs, he takes us with him into the realm of exile, making strange the familiar. Consider, for instance, the closing lines to an untitled poem from *A Part of Speech:*

> A morning milkman, seeing the milk that's soured,
> will be the first to guess that you have died here.
> Here you can live, ignoring calendars,

> gulp Bromo, never leave the house; just settle
> and stare at your reflection in the glass,
> as streetlamps stare at theirs in shrinking puddles.

Here the milkman is made into a reader of signs, and death is presented as that form of living which is void of dwelling. Never leaving the house, the man is never at home; staring only at his reflection, he never sees himself. In these lines we have an inversion of the sign made visible in the lentils and iron pots above. Here the sacred is revealed under the inverted sign of sickness, made present by its absence: the milk sours as the man guzzles Bromo, medicating himself to death. The light that would illuminate the road into a community, through which the man may seek a return home, is swallowed up in a shrinking puddle that sullies the path. Once again, however, there is an "and yet" underlying the poem: the reflection of the light that catches the poet's eye rises upward, and in this rising upward the sanctity of the word manifests itself. The reflection is in the puddle, but the light comes from above. Poetry, says Brodsky in *Less Than One,* "is language negating its own mass and the laws of gravity; it is language's striving upward—or sideways—to that beginning where the Word was." That beginning is where the poem both begins and seeks its end. What is it that negates the laws of gravity and the mass of language, levitating even iron pots? It is the sacramental sign.

Brodsky illustrates this point very effectively in the last few lines of his **"Ekloga 4-aya: Zimnyaya"** (**"Eclogue IV: Winter"**), where we read:

> That's the birth of an eclogue. Instead of the
> shepherd's signal,
> a lamp's flaring up. Cyrillic, while running witless
> on the pad as though to escape the captor,
> knows more of the future than the famous sybil:
> of how to darken against the whiteness,
> as long as the whiteness lasts.
>
> (*To Urania*)

In this poem the sacramental sign that flares up is not simply the iron pot or the streetlamp but is the poem itself, made of the imposition of black on white, as if the flame that burned were a dark one. Nonetheless, it is the dark letter carved into the wilderness of white that makes the wilderness visible, transforming it from an expanse of emptiness into a *page.* The pastoral presence is eclipsed by the Cyrillic scrawl that signifies an absence; it is as if the very letters of which the word is made get in the way of its contact with meaning. The word thus struggles to escape the letters that confine it, struggles, in a sense, to escape itself in the poet's effort to capture it. The scrawl takes on the significance of sacramental sign, however, not so much in its making visible a lack or an absence as in its opening up the yet-to-be: it knows more of the future—that is, it bears a deeper memory of the future, of the *afterward*—than the sybil. Like the Word that was in the beginning, the end of the poem about to be written precedes it. Here one may recall Brodsky's statement in *Less Than One* that "words, even their letters—vowels especially—are almost palpable vessels of time." The capacity of the word to contain this time is its capacity to convey meaning. Meaning, then, happens in transit, eternally on the way to a place where it has yet to be fulfilled. The poet in exile, however, has no star to guide him as his word carries him along this path. The flaring up of the poem takes the place of a star, as we see upon an examination of the Russian version of these lines. There the lamp replaces not the shepherd's signal but the "svetilo," which means 'light' or 'star'; taking the place of this light, the poem takes on the sacred. What the Cyrillic knows, moreover, it knows through a "greshnym delom" or through a 'sinful affair,' because it usurps the signal or sign that is forever yet to be revealed. The prospect of redemption arises from the realization of this usurpation; the light is perceived as a presence displaced; and the return homeward that always comes *after* happens from within a condition of exile.

What is perhaps most striking about these lines from Brodsky's **"Eclogue IV: Winter"** is that the Cyrillic stuff of writing has a certain life of its own. The word is sacred for Brodsky because it is alive; it speaks and is not merely a tool used by the speaker. Brodsky makes this explicit in *Less Than One,* where he declares, "Writing is literally an existential process; it uses thinking for its own ends, it consumers notions, themes, and the like, not vice versa. What dictates a poem is the language, and this is the voice of the language, which we know under the nickname of Muse or Inspiration." It is the voice of language that sanctifies the sign, not the other way around, and in its sanctification the sign signifies the living presence of another—the Muse or the Spirit—who casts the poet at a distance from himself. Announcing his distance, the voice of the other in the midst of language proclaims the poet's distance from a world in which he might dwell. Thus in **"Venetsianskie strofy 2"** (**"Venetian Stanzas II"**) the exiled poet writes:

> I am writing these lines sitting outdoors, in winter,
> on a white iron chair, in my shirtsleeves, a little
> drunk;
> the lips move slowly enough to hinder
> the vowels of the mother tongue,
> and the coffee grows cold. And the blinding lagoon
> is lapping
> at the shore as the dim human pupil's bright
> penalty
> for its wish to arrest a landscape quite happy
> here without me.
>
> (*To Urania*)

The poet's distance from himself, from the sacred, and from

a dwelling place is proclaimed in images of disjuncture: shirtsleeves in winter, cold coffee, a landscape there without him. The time is out of joint and the man is out of place, drunk enough so that the vowels that might be the vessels of time, and therefore of the sacred, elude him. Like the eye that would arrest the landscape, the word would capture meaning, but the verb is no sooner off the tongue and onto the page than the man has slipped behind.

While Brodsky may have the ability to perceive the sacramental sign, the sacred itself necessarily escapes him. The poet in exile, the poet of exile, is forever adrift. Commenting on the poet in the *Phaedrus,* Plato asserts that there is a "form of possession or madness of which the Muses are the source." In this case the poet has much in common with the madman, especially as Michel Foucault describes him when he writes, "Confined to the ship, from which there is no escape, the madman is delivered to the river with its thousand arms, the sea with its thousand roads, to that great uncertainty external to everything. He is a prisoner in the midst of what is the freest, the openest of routes: bound fast at the infinite crossroads. He is the Passenger *par excellence:* that is, the prisoner of the passage." What Foucault articulates Brodsky illustrates in these lines from **"Lullaby of Cape Cod"**:

> Preserve these words. The paradise men seek
> is a dead end, a worn-out, battered cape
> bent into crooked shape,
> a cone, a finial cap, a steel ship's bow
> from which the lookout never shouts, "Land ho!"
>
> [*A Part of Speech*]

The poet sketches the signifier, but the signified remains beyond the horizon of his vision; the homeland, like the word beneath the word, remains forever hidden in silence. Hence it is sacred. In the Russian text the term rendered as "Land ho" is the single word "Zemlya," which means "earth," as well as "land." As the Passenger *par excellence,* the poet is continually in search of this center, or this origin and organ of life, of the mother and the mystery: the earth. That is what the signifiers of exile struggle to signify. And that is what abides in the silence of the "other" language, the silence of all tongues, to which the poet strives to give voice and which gives it voice to the poet. The bearer of the sacramental sign thus bears something more than the sign can bear: he is the messenger of silence.

We have seen that the sacramental sign signifies not only the sacred but a distance from the sacred, and that the sign positions the sacred beyond the horizon of the yet-to-be. This beyond is the realm of silence, where the voice of language no longer speaks—or rather speaks in the mode of silence, in the mode of non-speaking: in the mode of death, for death is the one certainty situated in the yet-to-be. Death defines and delineates the realm of exile. In his article "Variations on the

Theme of Exile" George Kline comments on Brodsky's poetry, saying, "The increasing deafness of the old is a rehearsal for the non-speaking which is death, the silence which is eternity." If words are the vessels of time, then silence is, indeed, the vessel of eternity, the path to which leads through death. Brodsky, of course, is aware of this element not only in his own poetry but in any art that might bespeak this non-speaking. "Art," he asserts, "'imitates' death rather than life; i. e. it imitates that realm of which life supplies no notion: realizing its own brevity, art tries to domesticate the longest possible version of time." That realm of which a life steeped in language supplies no notion is the realm of silence; imitating death, the poet becomes the messenger of silence.

"Death as a theme," Brodsky notes, "always produces a self-portrait." In the condition of exile, moreover, the portrait of the self is sketched along the lines of separation from the other; home is made not only of familiar places but of familiar faces. The separation from those human relations determines a certain relation of the poet to his poetry. The messenger of silence is the messenger of separation and thus of infinite longing for the other, for silence is the stuff of which separation and exile are made. A poem about the end of love, for example, may have its links to a deeper existential concern, especially when it appears not only in the context of two lovers but in the context of exile, which Brodsky himself, again, identifies as the "natural condition of the poet." As a lover he separates; as a poet he writes of the separation that has deeper implications. Consider, for instance, a poem titled **"Stanzas"** from Brodsky's *Selected Poems:*

Let our farewells be silent.
Turn the phonograph down.
Separations in this world
hint at partings beyond.
It's not just in this lifetime
that we must sleep apart.
Death won't bring us together
or wipe out our love's hurt.

     . . . . .

As our union was perfect,
so our break is complete.
Neither panning nor zooming
can postpone the fade-out.
There's no point in our claiming
that our fusion's still real.
But a talented fragment
can pretend to be whole.

Swoon, then, to o'erflowing,
drain yourself till you're dry.
We two halves share the volume,
but not the strength, of the wine.
But my world will not end if

in future we share
only those jagged edges
where we've broken apart.

No man stands as a stranger.
But the threshold of shame
is defined by our feelings
at the "Never again."
Thus, we mourn, yet we bury,
and resume our concerns,
cutting death at its center
like two clear synonyms.

     . . . . .

Let our farewells be silent.

The parting from the other is a tearing away of the self from its soul and a rending of meaning from the word, and the messenger here conveys what he has retrieved from the bleeding silence of that gaping wound. Separation hints at a parting beyond because the volume constituted by self and other contains a world, a time yet to come, and therefore a home. The separation is silent because it is a form of death, and, as Brodsky says, this death culminates in a portrait of the self left to the frayed edges of itself. The poet of exile moves along this jagged edge that traces the silhouette of death. The difficulty confronting him is to fetch the word from that grave without tumbling into it.

The struggle of life with death, of exile with homeland, is a struggle of the word with silence. One poem in which this struggle unfolds most explicitly and most thoroughly is **"Gorbunov and Gorchakov,"** which is an extended dialogue between two patients in a psychiatric hospital outside of Leningrad. In this poem the messenger of silence joins his voice to the voice of the madman to make silence itself speak. Listen:

"And nothing can be more impenetrable
than veils of words that have devoured their things;
nothing is more tormenting than men's language."
"But if we view things more objectively
it may be that we'll come to the conclusion
that words are also things. And thus we're saved!"
"But that is the beginning of vast silence.
And silence is the future of all days
that roll toward speech; yes, silence is the presence
of farewells in our greetings as we touch.
Indeed, the future of our words is silence—
those words which have devoured the stuff of
things
with hungry vowels, for things abhor sharp corners.
Silence: a wave that cloaks eternity.
Silence: the future fate of all our loving—
a space, not a dead barrier, but space

that robs the false voice in the blood-stream throbbing
of every echoed answer to its love.
And silence is the present fate of those who
have lived before us; it's a matchmaker
that manages to bring all men together
into the speaking presence of today.
Life is but talk hurled in the face of silence."

[*Selected Poems*]

It bears repeating: silence is not a barrier but a space, the place of exile, the poet's point of departure and return. And in silence we are gathered together with him, confronted with our own exile. Just as the theme of death ends in a self-portrait, the pursuit of silence leads to a collision with the self. And yet, once again, the thing that posits the separation also implies a union: silence is a matchmaker that brings us together in a speaking presence, and the poetic word enables us to hear it. Like the death that accentuates life, silence calls forth the spoken part of the human being, as part of speech, that vibrates on the breath of life. Human presence is a speaking presence that harbors a non-speaking.

"The absence of response," says Brodsky, "has done in many a poet, and in so many ways, the net result of which is that infamous equilibrium—or tautology—between cause and effect: silence." The silence that threatens the poet is not the silence that gathers human being unto human being but the blank silence born of the collapse of difference into indifference. The one who is faced with the translation of silence into utterance is faced with the transformation of this emptiness into eloquence. Recall in this connection Brodsky's lines in **"Pen'e bez muzyki" ("A Song to No Music")**:

the embrace's stifling blindness
was in itself a pledge of an
invisibility that binds us
in separations: hid within
each other, we dodged space . . .

[*A Part of Speech*]

Once again the lover separates from the beloved, but the poet pursues deeper implications of the separation. Seeking the word hidden beneath the word, the silence beneath the vocable, the poet seeks the other within the self, the one who is drawn into the self in the act of embrace. This movement, this response of non-indifference, creates the proximity that might, if only for a moment, dodge space and span the distance that constitutes exile. The point is perhaps better made in the Russian line, "my skryvalis' ot prostranstva" or `we were hiding from space,' suggesting a hiddenness in a place beneath the word or beyond the word where meaning happens—silently. In that place beyond space the silence of emptiness is transformed into the silence of eloquence. From the

place beyond space the messenger of silence bears his message of embrace.

And yet, in his exile, the poet is invariably thrown back to the message of what has been lost to exile, of what is felt only as pain. One passage in which the pain of isolation is most strongly felt appears in the last two lines of **"I Sit by the Window"**:

I sit in the dark. And it would be hard to figure out
which is worse: the dark inside, or the darkness
out.

[*A Part of Speech*]

For "dark" and "darkness" we may read "silence." This is the darkness that the flaring up of the lamp of poetry endeavors to illuminate; this is the silence, the non-speaking, that drives the poet to speak or die, or to die in the speaking. What is left of the messenger's message? Brodsky tells us in **"Chast' rechi" ("A Part of Speech")**:

. . . and when "the future" is uttered, swarms of mice
rush out of the Russian language and gnaw a piece
of ripened memory which is twice
as hole-ridden as real cheese.

. . . . .
What gets left of a man amounts
to a part. To his spoken part. To a part of speech.

[*A Part of Speech*]

In the Russian text the penultimate line contains an important word left out of the English translation. It is a dative of the second-person pronoun *vam*: what is left of a man for you is a part of speech, that part which remains of the soul that the poet offers to you, his reader. And it is not his spoken part, exactly, but "chast' rechi voobshche" `a part of speech in general,' of speech as such. The messenger of silence is one who, in the end, cannot deliver his message. Brodsky reiterates this lament, this message, in **"Dekabr' vo Florentsii" ("December in Florence")**, where he writes:

A man gets reduced to pen's rustle on paper, to
wedges, ringlets of letters, and also, due
to the slippery surface, to commas and full stops.

[*A Part of Speech*]

Hence we see the poet addressing in his poetry the very thing that threatens it. The message is that the word is inadequate to the message, that the You who is addressed must find some way not to stop at the full stop, some way to dodge space and step through the ringlets of letters that occlude the word.

These, then, are the signposts of exile: wedges and ringlets of letters, commas and periods of punctuation. But, just as the word that comprises a poem bespeaks the silence from which it is born, so do the signposts pointing in one direction posit another. Brodsky etched such a sign for himself on 4 June 1977, the fifth anniversary of his exile from his homeland, when he wrote:

> I don't know anymore what earth will nurse my
> carcass.
> Scratch on, my pen: let's mark the white the way it
> marks us.
>
> (*To Urania*)

The poet is marked by the white in his marking of it; the sign he imposes on the emptiness is imposed on him, making him into who he is: a poet. Recall in this connection the lines from his **"Litovskii noktyurn" ("Lithuanian Nocturne")**:

> . . . nobody stands to inhabit
> air! It is our "homeward!" That town
> which all syllables long
> to return to. . . .
>
> . . . . .
>
> That is why it is pure!
> In this world, there is nothing that bleaches
> paper better (except
> for one's dying) than air.
> And the whiter, the emptier, which is
> homelike. Muse, may I set
> out homeward?
>
> (*To Urania*)

The very thing that the poet would convey on his page places it under erasure, "bleaches" it back into silence. Here we see that the shore from which the messenger sets out is precisely the place he seeks: it is a certain elsewhere hidden in the emptiness of the air, for even the emptiness has its secret side. It is home. Looking at the Russian text, we notice that in both of these stanzas the word "Domoi" `homeward,' is immediately followed by the word "vosvoyasi," which is translated as `town' but means `home' or `go home.' Home takes on its sense through the movement toward it, and yet it recedes as it is approached, `bleached' into a distant elsewhere. It should also be noted that the word rendered as "emptier" is "beschelovechnei," which in usage means "more ruthless" but literally means "without human beings": the emptiness is the signifier of exile, while home is where humaneness and humanity dwell.

The exile's absence from home, then, must come to signify and thus affirm the presence of a home in a place that is eternally elsewhere, forever under erasure. Brodsky himself makes this point when he writes, "Absence, in the final analysis, is a crude version of detachment: psychologically it is synonymous with presence in some other place and, in this way, expands the notion of being. In turn, the more significant the absent object, the more signs there are of its existence." Let us consider more closely now the significance of the absent home and the poet's affirmation of the elsewhere that harbors it.

Polukhina points out that "as the material means and goal of poetry, the word becomes the bearer of the spiritual content of human life," and, in the words of Jacques Lacan, "the spirit is always somewhere else." Why? Because the material means of capturing the spiritual invariably ends by displacing it. For the material traces the spatial, and the spatial is the opposite of the spiritual. Where dwelling happens, space is transformed into spirit. That is why, in the human realm, it is the body that brings the spirit to bear: a spiritual dimension of life can be an issue only for a creature of flesh and blood, only for one who eats. The absence of the body that Brodsky proclaims in *K Uranii* (*To Urania*), then, is a spiritual absence; that is, the poem uses a material means to declare that the spirit is elsewhere, particularly where we read:

> And what is space anyway if not the
> body's absence at every given
> point? That's why Urania's older than sister Clio!

Urania is the Muse of the heavens and the contemplation of the heavens, while Clio is the Muse of history. Urania is older because it is the longing for the heavens that gives rise to history. History is the tale of the human effort to reach the heavens in the vain construction of one Tower of Babel after another. The heavens comprise the realm of the Great Elsewhere that reveals to us where we are *not*.

In a poem titled **"Meksikanskii romansero" ("Mexican Romancero")**, Brodsky affirms the elsewhere of home by way of this "nowhere" when he writes:

> Something inside of me went slightly
> wrong, so to speak—off course.
> Muttering "God Almighty,"
> I hear my own voice.
>
> Thus you dirty the pages
> to stop an instant that's fair,
> automatically gazing
> at yourself from nowhere.
>
> [*A Part of Speech*]

While the English phrases "slightly wrong" and "off course" imply a loss of direction, the corresponding Russian words in the original are much stronger. They are "sorvalos'" and "raskololos'," meaning `torn apart' and `broken to pieces.' The soul has not just gone off course; it has lost the wholeness of what it is. It has lost itself and therefore is broken off from the divine: in the outcry of "God Almighty" that would make heard the voice of God the man hears only his own voice. And there is no deeper, more dreadful isolation. To be nowhere is to hear only your own voice; that is what defines the condition of exile. And yet the self upon whom the man gazes from nowhere is . . . elsewhere. Although the soul has lost its home, something of the home remains in the soul, "radi melkogo chuda" `for the sake of a small miracle,' as the Russian line reads; in the English text it is rendered by the much weaker "to stop an instant that's fair." The invocation of the small miracle entails an affirmation of the elsewhere from which the miracle stems; it amounts to the declaration that even though I am nowhere, there is a place of presence somewhere, a place where God dwells in lentils and iron pots in a land that a man can regard as native.

For the poet, however, that place remains elsewhere as long as he is a poet. Exile is his essential condition, as Brodsky has said, because there is always a distance between word and place; the exile of the man is an exile of the word. As a poet, all he has is the native tongue that strands him in a strange place from which he affirms the elsewhere. Recall, for example, the lines from Brodsky's **"1972,"** the year in which he was sent into exile:

> Listen, my boon and brethren and my enemies!
> What I've done, I've done not for fame or memo-
> ries
> in this era of radio waves and cinemas,
> but for the sake of my native tongue and letters.
> For which sort of devotion, of a zealous bent
> ("Heal thyself, doctor," as the saying went),
> denied a chalice at the feast of the fatherland,
> now I stand in a strange place. The name hardly
> matters.
>
> [*A Part of Speech*]

In this poem it is not so much the fatherland as the feast that designates the elsewhere. To be at home, on one's native and natal soil, is to sit at the table and consume the bread born from that soil, the bread that joins the man to the native land. The poet in exile and of exile is hungry. Hunger makes the place strange. It is a hunger that derives not only from what might be received but from what might be offered to the other. The distance from home is a distance from the other, from one's brother. Reaching for the chalice forever out of reach, the poet extends a hand to his fellow human being, seeking that proximity to the human reality that is the opposite of irreality. For the bread we break and share at the feast of the fatherland joins us not only with the native soil but with our brethren, those with whom we share our native tongue and for whom we answer.

Again, the affirmation of the elsewhere lies not just in the articulation of emptiness but in the stretching forth of the hand.

The hand that descends to the page to grope for the word reaches up for the elsewhere and for the other. Consider how these images work in **"Iork" ("York")** a poem written in memory of W. H. Auden:

> The emptiness, swallowing sunlight—something in
> common with
> the hawthorn—grows steadily more palpable
> in the outstretched hand's direction, and
> the world merges into a long street where others
> live.
>
> [*A Part of Speech*]

Once again we see that the distance from home lies in the distance from others; home is constituted by a human community. The emptiness described in these lines is the emptiness of the outside, of exteriority, of being left to a place that has no proximity to the human other. To be sure, the word translated as "emptiness," *pustota,* is a cognate of *pustynie,* which means "wilderness." The wilderness is that place which is external to the human community where others live. The affirmation of the elsewhere, then, is the affirmation of an interior, the kind Levinas refers to when he says, "Isn't . . . the alienation of man primarily the fact of having no home? Not to have a place of one's own, not to have an interior, is not truly to communicate with another, and thus to be a stranger to oneself and to the other." And: "There is no salvation except in the reentry into oneself. One must have an interiority where one can seek refuge. . . . And even if `at home'—in the refuge or in the interiority—there is `terror,' it is better to have a country, a home, or an `inwardness' with terror than to be outside." This is the interior that the poet seeks through his affirmation; it lies not in the isolation within oneself, where all a person hears is his own voice, but leads through the other. Interiority is to be found in the space *between* self and other.

Brodsky provides us with a poem about the poetry's affirmation of an interior elsewhere, once again, in his **"Lullaby of Cape Cod."** In connection with the matter at hand we note particularly those lines where he writes:

> Preserve these words against a time of cold,
> a day of fear: man survives like a fish,
> stranded, beached, but intent
> on adapting itself to some deep, cellular wish,
> wriggling toward bushes, forming hinged leg-
> struts, then
> to depart (leaving a track like the scrawl of a pen)
> for the interior, the heart of the continent.
>
> [*A Part of Speech*]

Here we acquire a better sense of the terror of the interior. In order to initiate a movement of return toward the elsewhere, toward this other place, the man himself must become other than who he is. This process of becoming, of course, links the elsewhere to the yet-to-be that was discussed above. And the two are linked by silence. As Brodsky puts it in his **"Strofy" ("Strophes")**:

> You won't receive an answer
> if "Where to?" swells your voice.
>
> [*A Part of Speech*]

If there is an answer or, better, a response to this question, it is "elsewhere." Since the approach toward, and affirmation of, the elsewhere entails taking on a new being, the terror that lurks in the interior is the terror of non-being, of the loss of what I am in order to become other and thus to become my own answer to the question of "Where to?" And in order to sustain that process of becoming, I must overcome the fear of no longer being who I am. The elsewhere is not only *where* but *what* I am yet to be.

Brodsky demonstrates his insight into this aspect of the condition of exile in the closing lines of **"Na vystavke Karla Veilinka" ("At Karl Weilink's Exhibition")** where we read,

> This, then, is "mastery": ability
> to not take fright at the procedure of
> nonbeing—as another form of one's
> own absence, having drawn it straight from life.
>
> (*To Urania*)

From the depths of these lines the abyss into which the man gazes peers back into the man. For here he discovers that not only is he *in* exile, but he *is* exile: not only is his home elsewhere, but he is himself elsewhere, clutching at mere traces of himself along the jagged edges of his art. The poet struggles to regain his soul by offering it up to the other, both human and divine, through his song, but the song ends by eclipsing the offering. Thus the poet no sooner speaks than he is thrown back to that position of absence from which he must once again listen for the voice that comes both from within and from beyond. In this eternal repetition, this repeated affirmation of the elsewhere, we catch a glimpse of the infinite at work in poetry. In *Less Than One* Brodsky explains: "Love is essentially an attitude maintained by the infinite toward the finite. The reversal constitutes either faith or poetry." A poem, like the home that the exile seeks, is a finite vessel of the infinite; home, like a poem, is the place where iron pots can contain the Infinite One. And love opens up the path to the elsewhere that is home, where the life of the soul unfolds in the affirming embrace of the other.

Perhaps now we may have a better sense of that life which silently abides in the sanctity of the elsewhere. The sacramental signs that go into the making of Brodsky's poetry silently convey a message that is otherwise left to mere silence. And even if the message tells us that we have no answers to the question of "Where to?" it nonetheless affirms the urgency of the question and of what is at stake in it. "When it comes down to it," Brodsky raises the question for himself, "where am I from?" This is the question that points to a place where he has yet to arrive. It is the question for which the poet expresses his defiant gratitude in a poem written on his fortieth birthday titled **"May 24, 1980"**:

> I've admitted the sentries' third eye into my wet
> and foul
> dreams. Munched the bread of exile: it's stale and
> warty.
> Granted my lungs all sounds except the howl;
> switched to a whisper. Now I am forty.
> What should I say about life? That it's long and
> abhors transparence.
> Broken eggs make me grieve; the omelette, though,
> makes me
> vomit.
> Yet until brown clay has been crammed down my
> larynx,
> only gratitude will be gushing from it.
>
> (*To Urania*)

This, then, is mastery: to give thanks for the thing that wounds the soul. For the soul is animated and known by its wounds, by the questions that emerge, like life, from broken eggs, and not by answers which, in this poem, are omelettes. The soul is punctuated not by full stops but by question marks and speaks through the howl it holds back. Thus it transforms the howl into words and silences that breathe words like a whisper. Here we see poetry's link to faith and gratitude's link to poetry: I shall sing my song even—or especially—when, by every right, it should not be there. I shall affirm the sanctity of the silent elsewhere even from within the confines of this noisy, alien nowhere.

Jacob Weisberg (review date Spring 1994)

SOURCE: "Brodsky's Venice," in *Partisan Review,* Vol. LXI, No. 2, Spring, 1994, pp. 325-27.

[*In the positive review of* Watermark *below, Weisburg discusses Brodsky's metaphorical treatment of Venice.*]

Since the publication of his 1986 collection *Less Than One,* Joseph Brodsky has continued to develop his mastery of an idiosyncratic form that defies literary genre. Brodsky's prose pieces superficially resemble familiar or critical essays, but they lack the clarity and analytic pointedness one expects from those forms. Willfully opaque and meandering, they often leave more music and texture than the sense of an argument understood. Their structures invisible, Brodsky's nonfiction writings veer often into aphorism and apostrophe, as they mine autobiographical and philosophical veins tenuously related to the topic at hand.

So it is with *Watermark,* a slim volume whose intent seems not so much to propound a thesis as to complicate and deepen an intellectual relationship, creating dazzling plays of metaphor and paradox in the process. Brodsky's is a murky, beautiful, frustrating work, which draws the reader closer to his subject without attempting definitive judgements, or really any judgement about it at all. Simultaneously absorbing and elusive, it is a literary hybrid that may be best appreciated if thought of as a kind of thematic prose-poem, or a dramatic monologue, rather than an essay.

Venice, as Mary McCarthy commented, is a phenomenon about which "the rationalist mind has always had its doubts." Her own novella-length essay on the subject, *Venice Observed,* however, constitutes an effort to see what the rationalist mind can do with the city after all. Brodsky, on the other hand, goes with the flow of the place. There is little to say about Venice as urban curiosity that has not been said already, and he is not interested in matching art-historical or architectural wits with Ruskin and Bernard Berenson (though he does steal a line from Prince Charles, blaming modern architects for doing "more harm to the European skyline than any Luftwaffe"). Rather, Brodsky uses the city as departure points for a series of watery meanderings. "If I get sidetracked," he writes, "it is because getting sidetracked is literally a matter of course here and echoes water."

Those anticipating a kind of exalted travel book, the kind a Nobel laureate might toss as a bouquet to his fans, will be disappointed. Brodsky fails to even note most of those sights beloved of tourists and neglects as well the city's politics, economics, cultural life, even its currently consuming questions of conservation. Nor does he make an effort to capture its indigenous social milieu, which is largely closed-off to short-term visitors. McCarthy made much of the materialism and matter-of-factness of the Venetians. But Brodsky's only discussion of the city's habitants is his brief aside that "no tribe likes strangers, and Venetians are very tribal."

The sole Venetian characters in his book appear almost as ghosts. The first is a minor aristocrat, "the umpteenth," who throws a party crashed by the author in a mildewed palazzo. Brodsky's *discursus* on the gala neglects the guests for the putti, and it wanders off into a meditation on time and space. The only other local in his account is not a native Venetian at all, but an American, Olga Rudge, Ezra Pound's widow, whose flat Brodsky visits with his friend Susan Sontag. Rudge feeds him tea and "garbage" and reminds him of the old CP members he dealt with as a young dissident in the Soviet Union. But she too is an anachronism, less meaningful to

Brodsky than the lifeless stones—which bring him closer to the ethereal realm he seeks.

What, we might ask, draws him to the city? Brodsky credits his visits to "visual reasons." He calls Venice "the city of the eye," and again a place where the body "starts to regard itself as merely the eye's carrier." But physical beauty, though often noted, seems a happenstance, rather than that which the poet seeks in his sojourns. Brodsky is purposeful in limiting his visits to winter, during which the days are short and the clouds hang low. This is not just a strategy for avoiding German tourists. It is during this "abstract season," as he calls it, when things are paradoxically at their most real. Venice, where Brodsky has been traveling each winter for almost twenty years, becomes a way for this self-described "cardiac cripple" to transcend the confines of the body. Venice in winter is for him a head-clearing experience, a catalyst for deeper thoughts.

> *Watermark* is a murky, beautiful, frustrating work, which draws the reader closer to his subject without attempting definitive judgements, or really any judgement about it at all. Simultaneously absorbing and elusive, it is a literary hybrid that may be best appreciated if thought of as a kind of thematic prose-poem, or a dramatic monologue, rather than an essay.
>
> —*Jacob Weisberg*

Brodsky's most pungent descriptions are often metaphorical inversions: concrete things articulated through comparison to incorporeal ones. Arriving for the first time, he writes: "The boat's slow progress through the night was like the passage of a coherent thought through the subconscious." Opening a window on Sunday, his room is flooded with a "pearl-laden haze, which is part damp oxygen, part coffee and prayers." Through the book, Venice itself appears as a dream or a reflection rather than a solid presence. And the author is a dreamer within a dream. Venice is a city to which for years he has been returning "or recurring in it, with the frequency of a bad dream." This conceit helps explain the book's apparent lack of direction. If dreams were a genre, Brodsky cracks, "their main stylistic device would doubtless be the non sequitur."

Thus the author seems as much a connoisseur of the idea of Venice as of the city itself. He describes the place almost as if it were one of Italo Calvino's magical, invisible cities. The only thing better for his purposes than a city built on water would be a city built on air, as he paraphrases Hazlitt. The Venice he loves is both the real city and the unreal one that lends itself to transcendent thoughts. The deepest theme of his essay is the passage from the real to the unreal, from the physical to the metaphysical.

Brodsky's distinctive, unidiomatic English, which reveals and conceals at the same time, is particularly appropriate to his task. Unlike Nabokov, whose adoptive language aimed to dazzle with its fluent precision, Brodsky's remains contentedly foggy. When a term sticks in his head, he repeats it more times than conventional style allows, and he relies heavily on figures of speech—"not to say," "not to mention," "better yet"—to connect his peregrinations. At the same time, he is wonderfully inventive, devising collective nouns like "a parthenon of candles" or the "kremlin of drinks" he imagines upon a table. This vernacular, too, reflects his theme; his meanings shimmer just beneath the cloudy surface of his writing.

It is in this context that Brodsky's title begins to make sense. At one level, his is a book about the actual Venice, a city which is marked by water, both historically and aesthetically. But at another level, Brodsky is writing about the watermark familiar to stamp collectors, a translucent image imbedded in paper, which becomes visible to the naked eye only when it is held up to the light or wetted. Venice for him is such an emblem; it is a physical dimension containing a metaphysical essence; a place where what goes unseen becomes visible, upon immersion in the author's own depths.

Robert D. McFadden (obituary date 29 January 1996)

SOURCE: "Joseph Brodsky, Exiled Poet Who Won Nobel, Dies at 55," in *The New York Times,* January 29, 1996, pp. A1, B5.

[*In the obituary below, McFadden provides an overview of Brodsky's life and career.*]

Joseph Brodsky, the persecuted Russian poet who settled in the United States in the early 1970's, won the Nobel Prize for Literature in 1987 and became his adopted country's poet laureate, died yesterday at his apartment in Brooklyn Heights. He was 55.

The cause was believed to be a heart attack, said Roger Straus, Mr. Brodsky's friend and publisher. Mr. Brodsky had open-heart surgery in 1979 and later had two bypass operations, and had been in frail health for many years.

The poetry of Joseph Brodsky, with its haunting images of wandering and loss and the human search for freedom, was not political, and certainly not the work of an anarchist or even of an active dissident. If anything, his was a dissent of the spirit, protesting the drabness of life in the Soviet Union and its pervasive materialist dogmas.

But in a land of poets where poetry and other literature was officially subservient to the state, where verses were marshaled like so many laborers to the quarries of Socialist Realism, it was perhaps inevitable that Mr. Brodsky's work—unpublished except in underground forums, but increasingly popular—should have run afoul of the literary police.

He was first denounced in 1963 by a Leningrad newspaper, which called his poetry "pornographic and anti-Soviet." He was interrogated, his papers were seized, and he was twice put in a mental institution. Finally he was arrested and brought to trial.

Unable to fault him on his poetry's content, the authorities indicted him in 1984 on a charge of "parasitism." They called him "a pseudo-poet in velveteen trousers" who failed to fulfill his "constitutional duty to work honestly for the good of the motherland."

The trial was held in secret, though a transcript was smuggled out and became a cause célèbre in the West, which was suddenly aware of a new symbol of artistic dissent in a totalitarian society. Mr. Brodsky was found guilty and sentenced to five years in an Arctic labor camp.

But amid protests from writers at home and abroad, the Soviet authorities commuted his sentence after 18 months, and he returned to his native Leningrad. Over the next seven years he continued to write, with many of his works translated into German, French and English and published abroad, and his stature and popularity continued to grow, particularly in the West.

But he was increasingly harassed for being Jewish as well as for his poetry. He was denied permission to travel abroad to writers' conferences. Finally, in 1972, he was issued a visa, taken to the airport and expelled. He left his parents behind.

With the help of W. H. Auden, who befriended him, he settled in Ann Arbor, Mich., where he became a poet-in-residence at the University of Michigan. He later moved to New York, teaching at Queens College, Mount Holyoke College and other schools. He traveled widely, though never back to his homeland, even after the collapse of the Soviet Government. He became a United States citizen in 1977.

Meanwhile, his poems, plays, essays and criticisms appeared in many forums, including *The New Yorker, The New York Review of Books* and other magazines. They were anthologized in books in a growing canon that garnered the 1981 MacArthur Award, the 1986 National Book Critics Circle Award, an honorary doctorate of literature from Oxford University and, in 1987, the Nobel Prize in Literature.

The Swedish Academy, which awards the prestigious prize, said he had been honored for the body of his work and "for all-embracing authorship, imbued with clarity of thought and poetic intensity." It also called his writing "rich and intensely vital," characterized by "great breadth in time and space."

In 1991, the United States added to his honors, naming him poet laureate. The rumpled, chain-smoking Mr. Brodsky had for 15 years been the Andrew Mellon Professor of Literature at Mount Holyoke College, in South Hadley, Mass., and had been scheduled to return there today to begin the spring semester.

Joseph Ellis, a former faculty dean who brought Mr. Brodsky to the college in the early 1980s, recalled yesterday how his friend often was seen speeding around the campus in an old Mercedes. He would interrupt conversations with students and colleagues to jot down notes on bits of paper he carried in his pocket. "He thought out loud in front of his students in a way that was inspirational," Mr. Ellis said.

Mr. Brodsky, who wrote in English as well as in Russian, though his poems were composed in Russian and self-translated, was a disciple of the Russian poet Anna Akhmatova, whom he called "the keening muse." He was also strongly influenced by the English poet John Donne, as well as Mr. Auden, who died in 1973. One volume of Mr. Brodsky's poetry, *Elegy to John Donne and Other Poems,* was published in London in 1967. His *Selected Poems* had a foreword by Mr. Auden.

But Mr. Brodsky was best known for three books published by Farrar, Straus & Giroux: a volume of poetry called *A Part of Speech* (1977); a book of essays, *Less Than One* (1986), which won the National Book Critics Circle Award, and a book of poems, *To Urania* (1988). Other recent works include a play in three acts called *Marbles* (1989) and a book of prose, *Watermark* (1992).

Mr. Straus remembered Mr. Brodsky as "very warm, very caring, very willing to give his friendship," especially to young writers and other exiles, some of whom he championed selflessly.

Robert Silvers, co-editor of *The New York Review of Books,* also spoke in glowing terms of Mr. Brodsky and his work. "It was astonishing that a Russian poet should have emerged as also one of the most powerful writers in the English language in just these years of exile," he said.

In Russia, Yevgeny Kiselyov, host of the weekly news program Itogi, told the nation's television viewers: "He was the only Russian poet who enjoyed the right to be called `great' in his lifetime."

It was also reported in Moscow that Gleb Uspensky, a senior editor and co-publisher of the Russian publishing house Vagrius, had met Mr. Brodsky in New York last fall and asked him to return to Russia for a tour as part of a deal to republish some of his works in Russian. Mr. Uspensky was quoted as saying that Mr. Brodsky seemed interested, but was torn by the prospect and did not agree.

Joseph Aleksandrovich Brodsky—whose first name is sometimes given as Josip or Iosif—was born in Leningrad on May 24, 1940, to Joseph Aleksandrovich Brodsky, a commercial photographer, whose status as a Jew kept him often out of work, and Maria M. Volpert Brodsky, who was linguistically gifted and often supported the family.

The redheaded boy spent his early years living in a communal apartment shared with other families. His parents gave him a Russified, assimilated upbringing, and he himself made little of his religious lineage, but as he later recalled, his teachers were anti-Semitic and treated him negatively.

The poetry of Joseph Brodsky, with its haunting images of wandering and loss and the human search for freedom, was not political, and certainly not the work of an anarchist or even of an active dissident. If anything, his was a dissent of the spirit, protesting the drabness of life in the Soviet Union and its pervasive materialist dogmas.

—Robert D. McFadden

However, he was something of a spiritual dissenter, even as a boy. "I began to despise Lenin, even when I was in the first grade, not so much because of his political philosophy or practice . . . but because of his omnipresent images," he recalled.

He quit school at the age of 15 and began working in what proved to be a series of jobs, including laborer, metal worker and hospital morgue attendant. Literature provided an alternative to the drabness of his life. He learned Polish so he could translate the works of Polish poets like Czeslaw Milosz, and English so he could translate Donne.

Beginning in 1955, he began to write poems, many of which

appeared on mimeographed sheets, known as samizdat, and were circulated among friends. Others were published by a fringe group of young writers and artists in the underground journal *Sintaksis.*

He began joining street-corner recitations, rendering his poems in a voice that was soft yet dramatic, reflecting the weariness and vibrancy in his verses. "He recited as if in a trance," one friend recalled. "His verbal and musical intensity had a magical effect." As his popularity began to grow, he also made enemies among older, more entrenched Leningrad writers.

In 1963, after a Leningrad newspaper denounced the 23-year-old poet as "a drone" and "a literary parasite," harassments began in a pattern that seemed to confirm that they had official backing. These led to a trial that began in February 1964. A transcript sent to the West contained this colloquy:

> Judge: What is your profession?
>
> Brodsky: Translator and poet.
>
> Judge: Who has recognized you as a poet? Who has enrolled you in the ranks of poets?
>
> Brodsky: No one. Who enrolled me in the ranks of the human race?

Found guilty and given a sentence of five years, Mr. Brodsky was sent to a labor camp near Arkhangelsk where he chopped wood, hauled manure and crushed rocks for 18 months. At night, in his bunk, he read an anthology of English and American poetry.

After his release and return to Leningrad, the harassment resumed, but so did his work, and some of it began appearing in the West. *Verses and Poems* was published by the Inter-Language Literary Associates in Washington in 1965. *Elegy to John Donne and Other Poems* was published in London in 1967 by Longmans Green, and *A Stop in the Desert* was issued in 1970 by Chekhov Publishing in New York.

Despite his growing stature, however, he was denied permission to attend writers' conferences abroad. In 1971, he received two invitations to immigrate to Israel. In May 1972, he was summoned to the Ministry of the Interior and asked why he had not accepted. He said he had no wish to leave his country.

Within 10 days, authorities invaded his apartment, seized his papers, took him to the airport and put him on a plane for Vienna. In Austria, he met Mr. Auden, who arranged for his transit to the United States. After a year at Michigan as poet-in-residence, he taught at Queens College (1973-74), returned to the University of Michigan (1974-80) and then accepted a chair at Mount Holyoke.

Mr. Straus recalled that he was with Mr. Brodsky in London when they learned about the Nobel Prize. "He was overjoyed," Mr. Straus recalled. "It was fairly amazing that Joseph should win at that young age." But publicly, Mr. Brodsky made light of it. "A big step for me, a small step for mankind," he joked.

In naming him United States poet laureate in 1991, James Billington, the Librarian of Congress, said Mr. Brodsky "has the open-ended interest of American life that immigrants have. This is a reminder that so much of American creativity is from people not born in America."

Mr. Brodsky is survived by his wife, Maria, and his daughter, Anna, who were with him when he died.

Martin Well (obituary date 29 January 1996)

SOURCE: "Nobel-Winning Poet Joseph Brodsky, 55, Dies," in *Washington Post,* January 29, 1996, p. B4.

[*Below, Well discusses Brodsky's life, particularly his experiences in the former Soviet Union.*]

Joseph Brodsky, 55, a poet exiled from the Soviet Union who went on to win the Nobel Prize for literature and become poet laureate of the United States, died Jan. 28 at his home in New York City.

Mr. Brodsky's longtime publisher, Roger Straus Jr., said the world-renowned poet, who had suffered for years from severe heart problems, had died of a heart attack at his apartment in Brooklyn Heights.

As much as any of his contemporaries, Mr. Brodsky seemed to typify the romantic image of the artist struggling against nature and human institutions on behalf of his poetic vision.

He grew up in a communal apartment in Leningrad. He dropped out of school at age 15, and he became one of the underground poets whose work was copied and passed from hand to hand. Brought into a Soviet Court, he defied his judge in a now-celebrated exchange and was sentenced to crush rocks near the Arctic Circle.

Exiled from the Soviet Union years later, he came to the United States and in 1977 became a U.S. citizen. He was awarded the Nobel Prize in 1987 and was named to serve at the Library of Congress as poet laureate in 1991. The first foreign-born person to win the post, he used it to plead for

American poetry and for the place of poetry in the United States.

Meanwhile, he continued to teach at Mount Holyoke College, in Massachusetts, and to write the poems that critics hailed as brilliant, individualistic and filled with complex imagery and intellectual intensity. The works were demonstrations of a technical genius that transmuted mere words into haunting music.

For years he wrote mainly in Russian, often translating afterward into English. Known for mastery of rhythm and meter, his poems frequently spoke of exile and loss. A fellow poet called his lifework "no less than an attempt to fortify the place of man in a threatening world."

Although he was ill—he had suffered three previous heart attacks, undergone two heart-bypass operations and been advised to have another—he kept writing.

He was writing "right up to the end," Straus said. On Thursday, he was in the publisher's New York office, "correcting the last few poems" for a book that is to appear shortly, Straus said.

He was "a great man and a magnificent poet," said Anthony Hecht, who was a predecessor to Mr. Brodsky as poet laureate. "All his friends have been concerned for his health for a very long time."

Joseph Alexandrovich Brodsky was born May 24, 1940, in Leningrad, the only son of a commercial photographer who served in the Soviet Navy. His mother was described as linguistically gifted. Although he was given what a friend described as an assimilated upbringing, the family suffered harassment because they were Jewish.

Mr. Brodsky showed an independent streak early on. He once recalled taking a dislike to Lenin, not so much because of the Soviet leader's policies but because his picture was inescapable in Soviet schools.

In *Less Than One,* a 1984 memoir, which won a National Book Critics Circle award, Mr. Brodsky told of why he walked away from school. He said it stemmed from a "gut reaction" in that he "simply couldn't stand certain faces in my class . . . mostly of teachers."

Afterward, he held many manual labor jobs. But at the same time, he learned Polish to translate Czeslaw Milosz and other poets, and English to translate John Donne. He made a living briefly as a translator. He began writing poems in his midteens, soon winning a reputation among the underground poets who read on street corners and whose typewritten verses were quietly passed among admirers.

As his poems gained attention, he was viewed warily in establishment cultural circles. A Leningrad newspaper denounced him in 1963 for "anti-Soviet" work, and he was subjected to harassment that included being put in a mental institution twice.

The climactic moment came in early 1964, when he was brought to court on charges of being a social parasite.

> **As much as any of his contemporaries, Mr. Brodsky seemed to typify the romantic image of the artist struggling against nature and human institutions on behalf of his poetic vision.**
>
> **—Martin Well**

Asked about his job, he told the judge that he was a poet. When asked whether he had a permanent job, he said, "I thought this was a permanent job."

"Who said that you were a poet?" the judge demanded. "Who included you among the ranks of poets?" "No one," Brodsky replied. "And who included me among the ranks of the human race?"

The sentence was five years at hard labor for shirking the duties of a Soviet citizen.

In the camp at Archangel, Mr. Brodsky had a copy of Louis Untermeyer's anthology of British and American verse. As an exercise, he would read the first and last lines of the poems and "try to imagine what would come between."

Meanwhile, a journalist had made a transcript of his hearing, and his insouciant defiance became widely known in the West. Other Soviet poets protested his sentence. Released from the labor camp after 18 months, he was allowed to return to Leningrad.

At the same time, some of his works, translated into English, German and French, were appearing in the West, winning favorable attention. But at home, the harassment continued; he was called to a government office in 1972 and asked why he had not accepted invitations to emigrate to Israel. He said he did not wish to emigrate, but it was made clear that he had to go.

In a few days, he was issued a visa and summoned to an airport. After the poems he was carrying were seized, he was put on board a flight to Vienna. Shortly afterward he came to the country where he said life was "terribly good to me" and became a poet-in-residence at the University of Michigan. He continued to write and publish works that led to the award of the Nobel Prize. The Swedish Academy cited him for his "all-embracing authorship, imbued with clarity of thought and poetic intensity."

"I'm the happiest combination you can think of," he said when he learned of the award. "I'm a Russian poet, an English essayist and citizen of the United States."

Mr. Brodsky traveled widely, but never returned to Russia, his publisher said last night.

Hecht said Mr. Brodsky had a son in Russia. Survivors include his wife, Maria, and their daughter, Anna.

J. M. Coetzee (review date 1 February 1996)

SOURCE: "Speaking for Language," in *The New York Review of Books,* Vol. XLIII, No. 2, February 1, 1996, pp. 28-31.

[*Coetzee is a South African writer. In the mixed review of the essay collection* On Grief and Reason *below, he examines Brodsky's views on poetry and discusses the poet's relationship to Russian literature.*]

In 1986 Joseph Brodsky published *Less than One,* a book of essays. Some of the essays were translated from the Russian; others he wrote directly in English, showing that his command of the language was growing to be near-native.

In two cases, writing in English had a symbolic importance to Brodsky: in a heartfelt homage to W. H. Auden, who greatly helped him after he was forced to leave Russia in 1972, and whom he regards as the greatest poet in English of the century; and in a memoir of his parents, whom he had to leave behind in Leningrad, and who, despite repeated petitions to the authorities, were never granted permission to visit him. He chose English, he says, to honor them in a language of freedom.

Less than One is a powerful book in its own right, worthy to stand beside Brodsky's principal collections of verse: *A Part of Speech* (1980) and *To Urania* (1988). It includes magisterial essays on Osip Mandelstam, Anna Akhmatova, and Marina Tsvetaeva, the poets of the generation before Brodsky to whom he feels closest, as well as two brief masterpieces of autobiographical recreation: the memoir of his parents, and the title essay, on growing up amid the stupefying boredom of Leningrad in the 1950s. There are also travel essays: a trip to Istanbul, for instance, gives rise to thoughts on the Second and Third Romes, Constantinople/Byzantium, and Moscow,

and hence on the meaning of the West to Westernizing Russians like himself. Finally, there are two virtuoso literary-critical essays in which he explicates ("unpacks") individual poems that are particularly dear to him.

Now, nine years later, we have *On Grief and Reason,* which collects twenty-one essays, all but one written since 1986. Of these, some are without question on a par with the best of the earlier work. In **"Spoils of War,"** for instance—an essay classical in form, light in touch—Brodsky continues the amusing and sometimes poignant story of his youth, using those traces of the West—corned-beef cans and shortwave radios as well as movies and jazz—that found their way through the Iron Curtain to explore the meaning of the West to Russians. Given the imaginative intensity with which they pored over these artifacts, Brodsky suggests, Russians of his generation were "the real Westerners, perhaps the only ones."

In his autobiographical journey, Brodsky has yet to arrive at the 1960s, the time of his notorious trial on charges of social parasitism and his sentencing to corrective labor in the Russian Far North. Perhaps he never will: a refusal to exhibit his wounds has always been one of his more admirable traits ("At all costs try to avoid granting yourself the status of the victim," he advises an audience of students).

Other essays also continue where *Less than One* left off. The dialogue with Auden begun in **"To Please a Shadow"** is carried on in **"Letter to Horace,"** while the long analytical essays on Thomas Hardy and Robert Frost can stand beside the earlier readings of poems by Tsvetaeva and Auden.

Nevertheless, as a whole *On Grief and Reason* is not as strong as *Less than One.* Only two of the essays—**"Homage to Marcus Aurelius"** (1994) and **"Letter to Horace"** (1995)—mark a clear advance in Brodsky's thought, and a deepening of it. Several are little more than occasional: a jaundiced memoir of a writers' conference (**"After a Journey"**), for instance, and the texts of a couple of commencement addresses. More tellingly, what in earlier essays had seemed no more than passing quirks now reveal themselves as settled elements of a systematic Brodskian philosophy of language.

The system can best be illustrated from the essay on Thomas Hardy. Brodsky regards Hardy as a neglected major poet, "seldom taught, less read," particularly in America, where he is cast out by fashion-minded critics into the limbo of "premodernism."

It is certainly true that modern criticism has had little of interest to say about Hardy. Nevertheless, despite what Brodsky says, ordinary readers and (particularly) poets have never deserted him. John Crowe Ransom edited a selection of Hardy's verse in 1960. Hardy dominates Philip Larkin's widely read *Oxford Book of Twentieth-Century English Verse*

(1973), with twenty-seven pages as opposed to nineteen for Yeats, sixteen for Auden, a mere nine for Eliot. Nor did the Modernist avant-garde dismiss Hardy en bloc. Ezra Pound, for instance, tirelessly recommended him to younger poets. "Nobody has taught me anything about writing since Thomas Hardy died," he remarked in 1934.

Brodsky chooses to present Hardy as a neglected poet as part of an attack on the French-influenced modernism of the Pound-Eliot school, and on all the revolutionary -isms of the first decades of the century, which, to his mind, pointed literature in the wrong direction. He wishes to reclaim leading positions in Anglo-American letters for Hardy and Frost, and in general for those poets who built upon, rather than broke with, traditional poetics. Thus he rejects the influential anti-naturalist poetics of the Russian critic Viktor Shklovsky, which are based on unabashed artificiality, on the foregrounding of the poetic device. "This is where modernism goofed," he says. Genuinely modern aesthetics—the aesthetics of Hardy, Frost, and, later, Auden—uses traditional forms because form, as camouflage, allows the writer "to land a better punch when and where it's least expected."

Everyday, common sense language of this kind is prominent in the literary essays in **On Grief and Reason,** which appear to have had their origin as lectures to classes of undergraduates. Brodsky's readiness to meet his audience on their own ground produces some unfortunate effects, including bathetic inflation (some lines by Rilke become "the greatest sequence of three similes in the entire history of poetry"). It is not clear that Brodsky appreciates the social significance of slang, much of which is created by powerless groups, particularly the young, to exclude outsiders. Precisely because it marks a boundary, politeness suggests that outsiders *not* trespass.

Strong poets have always created their own lineage and, in the process, rewritten the history of poetry. Brodsky is no exception. What he finds in Hardy is, to a degree, what he wants readers to find in himself; his reading of Hardy is most convincing when in veiled fashion it describes his own practices or ambitions. He writes, for example, that the germ of Hardy's famous poem "The Convergence of the Twain" (on the sinking of the Titanic) probably lay in the word "maiden" (as in the phrase "maiden voyage"), which then generated the central conceit of the poem, ship and iceberg as fated lovers. The suggestion, dropped almost in passing, seems to me a stroke of genius. But beyond that it gives an insight into Brodsky's own creative habits.

Behind Hardy's "The Convergence of the Twain" Brodsky also points to the presence of the Schopenhauer of *The World as Will and Idea:* ship and iceberg collide at the behest of a blind metaphysical force devoid of any ultimate purpose, a force that Brodsky calls "the phenomenal world's inner essence." In itself this suggestion is not novel: whether or not

Hardy had Schopenhauer in mind, Schopenhauer's brand of pessimistic determinism was clearly congenial to him. But Brodsky goes further. He recommends to his audience that they read Schopenhauer, "not so much for Mr. Hardy's sake as for your own." Schopenhauer's Will is thus attractive not only to Brodsky's Hardy but to Brodsky himself.

In fact, through his reading of five Hardy poems, Brodsky intends to reveal Hardy as a vehicle for a Schopenhauerian Will acting through language, more like a scribe used by language than an autonomous user of it. In certain lines of "The Darkling Thrush," "language flows into the human domain from the realm of nonhuman truths and dependencies [and] is ultimately the voice of inanimate matter." While this may not have been what Hardy intended, "it was what this line was after in Thomas Hardy, and he responded." Thus what we take to be creativity may be "nothing more (or less) than matter's attempts to articulate itself."

What is here called the voice of inanimate matter more often becomes, in Brodsky's essays, the voice of language, the voice of poetry, or the voice of a specific meter. Brodsky is resolutely anti-Freudian in the sense that he is not interested in the notion of a personal unconscious. Thus to him the language that speaks through poets has a truly metaphysical status. And since it sometimes spoke through Hardy, Brodsky makes clear, it is capable of speaking through every real poet, including himself. In a disconcerting way, Brodsky here finds himself not at all far from the kind of reductive cultural critique that claims that speakers are little more than the mouthpieces of dominant discourses or ideologies. The difference is that, while the latter critique is based within history, Brodsky's idea is that language—the time-marked and time-marking language of poetry—is a metaphysical force operating through and within time but outside history. "Prosody . . . is simply a repository of time within language," he wrote in **Less than One.** "Language is older than state and . . . prosody always survives history." Brodsky is unequivocal in taking away control of the history and development of poetry from the poets themselves and handing it to a metaphysical language—language as will and idea. In Hardy's poetry, for instance, having acutely pointed to a certain absence of a detectable speaking voice, to an "audial neutrality," he suggests that this apparently negative attribute would turn out to have great importance to twentieth-century poetry—would, indeed, make Hardy "prophetic" of Auden. But, Brodsky maintains, it was not so much the case that Auden or any other of Hardy's successors imitated him as that Hardy's voicelessness became "what the future [of English poetry] liked."

As an assertion about Hardy or Auden or poetry in general this may be unverifiable and to that extent meaningless. In relation to Brodsky's own poetic practice, however, it has an interest of its own. Yet for an idea so fundamental to his philosophy of poetry, it is oddly absent from his own poetry. In only one or two poems, and there only fleetingly, does Brodsky directly take as a theme the experience of being spoken through by language (of course he may claim that all his poems *embody* the experience). One explanation may be that the experience is more appropriately treated at a respectful remove in discursive prose. A more interesting explanation is that the metapoetical theme of poetry reflecting on the conditions of its own existence is absent from his own work precisely because to attempt in his own poems to understand and thus master the force behind him would strike Brodsky as not only impious but futile as well.

But even within the discourse of vatic poetry there remains something odd, even eccentric, in the elevation of prosody in particular to metaphysical status. "Verse meters in themselves are kinds of spiritual magnitudes for which nothing can be substituted," writes Brodsky. They are "a means of restructuring time." What precisely does it mean to restructure time? Brodsky never explains fully, or fully enough. He comes closest in the essay on Mandelstam in *Less than One,* where the time that utters itself through Mandelstam confronts the "mute space" of Stalin; but even there the core of the notion remains mysterious and perhaps even mystical. Nevertheless, when Brodsky says, in *On Grief and Reason,* that "language . . . uses a human being, not the other way around," he would seem to have the meters of poetry above all in mind; and when—particularly in his lectures to students—he pleads for the educative and even redemptive function of poetry ("love is a metaphysical affair whose goal is either accomplishing or liberating one's soul, . . . [and] that is and always has been the core of lyric poetry"), it is submission to the rhythms of poetry he is alluding to.

If I am right, then Brodsky's position is not far from that of the educators of ancient Athens, who prescribed for (male) students a tripartite curriculum of music (intended to make the soul rhythmical and harmonious), poetry, and gymnastics. Plato collapsed these three parts into two, music absorbing poetry and becoming the principal mental and spiritual discipline. The powers Brodsky claims for poetry would seem to belong even more more strongly to music. For instance, time is the medium of music more clearly than it is the medium of poetry (we read poetry on the printed page as fast as we like—faster than we should—whereas we listen to music in its own time). Music structures the time in which it is performed, lending it purposive form, more clearly than poetry does. Why then does Brodsky not make his case for poetry along Plato's lines, as a species of music?

The answer is of course that, while the technical language of prosody may derive from the technical language of music, poetry is not a species of music. Specifically, it works through words, not sounds, and words have meaning: whereas the semantic dimension of music is at most connotational and therefore secondary.

Since antique times we have had a well-developed account, borrowed from music, of the phonics of poetry. We have also elaborated a host of theories of the semantics of poetry. What we lack is any widely accepted theory that marries the two. The last critics in America who believed they had such a theory were the New Critics; their rather arid style of reading ran out in the sands in the early 1960s. Since then, poetry, and lyric poetry in particular, has become an embarrassment to the critical profession, or at least to the academic arm of that profession, in which poetry tends to be read as prose with ragged right margins rather than as an art in its own right.

In **"An Immodest Proposal"** (1991), a plea for a federally subsidized program to distribute millions of inexpensive paperback anthologies of American poetry, Brodsky suggests that such lines as Frost's "No memory of having starred / Atones for later disregard / Or keeps the end from being hard" ought to enter the bloodstream of every citizen, not just because they constitute a lapidary *memento mori,* and not just because they exemplify language at its purest and most powerful, but because, in absorbing them and making them our own, we work toward an evolutionary goal: "The purpose of evolution, believe it or not, is beauty."

Perhaps. But what if we experiment? What if we rewrite Frost's lines thus: "Memories of having starred / Atone for later disregard / And keep the end from being hard"? At a purely metrical level the revision is not, to my ear, inferior to Frost's original. However, its meaning is opposite. Would these lines, in Brodsky's eyes, qualify to enter the bloodstream of the nation? The answer is no—the lines are false. But to show how and why they are false entails a poetics with an historical dimension, capable of explaining why it is that Frost's original, coming into being at the moment in history when it does, carves out for itself a place in time ("restructures time"), while the alternative, the parody, cannot. Such a poetics would have to treat prosody and semantics in a unified *and* an historical way. For a teacher (and Brodsky clearly thinks of himself as a teacher) to assert that the genuine poem restructures time means little until he can show why the fake does not.

In sum, there are two sides to Brodsky's critical poetics. On the one hand there is a metaphysical superstructure in which the language-as-Muse speaks through the medium of the poet and thereby accomplishes world-historical (evolutionary) goals of its own. On the other there is a body of insights into and intuitions about how certain poems in English, Russian, and (to a lesser extent) German actually work. The poems Brodsky chooses are clearly poems he loves; his comments on them are always intelligent, often penetrating, sometimes dazzling. I doubt that Mandelstam (in the essay in *Less than One*) or Hardy (in this collection) have ever had a more sympathetic, more attentive, more cocreative reader. Fortunately the metaphysical superstructure of his system can be detached and laid aside, leaving us with a set of critical readings which in their ambitiousness and their fineness of detail put contemporary academic criticism of poetry to shame.

Can academic critics take a lesson from Brodsky? I fear they will not. To work at his level, one has to live with and by the great poets of the past, and perhaps be visited by the Muse as well.

Can Brodsky learn a lesson from the academy? Yes: not to publish your lecture notes verbatim, unrevised and uncondensed, quips and asides included. The lectures on Frost (forty-four pages), Hardy (sixty-four pages), and Rilke (fifty-two pages) could with advantage have been cut by ten to fifteen pages each.

Though *On Grief and Reason* intermittently alludes to, and sometimes directly addresses, Brodsky's own status as an exile and immigrant, it does not, except in an odd and inconclusive exercise about the spy Kim Philby, address politics pure and simple. At the risk of oversimplifying, one can say that Brodsky despairs of politics and looks to literature for redemption.

Thus, in an open letter to Václav Havel, Brodsky suggests that Havel drop the pretense that communism in Central Europe was imposed from abroad and acknowledge that it was the result of "an extraordinary anthropological backslide," whose basis was no more and no less than original sin. The President, he writes, would be well advised to accept the premise that man is inherently evil; the reeducation of the Czech public might begin with doses of Proust, Kafka, Faulkner, and Camus in the daily papers. In *Less than One* Brodsky criticized Aleksandr Solzhenitsyn on the same grounds: for refusing to accept what his senses plainly tell him, that humankind is "radically bad."

In his Nobel Prize lecture Brodsky sketches out an aesthetic credo on the basis of which an ethical public life might be built. Aesthetics, he says, is the mother of ethics, in the sense that making fine aesthetic discriminations teaches one to make fine ethical discriminations. Good art is thus on the side of the good. Evil, on the other hand, "especially political evil, is always a bad stylist." (At moments like this Brodsky finds himself closer to his illustrious Russo-American precursor, the patrician Vladimir Nabokov, than he might wish to be.)

Entering into dialogue with great literature, Brodsky continues, fosters in the reading subject "a sense of his uniqueness, of individuality, of separateness—thus turning him from a social animal into an autonomous `I.'" In *Less than One* Brodsky commended Russian poetry for setting "an example of moral purity and firmness," not least by preserving classical literary forms. Now he rejects the nihilism of postmodernism, "the poetics of ruins and debris, of

minimalism, of choked breath," holding up instead the example of those Eastern European poets of his generation—he does not name them—who, in the wake of the Holocaust and the Gulag, took it as their task to reconstruct a common world culture, and hence to rebuild human dignity.

It is not Brodsky's manner to attack, discuss, or even mention the names of his philosophical opponents. Thus one can only guess how he would respond to arguments that artworks (or "texts") construct communities of readers as much as they construct individuals, that an emphasis such as his on a highly individualistic relation between reader and text is historically and culturally bounded, and that what he (following Mandelstam) calls "world culture" is merely the high culture of Western Europe in a particular phase of its history. There can be no doubt, however, that he would reject them.

The prestige enjoyed by the poet in Russia since Pushkin, the example of the great poets in keeping the flame of individual integrity alive during Stalin's dark night, as well as deeply embedded Russian traditions of reading and memorizing poetry, the availability of cheap editions of the classics, and the near-sacred status of forbidden texts in the *samizdat* era—these and other factors have contributed to the existence in Russia of a large, committed, and informed public for poetry. The bias of literary studies there toward linguistic analysis—in part a continuation of the Formalist advances of the 1920s, in part a self-protective reaction to the ban, after 1934, on literary criticism not in line with socialist-realist dogma—has further fostered a critical discourse hard to match in the West in its level of technical sophistication.

Comments on Brodsky by his Russian contemporaries—fellow poets, disciples, rivals—collected by the poet and critic Valentina Polukhina prove that, despite nearly a quarter of a century abroad, Brodsky is still read and judged in Russia as a Russian poet.

His greatest achievement, says the poet Olga Sedakova, is to have "placed a full stop at the end of [the Soviet] literary epoch." He has done so by bringing back to Russian letters a quality crushed, in the name of optimism, by the Soviet culture industry: a tragic perception of life. Furthermore, he has fertilized Russian poetry by importing new forms from England and America. For this he deserves to stand beside Pushkin. Elena Shvarts, Brodsky's younger contemporary and perhaps his main rival, concurs: he has brought "a completely new musicality and even a new form of thought" to Russian poetry. (Shvarts is not so kind to Brodsky the essayist, whom she calls "a brilliant sophist.")

The Russians are particularly illuminating on technical features of Brodsky's verse. To Yevgeny Rein, Brodsky has found metrical means to embody "the way time flows past and away from you." This "merging of [the] poetry with the movement of time," he says, is "metaphysically" Brodsky's greatest achievement. To the Lithuanian poet Tomas Venclova, Brodsky's "giant linguistic and cultural reach, his syntax, his thoughts that transcend the limits of the stanza," make his poetry "a spiritual exercise [which] extends the reach of [the reader's] soul."

There is thus no doubt that Brodsky is a powerful presence in Russian literature. Receptive as his fellow writers are to his innovations, however, all except Rein seem skeptical about the metaphysics behind them, a metaphysics that makes the poet the voice of a Language understood as having an independent reality. Lev Loseff dismisses this "idolization" of language out of hand, attributing it to Brodsky's lack of formal education in linguistics.

At the risk of oversimplifying, one can say that Brodsky despairs of politics and looks to literature for redemption.

—J. M. Coetzee

Brodsky is not a well-loved poet, as (say) Pasternak was well loved. Russians look in vain to him, says Venclova, for "'warmth,' . . . all-forgivingness, tearfulness, tenderheartedness, or cheeriness." "He does not believe in man's inherent goodness; nor does he see nature as . . . made in the image of God." The poet Viktor Krivulin expresses doubts about the very un-Russian irony that has by now become habitual to Brodsky. Brodsky cultivates irony, suggests Krivulin, to protect himself from ideas or situations that may make him uncomfortable: "A fear of openness, possibly a desire not to be open . . . has grown deeper so that every poetic statement already exists inherently as an object for analysis and the following statement springs from that analysis."

Roy Fisher, one of Brodsky's best English commentators, points to something analogous in the texture of Brodsky's self-translations from Russian, which he criticizes as "busy" in a musical sense, with "lots of little notes and pauses." "Something is running about in the way of the poetry."

This "busyness," together with a continual ironic backtracking, has become a feature of Brodsky's prose as much as of his verse, and is likely to irritate readers of *On Grief and Reason.* Brodsky's logic has acquired a jagged quality: trains of thought have no time to develop before being halted, questioned, cast in doubt, subjected to qualifications that are in turn, with mannered irony, interrogated and qualified. There is a continual shuttling back and forth between colloquial and formal diction, and when a *bon mot* is on the horizon, Brodsky can be trusted to scamper after it. In his fascination with the echo-chamber of the English language, he is again not unlike Nabokov, though Nabokov's linguistic imagination was more disciplined (but also, perhaps, more trammeled).

The problem of consistency of tone becomes particularly marked in essays that have their origin in public addresses, where, as if in an effort to suppress the habitual sideways movement of his thought, Brodsky goes in for large generalizations and hollow lecture-hall prose. (Specimen: "Since the general purpose of every society is the safety of all its members, it must first postulate the total arbitrariness of history, and the limited value of any recorded negative experience.")

Brodsky's difficulties here may in part be temperamental—public occasions clearly do not fire his imagination—but, as the American critic David Bethea has observed, they are also linguistic. Brodsky, says Bethea, has yet to command the "quasi-civic" level of American discourse, as he has yet to entirely command the nuances of ironic humor, the very last level of English, in Bethea's view, to be mastered by foreigners.

An alternative approach to Brodsky's problem with tone is to ask whether his imagined interlocutors are always adequate to him. In his lectures and addresses there seems to be an element of speaking down that leads him not only to simplify his material but also to wisecrack and generally to flatten his emotional and intellectual range; whereas, once he is alone with a subject equal to him, this uneasiness of tone vanishes.

We see Brodsky truly rising to his subject in the two Roman essays in *On Grief and Reason.* In its emotional reach, the essay on Marcus Aurelius is one of Brodsky's most ambitious, as though the nobility of his subject frees him to explore a certain melancholy grandeur. Like Zbigniew Herbert, with whose stoic pessimism in public affairs he has more than a little in common, Brodsky looks to Marcus as the one Roman ruler with whom some kind of communion across the ages is possible. "You were just one of the best men that ever lived, and you were obsessed with your duty because you were obsessed with virtue," he writes movingly. We ought always to choose rulers who, like Marcus, have "a detectable melancholic streak," he adds wistfully.

The finest essay in the collection is similarly elegiac. It takes the form of a letter from Brodsky the Russian or (in Roman terms) Hyperborean to Horace in the underworld. To Brodsky, Horace is, if not his favorite Roman poet (Ovid holds that place), then at least the great poet of "melancholic equipoise." Brodsky plays with the conceit that Horace has just completed a spell on earth in the guise of Auden, and that Horace, Auden, and Brodsky himself are thus the same poetic temperament, if not the same person, reborn in successive Pythagorean metamorphoses. His prose attains new and complex, bittersweet tones as he meditates on the death of the poet, on the extinction of the man himself and his survival in the echo of the poetic meters he has served.

Tatyana Tolstaya (essay date 29 February 1996)

SOURCE: "On Joseph Brodsky (1940-1996)," in *The New York Review of Books,* Vol. XLIII, No. 4, February 29, 1996, pp. 7, 53.

[*Tolstaya is a Russian writer. In the following tribute, she discusses Brodsky's impact on Russian writers and literature, stating "Russian literature . . . has lost the greatest poet of the second half of the twentieth century."*]

When the last things are taken out of a house, a strange, resonant echo settles in, your voice bounces off the walls and returns to you. There's the din of loneliness, a draft of emptiness, a loss of orientation and a nauseating sense of freedom: everything's allowed and nothing matters, there's no response other than the weakly rhymed tap of your own footsteps. This is how Russian literature feels now: just four years short of millennium's end, it has lost the greatest poet of the second half of the twentieth century, and can expect no other. Joseph Brodsky has left us, and our house is empty. He left Russia itself over two decades ago, became an American citizen, loved America, wrote essays and poems in English. But Russia is a tenacious country: try as you may to break free, she will hold you to the last.

In Russia, when a person dies, the custom is to drape the mirrors in the house with black muslin—an old custom, whose meaning has been forgotten or distorted. As a child I heard that this was done so that the deceased, who is said to wander his house for nine days saying his farewells to friends and family, won't be frightened when he can't find his reflection in the mirror. During his unjustly short but endlessly rich life Joseph was reflected in so many people, destinies, books, and cities that during these sad days, when he walks unseen among us, one wants to drape mourning veils over all the mirrors he loved: the great rivers washing the shores of Manhattan, the Bosporus, the canals of Amsterdam, the waters of Venice, which he sang, the arterial net of Petersburg (a hundred islands—how many rivers?), the city of his birth, beloved and cruel, the prototype of all future cities.

There, still a boy, he was judged for being a poet, and by definition a loafer. It seems that he was the only writer in Russia to whom they applied that recently invented, barbaric law—which punished for the lack of desire to make money. Of course, that was not the point—with their animal instinct they already sensed full well just *who* stood before them. They dismissed all the documents recording the kopecks Joseph received for translating poetry.

"Who appointed you a poet?" they screamed at him.

"I thought. . . . I thought it was God."

All right then. Prison, exile.

> Neither country nor churchyard
> will I choose
> I'll come to Vasilevsky Island to
> die,

he promised in a youthful poem.

> In the dark I won't find your deep
> blue façade
> I'll fall on the asphalt between the
> crossed lines.

I think that the reason he didn't want to return to Russia even for a day was so that this incautious prophecy would not come to be. A student of—among others—Akhmatova and Tsvetaeva, he knew their poetic superstitiousness, knew the conversation they had during their one and only meeting. "How could you write that. . . . Don't you know that a poet's words always come true?" one of them reproached. "And how could you write that . . . ?" the other was amazed. And what they foretold did indeed come to pass.

I met him in 1988 during a short trip to the United States, and when I got back to Moscow I was immediately invited to an evening devoted to Brodsky. An old friend read his poetry, then there was a performance of some music that was dedicated to him. It was almost impossible to get close to the concert hall, passersby were grabbed and begged to sell "just one extra ticket." The hall was guarded by mounted police—you might have thought that a rock concert was in the offing. To my utter horror I suddenly realized that they were counting on me: I was the first person they knew who had seen the poet after so many years of exile. What could I say? What can you say about a man with whom you've spent a mere two hours? I resisted, but they pushed me on stage. I felt like a complete idiot. Yes, I saw Brodsky. Yes, alive. He's sick. He smokes. We drank coffee. There was no sugar in the house. (The audience grew agitated: Are the Americans neglecting *our* poet? Why didn't he have any sugar?) Well, what else? Well, Baryshnikov dropped by, brought some firewood, they lit a fire. (More agitation in the hall: Is *our* poet freezing to death over there?) What floor does he live on? What does he eat? What is he writing? Does he write by hand or use a typewriter? What books does he have? Does he know that we love him? Will he come? Will he come? Will he come?

"Joseph, will you come to Russia?"

"Probably. I don't know. Maybe. Not this year. I should go. I won't go. No one needs me there."

"Don't be coy! They won't leave you alone. They'll carry you through the streets—airplane and all. There'll be such a crowd they'll break through customs at Sheremetevo airport and carry you to Moscow in their arms. Or to Petersburg. On a white horse, if you like."

"That's precisely why I don't want to. And I don't need anyone there."

"It's not true! What about all those little old ladies of the intelligentsia, your readers, all the librarians, museum staff, pensioners, communal apartment dwellers who are afraid to go out into the communal kitchen with their chipped teakettle? The ones who stand in the back rows at philharmonic concerts, next to the columns, where the tickets are cheaper? Don't you want to let them get a look at you from afar, your real readers? Why are you punishing them?"

It was an unfair blow. Tactless and unfair. He either joked his way out of it: "I'd rather go see my favorite Dutch." "I love Italians, I'll go to Italy." "The Poles are wonderful. They've invited me." Or would grow angry: "They wouldn't let me go to my father's funeral! My mother died without me—I asked—and they refused!"

Did he want to go home? I think that at the beginning, at least, he wanted to very much, but he couldn't. He was afraid of the past, of memories, reminders, unearthed graves, was afraid of his weakness, afraid of destroying what he had done with his past in his poetry, afraid of looking back at the past—like Orpheus looked back at Eurydice—and losing it forever. He couldn't fail to understand that his true reader was there, he knew that he was a Russian poet, although he convinced himself—and himself alone—that he was an English-language poet. He has a poem about a hawk (**"A Hawk's Cry in Autumn"**) in the hills of Massachusetts who flies so high that the rush of rising air won't let him descend back to earth, and the hawk perishes there, at those heights, where there are neither birds nor people, nor any air to breathe.

So could he have returned? Why did I and others bother him with all these questions about returning? We wanted him to feel, to know how much he was loved—we ourselves loved him so much! And I still don't know whether he wanted all this convincing or whether it troubled his troubled heart. "Joseph, you are invited to speak at the college. February or September?" "February, of course. September—I should live so long." And, tearing yet another filter off yet another cigarette, he'd tell another grisly joke. "The husband says to his wife: 'The doctor told me that this is the end. I won't live till morning. Let's drink champagne and make love one last time.' His wife replies: 'That's all very well and fine for you—you don't have to get up in the morning!'"

Did we have to treat him like a "sick person"—talk about the weather and walk on tiptoe? When he came to speak at Skidmore, he arrived exhausted from the three-hour drive, white as a sheet—in a kind of condition that makes you want to call 911. But he drank a glass of wine, smoked half a pack of cigarettes, made brilliant conversation, read his poems, and then more poems, poems, poems—smoked and recited by heart both his own and others' poems, smoked some more, and read some more. By that time, his audience had grown pale from his un-American smoke, and he was in top form—his cheeks grew rosy, his eyes sparkled, and he read on and on. And when by all counts he should have gone to bed with a nitroglycerin tablet under his tongue, he wanted to talk and went off to the hospitable hosts, the publishers of *Salmagundi,* Bob and Peggy Boyers. And he talked, and drank and smoked and laughed, and at midnight when his hosts had paled and my husband and I drove him back to the guest house, his energy surged as ours waned. "What charming people, but I think we exhausted them. So *now* we can really talk!" "Really," i. e., the Russian way. And we sat up till three in the morning in the empty living room of the guest house, talking about everything—because Joseph was interested in everything. We rummaged in the drawers in search of a corkscrew for another bottle of red wine, filling the quiet American lodging with clouds of forbidden smoke; we combed the kitchen in search of left-over food from the reception ("We should have hidden the lo mein. . . . And there was some delicious chicken left . . . we should have stolen it.") When we finally said goodbye my husband and I were barely alive and Joseph was still going strong.

He had an extraordinary tenderness for all his Petersburg friends, generously extolling their virtues, some of which they did not possess. When it came to human loyalty, you couldn't trust his assessments—everyone was a genius, a Mozart, one of the best poets of the twentieth century. Quite in keeping with the Russian tradition, for him a human bond was higher than justice, and love higher than truth. Young writers and poets from Russia inundated him with their manuscripts—whenever I would leave Moscow for the US my poetic acquaintances would bring their collections and stick them in my suitcase: "It isn't very heavy. The main thing is, show it to Brodsky. Just ask him to read it. I don't need anything else—just let him read it!" And he read and remembered, and told people that the poems were good and gave interviews praising the fortunate, and they kept sending their publications. And their heads turned, some said things like: "Really, there are two genuine poets in Russia: Brodsky and myself." He created the false impression of a kind of old patriarch—but if only a certain young writer whom I won't name could have heard how Brodsky groaned and moaned after obediently reading a story whose plot was built around delight in moral sordidness. "Well, all right, I realize that after *this* one can continue writing. But how can he go on living?"

He didn't go to Russia. But Russia came to him. Everyone came to convince themselves that he really and truly existed, that he was alive and writing—this strange Russian poet who did not want to set foot on Russian soil. He was published in Russian in newspapers, magazines, single volumes, multiple volumes, he was quoted, referred to, studied, and published as he wished and as he didn't, he was picked apart, used, and turned into a myth. Once a poll was held on a Moscow street: "What are your hopes for the future in connection with the parliamentary elections?" A carpenter answered: "I could care less about the parliament and politics. I just want to live a private life, like Brodsky."

He wanted to live, and not to die—neither on Vasilevsky Island, nor on the island of Manhattan. He was happy, he had a family he loved, poetry, friends, readers, students. He wanted to run away from his doctors to Mount Holyoke, where he taught—then, he thought, they couldn't catch him. He wanted to elude his own prophecy: "I will fall on the asphalt between the crossed lines." He fell on the floor of his study on another island, under the crossed Russian-American lines of an emigré's double fate.

> And two girls—sisters from un-
>   lived years
> running out on the island, wave to
>   the boy.

And indeed he left two girls behind—his wife and daughter.

"Do you know, Joseph, if you don't want to come back with a lot of fanfare, no white horses and excited crowds, why don't you just go to Petersburg incognito?" "Incognito?" Suddenly he wasn't angry and didn't joke, but listened very attentively.

> Yes, you know, paste on a mustache or something. Just don't tell anyone—not a soul. You'll go, get on a trolley, ride down Nevsky Prospect, walk along the streets—free and unrecognized. There's a crowd, everyone's always pushing and jostling. You'll buy some ice cream. Who'll recognize you? If you feel like it you'll call your friends from a phone booth— you can say you're calling from America, or if you like you can just knock on a friend's door: "Here I am. Just dropped by. I missed you."

Here I was, talking, joking, and suddenly I noticed that he wasn't laughing—there was a sort of childlike expression of helplessness on his face, a strange sort of dreaminess. His eyes seemed to be looking through objects, through the edges of things—on to the other side of time. He sat quietly, and I

felt awkward, as if I were barging in where I wasn't invited. To dispel the feeling, I said in a pathetically hearty voice: "It's a wonderful idea, isn't it?"

He looked through me and murmured: "Wonderful . . . Wonderful . . . "

Jessica Greenbaum (review date 12 February 1996)

SOURCE: "Name-Dropping the Ancients," in *Nation,* New York, Vol. 262, No. 6, February 12, 1996, pp. 32-4.

[*In the following review of* On Grief and Reason, *Greenbaum faults what she considers Brodsky's obscurity, sexism, and didacticism in the volume.*]

It starts innocently enough. Perusing a book of poems or essays by Joseph Brodsky you think, "A Nobel Prize winner. He must be something." Soon on, the author mentions his friendship with Anna Akhmatova. "He must be *really* something," you correct yourself. Throughout the next pages Brodsky confirms this, letting on—through a lyricized avalanche of name-dropping—that he is intimate with every literary tradition since Genesis. You want to follow such intelligence to its zenith! But, oddly, you feel stranded by the work. Every now and then—sweating, bushwhacking your way through thickets of allusion-laden, sexist, self-indulgent, self-congratulatory prose—you wonder why a celebrated man of letters like Joseph Brodsky is largely unreadable.

On Grief and Reason, Brodsky's new collection of essays, is clearly the work of a ravenous, driven, history-drenched mind. Unlike the essays of Eavan Boland . . ., William Hazlitt, Philip Lopate or James Baldwin, his do not wander an expanding path, courteously leading the reader into widening revelations. Rather, Brodsky buckles you in with his credentials, then takes you on a joy ride into his own thickly rhetorical, associative, lint-collecting consciousness, dropping you in unmarked wilderness much of the time. This may appeal to adventurous readers. Depending on your temperament and on your ability to stomach an imperious posturing that *never* flags, you can isolate prize moments from the trip.

The first essay, **"Spoils of War,"** starts: "In the beginning, there was canned corn beef." Brodsky's bible then re-creates, with wry impressionism, the world that the war created. This passage describes the era's Philips radio:

> Through six symmetrical holes in its back, in the subdued glow and flicker of the radio tubes, in the maze of contacts, resistors, and cathodes, as incomprehensible as the languages they were generating, I thought I saw Europe. Inside, it always looked like a city at

night, with scattered neon lights. And when at the age of thirty-two I indeed landed in Vienna, I immediately felt that, to a certain extent, I knew the place. To say the least, falling asleep my first nights in Vienna felt distinctly like being switched off by some invisible hand far away, in Russia.

The metaphor's an ace—vibrant while cross-indexing the subconscious and the outer world. Brodsky, a simultaneous translator of language and language's relationship to experience, enjoys these nuggets. In his essay about the inveterate traveler, **"A Place as Good as Any,"** he describes the singularly detached observations of the tourist: "Linger by well-lit shop windows, especially those selling watches. . . . It's not that you need a new watch; it's just a nice way of killing time." The observations seem haunted by the blank space around the traveler, and end: "Admire the clean-swept pavement and perfect infinity of avenues: you always had a soft spot for geometry, which, as you know, means 'no people.'" It is a free translation, complete with poetic shadow.

Brodsky's infatuation with the experience and texture of English—he seems to drape his thoughts in huge bolts of it—is partially described in his essay titled **"The Condition We Call Exile"**: "In a manner of speaking we all work for a dictionary," he says; "Because literature *is* a dictionary, a compendium of meanings for this or that human lot, for this or that experience. It is a dictionary of the language in which life speaks to man. Its function is to save the next man, a new arrival, from falling into an old trap."

Sometimes the actual information is the only engaging portion of an essay. In **"Homage to Marcus Aurelius"** (*On Grief and Reason* often addresses the ancients), Brodsky does a fun riff on good old equestrian statuary—what it insinuated and how superior it remains to anything modern day sculptors could imply with bronzed autos. After noting that one of the few visible equestrians of our day is Prince Philip, whose given name "is of Greek origin and means *philo-hippoi:* lover of horses," he writes:

> Actually, there is a whole etiquette of equestrian statuary, as when a horse, for instance, rears up under the rider, it means that the latter died in battle. If all four hooves rest on the pediment, that suggests he died in his four-poster. If one leg is lifted high up in the air, then the implication is that he died of battle-related wounds; if not so high up, that he lived long enough, trotting, as it were, through his existence. You can't do that with a car.

Unfortunately, little else in the piece reads nearly as pointedly or engagingly. The long essay ends with choice passages from Aurelius's *Meditations,* including one especially suited to Brodsky: "Men have come into the world for the

sake of one another. Either instruct them, then, or bear with them."

Not only does the author thrive on "instructing men," he thrives on instructing *men.* Brodsky's overt sexism, especially annoying when partnering his moral posture, breeds in his grammar and swarms the book like kudzu. The poet is male, the muse female; the artist is male, the model female, blah blah. The reader, too, is presumed male. Female companions are his "young lady," his "charge" or his "distraction," and the tone is dispassionately patronizing. Although the book conjures enough literary players to fill a stadium, Brodsky mentions—fleetingly—only three women: Akhmatova and (our sluggers!) Elizabeth Bishop and Marianne Moore.

Brodsky likes *creating* information, too. Pronouncements punctuate the essays: "The most definitive feature of antiquity is our absence"; "A poet is always a conceptualist rather than a colorist"; "Of course a writer always takes himself posthumously"; "On the whole, every new aesthetic reality makes man's ethical reality more precise. For aesthetics is the mother of ethics"; "Evil, especially political evil, is always a bad stylist"; "Mimicry is the defense of individuality, not its surrender." You have to assume some are just for the heck of it, like, "A nervous person should not, and in fact cannot, keep a diary." (Exit Cheever.) Some of the proclamations ring true—like the passages about ethics and aesthetics (which Keats said differently). But most sound like pedantry or the arbitrary entitlements of The Big Thinker—the academically convoluted statement about mimicry defending individuality, for example, which doesn't seem to square with his rule about aesthetics. (Consider Nazis.)

I found the most provocative statements in **"Uncommon Visage,"** Brodsky's Nobel Lecture. "If art teaches anything—to the artist, in the first place—it is the privateness of the human condition," Brodsky writes. He then places this relationship in the context of the state:

> Language and, presumably, literature are things that are more ancient and inevitable, more durable than any form of social organization. The revulsion, irony, or indifference often expressed by literature toward the state is essentially the reaction of the permanent—better yet, the infinite—against the temporary, against the finite. To say the least, as long as the state permits itself to interfere with the affairs of literature, literature has the right to interfere with affairs of the state.

This eloquent thesis reflects some of the collection's general concerns. Brodsky considers books to be "an anthropological development, similar essentially to the invention of the wheel . . . a means of transportation through the space of experience, at the speed of a turning page." Poetry distinguishes itself from other literature, he says, by using all three modes of cognition—analytical, intuitive and prophetic—at once. Wit relieves the work sometimes. Finding the thread between dictators who committed genocide despite their literacy, he writes that what Lenin, Stalin, Hitler and Mao Zedong had in common "was that their hit list was longer than their reading list."

Brodsky's other major concern is, of course, poetry, poets and poems. The book contains painstaking treatises on Frost, Rilke, Hardy and Horace, as well as a personal remembrance of Stephen Spender, who died in July 1995. The essays on the four older poets are all deeply felt, scholarly examinations—but their development is intractable. Even the devoted will have to return with microscope and tweezers. It shouldn't be the sign of intelligence to make one do so.

Brodsky's comparison of Hardy's "The Darkling Thrush" to Frost's "Come In" may shed some light on why this happens. Brodsky notes that both poems use the same bird as an extension of the poet's psyche. While Hardy waits until the sixteenth line to introduce his thrush, Frost "gets down to business in the second line." Brodsky remarks: "On the whole, this is indicative of the difference between the Americans and the British—I mean in poetry. Because of a greater cultural heritage, a greater set of references, it usually takes much longer for a Briton to set a poem in motion."

A fascinating premise (although British sonnets work pretty fast), but more true of the author himself, who seems to want to inhale all origins for a given thought, then exhale them into the essay.

Is it impossible, linguistically, to convey kaleidoscopic thinking clearly, or does Brodsky's unedited rhetoric just get in the way? Consider this passage, for example, from **"Collector's Item,"** a baggy forty-six-page essay whose *raison d'être* I have yet to discern: "All of this leaves our author at the close of the twentieth century with a very bad taste in his mouth. That, of course, is to be expected in a mouth that is in its fifties. But let's stop being cute with each other, dear reader."

Dear reader yourself! Brodsky's language often bespeaks his indulgence. He admits to vagary or mixed metaphors without bothering to quit them. Instead he says, "I understand that I am out of my depth here. All I am trying to say is that. . . . "; or "I am mixing metaphors here, but perhaps I can justify this. . . . " He writes, "One shouldn't bother with such subtleties," then continues to do so.

Perhaps Brodsky should pay even more attention to himself than he does. In **"How to Read a Book,"** he states, "The more one reads poetry, the less tolerant one becomes of any sort of verbosity. . . . Good style in prose is always hostage to

the precision, speed, and laconic intensity of poetic diction." Yes.

Michael Harris (review date 19 February 1996)

SOURCE: "When Society Chooses to Ignore Poetry," in *Los Angeles Times,* February 19, 1996, p. E3.

[*In the following positive review of* On Grief and Reason, *Harris discusses Brodsky's views on poetry.*]

An enigma strikes anyone who has read Russian literature and pondered Russia's history: How could the same country give birth to so many people of outstanding humanity—and, at the same time, as if to a wholly different species, so many murderous goons?

In these 21 essays [in ***On Grief and Reason***], Joseph Brodsky, the Nobel Prize-winning poet who was expelled from the Soviet Union in 1972 and lived in the United States until his death on Jan. 28, not only proves himself, unsurprisingly, to be one of the good guys but comes up, quite unexpectedly, with an answer.

Poetry.

Haven't the Russians always taken poetry more seriously than anyone else? Yes and no, Brodsky says. The "celebrated Russian intelligentsia" of the 19th and early 20th centuries did, but not the mass of the nation. "Reduced . . . to a crude formula, the Russian tragedy is precisely the tragedy of a society in which literature turned out to be the prerogative of the minority."

The goons, in other words, never got the message. And in that sense—in failing to absorb what literature, the most highly evolved form of human speech, could have taught them—they really *were* a different, and inferior, species.

What about us—the democratic West? The Cold War enabled us to "externalize evil" by identifying it with communism, Brodsky warns. We forgot that "man isn't that good," that we, too, are capable of evil—as America's poets, a numerous, productive and talented tribe, a "natural resource of endurance," have been reminding us all along, if only we would listen.

Brodsky ranges widely in these essays, in a supple, pungent, idiomatic English that puts most native speakers of the language to shame. He explicates and appreciates other poets—Robert Frost, Thomas Hardy, Rainer Maria Rilke, W. H. Auden, Stephen Spender; he addresses a graduating class at the University of Michigan and (in an open letter), Czech

President Vaclav Havel, a fellow writer; he discusses the Stoic *Meditations* of Marcus Aurelius, superspy Kim Philby and the shifting terrain of exile. He is serious and funny, blunt and indirect by turns.

> **By failing to read or listen to poets, a society dooms itself to inferior modes of articulation—of the politician, or the salesman, or the charlatan—in short, to its own. It forfeits its own evolutionary potential.**
>
> —*Joseph Brodsky*

He keeps coming back, though, to the idea that "aesthetics precedes ethics," that literature, in the words of his 1987 Nobel acceptance speech, is "moral insurance," and that we all need it desperately, lest we be goons too.

Is this true? Right now, it almost doesn't matter; it's so exhilarating just to hear such a blithe and fearless assertion at a time when poetry is considered, at best, a frill in educating the work force of the 21st century to "compete."

Brodsky sees a different kind of competition:

"The old adage about the poet's role in, or his duty to, his society puts the entire issue upside down," he insists.

> By writing . . . in the language of his society, a poet takes a large step toward it. It is society's job to meet him halfway, that is, to open his book and read it. . . .
>
> By failing to read or listen to poets, a society dooms itself to inferior modes of articulation—of the politician, or the salesman, or the charlatan—in short, to its own. It forfeits . . . its own evolutionary potential. . . .
>
> The charge frequently leveled against poetry—that it is difficult, obscure, hermetic and whatnot—indicates not the state of poetry but, frankly, the rung of the evolutionary ladder on which society is stuck.

Seamus Heaney (essay date 3 March 1996)

SOURCE: "The Singer of Tales: On Joseph Brodsky," in *The New York Times Book Review,* March 3, 1996, p. 31.

[*Heaney is an Irish poet who was awarded the Nobel Prize in Literature in 1995. In the tribute below, he fondly remembers Brodsky's passion for language and poetry.*]

Those who knew Joseph Brodsky were well aware that his heart disease was serious and that it would probably be the death of him, but because he always existed in his friends' minds not just as a person but as some kind of principle of indestructibility, it was difficult for them to admit that he was in danger. The intensity and boldness of his genius plus the sheer exhilaration of being in his company kept you from thinking about the threat to his health; he had such valor and style, and lived at such a deliberate distance from self-pity and personal complaint, you were inclined to forget that he was as mortal as the next one. So his death in January at the age of 55 was all the more shocking and distressing. Having to speak of him in the past tense feels like an affront to grammar itself.

There was a wonderfully undoubting quality about Joseph, an intellectual readiness that was almost feral. Conversation attained immediate vertical takeoff and no deceleration was possible. Which is to say that he exemplified in life the very thing that he most cherished in poetry—the capacity of language to go farther and faster than expected and thereby provide an escape from the limitations and the preoccupations of the self. Verbally, he had a lower boredom threshold than anyone I have ever known, forever punning, rhyming, veering off and homing in, unexpectedly raising the stakes or switching tracks. Words were a kind of high octane for him, and he loved to be propelled by them wherever they took him. He also loved to put a spin on the words of others, whether by inspired misquotation or extravagant retort. Once, for example, when he was in Dublin and complaining about one of our rare heat waves, I suggested jokingly that he should take off for Iceland, and he replied in a flash, with a typical elevation and roguery, "But I could not tolerate the absence of meaning."

His own absence will be even harder to tolerate. From the moment I met him in 1972, when he was passing through London on the second leg of his journey from dissidence in Russia to exile in the United States, he was a verifying presence. His mixture of brilliance and sweetness, of the highest standards and the most refreshing common sense, never failed to be both fortifying and endearing. Every encounter with him constituted a renewal of belief in the possibilities of poetry. There was something magnificent in his bewilderment at the sheer ignorance of the demands of the art evident in the work of many poets with big reputations, just as there was something bracing about what he called "doing the laundry list" with him, which meant going over the names of contemporaries, young and old, each of us sticking up for the ones he regarded most. It was like meeting a secret sharer.

But that was a personal bonus, and in the end it is less important than what might be called his impersonal importance. This had to do with Joseph Brodsky's total conviction about the trustworthiness of poetry as a force for good—not so much "for the good of society" as for the health of the individual mind and soul. He was resolutely against any idea that put the social cart before the personal horse, anything that clad original response in a common uniform. "Herd" for Joseph would have been the opposite of "heard," but that did not lessen his passion to reinstate poetry as an integral part of the common culture of the United States.

Verbally, Joseph had a lower boredom threshold than anyone I have ever known, forever punning, rhyming, veering off and homing in, unexpectedly raising the stakes or switching tracks. Words were a kind of high octane for him, and he loved to be propelled by them wherever they took him.

—*Seamus Heaney*

Not that he wished to use the sports stadiums for poetry readings. If anyone happened to bring up the huge audiences that attended such events in the Soviet Union, there would be an immediate comeback: "Think of the garbage they have to listen to." In other words, Brodsky decried the yoking together of politics and poetry ("The only thing they have in common are the letters p and o"), not because he had no belief in the transformative power of poetry per se but because the political requirement changed the criteria of excellence and was likely to lead to a debasement of the language and hence to a lowering of "the plane of regard" (a favorite phrase) from which human beings viewed themselves and established their values. And his credentials for such a custodianship of the poet's role were, of course, impeccable, since his arrest and trial by the Soviet authorities in the 1960's and his subsequent banishment to a work camp near Archangel had specifically to do with his embrace of poetic vocation—a socially parasitical vocation, according to the prosecution. This had turned his case into something of an international cause célèbre and insured him immediate fame when he arrived in the West; but instead of embracing victim status and swimming with the currents of radical chic, Brodsky got down to business right away as a teacher at the University of Michigan.

Before long, however, his celebrity was based more on what he was doing in his new homeland than on what he had done in the old one. To start with, he was an electrifying speaker of his own poems in Russian, and his many appearances at universities all over the country in the 1970's brought a new vitality and seriousness to the business of poetry readings. Far from cajoling the audience with a pose of man-in-the-street low-keyness, Brodsky pitched his performance at a bardic level. His voice was strong, he knew the poems by heart and his cadences had the majesty and poignancy of a cantor's, so his performance never failed to induce a sense of occasion in all who attended. He therefore gradually began to be regarded as the figure of the representative poet, sounding prophetic even though he might demur at the notion of the prophetic role, and impressing the academics by the depth of his knowledge of poetic tradition from classical times up through the Renaissance and in modern European languages, including English.

Still, if Joseph was uneasy about the prophetic, he had no such qualms about the didactic. Nobody enjoyed laying down the law more than he, with the result that his fame as a teacher began to spread and certain aspects of his practice came to be imitated. In particular, his insistence that students learn and recite several poems by heart had considerable influence in creative writing schools all over the United States, and his advocacy of traditional form, his concentration on matters of meter and rhyme, and his high rating of nonmodernist poets like Robert Frost and Thomas Hardy also had the general effect of reawakening an older poetic memory. The climax of all this was to come with his **"Immodest Proposal,"** made in 1991 during his term as poet laureate. Why not print poetry in millions of copies, he asked, since a poem "offers you a sample of complete . . . human intelligence at work" and since that same poem also tells its readers, "Be like me"? Moreover, because poetry employs memory, "it is of use for the future, not to mention the present." It can also do something for ignorance and is "the only insurance available against the vulgarity of the human heart. Therefore, it should be available to everyone in this country and at a low cost."

This mixture of barefaced challenge and passionate belief was typical of him. He was always putting the slughorn to his lips and blowing a note to call out the opposition—even the opposition within himself. He was, indeed, a walking, talking example of Yeats's notion that poetry comes out of that inner quarrel. It manifested itself in everything he did, from the urgency of his need to go into overdrive when rhyming to the incorrigible cheek of his duel with death itself every time he bared his teeth to nick the filter off a cigarette. He burned not with the hard, gemlike flame that Walter Pater proposed as an ideal but rather with a kind of flame thrower's whoosh and reach, supple and unpredictable, at once a flourish and a menace. When he used the word "tyrant," for example, I was always glad that he wasn't talking about me.

He was all for single combat. He took on stupidity as eagerly as tyranny (in his understanding, after all, the former was only another aspect of the latter), and he was as bold in conversation as he was in print. But the print is what we have of him now, and he will survive behind its black lines, in the pace of its poetic meter or its prose arguments, like Rilke's panther pacing behind black bars with a constancy and inexorability set to outpace all limit and conclusion. And he will survive too in the memories of his friends, but for them there will be an extra sweetness and poignancy in the pictures they carry—which in my own case will include that first sight of him as a young man in a red woolen shirt, scanning his audience and his fellow readers with an eye that was at once as anxious as a hedge creature's and as keen as a hawk's.

Hugh Kenner (review date 14 April 1996)

SOURCE: "Between Two Worlds," in *The New York Times Book Review,* April 14, 1996, p. 14.

[*In the positive review of* On Grief and Reason *below, Kenner praises the title essay of the collection, stating that it is "probably the best piece ever written on the poetry of Robert Frost."*]

The vital information: Joseph Brodsky was born in 1940 and came to the United States in 1972 as an involuntary exile from the Soviet Union. He was awarded the Nobel Prize in Literature in 1987 and was Poet Laureate of the United States in 1991 and 1992. He died early this year. The essays and lectures collected in **On Grief and Reason** are mostly post-Nobel. A writer, then, who spent nearly half his life immersed in a language he hadn't grown up speaking.

That can be enabling; the example of Samuel Beckett in Paris comes to mind, or of Joseph Conrad in London. Conrad, who'd grown up with Polish, even had to choose whether the language for his novels would be French or English, each of which offered a stable and literate public. He is said to have chosen English because he judged the competition less formidable: no British Stendhal or Flaubert to be threatened by. Though his spoken English is reported to have been often impenetrable, his fiction abounds in local brilliances no native speaker would have thought of, like "He was densely distressed."

And Brodsky? How did he navigate between the spoken and written modes of American English? Neither offers much guidance to the other. What you say and what you write are apt to be somewhat different. To add complexity, many pieces he wrote were intended for speaking—for instance, in a football stadium at the University of Michigan. He told the 1988 graduating class, "To say the least, you were born, which is in itself half the battle, and you live in a democracy—this halfway house between nightmare and utopia—which throws fewer obstacles in the way of an individual than its alterna-

tives." Whether the first half of that sentence grins a feeble grin or encodes a Russian profundity depends perilously on how the spoken phrases are cadenced. Verbose buffoonery of that order infests many of Brodsky's paragraphs.

But suspension between two worlds also empowered some incomparable pages. The title essay here is probably the best piece ever written on the poetry of Robert Frost. Brodsky ends a brief summary of Frost's life by proposing that both the adulation and the resentment he received had in common

> a nearly total misconception of what Frost was all about. He is generally regarded as the poet of the countryside, of rural settings—as a folksy, crusty, wisecracking old gentleman farmer, generally of positive disposition. In short, as American as apple pie. He was indeed a quintessential American poet; it is up to us, however, to find out what that quintessence is made of, and what the term "American" means as applied to poetry and, perhaps, in general.

It is enthralling to listen to Brodsky's mind at work on what the term "American" means. He very quickly separates Frost from "the continental tradition of the poet as tragic hero." No, Lionel Trilling had it right when he called Frost "terrifying." For tragedy looks back on what has happened, whereas terror pertains to what may happen. Brodsky transcribes a Frost poem, "Come In," and devotes seven pages to guiding us through it. By the time we have assented to those pages we'll have ceased to think of Frost as a folksy farmer. "The 20 lines of the poem constitute, as it were, the title's translation. And in this translation, I am afraid, the expression `come in' means `die.'" But the essay still has 32 pages to run, and in them Brodsky turns from Frost "at his lyrical best" to confront "his narrative best": the poem "Home Burial." He commences by proposing that Frost is "a very Virgilian poet," though not the Virgil of the *Aeneid,* not the Virgil of the *Eclogues* and *Georgics.* "With few exceptions," Brodsky ventures, "American poetry is essentially Virgilian, which is to say contemplative."

"Yet Frost's affinity with Virgil is not so much temperamental as technical," he says.

> Frost and Virgil have in common a tendency to hide the real subject matter of their dialogues under the monotonous, opaque sheen of their respective pentameters and hexameters. A poet of extraordinary probing and anxiety, the Virgil of the *Eclogues* and the *Georgics* is commonly taken for a bard of love and country pleasures, just like the author of *North of Boston.*

Frost's "Home Burial" begins: "He saw her from the bottom of the stairs / Before she saw him"—on which Brodsky confers the adjective "Hitchcockian." He'll have us imagine this line and a half "sitting on the page all by itself, in minimalist fashion." Now "place yourself in either position—better in his—and you'll see what I mean. Imagine yourself observing, watching somebody or imagine yourself being watched. Imagine yourself interpreting someone's movements—or immobility—unbeknownst to that person. That's what turns you into a hunter, or into Pygmalion." What renders this account gripping is that its author speaks with the authority of experience. This is how poets work: they set up tensions in a dozen words, for the next half-dozen words to interact with. A familiar instance: "Let us go then, you and I, / When the evening is spread out against the sky." That unnerves with portent. Who speaks? And does the "you" address me, the reader? Or someone other than the speaker and me? And go where? Whereupon a third line impinges abruptly on our unease—"Like a patient etherized upon a table." So poems proceed; and attention must regroup, redeploy itself, in very brief stretches. The familiar "Yes, but what does it mean?" derives from an assumption that meaning exists only once the poem is complete. But if our way of reading is to wait impatiently for that moment we'll have experienced nothing.

For this essay on Frost, for an equally probing one on four poems by Thomas Hardy, for an **"Homage to Marcus Aurelius"** for half a hundred pages on an English translation of a poem Rainer Maria Rilke wrote in German 90 years ago, and for many scattered felicities, this collection is occasion for gratitude. It is rare for someone so advantageously situated, within poetry but both within and outside of American speech, culture and experience, to confide in us with such pedagogic confidence.

FURTHER READING

Criticism

Billington, James H. "The Poet Who Proved the Power of Words." *Washington Post* (January 30, 1996): D1.
    Tribute by the librarian of Congress who appointed Brodsky poet laureate of the United States.

Phillips, William. "Intellectuals and Writers since the Thirties." *Partisan Review* LIX , No. 4 (Fall 1992): 531-58.
    Transcript of a panel led by Phillips with writers Saul Bellow, Ralph Ellison, Czeslaw Milosz, and Brodsky. The writers discuss such subjects as the role of writers and intellectuals, history, Eastern European literature, and the influence of religion on society.

Additional coverage of Brodsky's life and career is contained in the following sources published by Gale Research: *Contemporary Authors,* Vols. 41-44R; *Contemporary Authors New Revision Series,* Vol. 37; *DISCovering Authors Modules: Poetry; Major Twentieth Century Writers;* and *Poetry Criticism,* Vol. 9.

George Mackay Brown

1921-1996

Scottish poet, novelist, short story writer, essayist, dramatist, scriptwriter, journalist, librettist, and author of children's books.

The following entry presents criticism on Brown's works through 1996, including reviews of two posthumously published collections. For further information on his life and career, see *CLC,* Volumes 5 and 48.

INTRODUCTION

One of Scotland's foremost contemporary authors, Brown incorporated in his writings elements from Norse sagas, Scottish ballads, medieval legends and myths, and Roman Catholic ritual. He commonly employed simple language and syntax and explored themes of history, religion, mysticism, and the people and life of his native Orkney Islands. Deeply committed to the values inherent in the elemental existence of Orkney's farmers and fishermen, Brown extolled the virtues that can be gained through hardship and emphasized the damaging effects of the forces of progress on Orkney society. While Brown's antiquated prose style and his preoccupation with Orkney were sometimes faulted for failing to engage contemporary realities, most critics complimented his intimate portrayal of a specific locality and his fundamental insight into the common concerns of human existence.

Biographical Information

Brown was born in the seaport town of Stromness on the island of Orkney, attended Stromness Academy from 1926 to 1940, and received bachelor's and master's degrees in English from Edinburgh University. Throughout his career, Brown was the recipient of a number of awards and honorary degrees, including fellowship in the Royal Society of Literature and officer's rank in the Order of the British Empire. Brown never married and remained a dedicated Orcadian throughout his life—he rarely traveled, and visited England only once. Brown died on April 13, 1996, in a Kirkwall hospital at the age of 74, and was buried near Stromness on April 16, the Feast of St. Magnus, a figure significant in his life and work.

Major Works

Brown began publishing his work at the suggestion of Scottish poet and fellow Orcadian Edwin Muir. In his introduction to Brown's initial collection of verse, *The Storm and Other Poems* (1954), Muir stated: "[Brown writes] beautiful and original poems, with a strangeness and magic rare anywhere in literature today." Using metrical unrhymed verse and images of arrested action that critics have compared to Muir's poetry, Brown introduced in this volume his contemplation of Orkney and his concerns with religious symbolism and myth. In his next volume, *Loaves and Fishes* (1959), which was praised for is mature themes and outlook, Brown displays his interest in Icelandic legend, Christianity, martyrdom, and Orcadian history. The pieces in *The Year of the Whale* (1965) employ evocative symbolism and are endowed with a vivid sense of character and place. Combining secular and religious themes, local and epic subjects, these poems range in setting from Orkney during the Viking era to the United States during the presidency of John F. Kennedy. Brown's conversion to Roman Catholicism in 1961 emerges in this volume through his use of litanies and his preoccupation with birth, love, death, resurrection, and religious ceremony.

Fishermen with Ploughs: A Poem Cycle (1971), a sequence of loosely connected lyrics and sections of prose, is often considered Brown's most impressive poetic achievement.

Extending his stylistic forms to include triadic runes and incantations and utilizing poetic structures derived from the months of the year, the days of the week, and the Roman Catholic stations of the cross, Brown depicts Orkney life from its first settlements in the ninth century through its present depopulation and imagines future resettlement following a nuclear holocaust. Replete with apocalyptic despair and disillusionment, these poems solidify Brown's position against materialistic progress and exemplify a central idea in philosophy: "It could happen that the atom-and-planet horror at the heart of our civilization will scatter people again to the quite beautiful fertile places of the world." *Winterfold* (1976) contains a series of rune-like variations on the stations of the cross and "affirms [Brown's] belief that the journey of Christ parallels the fruitful journey of all things that follow nature to death, and resurrection in harvest," in the words of Dennis O'Driscoll. This volume has been interpreted as an optimistic postscript to the dark vision prevalent in *Fishermen with Ploughs*. *Voyages* (1984) continued Brown's interest in history, Norse medievalism, and the Orkneys. *The Wreck of the Archangel* (1989) confirmed Brown's position as an important poet.

Brown was also a prose writer, and produced a number of short story collections, novels, and essay collections. His first novel, *Greenvoe* (1972), describes the gradual decimation of a mythical Orkney fishing village after the construction of a secret military establishment on the island. By detailing the events of the five days preceding its final demise, Brown suggests that the banal existence of its inhabitants inadvertently contributed to the destruction of the village. Despite its bleak theme, *Greenvoe* concludes with an ambiguous but uplifting promise of resurrection. In *Magnus* (1973), Brown combines the starkness of Norse saga with the ornamentalism of the Roman Catholic mass. The story of the martyrdom and sanctification of twelfth-century Earl Magnus of Orkney, who was killed by his cousin and rival for supreme control of the Orkneys, *Magnus* extends Brown's fascination with the Christian theme of redemption. Brown's third novel, *Time in a Red Coat* (1984), is a fable that chronicles the experiences of a young Eastern princess as she journeys through distant countries and flees the devastation of her homeland by marauders. An innocent figure, the princess begins her travels in a white coat that gradually turns red due to the human folly and injustice she encounters. In *Vinland* (1992) "Brown has returned to the world of his beloved *Orkneyinga Saga,* that astonishing, bloody and darkly humorous chronicle of early Orkney which also provided material for his novel *Magnus,*" Jonathan Coe remarked. *Vinland* chronicles the spiritual development of it hero, Ranald Sigmundson, from youthful seafaring adventures to old age. The fictional locale of Vinland "comes to symbolise a hope of release from the grip of the Orcadians' primitive, fatalistic Christianity, as well as providing a model of man in harmony rather than conflict with the physical world—a natural equivalent of the 'Seamless Coat' after which

St Magnus was searching in the earlier novel," Coe noted. *Beside the Ocean of Time* (1994), which was shortlisted for the 1994 Booker Prize, again presents an island hero, a young dreamer named Thorfinn whose adventure fantasies illuminate the Orkney lifestyle.

An eminent chronicler of Orkney life and geography, Brown has published numerous collections of essays, including *An Orkney Tapestry* (1969), which Seamus Heaney described as "a spectrum of lore, legend, and literature, a highly coloured reaction as Orkney breaks open in the prisms of a poet's mind and memory." In *Portrait of Orkney* (1981), Brown intertwines contemporary descriptions and facts with history, legend, and anecdote. Brown's works for the stage include *A Spell for Green Corn* (1970), which is concerned with symbolism, ritual, and the supernatural, and *The Loom of Light* (1972), an adaptation of *Magnus.* He has also written radio and television plays and published several children's books, including *The Two Fiddlers: Tales from Orkney* (1974) and *Pictures in a Cave* (1977), and a biographical work, *Edwin Muir: A Brief Memoir* (1975).

Critical Reception

Most essays about Brown and his work describe him as a writer of unparalleled importance to Orkney society, and significant as well to readers of all nations. Although some critics have found his chosen narrowness of topics and locales limiting, others have praised Brown's body of work as valuable in its depth rather than breadth, agreeing with his assessment of Orkney as "a microcosm of all the world." Obituaries and tributes described Brown as "one of the great poets of place" (Ray Olson), "a giant of literature and much loved" (The London *Tablet*), "a major influence" and a leader of "the Scottish literary renaissance" (*The Guardian*).

PRINCIPAL WORKS

The Storm and Other Poems (poetry) 1954
Loaves and Fishes (poetry) 1959
The Year of the Whale (poetry) 1965
A Calendar of Love and Other Stories (short stories) 1967
A Time to Keep and Other Stories (short stories) 1969
Fishermen with Ploughs: A Poem Cycle (poetry) 1971
Poems New and Selected (poetry) 1971
Greenvoe (novel) 1972
Magnus (novel) 1973
Hawkfall and Other Stories (short stories) 1974
Winterfold (poetry) 1976
Andrina and Other Stories (short stories) 1983
Time in a Red Coat (novel) 1984
The Wreck of the Archangel (poetry) 1989
Selected Poems, 1954-1983 (poetry) 1991

Vinland (novel) 1992
Beside the Ocean of Time (novel) 1994
Winter Tales (short stories) 1995

CRITICISM

Glyn Maxwell (review date 11-17 May 1990)

SOURCE: "Island Voices," in *The Times Literary Supplement,* No. 4545, May 11-17, 1990, p. 495.

[*In the following review of* The Wreck of the Archangel, *Maxwell praises Brown as a creator of "pure and unadulterated" poetry.*]

There can be few poets anywhere in the Western world writing as pure and unadulterated a poetry as that of George Mackay Brown. His line of descent begins with the Wanderer/Seafarer, alone with his language. But Mackay Brown is very much at anchor, partaking of what his mournful ancestor dreamed: "a fire, autumn beef and ale, welcomings there, / they warmed and worded them well". There is something wondrous about a contemporary poet who is not only alert to the chances given by the kenning, the compound, the archaism, but takes them—"wavecrash", "sunbright"—and, by dint of that awareness, enables the compounds we already have ("sweetheart", "starlight", "blackbird", "nightfall") to split and reform with freshened power.

Mackay Brown's phrases are hewn and stripped [in *The Wreck of the Archangel*], the whole poem an act of fierce reclamation from an unending sea that is not, like the one Crichton Smith sees, a call to memory or the imagining of what is beyond, but a dreaded entity: a man's feet are "in thrall always / To the bounteous terrible harp", and a life of craggy solitude on the bleak island is harvesting merely to survive. Whether aboard ship or on land, the hard sounds of the poet's farmers and fishermen are isolated by the ocean's sibilance. Mackay Brown possesses the great gift without which alliteration is merely decorative. He uses it to colour in, to point, to focus:

> The seamen stopped their lading. Poets are welcome,
> They remind men of the great circle of silence
> Where the saga sails forever.

His capacity to invigorate the limited scope of what is about him allows his religious conviction to come alive in the simplest of pieces. After all, one of the great joys of island life must be arrival at a warm inn; but this homely scene can absorb stars, shepherds, kings: "Far on, they saw what one took to be a star, / Or a man with a lantern", or the voice of the poet himself: "By midnight, I had stood at every door / In the island but one, / And it is a shelter for sheep."

Andrew Wawn (review date 28 August 1992)

SOURCE: "Access to Eden," in *The Times Literary Supplement,* No. 4665, August 28, 1992, p. 18.

[*In the following review, Wawn remarks favorably on the imagery employed in* Vinland.]

[*Vinland*] is a strange and striking saga-novel by an Orcadian who long ago earned an honoured place on the runic roll of those post-medieval writers who have sought to recreate and respond to the world of the ancient Viking north. George Mackay Brown writes of feeling like "Aladdin in the enchanted cave", as he surveyed the huge deposits of Norse-related narrative over which his imagination could range. It seems an appropriate image, much favoured by early nineteenth-century Scandinavian writers as they discovered the genie within the long neglected lamp of Eddic poem and saga. Some of the accumulated textual tarnish was polished off by the great Arnamagnæan Commission series of editions, each with a facing-page Latin translation, which reached out to educated readers throughout Europe in the nineteenth century. British Icelandophiles, among them Sir Walter Scott, began to acquire these volumes; his splendid Orcadian novel *The Pirate* draws heavily on the painstakingly accumulated Icelandic holdings in his Abbotsford library.

The sagas used by Scott are among the identifiable impulses behind Mackay Brown's novel: *Brennu-Njáls saga, Orkneyinga saga,* the so-called Vinland sagas. The contrasting voices of the medieval Celtic lyric and Hans Christian Andersen also seem to catch the ear. The sour-spirited critic may grumble about inadequately assimilated sources. The specialist reader is much more likely to enjoy identifying the provenance of the oneliners, the gnomic saws, the motifs and the incidents with which the narrative is flecked; there is a convincing sense that the novelist has husbanded the material shrewdly and made it securely his own. The general reader will find many other features by which to be challenged, intrigued and moved, as the narrative pursues its laconic way in sinewy language and syntax which seeks constantly to challenge stale colloquial expectation.

At first sight, *Vinland* seems taken up with moods, gestures and epiphanies; it does not signal excitedly when important ideas appear in its narrative. Thus, at one level, we follow the fortunes of Ranald the hero, as he moves determinedly but uncertainly from a sea-roving youth, through agrarian middle age and on to visionary and rheumatic senility. We register, too, the narrative fate of other young men, "splits" of the protagonist, who were either less fortunate or more rebellious—as when Ranald the dutiful son fathers Einhof the runaway heir. Gradually, a pattern of ideas—of themes and variations—emerges. Ranald roves the seas between Greenland, Vinland, Iceland and Orkney, but the dilemmas of Viking life follow him like porpoises. For all the novel's gloomy sense of fate's tight fist, the North Atlantic hero has endlessly to exercise his (all too) free will in making hard choices: heroic enterprise or agrarian domesticity, lobster-fishing or learning Latin, ship or farmhouse, crew or family. He might also decide between the conflicting wishes of father and mother and loyalty to foreign king or to homeland—a fraught choice in a homeland in which "there are always two earls, sometimes three". Are the prizes worth the prices? Is civilization really just like old age; that is, tolerable only when you consider the alternative? It is no wonder that many a grizzled Orcadian soul took refuge in the strong libations supplied by Ord, the surly malt-maker of Papa Stronsay.

As Viking society struggles on stubbornly and unstably through days of fair and foul, feast and famine, the narrative generates consolatory images of permanence—poetry, memory, and religion. Poetry—a vision of the "Fatal Sisters"—is as powerful now in Mackay Brown's Orcadian vision as it formerly was with Scott, Thomas Gray, and on back via Torfæus's *Orcades* to the great Battle of Clontarf poem in *Njáls saga*. Indeed, as this seven-hundred-year span of literary continuity proves, poetry can offer permanence. Hence the novel's investigation of the creative processes of its poets; there are some half-a-dozen arresting poems among the sections of taut and gritty semi-alliterative prose.

While poems can outlive the poet, Ranald's dreams and memories go to the ship-shaped stone chapel of death with him. At least such visions had helped to make endurable the thistle-strewn path through old age. Ranald's youthful voyage to Vinland provided a crucial imaginative reference point for the rest of his life. In his dotage, he still ponders distractedly but obsessively the possibility of having a boat built which might take him back to make his peace with that wondrous land of grape and butter-nut. Vinland was an Edenic world, an earthly emanation of some divine harmony; and it was tainted by Viking man—by accident and fear as much as by malevolence.

Earthly access to true paradise is available to Ranald through the sacramental system of the Christian church, towards whose witness he turns with ever increasing intensity in his last isolated and ascetic years. For some Victorian recreators of the North—Sir George Dasent, for instance—the Christian religion in medieval Scandinavia had been a baleful authoritarian influence on the democratic, muscular-pagan world of the Viking sea-pirate. The new faith had led people to sit down and think, rather than go out and do; this was not the way to

win—or retain—an empire. Mackay Brown's novel is more sympathetic. Its Christian vision is powerful, but its voice is not that of medieval Christendom. Both faith and language are rooted in the strakes and thwarts and wave-crests of the real boats of real sailors.

It is with such images that the book ends—and it is in this sensibility that the linguistic as well as the spiritual heart of the book lies. The author has clearly relished looting the neglected granaries of language, for the seductive delights of chidden dogs, unthonged bags, unbunged casks, slugabeds, gluttings, reeks of scorchings, crepitations of cinders, word-storms, boat-nousts, dottled farmers, blackavized ruffians, and the rest. Philology and literary creativity are thus fruitfully united by Northern enthusiasms.

Jonathan Coe (review date 24 September 1992)

SOURCE: "Sydney's Inferno," in *London Review of Books,* Vol. 14, No. 18, September 24, 1992, p. 22.

[*In the following excerpt, Coe discusses Brown's exploration of "the riddle of fate and freedom" in* Vinland.]

If you want to consider the struggle of the individual in the face of supernatural forces, to address what George Mackay Brown calls 'the riddle of fate and freedom', then you are best-off retreating into the distant past, as he has done in his fifth novel, **Vinland.** Here Brown has returned to the world of his beloved *Orkneyinga Saga,* that astonishing, bloody and darkly humorous chronicle of early Orkney which also provided material for his novel **Magnus** in 1973. This time, instead of drawing modern historical parallels, Brown has confined himself to putting fictional flesh onto historical bones, in a narrative which switches back and forth from the diplomatic warring between the rival Earls of Orkney and their sovereigns, the Kings of Norway, to detailed imaginative re-inventions of the lives of ordinary farmers, merchants and seamen forcing out a living from the islands.

On the face of it the book has an obvious structural flaw. It begins as a thrilling adventure story, with a young seafarer, Ranald Sigmundson, stowing away on a ship from Greenland which sets its course for the edge of the world and manages to end up in North America, which the explorers dub 'Vinland' on account of the lushness of its grapes. Initially friendly relations with the American Indians are promptly ruined by a callous act of violence from one of the seamen, and the colonisers are obliged to sail home, vowing to return one day and in the meantime cherishing a lifelong image of the newfound country as earthly paradise. After that, Ranald is introduced at the Norwegian court, returns to Orkney, grows up, becomes a respected farmer and travels to Ireland to assist at the disastrous battle of Clontarf, which takes place on Good Friday 1014 and from which he emerges mercifully unscathed. At this point Ranald, filled with a healthy disgust for politics and warmongering, beats a high-minded retreat to his farm: but 'those blood-splashed men in high places, and . . . their plots and counter-plots' continue to form the main substance of the narrative, while the protagonist who is clearly intended to channel our sympathies stands back, uninterested and aloof, and so the book becomes curiously diffuse, dwindling to a series of breathlessly disconnected episodes which remain colourful and exciting but fatally lacking in any central focus.

To insist upon this awkwardness, all the same, is to forget the thematic strands which hold the novel together, and to ignore the fact that, while it masquerades as an adventure yarn, its subject is really Ranald's spiritual development. With grace and economy, Brown draws a trajectory which transforms his hero from a golden-haired youth, brimful of hope, steaming ahead in the world of business and drawing the admiration of all who meet him, into a wise old dotard, groping his way towards a final understanding even as his mental and physical abilities are on the wane. In this way *Vinland* reminded me strongly of Hrabal's marvellous (though far jokier and more worldly) *I served the King of England*. Such a reading, however, makes the American prologue at first something of a puzzle. There's no authority for it in the saga which Brown uses as his source for most of the novel: could he simply have included it to make the opportunistic point, in this anniversary year, that the Orcadians' Nordic ancestors got there five hundred years before Columbus? Only in the closing pages do we realise that Ranald's boyhood memory of Vinland is central to his chances of redemption: 'every man born,' a priest tells him, 'is aware, now and then in the course of his life, of . . . a wild sweet freedom when all seems to be possible and good.' For Ranald, this awareness is 'lost somewhere in the dream of childhood' and represents 'a state beyond the dark operatings of fate, a place of light and peace'. Vinland, then, comes to symbolise a hope of release from the grip of the Orcadians' primitive, fatalistic Christianity, as well as providing a model of man in harmony rather than conflict with the physical world—a natural equivalent of the 'Seamless Coat' after which St Magnus was searching in the earlier novel. This symbolism may leave Brown in the position of idealising the American Indians, observing that they had 'entered into a kind of sacred bond with all the creatures, and there was a fruitful exchange between them, both in matters of life and death', but there is no denying the lethal accuracy and economy with which he portrays the hotheadedness of their invaders. When a seaman called Wolf misinterprets their ceremonial war dance and kills one of the Indians on the spot, his actions echo throughout the entire book: 'It's some great fool like you,' says his captain, 'that will bring the world to an end.' Brown's coolly horrified unravelling of the cycles of violence and acquisitiveness which follow from such

behaviour mark *Vinland* as not only the work of a master storyteller, but a novel of fierce contemporary relevance.

Jane Roscoe (review date 24 June 1994)

SOURCE: "Northern Light," in *New Statesman & Society*, Vol. 7, No. 308, June 24, 1994, p. 39.

[*In the following review, Roscoe compares* Vinland *and* Beside the Ocean of Time.]

John Donne once said in a sermon that if your mind wanders to other places, then that is where you are; you are no longer in the present. Thorfinn, the hero in George Mackay Brown's new novel [*Beside the Ocean of Time*], spends much of his childhood daydreaming. Through these dreams, Brown is able to dislocate time, mingling the past and the mythology of the Orkneys with the present, the 1920s and 1930s. Each dream is a tale that takes us into another time and world, from Vikings, broch builders and Robert the Bruce to press gangs and the legendary seal folk.

Thorfinn Ragnarson is known on his island of Norday as a "lazy idle useless boy". But his dreams tell us that he is a storyteller, the ancient bard; he has the "gift of language". His island world is abruptly destroyed when the government decides to build a military aerodrome on it. Crofters are served with notice to vacate land that has run through families for generations; crops are flattened by Nissen huts and concrete.

We next come upon Thorfinn in the role of Private Ragnarson, a prisoner of war. He is now writing in earnest. After the war Thorfinn spends several years in Edinburgh, becoming a successful writer, his books based on his childhood dreams. Yet he is dissatisfied with his work, and realising that he needs quiet and solitude to develop his writing, he returns to Norday.

> No one could say that Brown himself has not been close to the "mythical past" of the Orkneys; he is in fact a master of this kind of writing, and his poems and stories brilliantly evoke the "rich and strange" of Orkney history.
>
> —*Jane Roscoe*

Brown was born on Orkney in 1921 and still lives there. Those familiar with his work will recognise many of the themes that have always fascinated him, but it is the last chapter of this book that cannot help but bring its author into the foreground.

The success of one of Thorfinn's novels echoes the success of Brown's *Greenvoe,* which also focused on the island community destroyed by modern technology. Thorfinn sadly comments that his one successful work was based on the life of an Orkney islander and "who nowadays is interested in the life of a poor islander?" Yet this is precisely what Brown's success is based on. But even while we jump to his defence, we know that it is really Brown's unique way of representing such lives that continually draws readers back to his work.

The title *Beside the Ocean of Time* links this book with Brown's last novel *Vinland.* In *Vinland,* the protagonist dwells at the end on an imaginary ship, a ship that will carry him on his final voyage: death. The voyage in this new work is one of life; a man's life is a voyage over the ocean of time.

Brown's hand has, I feel, been lighter, more subtle in his previous work. Although the language is as usual terse and austere, there are the odd times when he seems to be labouring his point. In his earlier short stories, one *felt* that the fire in the croft was life and must never go out. You did not need to be told.

The soul-searching of Thorfinn raises the question of whether Brown is dissatisfied with his own achievements. Thorfinn sees himself in search of the "grail of poetry"; he wants to "dredge something rich and strange" out of the mythology of the islands. In the end he appears to admit defeat. The prose poem he wants to write will be, for him at least, unattainable. No one could say that Brown himself has not been close to the "mythical past" of the Orkneys; he is in fact a master of this kind of writing, and his poems and stories brilliantly evoke the "rich and strange" of Orkney history.

Publishers Weekly (review date 29 August 1994)

SOURCE: A review of *Beside the Ocean of Time,* in *Publishers Weekly,* Vol. 241, No. 35, August 29, 1994, p. 63.

[*In the review below, the critic offers a mixed assessment of* Beside the Ocean of Time.]

[*Beside the Ocean of Time,*] Brown's sweet coming-of-age novel about a fantasy-prone adolescent growing up in the Orkney Islands just before WWII offers some moving passages and fine, delicate prose but is sabotaged by a paucity of plot and narrative drive. Thorfinn Ragnarson is the daydreaming son of a tenant farmer, avoiding both work and school despite the best efforts of family, friends and neighbors. Instead, the boy dreams up elaborate historical fantasies. In a series of odd yet intriguing chapters, Brown (*Vinland*) transforms Thorfinn into a Viking traveler, a freedom-fighter for Bonnie Prince Charlie and the colleague of a Falstaffian knight

who participates in the Battle of Bannockburn. The author then hurls his protagonist into the future as Thor, who returns to the Orkneys as an adult and recalls his internment in a German POW camp, where he discovered his writing skills. Thor also reflects on the history of the islands, the links between dreaming and writing and the whims of fate. Brown's lyrical descriptions and gift for local color capture the flavor of the Orkneys (where he was born), but his thin and choppy story line undermines this otherwise worthwhile effort.

Publishers Weekly (review date 26 June 1995)

SOURCE: A review of *The Wreck of the Archangel,* in *Publishers Weekly,* Vol. 242, No. 26, June 26, 1995, p. 103.

[*In the following review, the critic describes the poems in* The Wreck of the Archangel *as "stout fare."*]

A poet of the Orkney Islands of northernmost Scotland, Brown (*Voyages*) is something of a relic. The stuff of these poems is stout fare: legends of the sea, fish and corn, crumbling kirks and stone jars full of ale. Elemental rewards are discovered in these provincial tales and evocations, as in the title poem, which opens the collection: "Then, under the lamentation of the great sea harp, / Frailty of splintering wood, scattered cries, / The Atlantic, full-blooded, plucking / And pealing on the vibrant crag." As clear images of historical and contemporary Orcadian life appear, so does the ripe intelligence of the collection; here is a real if pre-industrial culture, preserved by a skilled poet's fervent art in a variety of styles. A number of meditations and seasonal songs close the book with a sense of religious authenticity.

Ray Olson (review date July 1995)

SOURCE: A review of *The Wreck of the Archangel,* in *Booklist,* Vol. 91, No. 21, July, 1995, p. 1855.

[*In the following review, Olson finds that Brown's poems "telescope the centuries."*]

Although not old-fashioned, Brown's poetry frequently seems ancient. [In *The Wreck of the Archangel*] Brown recalls the earliest history of his homeland—Orkney is the first archipelago north of the Scottish mainland and boasts some of the oldest Stone Age buildings in the British Isles—in verses that advert to Norse Vikings, the Romans before them, and, yet earlier, the semilegendary Picts. He often writes the oldest kinds of poems in English: calendar poems, riddling or question-and-answer poems, bestiaries, songs about the saints and holy days, verses on the most elemental things—a whole suite of poems here is about stone—in which the normally voiceless subjects speak their thoughts. He also writes splendidly of the experiences of the farmers, fishers, sailors, and children who are the principal actors in the long human drama of Orkney (see especially **"Rackwick: A Child's Scrapbook"** and **"The Horse Fair"**). Brown's poems telescope the centuries, returning us to an archetypal northern Europe as lively as the modern American rat race but far more significant.

Brown's poems telescope the centuries, returning us to an archetypal northern Europe as lively as the modern American rat race but far more significant.

—Ray Olson

Richard Henry (review date Autumn 1995)

SOURCE: A review of *Beside the Ocean of Time,* in *World Literature Today,* Vol. 69, No. 4, Autumn, 1995, pp. 790-91.

[*In the following review, Henry describes Brown's chronicling of island life in* Beside the Ocean of Time.]

George Mackay Brown's **Beside the Ocean of Time** might have been subtitled "A Writer's Life." The novel recaps Brown's continuing preoccupations as expressed in his weekly columns in the *Orkney Herald* in the 1940s and 1950s and the *Orcadian* in the 1970s, 1980s, and 1990s, and in nearly two dozen volumes of poetry, ten collections of short stories, and a handful of novels. This substantial body of work rarely looks beyond the islands for its material and has earned him the unofficial status of chronicler of the Orcadian experience. It also serves as a sequel to that earlier and anonymous chronicle of the islands, the *Orkneyinga Saga.* Just as the earlier saga draws deeply from the past to demonstrate an essential "Orkney" experience validating its current chronicle, **Beside the Ocean of Time** further demonstrates this continuity by incorporating 800 years of Orkney history into a twentieth-century narrative on the life of Thorfinn Ragnarson.

The experience has changed little despite the technological upheavals of the past ninety years. Life on the islands remains sharply tuned to a number of cycles: those of the seasons, those of men and women from birth to death, and the inevitable series of invaders who surge and recede like the ocean tide. The cyclic nature of the Orcadian experience has provided ample material for Brown and serves as one structural frame upon which he builds his narratives. It also provides him with his most powerful means of asserting the continuity of Orcadian experience: argument by association. In the juxtaposing of two or more events, their shared features are made fully manifest despite the centuries separating them.

Beside the Ocean of Time comprises eight episodes from Ragnarson's life, from his childhood in the 1920s and 1930s, through the war of the 1940s, to a reflective look backward from the late 1960s. Despite the focus on Ragnarson, Brown is generally concerned with the social, historical, and natural facets of the islands. These concerns are explored in full as Brown reprises eight centuries of Orcadian history in the lives of the twentieth-century islanders. The distinction between past and present is most heavily maintained in the opening episodes, "The Road to Byzantium" and "Bannockburn," where a young Thorfinn dreams his journey with a band of Norsemen traveling down the Volga to Constantinople in the 1100s and his journey as squire to the Battle of Bannockburn (1314). In these opening stories the past is romantically figured and framed by an ordinary and mundane present. The distinction between past and present is not complete, however, nor is the past the only shaping force. In "Bannockburn," for example, the present informs the past—Thorfinn peoples his dream with the local innkeeper and the horse the blacksmith is shoeing.

One of the experiences running through **Beside the Ocean of Time** is that of displacement—from the displacements of the islands' "original" people by emigrants from Alba, Cornwall, and Sicily nearly two thousand years ago, the conscription of young men by the press gangs of King George III, and the displacements initiated by the British government during World War II, when it requisitioned the entire island of Norday for an air force base (an event treated more fully in Brown's 1972 novel **Greenvoe**). Resistance is often passive and, with time, often successful. The emigrants from Alba, for example, build an impregnable castle and stow themselves away in it when invaders arrive. The islanders hide their young men in smugglers' caves until the press gangs leave. Even the commandeering of the island by the British is temporary. The islanders begin returning soon after the base is abandoned.

In addition to nicely juxtaposing two moments in time to expose their essential similarities, the tales are enriched by subtly juxtaposing Thorfinn with other members of the community. This further heightens Brown's assertion of the continuity of the Orcadian community in spite of, or even in the face of what appears to be utter annihilation. Like John Eagle in the novella **"The Golden Bird"** (1987), the Skarf in **Greenvoe** (1972), and Einhof Sigmundson in the novel **Vinland** (1992), Thorfinn, the dreamer/writer, is often physically and socially outside the normal sphere of his tribe. The locations of his fancies, the prow of a boat in a shed, on an isolated rock on the beach when everyone else is up on a ridge, as well as the status accorded him by his fellow human beings, the teacher's labeling him a lazy and useless boy or as a prisoner of war, permit him the special perspective from which he can describe the islands and his people. This perspective, both inside and outside the community and inside and outside the constraints of time, no doubt led to the shortlisting of *Beside the Ocean of Time* for the 1994 Booker Prize.

Patrick Crotty (review date 6 October 1995)

SOURCE: "Orcadian Epiphanies," in *The Times Literary Supplement,* No. 4827, October 6, 1995, p. 26.

[*In the following review, Crotty offers a mixed assessment of* Winter Tales.]

The Orkney of George Mackay Brown's poems and fictions has always been an ideal glimpsed behind a contemporary island reality he finds unsavoury, if not quite so unsavoury as life on the mainland. Consumerist values infect even the furthest corners of his archipelago, threatening the harmony with elemental rhythms celebrated in each of the three dozen or so books he has published since 1954. The forces of modernity are connected in the author's mind with the Calvinist assault on "wonderment"—a term few other writers would dare employ—so that the primitive becomes synonymous with the sacramental, and the imagined, ulterior Orkney of the writing takes on an aspect simultaneously pagan and Catholic.

"The Paraffin Lamp", one of the shortest of the eighteen pieces in *Winter Tales,* brings a moralizing satisfaction to its account of an ageing islander's grudging acceptance of electric light: "He said that was a very handy thing, the electric light. He could see by it to fill his old lamp, and trim the wick, and light it with a wisp of straw from the fire." There may be a paradigm here for Mackay Brown's cussedly conservative art. This is a collection not of short stories—too literary a term—but of tales, tales born of innumerable northern winters when the harshness of the struggle for subsistence was relieved only by the exchange of narratives round the fire. Mackay Brown's "ballads in prose" derive from the oral traditions of Orkney; they do not, however, extend them. They are written fictions addressed less to a northern community—as eager as any in Glasgow or London for electronic entertainment in the evenings—than to a sophisticated metropolitan readership which needs to be reassured that ancient patterns of living persist at the latter end of the world. (The representatives of that readership put *Beside the Ocean of Time* on last year's Booker short-list.)

An encounter between the old Orcadian ways and the more

powerful surrounding world lies at the heart of most of these tales (only **"The Road to Emmaus"**, an over-explicit updating of the New Testament in the manner of school-magazine fiction, makes no reference to the islands). The precision and lucidity of Mackay Brown's style—or styles; he varies his idiom according to temporal setting—gives his writing more interest than its predictable and even static vision promises. Thus the diary-narrative of the protagonist's education in simplicity in **"The Laird's Son"** is enlivened by some finely realized detail of eighteenth-century Edinburgh. **"Lieutenant Bligh and Two Midshipmen"** elaborately fictionalizes the meeting, in 1780, in Stromness (always Hamnavoe in Mackay Brown's work), between Bligh and George Stewart, an Orkney man who was to end up on the wrong side of the Bounty mutiny and drown on his way home to face trial. Prompted by an authorial note external to the story itself, the reader's consciousness of the future course of the relationship between the two men lends the proceedings a genuine pathos. The pieces set in the Middle and Dark ages, where the antagonists are Norse crusaders and Spaniards, Celtic monks and Vikings, supply a validating historical context for the qualities of lyricism and simplicity which can seem mannered in some of the other stories.

The constantly shifting temporal focus underlines the permanence of Orkney in contrast to the fleeting human lives which replicate their patterns across the centuries. Mackay Brown's view of history is familiar from many of his earlier books, as is the maritime imagery he uses to render it. Remarkably, he can still make this imagery sound new-minted. In **"Dancey"**, for instance, we were told that "Andrew Crag came home from the sea day after day and a wave of children broke about his knee".

For the Christian, the wave of time is steadied by the Incarnation: Christ's arrival on earth is the greatest of all winter tales. Story after story here makes reference to Christmas and the failure of Calvinistic Orcadians to celebrate it as their forebears did. Intimations of the eternal hover at the edges of island life, but though registered by the author's eye, they remain invisible to his characters. **"A Boy's Calendar"** ends with the report of a baby who survived the wreck of a ship called the Archangel to be brought up by crofters. "Since there was no way of knowing the child's name, they had called him Archie Angel." Another calendar story, **"Ikey"**, concludes with a young tinker's breaking the window frame of a ruined inn to make kindling for a mother who has just given birth to a child in an adjacent byre.

Mackay Brown arranges his epiphanies with skill, but they can seem decorative and even sentimental to the secular reader. The other-worldly music of this fiction is haunting, certainly; it needs more of the ground bass of the contemporary to be fully convincing.

Kirkus Reviews (review date 15 January 1996)

SOURCE: A review of *Winter Tales,* in *Kirkus Reviews,* Vol. LXIV, No. 2, January 15, 1996, p. 82.

[*In the following review, the critic describes the stories of* Winter Tales *as "always luminous if sometimes lifeless."*]

Noted Scottish poet, novelist, and playwright Brown (*A Time to Keep,* 1987, etc.) celebrates the dark season of the year in the Orkney Islands with 18 always luminous if sometimes lifeless stories.

Suffused with old Norse and Christian beliefs, the tales are all set in the northern islands once ruled by the Vikings. Many characters, like the stubborn farmer in **"The Paraffin Lamp,"** who uses the electric light only when he needs to fill his old lamp, still observe the traditional rituals, especially those of the Yule season, that ease the passing of winter. Inured to hardship and frugality, the islanders must contend with weather that is always changing ("one day is wind and flung spindrift, the next is loveliness beyond compare"). And this protean weather is sometimes center stage, as storms and blizzards dramatically take lives: In **"A Boy's Calendar"** and **"Dancey,"** two babies, the sole survivors of ships wrecked by terrible storms, are adopted by childless women and become islanders. In other pieces, the weather is simply part of the fabric of daily life: Men and women race to harvest crops before the rain comes, or to harvest fish before a blizzard strikes. Three notables are **"Lieutenant Bligh and Two Midshipmen," "The Woodcarver,"** and **"A Boy's Calendar,"** in which, respectively, Bligh, of *Mutiny on the Bounty* fame, visits the islands and signs on two local men; an imaginative husband, who finds refuge from his acerbic wife in drink and carving, becomes an unwilling cultural icon; and a young boy describes the round of work and celebration in a typical year. Stories such as **"St. Christopher"** and **"The Road to Emmaus"** give the saint's life and the Crucifixion a local setting, while **"A Crusader's Christmas"** recalls the Viking era.

Cumulatively, an affectionate but muted portrait of a far place where both heart and spirit are strong, though the days are often short and bitter.

Ray Olson (review date 1 February 1996)

SOURCE: A review of *Winter Tales,* in *Booklist,* Vol. 92, No. 11, February 1, 1996, p. 916.

[*In the following review, Olson finds the stories of Brown's* Winter Tales *"as poetic as any of his verse."*]

These 18 stories [in *Winter Tales*] by Orkney poet Brown are as poetic as any of his verse; indeed, the shortest, especially **"Shell Story,"** about the widows of lost fishermen tossing scraps to gulls, are prose poems, although in the manner of folktales rather than the meditation or wry jape usual for the form. Several stories are, like many Brown poems, calendars consisting of 12 monthly sections, always ending at Yuletide. They range in style from the 12 tiny impressions that add up to **"A Nativity Tale"** to long character sketches, such as **"Ikey,"** about a tinker (itinerant) boy who is a mascot to the stabler folk of the islands he tramps, and **"The Woodcarver,"** a dourly comic look at a genuine folk artist. A few stories are sui generis, **"Lieutenant Bligh and Two Midshipmen"** outstandingly so; read it to learn what historical fiction ought to *sound* like—an aural slice of its era, not modern speech dressed, as it were, in period drag. This collection, like the star associated with its season, shines with gentle brilliance.

Mel Gussow (obituary date 16 April 1996)

SOURCE: "George Mackay Brown, 74, Dies; Poet Steeped in Orkneys Lore," in *The New York Times,* April 16, 1996, p. B7.

[*In the following obituary, Gussow recaps Brown's life and career.*]

George Mackay Brown, a poet, novelist and short story writer whose work evoked the rugged life and the history and culture of the remote Orkney Islands in Scotland, died on Saturday in a hospital in Kirkwall in the Orkneys. He was 74.

Writing in the British magazine *The Listener,* Seamus Heaney said that Mr. Brown's imagination "is stirred by legends of the Viking warrior and Christian saint," and added, "It consecrates the visible survivals of history, and ruins of time, into altars that are decked with the writings themselves." Mr. Heaney said he had never seen Mr. Brown's poetry sufficiently praised.

Mr. Brown was born and remained rooted in the Orkneys, and his art was filled with the rich lore and humanity of the people he knew so well. He also explored Scottish myths and mysticism as well as rituals of the Roman Catholic faith. At the same time, he expressed a social consciousness, as in his first novel, **Greenvoe,** which described the death of a 1,000-year-old village at the hands of a military-industrial establishment.

Reviewing the author's collection *A Time to Keep and Other Stories* in *The New York Times Book Review* in 1987, Sheila Gordon wrote that in his "marvelous stories," the author "holds us in the same way the earliest storyteller held the group around the fire in an ancient cave."

Mr. Brown spoke with modesty about his own writing. He said he believed in "dedicated work rather than in 'inspiration,'" and added that writing was "a craft like carpentry, plumbing or baking; one does the best one can." With his thick thatch of hair and his strong jaw, and wearing the clothes of a workingman, he looked very much like the farmers and fishermen who populated his poems and stories.

He was born in the fishing town of Stromness. Leaving school at an early age, he worked as a journalist. At 30, he resumed his education at Newbattle Abbey College on the mainland, where he came under the tutelage of the poet Edwin Muir, who was also from the Orkneys. In 1954, Mr. Muir wrote the introduction to Mr. Brown's first collection of poetry, *The Storm and Other Poems. Loaves and Fishes* was published in 1959, followed by *The Year of the Whale* and *Fishermen With Plows: A Poem Cycle,* often regarded as his finest poetic work. His other books of verse include *Winterfold* and *Poems New and Selected.*

In the late 1980's he also began publishing books of short stories, beginning with *A Calendar of Love and Other Stories.* Among his other anthologies are *Hawkfall and Other Stories* and *Andrina and Other Stories.* The story **"Andrina"** was made into a television film by Bill Forsyth. In 1994, his novel *Beside the Ocean of Time* was one of six works of fiction shortlisted for the Booker Prize.

He collaborated with the composer Peter Maxwell Davies on a variety of musical works, including the opera **"The Martyrdom of St. Magnus."** In addition, he wrote plays, stories for children and essays about the Orkneys.

Christopher Andreae (review date 8 July 1996)

SOURCE: "Orkney," in *The Christian Science Monitor,* July 8, 1996, pp. 16-17.

[*In the following review, Andreae considers Brown's posthumously published* Following a Lark *and* Orkney: Pictures and Poems.]

In an island, time is a simple pure circle.

The line is from a recently published poem by George Mackay Brown (1921-1996). Brown, a prolific source of poems, novels, short stories, and other forms of writing all closely connected with his native Orkney, had islands—and the concept of pure circles and cycles of time—in his veins.

Orkney, at the northeastern tip of mainland Scotland, across the Pentland Firth, is not, strictly speaking, "an" island. It is 67 islands. Sixteen of them are inhabited by people and cows; many more by birds. Even a hasty visitor (the only kind of visitor I have so far been) to this remote outpost of Britain immediately senses that to Orcadians, the archipelago is unquestionably the center of the known universe. It makes all those *other* places elsewhere seem peripheral and distant.

Brown was no visitor: He was virtually the one-man literary genius of Orkney, its voice.

Two books of poems by GMB (as he is familiarly known) have been published this year: *Following a Lark* and *Orkney: Pictures and Poems.* Both books have turned out to be posthumous. (Both are available only in Britain.)

The second book was unusual in its genesis. Brown's writing and Gunnie Moberg's photographs have been published side-by-side before. But on this occasion, the poems were written in direct response to the photographs. The Swedish-born photographer, who has lived on Orkney for 20 years (and in Scotland for almost 30) was not asked to illustrate a text; the procedure was the other way around.

For about six months, she lent Brown prints of the photographs she had chosen for the book, which was to be published at the opening of a first retrospective of her work. . . . The images were propped on an easel, several at a time, in Brown's sitting room. Moberg had asked him just for short captions. But secretly—until the final drafts—he wrote full-fledged poems, 48 in all.

Photographs and words together form an unusual procession of contemplative insights into the small part of the world that poet and photographer know so intimately.

There is a certain rightness about the Scandinavian nationality of the photographer. Although the Orkney Islands have been Scottish since 1468, their links before that were all with Scandinavia. As with Shetland, farther north still, Gaelic is not spoken in Orkney. Most of the place names here have a Norse ring to them. (Hypothetically, the Viking occupation was preceded by Piets and the "first Orcadians" spoke a Celtic language.) The main island used to be called "Hrossey." Norse for "horse island." GMB's poems are punctuated with such local names as Scapa Flow, Rinansay, Swona, Hamnavoe, and Egilsay.

Even though Orkney is the theme of the book, there is an intriguing counterpoint between its two covers. Brown could never be called an abstract writer. But Moberg's photographs do sometimes tend in that direction, as if the scale or specificity of a close-up rock pool or an aerial view over the land—an isolated church casting long morning shadows—have taken on a new and independent life of color and texture and light as photographs.

Brown rather literally brings them down to earth. He sees them as places. His verse is quietly informative, as if he realized the need to make these poems act as captions.

Brown was a poet who looked across modern Orkney with a sense of history, a preference for the past, and the persuasive idea that time will tell.

—*Christopher Andreae*

It is interesting to know that while Moberg recently had a period when she gave up photography because she felt it was too tied to "what's there," Brown was preoccupied undeviatingly with a theme and a subject, and he knew it. He never ceased to explore and re-explore its meanings and implications.

While Brown's concerns are the times and history—the folk history above all—of the place that absorbed him, Moberg mainly provides a sense of the landscape, both near and far.

Although much of the Orkney coastline is composed, spectacularly, of caves and sea-stacks and wave-cut inlets, the islands are not ruggedly mountainous; the hills are mainly low and rounded, the land fertile and green. There is heather. And there are pastures for sheep and cows.

But there are also rocks: flagstones of varying color, some making highly durable building material. Having been populated for an exceptionally long time by stone builders, Orkney is a paradise for archaeologists. Amazing discoveries continue to be made, as if the renowned prehistoric riches of the Skara Brae village, the brochs (or fortified towers) of Midhowe or Gurness, the burial cairn of Maes Howe, and the henges or stone rings of Stenness and Brodgar were not enough.

These have all become essential parts of modern Orkney and its tourism. Yet Brown and Moberg have not pieced together some trite tourist brochure, anything but. They potently insist that in spite of daytrippers and vacation-home dwellers, in spite of traffic and technology, Orkney survives as an ancient place of deep meditation.

Brown was a poet who looked across modern Orkney with a sense of history, a preference for the past, and the persuasive idea that time will tell.

The line quoted at the beginning of this article is from a poem in the book called ***Churchill Barriers.*** These barriers were built during World War II, partly to protect Scapa Flow, where a Nazi submarine had torpedoed a British battleship with great loss of life, and partly to make road crossings (instead of boat crossings) between several of the southern islands.

A guidebook today comments that the barriers have "probably saved these isles from postwar depopulation."

But Brown's poem suggests that these feats of engineering (built by "Italian prisoners, Glasgow navvies") meant that every islander woke one morning to say, "I am an islander no more!" and consequently that an "enchantment is gone from his days."

Characteristically, though, the poet ends by seeing time as coming full circle:

> What does Time say, in its circuits?
> Spider-web, Earl's Palace, sea stack—
> I bring all to ruin
> And to new beginnings.
> Will the stars shine over islands again?
> Will sails fly from shore to shore to shore?

> Although George Mackay Brown forever asked such questions, there was something in the grit and foresight of his writing that suggests he knew that sometime, somehow, the answer would be yes.

Joseph J. Feeney (essay date 3 August 1996)

SOURCE: "An Island World of Vastness: George Mackay Brown (1921-96)," in *America*, Vol. 175, No. 3, August 3, 1996, pp. 24-5.

[*In the following tribute, Feeney explores Brown's career, noting Seamus Heaney's remark that Brown could "transform everything by passing it through the eye of the needle of Orkney."*]

His work is craggy, granitic, primitive, as stark as the wind-seared rock of his native Orkney. Rarely leaving the "oyster-grey" islands north of northmost Scotland, George Mackay Brown found there a world of local vastness, where he word-carved novels, stories and poems about prows and rudders, "sea sounds" and stars, wars and murders, and island chieftains for whom "Roots / cried, stars sang, / gulls wrote a name in the air and in water."

Though Brown thought himself a mere craftsman, his death this year in Kirkwall, Orkney's capital, brought tributes proper to an artist. In London, *The Tablet* called him "a giant of literature and much loved"; *The Guardian* found him "a major influence" and a leader of "the Scottish literary renaissance"; *The Times* named his last novel "a magisterial summing-up of the purpose and meaning of man's life."

"By drawing his boundaries tightly around himself," continued *The Times,* "Brown freed his imagination to sweep through time and space." Perhaps *The Economist* best caught his quirky localism: "He found all he wanted in Orkney, especially in its timeless traditions of farming and fishing, its handed-down stories and the long history of its inhabitants, whose physical legacies stretch back 6,000 years and are never far from sight in the islands."

I first read George Mackay Brown ("Mackay" rhymes with "sky") in 1990, when a Jesuit friend, a Scot, urged the novel *Magnus* on me. It proved a feast: the 12th century reimagined; wildlands made vivid; places and persons starkly named (Birsay, Egilsay, Skail, Stedquoy; Mord Clack, Hold Ragnarson, Jorkel Hayforks); the peace-seeking earl Magnus Erlendson darkly murdered (to become St. Magnus Martyr); and—a final pleasure—Brown's craggy, lyrical prose: "I will speak first of the coat that is beautiful and comely, yet subject to the mildew and mothfall of time."

I also admired the novel's highly physical yet deeply religious sense of sacrifice, both primitive and Christian. In ancient Orkney, Brown wrote, "the animals honoured the god . . . with their broken flesh and spilled blood . . . I speak of priests, a solemn sacred ritual, lustrations, sacrifice. The kneeling beast, the cloven skull, the scarlet axe, the torrent of blood gurgling into the earth at the time of the new sun, the hushed circle of elders." And "when the hands of the priest and the elders dabble in the blood, the whole tribe is washed clean of its blemishes." Centuries and civilizations later, a newer and ultimately similar sacrifice graced a 12th-century kirk:

> The old priest peered closely into the parchment that he held in front of him, and he read the Latin [of the Gospel] in a faded voice. Candle-light splashed the worn parchment. . . . [Then began] a slow cold formal dance with occasional Latin words—an exchange of gifts between God and man, a mutual courtesy of bread and wine. Man offers . . . the first fruits of his labour to the creator of everything in the universe, stars and cornstalks and grains of dust. . . . The bread will be broken, and suffused with divine essences, and the mouths that taste it shall shine for a moment with the knowledge of God. For the generations, and even the hills and seas, come and go, and only the Word stands, which was there . . . before the fires of creation, and will still be there inviolate among the ashes of the world's end.

Bardic and mystical, Brown found Orkney a "microcosm of all the world." Born in 1921 in the town of Stromness, he developed tuberculosis at the age of 20. Only a decade later could he resume his formal education, studying under the Orkney poet Edwin Muir at Newbattle Abbey near Edinburgh. Despite recurring illness, he did an English degree at Edinburgh University (1956-60) and graduate work on the poetry of Gerard Manley Hopkins (1962-64). In 1961, rejecting what he called a "life-denying" Scots Calvinism, he became a Roman Catholic—a rarity in Presbyterian Orkney— and deepened his sense of sacramentality and of liturgical festival.

Returning to his native Stromness in 1964, he wrote with quiet discipline. Six days a week, he sat at his kitchen table from 9 A.M. to 1 P.M., ball-point pen in hand, bond paper before him, his back to the window to avoid distractions. To fend off visitors, he posted a note on his front door, "Working all day. GMB." Brown never married and rarely left Stromness. Though granted a Travel Award in 1968, he got no farther than Ireland, where he stayed with his friend and admirer, the poet Seamus Heaney. He visited England just once, in 1989.

Writing came easily to him. "He was amazed," said a friend, "at the effortlessness of his writing, incredulous that anything so easily accomplished could have any value." Slipping smoothly between past and present, he linked ancient sagas and modern events. Yet though he wrote of Nazi Germany and Eastern desert kings, he was at his best when telling about Orkney's people—a "mingled weave" of Norsemen, Picts, Icelanders and Scots with "stories in the air." He devoted two books to his islands—*An Orkney Tapestry* (1969) and *Portrait of Orkney* (1981)—but all his novels, poems, stories, plays and children's books reveled in Orcadiana. Over 20 of his works were set to music by the Orkney composer Sir Peter Maxwell Davies—most notably the opera "The Martyrdom of St. Magnus" (1977)—and together Brown and Davies founded the annual St. Magnus Festival in Kirkwall.

George Mackay Brown could transform everything by passing it through the eye of the needle of Orkney.

—*Seamus Heaney*

Never a self-promoter, Brown still won quiet fame through his poetry, his novels *Greenvoe* (1972) and *Magnus* (1973), his consequent O.B.E. award (1973) and Bill Forsyth's television film of his story **"Andrina."** (The filming of *Greenvoe* will soon begin.) Brown received honorary doctorates from the universities of Dundee and Glasgow, and his work has been translated into such languages as Polish, Hebrew and

Japanese. He published 34 books, and his last novel, *Beside the Ocean of Time* (1994), was shortlisted for the Booker Prize, Britain's major literary award, and won the Saltire Award for the best Scottish book of 1994.

This theme of time—"the ocean of time"—in a way defines him. "Haunted by time," Brown delved into Orkney's various pasts, while distrusting the modern technologies of North Sea oil drilling and uranium mining. Rigs and mines marred Orkney's sea and land, he felt, just as television corrupted storytelling, telephones distracted thought, and modern conveniences masked the rhythms of nature and life and language.

Since for Brown events of a thousand years past were as present as those of his own boyhood, in his poems history, both great and little, comes to singing life.

Ray Olson

His poems keep these primal rhythms alive. Island women "have the silence of stones under / sun and rain." A local chief "died one shearing time, / webs of winter on him." After school, a boy "leaves / the sea smells, creel / and limpet and cod" to meet a girl with "cornlight / in the eyes, smelling / of peat and cows / and the rich midden." August is the "month of the sickled corn," and December brings "flute song, / star in the solstice tree." At Epiphany-time, "The three kings / met under a dry star. / There, at midnight, / the star began its singing." In spring, the crucified Christ was reduced to "flake of feather and slivers of bone," and "suffered himself to become, on a hill, / starker than seed or star." Such phrases as the above catch Brown's style: economy of words, sharp stresses, vivid images, Anglo-Saxon alliteration ("starker than seed or star"), Hopkinsian word-surprise ("pilgrim" as a verb) and old words and localisms ("skirls," "cuithe," "querns," "cruisie," "nousts"). His poems are minimalist—pared to verbal bone and forged image—and are often modernist as, while careful of form, he heaps up vivid fragments. He can make even a poet's fallow day poem-worthy: At day's end the poet's "seaward window smouldered, black and red. / Would a poem come with the first star? / Lamplight fell on two white pages."

On April 13, 1996, George Mackay Brown died in a Kirkwall hospital at the age of 74. The man who, according to Seamus Heaney, could "transform everything by passing it through the eye of the needle of Orkney," was himself transformed by death. After a funeral Mass at St. Magnus's Cathedral, Kirkwall, he was buried near Stromness on April 16, the feast of St. Magnus. But his work remains, for richness and delight. New work is also promised. His last poetry collection,

Following a Lark, was published in May; and he left a trove of unpublished manuscripts: more poems and stories, one may hope, of ancient ships and heroes, of primal feasts and ceremonies, and of things—to use his words—as "ordinary as pebbles, shells, seapinks, stars."

Publishers Weekly (review date 30 September 1996)

SOURCE: A review of *Selected Poems, 1954-1992,* in *Publishers Weekly,* Vol. 243, No. 40, September 30, 1996, p. 84.

[*In the following review, the critic describes Brown as gifted in "sharpening one's interest in genuinely rustic activities."*]

Gathering the best-known work of one of the leading poets in the Scottish Literary renaissance, this volume displays Mackay Brown's gift for sharpening one's interest in genuinely rustic activities. In his world, a rough-hewn, remote island off the shore of Northern Scotland marked by anvils, spades and nets, stone kirks and bowls of ale, seasonal imagery and the lusciousness of agrarian life are explored with vigor and depth. After a day-long trip to the market: "The sun whirled on a golden hoof. It lingered. It fell / On a nest of flares." In another song, the poet recounts a blinding storm: "In summer's sultry throat / Dry thunder stammered. / . . . Next morning in tranced sunshine / The corn lay squashed on every hill; / Tang and tern were strewn / Among highest pastures." Mackay Brown (1921-1996) conjures the potent goodness of the pure, unsmogged world, and he allows the old, solid things of the earth to commerce freely with the world of song, and with the dance of English speech. Some of the poems are even directly religious, such as **"Daffodils,"** which eulogizes three women who stayed at the base of Christ's cross while he died. Rhythmically, much of this work returns to the broken power of ancient "sprung" rhythms for its musical force. Mackay Brown's assertive, beautiful poems make this a collection worth having.

Ray Olson (review date 1 November 1996)

SOURCE: A review of *Following a Lark* and *Selected Poems, 1954-1992,* in *Booklist,* Vol. 93, No. 5, November 1, 1996, p. 475.

[*In the review below, Olson praises Brown as "one of the great contemporary poets of place."*]

When Brown died on April 13, 1996, one of the great contemporary poets of place died. Nearly 75, he had spent virtually his entire life in Orkney, the islands directly north of Scotland, refusing even invitations to be honored in England, which he visited only once. As he lived in Orkney, so he wrote of Orkney, whose history and perennial occupations, farming and fishing, were, together with the Christian holidays, the stuff of his writing. These books [***Following a Lark*** and ***Selected Poems, 1954-1992***] are the last new collection and the last retrospective selection of his verse that he made. The work in them is modern in its specific vocabulary, its combinations of austerity and sensual vividness and of conversational and formal tones, and its sharp imagery. It is formal verse, often stanzaic and rhymically intentional, yet it seldom rhymes. Since for Brown events of a thousand years past were as present as those of his own boyhood, in his poems history, both great and little, comes to singing life. Here is King Macbeth talking with the earl of Orkney, and here, over and over, are seasonal labors in the fields and at sea and children going to school or to town on Saturday. And here, too, are the events of Easter and Christmas reset in Orkney with amazing power and cogency. "I hoard," Brown wrote, "before time's waste / Old country images." His hoarding is our treasure.

FURTHER READING

Criticism

Kernochan, Rose. A review of *Winter Tales. New York Times Book Review* (31 March 1996): 18.

Brief review of *Winter Tales.*

Longley, Edna. "What the Doctor Said." *London Review of Books* 12, No. 6 (22 March 1990): 22-3.
    Review of a number of works, including *The Wreck of the Archangel.*

McDuff, David. "Poetry Chronicle II." *Stand Magazine* 32, No. 1 (Winter 1990): 64-5.
    Brief commentary on Brown's work.

McDuff, David. "Poetry Chronicle I." *Stand Magazine* 33, No. 2 (Spring 1992): 63-4.
    Brief commentary on Brown's work.

O'Donoghue, Bernard. "Under the Rooftrees." *The Times Literary Supplement,* No. 4627 (6 December 1991): 24.
    Positive assessment of *Selected Poems, 1954-1983,* drawing comparisons between Brown and other poets.

O'Donoghue, Bernard. "Orkney Idylls." *The Times Literary Supplement,* No. 4748 (1 April 1994): 20.
    Discusses the main character's exploration of history in *Beside the Ocean of Time.*

Crotty, Patricia. "Et in Orcadia Ego." *Spectator* 275, No. 8723 (16 September 1995): 38-9.
    Discusses the poems of *Winter Tales.*

Additional coverage of Brown's life and career is contained in the following sources published by Gale Research: *Contemporary Authors,* **Vols. 21-24R, 151;** *Contemporary Authors Autobiography Series,* **Vol. 6;** *Contemporary Authors New Revision Series,* **Vols. 12, 37;** *Dictionary of Literary Biography,* **Vols. 14, 27, 139;** *Major Twentieth Century Writers;* **and** *Something About the Author,* **Vol. 35.**

Richard Condon
1915-1996

American novelist.

The following entry provides an overview of Condon's career. For further information on his life and works, see *CLC,* Volumes 4, 6, 8, 10, and 45.

INTRODUCTION

A prolific and popular author, Condon blended satire and suspense to create entertaining, often humorous novels that comment on contemporary society. Characterized by intricate plots, an abundance of factual information, and sumptuous meals, Condon's fiction concerns paranoia, greed, and the exploitation of power, usually within a political context. Although critical opinion of his novels varied throughout his career, Condon perhaps is best remembered for *The Manchurian Candidate* (1959), *Winter Kills* (1969), and *Prizzi's Honor* (1982), each of which were adapted for film. Herbert Mitgang observed: "The singular Condon genre combines American politics, scoundrels in various corners of the world, linguistic shenanigans, cholesterol-loaded meals, cold warriors in intelligence agencies, legalized thievery in Washington and put-downs of the high and mighty everywhere."

Biographical Information

Born March 18, 1915, in New York City, Condon graduated from De Witt Clinton High School, but because his grades there were so bad, he never attended college. He worked as an elevator operator, a hotel clerk, a waiter, and briefly as a copywriter at an advertising agency. Copywriting led him into movie publicity, and he joined Walt Disney Productions in 1936. During the 1940s and 1950s Condon worked as a movie publicist at nearly every major Hollywood studio, where he observed the art of storytelling. In the late 1950s Condon returned to New York to become a novelist. The commercial successes of *The Oldest Confession* (1958), his first novel, and *The Manchurian Candidate*, which was adapted for film in 1962, allowed Condon to devote himself to writing. In 1959 he left the United States, living first in Mexico for a few years, then in Switzerland, and finally in Ireland, where he arrived in 1971. During the 1960s and 1970s some of Condon's novels received more critical attention than others, notably *An Infinity of Mirrors* (1964) and *Winter Kills.* In 1980 he returned to the United States and settled in Dallas, Texas. Condon's literary career revived upon publication of *Prizzi's Honor*, the first of four novels about the mobster family Prizzi. John Hurston directed the hit film version of the novel, which starred Jack Nicholson, Kathleen Turner, and

Anjelica Huston; the screenplay, which Condon co-wrote with Janet Roach, earned an Academy Award nomination. Condon wrote several other novels, notably *The Final Addiction* (1991) and *The Venerable Bead* (1992) before he died in Dallas in 1996.

Major Works

Condon's earliest novels feature satiric attacks on contemporary culture, while parodying the suspense genre. *The Oldest Confession* tells of an international art theft; *The Manchurian Candidate,* set during the Korean War, details the capture of an American GI who is brainwashed by communists and programmed to assassinate the Republican presidential candidate modeled on Senator Joseph McCarthy. Statistical and historical details and preposterous plots form many of Condon's novels during the 1960s and 1970s, including *An Infinity of Mirrors* (1964), which relates the experiences of a German colonel who falls in love with a French Jewish girl during World War II; *The Ecstasy Business* (1967), which satirizes the American film industry; and *Mile High* (1969), which represents a fictional account of the Prohibition era.

Condon's next novels raise paranoia to its highest level in his art. Set in the early 1960s, *Winter Kills* recounts the CIA-influenced assassination of U.S. President Tim Keegan, a character based on John F. Kennedy, and *The Whisper of the Axe* (1976) recounts a conspiratorial group of wealthy men who instigate urban terrorism to trigger another American revolution. Condon's later fiction emphasizes the abuse of power and features some of his most entertaining characters, especially the members of the Prizzi family of mobsters in Brooklyn. *Prizzi's Honor,* which relates the adventures of henchman Charley Partanna and his marriage to Maerose Prizzi, granddaughter of don Prizzi; *Prizzi's Family* (1986), a "prequel," which recounts Charley's formative years; *Prizzi's Glory* (1988), which concerns a deal between Maerosa and the don to achieve respectability for the next generation of Prizzis; and *Prizzi's Money* (1994), in which Maerosa gains control of the entire Prizzi family fortune. *The Final Addiction,* a political satire about "image," targets a number of American presidents and institutions, including the CIA, FBI, and NRA. *The Venerable Bead* lampoons American business practices, especially its influence in national politics.

Critical Reception

Although critical reception of his twenty-six novels has varied throughout his career, Condon maintained a large, loyal readership, sometimes referred to as the "Condon Cult." Charles McCarry called *The Manchurian Candidate* "arguably the best thriller ever written," observing that Condon "was to paranoia what Tennyson was to melancholy, a writer of powerful and utterly unique imaginative gifts who transmuted a form of madness into the intellectual coinage of his time and place." Commentators praised Condon's ability for wildly funny, mesmerizing storytelling and maniacal characterization, often citing his mastery of English sentence structure. Others found some of Condon's works burdensome or overly lengthy, faulting his highly dense, detail-oriented narrative structure and convoluted plots. Mel Gussow summarized Condon's literary achievement: "Novelist is too limited a word to encompass the world of Mr. Condon. He was also a visionary, a darkly comic conjurer, a student of American mythology and a master of conspiracy theories."

PRINCIPAL WORKS

The Oldest Confession (novel) 1958
The Manchurian Candidate (novel) 1959
Some Angry Angel: A Mid-Century Fairy Tale (novel) 1960
A Talent for Loving; or, The Great Cowboy Race (novel) 1961
Any God Will Do (novel) 1964
An Infinity of Mirrors (novel) 1964
The Ecstasy Business (novel) 1967

Mile High (novel) 1969
The Vertical Smile (novel) 1971
Arigato (novel) 1972
The Star-Spangled Crunch (novel) 1974
Winter Kills (novel) 1974
Money Is Love (novel) 1975
The Whisper of the Axe (novel) 1976
The Abandoned Woman (novel) 1977
Bandicoot (novel) 1978
Death of a Politician (novel) 1978
The Entwining (novel) 1980
Prizzi's Honor (novel) 1982
A Trembling Upon Rome (novel) 1983
Prizzi's Family (novel) 1986
Prizzi's Glory (novel) 1988
Emperor of America (novel) 1990
The Final Addiction (novel) 1991
The Venerable Bead (novel) 1992
Prizzi's Money (novel) 1994

CRITICISM

John F. Baker (interview date 24 June 1983)

SOURCE: "Richard Condon," in *Publishers Weekly,* Vol. 223, No. 25, June 24, 1983, pp. 66-7.

[*In the following interview, Baker presents Condon's comments on his writing career, including highlights from his personal life.*]

Richard Condon, who has been writing novels for 26 years—and living in various overseas parts of the world for much of that time—was astonished recently to find the American Booksellers Association convention right on his doorstep, where he now lives in Dallas. "I don't get out of the house much," he said with his rather inscrutable smile. "But I couldn't resist just taking a look, and it was terrifying: all those people, all those books, all those computers!"

Since Condon is known as one of the first name authors ever to go the word processor route—he has been using one for at least seven years now, which makes him practically one of the Wright Brothers—his alarm at the electronicization of books seems excessive. But he specializes in keeping his hearers, like his readers, slightly off balance. The scene of the meeting with *PW* is The Mansion, Dallas's most exclusive restaurant, and he describes with conspiratorial glee how the city's wealthy elite breakfast there often. "At 6.30 A.M. the driveway will be full of Cadillacs and Mercedes, and an hour later, long before you or I get to breakfast, they'll all be gone!" The unexpected has always been his trademark, and after a series of contemporary and sometimes even futuristic thrillers, he has now come up with a book completely out of left field: a papal historical novel called *A Trembling Upon Rome,* which is coming out in a few weeks from Putnam.

The idea has haunted Condon, he says, ever since 1967, when he first became interested in the fact that for a time, during the late 14th and early 15th centuries, there were three different popes sitting simultaneously in the Roman Catholic world—in Rome, in Avignon, in Pisa and, finally, Constanz. "The Catholic Church has always been powerful, but when you're talking about it in that period, you're talking law, you're talking international finance and, above all, government. The popes then were stronger than kings." The picture Condon draws is one of ruthlessness, cruelty, greed and opportunism, with questions of faith far at the back of the minds of all his scheming popes, cardinals and bishops.

He acknowledges that there is a lot of historical background to grasp before his plot becomes clear and that "perhaps it's a hard book to get into. But," he adds mischievously, "I guess I'm relying on a number of professional Catholics who will read it in outrage. Perhaps the 'Phil Donahue Show'...."

Does he see the book's picture of a corrupt and worldly Church as relevant to today? "Well, no religion can exist without money, and the Vatican still has its banking problems, doesn't it? I wanted to show that things were much the same in the 15th century." One of the things Condon discovered in his research was that one of the most venal of the Schism Popes was John XXIII; when the Church bestowed that name and number on one of the most beloved of recent popes, he saw it as a deliberate attempt to obliterate the memory of the previous John XXIII.

Where do all Condon's often offbeat ideas come from? Ranging as his novels do from right-wing political plotters (*The Manchurian Candidate,* still probably his best-known book) through a presidential assassination (*Winter Kills*) to Mafia machinations (*Prizzi's Honor*) and a dark feminist future (*Whisper of the Axe*), and now to Church history, he probably covers a wider range of subjects in his fictions than any popular novelist. "Well," he says, "if you spend eight hours a day thinking about something obsessively, you're bound to be ahead of anyone else. Then once you're ahead, in terms of what you know about the subject, you add a dash of melodrama, and there you are."

He has an entertaining presentation of his life which he has now polished, through interviews and self-sketches, to perfection: a faintly bemused man who has simply stumbled from one thing into another without any very clear sense of direction. He grew up in New York, went to sea on a cruise liner as a waiter, later became a movie publicist (most notably for Walt Disney at the height of the Disney success in the late '30s and early '40s). "From the time I joined Disney in 1936

to the time I finally left the film industry in 1957, I worked for all the major companies except Warner and Metro." The occupational disease of that profession, duodenal ulcers, finally caught up with him, and, "since the only other thing I knew how to do was spell, I decided to write novels."

There have now been 20 of these, beginning in 1958 with *The Oldest Confession.* As for publishers, after a few books in the first years of his writing career with McGraw-Hill and Random House, he settled in with Joyce Engelson at Dial and stayed for 14 years, following her to Richard Marek when that imprint went to Putnam and staying on there, contractually, after Marek and Engelson left for St. Martin's.

Apart from his fiction, he writes extensively on food (he now has, he says, seven pieces in the backlog at *Gourmet* magazine and remembers fondly as the best title ever put on a piece of his, an article about cooking spaghetti called "Remembrance of Things Pasta," which appeared in *Venture* magazine in the '60s). His only book in this vein, *The Mexican Stove,* he wrote with his daughter Wendy Bennett; it was originally published by Doubleday and, he says, is about to be reissued next year.

He is, as always, working on his next book. It will be called *The Averted Eye* and will, he says, be about a womanizing TV anchorman who becomes involved in national politics and soap opera ("How else would you get to be president today?" the novelist asks, not entirely rhetorically).

One of Condon's favorite jokes is to put people he knows, by name, into his books as minor characters, in much the way Alfred Hitchcock always inserted shorts of himself into his movies. This has happened so far to no fewer than 130 of Condon's friends and acquaintances, and he calls them the International Confederation of Book Actors. The longest-lived of them, a friend called Franklin Keller, he calls his "hiring chief," and he has appeared in most Condon books. Putnam's vice-president for public relations, Harriet Blacker, is, he says, one of the latest additions to the roster. "She'll be a tough Wall Street lawyer," he grins, to Blacker's rather dubious delight.

Since many moviegoers first became familiar with Condon's name through the brilliant movie made of *The Manchurian Candidate,* and he has been around movies for so much of his adult life, it's only natural to talk about films of his books. There have been four so far, "and a lot of expensive options," but the movie version of *Winter Kills* released in 1979 makes by far the oddest story (and one that Condon himself tells, at fascinating length, in the May issue of *Harper's*).

To recap his tale very briefly, the producers who originally put up the money are now, respectively, dead (murdered) and behind bars for cocaine smuggling. The movie was finished, after horrendous difficulties, only because many of the all-star cast and crew agreed to forfeit their salaries. It opened to audience and critical enthusiasm and was then abruptly withdrawn (it was never shown in many overseas markets at all); recently it resurfaced briefly to equal enthusiasm and disappeared again. It seems to be currently in limbo—and is meanwhile on the way to becoming a sort of cult classic. Condon hints darkly that his theme, that a presidential assassination is in the interests of many of the world's most powerful people, may be behind the movie's strangely checkered career to date.

But withal he is cheerful. "In the course of writing seven hours a day seven days a week, I have piled up four- or five-million words and have made about $2 1/2-million. That sounds like a lot, but it's only about what someone in middle management would have made over the same period in salary. The difference—and it's an important one—is that I've lived wherever I wanted to, and I didn't have to drive to the office every day."

John Skow (review date 22 September 1986)

SOURCE: "Mafioso," in *Time,* Vol. 128, No. 12, September 22, 1986, p. 95.

[*In the following review, Skow comments on the characters of* Prizzi's Family.]

"Prequel" is one of those smarmy coinages, like "brunch," that make a self-respecting user of language want to wash his mouth out with whisky. Brunch can be avoided by not getting out of bed before noon on Sundays, but prequel—*ptui!*—probably is inevitable for works such as Richard Condon's rowdy new novel, a report on the formative years of the author's lovable but dumb Mafia assassin Charley Partanna.

Condon's book [*Prizzi's Family*] is not so stirring an achievement as to be inevitable, but it is cheerful and funny, and no effort should be made to avoid it. Charley, of course, is the hero of *Prizzi's Honor,* the 1982 Condon novel that Director John Huston turned into one of Jack Nicholson's better films. There Charley was seen at mid-life, and his crisis was that his wife (Kathleen Turner in the film) turned out to be not only a Mob hit woman but a boodler who tried to grab some Mafia loot. Wistfully but dutifully, Charley killed her, after she was set up by his old and still smoldering sweetheart Maerose Prizzi (Anjelica Huston).

The new novel precedes *Honor* by a few years and more or less explains Charley's problem: he is girl-simple, as his associates accurately put it. He could be content with living the good life as a respected professional man, blasting some slob with an assault rifle here, acing out several losers with cya-

nide grenades there, and studying hard for his high school diploma at night school, where he earns the respect of all and is voted secretary-treasurer of his class.

Instead he becomes involved, in the manner of horsemeat becoming involved with lions, with a jumbo showgirl named Mardell and with the volcanic Maerose. "It was like being locked in a mailbag with eleven boa constrictors . . . His head came to a point where it suddenly melted and flopped all over his shoulders and out all over the bed. His toes fell off." This is sex with Maerose—all very well, except that she is the granddaughter of Don Corrado Prizzi, a Mafia eminence not to be messed with.

Complications ensue like crazy. One of them is a candidate for the New York City mayoralty, who made his pile in the TV tabernacle dodge. He is an out-of-towner, really, who does not understand how things work in New York, and he wants to have Charley indicted for his sixth-to-last murder. Maerose, a more serious troublemaker, wants to take over her grandfather's operation. As usual with the author's recent entertainments, the fact that none of this makes much sense becomes a literary metaphor on the order of Melville's white whale, implying as it does that the entire world is nuts. This is clearly Condon's view, and he is mightily persuasive as he defines human character: foaming perversity, rascality, obsessional lunacy, wowserism, religious mania, assault and battery, and our old friends greed and lust. No sloth, though; Charley and his chums sure do keep active.

Michael Neill (essay date 8 December 1986)

SOURCE: "His Years of Self-Imposed Exile Over, Richard Condon Is Back in America, Sitting Prizzi," in *People Weekly,* Vol. 26, No. 23, December 8, 1986, pp. 129, 131, 133.

[*In the essay below, Neill reviews Condon's life and literary accomplishments.*]

Like Don Corrado Prizzi, Richard Condon believes in family. For the Don—venomous and ancient, the spider at the center of Condon's *Prizzi* novels—family has to be protected; family is reason to kill. For Condon, affable but getting on in years himself, family is a reason finally to settle down in America after 19 years living in various spots around the world. And family is the reason he keeps writing at 71, despite the estimated $2 million he has made from his books and despite the two recent abdominal operations.

"A friend asked, 'Why does one still do it?'" Condon says with a laugh in the art-filled living room of the Dallas home he has lived in since 1980. "I said, 'One does it for one's estate.'" Condon's latest estate-fattening effort is *Prizzi's*

Family, a prequel to his best-selling *Prizzi's Honor* and the 21st in a line of novels stretching back to 1958. The sixth of Condon's novels to be brought to the screen, *Prizzi's Honor* earned eight Academy Award nominations. Condon co-authored the screenplay and says, "I loved the movie. John Huston [the director] is the best cinematic storyteller we have."

Condon has written his novels while living in Mexico, France, Spain, Switzerland and, for 10 years, Ireland. Now Condon and Evelyn, his wife of 48 years, live in Texas to be near their younger daughter, Wendy Jackson, and her two children. Their other daughter, Deborah, lives in England. In Dallas, Condon combines his dual roles of family man and grand old man, producing a book every 11 months or so.

Condon has a theory about why writing comes so easily to him. "I'm a stutterer," he says. "Words fascinate me. I've had to have six synonyms ready at all times while talking, because if I know I'm going to stutter, I can make those interchangeable shifts." However much the critics praise his work, though, he has his own ideas about what he's doing. "I have never written for any other reason than to earn a living. This is most certainly true of other writers, but some poor souls get mightily confused with art. I am a public entertainer who sees his first duty as the need to entertain himself."

The family warmth Condon now enjoys was missing when he was a child in New York City, the eldest son of a successful lawyer who had high ambitions for him. "My father was a shouter," remembers Condon. "I became a stutterer, and I was stuck with it the rest of my life. I think, unconsciously, knowing how his shouting hurt me, I wanted to wound him [by stuttering]—and it worked out that way."

Condon found another way to rebel, too. At DeWitt Clinton High School in the Bronx, he says, "I finished so far down in my class that no university in the country would accept me." Much to his father's dismay, Condon worked as an elevator operator, a bellboy and a waiter on a cruise line.

Condon eventually got a job writing package inserts, which he describes as "those little scraps of paper tucked inside product boxes that nobody ever reads." That led to writing copy for an advertising agency, and that in turn led him to marriage. As Condon tells it, the agency needed to fill a hotel dining room with elegant-looking people for a photographic shoot. Five professional models sat up front, close to the cameras. The rest of the diners were agency employees, including a tuxedoed Condon. One of the models was Evelyn Hunt, then with the Powers Agency. They met that night; they were married a year later.

From advertising, Condon made the leap into public relations, working for the Disney studio and handling the publicity for such movies as *Pinocchio, Fantasia* and *Dumbo.* He also wrote a play called *Men of Distinction* that had a four-performance run on Broadway in 1953. Four years later Condon decided the publicity business wasn't fun anymore. As he told Evelyn at the time, "The only thing I know how to do besides publicity is spell," so he started writing. His first novel, *The Oldest Confession,* was published when Condon was 42. He immediately sold both paperback and film rights and says, "I've never had to look back."

Condon already is planning a third Prizzi novel—to be called *Prizzi's Glory*—which will be set a few years in the future. "I believe that in about 30 years, the survivors of what we know as the Mafia will be our leaders," he says. "Money demands respectability. Go back to the 1860s, with the robber barons—the Rockefellers, the Mellons, the Vanderbilts, the Astors. They were vilified, yet today they are the social, political and business leaders of the nation."

That sort of transition is not so different from that of a New York City kid with a bad stutter who couldn't get into college and became one of America's best-selling authors.

Roderick Mann (essay date 16 August 1987)

SOURCE: "Condon Still Waiting with 'Prizzi' Prequel," in *Los Angeles Times,* August 16, 1987, p. C37.

[*In the following essay, Mann relates the difficulties of transforming Condon's novels into screenplays*]

Because his novel *Prizzi's Honor* was such a success, both as a book and a movie, Richard Condon finished his follow-up book *Prizzi's Family* confident that the phone soon would ring with Hollywood offers.

They didn't come.

And now, almost a year since hardcover publication and with the paperback on sale, the book still has not been picked up.

Condon is mystified.

"There've been no overtures at all," he said the other afternoon on a visit to Los Angeles from his Dallas home. "Very surprising."

Prizzi's Family is a prequel to *Prizzi's Honor* in which Condon fills in the background to the people involved in this organized-crime story. In it Charley Partanna, the hit man played so splendidly by Jack Nicholson in the movie, is just 30.

"And that seems to be the problem," said Condon. "Nicholson

is so firmly entrenched in people's consciousness as Charley that they can't see anyone else playing it. And they don't see him passing for 30."

But Condon, whose 21st novel this is, is far from down-hearted.

"Remember," he said, "the first book took 14 months to sell. Though that was because the copy I sent [director] John Huston never reached him in Mexico. Finally, I had the book hand-delivered to him and he called me and said yes within two days."

It was Huston who had to convince Condon that Nicholson (who starred in the movie with Kathleen Turner) was right for the role.

"I don't mind admitting I opposed Jack's casting," said Condon. "I felt he looked too German-American to play a Sicilian. I was proved wrong, of course. He did a smashing job.

"Not only did he dazzle me in the movie, but he changed the contours of Charley Partanna when I came to write the second book. I had a different Charley in mind when I wrote *Prizzi's Honor.* When I wrote *Prizzi's Family,* the image of Jack kept crowding into my mind."

Prizzi's Honor was the sixth Condon novel to be made into a movie (some of the others: *The Manchurian Candidate, A Talent for Loving, Winter Kills*). But it was the only one for which he wrote the screenplay.

"I lived out of the country for so many years that always before I was just glad to take the money and forget about the projects," he said. "But when this came up, I'd moved back to Dallas so I was available.

"Then when I was writing the screenplay, I was hit with an aneurysm of the aorta, which put me out of business for nearly six months. It's a fairly big number, that operation. The survival rate is only 3%, they tell me. For months, all I could do was sit in a chair, I felt so weak. Now I have a Dacron aorta."

Condon decided to live abroad after spending years in movie advertising and publicity, a calling that eventually earned him several ulcers. He has lived in Mexico, Spain and France, though the majority of his years overseas were spent in Switzerland (9 years) and Ireland (almost 10).

Condon liked Switzerland and this month, in *Travel and Leisure* magazine, writes a paean of praise to its railways.

"I don't understand why people always say it's boring," he said. "The Swiss have a good sense of humor, though they

are serious about their work. I think people's attitude stems from that sneer of Orson Welles' in *The Third Man* in which he dismissed them as a race that had produced nothing more interesting than the cuckoo clock."

Ireland, too, he enjoyed. He lived there in a Georgian house, Rossanarra, which was designed by the architect responsible for the White House, James Hoban.

And he says his return to the United States in 1980 was prompted not so much by homesickness as a desire to spend time with his two grandchildren in Dallas.

"I miss Europe," he said. "Next month, Evelyn [his wife of 48 years] and I are going over to look for a flat in London."

Did he find writing easier when he lived abroad?

"Only because I don't speak any foreign languages, which means I don't have to go to any dinners or cocktail parties and can devote more time to writing. To me, two women sitting behind me on the bus chattering away sound interesting because I've no idea what they are saying. The fact that they are probably grumbling about the quality of the meat some butcher has given them doesn't concern me."

In Ireland, of course, he could understand. . . .

"Yes. But there I lived in such an isolated place it didn't make any difference. I never saw anyone."

At his home in a Dallas suburb—"It's all white houses with picket fences, rather like the back lot at Metro must have been when they were making those *Andy Hardy* movies"—he is at work on his 23rd novel.

The 22nd—*Prizzi's Glory,* the sequel to *Prizzi's Honor* and the final book in the trilogy—is already set for publication next year.

"My only contact with the world is looking out of the window at the occasional automobile passing by," the 72-year-old author said. "I know of no indulgence like being an author. When a chap writes a novel he runs the show."

And there's another thing: Since becoming a novelist, Condon has not had one ulcer.

Charles Champlin (review date 18 September 1988)

SOURCE: "Bloody Sunday," in *Los Angeles Times Book Review,* September 18, 1988, p. 13.

[In the following excerpt, Champlin finds Condon's "gift for the preposterous undiminished" in Prizzi's Glory.*]*

After *Prizzi's Honor* and a prequel, *Prizzi's Family,* Richard Condon concludes his trilogy with *Prizzi's Glory,* a sequel that takes us into years not yet born and into the higher reaches of respectability.

By now the Prizzis are unthinkably rich. Their holding company grosses nearly $17 billion annually, owns among other items 32 law firms, 137 hotels and 381 hospitals and has 9,208 senior executives, lawyers and accountants. It has respect but not respectability, for which Maerose (the Angelica Huston character in the film) is aiming with a drive that has overwhelmed even the old Don himself.

Paving the road to respectability, Maerose takes husband Charlie Partana away from his killing chores and, against his better judgment, sees that he has a new name, face, voice and MO. When last seen, he is rushing up a veritable peak of propriety, uttering curses like "What in tunket!" and "Great Godfrey!"

Condon, as usual, wields a pen that is part scalpel, part Samurai sword. The legitimatizing of criminal money and the illegitimizing of the higher (and lower) reaches of government are equal themes.

Prizzi's Glory is with all else a hymn book in favor of Italian cooking. Too, it is also a satirical litany of the trappings of success. It is not kind to the incumbent Administration or televised religion, but it does celebrate family togetherness. Condon's powers of invention and expression and his gift for the credibly preposterous are undiminished.

Vincent Patrick (review date 9 October 1988)

SOURCE: "Prizzi for President," in *The New York Times Book Review,* October 9, 1988, p. 24.

[In the review below, Patrick praises Condon's characterization in Prizzi's Glory.*]*

The final volume in the Prizzi trilogy, *Prizzi's Glory,* opens in 1985 with the family doing business as usual in Brooklyn under the skilled stewardship of its 48-year-old C.E.O., Charley Partanna, whom Richard Condon fans know as the Mafioso whose single venture into matrimony, with a hit woman for the mob, ended with her tragic death in California.

At the start of the present volume Charley marries Maerose Prizzi, a great beauty and granddaughter of Don Corrado,

bringing to fruition their 19-year engagement. The most Sicilian of the Don's offspring, she paradoxically longs for respectability and acceptance into New York's nouvelle society. To this end, Charley—who runs the Prizzis' street operations and who is "not an originator" but a man who "could carry out orders with the dedication and mindlessness of a lieutenant colonel of the U.S. Marine Corps"—is made over with a new name, face and background as well as British elocution lessons. As Charles Macy Barton, he replaces Edward S. Price (the Don's son, Eduardo Prizzi, himself made over years earlier) as head of America's largest conglomerate.

Eduardo is a man so attuned to public relations that the interior of his private DC-10, acquired from his late, great friend, the Shah of Iran, is as austerely decorated as a turn-of-the-century Vermont store, complete with cracker barrel and roll-top desk. He also keeps several sets of dentures for different occasions. To indicate total submission at meetings with the Don, he has a copy of George Bush's teeth made from photographs taken on the day the Iran-contra scandal broke. Since Charley is to replace him, a suitable slot needs to be found for Eduardo—the family runs him for President of the United States in the 1992 election. The Prizzis' street operations (loan sharking, extortion, etc.) are franchised out to the highest bidders, thus getting the family off the street completely and into the far more lucrative area of politics.

The plot gives Mr. Condon ample elbow room for political and social satire that is always funny. Much of it is based on observations from the point of view of Charley Partanna or his cohorts, clear-thinking, pragmatic Sicilians whose values aren't learned from this season's television series. We like them for that, and Mr. Condon doesn't invest his characters with cute, endearing qualities; rather, the Prizzis' charms stem from their complete lack of hypocrisy.

Toward the end things take an unexpectedly serious turn and a touch of tragedy leavens the humor, a feature of the Prizzi novels that works perfectly here. We close the book with a sense of loss for Charley and for ourselves. We are going to miss these Prizzis.

Jonathan Yardley (review date 7 February 1990)

SOURCE: "Condon's Hilarious Nightmare," in *Washington Post,* No. 64, February 7, 1990, p. C2.

[Below, Yardley applauds the accuracy of Condon's satire in Emperor of America.*]*

Richard Condon's 23rd work of fiction isn't so much a novel as a jeremiad, but that is scarcely likely to scare away his many admirers. *Emperor of America* is, so far as plot and characterization and other such trifles are concerned, rather short of the mark; but as a sendup of the Reaganite nightmare and the televidiotic culture upon which it fed, *Emperor of America* is bang on from first page to last—a mean, nasty and thoroughly hilarious piece of social and political lampoonery.

Its underlying premise is that, as "Ronald Reagan had very nearly broken his heart in trying to warn America," Nicaragua is "out to conquer the world." The Sandinistan designs are ghastly:

> In 1980, Nicaragua had a population of 3 million people, but by practicing advanced breeding techniques, they had been able to swell to 21 million by CIA estimate, almost all of them fierce males who wanted to invade and occupy the United States, rape the flower of American womanhood, desecrate the flag, and ban the Pledge of Allegiance from all American schoolrooms, while making it part of martial law that all women have abortions regardless of race, creed or color.

All across the globe the Nicaraguan hordes are on the march, waving the banner of godless communism and launching invasions of strongholds of "the Free (Anti-Nicaraguan) World." One of these is against Portugal, but it is repelled by American forces led by Col. Caesare (Chay) Appleton, "a spit-and-polish soldier who had very little understanding of almost everything all other people took for granted," a 37-year-old career officer who suddenly finds himself, thanks to this famous victory, an American hero.

As a sendup of the Reaganite nightmare and the televidiotic culture upon which it fed, *Emperor of America* is bang on from first page to last—a mean, nasty and thoroughly hilarious piece of social and political lampoonery.

—*Jonathan Yardley*

One thing leads very quickly to another. The District of Columbia is leveled by a nuclear explosion that "vanished the White House, demolished the Capitol, and caused all but one national government building, the headquarters of the Central Intelligence Agency at Langley, Virginia, to disappear." The culprit is neither Nicaragua nor the Soviet Union but the enemy within, the Royalist Party, which stands for "strictly PR and looting all the way" and which is masterminded by Chay Appleton's brother-in-law, Wambly Keifetz IV, "the second-richest man in the world, lacking only that extra two

billion to overtake an octogenarian Bochica Indian in Colombia who was El Supremo in cocaine production."

Keifetz needs a figurehead, and Chay is the perfect foil. Good military man that he is, he obeys orders and accepts the job of CINCAFUS-CIAFBIANSA: "Commander-in-Chief of the Armed Forces of the United States, the Central Intelligence Agency, the Federal Bureau of Investigation and the National Security Agency," which makes him "one of the most powerful men in the world, outranking his mother." In time he rises still higher, after "the American Republic had been transformed into an Imperial government over which Caesare Appleton, then Chairman/CEO/World Hero, had been named as the nation's first monarch, Emperor Caesare I, absolute ruler of the American people."

With that Condon is off and running, heaving grenades right and left as he polishes off just about every target offered to the satirist by this age of self-indulgence and excess. The list is recited by Wambly Keifetz:

> Ronald Reagan was the greatest President this country has ever produced. He gave us the FBI race wars, the Qaddafi bombings, the Star Wars flapdoodle, the Grenada farce, the Bitburg shaming, the endless bank failures, the Lebanon disasters, the crumbling national airlines, the rape of HUD, the oligarchy of Big Oil, insured inflation, and the shoring-up of sinister Israeli politicians—all to keep our people diverted and entertained until the Royalty Party could consolidate its position. He fought for an end to legal abortion so that the market for our hard-ticket items would never be jeopardized but always expand beyond the food supply. He taught our people to *get the money*.

If it's all a bit on the broad side, from time to time crossing the line that separates satire from slapstick, who cares? Sex, drugs, the Mafia, the CIA, momism, television, Texas—you name it, Condon has an unkind word for it. His characters are caricatures and his plot is preposterous, but who cares about that, either? *Emperor of America* may be a pie-throwing exhibition, but say it for Condon that most of his meringues land right smack on target.

Ray Blount Jr. (review date 11 February 1990)

SOURCE: "Fat Cats in the Driver's Seat," in *The New York Times Book Review,* February 11, 1990, p. 34.

[*In the review below, Blount finds* Emperor of America *not representative of Condon's usual fiction.*]

The imminent legacy of Reaganism: an America governed

so effectively by fat cats and image-mongers that the Constitution is abandoned, the District of Columbia is obliterated by a private-sector nuclear device, royalty is instituted and the figurehead chief of state is Caesare (Chay) Appleton, a Reaganesque and Ollie Northern hero of the Nicaraguan Conflict, whose trademark is a homburg hat worn—even into battle—sideways.

Richard Condon has a new novel, *Emperor of America.* Its premise is the above, all of which I buy, except for the hat.

In my view, a popularly tenable vision of national Republicanism as both ludicrous and menacing is at least 10 years overdue. And who better to provide such a vision than Mr. Condon, whose witty and highly readable novels have included *The Manchurian Candidate, Winter Kills* and *Prizzi's Honor,* all three of which have been made into memorable movies. I welcomed this book with open arms.

Then, after bringing those arms somewhat closer together (as befits a reviewer), I started reading. The first thing that tempted me to open my arms again, and drop the book, was a bit of military communications confusion caused by someone's name being Roger Over. That sounds like a joke Ronald Reagan might *tell*.

The second thing was the hat.

How can the same man who created Maerose Prizzi have also created a mediagenic man-on-horseback character who wears a homburg sideways? Surely such a trademark would look dumb and forced to any viewer, however credulous, and would wobble. I regret to report that the hat characterizes the book.

Of Wambly Keifetz IV, the greedhead power broker whose machinations shape the new America, Mr. Condon writes: "He was ardently committed to the Flag to which he referred affectionately as 'Old Tootsie,' and he led the sixty-seven-person staff at Keifetz Hall, Greenwich, each morning in singing the national anthem, controlled by pitch pipe, followed by a massed Pledge of Allegiance in Latin, the original form of the oath as it had been taken daily by the Roman legionaries under Julius Caesar in 40 B.C. with: 'I pledge allegiance to the balance of trade and to the Export-Import Bank for which it stands. For tax loopholes indivisible with a kiss-off and a promise for all.'"

This is high school level sardonicism, and not at its most accessible. In *Emperor of America,* for some reason, the heretofore deft Mr. Condon becomes not only heavy-handed but airily hard to follow. Only professional doggedness kept this reviewer wading back and forth through sentences like "Jon's fiancee, Elizabeth, had moved him even beyond his own be-

lief in any conceivable extent that a woman had ever moved any man."

Occasionally, out pops an arresting, Chandleresque line ("a jaw like a hammock filled with fat people"). Other passages have their own peculiar charm: "'I am not a politician,' he said with the odd sincerity of the overweight."

But how do you like this for an image: "Chay used his expressive eyes for television. . . . With the right television makeup, they seemed to leak out of his face like pieces of canned fruit."

Here is a sentence that I can't get out of my mind, somehow: "She experienced the terror of possibly falling out of the chaise longue."

The plot, in my judgment, is too slapdash to go into.

The hell of it—well, part of the hell of it—is that Mr. Condon makes some good points. The big-money forces behind Emperor Appleton supply him with a self-image consultant (formerly an assistant to Michael Deaver), whose job is to convince Appleton, as the aforementioned Keifetz puts it, "that his magic came to him in the form of his immeasurable luck. If he believes that, everything has to come out right and he will do anything we tell him because he won't be interested in thinking for himself, he'll let his magical luck come up with the solutions. . . . And God knows that if they are told about his magic, the people will absolutely believe in him, and we'll stay where we belong, in the driver's seat." I don't think I have encountered anywhere else such a plausible sinister analysis of the Reagan dynamic.

In our time, this book insists, the consent of the governed is best obtained and retained by what we might call govertainment. Or, in the words of Keifetz: "Television! The key to all minds and all hearts because it permits the people to be entertained by their government without ever having to participate in it. . . . Representation is fiction."

This fiction, however, is not representative—of Mr. Condon's litertainment or, I like to think, of anti-Reaganism. Can it be the work of some impostor, a Republican dirty trickster?

Other possible explanations:

· What the author refers to rather nicely as Ronald Reagan's "Harold Teen manner" somehow scuttles satirical attacks on the old phenom. Only Garry Trudeau slashed away at Mr. Reagan steadfastly throughout the 1980's, and as a result "Doonesbury" was widely criticized (though not by me) as no longer funny.

· Mr. Condon has given vent to a kind of nausea brought on

by the corruption of political discourse in the Reagan-Bush years. Consider this outburst, which has to do with the unhealthy magic of television viewing: "Does it not seem passing strange? The mayhem there, the palmistry of lewdness produced at such low cost? A pod of wattage for a chair, to enjoy, in congress, busts of stellar consequence? Villains into shining heroes, tailored changelings by the magic wands of light? But wait! Keyholes for pain are not all it reaches. It proves that the possession of money, reason for such Eden, is why we're here." Surely no one who has ever written well could write this badly except on purpose. Can it be a hint that the novel's opening scene is in a town called Almódovar, which is the name of the director of *Women on the Verge of a Nervous Breakdown*?

· The author decided he was going to be wildly fanciful in this one, and therefore didn't have to be rigorous. Actually, of course, the wildly fanciful has to be more rigorous than anything.

· Mr. Condon, like his Manchurian candidate, was programmed years ago by the Republicans to establish himself as a trenchant observer and then, when the time came, to render the truth about Reaganism in self-discrediting form.

· Luck.

Herbert Mitgang (review date 14 February 1990)

SOURCE: "A Twisting Road of Humor to an Imperial America," in *The New York Times,* February 14, 1990, p. C19.

[*In the following review, Mitgang reviews Condon's strong political opinions in* Emperor of America, *"even if they come across like rabbit punches."*]

Who would dare to combine the styles of the *Manchurian Candidate* and *Prizzi's Honor,* more or less, and invent a character who heads the Royalty Party, not in Naples but in the United States? None other than Richard Condon in his latest sendup of the American scene and Presidency.

In *Emperor of America*, his 23rd novel, Mr. Condon is a little more hortatory than usual. He seems to be warning readers against electing a kingly ruler, as Sinclair Lewis once did in his cautionary anti-dictator novel, *It Can't Happen Here,* about a flag-waving general in the White House. Mr. Condon obviously aims to be serious, but he can't help it if his writing is outrageous. He keeps putting English on the eight ball, giving his story screwy turns.

Emperor of America is written with a wink and a smirk and the confidence of an author who has resolved that he's not

going to hold back his strong opinions, not at his exuberant age of 74, even if they come across like rabbit punches.

Without giving away every detail of the convoluted plot, it can be revealed that Mr. Condon is not an admirer of the former President and First Lady, Ronald and Nancy Reagan, who play more than cameo roles in his satire. He doesn't even like their pet, whom he calls a "dear little rented dog." They are mentioned at least a dozen times during the establishment of the fictional imperial presidency.

The time is March 18, 1990. At 11:04 A.M. on that day next month, a nuclear device is exploded in Washington, wiping out the District of Columbia and evaporating 1,397,200 people. The catastrophe causes the White House to vanish, demolishes the Capitol and destroys every national building but the headquarters of the Central Intelligence Agency. The Royalist Party shares responsibility with the National Rifle Association for causing the atomic explosion.

Afterward, news is sent out by the television networks in the form of daily mass exorcisms that were started, Mr. Condon writes, "by the Reagan Administration (1981-1989): the constant moral bloopers; the Grenada mockery; the Lebanese disasters; the Iran-contra scandals; the Persian Gulf debacles; the Libya fixation; the Supreme Court appointment messes; Congressional committee exposures; the charges, arraignments and indictments of high Federal officials beyond any count of corruption in White House history."

Here is the country's mood after the bomb: "The Royalists had best access to where the American people lived; that vast diamond-bright area of daytime television and prime-time soap." He continues, "The Reagan Administration—that shining definition of reigning glamour and romance associated with queens, big money, great dressmakers, great poverty, colorful (moderate) mullahs, glamorous (if shocking) scandals and entertaining South American drug lords—had overtaken the national imagination of a society which had been compartmentalized by money." Naming names, "The yuppie virus, which had been fed by the decade of Ron and Nancy, the bull market and eight unrelenting years of political fantasy, struck as AIDS had struck."

But follow the money and the military. How does an Army colonel, Caesare Appleton, become the first Chairman and Chief Executive Officer of the United States and then Emperor Caesare I? Blame Nicaragua, which the author calls "an evil empire," for his rise to power. With breeding techniques, the Sandinistas swell their population from 3 million in 1980 to 21 million people, "almost all of them fierce males who wanted to invade and occupy the United States, rape the flower of American womanhood, desecrate the flag and ban the Pledge of Allegiance from all American schoolrooms."

Colonel Appleton beats the Sandinistas on the battlefields of Portugal and Southeast Asia, becomes a national hero and takes over as a Royalist. It helps, of course, that his manipulative mother gets him to sign up with the William Morris Agency to make money and a name for himself.

In case of doubt about how Mr. Condon feels about the former President some of his characters pause now and then to emphasize his views indelicately: "Ronald Reagan was the greatest President this country has ever produced. He gave us the F.B.I. race wars, the Qaddafi bombings, the 'Star Wars' flapdoodle, the Grenada farce, the Bitburg shaming, the endless bank failures, the Lebanon disasters, the crumbling national airlines, the rape of HUD, the oligarchy of Big Oil, insured inflation and the shoring up of sinister Israeli politicians—all to keep our people diverted and entertained until the Royalty Party could consolidate its position."

Emperor of America is written with a wink and a smirk and the confidence of an author who has resolved that he's not going to hold back his strong opinions, not at his exuberant age of 74, even if they come across like rabbit punches.

—Herbert Mitgang

And that's not all. The novel also includes cocaine, rape, the mafia, abortion, a House of Lords in Dallas (where the author lives), sibling rivalry, momism and a huge statue erected on Government grounds to former Vice President Spiro T. Agnew. By the end of *Emperor of America,* Mr. Condon has had more fun than anybody; most of the time his humor is wild enough to work.

Carolyn See (review date 26 February 1990)

SOURCE: "Words—and Satire—Fail in Novel," in *Los Angeles Times,* February 26, 1990, p. E5.

[*In the following review, See faults* Emperor of America *for its lack of genuine satire, claiming the novel "is funny as a crutch."*]

The time is 1990; the place, America. The international situation is, as usual, exciting.

Col. Caesare Appleton has succeeded in bravely fighting back another bloodthirsty wave of Sandinistas, this time in southern Portugal. Those pesky Nicaraguans in 1980 had only a population of 3 million people. But by "practicing advanced breeding techniques, they had been able to swell to 21 million by CIA estimate, almost all of them fierce males who wanted to invade and occupy the United States, rape the flower of American womanhood, desecrate the Flag, and ban the Pledge of Allegiance from all American schoolrooms, while making it a part of martial law that all women have abortions, regardless of race, creed or color."

So . . . Col. Appleton, hereinafter referred to as Chay, has become a great American military hero. Our former President, Ronald (The Great Waver) Reagan, and his lovely wife, Nancy, have instilled so many royalist yearnings in our vast population that scarcely anyone notices when Chay's brother-in-law, a corporate-wizard, Donald Trump kind of guy, more or less absentmindedly blows up Washington, D.C., with one well-placed nuclear weapon, builds a "Pink House" out in Southern California to replace the White House in our former capital, and installs Chay and his wife as Emperor of America and his consort—both part of a handsome puppet-couple, tools of a capitalist consortium, and the logical human sequels to our fabled Reagan Legacy.

Why is Chay such a vacant, lobotomized jerk? Richard Condon, whose earlier works include *The Manchurian Candidate* and other masterpieces about the effects of brainwashing on various luckless individuals, takes the position that Col. Caesare Appleton has become the militaristic moron he is because his mother, a venal, vicious, venomous mom who comes straight out of Philip Wylie's *Generation of Vipers*, sent her son away to military school when he was only 5, forever depriving him of the consolations of female company and making him a patsy for whatever woman comes along in his adult life.

(Thus, Chay's corporate-king brother-in-law can control him by means of women, which makes for some pretty tasteless and heavy-handed satire—not quotable in a family newspaper.)

So it's hard to tell what or whom the author hates most here—smothering mothers, Corporate America, former President Reagan or the total overall degeneration of American civilization.

For instance: "Television, of course, is everything. Pictures, and their seldom-relating commentary, crowd out thought. With television paving his way, Napoleon could have taken Moscow. Hitler could have had a Hollywood contract. With television, the French Revolution need never have happened. Marie Antoinette would have chatted glamorously on the 10 highest-rated talk shows. Cake would be in. Bread would be out. After all, we have only to look at Reagan." So says one of Chay's scheming lady friends, part of the devilish plot to place this creation on the throne of the United States.

But *Emperor of America* runs into trouble. It's more than a little difficult to satirize modern American life, for one thing. When Chay decides to invade Nantucket Island to continue the war with the Sandinistas, and the author reports that "the 70,000-man combined U.S. Task Force easily overcame the 679-man Nicaraguan labor battalion," it's just not funny, somehow, not after Operation Just Cause. This kind of military operation is what America does to spend time these days.

It is funny, maybe, but funny as a crutch. When Condon goes on to write, "In the popular imagination, over the 13 years since Ronald Reagan had invented it and Col. North had made it famous throughout Iran, Nicaragua had become a gigantic country, about the size of China, having a population of nearly 22 million people, all bloodthirsty fighters and dangerous Communists," he's not only failing at satire (since he says no more than the unadorned truth) but he's being repetitive (see earlier quote).

A little desperately, Condon falls back on other things to satirize: All those grasping ladies, and the fact that in northern Australia, in every plane that lands, the passengers are sprayed with pesticide. Again, that's not satire—it's no more than the truth.

Emperor of America finally does no more than illustrate why Reagan really *was* the "Teflon" President: In the eyes of his supporters, he could do no wrong. To his detractors, his action became almost literally unspeakable, far beyond the reach of any satire.

In Condon's case, the worst thing that can happen to a writer occurred. Words failed him.

Sarah Booth Conroy (review date 10 May 1990)

SOURCE: "From 'Prizzi' to Politics, Slippery Satire," in *Washington Post*, May 10, 1990, pp. D1, D6.

[*In her review of* Emperor of America *below, Conroy questions Condon on a variety of topics, including his politics, his writings, and his future plans.*]

> Each time Chay would make a plan to slip into New York incognito, Keifetz and Grogan would increase the mood-altering drugs, which led to more hypnosis, which led to more biofeedback, which led to making him feel more and more and more that he was actually Ronald Reagan, until he began to reach the point where he ran the country's foreign affairs and Defense Department purchasing by astrology.
> [*Emperor of America*]

"Strident, venomous, punitive, mean"—that's the way Richard Condon characterizes his new book, *Emperor of America*, a rough, ready and raucous satire on Ronald Reagan, and on Lt. Col. Oliver North and co-conspirators.

In which: A businessman drops a nuclear bomb on Washington. An army colonel becomes a national hero battling Nicaraguans bred to fight. The CIA flies Colombian cocaine to Nantucket. And the colonel is crowned Emperor of America.

Well, it's not as though any of his earlier 22 novels were *Anne of Green Gables*.

The Manchurian Candidate eerily predicted the character of John F. Kennedy's assassin and Lee Harvey Oswald's death.

In *Winter Kills,* Condon went back to a presidential assassination, presenting another plausible plot; in *Death of a Politician* he fantasized a Sen. Joe McCarthy-like character.

Condon's most recent hits have been his three *Prizzi* books—*Prizzi's Glory, Prizzi's Family* and *Prizzi's Honor*, from which the magnificent John Huston movie was made.

"If you're writing about the Mafiosi, it's based on a rock bed of reality. If you're writing about politicians, you're writing about marshmallows and smoke," he said. In any case, money is both the villain and the unifying theme in all his books. The constant reader may suspect he prefers the Mafiosi—hit men and women (equal opportunity employers), gangsters, gamblers and cooks (does Prizzi come from Pizza?)—he seems to find them more principled. But then he grew up in Manhattan.

"Because of the universally popular concept of the Mafiosi, I was able to maintain the realism of who and what they were and where they lived while satirizing them."

Condon does not look as though he has ever committed assassination, murder, orgies, coups etc., although those are some of the crimes that he's written about. Not long ago, Condon—ensconced in the ultra-respectable Hay-Adams Hotel—was disguised as a nice 75-year-old author. He drank pitcher after pitcher of—steel yourself—iced tea and explained why he doesn't need Russians to play villains in his stories as long as he has corrupt American politicians.

Emperor of America resulted from Condon's coming back to the United States from Ireland during the 1980 election, at the beginning of Reagan's first term.

On April 26, 1982, the book began to ferment—maybe mold is a better word—in the novel factory in Condon's head. That date was when he was traumatized by reading in *Time* magazine a full-page story about the visit of the Reagans to Claudette Colbert in Bermuda.

"The story said that the trip was backed up with a fully equipped hospital ship, four helicopters, two fire engines, a new telephone cable for 50 telephones, 110 drivers, 518 people, including 200 journalists. And that slammed home to me that whoever was doing the thinking for Reagan had decided that now was the time for an American monarch. After all, the Divine Right of Kings is the same as the Teflon effect—the king can do no wrong. My book just takes it one step further."

Not until the last year of Reagan's second term did Condon write *Emperor.* He can't believe "that two days after Reagan left the White House, the New York Times reported he was the most popular president in history. I elected myself as the person to say, 'There's no reason for this man to be a popular president and here's why. . . .' I felt I had to raise my voice, and say, 'Damn it, how can you possibly accept this idiot as your great leader in history?'"

As a character says in *Emperor*:

> Television and only television elected Ronald Reagan, did it not? His lovely tailoring, his Harold Teen manner, his acknowledged genius as a waver— why else would the owners of the country have chosen a failed movie actor to fill the presidency? Television! The key to all minds and hearts because it permits the people to be entertained by their government without ever having to participate in it.

The novelist believes that "the manipulators—I should say the custodians of law and order, our lives and government— have decided that the attention span of the American people is limited to three days. When you think of all the things people have to get done in a day, plus the engulfment of television, all they can do is to view politics as entertainment.

"I think of the American people as sitting on bleachers by the river. Around comes a float—the Iran-contra float; here comes another: our brave president daring to go to Colombia to solve the drug problem. You can't get any more satirical than that. . . . Satire can only survive by holding a very slippery thin edge of reality. You have to try to make people believe in what you're writing about, even if you're mocking what they have accepted."

Condon expected opinions—literary and political—to be divided on *Emperor.* He was right. Roy Blount Jr. in the *New York Times Book Review* wrote that he finds the "hithertofore deft Mr. Condon becomes not only heavy-handed but airily hard to follow." And he postulates, "Mr. Condon, like his Manchurian candidate, was programmed years ago by the

Republicans to establish himself as a trenchant observer and then, when the time came, to render the truth about Reaganism in self-discrediting form."

Jonathan Yardley in the *Washington Post Book World* said the book isn't so much a novel as a jeremiad, but he added that "as a sendup of the Reaganite nightmare and the televidiotic culture upon which it fed, *Emperor of America* is bang on from first page to last—a mean, nasty and thoroughly hilarious piece of social and political lampoonery."

"This is a black book—devastating," says Charles McCarry, a novelist and ghost writer of the biographies of Donald Regan and Alexander Haig. "Inside every cynic is an evangelist," says McCarry. "Richard struggles to keep it corked. And when he does, any writer would be proud of that absolutely original voice."

As you might guess, McCarry is a good friend of Condon. "When I write him, I address him as '*Cher Maitre.*'" With Len Deighton and Rod MacLeish, McCarry and Condon name characters after each other. Condon invented the International Confederation of Book Actors—he says it's composed of people "who would have acted in movies, radio or opera if we hadn't been too busy writing." But all he really means is that they borrow each other's names to use for their characters. Condon sends the friends so honored (?) a certificate of performance when he uses their names in a book.

He also sometimes uses allusions to his friends as real people; for example, as a way of chiding McCarry for ghosting political biographies instead of sticking to his great novels, Condon writes in *Emperor*:

> Since the night he had entered his sister's bed, Chay had not wanted anyone to know the true facts about anything in his past . . . working with such distinguished biographers as Abner Stein and Charles McCarry, or rearranging the facts of his life for the ghost writers who assisted him with his autobiographies, Chay always needed to change the truth to something else.

To confound his fans, who might confuse him with his characters, let it be explained that readers often think that writers have the same sexual adventures, physical characteristics, etc. of their characters, while in truth, writers are usually fatter, more chaste and less murderous than their characters. Hot-footing it all over seven countries in 27 years, Condon perched in, among other roosts, what he calls "gringo heights" in Mexico City; in a palazzo in Lugano; and Rossenarra, an 1824 country house in Ireland. These and all other exotic places he used as settings for his life and his books. He came back to the United States with the wife he skipped the country with,

Evelyn Hunt Condon. After 53 years of careful inspection, he still counts the former Powers model as a great beauty.

He's hiding out now in a safe house—the innocuous sort of place you'd expect if he were a federal grand jury witness, relocated under a new identity: in a semidetached house in a suburb of Dallas. (Condon, who grew up in Washington Heights, Manhattan, calls Dallas the most foreign of all his venues.)

"It's like living on the back yard of Metro [Goldwyn-Mayer]—trees and picket fences. Judge Hardy goes by every hour on the hour. We're very tame. Our car is 10 years old and has 19,000 miles. We take long tours of the supermarket."

"We thought about heading out to Timbuktu or the Amazon, but we weren't sure they'd accept our Medicare card," said Condon. There are other attractions on this side of the Atlantic for Condon and his wife: the two Condon daughters (who speak five languages as a result of his travels) and three grandchildren. Imagine! Condon as a grandfather, not a godfather!

Evelyn Condon serves as his first editor. "I'm weak on punctuation," he said. "She makes check marks by what I should change." Condon uses an Olivetti computer—"I was the second professional writer to use a computer, John Hersey was the first. But his was borrowed—in 1976 I was the first writer to buy one." Condon says he's slowing down—"always before, I had two books ahead in my mind."

His 24th novel, not long finished, is even now up for auction. Condon prefers the advance he gets when three publishers bid against each other. "Publishers love to call writers disloyal. But Ronald Wilson Reagan taught us to 'Get the money.'" The 24th, *Get out of My Dream* [later called *The Final Addiction*], is a political satire too—set in the 1992 elections—about the entanglement in cocaine dealing of a frankfurter salesman.

Five of Condon's books have been filmed—most recently the block-buster *Prizzi's Honor,* for which he wrote the script. "Never ask a writer advice on casting," he said with a shake of his head. "I opposed Jack Nicholson bitterly. 'He isn't Italian,' I said. 'He looks German.' Anjelica Huston was the only one in the movie who looked right. But I was wrong. Nicholson was wonderful."

Condon admits that movies sell books. *The Manchurian Candidate* only sold 14,000 in hard copy. My wife said there must have been only four copies bought and those passed hand to hand. Not until the film was a hit did the softback make back the advance."

Frank Sinatra (who stars in the movie along with Laurence

Harvey and Angela Lansbury) and two others owned the film rights to *Manchurian Candidate,* Condon said. "In the first place, people were nervous about making a movie about a presidential assassination. Sinatra flew in to the Kennedy compound to see how [Kennedy] felt about it—and Kennedy said he had no objection."

After the film was withdrawn from distribution after the Kennedy assassination, Sinatra bought it from the other owners. "And he wouldn't allow it to be shown again until the distributor straightened out the bookkeeping on it—till then it hadn't made a profit," Condon said. The current re-release helped sell the paperback.

Condon, who once wrote that it takes more than 50 novels to equal the take on two screenplays (but he claimed the proceeds of the film rights to *The Manchurian* barely covered his Mexican move) is gleeful at the thought of a recent inquiry from a movie company that wants to film one of his best, *Infinity of Mirrors,* where his wrath is turned to denouncing Nazism. "Even in Texas, there's some consternation about the reunity of Germany. Film people have to be opportunists."

In *And Then We Moved to Rossenarra or The Art of Emigrating,* Condon admits to only "three out of the seven deadly sins: greed, wrath and gluttony."

Condon, with the intention of living forever, now enjoys food mostly as a voyeur, feeding his heroes and villains well. *Emperor* is fixated on *kalbsbratwurst,* a German sausage.

One of his most charming books, *The Mexican Stove—Words by Richard Condon, Food by Wendy Bennett* [a daughter]—has recently been reissued by a Texas publisher with Condon's original choice of title, *Ole', Mole'.* Condon makes two claims for the book: It's the only Mexican cookbook written (and test cooked and eaten) in Ireland, and it has the longest introduction (55 pages, also autobiographical) ever written for a cookbook.

After the pouring out of the invective in *Emperor of America,* no wonder Condon says: "I'm so tired of writing political satire. I think my next one will be about a nice collie—better a dachshund, maybe a hunting dachshund."

You can hear the dog story pawing through his mind.

Who knows, the next book may be about a politician who becomes a weredog at the full moon and is bribed by the Mafioso with feinbratwurst.

Alex Heard (review date 10 September 1991)

SOURCE: "As the Political World Turns," in *Washington Post,* September 10, 1991, p. F3.

[*In the following review, Heard profiles the central characters in* The Final Addiction, *concluding that Condon "keeps things running nicely."*]

As fans of **The Manchurian Candidate** will recall, when Richard Condon puts on his political-satire hat, he has a thing for extremely stupid, cardboard male politicians who are backed by wily women. In **The Final Addiction,** a broad tour through the barrens of contemporary politics, the viper's nest of the global spy game, the void of Our National Mind and the shadowy controlling presence of organized crime (yes, the good old Prizzis make an appearance), there are two of these guys. Both are so insipid that you worry—repeated contact may be too much like mainlining marshmallow paste. But Condon, pro that he is, works that out satisfactorily. One of them appears only in tolerably brief scenes. The other mutates into a new, higher, more interesting stupidity life form.

The first is Osgood Noon, a presidential candidate. Take President Bush, liposuction his brain, and you've got Noon. He entered Republican politics by convincing his skeptical father that "this move could help business." Rising through the appointive ranks—ambassador to Monaco, chairman of the National Energy From Toxic Waste Commission, State Department, Reagan's "short list" of 91 candidates for running mate—he's being positioned by his brilliant wife, Oona, to run in 1992 on a pro-flag, pro-Pledge, pro-gun ticket. Downplaying his inherited wealth, "Goodie" claims not one but four heartland states as his home. "I am a working stiff," he says, "a tool handler from the oil fields of Texas who gets by with the sweat of his brow." This dolt's favorite hobby is pecking out "typewriter portraits" of former presidents.

The Final Addiction, like many a Washington lampoon before it, attaches a bicycle pump to current and recent events, and works it until they reach parade-float proportions.

—Alex Heard

The second is Owney Hazman, son of an American triple-agent and an Iranian double agent, who grows up harboring one obsession: to find his mother, who went into hiding when the father's house of cards collapsed in 1969. To that end, young Owney starts greedily hoarding a sizable financial nut, which he gathers first as a novelty salesman, then as a frankfurter salesman working for his wife's father. Owney is certainly an idiot—at one point he says to a much wiser character who is fleeing drug lords, "You don't really think, in this day and age, that anyone would think of killing anyone for four billion six hundred and twenty million dollars?" But he at least is capable of tying his shoes and "growing." His ambition is to become a network anchorman—the hope being that his mother will see him, rich and famous, and return at last to his side. Before it's over he lands something much, much bigger, in an ending that takes all the novel's themes way beyond their logical extreme.

As matters turn out—this is revealed very early, so I'm not giving anything away—Oona Noon is Owney's mother. She has her own agenda. She was a fanatic follower of the Ayatollah Khomeini, and her mission is to undermine the United States by flooding it with cocaine, which she smuggles in using a fleet of 79 supertankers inherited from her second husband, Nicky Nepenthe. Oona covets the presidency for her husband and herself. ("A five-day vacation for two people costin' five million dollars" is how she shrewdly appraises a recent official presidential visit to Barbados.) She's also determined to mother Owney along life's path without his knowing her true identity. Initially she pays for his anchorman lessons, but he proves hopeless; among other shortcomings, he can't get the knack of saying "I'll see you tomorrow" to the camera with the right degree of fake sincerity. Then she paves the way for a congressional seat, but that's scuttled when Owney, temporarily estranged from his wife, is taped by the CIA in a carnal engagement with a notorious IRA terrorist.

You're probably beginning to get the idea. **The Final Addiction,** like many a Washington lampoon before it, attaches a bicycle pump to current and recent events, and works it until they reach parade-float proportions. Normally I find this approach boring, especially since it has evolved into the iron-clad formula for satirists aiming to "blast" contemporary public life. Even so, Condon is better at it than most. He relentlessly hits you with a denser (and dumber) supply of gags, leaving you with a sort of dizzy satisfaction—think of it as authoritative slapstick. He's strongest with the description of his very large cast of shameless characters. Here's our first sight of Oona:

A long robin's-egg blue car with a two-seater body by Figoni e Filaschi . . . drove up slowly . . . The Figoni vision was driven by a striking woman of an interesting age, Owney decided. She had a golden tan and wore a V neck yellow sweater over a scarlet blouse. Her eyes were like Delft dinner plates on a snowfield . . . She had cheekbones as high and flat as an Inuit medicine man's and short yellow hair which fit her like an Aztec feather helmet. He made a vivid note to stay out of her way . . . She wore clothes as if van Dongen had painted them on her, and she had a mouth that looked like a meal in itself.

Novels that "romp" through modern politics are usually driven by kooky plots. (Make no mistake, *The Final Addiction* is too.) But they survive from moment to moment on the basis of sharp, funny writing. Except for the final pages, when he flies too far into the wackysphere, Condon keeps things running nicely.

Herbert Mitgang (review date 18 September 1991)

SOURCE: "Insulting without Libel in a Satirical Novel," in *The New York Times,* September 18,1991, p. C18.

[*In the review below, Mitgang discusses the targets of Condon's satire in* The Final Addiction.]

There's nobody else quite like Richard Condon writing satirical novels today. The singular Condon genre combines American politics, scoundrels in various corners of the world, linguistic shenanigans, cholesterol-loaded meals, cold warriors in intelligence agencies, legalized thievery in Washington and put-downs of the high and mighty everywhere. As the comedian Mort Sahl used to say in his nightclub act at the Hungry I in San Francisco. "Is there anyone here I haven't offended?"

The Final Addiction, Mr. Condon's 24th novel and may he go on forever, could be categorized as a Reagan-Bush-Quayle-era thriller. It's not so deliberately plotted as *The Manchurian Candidate* or *Prizzi's Honor,* but it's nearly as imaginative and even more outrageous. The remarkable achievement of Mr. Condon's recent novels, including his new one, is that they are insulting without being libelous. A neat trick.

American Presidents often provide the background music for Mr. Condon's novels. *Winter Kills* featured a libidinous young President who is assassinated. *The Star-Spangled Crunch* included a big-time operator who is forced to leave office because of a scandal. In *The Final Addiction,* there are references to Calvin Coolidge, Jimmy Carter and, coming up to the 1980's and 1990's, a dimwitted President who loves sending arms to the Nicaraguan rebels and another who is best remembered for hating broccoli.

The real and the unreal all flow together in Mr. Condon's mad, mad, mad Presidential whirlpool. A future White House hopeful's wife, Mrs Goodie Noon (sounding like Finley Peter Dunne's humorous political observer, Mr. Dooley), says:

"Oh, it's nice bein' a President, I can tell you. Look at the time the Reagans went down to Barbados for a little five-day visit. Three hundred and eighteen people had to go along with him an that ain't countin the crews on the hospital ship and the light cruiser filled with marines ready to swarm ashore in case they had to rescue him from the tourists, and the 700 members of the international press media." After saying that the Reagans knew how to do it "better'n bein' a king and queen," she goes on: "Sure, the five days on Barbados for two people in love cost the taxpayers $5 million, but think what Truman or Kennedy or Johnson or Ford or Carter woulda given the people. Jes' the same old thang—gettin' on an off Air Force One. Lemme tell you no other ruler in the world comes even close to the Reagans when they travel on the taxpayer."

The character named Goodie Noon does succeed President Reagan. Instead of going to Camp David, the Marine helicopter takes Mr. and Mrs. Noon to the family pad on "Bland Island." In case the reader is in doubt about who the author means, Goodie has the Presidential helicopter, which he calls his Herkybird, fitted out like the interior of the ranch house to the movie *Giant,* with "several really good paintings by Grant Wood." Even though Goodie was born "a Connecticut man, he lived and breathed Texas" and claimed four states as his home.

Goodie, who at one point is described as the education President, has a hero: Calvin Coolidge. The author compares their speaking styles: "Goodie Noon's voice, had Calvin Coolidge ever spoken, which he had not, could have been a nasal match of his hero's speech. It was as though trained people came in every morning, before both men arose, to pack their sinuses with hot sand through which a dissonant treble wind whistled." Goodie often uses his voice to declaim, "Promote the flag, and the flag will promote you."

Among the novelist's other targets are the National Rifle Association, Klaus Barbie, Barbara Walters, his own fictional Prizzis ("a kinder and gentler Mafia"), the C.I.A., the F.B.I., the K.G.B., the Chinese Foreign Intelligence Department, frankfurters containing monosodium glutamate and other additives and preservatives, the Concorde, the savings and loan industry, the New York City subway system, Star Wars, wigs worn by United States Senators and Walter Cronkite's mustache.

Oh, yes, there's a plot in *The Final Addiction.*

A young man is a successful frankfurter salesman, specializing in novelty franks, which the trade says should never be called hot dogs. His wife is beautiful and his father-in-law is wealthy. But there is something nagging at his mind as he grows up. His mother left him at an early age, leaving only a note saying that there's hamburger in the fridge. His wife has a blooming career as a pop singer. He meets a woman who is supporting her simpleton husband for President, using her billions of dollars from her cocaine empire. How is the young man going to find his long-lost mother and what has she been up to? The way to track her down is to become a television anchor, make several million a year and be seen on screens all over the world and be spotted by Mom.

Meantime . . . the Chinese, the Syrians, the Afghans, the Mafiosi and disguised intelligence agents from the fisheries and wildlife services of nine nations are watching the anchor's every move. And the frankfurter business begins to expand.

All more or less clear?

In the final chapter of *The Final Addiction,* Mr. Condon wraps it up: "That is the full (if amazing) story of the profound national mystery of how an unknown, inexperienced 32-year-old man came to be nominated as candidate for Vice President of the United States of America at the Republican Presidential nominating convention at New Orleans, the youngest and, some would say, the callowest man ever to be chosen for that high office, which, as every American child knows, is only a heartbeat away from the Presidency. The man named to be Vice President had had no experience beyond the field of frankfurters."

Richard Condon has done it again. As they say in Hollywood, *The Final Addiction* is high concept.

Kirkus Reviews (review date 15 September 1992)

SOURCE: A review of *The Venerable Bead,* in *Kirkus Reviews,* Vol. LX, No. 18, September 15, 1992, p. 1144.

[*Below, the critic briefly summarizes the major themes of* The Venerable Bead.]

Galloping satire whose hairpin turns can be followed only by God (the *Bible*) and Condon (*The Manchurian Candidate,* etc. etc.), and one of those may still be in the dark.

Condon veterans will brace themselves for the same gaudy density of higgledy-piggledy jokery that filled 1991's *The Final Addiction*—but this time Condon outdoes himself. Set in the early 70's, [*The Venerable Bead*] finds the Commie menace in full bloom. Any theme laid bare by the book's readers, however, may well suddenly be swallowed like oyster meat by another theme. One leading theme is about polymorphous human appearances, a subject that at last gets so complicated that one loses track of which physical body the heroine is wearing—as does her lover, who also wears a series of bodies. A second theme is about immortality, or the extension of human life by way of a secret Albanian yogurt formula passed on to the hero, Joseph Reynard, by his departed 134-year-old great-grandfather (Joseph himself was sired by an 80-year-old father). Will Joseph and his beloved Leila Aluja—an Iraqi-American superspy for the Sino-Alba-

nian spymaster Josef Shqitonja (really Joe Reynard himself)—get out of the spy business and become billionaires with this fast-food recipe? Quite possibly, since Leila owns The Venerable Bead—a huge, legendary ruby whose bearer is fated to have faultless good luck and great power. A third theme involves the corruptions of celebrityhood and the media, with Leila transformed into rock superstar Meine Edelfrau ("Ma Donna" in Albanian), and a fourth is about gun control and arms dealing. Hey, Joe wonders, won't a geriatric world population quintupled by long-life yogurt overburden the planet with ghastly survival problems? Condon smiles, nodding.

Betrayal of love and trust leads to a repeat ending of *Prizzi's Honor* that's even wilder than the original.

Jay Cantor (review date 29 November 1992)

SOURCE: "Whatever Leila Wants...," in *Book World—The Washington Post,* November 29, 1992, p. 9.

[*In the review below, Cantor analyzes the plot of* The Venerable Bead.]

Even in the more than 10,000 words *The Washington Post* has provided for me to review Richard Condon's new novel, *The Venerable Bead,* I couldn't possibly summarize the plots within plots that Condon invents in order to reveal what is really already happening to us, those open secrets and purloined letters that are the nightly news.

Leila Aluja, our main character (or should I say characteroid, or center of narrative interest?), is first of all a secret agent for the international security firm that runs the recently privatized FBI, CIA and KGB. In her efforts to crack the Albanian spy network that runs Hollywood talent agencies on behalf of the Communist Chinese, she becomes a movie star; and then a pop queen; and then a powerful Washington lawyer-lobbyist for the NRA and the Mafia; and then a public relations czarina who pre-sells easy-win wars to keep the Pentagon five-sided; and then a fast-food mogul of pre-cooked haggis, tofu pizza and other delights; and then she goes on the trail of a yogurt that will make us live nearly forever, so the planet will split its sides laughing; and then . . . and then . . . and then. All these doings are recounted with sly digs, word play, an amiably mean ragtag style and a sufficient number of brand names to make you gag on what you are already daily swallowing.

Leila isn't (but in this sort of world who could be?) a rounded character with whose loves and losses you identify. She is, rather, the floating center of a delirium of fantasies that we call ours, though they are as pre-sold to us as the wars whose heroes then stalk our pre-fab dreams. In our personal and national fantasy life—or so Condon avers—we are an amalgam of tabloid elements, and *The Venerable Bead* is a snappy sample of that internal film strip, until in the last judgment (and this deeply moral book provides one) we see a country, perhaps ours, that has become a serial of sinister plots, populated by personalities that are themselves made (like Leila's) of false memories and programmed desires that don't belong to us, things we've "seen on television or read as headlines in *The National Enquirer* or in one of those commercials with soap opera plots." And so "from the ten thousand things she had heard or imagined about other people while her past was dying, she had built a memory." Which memory is this book, or, I guess, this newspaper, which will then become a part of your and my seemingly personal memory.

That all seems about right to me on a bad day, so it is perhaps not the whole truth, or how would this novel have gotten written? Still, was it Condon, author of *The Manchurian Candidate* and *Prizzi's Honor* and many other novels, who also wrote the Watergate Cover-Up and Pat Buchanan's speech at the Republican Convention (which was no doubt a Demo dirty trick)? Was it Condon who, on a sour day, scripted the election that just was, in which (but could this really have happened?) the president of the United States—called Goodie Noon when he appears in this novel—appeared on a television talk show with a wide-suspendered host, and implied that his opponent, Gov. Bozo Waffle, had been programmed in Moscow to take deep cover as a good old boy, become president of the United States, and invite his old bolshy comrades (who knew that the jig would soon be up for them in the U.S.S.R.) to high U.S. government positions (like head of the National Rifle Association), where they could transfer our assets to already bulging Swiss bank accounts? Did Condon invent Skadillionaire Uncle Scrooge Perot, who accused President Goodie Noon of sneaking LSD into the punch bowl at his daughter's wedding to Sean Penn?

Which is to say that *The Venerable Bead,* which reports Condon's (or his allies') other doings during the Reagan-Noon years—and delivers the goodies on the movie business, the public relations firms that now schedule our wars' victory parades in advance, the NRA, our also murderous fast food, and the last opera buffo minutes of the communist conspiracy—has a hard time keeping up with the excesses of our current events. Almost forcing sentences like my last one to go on and on excessively, like Condon's delightfully excessive plots, trying to keep ahead of the curve, taking on an increasingly shrill tone as the engine of outrage goes into overdrive when (for example) the Brady Bill (named by Condon—or was it someone else?—for a man who was shot in an attempt to assassinate his best friend, conservative Ronald Reagan) is nixed by the conservative NRA, which in this outrageously outraged novel (or is it real life?) has bought the Congress, lest our constitutionally guaranteed right to commit murder ever be abridged.

This adds to history the kind of irony that at one time only novelists provided. Any engine might whine from the pressure of trying to keep up with such history. Or perhaps (as Condon himself implies) the shrill sound we dogs sometimes hear is the screams of souls in torment, in this case particularly our main character, Leila Aluja, who finds as she dies that her memory "bobbled like a cork upon a chaotic sea of deals, money, power, celebrity, sex, television, greed, and politics, the tarnished threads of the true flag. She relived what she had been trained to dream but had never seen, lifetimes flashing past in nanoseconds . . . She remembered her life . . . which was the price she had paid for her constant betrayal of love and trust. Suddenly she knew where she was. She was in hell."

Herbert Mitgang (review date 2 December 1992)

SOURCE: "Intrigue in the Business World and in Suburbia," in *The New York Times,* December 2, 1992, p. C22.

[*In the following excerpt, Mitgang lauds Condon's mockery of the politically powerful in* The Venerable Bead.]

The heroine of Richard Condon's 25th novel—his deadliest satire on the underbelly of American life since his series of Prizzi novels—starts out as Leila Aluja, the canny daughter of Iraqi immigrants, who acquires the rights to Tofu Pizza, the taste sensation of Europe and Asia. She advances from demonstrating pre-packed lunches at a trade school in Michigan to become the billionaire head of the world's largest fast-food conglomerate. Her companies own 114,720 outlets in 31 countries, a national evangelical television network; casinos in Nevada, Aruba, the Bahamas and Puerto Rico; a chain of ballroom dancing schools, and "7 U.S. senators and 61 congressmen."

Leila's aphrodisiac is power, which she gains and exercises ruthlessly. Her ambitions are fulfilled with the help of a good-luck talisman, the ancient ruby that inspires the novel's title. Along her crooked road to wealth and fame, Leila acquires and divorces four husbands, at least one of whom, a Chinese-Albanian spy-master, she probably loves. Before succeeding in the fast-food game, she becomes an American counterspy, a Washington lawyer and lobbyist, and a film and recording star. Her theatrical name, which becomes better known than Madonna's, is Meine Edelfrau.

Describing his heroine as a Washington spy and propagandist during the Persian Gulf war, Mr. Condon writes: "Leila had the knack of believing in whatever she was paid to do. She sold war with the same high purpose and zeal she brought to her crusades for cigarettes. If the crack industry had been better organized or had any goals beyond making money by killing people, she would have sold the meaning of its effect, slightly modulated from a chemical which produced insanity, to the stuff that dreams are made of."

Mr. Condon stops the action now and again to ridicule real people and imaginary organizations. Senator Joseph R. McCarthy is described as a man "who had given up his life mostly to booze" while hunting Reds. The director of the Federal Bureau of Investigation, J. Edgar Hoover, is nailed for maintaining that "there is no such thing as the Mafia," one of the author's favorite targets. President Ronald Reagan is reviled for stating that the burden of decreased charitable works would be taken up happily by the private sector. Among the lobbying groups attacked are the "National Gun Carriers' Association" and the "Center for American National Cigarette Education and Research (C.A.N.C.E.R.)."

Happily, we are back in familiar Condon country, a fictional land where political lions dwell, scoundrels thrive and greed trickles upward. With outrageous humor, the author mocks the power brokers behind the Manchurian candidates who dominate everything from Hollywood to Washington. Should we laugh at his puns and inside jokes, or shudder at the people who rule his American rookery? In *The Venerable Bead,* Mr. Condon has the singular ability to make readers do both.

Donald E. Westlake (review date 13 December 1992)

SOURCE: "Stalin Goes Hollywood," in *The New York Times Book Review,* December 13, 1992, pp. 9, 11.

[*Below, Westlake calls* The Venerable Bead *"a lot of fun, loose-jointed, manic, over the top from first word to last."*]

Richard Condon has always been way out there on the cutting edge between prescience and lunacy. In toughly comic novels from *The Manchurian Candidate* to *Prizzi's Honor* and beyond, he has reflected the real world through a slightly distorting mirror in which our near future grins back at us, without comfort. In such books, there's a tight and brilliant control over story, over character, over Mr. Condon's own savagely satirical instinct. But from time to time his irritation boils over, and out of him comes whirling a fictional dooms-day machine, mowing down everything in its wake, from our most pious political platitudes to the entire best-seller list. Now, in the twilight of spydom, with sovereign nations everywhere cracking like the glassware in a coloratura's hotel suite, comes the spy novel not to end all spy novels but to bury them, and then do something raucous on their graves.

The Venerable Bede was an English monk and historian, born in 673. He wrote *Historia Ecclesiastica Gentis Anglorum,* among other works, introduced the concept of dating back-ward into antiquity from the birth of Christ, and died in 735 without ever knowing about Richard Condon's latest novel. The Venerable Bead in *The Venerable Bead* is the Ahmadabad Ruby, a stone that—but let Mr. Condon tell you:

> "It was so old and so priceless that its name had been changed to the Venerable Bead. It had been a gift to Leila on her wedding night from her second husband, the most powerful man in the history of Hollywood, who had inherited it from his father, a close comrade of Joseph Stalin. It weighed 97.643 carats. . . . It was valued at $1,483,700." The juxtaposition of Hollywood and Stalin, and the combination of utter absurdity with finicky numerical exactitude, are what this book is all about, if it's all about anything. It isn't about the Venerable Bede, of course, but then again it isn't about the Venerable Bead, either.

In the novel, the ruby is not stolen, not lost, not pawned, not traded, not a plot point, not a Maguffin, not an issue, not even referred to except at the beginning and the end. It's merely the red thing Leila carries on a thin gold chain around her neck.

Ah, Leila. If this novel had a heroine, which it hasn't, Leila would be it. Her history is so complex that we are given an entire chapter just to list her careers. The daughter of a Mafia-connected Congressman, she has been at one time or another a counterspy for the United States Government, a movie star, a rock singer who earned an average of $63 million a year—"Her second record album on the Cacophony label, *I Stand Alone,* from her hit film *Nobody Stands Alone,* sold 7,450,000 copies"—and also a dominant Washington lawyer for the weapons industry, the cigarette industry and the mob. In addition, she is the sometime head of her own powerful New York public relations firm, the closest adviser to the President and a sexual athlete who hip-flips men into the air when she's in the mood.

> **Now, in the twilight of spydom, with sovereign nations everywhere cracking like the glassware in a coloratura's hotel suite, comes [*The Venerable Bead,*] the spy novel not to end all spy novels but to bury them, and then do something raucous on their graves.**
>
> **—*Donald E. Westlake***

When we first meet Leila, aboard a Florida-bound passenger liner called Eros, she's in her early 40's and is president of the largest fast-food company in the world. She's also beautiful—wouldn't you know it?—and she had "big hair"; hair apparently so big it could be (but isn't) rented to the underclass as living space. If the heroine of a Jackie Collins novel were to meet Leila, Leila would merely laugh, but the other girl would be so envious her eyelashes would catch fire.

Leila has had four husbands, the first of whom nobody can remember. The second was a Hollywood agent and a spy, the third the cocaine-snorting head of the National Gun Carriers' Association, and the fourth a professor of Gaelic studies at Columbia University. His propensity to speak only in Gaelic, particularly in bed, is what drives the poor woman into the arms of a sports dentist; trust me.

I'm not going to give a plot summary here. If Mr. Condon could get along without one, so can you. I'll just say that manic scenes come flying out of nowhere, divert us and self-destruct. There's the hilarious conversation between Leila and her third husband about legalizing flamethrowers for civilian use: "Sure, it's possible that some kids loitering in schoolyards could get a little charred—but the greater good is the safety and protection that flamethrowers can give us by allowing each citizen, armed and ready, to defend his rights under the Constitution." Again, when the Chinese disguise their spies with four-inch elevator shoes, American know-how beats them with "Manhole Shoes," to make our spies four inches shorter.

It is one of this book's conceits that virtually all Hollywood agents are actually in deep cover, that they are, in fact, Albanian spies working for China. When the F.B.I. swoops up more than 300 of them, we get this: "Only three people were left throughout the entire craft of film making who knew how to make deals, get the right tables in restaurants, actually read a script, or to help an actor write a letter home to mother—in sum, how to make movies. This accounted for such films as *Ishtar, Hudson Hawk* and *Howard the Duck.*"

The free-floating rage behind such commentary is not always under control, nor is it always used to fuel a comic intent. For instance, the fourth (but not the last) time Mr. Condon informed me that "PAC's, or political action committees, had been invented by the U.S. Congress so that it could be bribed legally," without then putting any comic spin on the idea, I gave up hoping he'd find the satire inside the concept. (He never did.) This is merely reportage, realistic pastel inappropriately amid the pyrotechnicolorics.

Still, despite the author's occasional confusion as to which side of the looking glass he's on, *The Venerable Bead* is a lot of fun, loose-jointed, manic, over the top from first word to last. Pending the arrival of a rational world, Richard Condon is among the most accomplished and witty ranters in the bedlam we've got. Just don't ask him to make sense until the rest of us do.

Joe Queenan (review date 6 February 1994)

SOURCE: "Swept Away by the Hit Man's Daughter," in *The New York Times Book Review,* February 6, 1994, p. 9.

[*In the review below, Queenan finds* Prizzi's Money *"riotously funny," emphasizing Condon's "acid prose."*

Measles rarely plays a pivotal role in books about the Mafia. But when Charley Partanna, hit man's hit man, is suddenly afflicted by a severe case of the measles 49 pages into Richard Condon's hilarious novel **Prizzi's Money,** he finds himself incapable of accepting a mob contract to go to London to murder Julia Asbury, a brassy woman who is trying to steal $1.4 billion from the infamous Prizzi family. By the time Charley is feeling well enough to ice the truculent whackee, the Prizzis have discovered that Mrs. Asbury is actually Julia Melvini, the daughter of another top Prizzi hit man, known as the Plumber "because of his signature threat to flush recalcitrants down the toilet." In fact, the Plumber's most recent victim was his son-in-law, Henry, husband of Julia, who hired the Prizzis to stage his own kidnapping so he could keep the $75 million ransom—but who now must die because his wife has become so annoying.

Since industry ethics deem it dishonorable to hit the daughter of a hit man while the hit man is still doing hits for the family that authorized the hit, Don Corrado Prizzi, *capo di tutti capi,* orders one of Charley's aides, Pino Tasca, first to whack the Plumber—taking care of any problems on the offense-to-*omerta* front—and then to whack the Plumber's daughter. But Pino complicates everything by falling in love with the hit man's daughter, then bungling the hit on her hit man dad and then getting hit himself.

In the end, the only way the don has any hope of getting his money back is by arranging for his son Eduardo, a financial genius with blue hair "by Albert of Warsaw," to marry Julia and then trick her into running for the United States Senate, which will require her to relinquish control of the 137 companies her whacked husband used to own and fork them over to the Prizzis. Which seems like a wonderful solution to everyone but Julia, who couldn't care less about the Senate, and Charley Partanna, who despite being engaged to Maerose Prizzi, the granddaughter of the *capo di tutti capi* who authorized the contract on Julia in the first place, has now fallen madly in love with the woman he would have iced 120 pages earlier if he hadn't come down with the measles. Mr. Condon writes:

> They were in love, as much as Charley detested the transience of that phrase. They loved in the way the great ones had loved, Charley insisted, the way Bogie and Ingrid had loved, and Ingrid and Bogie. With all his heart he knew that he and Mrs. Asbury were one

being. They made cosmic music together. Why else, Charley asked himself, did he always wear a jacket and a necktie when he saw her?

Why ask why?

Prizzi's Money is the latest riotously funny installment in a series of novels that includes *Prizzi's Glory, Prizzi's Family* and *Prizzi's Honor,* the last of which was the basis for a fine movie starring Jack Nicholson as the likable hit man Charley Partanna. As was the case in *Prizzi's Honor,* the infamous don, his vile sons and their assorted *vindicatori, intimidatori* and even what Mr. Condon refers to as "assistant *intimidatori*" and "apprentice *vindicatori*" now find themselves confronted by a force of nature that they are culturally unequipped to deal with: a perfidious woman 10 times more cunning and determined than they are. As the long-suffering don gloomily laments: "Sixteen months ago this Asbury woman was a simple housewife, now she runs 137 companies and wants to take over the biggest conglomerate in America. It's that . . . woman's movement that puts these crazy ideas into their heads."

The delicious notion that the Cosa Nostra could somehow be subverted by Naomi Wolf-style power feminism is only one of the gloriously crackpot ideas that appear in *Prizzi's Money.* There is also a memorable scene in which the Prizzis pay a shady butler $50,000 to murder Mrs. Asbury, but insist on getting a receipt. In another set piece, Don Corrado's son Vincent, whose daughter Maerose is engaged to marry Charley Partanna, is seen at his desk fuming at how hard it is to fill out his I.R.S. forms. And the book is also liberally supplied with such shadowy organizations as the Little Sisters of Pain and Pity and churches with names like St. Philip of the Wounds.

Of course, what really makes the novel work is Mr. Condon's acid prose. "If taxis wore clothes they would resemble Charley," he writes. Of Julia, he says, "She had a passionate Sicilian nose and—God!—what a mouth—an army could feed on that mouth and be able to march for 10 days." Finally, summing up the unconventional love affair between the attractive psychopaths, he writes:

> Charley went head over heels about Mrs. Asbury. At her insistence he shaved off the mustache and went back to wearing an ordinary felt fedora. No matter how busy he got with his work and, what with subverting the labor movement, going through all the intricate moves of bribing politicians and police officials, assigning contracts for hits, keeping up with the public's relentless demand for cocaine and adding to the American cost of living by his chains of tributes that took effect as soon as the goods were moved into the cities, tributes that were then added

to the cost of almost everything to be passed on to the consumer, Charley was always thinking about Julia Asbury and how, despite his engagement to Maerose Prizzi, he could ask a classy woman like that to marry him.

Chris Petrakos (review date 20 February 1994)

SOURCE: "Appraising Condon's Latest 'Prizzi'," in *Chicago Tribune,* February 20, 1994, sec. 14, p. 7.

[*In the following excerpt, Petrakos gives a brief, favorable review of* Prizzi's Money.]

Malice, greed, violent death, betrayal, conspiracy—only Richard Condon can write about such matters and leave his readers feeling cheerful and refreshed. While Condon's new book, *Prizzi's Money,* is not quite up to his previous volumes on the first family of crime, it still delivers enough jabs to the bloated gut of American culture to keep the pages turning at high speed.

The book begins with the spectacular kidnapping of political heavyweight Henry George Asbury, a man who has "been seriously involved with every mirror he ever met." But the kidnapping is simply a money-making scheme hatched by Asbury and his very cunning wife, Julia, who also happens to be the daughter of a Mafia hitman, the Plumber.

Henry has made a big mistake, however; he's double-crossed his wife and cut the Prizzi family into the deal. Julia's subsequent fury, her icy resolve and her absolute skill as a financial and sexual manipulator sets the plot running in several directions and threatens to pull down the Prizzi empire.

As usual, Condon spins a bunch of insane variations off of this already manic scheme, introducing old characters like Charley Partanna and Maerose Prizzi, as well as new ones like Pino Tasco, the killer with the beautiful teeth. His manic plotting is as entertaining as always, as are his lightninglike guerrilla attacks on politicians and the Catholic church. And I'm always astonished by how much Condon can pack into a descriptive statement: "Vincent had a totally closed face, like a bank vault shut impenetrably by a system of time locks."

Lorrie K. Inagaki (review date Summer 1994)

SOURCE: A review of *Prizzi's Money,* in *The Armchair Detective,* Vol. 27, No. 3, Summer, 1994, pp. 361-62.

[*In the review below, Inagaki claims that* Prizzi's Money *is "enjoyable reading."*]

George Asbury, a billionaire businessman who has served as "advisor to presidents", is kidnapped while accompanied by two men on a boat in the open sea. Amazingly enough, neither of the two men on board remember anything about Mr. Asbury's disappearance. One moment they were all on board and the next, Mr. Asbury was gone. Julia, his young wife, appears grief-stricken in public but privately knows that she and her husband had planned the kidnapping in order to escape with the ransom money and the $1.4 billion illegally siphoned from his failing companies. What she doesn't know is that her husband had secretly made a deal with the Prizzi crime family. When Julia discovers that the Prizzi family is after her for the money, she devises a bold and elaborate scheme to pull the wool over their eyes and escape with a new identity. This takes a bit of doing, however, especially when hit man extraordinaire Charley Partanna is ordered to do away with her. Julia also doesn't expect to fall in love with Charley.

Fourth in the continuing saga of the Prizzi crime family (following **Prizzi's Glory, Prizzi's Family** and **Prizzi's Honor),** **Prizzi's Money** brings back the now familiar members of the family including Charley Partanna, Don Corrado Prizzi, Maerose Prizzi and Edward Price. The main character, however, in this one is Julia Asbury, nee Julia Melvini, the daughter of another Prizzi hit man. Julia is brainy and brash, and clearly more than a match for anyone in the Prizzi family. Supporting characters include Julia's twin brother, a tenacious newspaper reporter, and Julia's father. Every character is entertaining, although none of them could be considered admirable. The plot is outrageous and moves at breakneck pace. The writing is witty, smooth and replete with offbeat and black humor. All these elements work together to make this book enjoyable reading.

Mel Gussow (obituary date 10 April 1996)

SOURCE: "Richard Condon, Political Novelist, Dies at 81," in *The New York Times,* April 10, 1996, p. A16.

[*In the following obituary, Gussow reviews Condon's literary career and life.*]

Richard Condon, the fiendishly inventive novelist and political satirist who wrote **The Manchurian Candidate, Winter Kills** and **Prizzi's Honor,** among other books, died yesterday at Presbyterian Hospital in Dallas. He was 81.

Novelist is too limited a word to encompass the world of Mr. Condon. He was also a visionary, a darkly comic conjurer, a student of American mythology and a master of conspiracy theories, as vividly demonstrated in **The Manchurian Candidate.** That novel, published in 1959, subsequently became a cult film classic, directed by John Frankenheimer. In this spellbinding story, Raymond Shaw, an American prisoner of war (played in the film by Laurence Harvey), is brainwashed and becomes a Communist agent and assassin.

When the 1962 film was re-released in 1988, Janet Maslin wrote in *The New York Times* that it was "arguably the most chilling piece of cold war paranoia ever committed to film, yet by now it has developed a kind of innocence."

Mr. Condon was a popular novelist who earned serious critical attention, although he did not always win favorable reviews. His response "I'm a man of the marketplace as well as an artist." And he added. "I'm a pawnbroker of myth." Though others made claims that his novels were prophetic he admitted only that they were "sometimes about five and a half minutes ahead of their time."

In **Winter Kills,** a President, evidently modeled on John F. Kennedy, is assassinated in a conspiracy involving the Central Intelligence Agency and the underworld. Obsessed by politics, Mr. Condon once said, "Every book I've ever written has been about the abuse of power. I feel very strongly about that. I'd like people to know how deeply their politicians are wronging them." That abuse could be in contemporary life or as long ago as the 15th century, as in his novel *A* **Trembling Upon Rome.**

Politicians like Senator Joseph R. McCarthy and President Richard M. Nixon appeared in various guises in his work, Nixon as Walter Slurrie in **Death of a Politician.** Speaking about politics and political thrillers, Mr. Condon once said, "It's the villains that make good literature, because they're the only ones in the story who know what they want."

He did not write his first novel until he was 42, but, once started, he never stopped. The first, **The Oldest Confession** (1958), was filmed as *The Happy Thieves,* starring Rex Harrison and Rita Hayworth. The novel was a success, but the film was a failure, whereas the second, **The Manchurian Candidate,** was popular in both forms. Eventually he wrote 26 novels and two works of nonfiction, **And Then We Moved to Rossenarra,** a memoir of the years he lived in Ireland, and **The Mexican Stove,** a cook book he wrote with his daughter Wendy Jackson.

When asked how he knew so much about crime families he said he first learned about the subject as a boy on the streets of Washington Heights. He was born in Manhattan and graduated from De Witt Clinton High School. Because his grades were so poor, he never went to college. He worked as an elevator operator, a hotel clerk and a waiter, then sold an article to *Esquire* magazine. While working as a copywriter for an advertising agency, he met a model named Evelyn Hunt, whom he married in 1938. Copywriting led him into movie publicity, with his first stop the Disney organization.

For 22 years, he was a movie publicist, working for almost every major Hollywood studio. With characteristic panache, he later described himself as "a drummer boy for the gnomes and elves of the silver screen." During this period, he saturated himself with movies, watching eight a week. They were, he said, mostly bad films, but they taught him the art of storytelling and the need for the novelist to be entertaining.

In the late 1950's, he left Hollywood and returned to New York to become a novelist. The idea for **The Oldest Confession** came while he was on location with *The Pride and the Passion* at El Escorial, outside Madrid. Fascinated by Old Master paintings, he wrote his book about art thievery. The consecutive success of **The Oldest Confession** and **The Manchurian Candidate** enabled him to devote himself to fiction.

In 1959, he began a series of migrations, first to Mexico, then to Switzerland, finally to Ireland. His travels added to his backlog of knowledge, but he continued to set most of his novels in the United States. Through the 1960's and into the 70's, his books received mixed reviews, with some of the more admiring notices going to **An Infinity of Mirrors** in 1964. **Winter Kills,** in 1974, drew favorable attention, with Christopher Lehmann-Haupt saying in his review in *The Times* that it was "a grand entertainment" and "the best book Mr. Condon has written since **The Manchurian Candidate.**"

After writing a series of novels in Ireland, Mr. Condon moved back to the United States, settling in Dallas in 1980. In Texas, he had his next comeback, with **Prizzi's Honor,** about the Prizzi family of mobsters in Brooklyn. John Huston turned the novel into a hit film, starring Jack Nicholson, Kathleen Turner and Anjelica Huston. The screenplay, by Mr. Condon and Janet Roach, was nominated for an Academy Award. Several years later, Mr. Condon completed the fictional cycle with **Prizzi's Family, Prizzi's Glory** and **Prizzi's Money,** published in 1994.

Among his other novels are **Some Angry Angel, A Talent for Loving, Arigato** and **Emperor of America.**

Throughout his life, Mr. Condon displayed a wry, even diabolical streak. He often named his characters after real people. For example, the characters in Raymond Shaw's infantry squad in **The Manchurian Candidate** were named for people associated with the Phil Silvers television show, *You'll Never Get Rich.* His longest-running character, Dr. Weller, was named after A. H. Weller, a former film critic for *The Times.* In various Condon novels, Dr. Weller turns up as

an obstetrician, a cardiologist, a psychiatrist and the royal physician.

Charles McCarry (obituary date 10 April 1996)

SOURCE: "Storyteller for a World Gone Mad," in *Washington Post,* April 10, 1996, p. C1.

[*Below, McCarry reminisces about Condon's most significant novels and his contribution to the genre.*]

Richard Condon, who died yesterday in Dallas, the city of cities in the world atlas of conspiracies, was to paranoia what Tennyson was to melancholy, a writer of powerful and utterly unique imaginative gifts who transmuted a form of madness into the intellectual coinage of his time and place.

In his second novel, **The Manchurian Candidate,** arguably the best thriller ever written, Condon turned the certainties of Eisenhower-era America upside down with a tale of a made-in-China political assassin with an Electra complex. Like insanity itself, the story was deeply terrifying but also wildly funny.

What had seemed merely a good, amusing read when the book was published in 1959 became all too plausible with the violent, incomprehensible death of President Kennedy only four years later—a kind of death that only Condon had been able to imagine and, more than that, had been able to explain in terms of an airtight scenario in which certain powerful people profited from the murder of the living symbol of the nation.

America never quite regained its psychic feet after Dallas, which meant, in a sense, that it increasingly began living with Condon's reality. This reality, fictional to be sure though not for long, was based on the idea that there was a second America hidden inside the visible America, and that the hidden one was the real one. This dark inner country, in Condon's many subsequent books, was run by characters who enjoyed the purified serenity of the truly insane, men and women who pursued monstrous ends by rational means, people who were first, last and always motivated by one thing: money.

Money bought power, money bought fame, money bought love, money bought happiness. Money, in Condon's brilliantly realized world, bought everything except the totally irrelevant thing that no one in his right mind was interested in—sanity.

Wonderfully dotty characters, instantly recognizable to any '90s reader as the folks we elect and appoint and televise to the highest offices in the land, fall out of Condon's books like figures from a storybook in the titles of a Disney film.

The original, the ur-nut, is the mother of Raymond Shaw, the tortured, brainwashed assassin of *The Manchurian Candidate.* This is how Condon introduces her, at a White House ceremony at which Raymond is about to be awarded the Medal of Honor for heroism in Korea: "Raymond's mother was across the {Rose} Garden . . . hand[ing] out cigars to press people whether the press people wanted them or not. Raymond's mother was dressed up in about eight hundred dollars of the best taste on the market. . . . She would have given the press people money, Raymond knew, but she had sensed somehow that it would be misunderstood."

Immediately the reader knows how Raymond feels. And he recognizes that something funny, something awful, something beyond the usual excesses of motherhood is going on here. It is a Freudian rule of thumb that you can't trust your own mother. Soon the reader will find out that Raymond, winner of the nation's highest award for valor, is an assassin. But wait—Raymond does not know that he is an assassin, and he does not know who controls him. When Raymond realizes the whole appalling truth, 250 scintillating pages later, the reader will understand for the first time how little Freud really knew.

Apart from his spellbinding gift as a storyteller and his infallible instinct for character—he never met a maniac he could not in his own heart love and render lovable—what the writer admires in Condon is his mastery of the English sentence. No one since Gertrude Stein has done it better, and Condon has the edge on Stein in that his sentences hang together to form paragraphs, pages, chapters and whole novels in which there is rarely a cuttable word or punctuation mark.

Every Condon sentence in every one of his books is a quintessential Condon sentence. No one else could possibly have written this one, from his last novel, *Prizzi's Money,* which I am opening at random. "Nuela had a long farewell dinner with Lieutenant Zendt, her longtime companion from NYPD Homicide, who armed her with a note to a Superintendent of Police at Scotland Yard because he knew all the good restaurants."

Thirty-six words, two commas, one period . . . and a color snapshot of a character's whole world.

Condon, who was 81, will be remembered in his obituaries for *The Manchurian Candidate* and *Prizzi's Honor,* partly because both were made into memorable movies and mostly because they were such good books.

My own favorites among his more than two dozen novels are two that stand somewhat apart from the main body of his work. First, *Some Angry Angel,* in which a heartless gossip columnist is redeemed by the love of the wife to whom he

has just been reconciled, only to lose her to blind fate in one of the most wrenching scenes every written.

Most of all, *An Infinity of Mirrors,* a story about a French girl, a Jew, and a German officer who fall in love in Paris in the days just before the outbreak of World War II. Here is a passage:

> How could there be time for him to find the truth that she represented, or her magic, which glimmered and then concealed itself? How could she find him? How could he show himself? How could he know what his life meant until he had lived it and then could say, I am a particle of the love that I felt for you.' He felt that he and Paule were figures facing and reflecting each other endlessly in an infinity of mirrors, which were the past and the future.

Condon wrote just like that in the dozens of letters he and I exchanged over half a lifetime. Particle of genius that he was, standing between past and future, understanding monstrosity, understanding love, understanding the partnership between the two.

He just couldn't help it.

Myrna Oliver (obituary date 10 April 1996)

SOURCE: "Richard Condon; Best-Selling Novelist," in *Los Angeles Times,* April 10, 1996, p. A12.

[*In the obituary below, Oliver presents a summary of Condon's life and career.*]

Richard Condon, best-selling author of about two dozen novels—including *The Manchurian Candidate* and *Prizzi's Honor,* which were made into popular films—died Tuesday in a Dallas hospital. He was 81.

Condon, who spent 27 years in Mexico and Europe, had lived in Dallas for the past 16 years to be near his family. He had suffered from heart and kidney problems.

His 1959 novel *The Manchurian Candidate* featured an American prisoner of war in Korea who is brainwashed by communists to kill a powerful Joseph McCarthyesque presidential candidate in the United States. The film, starring Laurence Harvey as the prisoner and Frank Sinatra as a fellow soldier who tries to stop him, was seen as a liberal sendup of political paranoia when it was released in 1962.

But it was still playing when President John F. Kennedy was assassinated in Dallas in November 1963, and its similarities to real life prompted its quick withdrawal from circulation. Some people suggested that the slaying was inspired by the film—an astounding idea to Condon.

Originally, the acclaimed motion picture did not fare well at the box office, especially outside urban areas. It had greater success when it was re-released by Sinatra and its co-owners 25 years later.

"The audience did not know if it was coming from the left or the right," Condon said in 1988 of the original release. "In the first week, it was picketed by communists in Paris and the American Legion in Orange County."

Condon also wrote a series of novels about the Prizzi organized crime family, but only the first, *Prizzi's Honor,* was filmed. Condon, with Janet Roach, adapted his 1982 novel into the screenplay for the 1985 film starring Jack Nicholson and Anjelica Huston. Their script was nominated for an Academy Award, and Huston won the Oscar for best supporting actress. The screenplay also won awards from the Writers Guild of America and the British Motion Picture Academy.

Former *Times* entertainment editor Charles Champlin wrote in praise of the novel: "Richard Condon stands among the American popular novelists of his generation like a borzoi among retrievers. He may not (but may) be better or more efficient at what he does, but he is indubitably and refreshingly different."

The novelist's sense of humor, Champlin said, included "an eccentric vision of the real world as requiring only the slightest push to expose all that is preposterous and bizarre in it."

"He begins with observable reality—brainwashing, an Asian war, geopolitics, the Kennedy family, the Mafia—moves up one floor and starts imagining."

Condon's first novel, *The Oldest Confession* in 1958, was about bullfighting and thievery in Spain. It was made into the 1962 film *The Happy Thieves* starring Rex Harrison and Rita Hayworth.

Another novel, *Winter Kills,* was made into a film in 1979 starring Jeff Bridges as the younger brother of an assassinated president investigating the murder.

Condon said that all his books, usually seen as black comedies, focused on the abuse of power.

Other novels included *A Talent for Loving, Any God Will Do, Money Is Love, Death of a Politician, Prizzi's Family, Prizzi's Glory* and *Prizzi's Money.*

Condon began writing novels when he was in his 40s. A na-

tive New Yorker, he spent 22 years as a New York-based film publicist for Walt Disney Productions and other major studios.

He joked that he became a novelist after the motion picture business gave him an ulcer and he realized that "all I could do was spell."

Hollywood moguls were surprised when the publicist began publishing successful novels. "You mean," exclaimed one producer, "this is that fat guy who used to meet our plane in Paris?"

FURTHER READING

Criticism

Bandler, Michael J. "The Laundering of the Prizzi Family." *Chicago Tribune* (24 October 1988): sec. 5, p. 3.
    Favorable review of *Prizzi's Glory.*

Breslin, Jimmy. "Charley and Maerose: The Early Years." *The New York Times Book Review* (28 September 1986): 13.
    Favorable appraisal of *Prizzi's Family.*

Champlin, Charles. "Criminal Pursuits." *Los Angeles Times Book Review* (17 January 1993): 10.
    Reviews *The Venerable Bead,* noting Condon's fetish for weird names and precise numbers.

Coates, Joseph. "Nicaraguans Out 'to Take Europe'?" *Chicago Tribune* (22 February 1990): sec. 5, p. 3.
    Praises the action and language in *Emperor of America.*

Coates, Joseph. "Reality Set to Satirical Music." *Chicago Tribune* (26 September 1991): sec. 5, p. 3.
    Favorable review of *The Final Addiction,* suggesting that Condon is "right on target when he identifies America's fatal addiction as the image."

Dooley, Susan. "Fiction." *The Washington Post—Book World* (23 January 1994): X6.
    Summarizes the plot of *Prizzi's Money.*

Epps, Garrett. "The Life and Loves of a Hit Man." *Book World—The Washington Post* (24 August 1986): 1-2.
    Compliments Condon's sense of humor and irony in *Prizzi's Family.*

Firth, Brian. A review of *Emperor of America,* by Richard Condon. *West Coast Review of Books* 15, No. 3 (1990): 26.
    Asks if "we today are repeating the mistake made by the

critics of [Jonathan] Swift, and taking masterly satire for mere entertainment?"

Greenwell, Bill. "Sledgehammers." *New Statesman and Society* 3, No. 96 (13 April 1990): 40.
> Calls *Emperor of America* "a wicked little spoof that should have been wrapped up in a shorter story."

Jeffery, Keith. "Moving among Powerful People." *The Times Literary Supplement,* No. 4607 (19 July 1991): 21.
> Describes *The Final Addition* as "many things," including a satire, a parable, and a feminist tract.

Kent, Bill. A review of *The Final Addiction,* by Richard Condon. *The New York Times Book Review* (17 November 1991): 20.
> Claims the novel "churns up absurdities into a fizzy froth of political satire, melodrama, and gratuitous silliness."

A review of *Prizzi's Family,* by Richard Condon. *Kirkus Reviews* LIV, No. 14 (15 July 1986): 1040.
> Mixed assessment, faulting Condon's "gross rather than pointed satire."

A review of *Prizzi's Glory,* by Richard Condon. *Kirkus Reviews* LVI, No. 14 (15 July 1988): 991-92.
> Notes the "vitriolic swipes at US politics" and "Condon's inventive and literally tasty prose."

A review of *Emperor of America,* by Richard Condon. *Kirkus Reviews* LVII, No. 23 (1 December 1989): 1693-694.
> Finds the novel "both heavy and tedious."

A review of *The Final Addiction,* by Richard Condon. *Kirkus Reviews* LIX, No. 13 (1 July 1991): 805-06.
> Highly favorable review, observing that "the 'final addiction' is to the public's stupidity."

A review of *Prizzi's Money,* by Richard Condon. *Kirkus Reviews* LXI, No. 22 (15 November 1993): 1407.
> Claims that Condon is "in top form" with this novel, calling it "a tangled web!"

A review of *Prizzi's Glory,* by Richard Condon. *The New Yorker* LXVI, No. 45 (26 December 1988): 96-7.
> Praises Condon's satirical skill, comparing the novel to a "feast of cheerful mordancy."

Lyons, Gene. "Married to the Mob." *Entertainment Weekly,* No. 208 (4 February 1994): 48-9.
> Summarizes the plot of *Prizzi's Money.*

A review of *The Final Addiction,* by Richard Condon. *The New Yorker* LXVII, No. 36 (28 October 1991): 119.
> Comments on "the deadpan precision with which the author marries completely outlandish and surreal plot developments of accurate but equally surreal descriptions of public service."

Petrakos, Chris. "Richard Condon Takes on the CIA, the NRA and Madonna." *Chicago Tribune* (8 November 1992): 8.
> Detects "a genuine sense of indignation and anger" behind Condon's satire in *The Venerable Bead.*

Pinsky, Mark I. A review of *Prizzi's Family,* by Richard Condon. *Los Angeles Times Book Review* (16 November 1986): 4.
> Brief favorable assessment, calling the novel "a tasty morsel."

A review of *The Final Addiction,* by Richard Condon. *Publishers Weekly* 238, No. 31 (19 July 1991): 45.
> Finds "Condon's satirical eye is as wickedly sharp as ever."

A review of *The Venerable Bead,* by Richard Condon. *Publishers Weekly* 239, No. 40 (7 September 1992): 76.
> Notes that "Condon here afflicts the comfortable to hilarious effect."

A review of *Prizzi's Glory,* by Richard Condon. *Time* 132, No. 12 (19 September 1988): 95.
> Negative review, observing that "there is too much stuff and not enough funny."

Sanders, John. "The Fantastic Non-fantastic: Richard Condon's Waking Nightmares." *Extrapolation* 25, No. 2 (Summer 1984): 127-37.
> Examines Condon's spy novels in terms of what the critic calls "'borderline' fantastic literature."]

Wilkinson, Burke. A review of *The Venerable Bead,* by Richard Condon. *The Christian Science Monitor* (7 June 1993): 13.
> Brief positive review.

Additional coverage of Condon's life and career is contained in the following sources published by Gale Research: *Bestsellers,* Vol. 90:3; *Contemporary Authors,* Vols. 1-4R, 151; *Contemporary Authors New Revision Series,* Vols. 2, 23; *Contemporary Authors Autobiography Series,* Vol. 1; *DISCovering Authors Modules: Novelists;* and *Major Twentieth Century Writers.*

Marguerite Duras
1914-1996

(Born Marguerite Donnadieu) French novelist, playwright, scriptwriter, short story writer, and essayist.

The following entry provides an overview of Duras's career. For further information on her life and works, see *CLC,* Volumes 3, 6, 11, 20, 34, 40, and 68.

INTRODUCTION

Hailed as one of France's most original and controversial contemporary writers, Duras utilizes fiction, drama, and film to explore the nature of love and the existential conflicts of the individual. While her early novels were considered realistic and stylistically conventional, Duras's later experiments with form, repetition, allusive dialogue, and fragmentation led many critics to label her as one of the French *nouveaux romanciers,* or New Novelists. Juxtaposing biographical and fictitious elements within shifting time frames and questioning the reliability of memory, Duras challenged the boundaries between fact and fiction. Two of her works of autobiographical fiction, *L'amant* (1984; *The Lover*) and *L'amant de la Chine du Nord* (1991; *The North China Lover*) attracted a large international audience. Duras has also been singled out as one of the best experimental filmmakers of the twentieth century, particularly for her screenplay for the film *Hiroshima, mon amour* (1960).

Biographical Information

Duras was born Marguerite Donnadieu on April 4, 1914, near Saigon, Vietnam, then known as French Indochina. She was one of three children; her father, who died when she was four, was a mathematics professor. Her mother unwittingly bought a worthless piece of farm land which was annually flooded by the Pacific Ocean. Despite the family's poverty Duras was able to study Vietnamese and French in the prestigious Lycee de Saigon. At the age of seventeen Duras left Cambodia for France and eventually earned a *licence* in law and political science at the University of Paris, Sorbonne. She worked as a secretary for the Ministry of Colonial Affairs until 1941 and during World War II served as a member of the Resistance, working with François Mitterrand. In 1946 she divorced her first husband, Robert Antelme, whom she had married in 1939. She later married Dionys Mascolo, with whom she had a son, Jean. She published her first novel, *Les Impudents,* in 1943 and went on to publish more than 70 novels, plays, screenplays, and adaptations in her lifetime. In her later life she lived with a young homosexual writer, Yann Andrea Steiner. In 1984, while recovering from alcoholism in a treatment

center, Duras wrote *The Lover,* for which she won the Prix Goncourt in 1984. In poor health as a result of her life-long problem with alcoholism, she died on March 3, 1996, in Paris.

Major Works

Duras's work has spanned many genres and styles, but it has remained constant in its emotional intensity and its themes of love, solitude, desire, and despair. Commentators on Duras's work often divide her literary career into four periods. The novels from her first period have been described as her most realistic and conventional. Her most significant novel from this period, *Un barrage contre le Pacifique* (1950; *The Sea Wall*), is set in Indochina and reflects both the author's interest in East Asian culture and in issues of social injustice and oppression. Like many of her acclaimed novels, the book is loosely based on an incident which occurred in Duras's childhood. The works from Duras's second period are marked by a shift from linear plots and abrupt, obscure dialogue to a more personal and ironic idiom. The primary works from this period—*Le marin de Gibraltar* (1952; *The Sailor from*

Gibraltar) and *Les petits chevaux de Tarquinia* (1953; *The Little Horses of Tarquinia*)—are considered more concentrated than Duras's previous novels because they focus on fewer characters, events, and relationships. *The Sailor from Gibraltar* concerns a woman who travels on her yacht throughout the Mediterranean in search of her former lover. Duras suggests that the protagonist's persistence gives meaning to her otherwise empty life. *The Little Horses of Tarquinia* similarly reflects Duras's increasing interest in individual characters and their varying moods and emotions. Duras's next literary cycle includes works often described as antinovels, in which she employs minimalist techniques to accent particular experiences or emotions. *Le ravissement de Lol V. Stein* (1964; *The Ravishing of Lol Stein*), for instance, describes a woman's descent into madness after being rejected by her fiance. Considered an antinovel because of its stark narrative, unreliable narrator, and fragmentary contrast and insights, *The Ravishing of Lol Stein* has also been described as an investigation into human consciousness. *The Vice-Consul*, considered the last of Duras's antinovels, simultaneously focuses on a young Oriental girl who is abandoned by her mother after becoming pregnant and a government official who becomes involved in the glamorous diplomatic life of Calcutta, India. Her fourth and most eclectic literary period is evidenced in such novels as *La maladie de la mort* (1982; *The Malady of Death*), *The Lover,* and *The North China Lover. The Malady of Death* is a minimalist account of an asexual man who pays a prostitute to live with him for a week and addresses his overwhelming sense of isolation and inability to love. *Emily L.* (1987), another novel from this period, also addresses how one's inability to love can lead to self-destruction. Often considered a revised version of *The Sea Wall, The Lover* explores more completely Duras's childhood experiences in French Indochina and her debilitating relationships with her overbearing mother and indolent brothers. While *The Lover* is recognizably autobiographical, Duras focuses on the recollection of events and their emotional significance rather than on the events themselves, thus creating a complex structure that conveys the illusions of simplicity. In 1985, Duras published *La douleur* (1985; *The War: A Memoir*), a collection of six narratives believed to have been written during World War II and forgotten for forty years. In the title story, Duras recounts her experiences with the French Liberation Movement during the war. She also describes the mental agony she endured while waiting for her husband, Robert Antelme, to return from a German concentration camp. *The North China Lover,* which began as a screenplay for Jean-Jacques Annaud's adaptation of her novel *The Lover,* tells the same story as the novel but in a very different style and tone. In addition, Duras provides cinematic directions—how a scene could be shot, what kind of actress should play a role—creating a work that is part novel, part screenplay. The publication of *The North China Lover* is in large part due to the disagreements between Duras and Annaud over the script for *The Lover.*

Critical Reception

Critical commentary on Duras's work has focused on several major themes. These include the relationship between love and self-destruction, the metaphysics of boredom and inactivity, and the pain of solitude and despair. As Germaine Brée has observed: "The very title of [*The Sea Wall*] suggests a dogged, unequal battle against a superhuman force. This was to remain one of Duras's basic themes: barrage against the immense solitude of human beings, barrage against the pain of all involvements, barrage against despair." Scholars have also noted Duras's movement away from the realism of her early novels to the minimalist techniques and focus on emotional experience of her later works. Considered one of her most abstract and impressionistic works, *The Vice-Consul,* notes Alfred Cismaru, contains "standard [antinovel] devices: unfinished sentences, subconversations, hidden allusions . . . [and] mysterious and unexplained situations." At the time of its publication, many critics argued that *The Lover* was Duras's most effective synthesis of her themes and minimalist style. With the publication of *The North China Lover,* however, many critics argued that the latter was the better of the two closely related novels. In *The North China Lover,* Duras writes in the third person, a technique which she uses to distance her characters from the reader, instead of switching between first and third person as she did in *The Lover.* While the second novel is more explicit and shocking, critics believe it is more humane, lyrical, and compelling.

PRINCIPAL WORKS

Les impudents (novel) 1943

La Vie tranquille (novel) 1944

Un barrage contre le Pacifique [*The Sea Wall*] (novel) 1950

Le Marin de Gibraltar [*The Sailor from Gibraltar*] (novel) 1952

Les petits chevaux de Tarquinia [*The Little Horses of Tarquinia*] (novel) 1953

Des journees entieres dans les arbres [*Whole Days in the Trees and Other Stories*] (short stories) 1954

Le square [*The Square*] (novel) 1955

Moderato cantabile [*Moderato canatabile*] (novel) 1958

Les viaducs de la Seine-et-Oise [*The Viaducts of Seine and Oise*] (play) 1959

Dix heures et demie du soir en ete [*Ten-Thirty on a Summer Night*] (novel) 1960

Hiroshima, mon amour [*Hiroshima, mon amour*] (screenplay) 1960

Une aussi longue absence [with Gerard Jarlot] (screenplay) 1961

L'apres-midi de Monsieur Andesmas [*The Afternoon of Monsieur Andesmas*] (novel) 1962

La ravissement de Lol V. Stein [The Ravishing of Lol V. Stein] (novel) 1964

Theatre I: Les eaux et forets; Le square; La musica [The Rivers in the Forests; The Square] (plays) 1965

Le vice-consul [The Vice-Consul] (novel) 1966

*La musica (screenplay) 1966

L'amante anglaise [L'amante anglaise] (novel) 1967

L'amante anglaise (play) 1968

Theatre II: Suzanna Andler; Des journees entieres dans les arbres; "Yes," peut-etre; Le shaga; Un homme est venu me voir [Suzana Andler; Days in the Trees] (plays) 1968

Detruire, dit-elle [Destroy, She Said] (novel) 1969

Abahn Sabana David (novel) 1970

L'amour (novel) 1971

*Jaune le soleil (screenplay) 1971

*Nathalie Granger (screenplay) 1972

*La femme du George (screenplay) 1973

*India Song (screenplay) 1974

Les parleuses [Woman to Woman] (interviews) 1974

*Baxter, Vera Baxter (screenplay) 1976

*Son nom de Venise dans Calcutta desert (screenplay) 1976

*Des journees entieres dans les arbres (screenplay) 1976

*Le camion (screenplay) 1977

L'eden cinema (play) 1977

*La navire night (screenplay) 1978

*Aurelia Steiner, dite Aurelia Melbourne (screenplay) 1979

*Aurelia Steiner, dite Aurelia Vancouver (screenplay) 1979

*Cesaree (screenplay) 1979

*Les mains negatives (screenplay) 1979

L'homme assis dans le couloir [The Seated Man in the Passage] (novel) 1980

Agatha (novel) 1981

*Agatha ou les lectures illimitees (screenplay) 1981

*L'homme Atlantique (screenplay) 1981

Outside (essays) 1981

*Dialogue de Rome (screenplay) 1982

L'homme Atlantique (novel) 1982

La maladie de la mort [The Malady of Death] (novel) 1982

L'amant [The Lover] (novel) 1984

*Les enfants (screenplay) 1984

La douleur [The War: A Memoir] (novel) 1985

Le vie materielle [Practicalities: Marguerite Duras Speaks to Jerome Beaujour] (recorded conversations) 1986

Les yeux bleus, cheveux noirs [Blue Eyes, Black Hair] (novel) 1986

Emily L. [Emily L.] (novel) 1987

La Pluie D'Ete [Summer Rain] (novel) 1990

L'Amant de la Chine du Nord [The North China Lover] (novel) 1991

Le Monde Exterieur (essays) 1994

That's All (essays) 1996

*Duras also directed these films.

CRITICISM

Gabriel Josipovici (review date 9 March 1990)

SOURCE: "Risking an Opinion," in The Times Literary Supplement, No. 4536, March 9 & 15, 1990, p. 248.

[In the following review, Josipovici claims that Practicalities is surprisingly boring and uninformative given the high quality of Duras' fiction.]

Throughout the autumn and winter of 1986 Marguerite Duras talked to Jérôme Beaujour about anything that took her fancy. The conversations were transcribed, then edited by Duras into a series of distinct pieces ranging from one to ten pages. Beaujour is a mere ghostly presence, someone who is being talked at rather than an active questioner. "At most the book represents what I think sometimes, some days, about some things", Duras writes. In French the book was called La Vie materielle, but for some reason Barbara Bray has removed the Marxist echo and given English readers the meaningless title, Practicalities.

This is particularly unfortunate because the personality and life that come through are the antithesis of practical. We learn here about Duras's recurrent alcoholism; about the horrors of her periodic efforts at drying out; about her improbable love affair at sixty with an unstable young homosexual (which has been examined from his point of view in Yann Andrea's M.D.); about her house in the country and her flat at the seaside; about her past, her views on men, women, life, love and writing. It does not add up to much, and the personality that comes through is neither interesting nor appealing.

Duras's recent burst of memoir-writing and autobiographical fiction has raised once again the question of the relation of a writer's life to her work. In this case we have the curious phenomenon of someone who cannot write a dull sentence and yet whose comments outside fiction range from the embarrassing to the banal. The puzzle is compounded by the fact that so much of her fiction, it turns out, is autobiographical in inspiration, from her early novel about her mother, Barrage contre le Pacifique, to her recent novel about her infatuation with Yann, Yeux bleux, cheveux noirs. Yet the point here is that for the reader it could not matter less whether these were "true" or "invented". Duras's novels create their own mood and space from the first sentence. No one else writes in the least like her; she fits into no category or school. The only thing to be said about her work is that it has the stamp of complete authenticity when it comes off, and can be excruciatingly mannered when it does not. This is because she is always prepared to take risks. And because, despite the vagaries of her private life, she continues to produce novels (and films) at an amazing rate.

Practicalities does not reveal where her best works get their power from, nor why her recent work has been so uneven. Instead it reveals a rather pathetic yet also rather smug and opinionated woman. Too much of it consists of sentences like: "I've noticed that writers who are superb at making love are much more rarely great writers than those who are scared and not so good at it." And: "There's one thing I'm good at, and that's looking at the sea." Our culture is hungry for personalities and opinions. It usually gets what it deserves.

Alan Riding (essay date 26 March 1990)

SOURCE: "Duras and Her Thoughts of Love," in *The New York Times,* March 26, 1990, pp. C11, C16.

[*In the essay below, which is based on an interview with Duras, Riding discusses the autobiographical nature of her writing.*]

To describe Marguerite Duras as a little old lady, even though she is all three things today, is to ignore the flirtatious twinkle in her eye that perhaps helps explain why, at the age of 75, she keeps on writing and thinking about sex and love.

She reveals herself only slowly, though. Photographs make her seem severe, even intimidating, while in person her small body, ravaged by alcohol, cigarettes and a few natural illnesses, looks as crumpled and shapeless as a mistreated doll.

Yet, as one sits close enough to hear her thin voice and its accompanying silences, her eyes can be seen sparkling with mischief as she throws out words and phrases, like lassos to tease and then capture her listener.

"I write about love, yes, but not about tenderness," she said, as if to do so were a literary sin as unpardonable as sentimentality. "I don't like tender people. I myself am very harsh. When I love someone, I desire them. But tenderness supposes the exclusion of desire."

So sexual love it is in her books, usually young love, love plucked from her past or her imagination, love that may or may not be consummated, love wrapped in her own memories of war, of death, of poverty, even of happiness, love that must be besieged by desire to be real.

Her main raw material is of course herself, an extraordinary life cut like cord into sections and variously displayed in her books as elegant bows or tight knots. "Even when my books

are completely invented, even when I think they have come from elsewhere," she explained, "they are always personal."

Ranging from her childhood of hardship in Indochina and her war years in Paris to her fight against alcoholism and her autumnal love for her young homosexual companion, her life is therefore an open book, its episodes told and retold, yet transformed each time by language that can be terse or erotic, painful or violent.

To look at her works, be it ***Hiroshima Mon Amour***, her best-known screenplay, or ***The Lover***, her most successful novel, is always to learn more about her, to be drawn—much as cinemagoers might be to famous actors—to see what she has done next. To French readers, the question is simply, do you or do you not like Duras?

Few of her several dozen books, plays or screenplays could be considered more personal than ***Practicalities***, to be published this month in English by Grove Weidenfeld. In this case it is not even a novel, but a collection of opinions and reflections, a sort of interview in which questions are omitted and answers are edited.

First published in France in 1987 as ***La Vie Matérielle***, the 143-page book is described as "Marguerite Duras speaks to Jérome Beaujour," a friend of her son who is "like another son to me." But, with no sign of Mr. Beaujour in its pages, ***Practicalities*** is simply Duras the author talking about Duras the life.

Some themes are familiar, like her belief that in cinema and theater, art forms in which she has had notable success, the word is supreme. "Acting doesn't bring anything to a text," she writes. "On the contrary, it detracts from it—lessens its immediacy and depth, weakens its muscles and dilutes its blood."

She writes about writing as "a matter of deciphering something already there, something you've already done in the sleep of your life, in its organic rumination, unbeknown to you." And she plays games: "Writing isn't just telling stories. . . . It's the telling of a story, and the absence of the story. It's telling a story through its absence."

She talks about writing in much the same way. "I don't know where I'm going when I start to write," she said in a recent interview. "You shouldn't have a subject. You have to go into the forest; you shouldn't be afraid, and it comes, all alone; stories of love, of foolishness, they come on their own, as if you were walking like a blind man before they arrived."

When she writes about the women in her novels, she seems to be describing herself. "They all see quite clearly and lucidly," she said. "But they're imprudent, improvident. They all ruin their own lives. They're very timid; they're afraid of streets and public places; they don't expect to be happy."

Miss Duras admitted she, too, was now afraid of going out. She owns a country house and a place by the sea, but when she is in Paris she rarely leaves her apartment in St.-Germaindes-Prés. "Until *The Lover*, I was never on television, but afterward everyone recognized me," she recalled. "'That's her from the TV.' they'd say, and it was hell. I was scared, physically scared."

A former member of the French Communist Party who still describes herself as a Marxist, Miss Duras said she had other reasons for fear. "All this talk of German reunification worries me," she said. "It worries everyone who lived through the last war. I'm afraid that German youth has not been taught the truth about their own country."

Her memories of the war remain strong, both her years in a Resistance group headed by Francois Mitterrand, now France's President, and her weeks waiting for her husband to return from Dachau concentration camp, described so movingly in her book *The War*, Her dislike for Gen. Charles de Gaulle dates from that time. "He never pronounced the word 'Jew' after the war," she said, "Many people think I am Jewish and that always pleases me."

Sex, too, is naturally present in her new book, not least in a chapter called **"The Train From Bordeaux,"** when she remembers an erotic encounter during an overnight train ride to Paris when she was 16 years old. "The man and I were the only two still awake," she recalled or imagined. "And that was how it started, suddenly, at exactly the same moment, and with a single look."

A conversation with Miss Duras in fact in many ways resembles *Practicalities.* In her book she returns time and again to her fight against alcoholism. almost obsessively trying to fathom her own addiction. "Alcohol is a substitute for pleasure though it doesn't replace it," she writes, "Alcohol doesn't console, it doesn't fill up anyone's psychological gaps, all it replaces is the lack of God."

In a final chapter called **"The People of the Night,"** she describes the deliriums that accompanied her last, alcoholic crisis and the loving way her companion, Yann Andrea, helped her through it. And as he brought her a glass of pomegranate juice one recent afternoon, the conversation also turned naturally to alcoholism.

"Three times I have stopped and three times I have started again," Miss Duras said. "You know, a few days ago I was given a prize at the Austrian Embassy and when I arrived, the first thing I saw was the Champagne. Yann immediately

looked at me sternly and I didn't have any, but I'm still an alcoholic."

"Do you drink?" she asked, as if looking for understanding. "When you drink, you can do without everyone. It's horrible. Out of love for me, Yann also began to drink. What are your weaknesses? Do you take drugs?"

Her questions serve as her lassos, reaching out to her interviewer—Where were you born? Where have you lived? Have you read Marx?—in order to pull him toward her, to disarm him perhaps, certainly to disrupt the relationship between interrogator and interrogated. Satisfied, she then awaits the next question.

At the moment she is not writing, she said. She finished her most recent book, *La Pluie d'Eté*, last November and it was published in French last month. Before that, she completed the screenplay for *The Lover* and, to be directed by Jean-Jacques Annaud, whose films include "The Name of the Rose" and "The Bear," shooting will begin here this summer.

"I must go back to my books," she said, nodding toward her study where for decades she has written her novels, plays and screenplays in long-hand. "But at the moment I'm buried in taxes, bills, contracts, requests and letters. Still, at least I've started to read newspapers again."

Asked if she read other authors, she pulled a face of embarrassment. "I've read things, classics and so on," she said, "But we didn't have books when I was young. My inspiration has been what I've lived, the terrible misery my mother knew, the rice plantations in Indochina. But yes, I've done my homework."

The subject of her health, though, seems more relevant today, since she emerged only last June from nine months in the hospital. "The first time, 20 years ago, it was for cirrhosis of the liver; nine years ago it was for alcoholism; this time it was for cigarettes," she said, "but happily it wasn't cancer."

And her health now?

"It's O.K.," she said with a smile. "I've got a good head."

Leslie Garis (essay date 20 October 1991)

SOURCE: "The Life of Marguerite Duras," in *The New York Times Magazine,* October 20, 1991, pp. 44-6, 52-3, 60-1.

[In the following essay, which is based on an interview with

Duras, Garis discusses how the author's views and life experiences have impacted her writing.]

Novelist, playwright, film maker, Communist, outrageous social commentator, Marguerite Duras has awed and maddened the French public for more than 40 years. Considering her impoverished childhood in Vietnam, her participation in the French Resistance, her Communism and ultimate disaffection with the Party, her two marriages and many liaisons, the near-fatal cure she underwent for alcoholism in 1982, and, especially, her miraculous recovery from a five-month coma induced by complications from emphysema in 1988, it is reasonable to suggest that Marguerite Duras is a force of nature.

Her 48th work, *The Lover*, published in 1984 when she was 70, was a best seller not only in France and throughout Europe, but in the United States as well. According to the French publisher Jerome Lindon, whose Les Editions de Minuit brought out *The Lover*, it is one of the few contemporary French books to have an international impact. He knows of at least 29 foreign editions, including 3 in separate Chinese dialects. It won France's most prestigious literary award, the Prix Goncourt.

Set in prewar Indochina, where Duras spent her childhood, *The Lover* is a despairing, sensuous novel about an affair between a 15-year-old French girl and a 27-year-old Chinese man. The consuming infatuation and brutal shifts of power between the lovers echo many issues of modern colonialism. Although Duras's work is avidly followed by a coterie of intellectuals, and her 1960 film script of Alain Resnais's *Hiroshima Mon Amour* has become a cult classic, it wasn't until *The Lover* that she reached a mass audience. Duras stated publicly that it was completely autobiographical—an assertion that made her a media star.

Now, at 77, she has again captured center stage by publishing *L'Amant de la Chine du Nord* (*The North Chinese Lover*), a book the newspaper Le Point calls "stunning and diabolical." With the audacity for which she is famous, this book is an end run around the film director Jean-Jacques Annaud, who has shot his version of *The Lover*, scheduled for European release in January. Until she and Annaud argued, Duras was the screenwriter, eventually Gérard Brach, whose credits include the screenplays for "The Name of the Rose" and "The Bear," adapted the novel with Annaud. (Annaud will not speak to the press about the film.) Meanwhile, Duras recast her best seller into a new version, which is a fuller telling of the original, including many new shocking details, and—always mischievous—camera angles and directions for the soundtrack. Duras says her new book is *more* true than *The Lover*.

Truth, in the Durasian universe, is a slippery entity. After *The Lover*, Duras said, in *Le Nouvel Observateur*, that the story of her life did not exist. Only the novel of a life was real, not historical facts. "It's in the imaginative memory of time that it is rendered into life."

Between *The Lover* and *The North Chinese Lover*, Duras has written and directed her 18th film and published a collection of essays, three novels and **"The War,"** a vivid account of waiting for her husband, Robert Antelme, to return from Dachau during the Liberation, then nursing him back to health from near starvation.

Keeping in mind her special relationship to truth, I visited her in her apartment in Paris to talk about her work and her long life. At that time she had almost completed *The North Chinese Lover*. Monique Gonthier, a bilingual French journalist, accompanied me for linguistic emergencies.

In the dark, cramped hallway of their apartment stand a tiny woman bent with age and a handsome, middle-aged man—Marguerite Duras and her companion of 11 years, Yann Andréa. She wears a plaid skirt and green stockings, he wears leather pants and has a mustache; together they evince images of whimsy, intellect and danger.

We walk into a small, dusty room filled with strange objects: a broken candleholder that is a model of the Eiffel Tower, a box of old postcards, little tins of tea next to a piece of curled red ribbon. There are piles and piles of paperback books and a round table in the middle of the room where Duras seats herself in front of some blank pages and three pens.

[In *The Lover*,] the consuming infatuation and brutal shifts of power between the lovers echo many issues of modern colonialism.

—Leslie Garis

Her head is so large that her cheeks spread out toward her narrow shoulders. She must be less than five feet tall. She wears many rings and bracelets.

"Let me tell you something," she says. Her voice is gruff, energetic and frank. "I am finishing a book. I am going to pick up the story of *The Lover* without any literature in it. The fault I have found with *The Lover* was its literariness, which comes very easily to me because it's my style. But you won't understand that."

"Even I am struggling to understand," says Yann, smiling. "Another version of *The Lover* without the style of *The Lover*? It's the same story."

"Not exactly. Another novel. It is between the little girl and the Chinese."

"Why go over the material again?" I ask.

"Because there is a film maker who is one of the greatest in the world, whose name is Jean-Jacques Annaud, who took on *The Lover*. He told a story that I didn't recognize, so I said: 'Now you're going home, it's finished. I don't want to work with you anymore.' I was a little nasty."

The film is being made in English with two unknowns playing the leads: an English girl and a man from Hong Kong. Duras waves her hand in dismissal when I ask her if she will watch the shooting. "It doesn't interest me," she says, But, of course, she has her new book, which more or less throws down the gauntlet to Annaud.

As Yann plays with a piece of ribbon like the one on the table, twisting it through his fingers, she looks at me expectantly, and I begin by asking about early literary influences. She denies having any. "My mother was a farmer," she says bluntly. "She had no idea what literature was all about."

"Did you know you were a writer when you were young?"

"I never doubted. I wrote when I was 10. Very bad poems. Many children start out writing like that, with the most difficult form."

The form of a typical Duras novel is minimal, with no character description, and much dialogue, often unattributed and without quotation marks. The novel is not driven by narrative, but by a detached psychological probing, which, with its complexity and contradictory emotions, has its own urgency.

I ask her why she has said in interviews she feels suffocated by the classical novel, especially Balzac.

Balzac describes everything, everything. It's exhaustive. It's an inventory. His books are indigestible. There's no place for the reader."

Yann says gently: "There is pleasure too, in reading Balzac. You're very reassured."

"If you read it at 14," Duras barks back. "Balzac was my earliest nourishment. But I am a part of my own time, you have to be a part of your own time. One can no longer write as Balzac does. And Balzac could never have written 'Lol Stein.'"

The Ravishing of Lol Stein (1964) is one of Duras's seminal works. Nineteen-year-old Lol Stein is engaged to Michael

Richardson. They go to a ball in S. Tahla, an imagined town on the north French coast, similar to Trouville, where Duras owns a house. Anne-Marie Stretter, a glamorous older woman, arrives and steals away Michael Richardson. Lol Stein goes mad. Ten years later she is back in S. Tahla as a married woman. She walks incessantly, seldom talking. One day she follows a man who has a clandestine meeting with a woman from Lol Stein's youth. Later, the three of them meet socially, and eventually Lol Stein lies in a field outside a hotel in which the man and woman are making love. She occasionally sees her woman friend, naked, cross in front of the window, oblivious of being watched. The man, however, knows, which heightens Lol Stein's pleasure. An odd, obsessive longing she had felt to follow Michael Richardson and Anne-Marie Stretter when they left the dance is now fulfilled by this act of voyeurism.

I ask her what sort of state she was in when she wrote *Lol Stein*, and she tells me a curious story.

"With *Lol Stein*, I screamed. I was by the sea, in a house in Trouville. I was in the living room, and at a little distance was my lover. I heard a cry. I leaped up. I went to see the young man. I said, 'What's the matter?' He said: 'What are you talking about? I'm the one who should ask why you screamed.' I'd cried out, without even . . . it's funny."

"Have you ever known someone like Lol Stein?"

She picks up the papers before her, stands them upright and taps the edges to align them. She is so small that her face disappears behind the pages. I hear a deep sigh.

"One day I took care of a madwoman. I went to a psychiatric hospital and asked for a young woman who had attracted me. She was very beautiful, very elegant. I took her out in the car. She didn't say anything. We simply went to a cafe. She ate and ate and ate—like a clochard, crudely, with her hands. At her core she was very sick. I wanted to see it physically. I saw it in her. The gaze. That's Lol Stein.

"I've been thinking about this character for 10 years. I have an image. Not another book. Maybe a film. She is on the beach at Trouville. She is in a rickshaw. There's no roof, she's exposed. She is very made up, like a whore. She's wearing dirty dresses, and it's as if she grew old in an asylum. And you know where she's going? She's going to the dance."

"Terrific!" says Yann. "You have to do it! Write it!" She turns to him with a distant look in her eyes and a faint smile. Silence prevails.

Marguerite Duras was born in Giadinh, near Saigon, in 1914. Her father, Henri Donnadieu, was a professor of mathematics at a school in what was then French Indochina. He died in

1918, leaving Marguerite, two brothers and her mother practically destitute.

Until she went to the Sorbonne in France in 1932, Duras lived like an Asian child and spoke fluent Vietnamese.

In 1924 her family moved to Sadec, then to Vinhlong, villages on the Mekong River. In Vinhlong a new French governor arrived from Laos with his wife, a pale beauty named Elizabeth Striedter. It was rumored that the wife had a young lover in Laos who killed himself when she went away. The news of this suicide had a searing effect on the imagination of Duras, for whom the woman came to represent a dark, mythic feminine power. She was the model for Anne-Marie Stretter (who reappears in *The North Chinese Lover*). "Many times I have said to myself," Duras told the critic Michelle Porte, "that I am a writer because of her."

There was another event in Vinhlong that changed Duras forever. Her mother, the daughter of poor French farmers, had saved for 20 years to buy arable land in Indochina. At last she purchased a farm from the French colonial government, not realizing that without a bribe she would be cheated. With the help of her children, she built a bungalow and planted rice. But as soon as the rainy season started, the sea rose to the house, flooding the fields, ruining the crops. Every penny of her savings was lost. She fought against the sea for years, building dikes that washed away, until finally her health was broken. Marguerite, herself, at age 12, had an emotional crisis serious enough to be called madness. After that, for the rest of her life, she was preoccupied by insanity and convinced that the world was fundamentally unjust.

Her childhood was also full of a wild freedom. With no supervision she played in the rain forest and hunted for birds and small game that, in her extreme poverty, she brought home to eat.

In a 1974 booklength interview with Xaviere Gauthier, Duras said: "I have a bedazzled memory . . . of the night in the forest when we'd walk barefoot, barefoot while everywhere it was teeming with snakes! . . . I wasn't afraid at 12, and then, as an adult, I've said to myself, 'But how did we get out alive?' We would go to see the monkeys, and there were black panthers too. I saw a black panther fly by a hundred meters away. Nothing in the world is more ferocious than that."

Thinking about that panther, I ask her: "There seems to be a chronic underlying panic in your books. Did that come from your childhood?"

"Who can say? It's true that it exists. Endemic, as they say."

During another long silence I gaze at a strange tableau on a table. A mirror with dried flowers drooping from the top is propped against the wall. In its reflection is a poster of "Destroy She Said," her first independent movie. Leaning against the mirror is another, smaller mirror.

"There was a sexual fear, fear of men, because I didn't have a father. I wasn't raped, but I sensed rape, like all little girls. And then afterwards I had a Chinese lover. That was love."

Yann serves us grenadine. I remember French friends telling me, with eyebrows raised, that between them is *un vrai amour,* even though he is a homosexual.

"Do you think most people live with continual fear?"

"Only the stupid are not afraid."

Fear, despair, alienation are themes that seized her in her childhood; later Duras became fascinated with crimes of passion. In the 1958 novel *Moderato Cantabile*—Duras's first major success—a crime is committed: lying on the woman he has just killed, a man sobs: "Darling, My darling." Two witnesses, a man and a woman, later drink together and reconstruct in repetitious and incantatory dialogue a passion so intense that its climax was murder. This mix of eroticism and death runs through her work like a river that feeds everything it passes. Certainly one of its sources was the French governor's wife, but an even stronger one was a savage conflict within her family circle.

Duras passionately loved Paulo, the younger of her two older brothers (both of whom are now dead). Paulo was slightly retarded and was deathly afraid of Pierre, the older brother, who tormented and physically battered Paulo. One of the most jarring revelations in "The North Chinese Lover" is that Duras had sex with Paulo. In the book he begins to crawl into her bed when they were both very young, precipitating terrifying rages from Pierre. That intimacy eventually leads to consummation, just before the family leaves Vietnam. This new slant on her childhood might explain why she hated Pierre so much that she wanted to kill him.

"I should have," she cries today. "There was only one solution. That was murder. And one didn't adopt that solution. And it went on throughout my whole childhood. Hate grows. It's like a fire that doesn't go out. When he was 17 and I was 13, during a nap one day I got a knife to kill him."

"Why?"

"For everything, for the sake of killing him. So he wouldn't beat the little one anymore. I can't talk about the little one because I'm going to cry."

"Why didn't you kill the older one?"

"He woke up. He laughed." She imitates horrible laughter. It's a bizarre moment. "He got hold of the knife. He flung it away. I picked it up. He called my mother. He told her. They laughed uproariously. And I cried, I cried."

"What did your mother do?"

"She was very hard on me. She didn't love us, the little one and me. I've never seen anything like it in my life, my mother's preference for my older brother. She was proud of me because I did well in school. My little brother wasn't altogether normal, and that's why my older brother persecuted him. And as for me, I was going mad with pain because above all I loved my little brother. I wanted to kill myself when he died."

Self-destruction for love is a particularly Durasian obsession. "You destroy me. You're so good for me," repeats the woman in **"Hiroshima Mon Amour"** to her lover. I ask her today why sex and death are always entwined for her.

"It's difficult to articulate. It's erotic." She takes a deep breath. "I had a lover with whom I drank a lot of alcohol." She pauses, staring straight at me. Her face is expressionless, her dark eyes are absolutely still. "I'm acquainted with it, the desire to be killed. I know it exists."

In *Practicalities*, a 1987 book of essays, Duras writes about a violent affair. "We took a room by the river. We made love again. We couldn't speak to one another any more. We drank. He struck me . . . in cold blood. We couldn't be near one another now without fear and trembling. . . . We were both faced with the same strange desire." It was after that experience that she wrote *Moderato Cantabile*.

Is Duras's attitude toward eroticism an anomaly, or is it particularly French? Jennifer Wicke, an associate professor of comparative literature at New York University, told me that while the English may write about a languid conversation in front of a fire, the French are entirely different.

"Duras's writing is always at an extremity, and that is quite French," she said. "I see her as carrying on the tradition of *l'amour fou,* the crazed love. It's a bleak world view, the opposite of a lyrical text. It proposes a tragic end, because desire can't be sustained. It will either turn into obsession and, thus, ultimately destroy its object, or it will see itself be deflated by the very cruel contingencies of history, or death."

Duras is associated with the Nouveau Roman (literally "new novel"), a movement born in the 50's, whose members include Nathalie Sarraute, Alain Robbe-Grillet, Michel Butor and Claude Simon. The Nouveau Roman rejects the classical novel as an inappropriate medium to express the chaotic, morally ambiguous postwar world. Although Duras shares many of the movement's stylistic hallmarks—the free flow of time and the use of silence—she is the least obsessed with literary principles, and the most inspired by her own inimitable sensibility.

Peter Brooks, the Tripp Professor of Humanities at Yale University, commented to me that the other Nouveau Roman writers got more attention than Duras when the movement began because there was "something more technicolor about their technique. Their theorizing and their break with the traditional novel were overt and total. But Duras is the one from that whole generation who really is going to last."

Duras looks at Yann, and he takes her hand. During our conversation he has been shuffling around, walking in and out of the room, one hand on his hip, flipping his hair back with a toss of his head—a movement that must be, in other circumstances, flirtatious. I ask how they like to spend their time.

"The thing we like most in life is to be in a car together," she says, "to go in bistros, cafes, and make stories from what we see."

"Do you ask a lot of questions?"

"All the time. People talk to us. I go out every day in the car." Then she adds: "I had chronic bronchitis. You can hear my voice very well, even so. I still have vocal cords. I was in a coma for five months."

In October 1988, Duras fell into a coma from which she miraculously awoke intact. She now has a tracheostomy and wears a necklace of wire with a silver button in the middle. At times she adjusts it, which seems to alter the force of her voice.

The most difficult storm Duras weathered was her cure from alcohol in 1982. Yann wrote a harrowing account, which has not yet been translated into English, called simply "M.D." She tells me Yann's book is "magnificent."

"I drank because I was an alcoholic. I was a real one—like a writer. I'm a real writer, I was a real alcoholic. I drank red wine to fall asleep. Afterwards, Cognac in the night. Every hour a glass of wine and in the morning Cognac after coffee, and afterwards I wrote. What is astonishing when I look back is how I managed to write."

Her small, bejeweled hands lie on the table before her, one resting on the blank paper.

The next day we talk about criminals. Duras has never shunned conflict—as a Resistance fighter, as a Communist or as a woman who speaks out in defense of murderers if she imagines the killer is an anti-establishment figure.

"I became great friends with Georges Figon," she tells me. "He had stolen diamonds and he had killed people. And afterwards he had kidnapped people, with ransom. He was a dear friend. I got him a television interview. He was amazingly intelligent. I even went away for the weekend with him."

"A romantic weekend?" Monique immediately asks.

"No. We never slept with each other. Never. And he never tried to sleep with me."

What is the allure of a criminal for her?

"It exerts a fascination for me—all the people who abandon the golden rule of good conduct. Criminals are heroes for me."

In 1985 Duras wrote an article about Christine Villemin, who was accused of murdering her child. Although conceding Villemin's guilt under the law, she justified the murder as a natural result of social injustice. The article caused a furor.

Duras's pronouncements in the press have given her a notorious reputation. In 1988 she was interviewed on television for some four hours. Duras alternately spoke and stared speechlessly into the camera. Very little of it was comprehensible to the general public. It was just before her coma.

During my interview I was disconcerted by her habit of jumping disconnectedly from subject to subject, and it wasn't until I was back in America and spent many weeks studying the transcript of the interview (which Nancy K. Kline, of Barnard College, translated for this article) that I gradually understood the connections she was making. In New York I spoke to Tom Bishop, chairman of the French department at New York University, a Beckett scholar and a friend of Duras's for 25 years. It had occurred to me that she had sustained brain damage in the coma.

> **She used to say that as a film maker she wanted to "murder the writer," and recently she said she wants to "kill the image."**
>
> **—*Leslie Garis***

"She was always like this," he declared. "I don't think she was ever any different. I would doubt that it's the coma." He described the scattershot exchanges of ordinary friendship, which often went something like this:

Bishop: "Let's have lunch."

Duras: "I never have lunch."

Bishop: "O.K."

Long pause.

Duras: "Where would you want to have lunch if we had lunch?"

Bishop: "I was thinking of the Rue de Dragon."

Duras: "Well, O.K., fine, let's do that."

"I think she's a fabulous writer who should just write and not talk about what she's thinking," Bishop said. Like her talk, her work doesn't make "a lot of sense," but it does "something else. It allows me to have an insight into the human psyche that I have found unique. I have learned things about humanity through her that others don't teach me."

A good example of meaning in ambiguity is Duras's work in the cinema, where she is almost as important to 20th-century experimental film as she is to literature. Annette Michelson, a professor of cinema studies at New York University, told me that one of Duras's most important contributions is her realization that "the cinema is made of relations." "And when you change the relations between sound and image," she says, "you have something new."

In ***India Song*** (1975), the actress Delphine Seyrig and various men walk through a room furnished only with a grand piano. They dance, lie down, sleep, weep, while off-screen voices comment on the unbearable heat, a man shrieks and sobs, a woman chants in Cambodian and jazz melodies pulse. Sounds never emanate from the actors. And yet the audience feels despair, longing, sensuality, the presence of death, colonialism, the impossibility of human communication—a welter of specific impulses that elude verbal definition.

Of course, a writer who concerns herself with disjunction and alienation is difficult to pin down in conversation. She used to say that as a film maker she wanted to "murder the writer," and recently she said she wants to "kill the image." I wonder how it is possible to make a film without image.

She answers: "With words. To kill the writer that I was."

All right. Suddenly she picks up the pen that has been in front of her for two days and begins to write on the paper. "I'm thinking of something." She looks up. "Sensitivity depends on intelligence. It's completely connected. There's an innocence also. Luckily." She puts down the pen. I record it as it happened. I do not fully understand.

To ground us a little, I introduce the subject of politics. Her hatred of de Gaulle springs to the surface.

"When de Gaulle arrived in France, I became an anti-Gaullist instantly. I saw through his power game. I saw he was an arriviste, with a special gift for language. And at just that moment they opened the camps, and my husband had been deported. I never got over it, the Jews, Auschwitz. When I die, I'll think about that, and about who's forgotten it."

"De Gaulle never said a word on the Jews and the camps," Yann adds quietly. "If de Gaulle had not been as big as he was," Duras says angrily, "no one would have noticed him. Because he was taller than everyone, he was boss. But why this arrogance? As far as I'm concerned, he's a deserter. He's horrible, horrible."

In *The War*, Duras describes her days in the Resistance, working with François Mitterrand, keeping records of deportees, trying to coax information from Germans stationed in Paris. It was Mitterrand who went to Germany with Dionys Mascolo, the man who would be her second husband and the father of her son, Jean. They rescued Antelme from Dachau in the first days after the German surrender. Antelme, nearly unconscious, was consigned to a quarantine section for hopeless cases. Mitterrand and Mascolo smuggled him out.

"Mitterrand is wonderful. I worked with him in the Resistance. I protected him in the street. We never met in a house or a cafe. We liked each other so much we could certainly have slept with each other, but it was impossible. You can't do that on bicycles!" She laughs.

"Are you still a Communist?"

"I'm a Communist. There's something in me that's incurable."

"But you left the Party."

"The Party is not Communism." Her mouth hardens into a straight line across her wide face.

"Has there been any true Communist government over the years?"

"Not one. There was one Communist year: 1917."

"Do you hope to see that sort of Communism return to the world?"

"I don't know. I don't want to know. I am a Communist within myself. I no longer have hope in the world."

Yann begins to laugh. "And the other?" he asks. "Do you have hope for the next world?"

She is not amused by his question. "Zero. Zero."

Marguerite Duras with Alice A. Jardine (interview date 1991)

SOURCE: An interview with Marguerite Duras, translated by Katherine Ann Jensen, in *Shifting Scenes: Interviews on Women, Writing, and Politics in Post-68 France,* edited by Alice A. Jardine and Anne M. Menke, Columbia University Press, 1991, pp. 71-8.

[*In the following interview, Duras remarks on feminism and how the response to her work has differed in France and the United States.*]

[*Jardine:*] *Question 1: What does it mean to you to write at the end of the twentieth century?*

[Duras:] Writing . . . I've never asked myself to be aware of what time period I was living in. I have asked myself this question in relation to my child and his future activities, or in wondering what would become of the working class—you see, in relation to political considerations or issues. But not as concerns writing. I believe writing is beyond all . . . contingency.

Question 2: Is it valid/of value to write as a woman, and is it part of your writing today?

I have several opinions about that, several things to say. Perhaps I should give a personal example. I don't have any major problems anymore in terms of the reception of my books, but the way men in society respond to me hasn't changed.

That hasn't changed at all?

No, each time I see critics who are . . . Misogyny is still at the forefront.

Only in France or . . .

I haven't read the foreign papers. *The Lover,* you know, has been translated in twenty-nine countries. There have been thousands and millions of copies sold. I don't think that in America there's been as much [misogyny] . . . because a lot of women write articles [on my work]. I don't think there's been any misogyny, strictly speaking, aimed at me in America.

I have the same impression.

No, actually, there is someone at the *New York Times* who doesn't like me at all, because I was once rather nasty to him. It was after a showing of **India Song.** The auditorium was full, I remember that, and at the end the students were really pleased and gave me a big ovation. The audience was asked to speak; I was there to answer. So this guy got up, you know, from the *Times,* very classic, old. He began, "Madame Duras, I really got bored with your . . ."

He said that?! in public?

Yes, it was a public thing. So I said: "Listen, I'm really sorry, but it's hardly my fault. There must be something wrong with you." He just looked at me. (Usually this works well.) "Please excuse me, but I can't do anything for you." It was really terrible. Since then, people tell me, "I can't invite you anymore because he'll never forgive you." It doesn't matter to me. I'm very happy.

I have the impression that misogyny, in the most classic sense of the term, exists in France much more than in the United States. Even if it's on the tip of American men's tongues or the tip of their pens, they stop themselves now because there's been so much . . . They swallow their words because they know what will happen afterward if they don't; whereas here in France, it seems to me that they get away with it. No one says anything. And that's why, for me, to write as a woman in France begins to have a very different meaning. . . .

But I have safety valves. That is, from time to time, I write articles about critical theory, and that scares the critics.

I can imagine.

But . . . it scares women too. It has to do with *écriture féminine.* There are a lot of women who align themselves with men. Recently, a guy did a whole page in a journal about me to say that I don't exist, that I'm . . . I don't remember what. So in that instance, I said that he was the victim of great pain at the thought of my existence. And I can't do anything about that.

It's not worth the energy.

No. It's not a question of energy. It's just that in France, if you don't pay attention, you can get eaten up.

As a woman or as a writer generally?

As a woman writer. There are two potential attacks: those from homosexuals and those from heteros.

And they're different?

At first, no; but in the end they each think that they do such different things, although it's not true at all. They do the same things. It's about jealousy, envy . . . a desire to supplant women. It's a strange phenomenon. I write quite a lot about homosexuality . . . because I live with a man who's homosexual . . . as everyone knows . . . but I write outside all polemic. You see, **Blue Eyes, Black Hair** is outside any polemic. Homosexuals are often not interested in their experiences, they think they've said everything there is to say. That's a limitation. They're not interested in knowing what a woman can get from that experience. What interests them is knowing what people think about homosexuality, whether you're for or against it, that's all.

You have been describing men's reactions to your work as a woman writer. I too have been intrigued by the question of how men respond to woman and women. My latest book, Men in Feminism, *coedited with Paul Smith, is a collection of articles addressing the complicated relationship men have to feminism, and women have to feminist men. My book* Gynesis *intervenes in this debate by examining how the metaphor of woman operates in several key French texts by men from the last twenty-odd years, for example, those by Blanchot, Deleuze, Derrida, and Lacan.*

You know, even before those writers, there was Beauvoir. She didn't change women's way of thinking. Nor did Sartre, for that matter. He didn't change anything at all. Is *Gynesis* coming out in France?

Yes. One of the interesting problems that has come up with my translator is how to find an expression for the term "man writer." In the United States, you see, we're trying to deuniversalize: we say woman writer. We try to give terms genders. But in French, it doesn't work at all. If my translator uses "man writer," everyone will say it's horrible.

It's too late.

Yes, it's too late. But I can't just put the gender of the writer in the footnotes either. When I say "writer," I mean "man writer" because that's how the universal returns.

Because "writer" historically means male, is that it?

Yes, the universal.

But even when they were making distinctions between men and women writers twenty-five years ago, in newspaper headlines, there were no women writers or men writers. There were "novels by women," "novels by men," and books by women or books by men. But that was always a minor distinction, always in a footnote.

It's odd, in French you can get woman out of the universal, but not man (you can say woman writer [femme écrivain] but not man writer [homme écrivain]).

Question 3: Many women writing today find themselves, for the first time in history, at the center of such institutions as the university or psychoanalysis. In your opinion, will this new placement of women help them to enter the twentieth-century canon, and if so will they be at the heart of this corpus or (still) in the footnotes?

I think that the women who can get beyond the feeling of having to correct history will save a lot of time.

Please explain.

I think that the women who are correcting history, who are trying to correct the injustice of which they're victims, of which they always were and still are victims—because nothing's changed, we have to really get that: in men's heads everything's still the same. . . .

You really think so?

I'm sure, yes. The women who are trying to correct man's nature, or what has become his nature—call it whatever you want—they're wasting their time.

What you're saying is really depressing.

I think that if a woman is free, alone, she will go ahead that way, without barriers; that is how I think she'll create fruitful work.

All alone?

Yes. I don't care about men. I've given up on them, personally. It's not a question of age, it's a question of intellectuality, if you like, of one's mental attitude. I've given up on trying to . . . to put them on a logical track. Completely given up.

It's true that in the United States, after so many years, especially in the university, after so much effort to change what and how we read, what and how we interpret, etc., the new generations may be feeling a sort of exhaustion and boredom with that struggle.

That's what I think.

Yes, but it's really complicated . . . this desire not to be always criticizing, always in negation.

Yes, it's an impasse.

I have always believed in the importance of this struggle, but I recognize more and more why young women can say that the struggle isn't for them.

I'm certainly not leading it.

But you did lead it at a certain period, didn't you?

No. Maybe you're thinking about a woman from the women's movement who interviewed me. I don't remember anymore. I said there was a women's writing, didn't I?

Yes.

I don't think so anymore. From the position I have today, a definitive one, the most important writer from the standpoint of a women's writing is Woolf. It's not Beauvoir.

Yes, but for me, there's more of a schizophrenia to it, because when I think of my intellectual, institutional, political life, Beauvoir is the one who plays the part of the phantasmatic mother . . . I must do everything, read everything, see everything . . . but in my desire for writing, it's Woolf. They go together.

Yes, exactly. It's not all of Woolf. *A Room of One's Own* is the Bible.

And in my imagination, Marguerite Duras, you are there with Woolf.

Yes, well, still. You know, when I was young, I was very free. I was part of the Resistance during the Algerian War. I took a lot of risks, I risked . . . even with Algeria, I ran the risk of being imprisoned. Maybe it's in that sense that I'm still free.

That is, because you've already taken risks.

Because I haven't written on women. Or very little. I see women as having pulled themselves through. That is, they've taken the biggest step. They're on the other side now. All the successful books today are by women, the important films are by women. The difference is fabulous.

So perhaps, according to you, we have to turn away somewhat from the reactive struggle and move instead toward creativity.

Yes, that's what I think.

Do you think this is going to happen by itself? I'd like to believe it, but I'm not sure.

I believe that a book like **The Lover**—which was a slap in the face for everyone, for men—is a great leap forward for women, which is much more important. For a woman to claim international attention makes men sick. It just makes them sick.

I didn't see it like that from the United States.

That's how it was. I don't know how it was for Americans because I got an important American prize . . . and six Americans voted for me. You see, there were 700 voters, then 500, then 300, and finally 70 and then less—you know at different stages of the competition. In the end, there were nine voters. The six Americans all voted for me. The three Frenchmen (France has never had a prize in America) all voted *against* me.

You're kidding?

Some papers, and probably they were right . . . said that they didn't want a writer from the Left to have the first American prize. But that's not it. It's because I was a *woman* writer. Of course, we must recognize that those three people were on the Right. I think that women on the Left are less alienated; whereas on the Right, so many women with government responsibilities are just followers. It's striking how visible that is.

Question 4: Today we are seeing women produce literary, philosophical, and psychoanalytical theory of recognized importance, and parallel to this, we are seeing a new fluidity in the borderlines among disciplines and genres of writing. Will this parallelism lead only to women being welcomed alongside men, or to a definitive blurring of these categories?

I don't know, it's dangerous. Because men's criteria have been tested a long time, and men manipulate them astutely and diplomatically. Men aren't politicians, they're diplomats, and that's a degree lower.

Question 5: Given the problematic and the politics of the categories of the canon, and given the questions we've been dealing with here, do you think your oeuvre will be included in the twentieth-century canon, and if so, how will it be presented? In your opinion, what will be the content of the canon?

This is an indiscreet question. . . .

No it isn't. I don't know what it will be, I don't know, how can I say this, who will be deciding. The only thing that reassures me is that, now, I've become a little bit of an international phenomenon—even a pretty big one. And what France won't do, other countries will. So I'm safe. But those are the terms that I have to use. I'm not safe in France. I'm still very threatened.

You think so really?

Yes, I'm sure, I know, I'm sure.

For me though, coming from the outside, that's incredible, incomprehensible even.

But they never attacked Simone de Beauvoir.

What do you mean?

They never attack Simone de Beauvoir. They never attack Sarraute. But in my case, I've been involved in men's things. First, I was involved in politics. I was in the Communist Party. I did things that are considered in bad taste for a woman. That's the line England took for a long time. In England, they said that Marguerite Duras could never be a novelist because she was too political. Now, my literary oeuvre, my literary work has never gotten mixed up with politics. It never moves to rhetoric. Never. Even something like *The Sea Wall* remains a story. And that's what has saved me. There's not a term, not a trace of dialectic in my fiction. Well, there might be some in *The Square*, perhaps, a kind of theory of needs from Marx that was figured in the little girl, the maid who did everything, who was good for everything, but that was the only time, I think.

But still, your book **Les Parleuses** *has come out from Nebraska Press with a great deal of success.*

How was that translated?

Woman to Woman.

Isn't that a little outmoded now, *Les Parleuses?*

Not in the United States. Here maybe. No, not even here; people recognize that there are really beautiful things in it.

The speaking women, that is?

Yes, the image of two women engaged in speaking to each other.

You know, when I gave that title to my publisher, he was afraid it would have a negative effect. But I said I wanted it because others would say that women just gossip.

Right. . . .

Question 6: And a last question just for you: we are asking you these questions about the future destiny of the work of contemporary women, when, in fact, your work seems to have been canonized already. Actually, you are one of the few people who has been able not only to see her work emerge from an unfair obscurity into the limelight but who has seen it attain worldwide recognition. How has becoming a celebrity influenced a vision that was intentionally critical and other?

You know, *The Lover* came late in my life. And even its fame wasn't something new for me. I had already had two things make it on the worldwide scene, and so I was used to that phenomenon—of something operating totally independently of you. It happens like an epiphenomenon, it takes place in inaccessible regions. You can't know why a book works, when it works that well. First, it was *Hiroshima, mon amour,* which was seen all over the world. And then I had *Moderato cantabile,* which must have had the same effect as *The Lover,* for it was translated everywhere. Such a small book that was a worldwide hit, it's strange. Well, I was no young girl in the face of those events. As for the end of your question, "a vision that was intentionally critical and other"—that doesn't have anything to do with it. I understand the implication in your question that being famous somehow intimidates, inhibits. No, no, on the contrary. . . .

But there's a mythology that says that being famous is a defeat in mass culture.

Yes, I know that. . . . That reminds me of what Robbe-Grillet told me one day. He said, "When you and I have sold 500,000 copies, that will mean we don't have anything else to say." Well, so I don't have anything else to say—and he has another book.

Ginger Danto (review date 23 February 1992)

SOURCE: "A Man, a Woman and a Voyeur," in *The New York Times Book Review,* February 23, 1992, p. 12.

[*Below, Danto reviews Duras' novella* The Man Sitting in the Corridor *and compares it to her earlier novel* The Ravishing of Lol Stein.]

In *The Ravishing of Lol Stein*, a 1964 novel with which Marguerite Duras began to skirt the celebrity she would encounter exponentially 20 years later with *The Lover*, the protagonist is a woman whose resilient memory of lost love festers into a form of insanity. The narrative moves from before, when Lol Stein is young and borne by love, to after, when she is older, spent by residual grief and mad. In the last state, Lol Stein returns to roam the scene of her youthful tryst, a village in Normandy, where she sees a man with a woman who resembles her onetime rival. Later Lol Stein lies in a field from which she can see the couple making love and experiences a vague voyeuristic pleasure that supplants her nostalgia for a severed past.

In many ways, this early novel served as a blueprint for episodes in Ms. Duras's subsequent stories, in which love shifts, like mercury, in and out of once true hearts suddenly reoriented. And while Ms. Duras's intermingled themes of desire and disappointment perennially resurface, what disappears in successive works is detail and description, like so much

excess carved away to yield an increasingly lean, essential plot.

Ms. Duras's 1980 novella *The Man Sitting in the Corridor*, whose superb English translation by Barbara Bray is only now appearing, was such an exercise in the author's progressive distillation of her prose. Here it is so spare that at most several sentences (and once a mere 15 words) occupy an entire page. Thus unencumbered, the rare bits of writing gain resonance, like a lone voice echoing through a tunnel. Moreover, by writing less—and thereby suggesting more—Ms. Duras invests her information with a power unavailable to more copious, if still evocative, forms of literary expression. More than in her other fiction, however, the style of *The Man Sitting in the Corridor* suits its similarly thrifty scenario of a protracted sexual exchange between a man and a woman, as told by a voyeur.

In the context of Ms. Duras's *oeuvre,* which continually recasts, in variously altered guises, intermittently abandoned persons and plots, *The Man Sitting in the Corridor* can be considered a close-up of the scene of Lol Stein's vicarious encounter. And, like a camera lens that magnifies fine details at the expense of a contextual blur, the novella focuses on the deconstructed inventory of its erotic action, stripped of situational clues and elaboration. There is no history attached to these people, who have no names. There is only the present, and a cast that includes the narrator's "I," as well as "he" and "she," along with references to the male sexual organ—indeed an essential character—as "it," Nor are we anywhere specific, but in a generic landscape of sun, sea and clouds, with somewhere a house that has a corridor.

As a film maker, Ms. Duras is also acquainted with close-ups that magnify to unrecognition, rendering even beautiful images unexpectedly grotesque. The same distortion occurs in this brief text, where the closely chronicled denouement of passion is possibly fatal pain. We watch this process, voyeurs ourselves, by way of a witness whose faithful, frame-by-frame narrative unfolds page by page, so that even when nothing "happens," something is going on. Indeed, a third of the way through the book we're told, "The man would go on waiting." Until then the surveyed couple remain inert: he seated in some corridor, she sprawled outside within his (and our) vision.

But despite their inertia, or perhaps because of it, a slow, pre-erotic tension fills the air between them. Thus Ms. Duras's meticulously chosen words, which do little more than deploy two people in proximity, mimic the still form of foreplay for what these people will ultimately do—so that when the woman cries out and the man moves toward her, there is a sense of relief, but also of disappointment. Perhaps the most erotic moment of this interlude was one of anticipation.

For soon the woman becomes inanimate in her submission. The man treats her as if she isn't human, and as if he too is "mechanical." It is only when the man says "I love you" that we recognize him as the woman's lover, and it is only when she begs to be beaten that we realize this is the only kind of love she wants: "She says she wants him to hit her, in the face she says, she asks him to, Come on He does, he comes and sits by her and looks at her again. She says she wants him to hit her, hard, as he did her heart just now. She says she'd like to die."

In her own story, Lol Stein never saw the suspect woman destroyed like herself. Perhaps Ms. Duras, who has said in interviews that the character of Lol Stein haunted her for years, wrote *The Man Sitting in the Corridor* to afford Lol Stein this belated opportunity. On its own, the novella paints the most searing abstract yet of the Duras heroine—a woman who seeks love only to be charred by at like someone who willingly puts her hand into a flame.

Ron Grossman (review date 27 May 1992)

SOURCE: "Marguerite Duras Makes No Sense, Compellingly," in *Chicago Tribune*, May 27, 1992, p. 3.

[*In the following review, Grossman states that despite its unusual and sparse style, somber mood, and difficult subject matter,* Summer Rain *is a compelling novel.*]

It would be foolish to argue with Marguerite Duras that her novels don't make sense.

The grande dame of contemporary French letters would take the reproach as a compliment. For half a century, Duras has fascinated her fans with books in which she set aside most of the novel's conventional devices: plot, characterization, description and action.

Summer Rain, the most recent of her works to be translated into English, doesn't just leave readers scratching their heads. The characters don't seem to know what's up either.

"You're as beautiful as Hanka Lissovskaya," one character tells his daughter.

"Who's she?" the daughter asks.

"Your mother."

Because of that disdain for logic, Duras has often been considered a member of the nouveau roman movement, which introduced mimimalist storytelling to the French reading public. But for novelists like Nathalie Sarraute and Alain Robbe-Grillet, the less-is-more technique was an aesthetic device.

For Duras, it is a philosophy of life. She is convinced that the world is simply absurd.

Considering her biography, it would have been hard to her to come to another conclusion. Duras was born in 1914 in IndoChina, then a French colony. Her father died when she was a child, and her mother saved for years to buy a small farm with which to support Duras and her two brothers. Unfortunately, she was tricked into buying a piece of worthless land that flooded during the rainy season, leaving the family penniless. Duras drew upon the experience for *The Lover*, the novel for which she is best known in America.

Making her way to France, Duras studied mathematics at the Sorbonne, then served with the Resistance during World War II. Aided by Francois Mitterrand, who went on to become president of France, Duras rescued her husband from a Nazi concentration camp. Then she promptly divorced him.

A distinguished filmmaker, best known for her script for *Hiroshima Mon Amour*, she has published dozens of books between bouts of depression and a lifelong struggle with alcoholism.

Summer Rain takes place on the other side of the tracks in a large, impersonal suburb of Paris. By some fashion or another, an Italian man and a Russian woman have made their way there and had seven children, supporting their brood on the public dole. Evenings, the parents go off to the shanty town's taverns, leaving the eldest children, Ernesto and Jeanne, to take care of the younger ones.

Ernesto decides he doesn't want to go to school, arguing with perfect logic: "They teach me things I don't know."

Nonetheless, he not only learns to read, but by the time he's 12, he has become a prodigy. Listening outside schoolrooms, he teaches himself virtually the whole body of mankind's knowledge. At the novel's end, he goes off to study mathematics in America, just as Duras once went to France to study that subject. But just before leaving, he and his sister become lovers.

Whatever else can be said of Duras, she doesn't expect her characters to do that which she herself wouldn't. In another book, *The North Chinese Lover*, she obliquely reported having had an affair with her younger brother.

Only Duras can take such unpalatable material, pass it through the filter of her bleak philosophy and produce novels of such compelling presence that the reader wants to devour them at a single sitting.

Lauren G. Munn (review date 5 January 1993)

SOURCE: "If Revenge Is Duras' Aim, Then It's Also Her Muse," in *Chicago Tribune,* January 5, 1993, p. 3.

[*In the following review, Munn compares* The North China Lover *to* The Lover *and argues that despite their similar subject matter* The North China Lover *is a more personal and a better-written account.*]

In *The North China Lover*, Marguerite Duras rewrites a story she has told over and over, most notably in her 1984 novel *The Lover*. She has never told it better than here.

Replete with haunting images of forbidden passion, familial violence, hatred and love, *The North China Lover* strikes an emotional chord that Duras' other works have sought to destroy. Known for alternating between first-person and third-person narration, Duras deliberately distances readers from her characters. Their emotions appear on the page but are never shared. Yet by maintaining the third-person voice throughout this autobiographical confession, Duras forges a new connection, one that is rewarding and deeply affecting.

The novel began as notes for the screenplay Duras was to write for French director Jean-Jacques Annaud's film adaptation of *The Lover*, now at area theaters. It developed into a story of its own when she was replaced by another writer after a falling-out with Annaud. Whether or not Duras published this book in retaliation (which seems likely, considering its cinematic quality), what she has created far surpasses Annaud's film and the novel on which it is based.

Duras illuminates the wretched poverty of her family in 1930 French Indochina, the violence they suffered at the hands of her opium-addicted brother and the passion that threatened to consume her at 14 when she embarked on a scandalous affair with a 27-year-old Chinese man. She intensifies the already concentrated sensuality of both the book and film versions of *The Lover*. She lays bare her incestuous relationship with her younger brother, Paulo—a relationship she only hinted at in *The Lover*. But the main difference dwells in the explanation behind her affair with "the Chinese," as she refers to her lover.

In both the film and the earlier novel, it is the wealth of the Chinese man that propels her into his arms. She trades her body for money—enough to pay off her brother Pierre's opium debts and to buy them passage back to France on an oceanliner. The possibility that she may love him is only entertained at the end as she watches him watch her sail away.

In *The North China Lover*, "the child," as Duras refers to herself, seems motivated less by money than by desire. Throughout the narrative, she questions her feelings, testing their true depth. Their relationship, while still based on power, is complicated by the intensity of their emotions. Much more a tragic love story than *The Lover*, this novel reveals the depth of Duras' love for the Chinese-a love that continues to sustain and influence her work.

Duras further eroticizes that love through the film-like quality of her writing style, which transforms the reader into a voyeur. "She isn't alone in the picture anymore. He is there. Beside her," Duras writes. "He gently rolls onto that skinny, virgin body. And as he slowly covers it with his own body, without touching it yet, the camera might leave the bed; it might veer toward the window, might stop there at the drawn blinds."

This cinematic style lends credence to the belief that Duras wrote *The North China Lover* as a direct affront to Annaud. Heightening such suspicions are the sporadic footnotes advising on the use of lighting, music and casting "if this book is made into a film."

Whatever her motivation, Duras has written an original and powerful book, with the brutal honesty of a black and white documentary.

Melanie Rae Thon (review date January/February 1993)

SOURCE: A review of *The North China Lover,* in *Boston Review,* January/February, 1993.

[*In the following review, Thon contends that* The North China Lover *is less distant and more humane than the earlier novel* The Lover.]

Spare and erotic, *The North China Lover* is not merely the story of *The Lover* retold: it is a haunting transformation of Marguerite Duras's original vision, more tender and more terrifying, more devastating because it is more humane.

In pre-war Indochina, a wealthy Chinese man meets an adolescent girl on a ferry and offers her a ride in his limousine. She's poor and white, a child, but they are bound to each other from the start, "shut in together, in the twilight of the car." The lover is "more solid" than he was in the first book, "less timid facing the child." The balance between them has shifted. Though the child still can be cruel, she's too vulnerable to be callous, too immersed in her own desire to pretend she wants the Chinese only for his money.

Crossing one boundary allows the child to cross all others. She loves everyone too much: the man, her beautiful friend Hélène, her brother Paulo. It's dangerous, living this way. Despair and insight come with passion, the child says, and it's true: fears intertwine; one threat exposes another. Thanh, her mother's chauffeur, is the only one to refuse her. "He says inside him he has the fear of killing the men and women with white skins, that he has to beware."

His words echo. All her life the child has been tormented by her older brother, Pierre, afraid of what he'll do to her and Paulo if he finds them together. She imagines being killed by tigers, or a stranger, or a brother—she asks the lover how *he* would kill her at Long-Hai, and he says, "Like a Chinese. With cruelty on top of killing." These fantasies have a terrible logic. There is a place where desperation and desire collide, where the fear of being destroyed and the fear of being abandoned are one.

For those who live inside this novel, love is forbidden: the love of a grown man for a child, a mother for a brutal son, a sister for a fragile brother. But Duras's people transcend judgment. The mother tells the Chinese man, "You ought to know, Monsieur, that it is sacred even to love a dog. And we have the right—as sacred as life itself—not to have to justify it to anyone."

Originally written as notes for a filmscript, *The North China Lover* is elliptical, sometimes eerie: the child "dissolves in the moonlight, then reappears." The "I" of the first novel has stepped out of our way, has become an *eye* instead, lingering on a hand that seems "charmingly crippled," or on the "fabulous, silken flatness of the delta." Again and again, the eye focuses on the skinny body of the child, so we can never forget how young and small she is.

Duras is re-imagining her own work, giving directions. In a footnote, she tells us Hélène has died of tuberculosis. In another she says the actress who plays the child can't be too pretty. "Beauty doesn't act. It doesn't look. It is looked at."

The effect of these details is surprising. They don't distract us. Our awareness of Duras's process only pulls us closer. We are with a woman trying to reveal the experience at the center of her life, participating in her fierce desire to get it right.

Marguerite Duras knows the lover is dead when she begins the second novel. She's learned that the people of Sadec loved him for his kindness and simplicity, that toward the end of his life he was very religious. He's become human and real to her in ways he wasn't when she told her story the first

time. In the introduction, she says: "Writing this book made me deliriously happy. The novel kept me a year, enclosed me in that year of love between the Chinese man and the child."

The final section of *The North China Lover* is a list of suggested shots for the filmmaker that reads like a poem. The story unfurls one last time, and we see everything quickly, in bursts: "The straight monsoon rain and nothing more, that straight rain across the entire frame. Straight, like no place else." The lovers are absent but seem to move in the white space, between the images, between "a day of a different blue" and the surface, the "skin" of the dark river "very close up." Like Duras, we feel a sense of awe and joy, plunged into the world of the child and her Chinese lover again.

Elaine Romaine (review date Spring 1993)

SOURCE: "The Telling Remains," in *Belles Lettres: A Review of Books by Women,* Vol. 8, No. 3, Spring, 1993, p. 9.

[*In the following review of* The North China Lover, *Romaine discusses how repeating essentially the same story over again in her work allows Duras to perfect the telling of this tale.*]

In the hands of a French male director, Marguerite Duras's *The North China Lover* could become a voyeuristic film of another Lolita. In fact, it has. Sex in all its variations certainly pervades the novel, sometimes gratuitously. But, unlike many of Duras's previous novels with the same plot and characters, the girl in this novel is not defined only in sexual terms. Duras has other more central themes: memory and fiction itself.

Written first as a film script, this autobiographical work takes place in 1930 Indochina. A poor, half-caste 14-year-old girl has an affair with a wealthy, 27-year-old Chinese man. Her brothers, Pierre and Paulo, know of the affair, while her mother, "killed by life," views her daughter's sexuality almost indifferently. The Chinese lover, who feels the "despair at the happiness of flesh," redeems the family debt, thinking the girl will leave for France.

Happily, Duras subverts convention by demanding in a wry footnote that the film actress not be pretty: "Beauty doesn't act. It doesn't look. It is looked at." And here lies the crux of the novel. Much is made of the girl's "looking," of her need to observe the cold truth of every detail. "She gives him a straight look. A look you could call unabashed. Fresh. Not right, her mother calls it." At 14, poverty and incest have made her neutral, vigilant, unsentimental. She survives by desiring a man "who loves a woman and the woman doesn't love him." Observing her passion much as a writer might, she strips it of prettiness. She does what she does, "just to see." And it is *her* gaze, not the lover's, that names and defines her experiences.

The girl, as Duras remembers herself, is already writing her own life. The novel, which Duras calls both a book and a film, contains wide spaces between short paragraphs, directions for a camera, and even chapters devoted to single line images—very much in the tradition of the *nouveau roman.* In fact, the girl's eye clicks like a lens. "The canvas shade against the heat. The blood on the sheets. And the city, always invisible, always external—those things she remembered." Her eye is nonjudgmental, mirroring obsession through simple repetition: "She sees him. She lowers her eyes. She looks at him, too. She sees him. She pulls back." Sometimes tedious, the repetition mostly proves hypnotic, drawing the reader from passion to ennui to the "frightful pain of (the lovers') need. . . ." It is an elemental fable where the main characters are nameless: The Girl or The Child, The Man or The Chinese, The Mother.

Yet why recount this same story in novel after novel? Each retelling brings Duras closer to the truth of a memory that haunts her. We remember so we do not forget. Quite simple. But if I record precisely what I remember, the memory becomes fixed; it is not tied to a memory that will die when I die. For Duras, fiction is memory made (dare I say it?) immortal. She remembers her passion but she also remembers the girl who became a writer at that moment. The girl cries at the end, "talk about everything, the happiness as well as the suffering. . . . In order for people—anyone who wanted to, she says—to tell it over and over again, for them not to forget the whole of the story, for something very precise to remain."

And what remains? The telling remains. Duras writing year after year, recapturing what has compelled her to write. The significance of the affair (ignore the patriarchal French film!) lies not in sexual passion, but in what it produced: Duras as writer. Her fictional self has transformed the real self whose story "demanded to be written—until she reached that moment of clear memory in the forest of writing."

Daniel Gunn (review date 25 February 1994)

SOURCE: "Eternally Unpredictable," in *The Times Literary Supplement,* No. 4743, February 25, 1994, p. 24.

[*Below, Gunn reviews two of Duras' works,* Le Monde Exterieur *and* Ecrire, *as well as Christiane Blot-Labarrer's* Marguerite Duras *and Leslie Hill's* Marguerite Duras, *both biographies.*]

Who gets closest to Marguerite Duras? Who writes most illuminatingly of her, the author herself or her critics? All four books under review, even that entitled *Le Monde extérieur,* are trying to get close to Duras, though they do not agree on how best to do so. Does one get closest by becoming intimate, or rather by maintaining some distance? Christiane Blot-Labarrère tries the former approach, Leslie Hill the latter; and, perhaps unsurprisingly, their works argue respectively for Duras the destroyer of boundaries, and Duras the advocate of the impossibility of encounter. While Duras herself goes both inside, in *Ecrire,* which is concerned in part with her house, and "outside" (*Le Monde extérieur* is subtitled *Outside 2*), in an attempt to write about herself as one who claims she cannot write, yet who writes notwithstanding (and prolifically).

The final chapter of Blot-Labarrère's book is called "Duras telle qu'en elle-même", and in it she tries to show what has been her conviction throughout, that Duras is "in herself" most when in her work; or that, since all her work is about herself, Duras is most herself when most inventive. Taking a lead from Duras's statement in her novel *L'Amant,* that "L'histoire de ma vie n'existe pas", Blot-Labarrère largely eschews a chronological overview of the *oeuvre* (though interestingly not in the photographs which accompany the text), and works with prominent Duras themes and loci. Childhood, then, if it is the origin of many major Duras preoccupations—the family, incest, ambivalence, the margins, the sea, the outsiders—is most important not as a period of time but as a myth re-created in support of ever-contemporary desires.

As Blot-Labarrère's book progress, with some useful discussion of Jewishness, the colonies, weather and the seasons, it becomes clear that Duras is herself mythic for her critic. And it is perhaps because the intensity of the author's admiration of Duras militates against her essentialist desire to grasp the writer, that she chooses to graft her text, stylistically, so closely on to that of its subject. So she concludes her work with a summons to "franchir les passes et, Navire Night, partir pour une écriture au long cours, sur la mer d'encre noir". We are just a step away, here, from Duras on Duras; but we are also only two steps from the mimicry of Alain Vircondelet's lamentable biography of Duras (1991), in which the biographer dispensed with independent research by invocation of his subject's disregard for chronology; or three steps from the hilarious book parodying Duras, *Virginie Q* (1988), which is full of such invocations.

Nor is one reassured as to the critic's role, on reading in *Le Monde extérieur* Duras's tribute to Blot-Labarrère (who has edited this volume, though to a system I cannot begin to fathom), which asserts that "C'est merveilleux que Christiane Blot-Labarrère existe pour raconter l'écriture". Such critical doubling can, at its best, give the reader a taste of the excitement Duras offers. But it does not help in demarcating the line between Duras "in herself" and Duras as the object of what may be called (using Leslie Hill's term) "transferential love"; the line between Duras and Duras parody; or the fine line between Duras at her best and Duras at her worst. Hill also chooses not to explain why good Duras is very good and bad Duras awful, but there is enough in his book to give the reader some indications. With his greater distance, and his willingness to explore her "mythifying—if not, indeed, mystifying" writing, he introduces a Duras who has very self-consciously created a myth around herself. Hill's study of Duras's "image", and of her journalism and television appearances, which he suggests should be viewed less as comments on her work than as part of the work itself, makes a peculiarly appropriate opening. This is particularly so since he never exaggerates his case, and shows that Duras has a 100 per cent commitment to her every utterance, no matter how alarming it may be.

Hill presents a paradoxical Duras, with his key concept of "apocalyptic desire" (and of incest) leading to "epistemological frustration", exhaustion, loss, paucity, blankness, dissolution, sublime excess and impossibility. Hill follows a more or less chronological scheme, and in a broad sweep takes in Duras's films, plays and fiction. At times, it is hard, reading his book, to grasp how the passage from apocalyptic concept to immensely charged text comes about; and Hill's own style, never emulating that of its subject, gives no help here, nor do his quotations, since (and the contrast with Samuel Beckett, the subject of Hill's previous book, is striking here) Duras appears curiously weak in quotation. But the term "apocalyptic desire" allows Hill to account for much that is formally innovative in Duras: in her films, for example, the disjunction between image and word. And, especially in an analysis of Duras's most fascinating works, Hill does give a strong sense of the stakes involved; not least when he takes the risk, with his view of destruction-in-revelation and revelation-in-destruction, of reducing the critic's position to a very fine margin—upon which margin he must then balance.

Given the ambivalent and paradoxical nature of Duras's world, it is perhaps to be expected that, when speaking of *Le Monde extérieur,* Duras in fact speaks of herself, and in a way which confirms Hill's contention that her journalism should be considered as part of her literary output. From the occasional pieces collected here—magazine articles, prefaces, comments on photographs, film production, lovers, films and on much else besides—certain of her more incendiary articles have been omitted. Yet there is more than enough here to confirm that Duras's views are never predictable, always controversial, sometimes aberrant. From her support for the sinking of the Rainbow Warrior, for the American bombing of Tripoli, for Amnesty International and for various artists and painters, to her denunciation of the French right, of drugs, of the Communist Party, of Gorbachev, consistency and objectivity are surely the least of Duras's concerns. She often breaks off from some topical or political question to interject an in-

tensely personal reflection, memory or analogy, so finding herself "in herself" when on the "outside". At one point, she launches a tirade against men, who are "fatigués . . . malades . . . suicidaires", only to follow it with: "J'aime les hommes, je n'aime que ça."

It is love for one man in particular—love more than respect or admiration—which marks this collection most boldly, and that man is François Mitterrand. The love, which has its origins in the Resistance (as readers of *La Douleur* will recall), leads here to many of the most extraordinary judgments, since Mitterrand must, at all costs, be defended; to the point that he is grouped with Robert Badinter and Pierre Mendès France as the only ones worthy of power, because they are the only ones who don't give a damn about power. In *Ecrire,* which collects transcripts from three short films on or by Duras, the turn inwards to the principal preoccupations appears to have results for the style, which often out-Durases Duras. Never negligent of an opportunity to use the word "ça", Duras writes (of a pilot killed in the Second World War): "ça a vingt ans. L'âge, le chiffre de l'âge s'est arrêté à la mort, ça aura toujours vingt ans, ça que c'est devenu." In transcribing her discourses from the films, Duras gives free rein to the "ça", almost as if she were caricaturing herself.

Nor do the subjects of the two main pieces strike one as anything less than extreme Duras. A British pilot of twenty (to whom the collection is dedicated), shot down and killed in the final days of the war, permits an invocation of his grave, a lament for youth and a venting of abiding hatred of the Germans. Writing, here, as tomb-building and tomb-preservation, evoking hopelessness, heroism and, of course, the loss of the author's own brother; and all these packed into a short narrative which is as full of blanks as it is of the word "ça".

The other main piece evokes Marguerite Duras's house at Neauphle-le-Château, where, among other things, she recalls observing the death of another aviator, this time a common house fly, whose end she narrates at some length. In this house too, most importantly, she feels the real break through in her writing career occurred, and here she is able most fully to experience the states which for her befit the writer (and all of which are reminiscent of Samuel Beckett on the painter, Bram van Velde): complete uncertainty, want of subject before "une immensité vide", impossibility of writing and surprise at writing which emerges none the less. By turns magnificent and infuriating, Duras turns in upon herself, and threatens thus to lose or parody herself. But then she turns half an eye on the "outside", and brings it, and herself in the process, to life again; even if this world has been reduced—or perhaps Duras would say *magnified*—to the agonies of a young pilot, or, indeed, of a fly.

Raylene Ramsay (essay date February 1994)

SOURCE: Writing Power in Duras' *L'Amant de la Chine du nord,*" in *College Literature,* Vol. 21, No. 1, February, 1994, pp. 46-62.

[*In the essay below, Ramsay considers the autobiographical fiction genre and analyzes the language and structure of Duras' works.*]

It has been a matter of theoretical concern that "difference" or the "feminine," like the principle of "carnival" or of the disorderly woman, might remain a simple reversal of values, reversal that ultimately serves to reinforce the power structures in place. The transgression of the law—or of narrative— might simply confirm the power of the law or of the language that it transgresses.

The question of whether writing has the power to enter and recover a "wild country" of "difference" (another kind of power) through reversals or transgressions of traditional frames of reference is necessarily at the heart of any critical reading of the "new autobiographies" (*L'Amant, Emily L.*) of Marguerite Duras. Nathalie Sarraute's "new autobiographies," too (*Enfance, Tu ne t'aimes pas*), seek to move toward the unknown (the unsayable) in the self through the prodding, the squeezing inside and the exposing of the meanings of conventional expressions. These works remain self-consciously aware of the compromised nature of the language that serves as their instrument of investigation. Duras attempts to recover the power of the "wild country" through a "chaotic" text that models regression to the brutality of primitive states, a text marked by the cry, gesture, silence, and obsessive repetition of founding scenes of desire. Sarraute is embroiled in a struggle between a unified, polished, surface order of language as it fixes and limits sensations and self and the swarming undersides of these structures, the multiple selves that can be forced for a moment into view in a war of the words. Both writers have undertaken this "impossible" movement between feeling and saying through the medium of a literary excavation without much certainty of success and with a paradoxical sense of powerlessness/new power.

The "new" power sought in the "new" autobiographies resides in just this apparent contradiction, the impossible movement, both in and yet somehow reaching beyond the postmodern bind in which self, desires, sensations, fantasies are a construction by language, discursive formations, always already there. As they transform traditional autobiography, science, and gender, the new autobiographies rewrite the apparently dialectical oppositions (the logic of contradictions) lurking in the very designation of the reversals they effect: feminine for masculine, or powerlessness for power. They write a new "chaotic" character into the circulation between power and resistance to power.

For Michel Foucault, power and knowledge are situated within a social dynamics of control characterized by a movement from subversion to containment. Such a movement is essentially a self-canceling equilibrium process: subversion remains within power. In Duras' work, however, power/language/ knowledge are abused and used to forge connections with what is not (in) power. This is, Duras expresses it in *Emily L.,* the unsayable or unreadable "minimal difference, where the meanings are" sensed in the unmaking and remaking of knowledge. In Sarraute, the unsayable is identified with the tiny, affective, tropistic "differences" underlying and deferred in speech yet detectable through the speaking voice. Although they participate in the circulation of power/resistance to power that constructs both the individual and the truth, a circulation that is, for Foucault, at once an effect of power and its mode of domination, the "differences" in the new autobiographies also introduce something new (local, approaching agency). These local, unpredictable, mobile truths move the ordered Foucault system in equilibrium through minute but recursive changes toward the fluctuating non-equilibrium states and the bifurcation points of random change that may create event or new knowledge. The forms of the new autobiographies are close to the models of a new science (chaos theory, Ilya Prigogine's "dissipative systems," catastrophe theory) that contests reductive determinism. They move beyond the Foucault model to the extent that the circulation Foucault envisages leaves no place for change or agency.

It has become a commonplace that pre-oedipal identification is the most obvious route to significations unassimilable to the Patriarchal Law in place. The originality of *L'Amant de la Chine du nord,* I argue, is that as it experiments with the forms through which the capture of the unconscious or the prelinguistic might indeed be possible (the psychoanalytic domain), it simultaneously struggles with the question of whether the unconscious is indeed structured like a language, as Jacques Lacan claims (the domain of the semiotic). The character of the "beyond" (beyond the prison-house of language or readymade Law, beyond dialectic, beyond deterministic closed systems, beyond conventional notions of power as juridical sovereignty, social contract, or right) that the new texts model is not simply a regression to the pre-oedipal. The "minimal difference" of which Duras speaks must participate in the sphere of language as much as in the pre-linguistic. Its nature—that of the body made word—is contradictory.

Nor does the pre-oedipal or the "minimal difference" simply recover a traditional essence. In her study of Italian feminism, Teresa de lauretis argues that a certain form of essentialism, based on the individual contexts and experiences of women, is not incompatible with constructionism (woman as readymade ideological or linguistic product), despite the mutual exclusion of essentialism and constructionism in current theory. Change, agency, the touching of a beyond might derive, her thesis suggests, from the very specificity and uniqueness of female contexts and experiences and within local inter- and intra-personal hierarchies, differences, and relations of force as much as from global equal rights. Agency might manifest itself in choice and individual style.

For Foucault too, the local and the singular have particular significance: "Power is constructed and functions on the basis of particular power myriad issues, myriad effects of power" (*Power/Knowledge*). The traditional relation between the global (as cause and dominance) and the local (as effect and submission/reaction) undergoes a radical change. As in the principle of "sensitive dependence on initial conditions" in chaos theory (a principle that emerged from the study of non-mechanical, non-traditional dynamical physical systems), small local dislocations or effects of power, magnified through the system, can initiate major change in global relations. In the Lorenzian hypothesis of "the butterfly effect" in weather systems, for example, the movement of a butterfly's wings in Peking, repeated through the system, might produce a storm in Florida. In the new autobiographies, as in postmodernism and feminism, the dissolution of "Man" and the subsequent lack of any absolute principle or paternal legitimation to give meaning to the self and to the world constitute the starting points for the exploration of the chaotic and generative impulses and the complex, sado-masochistic relations of power concealed within this "void." These relations do not exist in perfect equilibrium or symmetry and are far from predictable—not unlike those of most complex living systems.

Foucault chooses, much as the new autobiographers do, to investigate the network of relations from the bottom, or at the lowest level. But arguing that power is always already there, that one is always inside power, the philosopher limits his enterprise of knowledge to an intellectual modeling of the ways in which the mechanisms and effects of power have been able to operate. The new autobiographers are writing from within similar power relations and discourses but they do not seek to elaborate a distancing archaeology of knowledge or a history of sexuality as Foucault does. Rather, at the limits of their own intimate affective experience, they seek to sound the unsaid or unsayable, the more mobile "chaotic" laws of intimate power, sexuality, and knowledge. Resistance, for Robbe-Grillet, cannot be simply a question of opposition to the Law, of cutting off the King's head, or indeed of casting bright light on his own fantasies of the beautiful captive. In Robbe-Grillet's work, Boris, the regicide, is also the King; as his old head rolls, the "hydra-monster" of theory simply sprouts new heads, Stalin replaces the Czar, and the marine monster who both devours little girls and flees the devouring sea/mother (mer/mère) makes confession of his fantasies—but in a self-conscious linguistic pirouette. In the new interchangeable non-dialectical figures that they create and in the movement that breaks down the limits between inside and outside, language and life, sadism and masochism, there is,

however, a recording of the relations of power that may alter them.

The limitation of Foucault's poststructuralist formulation of the question of the relation to power (even in resistance, one is inside power) is highlighted by a number of new forms emerging into the general cultural climate. These appear in art, in the work of Magritte (paintings of landscapes/landscapes painted that are simultaneously inside and outside the room in *The Human Condition* or *The Beautiful Captive*) for example. They are present also in the scientific discourses that Foucault himself sees as dominant in contemporary society, in the reversibility of the new topological figures of the Möebius strip or Klein worms where inside and outside are indistinguishable, in Heisenberg's "complementary relations" (matter as both particle and wave), and in the unpredictability *and* pattern in the dynamical systems of chaos theory. De Lauretis, too, formulates the hope that struggle against repressive or disciplinary power might take place not in the name of juridical sovereignty or right—that is, of the other face of global power—but rather in the search for a new kind of right.

Foucault claims, however, that the play of power and resistance that generates itself at each moment, at specific points, and in every relation (between male and female, adult and child, etc.) allowing the emergence of "subjugated knowledges," including those of the body, nonetheless remains within power. According to the Foucault model, then, Duras' resistance would necessarily function within a sexuality constructed by a productive power exercised in both the repression and the stimulation (by advertising, pornography, etc.) of bodies and desires and in the production of effects at the level of desire and knowledge. Duras' work, however, is an attempt to dramatize such internalized oppressions and to go beyond the effects of the matrix of received sex/text. Her text seeks stubbornly, persistently, passionately, outside the mainstream tradition of rationality, to write her desire in spite of its mixed nature and the problematic gap between text and life. Foucault, who, as Jana Sawicki argues, sees the body as the target and the vehicle of modern disciplinary practices, calls for a displacement in relation to the sexual centering of the problem of power, and argues against the thesis of repression.

In Duras' work, too, of course, the Law may be constitutive of desire. "Difference" is perceptible only through the rhythms, semiotic flow, and breaks of the texts that obscure it. It is the lost, pre-verbal, desiring other side of the repressive and formative social structures in place. But sign-posted in linguistic, thematic, and structural inversions, and in the writer's metatextual observations and the fracturing effect of metalepsis (illicit slippage between levels of the text, between fiction and metacommentary), desire in Duras is a complex, non-linear, non-dialectical product of a pleasure-inducing network of power relations and conflicts and not simply an opposite reaction to repression or disciplinary normalization of the body. It maintains tensions and interactions at all levels of functioning of the text between the pre-oedipal or pre-linguistic (maternal fusion, oceanic beatitude, emotion) and the oedipal (the separation, identification with the father's authority [the Phallus], loss, individuation, and rationality of the symbolic or linguistic).

One new autobiography (also a novel and a film scenario), Duras' 1991 *L'Amant de la Chine du nord,* illustrates precisely the existence of a power of writing in Duras that cannot be wholly contained as in the Foucault model. In this rewriting of a first autobiographical fiction—a local re-writing of the story of the lover (brother, mother) already present in *Un Barrage contre le Pacifique* (Gallimard, 1950) and *L'Amant* (Minuit, 1984)—Duras seeks once again, stubbornly, passionately, to write intense and buried desire from her own hysterical body at once given voice by, and filtered through, a text that seeks new forms of community and economies of power and pleasure. The fictional truth that Duras attempts to produce, as writing gives form to her life and her life takes on the form of art, goes beyond the role that Foucault assigns truth, that of reflecting and sustaining social systems. In this respect, it may engender something new, not embedded in the circulation of power relations in place. Duras has presented *L'Amant de la Chine du nord* as the most truthful of her autobiographies. At first sight, an aging writer appears to be at pains to retell the stories of institutional colonial power and of the play of power within familial and sexual relations that have already appeared in her earlier texts in order to set the record still straighter.

Rather than simply demonstrating improved recall of real events or greater sincerity, however, the re-writing of *L'Amant* "without literariness' introduces a number of small and only apparently inconsequential local changes in the stories recounted in the earlier works. These differences magnify through the intertextual "system" of Duras' work, introducing uncertainty and disorder—not unlike the principle of sensitive dependency on initial conditions that creates the butterfly effect in chaos theory. The modification of details and the addition of a number of new scenes also alter previous relations of power within familial relations and between the former and the present works.

One such "new" and very cinematographic or visual scene is situated in early childhood at Vinhlong, one evening after house-washing when the younger brother Paulo has been chased away by Pierre. The mother is braiding the child's hair for the night under the mosquito net in the bed they share to prevent the young girl from sneaking into Paulo's bed. The daughter initiates a dialogue with the mother, accusing her of blind preference for the bullying older brother and neglect of the dominated and slightly retarded younger son.

Despite the new diegetic frame, this is, once again, the primal Durassian scene of the family romance, the triangulation or circulation of desire through the mother's unjustified and passionate preference for the violent profligate brother, the daughter's desire to be loved by the mother (and brother) and protective, possessive love for the "little" brother. However, although the scene is still colored by the young girl's accusing and demanding cries of pain, it is marked by an attempt on the part of the (adult?) narrator to speak also from the mother's position. She recalls the mother's protest that she loves all her children, and her admission of the danger posed by Pierre. In this context, Pierre takes on the form of the negative archaic father of the Oedipus myth, a powerful and tyrannical Laios who would kill any son who threatened to replace him.

The daughter's rage at the mother's preference for the older brother is permeated in this scene by a new understanding, an apparent intimacy and an empathetic affective power moving within the mother-daughter relationship. Such minor changes in the writer's still complex and contradictory remembering and re-writing of youthful desire, out of the devastation of age, evoke a more intense identificatory relation with the mother than the scenes of *Un Barrage contre le Pacifique* or *L'Amant.* The fluctuations between the child's individuation and separation from the mother and her need for recognition of and by the mother that marked the account of the mother-daughter relation in *L'Amant* are resolved in this work on the side of a movement toward mutual recognition and a kind of interchangeability. Translating this within a psychoanalytic frame, in *L'Amant de la Chine du nord* there seems to be an attempt to resolve the conflict between a pre-oedipal stage of unity with the mother and a situation of oedipal conflict in which identification with the mother (as inside, lack of desire, lack of agency and of power) requires renunciation of outside "phallic" desire, excitement, power. Duras is seeking a border territory, margins in which it is possible to renegotiate the apparent opposites of a pre-oedipal, "feminine" space of freedom from linguistic and patriarchal constraints in "maternal waters" (similar to the space outside language posited by object-relations models of analysis) and an oedipal, ready-made, "masculine" language.

Toward the end of the novel, the ambiguities already present in the earlier portraits of the mother in *L'Amant* as punitive and yet, at some level, complicitous with her young daughter's transgressions of the law (her conversation with the Director of the Pensionnat Lyautey in which she explains her daughter's need to come and go as she pleases) are also given a new focus by the addition to the story of a meeting between lover and mother. The lover comes to the mother's house as envoy for his wealthy father who has been solicited by the older brother for compensation for his sister's "dishonor." He is initially indistinguishable from the Chinese creditors waiting for payment of Pierre's opium debts and perhaps represents a similar dishonor, a client come to pay for the daughter's favors.

The new dialogue between the mother and the Chinese man could be described as "scattershot," a term that Tom Bishop uses to talk about his own disconnected exchanges with Duras, punctuated by silence or repetition, and unconcerned with making clear immediate sense. It succeeds in establishing intimacy between the mother and the lover indirectly, using rhythm, break and repetition, through the shared interest in the young Marguerite and the mother's empathetic understanding of the lover's suffering. The subsequent new scene between mother and daughter also turns around the daughter's emotional involvement with the Chinese man and her probable future abandonment in favor of a traditional Chinese bride. The mother appears to have an intuitive understanding not only of the desire and empowerment inherent in the daughter's transgressions, freedom, and socially marginal status, but also of the daughter's fierce desire for the power (the money) to compensate her mother as defrauded and powerless woman. In this scene, then, it is together that the mother and the daughter ("Elles") took ("ont pris") the money that the too wealthy Chinese father had to offer in an act that reversed self-abasement to make it self-empowerment: "Avec la mère elles ont fait ça: elles ont pris: l'argent" [They did it: she and the mother: they took: the money].

Although Duras' own obsessive relationship with money is indeed "common knowledge," money/power is not modelled here as simply serving the economic circulation of commodities or as something one acquires or possesses. A metatextual or omniscient commentary claims that the North Chinese lover, too, had understood intuitively the true and double nature of the desire elicited by the diamond in the pivotal scene of seduction on the ferry crossing the Mekong: "Le Chinois avait su qu'elle avait voulu la bague pour la donner à la mère autant qu'elle avait voulu sa main sur son corps" [The Chinese man had known that she had wanted the ring to give it to her mother as much as she had wanted his hands on her body].

It would not have been possible for the daughter/narrator to have been present at a meeting between the lover and the mother. This could only have been imagined, or, at best, recounted second-hand. It seems improbable that these additions to the novel of childhood in Duras' mature years have their origin in any single scene lived more than fifty years earlier. They are in apparent contradiction with certain other earlier fictional portraits of the mother's law-enforcing codes and attitudes—scenes, for example, in which the child, suspected of sexual precociousness, is stripped, humiliated, and beaten by a suspicious, desperate mother egged on voyeuristically by the brutal older brother in order to "correct" (*"dresser"*) her daughter's sexual promiscuity and save her social reputation. By emphasizing the complicity between mother and lover in the first dialogue, or mother and daughter in the second, Duras may be rewriting one more time, and with a more positive resolution, the complex scars left by this other recursive scene of the mother's anger and despair, the daughter's physical humiliation, and the brother's sexual voyeurism.

The truth of the scenes of the mother's direct complicity in the daughter's affair and "prostitution" added in *L'Amant de la Chine du nord*, and the knowledge that these scenes invoke, derive less from a recovery of a factual past event than from its invention, in the present, where the body is, in a movement between past desire remembered in the present and desire created through the act of writing. Duras has said explicitly in a number of interviews that the mother could not have been told of, and could not have accepted, an affair between her adolescent daughter (fifteen and a half in *L'Amant*, fourteen in *L'Amant de la Chine du nord*) and a twenty-seven year old Chinese man. In the final lines of the interview with Bernard Pivot for the *Apostrophes* program televised after the appearance of *L'Amant*, Duras reiterates this claim that neither her mother nor her brother ever knew of the lover's existence:

> Bernard Pivot: "Est-ce qu'elle, elle avait honte de votre liaison avec le Chinois?"
>
> Marguerite Duras: "Elle ne la connaissait pas . . . ça aurait été pire encore si elle avait appris que sa fille couchait avec un Chinois, pire que le barrage . . . Elle ne l'a jamais su."
>
> [Bernard Pivot: "Was she ashamed of your affair with the Chinese man?" Marguerite Duras: "She didn't know about it. That would have been even worse if she had learned that her daughter was sleeping with a Chinese, worse than the sea-wall . . . She never knew."]

There is no reason to doubt the sincerity of this assertion, but it is contradicted in *L'Amant de la Chine du nord*. The truths of Duras' relationships always turn out to be more local, relational, multiple, contradictory, and shifting than any single or global statement can suggest. Perhaps this is because Duras' text has no power to say anything not known directly and locally, that is, through the body in the dialogic act of writing.

The scenes of reconciliation between mother, daughter, and lover do not eliminate the daughter's rage against the injustice of the mother's exclusive love for a "criminal" son. However, the fiction of a complicity on the part of the mother with a lover himself now identified more strongly with the maternally beloved "little" brother also changes the relations of power that existed in previous texts. In *L'Amant*, at the dinner he offers the young girl's family in an expensive restaurant, the rich Chinese lover is ignored, exploited, and humiliated. He is presented as weak and ineffectual before the older brother in this scene where the young Marguerite joins cruel ranks with her poor, but scornfully racist white family. The adolescent participates in the mother's fascination with the toughness of her farming brothers and the brute strength of the older brother against the weakness of the lover, although she does resist the brother's absolute tyranny. Annaud makes this ugly scene a central one in his film, pushing the family's vulgar disdain and the young girl's provocative bravado to burlesque lengths and inventing a subsequent scene of sexual violation in which the lover takes revenge for his public humiliation. In the version of the dinner and its nightclub sequel in *L'Amant de la Chine du nord*, on the contrary, the lover is tacitly accepted by the mother and the little brother. Pretending to be adept in Kung-Fu, he stands up to and defeats the bullying older brother. Indeed, a taller, more confident, less weak and fearful lover is prescribed by Duras to play the lead part of "her" film.

Although all the elements of potential abuse of power are put provocatively into play in this text in characteristic Durassian reversals—the nymphet, the older man, a diamond, inequality of power—the lover himself in *L'Amant de la Chine du nord* moves between positions of power and of weakness that are linked not only to virility or impotence, or to wealth and social situation, but also, and especially, to states of desire. The lover from North China is in the power of his father's law, in the power of the fear of death, and in the final instance, as much in the desperate power of money ("un désespéré de l'argent") as is Duras' mother, otherwise burdened with her son's gambling and opium debts, and her family's material survival. The lover is also, and most particularly, in the power of his exclusive, excessive passion for the under-age white girl.

Voluntarist attitudes in the De Beauvoir style, claims Marcelle Marini, are explicitly refused by Duras ("Je [ne] veux pas être déclarative" [I don't want to make statements]) (Duras and Gauthier) or undermined by other involuntary movements of the body. Truth and power for women, according to Duras, derive from desire: "On n'écrit pas au même endroit que les hommes. Et quand les femmes n'écrivent pas dans le lieu du désir, elles n'écrivent pas, elles sont dans le plagiat" (Porte, qtd. in Marini, *Territoire*) [We don't write from the same place as men. And when women don't write from the place of their desire, they do not write, they plagiarize]. Duras, says Marini, takes the figures that De Beauvoir's analysis lays bare—the man who exults in feeling sexually powerful and the woman who is affectively dependent and dispossessed— and explores their underside, their indecency. Her writing removes the taboo on the aggressive violence within us and permits investigation of dereliction, the horror of loss, suicidal crisis, desire to massacre those one loves, or to destroy

the sex desired in the body of the other ("L'autre corps"). These undersides reveal unexpected new relations of gender, close to an *entre-deux* or to what Julia Kristeva in *Powers of Horror* has called "abjection": an *entre-deux* that the lover comes to embody and that once again incorporates new relations of power/lack of power.

Madeleine Borgomano's readings of the novels of Duras could be extended to the autofictional stories of the power/powerlessness of the mother and of the power/lack of power of money to see the latter as also deriving from a passionate story of the painful and regressive desire for a male body that has disappeared ("le significant absent du corps masculin participe de ce vide central du texte durassien" [the absent signifier of the masculine body is part of this central void in the Durassian text]). In this reading, the fables of the loss of Duras' own child-lover-little brother would appear to be a traditional Freudian or Lacanian story of loss (of the Phallus).

> **Although all the elements of potential abuse of power are put provocatively into play in this text in characteristic Durassian reversals—the nymphet, the older man, a diamond, inequality of power—the lover himself in *L'Amant de la Chine du nord* moves between positions of power and of weakness that are linked not only to virility or impotence, or to wealth and social situation, but also, and especially, to states of desire.**
>
> *—Raylene Ramsay*

But, in *L'Amant de la Chine du nord*, the little brother's desired body, like the lover's, is feminized and sexualized. Paulo is also a (post-Renaissance) Christ-like figure, described as a martyr dying of despair and pain. The passionate, protective and possessive maternal love for Paulo ("C'est comme mon fiancé, Paulo, mon enfant, c'est le plus grand trésor pour moi" [29; He's like my fiancé, Paulo, my child, he's my greatest treasure]) is paralleled by a fierce rejection of the kind of cruel and tyrannical paternal power exerted by the older brother Pierre.

In *Un Barrage contre le Pacifique*, a single brother who exerts a strong fascination on the young girl concentrated aspects of the two brothers. It seems clear that Duras' rage against and refusal of the fascination of the older brother's power was less intense or less conscious at the time of the writing of *Un Barrage* than it had become almost forty years later. In *L'Amant de la Chine du nord* on the other hand, the daughter's fierce love for her victimized brother, first clearly evoked in *L'Amant,* has been pushed to its extreme limits and become explicitly incestuous.

What was telescoped into a single character in the fictional *Un Barrage* is polarized in the autobiographical *L'Amant* and its sequel, suggesting that the turbulent extreme states of love and hate, of rage and tears, may be "complementary." The poles of pain and pleasure, sadism and masochism, power and lack of power, love and hate are contradictory but not mutually exclusive and as troubling in the circulation of their distinctive features as the meaning of the accompanying tears that link the lover "taking" the little white girl and those of the little brother "taken" by the sister.

The verb "to take" is used to express the reciprocity of love in the incestuous relation with the younger brother: "C'avait été là qu'ils s'étaient pris pour la seule fois de leur vie" [It was there that they took each other the only time in their life] and the triangulation of passion in the desire to give Hélène to the lover: "Je voudrais beaucoup ça, que tu la prennes comme si je te la donnais" [I would like that a lot, for you to take her as if I were giving her to you]. The potential self-discovery in self-dispossession is implied in the scandalous being "taken" in the ditches along the roadways, or being "taken for another" by men who do not love her like the schoolgirl "prostitute," Alice. Duras exploits the contexts in which the verb to take ("prendre") recurs to create a network of significations that undermine the traditional semantic distinctive features (+ active + virile) of its active form ("to take") as well as its conventional binary relationship (active/passive) with the passive "taken." In the repetitions of the verb "to take," desire is made to circulate between the passivity and the sexual violence, the voyeurism and the exhibitionism, the control and the renunciation of control that lie at the paradoxical heart of the work of Duras. Again, conventional binary opposition is rewritten.

Similarly, the repetition of the verb "to look" is used to effect shifts between seeing and being seen, between being the subject or the object of the gaze. The two are telescoped into a non-contradictory interactive process in which relations of domination have been reconfigured but have not disappeared. On the ferry: "Il la regarde. Ils se regardent . . . Elle le regarde fort" [He looks at her. They look at each other . . . She looks hard at him]. In the Morris Léon Bollée, driving towards Saigon: "Lui, il regarde alors les signes de misère" [*He* looks at the signs of poverty, then]. Later, "Il la regarde très fort" [He looks very hard at her]. "Le Chinois la regarde: Tu pleures" [The Chinese man looks at her: You're crying].

The "child" accepts being the object of the gaze and the object of a seduction, but her own looking is also determinedly active. In the bedroom in Cholen, "Elle le regarde. Ce n'est pas lui qui la regarde. C'est elle qui le fait. Elle voit qu'il a peur" [She looks at him. It is not he who looks at her. She looks. She sees that he is afraid]. "C'est elle qui veut savoir . . . " [It is she who wants to know . . .]. The verbal repetitions may correspond to directions for the camera but these movements of oscillation and reversal are something more. Significantly, the Chinese fiancée who does not yet have the right to look at the lover plays no active part in the story. What does not permit circulation of power and powerlessness, taking and being taken, looking and being looked at, what is passive only, is rejected. In a footnote that describes the requirements for casting the protagonist of the film, beauty is excluded because: "La beauté ne fait rien. Elle ne regarde pas. Elle est regardée" [Beauty does nothing. It does not look. It is looked at]. At the end of the book in a similar and now characteristic conflating of opposites, of strength and weakness, the lover "avait pleuré. Très fort. Du plus fort de ses forces" [had cried. Very hard. With all his strength]. The breaking down of the conventional opposition between the intimate and the public, the movement that characterized *L'Amant,* is also continued here in the repetition of the "openness" of the room, the "exposure" of the lovers " . . . dans ce passage du dehors dans la chambre" [. . . in the passage from the outside into the bedroom].

It can be argued that the relative positions of the writer and the young girl she once was are involved similarly in a circulation of opposing elements. Duras' relation with her character/adolescent self is sometimes that of a fascinated or admiring mother gazing at "la petite" [the little one], sometimes that of empathetic regression to the child's state "je" [I]. The text moves between a polyphony of first persons, "Je" [I] the writer and "Je" [I] the child, and third persons, "elle" [she], "la petite" [the little one], "la petite blanche" [the little white girl], "la jeune fille" [the young girl], and "elle" [she], the writer. Other subject designations operate a circulation between characters and between narrator and character. The words used to designate Paulo by the sister, the mother, and the narrator, "le petit frère" [the little brother] or "l'enfant" [the child], are used to refer to the protagonist/child that the narrator once was, also described as "la petite" [the little one] or "l'enfant" [the child]. The fluidity of these movements breaks down the boundaries of a clear and distinctive, single, powerful self. Past unconscious desire or what Duras has called the "ombre interne" [inner shadow] surfaces in the poetic devices of the rhythmic, repetitive writin . At the same time, there is a narrative stance of present and artful (conscious) control over complex textual relations and intertextual reference.

The extreme masochistic thematics so troublingly present in Duras' earlier works recur in this re-writing of power. The fascination exerted by the *crime passionnel,* the fantasy of self-loss or dissolution of the self in the other and the text's own uncertainties and self-cancelings are all reinforced by the use of diminutives with shifting reference. In the drama of the opening of the body to the other/the outside in the scene of the "little one's" deflowering, the "taking," the "bleeding," and the "mind-numbing pain" are presented as a kind of ecstasy. Suffering transforms to pleasure and vice-versa in this place where one is lost (*"naufragé"*) and thought is defeated (*"terrassée"*), where the ecstasy of the flesh is also longing and despair ("ce désespoir du bonheur de la chair") perhaps because, to echo Duras, no love can take the place of Love. The words that weave the thread of a masochistic mysticism in this scene ("prendre," "naufragé," "terrassée") are repeated at other moments of *L'Amant de la Chine du nord* and in other Durassian texts.

The child is "emportée par le chauffeur à son amant. Livrée a lui" [carried off by the driver to her lover. Delivered over to him]. "Elle devient objet à lui, à lui seul, secrètement prostituèe ... Livrée comme chose, chose par lui seul, volée. Par lui seul prise, utilisée, pénétrée" [She becomes his object, his, his alone, secretly prostituted ... Delivered like a thing, his thing alone, robbed. Taken by him alone, used, penetrated]. Her identity becomes "celle de lui apartenir à lui, d'être à lui seul son bien, sans mot pour nommer ça, fondue à lui, diluée dans une généralité ... celle depuis le commencement des temps nommée à tort par un autre mot, celui d'indignité" [that of belonging to him, of being his thing only, with no word to name this, merged with him, diluted in a generality ... that named erroneously from the beginning of time by another word, indignity]. He "lovingly" insults her: "—Une petite Blanche de quatre sous trouvée dans la rue" [—A poor little White girl picked up in the street].

In this more recent text, however, there are small changes in the re-writing of the passionate relation with the lover and of the gender associations of the pairs of strength and weakness, outside and inside, domination and humiliation that go further than *L'Amant* in the modification of the traditional "feminine" connotations of weakness, inside, and humiliation.

She, in her turn, insults and degrades him in erotic play as an "espèce de petit Chinois de rien du tout, de petit criminel" [worthless little Chinese, little criminal]. Earlier, she had called him "un voyou" [a wastrel], the word that designated the older brother. The text comments on the inversions it employs: "C'est là, ç'avait été là, après ce fou rire-là, que s'était inversée l'histoire" [It's there, it was there, after that uncontrollable laughter, that the story had reversed]. She had taken the hand of the Chinese man, weak, unresisting, and naked, and looked at it before putting it aside: " ... ça s'infléchit vers les ongles, un peu comme si c'était cassé, atteint d'adorable infirmité, ça a la grâce de l'aile d'un oiseau mort ... Elle la regarde. Regarde la main nue ... La main, docile, laisse faire" [It curves in towards the nails, a little as if it were broken, af-

fected by an adorable infirmity, it has the grace of the wing of a dead bird ... She looks at it. Looks at the naked hand ... The hand is docile, does not resist]. In the bedroom, initially, the lover seems to control the scenario "avec une sorte de crainte comme si elle était fragile, et aussi avec une brutalité contenue" [with a kind of fear as if she were fragile and also with restrained brutality] but he is awed, overwhelmed by his "violation" and, as in *L'Amant,* the child also dominates the lover's abandoned, weak, and unresisting body: "Et c'est alors qu'elle le fait, elle. Les yeux fermés, elle le déshabille" [And it is then that *she* does it. With her eyes closed, she undresses him]. When the lover returns from the visit to the mother at Sadec, "Elle le savonne. Elle le douche. Il se laisse faire. Les roles se sont inversés" [She soaps him down. She showers him. He does not resist. The roles are reversed]. She protects him, maternally. He is her impotent "child" "without strength" who "fait ce qu'elle veut" [does what she wants], much as she has been "sa soeur de sang. Son enfant. Son amour" [his blood sister. His child. His beloved]. He is killed by her, martyred: "Mort du désir d'une enfant. Martyre" [Dead from desire for a child. A martyr] as she, too, becomes fascinated by the fear of martyrdom, "D'être tuée par *cet inconnu* du voyage à Long-Hai" [of being killed by *this stranger* of the Long-Hai journey]. As her departure and his marriage approach, his despair and erotic impulse towards death increase:"—il dit: Désespéré, fou, à se tuer" [—he says: Despairing, mad, to the point of suicide]. On the boat, the young girl closes her eyes to rediscover the smell of the silk suit, the skin, his captive look: "L'idée de l'odeur. Celle de la chambre. Celle de ses yeux captifs qui battaient sous ses baisers d'elle, l'enfant" [The idea of his smell. The smell of his bedroom. The idea of his captive eyes fluttering beneath her kisses, she, the child]. Her body is a center of power.

The thin child, almost without breasts, is "cruel". But, so, too, in this oscillating movement that is not an equilibrium, is the North Chinese lover. Unable to keep the child through fear of his father and weakness before the force of Chinese family law that would have him marry the sixteen-year-old Chinese girl betrothed to him in childhood to unite the family fortunes, he fantasizes the murder of the little white girl at Long-Hai, a place of primitive impulse and madness and of her cruel sacrifice in jealous love. In spite of her fear, the young girl shares, but asymmetrically, the fascination of this fantasmatical beach-site of loss of power, where the mad beggar-women and the dispossessed laugh at the same time as they cry.

In earlier work, I interpreted the recurring thematic of "feminine" self-loss and "masculine" violence and domination (ravishing) as the textual imaging of a sado-masochistic (master-slave) structure of the psyche that Jessica Benjamin, for example, sees as characterizing quintessentially the "bonds of love." The remembering of the incestuous nature of the fierce love for the little brother that was not present in

L'Amant might be emblematic of a struggle within the psyche against the superego and its burying ("enfouissement") of powerful impulses. While there is no substantive evidence of the real existence of a Chinese lover or of an incestuous relation with one brother, autofiction seeks the recovery of such desires from repression or from the kind of projection that seems to be at work, for example, in *Agatha* in the invention of the meeting between a brother and a sister and their indirect evocation of an earlier incestuous love. Lacan has claimed that Duras' poetic discourses unconsciously repeat his own psychoanalytic constructs ("Elle s'avère savoir sans moi ce que j'enseigne" [It turns out that she knows, without me, what I teach; qtd. in Marini). Yet Duras' re-writing of the non-dialectical, asymmetric, unpredictable structures of an intra- and inter-psychic sado-masochistic desire is surprisingly conscious. It seems to go beyond the fetish of the lost Phallus or, indeed, beyond even the primal Lacanian "mirror" stage or scene in which the jouissance of (self)recognition through the other is also (self)loss as anguished captive of the dislocated image of the other(self), loss accompanied by aggressive tension toward the other(self). And whereas Lacan takes for granted the primacy of the theoretical discourse, in Duras' text the conscious character of the structuring of the "I" as a fiction, the systematic breakdown and proliferation of traditional meaning, the silences and gaps that demonstrate loudly that conscious language is holed or flawed ("lacunaire") and allows the activity of the imagination to penetrate only in a veiled and incomprehensible form, infinitely repeated, alter traditional power relations between writing from the body and theory. These different kinds of discourse become "complementary" and similarly narcissistic. The logic of the unconscious, which, for Freud, ignores the dialectic of alternatives much as dream brings together opposites (the hunter is also the hunted) influences this Barthesian "mixing" of every language.

Duras' explicit, repetitive intratextual paradigms of sexual violence and masochism are troubling. But the conflating or telescoping of opposites to show their connections in a chaotic and dynamic non-dialectical structure changes conventional relations. Such a structure makes new sense out of the scenes of excess and contradiction that recall Lol who "devait délicieusement ressentir l'éviction souhaitée de sa personne" (*Le Ravissement*) [who must have experienced the desired eviction of her person with delight]. At the same time, the small changes in the gendering of the dominator and the dominated in the shifting relations of power between the little white girl and her Chinese lover have moved in the direction of an increased association of the "feminine" with active and enjoyed power.

My staging of the sado-masochistic thematics that mark the new autobiographies and, indeed, characterize postmodern texts in general suggests the lines of intersection of what Foucault sees as the two dominant views of the domain of sex: at once the place where the "ineluctability of the master" is established and the source of the most radical of all subversions. Power and resistance to power converge at this intersection. Foucault argues that the figure is dialectical, reducing power to a negative law of prohibition that is homogeneous at every level (the family and the state). It enables power never to be considered in other than negative terms, and the fundamental operation of power to be thought of erroneously as a speech act (enunciation of law, discourse of prohibition), while its origin is subjectivized and located in the sovereign.

The relations of domination, like resistance, in the new autobiographical texts, however, are multiform and largely interchangeable. The writer becomes the child and the child the writer in a telescoping of present and past, history and story, ignorance and rhetorical mastery as Duras claims to have rediscovered and relived the formative age of her own crossing of the Mekong River during the year she re-wrote this new autobiography. The portrait of the film's heroine is evidently a function of the writer's present images of herself and her "others" as well as a product of her previous works and of her personal past. The images of early childhood with the mother in Vinhlong give way to the crossing of the Mekong in which the child is both the heroine of the fictional autobiography *L'Amant* and aspects of the self-portrait that Duras chooses to elaborate in 1991.

But writing, as for Peter Morgan in *Le Vice-Consul,* is also an act of desire and an act of knowledge whose vehicle is empathy with pain and non-knowledge. "Peter Morgan est un jeune homme qui desire prendre la douleur de Calcutta, que ce soit fait, et que son ignorance cesse avec la douleur prise" [Peter Morgan is a young man who desires to take on the pain of Calcutta, who wants this to be done, and his ignorance to cease with the pain assumed]. The verb "prendre" here takes on the meanings of "apprendre," but taking and being taken, knowing and non-knowing, like power and powerlessness, are, once again, telescoped.

Such a concern with the nature of verisimilitude and truth as ready-made, originating in common knowledge and in texts (that is, as effect of power and mode of domination in Foucault's model or as entry into the Symbolic in Lacanian terms), has characterized both *nouveau roman* and new autobiography from their poststructuralist beginnings. The writer remembers her childhood: "Elle se souvient . . . Elle entend encore le bruit de la mer dans la chambre" [She remembers . . . She can still hear the sound of the sea in the bedroom]. Sensation, as in Sarraute or Robbe-Grillet, seems to provide some guarantee of truth. But the memory of the sound of the sea recalls, indistinguishably, her past writing of her childhood: "D'avoir écrit ça, elle se souvient aussi, comme le bruit de la rue chinoise. Elle se souvient même d'avoir écrit que la mer était présente ce jour-là dans la chambre des amants"

[Writing that, she remembers too, something like the sound of the Chinese street. She even remembers having written that the sea was present that day in the lovers' bedroom].

There is an author(ity) controlling and commenting metatextually on these slippages. The writer calls attention in footnotes to the intertextual origins of a number of scenes, for example, the "ghostly ball" ("bal exsangue") on the deck of the liner that had "already" appeared in *Emily L.,* now watched by the Chinese lover and the little white girl. She corrects the details of scenes from earlier texts—the rattle-trap family car, the B12, from *Un Barrage contre le Pacifique* was not in such bad condition, after all. Referring to herself in the third person, Duras, narrator, also plays critic for her reader, analyzing, for example, the nature of the dialogues while again pointing to their unnatural, factitious, but artful character that paradoxically re-creates naturalness: "L'auteur tient beaucoup à ces conversations 'chaotiques' mais d'un naturel retrouvé. On peut parler ici de couches de conversations juxtaposées" [The author attaches great importance to these "chaotic" conversations with their constructed natural-ness. You could say that they are layers of juxtaposed con-versations].

Memory, like writing, is the recapture of a past (body/text) but triggered by a present body and entrusted to a present text that frames and transforms it. Here again, the relations of power put into play in Duras' latest work in the movement between feeling and saying, life and text, go beyond any simple resistance to traditional narrative. There is at once a contesting and reversal of narrative conventions (mimesis is not life) and an affirmation of the writer's power for change (writing brings life to mind/text and alters it).

The relations of power that the thematics and the forms of Duras' text trace are analogous to "complementary relations" in particle physics (association of opposites, matter as both particle and wave) or certain models of the new sciences of complex systems mentioned at the beginning of this essay that incorporate a plurality of simultaneous, self-ordering physical processes. Equilibrium, predictability, and symme-try, like classical determinism, give way in these complex physical systems in far from equilibrium states to probabilis-tic processes, recursive and self-similar asymmetry, sponta-neous local activity, disordered order, and, more generally, to new "complementary" orders within disorder and random-ness. Within science, such new models represent change in traditional binarism and determinism. In writing, too, they suggest new kinds of sovereignty.

The fluctuating, local movements toward identification with the mother as intuitive and non-phallic and the imagining of the mother's empathetic, self-giving understanding of the power of her daughter's transgressive desires effect changes in intimate relations of familial and sexual power. So, too,

does the writing off, or writing out, of the self-assertive power and attraction of the older brother, the settling of accounts with brutal physical power in favor of the interaction with a feminized, beloved little brother identified increasingly with the lover. These shifts in the relations with the mother, brother(s), and lover, and with the child she once was, do suggest local and specific agency (the writer seeking present resolution of her own past [selves], the mind evoking the senses of the body's responses, in the present, to these fic-tional "memories"). I have argued that the to-and-fro move-ments and the gendering of relations of domination and submission both stage and begin to subvert relations of power. Like the "complementary" and "chaotic" forms that carry them, these changes are not always already there. Perhaps we are not always within power as Foucault would have it. What is filtered through the gaps in the text does take Duras fur-ther, beyond her ready-made "self." The forms of these modi-fications may indeed go beyond the already said to represent not only a staging of previously existing power (and gender) relations but also a rewriting of the conventions of traditional autobiography, science, and gender that is both the power of this writing and a re-writing of power.

Alberto Manguel (review date 27 January 1995)

SOURCE: "Deja Vu Again," in *The Times Literary Supple-ment,* No. 4791, January 27, 1995, p. 23.

[*In the following review, Manguel considers the autobio-graphical nature of* The North China Lover *and concludes that a clear, factual biography would aid the reader in inter-preting Duras' works.*]

Marguerite Duras's novel, *The North China Lover* (1991), can be read in at least two ways. Read in the order in which it was written—that is to say, after *The Lover*—it has the qual-ity of *déjà vu,* an extended annotation or correction of the original story. But read on its own, without reference to its best-selling precursor, *The North China Lover* unfolds as one of the most intense, controlled, quietly moving stories Duras has written.

L'Amant was published in France in 1984. It won the Prix Goncourt, was translated into a dozen languages and, a few years later, it was made into a slick, sunset-coloured film di-rected by Jean-Jacques Annaud. It was obvious to anyone who knew anything about Duras's own experience of film-making, that she would not approve of Annaud's interpreta-tion. At first, out of a sense of duty, or false hope, Duras collaborated with Annaud, supplying him with several scripts, none of which satisfied him. At length, she dissociated her-self from the production, explaining later that Annaud had mistakenly read *L'Amant* as an autobiographical memoir rather than a piece of literary fiction. Partly to show the kind of film she would have made instead, Duras wrote *L'Amant de la Chine du Nord*.

Not that Annaud should be blamed for confusing Duras's facts with Duras's fiction. Set in colonial Indo-China, where Duras was born in 1914, *L'Amant* tells the story of an affair between an adolescent French girl and a Chinese man—an affair Duras has always claimed as hers. The girl's passionate mother, her two brothers—one older and sadistic, the other younger and fragile—belonged also to Duras; "the small cast of my life" as she called them, returning to them in novel after novel and film after film. *L'Amant* began as a running commentary on a family photo-album. After *The Lover, The North China Lover* can be read as a commentary on that commentary.

Certainly Duras needed no excuse to rewrite the story. The film-marker who took the soundtrack from one film (*India Song*) and superimposed it on another, different film (*Son Nom de Venise dans Calcutta désert*) would have no qualms about going back to the same childhood territory of *The Sea Wall*, of *Whole Days in the Trees*, of *The Lover*, conjuring up the characters and having them act out their passions once again.

Read for its own sake, however (in Leigh Hafrey's precise translation), *The North China Lover* becomes an extraordinary love story that changes subtly in the telling, as it follows the vagaries of the author's memory. In her foreword to the novel, dated 1991, Duras says (but, in light of her complaint about Annaud, are we to believe her?) that she began writing *The North China Lover* after learning that the Chinese man of her adolescence had died, and she names him for the first time: "In the blinding light of the retelling, Thanh's face suddenly appeared." And she adds: "I became a novelist all over again", as if the death in real life had caused her to turn, once more, to fiction.

To constrain the uncertainty between imagination and memory, Duras has set up a number of instructions for the reader, so that the text becomes something between an annotated journal and an outline for a film-script. The most obvious device is that of using the author's eyes as a camera (hardly surprising in someone like Duras, for whom the passage from book to screen is so frequent), closing in on certain scenes, panning out over others, with notes that make clear the author's wishes if ever the novel is filmed. Duras is quite unabashed about her intentions. At the beginning of a scene in which the mother talks about the wicked elder brother, Duras intervenes at the foot of the page: "For a motive, we can choose. We can stay with the face of the mother as she talks. Or we can see the table and children as the mother *talks about them*. The author prefers the latter option." In spite of this device, the uncertainty remains and lends the story an

uneasy power. *The Lover* told a story with conviction; *The North China Lover* is far more hesitant in the telling, forcing the reader to make decisions, "compromising" them (the word is Duras's) in the text. "They may be sleeping", writes Duras of the girl and her lover. "We don't know." The reader has to guess.

Duras's public knows that, more than most writers, she has always claimed correspondences between the experiences of her past and present, and her books and films. For that reason, and to avoid a *faux pas* such as Annaud's, it might be useful to have a sensible, factual biography that would not interpret but simply clarify the inspiring events of her life. However, *Duras,* by Alain Vircondelet, Professor at the Institut Catholique in Paris, is little more than one long exclamation: "O vanity of biographies", he laments, "that claim to restore day after day the slow, furious groping of time, arrange days and nights of tumult and silence, organize events!" Vanity or not, this restoration of order is what is needed and what Vircondelet has largely failed to deliver. In its absence, we must rely on Duras's shifting memories, and be satisfied with their double allegiance to both fiction and fact.

Robert L. Mazzola (essay date Winter 1995)

SOURCE: "Emerging from the Shadows: Fratricidal Moves in Marguerite Duras' Early Fiction," in *Dalhousie French Studies*, Vol. 33, Winter, 1995, pp. 113-23.

[*In the following essay, Mazzola discusses the relationship between gender and familial roles in Duras's fiction.*]

Brothers form bridges and barriers between mothers and daughters in much of Marguerite Duras' fiction, especially in early novels such as *Les impudents* (1943), *La vie tranquille* (1944), and *Un barrage contre le Pacifique* (1950), all of which foreshadow the tragedy of the two brothers in *L'amant* (1984). Brother *figures,* in the guise of husbands and lovers, inform this bridge/barrier motif in these and other books (*récits, romans*) in which actual brothers are not alluded to directly (*Les petits chevaux de Tarquinia* [1953]). The allusion to familial ties—all important for Duras' cosmogony—borne by *men in general,* both absent (dead, missing or silent fathers) and present (secondary male characters such as the *caporal in Un barrage contre le Pacifique*), reinforces the bridging/barring procedure which culminates in *fratricide.* This term takes on special significances when applied to Duras and therefore requires clarification and definition before its implications for the mother-daughter relation investigated here can be fully actualized in a reading which sees the annihilation of the brother or brother figure as essential to the exploitation and redefinition of the whole maternal-filial bond.

The usual acceptation of fratricide—killing a brother—has already been repressed by the time later novels have undergone certain stylistic and content modifications through the *optique* of Duras' 1962 *L'apres-midi de Monsieur Andesmas* in which father-daughter relations are examined. The less literal but no less powerful symbolic meaning of fratricide—eliminating the brother-barrier by means of denial, assimilation or escape—is the alternative definition of this phenomenon that I intend to explore.

To facilitate this exploration, we can turn to the history of Sophocles' *Antigone* in which the *idea* of fratricide is exposed covertly in the character of Antigone herself. Her enterprise has traditionally been considered the antithesis of fratricide in that she works to honor and thus perpetuate, i.e., give *further life* to, her dead brother Polyneices, that vilified—principally by their uncle/great-uncle Creon—prince and brother of the honorably slain Eteocles. But it can be argued that by sprinkling dust upon his corpse in a rite that would propitiate the chthonic gods, she covers over and thereby reinforces a denial of Polyneices' status as brother, would-be ruler and man. His death is *her* opportunity for self-assertion. She speaks as a man might speak, defying both authority and propriety; she rejects the lover/husband brother substitute Haemon, whose very name suggests the blood-tie, tainted by her father's sin, which she must rupture in order to assert her new-found status as a *woman who speaks*. In so doing, she usurps the Polyneices role and alters the notion of the gender-specific speech act. Fratricide, the symbolic act, becomes a praxis that ultimately, at least, eschews actual killing and manages concomitantly to remain compatible with real sibling love. This paradox arises in the Antigone story as well as in Duras' treatment of women who in the formative stage of girlhood learn to speak in a way new for them. They capitulate less to the dead father who often speaks through the mother, the brother, or a substitute (e.g., an uncle). Jocasta is, of course, the prototypical conduit for the absent father's speech.

Paradoxically, Jocasta is both this conduit for the mythologizing speech of the absent male and the one who cuts it short, thus obviating its paternal content. The Durassian mother figure is a Jocasta stand-in, performing rites of silence (hiding certain truths from the child), of expiation (blood-letting as sacrificial atonement), and of murder (suicide, either by act or omission as in the case of the mother in *Un barrage contre le Pacifique*). In that text, a mother accomplishes her own death not through an overt act but by omitting those possible speech components which, if uttered, might free her children from the unviable myth of the barrier she has attempted, successfully and *un*successfully, to construct. So that, while she is a would-be builder (of the seawall doomed to failure), she

is also a destroyer of possibilities that her son and daughter might have actualized if they had been given the knowledge with which to begin constructing their own separate existences. Where she succeeds, she destroys: in her son Joseph, she helps to create an individual (a brother whose parentage in Duras' fiction we will shortly begin to trace) in whom the act of separation and autonomous existence leads from silence to rebellion (with and without words) and, finally, to the despair of guilt at the mother's death. As the novel ends, no new identity has been forged for either Joseph or Suzanne. They depart without leaving behind them those destructive elements which later in Duras' work will lead to the asylum (*Détruire, dit-elle*). Their "escape" is as illusory as the prospect of holding back the rising ocean with logs held together by ties that tiny crabs can gnaw.

Antigone's own "escape" is effected through death (suicide) thus echoing her mother's fate. What about Duras' heroines? Can they be said to repeat a maternal pattern? Is that pattern conditioned, wholly or in large part, by the triangular mother-brother-daughter (sister) relation? Bearing these questions in mind, it is possible to weave into this pattern the fratricidal *moves*—denial, assimilation, escape—which drive the Durassian woman.

My thesis here—that what "drives" the woman Duras creates derives reactively from the dynamic which the triangular relation(s) set(s) up—necessitates a tracing of the influence exerted on that woman by her brothers. In *Les impudents* Maud's older brother Jacques stands in for the dead father. He is twenty years her senior, and his presence throughout the novel is patriarchal and shadowy as such presences without depth (usually male presences) often are in Duras' fiction. Duras' Deleddian ruralness and primitive social patterning in this early work serve to isolate the young (twenty-year-old) heroine, thus adding further menace to the shadow cast by the present/absent father figure transformed into a brother who, typically for Duras, is troubled and troubling. The younger brother, Henri, is portrayed as weak and ineffectual (perhaps retarded) as all *petits freres* are in Duras (cf. *L'amant*).

This 1943 text sets the stage for, and initiates, the fratricidal trace ultimately sustained through (now) fifty years of a saga without resolution, without emergence from Duras' *selva oscura* in which the *three beasts of resistance* are internalized as moves toward sublimated murder. This interior praxis (to the extent that this obvious contradiction can bear the weight of guilt which is inevitably imposed when sibling love and sibling rivalry lead to the much discussed Durassian "violence") produces the confrontation at the edge of shadowy forests and remote locales that mark Duras' mental and emotional landscape from this "war novel" to *Détruire, dit-elle* and beyond. The three impositions which test the mettle of the lost soul still seeking salvation, coincide with the denial (this can't be happening), the assimilation (by becoming like the *he* I continue the first move and perpetuate the denial), the escape (mental and emotional, rather than actual, i.e., external, as I have already asserted). At the end of ***Les impudents*** Maud and Mme Taneran, her mother, come close to a level of "violence" which will mark all future mother-daughter relations in Duras' *Æuvre*. Any confrontation between mother and daughter is mediately traceable to the older brother who combines the twin warring aspects of the dyad formed by his precursor, Eteocles-Polyneices. A sometime hatred brings the mother's rapport with her daughter dangerously close to shattering, once the formula which runs that relation touches, as it always must, upon the irrational defense posture the mother assumes vis-a-vis the son. The daughter's "violent" reaction in Maud's case is the creation of an imaginary "death-of-the-(br)other" and the death mask that accompanies and covers over such unacceptable fantasizing. Jacques must "die" if Maud will live, and mother must hate the daughter who imposes such an unresolvable choice. This existentialist moment conditions every daughter-mother relationship in Duras' work and moves to deconstruct Sartrean choice at its most apparently vulnerable point: the question of *viability of choice.*

Maud and her mother "s'étaient évitées à cause de Jacques et d'Henri". Avoidance and inevitability set the scene for the imaginary escape that caps the thwarted denial and assimilation which Maud has attempted. The two sons (wittingly and unwittingly) contrive to separate, dissociate, her from the mother. As always, the mother defends, this time the younger brother as "le plus gentil de vous trois". Once Duras makes it clear that no choice worth the name 'viable' can come of this confrontation, Maud "escapes" through the fantasy of the death scenario. This immediately recalls the same, nearly exact, scene recounted at the end of *L'amant*, where the burial of the mother with the older brother becomes a memory for the protagonist, obfuscated consciously or unconsciously through the loss of definition (as in photographic definition) wrought by the intervening years and events between Cochin China and Paris.

A few pages before the confrontation which so sharply divides mother and daughter, the imagination of death takes over and Jacques' face, transfigured by several levels of crime, becomes submissible to an act of coverage that denial alone could not make accessible to Maud in her quest for self-definition. It becomes for her "[u]n visage défiguré,"

> [u]n visage faiblement balancé au-dessus de la vraie tristesse et qui pour la première fois rappellerait celui de son enfance, son enfance enfin surgie et éblouie par la mort toute proche. De ce visage volerait en éclats toute la vanité si vivante, la sempiternelle complainte du plaisir, la très belle laideur.

It is fortuitous that this late chapter exhibits through the use of a telling oxymoron the driving motive of Duras' fiction, especially in these early texts. The same altered pleasure principle which comes to such full fruition in *L'amant* juxtaposes the beauty of the moment with the ultimate and ulterior betrayal of that beauty in death. Death either stands as that corruption of an eternal ideal, or it is incorporated into the ideal, literally made part of its body. The oxymoronic relation between Antigone and the brother resolves the conflict that ends in so much death by denying death its sting. If the gods of the Underworld whom Antigone says she wishes to propitiate become participants in her act of self-assertion, then finality as a concept is brought into question and recourse to the eternal and its seat of justice brings about the displacement of Creon's earthly sway. The separation motif alluded to in ***Les impudents*** is vital to the enactment of this displacement since the mother will not (cannot?) allow herself to be separated *off* from the image of the son. The separation, therefore, comes about between the true combatants, mother and daughter, and alienation and despair are the result:

> C'est parce qu'elle [Mme Taneran] croyait en son fils qu'elle vivait dans un songe inaccessible à aucun démenti de la réalité.
>
> À certains moments elle haïssait Maud. Avec brutalité, cette enfant défigurait l'objet de son amour. Et que lui resterait-il en face de cette seule souffrance sans fraîcheur de sa foi?

A year after the publication of ***Les impudents***, Duras dedicates her second novel of her mother: the combat toward an unattainable resolution of maternal-filial conflict continues. She had dedicated ***Les impudents*** to "mon frère Jacques D. que je n'ai pas connu," and the order of her dedication in fiction does in fact take her from the brother toward, not *to,* the mother whose presence is as inexplicable as a father's "absence." Death explains nothing, and especially so to a child. The irony of that second title, ***La vie tranquille***, serves to place in a now sharper relief than was true in the earlier text the immanent "violence" the author nurtures within that absence. As the mother rejected anyone who attempted to dispel the illusion she had built up around a recalcitrant son who had usurped all but one of the father-husband's privileges, so the daughter finds herself in a web of self-deception which she must help to weave in order to compete with the object of that maternal illusion.

La vie tranquille illustrates the impossibility of this competition and at the same time its magnetic lure. Françou Veyrenattes, whose uncle Jérôme dies at the beginning of the novel, extends Maud as a stronger Antigone figure and adds to the formula the element of guilt (a component of underestimated importance in Duras' *douleur,* variously rendered as 'sorrow,' 'grief,' 'despair'). The life of les Bugues, another

Deleddian primitive rural location in northwestern France, is contrasted with the coastal town of T. to which Françou "escapes" in part two of the book. The shadowy brother, Nicholas, has now been consigned to the shadow realm of death; he is *already* Polyneices as the story of guilt unfolds (Jérôme may have died as a result of an episode in which his niece played a part). The life she tries to escape is, in reality, *une vie tourbillonnée* ("désordre, ennui, désordre") and the respite on the Atlantic coast represents the only tranquil part of the text.

Françou's lover Tiène becomes her safe harbor and in him she manufactures a tranquility to offset the boredom and disorder, a sort of quotidian chaos, that envelops all rural life in Duras' writing. As a more pronounced Antigone figure than Maud, she takes risks (leaving home *and* returning) and attempts to "bury" the brother, to lay his ghost. While he lives to speak, her mouth is mute, and so she fantasizes a state of mind in which she is *unbrothered*: "il évitait de me regarder . . . et c'est pourquoi, très loin, au delà de ma joie, je me sentais un corps triste, sans frère". Her body is sad because even the consolation of a lover cannot replace the lost brother (he has become more involved with Luce Barragues, the mother of his child). Yet his absence is necessary to Françou's ability to extricate herself from the morass represented by les Bugues. Here the mother and father hover but remain ineffective. The father says and does little, while the mother is cast in the most Jocasta-like role of any Durassian mother. Her brother has been killed (seemingly unintentionally) by her son, thus enacting the violent solution (death of a tyrant) which Sophocles eschews in *Antigone*. Françou as a heightened Antigone has prompted the brother's actions rather than followed and apologized for them as did the prototype of the woman in search of her own voice.

If Polyneices had been victorious against Thebes, would not Creon have fallen as did Eteocles? Such speculation serves the argument that places Antigone and the Durassian woman at the antipode to the traditionally acceptable heroine whose voice serves, outside of comedy, of course, only to reinforce that of her father, brother, uncle or husband (sometimes that of a son-husband).

The fraternal link in the early and later fiction of Marguerite Duras does more than oppose than link's bridging function to its status as a barrier that the sister must surmount. Somehow, and in ways I have suggested here, the author conveys the interrelatedness of these two vital aspects of the relation without apparently submerging one in the other. When the mother in *L'amant* beats her daughter in the presence of the sons/brothers, she reinforces both functions which her role as mother has created. Maud, Françou and Suzanne forge a *resistance* to the filial illusion on which the mother feeds but fails to thrive, so long as the bridge that the mother made possible by birth and nurture holds son and daughter to her

via the son's adopted paternal authority in the mother's household. That is the two-span bridge.

The barrier that the bridge as procedure necessarily implies in Duras prevents significant movement on the part of both mother and daughter. They can move only by way of the bridge-link the one has forged and the other has been forced to maintain under her mother's careful (and often care*less*) supervision.

To the extent that this arrangement fails to move the novels' characters, making change viable and letting past be past, the fiction itself may be seen to fail in convincing us that an endless memoir, confession or expiation is ever able to do more than suggest the inevitability of stagnation once the past *becomes* the future, and not just any future but the *only* future. It is at this point that the notion of a bloodless fratricide as three-pronged approach to salvaging some part of the past in order to create a new future emerges from the shadowland of Antigone's walled-up grotto. The Durassian *W*oman is also, and this is her strength, a *w*oman: not a virtue incarnate, but rather an individual seeking an individual's voice to help stave off madness and emerge from the shadowy forests of the mind. Ultimately in these and other, later texts, we do not sense a failure in the writing, in the expression. The *douleur* of creativity, the despair without sadness, the flight *into* and then *out of* the mind's shadows form the essential Durassian enterprise at the center of which is a woman.

Perhaps no other female character epitomizes this ambiguity of purpose, this ill-defined search, better than the *mendiante* of *Le vice-consul* and *India Song*. Attempting to de-fine her, Duras brings us back to our earlier question: Is there a pattern that unites and identifies the Durassian woman? Is it repeatable? *Le vice-consul*, which Duras describes as "le travail le plus difficile de ma vie" (*Écrire*), may hold the answer, with its depiction of this peripatetic woman who has been forced by circumstance to abandon her daughter:

> Elle reste une dizaine de jours dans la cour d'un poste sanitaire, nourrie, mais elle se sauve encore, après le pied finira par guérir, il y aura un mieux-être. Après c'est la forêt. La folie dans la forêt. C'est toujours près des villages qu'elle dort. Mais parfois il n'y en a pas, alors c'est dans une carrière ou au pied d'un arbre. Elle rêve: elle est son enfant morte, buffle de la rizière, parfois elle est rizière, forêt, elle qui reste des nuits dans l'eau mortelle du Gange sans mourir, plus tard, elle rêve qu'elle est morte à son tour, noyée.

The woman who becomes her own child and dreams of joining that other self in a death by water that mimes a return to the womb, recalls the fates of Maud, Françou and Suzanne, and calls ahead to Valérie Andesmas and the 'girl' of *L'amant*. Because the family center will not hold, that family turns out the pregnant girl who then becomes the beggar woman of *Le vice-consul*. While that text does not deal with the mother or brothers in any developed way, the parallel between one kind of familial abandonment and another is clear. What continues to bind the beggar to her lost child is precisely the bridge as barrier that will always link her to lost family while distancing her from them. And for Duras this beggar *must* be a woman. She *bears* the child she *is*. The pattern is that very ontological acknowledgement, that simple yet complex weave that forms the paradox of life. Through *immersion* in it one lives but risks madness; by *emerging* from it one sees clearly and courts death.

Killing, in actuality or figuratively, combines the moves utilized by the women of Duras' early novels in dealing with the intractabilty of this human paradox epitomized as man (absent father, present brother) and by the other woman (now viewable as the other self) represented by the Durassian mother. Through thought and dream, this child-woman first denies that the paradox truly is one (Françou's "hope"), then she assimilates the other, becomes like him, seeks him incestuously in other men (Françou with Tiène, Suzanne with Monsieur Jo but ultimately back with Joseph, Maud with Jean and Georges, stand-ins for Jacques). Finally, an escape of one kind or another is attempted but fails. To escape the other the heroine must "kill him off." It will take the revelation of those "autobiographical" insights to which we are made privy in *L'amant* to effect a true departure, a killing-off of the past, flight to France and to the art of writing. But the fratricide is, of course, never complete. The writing resurrects and reenacts it with the genesis of each new text.

Alan Riding (obituary date 4 March 1996)

SOURCE: "Marguerite Duras, 81, Author Who Explored Love and Sex," in *The New York Times,* March 4, 1996, p. C10.

[*In the following excerpt, Riding remarks on Duras's life and literature.*]

Marguerite Duras, author of the best-selling novel *The Lover* and one of the most widely read French writers of the postwar era, died today at her home in Paris. She was 81.

Miss Duras, who was also a prolific playwright, film maker and screenwriter, was best known for the way she used her early life in French Indochina as the inspiration for many of her works, including *The Lover*, the story of her clandestine teen-age romance with a wealthy young Chinese man. . . .

[H]er plays continue to be performed regularly in France.

However, despite the enormous success of her screenplay for Alain Resnais's 1960 classic, **"Hiroshima, Mon Amour,"** few of the 19 movies she wrote and directed herself did well, not least because words often entirely replaced action. Until her 70th birthday, her novels had a loyal albeit small readership. With the publication of *The Lover* in 1984, however, Miss Duras reached a mass audience in France and abroad. The book sold more than two million copies and was made into a well-received film in 1992 by Jean-Jacques Annaud.

Because she considered her words to be sacrosanct, she often had stormy dealings with movie directors who adapted her novels, among them Peter Brook, Tony Richardson and Jules Dassin. And when Mr. Annaud altered her screenplay for *The Lover*, Miss Duras broke with him and turned her text into yet another semi-autobiographical novel, *The Lover From Northern China.* She described that book, published in 1991, as a "reappropriation" of *The Lover,* yet once again she seemed to be reinventing her life to a point where it became impossible to know whether her original novel, Mr. Annaud's film or her second version of the story was the closest to reality. To Miss Duras, of course, this did not matter.

She was born on April 4, 1914, in Gia Dinh, near Saigon. Her parents, Henri and Marie Donnadieu (she changed her name to Duras in the 1930's), were teachers in France's colonial service. She was only a child when her father died, and her first memories were of economic hardship, above all after her mother invested the family's savings in a disastrous rice-farming venture.

After attending school in Saigon, Miss Duras moved to France at the age of 18 to study law and political science. After graduation, she worked as a secretary in the French Ministry of the Colonies until 1941, but by then Nazi Germany had occupied France. In 1943, she joined the Resistance in a small group that included Françoïs Mitterrand, who remained a friend until his recent death.

In 1939, Miss Duras married the writer Robert Antelme, who was arrested and deported to Germany during the war. By the time he returned from Dachau concentration camp in 1945 (he was the subject of her 1985 book *La Douleur,* later published in the United States as *The War*), she was already involved with Dionys Mascolo, who was to become her second husband and with whom she had a son, Jean.

In the late 1940's, Miss Duras joined the French Communist Party, and though she later resigned, she always described herself a Marxist. Yet perhaps her strongest political stance was her contempt for Gen. Charles de Gaulle. . . .

Her first book, *Les Impudents*, was published in 1943, and from that time, she lived off her writing, gradually building a body of work that included more than 70 novels, plays, screenplays and adaptations. She eventually acquired a country home in Normandy, but her book-lined Left Bank apartment on the Rue St.-Benoit remained her Paris home from 1942 until her death.

For many years, she struggled with alcoholism—a subject she frequently addressed in her writings—and her health was further shattered by emphysema. But in the 1980's, long separated from Mr. Mascolo, she also found love again in an unusual relationship with a young homosexual writer, Yann Andrea Steiner, with whom she shared her final years.

Late last year, struggling again with illness, Miss Duras published *That's All,* a tiny 54-page book that seemed intended to be her literary adieu to her readers, to Mr. Steiner and to herself. Written between November 1994 and last August, with each occasional entry carrying a date, it consisted of poetic bursts of love, fear and despair, as if all too aware that her death was near.

The very last entry, on the afternoon of Aug. 1, 1995, read:

"I think it is all over. That my life is finished.

"I am no longer anything.

"I have become an appalling sight.

"I am falling apart.

"Come quickly.

"I no longer have a mouth, no longer a face."

She is survived by her son and Mr. Steiner.

FURTHER READING

Criticism

"Writer's Life Inspired Novels, Films." *The Globe and Mail* (4 March 1996): C1.
> Summarizes Duras's life and her contribution to modern literature.

Goodman, Richard. A review of *Summer Rain,* by Marguerite Duras. *New York Times Book Review* (14 June 1992): 20.
> Reviews *Summer Rain* and compares Duras unfavorably to Samuel Beckett.

Harris, Michael. A review of *Summer Rain,* by Marguerite Duras. *Los Angeles Times Book Review* (14 June 1992): 6.
> Comments on Duras's sparse writing style, which he finds very effective.

Hirsch, Marianne. "Inside Stories." *Women's Review of Books* VIII, No. 1 (October 1990): 19-20.
> Argues that *Practicalities* and *Emily L.* deliver a feminist message and contends that the personal and political are interconnected in Duras' writing.

Marcus, James. "Between Herself and Herself." *New York Times Book Review* (20 May 1990): 30.
> Reviews *Practicalities* and argues that the same disjointed autobiographical renderings which make her fiction powerful are distracting in this nonfiction work.

Soloman, Charles. A review of *The Man Sitting in the Corridor,* by Marguerite Duras. *Los Angeles Times Book Review* (12 January 1992): 10.
> Argues that *The Man Sitting in the Corridor* is fragmentary and too short to appear outside an anthology.

Wilmington, Michael. "Duras Series Reveals Filmmaker's Voice." *Chicago Tribune* (15 September 1995).
> Reviews Duras's work as a filmmaker.

Additional coverage of Duras's life and career is contained in the following sources published by Gale Research: *Contemporary Authors,* Vols. 25-28R, 151; *Contemporary Authors New Revision Series,* Vol. 50; *Dictionary of Literary Biography,* Vol. 83; and *Major Twentieth Century Writers.*

Odysseus Elytis
1911-1996

(Also transliterated as Odysseas; born Odysseus Alepoudelis)
Greek poet, essayist, graphic artist, translator, and critic.

The following entry provides an overview of Elytis's career.
For further information on his life and works, see *CLC*, Volumes 15 and 49.

INTRODUCTION

A Nobel laureate, Elytis gained international acclaim for his
poetry, which combines elements of surrealism, eroticism,
and lyricism. His poems attempt to define the Greek identity
and, more universally, to help man cope with the dualism of
life. The sun is a central symbol in his work; he often referred
to himself as a "solar metaphysician."

Biographical Information

Elytis was born in Iraklion, Crete, to a wealthy industrialist
and his wife. In 1914 his family moved to Athens, where he
attended primary and secondary schools and briefly attended
the University of Athens School of Law. Elytis spent his summer vacations on the Aegean Islands, and the landscape and
imagery of the islands infuses his poetry. The free association of surrealism, especially the French Surrealism of such
artists as Paul Eluard, was also a major influence on his art
and his poetry. After leaving law school in 1935, Elytis displayed several visual collages at the First International Surrealist Exhibition in Athens. At this time he also began
publishing poems in various Greek periodicals under the name
Odysseus Elytis. "Elytis" is a combination of the Greek words
for Greece, hope, freedom, and Eleni (a figure in Greek mythology representing beauty and sensuality), which are all
elements in his poetry. He chose not to publish under the
name of Alepoudelis to avoid associations with his family's
popular soap-manufacturing business. Elytis was hailed as a
poet of the avant-garde and was part of the generation of the
thirties including other important Greek writers such as
George Seferis and Yannis Ritsos. He served on the Albanian front during the World War II as a second lieutenant in
Greece's First Army Corps, an experience which became the
basis for *Azma iroiko ke penthimo yia ton hameno
anthipologhaghotis Alvanias* (1945; *Heroic and Elegiac Song
for the Lost Second Lieutenant of Albania*). From 1948 to
1953, Elytis lived in Paris, where he studied at the Sorbonne
and wrote articles in French for *Verve* magazine. After returning to Greece, Elytis wrote his famous *To Axion Esti*
(1959; *The Axion Esti*), which won Greece's First National
Award for Poetry. Elytis won the Nobel Prize in 1979, which

garnered him international attention. Elytis never married
because he claimed his poetry would suffer, and for the same
reason he did not change his lifestyle upon winning the Nobel
Prize with its accompanying $190,000 award, instead con-
tinuing to live in a small apartment in Athens. Elytis died on
March 18, 1996, at the age of 84.

Major Works

Aspects of surrealism and the landscape of the Aegean Islands dominate Elytis's poetry. Sensual imagery and Eros in
its physical and spiritual sense fill his earlier work such as
Prosanatolizmi (1939; *Orientations*) and *Ilios protos* (1943;
Sun the First). Darker themes of death, age, and mortality
crept into Elytis's poetry after he served in World War II. His
*Heroic and Elegiac Song for the Lost Second Lieutenant of
Albania* centers on the death of a young Greek soldier whose
transfiguration and resurrection serves as an affirmation of
justice and liberty. The work advances Elytis's concerns with
the merging of physical and spiritual existence and celebrates
the defense of freedom and victory over oppression. Considered one of the poet's greatest works, *To Axion Esti* has been

called Elytis's "spiritual autobiography." The collection borrows much of its symbolism from the Greek Orthodox Church, along with folk tradition and other elements which Elytis fused to create his own version of Greek tradition. While it identifies the defeat and alienation of Greece after World War II, it also affirms the regenerative power of living in the present. In *Exi ke mia tipsis yia ton ourano* (1960; *Six and One Remorses for the Sky*) Elytis furthers his effort to reconcile elements of the dualism of human existence. Both *Thanatos ke Anastasis tou Konstandinou Paleologhou* (1971; *Death and Resurrection of Konstandinos Paleologhos*) and *To Fotodhendro Ke i Dhekati Tetarti Omorfia* (1971; *The Light Tree and the Fourteenth Beauty*) center on the triumph of hope over despair, the union of spirit and flesh, and the richness of Greek culture and tradition. While most of Elytis's poems are inspired by real life, they do not transcribe actual events. A real woman Elytis met inspired *Maria Nefeli* (1979; *Maria Nephele*), who represents a departure from his typical female character. Maria is a modern, urban woman who is fighting for recognition, not protection. The setting is the polluted city instead of the open country of purity and fresh air usually at the center of Elytis's work. The dialogue between Maria and the poetic persona illuminates Elytis's preoccupation with humanity's ability to attain harmony amid the chaos of the modern world. By the time Elytis wrote *Ta elegia tis Oxopetras* (1991; *The Elegies of Jutting Rock*), the darker images became a stronger element in his poetry. Death becomes just another step in the journey instead of something to overcome. However, there is acceptance on the part of the poet rather than defeat or despair.

Critical Reception

Elytis did not receive international attention for his work until the publication of *The Axion Esti*. Critics praised his formidable technical skill and his merging of the demotic and classical aspects of the Greek language. Reviewers lauded his lyricism, musicality, and imagery. Much of the criticism of Elytis's work centers on the skill of his translators. The dense linguistic structure of Elytis's poetry makes it difficult to translate, and critics faulted many who have tried for losing the lyricism of his work.

PRINCIPAL WORKS

Prosanatolismi [*Orientations*] (poetry) 1940

Ilios o protos [*Sun the First*] (poetry) 1943

Azma iroiko ke penthimo yia ton hameno anthipologhagho tis Alvanias [*Heroic and Elegiac Song for the Lost Second Lieutenant of Albania*] (poetry) 1945

To Axion Esti [*The Axion Esti*] (poetry) 1959

Exi kai mia tipsis yia ton ourano [*Six and One Remorses for the Sky*] (poetry) 1960

To Fotodhendro Ke i Dhekati Tetarti Omorfia [*The Light Tree and the Fourteenth Beauty*] (poetry) 1971

O ilios o iliatorus [*The Sovereign Sun: Selected Poems*] (poetry) 1971

Thanatos ke Anastasis tou Konstandinou Paleologhou [*Death and Resurrection of Konstandinos Paleologhos*] (poetry) 1971

The Monogram (poetry) 1972

Ta Ro tou Erota (poetry) 1972

O Fillomandis [*The Leaf Diviner*] (poetry) 1973

Anihta Hartia [*Open Papers*] (essays) 1974

Ta eterothale (poetry) 1974

Sappho—Anasinthesi ke apodosi [translator] (poetry) 1976

Simatologion [*The Siblings*] (poetry) 1977

Maria Nefeli: Shiniko Puma [*Maria Nephele: A Poem in Two Voices*] (poetry) 1978

Tria poiemata me simea efkerias [*Three Poems under a Flag of Convenience*] (poetry) 1982

To imerologio enos atheatou Aprilou [*Diary of an Invisible April*] (poetry) 1984

O mikros naftilos [*The Little Mariner*] (poetry) 1986

What I Love: Selected Poems of Odysseas Elytis, 1939-1978 (poetry) 1986

Ta Demosia ke ta Idiotika (essays) 1990

Idiotiki Odos (essays) 1991

Ta elegia tis Oxopetras [*The Elegies of Jutting Rock*] (poetry) 1991

CRITICISM

Peter Green (review date 26 June 1980)

SOURCE: "The Poets' Greece," in *The New York Review of Books,* Vol. XXVII, No. 11, June 26, 1980, pp. 40-4.

[*In the following excerpt, Green traces Elytis's relationship to the tradition of Greek poetry.*]

When the Swedish Academy announced its choice for the Nobel Prize in literature last year, the general reaction was one of bewilderment. Who on earth, people asked, was Odysseus Elytis? Some students of the international literary scene ("irritated," as a friend wrote me, "at the selection of a man who hadn't been published by Penguin") hinted that the Academy's recent habit of honoring elderly obscure poets such as Vicente Aleixandre or Harry Martinson was rapidly becoming an affectation. This is unfair to Elytis, a poet of large achievement; but it does pinpoint, with some force, the problems involved in getting Greek poetry across to a Western audience. An unfamiliar alphabet and language are only the first hurdles to be overcome. Behind them lie an attitude to life and a cultural tradition that are at odds with the Anglo-American literary scene.

Poetry in Greece remains a natural part of popular life in a way that has long ceased to be true in the West. The editors of *Twenty Contemporary Greek Poets* claim that, on average, Greece sees two new volumes of poetry published daily, and from my own experience I would think their estimate no exaggeration. A spate of literary periodicals, some shorter-lived than others and with names like *Tram* and *Parallax,* provides a regular forum for young writers. What is more, they sell. One of the best-known and most popular recent Greek songs was a setting of a short lyric by George Seféris—another Nobel Prize winner, Greece's second in only thirteen years.

Nor is this efflorescence exclusively urban or intellectual. Today, despite the destructive inroads made on local culture and dialects by the transistor radio and, latterly, television (still, luckily, hard to beam to some of the more remote islands and mountain fastnesses), Greece preserves, to a surprising degree, her tradition of oral poetry. In Crete, peasants continue to learn by heart long sections (sometimes all) of the 10,000-odd lines of Kornaros's seventeenth-century epic, the *Erotókritos,* and couplets from it are printed on the back of the tear-off sheets of the little religious calendars that hang in almost every Greek home. Memory is reinforced by spontaneous composition: this is especially true of the ritual lament for the dead, the *moirológhi,* which has its roots deep in antiquity, and still flourishes in certain rural areas, above all the Deep Mani of the southern Peloponnese, where Patrick Leigh Fermor recorded a *moirológhi* composed for an English airman shot down at Limeni during World War II.

Greek poetry stands in a curious and ambivalent relationship to the literary traditions of the West: at once their ancient fountainhead and, more recently, an odd tributary that, ever since the Greek War of Independence (1821-1830), has been moving uneasily back toward the main cultural tradition. On the one hand, Greek poetry offers the virtually unique phenomenon of a language and a poetic tradition that have evolved, unbroken, over three millennia. (To grasp this one need only leaf through a comprehensive anthology such as the bilingual *Penguin Book of Greek Verse,* which starts with the *Iliad* and ends with the early surrealist verse of Odysseus Elytis.) On the other, the impact, first of Byzantium, and then of the long Turkish occupation, effectively cut Greece off from the Renaissance, with all the impoverishment of language, parochialism, and subjugation that that implies. What other Western country, as Kimon Friar rightly asks, has retained so clear an identity and integrity under such crushing odds?

This isolation brought, nevertheless, certain unpredictable advantages. It threw the Greeks back on their own idiosyncratic resources, sharpened imagination, bred suspicion of fashionable trends. Elytis, himself an accomplished painter and art critic as well as a poet, was one of the first to point out

how, in the visual arts, Greece, unconscious of experiments in chiaroscuro and perspective, "still clung to the flat ideography of Byzantine icons and mosaics, which in their clear linear shapes and colors . . . were flattened out as though in a blazing and absolute light." Those bright flat colors, that scouring sun, those mosaic fragments recur again and again in Greek poetry no less than in Greek art. Obsessions with freedom and death, both heightened by alien domination and incessant wars; the complex liturgical forms of the Eastern Orthodox Church: the vigorous oral tradition of folksong, epic, and ballad—these form the core of the modern Greek poetic tradition, on to which such latterday influences as Marxism or French surrealism have merely been grafted.

Another problem unique to Greece—at least in so exacerbated a form—has been the emergence of two competing literary languages, the demotic tongue, spoken on every street, and the so-called *katharévousa,* or "purist" speech. The latter, a largely artificial construction based on ancient Attic, was developed shortly before the Greek War of Independence, at the insistence of those philhellenes, both Greek and foreign, who dreamed of restoring Greece's classical heritage, and found the common spoken tongue, with its slang, borrowed words, and lack of abstract terms, singularly inadequate for this purpose. Inevitably, having two languages not only created confusion in Greek education and literature, but also very soon acquired political connotations: advocates of *katharévousa* tended to be conservatives of the right, demoticists to be populists, liberals, ethnic idealists. Demotic was first recognized by Venizelos's Ministry of Education in 1917, and has been in and out ever since, depending on the political views of those in power. George Papandhréou had school texts put in demotic Greek; the Colonels switched them back to *katharévousa.*

The best compromise, known as *kathomilouméni,* or "daily speech," is a flexible blend of the two employed by some daily papers, based on demotic, but freely introducing abstractions and coining neologisms from the ancient tongue. It has, typically, attracted nothing but scornful criticism from purists in either camp. Ultimately, every serious Greek writer is, in effect, forced to invent his own language. Kalvos experimented with *katharévousa,* and so, surprisingly, did Cavafy, revealing "cunningly placed bits of whalebone in the more sinuous demotic."

But this linguistic ambivalence was also a sign of a far deeper fission, and conflict, in the body of Greek society. For over a millennium, after the division of the Roman Empire into East and West by Theodosius (AD 395), Byzantium, renamed Constantinople in honor of Constantine, the first Christian emperor, had preserved the Roman tradition in the shape of a proud, indeed unique, Christian theocracy. After the Great Schism of 1054 over the nature of the Holy Ghost, Eastern Orthodoxy's links with the West were severed. The

Byzantines did not think of themselves as Hellenes: to them "Helléne" was rather an opprobrious synonym for "pagan." In their own eyes they were, rather, Romans (*Romaioi*). Ethnically, the mainland Greeks, whom they called "Helladics," were no more than the occupants of an unimportant province of the Byzantine Empire. Apart from a brief Hellenizing movement in the early fifteenth century, shortly before the fall of Constantinople (1453), the notion of recovering, let alone emulating, the glories of ancient Greece gained no real ground until after the French and American revolutions, about 1800. Its chief proponents were Greek intellectuals educated, and for the most part resident, abroad, encouraged by romantic foreign philhellenes such as Shelley and Byron.

The idea of "Hellenism" was thus anathema, not only to the Orthodox Church but also to those countless simple, devout Greeks for, whom patriotism meant the latterday revival of Byzantium: *their* talisman was not the Parthenon, but the great Church of the Holy Wisdom in Constantinople. (Even today travel agencies in Athens offer packaged Easter tours "to the City": no need to name it, for a Greek only one city is worth consideration.) Their contempt for the ancient past was reinforced by ignorance. When one klephtic (guerrilla) leader heard himself compared to Achilles, he snapped: "Who is this Achilles? Did the musket of Achilles kill many?" Was the long, proud tradition of survival under the Turks, with its religious separatism, its klephtic ballads, its fighting priests, even its Karaghiozi shadow-theater, to be jettisoned in favor of some pagan dream foisted on the *Romaioi* by godless foreigners, who—brought up on Gibbon—dismissed Christian Byzantium as a barbarous, obscurantist medieval aberration?

Yet despite all this the notion of Hellenism took root. No one could deny that it played a vital role in winning the War of Independence, or that (with Constantinople still in Turkish hands) it offered a focal point, in Athens, for the nationalist aspirations of the new state. However much populist heroes of the anti-Turkish resistance like Kolokotronis and Makriyannis might grumble, Hellenism was from now on a permanent factor in Greek life. To encompass the tensions between Hellenism and *Romaiosyne* has ever since been an overriding concern of all Greek writers, a problem as difficult to ignore as to resolve.

The work of Elytis demonstrates that the closest links between modern and ancient Greece have little to do with intellectual theory or refurbished myth. The true perennial factor is Greece itself: that mountainous, harsh, limestone peninsula, with its scatter of islands, its violent storms, its whitewashed chapels, its poverty, its superstitions. In their isolation, the Greeks have preserved, below the threshold of public history, a peasant culture of extraordinary tenacity and complexity that reaches back into the remote pre-Christian past. Countless modern superstitions, legends, and beliefs have survived intact. A modern Boeotian farmer working the land

around Mt. Helicon could feel a sense of kinship with his Hesiodic ancestor of the *Works and Days* (c. 700 BC), and indeed still shares many of his legends and agricultural observances. The liturgical fabric of the Orthodox Church is seamed with a rich assortment of pagan symbols and ritual. That intricate modern taverna dance the *zeïbékiko* is directly descended from the classical Pyrrhic dance, while Lydian and Dorian modes still survive in the music that accompanies it.

Metternich once remarked, scornfully, that it was impossible to define what the word "Greek" meant, whether ethnically, politically, or geographically. In the climate engendered by the Congress of Vienna (1814-1815) this attitude was understandable, but it provided an agonizing legacy for the Greeks themselves, of which their imposed Bavarian monarchy was only the most obvious symptom. Inevitably, much of their new literary theory was imported, for the most part from France. The educated Phanariot Greeks from Constantinople, who after 1830 flocked to the new capital in Athens, were French-speaking cosmopolitans, accustomed to high office, often in key diplomatic posts; not surprisingly, they had romantic visions of a rejuvenated classical Greece, in the style of Hugo or Byron. They also wrote in *katharévousa*—"the ugly purist screech," as a distinguished (but far from impartial) contemporary critic describes it.

Equally foreign in its antecedents was the remarkable school of poetry that developed in the Ionian islands, Zakynthos in particular, off the west coast of Greece. Since these islands had never come under Turkish domination, their links with Western Europe, in particular with England and Italy, were strong. It is one more paradox in the odd story of modern Greek poetry that the two main representatives of the Ionian School, Dionysios Solomos (1798-1857) and Andreas Kalvos (1792-1869), both began their poetic careers writing in Italian, and in fact never acquired perfect fluency in Greek. Both, further, wrote passionately patriotic poetry (the first few verses of Solomos's *Ode to Liberty* were adopted as the Greek national anthem) while for the most part living abroad. It is doubtful whether Solomos ever set foot on the Greek mainland at all. Kalvos's brief and disastrous encounter with the ugly internecine factionalism of the Greek resistance movement at Náfplion not only sent him scuttling back posthaste to Corfu and thence to England, but seems to have fatally damaged his poetic impulse. Yet it is in Solomos and Kalvos that we first catch that characteristic sensuous celebration of the light and landscape that has haunted Greek poets ever since, and that reaches its apotheosis in the work of Elytis.

Born in 1911, on Crete, of Mytileniot descent, Odysseus Alepoudhelis took the pen name "Elytis," compounding it from the Greek words "Ellas" (Greece), "Eleni" (Helen), "elpidha" (hope), and "eleftheria" (freedom). Hope proved the dominant element in this conflation. Although Elytis became a mature writer during the Thirties, he stayed apart from the fashionable Angst and pessimism of the time—in sharp contrast to many of his contemporaries who affected *poésie maudite* in the manner of Baudelaire, above all Kostas Karyotákis, with whose highly public suicide in 1928 "despair, loneliness and anxiety erupted into Greek poetry." Elytis saw that the Smyrna disaster of 1922 effectively killed the "Great Idea" of a revived Byzantine Empire centered on Constantinople, but his work, from his first collection, *Orientations* (1939), to the magnificently orchestrated personal and ethnic testament, *The Axion Esti* ("**Praised Be**" or "**Worthy it is,**" a phrase from the Liturgy), published twenty years later, has a kind of passionate optimism about the possibilities of his small Aegean world.

Yet he has never been a mere romantic sentimentalist: his **"Heroic and Elegiac Song for the Lost Second Lieutenant of the Albanian Campaign"** (1943) would alone suffice to disprove that. It is true that one of his most lyrical collections, ***Sun the First,*** was actually published during the German-Italian occupation of Greece (the **"Heroic and Elegiac Song,"** for obvious reasons, had to wait until 1945). Asked why, in a time of darkness and loss, he wrote poems of exaltation, he replied that "it was not the events of the age that interested him as poetry but the emotions with which these events were confronted and transfigured." His hope springs from inner spiritual certainty.

The beauty and lyricism of Elytis's work, so imbued with the Greek *genius loci,* at once bring it within reach of the sympathetic European or American reader—especially those who have experienced a Greek summer.

—*Peter Green*

The beauty and lyricism of Elytis's work, so imbued with the Greek *genius loci,* at once bring it within reach of the sympathetic European or American reader—especially those who have experienced a Greek summer.

> In these whitewashed courtyards
> where the South Wind blows
> Whistling through vaulted arcades,
> tell me is it the mad pomegranate
> tree
> That frisks in the light scattering
> her fruit-laden laughter
> With a wind's caprice and murmur-
> ing, tell me is it the mad
> pomegranate tree
> That quivers with newborn foliage

> at early dawn
> Unfolding all her colors on high
> with a triumphant tremor?

There's a touch of Dylan Thomas in such lines of Elytis, and more than a touch of French surrealism (in his case by way of Paul Eluard), something which, after André Breton's famous Manifesto of 1924, took root and flourished with peculiar vigor in Greek soil.

What I find really remarkable about French surrealism in Greece is the diversity of poets whom it influenced, from an out-and-out romantic like Nikos Gatsos to the dedicated communist Yannis Ritsos. Gatsos (b. 1911) wrote his extraordinary poem *Amorghos* (the name of a Greek island, which Gatsos had never visited, nothing to do with his poem, and chosen as its title merely for euphony) in a single night, surfing on a wave of imagery that never quite slips out of control:

> Only if birds should ripple amid the
> masts of the lemon trees
> With the firm white flurry of lively
> footsteps
> Will the winds come, the bodies of
> swans that remained immaculate,
> unmoving and tender
> Amid the streamrollers of shops and
> the cyclones of vegetable gardens
> When the eyes of women turned to
> coal and the hearts of the
> chestnut hawkers were broken
> When the harvest was done and the
> hopes of crickets began . . .
>
> [translated by K. Friar]

In the hands of Ritsos (b. 1909) surrealism becomes an effective political weapon. After describing a nocturnal interrogation, with its floodlights, cigarette butts, and forced confessions, he picks up a surprising scene through the window:

> Close by, in the big well-swept
> sportsground, with its wire net-
> ting,
> They saw the three diplomats, in
> tophats and starched shirts,
> Collecting eggs from the floodlit
> chickenhouse. The hens,
> Up and awake (white, for the most
> part) weren't clucking,
> Just peering carefully at their glint-
> ing cufflinks, well aware,
> Like expert pawnbrokers, that these
> weren't genuine diamonds.
>
> [translated by P. Green]

There is something about the sharp Greek contrasts of light and shade, the unpredictable paradoxes of the Greek mind, that makes surrealism seem a natural mode of expression: one with which both Aeschylus and Pindar were already, each in his own way, familiar.

The poem by Elytis quoted above goes on to rhapsodize about naked sunburned girls in the meadows. This motif, a recurrent feature of Greek poetry ever since the days of Kalvos and Solomos, stands out as pure Hellenizing fantasy, since the contrast with actual social mores, despite modernizing trends in the last two decades, remains absolute. Greek women (as the number of secretaries' parasols in Athens eloquently testifies) hate getting sunburned, and blush at the very thought of public nakedness. Such literary conceits are more likely to score with visiting foreigners than with the Orthodox Church, still the most all-pervasive spiritual and moral force in Greece, and not noted (to put it mildly) for egalitarianism or permissiveness toward women. So a classic tension develops in Elytis's work, not only between the demotic and the Hellenizing traditions, but also between the sensuousness and the equally passionate spiritual instinct that hold the Greek psyche in an uneasy balance.

This tension is most clearly expressed in *The Axion Esti,* the work above all on which Elytis's reputation rests, and which almost certainly won him the Nobel Prize. One measure of its achievement is the degree to which Elytis succeeds in reconciling fire and rose, the world of the senses and the world of the spirit. Just as he did in an earlier poem **"The Autopsy"** (1957)—where "it was found that the gold of the olive root had dripped into the leaves of his heart"—Elytis here merges and symbolically identifies his own being and history with that of Greece. He wants his childhood to become that of all poets, of Greece, of the Creation. The sufferings he observed as an adult, from the Albanian campaign of 1940 to the terrible civil war of 1946-1949, he wants to make universal in a formal liturgical setting. The poem closes with a doxology of praise that seeks to transfigure and sanctify the simple, eternal features of Aegean life that recur in Elytis's verse.

The tripartite structure of *The Axion Esti*—**"Genesis," "Passion," "Gloria"**—not only echoes in its symbolism the Orthodox Liturgy, but even suggests the architecture of a Christian basilica. Linguistically, Elytis's supple Greek exploits an equally wide, and symbolically apt, range of usage, from the formal vocabulary of the Septuagint or ecclesiastical hymnology to demotic folk ballads, from Cretan epic (the *Erotókritos*) to the simple vernacular prose of General Makriyannis (1797-1864), the homespun autodidact hero of the War of Independence, whose *Memoirs,* now a kind of demoticists' bible, have provided stylistic inspiration for several generations of Greek writers. Elytis echoes Makriyannis not only in passages describing the drizzle and sweat and lice-

ridden exhaustion of the Albanian campaign, but also, with horrific effect (and, again, a touch of surrealism) as a postlude to a wartime execution:

> And the boys were very frightened; and the men,
> with leaden faces, straw hair,
> and black boots, turned waxen. Because the shacks
> all around shook as in an
> earthquake, and in many places the tarpaper fell off
> the walls, and far off, behind
> the sun, women appeared weeping, kneeling down
> in a vacant lot full of nettles
> and black clotted blood. While the great clock of
> angels chimed exactly twelve.

It is impossible to convey, except through extended quotation, the complexity and power of this great poem, at once so universal and so quintessentially Greek.

> Take away my sea with its
> white north winds,
> the wide window full of lemon
> trees,
> the many bird songs, and the
> one girl
> whose joy when I merely touched
> her was enough for me,
> take them away, I have sung!
> Take away my dreams, how can
> you read them?
> Take away my thoughts, where
> will you utter them?
> I am clean from end to end.
> Kissing, I enjoyed the virgin
> body.
> Blowing, I colored the fleece of
> the sea.
> All my ideas I turned into
> islands.
> I squeezed lemon on my conscience.

The poet's early years blend into the dawn of the world; the Greek islands, irradiated with sunlight, become a primal Eden; while the final Gloria—that exultant paean to earth and sky, winds, mountains, love, all moments of bright perception: "nine in the morning like fragrant bergamot," "the wooden table, / the blond wine with the sun's stain / the water doodling across the ceiling," "conscience radiant like a summer"—recalls, in its innocence and intensity, nothing so much as Christopher Smart's *A Song to David.*

The only modern work I know with which it is remotely comparable, in spiritual force, complex verbal beauty, length, structure, and doxological allusiveness, is David Jones's *The Anathemata,* and *The Axion Esti* seems to me the better poem.

Not only is the feeling deeper, the structure more intricate, the imagery more intense; it also possesses a natural depth of perspective that the *Anathemata* cannot match, since beyond Orthodox Byzantium lies the whole rich Hellenic tradition reaching back to Homer, whereas the Catholic "Matter of Britain" rests on a Roman military occupation, woad-covered warrior tribesmen, and Druidic sacrifices at Stonehenge.

When Elytis made his acceptance speech at the Nobel Prize ceremony he said: "I would like to believe that the Swedish Academy wants to honor in me the entire canon of Greek poetry." Whether or not we agree with Constantine Trypanis's claim that "in the last hundred years much greater and more original poetry has been written than in the fourteen centuries which preceded them," no one can deny the amazing richness and diversity of Greek poets in this century: Sikelianos, Caváfy, Seféris, Kazantzakis, Yannis Ritsos, and Elytis alone would constitute a quite exceptional list for so small a country. Of these, it is perhaps Anghelos Sikelianos (1884-1951) who best exemplifies the near-schizophrenic dilemma of the Greek intellectual committed to neo-Hellenism. Like Eliot, he saw the modern world as a wasteland, in his case to be redeemed by a reversion to the supposed values of the pre-Socratic thinkers, and, beyond them, to that universal feminine principle he saw at the heart of Aegean civilization. Yet his attempt to by-pass two millennia of Christian belief was doomed to inevitable failure, and there was a sadly appropriate irony in the fact that his Delphic festival of the arts had to be financed by his rich American wife. What would a modern Spartan peasant see in his passionate "Hymn to Artemis Orthia"? Plain blasphemy, I suspect; the syncretism he aimed at ("sweet child, our Dionysus and our Christ") never really took, and only Elytis has ever come near achieving it.

Anyone who dips into Kimon Friar's huge anthology, *Modern Greek Poetry,* will soon realize that the poets I have discussed form only a small fraction—if, arguably, the most distinguished—of those whose work has left its mark on modern literature: while the gifted young writers represented in *Twenty Contemporary Greek Poets* show very clearly that the Greek tradition has great vitality, and, incidentally, that under Valaoritis's influence French surrealism is still flourishing in Athens: Vassilis Steriadis can write:

> Dear Tassos
> my dying and coming is out of
>   question
> Katia won't let me
> But Katia is full of holes and a bit
>   mad
> as she falls from the clouds
> into a box of sugared almonds

If these young poets use traditional myths, it tends to be with a conscious off-handedness. When Yorghos Chronas's mermaid asks a sailor, in a storm at sea, if Alexander the Great still lives, and gets the ritual answer (to avert shipwreck) "He lives!" the poet comments:

> Maybe he lived, maybe he didn't,
>   how did he know?
> he was just a sailor by himself at
>   sea . . .

For Yannis Yfantis the Achaean siege of Troy resembles spermatozoa assaulting an ovum, till "like a penis that old horse entered her." The scars of occupation and civil war recur grimly among the pop-culture American icons (TV, refrigerators, Marilyn Monroe). Greece has suffered more than most countries in the course of her history, and put her bitter experiences to better poetic use. Elytis himself should have the last word:

> The noon bell chimes
> and slowly on the scorching stones
>   letters are carved:
> NOW and FOREVER and
>   PRAISED BE.
> Forever forever and now and now
>   the birds sing
> PRAISED BE the price paid.

Andonis Decavalles (review date Winter 1980)

SOURCE: A review of *I Mayia tou Papadhiamandhi,* in *World Literature Today,* Vol. 54, No. 1, Winter, 1980, pp. 149-50.

[*In the following review, Decavalles praises Elytis's rediscovery of the turn of the century prose writer Alexandros Papadhiamandhis in his* I Mayia tou Papdhiamandhi.]

Deep intellectual and emotional affinity has obviously inspired this perceptive and brilliant, touching and revealing evaluation of Alexandros Papadhiamándhis by the outstanding contemporary Greek poet and 1979 Nobel laureate. Papadhiamándhis was a saintly man from the island of Skiathos whose several narrative tales, written around the turn of the century, made him the first original and unsurpassed master in modern Greek prose. His stories were all drawn from that Aegean island, the integrity of its closed and tiny world, its rocky natural beauty, its simple, unsophisticated and religiously inspired people, the picturesqueness and tragic nature of their lives. A poetic genius and a wise innocence in their author lent those narratives, in their strange mixture of elevated language and the demotic tongue, of exquisite art and careless journalistic improvisation, an irresistible charm. In subsequent years the prosaic narrow-mindedness of critics failed to see the inherent greatness and lasting universality of the stories.

Hence Elytis's affectionate concern to rediscover, reveal and defend, in his forty-five-page essay and the seventy-page selection that follows it, the personality and peculiar genius of the old master with whom he shares much in many respects; this fact makes the defense of Papadhiamándhis very much Elytis's own self-defense. Elytis too has suffered from the narrow-mindedness and prejudice of his younger critics. What he reveals and stresses in Papadhiamándhis is his love of life in its universality, its closeness to nature and its cycles—the things that make it stand beyond what is perishable in temporality. Papadhiamándhis is the last survivor and reporter of a small, marvelously integral, materially poor but spiritually rich world destined to die culturally in the experience of two world wars and what they brought.

Totally identifying himself with Skiathos, he raised that island into a poetic reality untouched by time's ravages. Out of quantities he built a world of quality in his mixing inseparably the physical with the spiritual essence. In his stories he dealt with "pure units," the souls "sculpted by the winds" and made "imperishable like sea-cliffs." He lent that reality his dream in its "continuous contact with the world beyond." His so-called "saintliness," his wise and tested innocence, never lost its humanity, its sensual desires, its eros for beauty in nature and in lovely girls, an eros for the physically unattainable (*afthasto*) which only imagination can reach. Apart from his undeniable poetic gifts, it was his human sensuality itself for physical and spiritual beauty and the beauty of words in their marvelous weddings that strangely made him the more saintly and the more pure.

Roderick Beaton (review date 9 October 1981)

SOURCE: "On the Parnassian Slopes," in *The Times Literary Supplement,* No. 4097, October 9, 1981, p. 1175.

[*In the following excerpt, Beaton finds fault with the contemporary language of Edmund Keeley's and George Savidis's translation of Elytis's* The Axion Esti, *but asserts that they have achieved a readable version of a complex poetic work.*]

A consequence of Greece's recent accession to the EEC predicted in a light-hearted mood by an academic colleague was the likely establishment of a Greek "poetry mountain". With a population of less than a fifth of that of Great Britain, Greece nonetheless produces annually a greater volume of published poetry. Who reads it all is another matter; but it is not only in quantity of published work that Greek poets excel. Since the time of Constantine Cavafy in the early part of this century, several of them have established international reputations,

while others have produced work of exceptional quality which remains little known abroad.

Odysseus Elytis was surprisingly little read in this country until the award of the Nobel Prize for Literature in 1979 brought him into the international limelight. This is not wholly the fault of translators—he is well represented in the early translations of Greek poetry by Edmund Keeley and Philip Sherrard, translations of his poetry have been appearing in magazines such as *Agenda* for many years, and Kimon Friar's book-length selection, *The Sovereign Sun,* was published in America in 1974. The truth seems to be that poetry which is lyrical, optimistic and which exults in the possibilities of language does not so easily find favour with British readers as it does say, in France, where Elytis is much better known. Be that as it may, it is a sad reflection on British publishers and readers that the translation by Keeley and George Savidis of Elytis's greatest work, *The Axion Esti,* has only recently been brought out in this country, six years after it appeared in a limited edition in the United States.

Edmund Keeley is a veteran translator of Greek poetry, having collaborated with Philip Sherrard on the now classic *Collected Poems* of Seferis and more recently on translations of Cavafy and Sikelianos, while Savidis is one of Greece's foremost editors and textual scholars. The result is a translation of a high degree of accuracy, with a useful explanatory preface and an excellent and wisely selective set of notes, many of them based on the poet's own unpublished commentary, and a valuable adjunct to the original Greek text, which is unannotated. The English translation aims above all to be faithful to the Greek, and it is a pity from this point of view that the publishers have not been able to retain the parallel-text format for which the translation was originally intended, and to which reference is still made in the preface.

As the translators themselves concede in this preface, no English equivalent can do complete justice to the linguistic exuberance and allusiveness of Elytis's text, and it must be admitted that they have not always risen fully to its challenge. In particular the decision, explained in the preface, to avoid echoes of the King James Bible is arguably a mistaken one, in that the enrichment of the contemporary poetic language by judicious allusion to the language of earlier periods is one of the major achievements of the poem. The language of the translation is too consistently contemporary, and in the prose passages the introduction of modern slang to reproduce the "early nineteenth-century demotic" of the original obscures the deliberate datedness of that idiom, and of Elytis's inspired exploitation of the common elements between the styles of General Makriyannis and of the Greek New Testament. Similarly, the inclusion of one each of the best known Anglo-Saxon four-letter words may have seemed to the translators obligatory for publication in America in the mid-1970s, but jars a little today. Elytis is a poet who calls a great many things by their names without prurience, but without vulgarity either.

These are small criticisms, however, when set beside the very considerable achievement of the translators in giving us a fresh and always readable version of a poetic work of such magnitude and complexity.

Karl Malkoff (essay date Summer 1984)

SOURCE: "Eliot and Elytis: Poet of Time, Poet of Space," in *Comparative Literature,* Vol. 36, No. 3, Summer, 1984, pp. 238-57.

[*In the following essay, Malkoff compares and contrasts Elytis's* To Axion Esti *to T.S. Eliot's* Four Quartets *and asserts that both poets are seeking a unity of being in their work.*]

In this essay I propose to explore the differences between T. S. Eliot's *Four Quartets* and Odysseus Elytis' *To Axion Esti,* in the hope of discovering patterns that may contribute to an understanding of their poetry in general. As a preliminary to such an investigation, it would be prudent to establish a common ground of discourse for two poems that are only rarely mentioned in the same breath, and which, at first glance, may seem quite unrelated. Is is a commonplace in criticism of modern Greek literature to note that while George Seferis, Greece's first Nobel Prize-winning poet, came very much under Eliot's spell, her second, Elytis, though admiring his American contemporary, has gone out of his way to characterize Eliot's work as being far too despairing. Nonetheless, the *Quartets* and the *Axion Esti* often coincide in theme—that is, in historical focus, and in the attempt to bridge the gap between man and God—and in form, as Eliot and Elytis use strikingly similar structural principles in their struggle to perceive order in the world's apparent chaos.

I use the word "historical" in two senses. First, and more generally, I refer to the concern of each poet with the nature of man's involvement in time. In "Burnt Norton" Eliot is preoccupied with the irredeemability of time, with an irrevocable past and a determined future. To participate in eternity, perhaps mystically, offers the only release; but we still face the paradox that "Only through time time is conquered." It is hardly necessary to document the importance of the idea of time to the *Quartets,* so frequently and explicitly does it appear. Time is sometimes linear or progressive, sometimes cyclical, sometimes chaotic; it is often understood, though not necessarily experienced, as a function of eternity. It is also noteworthy that while Eliot begins with emphasis on the individual's experience of time, there is a movement through the *Quartets* toward a more public context, from the Rose Garden to the streets of London. In fact, the final formulation

of the paradox that time can be conquered only through time reads:

> A people without history
> Is not redeemed from time, for history is a
>   pattern
> Of timeless moments.

Although Elytis is far less concerned with the *idea* of time, with its abstraction (a point important later in this essay), he gives ample attention to the experience of time. In the first section of *To Axion Esti,* **"Genesis,"** which is at once about the creation of the universe, the Greek people, and the poet himself, the hours of the day—the precise o'clock is important enough to be referred to three times—tick away as well as the months of gestation and the seven days of the Creation. The passing seasons are almost characters in the poem, so forcefully do they participate in its actions. And just as ontogeny is said to recapitulate phylogeny, in Elytis' world the individual Greek seems destined to bear the burden of his race's history. When, for example, in **"The Passion,"** the poem's second section,

> They came
> dressed up as "friends,"
>   came countless times, my enemies,
> trampling the primeval soil,

the language is equally appropriate to the innumerable invasions of Greece through the centuries, to the wars of the poet's own time, or to even some incident in his private life. In *To Axion Esti's* third and final section, **"Gloria,"** Elytis most nearly approaches Eliot's concern with the idea of time. The section concludes with seven couplets, each first line praising the *now*—the ephemeral world—and the second the *always*—the eternal. This sense of the dual nature of things is related to Eliot's "still point of the turning world." Although there are important differences in means of expression, both poets are seriously concerned with the notion that our lives take shape at the point where time and eternity intersect.

The second sense of "historical" has to do with a specific cataclysmic event in the lives of both poets: the Second World War. We have already noted Eliot's tendency toward the abstract and therefore should not be surprised to find a less consistent preoccupation with the particular. Nonetheless, the war, frequently the unspoken but crucially implied backdrop to Eliot's speculations, becomes increasingly important as he moves from his exploration of time as a universal to the historical moment. "Burnt Norton" (1935) was written before the start of World War II (though not before Hitler's rise to power). By the time "East Coker" (1940) was published, the war had begun, and though the suggestion of its opening lines that houses rise and fall may be influenced by that fact, the only certain reference to the war is in Section V, where Eliot mentions his wasted "years of *l'entre deux guerres.*" "The Dry Salvages" (1941) is even less explicit, but two movements of "Little Gidding" (1942) focus specifically on the war. In Section II, in lines whose form and content evoke Dante's *Inferno,* air-raid warden Eliot walks through the hellish streets of London during the Blitz, encountering there a ghostly poetic ancestor, while "the dark dove with the flickering tongue," the war plane, passes overhead. Section IV is devoted wholly to that dove "With flame of incandescent terror," at once war plane and Holy Spirit, creature of both time and eternity. Eliot patrolling the wartime streets is perhaps the most eloquent testimony of all to his dictum that "only through time time is conquered"; though the path of the mystic beckons, there is no escape from the world of the particular. Or, to borrow (steal?) Dante's formulation, in order to see God we must first descend into Hell.

Although the threat to Europe's survival is the *Quartets'* most pressing historical context, Eliot pursues a more private historical quest through the poems: the establishing of his roots in England. That they require establishing is acknowledged tacitly in "The Dry Salvages," a quartet which takes its title from the scene of Eliot's childhood vacations in Massachusetts and opens with a mediation on the Mississippi, near whose banks the poet was born. However, the titles of the other three *Quartets* refer to places in England, including East Coker, the village from which the Eliots emigrated in the seventeenth century. In this context, Eliot's birth in America comes to seem an accident of exile; the *Quartets,* insofar as they partake of time, are grounded on English soil—"History is now and England."

In *To Axion Esti,* where Greece is the link between microcosm and macrocosm, between the individual and the universe, there is no similar complication: this is a national poem. And there is no need to scour the text for allusions to World War II. The heart of the poem is its series of six Readings, whose architectural functions we shall soon have occasion to clarify. They consist of a generalized prose account of Elytis' experiences during the Albanian campaign, the Occupation, and finally the Civil War that without respite followed the liberation of Greece. These Readings literally provide the text that the contemporary Greek must interpret in order to understand his place in the universe. Elytis is not coy about giving the temporal its due; it is around the major historical events of his time that *To Axion Esti* coalesces.

The search for God, which involves doing business with eternity, is nonetheless pursued under the pressures of history. By what path does one reach the God who has either presided over the horrors of our world or has ceased to preside over anything? Enmeshed in time, how do we taste eternity? For both Eliot and Elytis, the solution—if solution it can be called—lies in immersion in the destructive element, whether that element be called Time or War or the Dark Night of the Soul. In "East Coker," Eliot says:

> O dark dark dark. They all go into the dark, . . .
> I said to my soul, be still, and let the dark come
>   upon you
> Which shall be the darkness of God.

In Elytis' Second Reading, the soldier (whose name means "Freedom") says that "only he who wrestles with the darkness inside him will find his own place in the sun someday." Of course, the mystic's Dark Night is Eliot's concern, while Elytis, whose religious forms sometimes seem like empty shells, is far more secular. But in each case there is the notion of sacrifice, of denial, as the path to salvation; and in each case the instrument of salvation is a love whose darker implications are scarcely disguised. Our only hope, insists Eliot, is "To be redeemed from fire by fire. / Who then devised the torment? Love." And for Elytis, *"The blood of love has robed me in purple / And joys never seen before have covered me in shade."*

Ultimately most significant, if not most immediately obvious, are the similarities in structure between the *Four Quartets* and *To Axion Esti.* It is arguable that a poem's form is its most important statement about the nature of reality, that content is simply a commentary on form's assertions. In any case, if we suggest that two works embody similar visions of reality, we may look to form as a promising source of confirmation. The structure of the *Four Quartets* is far more familiar to English-speaking readers. Each of the *Quartets,* modeled loosely on the last quartets of Beethoven, has five movements. The first is always a verbal equivalent—if we can speak of such a thing—of a sonata; the second, a lyrical mode shifting abruptly to the prosaic; the third, development of a theme; the fourth, a relatively brief lyric; and the fifth, a further variation on themes suggested by the opening movements. Perhaps most important is the simple fact that in the *Four Quartets* form is repeatable and recognizable. Although Eliot may have labored long hours inventing his verbal equivalents to musical form, the effect of using the same formal sequence in each of the *Quartets* is to reinforce the illusion that the poem's structure precedes its content (this is, in fact, literally true for the last three poems, some of whose materials—e.g., the Blitz—could hardly have been foreseen when "Burnt Norton" was written, but whose basic shapes had already been determined by that earlier poem). This may not seem extraordinary in itself, but if the composition of the *Quartets* is placed in its proper historical context, their shapeliness becomes noteworthy. In the mid-1930s, Ezra Pound was well into the *Cantos,* an open-ended poem in free verse, almost entirely devoid of repeated formal patterns. Eliot's previous major poem, *The Waste Land* (1922), written with substantial editorial help from Pound, and whose subject may be described as the fragmentation of western culture, eschewed symmetry. Since there was ample precedent for the "open" poem, and since *The Waste Land* seems to exhibit an interdependence of form and content, one might expect the form of *Four Quartets* to be similarly mimetic.

The very title of **To Axion Esti** suggests that its organizational principles will be ecclesiastic. The phrase "Worthy it is" is drawn from the Greek Orthodox liturgy, where, as in Elytis' poem, it is a frequently recurring refrain. The poem has three—obviously theologically significant—broad divisions, **"Genesis," "The Passion,"** and **"Gloria,"** which reflect the Christian itinerary of birth, suffering and death, and rebirth.

The first section, **"Genesis,"** is divided into seven "hymns," each corresponding to a day of the biblical creation. The Genesis itself, however, applies simultaneously to the cosmos, eons in the making, the Greek people, and the poet himself. In fact, a tension persists, not only through this section but through the entire poem, between theologically inspired form and generally secular content. This has the effect of utilizing Christianity as a source of myth, and therefore of metaphor, much in the way that William Butler Yeats used his *Vision* to inform his poetry (with the significant difference that Elytis' myth is immediately and emotionally available to his audience).

By far the most substantial segment of the triptych, as well as the most complexly structured, is part two, **"The Passion."** It is as if the experiences of the war years, unless subjected to rigid discipline, could yield no more than an undifferentiated cry of pain and terror; only under the most formal circumstances can the emotions provoked by those years be revisited. The matter of **"The Passion"** is contained in its Readings, prose passages stylistically reminiscent of General Makrigiannis (whose *Memoirs* of the war of liberation against the Turks—an adumbration of World War II—have become a touchstone of demotic prose). As in the Greek Orthodox liturgy, whose general structure is suggested by **"The Passion"** (just as Beethoven's quartets are suggested by *Four Quartets*), the Readings are centerpieces for liturgical music, represented here by Psalms and Odes. Each Reading is preceded and followed by an Ode, a strictly metrical lyric (although the meter varies from Ode to Ode). The unit of Ode-Reading-Ode is itself preceded and followed by two Psalms, poems in free verse. Two Readings, with their attendant poems, form a structural unit, of which there are three all told, so that **"The Passion"** may be represented as follows:

PPOROPPOROPP PPOROPPOROPP
PPOROPPOROPP

The precise nature of these intricacies is less important than the fact that they exist at all. And though the need to contain

the experiences of the Readings, which are absorbed and transformed by the encompassing lyrics, partially justifies such form, we may still hope to find further support for such complexities.

"Gloria" has a less obvious, but in its own way intricate, structure which, as Edmund Keeley and George Savidis point out, serves to prevent "this section . . . from degenerating into a random enumeration of things 'worthy of praise,'" though, again, other explanations are possible. This section of the poem is also divided in three, with the arrangement of quatrains, triplets, and couplets of the first and third sections identical to each other, and similar to that of the second section. There are further refinements: for example, the triplets always provide specific instances—specimens. I am tempted to say—of the generalizations made in the quatrains preceding them; the groups of seven couplets, always introduced by a quatrain headed by "Axion esti," in turn echo the *Ave,* praise Him, and distinguish the Now from the Always.

To this point, both similarities in theme and complexities in structure have been observed in the two poems. Do their structural complexities also share some common characteristic? One way of approaching this question is suggested by George Savidis' remark in his essay "'Axion Esti' To Poiema tou Elyti": "The numbering of the sections by Elytis, not according to their typographical order, but distinguished by each genre . . . permits us also to read in their own order all the corresponding sections." In other words, all the Psalms can be taken from their sequential place in the poem and read together, as can the Odes and the Readings; most important, the new groupings have unity and coherence. Curiously, the same is true of Eliot's *Quartets.* For example, excerpting the fourth movement from each *Quartet* would give us a series of lyrics devoted to God the Father, Christ the Redeemer, the Virgin, and the Holy Spirit; the sequence as a whole could comprise Eliot's vision of Godhead. A cross-section of the opening movements would reveal the range of his perspectives on time: linear, cyclical, chaotic (in flux), and as a function of eternity. In neither poem, of course, would the aesthetic wholeness of the original work survive. We can nevertheless learn a great deal about the *Quartets* by reading the fourth movements in sequence, or, in **To Axion Esti,** all of, say, the Readings.

We now face the task of interpreting this similarity in structure. I acknowledge at once that it is futile to attempt to put into words what is expressed by a poem's form; the material will be too complex, or too subtle, or both. Nonetheless, statements general enough not to do violence to the form, but specific enough to shed light on its purposes, are not out of the question. By facilitating readings of their poems in other than typographical order, Eliot and Elytis invite their readers to recognize the spatial, as well as the more obvious temporal, aspects of poetry. That is, to borrow the notion E. M. Forster applied to the novel, the poem exists not only in time insofar as we are in the process of reading it but also in space insofar as we can apprehend it as a whole, a pattern. Eliot, whether or not he had Forster in mind, is quite explicit about this dimension of poetry:

> Only by the form, the pattern,
> Can words or music reach
> The stillness, as a Chinese jar still
> Moves perpetually in its stillness.

Although we can only experience one moment at a time, our awareness of pattern, as it is pressed on us by Eliot and Elytis (not only in passages like Eliot's cited above but continuously in the structures of their poems as well), reminds us that every moment of the poem exists simultaneously. The analysis of any complete poem implies recognition of its spatial dimension, but few poems suggest so clearly their own reordering, insist so strongly on their existence in space as well as time.

What makes this hypothesis especially interesting is that both poems are deeply involved in the exploration of the relationship between time and eternity, which, as Eliot's metaphor makes evident, correspond to typographical sequence and pattern respectively. In addition, both poets deal with the tension between place and infinity ("England or nowhere" in Eliot, the microcosm and macrocosm in Elytis), between the one and the many. If we look at the epigraphs—taken from fragments of Heraclitus—to Eliot's *Quartets,* we find that they have as their common theme the resolving of dichotomies:

> Although there is but one Center, most men
> live in centers of their own.
>
> The way up and the way down are one and the
> same.

The epigraphs would not be out of place affixed to the beginning of *To Axion Esti.* In content as well as form, both poems are committed to the recognition and resolution of dualisms.

Dualism, the perception of such dichotomies as time and eternity, the one and the many, spirit and matter, body and soul, may be either cause or symptom of man's separation from God or of the alienation of the individual from his society. The dualistic perception of reality has been a characteristically Western way of—or obstacle to—looking at the world, but at certain times in history it has been felt as more particularly painful. Clearly, the Second World War, when man had even more reason than usual to suspect God's absence and the very fabric of society was in danger of disintegrating, was one of those times. But our century as a whole has been preoccupied with the apparently widening gap between man and God and the fragmentation of Western culture; in fact, we have had to confront the waste land given mythic reality by Eliot in the 1920s, and to which both the *Four Quartets* and *To Axion Esti* are answers, assertions that in spite of apparent difficulty—or impossibility—the isolated individual can experience his existence as part of a greater whole.

It is now clear that in certain themes, and in principles of structure as well, there are important similarities between *Four Quartets* and *To Axion Esti.* Both are located in the mainstream of a poetic tradition which has had as its chief concern the identification and reconciliation of dualisms. It reached its greatest notoriety in the French *Symbolistes,* but also included such poets as John Donne, William Blake, William Butler Yeats, and Wallace Stevens. Eliot and Elytis stand out because they have made the structure of their poems directly bear the weight of their visions of reality. The nearly contemporary appearance of these poems—little or no direct influence is involved—helps argue the existence of a common European literary tradition, not simply in the more obvious sense that in an age of relatively accessible translations international contemporaries affect one another, but in the more profound sense that they have emerged from a common store of preoccupations and strategies (rather as breakthroughs in science sometimes occur independently in two or more places, based on a common body of understanding, instead of on the more usual collaborations). There are, however, crucial differences between Eliot and Elytis which should not be overlooked.

My preliminary remarks, designed to emphasize similarities, have nonetheless touched on contrasts. I have said in passing that in Eliot an emphasis on time and eternity is accompanied by a tendency toward the abstract, while in Elytis an emphasis on the one and the many is accompanied by a tendency toward the concrete. I shall develop these propositions in greater detail. At the same time I shall be interested in determining whether the differences are accidental or are an inevitable and orderly consequence of distinct sensibilities being applied to the same problem.

I shall begin by examining how Eliot and Elytis treat the paradox that is important to both their works (although more nearly central to Eliot's): that salvation comes from the awareness that time and eternity are in contact with each other, and consequently that only through time can time be transcended. Eliot characteristically expresses this paradox in abstract language:

> Time past and time future
> What might have been and what has been
> Point to one end, which is always present.
>
> . . . . .

> the light is still
> At the still point of the turning world.
>
> . . . . .
>
> Time the destroyer is time the preserver.
>
> . . . . .
>
> Here, the intersection of the timeless moment
> Is England and nowhere. Never and always.

These examples could, of course, be multiplied considerably. They are nevertheless sufficient to indicate that Eliot's vision of reality invites abstract formulation, and that a good deal of the appeal of his verse is to the conscious, logical intellect. If it were entirely that, Eliot need hardly have bothered to write a poem; an essay would have sufficed. (Indeed, Eliot's Ph.D. dissertation was a study of the philosopher F. H. Bradley.) There are, however, at least two reasons why these abstractions are distorted when removed from context.

First, Eliot uses ideas the way other poets use images; they do not appear in an absolute sense, but rather are juxtaposed with other, often contradictory, ideas, so that the poem's significance lies not in the idea but in the tension between ideas. For example, the proposition offered by Eliot at the start of "Burnt Norton" has sometimes been taken as the poet's unambiguous assertion about the nature of reality.

> Time present and time past
> Are both perhaps present in time future,
> And time future contained in time past.
> If all time is eternally present
> All time is unredeemable.

The key words in this passage are "perhaps" and "if." But even if the syllogism stands on its own feet logically—because time present and time past *are* both present in time future—the conclusion is nonetheless seriously challenged by the rest of the poem. Time *is* redeemable poetically by the imagination and theologically by the Redeemer and the mystery of the Incarnation, that is, by the paradoxes central to the *Quartets.*

Second, the poems are hardly devoid of imagery, and the images, in juxtaposition to the abstract statements, alter the abstractions. In the example given above, the images of rose garden, birds, children, and light which fill the first movement of "Burnt Norton" do not so much illustrate as explore the opening lines, so that the abstractions do not limit the meanings of the images, which retain a fine mysteriousness. In some cases, as when Eliot refers to the light that is "At the still point of the turning world," imagery and abstractions are thoroughly entwined, as in the Metaphysical poets.

Still, in Eliot, as in the Metaphysicals, it is the abstract mode that organizes and dominates the poem. The poet appeals to the conscious intellect, and he must supply in condensed and rationally apprehensible form his vision of reality. This emphasis on the abstract does not necessarily amount to that "dissociation of sensibility," the splitting of intellect and emotion that Eliot felt the Metaphysicals had been the last to avoid. But it does entail enough condensation for the conscious intellect to grasp in a given moment what is placed before it. Ezra Pound's well-known definition of an "Image" can be applied to the "conceits" used by Eliot in *Four Quartets:* "that which presents an intellectual and emotional complex in an instant of time."

In Elytis, the convergence of time and eternity is rarely expressed so abstractly, so baldly as in Eliot. In **"Genesis,"** the *persona* of **To Axion Esti** describes himself as "the One I really was, the One of many centuries ago, / the One still verdant in the midst of fire, the One not made by human hand." The convergence of time and eternity is implicit in the notion that the self in the present is also the Self that has always existed; but it is characteristically in terms of the merging of selves, of the One and the many, that the paradox is expressed—abstraction is given bodily form.

In **"The Passion,"** the eternal is overshadowed by immersion in time. The war makes one painfully aware of accident and chaos, and obscures visions of underlying permanence and harmony. Only—as Eliot might have put it—the pattern imposed by the poem's structure stands up to the welter of events. In **"Gloria,"** which is unmistakably an assertion of underlying harmony, the connection between time and eternity again comes to the fore. The poem ends with seven couplets, each celebrating the *now* in its first line, the *forever* in its second. For example, "Now the Moon's incurable swarthiness / Forever the Galaxy's golden blue scintillation." The first line depicts the heavens in terms of the mutability of their separate parts, the second the everlastingness of the totality. Elytis works paratactically rather than through the syntax of metaphor, by accretion rather than concentration. It is by the piling up of images rather than the distillation of ideas that his perspective takes shape.

As noted earlier, the dominant dualism in the *Quartets* is temporal, that is, it involves the tension between time and eternity. But spatial dualism is unquestionably important, if only because imagery is by necessity spatial, even when it is used metaphorically to express temporal duality, as, for example, in "the still point of the turning world." At times Eliot is also interested in spatial imagery for its own sake, in the relationship between microcosm and macrocosm, and in the ancient Hermetic formula—"As above, so below"—which unites them. For instance, the first stanza of "Burnt Norton" 's second movement begins in mud—its first word, "garlic," is symbolic of whatever is at home in the earth's embrace—and ends with "stars." In between, Eliot spells it out:

> The dance along the artery
> The circulation of the lymph
> Are figured in the drift of stars.

In short, "as above, so below," with one proviso. Below is war, below is conflict: above is reconciliation. Even here temporal dualism is implied—below is the world of time, above, eternity. The "bedded axle-tree" of the first stanza will soon become "the still point of the turning world" of the second.

For Eliot, the individual's relationship to God is at the heart of things. From this perspective, space is nearly illusory. What principally separates man from God is the former's existence in time. His chief problem is how to bridge this gap. God managed it in the Incarnation. For man, it is indeed an imposing task. To achieve it, it seems that one must escape rather than celebrate the physical world.

> Descend lower, descend only
> Into the world of perpetual solitude,
> World not world, but that which is not world,
> Internal darkness, deprivation
> And destitution of all property,
> Desiccation of the world of sense.

This is a dominant—if not exclusive—mode in the *Quartets:* to escape from space in order to be able to escape from time through time. Eliot's poetry, as I have already noted, contains a good deal of imagery, which by nature is spatial. However, I have also observed that these images are often temporal metaphors. Even in one of the *Quartets'* most impressive (spatial) images, the evocation of the Mississippi which begins "The Dry Salvages," Eliot soon reveals that the river corresponds to time, as the ocean into which it flows corresponds to eternity: "The river is within us, the sea is all about us."

Far more secular, Elytis hopes not to transcend time—he seems unable, in this poem, even to imagine transcending it—but to be aware of his existence as part of an entity (or series of entities) greater than himself, which is, for all practical purposes, eternal: Greece, the human race, the cosmos. For him, the relationship between microcosm and macrocosm is central. Indeed, each of the last six hymns of **"Genesis"** concludes with the following formula:

> THIS
> the small world, the great [world].
> (AE, p. 6, etc.)

At times the distinction between great and small seems to

break down. In Psalm XV, which compares the poet's self to God, Elytis writes:

> Look, it is you who speak and I who come true,
> I hurl the stone and it lands on me.
> I deepen mines and elaborate the skies.
> I hunt the birds and lose myself in their weight.
> I was your will, my God, and here I pay you
> back.
>
> (AE, p. 99)

It is not inconsistent with the distinctions I have been developing between Eliot and Elytis that the former's god disappears into the featurelessness of undifferentiated being and seems, like the god of the *via negativa,* describable only in terms of what he is not, while the latter's god is close enough and definite enough to be addressed face to face, superior but somewhat fathomable, perhaps to be argued with, certainly to be appealed to. This god is not always distinguished from the poet's self and sometimes seems to be the self's creation. Clearly, in Elytis' world, man performs many of God's functions, for example, in the poet's sanctification of the things of this world by naming them in **"Gloria."** In general, Elytis' poet shares with God the title of "Master-builder." For Eliot, the vastness of the gulf between the poet on the one hand and God and his universe on the other is far more important than what they might have in common. Eliot's view of the poet as creator can be understood as a function of this belief.

Throughout the *Four Quartets,* the theme of creativity, of art, is always near the surface. The arrangement of what is essentially a search for God in the form of a musical composition says volumes about art's relevance to that quest. But on at least three occasions, Eliot turns directly to confront the shortcomings of art, and most particularly of literature:

> Words move, music moves
> Only in time; but that which is only living
> Can only die. Words, after speech, reach
> Into the silence. Only by the form, the pattern, .
> Can words or music reach
> The stillness, as a Chinese jar still
> Moves perpetually in its stillness.
> Not the stillness of the violin, while the note lasts,
> Not that only, but the co-existence,
> Or say that the end precedes the beginning,
> And the end and the beginning were always there
> Before the beginning and after the end.
> And all is always now. Words strain,
> Crack and sometimes break, under the burden,
> Under the tension, slip, slide, perish,
> Decay with imprecision, will not stay in place,
> Will not stay still.

The first twelve and a half lines of this passage provide still another metaphor for **"Burnt Norton"**'s main theme. The pattern is the conception of the work as a whole; but at any given instant only one finite point in the work, rather than its wholeness, can be experienced. In other words, the reading of the poem (or listening to the piece of music) is to time as pattern is to eternity. As part of man's world, art participates in the temporal paradox and assists greatly in helping us to understand it. However, the last four and a half lines develop the linguistic consequences of the gap between time and eternity. Like the individual grappling with the implications of his distance from God, words—timeborn creatures—are in danger of collapsing under the burden of sustaining the timeless pattern. In a sense, it cannot be done. Poetry is an attempt to get around the imposing task of abstracting truth from reality. But even poetry is only a relative improvement.

In **"East Coker,"** the critique of language continues:

> That was a way of putting it—not very
> satisfactory:
> A periphrastic study in a worn-out poetical fashion.
> Leaving one still with the intolerable wrestle
> With words and meanings. The poetry does not
> matter.

It is somewhat ambiguous whether this discouraging conclusion applies merely to the lyric passage which immediately precedes it in the text or to poetry in general. What follows, however, is an explicit indictment of language, and particularly of the attempt to embody an understanding of the world in language. Wisdom, we learn, "is only the knowledge of dead secrets." Experience seems to teach us to impose patterns on reality, but the patterns are necessarily false.

> For the pattern is new in every moment
> And every moment is a new and shocking
> Valuation of all we have been.

Language, striving to capture the passing moment, the now, falls into the trap of time's continual movement. Not only does the moment remain tauntingly out of reach, but even the past is beyond our mastery, since the inexorable wave of new presents cannot fail to modify whatever pattern we think we have seen—a more pessimistic application of the position Eliot had taken earlier in "Tradition and the Individual Talent" (1919).

Eliot returns once more to this theme in the fifth movement of the same Quartet.

> So here I am, in the middle way, having had
> twenty years—
> Twenty years largely wasted, the years of
> *l'entre deux guerres*—
> Trying to learn to use words, and every attempt

> Is a wholly new start, and a different kind of
> failure
> Because one has only learnt to get the better of
> words
> For the thing one no longer has to say, or the
> way in which
> One is no longer disposed to say it.

As significant as the fact that the world the poet observes exists in time is that he himself is subject to time and change. How to give permanent shape to experience, when both the experiencer and the world experienced simply will not stand still, is yet another version of the problem of reaching the still point of the turning world while still a part of that changing world. If there is any solution to this apparent dilemma, it must lie in paradox, beyond ordinary logic and analysis. The still point, for example, may be reached mystically, in the place where "the fire and the rose are one." Perhaps the pattern that is permanent yet reflects change can exist in the poem grasped as a whole. Surely nothing less, no mere part of it, would do, nor would analysis demonstrate adequately that it had succeeded. It is arguable, of course, that neither solution can be realized. One may contend that mysticism has no connection with the affairs of time, and that one is therefore left with existential hope and anguish, and that the struggle of words and with words must continue without final victory and be its own reward. However we read the poem and interpret Eliot's final position—if, indeed, he has one—on the feasibility of such final victories, time remains language's chief tormentor.

In Elytis, although the passing of time may evoke occasional nostalgia—as in the naming of women in the poet's past—this aspect of reality is not poetry's signal enemy. Elytis' decision to confront experience not as an individual but rather as part of a greater whole results in a far more relaxed—though not less respectful—attitude toward language. While Eliot addresses the difficulties of using words throughout the *Quartets,* Elytis only once self-consciously considers his language, in Psalm II of **"The Passion,"** and here not to wrestle with words but to establish their connections with those greater entities, cosmos and country.

Elytis' Greek language is seen in connection with the Greek people and their history, from Homer, whose great epics fathered classical civilization, and the Byzantine hymns which are the backbone of Greek orthodoxy—not to mention of *To Axion Esti*—to the first words of Dionysios Solomos' "Hymn to Liberty," the national anthem of Greece, grounded in that nation's war of independence from the Turks.

Words, however, are connected not only with things Greek but also with the universe at large; they are creatures in nature. Bream and perch are "wind beaten verbs," the songs of the sirens "rosy shells with the first black shivers," and sweet psalms to God "the first chirping of finches." It is out of this intimate relationship between words and things that a definition of the poet emerges which does not arise in Eliot's work: the poet as namer. As **"Genesis"** is given over to the creation of the world, so **"Gloria"** is devoted to the naming of its representative features. In the first instance, it is God or the powers of nature which do the making; in the second, it is the poet. Elytis will become a *"monk of things verdant, / And reverently serve the order of birds."* He names and praises winds, islands, flowers, women, ships, mountains, and trees, a selection with universal applicability, but in its particulars characteristically Greek. In addition, there is for each category a stanza made up of proper names of eight or nine items in that class. The name—the poet's contribution—is a palpable entity in its own right, not quite separable from the object it designates.

Concern with words leads each poet into the past of his language; but here, too, differences in their approach to that past conform to the general pattern. Eliot, in "East Coker," quotes from *The Governour* of Sir Thomas Elyot, originally published in 1531:

> Two and two, necessarye coniunction,
> Holding eche other by the hand or the arm
> Whiche betokeneth concorde.

This passage, of course, evokes a particular moment in English history. It is equally significant that Elyot is an Eliot— or Eliot an Elyot—an ancestor of the poet, a part of his personal past. This is perfectly in keeping with the *Quartets'* emphasis on the individual's struggle as an individual to overcome the constraints of time.

For Elytis, on the other hand, language is the instrument of a people, in this case the Greek people, which leads him both to a sense of language in history, in time, and of its overriding unity—that is, of both the movement and the pattern. In addition to acknowledging the past in a number of allusions (such as the one to Solomos mentioned above), Elytis also seems to deny time's effects in his use of words drawn from the full range of the Greek language. *Okypoda, agkhemakhos,* and *simantores,* for example, are Homeric; *ikthyophores,* classical; *ta Minaia ton Kipon,* Byzantine; *Thee protomastora,* from folk tradition. By combining such words and phrases with contemporary demotic Greek, e.g., *okypoda philia* 'swiftfootedkisses,' Elytis downplays the fact that those words are archaic and makes them part of a continuous, living language. The tension between demotic Greek and *katharevousa*—between the language as it is commonly spoken and the scholarly attempt to preserve as many as possible of the characteristics of the ancient tongue—has existed since the Greeks achieved their independence from Turkey and has always had strong sociological and political overtones. It has resulted in a sensitivity to language on all levels of society quite unparalleled in the modern English-speaking world. The sense of continuity is also unique. Despite the far greater time span, there is less difference between Homeric and Modern Greek than there is between Middle and Modern English. The Greek persistence in pronouncing all Greek from Homer on— to the horror of most non-Greek classicists—in the same (that is, modern) way, has also served to reinforce this sense of wholeness of the language—a sense that Elytis has taken full advantage of.

Not surprisingly, then, Eliot's and Elytis' attitudes toward language turn out to be special instances of their broad visions of reality. Eliot, who must in a single instant capture an essence which partakes of both time and eternity, is, at least on the surface, humble in his inability to make words do what he demands of them (although we may well suspect a certain coyness in such protestations); Elytis exults in the godlike power to name and sanctify, and, although respectful of the formidable tradition to which he belongs, is consequently far less critical of language's ability to perform as required.

For Eliot, struggling with time, the most significant confrontations of words are with the abstract. Time is an experience of the intellect rather than of the senses (except for the present; but without an awareness of past and future, the present has nothing to do with time); language, which originates in concrete experience, must always borrow from the spatial world of the senses in order to express the abstract. Such borrowing (more commonly known as metaphor) is not without special power, but used extensively it risks diminished impact. Elytis, committed to space, can push language back to its sources, where, like the giant Antaeus, it gains strength by making contact with the ground from which it sprang. This does not, of course, necessarily make Elytis a better poet than Eliot (even if his work were utterly free of the abstract, which it is not); but it helps to explain Eliot's sense of struggle and tension with regard to language as opposed to Elytis' sense of sheer pleasure.

There is a relationship between the two poets' preferred locations along the space-time continuum and the respective literary traditions where they sought support early in their careers. Eliot's well-known essay "The Metaphysical Poets" (1921) has long been taken as an accurate signpost identifying the poetic preoccupations of that stage of his development. He complained of the dissociation of sensibility that has taken place since the seventeenth century, of poets who do not "feel their thought as immediately as the odour of a rose." In a sense, all of Eliot's poetry has been an attempt to counter that long-dominant tendency by reuniting feeling and intellect; indeed, such conceits as Christ the wounded surgeon (in the fourth movement of "East Coker") healing us with "sharp compassion" are closer in sensibility to John

Donne—for example, in the paradoxes of Donne's Holy Sonnet XIV, "Batter My Heart"—than to most of Eliot's contemporaries. Though the purpose of such poetry may be the joining of feeling and intellect, it is through intellect that feeling must be reached (just as eternity must be reached through time), both in Metaphysical poetry and in *Four Quartets*. It is not illogical to suppose that Eliot's concern with time contributed to his predilection for this poetic mode.

Elytis, on the other hand, is known for his early interest in (especially) French surrealism. Surrealism, of course, rather than emphasizing the claims of intellect as a means of organizing one's response to experience, pays homage to the irrational, or at least to the nonrational. Logical distinctions between inner and outer realities (including the one and the many), conscious and unconscious, fantasy/dream and objective perception are broken down. Even more important, the "reality" of surrealism is fully available to the senses. When Elytis follows Paul Eluard's "blending of the human body and the nature of the world" in a poem like "Body of Summer," he is not simply exploring a rich source of metaphor but also anticipating the emphasis of *To Axion Esti* on spatial rather than temporal relations. As in *To Axion Esti* the individual is not clearly distinguishable from his surroundings. While he may be subject to the cyclical time of nature, he is oblivious to linear, irredeemable time.

Unity of being. In the end, that is what both Eliot and Elytis, like so many of their contemporaries, seek. Of all dualities to be resolved—thought and feeling, time and space (with the crucial subdivisions of time and eternity, the one and the many), body and spirit—none is more imposing than the alienation of the individual from that which is greater and more enduring than himself. The Second World War, bringing to the forefront of consciousness the often repressed awareness of death, superseding with its peculiar chaos the ordinary structures of society, questioning by giving shape to human evil the very notion of a divinely ordered universe, makes even more pressing than usual the need to escape from accident to necessity, from helplessness to strength. What similarities in structure and theme between *Four Quartets* and *To Axion Esti* possess are due to this underlying sameness of purpose.

As important to the poems' final nature as their creators' need to resolve dualities is the difference in sensibility which determines from which end of the continuum the attempt to bring unity will begin. Eliot struggles to give body to his abstractions; Elytis must impose intelligible order upon the sensory world. It is arguable, then, that Eliot and Elytis not only define the chief preoccupations of twentieth-century European poetry but also establish the boundaries within which poets so preoccupied may operate.

Andonis Decavalles (review date Spring 1985)

SOURCE: "Elytis's Sappho, His Distant Cousin," in *World Literature Today,* Vol. 59, No. 2, Spring, 1985, pp. 226-29.

[*In the following review, Decavalles asserts that although Elytis and Sappho were separated by time, their common language and culture enabled Elytis to bring new life to Sappho's work.*]

To those familiar with Odysseus Elytis, it is no surprise that the 1979 Nobel laureate has now lent his modern voice to that old "distant cousin" of his, as he calls Sappho. This was almost bound to come. After a lengthy flirtation, these two representatives of a three-millennia poetic tradition have finally joined in a poetic-erotic embrace, an identification through which the younger poet has poured new life and voice into the older one. Elytis has even restored the much-fragmented Sappho to her inherent fullness.

The fate of Sappho and her poetry through the ages is well known. The originality she once brought to poetry and the popularity and fame she gained and enjoyed in the ancient world were later darkened by defamation, persecution, and even extinction, first through the zeal of the early Christians and later through others and through historical events from the third to the thirteenth century. She was for a while painstakingly and partially restored during the Renaissance, only to disappear again, then later be recovered once more, mostly in fragmentary quotations, papyri, and mummy wrappings from the late nineteenth century onward. Ever since, scholars and poets have felt the challenge to discover Sappho in her fragmented self, to decipher her and her message, and even to derive a spark of inspiration from that message and its manner. The restoration has ranged from textual editing and literal renderings by J. M. Edmonds, Theodore Reinach, Denys Page, and Edgar Lobel—to mention some of her most distinguished restorers—to freer and more or less imaginative treatments by such writers as Hilda Doolittle, Ezra Pound, and, more recently, Mary Barnard and Willis Barnstone, among others. There have, besides, been understandings and intentional misunderstandings, as well as moralistic, often perverse "purifications" and "justifications" of her where she was found "offensive" to the purity of certain social standards and tastes. Fortunately, these have been counterbalanced by the honest longing of more liberated minds wishing to find and restore her true essence: not a priestess and a schoolmistress of manners for wealthy girls, but a passionate, freeminded, down-to-earth, sincere and frank lover speaking her own truth, admiring and loving beauty in nature and her female comrades, and not free of envy, jealousy, bitterness, or vengefulness toward her betrayers and enemies. All these did not, however, reduce her wish for affection, trust, innocence, purity, even virginity.

There was a remarkable individuality in Sappho, and she was gifted with an extraordinary zest for life, a bright and playful mind, and an originality and creative skill that combined to voice the honest truth concerning herself and her experience. If we may accurately judge from what we can sense, there was little if any artificiality in her diction and her manner. She spoke and wrote in the language of daily life to worship her preferred gods, Aphrodite and Eros, to celebrate social festivities and events (much of her poetry is occasional), and to address her sweethearts in letter form to tell them of her feelings toward them.

The systematic grammarians of Alexandria divided her poems into nine books according to their metrical arrangements, a practice followed by most of her editors ever since. The more imaginative her presentation, particularly by poets, the more it has tried to deviate from that technical rule. All this until Elytis came to lend his mind, heart, and skill to restore her to what he thought was her true essence and voice. His connection and relation with her has been long and intimate, based on deep-rooted ties. There is first of all their common origin, the Aegean, Elytis's poetic realm, and there is more specifically the Aeolian island of Lesbos, Sappho's Lesbos and Elytis's own cultural and ancestral origin, the shaper of much of his intellectual and emotional personality and his view and interpretation of life, besides being the storehouse of his imagery—in short, the motherlode of his poetic creativity. The Aeolian Sappho was once the poetic voice which Elytis found the closest to his own mind and heart, next to that of the Ionian Homer.

The most extensive prose commentary Elytis has written on Lesbos is the article he published on his fellow countryman, the folk painter Theophilos, compiled in 1967 yet begun as early as 1947. The first part, subtitled "The Other Lesbos," speaks of the island as a realm of fascinating individuality, shared equally by its rulers the sun and the moon, who impose equal justice on it. In Elytis's poetry, it is **"The Light Tree and The Fourteenth Beauty"** which clearly has Lesbos as its setting, a locale of physical as well as spiritual experience, of growth from childhood to full poetic maturity. As for his connection and references to Sappho herself, his **"Open Book"** is full of them. There we are told that a fragment of Sappho he once came upon by chance in the British Museum made him conscious for the first time of the origin of his love for poetry. Elsewhere he tells us how Sappho—among other poets, including even Dylan Thomas—made him feel that when divine myths are lost, it is the ego of the poet which must shape the world. In the midst of a nature bestowed upon him by his ancestors, he was once made to feel that "the old voices of Sappho" were one of the two main "currents starting from remote springs" and bound to intersect in him, the other current being "the passion to cross out and to rewrite

from the beginning at the point where Eros should be the real Eros, true and free." He adds elsewhere that it was she, Sappho, who taught him how to see the blue of the sky and how to listen to the sound of the sea. Where her name is not clearly mentioned (as on page 21 of **"Open Book"**), we sense the sound of her Aeolian voice echoed in the musically fascinating nonsense verse that he believes he hears coming out of the mouth of an angelically beautiful girl, whose voice mingles with the noise of the sea and the foliage.

> **To those familiar with Odysseus Elytis, it is no surprise that the 1979 Nobel laureate has now lent his modern voice to that old "distant cousin" of his, as he calls Sappho.**
>
> —*Andonis Decavalles*

This is the least we can say as to connections and references. Need we add that whatever liberating and self-liberating force Elytis felt he found in surrealism as springing from one's deeper, intuitive, unimpeded self, he undoubtedly, felt he found also expressed in Sappho? In the introduction to *Sappho* he speaks of her as follows in connection with the world that produced her:

> Historians have spoken about the exquisitely refined yet plush manner of life developed on Lesbos in the seventh and sixth century B.C. A mixture of free morals and customs based on models of worship where nature and Eros had a leading position. If one adds the facing yet not distant Asiatic hinterland, the site of Lydia, renowned like Sardis for women's cosmetics and clothing, one would understand that, near the Paris of that time, the women of Mytilene might speak the way Sappho spoke.

There was no shame in their being true to themselves and frank concerning their passions and desires. No puritanical moralism impeded them. As to Elytis's own poetry itself in this connection, anyone familiar with it should know how much, from its very beginning, in its lyricism, its musicality, its erotic content, its positing of life's full enjoyment and transcendence in the process, always in the name of love, it does not lie far from that of Sappho. The work of both poets has been to a great degree the spring blossom of the same soil under the same sky, the same sunlight, despite the huge expanse of time between them.

What was then still left for Elytis to do with Sappho? If her other, mostly foreign translators-interpreters were bound inescapably to approach her from their respective distances in time and culture and language, doing variously the best they could under the circumstances, Elytis, for several reasons, could easily reduce that distance thanks to his multiple affinities with her. His only separation was that of time, and even that was only apparent. Their languages had common roots and common natures, the one being much the heir of the other. Technically speaking, a strong link between them was the common idiom of the spoken Greek rendered marvelously lyrical through demotic songs of loves, joys, and sorrows, through virginal songs, prothalamia and epithalamia, or wedding songs. Of that stock Elytis could take wonderful advantage, yet little echoing the demotic songs themselves, for the language in his Sapphic renderings is the everyday, contemporary, spoken Greek in its lively richness. The voice here may be said to be the translator's as well as Sappho's, for it has grown through long years of poetic creativity to the point where these renderings unfailingly sound like original poems, Elytis's own.

It is gratifying, moreover, to see that Elytis has taken the additional original step of attempting to overcome the fragmentariness of the historical record and augment the seven hundred surviving lines of Sappho's verse. Where he found complete poems, he faithfully reproduced them; but where he met with fragments, he took them as pebbles to produce faithful, uncompromising, and only slightly altered poetic mosaics as full as those fragments allowed him, combining their thematic and emotional aspects where they could be fit together. One naturally wonders whether such combinations might not allow endless variety, decided by the taste and personal inclination of the one who attempts them. Elytis's choices and his skillful practice with Sappho's fragments leave no doubt that, for the most part at least, he has been faithful to her spirit and art.

The number 7 has long been Elytis's favorite as a structural element in his poetry. In most of his later collections the poems are grouped by sevens and multiples of seven. Sappho followed the same practice. Her entire extant work is divided, arranged, and organized in seven thematic groups under headings drawn from that oeuvre. The first group, entitled "Aeríon epéon árhome" (I Start with Airy Words), is composed of four poems in which, by way of introduction, she speaks of being inspired by the Muses to serve beauty and tell the truth, so to be remembered in times to come. She is haunted by Aphrodite, and so she burns with desire and pain. She is not filled with wrath against her enemies and does not wish revenge; although she has done only the best for others, she has received only the worst in return, but complaints and laments should not be heard in poets' homes. In her mortality, she does not aspire toward touching heaven. Her mind is innocent and pure, and she wishes to stay eternally virginal.

In the second group, entitled "Iros ángelos" (Messenger of Spring) and comprising eight poems, spring is announced by the nightingale, Cretan girls dance and step on little flowers, and Hesperus eventually restores what the Dawn has dispersed. The Moon in her bright light effaces all the stars, and Sappho in her loneliness suffers the pains of Eros, who is summoned to come down from heaven, since he has always been eager to respond kindly to her wishes and entreaties. The group closes with Sappho's fullest and best-known poem, the prayer to Aphrodite to descend from her heavenly throne and give solace to the suffering poet, victim of love's traps and machinations, and to bring back her beloved.

> **The number 7 has long been Elytis's favorite as a structural element in his poetry. In most of his later collections the poems are grouped by sevens and multiples of seven. Sappho followed the same practice.**
>
> **—Andonis Decavalles**

The most extensive group is the third, containing sixteen poems under the heading "Tais émes etíres" (To My Beloved Girl Comrades). These are invitations to Sappho's sweethearts to come and join her in songs and festivities and love embraces, wishing that her nights with them could be twice as long, remembering their youthful beauty, complaining of their unfaithfulness, admitting her jealousy of them, and reminding them of their mortality. In the most outstanding among these poems the poet suffers ecstatically, in a frantic seizure, all the physical and mental pangs of envy toward the man who is privileged to contemplate the beauty and enjoy the sweetness of voice and the laughter of her own beloved. Much is said of the unsurpassed power of Eros, to which women are the most vulnerable; Helen was its victim when she deserted her husband to follow her beloved to Troy. The section closes with another of Sappho's most memorable pieces, her poem to Anaktoria, who has departed to Sardís, in Lydia; there Anaktoria distinguishes herself among the Lydian women, whose beauty pales all stars and light and gives life to plants and flowers. She, however, must still be thinking nostalgically of Atthis, and her inviting voice seems as if conveyed across the distance.

The seven poems under the heading "Imináon" (Wedding), in the fourth group, are wedding songs, prothalamia and epithalamia, introduced by a lament for the death of Adonis. Bridegrooms and brides are alternately addressed in praise or invitation to prepare for their union, for the loss of their virginity. The fifth group, containing five poems and titled "Kípri ke Niriídhes" (Cypris and Nereids), opens with Sappho's bitterness for her misbehaving, corrupt, wasteful, and insulting brother, whom she implores Aphrodite and the Nereids to bring back from abroad, purify, and make once again a joy to his friends and a bane to his enemies. After a short yet affectionate address to her daughter Kleis, she offers a young lover of hers the equally affectionate advice to look for another, younger companion more suitable to his age. Lastly she tells us of her mother's instructions as to how a young woman should take care of her coiffure and headdress.

Two poems under the joint title "Plásion dhi mi pot ónar" (Come Close to me in My Dream) make up the sixth group; one is a prayer to Hera, the other a celebratory account of how young Hector brought Andromache as his bride from her native Plakia to Troy for the first time and the warm welcome they received. The seventh and final group, "Pantodhápesi memihména" (Mixed in All Manners), comprises what still remains of Sappho's fragments, including the most mutilated selections. Elytis combines these into nine still-fragmentary poems, or rather parts of poems, with numerous gaps which the boldest imagination might attempt to fill. The resulting compositions are riddles of defective syntax, shards of sentences, portions of words, clusters of unclear references and unclear meaning. They constitute mostly sounds, with their mysterious Aeolian musicality, like those that Elytis once heard from the mouth of that angelically beautiful young girl somewhere on Lesbos, near the sea. In the introduction to *Sappho* the poet tells us:

> Two and a half millennia ago, in Mytilene, I still see Sappho, like a distant cousin with whom I played in the same gardens, round the same pomegranate trees, above the same cisterns. She was somewhat older than I, a brunet, with flowers in her hair, and secret album full of verses that she never let me touch.

> Of course we lived on the same island. We had the same sense of the physical world, a characteristic one, which continues unalterable, from that time until today, to follow the children of little Aeolia.

Did that young brunet ever suspect, or even hope, that this younger cousin of hers, her playmate in several deeper respects, would at some future time get hold of her secret album and learn all her secrets, in full or in part, in order to lend them his own Aeolian voice and thus restore and revive her as our contemporary? With no little fascination, she would have seen her words sumptuously printed in a beautiful edition face to face with their modern echo, and she would also have seen herself, her beloved comrades, and her Aeolian world in bright colors as drawn by her younger cousin in his illustrations.

Andonis Decavalles (review date Summer 1986)

SOURCE: A review of *O mikros naftilos*, in *World Literature Today*, Vol. 60, No. 3, Summer, 1986, p. 500.

[*In the following review, Decavalles praises Elytis's* O mikros naftilos *stating that it "stands unquestionably on a level with Elytis's other major poems and also constitutes a comprehensive summation of his life and creativity."*]

Odysseus Elytis has dominantly and insistently been the poet of the bright and affirmative view of life. A worshiper of the sun, he has seen its light bathe and make lucid and diaphanous his eternally youthful Aegean world, which he has wished to see inspired, purified, and sanctified by Eros or Love in both its physical and its spiritual sense. Hence his "solar metaphysics."

Increasingly, however, personal and historical experience, age, mortality, and the approach of death have brought into Elytis's vision the darker, more pragmatic aspects of life as well, to which he constantly opposes his heavenly light. In one major poem after another—e.g., *The Axion Esti* (1959), **"The Light Tree and the Fourteenth Beauty"** (1971), *Maria Nephele* (1979), and now **"The Little Mariner"**—he has given an account of that struggle. What varies most in these poems is the form, manner, tone, and range of his craft in expressing an unswerving faith in his convictions, yet with an increasing and deepening recognition and consideration of the darkness that must be countered and transcended by spiritual wisdom. In Elytis's later poetry the Platonic belief in the existence of an "upper earth" that is truer than the one on which we live provides solace in the face of approaching death.

In **"The Little Mariner,"** as in Elytis's previous poems, the Pythagorean number seven and its multiples serve as a structural unit in the complex ordering of the fifty-eight pieces that make up the poem, pieces widely divergent in nature, manner, and content, ranging from mostly personal lyricism, to prose accounts, to lists of various kinds—the latter making their first appearance in his poetry. The title itself reminds one of the "sailor boy in the garden" of Elytis's early verse, who, however, now approaches the end of his odyssey.

A short opening selection titled **"Entry"** asks, "Golden air of life, why don't you reach us?" What follows is arranged in four major sections, three long and one somewhat shorter. The former are each divided into four parts under identical headings, whereas the latter has only two divisions. Under the first heading, **"The Little Mariner,"** a "Projector" speaks in each major subsection, enumerating prominent injustices and political crimes committed throughout Greek history from ancient times to the present. This is the guilty side of life that needs purging. Under the second heading, **"Smelling the**

Best," four major subsections, each containing seven poems, provide the mariner's account of his growth through experience and the attainment of the wisdom necessary to combat the evil inherent in life. Under the third heading, **"With Life and with Death,"** three of the four subunits contain seven poems each, in which the forces of light clash with the forces of darkness, then eventually merge on a higher plane of transcendence. Finally, in the first three of the four, the common heading "Whatever One Loves" unites the poems **"Traveling Bag," "Guide through the Aegean,"** and **"Snapshots."** Each selection provides lists of literary and artistic works, quotations, vocabulary, and a view of different places and women, all of which represent the indispensable treasures that the Little Mariner has gathered during his life's journey. The poem ends appropriately with a piece titled **"Exit."**

"The Little Mariner" stands unquestionably on a level with Elytis's other major poems and also constitutes a comprehensive summation of his life and creativity.

Joseph Garrison (review date July 1986)

SOURCE: A review of *What I Love,* in *Library Journal,* Vol. 111, No. 12, July, 1986, p. 88.

[*In the following review, the critic praises Elytis's* What I Love.]

This selection, covering the years 1943 to 1978, will please readers already familiar with Greece's 1979 Nobel Laureate and serve as a good introduction to those reading him for the first time. Elytis has said that Paradise and Hell are made of the same materials and that "only the perception of the order of the materials" differs, an idea illuminated here. If we perceive the moon as "hemorrhaged" or believe that "the beautiful can't happen twice," we have perceived wrongly. To perceive rightly, we must look at "the shells," "the leaves," and "the stars" in the right way. Elytis thus takes us back beyond the Latin word *ars* to its Greek root *harmos*—that is, to the weaver's loom, where, in the warp of reality, we perceive our realities and create our human designs.

Booklist (review date 1 September 1986)

SOURCE: A review of *What I Love: Selected Poems,* in *Booklist,* Vol. 83, No. 1, September 1, 1986, p. 22.

[*In the following review, the critic complains that much has*

been lost in Olga Broumas's translation of Elytis's What I Love.]

Eternal freshness, clarity, the ability to convey the abstract through the concrete, even the mundane, a sheer musicality—these are among the gifts the Greeks have given to poetry, from earliest times. One of the most famous of post-World War II Greek poets, Elytis maintains this great tradition, but he does so with a personal voice, especially in his love lyrics. In this selection of about two dozen poems, translator Broumas presents a range of the poet's interests and styles, some of which borrow heavily (perhaps too much so) from French surrealism of the early part of the century. The result is a curious amalgam of sensual particulars set amid almost mythic frames. Broumas has attempted high fidelity to Elytis' music and rhythms, but somehow, perhaps inevitably, much seems to have been lost in translation.

C. E. Fantazzi (review date December 1986)

SOURCE: A review of *What I Love: Selected Poems,* in *Choice,* Vol. 24, No. 4, December, 1986, p. 632.

[*In the following review, Fantazzi states that Olga Broumas's translation of Elytis's* What I Love *loses the music, the images, and sometimes the sense of the original.*]

Broumas, who translated these poems, has an obvious devotion to her fellow countryman, Odysseas Elytis, whose voice she professes to recreate in English, "with an accent, idiosyncratic," as she states in her prefatory note. She does indeed give him a distinct voice in English, but the accent and the idiosyncrasies are so pronounced that the renditions are often incomprehensible. Elytis is a difficult poet in Greek, shunning punctuation, running words into one another in clusters with little syntactic joining, but one can catch the sense, and the music of his language is enchanting, the imagery limpid and luminous, reflecting the effulgence of the Greek air and the sparkling waves of the Aegean. The same cannot be said of the facing English translation. The music is gone, the images faded, the sense often lost altogether or mutilated beyond recognition. The first line of the first poem from **"Sun the First"** may serve as an illustration: "I don't know anymore the night terrible anonymity of death." Add a little rhythm and punctuation and the line begins to make sense: "I no longer know the night, death's terrible anonymity" (translation of Edmund Keeley in *Voices of Modern Greece,* ed. by Edmund Keeley and Philip Sherrard, 1981). The instances of outright errors of translation and infelicities mar every page. Broumas's heart was in the right place, but she should have made use of an English interpreter.

Karl Malkoff (review date January-February 1987)

SOURCE: "Poetry with an Accent," in *American Book Review,* Vol. 9, No. 1, January-February, 1987, pp. 22-3.

[*In the following excerpt, Malkoff discusses some of the problems of Olga Broumas's translation of Elytis's* What I Love, *but asserts that it does shed light on the original work.*]

New translations of poems (which, like most of those selected by Olga Broumas for *What I Love,* have been recently rendered into English by more than competent translators) promise something new. In this respect, Olga Broumas, for better and for worse, does not disappoint. She informs us at the outset that she intends to preserve the strangeness, the foreignness of Elytis's texts. It ought to be, she asserts, "English with an accent."

This raises basic questions. In the very first poem, **"Sun the First,"** a critical sentence is translated: "I don't know anymore the night." Clearly, English with an accent. Broumas's line indeed follows the original word order. To the Greek reader, however, this order is natural and idiomatic, as other translators have more or less made clear (Edmund Keeley and Philip Sherrard: "I no longer know the night"; Kimon Friar: "I know the night no longer"). Sometimes the point of reproducing Elytis's foreign accent seems to make sense. For example, another section of **"Sun the First"** begins, "Day shiny shell of the voice you made me by. . . . " The ambiguous positioning of "shiny" between "Day" and "shell" reflects the fact that in Greek adjectives may come before or after the nouns they modify. On the other hand, in poems like **"Helen,"** when we read, "With her existence alone/ she annihilates off [sic] half the people," it is difficult to avoid at least considering the possibility that the choice of language is uninformed rather than intentional, possibly a confusion generated by the expression "finishes off." This is not the place to answer the question of what the translator's chief goal ought to be: the most literal possible (yet still idiomatic) reproduction of the text, the freer attempt to reproduce as nearly as possible the impact the work has made in the original, or a refusal to allow the translation to make what ought to seem strange familiar. But Olga Broumas's translations provocatively raise that question.

Somewhat more disturbing to the reader who, having been assured that "Line by line, the poems nearly match their original," is willing to give up the idiomatic are the liberties Broumas seems to take in the "literal" translation of certain words. The first of the prose poems—surely suitable material for the literalist—of **"The Hyacinth Symphony"** is a striking example of this. Here the night is "drawing her naked body" while in the original it "dreams" it (*onirevetai*); here the night has many "composers" while in the original it has many "compasses" (*piksides*); here an anchor "regales the

depths" while in Greek it "leads" them (*iyemonevei*). It is *not* that such variance is never acceptable in translation (it may sometimes be preferable); it is simply that if Broumas claims to offer the literal, it is difficult to justify these departures.

Having gotten the worst of it off my chest, and without denying some lack of confidence in the text produced by the contradictions cited above, I nonetheless had a certain amount of pleasure reading this volume. First of all, whether one agrees with it entirely or not, Broumas has a point. Not only is Elytis a speaker of Greek rather than English, he is also a surrealist, who sees the world in terms of its odd juxtapositions which the rational, conscious mind attempts to smooth out, to rationalize just as, Broumas might say, the conventional translator is a rationalizer of the strangeness of other languages and the unique approaches to reality those other languages contain. On at least some occasions, she captures Elytis's special music with accuracy and intensity (I am thinking of a poem like **"The Kite,"** from the *Maria Nefele* sequence: "In the bath next door the faucets open / face down on my pillow / I watched the immaculate white fountains splashing me; / how beautiful my god how beautiful / foot-trampled on the ground / to still hold in my eyes / such mourning for the distant past."

Second, although Sam Hamill's "Afterword" seems at first glance an attempt to give the appearance of predetermined purpose to a relatively accidental selection of poems—the theme of love, cited in the title, is ubiquitous in Elytis—the fact is that Hamill does point to a particular characteristic of Elytis's work which is effectively highlighted by Broumas's translations. Hamill writes: "Like the presocratics Elytis is far more interested in the origins and sources of mythology (in the *mechanism,* to use his own term), than in the figures themselves." All poets make myths, more or less, but this aspect of the poet's art is of special importance to Elytis's poetic powers. From the body-island of **"Sun the First"** to the girl-cloud of *Maria Nefele,* Elytis's ability to see the relationships between microcosm and macrocosm, between inner reality and outer, as literal rather than metaphorical bonds, is lucidly on display and is revealed as one of the essential components of man's myth-making capacities.

To answer the question implied at the very start of this review (why another translation of these poems?): Elytis is a major poet, expressing with clarity and passion one of the sensibilities of modern Greece. He not only *deserves* a variety of perspectives on his work, he *needs* them, so that in turn its various dimensions can be emphasized for English-speaking readers; to get them all at once, that reader must learn Greek. Olga Broumas's translation is not without its flaws, but it is interesting work and unmistakably sheds light on the original poetry.

Jeffrey Carson (review date Winter 1987)

SOURCE: A review of *What I Love: Selected Poems,* in *World Literature Today,* Vol. 61, No. 1, Winter, 1987, pp. 139-40.

[*In the following review, Carson criticizes Olga Broumas's translation of Elytis's* What I Love *for its inaccuracy.*]

Odysseas (or Odysseus) Elytis's great poetry is so rooted in the Greek language that transplantation into the alien soil of English is unlikely to take. How can one make readers unrooted in his Aegean world feel his seeming abstractions as emotions or respond deeply to "olive-tree," "whitewash," "Kore"? Each new graft by a serious translator brings fresh hope that the shoots will live, that more of Elytis will leaf in our foreign air.

Elytis's Greek varies, often in a single strophe, from literary to slang, from rhetorical to simple, from learned to folk-song-like. Profoundly personal without being at all confessional, he requires us to make the harsh and timeless Hellenic world of the poems into our own truth, and so professes a Shelleyan belief in Poetry's transforming magic. His poetry depends on musical values for its urgency and to conjoin word and inner feeling, so to change us through our relationship with language—something like a mixture of Stevens and the Pound of "Drafts and Fragments."

Thus Elytis demands more than the translator's usual patience and discipline, a discipline to which Olga Broumas has evidently not submitted herself. Since all but two early pieces in *What I Love* have been accurately translated by others, one wonders why her translations are shockingly inaccurate. There is not one poem in the book that is carefully or skillfully rendered. Examples of lapses in simple accuracy, giving one per page (there are many more on each page cited here, as on every page) from the first four pages: "greens" for "garden-patch" (p.5), "arbor" for "grapevine" or "vineyard" (7), "drawing" for "dreaming" (9), "sharing" for "portioning out" (11). Printing the Greek en face amounts to hubris.

Such inaccuracy would be somewhat less culpable if the translations captured Elytis's rich, allusive poetic sensibility or were themselves at least good English. They fail in both respects. Let us examine one of Elytis's most graceful lyrics, the twenty-two-line **"Small Green Sea"** (translated by others twice before). The image of Kore, the maiden, is crucial to all of Elytis's books. She embodies the beginnings of fertility, fresh and virginal: she is Poetry herself. He calls her by many names. Here she is Sea (*Thalassa*), whom he wishes to educate in Ionia, where so much of the Greek miracle began. He would have her inspire him through all of Greek history with divinity, to be communicated in a sexual embrace. In the second line Broumas tones down Elytis's urgent phrasing: her "I want to adopt you" ought to be "How I would like

to adopt you." Four lines later Broumas renders the simple word for "little tower" as "tight tower," whatever that may mean. Two lines later Elytis wants Sea to learn "to turn [rotate] the sun," not, as Broumas has it, "turn to the sun." In line 14 Broumas writes, "Go through Smyrna's window" for Elytis's "Enter Smyrna by the window." Her line 17 reads, "With a little north a little levantine." What she wants with the north and a diminutive Eastern gentleman I cannot tell: Elytis wants Sea to return "With a little bit of Northwind a little Eastwind." When the poet sleeps with Sea to get the essence of Ionia, Broumas either misunderstands or (as I suspect) suppresses this act. Broumas's "come back / Illegally to me to sleep / To find deep in your keep / Pieces of stone the talk of the Gods" (the clanging rhymes are gratuitous) should be something like "come back / Little Green Sea thirteen years old [this line is omitted by Broumas] / So I may sleep with you illicitly / And find deep in your arms / Pieces of stones the words of the Gods." Broumas has lost the poem. This is not an isolated instance of bowdlerization. In the last stanza of **"Ode to Picasso"** and in the biting fourth stanza of **"Maria Nefele's Song"** (whose astringent meter and rhyme are not even suggested), Broumas again alters the sexual imagery Elytis clearly intends, and on page 71 she translates "buttocks" as "thighs." If Elytis's sexuality discomfits or offends her, she should leave his work, drenched in the erotic, alone.

Half of **What I Love** is made up of out-of-sequence selections from Elytis's book-length poem *Maria Nefele.* Broumas strives for a punchy style; this could have been appropriate here. To see why it is not, let us look at **"Nefelegeretes"** (Cloud-Gatherer). The ancient Greek word is a frequent Homeric epithet for Zeus. The first line literally is, "Ah how beautiful to be cloudgatherer." Broumas translates this as "Ah how beautiful to hang out with the clouds." The slang does not fit. In the next line her word-for-word translation "on old shoes" misses the idiomatic meaning Elytis intends, "for the heck of it." In the first line of this poem's second stanza, Broumas's "to reap unpopularity" should be "enjoy unpopularity." Nine lines later, "the fat people" should be subject, not object, as here. Broumas's penultimate line, "and with large leagues open yourself freely to cry," is incomprehensible; an idiom, the Greek means, "and with great strokes you swim out to weep freely." As translated here, the poem is unintelligible. Broumas has not worked out the poem's meaning before translating.

Perhaps Broumas's own grammar is insecure: "don't be afraid / of what is written you to feel" (89); "I they threw me from the doors outside" (87). Her "It's me to who shouts" (43) must be making Elytis sad. If sometimes her style is usefully crisp and direct, as in certain lines of the difficult piece titled **"The Monogram,"** in no poem is her version superior to her predecessors', although improvement is the point of retranslation.

What I Love has a handsome cover, but the words "Nobel Laureate" on it may mystify the reader who finds the book's contents unworthy of that award. May I recommend Kimon Friar's Elytis translations *The Sovereign Sun,* which is what the Nobel Committee read?

Publishers Weekly (review date 22 April 1988)

SOURCE: A review of *The Little Mariner,* in *Publishers Weekly,* Vol. 233, No. 16, April 22, 1988, p. 79.

[*In the following review, the critic asserts that Elytis's* The Little Mariner *is about a journey.*]

This major work by Nobel laureate Elytis is composed in an elaborate symphonic form but has the simplest and oldest of story lines: a journey or quest—in this case, as the poet writes, "to find out who I am." The "I" is multipartite—representing not just the poet or the Greek nation but all humankind; and the journey takes place on many levels—geographical, historical, philosophical, linguistic, spiritual—alternating among four different kinds of "movements" that approach the problem of human self-realization from various angles using multifarious styles of verse. The poems are by turns lyrically luminous and simply direct; the sheer beauty of the Aegean pelago shimmers throughout as does the tradition of Greek ideals, which are set counterpoint to a millennium of political injustices and betrayals. The translation by Broumas, Greek-born and -bred and a Yale Series of Younger Poets prizewinner, is a wonder in itself. Where the poems are not quite translatable (because they are written in ancient or demotic Greek, for example), Broumas supplies notes to clarify Elytis's intention.

The Virginia Quarterly (review date Autumn 1988)

SOURCE: A review of *The Little Mariner,* in *The Virginia Quarterly Review,* Vol. 64, No. 4, Autumn, 1988, pp. 134-35.

[*In the following review, the critic states that Elytis's* The Little Mariner *is "more interesting for its experiments in form than for its lyrical content."*]

Elytis, winner of the 1979 Nobel Prize for literature, is the last in a distinguished line of modern Green poets, beginning with Cavafy and including George Seferis and Yannis Ritsos. This book includes, as the jacket tells us, his major work since he received the prize. It is also the second translation of his poetry by Olga Broumas since *she* won the Yale Younger Poets Award. All honors aside, I found the book more inter-esting for its experiments in form than for its lyrical content (is this Elytis or is it the translation?). The book is framed by an "Entrance" and an "Exit"; and each section entitled "The Little Mariner" opens with a "Spotlight," or a series of scenes from Greek history. Elytis includes prose poems, lists of his favorite words, his favorite places, and his favorite cultural artifacts (for better or worse, this reader was reminded of E. D. Hirsch's lists for the culturally literate). He has even written his own Sapphic fragment, in parts of words strewn over a page; and one poem in Ancient Greek, rendered by Broumas in slightly archaic English. This poet believes that Paradise "was a right," but his tone throughout is elegiac. The best poems express a sense of loss, even as they refuse nostalgia.

Andonis Decavalles (essay date Winter 1988)

SOURCE: "Time versus Eternity: Odysseus Elytis in the 1980s," in *World Literature Today,* Vol. 62, No. 1, Winter, 1988, pp. 22-32.

[*In the following essay, Decavalles discusses the themes of death and eternity in Elytis's* Diary of an Invisible April *and asserts that this poem is darker than the poet's other work.*]

For close to five decades, the poetry of Odysseus Elytis grew and blossomed with unaging and hopeful youthfulness in its battle against time and decay. It kept its undiminished commitment to extend and raise the material world to a higher sphere, to its pure, immaterial, imperishable essence. It kept alive its power to transform sorrow into joy, darkness into light, and negation into affirmation of life. Insistently it repeated its belief in man's potential and capacity to detect, to discover in the world of matter the lasting, spiritual, visionary messages that reveal a superearthly realm abiding within it. It created its own universe through Eros, the beauty of nature, and the Aegean sunlight as embodiments and expressions of an ancient yet still-vital Greek spirit of which they are the forces and analogies.

That youthfulness matured in wisdom through experience and the increasing awareness of sufferings—personal, racial, historical—the products of time that poetry needed to face, purge, and surpass through its belief in the existence of a paradise made of exactly the same elements that also constitute hell, where Heraclitan conflicts and antitheses meet in their extension. To quote the ancient thinker: "Opposition brings concord. Out of discord comes the fairest harmony." The battle with time, in Elytis's verse, gave birth to a continuous series of scintillating, timeless poetic "moments," instantaneous "meteoric" uplifts, "signals" witnessing the "lastingness" of a "real Earth," the "Earth of an upper world," a "second Greece" as the realm of poetry itself.

However, our individual mortal nature has its decline and end as well. Time, that *vrotolighos* or "destroyer of men," has not left the aging Elytis (b. 1911) unaffected. Together with developments in world affairs and circumstances and the spiritual and moral decline of our day, it has increased in the poet a certain awareness, a need to defend himself and the values that are part of his longtime creed, his message: first against those who have challenged, negated, or ignored it; and then against his own deeper, growing wonderings. Preaching his own gospel, he has long repeatedly expressed sorrow and militant complaint that his message of redemption has not borne the fruit expected through its wider acceptance and response, specifically in his own country, for which it was meant. On the other hand, the reality of human passions, life's darker side, which he has believed inseparable from the brighter one, has, in declining times, caused him increasing consternation, and the poetry of his full maturity has had to submit its faith to the test of nostalgic recollection and introspective reevaluation in order to deepen and widen the meaning of its "weapons."

With regard to death's challenge, that was initially met with its reversal in the *Heroic and Elegiac Song for the Lost Second Lieutenant* (1945) and *The Axion Esti* (1959). Later, in "The Autopsy" from *Six and One Remorses for the Sky* (1968), that autopsy of his own body revealed what was imperishable and eternal in his elemental self and gave signs and promise of regeneration. In "The Sleep of the Valiant" from that same book it was life that was miraculously the victor in a spiritual sense despite the death of the heroes. Soon thereafter, the poems in *The Light Tree and the Fourteenth Beauty* (1971) were to recollect nostalgically Elytis's entire spiritual life in terms of "meteoric," instant, revealing communications with the "sovereign sun," yet with an already painful eventual realization that the "light tree" of youth had become difficult to recover, if at all, and that the sun of life was also bound to set, leaving behind the darkness of the night sky. Still, the aged poet, not yielding to final despair, passed ingeniously to the lunar, mystical, occult, internal, meditative reflection of his "solar metaphysics," thus moderating the sorrow for the losses that time had brought. That reconsideration concluded with "Silver Gift Poem" as the only lasting final gain from life's losing game—silver being both the poet's age and the coloring of the trees of paradise.

Among Elytis's poems published in the 1970s, history and an old legend of the Greek people inspired 1971's "Death and Resurrection of Constantinos Paleologhos" (the last, tragic emperor of the Byzantine Empire), whereas in *The Monogram* (1972) it is love that sings the hope of its continuation and fulfillment in paradise. In *Maria Nefeli* (1978), on the other hand, Elytis embraced in his verse the word and mind of postwar youth in its nightmarish, urban, technological world estranged from nature, so as to argue that behind the apparent change life still remains changeless in its deeper

essence. The hippie girl Maria, the suffering victim of what surrounds her, demonic as she appears, still maintains within her the angelic and transcendental elements and virtues Elytis has always bestowed upon his "girls."

The awareness of time, as decay and death, and of its encounter were to become central, prominent, in Elytis's three poetry books published in the 1980s. Their proper consideration as stages of development requires our taking them in the sequence of their composition rather than that of their publication. Architecturally conceived and mathematically ordered as wider thematic units, as larger poems in parts—where, however, the parts are full individual poems in themselves—these books, or rather long poems, varied in the length of time required for their completion. This explains why *O mikrós naftílos* (The Little Seafarer), one of the three poems under consideration, mostly composed between 1970 and 1974, according to the poet's testimony, was not published until 1985, following *Tría piímata me siméa efkerías* (Three Poems under a Flag of Convenience; 1982) and *Imerológhio enós athéatou Aprilíou* (Diary of an Invisible April; 1984)—the last volume being, by all indications, a product of 1981.

The content, manner, style, context, and issue of each of these long poems are different as they all face time's challenge. Of the three, "The Little Seafarer" and "Three Poems" recapitulate at least in part much of the Elytian creed, though in different ways, in the fight against the odds they face, and they both end in doubt as to whether the poet has succeeded through his lifelong message in becoming the enlightener and savior he aspired to be. In times of turmoil the darker side of reality, previously repressed, overcome, and surpassed, needs now to be more frankly recognized and more painfully combatted, and with perhaps not as much certainty as before. Harder questioning succumbs to an invading despair, although resisted to the utmost. The "Diary," on the other hand, opens a new realm in Elytis's poetry. Death is met face to face as "imminent" and inescapable. The poet himself is not exempted from that final share of mortality.

The remote precedent of "The Little Seafarer" was certainly "Sailor Boy of the Garden" from *Ilios o prótos* (Sun the First; 1943). That was the poet's initial youthful self. Even since, Elytis has often projected himself as a mariner (in the Homeric if not the Coleridgean or the Rimbaldian sense), with that seafarer's appearances reflecting the gradual stages and moments in his life's spiritual journey. There is an "Odyssey" in *The Light Tree* (1971) emotionally influenced by the painful feeling of self-exile and nostalgia during Greece's sufferings under the colonels' junta of 1967-74.

"The Little Seafarer" has its factual challenge in the memory of Greek history considered in its darker aspects. That history had already provided the "mythical" basis of *The Axion Esti,* but there "the Passion" in it, the sufferings of the war decade of the 1940s, and all the long travails of the past were eventually overcome through the poet's still-youthful hopefulness, his sunlit affirmation of life, and his expectation of recovery of an earthly, physical, yet spiritual paradise made possible through what he deemed "worthy" in the Greek realm and the Greek soul. On the contrary, in **"The Little Seafarer"** a different predisposition, awareness, and circumstance makes him view Greek history in the light of political and other injustices and murders committed there for centuries, crimes which no sunlit limpidity can purify in their stark truth and perpetuity.

The poem consists of fifty-eight pieces (structured mostly around multiples of seven, as usual in Elytis) plus a short "Entrance" and "Exit" which frame the poem emotionally as well as physically, summarizing it in terms of its desperately expectant struggle and frustrating outcome. The "Entrance" reads:

> SOMETIMES IT'S
> no more than a glow behind the
> mountains—there toward the sea. Sometimes again
> a strong wind that stops suddenly just outside the
> harbors. And those who know, their eyes fill with
> tears
>
> *Golden wind of life why don't you reach us?*
>
> No one hears, no one. They all go holding an
> icon and on it fire. And not one day, one moment
> in this place when injustice doesn't occur or some
> murder
>
> *Why don't you reach us?*
>
> I said I'll leave. Now. With whatever: travel
> bag on my shoulder; Guidebook in my pocket;
> camera in my hand. Deep in the earth and deep in
> my body I'll go to find out who I am. What I give,
> what they give me and left over is injustice
>
> *Golden wind of life . . .*

The concluding "Exit" adds:

> BUT INCOMPREHENSIBLY
> no one hears. The burning
> bird of Paradise goes ever higher. The voice was
> turned elsewhere and the eyes remained
> unmiracled.
>
> *Helpless are the eyes*

> One among thousand of murderers, I
> lead the innocent and powerless. I wrap myself in
> an ancient cloak and again descend the stone stairs
> beckoning and exorcising
>
> *Helpless are the eyes, that you beckon to*
>
> centuries now above the blue volcanoes. Far on
> my body and far on the earth that I tread I went to
> find out who I am. I stored up small happinesses
> and unexpected meetings, and here I am: unable to
> learn what I give, what they give me and left over
> is injustice
>
> *Golden wind of life . . .*

The italicized verses are from one of the fragments of *The Free Besieged,* the unfinished final masterpiece of modern Greece's first national poet, Dionysios Solomos (1798-1857), where the "free besieged" were the starving population of Mesolonghi, who, after successfully resisting a Turkish siege in 1825-26 during that country's war of liberation, made a heroic sortie in which most of them perished under the guns of the enemy. (As is well known, it was at Mesolonghi that Lord Byron died in 1824, and Solomos wrote a long ode on his death.) The body of the poem is in four major parts, with the first three containing four sections each and the fourth containing two sections. In the first section of each part, "scenic" in nature, a *provolefs* or "speaking projector" gives short prose accounts in chronological order of seven major political injustices and murders—a total of twenty-eight—committed in Greek history from antiquity and the classical era, through the Hellenistic and Byzantine periods, to the present. The awareness of this grim reality is what instigates, in the following three sections, the seafarer's recollective journey in search of his Aegean identity to fight against the evils.

The common title of the four separated sections of the second part, **"Myrisai to áriston"** (To Scent the Excellent), is taken from the sixth-century Byzantine hymnist Romanos the Melode's "Hymn to the Whore" with its allusion to Matthew 26:6-13, where the whore pours her precious ointment on Christ's head. The analogy to Elytis's "girls," on the one hand, and to the objective and function of his poetry on the other as insinuated in the twenty-eight prose pieces of these four sections is obvious. The poet recapitulates his spiritual growth through the discoveries he made of life's essence and its redeeming truth, notions long familiar to his readers. There is the "material of feelings" which he "touched" in his struggle to restore the "innocence" he found everywhere, "so powerful that it washes away blood." "I resided," he says, "in a country that came from the other, the real one, as the dream comes from the facts of my life. It too I named Greece and I drew it on paper so I could look at it. It seemed so little; so elusive." In its extension, "with a blissful light above the sea," that "true Greece" came to reveal "the real grandeur of this littleness," this "second world that always comes first within me." Poetry gave him "a kind of special courage" to win his own "transparency," the movement within the moment which gives it "duration," whereupon "Sorrow becomes Grace and Grace an Angel."

The awareness of time, as decay and death, and of its encounter were to become central, prominent, in Elytis's three poetry books published in the 1980s.

—Andonis Decavalles

As for time, "The clock that concerns us is not that which counts the hours but that which allots the portion of things' decay and indestructibility, in which, in any case, we participate, as we participate in youth or age." He has refused to accept death as "hooded in black," as he was told when a child, for "he who chewed bayleaf [this must be the Pythia at Delphi] said something else." Also, "Man is never so great, or so little, as the concepts he conceives, starting from Angel up to Demon. He is equal to the part that remains when the two opposing forces neutralize each other." With regard to death, "If there is a way to die without disappearing—it is this: a transparency in which your ultimate components— dew, fire—become visible to all, and one way or another, you shall exist forever." As to paradise, all religions have lied about it: "Yes, Paradise was not a nostalgia. Nor, even more, a reward. It was a right." Things change and we change with them, yet our nature will stay "irreparably engraved on the geometry that we disdained in Plato." The external things in nature are "the same natural and spontaneous movements of the soul that give birth to matter and set it in a certain direction; the same reformations, the same risings toward the deepest meaning of a *humble Paradise,* which is our true self, our right, our freedom, our second and real ethical sun"—an obvious affinity with Plato's notions.

These and other substantial components of Elytis's creed are recalled and newly expressed as his defense against an acrid awareness of time as a dark historical inheritance, and several ideas here will find their poetic expression in the third part of the poem as well, whose separate sections bear the common title **"With Both Light and Death"**—taken from the ode "To Death" by Andreas Kalvos (1792-1816), Solomos's contemporary and a major poet whom the latter apparently ignored. As early as 1942, in his essay **"The Lyric Physiognomy and Lyric Daring of Andreas Kalvos,"** Elytis had voiced his admiration for his short-lived predecessor and the technical skill in the sui generis, unorthodox, strange individuality of his language, his stanzaic form, his sound and rhythm. In the cited ode the ghost of the poet's mother, like the Homeric Antikleia, appears to him to tell him "not to investigate the inexpressible mystery of death," adding that life is "unbearable toil" whereas the dead enjoy "endless peace, with no fear, sorrow, or dreams." The quoted stanza reads: "My son, you saw me breathing, / The sun, chasing in cycles / like a spider, enfolded me / unceasingly with both light / and death." Again the relevance and affinity with Elytis's circumstance and concerns are obvious here.

In a variety of forms, manners, and tones, the twenty-one (three times seven) mostly lyric pieces of **"With Both Light and Death"** summon as a solace and defense all they can recall in facing the increasing nearness of death itself. In the opening selection the hopeful expectation of a celestial transformation still exists.

> I turned death toward me like a gigantic
>   sunflower:
> Adramyttion Bay appeared with the
>   northwester's curly
>   strewing
> A moveless bird between sky and earth and the
> mountains
>   Lightly set one in the other. The child appeared
>   who ignites
>   Letters and runs to turn back the wrong in my
>   breast
>   In my breast where appeared the second Greece
>   of the upper world.
>
> This I say and write not to be understood
> Like a plant satisfied in its poison until the
>   wind
> Turns it to fragrance which it scatters right to
>   the world's
>   four points:
> My bones will appear later phosphorescing an
>   azure
> Which the Archangel carries in his arms and
>   lets trickle
> As with great strides he traverses the second
>   Greece of the upper world.

There is still expectation of the "mercy-giving orchard."

> I await the hour when a
> Mercy-giving orchard will assimilate
> The refuse of all centuries—when a

Girl will declare revolution in her body
Beautifully with tremulous voices and glisters
Of fruit bringing history back again
To its starting point
                                    in which case
Probably even Westerners will go Greek
Reaching all the way to the figtree's liver
Or the perfection of waves will be dictated to
          them
While asleep
                    and from a breach in their thought
          the
                    fumes
Of a certain courageous lavender encountered
          in childhood
Will propitiate the starry spaces full of angers.

One selection will ask, "where is the meaning that fell from your hands / . . . / . . . what burning / Dress is this that detaches your flesh," recalling the "Youth kneeling in the transparent deep / . . . / Biting as if a coin [the funereal obol] the same sea that / Gave you the very shining the very light the meaning you seek." Another has truncated words and phrases like those in the Sapphic fragments. Still another says:

I speak with the patience of the tree that rises
Before the window just as old
Whose shutters the wind has dilapidated
And keeps pushing it open and getting it wet

With water of Helen and with words
Lost in the dictionaries of Atlantis
I alone—and earth from the opposite place
The place of destruction and of death.

The poet will imploringly address the Holy Virgin, the Mother, in the language of Byzantine hymns, calling her by the numerous imaginative, poetic names that the Greek people have given her, beseeching her to come to him in his loneliness.

Some inherited bitterness in the Greek temper, the product of long historical suffering, Elytis has constantly decried and opposed. It becomes again the subject of some lovely, sorrowful lyricism in this series of sections.

Where shall I say it—night in the air
To the stars' medlars to the blackness smelling
          of
The sea. Where shall I speak the Greek of
          bitterness
With trees for capitals where shall I write it
That the sages know to decipher
Between the second and third wave

Such an anguish heavy with stones that did not
          sink.

Saint Sozon—you who watch over storms
Raise me the eye of the sea
That I go miles in it to the green translucence
That I arrive there where the sky's
          masterworkers dig
And may I find again the moment before I was
          born
When the violets were fragrant when I didn't
          know
The way the thunderbolt doesn't know its
          lightning
But doublestrikes you—all luminous!

The section's final piece, an elegy, appears to have been inspired by a dear dying friend, whom the poet wishes and begs to be his forerunner, to guide and welcome him when he too goes across.

And most important of all: you will die.
The other Golden Horn will open
Its mouth for you to pass with white face
While the music continues and on the trees
Which you never turned to see the hoarfrost
          will release
One by one your works.
                              Well then! Think now
If the truth gives off
Drops if the Milky Way widens
Substantially: then wet gleaming with your
          hand upon
Noble laurel you leave even more Greek
Than I who blew for you the propitious wind in
          the strait
Who packed for you bags of whitewash and
          bluing
The little icon showing gold July and August
And you know I being a lost
Voyager when to give me hospitality
Setting on the tablecloth
The bread the olives and the consciousness
Day first for us in the second homeland of the
          upper
world.

Sappho provides the common title **"Otto tis erate"** (Whereof One Loveth) of the three sections that make up the fourth and final part of the poem. Their individual subtitles are the three items of luggage and equipment mentioned in the "Entrance" which the seafarer takes with him on his journey in search of his identity. **"The Traveling Bag"** contains the names of fifty-four poets, writers, thinkers, artists, and composers, with three or four of their verses, phrases, works of art, musical compositions, and some monuments, "only what's necessary" from things he has gathered throughout Greece and the Western world through all times since prehistory. **"Aegean Route"** is an alphabetical list of some four hundred Greek nouns and names, "Only Words. But words to guide with precision to what I was looking for. So, bit by bit, turning the pages I saw the place take on form like the tear from emotion." **"Snap-shots,"** finally, includes thirty-one short prose sketches, images that the camera of the poet's eye and sensibility and preference has caught in various parts of Greece and elsewhere as instantaneous revelations.

All those have been his equipment and wealth, found as he went "deep in the earth and deep in my body." As the "Exit" implies, however, these have brought him no final redemption, apparently leaving him estranged and uncomprehending, deprived of the response he was expecting. The "small happinesses and unexpected meetings" have left him "unable to learn what I give, what they give me and left over is injustice." For the first time a poetic work by Elytis ends in despair, without a "meteoric" reversal. The uncured evils still thrive.

When we turn to the **"Three Poems under a Flag of Convenience"** (1982), we may possibly understand the evoked *efkerías* (opportunity, convenience) as another chance, another try to admonish and so to break the isolation, the increased loneliness always extant in Elytis's admonitions. In their unity and sequence the three poems here, each divided into seven parts, bear the individual titles **"The Garden Sees,"** **"The Almond of the World,"** and **"Ad Libitum."** The viewing garden is obviously the paradise-oriented angle of vision, detecting through sunny lucidity and projecting through instantaneous revelations life's real essence and truth. The "almond of the world" must be that real essence and truth itself, Elytis's equivalent of Plato's *to agathon,* yet bitter at times, as almonds are. As to the phrase "ad libitum," ironically enough, instead of pleasurable ease it expresses the strain in a losing battle of the poet's identity against the odds that time has brought.

No less the *vates* that he has always been, the poet has the garden's eye detect and reveal ingredients of his transcendental creed and its salvatory potential, as yet unfortunately ignored by those to be rescued.

>   1. Maybe
>   if we except Anchorites
>   I might be the last player
>   to exercise his rights
>
>   presumption
>
>   I don't understand
>   what profit means

a Panselinos who paints though God does not
>   exist
and proves exactly the opposite

>   stream

>   what water
>   blue with sparks

beyond the barrier of the Sirens' sound
signals to me

>   leaping

>   come on

somewhere

>   Perfection lies completed
>   and lets a rivulet roll up to here

Art makes real the unreal; it even creates God where He does not exist. Perfection is *there,* accomplished for those who care for it. There are always its "raging" messages, one after another, but "what to do / no one knows." As to the future:

>   So what will happen when
>   sometime social struggles stop when inventions
>   obsolete themselves when all demands are
>   satisfied

>   void

>   inside which will fall those (serves
>   them right)
>   who turn the wheel for the sake of
>   the Wheel

>   dazzle

>   we others
>   shall commence to live initiates in the body's
>   Sanskrit
>   essentially and metaphorically speaking

We are the microcosms of a macrocosm, a universe made of "antimatter," and there are "a million signs / omega zeta eta [i.e., zoe or 'life'] / and if these don't form a word for you / tomorrow / will be yesterday forever." If the words will raise life to its affirmation, then "at a second level wars will recur / without anyone's being killed / there are sufficient reserves of death," where war gains its Heraclitan meaning. The garden then "starts off the countdown / withering / acme / waking / a young woman's breast is already / an article of the future's Constitution."

It is in this spirit that the poem unfolds to its end with the belief that "the decay of time at last will turn against it." The urging comes with a reference to Oedipus's reaching his transcendence at Colonus.

> . . . advance
>> you encounter the famous grove of
>>> Colonus
>> you follow Oedipus
>
>>> coolness
>>> peace
>>> nightingales
> suddenly daybreak
>> the cock on the weathervanes
>> it's you in the church
>> the icon-screen superb with pomegranate
>>> trees
>
> Kore stepping on the waves
>> a gentle westerly
>>> wafts
>
> your hand copies
>> the Inconceivable.

But this is not easy. As the second poem states:

> *the almond of the world*
>> is deeply hidden
>>> and still unbitten
>
> a myriad possibilities shudder
> around us which we idiots wouldn't
>>> even touch
>
> we never understood how pigeons think
> two hand-spans above our head
>>> what we have lost already is in
>>>> play

No doubt, "*the almond of the world* / is bitter and there's no way / you can find it unless / you sleep half outside of sleep." That he himself has strived for.

> at night
>> when I speak as if to stir up constellations
> in the upper embers for a moment the face
>> is formed that God
>> would give me if he knew
>> how much the earth in truth cost me
> in desperation
>> in "it was destined" whispered variously
>>> at night

> in cypresses
> centuries old like poems
> during the making of which I was
>> disrealized.

Though his strife has caused him isolation and loneliness, and despite the dislike he may have encountered, he would not give up. He would continue his "course / against this society / against inhibiting idiocy." Poetry needs to produce a spark in its fruit, for "something surely / must surreptitiously have been subtracted / from the terraqueous globe / for it to pant so / to turn pale / and for mourning to spread itself" The sad truth is that "Even if you have it all / something's always lacking / it's enough the Integral not be accomplished / and Fortune feel fortunate."

Never before has Elytis spoken in a language of such stark and hopeless pragmatism about time's advance and the accompanying physical, mental, and moral decline, where death is in view.

—*Andonis Decavalles*

Man's longing for perfection is always plagued by limited potential, as was earlier expressed in *The Light Tree.* "We always sought / precisely that which cannot be"—one of heaven's sins which led to the *Six and One Remorses.* As you strive to cut "the almond of the world," you have your hand scorched and end up writing "some white / poems on the black page." Further on are implications of Plato's notion of our preexistence, forgotten upon birth, to be recollected and regained in a lifelong struggle: "man is as if coming from elsewhere / and so he sounds out of tune / with a memory all fragmented." Loneliness is the price, with only instantaneous gratifications.

> all alone
>> I am hanging
>>> since Heraclitus' time
> like *the almond of the world*
>> from a branch of the North Aegean
>> an ancient fisherman with his trident
>> who has known many gales until there:
>> sometime the moment arrives
>
> the waters around him become
>> brilliant
>> chilly
>> rosy
> he squints his eyelids
>> it's because the reflection

all absolute beauty
shows with whom it briefly had with no
intention on his part

a confidential meeting.

An expectation of a kind of afterlife can be seen in the lines "axiomatically I am living beyond the point where I find myself / besides / continuing along my mother / you will meet me even after death." Such still-inherent hope for spiritual timelessness, for eternity, carries on in dialectical fashion its desperate battle against increasing doubts and questionings as we reach the third poem, **"Ad Libitum,"** which represents a more pragmatic encounter with and consideration of temporal reality. Much as in *The Axion Esti,* the poet begins here by defining his personal yet ethnic and historical identity, but with a more painful awareness of the present and the future.

I am alpha years old and European to the
middle
of the Alps or Pyrenees
I never never touched the snow

there's not one who can represent me
war and peace ate at me on both sides
what remained endures still

till when
friends

must we lift up the excommunicated past
filled with kings and subjects

myself
I feel like a seduced cypress

to whom not even a tombstone remained
only empty plots rocks stone-enclosures
and the inconsolable northwind
beating yonder on the factories' high walls

all of us enclosed there we work as
elsewhere in History

the

Future

years say spilled crude oil
set ablaze

help

Rintrah roars and shakes
his fires in the burdend air

my unfortunate allalone *one*

what's to become of you
five or six zeroes on the side will eat you up

and it is finished

there already now
Authority dresses as Fate and whistles to
you

Ad libitum.

Never before has Elytis spoken in a language of such stark and hopeless pragmatism about time's advance and the accompanying physical, mental, and moral decline, where death is in view. Rilke had wished one's death to be individual, chosen, one's own, in agreement with the identity of his soul. Here instead we read:

fortunately the ambient wind has no memory
it persists in smelling of rose
and in punishing you
while you die wretchedly

ready in line behind the others
for passport control
with an airline bag on your shoulder

You resist such impersonal, mechanical, mass departure, where "you call to mind your limits / always in the dark / conducted by a ground-stewardess / completely uninterested in your personal luck." The air-flight scenery and much else was part of Maria Nefeli's world as well, but in that poem was eventually redeemed through the revelation of Maria's deeper purity and victimized innocence and through the poet's still-solid faithfulness, whereas here it remains unpurified and unredeemed. The "girl" in this poem seems to have lost her old, gratifying nature, remaining strange and indifferent as to the traveler's movement toward "the cryings of birds-of-prey / and the complete petrification / wherein you shall be enlisted / thee little one / how can you magnified by thought / defy natural phenomena."

The poet had been deemed a "phenomenon" by those who heard at night a pen scratching "like a cat on the closed / door of the Unknown" guarded by "infamous / personae turpi." The victims of our times, "amid revolutions and wars we all grew up / that's why on our foreheads / the mark of the bullet not shot / at all times continues to cause death." Confronting such despairing circumstances, the "final conclusion" asks:

what can one say

until we become men whom health does not bore
some Beauty will be traveling in space
camouflaged never struck by anyone

an idol that still

knows to preserve the olive-tree's aspect
among the Scythians

and that will be restored to us
like a lovely echo from the Mediterranean
smelling still of a deepsea goat

one for the other Odysseus
upon a raft

centuries now

I cry out in Greek and no one answers me

it is that no one knows any more
what noon reflection means
how and whence leans omega to alpha
who finally disunites time

Ad libitum.

How much hope is there still left for time's transcendence? The highly unexpected and puzzling postscript reads: "P.S. But there is a different version: don't believe me / the more I age the less I understand / experience untaught me the world." Is this only an ironic joke, or a moment's mood, or a way to say that negation too has not been overlooked or omitted? Or does it express the poet's utter bitterness for the lack of response he feels he has received? Or does it say that even he himself has not been left untouched by doubt as to the validity, the truth, of his message? The fact remains that even if this postscript comes gently, sotto voce, as an epilogue, an afterthought, it is still the last word of the poem, its conclusion, with an emotional precedent in the "Exit" of **"The Little Seafarer."**

The next step in the confrontation with time comes in **"Diary of an Invisible April."** When the book appeared in 1984, its tone and spirit caused no little surprise and perplexity as well as debate among critics. The poet's subsequent comments on it in an interview with the Athenian daily *To Vima* (3 February 1985) added to the controversy. In the preamble to that interview Nikos Dimou said he found in the poem "a goodbye, a foreboding of death, a pessimistic lyricism," adding, however, that "this perhaps most difficult of Elytis's poems so far . . . does, on a second, secret level, certainly still *recall eternity.*"

Elytis objected to the poem's being called "pessimistic," as he has always objected to the optimism attributed to his previous poems. Optimism and pessimism, he has said, are only a matter of tone as required by the subject that concerns him each time he writes. His point has always been that a poem, as a work of art, is autonomous and self-subsistent, independent of its creator's personal experience and feelings—a view theoretically not all that far from T.S. Eliot's contention (in "Tradition and Individual Talent") that *significant* emotion "has its life in the poem and not the history of the poet. The emotion of art is impersonal." The meaning and extent of such "objectivity" in the work of the two poets, however, would require careful consideration. At present, I would only say that, whereas Eliot was fervently antiromantic, the same is not true of Elytis's temperament and practice. The latter has been above all the lyric poet speaking in the first-person singular, powerfully expressing and projecting his own experience, views, feelings, and emotions. This does not deny the fact that he has been an extraordinary craftsman with an almost unfailingly conscious and masterful, "classical" control of his means and objectives. Moreover, he has always aimed at widening the personal to embrace the traditional, the ethnic, the human, the universal. His work, to a considerable extent, can be viewed as his spiritual autobiography, encompassing the conscience of the world within which he has grown and out of which he has shaped his own world. As to the **"Diary"** in particular, no matter how universal it may be in the experience it reflects, it is emphatically a personal poem, in fact Elytis's most sincerely, most intimately personal work.

> **Elytis objected to ["Diary of an Invisible April"] being called "pessimistic," as he has always objected to the optimism attributed to his previous poems. Optimism and pessimism, he has said, are only a matter of tone as required by the subject that concerns him each time he writes.**
>
> **—Andonis Decavalles**

The view that **"Diary of an Invisible April"** "still recalls eternity" has caused most of the controversy among its interpreters. Such a view would have to draw its support from the spirit of long precedents in Elytis's poetic world. However, whether the notion of eternity is still positively viewed in the **"Diary"** itself is what has been questioned. Disagreeing with Dimou's view in several vital respects, Stratis Berlis has remarked: "Elytis in the **'Diary'** changes *manner*. It is not a simple change of atmosphere—cloudiness taking the place of the sun. . . . It is a change (or at least an intense differentiation) of attitude, view, and function. An essential change that goes much deeper. . . . There is a change of soul and spirit." In a well-taken and interesting comment, Berlis adds that the **"Diary"** should be viewed as

> . . . a "marginal work" in Elytis's poetry which has no precedent in his oeuvre.
> Such boundary works, almost confessional records of extreme experiences, we
> find in other great poets as well, especially in the romantic and idealistic ones
> (e.g., *Igitur, Une saison en enfer,* and others). In all these there are projected
> situations which the poets had previously rejected because of their inclination
> toward an absolute purity, an ideal rendering of the world. They project, that is,
> the antipode of their poetic ego, the "demonic" side of an "angelic" world as
> shaped in the rest of their work. . . . The poet does not simply reveal the dark side
> of his luminous self: i.e., he does not let what is repressed in him come out, but he
> goes deeper; he questions and even negates in a way what he has accomplished,
> thus giving it its true meaning.

"Diary of an Invisible April" does indeed have the "marginal," private, intimate, confessional nature described by Berlis. It consists of forty-nine (seven times seven) entries or short poems varying widely in form and manner—some in poetic prose and some in verse—preceded by an introit and closed by an epilogue. Chronologically, it covers the period from Wednesday, 1 April, to Thursday, 7 May of 1981. Commenting on his choice of April, the poet has said, "The actual April serves as the body of the 'poetic' one." Containing Holy Week, April implies (as Elytis has conceded) the notions of death, rebirth, and resurrection as well as the mystery cults of the fertility gods, Christ's Passion, Eliot's "cruelest month," and also April Fool's Day to serve as a "safety valve to keep the reader in a mysterious uncertainty." Still, considering the poem's tone and the power of its emotional, intimate sincerity, one wonders whether that "safety valve" was genuinely part of the work's original conception and composition or appeared more as an afterthought.

What is technically new in this poem in terms of Elytis's oeuvre is the "cinematic" nature of the work's structure and development, which, according to the poet, makes the **"Diary"**

> . . . a "serial of the soul" in which every episode has its own self-sufficiency, no

matter how short the episode happens to be. Besides, my reference, in the first
> poem, to "a worn-out movie reel" is not a random one. . . . The motions of things
> are given the way a camera lens would record and project them. Such a technique
> has helped me, thanks to a bold decoupage, to maintain the notions of lastingness
> which does not coincide with the current time.

As he has explained, "The notion of eternity is not identical with the notion of duration in our personal life, as some would like to think." The "worn-out movie reel" is probably to be understood as his message, repeated for so long, like a movie "once filmed secretly and which nobody has even seen."

The short prologue reads: "Come now my right hand / paint that which demonically pains you, / but also strike it / The Madonna's silvering / that wildernesses have at night in the marsh-waters." (Worshipers in Greece cover parts of the Virgin's icons with silver engravings as offerings to her grace.) Summarizing much of Elytis's poetic objective, the prologue tells symbolically of his desperate, painful struggle against the "demonic" in life, against sorrowful reality and circumstance, against the corruption and decline that time brings, with death as their climax. Poetry once again strives, yet with less success, to turn the demonic into the angelic. Images and references show the struggle waged on several levels, external and internal, where death is "imminent."

In the nightmarish opening "The horses keep on chewing white sheets and keep / on penetrating triumphantly into the Threat," recalling instances in his previous verse (*The Light Tree,* for example) where images of horses were used to evoke the Apocalypse. Next, the coming of April, as *"flora mirabilis,"* makes her "victims" bend and take "the position they / had before separating from the Mother." Such a return, rather than alluding to the Platonic immortality of the soul, is meant by the poet to be a descent to nonexistence, to the chthonic realm. The position itself reminds one somewhat of that in Dylan Thomas's "Twenty-Four Years," where "in the groin of the natural doorway I crouched like a tailor sewing a shroud for a journey," thus implying, however, that birth itself is the beginning of the macabre journey toward death.

Whereas in ode k of **"Passion"** in *The Axion Esti* the poet said, "I will tonsure my head, monk of things verdant," here he wonders, "but for what / tribe of people then is this funeral?," adding, "I must / take off the vestments to wear again my golden / breastplate and go forth with sword in hand," for "There are certain frightening facts that God is / taking away from me and my mind giving back to me." Further on, a sense of exhaustion is evident: "The percentage of beauty that was mine goes, / I've spent it all. / So I want the coming winter to find me, without / fire, with ragged trousers, shuffling blank paper / as if I were conducting the deafening orchestra / of an ineffable Paradise." Mixed feelings, prevalently of despair, make him feel that he is "ready for the worst."

Gloom causes the poet's need to escape into ancestral memory, where Theotokopoulos (El Greco) comes with two gigantic wings to lift him "high in his heavens"—an attempt to idealize death as redemption. But other ancient memories come too: of "ancestors, wild and tormented," of the fighters in the Greek war of independence and those who suffered the holocaust of Ionia in 1922, of the "little church" he longed for years to build as a shelter for his soul; only its image remains to hang now on the wall as a solace. As for the "girl" who was forever his cherished embodiment of love and beauty, of life itself, its catalyst:

> I saw her come straight to me from afar. She
> wore canvas shoes and advanced light-footed
> and in black-and-white. Even the dog behind
> her was half-immersed in black.
>
> I got old waiting, truly.
>
> And now it's too late for me to understand that
> as she advanced, so the void grew larger, and
> that we were never supposed to meet.

It sounds as if her loss is final. In her stead there is now the wild figure of a hag "with her loosened hair and / cat's eyes painted on the window pane." There is longing for his mother to come and see that

> . . . as I was
> born, I left. I was so very little—who knows
> these things?—and so many monsters crawled
>   by
> on splayed, greasy paws.
>
> Thus, in a life set up with such difficulty,
> there is nothing left except a half-ruined
> door and many big rotting water-anemones.
>   There
> I pass and go—who knows where?—to a belly
> sweeter than the homeland.

A bitter account of life. Introspection will grant its revelation.

> Past midnight my room moves about over all
>   the
> neighborhood and shines like emerald.
>   Somebody
> within it searches—and the truth continually
> escapes him. Hard to imagine that this truth
> is found lower down

> Much lower down
>
> That death also has its own Red Sea.

Not ascent but descent is the process; but is there still an expectation of a Promised Land in that descent?

Through sundry recollections, furtive and vanishing visions offering no solace at a time "full of revolutions, uprisings, / blood," where "God is away," the poem reaches its core. We find memory alphabetically recalling names of people, places, and events in Greek history, myth, and legend, from the Pelasgians and Homer to the unknown Master Anthony, covering the whole alphabet and the whole expanse of time, concluding with the sad comment: "Dawn found me having run through the history of / the death of History, or rather the history of / the History of Death (and this is not wordplay)."

I have already mentioned the two previous stages in Elytis's consideration of Greek history: the one in *The Axion Esti*, where the vision of hopeful expectation was to transcend its passions; the other in **"The Little Seafarer,"** where that history's grim side apparently remained unpurged, unsurpassed, unredeemed. In this present third stage, history, the product of time, is identified with death itself. Elytis's coping with time and history would naturally again bring to mind T. S. Eliot, who made those his supreme concern and subject matter. One would perhaps hardly associate the Mediterranean Elytis, poet of the Aegean, worshiper of youth, of Eros, and of the sensual world, with the Northern, meditative, abstractionist, and rather stern Eliot. Karl Markoff, in the 1984 essay "Eliot and Elytis: Poet of Time, Poet of Space," was the first, so far as I know, to attempt an interesting comparison of the *Four Quartets* with *The Axion Esti* and to indicate temperamental and ideological similarities and differences between the two poets, and his perceptive remarks may have encouraged further comparative studies by Greek critics, studies instigated mostly by Elytis's insistent defense of his notion of timelessness and eternity as increasingly challenged by time in the years of his full maturity.

Different temperaments, different cultural backgrounds, different ideological foundations and traditions made the two poets create two considerably different worlds. Central in both is the notion of love as the supreme means of transcending time; yet whereas in Elytis love has had its foundation in ancient, primeval Eros, Eliot's verse drew its essence almost exclusively from Christian dogma, morality, and metaphysics. To the latter, Elytis has counterposed his "solar metaphysics," including a belief in eternity derived from ancient, pre-Socratic, and Platonic sources and their later transformation and extension in the Byzantine world and its mysticism.

As to history and its value for the living, the early Eliot expressed his reservations about it. Already in "Gerontion" he was to state:

> History has many cunning passages, contrived
>> corridors
> And issues, deceives with whispering ambi
>> tions,
> Guides us by vanities. Think how
> She gives when our attention is distracted
> And what she gives, gives with such supple
>> confusions
> That the giving famishes the craving. Gives too
>> late
> What's not believed in, or if still believed,
> In memory only, reconsidered passion. . . .

Later on, in *Murder in the Cathedral,* he has Thomas à Becket say: "I know that history at all times draws / The strangest consequence from the remotest cause"; and through stages of development, years later still, time and history receive their full and final consideration in the *Four Quartets,* where memory—personal, ancestral, historical—and human experience all together, when liberated from time, confer "freedom" if they equip one with "another pattern" instead of bending one to dead imitation and repetition. Factions, opposites, conflicts, enmities, and divisions need to be reconciled and surpassed in that supratemporal, timeless, eternal pattern. To quote "Little Gidding":

> This is the use of memory:
> For liberation—not less of love but expanding
> Of love beyond desire, and so liberation
> From the future as well as the past.
>> . . . .
> History may be servitude
> History may be freedom
>> . . . .
> We die with the dying:
> See, they depart, and we go with them
> We are born with the dead.
> See, they return, and bring us with them.
> The moment of the rose and the moment of the
>> yew tree
> Are of equal duration. A people without history
> Is not redeemed from time, for history is a
>> pattern
> Of timeless moments.

There are obvious analogies between what is stated here and Elytis's belief in eternity as made of "timeless moments" within time. Such moments have been the spark of most of his poems, and their memory has been his poetic storehouse, his transcendental resource, until the present summoned history as a series of "injustices and crimes" perpetuated, which his "solar metaphysics" has failed to transform. The inescap-

able reality of death's approach was next, in the **"Diary,"** to equate, to identify "the history of the death of History" with "the history of the History of Death." The identification as stated might cause some perplexity as to its meaning. Does the death of History, as identical with the History of Death, still leave eternity unaffected as separate from time, liberated from it? Or does it all end with death? It was within time, after all, that the eternal moments flourished. Only the context would encourage one understanding or another.

What prevails in the **"Diary"** are the low spirits of a soul contrite, bent by the burden of the inescapable, by life's finality; the desperate search for solace still continues, but it all seems in vain: "Death is an imminent event / burdened with some old happinesses / and that very well-known (bleached in wild deserts) despair." If Palm Sunday, opening ***The Light Tree,*** was soaked with recollected sunlight, "as when after someone sprinkled holy water and the new things they too seemed old," uniting past with present in an endless continuity, here

> Arriving the ship grew larger and blocked the
>> harbor. No movement on the decks.
> Maybe it's transporting the new midnights,
>> compact and boxed. Maybe just one
> soul, delicate as smoke and recognized by the
>> odor of burning.
>
> However it may be, there are many animals that
>> haven't yet managed to emerge
> from the Ark and they are showing impatience.
>> Even the crowd that floods the
> breakwater and casts uneasy glances, little by
>> little becomes conscious that the all
> depends upon a moment—
>
> the moment exactly when, just as you're about
>> to seize it, it vanishes.

The death summons brings up a teleological question: "Some unknown Gabriel signals to me / —Agreed, we shall all die; but for what? / . . . / The others sleep supine, either temporarily / or eternally, with faces uncovered to the sky. / I follow my remaining days / —Agreed, yes; but this life has no end." Is there resistance in the last line, or is this merely a positing of life's endlessness?

The Holy Week we enter at this point in the **"Diary,"** the Week of Passion, does not end in reversal, in resurrection. On Holy Tuesday the poet will uncover the "little garden" of memory "like a coffin." On Holy Wednesday "the cactuses keep on growing and men keep on dreaming as if they were eternal," but "the inner part of Sleep," the liberating dream, has been darkened too by the "black bulk that moves," by the "black century." On Good Friday, "In Place of a Dream," in the "mournful meek sky in the incense / arise ancient Mothers upright as candlesticks," where the poet feels "As if I were, say, death itself though / still a beardless youth just setting out / who hears for the first time in the candles' penumbra / the 'come and receive the last kiss.'" This "last kiss," in the Orthodox funeral service, is given to the deceased before burial—for the poet, his first youthful acquaintance with death. Bitter is the realization, on Holy Saturday, of "Lost ones caught by the Uncaught," apparently contradicting the "signal" given in *The Light Tree:* "Unless you prop your foot / outside the Earth / you shall never manage / to stand on it." In his own attempt to do so, as he now confesses, "my lovestruck soul poured out of the earth." As to Easter Sunday, "You feel like flying high and from there to / freely share out your soul," then "you'd take the place in the / tomb that is yours." The 1st of May, when it comes, will not change the mood. Crushing, like the preceding *"flora mirabilis,"* it advances with "many crawling or flying / bugs, snakes, lizards, caterpillars and other gaudy monsters," the offspring of nightmare rather than of paradise. In the same oppressive spirit comes the realization or rather impression that "My life (a tiny piece of my life) falling on / the life of others, leaves a hole." The epilogue then reads: "—Everything vanishes. To each comes his hour. / —Everything remains. I leave. We'll see about you," with the last statement meant by the poet as "a challenge by one who has passed the test."

What might we conclude as to whether the **"Diary"** "on a second, secret level, still recalls eternity"? And how is *eternity* to be understood here? The third Palm Sunday entry states that "we shall all die," but also that "this life has no end," and the epilogue distinguishes again between individual mortality ("Everything vanishes") and life's eternal nature ("Everything remains"). Spiritual eternity as immortality of the soul reaches its lowest point in the **"Diary."** It is mostly recalled with much longing, yet as inaccessible and fading under death's shadow. In this poem much of Elytis's preceding fervent affirmation seems undermined by doubt, uncertainty, a sense of loss in the awareness of decline and of death as inescapable. Sorrowful, nostalgic recollection increases the sense of loss itself. Resistance and self-defense recede. As to death, that is personal yet more than personal, being the reflection of the dying spiritual world of our times.

Viewed in the context of Elytis's entire poetic realm, the **"Diary"** is the darkest, most painful, and most desperate of all its moments. It is a de profundis questioning of the outcome of a life's effort, which seems to shake the truth and value of the poet's very message and its trust in eternity. Utter sincerity in its memorable utterings gives the poem its surpassing power. Correctly, the poem has been called *oriako*—i.e., the uttermost limits that the soul reaches in its naked sincerity, with no subterfuge. Thematically considered, as desired by the poet, it adds its extreme moment of doubt and depression, if not necessarily negation, to the brighter, sunnier moments in Elytis's poetry. It adds its own different poetic eternity, its own truth. Death is an end which poetry surpasses in its own eternity. One might say that the poem's closeness to the dark reality of death triggers exquisite reactions still springing, no matter how indecisively, out of life's affirmation. It should be added that the **"Diary"** is not to be taken as the poet's final word. A new volume, "Elegies of Exopetra," has already been promised and is now taking shape.

R. A. Picken (review date February 1989)

SOURCE: A review of *The Little Mariner,* in *Choice,* Vol. 26, No. 6, February, 1989, pp. 946-47.

[*In the following review, Picken calls Elytis's* The Little Mariner *his "most important work since he was awarded the Nobel Prize for Literature," but complains that Olga Broumas's translation fails to convey the musicality and imagery of Elytis's poetry.*]

The Little Mariner, published in Greece in 1985, and here translated into English for the first time, is quite clearly Odysseas Elytis's most important work since he was awarded the Nobel Prize for Literature in 1979. In it he attempts, as he has done in so much of his poetry, to correlate his ecstatic, lyrical response to the physical world with a somber, reflective, even philosophical meditation on his country's long history. It is a highly structured work, in which alternating prose poems and lyrical passages are separated by four "spotlights," shining into dark corners of Greek history and illuminating scenes of injustice and betrayal. Olga Broumas, who has already translated a selection of Elytis's poems (*What I Love*), fails to convey in English very much of the poet's celebrated musicality, verbal magic, or sparkling imagery. More lamentably, certain passages of her translation are quite incomprehensible, while the Greek text always makes sense despite the poet's sometimes obscure use of language. There is a preface by Carolyn Forché, which gives the reader guidance on how to approach the poem, and brief notes that explain several possibly unfamiliar references and some of the linguistic choices the translator made.

Hugh M. Crane (review date June 1989)

SOURCE: A review of *The Little Mariner,* in *Small Press Magazine,* Vol. 7, No. 3, June, 1989, pp. 47-8.

[*In the following review, Crane complains that there are problems with the structure of Elytis's* The Little Mariner.]

Out of his long life Odysseas Elytis has made a long poem, *The Little Mariner.* Ironically, it consists mostly of prose, as even a poet's life must. Another imbalance, in the structure, sharpens this point. Four types of sections—**"The Little Mariner," "Anoint the Ariston," "With Light and Death,"** and **"What one Loves"**—are presented in succession three times, but with one more each of **"The Little Mariner"** and **"Anoint the Ariston"** rounding out the total to fourteen. Only the three sections of **"With Light and Death,"** together with the **"Entrance"** and **"Exit,"** are written in verse. The remaining prose modulates from **"The Little Mariner"** sections—where it reads like the captions of a bitter slide show of Greek history—through the ethical meditations in poetic prose of **"Anoint the Ariston,"** to the catalogs of **"What One Loves,"** a checklist of cultural literacy, a glossary of Elytis' poetic vocabulary, and "Snapshots" of islands and ports. Prose is, thus, the mode of the temporal and of defeat. The losses of **"The Little Mariner"** sections literally surround and outnumber the personal experiences of **"What One Loves."** But the final image of the former, the escape of Bishop Makarios from assassins, suggests a way out, leading to the last section of **"Anoint the Ariston,"** where a discussion of poetry, the mode of the immortal, is laid in the scales. Throughout the poems of **"With Light and Death"** Elytis has been developing images of eternal youth, powerful yet innocent, of androgynous but undeniable sexuality, and the **"Exit"** offers some grounds of assurance that we may return to the beginning.

The difficulties posed by the poem's structure, which is even more elaborate than this sketch suggests, do not arise from its complexity, although there is the weakness of summation, of an attempt to reconcile long accounts in shorthand. More problematic are the long, dull sections of **"What One Loves,"** particularly **"The Travel Sack"** and **"Aegeodrome."** The former inventories a personal museum of Elytis' favorite masterpieces, right down to the Kochel numbers of Mozart's works. If this is to escape pedantry, if by its flatness we are meant to see the inadequacy of high culture in balance against injustice, we have a clear example of the fallacy of imitative form. Likewise with the lifeless lexicon of **"Aegeodrome."** Furthermore, the overall metaphor of journey and return produces too little sense of motion to raise it above the triteness and limpness of convention. And the central image of innocent sexuality is shaded at times by voyeurism.

Elytis' verse can excite the verbal imagination. His imitations of Greek epigraphy and of Sappho generate ambiguity at several levels, even about the identity of individual words; the second plays fully with Sapphic lacunae. Whatever form Broumas' pun on the "Greek state" takes in the original, it wonderfully encapsulates the forces pitted against each other.

Despite his inclusion of Mozart *et al.,* however, Elytis' "Greek state" is no symbol for Western culture. Europeans, never mind Americans, will sense a call for Greek cultural hegemony ("a lost Greek empire. For the sake of language, not anything else"), a hope that "Even the Franks might Hellenize," and admiration for a "small Alexander the Great."

Robert Shannan Peckham (review date 26 April 1991)

SOURCE: "Encounters on a Voyage," in *The Times Literary Supplement,* No. 4595, April 26, 1991, p. 24.

[*In the following review, Peckham discusses the themes of voyaging and seafaring found in Elytis's* Idiotiki Odos.]

"The first thing God made", George Seferis once observed, "was the long journey." Images of voyaging and seafaring abound in modern Greek poetry, from Solomos to Cavafy and Seferis, and they also pervade many of Odysseus Elytis's own collections. Elytis has published a critical appreciation of the writer Alexandros Papadiamantis (1976), whose masterful short stories evoke the sea and coastline of his native Skiathos, and from Elytis's early volume *Prosanatolismi* (1940), through to his celebrated poem *To Axion Esti* (1959), and his more recent *Anichta Chartia* (1974) and *O Mikros Naftilos* (1985), a preoccupation with travelling and the sea is conspicuous.

The motif of sea and navigation is manifest in Elytis's new book, *Idiotiki Odos,* which consists of two prose meditations on poetry and painting. As the title suggests, many of its themes echo those of his previous booklet, *Ta Demosia ké ta Idiotika,* (1990). While the phrase "private way" itself carries connotations of travelling, the heading of the second section "Full and By" is explicitly nautical (as are many of the thirty-five coloured illustrations by the poet which accompany the text). In *Idiotiki Odos,* Elytis declares that "there are times when I feel like a boat in a garden" ("Iné phorés pou ésthanomé varka sé kipo") a phrase reminiscent of the "small sailor of the garden" of his earlier poetry. In *"The Odyssey",* from an earlier collection (1971), the protagonist fantasizes about a series of voyages and in the process his house is transformed into a boat, which he pilots through an imaginary landscape. The poet's hallucinatory journey recalls Rimbaud's "Le Bateau ivre" and becomes a fantastical expedition through the currents and undercurrents of a vast poetic tradition.

For Elytis, as for Seferis, the "long journey" is erotic. The foam of the ship's prow is associated with sexual energy; in *Idiotiki Odos* words jostle at the tip of the artist's pen, "as if they are looking for something, spring up to the point of sprinkling the face" ("San kati na zitané anapidoun os to simio na sé pitsilnané ké sto prosopo"). Many of Elytis's travel poems are punctuated by erotic encounters, whether actual or conjectural, just as the protagonist in **"The Odyssey"** fantasizes about a woman exposing her "sea urchin . . . in sea-depths unexplored". The poet is an explorer who manages the boat as best he can.

"The great sea is five to six thousand words", Elytis notes in *Idiotiki Odos,* "and my vessel a space of up to fifteen steps in length which goes up and down continually". With the standard Greek *dekapentasyllavos,* or fifteen-syllable line, as his measure, the poet must negotiate his passage through the turbulent history of the Greek language. This witnessed the contest for supremacy between demotic and purist. In 1976 the struggle formally ended when standard modern Greek was adopted as the official language, with *dimotiki* as its core. Elytis himself is a member of the "Greek Language Society" which was established in the early 1980s to promote the reciprocity of purist and demotic. In the same way Elytis's poetry moves between popular speech and highly stylized verse. As the poet himself asserted in a recent interview, he exploits the many linguistic registers, ancient, Byzantine, ecclesiastic, contemporary, idiomatic, purist and demotic. It is precisely this dense linguistic texture that makes his poetry so difficult to translate.

The motif of sea and navigation is manifest in Elytis's . . . *Idiotiki Odos,* **which consists of two prose meditations on poetry and painting.**

—*Robert Shannan Peckham*

The travelling metaphor in *Idiotiki Odos* becomes progressively polysemous as it extends, not only to an itinerary through an imaginary geography, but to Elytis himself as he paces the constricted space of his Athenian apartment. There are references to painters such as Braque, Juan Gris, and Picasso, whom the poet befriended on his *séjours* in France from 1948 to 1952; and the relationship between painting and travel is expressed in a remark made by Picasso. When Elytis asked him about the fact that he never went on journeys, Picasso answered: "Instead of running after the world, isn't it better to get it to come close to you? . . . all five continents, I have them inside my atelier." In *To Axion Esti* painting, sea and poetry are inextricably bound up, as the poet dips his brush "into the humble bucket and paint: / the new hulls, / the new gold and black icons!" Just as Cavafy maintained that he felt a hundred and twenty-five voices telling him he could write history, Elytis has admitted that "a million voices inside me were saying yes—I could be a painter". It was Elytis's relationship to painting, as well as his many

ties with France, that formed the basis of an exhibition held in 1988-9 at the Pompidou Centre, dedicated to the poet.

An admirer, like George Seferis, of the Greek artist Theophilos, who died in the year Elytis's first poems were published (1935), and about whom he has written, Elytis was also a close friend of the art-collector Tériade. It was Tériade who converted his Villa Natacha into an art centre, as well as inaugurating a museum dedicated to Theophilos in Mytilini; and who introduced Elytis to Matisse and Picasso, in 1948. It was during his first trip to Paris also in 1948, that Elytis made the acquaintance of André Breton, René Char, Paul Eluard, Pierre-Paul Jouve and Tristan Tzara. But although he was greatly influenced by French poetry, it was painting that proved a more decisive influence on his own work. Throughout *Idiotiki Odos* Elytis is intent on revealing the correspondences and equivalences of poetry and art. He is fascinated by what he calls "geometries", a preoccupation which relates to his interest in Cubist art. The complex architectonic form of poems like *To Axion Esti,* which alternates between odes, hymns, and prose passages, or *The Monogram* (1970), might be elucidated with detailed numerical charts, as Andreas Kalvos provided for his odes in *I Lyra* (The Lyre, 1824). A collage technique, including extracts from numerous writers, among them lines from another poet-artist, Blake, is employed in *The Little Sailor.*

Finally, Elytis's pseudonym itself constitutes a linguistic collage, incorporating four major components of his mythology: "Ellas" (Hellas), "Elpida" (Hope), "Eleftheria" (Freedom), and "Eleni" (Helen). At the same time the name *Elytis* puns on the modern Greek word *alytis,* meaning vagabond; the epithet, in fact, which Homer employs to describe the disguised Odysseus. The poet adopted the name Elytis as a way of evading the connotations of his own name, Alepoudelis, which had become inextricably linked with the brand of soap manufactured by his family. As Elytis observes in *Idiotiki Odos:* "Love for the material doesn't have any relation to the materialistic perception of life."

Jeffrey Carson (review date Summer 1992)

SOURCE: "Elegiac Elytis: 'Elegies of Jutting Rock'," in *World Literature Today,* Vol. 66, No. 3, Summer, 1992, pp. 445-46.

[*In the following review, Carson discusses Elytis's use of elegy as the form for his* Ta elegia tis Oxopetras.]

Odysseus Elytis's eightieth birthday, on 2 November 1991 was widely celebrated in Greece. Literary journals undertook dedicatory issues, television and radio produced special programs, concerts were given. Elytis answered us with the best gift of all, a new volume of poems, *Ta eleyía tis Oxópetras* (The Elegies of Jutting Rock), his fourth since his Nobel Prize in 1979.

Jung suggests that the artist in old age must reverse the expansions of youth and focus on what is most meaningful and permanent. The aged Rembrandt's sitters radiate a dim halo of inner, unnatural light, and Titian's later backgrounds smolder with sanguine brushstrokes. The old Yeats climbs in his last works toward a joyful simplicity based on reality's archetypes, and the euphonious Stevens grows harsher in his imagination's recasting of memory and desire. Beethoven's mysterious late quartets plumb imagination and introspection as a deliverance from the tragedy of experience, and Bach wrote fugues in his last year that to this day no one is sure how to execute. With the concentration and ardent assurance of his recent period, Elytis joins this group.

In his collected prose Elytis, describing his paradise, invokes the *kore* poetry and "birds which even amid the truth of death insist on warbling in Greek and on saying 'eros,' 'eros,' 'eros.'" Elytis's first great poem, **"Anniversary"** (from his 1939 book *Prosanatolizmí* (Orientations) is a meditation on death. Eros and thanatos continue to be his theme. The Elegies, however, are not "about" death; rather, Elytis peers through death to eternal values as he used (and continues) to peer through pelagic waters and crisp ethers. Thus the title is apt, since an elegy is a lyric whose formal lament meditates on the death of a person or the tragedy of existence and finds solace in the contemplation of eternal values. "Jutting Rock" translates the Greek *Oxópetra,* the name of a deserted rocky promontory on the island of Astypalaea; the poet has in mind the sound and image rather than the place.

Elytis is doing nothing else than trying more concretely than ever to get into words the ultimate diaphaneity he has always attested. The difficulties of the book are not in the writing but in the subject. That is why Elytis has developed, yet again, a new style, different from the many he has previously found useful.

For a model, Elytis took Hölderlin's elegies, which deal with the impossible ideal and golden youth. The look of Hölderlin's lines and techniques of construction deliberately recall Pindar, always one of Elytis's exemplars. (Like Elytis, Pindar thinks perceptually, not conceptually, and, with one exception, no two of his elaborate meters are identical.)

In the third Elegy, **"Cupid and Psyche,"** Elytis remembers how Hölderlin transformed his love for a real girl into poetry (called "Diotima"), and, like Hölderlin, he affirms that "within the Futile and the Nothing" exists "that unascertained something": this is the thesis of all fourteen of the Elegies. "Cupid" in Greek is *Eros; Psyche* is the word for "Soul." Their story was probably first told in Apuleius' Latin romance *The Golden Ass* (after 125 A.D.). After the girl Psyche lost her god-lover by looking at him, Venus set her many tasks, one of which was to bring back from Persephone a box containing Beauty; opening it, Psyche found nothing; Cupid eventually married her. In Plato's *Symposium* Socrates says that the priestess of Mantinea, Diotima, taught him his metaphysic of Eros. The disastrous end of Hölderlin's love affair with Susette Gontard (whom he called "Diotima") upset his fragile psyche; when he heard of her death in 1802, he went mad. Caught permanently in the "Harpy's claws" of madness, Hölderlin, who was Swabian, often signed his name "Scardanelli."

Elytis calls Dionysios Solomos "my master" and often invokes him in his poetry, always heroically. Solomos (1798-1857) is the founder of modern Greek poetry. Born on the Ionian island of Zakynthos, then part of Italy while most of Greece belonged to Turkey, he was educated in Italian, and so he did not know the purist Greek in which other writers waxed poetic. Though he never visited the Greek mainland, he proved that the spoken language was capable of great subtlety and exaltation in a poetry of national, ethical, and stylistic struggle. In his verse romantic emotion is controlled by exquisite diction, rigorous form, and undoubted sincerity. Because he was forging something new, he completed little, but every one of his fragments has seeded much Greek poetry. The short poem "Glory," for example, on the Ottoman slaughter of the populace of tiny Psara, showed how the demotic tongue could rival Simonides for grave brevity: "On the deepblack ridge of Psara / Glory walking in solitude / meditates on the bright young heroes / and on her hair she wears a wreath / woven of the scanty grasses / remaining on that desolate land."

Solomos's most famous longer poems are "The Hymn to Liberty" (whose first stanzas are the Greek national anthem), "On the Death of Lord Byron," and his masterpiece, the fragmentary work "The Free Besieged," in which the starving Greeks of Missolonghi heroically resist the Turks during the War of Independence. In his great 1985 sequence *The Little Seafarer* Elytis imagines the poet's spirit at Missolonghi, and in a set of epiphanies called **"Snapshots"** he recalls a visit to Solomos's house: "Late afternoon in Akrotiri, at the old house of Dionysios Solomos. In front of the large, round, stone table in the garden. Awe and silence. And also a muffled, strange consolation." These words are the starting point for **"Awe and Devastation of Solomos."**

What Yeats called Byzantium and Pound Ecbatana, Elytis calls **"Lost Commagene,"** which in daily life is unattainable. Commagene was a small Hellenistic kingdom founded in 162 B.C. in northern Syria, later annexed to Roman Syria by Vespasian. Eupalinus of Megara built the underground aqueduct on Samos—a remarkable engineering feat—during the reign of Polycrates (d. 522 B.C.). (Possibly the association was triggered by the founder of Commagene's capital [150 B.C.], King Samos.)

The concluding elegy, **"The Last of Saturdays,"** allows an ascension into the pellucid sea depths and sunlight of the other side. Socrates was warned by invisible powers to prepare for the ascension by writing poems. The line "the stone and the tomb and the soldier" refers to icons of the Resurrection. This is the Elegies' permanent principle of hope, tragically metaphorical. The last line is "Death the sun without sunsets." The last line, that is, of **"The Elegies of Jutting Rock";** Elytis is still writing, and, as he has said, there is a different version waiting to be built on Homer's beaches.

Ostensibly, these five essays by the Greek poet Elytis, winner of the 1979 Nobel Prize in Literature, explore his development as a poet and his continuity with classical and modern Greek and European literature and myth. In a deeper sense, the selections represent autobiographical prose poems that reproduce the poetic process as Elytis meanders from an awareness of light and nature to passion and ecstasy, from the possibilities of metaphor in Greek to the influences of Rimbaud, Jouve, Lautréamont, Lorca, Ungaretti, and others. Joining the ranks of George Seferis and Yannis Ritsos, Elytis attempts to establish the contours of an authentic modern Greek poetry that is true to the Hellenic spirit. Of interest to students of modern poetry in general.

Publishers Weekly (review date 3 October 1994)

SOURCE: A review of *Open Papers,* in *Publishers Weekly,* Vol. 241, No. 40, October 3, 1994, pp. 64-5.

[*In the following review, the critic discusses how Elytis's* Open Papers *tells of a career guided by luck, risk, and a belief in modernism.*]

Part autobiography, part statement of artistic principles, the five essays collected here cover Elytis's journey to poetry, from discovering the works of Sappho at age 16 to winning the Nobel Prize in 1979. Born in Crete in 1911, at 18 Elytis heard "a secret voice" that led him to abandon everything for his art. As a student in the 1930s he was totally absorbed in the Surrealists with Éluard, Breton and Lorca offering new perspectives to a young man already influenced by Freud, Baudelaire and Novalis. He pays tribute to these and other writers in the essay **"For Good Measure,"** which also honors Picasso for his insistence on turning upside down one's view of the natural world. In the most interesting section of the book, **"Chronicle of a Decade,"** Elytis recounts the time spent seeking out writers and periodicals that would be sympathetic to newfound passion for a lyrical and mystical vision of life. Elytis's credo is set forth in the title of the last essay—**"Art-Luck-Risk."** If, through the decades, Elytis did take political and artistic risks, this clear articulation shows that his art was not guided by luck or risk alone but by a real belief in modernism.

T. L. Cooksey (review date December 1994)

SOURCE: A review of *Open Papers,* in *Library Journal,* Vol. 119, No. 21, December, 1994, p. 91.

[*In the following review, Cooksey praises Elytis's* Open Papers.*]*

Christopher Merrill (review date 1 October 1995)

SOURCE: "The Voyages of a Poet," in *Los Angeles Times Book Review,* October 1, 1995, p. 9.

[*In the following review, Merrill discusses Elytis's development as a poet which the artist traces in his* Open Papers.]

The flowering of Greek poetry in the 20th Century is one of the most interesting counterweights to the endless tragedy named modern European history. Constantine Cavafy, Angelos Sikelianos, George Seferis, Yannis Ritsos, Odysseus Elytis—these poets have shaped the international literary landscape. And none is more exuberant in praising the things of the world than Elytis, about whom Lawrence Durrell wrote, "The Greek poet aims his heart and his gift at the sublime— for nothing else will do." Elytis calls himself a solar metaphysician; in the essays that make up ***Open Papers,*** his primary statement on poetry, he explores "the mystery of light," the dazzling heart of his work.

Born in 1911 on the island of Crete, Elytis has spent most of his life in Athens, writing poetry and creating collages. In the 1930s he helped introduce French Surrealism into Greek poetry—a signal event in contemporary letters. Elytis adapted the ideas of André Breton and Paul Eluard to the Mediterranean world, and thus he heard that "secret voice [moving] within and beyond reasonable order, above and independent from time and in constant duration. To render its presence sensible even for a moment," he realized, "was the poet's mission." This he has achieved in books of poems bearing such titles as ***Sun the First, Heroic and Elegiac Song for the Lost Second Lieutenant of the Albanian Campaign, The Axion Esti*** and ***The Light Tree and the Fourteenth Beauty.*** In 1979 he was awarded the Nobel Prize in Literature.

Open Papers, first published in 1974 and translated now by Olga Broumas and T. Begley, is a hymn to his poetic sources. Here are sketches of the Greek landscape, memories of his first encounters with Surrealist writings and appreciations of pivotal figures like Rimbaud, Lautréamont, Eluard, Lorca, Reverdy and Picasso. This last Elytis wrote in French, in one sitting in 1951, after lunching with the great artist, who "seemed a rascal of 17, not a personage in his 70s."

Picasso was "a deep breath" for the poet, who in the wake of World War II, "in the huge hospital that Europe had become," was struggling to find his bearings. He had traveled to Paris in search of the most unfaithful of lovers, Poetry. Albert Camus and René Char among others befriended him, but it was at Picasso's table—where the artist's "analogies to life, to how we love or hate, danced before my eyes," Elytis writes that he learned a central truth: "What must be practiced—assiduously, infinitely and without the slightest pause—is anti-servitude, noncompliance and independence. Poetry is the other face of Pride."

These lines conclude his autobiographical **"Chronicle of a Decade,"** a sweeping essay of nearly 80 pages charting the growth of the poet's mind. From his earliest university days to his excursions around Greece and thence to life during the Nazi occupation of his homeland, we see Elytis come of age.

Now he is reading the Surrealists, "[breathing] in what was perhaps the last pure oxygen" available to the spirit in the years before the world was plunged into war. Now he is pinned down by artillery fire, unaccountably thinking about Cavafy's ability to adapt to anything.

"Deep down we knew, we felt it," Elytis says of his literary circle's wartime experience, "poetry was hope's ultimate refuge from general scorn, its only free stronghold against dark forces."

He recalls Matisse painting "the juiciest, rawest, most enchanting flowers and fruits ever made, as if the miracle of life itself discovered it could compress itself inside them forever," even as the ovens of Buchenwald and Auschwitz were burning.

If at times Elytis' sentences seem tangled, that is because he believes that even in prose, "it is the poet's duty to risk sudden and uncontrolled *coups d'esprit,* to provoke new oscillations by syntactical intervention and to acquire, in style and speech, something of a young organism's shimmer or the carriage of a bird toward the heights." Indeed, in many places in **"First Things First"** and **"The Girls,"** the opening essays of Open Papers, Elytis' prose takes on both the color and accent of his verse:

> On death's eve, tell me, how is a body suffered?
>   On death's eve, tell me, how is a white voice written?

> We walked on some shore, not feeling each other. Someone's walking "was
>   bothered by angel's wings." Until suddenly everything turned dark, and it seemed
>   to him the far neck of the cove groaned deeply.

> It's that I couldn't bear to be half in this world;
> I went after Poetry as after a
>   woman, to give me child, as though from one to the other I might not die. I never
>   thought to cry that everything was dim. If it were possible to save a palmful of
>   clear water! I cried in front of waves and saw in poems the sky clear.

This version of **Open Papers** is roughly half the length of the original book; the missing essays are devoted to Greek poets and artists largely unknown in this country. This, then, is a selected edition of Elytis' most important prose work—a fact overlooked in Sam Hamill's introduction, which is notably short on information; a glossary would also have been useful. Nevertheless, readers will be grateful to Broumas and Begley for their labor of love.

"I want the first glimpse of the world," the poet declares. "May I never lose Columbus' emotion. There are so many little things no one has managed to explore." Fortunately, through all of his poetic voyages Elytis has kept that "rare excitement" Cavafy advised a certain traveler to cultivate on his way back to Ithaca. The record of his explorations—physical, spiritual and literary—is one of Greece's modern glories. In **Open Papers** we learn how and why that came to be.

Mel Gussow (essay date 19 March 1996)

SOURCE: "Odysseus Elytis, 84, Poet and Nobel Laureate Who Celebrated Greek Myths and Landscape," in *The New York Times,* March 19, 1996, p. D23.

[In the following essay, Gussow presents an overview of Elytis's life and career.]

Odysseus Elytis, a Nobel Prize-winning Greek poet celebrated for his lyrical and passionate evocations of his country's history, myths and rugged landscape, died yesterday at his home in Athens. He was 84.

When Mr. Elytis (pronounced ee-LEE-tis) won the Nobel Prize for Literature in 1979, the Swedish Academy said that his poetry, "against the background of Greek tradition, depicts with sensuous strength and intellectual clearsightedness modern man's struggle for freedom and creativeness." He was the second Greek poet to be named a Nobel laureate; the first was George Soferis in 1963. Both were part of a group of poets sometimes called the Generation of the 30's, and had a profound effect on Greek literature.

The Swedish Academy praised Mr. Elytis's most famous work, *The Axion Esti* (*Worthy It Is*) as "one of 20th-century literature's most concentrated and richly faceted poems." First published in 1950, it was his spiritual autobiography. In an appreciation in *The New York Times* at the time of the award, Edmund Keeley, who translated Mr. Elytis's work into English, compared him to Walt Whitman in his presentation of "an image of the contemporary Greek consciousness through the developing perspective of a persona that is at once the poet himself and the voice of his country."

Because sections of *The Axion Esti* were set to music by Mikis Theodorakis, the poet became especially popular with young people in Greece; they sing his songs in tavernas. Mr. Theodorakis called the epic poem a "Bible for the Greek people." Mr. Elytis once said, "I am personifying Greece in my poems. . . . All the beautiful and bitter moments beneath the sky of Attica."

Notably reticent, he lived modestly and avoided literary circles. The Nobel Prize, awarded in a year when Graham Greene was reportedly a favorite, brought him sudden international fame. As a result, he became an unofficial cultural ambassador for Greece. Although he published three books of verse in 1979, it was several years before he began writing again.

In one of the paradoxes of his life, he was called the "sun-drinking poet," because he often wrote about the themes of sun, light and purity, and also "the owl," for his habit of sleeping during the day and working at night.

Mr. Elytis was born on Nov. 2 1911, in Iraklion in Crete. His surname was Alepoudhelis. He took the name Elytis when he began writing poetry in his early 20's in order to avoid association with the family's prosperous soap-manufacturing business. The pen name, he said, was derived from a combination of Greek words meaning Greece, hope, freedom and Eleni, the figure in Greek mythology that personifies beauty and sensuality. All these elements appeared in his poetry.

In 1914, the Alepoudhelis family moved to Athens, where Odysseus grew up, spending his summers on islands in the Aegean Sea. As a young writer, he was greatly influenced by the Aegean experience and by the poetry of Paul Eluard, the French surrealist. He studied at the University of Athens School of Law, but left before he received his degree in order to devote himself to poetry. His first collection was published in 1930. In the early 1940's, he was an officer in the Greek army, fighting against Italian fascists in Albania. From that wartime experience came the poem, **"Heroic and Elegiac Song for the Lost Second Lieutenant of the Albanian Campaign,"** a tribute to the national consciousness.

In 1948, he began *The Axion Esti.* It was 11 years before the book was published, along with a collection of verse *Six and One Regrets for the Sky.* Together, the two books firmly established his reputation. In **"The Autopsy,"** one lyric in the collection, the central metaphor is that of Greece personified, surgically opened to reveal essential elements; the olive root, the heat, the sky and sand.

When he won the Nobel Prize at the age of 68, Mr. Elytis took the long, Homeric view of the award. He said: "The Swedish Academy's decision was not only an honor for me but for Greece and its history through the ages. I believe that it was a decision to bring international attention to the most ancient tradition in Europe, since from Homer's time to the present there has not been a single century during which poetry has not been written in the Greek language."

At the time, in characteristic Spartan fashion, Mr. Elytis was living in a two-room apartment in downtown Athens, and he vowed that the award and the $190,000 prize would not change his life. He said his life was based on the same laws governing poetry: "concentration on the basics, elimination of all superfluous things and of all falsehoods."

When two collections of Mr. Elytis's verse, *Maria Nephele* and *Odysseus Elytis: Selected Poems* (including **"The Axion Esti"**), were published in the United States in 1982, Rachel Hadas wrote in *The New York Times Book Review* that his "unique strength is the celebration of a landscape that is his protean theme, his finest invention." It is, she said, a terrain that "is both his beloved Greece and the human body, a vision rooted in the past and passionately imagined in a kind of floating, timeless present."

He also wrote many essays and created collages. Art was an important part of his life, and he frequently wrote about artists he had known, including Picasso, Matisse and Giacometti.

Mr. Elytis's doctor said that the poet had been hospitalized repeatedly in the last decade. He continued to write, however, and published a volume of poetry last year. A bachelor all his life, he said, "If I married, my poetry would suffer."

Dimitris Avramopoulos, the Mayor of Athens, said that the city was in mourning and that, as a result of Mr. Elytis's death, "Greece and the world are poorer in spirit, in creation, in inspiration."

FURTHER READING

Criticism

Deligiorgis, Stavros. "Elytis' Brecht and Hadzidakis' Pirandello." In *Modern Greek Writers,* edited by Edmund Keeley and Peter Bien, pp. 192-204. Princeton: Princeton University Press, 1972.

> Discusses the role of translation and foreign influences in the modern period of Greek writing, specifically using Elytis's Brecht and Hadzidakis's Pirandello.

Friar, Kimon. "The Imagery and Collages of Odysseus Elytis." *Books Abroad* 49, No. 4 (Autumn 1975): 703-11.

> Discusses the relationship between Elytis's painting and poetry.

Gregory, Dorothy M-T. "Odysseus Elytis." In *European Writers: The Twentieth Century,* edited by George Stade, pp. 2955-88. New York: Charles Scribner's Sons, 1990.

> Traces Elytis's career in light of his relationship with Greek poetry.

Ivask, Ivar. "Analogies of Light: The Greek Poet Odysseus Elytis." *Books Abroad* 49, No. 4 (Autumn 1975): 627-30.

> Asserts that Elytis is one of the three major modern Greek poets.

Ivask, Ivar. "Odysseus Elytis on His Poetry." *Books Abroad* 49, No. 4 (Autumn 1975): 631-45.

> Elytis discusses his poetry, including the place of surrealism and Greekness in his work.

Jouanny, Robert. "Aspects of Surrealism in the Works of Odysseus Elytis." *Books Abroad* 49, No. 4 (Autumn 1975): 685-89.

> Analyzes the aspects of surrealism found in Elytis's poetry.

Keeley, Edmund. "Elytis and the Greek Tradition." In his *Modern Greek Poetry,* pp. 130-48. Princeton: Princeton University Press, 1983.

> Analyzes Elytis's poetry in light of the full scope of Greek tradition.

Keeley, Edmund. "The Voices of Elytis' *The Axion Esti.*" *Books Abroad* 49, No. 4 (Autumn 1975): 695-700.

> Discusses the narrative voice in Elytis's *The Axion Esti.*

Keeley, Edmund, and George Savidis. "Preface." In *The Axion Esti,* by Odysseus Elytis, pp.xiii-xv. Pittsburgh: University of Pittsburgh Press, 1974.

> Provides an introduction to the translation of Elytis's *The Axion Esti.*

Additional coverage of Elytis's life and career is contained in the following sources published by Gale Research: *Contemporary Authors,* **Vols. 102, 151;** *DISCovering Authors Modules: Poets;* **and** *Major Twentieth Century Writers.*

James M. Gustafson

1925-

American theologian, educator, and author.

The following entry provides an overview of Gustafson's career through 1996.

INTRODUCTION

A theologian and the author of several books about Christian life and ethics, Gustafson is best known for his landmark *Ethics from a Theocentric Perspective,* Volume I: *Theology and Ethics* (1981) and Volume II: *Ethics and Theology* (1984). Theocentrism, according to Gustafson, focuses on human experience, the proper ethical evaluation of which must be consistent with empirical scientific data and God's overall plan for the whole of creation—a plan that, he asserts, exceeds purely human interests. Such a perspective is at odds with the scripturally dogmatic Judeo-Christian anthropocentric approach, which views humankind as the focus of creation and God's activity. However, even though Gustafson requires religious piety as a foundation for construing right ethical-moral conclusions, traditionalist Christian ethicians still condemn theocentrism as naturalistic and non-Christian.

Biographical Information

Gustafson was born and raised in Norway, Michigan. He served in Burma and India during World War II, and after returning home he received his Bachelor of Science from Northwestern University in 1948. He went on to receive a Bachelor of Divinity from the University of Chicago in 1951 and a doctorate from Yale University in 1955. For a time Gustafson served as the pastor of a Congregational Church. He taught at Yale from 1955 to 1972 and during that time he published his first book, *The Advancement of Theological Education* (1957). In 1972 Gustafson joined the faculty at the University of Chicago Divinity School, where he wrote his landmark work, the two-volume *Ethics from a Theocentric Perspective.* Since 1987 he has been the Henry R. Luce Professor of Humanities and Comparative Studies at Emory University in Atlanta, Georgia.

Major Works

Gustafson's principal writings focus on the development of a new methodology for analyzing contemporary ethical issues. In his *Treasure in Earthen Vessels: Church as a Human Community* (1961), he emphasized the pivotal importance of history and culture in the development of the Christian life. With the publication of *Christ and the Moral Life* (1968) and *On Being Responsible: Issues in Personal Ethics* (1968),

Gustafson began to examine various ethical approaches for moral-ethical decision-making. For example, *On Being Responsible* explores excerpts from the writings of Karl Barth, Martin Luther King Jr., Pope John XXIII, and Max Weber in order to clarify the role of personal responsibility in ethical decision-making. In *The Church as Moral Decision Maker* (1971), Gustafson calls for the Church to be a community that encourages moral discourse, while his essay in *Moral Education: Five Lectures* (1971) explores the notion of moral autonomy and accountability in contemporary ethics. Critically acclaimed for its careful scholarship, *Theology and Christian Ethics* (1974) examines moral education and discernment in moral decision-making, the role of the theologian and the scriptures in making moral decisions, the relationship between spiritual life and moral life, and the influence of history and science on moral decisions. The history of the development of various Christian ethical systems and their apparent convergence during the late twentieth century is the subject of *Protestant and Roman Catholic Ethics: Prospects for Rapprochement* (1978). Earlier in his writing he showed a preference for relativism as opposed to objectivism. According to relativism, moral good is relative to a particular group and time, while objectivism asserts that there is some unchanging moral good that anyone can attain. However, Gustafson did not like the tendency of relativism to yield to subjectivism, in which moral good becomes whatever particular people say it is. In ethical discussions subjectivism requires that the world exists only for the benefit of humankind. In religious discussions subjectivism turns God into the instrument to fulfill human wants. These pitfalls of subjectivism are part of what Gustafson refers to as anthropocentrism, or the view that human beings are at the center of things. In an effort to overcome anthropocentrism, Gustafson developed a new approach to ethics in his *Ethics from a Theocentric Perspective* in which he related four points: an interpretation of God, of the world, of persons as moral agents, and of how such persons should make moral choices. The theocentric perspective views human experiences as being part of God's grand design for the universe and promotes the consideration of empirical scientific and historical data in ethical-moral decision-making, while denying the dogmatic and doctrinal primacy accorded the scriptures, theology, and tradition in defining the morality of a situation.

Critical Reception

Gustafson's critics are varied in their reaction to his work, but they share a respect for the importance and erudition of his approach to ethics. Many critics question his explanations of faith, piety, and human suffering, while others wonder at his Christology and his notion of God. A common concern among traditionalist Christian ethicians is that Gustafson's work values empirical scientific data over and above traditionalist Christian anthropocentric theology, dogma, and doctrine. Most reviewers applaud the clarity of his scholarly style, and the thoroughness with which he covers the material. In addition, theologians and ethicians agree that Gustafson's work—especially his *Ethics from a Theocentric Perspective*—substantially contributes to the ongoing development of contemporary ethics.

PRINCIPAL WORKS

The Advancement of Theological Education [with H. Richard Niebuhr and D. D. Williams] (essays) 1957

Treasure in Earthen Vessels: Church as a Human Community (essays) 1961

Christ and the Moral Life (essays) 1968

On Being Responsible: Issues in Personal Ethics [editor with James T. Laney] (essays) 1968

Sixties: Radical Change in American Religion [editor with R. D. Lambert] (essays) 1970

The Church as Moral Decision Maker (essays) 1971

Christian Ethics and the Community (essays) 1971

Moral Education: Five Lectures [with Richard S. Peters, Lawrence Kohlberg, Bruno Bettleheim, and Kenneth Kenniston] (essays) 1971

Theology and Christian Ethics (essays) 1974

Can Ethics Be Christian? (essays) 1975

The Contributions of Theology to Modern Ethics (essays) 1975

Protestant and Roman Catholic Ethics: Prospects for Rapprochement (essays) 1978

Ethics from a Theocentric Perspective, Volume I: *Theology and Ethics* (essays) 1981

Ethics from a Theocentric Perspective, Volume II: *Ethics and Theology* (essays) 1984

CRITICISM

Charles E. Curran (review date 19 March 1971)

SOURCE: A review of *The Church as Moral Decision Maker,* in *Commonweal,* Vol. XCIV, No. 2, March 19, 1971, pp. 43-4.

[*In the following review, Curran states that although the material in Gustafson's* The Church as Moral Decision Maker *is a bit dated, the church needs "the type of careful, reflective, analytic moral discourse which Gustafson handles so well."*]

This slim volume [*The Church as Moral Decision Maker*] gathers together eight previously published essays by James M. Gustafson which are now grouped together around the two general themes of the church in society and moral perspectives on the church.

The subject matter of the essays is somewhat dated; for example, the first essay on Christian attitudes towards a technological society originally appeared over ten years ago. Since then there has been much theological discussion about technology and secularity. Likewise the essays on the church do not propose any radical new types of church community but rather assume that churches will continue to exist in the future much the same as they were a few years ago. One would never come away from reading this book with the impression that the church is experiencing any real crisis today.

This book does not attempt to suggest radical reforms in the church. No one would ever include these essays in any "futuristic symposium" on the church in the next century or even the church in the '70s. There are no sweeping criticisms of the present and no prophetic blueprints for the future, but this book does make a significant contribution to the discussion, if only to remind us of the continuing need for careful analysis in our discourse about the church and society.

In these essays Gustafson carefully pursues his critical analysis of the church as a voluntary association and of the society in which we live. The scholarly, analytical and unsensational approach so well illustrated in Gustafson's methodology must always be present in our theologizing about the church and society. Although such an approach appears to be dull and unexciting in comparison with other approaches to the same subject, often its value is more lasting.

An opening introduction by Charles M. Swezey, who assembled the collection of essays, sketches the later development of Gustafson's moral methodology and tries to relate these earlier essays to this methodology. Gustafson views the technological society in all its ambiguities which excludes canonizing technology as totally good or rejecting it as the product of evil. Perhaps Gustafson sees the ambiguity of technology too much in terms of a division between the inner and the outer in man so that technology is seen as a product of rationality and thus is somewhat opposed to the human.

A careful analysis of Christian social action examines the forms of such action under three different perspectives—as governed by the social structure itself, by personal faith, and by God's objective action. The essay on "Authority in a Pluralistic Society" starts from a sociological analysis of the pluralistic society to determine the role and function of authority. Perhaps the contemporary experience would move the author to change his emphasis on the civil law as providing "the clearest statement of the social and cultural consensus present in a pluralistic society. . . ."

The essays in Part Two emphasize the reality of the church as a voluntary association which as one of its purposes must become a community of moral discourse and then properly use its institutional power. Gustafson and others have seen the voluntary association as the model of the Protestant church in this country, but contemporary Roman Catholic ecclesiology understands the church in a very similar way. In the future, for example, the magisterial function in the Roman Catholic church should be exercised more in accord with the model of a community of moral discourse as sketched by Gustafson.

In these essays Gustafson alludes to two important moral themes which still interest him today—the model of responsibility and the concern of moral education and development. Gustafson examines the moral purposes and functions of the church and the best way to implement these. He often succinctly reviews past theological approaches and then carefully indicates guidelines and directions which the church should follow without presenting any detailed and concrete plan. As a good academician he tries to move the question forward step by step.

In sum, the impact of these essays suffers from the changes which have occurred in the church and society in the last few years. Gustafson stresses the need for the church to be a community of moral discourse, but moral discourse in the church needs a plurality of forms including a more prophetic dimension than is apparent in this volume. The church, however, needs today and always will need and profit from the type of careful, reflective, analytic moral discourse which Gustafson handles so well.

John F. Dedek (review date 24 October 1975)

SOURCE: A review of *Theology and Christian Ethics*, in *Commonweal*, Vol CII, No. 16, October 24, 1975, pp. 24-5.

[*In the following review, Dedek praises Gustafson's essays in* Theology and Christian Ethics.]

James Gustafson is one of the ablest theologians of our time. His writings have made a significant contribution to ethical clarity. They also reveal a man of penetrating intellect, wide reading, profound faith, a natural skepticism, openness and fairness, and a finely balanced judgment. He is one of the truly wise men of our age. The Christian world still awaits his development of a systematic ethics. It would be interesting to see how Gustafson would put together the profound insights found in his disparate essays and reviews and in par-

ticular how he would put together the Lutheran and Calvinistic streams in his own ethical thought.

In the meantime Charles M. Swezey again has collected some of Gustafson's essays to make up the present volume [*Theology and Christian Ethics*]. Swezey also has written an excellent seventeen-page introduction which gives us a fine summary of some of the basic ingredients in Gustafson's ethical thought. Also a bibliography of Gustafson's writings between 1951 and 1973 has been compiled by the Reverend Ms. S. Anita Stauffer and is appended to the book.

The fourteen essays which form *Theology and Christian Ethics* were written between 1968 and 1972. Since everything changes so quickly nowadays, it is no surprise that a few of the moral issues of the late 1960s no longer appear so urgent to us today. But even in his discussion of these issues his careful methodology is illustrated. His consideration of the 1970 U.S. invasion of Cambodia, for instance, serves as an apt illustration of how the scriptures are to be used—and not used—in critical ethical thinking.

> James Gustafson is one of the ablest theologians of our time. His writings have made a significant contribution to ethical clarity. They also reveal a man of penetrating intellect, wide reading, profound faith, a natural skepticism, openness and fairness, and a finely balanced judgment. He is one of the truly wise men of our age.
>
> —*John F. Dedek*

One of course does not look for unity or a systematic development of thought in a book such as this. But the disparate essays are organized in a coherent way. There are three main sections in the book: 1) "Perspectives on Theological Ethics" which considers problems *about* the discipline of theological ethics, 2) "Some Substantive Issues" which considers problems *within* the discipline of theological ethics, and 3) "Ethics and the Sciences" which considers the *relation* of theological ethics to other disciplines. The fourteen chapters cover diverse questions such as the importance and limitations of involvement and disinterestedness in making moral decisions, moral education, the proper role or vocation of the theologian, moral discernment in the Christian life, the place of scripture in Christian ethics, the relationship between the spiritual life and the moral life, the relevance of the historical context to a moral issue, the relationship between the empirical sciences and Christian ethics, and basic ethical issues in the biomedical field.

All of the essays are exceptionally good, but I would like to single out one for special comment. It seems to me that chapter twelve, "What is the Normatively Human?" is the most important in the book. Fifteen years ago the word *human* was seldom used in moral discourse. Today nearly everyone is talking about the "humanizing" and the "dehumanizing" and what makes and keeps human life human. Everyone is for the human and against the inhuman, and everyone assumes that he understands what everyone else is saying.

William Herr (review date July 1978)

SOURCE: A review of *Protestant and Roman Catholic Ethics: Prospects for Rapprochement,* in *The Critic,* Vol. 37, July, 1978, pp. 4-5, 8.

[*In the following review, Herr falls short of agreeing with Gustafson's theory, but he praises* Protestant and Roman Catholic Ethics: Prospects for Rapprochement *as well-written and informative.*]

Gustafson has earned the compliment which Goethe, with perhaps less justification, bestowed on Kant. Reading this short work [***Protestant and Roman Catholic Ethics: Prospects for Rapprochement***] is like entering a lighted room.

His basic thesis is fairly simple, though perhaps debatable: both Catholic and Protestant ethicians are becoming increasingly aware of the limitations of their respective traditions; this may make it possible to reestablish a basis for a truly Christian, as opposed to sectarian, ethics.

The principal support for this thesis is a remarkably clear and concise historical analysis which no mere summary can possibly do justice. For early Christianity, Gustafson argues, as for Judaism, the concept of law was central to moral theology because a body of law was needed to guide the confessor and the rabbi in carrying out their professional duties. In the Catholic tradition this "juridical" approach led to the development of natural law ethics (and here Gustafson gives an explanation of the natural law tradition, going back to Augustine, which is far more clear and reasonable than that found in many Catholic philosophy textbooks).

With Luther, however, the concept of sin changed, and the confessor's role lost its importance. If justification is by faith, then sin is basically unfaith—a religious problem rather than an ethical one in the traditional sense of that term. Here the emphasis is on sin rather than on sins, on a person's personal relationship with God rather than on the violation of specific

moral laws. For Protestantism, then, ethics became more pedagogical than juridical, more dependent on the acceptance of specific religious presuppositions and less open to acceptance on purely rational grounds by "all men of good will."

Gustafson has the rare and admirable ability to say what needs to be said about a given topic, and then stop.

—*William Herr*

But this apparent antithesis suggests its own resolution: since the will of God as revealed in scripture and the natural law as discovered through reason have the same ultimate source, they cannot conflict. As an example, Gustafson compares Catholic and Protestant writings on the living wage around the turn of the century. Those who argued that justice is demanded by the natural law and those who contended that it is required by the message of Jesus necessarily reached quite similar conclusions.

In a chapter worth reading for its own sake as an introduction to contemporary Christian ethics, Gustafson argues that many Protestant writers are now seeking a foundation for "perduring moral norms," while many Catholics (he cites John Noonan in particular) are stressing that law theory necessarily develops differently in different historical contexts.

These converging tendencies offer some hope for the development of a Christian ethics which will build on what is present and supply what is lacking in both the Catholic and Protestant traditions, rather than being merely "the least common denominator to which both traditions can give allegiance."

Whether or not he accepts this conclusion, the reader will probably not find a more informative and better written exposition of the issue than this one. Giving the volume added value, both as a textbook and as an introduction for the average reader, are the variety of sources Gustafson uses and his copious and unusually informative notes.

One thing more should be noted: Gustafson has the rare and admirable ability to say what needs to be said about a given topic, and then stop.

Daniel C. Maguire (review date 16 July 1982)

SOURCE: A review of *Ethics from a Theocentric Perspec-*

tive, Volume I: *Theology and Ethics,* in *Commonweal,* Vol. CIX, No. 13, July 16, 1982, pp. 408-09.

[*In the following review, Maguire criticizes the theocentric view of God that Gustafson sets forth in his* Ethics from a Theocentric Perspective, *Volume I:* Theology and Ethics, *but asserts that there are still good things in the book.*]

To embark upon elementary theological explanation is a very personal and generously self-revealing endeavor. It's also rare. Much theology settles for analysis of waves, leaving unexamined the unseen currents that define our direction and destiny. It is, therefore, an intellectual event when someone reaches for the radical metaphors and myths that sustain a dominant religious worldview and subjects them to bold scrutiny. When the author of such a venture is a well-known theologian whose work is admired by many, the significance of the event is extenuated.

James Gustafson's volume under review is the product of thirty years of energetic labor in the field of theological ethics. He has not undertaken previously a work of such scope nor, he says, will he do so again. He has given us a serious work meriting serious attention.

It is Gustafson's purpose to save us from our "egocentric predicament." His intention is that both Christian ethics and much of Western philosophical ethics have made humankind ("man," in his term) the measure of all things. Theologians in this traditional understanding seek ways of finding a "happy coincidence between the divine law and what fulfills human life." Gustafson earnestly departs from this tradition of happy coincidence." To do so, as he admits, is no minor move for a Christian theologian. Indeed, it may, in the opinion of many, put him outside recognizable Christian perspectives. To base one's "theocentric" ethics on the contention that we have been strapped with a Ptolemaic religion in a Copernican universe," signals an epochal change. It means, he allows, that "one moves closer to some aspects of the Stoic tradition than most of Christian theology and ethics has. One entertains the possibility that the 'law of God' does not guarantee benefits to oneself, to the perceived interests and good of one's community, or even to the human species as a whole." God is not nearly as "homocentric" or "anthropocentric" as we had assumed.

Gustafson comes to this theocentric God by way of nature. Christian theology, he claims, has been too intent on seeing history as the sacrament of God's purposes rather than nature. Gustafson calls for a stress on nature as well as on history, prescribing, specifically, some heliocentric correctives for historicized Christianity. He notes frequently in the volume the scientifically predicted demise of the sun and this solar system some billions of years down the trail. This total death is our terrestrial and cosmic destiny and what it says of

"the will of God" stirs more than a Calvinistic gloom in Gustafson's theological soul. "The 'Long Friday,' as the Scandinavians call what we call 'Good Friday,' is truer to human experience than the superficial Easters to which instrumental pieties of the present age seem to point." How do persons reassess their ultimate end in the face of this theocentric and not anthropocentric God? By accepting that their chief end is not salvation but simply to honor, serve, glorify, and celebrate God "as the Calvinists have always said but not always believed and practiced."

Clearly the implications of this Gustafsonian shift are seismic. For one thing, Gustafson gives us more badspel than gospel. Angelic choirs do not attend this book singing tidings of great joy. In no meaningful way can this theocentric and not a little eccentric God say: "I have called you friends!" (John 15:15) This God, to whom Gustafson assigns male gender, views us as "instruments" in his service, plans ultimate cosmic extinction for us, and then wants us to glorify and celebrate his grandeur. What's to celebrate?

Gustafson, it seems, has transferred "the egocentric predicament" from us to God. This is not a God who wants to gather us protectively as the mother hen would cherish her little ones. (Matthew 23;37) This is not a God who promises that the end of human life is not death but resurrection. This is not a "God of hope." (Romans 15:13) This God seems to have no more ultimate concern for us than he had for the dinosaurs.

Christian hope, I would urge, calls us to reach with stubborn confidence for the possibilities that lie beyond all current orthodoxies, scientific and theological, and to divinize no current state of any question. (That hope may be illusory but the surprises of both history and nature often support it in their fashion.) Is it patently absurd to hope that science which now reveals the sun's prospective end will, some billions of years from now, provide us the travel means to escape its terminal apocalypse or even the means to indefinitely refuel solar power? Gustafson indulges no hopes beyond current scientific promises. Like the natural-law ethicists he criticizes, he is too narrowly physicalist and partial in his assumptions.

He also finds no solace in Christian hope for immortality. "Christian eschatology, a theme used in our time to create conditions of hope for oppressed persons in the world as well as for those who aspire to immortality, must be questioned." Post-mortem survival is too anthropocentric for Gustafson's theocentric ethics. He does not sing with the ancient Christian hymn, *Dies Irae: "mors stupebit et natura."* (Death and nature will be stunned!) There will be no surprises for death. Its victory is assured and nature, as the arbiter of our hopes, enjoys hegemonic imperturbability.

Jesus is little consolation in all of this. While departing with many from a narrow Chalcedonic christology, (such incarnation is the essence of anthropocentrism) Gustafson replaces it with no christology. Jesus gets lost in the theocentric shuffle.

These criticisms of the foundational assumptions of this work must not blot out many good things in the book. He criticizes the rationalistic density of much philosophical ethics. He signals (without developing) the role of affect in ethical epistemology. He cites the vacuity of some of the "philosophy of theology" that parades as hermeneutics. He chastises the self-righteousness of some social reform movements. He criticizes ethical dogmatism and false absolutism. He defends the reformability of historically conditioned religious dogmas.

And yet, ultimately, his evacuation of hope seems his undoing. Hope is the parent of social justice and reform. His kind of theocentrism is tendentially quietistic. The ultimate unconcern of this God could be catching.

Barry J. Seltser (review date 15 May 1985)

SOURCE: A review of *Ethics from a Theocentric Perspective,* Volume II: *Ethics and Theology,* in *The Christian Century,* Vol 102, No. 17, pp. 503-4.

[*In the following review, Seltser lauds Gustafson's treatment of theological ethics in his* Ethics from a Theocentric Perspective.]

This long-awaited [***Ethics from a Theocentric Perspective***] is the second volume of a systematic work by one of the most influential and respected figures in the field of Christian ethics. In his earlier volume, James Gustafson presented his basic theological position, which is summarized again in the first part of this book. He then compares his approach to that of several theological and philosophical figures, before moving on to "apply" it to four spheres of social life (marriage and family, suicide, population and nutrition, and the allocation of biomedical research funding).

In a brief review it is impossible to do justice to the range and depth of Gustafson's project. I shall merely identify two particularly distinctive features of his approach. First, his central theological claim is embodied in the title of the two-volume set. He is arguing against what he rightly considers to be the anthropocentric tendencies of most recent Christian theology; he insists that Christians cannot continue to assume that God is concerned ultimately with human salvation, or that history is established for the sake of human good. Gustafson takes a basic theological assertion about God, summarized by his passionate insistence that "God does not exist simply for the service of human beings" but "human beings exist for the service of God," expresses and defends it clearly, and applies it rigorously to the world of human ac-

tion—all the while refusing to back away from its implications.

And the implications are staggering—for Christology, for eschatology, for theodicy and for social ethics. The almost ruthless integrity with which he faces up to where this theological position leads him is perhaps the single most important aspect of this book, and a feature which has always distinguished his work. Whether or not the reader accepts Gustafson's stance, no one will walk away from his book unchallenged.

> **The lack of absolute certainty and the inability to provide specific guidelines for each kind of moral problem follow from the very nature of life in this world. For those of us who agree with Gustafson on this point, his work provides one of the most painfully honest and challenging treatments of theological ethics in our age.**
>
> **—Barry J. Seltser**

Second, Gustafson does not supply specific point-by-point ethical prescriptions for the issues he addresses. This will frustrate those readers who want to be told what, as Christians, they should do. But Gustafson's understanding of the task of Christian ethics is at once more modest and more compelling; as he writes, "The function of the ethician is to broaden and deepen the capacities of others to make morally responsible choices." The notion of "discernment" is the central methodological key here, as it always has been in Gustafson's thought. The actor is called on to ask certain sorts of questions and to use broad moral rules, but never with the expectation that specific answers will follow syllogistically from theological premises or that moral ambiguity and tragedy can be driven from the field.

As a result, the book's discussions of specific moral issues reveal Gustafson's own ethical sensitivities and show how his theocentric perspective defines and clarifies the range of ethical options. (In particular, the chapter on suicide is a beautifully sensitive analysis of the inevitable problem of human despair.)

Gustafson's approach provides one of the few concrete efforts to recognize the complexity and specificity of ethical decision-making, without falling into a "situationist" or "relativistic" ethic. The lack of absolute certainty and the inability to provide specific guidelines for each kind of moral problem follow from the very nature of life in this world. For those of us who agree with Gustafson on this point, his work provides one of the most painfully honest and challenging treatments of theological ethics in our age.

Lisa Sowle Cahill (essay date Spring 1985)

SOURCE: "Consent in Time of Affliction: The Ethics of a Circumspect Theist," in *The Journal of Religious Ethics,* Vol. 13, No. 1, Spring, 1985, pp. 22-36.

[*In the following essay, Sowle Cahill summarizes the different points of Gustafson's argument from his* Ethics from a Theocentric Perspective.]

The two volumes of **Ethics from a Theocentric Perspective** demonstrate again and predictably the reasons for which Gustafson is widely respected by his colleagues in theological ethics, even those who disagree with his recent difficult theses. These volumes exhibit familiarity with major and minor theological figures ranging across the breadth of the Christian tradition, and exemplify an unerring talent for homing in on the crucial lines of division among central theological alternatives, those on which other authors are more slow to focus, or to address directly. Both volumes propose a "theocentric" position in contradistinction from the anthropocentrism which Gustafson judges to have characterized most Christian theology and ethics. By "anthropocentrism" he means an interpretation of religious experience, faith, and theology which centers on humanity, and considers the deity's existence primarily in relation to human welfare (1981:96-99). Gustafson's fundamental project is to develop a perspective on God which begins from historical, social human experience and in which the affective dimensions of specifically religious experience are emphasized. However, he gives priority in his theology and ethics to the divine object of this experience, rather than to its subject (1981:225-35). The definitive features of human and religious experience are interaction and relatedness of humans to one another, to the rest of creation, and above all to the Creator, in relation to whom all creatures are to be seen (1981:113, 327).

Gustafson draws on resources in the Reformed tradition to amplify the themes of the sovereignty of God, of God's glorification, and of ethics as relating to all things in ways appropriate to their relations to God. The chief characteristic of true religion is defined by Calvin's term "piety," meaning a sense of dependence on, awe of, and gratitude to God (1981:163-65). Evidence of God's existence and intentions emerges from what Jonathan Edwards calls the "religious affections," grounded in senses of dependence, gratitude, obligation, remorse, repentance, and hope (1981:113-35). God so experienced is the one who creates, sustains, orders, "bears down upon," and offers the possibility of human creativity and development. Gustafson reappropriates the classical symbols of God as Creator, Sustainer, Governor, Judge, and Redeemer of humanity, but repudiates suggestions that God has human fulfillment as a central purpose or even exists to fulfill human needs (1981:112).

Evidence about the universe from the empirical and natural sciences is crucial in Gustafson's analysis of religion, since he insists that religion and theology must be consistent with human experience in all its fundamental dimensions. Scientific criteria contribute to his rejection of certain central biblical and traditional themes, concepts, and images (1981:257). Gustafson's theocentrism excludes the privileged place of humanity in the universe, immortality of human persons, and the eventual rectification of injustice and compensation for undeserved suffering (1981:182-84). He also diminishes the religious centrality of Jesus, Jesus' "Abba" relation to the Father as a model for Christians, and the importance of the resurrection for understanding Jesus as Christ (1981:275-77). Especially stressed in Gustafson's position are the interdependence of humanity and creation; the inevitability of human suffering as part of a universe not particularly ordered to human ends; the possibility of radical moral conflict; and the normative nature of self-denial for the sake of other persons and of nonpersonal creation. These themes, proposed and defended in Volume I, are amplified in Volume II with reference to central representatives of the Western theological and philosophical traditions. They are applied to four realms of moral agency, from which their application to other realms may be analogized. The four are marriage and family, population and nutrition, suicide, and biomedical research funding.

One must offer critical responses to Gustafson's work circumspectly. The urgent impulse to counterargue is itself a tacit admission of the power of his accusation that "most modern theology" has made of God "a utility device" or guarantee of human well-being (1981:41). Even those who finally disagree with his conclusions will find credible Gustafson's own claim that he has meant "to find what can be most truly claimed about God rather than to defend traditional Christianity" (1981:279). Any critic is compelled to take with full seriousness the aim Gustafson proposes.

FUNDAMENTAL QUESTIONS

Gustafson's work poses three questions which I take to be of crucial importance for the discipline of theology in general, and for the contemporary significance of religion. They are (1) the problem of evil; (2) method in theology and ethics (what is to count as a decisive argument); and (3) the "doctrine of God," or the systematic articulation of images and concepts expressing human perceptions of God. My fundamental observation with regard to these questions is that the problem of evil is a key concern of the author, but that it is not addressed by him with a directness commensurate with its importance. The problem of method is given more explicit attention in Gustafson's argument that any adequate theology must take into account an adequate range of human experience, including the evidence about the human situation yielded by the natural sciences. However, one important motive for Gustafson's revision of theological method is the emptiness of traditional Christian answers to the reality of evil, answers which postulate supernatural solutions not persuasively confirmed in actual experience. Endorsing a conception of God which is more coherent with the human experience of suffering and with the relative indifference of the universe to human affairs, Gustafson ultimately offers a theism which is more consistent with a naturalistic view of the world than it is with standard Christianity. In the end, there remains a tension in his method between three factors which he affirms, but whose relation has not been entirely resolved: the truth and reliability of religious experience as an experience of a transcendent power; the relatively more "objective" quality of empirical information; and the Judaeo-Christian commitment to at least some realities which transcend scientific and logical verification. As a result, there is significant ambivalence, or at least ambiguity, in Gustafson's view of God.

THE PROBLEM OF EVIL

The existence of moral and physical evil and the nonexistence of an adequate theodicy have represented a major stumbling block for any monotheistic view of a benevolent creator. The most acute form of the problem of evil is the suffering of the innocent. The seriousness with which Gustafson takes this enigma and the inadequacy of traditional religion to deal with it are, I suspect, the source of the passion which underlies the analytical structure of this work. It is much more clearly an issue in the second volume, especially in the later chapters on moral problems. What I infer to be some of Gustafson's deepest theological concerns would be much more fully embodied and evident to his audience were the problem of suffering, mentioned again and again, lifted clearly to the surface as a central theme. In remarks to members of the American Society of Christian Ethics, Gustafson said what he has not said here in so many words: The church makes "excessive claims" in the face of human misery, and gives assurances which are not borne out by experience. The realities of human experience are not adequately caught up in "the first-order religious language of the church." "Superficiality" when confronted with the realities of human suffering on the part of the innocent is deep in the tradition. If the claims of the church cannot be sustained other than by appeals to eschatology, then this "disjuncture" must be faced.

It is striking how often in his major work Gustafson brings home the problem of suffering anecdotally, and how often anecdotes based on his own experience are relegated to the footnotes. In the first volume, Gustafson sparsely but movingly gives us his words at his father's deathbed: "Father, your sins are forgiven" (1981:184 n.68). In Volume II we are told in notes of Gustafson's experience at another deathbed, that of a colleague, and of how Gustafson with courage and realism endeavored to make the last few moments of his friend's life meaningful; (1984:118 n.46) as well as how Gustafson's own father went off to physical labor at the age of nine, while G. E. Moore indulged in reflections on the good and beautiful (1984:n.9). Gustafson's recollection of a Montana child's program recitation, "Jesus says we must forgive, we must forgive, we must forgive," makes it into the text (1984:211). Obviously, the teller has been much impressed by these incidents.

In *Can Ethics Be Christian?* Gustafson has suggested that their interpersonal and psychological experiences may dispose persons toward certain religious and moral perceptions and sensibilities: "religious belief and believing is refracted through the prism of what a person is becoming as the result of other experiences as well" (1975:64). Although a systematic theological ethics is not the place for personal testimonials, a more direct discussion of the pervasive human experience of suffering and its role in shaping this particular theological perspective would not be inappropriate from a theologian who at a theoretical level gives a great deal of emphasis to "the affections." In discussing Kant, Gustafson tells us, "For every writer of ethics, including the present one, no doubt one element in the way a position gets developed is a predisposition toward a particular cast of morality," even though the position is not thereby "totally relativized," nor "merely a rationalization for a moral inclination" (1984:131). If experience and the affections are real modes of knowing, and not sheerly subjective and relative to idiosyncratic circumstances, then one's "predisposition" needs to be taken into account in a systematic construal of one's ethics.

Many of the comments, almost tangential, which Gustafson makes in *Ethics from a Theocentric Perspective* about suffering, endurance, hope, and forgiveness are extremely suggestive, and indicate some ways in which more traditional or biblical images in Christian ethics could be developed to deal with the questions Gustafson raises. The discussions of marriage and suicide are replete with examples. Gustafson is eloquent on the "signs of 'suffering'" in marriage and family life (1984:163-66) and offers an analysis of suffering as related to failure to accept the conditions of finitude as well as to personal fault. In answer, he develops the notion of *forgiveness* as dependent on humility and resultant in renewal (1984:168). In the chapter on suicide, suffering in the form of despair is a major theme and also is connected with forgiveness and renewal (1984:206). Gustafson's sympathetic discussion of William Lynch's diagnosis of despair as a "failure of imagination" might have made an appropriate point of entry for biblical symbols of hope and promise, reinterpreted as part of a realistic and experientially supported human response to the problem of evil and suffering (1984:248; 1984:208-09). Gustafson speaks of "the moral task" as helping others to have hope, and says that the "first order of moral responsibility" is to "sustain and support" one another in times of "affliction" (1984:209, 212-13). These statements show just how crucial the reality of suffering is in Gustafson's conception of ethics. They also give tantalizing indications of how hopeful construals of human interdependence can respond to that reality, in ways consonant with at least some traditional Christian views of God and humanity. At the explicitly theological level, however, Gustafson responds to suffering with more resignation than hope. He judges that one "must consent" to the suicides of those for whom despair is realistic. "The tragedy of their deaths flows from conditions of life beyond their powers to control" (1984:209). He is extremely restrained in his interpretations of biblical symbols of transcendence, and, while not disallowing completely the existence of a transcendent God, is reluctant to define the divine attributes in ways which fly in the face of those aspects of common experience for which publicly acceptable evidence can be offered. Having abandoned religious accounts of suffering which rely on notions of a hidden divine "master plan," heavenly recompense, or punishment for past sins, he appears unconvinced that a religious perspective can endow suffering with either purposiveness or resolution.

THE SOURCES OF CHRISTIAN THEOLOGY AND ETHICS

In discussing Volume I with other Christian ethicists, Gustafson challenged those who dissent from his position to argue against him either on the grounds that the kinds of evidences he takes into account are irrelevant for theology or that the evidences he draws on are in error. He then called on them to show what kind of evidence would count for or against a more traditional theological position. The issue of evidence is indeed the crux of the matter, though it is virtually inextricable from that of our preunderstanding of the sort of reality about which we inquire.

Traditionally, the Bible (primarily) and central figures in the Christian heritage (secondarily) have been the key sources for Christian theology and ethics. Philosophical sources and "common human experience," including scientific observation, have also been used, but the ultimate court of appeal has been more specifically religious sources. There has existed a relative consensus about the importance of the constant reappropriation of the major themes of Bible and tradition, though this has inevitably been accompanied by disagreement about what exactly are these themes and about how they ought to be interpreted. As I observed above, Gustafson has abandoned this commitment to sustain and reinterpret the

"heart" of Bible and tradition, rejecting eschatology, eternal life, a personal deity, a purposive creation, and so on. In selecting as normative other themes, such as the sovereignty of God, the utter dependence and relative insignificance of humanity, and the interrelatedness of all creatures, he attributes great importance to the empirical sciences, especially the natural sciences. That is to say, the credibility of a theological proposal is contingent upon its consistency with evidence about the natural universe which can be verified by scientific (empirical) methods. The testing of theological claims against those of the natural sciences seems to be a necessary and decisive step in Gustafson's theological method (1981:257). This step is grounded in a firm commitment to take seriously both public intelligibility as an aim of theological discourse, and the socially established ways of understanding the universe in which human experience occurs. Gustafson's position is a reminder that appeals to special revelation and particularistic religious experience can conceal notions or images of God which are merely arbitrary, fanciful, or delusory.

However, since Gustafson's method represents a significant departure from the standard canons of theological discourse, it is important that its premises and implications be clarified. The question of sources and method is certainly not ignored (See especially 1981:chs. 3 and 5, 251-68; and 1984:143-44). However, Gustafson's language is very cautious, while the actual application of his method is very bold. We are told that the Bible has not been given the authority that it "normally" has (1984:144), and that Gustafson has "relied more heavily" on scientific sources (1984:144). Gustafson repeatedly makes statements to the effect that Christians must be exposed to "other ways of construing the world," especially scientific ones, and that the "varieties" of biblical literature must be judged according to whether or not they are "radically incongruous" with scientific theories about the physical universe (1984:291-92). The end result of this "heavy" reliance on scientific investigation is the repudiation of some themes or commitments which, it could be argued, are central to the religious tradition out of which Gustafson claims to work.

This position is provocative and worth a serious hearing. It does, however, lead to further questions. Many of them have to do with the nature of science as a mode of knowing, that is, with its epistemological claims, and with philosophical interpretations of those claims. Recent critical studies of scientific method indicate that the differences between scientific and religious construals of the world may not be as vast or as radical as we generally take them to be. For instance, what is the "objective" character or certainty of "scientific" knowledge? Is it less dependent on imagination and more securely linked to "reality" than religious, philosophical, or even aesthetic knowledge? Gustafson nuances his use of scientific criteria by allowing that scientific explanations are "socially interpreted and socially tested" (1981:125). Nonetheless, they seem to offer a foothold in verification which goes beyond that of theology, philosophy, and the social sciences.

Relevant analysis of the relations of scientific theories to our perceptions of "the overall scheme of things" is offered by Stephen Toulmin, a philosopher of science and a colleague of James Gustafson at the University of Chicago. *The Return to Cosmology: Postmodern Science and the Theology of Nature* (1981) incorporates publications and lectures spanning a thirty-year period (1951-1981). Taken as a whole, the collection calls into question the understanding of scientific knowledge apparently presupposed in Gustafson's theological method. Early on, Toulmin seems to assume the objective empirical character of scientific investigation, but expresses serious reservations about whether scientific evidence could be used to support such "ethico-political myths" as "the running down universe," "evolution" or "the Sovereign Order of Nature" (1982:34-35, 56). Generalizations or universalizations from specific areas of natural scientific study to the cosmos are, he thinks, extremely difficult to warrant. If Toulmin's initial suspicious are accurate, then they have obvious implications for Gustafson's stipulation of an empirical criterion for theological speculation about the power that orders (or declines to order) the universe.

More recently, Toulmin has shifted his position. Defining "postmodern" science as an enterprise which has yielded up the ideal of "detachment," Toulmin observes that the pure "spectator" position is available neither for philosophy *nor* for natural science (1981:238-54). He claims that the disappearance of the ideal of empirical verification will allow the pre-Newtonian interest in "cosmology," in the shape of the whole which includes humanity within it, to return. The contours this interest is likely to assume bear striking similarities to the religious and philosophical ideas of late antiquity, to Toulmin's eye. Of the two popular philosophies which tried to relate humanity to the cosmos,

> the Epicurean philosophy was primarily an inward-looking philosophy, teaching that self-command, that is, command over one's own inner, psychical resources, was more valuable than outward power, or command over the outward physical resources of the world. The Stoic philosophy resulted in a very similar set of ethical maxims, but it arrived at them from the opposite direction. It looked outward rather than inward: it taught its adherents to look for the sources of inner, human order and rationality in the external order of nature, and exhorted them to live in harmony with nature. By giving their own lives a *logos* that fitted harmoniously the *logos* of nature, they could . . . achieve both personal tranquility, or *apatheia,* and also good-spiritedness, or *eudaimonia.*(1982:261-62)

Today, in revised form, the Epicurean path is followed by the philosophy of "psychotherapy," while the Stoic one is followed, granting today's more historical or developmental view of the cosmos, by the philosophy of "ecology." Although Gustafson's theology is hardly reducible to environmental ecology, his advice for his own species is not dissimilar to that Toulmin attributes to the Stoics.

Toulmin, in fact, mentions Gustafson in connection with the returned plausibility of "cosmology" or "natural theology." Toulmin is particularly appreciative of Gustafson's commitment to discuss humanity and cosmos in terms of interrelatedness. Toulmin observes, correctly I think, that Gustafson's determination to "deal with . . . all created things in ways appropriate to their relations to God" may be translated "without too much distortion" into "'dealing with all our fellow creatures in ways appropriate to their places in the overall scheme of things'" (1981:269). "Natural theology" means simply, for Toulmin, putting the question about the shape of that scheme. Though Gustafson continues to use religious symbols of transcendence, it is unclear that he means more by them than Toulmin does by "natural theology." Furthermore, Gustafson is perplexing because he both insists that ethics must be based on the relations of things and expresses more skepticism than does Toulmin about whether those relations form any sort of cosmic order, pattern, or "scheme" at all. His reason for this, however, is *not* the impossibility of generalizing from particular forms of scientific evidence, but rather his confidence that that evidence contraindicates any comprehensive order, combined with his methodological requirement that any theological "cosmology" be in line with such evidence.

Science's "objectivity" has been questioned more recently in Langdon Gilkey's critique of the "establishment of science" at the center of Western culture, which has entailed the hegemony of its method in every discipline (1984:344-45). The view of human experience or the universe represented by, for example, the biblical book of Genesis, has come to be seen as "pre-scientific." All non-scientific worldviews are judged by the standards of modern science and found to be failures in the attainment of its peculiar ideals. Whether scientific ideals, methods, and explanation can account for human experience sufficiently, or even without misrepresentation, remains, however, an open question.

A more radical challenge to the ostensibly superior "objectivity" of science is represented by the insight that not only religious, but also scientific, thinking is metaphorical. In *Metaphoric Process: The Creation of Scientific and Religious Understanding,* Mary Gerhart (a theologian) and Allan Russell (a physicist) review both ancient and recent major contributions in this direction (1984). Using the idea of "metaphor," they develop the thesis that religion and science are epistemically similar and complementary, and that contrasts of them in terms of subjectivity and objectivity often result from too particularistic or narrow a view of both fields of knowledge.

While the early Toulmin has warned against unwarranted generalization from even so-called "hard scientific facts," the later Toulmin reintroduces the global questions but doubts the "hardness" of scientific reasons for—or against—them. Gilkey seems to concur that the scientific method construed as paragon of objectivity deserves to be challenged if not dislodged. Gerhart and Russell constructively nuance the meaning and method of science in a way which realigns it epistemologically with religion but does not obliterate their differences. Such attempts to examine critically science's modes of knowing support Gustafson's insistence that science is important and his demand that it become a dialogue partner of religion and theology. He sets before the theologian the task of interpreting science's claims and of discovering the languages which both scientist and theologian can speak. The unresolved question is whether either or both have a distinctive language which addresses realities not comprehensible within the other's worldview.

In one enigmatic and atypical passage, Gustafson himself says of all the world's religions that

> [h]owever they articulate that which is beyond the means of scientific investigation and proof, they nonetheless sense the reality of its presence. This is the moment, the time, and the point at which the religious consciousness moves beyond what radically secular persons feel. This is the step or the leap which distinguishes the religious consciousness from the secular. (1981:135)

If the experience of that which lies beyond scientific evidence is constitutive of religion, then it remains unclear in what sense a theology whose overriding test of coherence is experience scientifically described remains theistic. This is particularly the case if science is taken primarily to be natural science, and if scientific evidence is taken to be primarily of an empirical sort, and to have, if not an absolute, at least a privileged place of objectivity. Gustafson never explicitly rejects God's transcendence, even though he dispenses with many of the categories and images with which Christianity has elaborated it. His view of God remains unsatisfying to the extent that he declines to draw conclusions about the divine purposes and activity which would give that transcendence substance.

THE "DOCTRINE" OF GOD

What sort of deity do Gustafson's sources disclose? Gustafson does not deny that he may be "beyond the pale" of Christianity (1981:274), even though he continues to find many of its

symbols revealing expressions of religious experience. He downplays the role of Jesus, identified as *an* incarnation of theistic piety, and does not attribute to him ultimate status. Gustafson thus moves decidedly away from the Christocentrism which has characterized not only John Calvin's view of the divinity's self-disclosure, but also the view of most of the Christian tradition (See, for example, 1984:87). But even as Gustafson's commitment to Christianity diminishes, his commitment to theism remains, and his insistence on "theocentrism" increases. What or who is the "God" of Gustafson's theism?

Gustafson's perception that the innocent suffer, and are not recompensed, profoundly influences his view of the nature of God and makes him sympathetic to the critique of religion's "cultured despisers" (to borrow a phrase from Schleiermacher). This is demonstrated at the conclusion of Volume II, where Gustafson's view of the deity is recapitulated in terms which are not particularly Christian and are only minimally theistic, if by theism is meant faith in a god or gods known within but transcendent of human experience. The salient characteristic of God which there emerges is the fact that he (or it) is beyond human control (1984:319-20). This theme is amplified in forceful terms: "The desire to manipulate God is the temptation of religious persons. But God will not be manipulated. God will be God" (1984:320).

On the last two pages of the volume (1984:321-22), other divine characteristics are repeated, which have been defined many times before. God is the one who creates, sustains, bears down upon, and creates new possibilities. Much the same could be said of "the universe" or "the way things are," or "the overall scheme of things" (Toulmin), or of "nature" as a metaphor for the whole of what is. All things which nature includes or supports come into existence, continue to be, suffer and die or cease to exist, and are capable of change. At the same time, to use the term "nature" is not necessarily to imply any special internal coherence of the whole, or any predominance of life and change over suffering and death. The identity of or difference between nature and God deserves clarification. In exactly what ways does Gustafson's idea of "God" qualify or add to the common understanding of "nature"? In what ways does his idea of "theocentric piety" differ from the genuine appreciation of the natural scientist when confronted with the sheer fact that what is, *is,* whether or not human beings will it or control it or are especially served by it?

Earlier portions of the text lead to similar sorts of questions. In the chapter on suicide, Gustafson has told us that for "many," there are "good and realistic grounds for the deepest despair," and that "the powers that bear down upon them are greater than the powers that sustain them" (1984:209). Since he has said at many other places that God is the power that both bears down upon and sustains, (e.g., 1984:27) such a statement presses the issue of the author's "theocentric" conviction: What sort of God is it that is at the center of human experience? Gustafson even refers to the powers that bear down as "powers of destruction" and concludes that there is sometimes reason for "enmity toward" God (1984:216). In this conception, the will of God seems to go beyond lack of favoritism toward humans, beyond indifference even, and approach malevolence.

Although it would be difficult to argue that Gustafson's general portrait conveys a maleficent god, instead of or in addition to a benevolent one, the question at least remains whether the notion "God" is not the functional equivalent of "nature." God is frequently spoken of as an "ordering" or "governing" power, which implies a purposiveness not easily asserted of the natural world. Nonetheless, symbols of providence or order are in tension with other language which tends to indicate that "God" is simply the condition of possibility of everything that is *as* it is.

There occur many striking parallels in Gustafson's uses of the terms "God" and "nature." Nature is humanity's "enemy" as well as "friend"; nature both "threatens" and "sustains." Nature is the source of "the sustenance of life." And "in the end nature and God will not be defied" (1984:273). These words are repeated as a conclusion from the observation that "the powers that create and sustain human life also bear down upon it and destroy it" (1984:277). Gustafson comes close to saying that good does not predominate over evil in nature, and that the notion "God" implies no perspective beyond that of nature.

Early in Volume II, Gustafson draws theological support from the Reformed tradition by paraphrasing [John] Calvin's saying that "'nature is God' . . . if that is said with a reverent heart as Calvin prescribes" (1984:36). In a note we are given the relevant text from the *Institutes of the Christian Religion* (I, 5, 5): "I confess, of course that it can be said reverently, provided that it proceeds from a reverent mind, that nature is God" (1984:36n.24). What we are not given is the context, which is an argument for the immortality of the soul; and we are given only part of Calvin's addition: "but because it is a harsh and improper saying, since nature is rather the order prescribed by God, it is harmful in such weighty matters, in which special devotion is due, to involve God confusedly in the inferior course of his works." Calvin also reminds us in the *Institutes* (1955:H, 6, 1) that although "we cannot by contemplating the universe infer that he is Father," we are called "to the faith of Christ, which, because it appears foolish, the unbelievers despise."

It can be responded to Gustafson's undeniably incisive and commanding critique of self-serving "religion" that there is a paradox at the heart of the gospel: only those who repent and yield themselves up to the Kingdom will know the loving and merciful Father of Jesus. If religious experience with its affective foundations is, as Gustafson has insisted, a legitimate and reliable dimension of human experience, then it is plausible to claim that the testimony of religious persons constitutes a sort of verification of or evidence for *knowledge* of God's benevolent faithfulness, even if that benevolence can be known *only* through crucifixion and in purity of heart. This is the gospel paradox.

What is it that most of his critics find scandalous about Gustafson's position? Certainly, it is not merely his rejection of an afterlife, though this is mentioned frequently. Rather, it is something in support of which faith in resurrection life (not "immortality") often is adduced: belief in a personal God who creates, orders, forgives, and raises us from our suffering. As St. Paul warned, "But if there is no resurrection of the dead, then Christ has not been raised; if Christ has not been raised, then our preaching is in vain. . . . If Christ has not been raised, your faith is futile and you are still in your sins" (1 *Corinthians* 15: 13-14, 17; *Revised Standard Version*). It is no oversight that causes Gustafson to describe the significance of Jesus in terms of resignation to his cross, with no counterpoint of resurrection promise and fulfillment. The eschatological symbols of the New Testament are rejected in favor of an interpretation of Jesus in terms of struggle, suffering, doubt, and final consent to the inevitable, even when not perceived as a human good (1981:276-78). Gustafson revises Calvin's image of "piety," and Jonathan Edwards' of "consent" to mean courageous resignation to and cooperation with the cosmos on which humanity depends and to which it is subordinate. As the first volume [of *ETP*] concludes:

> Ethics in the theocentric perspective does not guarantee happiness, though it does not consign us to discontent. It requires consenting to the governance of the powers of God, and joining in those purposes that can be discerned. God does not exist simply for the service of man; man exists for the service of God (1981:342).

Gustafson's response to the infliction of underserved suffering and to the impression of divine arbitrariness is close to the agonized and aweful obeisance of a Job: "I know that thou canst do all things, and that no purpose of thine can be thwarted. . . . therefore I despise myself and repent in dust and ashes" (*Job* 42:2, 6). Contrast to this the more radiant gratitude of Rabbi Abraham Heschel, who, like Job and Gustafson, contends with human suffering and death (the Holocaust), seeks to illumine the meanings of service and piety, and refuses to take comfort in expectation of future reward:

> How can I repay unto the Lord all His bountiful dealings with me? When life is an answer, death is a homecoming. And the deepest wisdom man can at-

tain is to know that his destiny is to serve. . . . This is the meaning of death: the ultimate self-dedication to the divine. Death so understood will not be desecrated by craving for immortality, for the act of giving away is reciprocity on man's part for God's gift of life. For the pious man it is a privilege to die (1951:296).

FURTHER REFLECTIONS AND ATTEMPTED REPLIES

The chief fault of which Gustafson accuses Christianity is not its inclination to promote resurrection without embracing the cross, for that inclination is arguably intrinsic neither to the New Testament nor to the insights of those who have recalled the errant tradition to the biblical witness. Martin Luther and Dietrich Bonhoeffer are representative of those who have deplored the occasional sale of "cheap grace" in Christian history. More at issue is an archaic and very deep claim, even in the New Testament. That is the assurance that all crucifixion will be recompensed, the claim that the cross always is redemptive and divinely vindicated. "Cross" in the Christian religious sense means not merely innocent suffering, but suffering which is voluntarily and purposively appropriated, even if inevitable. The challenge of the cross is, in the midst of suffering, to affirm one's relatedness to others and one's service to them as the meaning of one's existence, and to do this out of love for and obedience to the encompassing and deliberate power sustaining and calling life.

Thus the *real* problem of the cross is neither that of facile compensation, nor even that of an afterlife; it is the appeal of this image to a self-sacrificial intention as an answer to the problem of evil. The limit of this appeal is its premise of mature, cognizant, and self-controlled will. The "residue" left by this answer is the bane of any theodicy: What of those for whom the integrative surmounting of suffering is not possible—children, for example? Here "eternal life" appears as possibly the only theistically cogent response. The sole alternative (besides a refusal to respond), the one by which Gustafson is persuaded, is to acknowledge conflict and injustice of an ultimate order. Since scientific systems of explanation seem to Gustafson to provide more forthright accounts of the radical disorder in experience than do traditional religious ones, he has shaped his "theocentrism" to fit their mold.

Perhaps Gustafson's choice can be countered only with the reply that it is not immediately evident why the rendering of human experience given by, say, a Carl Sagan is more persuasive than that of a St. Paul, or why Calvin was not right about whose "foolishness" is apparent and whose real. One's choice of authorities must finally depend on a conviction, arising out of one's own experience as part of the community

with whose life one identifies, about which symbol systems and explanatory concepts most authentically convey our human and religious reality. It is of the essence of the guilt of the church that it has distorted the biblical symbols of evil, repentance, promise, and hope into the paradigms of superficiality from which Gustafson recoils to the more honest "cosmologies" of the natural scientists. But whether these schemes should take priority in a satisfactory account of the whole of what it is that humans experience physically, affectively, and cognitively is the final question.

In a published lecture, Gustafson furnishes an anecdote about his maternal grandfather which may reveal a good deal about his own conception of his "calling" as a theologian, and about the sorts of commitments that forbid what appear to him comfortable theological evasions. In 1920, Nels Moody, an immigrant blacksmith, was written up in the company magazine as a "'model employee'" of John Deere, for which he had labored for forty-one years.

> During a protracted hot spell along about 1906, there were few men on the job in the blacksmith shop any day. On the hottest day of the period the men began dropping out at nine in the morning. At three in the afternoon the shop was practically deserted. At three-thirty the foreman walked through the shop to see that everything was all right before he shut down the plant for the day. He heard a noise emanating from the vicinity of Nels Moody's forge. He strolled over there and found Nels, unmindful of the heat, "turning out work in the accustomed manner." The foreman was perplexed, for it was not cost effective to keep the shop running with only one man on the job. He inquired from the superintendent what he should do. "Keep the plant running as long as Moody wants to work," were the instructions from the superintendent. "Nels finished out the day and then walked home." . . . Regarding the employee's pension plan, the report states, "Inasmuch as the pension is a gift of the company, [Moody] feels that he is not entitled to it." "He deems it a privilege to work." (Gustafson, 1982:505).

This story furnishes a perfect parable of the reception of *Ethics from a Theocentric Perspective* by Gustafson's colleagues. Many of a more empirical bent must be perplexed as to whether it is "cost effective" to reshape Christian symbols in pursuit of a realistic view of the world. Certainly many theologians question the cost effectiveness for their religious traditions of taking scientific hypotheses so seriously and so centrally. Yet a considerable proportion, like the superintendent, recognize not only fortitude but integrity in one whom others decline to imitate, giving what are considered generally to be excellent reasons.

Stephen Toulmin (essay date Spring 1985)

SOURCE: "Nature and Nature's God," in *The Journal of Religious Ethics,* Vol. 13, No. 1, Spring, 1985, pp. 37-52.

[*In the following essay, Toulmin discusses how Gustafson's* Ethics from a Theocentric Perspective *fits into the history of theological discourse, and he asserts that the author is both old-fashioned and revolutionary in his arguments.*]

I

Early in Volume I of ***Ethics from a Theocentric Perspective,*** James Gustafson quotes Alasdair MacIntyre's recent criticism of contemporary theologians: that they "are often more interested in other theologians than they are in God" (Gustafson, 1981:68). Nobody would ever criticise Gustafson himself in these terms. However unhappy some readers may be about his conclusions, the subject of his argument is never in doubt, and he never diverts us for long into the seductive byways of current theological debate, such as "method," "interpretation," and the "transcendental" nature of religious ideas. Not only James Gustafson's *"ethics"* is theocentric: the same is true of his whole way of thinking and feeling. So, again and again in the two volumes of this important work, he quietly but insistently draws his readers back to the specific issues that are the immediate topics of his reflections: about the nature of any approach to matters of conduct that places at its center the relationship of human agents to God.

Some readers will find the resulting argument confusing, for Gustafson's conclusions are, at the same time, both old-fashioned and revolutionary. They are old-fashioned, in being substantive and direct. James Gustafson uses the language of religion as it stands, without any apology or suggestion that we quieten our intellectual scruples about it, by treating it as an elaborate social fiction or *façon de parler*. He engages in no semantic byplay and shows no hesitation in speaking without gloss about the ways in which a belief in God can restrict and direct moral choices. On the contrary, he is ready to debate in their own terms and on their own conditions all his illustrious forerunners (whether Augustine, [John] Calvin or [Martin] Luther), and he is not inclined to take refuge in the transcendental and linguistic boltholes of the post-Kantian philosophers or their theological followers.

Yet Gustafson's conclusions are also revolutionary. Because he refuses to compromise the claims of his religion or explain them away as fictions or metaphors, he faces head-on issues that his contemporaries are prepared to fudge: notably, issues that arise out of post-Reformation changes in our scientific views about the world. He does not carry over without reconsideration sixteenth-century religious ideas, which took for granted a static order of nature and a *cosmos* limited in both size and duration: instead, he rethinks them in terms

appropriate to a time when the astronomical scale and antiquity of the physical world, and the evolutionary history of its inhabitants, have become established commonplaces. So, he takes new scientific ideas about the place of humanity in nature with deep seriousness, and addresses their meaning for theism generally—and, more particularly, for a theocentric approach to ethics—candidly and fearlessly.

Some will find the results disturbing; to others, they will be reassuring. As Gustafson reminds us (1981:251), Calvin himself confessed (with whatever careful and reverent qualifications) "that Nature is God," (Calvin, 1955: I, 58) and, in the same carefully qualified sense, his own theological conclusions may be read as an updated version of John Calvin's own. In discussing the relevance of science to human conduct, for instance, he writes (1981:273):

> To speak of God as a powerful Other, and to discern processes of the divine governance in the world, does not reduce human actions to the effects of describable and knowable sufficient causes. It does acknowledge the existence of conditions which both limit and sustain the possibilities of human action.

Contrasting his own Stoical position with H. Richard Niebuhr's views, which embody a markedly greater "confidence in the agency model of God," he continues (1981:273-74):

> I believe we can appropriately say only that we have capacities to respond to persons and events in an interactive way, and that through those actions we respond to the divine governance, to *the powers that bear down on us and sustain us*. (Italics added.)

As we read on, this last phrase becomes the *leitmotiv* of Gustafson's argument. We discover God, he argues (1981:197-204, 229-35), in all of our experience, notably in the ways in which experience mobilizes our affectivity, and a proper feeling for human finitude depends on our understanding of the world of Nature, since this is the stage on which our lives are lived out and all our actions performed. So, with Calvin's qualifications, respect for the findings of natural science has a legitimate part to play in "the retrieval and reconstruction of theology." (Gustafson, 1981:251). Above all, we shall be in a position to respond to these "powers that bear down on us and sustain us"—through which the "divine governance of the World" shows itself—as perceptively as is called for by a proper "discernment of the requisites for a moral ordering of life," only if we pay attention to the new scientific insights into nature that we owe to the astronomers and the geologists, the evolutionary biologists and the geneticists.

One last introductory remark. Because the powers in which

the divine governance of Nature can be seen are, for Gustafson, *there outside us,* their action is not some noumenal fiction, but is recognized in the course of phenomenal experience. He does not treat the conviction that the world is divinely ordered as a "social construct" or "regulative ideal." Quite the contrary: in his most challenging passages, he asks us concede that human beings may turn out *not* to have a uniquely important place in the "divine ordering" of the world.

> What we judge to be good for man, or for a human person, or some human group, may not be in accord with the ordering purposes of God, insofar as they can be discerned. . . . It may be that the task of ethics is to discern the will of God—a will larger and more comprehensive than an intention for the salvation and well-being of our species, and certainly of individual members of our species (Gustafson, 1981:113).

Certainly, nothing in our experience of the world warrants claims to the primacy of the human species, and it is a mistake for us to ask moral theologians for any such warranty.

For anyone who adopts a truly *theo*centric ethics, the basic moral imperative is, rather, "to conduct life so as to relate to all things in a manner appropriate *to their relations to God*" (my italics); and just what those relations will prove to be, in the whole scheme of divine governance, cannot be decided *in advance* but *remains to be seen.*

How does the truth about the whole scheme of natural powers and divine governance *show* itself in our experience? That is the central question in Gustafson's theology of nature, and we shall return to it later in this essay.

II

The reflections into which Gustafson's line of thought leads are fascinating and provoking in a dozen ways, and anyone who sets out to comment on them one faces an *embarras de richesses.* This essay focusses selectively on one notion that is central for both Calvin and Gustafson, *viz.,* "Nature." The specific sense in which Calvin understood this notion (I argue) was displaced, for the purposes of philosophy and theology, not long after his time, and it has been reincorporated into our general ways of thinking only in the mid-twentieth century. If James Gustafson's views appear both old-fashioned and revolutionary at the same time, therefore, this is no accident. For his ambition is to come to terms with a contemporary system of scientific cosmology that itself embodies a "revolutionary return" to scientific themes and a conception of piety toward Nature, of kinds that have been largely forgotten since the seventeenth century.

The essay takes up three issues in turn. We will look first

(1.1) at the historical transformations to which the idea of Nature was subjected by Descartes, Newton and the other "New Philosophers" of the seventeenth and eighteenth centuries, and then go on to show (1.2) how far, in the course of the twentieth century, natural scientists have undone these changes, and returned to attitudes more in harmony with those of the sixteenth-century humanists.

(2) Next, we shall see how hard it was for Immanuel Kant—working in the aftermath of Descartes' philosophical critiques, Newton's scientific triumphs, and [David] Hume's skeptical arguments—to preserve a robustly *outward*-looking interpretation of the "divine order" in natural phenomena, like that which Calvin held, and Gustafson would now revive; and recognize how this led Kant to take his own *inward*-looking, transcendental turn. If Kant's own philosophy was thus a response to the success of the seventeenth-century natural philosophy (notably, the ideas of Newton) we must ask how the current reversal of seventeenth-century ideas *within science* will affect our theological understanding of scientific ideas.

(3) Finally, we shall return to the basic question about Nature implicit in Gustafson's arguments, but to which he gives us no really full or explicit answer, viz.: If we seek to relate to all other things "in a manner appropriate to their relations to God," how can we know when we do, and when we do not, succeed in reading those relations aright?

There may no longer be unanswerable objections on the level of philosophical or scientific theory to seeing "evidences of divine ordering" in the world of Nature. But practical problems remain: especially in recognizing how particular constituents in that "divine ordering" relate to the larger whole of which they are parts, and in learning to order our conduct in ways appropriate to those relations.

Now as much as ever (we shall see) a neo-Stoic position has *general, theoretical* charms. But, for James Gustafson as much as for John Calvin, those charms are matched by the difficulties of knowing what *specific, practical* claims such a view of the world makes upon us in our moral and political lives.

III

(1.1) The seventeenth-century "scientific revolution" generated major changes in the idea of Nature current among educated men and women, both at the time and in the succeeding centuries. Its authors took pride in these changes: in their view, earlier conceptions had been filled with Aristotelian prejudices and superstitions, and were well abandoned.

Yet it is not easy to characterize the exact effect of these changes. In his massive and authoritative study, for instance, E. J. Dijksterhuis (1961) speaks of them as "the mechanization of the world-picture," and the image of the natural or physical world as a giant clock, and of God the creator as a cosmic clockmaker, is a recurrent theme in seventeenth-century debates about the relations between God and Nature. Still, reliance on this image of the universe as a "machine" was neither universal nor compulsory. An alternative commonplace treated Nature as a divine book, to be accepted—along with the Book of Scripture—as a source of evidence about God, the presumed author of both sacred texts. Galileo and Descartes both recognized that this "Book of Nature" was written in cypher, but it would have been malicious for God to have made his created world unintelligible to man. So the natural philosophers must simply accept the challenge and "crack" the mathematical code in which the Book of Nature was apparently composed.

Nor did the seventeenth-century philosophers see these alternative commonplaces as competing with one another, let alone as being inconsistent. Rather, they served in practice as parallel *topoi* or tropes, which the theorist could invoke as occasion demanded. Taken alone, neither image of Nature (as clockwork cosmos and as encrypted text) captured the crucial changes—intellectual and affective—that were embodied in the "new, mathematical and experimental philosophy of nature," which Galileo Galilei, Rene Descartes, and Isaac Newton built up over the years from 1600 to 1687. In order to identify those essential changes, we must dig deeper; and, if we do so, we shall find that the force of this scientific change of approach was, from the start, quite as much theological as methodological.

What essentially marked off seventeenth-century ways of thinking about Nature from their forerunners in the Aristotelian tradition was (I claim) neither the mechanization nor the mathematization of the world-picture. Rather, it was two features that are shared by all mechanical or mathematical views of Nature: the *deanimation* of Nature, and the associated *separation* of God the author of the Creation from Nature, its object. The philosophers of antiquity rarely saw any reason to set God apart from the natural world: in particular, Aristotelians were free to view the entire cosmos as "animate," even as "ensouled," and saw no more objection than Calvin did to equating God with the World of Nature in which and through which the divine life and mind were expressed. Taken as a whole, the Cosmic Soul (the final source of all changes in the cosmos) might be exempt from all change— "unmoved," according to the traditional scholastic translation. Still, as the "mover" of all "motions," the changeless ground of all change *in* the world could not ultimately be separated *from* the world in which those changes took place.

As a result, Aristotelian natural philosophy had no use for the sharp contrasts that we find in its seventeenth-century successor, in which a passive inanimate World of Nature composed of extended material objects was the locus of physical processes that were subject to rigorous causal laws and were describable in terms of mathematical equations and/or mechanical models. This World was set over against the active, animate World of Spirit, which alone had mentality and so can initiate actions in conformity with the demands of reason and in pursuit of the good. (See Descartes, 1637:*passim*).

Once this new view took root, in its classic Cartesian form, there was no longer any way of seeing God as being *in* the World of Nature, let alone as *being* that World. To be more exact, this could be done only at the price of great artificiality: as when Newton identified Space as the *sensorium Dei* in which God was aware of all natural events and treated "immaterial" fields of gravitational and electrical force as vehicles of God's action in Nature. So, for many of the "new philosophers," *deism* was the preferred theological destination (see Clarke, 1956, and Koyre, 1968).

This seventeenth-century transition—from the animated, active cosmos of the medieval natural philosophers to the inert, *de*animated material world of the new mathematical philosophy—was only one of a series of dichotomies, which ended not just by dividing Mind from Matter, rational thought from causal process, but by separating the realm of "values" from that of "facts" and setting *Humanity* over against *Nature*. It goes without saying that a world-view cut down the middle by such dichotomies was inhospitable to the ethical views that the Stoics had taught in Antiquity, and also to the quasi- or neo-Stoic doctrines that had been widely revived during the fifteenth and sixteenth centuries, in the wake of the Renaissance and the Reformation.

In this respect, Calvin's views are only one illustration of a more widespread view. In sixteenth-century French moral theory, for instance, one topic of debate was how to square accepted ideas about ethics with the Stoic view that a common *logos* informs both human conduct and the operations of Nature. When the Cartesian counter-revolution split the rational thoughts of human beings from the causal processes of material Nature, accordingly it also effectively divorced the "value" questions of ethics and moral theory from the "factual" issues of natural science, and so reenacted the Epicureans' rejection of the Stoic vision of Nature as the ideal or model for human thought and conduct.

The Epicurean implications of the New Philosophy were never allowed to become explicit. Throughout the Christian Era, the teachings of Epicurus were held in such discredit that Epicurean associations were as unwelcome to *bien-pensants* in the seventeenth and eighteenth centuries as they had been earlier on. So, we find Galileo and Descartes, Newton and Vico all of them playing down the Epicurean aspects of their philosophies. The only writers who were content to tolerate this reproach were the self-conscious innovators and dissenters, like Julien de la Mettrie in France and the Ranters and Levellers of Commonwealth England. (Why was Epicureanism for so long in disgrace? That question recurs later in our discussion, in connection with Gustafson's own views about the theology of nature.)

Rather than become allies of the Epicureans, mathematically-minded advocates of the new physical sciences turned rather to the Platonists. For instance: Descartes' central doctrine, that all speculative truths about the world are formal consequences of axiomatic ideas which are clearly and distinctly present to the philosophical intellect, has as obvious a Platonist ancestry as Galileo's doctrine that the Book of Nature is written in a hidden mathematical code. As for Isaac Newton, his correspondence with Henry More makes his sympathy for the "Cambridge Platonists" of his time quite evident (cf. Koyre, 1965).

This Platonist alliance reinforced the other theological implications of Cartesian and Newtonian natural philosophy. The "dualism" at its core was not merely a philosophical dodge: as Westfall's analysis of Newton's Arianism makes clear (Westfall, 1980), it also had a theological ancestry and significance. The incongruity in the new system between active rational Mind and inert mechanical Matter was a philosophical replay of a theological incongruity which had earlier caused the Trinitarians grief: the incongruity between the incorruptible perfection of God the Father and the corruptible nature of the historical, human, and material person, Jesus of Nazareth. Hence the pressing need to keep Divinity (and Mind, as its surrogate) separate from all bodily creatures (or Matter), as it had been in, e.g., the cosmological theory of Plato's *Timaeus*. As the rational Creator of Nature, after all, God the Father was no more embodied in his material Creation than the Demiurge was a physical part of the *ouranos* (the world of material necessity) for Timaeus or Plato (cf. Cornford, 1937).

To sum up: the "scientific revolution" gave rise to a view of the world in which *Nature* was both deanimated and devalued. One could no longer speak of Nature and God, as Calvin had done, in the same breath and similar terms. Now (*only* now) the divine realm became the World of *Super*nature rather than that of Nature; and "Acts of God" displayed their status through transcending the physical mechanisms of Nature, overriding its causal laws, and intervening in the physical phenomena of the material world *from outside*.

(1.2) The rigid lines of demarcation characteristic of the seventeenth-century mechanistic natural philosophy kept their hold over many hard scientists—at least in theory—well into the twentieth century. As a result, many philosophers and theologians still assume that the intellectual instrument they collectively know as *Science* remains committed, in practice, to some or all of the Cartesian dichotomies. This is a misreading of the situation. In fact, earlier hardline dichotomies and divisions were already beginning to weaken some time

in the nineteenth century, and by now, in the pragmatic decisions of working scientists, the original system carries very little serious authority.

If it still had practical force, indeed, both biology and psychology would be gravely impaired. As seventeenth-century writings on animal motion make clear, for instance, it was not just the rational thoughts and actions of the human mind that a mechanical natural science could not account for: the seemingly spontaneous phenomena of animal life were just as hard to digest (see Borelli, 1680:Introduction). On the seventeenth-century view, a "machine" was (by definition) an instrument which transmitted powers and actions that were initiated outside itself; so there was no room in the mechanism of nature for a "living" machine, let alone a "thinking" one. Just as mentality could be operative in human thinking, only through intervention of a "non-material" mind in the workings of the human brain, so the vitality of the animal frame could be maintained only by some equally "non-material" vital agency capable of operating within the animal brain. Paradoxically, therefore, a truly mechanistic physiology could not help being an animistic, or "vitalistic," physiology as well (see further Toulmin, 1969).

Early in the nineteenth-century, physiologists began to work for a relaxation of these constraints. Before 1870, Claude Bernard had demonstrated that physiological functions in the bodily frame, though physico-chemical in their material workings, could also be active (or "vital") in their own right. Thanks to his analysis of feedback systems in the body, the idea of a "machine" soon expanded to match, and the theoretical ideal of a "mechanistic" explanation followed suit [Clande Bernard. *Lecons sur la Chaleur Animale, Sur les effets de la chaleur et la fièrre,* 1876]. By now, this relaxation has gone much further. While many people still object to calling computers "thinking machines," their scruples do not extend to assuming that such mechanisms are activated by "non-material" spirits.

Nor is the taboo on mixing facts and values in the natural sciences enforced with its old rigor. Here too, the development of physiology made a crucial difference. Bodily *functions* cannot be explained without conceding the possibility of *mal*function and *dys*function; so the contrast between the healthy and unhealthy functioning of any organ carries with it implications about what is "for the *good* of" the individual whose health is in question. The *fact* that a bodily organ is malfunctioning cannot be one of those *value-neutral* facts that positivist philosophers of science used to point to as "building blocks" of an objective Science: quite the contrary, in physiology at least, facts and values are *inherently* interrelated.

This repenetration of natural science by value questions is strengthened by the intellectual heritage of Darwin's theory of organic evolution. At the core of Darwinism lies the image of living species *at home* in their natural habitats, and this idea is linked to a concept that is indispensable to biologists— the concept of *adaptation.* If it is self-evidently good to have (say) a normally functioning liver, it goes without saying also that it is "a good thing" for any population, whether human or animal, to live a life that is "well adapted" to the demands of its place and time. As Darwin himself showed in the concluding paragraph of *The Origin of Species,* about the botanical and zoological relationships exemplified in a "tangled bank," the evolutionary view of Nature is permeated with the forms of wisdom, balance, and harmony that had always entranced natural theologians [as in Charles Darwin. *The Origin of Species,* 1859].

The transition from Cartesian to post-Darwinian science thus takes us back from the Epicurean detachment of a "merely factual" Science to a new Stoicism, in which the observer sees "values" and "harmonies" within organic Nature itself. As a result, the assumptions of the scientific world-view are so transformed that Frederick Ferre can contrast seventeenth-century (or *"modern"*) science with late twentieth-century— or *"post-modern"*—science.

If this is so in the life sciences, it is all the more so in the human sciences: both those that study the mental activity of individual human beings and those that concentrate on social and cultural interactions among human populations. Descartes himself recognized quite accurately the reasons why a systematic study of human beings (psychology, say) would never amount to a "science," in the precise sense in which mechanics and optics are sciences: seen from his point of view, the force of the term "science" has been seriously weakened since his time, in extending it to make room for human sciences. As an outcome of this recent extension, in addition, most of the value considerations that were expelled from seventeenth-century Science, when "rational Humanity" was split off from "causal Nature" and "values" were divorced from "facts," are now back on the scientific stage.

IV

(2) By the late eighteenth century, the success of the scientific movement launched by Galileo, Descartes, and Newton had greatly limited the options for a "theology of nature." At that stage, only two possibilities apparently remained, and neither of these had any long term promise or attractiveness.

On one hand, there was "the theology of the sandbanks." The few remaining enthusiasts for the argument from design emphasized all those wonders of Nature for which the new Science had not—or, at least, had not *as yet*—found "mechanistic" explanations. This argument was a diminishing asset. Assuming that divine acts must involve supernatural violations of the order of Nature put natural theology at

risk, since the scope for such acts was cut down by every scientific advance: the "rising tide of Science" constantly threatened to submerge the remaining "sandbanks" and so destroy the room for miraculous manifestations of supernatural power in an otherwise mechanistic world.

That first alternative was rejected by Kant. He argued that the task of the physical science was to construct representations of the "empirical" World as the sphere of "causality," and these representations were in principle exhaustive. Rather than having to find a place within such empirical representations (still less in competition with them), theological accounts of experience must exist beside and in parallel with them. Hence, Kant's doctrine that the theological realm is not empirical but "transcendental": that theological discussion is concerned, not with the *content* of empirical experience, but with "necessary preconditions for the possibility of" our having such experience at all (Kant, 1781). Evidence of God's action is no longer to be found *in* experience: theism is, rather, an hypothesis about the *ground* of that experience. That thesis is still a familiar theological view: Gustafson considers it only to reject it. As he sees, the "transcendental" approach only threatens to dilute the belief that the order of Nature is the order of Creation also (Gustafson, 1981:65-66).

Taken by itself, neither of these positions is satisfactory; and, in any case, they share one questionable assumption. Kant may reject the Cartesian dichotomy, which treated causal matter and rational mind as distinct "substances," but in its own way his position is no less dichotomous than Descartes' had been. Specifically, "values" have no more place within Kant's empirical world than within Descartes' causal world of Matter or Nature. Rationality and Morality, God, Freewill and Immortality find a place only at the transcendental boundary of possible experience, where you could glimpse them out of the corner of your eye (Kant, 1781). So, despite their other differences, Kant and Descartes both saw the world of scientific phenomena as comprising bare "facts" among which "meaning" and "value" had no place, and in this view they were followed both by Schleiermacher, Dilthey, and other hermeneutic writers, and by their positivist opponents. (It is only in the last few years, for example, that Gadamer has begun to take seriously the idea that the natural sciences involve "hermeneutic" or interpretive elements, no less than the human sciences.)

The presuppositions of seventeenth-century natural philosophy thus banished everything of significance (e.g., value, meaning, grace and miracles) from the realm of Nature. Only two directions were left in which to look for evidence of God's action in the world: either among the few empirical phenomena that still resisted the naturalistic explanations of the sciences, or else quite away from empirical experience, among its "rational preconditions." And both approaches conceded, in effect, the positivists' thesis: that the natural sciences are wholly *factual,* and that statements about *values* originate only in human interpretations which go beyond the scientific facts about concrete cases.

V

(3) Were those conclusions ever more than temporary? Not at all: the twentieth-century expansion in the intellectual reach of the sciences has washed away the philosophical dikes that were so carefully erected three hundred years ago to separate "values" from "facts." As a result, there are no longer basic *scientific* objections to Gustafson's claim that we can discern, in empirical experience, evidence of the divine scheme of things, and so of the ways in which we and all other things both *do,* and *should,* relate to God. As a result, he obliges us to take seriously the surprising thought that the older-style "natural theologians" like Paley were not, after all, so misguided when they looked to scientific observations of nature for "evidences of God's Purpose and Wisdom."

True, Gustafson concedes, "the conditions for this discernment are not such as to provide absolute certainty about God's purposes. And thus, moral life will continue to have its risks [*ETP,* Vol. I]. But, at least, he "opens the way to the possibility" that God's purposes, and the focus of the moral life, may respect the needs of nature more than they do "human points of view," and he draws our attention to that possibility quite deliberately.

Once the underlying presuppositions of Gustafson's argument are stated, it becomes clear how deeply his ways of thinking are rooted in Stoicism. He is happy to stand alongside a Calvin whom he views—following John McNeill—as having links with the Stoics of antiquity, by way of Lactantius and Seneca, as well as alongside others who took the orderly operations of nature as signs of the power and presence of God: he refers particularly to Schleiermacher and the Deists, "the psalmists, Augustine, [Jonathan] Edwards, and many others" (Gustafson, 1981:251-53, especially 253).

These days, many other people—less scholarly, but just as serious-minded—find this aspect of Gustafson's moral theology congenial. The ecology movement has spontaneously led to the untutored revival of several Stoic themes: e.g., piety toward Nature (or the *cosmos*) and an obligation to harmonize our human actions with the order of nature. The Stoics saw a shared *logos* as underlying both the orderliness of Nature and the rationality of human experience: by understanding that shared *logos,* one could arrive at an ethics that brought Nature and humanity into harmony. For today's ecologists, the central moral imperative is likewise to *conform* and *conserve:* all human conduct is either "for" or "against" Nature, and actions that are not harmonious with Nature can only aggravate our conditions of life, and so recoil upon us.

If I read Gustafson aright, he would—like Lactantius—substitute God's purposes for the Stoics' universal *logos,* but,

with that one change, most of what followed then (and is still seen as following today) is acceptable to him just as it stands. In this, he is taking on a substantial intellectual burden: like the Stoics before him, he faces the task of explaining how we can infer the nature of the *logos*—or God's purposes for the *cosmos*—from the observable orderliness of our experience. In the two present volumes, he does little more than present these issues as a problem, but, if he addresses them more explicitly in future writings, they may take him further afield than he has yet fully explored.

At heart, the issues that confront Gustafson at this point are *epistemological* ones: Granted that we can speak of looking in our experience of Nature for "evidences" about the divine Scheme of Things and about how all the creatures involved in that Scheme relate to God: how can we *know* when we have correctly recognized that scheme and those relations?

This question may be asked either in a skeptic's deductivist tone of voice or in a more constructive and pragmatic spirit. But it is no less of a problem for being approached modestly. However we deal with this issue, we are playing for high stakes, risking no less than our understanding of the whole *cosmic* order on which the *moral* ordering of our lives finally depends: i.e., our feeling for how human life and concerns relate to the overall ordering of a cosmos that includes, not just our human species, but all other constituents in the scheme of Nature as well.

How does Gustafson deal with this epistemological question? His approach is, characteristically, level-headed. Like other prudent inquirers into concrete, substantive issues, he makes no attempt to state beforehand the procedures by which our ideas about God's purposes and designs for the worlds of Nature and Humanity are to be refined. If we rely on the critical use of our own natural perceptiveness, we shall find ways of making progress *ambulando,* as we go along, without the need to "justify" them in advance. For, apart from getting on with this task, no procedure exists to guarantee us a sure way of correctly identifying the patterns of relationships in which all the constituents of the world stand to God.

In any case (Gustafson asks [1981:113]) who are we to demand such a guarantee? A dozen roads exist by which, through confidence in the fruitfulness of honest hard work, we can move in directions that can *improve* and *refine* our understanding of those relations, even though none of them can be absolutely sure of leading, by itself, to that final destination. If we take up that challenge courageously, we may expect that faith to prove justified.

There is nothing specifically, or necessarily, *theological* in these roads. On the contrary, at this point Gustafson once again invites his colleagues in moral theology to be open to insights from the natural sciences. In a few cases (e.g., those raised by genetic counselling) it is clear enough that our moral problems can be resolved in "circumstantial" or "casuistical" terms only if we rely on the expert testimony of biological scientists (see, e.g., Gustafson, 1984:chap. 7), but, from Gustafson's point of view, the argument goes further. Considered against the largest background, our *moral* vision of Humanity and human conduct must be related to a *philosophical* vision of Nature and Nature's purposes; and that vision will be critically adequate, only if it accords with the reflective insights of contemporary physics, biology, and psychology. The theology of nature is thus inseparable from "cosmology," as the classical Greeks understood it: i.e., our vision of the physical orderedness of Nature, which serves as an example for the moral orderedness of Humanity and Society.

VI

James Gustafson's "theocentric ethics" accordingly presents a major intellectual challenge. For all its quiet-spokenness and modesty of statement, it is a challenge, not just to professional theologians and philosophers, but to the larger scientific and scholarly community also. Its most powerful challenge is perhaps not to his immediate theological colleagues, since he deliberately appeals over their heads to a wider circle. But that surely makes his arguments the more "challenging." During the twentieth century, the academic and religious worlds have won their way through to a point at which older scruples may be set aside: at which we can turn our eyes back from the mirror of the "transcendental" realm, and look for a direct insight into the scheme of things in our "empirical" experience of the human and natural worlds.

Let me speak personally, in conclusion. The new speculative license that Gustafson allows us is to me something of a relief. For some time, the new ways of thinking most typical of late twentieth-century science have been leading our scientific colleagues willy-nilly in *theological* directions: as a result, they have been raising questions that are cosmological, not just in the sense in which "physical cosmology" is a technical branch of physics, but in a more ancient, comprehensive sense. Meanwhile, professional philosophers and theologians—notably, *moral* philosophers and theologians—have mostly been blind to what is going on, so that the John Wheelers of the world have carried on one side of a potentially fruitful conversation without critical response from those who should have been most ready to listen to them and sift through their ideas and speculative innovations (cf. Wheeler, 1975).

After Gustafson's work theologians no longer have any excuse for delaying their reply to this revival of scientific cosmology and theology of nature. Nor are the implications of this revival merely speculative. Given the enlargement of human action *within* the world of Nature and the consequent

pressure of human activity on the natural environment, Stoicism in its contemporary form—viz., the ecology movement—is no longer a purely personal point of view. In addition, it has become big politics, not to say big business.

Up to now, the degree of consensus emerging from the debate about environmental protecting has been surprising, both about the intellectual considerations involved on which our theoretical view of the scheme of things depends, and about our obligations toward the other beings with whom we share the created cosmos. The nature and basis of that essentially *theological* consensus remain to be expounded, both for its moral significance and for its political consequences. And not the least among the merits of James Gustafson's new volumes is the powerful way in which his argument challenges us to start on that important work.

Richard McCormick, S.J. (essay date Spring 1985)

SOURCE: "Gustafson's God: Who? What? Where? (Etc.)," in *The Journal of Religious Ethics,* Vol. 13, No. 1, Spring, 1985, pp. 53-70.

[*In the following essay, McCormick analyzes Gustafson's* Ethics from a Theocentric Perspective *by questioning Gustafson in four areas: anthropocentrism, christology, revelation-inspiration, and practical ethics.*]

The name of James Gustafson is associated with voluminous reading, disciplined scholarship, and exacting analysis—in a word, with critical erudition. In combination these qualities have instructed all of us, especially where we are inclined by our biases, loyalties, other pressures, or simply myopia to oversimplify problems or take convenient shortcuts. Gustafson's contributions over the years have been enormous, perhaps most enduringly on his peers and students. Because his work has taken us beyond the privacy and limitations of our own insights, I feel certain that Gustafson would welcome attempts at a similar service.

There are two facets of *Ethics from a Theocentric Perspective* [Hereafter *Ethics from a Theocentric Perspective,* Vol. I or Vol. II will be referred to as *ETP,* Vol. I or Vol. II] that I want to note here. First, these two volumes constitute Gustafson's *Meisterstück*. By that I mean that they gather systematically and order the fragmentary pieces of some thirty years of work. He seems to regard the volumes as his ultimate statement, a kind of culmination.

Second, these volumes may be viewed as either a personal faith statement or a theological explanation of it open to public review. Inevitably they are, I believe, a bit of both, a faith statement theologically presented. The former dimension interests me more and is, from my perspective, the more significant dimension of the volumes. The proper response to a faith statement is respect and reverence, even if one must ultimately conclude that such faith is not in all respects one's own.

For these two reasons, I shall limit my reflections to *Ethics from a Theocentric Perspective* rather than attempt a ranging review of the entire Gustafsonian corpus. Furthermore, since I regard these volumes as above all a faith statement theologically presented, my reflections will take the rather unusual form of comparing my own faith, shaped within the Catholic tradition and symbol-system, to Gustafson's. The spirit of such a reflection is meditative rather than argumentative. It is "here is how I view things," not "here is where he is wrong and I am right." In such a spirit assertions should be read as questions put to the author. I underline this here because piety plays such a central role in Gustafson's theological analysis. At some point to find fault with the theology might appear to be faulting the nourishing piety. And that would be out of place, totally.

In a short essay one cannot possibly do justice to the breadth and subtlety, the wisdom and insight of Gustafson's *opus.* These qualities are there in abundance, as are honesty, openness, fairness, and an erudition that must be humbling to any critic. I acknowledge these with proportionate gratitude and thereby admit that there are many, many observations, analyses, qualifications with which I agree. If I attend to other dimensions in these remarks, no derogation is intended from the admissions stated here. Furthermore, it should need no saying that my questions to the author are made in fear and trembling born of respect for his work.

Gustafson writes: "For theological ethics . . . the first task in order of importance is to establish convictions about God and God's relations to the world. To make a case for how some things really and ultimately are is the first task of theological ethics" (1984:98). Two things stand out in this irreproachable assertion: first, "God's relation to the world . . . how some things really and ultimately are"; second, the phrases "establish . . . make a case for." Two questions might be put to *Ethics from a Theocentric Persepctive:* (1) Is this the way things really are? (2) Has Gustafson established it?

HOW THINGS REALLY ARE

Everyone who writes theology comes from somewhere. That somewhere may say more about a person's theology than any of us care to admit. So appropriately Gustafson tells us about his perception of the circumstances of our time. That perception may differ significantly from the reality of where he comes from. It is difficult for any of us to reflect on our own perceptions in a detached way. We are steeped in our culture, our temperament, our background and lineage, and shaped by these more than our discursive thought allows us to realize.

The name of James Gustafson is associated with voluminous reading, disciplined scholarship, and exacting analysis—in a word, with critical erudition.

—Richard McCormick, S.J.

Where Gustafson looks at cultures, he is impressed above all by our finitude and our inability to deal with it. When he looks at religion he sees above all instrumental religion or piety, the idea that religion is propagated for its utility value, that our pieties are aimed at our self-gratification. He excoriates "superficial Easters" as just another example of the deity being put into the service of our needs and gratifications.

When Gustafson looks at the theological scene (really, how we think about God), he derives "bearings" that will guide his subsequent reflection. These "bearings" are eruditely distilled from a critical reading of many sources (Rahner, Tillich, Moltmann, Lehman, H. Richard Niebuhr, process theology). They include the idea of a deity objective to us without being reduced to a categorical reality, a deity related to the natural world (the world described and explained by the natural sciences), and a deity whose actions in the world must be supported by some evidence, and more than popular piety and traditional theologies adduce. Gustafson's deity is not one who is chiefly or solely concerned with human benefits and well-being. Rather, the "ultimate Power" intends the well-being of the universe, and theological ethics must expand its vision to approach things in this way.

Gustafson rejects anthropocentric ethics, an ethics rooted in a notion of God who intends chiefly human benefits and salvation. What he rejects he states as follows (1981:82):

> Culturally, religiously, theologically and ethically, man, the human species, has become the measure of all things; all things have been put in the service of man. Man is always the *measurer* of all things; among the millions of forms of life only our species has developed the biological capacities to know, measure, evaluate, intend, experiment and test perceptions. This is the glory of the human species; this is the distinctiveness that can be described and is to be valued. But to be the measurer of all things does not necessarily imply that all things are to be in service of man.

This is the anthropocentric vision. Clearly Gustafson regards it as a distortion. Science has made it clear that human beings are miniscule developments in the overall universe and that our planet within the universe has a *finis,* a temporal end. This must lead us to question the place of humans as the crown and center of creation. It must also lead us to reject an ethic built on this assumption.

In the course of his rejection of such an ethic, Gustafson dismantles or throws into doubt a great deal traditionally associated with the Christian vision but for him associated with anthropocentrism: the personal nature of God, the centrality of Christ in Christian ethics, divine agency, salvation, the afterlife, and the efficacy of petitionary prayer, to mention but a few. In his theocentric ethic, the practical moral question is: What is God enabling and requiring us to be and to do in the patterns and processes of interdependence? The general answer to that question is: We are to relate ourselves and all things in a manner appropriate to their relations to God. What is this "manner appropriate to their relations to God?" We can discern, in a very general way, "the necessary conditions for life to be sustained and developed" (1981:339). These conditions remain general and do not provide the certainty we would like in complex circumstances; but they are "the bases of ethics" (1981:340). They form the shape of our conformity to the divine governance—a God Gustafson repeatedly describes as "the powers that bear down upon us and sustain us."

In impoverishing summary, this is "how things really are." How does Gustafson arrive at such a construal of God and the world? As I read him, his major sources are human experience and the sciences. Biblical materials must pass the tests presented by these twin sources. Similarly, if piety has no sound base in these sources, it must be regarded as deceptive and be reconstructed.

In these two volumes, a distinction can perhaps be made between what Gustafson writes (and intends) and the impressions his analyses create. It is always dangerous and perhaps even unfair to spin out impressions. Nevertheless, I shall do so because such impressions are unavoidable and can function as avenues to greater understanding.

"How things really are" strikes me as being remarkably bleak and grim in Gustafson's version of theocentrism. God is "the powers that bear down upon us and sustain us." His concern for us seems minimal. Jesus Christ did not save us in any traditional sense. Death is the tragic end. Jesus' resurrection—in traditional theology, the very cornerstone of Christian faith and hope—plays no significant role. What kind of theocentrism is this? Daniel Maguire (1982:257) calls it "post-Christian." Gustafson himself acknowledges that it departs in very significant ways from basic affirmations of traditional Christian faith. To me, it appears utterly gloomy and eventually hopeless. Whatever the case, it is not a construal of God

and His relations to the world that would sustain, attract, or inspire me at all. In other words, it is not "how things really are" from my experience of Christian living. And that brings me to the second question.

If one believes that Gustafson's gloomy account of "God's relation to the world" is not "how things really and ultimately are," then one must also assert that he has not established it. Such an assertion is itself difficult to establish. Indeed it is impossible. That is the nature of God-talk. All one can do is indicate dimensions that seem to have been overlooked or underplayed in Gustafson's account of things. This can take the form of questions put to Gustafson. I will do so in four areas of concern: anthropocentrism, christology, revelation-inspiration, and practical ethics.

ANTHROPOCENTRISM

The key move that Gustafson makes is the shift from anthropocentrism to theocentrism. Western moral and religious traditions have been based on the former. However, according to Gustafson, human beings are not the center and crown of the universe (1981:112). Salvation is not the chief or exclusive end of God (1981:110). In this sense human well-being is not the measure or focus of ethics. Human beings are only part of a broader governance.

Why does Gustafson make this move? Above all, he does so on the basis of scientific accounts of the origin of the universe, of life and its evolution, of the interrelatedness of aspects of nature and culture, and of the termination of our planetary system (1981:83, 111). Thus in a sense Gustafson consults and relies on the Book of Nature. The universe existed millions of years before the human race, and human life as we know it will have a *finis.* "If it were not for that knowledge, one might live contentedly with the traditional Western assurance that everything has taken place for the sake of man; that man is the crown of creation" (Gustafson, 1981-83).

But what exactly does that knowledge do? Gustafson argues that it decentralizes human beings. They can no longer be viewed as the center and measure. In this move, he distances himself from many of his "benchmarks," e.g., Barth, Aquinas, Rahner, Ramsey.

But could not one argue just the opposite conclusion? The fact (?) that the universe antedated human life by millions of years and will be around after life as we know it has disappeared can be read as God's lavish way of presenting human life precisely as the crown of the universe. The actor remains central even though and when the stage is empty and when the show is, so to speak, over. We have seen such lavishness throughout the natural kingdom. Lavishness may be viewed as highlighting rather than decentralizing human life.

This was the view of Barth, as Gustafson well knows. He viewed creation accounts as "comparable to the building of a temple, the arrangement and construction of which is determined both in detail and as a whole by the liturgy which it is to serve" (1958:98) Barth sees all of creation as a "theater of the covenant." Creation is "radically incapable of serving any other purpose" (1958:99) "It is the divine will and accomplishment in relation to man—and nothing else—which really stands at the beginning of all things. It was in this way—and no other—that heaven and earth originated." Thus creation is the "presupposition of the covenant" (1958:231) It was "foreordained for the establishment and the history of the covenant" (1958:231).

Gustafson may or may not agree with all of this. But that is not my point. The point is that the scientific evidence to which he appeals and which leads him away from classical anthropocentrism in Christian ethics seems to me to be quite compatible with such anthropocentrism. If it is not, why not?

To raise this question is in no way to endorse the utilitarian sentimentalities associated with abuses of anthropocentrism. Nor is it to deny that anthropocentrism could be placed on a larger cosmic stage. It is rather to suggest that cosmocentrism need not eliminate anthropocentrism. In this sense, it is rather to raise the question of the relevance of scientific data or opinion to religious concepts and convictions. While it would be a mistake to see the two as incompatible or contradictory, would it not also be mistaken to see one (scientific data) as simply determining the other? Unless Gustafson shows more clearly why the scientific data he cites lead away from anthropocentrism, unless he shows why Barth's reading (and that of traditional Christianity) is untenable, the basis for his type of theocentrism has been enormously weakened. Furthermore, he may not be totally protected from the accusation of "scientism."

Christology

Another way of approaching Gustafson's overall thesis (theocentrism vs. anthropocentrism) is via his christology. Gustafson formulates the following interesting sentence: "Christology is the most critical doctrinal issue for any Christian theology" (1981:275). I agree with that statement. It functions as an implicit invitation to test Gustafson's christology and then his central thesis in light of such a christology.

What is Gustafson's christology? It is contained in five pages (1981:275-279) and appears almost as an afterthought. Indeed the major directions and themes of *Ethics from a Theocentric Perspective* would stand without these pages. Gustafson acknowledges that he works out of the synoptic gospels rather than Revelation, John's gospel, and the Pauline corpus. He offers three reasons for this preference: (1) a strong sense of the priority of narrative over more abstract language in evoking and sustaining piety; (2) rejection of "biblicistic revelation"; (3) epistemological doubts about the meaningfulness of claims about the nature and activities of the "pre-existent Christ" of Colossians, Ephesians, etc. I am not sure what Gustafson is rejecting under the term "biblicistic revelation." But the overall effect of reasons two and three is quite clear. Gustafson refers to the "compelling power of Jesus' unique life and ministry, of his devotion to God" (1981:276). His qualities "powerfully show what human life, in fidelity to God and in openness to his empowering, can and ought to be." "His teaching, ministry and life are a historical embodiment of what we are to be and to do." In other words, Jesus is uniquely remarkable for his example.

That is true, of course; Jesus' example is unique. But it is not all of the truth. Raymond Brown (1971:612) points out that the phrase "as I have loved you" (John 13:14) emphasizes that Jesus is the source of the Christians' love for one another. In this sense it is effective, sc., "it brings about their salvation." Only secondarily does it refer to Jesus as the standard of Christian love. The implications of this are enormous. And Gustafson knows it; for he admits that his christology "does not meet the claims of many creeds and many Churches" (1981:278).

What claims? That Jesus is God become human, "the man who is not only man but God." Gustafson's omission (rejection?) of this central affirmation of the Christian faith leads him to "acknowledge that the particularity of the Christian story is more important for our individual and communal 'subjectivity' than it is for what we are finally able to say about the powers in whose hands are the distances of the worlds."

However, if one's christology takes fuller account of Colossians, Ephesians, and John's gospel (to say nothing of the early christological councils which Gustafson too quickly dismisses as "the votes of ecclesiastical councils"), it will tell us a good deal about "what we are finally able to say about the powers in whose hands are the destinies of the worlds." If Jesus is God-become-man, God's self-gift and self-revelation, the second person of the Triune God, then knowing Him is knowing God. His actuality is at once insight-injunction for us, insight into who God is and who we are, injunction as to what we should become. "'Lord,' Philip said to him, 'show us the Father and that will be enough for us.' 'Philip,' Jesus replied, 'after I have been with you all this time, you still do not know me? Whoever has seen me has seen the Father'" (*John* 14:8-9). Knowing Jesus' qualities, ideals, and injunctions is a direct insight into God's gracious governance of the world. More importantly, knowing *who He is* is knowing both the Godhead and ourselves in relationship with the Godhead, and therefore knowing some rather basic things about God's plan for us.

> Praised be the God and Father of our Lord Jesus Christ, who has bestowed on us in Christ every spiritual blessing in the heavens! God chose us in him before the world began, to be holy and blameless in his sight, to be full of love; he likewise predestined us through Christ Jesus to be his adopted sons—such was his will and pleasure—that all might praise the glorious favor he has bestowed on us in his beloved (*Ephesians* 11:3-6).

It was precisely oversight of this that Barth criticized in Calvin.

What is it that we know when we know *who Christ is?* What is this "every spiritual blessing in the heavens" bestowed on us in Christ? Once again, let me cite a passage from Barth's Gifford Lectures (1938:95).

> Jesus Christ is *Kurios*. What does that mean? It means that He is *the* great *change* in man's life. He changes it radically, because He changes it in its relation to God, because His work is the salvation of man and because this work of His is the work of God Himself. There is no greater or more radical change of man's life out of the rebellion of sin and the disaster consequent upon it into that new gratitude for his salvation which binds man once and for all and into the knowledge of the divine power of this divine work which has taken place for man and on him; and it consists in man's having the right in this gratitude and knowledge to understand his existence anew as grace and favour.

> Jesus Christ is this change in man's life. And that means that it is a *hidden* change. We think of the words "Your life is hid with Christ in God" (*Colossians* 3:3). If it is a visible life—and how else could it be a human life?—and if in this visible life there can be no lack of visible change of every kind, yet none of the visible changes in our life is *the* change, the *great* change which has taken place for us and on us in our relation to God. Jesus Christ is the great change and to seek this change even for a moment elsewhere than in Him, and hence to desire to see the change instead of believing it, is to confound two things and to deceive oneself, and by this one's salvation can be lost. But this fact that Jesus Christ is the great change in the life of man means also that it is a *real* change. God's decision and man's election, the death of Jesus Christ and the forgiveness of our sins, His resurrection and our justification—all this, as we have already seen, is beyond question irrevocable and cannot be undone, because

it is God who acts here. If we seek the change in our life, where we can *see* changes and hence somewhere else than in Jesus Christ, we shall certainly find it to be a very changeable kind of change! But if we seek it in *Jesus Christ,* and hence if we seek it by believing in Him, then we find it to be a change which we can no more go back on than God can cease to be God. The hiddenness of this change of life is therefore not to be separated from its reality nor its reality from its hiddenness. [Karl Barth. *The Knowledge of God and the Service of God According to the Teaching of the Reformation,* 1938.]

This "change in man's life," God's deed in Jesus Christ (to borrow from Joseph Sittler) tells us many things. The very first thing it tells us is that the dichotomy between anthropocentrism and theocentrism is a false dichotomy. Since *Theos* and *Logos* are one, being theocentric means being Christocentric—which means being anthropocentric in a way Gustafson cannot admit. The incarnation is necessarily affirmation about humanhood and is the Christian theological basis for asserting that "the glory of God is humanhood alive." After Jesus and because of what we know in Jesus, humans are indeed the measure of all things. To say less is to undermine the implicit affirmations of the incarnation.

Jesus is not the way, the truth, the life merely because he evokes and sustains certain personal and community pieties. He is God made present to us and therefore in Himself the revelation of God's presence and governance. He is not, through the narratives of his life and ministry, merely a sustaining basis for certain human subjectivities. He is the very ontological basis of our self-concept, of who we are, and therefore of who we should become and why. These hidden but real truths, which I take to be central to the Christian faith, are muted, perhaps even denied, in Gustafson's theocentrism. The exciting revelation (of God and ourselves) that is Jesus Christ pales into "the powers that bear down upon us and sustain us."

Why has Gustafson made this move from a classic or high christology in a way that allows him to compare and ultimately contrast anthropocentrism with theocentrism? One can only speculate here. There are several possibilities. One reason is that Gustafson reads anthropocentrism as selfish, individualistic, and utilitarian in character. He refers to it as "ego-centric" (1981:110). It is true that wounded, even if redeemed, human beings have a profound tendency to accommodate the truths of Christian faith to their own benefit and comfort, and to trivialize them in the process. We are always in danger of making the "Deity a utility device for the fulfillment of human aims" (1981:41). In this sense I can agree with much of what Gustafson says about "instrumental religion," about cheap grace and "superficial Easters."

But here Gustafson should be invited to be instructed by his own later, careful statements. "The fact that a symbol has been used excessively, or misused, in religious life is not a sufficient reason for eliminating it" (1981:243). The fact that anthropocentrism has been bent into distortions is no reason for its radical elimination.

Another reason for Gustafson's move may well be his emphasis on piety and its hermeneutical implications. He writes: "I am persuaded that the primary moment in a religious view of the world, and therefore an assumption in theology, is the affection of piety: a sense of dependence on, and respect and gratitude for, what is given" (1981:61). He describes it as a "basic disposition and attitude," "a settled disposition, a persistent attitude toward the world and ultimately toward God" (1981:201). Its fundamental characteristics are awe and respect. Gustafson prefers piety to faith for several reasons, one of the chief of which is that faith suggests a knowledge of God apart from the "experiential basis of all our knowledge" (1981:202).

Here the question must be raised about our knowledge of what Barth calls "the change" (Jesus) in our lives. It is a "hidden change." How could we possibly come to know the dimensions of that change experientially as Gustafson understands that term? As I read him, Gustafson's explanation of piety would exclude a high christology in principle. Why? Because piety does not include the type of faith required to affirm that reality. Why? Because all human knowing has an experiential basis and it is impossible to find such a basis for the assertion that Jesus Christ is God. Here we encounter another root of Gustafson's theocentrism: a univocal notion of human experience and knowledge. There is, for instance, little or no use made of the literature of mysticism in Gustafson. Is mystical experience without an experiential base?

I noted that if our Christology included John and the Pauline corpus, then such a christology would tell us a good deal about "what we are finally able to say about the powers in whose hands are the destinies of the worlds." It is perhaps the case that Gustafson has excluded this "good deal" by his treatment of faith and piety. But that leaves quite open, in my judgment, the question of whether his exclusion is appropriate. Obviously, I think it is not.

What, then, can we learn in and through Christ about the "ultimate powers?" Borrowing generously and unblushingly from two theologians (Joseph Sittler, Enrico Chiavacci) I would make the following suggestions.

Joseph Sittler has noted (1958:25) that the theme of the biblical narratives is God's "going out from Himself in creative and redemptive action toward men." Sittler refers to "God's relentless gift of himself," "the undeviating self-giving God,"

"the total self-giving of God," "God's undeviating will to restoration," the "history-involved assault of God upon man's sin," "the gracious assault of his deed in Christ." Jesus Christ is no less than God's self-giving deed.

The response of the believer to this person-revelation is the total commitment of the person known as faith. The term "faith" has had an uneven history in the hands of Christians. Too often it has been tied to a pale propositional understanding of God's deed in Christ. Once again, Sittler (1958:45):

> It is not possible to state too strongly that the life of the believer is for Paul the actual invasion of the total personality by the Christ-life. So pervasive and revolutionary is this displacement and bestowal that terms like influence, example, command, value are utterly incapable of even suggesting its power and its vitally recreating force. [*The Structure of Christian Ethics*]

The believer's response to this specific, momentous, and supreme event of God's love is total and radical commitment. For the believer, Jesus Christ, the concrete enfleshment of God's love, becomes the meaning and *telos* of the world and of the self. God's self-disclosure in Jesus is at once the self-disclosure of ourselves and our world. "All things were made through him, and without him was not anything made that was made" (John 1:3). Nothing is intelligible without reference to God's deed in Christ. The response to this personal divine outpouring is not a dead and outside-observer "amen." It is a faith-response empowered by the very God who did the redemptive and restorative deed in Jesus Christ, and is utterly and totally transforming—so much so that St. Paul must craft a new metaphor to articulate it. We are "new creatures," plain and simple. Faith is the empowered reception of God's stunning and aggressive love in Jesus. As theologian Walter Kasper summarizes it (1980:82), "Faith is not simply an intellectual act or an act of the will. It includes the whole man and every aspect of the human reality. . . . It embraces the whole of Christian existence, including hope and love, which can be seen as two ways in which faith is realized [Walter Kasper. *An Introduction to Christian Faith,* 1980]. This same point is underlined by Sittler when he notes that faith is the proper term "to point to the total commitment of the whole person which is required by the character of the revelation [*The Structure of Christian Ethics*].

Sittler has noted that "to be a Christian is to accept what God gives" [*The Structure of Christian Ethics*]. And what God gives is the going-out from himself in Jesus Christ. Something *has been done* to and for us and that something is Jesus. There is a prior action of God at once revelatory and response-engendering. Sittler correctly insists that the passive dominates the New Testament. "I love because I am loved; I know because I am known; I am of the Church, the body of Christ, because this body became my body; I can and must forgive because I have been forgiven" (Sittler, 1958:11). This prior action of God is reflected in the Pauline "therefore," which states the entire grounding and meaning of the Christian ethic.

The Italian theologian Enrico Chiavacci puts it this way (1980:291-92):

> In the New Testament the unique obligation of charity, which is the giving of self to God who is seen in one's neighbor, is grounded on the unique fact that God is charity.... "Walk in love *as* Christ has loved us and given himself." (Eph. 5:2) *"Therefore,* I exhort you brethren, through the mercy of God to offer yourselves.... "(Rom. 12:1) The fact that God—in his manifestation as philanthropy—is love does not refer to further justification; it is the ultimate fact. The obligation to love is based only on God's love for us.... It is true ... that in the "therefore" of Romans 12:1 we find the entire New Testament ethic. [Enrico Chiavacci. "The Grounding for the Moral Norm in Contemporary Theological Reflection."]

Here I want to make, as a part of my own faith statement, six points in a systematic way. First, as already noted, in Christian ethics, God's self-disclosure in Jesus Christ as self-giving love allows of no further justification. It is the absolutely ultimate fact. The acceptance of this fact into one's life (*fides qua*) is an absolutely originating and grounding experience.

Second, this belief in the God of Jesus Christ means to understand that "Christ, perfect image of the Father, is already law and not only law-giver. He is already the categorical imperative and not just the font of ulterior and detailed imperatives" (Chiavacci, 1980:288).

Third, this ultimate fact reveals a new basis or context for understanding the world. It gives it a new (Christocentric) meaning. As a result of God's concrete act in the incarnation, "human life has avilable a new relation to God, a new light for seeing, a new fact and center for thinking, a new ground for forgiving and loving, a new context for acting in this world" (Sittler, 1958:18).

Fourth, this "new fact and center for thinking" that is Jesus Christ finds its deepest meaning in the absoluteness and ultimacy of the God-relationship. The person of Jesus is testimony to the fact that "no effort of man to know himself, find himself, be himself, is a viable possibility outside the God-relationship" (Sittler, 1980:33).

Fifth, this God-relationship is already shaped by God's prior act in Jesus (self-giving). "To believe in Jesus Christ, Son of God, is identical with believing that God—the absolute, the meaning—is total gift of self" (Chiavacci, 1980:228). There-

fore, the "active moment of faith takes place in the recognition that meaning is to give oneself, spend oneself, and live for others" (Chiavacci, 1980:288). There is a German axiom that states: "Jede Gabe ist eine Aufgabe" ("Every gift constitutes an obligation"). That is profoundly true here. The very gift of God in Jesus constitutes or shapes the response; thus it is proper to refer at once to God's love-gift and command. Thus the Christian moral life must be viewed as "a re-enactment from below on the part of men of the shape of the revelatory drama of God's holy will in Jesus Christ" (Sittler, 1958:36). In this sense, it is the "following of Christ." It is a recapitulation in the life of the believer of the "shape of the engendering deed," to use Sittler's language.

Finally, the empowered acceptance of this engendering deed (faith), totally transforms the human person. It creates new operative vitalities that constitute the very possibility and the heart of the Christian moral life.

I mention and stress these points because there has been and still is a tendency to conceive of Christian ethics in terms of norms and principles that may be derived from Jesus' pronouncements. That there are such sayings recorded in the New Testament is beyond question. But to reduce Christian ethics to such sayings is, I believe, to trivialize it. In this sense I agree completely with Sittler when he states (1958:50-51):

> He (Jesus) did not, after the manner proper to philosophers of the good, attempt to articulate general principles which, once stated, have then only to be beaten out in corollaries applicable to the variety of human life.... His words and deeds belong together. Both are signs which seek to fasten our attention upon the single vitality which was the ground and purpose of his life—his God-relationship.

And in and through Jesus we know what that God-relationship is: *total* self-gift. For that is what God is and we are created in his image. To miss this is, I believe, to leave the realm of Christian ethics.

What would Gustafson make of this? From his *magnum opus* it is clear that he would not make much of it. He distances himself from Barth's christology and from Ramsey's emphasis on love. These distances are a formidable barrier to Gustafson's acceptance of what I regard as the heart of Christian ethics and Christian living.

Johannes D. Metz once noted (1978:39-40): "Christ must always be thought of in such a way that he is never merely thought of." Merely to "think of" Christ is to trivialize Him, to reduce Him to one more (among many) observable historical event, to an example of human benevolence. For the person of Christian faith, Jesus Christ is God's immanent presence, His love in the flesh. Unless I misread him, this Christic faith has disappeared in Gustafson's ethics. It has faded into the fog of an impersonal deism and seems to leave Gustafson "merely thinking about Christ." Why and how has this occurred? That brings me to my next point.

Revelation-Inspiration

Jesus Christ as God's self-revelation, as His total self-giving, as a deed engendering the shape of our response (total self-gift)—these are faith statements rooted in the biblical accounts. How would Gustafson react to such assertions? Early he states (1981:236): "The traditional language of God's love is not independently treated because, in my judgment, it is often used in an excessively vague way and many of the terms I shall employ could be developed as more precise specifications of it." I am sure that we all have heard love and God associated in ways that are as theologically meaningful as saccharine. But once again, is misuse a reason for abandonment?

In the biblical accounts, however, love is a symbol of God's way of self-revelation. This raises the much broader question of Gustafson's use of biblical materials. As I read him, he sees the Bible as a human record of the experience of God. In his words (1981:186): "I have indicated that the biblical materials are themselves human expressions of and reflections upon human experiences of a divine reality." Gustafson states that this requires "a qualification of the authority of Scripture." Early he does not expand on this except to say that his understanding of the authority of Scripture is not that of Augustine, Calvin, and Edwards.

In his second volume the matter becomes much clearer as Gustafson compares his position to that of four giants (Barth, Aquinas, Rahner, Ramsey). His summations, as always, are clear and fair. In fact Gustafson has been dining out on this type of thing for years, as witness his ***Christ and the Moral Life.*** He agrees with much that each puts forth but ultimately distinguishes his own position from each, and chiefly through the anthropocentric emphasis. And I believe this contrast traces to use of the biblical materials.

What interests me, then, above all in these accounts is Gustafson's use of biblical materials; for it is his use (or non-use) of such materials that will heavily determine his notion of God and God's relation to the world. And, as Gustafson repeatedly and correctly insists, it is such a notion that will determine the shape of one's ethics.

Two things stand out in Gustafson's use of biblical materials. First is his notion of revelation. He states (1984:28):

> For Barth we have knowledge of God only because God has chosen to reveal himself to man. And God has chosen to reveal himself in the life and events of

a particular people, and in Jesus Christ. Thus the biblical record and materials are the source of God's revelation, and thus of any reliable knowledge of God. I deliberately refrained from using the term "revelation" to characterize how humans become informed about God on the grounds that what is called revelation is reflection on human experiences in the face of the ultimate power and powers. The biblical records, in such a view, are an account of great importance, but not the exclusive source of our understanding of God. The term revelation could be used within the framework of my discussion only in a very weak sense, if at all.

Here we have Gustafson all but rejecting the biblical materials as revelation—as God's self-manifestation. The grounds for doing this: "what is called revelation is reflection on human experience in the face of the ultimate power and powers." Here Gustafson must be asked—and I believe exegetes first and foremost would urge the question—why reflection on human experience cannot be the vehicle of God's self-manifestation. In other words, is Gustafson's rejection of the biblical materials as containing revelation warranted? I think not. He says these materials are "an account of great importance." I fail to see what the importance is once biblical materials are reduced to mere reflection on human experience.

To claim a revelatory character to biblical materials is not to argue that they are the only sources of our knowledge of God. Not at all. But in Gustafson this revelatory character all but disappears. He is therefore left with a natural theology developed from the Book of Nature. This is, from a theological perspective, his key move.

The second noteworthy aspect of his use of biblical materials emerges when he compares his perspective to that of Paul Ramsey. For Ramsey the central ethical category in Christian ethics is obedient love, *agape*. For him, Christian ethics stands decisively related to Jesus Christ and issues in a love monism wherein all principles, virtues, and decisions are a working out of the love command. Gustafson rejects this (1984:86-7):

> But two questions can be asked about this to which I have given different answers than he does. The first is internal to the Bible: Within the biblical accounts, is the nature and activity of God as exclusively in focus on God's love as Ramsey's argument claims? I believe that it is not. The second question is: Does such knowledge as human beings can have of God's nature and activity depend so exclusively on the biblical material as Ramsey's does? The line of argument in Volume I is clearly that it does not.

Here I find myself much closer to Ramsey than to Gustafson.

That does not mean that one has to accept Ramsey's rule-deontological reading of the primacy of *agape*. Indeed, I do not. But I cannot read the New Testament literature in any other way than one that is a self-disclosure in Jesus Christ of a God of love and therefore a self-disclosure that gives primary and basic shape to the ethical lives of Christians. In other words, I agree with Ramsey that obedient love is the central ethical category in Christian ethics. I shall leave it to the exegetes to referee this difference with Gustafson. But it is a major difference and has a great deal to do with Gustafson's major move to theocentrism and away from Christocentrism—and *therefore* anthropocentrism. Gustafson's ethics is quite simply not decisively related to Jesus Christ, and he clearly acknowledges this. I cannot accept that, nor do I believe it warranted by biblical materials or the constant reflection on and appropriation of these materials over the centuries by the Christian community.

I am forced to conclude that Gustafson views Scripture as a *merely* human source. I say "merely" because it is clear that biblical inspiration cannot prescind from human instrumentality. But divine inspiration is not part of Gustafson's analysis or vocabulary. Neither, therefore, is the notion of biblical revelation.

All one can do at this point is to note that this is not the Christian, certainly not the Catholic understanding of Scripture. That understanding is succinctly stated by Vatican II (Abbott, 1966:112):

> 2. In His goodness and wisdom, God chose to reveal Himself and to make known to us the hidden purpose of His will (cf. *Ephesians* 1:9) by which through Christ, the Word made flesh, man has access to the Father in the Holy Spirit and comes to share in the divine nature (cf. *Ephesians* 2:18; 2 *Peter* 1:4). Through this revelation, therefore, the invisible God (cf. *Colossians* 1:15; 1 *Timothy* 1:17) out of the abundance of His love speaks to men as friends (cf. *Exodus* 33:11; *John* 15:14-15) and lives among them (cf. *Baruch* 3:38), so that He may invite and take them into fellowship with Himself. This plan of revelation is realized by deeds and words having an inner unity: the deeds wrought by God in the history of salvation manifest and confirm the teaching and realities signified by the words, while the words proclaim the deeds and clarify the mystery contained in them. By this revelation then, the deepest truth about God and the salvation of man is made clear to us in Christ, who is the Mediator and at the same time the fullness of all revelation. [*The Documents of Vatican II*, edited by Walter Abbott, 1966]

Here Scripture is seen as revelation. Scripture as revelation is, I believe, basic within the Christian community. As Roderick MacKenzie, S.J., notes (1966:108): Revelation "is a manifestation by God—primarily of Himself; secondarily of His will and intentions—granted to particular men at particular times" [*The Documents of Vatican II*]. This means, as MacKenzie notes, that Scripture *contains* revelation. It does not mean that all of Scripture *is* revelation. The notions of revelation and inspiration have disappeared in Gustafson's work and the effect of the disappearance is stunning.

Practical Ethics

This section can be very brief. In four chapters Gustafson treats four practical matters (marriage and the family, suicide, population and nutrition, allocation of biomedical research funding) to see what difference a theocentric ethics makes in the interpretation of morality. His treatment is, as usual, characterized by analytic thoroughness and depth, wide reading, and a sensitivity to the complexity of issues that does not trouble less complicated approaches.

There is a single dimension in these chapters that I found myself repeatedly noting: they could have been written independently of the theocentric perspective that Gustafson claims informs, induces, or backs them. Let a few instances of this suffice to make my point.

Speaking of those in a state of despair who might be suicidal, Gustafson asks (1984:208): "What is God enabling and requiring us to be and to do in these circumstances?" His response:

> We are to be faithful in our relations to others. We are to sustain relations with others which mitigate conditions that might lead to ultimate desperation. We are to relate to them so they sense possibilities for their lives, so that they can negotiate if not resolve conflicting loyalties, so that they can grasp realistic but satisfying aims. We are to keep company with the lonely, and be agents of forgiving and renewing powers. In these and other ways we relate to others in a manner appropriate to their relations to God; we contribute to the conditions which sustain life and create conditions of possibility for it.

There is nothing here that a thoroughgoing Christo- and anthropocentrist could not have written.

Or again, after noting that Kant rejects taking one's life to avoid misery, Gustafson states (1984:214): "I argue to the contrary; physical life is not of ultimate value; many persons who suffer acutely are in no way accountable for their sufferings. Suffering is inflicted upon them and it can be a morally proper choice to seek the relief of death for their own sakes and for that of others." Whether one agrees with that judgment or not, it is difficult to see how a theocentric perspective produced it.

Finally, in discussing the choices of families about their size, Gustafson argues that these choices should serve the wider ends of both present and future generations.

> Theocentric vision extends the range of considerations taken into account in family choices; it backs a moral consciousness of the consequences for others of choices that are made and can instill the motivation to take them into account in the conduct of family life. (1984:241)

One might easily respond to this that a Christo- and anthropocentric perspective with an appropriate social sensitivity would similarly "extend the range of considerations" and "instill the motivation." Similar reflections could be made at other key points. For instance, Gustafson notes (1984:247) that "theocentric ethics backs a preference for voluntary restraints" where family size is concerned. I believe a properly developed anthropocentrism would provide no less backing.

These considerations lead to the general question: what difference does theocentrism really make at the level of practical ethics?

These reflections on the Gustafson journey are above all theological. They have issued in several general questions. Does scientific evidence really topple traditional anthropocentrism? Do we really know as little about God through biblical materials and christology as Gustafson's christology asserts? Are the biblical materials really merely human accounts, without divine inspiration and revelation? Does Gustafson's theocentrism really make a practical ethical difference?

But let this reflection end where Gustafson begins, with the concept of God. The title of this brief article asks a question: "Gustafson's God: Who? What? Where? (Etc.)." The answer to that question—at the very heart of theological ethics, as Gustafson rightly insists—remains frustratingly elusive in Gustafson's *magnum opus.* Gustafson seems to know both far more and far less about Him/Her/It/Them than is warranted. More: God need not be personal. God does not intend our salvation nor our eternal life. Jesus Christ is not His self-disclosure nor is He central to Christian ethics. God does not act in history and clearly not in response to petitionary prayer. The record of human responses to God are not inspired and revelatory. Less: He is the "powers that bear down upon and sustain us." He is chiefly available to us through the Book of Nature, through the interdependencies of the cosmos in which humans are not central. Whatever God is, He is inaccessibly remote.

Gustafson's God? Not, I think, the God of Christian belief. Is Gustafson's, then, a Christian ethic?

James M. Gustafson (essay date Spring 1985)

SOURCE: "A Response to Critics," in *The Journal of Religious Ethics,* Vol. 13, No. 1, Spring, 1985, pp. 185-209.

[*In the following excerpt, Gustafson responds to five critics of his* Ethics from a Theocentric Perspective *including Stanley Hauerwas, Richard A. McCormick, Lisa Sowle Cahill, Stephen Toulmin, and Paul Ramsey. He asserts that his critics missed many of his important points and misconstrued others.*]

In 1981, I delivered the Ryerson Lecture at the University of Chicago, a lectureship which requires that a scholar present his or her work to an audience drawn from the entire university community. In that lecture, "Say Something Theological!", I stated the four major foci or themes of my work; it comes as close to a compact statement of my self-understanding, fully stated in *Ethics from a Theocentric Perspective,* as I have produced. I shall quote the lead sentences from each part of the lecture as a backdrop against which I can address my interpreters and critics.

"To say something theological is to say something religious. Theology has its deepest significance within the context of *piety,* and in the context of a historic *religious tradition.*"

"To say something theological is to say something about *how things really and ultimately are.*"

"To say something theological is to say something *ethical.*"

My work takes each of these with equal seriousness, and is constructed to show the interrelationships between them. The two volumes of *Ethics* are amplifications and developments of these themes and their interrelations.

All five of my critics fail satisfactorily to grasp how the four themes of piety, tradition, how things really are, and ethics interpenetrate in my work. Toulmin understands quite well how the last two are interrelated, but (perhaps for professional reasons) does not disclose the relations between piety and tradition to them. [Stanley] Hauerwas is quoted in a brochure as writing that my "critique of the anthropocentrism of Christian theology is a challenge so serious and well developed I do not think it will be possible for anyone to continue to do theology, and in particular theological ethics, in a 'business as usual' manner." I judge all my theological critics to want to do theological business as usual. They want nothing from other ways of construing the world to affect their theologies; indeed, I infer that they find that quite threatening. And none of them, as I shall develop below, does justice to the ways in which piety and tradition interpenetrate with my use of materials from the sciences. Nor are they very willing to be open to the possibility that some contemporary interpretations of how things ultimately are require some change in ethics. None of them is alert to the way in which I hold together our being and our doing in life, and thus the ways in which religious sensibilities evoked by the power and powers of God penetrate our modes of response to the world religiously, intellectually, and morally.

I shall not further develop the modes of interpenetration here; a careful reading of the *Ethics* makes them clear to perceptive readers. [Stephen] Toulmin comes closest to grasping the fundamental character of the vision I have articulated. I see the two volumes as a "whole" the parts of which are interrelated; I see it as being "organic" in its configuration. Alterations in one theme necessarily require alterations in the others. None of my critics faults the overall coherence of my *Ethics,* but at least my four theological critics basically ignore it, and Toulmin omits discussion of piety and tradition.

My response is divided into three parts: (1) themes they have ignored or inadequately taken into account in their interpretations of my work; (2) themes which they have misconstrued; and (3) remarks on each author separately.

I. MISSING THEMES

Apart from [Stephen] Toulmin, none of the authors takes into account my interpretation of the cultural and historical circumstances which I clearly indicate I am addressing. At least three of them take into account the interpretation of what I call utilitarian religion and seem to agree that there is some point to that. But what is left out is important. I am concerned about the effects of modern self-proclaimed human autonomy in relation to the natural world and potential dangers of this (as well as its benefits). The need to recognize human finitude or limitations in individuals, human communities, and institutions and in the species is a part of my argument throughout (see 1981:3-16). The failure to take into account what is for me a much deeper and longer range problem misses one of the marks of my recent work. What I write makes limited sense without taking seriously my arguments for a radical sense of dependence and interdependence not only in nature, but in history, society, and culture, and for the ways in which man participates in those patterns and processes of interdependence. Put differently, there is a theological and moral judgment in my work on the presumption of self-sufficiency that abounds in many places, and thus on the denial of God as the one whose ordering of life cannot be ignored or denied without courting perilous consequences. To me, this human presumption raises more serious religious and moral or theological and ethical issues than those addressed by my moral theological colleagues. In this respect I share some

measure the interpretation of modern life developed by Hans Jonas in *The Imperative of Responsibility* (1984), a book I hope other theologians and ethicians will respond to. To my critics: if I am incorrect in this, please show me the evidence. If I am correct, how do your various moral theologies address the issues? Do your theologies provide an ethical base that includes them? Can they be addressed without reliance on arguments from authority—biblical or theological—as your four papers very much do?

I am also concerned with the impact of many alternative ways of construing life in the world, i.e., to use a word I normally avoid, pluralism. There is a practical theological interest in my work; indeed, I state clearly that theology is a practical discipline. That practical interest is, in my view, a matter to be taken seriously by the churches. Neither clergy nor laity, at least among those with average education and above, is exempt from being affected by many different non-theological interpretations of life. Even if they do not watch *Nova* on public television, they are impacted by fictionalized versions of scientific interpretations on other television programs. The readers of the newsweeklies and daily newspapers know something about these alternatives. In addition, since childhood I have been impressed with different religious interpretations, and to have been stationed among Shans and Kachins, Khasis and Nagas, Assamese and Bengalis, Hindus and Muslims and Jains was enough to make me conscious of more radical religious pluralism than I knew in Norway, Michigan. A two-month return trip to India in 1978 and to other parts of Asia did not diminish my sense of the importance of these matters.

I believe that my work cannot be understood fairly without taking into account my interpretation of man and that serious misunderstandings result from not doing so. Any criticism, therefore, that does not demonstrate my errors in this regard is not cogent, and any profile that omits the anthropology necessarily distorts other aspects of my work.

James M. Gustafson

My concern in this respect is for the intellectual and moral life of the Christian community, its credibility, and its capacities to deal with alternative construals of life without retreating into intellectual and moral sectarianism. Indeed, in the face of these matters I was bold to say that I was more concerned for the truth claims, or at least the plausibility claims, of theology than with a defense of the Christian tradition. Among my critics only Toulmin, perhaps because his identity is not marked by membership in the Christian church, recognizes the importance of this aspect of my work.

A second theme that is quite missing is the interpretation of man that is essential to everything else in both volumes. Curiously, none of my critics thinks that the chapter "Man in Relation to God and the World," or the description of human experience that is given earlier, is important at many points for my argument. To be sure, some make general reference to my use of "experience" but as an abstraction and not a dense description. My arguments about man support the overcoming of dichotomies that are present in much of contemporary theology and particularly ethics: between religion and morality; reason and affectivity (an Edwardsian view that [Paul] Ramsey does not take into account in his own work); the is and the ought or fact and value; human nature and human history, etc. I shall not embellish this, but simply call attention to the sections "Natural Man" (1981:281-93) and "Convictions: The Priority of Human Experience" (1981:115-29). In the latter reference I request that they attend to the details and not simply the title. My account of "natural man" is defended, and what I say about a number of other things is not only coherent with it, but also is a necessary condition for understanding what I say, e.g., about the process of discernment; in the moves I make to explicate what I think is theologically defensible; and other places.

None of the authors attends to my discussion of "The 'Human Fault'" (1981:219-36). That has to be taken into account in order to understand my interpretation of other things I address. The moral fault is a deep religious fault; the deep religious fault has serious implications for our moral perceptions and actions. The afflictions of life that must be addressed practically are not only due to finitude, but to the human fault, the contraction of the soul, of vision, of rationality. I believe that my interpretation of the human condition necessitates a deeper and more radical conversion than is implied in any of the critical responses; perhaps Toulmin, in nonreligious language, understands this better than critics who cite biblical and other theological sources.

Thus I request that my critics attend to "The Correction." The correction requires not merely that one avoid becoming a "rule-utilitarian non-agapist" or any other jargonized position; it requires more than an orthodox set of Christian beliefs (a la [Richard A.] McCormick and [Lisa Sowle] Cahill), and more than identifying ourselves with Jesus and the church (Hauerwas) as our point of historical identity. It requires a more radical conversion than any of my theological critics. It demands an alteration and enlargement of vision, a reordering of the heart, and different standards for determining our human being and doing. (1981:308) It demands what the tradition calls repentence and salvation. I am, more radically than my critics, a conversionist in religion and morals.

I believe that my work cannot be understood fairly without taking into account my interpretation of man and that serious misunderstandings result from not doing so. Any criticism, therefore, that does not demonstrate my errors in this regard is not cogent, and any profile that omits the anthropology necessarily distorts other aspects of my work.

B. A. Gerrish has an article, "Theology Within the Limits of Piety Alone: Schleiermacher and [John] Calvin's Doctrine of God" [in *Reformatio Perennis: Essays on Calvin and the Reformation in Honor of Ford Lewis Battles,* edited by B. A. Gerrish and Robert Benedetto, 1981]. I cite the title to indicate a third and very fundamental theme which is not carefully addressed by my critics: the nature and significance of piety. I state very clearly over and over that the entire theological and ethical enterprise in which I am engaged makes sense only in the context of piety. Cahill, for example, does not note this in her criticisms of the ways in which I use materials from the sciences. (please see 1981:257, 1981:196, and elsewhere). Insofar as the charge of "scientism" (McCormick) implies a kind of rationalistic objectivism, it is grossly inaccurate. Insofar as the language of piety suggests to some an uncritical subjectivism, it is equally inaccurate.

Outside of piety, I cannot argue that the patterns and processes of interdependence are indications of *God's* ordering of the world; I cannot argue that the moral enterprise requires that we seek to discern the relations of all things to God (which is more complex than the application of moral rules). Outside of piety, I cannot argue for overcoming the dichotomies of reason and revelation, of morality and religion, and others which distort our capacities to comprehend properly both life in the world and our relations to God. I also argue for the use of the term piety rather than faith in order to overcome the dichotomy between faith and reason—a dichotomy which I infer is uncritically accepted by each of my theological critics. In short, outside of piety, the human relation to God evoked by the indications of the divine ordering in nature, history, and society and their interpretation in the Bible, I cannot, as Augustine, [John] Calvin, and [Jonathan] Edwards could not, say anything theological.

A fourth theme that certainly does not get serious attention by any of my theological critics, but is central to Toulmin's essay, is my statement that man is a participant in the patterns and processes of interdependence of life in the world. I hope I need not remind readers that I have argued that these patterns and processes are, in a strong sense, indications of the divine powers. The absence of attention to this in [Richard A.] McCormick's essay I find surprising. I would have thought that my use of this description would resonate with traditional Roman Catholic theology and with natural law as a basis for morality. It seems to me that what Thomas Aquinas did was similar to what I have done, namely to use a contemporary understanding of the relations of things to each other in nature, society, and culture as indications of how God is related to and is ordering the world and thus the ground of morality. McCormick's response to me is curiously Protestant and biblical; how the theology he portrays is related to the ethics he so carefully develops through his writings I cannot understand, unless we assume a sharp dichotomy between revelation and reason or faith and reason.

[Paul] Ramsey is correct to say that there are relational elements to his ethics, but his are more covenantal than mine. Nature seems to be dropped out of Ramsey's position; covenanted relations seem to be the only ones that count theologically and morally. He radically separates nature and history. He is willing to carry the distinction to what I find to be a logical but amusing, if not ridiculous, extreme when he justifies monogamy in Christendom on the basis of God's covenant with *one* people, Israel (many of whom had more than one wife after the covenant, if the biblical accounts are accurate) and Christ's covenant with one church. There, and not in nature, is where Ramsey sees the mind of God revealed about the order of marriage. Ramsey turns out to be more of a Barthian and biblicist than I thought. In contrast with Ramsey on this and other points, my descriptive statement enlarges the range of matters that are morally significant, provides a basis for addressing them which (on its descriptive premises about human participation) is generally accessible to Christians, atheists, and others in our pluralistic world (though that effect is not the motive for my arguing for the description). It also accounts for why I have to take into account outcomes of human action over a broader space and time than Ramsey does. On the basis of my theology, these outcomes necessarily are morally of great significance. I do not blush in shame for having consequentialist as well as deontic aspects of my ethics. The theology necessitates both. To undercut my position, Ramsey has to argue that this descriptive statement is incorrect; because he does not, apparently, perceive its significance for my project, his argument against me is not against the fundamental grounds of my work. Is God, for Ramsey, only important within the context of covenants? What is the theological and moral significance of natural interdependencies for Ramsey? Clearly my relationalism is not confined to the sphere of personal relations as Ramsey's is.

[Lisa Sowle] Cahill worries about my use of the sciences, and thus about an immanentism in my interpretation of how God is present in the world. McCormick, perhaps, has the opposite worry—that God is excessively transcendent for me. The divine powers are immanent in the ordering of life not only in nature, but in society and culture as well. The question for Cahill is this: can she develop theological *ethics* without inserting something like my description between her transcendent Deity and life in the world?

Since Cahill is so taken by my anecdotes from my family, I offer her another. At the time of this writing, my mother, age 94, in her third month of unconsciousness is sustained by a human invention called Ensure which goes from an electrically operated pump which holds a bag of that product and controls its flow to her stomach through a flexible tube passing through her nose. A catheter drains her urine, and attendants faithfully clean up her feces. My mother has become a biological organism that (not who) metabolizes Ensure into feces and urine and into sufficient energy to continue to metabolize Ensure into feces and urine. Her pastor prayed with my siblings and me, begging God to take our mother's life. When we returned to my mother's room, I pointed to the technology and said to my siblings, "God didn't put that damned thing up there and God can't take the damned thing down." How, pray tell, is God to take my mother's life if not through the ordering of nature? (In re: my casuistical colleagues, I interpret the issues in my mother's treatment not merely in medical casuistic terms [which I use to argue with her physician] but also in more radical religious terms: idolatry and failure to accept finitude. For an account of the former, read [Martin] Luther on the First Commandment in the Larger Catechism.)

Toulmin not only refers to my description of humans as interdependent and participants, but seems in general to approve of it. I take the critical point of his essay to be that I have not demonstrated how we can come to certitude about morality based upon these patterns and processes of interdependence. If I am correct, there is a Cartesian trace I would not expect to find in Toulmin. I have explained as thoroughly as I can at the present time both how we can seek certitude and why complete certainty is beyond our grasp, including the significance of development or change. But I find it ironic for Toulmin to be making that critical point against me, since I have been informed by much of his own philosophical work in developing my arguments about the limits of certitude.

Of course, [Stanley] Hauerwas's position simply rules out any concern for my descriptive statement. History (in a variety of senses, none of which are very clearly distinguished) is so exclusively the locus of whatever he wants to defend that we have a curious theology. To differentiate himself from me he writes: "I remain stuck with the claim that through Jesus' resurrection God decisively changed our history." (I don't know who is included and excluded from the "our.") "Therefore I believe we must continue to begin with the 'particular,' with the historical, not because there is no other place to begin but because that is where God begins." I say, harshly, that I find that sentence, even in context, to be ludicrous. I can only infer that nature is of no theological significance, and that God was absent, or something, until Jesus's resurrection. God is not sovereign over nature, I take it. Nature is also, then, of no ethical significance as a source of direction in Hauerwas's ethics. Hauerwas becomes a twentieth-century version of Marcion.

Before leaving this fourth theme, I wish to relate it to previous ones that my critics seem not to take seriously. The descriptive statement not only provides a cognitive basis for ethics to be defended only on rational grounds; it is an articulation of the experience of dependence and interdependence and the ambiguities of our capacity to be self-determining participants; it is a description *of our being* and not only a basis for our doing. In piety we find God inexorably present in these processes and patterns, and our participation in them is the locus of our fidelity and service to God.

II. MISCONSTRUED THEMES

The spheres of missing and underrated themes and that of misconstrued themes necessarily overlap. To write about the latter will, unfortunately, require some repetition of the former. Recall the themes of my Ryerson Lecture.

The theological enterprise is a religious enterprise in two dimensions. First, it exists within the context of piety; I have already indicated that my critics omit this theme. Second, it develops in the context of a historic religious tradition, unless it is a rationalistic theology or what is traditionally called "natural" theology. Of the theologians on whose work I comment in volume one, Ralph Burhoe comes closest to trying to develop a theology without significant reference to a particular religious tradition. On the context of piety and tradition, I believe some of my critics have both ignored and misconstrued what I have said; others disagree with how I have incorporated and differentiated myself from traditions. All of them have failed to grasp the mutual informing of piety and tradition.

Second, as McCormick accurately quotes me, theology seeks to say something about how things really and ultimately are. It is on the basis of this conviction (and it is argued for, not merely asserted) that I am theologically constrained to take more seriously than any of my critics, save Toulmin, some other disciplines that help us to understand how things really and ultimately are. This does not, however, relinquish the theological task to the scientist since, per definition, theology is reflection on the object of piety as piety is evoked by the powers that bear down upon us and sustain us.

Third, theology implies ethics; perhaps it even "entails" ethics. The ethical task is to discern what God is enabling and requiring us to be and to do. Only Ramsey has charged me with incoherence between what I say theologically and the ethics that follow from it; if I understand his critical argument I am not convinced by it. McCormick, in his addendum on special ethics, argues that one can come to the same conclusions (in the cases he cited) from ethics from an anthropocentric perspective as I do from a theocentric perspective. That, of course, does not surprise me because I never argued you could not and, as I shall illustrate later, I can suggest to McCormick some instances in which one's final judgment would be—and is—different.

I am misconstrued by my critics on the significance of piety and tradition in moving from experience and some aspects of science to what I affirm about the reality of God. Of course, insofar as my critics argue from authority—biblical or traditional theological—there is a significant difference between us, one which I have candidly stated and defended in my writings.

Both Cahill and McCormick, and [Gene] Outka behind Cahill . . . , do not state adequately the way in which I work from piety and the Christian theological tradition, and how I work within that tradition to interpret elements drawn from other sources. I have already adverted to the "scientism" charge; McCormick says I come "close" to it, and it is implied by Cahill and certainly by Outka's article ["Remarks and Theological Program Instructed by Science." *The Thomist,* Vol. 47, No. 1, October, 1983]. These critics seem to assume that I am trying to argue on purely cognitive (and not also affective) grounds, and that I am trying to argue rationalistically or nonhistorically, i.e., without reference to the Reformed tradition of Christianity. I can only beg, plead, cajole them to read with great care the argument of volume one and particularly chapter five. . . . For example, after I have argued for what sciences can contribute to our understanding of God, I say that I believe those contributions can sustain a general point, namely that "'God' refers to the power that bears down upon us, sustains us, sets an ordering of relationships, provides the conditions of possibilities for human activity, and even a sense of direction. The evidences from various sciences suggest the plausibility of viewing God in these terms. These terms, and any warrants for them from the sciences, however, find their full religious significance only within piety, religious affectivity" (1981:264). (I suppose if I had said only within "faith" it would not seem so offensive, but see my argument for the choice of piety rather than faith.)

In an earlier section of chapter five I show how traditional symbols—God as Creator, etc.—continue to be viable ways of speaking about God in relation to man and the world. These symbols do not come out of Buddhism, or Hinduism, or Teutonic religion, though there may be functional equivalents to some of them in other religions. . . . I give my reasons for preference for the Reformed tradition; true, I do not argue from its authority and am selective in relation to it, as I am sure my theological critics would have to admit that they are selective from their traditions, or more generally, the tradition. That Reformed tradition is of no mean significance in construing ethics from a theocentric perspective. Thus to interpret me as if I wished to move from evidences from science to an account of God on some presumptively purely nonhistorical, rational, cognitive basis without taking into the argument piety and tradition is simply wrong. As I said above,

I do not think that my *basic* move in drawing from the sciences (see McCormick, "The Book of Nature") is essentially different from that of Thomas Aquinas or Schleiermacher or others.

I also made it clear at several points that God remains mystery beyond our best efforts to say what we can honestly say about God. Great theologians, not merely Gustafson, have said that: an author of Genesis, the author of the Books of Samuel, Augustine, Thomas [Aquinas], Bonaventure, Luther, Calvin, [Jonathan] Edwards, Schleiermacher, [Karl] Barth, and many more. McCormick simply has a deaf ear if he cannot hear that in what I have written, and thus thinks I exclude all "mysticism."

To find out how things really and ultimately are, one has to read not only theology but also science. But the way things are, to the eyes of piety, has theological significance; it is an indication of God's ordering of the world. Cahill, Outka before her, and others appeal directly or implicitly to the limitations of scientific knowledge as those have been argued by recent historians and philosophers of science. I have read a great deal of that literature, and surely nothing in how I use evidences from science is based on a simple-minded Machian positivism.

An excursus is in order at this point. I find many theologians, who use [Thomas S.] Kuhn (and so many have read only him; cf. Kuhn, 1970) *et al.* to show that science is "softer" than is reputed, to be self-serving in the end. That is, if science is soft, there are warrants for theology being soft. And if science is soft, what we learn from it need not be taken seriously when we try to construe the world theologically, i.e., how things really and ultimately are. Or, another move is that the two realms of discourse are so different that they are incommensurable. Cahill comes close to affirming this when she writes that "the unresolved question is whether either or both have a distinctive language which addresses realities not comprehensive within the other's worldview." My criticism of Paul Holmer and others shows my response to that. But theologians do take recourse to scientific work, selectively; when it serves their interests, they use it and when it threatens them, they do not. I remind my readers that the fundamentalist creationists have also read their philosophy of science, and thus argue that the evolutionary accounts of nature are no more credible or incredible than the biblical account of creation as a scientific explanation. But most contemporary theologians are willing to accept the biblical account as mythic in part because they know there is a more defensible scientific account of how things have come to be. Maybe, then, they ought to ask themselves about other scientifically backed views, e.g., about the *finis* of things, and whether traditional eschatology can be held in the light of that.

Further, I have great respect for what can be known from the "soft" historical tradition and social framework of science. It is not so soft but what, e.g., a geneticist can determine precisely which chromosome is abnormal and thus the causal factor of a certain disease. That, I take it, is worthy of a lot of respect. And that has to be of theological significance if God is Creator and Orderer of nature.

I beg, plead, cajole my critics to read carefully the following, which is a conclusion to my discussion of ways in which theologians have related their work to science. I indicate my affinity with [Ernst] Troeltsch's statement (1981:251) and my differences from it. "First, piety (rather than 'belief') is a necessary condition for ideas of God to be subjectively meaningful and intellectually persuasive. . . . Second, the 'substantial content' of ideas of God cannot be incongruous with (rather than must be 'in harmony with') well established data and explanatory principles established by relevant sciences, and must 'be in some way indicated by these'" (1981:257). Ryerson Lecture themes are never separated. Moreover, it is our *ideas* of God that must be informed by relevant sciences. The sciences provide critical tests of traditional theological and ethical concepts; the impulse to test arises out of piety and not out of subservience to the sciences.

Of course, to Hauerwas the sciences are of no theological significance. We are somehow to begin with history or tradition and stay within them. His interpretation of my work goes back, as the other critics do not, to some things I wrote before 1979-1980. Hauerwas would be correct if what he is saying is the following: Gustafson has wrestled with social, cultural, and historical relativism all his career, and has rather consistently affirmed the inescapability of historical relativism. There have been changes in Gustafson's work, however, as he expands the criteria by which he tests, revises, and develops the historically relative base. But Hauerwas is saying something else. One has to be either a "historicist" or a "universalist." Somewhere on a continuum there is a gulf over which one has to pass; rather than a continuum to which ideas like universalism or relativisim have graded relevance, one has to be one or the other. And if you are one or the other then that is what you work from and dismiss all considerations from the other. Otherwise you are inconsistent. I, Hauerwas, begin with history and I stay with history.

One cannot read the long quotation Hauerwas has from 1981 accurately and come to his conclusion, "Yet, at times, Gustafson seems to suggest, in spite of his criticism of the philosophers, that it would be good if we could be so emancipated," that is, emancipated from the historical and cultural. The quotation says that to strive for the universal provides grounds for apologetic work, and for internal criticism and revision of the tradition. For Hauerwas, one has to be either a "particularist" or a "univeralist." To move from the more particular in order to explain or criticize it is, apparently, already for him to have made a theological error.

I think Hauerwas owes us clearer, more precise interpretations and defenses of a number of things for which he has become well known, but in this case for the following. I find history, particularism, and such words to run through his essay like a greased pig at the county fair contest. My mind thinks it grasps their meaning, but they slip away. These terms become abstractions that seem to me to have different referents at different places in the essay. Strangely, they point to little that is particular or historical except that God began with the particular, seemingly the resurrection of Jesus.

If Hauerwas thinks he can establish a defense of radical historicism, particularism, communalism, or what have you by making (for what are in one of his senses) only historical claims, he is mistaken. Subsequent to writing his essay on me I have seen two places in which he commends George Lindbeck's *The Nature of Doctrine* (1984). I read Lindbeck to be making some philosophical claims (universalistic?) about the nature of religious language and about the way one becomes religious or anything else—i.e., by learning to use a language. Certainly Troeltsch's and H. Richard Niebuhr's basis for being "historicists" is philosophically grounded. I do not see how one can make a claim for radical historicism on only historical claims.

Further, Hauerwas does not begin only with particular*ism;* he begins with something particular. And to show us why he begins with that particular and not some other possible particular surely involves arguing in a way that calls on criteria and justifications that are more general (if not universal). Why not begin with the cross rather than the resurrection? Why not with the creation? His criteria may be drawn from the Bible or the tradition, but he has to provide some kind of "non-particular" defenses for his choice. Otherwise he is left simply solipsistically confessing, and is likely to be quite unintelligible to others who want to start with a different particular.

The same issues are raised by his statement that the church is the context in which he does ethics; it is an abstraction. I can argue that the church is the context in which I do ethics. *What* church is Hauerwas's context, since it is such a crucial context? I do not recognize the Russian Orthodox Church in what he writes, nor the Roman Catholic Church; it certainly does not seem to me to be the Church of England or the Church of Sweden. By what criteria can we identify his "church?" Can it be done without some general (if not universal) claims? Maybe to be a radical particularist or historicist you have to be vague in order to avoid more expanded intellectual justifications or defenses (universalism?) for what you say.

If theology has to say something about how things really and

ultimately are, Hauerwas's theology is very narrow and confined. In this respect he and Ramsey are similar. If I understand Ramsey (and it is predictable that he does not believe I do), the covenant, not nature, is the theological basis for ethics. So where is, even in traditional Christian terms, the doctrine of creation? Hauerwas seems to me to be even more extreme than Ramsey, though it is not precisely clear what his claims are. Since God begins in history, according to him, everything else we do in ethics has to be confined in some way to the historical or particular. So of Hauerwas one also asks, where is the doctrine of creation?

I wonder what McCormick and Cahill think about Hauerwas's position. They seem to think I do not take tradition, history, or piety into account and thus rely too heavily on science and experience. Would they prefer Hauerwas? Hauerwas seems to me to take what they think is wrong about my work to an extreme position: only Christian faith, history, and tradition are theologically important. Hauerwas's is an intellectual and moral sectarianism of the most extreme sort; thus he keeps a clear distinction between Christianity and the rest of life alive but forecloses apologetics of any kind and limits the range of the ethical. Hauerwas's God becomes the tribal God of a minority of the earth's population. I could argue cogently, I believe, that this is very unbiblical in many respects.

My critics misconstrue what I say about Jesus Christ. Ramsey, McCormick, and Cahill are disturbed by what I do say; what I do not say disturbs them more. One difference between them and me is the authority of tradition. I am quite certain that if the early church had found its cultural environment in India of the first century of the common era, the philosophic explanations of the significance of Jesus would have been quite different than they became in the Hellenistic culture; Hinduism and Buddhism as context would have led to a different history of Christianity both in theology and ethics. Developments which, to me, can be explained as historically accidental are to them theologically determinative. I do not deny that there is value to the tradition of the West; indeed, clearly I affirm that the Reformed tradition perceived things in ways I think are of continuing validity. It is clear from the New Testament itself that Jewish Christianity was different from Pauline Christianity. But my arguments are not exegetical.

I do not make an exegetical argument . . . , as it seems that McCormick and Ramsey think I do. Cahill writes, "he downplays the role of Jesus, identified as *an* incarnation of theistic piety, and does not attribute to him ultimate status." I do not use "an," though it can be read in that way. I wrote, "Jesus incarnates *theocentric* piety *and fidelity* [please note, theocentric and not theistic, and note *fidelity;* Ramsey also misquotes this statement]. Through the gospel account of his life and ministry, we can see and know something of the powers that bear down upon us and sustain us, and of the piety and manner of life that are appropriate to them." Nobody seems to note the second sentence. I suppose if I had written, instead, "through the gospel accounts of his life and ministry God reveals something of the powers that bear down upon us and sustain and redeem us, and of the faith and life that is appropriate to them," it might have passed for orthodoxy, or at least avoided the charge of heresy that McCormick implies. But even if I chose to say that, which I cannot ("God reveals" being ruled out by me), I will never attribute to Jesus "ultimate status." Ultimate status, if I understand what Cahill wants that to refer to, is given only to God. If my theological critics claim that I have to adhere to the Chalcedonean formula to be a Christian, I do not agree. (Incidentally, I think a lot of contemporary Roman Catholic and Protestant theology, including Hauerwas's, does not deny Chalcedon; it just ignores it and practically follows a Christology closer to what I state.)

My theological critics do not develop my reasons for not saying "God reveals," and thus either do not understand the claims and limits of claims I make, or simply assert some view of revelation. McCormick asks "why reflection on human experience cannot be the vehicle of God's self-manifestation?" If he is willing to concede my description that what the Bible portrays is an interpretation of human experience, nature, history, culture, and self in the light of the communities' experience of the powers of God, the only issue is whether God made a choice to become manifest in those historical and natural events. If he concedes that, the distinction between revealed and natural theology is qualified, if not collapsed. I say that through those experiences the people confronted the reality of God, and could say that through them *they found* God manifest. Indeed, I think what I say is not terribly different from what my mentor, H. Richard Niebuhr, said in *The Meaning of Revelation,* but because he called it "revelation" (and meant it), it is not subject to McCormick's charge, I suppose.

The issue here is the use of personalistic language with reference to God. I discuss the significance of this for theological ethics in my section on Barth and Thomas. What is the proper language to use in construing God's relation to the world? Theological language designates relations which are "religious"; the term God refers to the powers that bring all things into being, sustain, and bear down upon us, etc. It is a linguistic construal. I avoid language like "God reveals himself" since it seems to suggest that the Deity, outside of our human construal of God, acts like a person. Even persons, for me, must be understood interrelationally, and not as "autonomously" as my critics seem to hold. To speak of God in personal terms seems to suggest that we can speak of God *in se.* I seek to avoid anthropomorphism in speaking of God. Thus I avoid the use of personalistic language about God. I have attempted to be precise in my thinking on this matter and thus to use language precisely. "God reveals himself" introduces an ambiguity I seek to avoid.

On this point it would have been worthwhile for my theological critics to have attended to my publications beginning with *Treasure in Earthen Vessels* and forward. Consistently my work has been motivated by a desire to force theologians to modify or correct exaggerated claims. *Treasure* was motivated by the writings on ecclesiology pouring forth in the 1950s, much of them under the auspices of the World Council of Churches Commission on Christ and the Church. To write about the church as a natural and political community, and as a community in which a historic tradition is maintained not by the "Spirit" but by social processes was offensive to some people when that book came out. The final chapter of *Christ and the Moral Life* is a very naturalistic proposal, as is what I say in *Can Ethics be Christian?* To repeat, I have all through my career been concerned about exaggerated claims of theologians, especially when those claims (as they often are) are tacitly empirical ones.

On this point, McCormick is an example of what I take to be exaggerated claims when he writes that faith "totally transforms the human person. It creates new operative vitalities that constitute the very possibility and heart of the Christian moral life." I take such an assertion to be testable, unless it is so tightly circular that it becomes tautological. It is very extravagant, more than Augustine, Thomas, Luther, Calvin, and even Schleiermacher claimed. And the limits of their claims were to a considerable extent drawn from observations that Christian people were not very transformed. Again, McCormick draws from Raymond Brown this point: "Jesus is the source of the Christians' love of one another." Jesus might well be *a* source, but my observation of Christians (and humbly, perhaps I might be included among them) is that their love for one another has a lot of sources, many of them very natural and shared by atheists, Muslims, Jews, Hindus, and animists, *et al.*

Even more egregious, and leaving me aghast, is McCormick's sentence, "Nothing is intelligible without reference to God's deed in Christ." That is an empirical claim. Perhaps since my beliefs are, according to McCormick not Christian, I have peculiar difficulties with it. But I think my scores of colleagues doing research on countless aspects of life and culture would be as surprised by it as I am. I really do not think McCormick believes what he said.

(Both orally and in writing I have been commended for being honest and courageous in writing *Ethics from a Theocentric Perspective.* I find those commendations to be alarming. Am I to draw the inference that many theologians and pastors are not being honest and lack in fortitude? The commendations only reinforce a point made earlier in this essay, namely my deep concern about the quality of intellectual and moral life in the Christian community.)

A further aspect of the theme of how things really and ultimately are is perhaps as much missed as misconstrued. I infer from all my theological critics that they still operate within a radical distinction between the sacred and the profane, the religious and the secular, faith and reason and others similar to these. My work intentionally interprets the relations of God to the world in ways which make those distinctions inadequate if not obsolete. To paraphrase a statement of [Dietrich] Bonhoeffer's, I never confront the reality of the world without confronting God, and I confront God through the reality of the world. It would not be inappropriate, except that it would invite misinterpretations, to say that the theology and ethics I have written are incarnational: God present in the world. If I confront God in the world, I confront God in natural and historical events that are both sustaining and destructive of the perceived good for human being.

Cahill writes, as if it is somehow shocking, "Gustafson even refers to the powers that bear down as 'powers of destruction' and concludes that there is sometimes 'enmity toward' God. In this conception, the will of God seems to go beyond lack of favoritism toward humans, beyond indifference even, and approach malevolence." If, in the two volumes, I ever ascribed either benevolence or malevolence to God, I was not careful. The impersonality of the Deity, to whom I am personally related, prohibits me from using (unless I am inconsistent) "—volence" as a suffix with reference to God. It denotes a capacity for intentional agency on God's part which I do not affirm. I can be thankful to God for his benefits to the world, just as [Abraham] Heschel can; but if I can be thankful for his benefits, I can have enmity toward God for the suffering of the world on precisely the same principle. I cannot expect families suffering from starvation because human obstacles keep them from getting food that exists on the earth to thank God for all his benefits to them. Enmity toward God is not without ambiguity; it can be justified and a sign of failure to consent.

Further, to recur to an earlier theme, because Cahill does not take seriously my dense description of religious affections she drops out altogether gratitude as one aspect of piety which moves humans to moral activity. Earlier she says that I appear "unconvinced that a religious perspective can endow suffering with either purposiveness or resolution." On purposiveness she is simply incorrect, unless that implies some grand metaphysical purpose. Suffering has many "purposes"; physical pain indicates the need for some attention to its cause; social oppression indicates the need for social justice, and so forth. Cahill resolves the issue of suffering by turning to biblical material. She finds in the New Testament "that all crucifixion will be recompensed," and "the claim that the Cross always is redemptive and divinely vindicated." For now I will grant that as a biblical claim, but I do not need to premise that biblical claim, curiously, to find little disagreement with the conclusion of her paragraph. "The challenge of the Cross is, in the midst of suffering, to affirm one's relatedness to others and one's service to them as the meaning of one's existence, and to do this out of love for and obedience to the encompassing and deliberate power sustaining and calling life." For me, the cross indicates and evokes a possible requirement of theocentric piety and fidelity; that fidelity requires that I be ready to be self-denying in service to others and the wide ordering of creation, not as *the* meaning of my existence, but in faithfulness to the powers that create, sustain, etc., etc.

Cahill wants to avoid "cheap grace," but it is a question of the reality and efficacy of grace in the world. At what point does the assurance that everything will come out all right in the end blur the Christian's perception of suffering in the world? At what point does it easily resolve the problem of being and value in favor of a dogmatic assertion that where there is being, there is value for man? And finally, does it lead to the slave morality that Nietzsche so powerfully depicts? Are the assurances of grace such that *no* experiential evidence can ever count against them?

Maybe I am too much a common sense thinker, but it seems to me that if I can be grateful to God for those things that are beneficial to humanity and life in the world, I can have enmity toward God for a lot of suffering. If this is not the case, Cahill and others perhaps ought to reintroduce the Devil into theology and ethics so they can relieve God of blame. Theoretical monotheists with a transcendent gracious God perhaps have to be practical Manicheans.

If God is like us, God must surely be suffering. I say this because if I could affirm a more anthropomorphic view of the Deity, much of the way in which I view the world could be stated in terms used by Moltmann and Kitamori. If I were persuaded by the arguments of the process theologians, toward whom there is clearly an opening in my work, I could explicate how events in the world, because of the internal relations with the Deity, have effects on the Divine. I can say that God is involved in both the benefits and sufferings of life in the world as the author, orderer, and end of all things. Perhaps the suffering of the world does somehow redound to the glory of God, but the manifestations of the presence of God in the world are not uniformly beneficial to the human species.

On the relations of God to the world, I find much of Edwards to be persuasive. Whether Ramsey or I am correct in interpreting Edwards is a matter for another time. Whether Edwards exerts a greater influence on Ramsey's or on my theology and ethics is also not a matter worthy of discussion; on that, however, I believe the greater influence is on my work. (Of course, Ramsey does not claim significant influence of Edwards on his own work; his Edwards studies are seemingly an important side venture from which we all reap great benefit.) The point with reference to this final theme in re: Edwards is this: my efforts to think about the relations of

God to the world have been more deeply informed by Edwards than by any other single theologian. If this theme is misconstrued, not seen for its importance, other aspects of my work cannot be adequately perceived. If Ramsey will permit me to cite a title from Edwards as a capstone for this theme, though it does not accurately encapsulate my view, it is this: "Images and Shadows of Divine Things."

This leads to the theme of the relations of theology to ethics. McCormick says that "cosmocentrism need not eliminate anthropocentrism." Theocentrism does not eliminate value for the human, but the two cannot be one unless it is proven that the "values" and "purposes" of (to use McCormick's term) the cosmos are identical with what fulfills human values and purposes, or more strongly, if the divine ends are identical with human fulfillment. Maybe one could have an ellipse with two poles—God and human—but I think there is no persuasive evidence that the Deity as the center of value and being is identical with the value of the human. I find his brief argument in which he comes to the conclusion that the late development of humanity can be read as God's lavish way of making human life the crown of creation to be implausible. I noted speculatively somewhere that life might have evolved elsewhere so that there are beings who would view us as we view animals. And our crowning capacities are such that we might be the destroyers of conditions that sustain life on this planet: humanity might be Siva.

I will not elaborate further on the relation of theology to ethics, but only remind my critics that this is developed in my two volumes in relation to piety, tradition, and how things really and ultimately are. Ethics is developed in the context of piety, the human fault, and conversion; moral reasoning is rooted in them as well as in the way things really are. I now turn to some comments on each of the articles and the letter.

III. REMARKS ON INDIVIDUAL CRITICS

The four articles each have a structure which enables me to respond to them in a way taht I have not in my discussion of themes. The letter, however, is impossible to respond to as a whole.

Hauerwas

I shall add little to what I have said. I read [Hauerwas's] article in simple terms. Gustafson was a "historicist," but is less one now than he once was. Therefore he aspires to be a "universalist." But he cannot quite make up his mind. One has to be either a universalist or an historicist. Hauerwas claims to be a consistent historicist because that's where God began. My previous responses to Hauerwas indicate my position in regard to his article. This position is theologically and religiously reductionistic and logically untenable, as I have argued earlier.

McCormick

McCormick chooses to read my two volumes as "a personal faith statement," though he admits that it is "a bit of both" that and "a theological explanation . . . open to public view." That is an interesting move. While he is moved to argue with it sometimes as a theological explanation open to public view, he has laid the ground for dismissing it because it is a "faith statement." I have addressed all I wish to his arguments against mine and have raised some questions about his "faith statement." He is really writing about *beliefs,* and shows that his, using Protestants more than Roman Catholics, are Christian beliefs. Mine are not Christian by his standards. Why his last remark is given in the form of a question I do not understand. His answer to it is clear. Gustafson's view of God is not Christian. Therefore his ethics is not Christian. That is clearly what he means. And he knows that nowhere in two volumes have I used the adjective Christian for the theological ethics.

For many reasons I am glad I do not belong to McCormick's Church, but particularly since he has seen fit to indict me for heresy. With my position clearly stated, his rebuttal of it and his own orthodox Christian view stated, and his weight as a responsible theologian for added authority, I would be surely summoned by some ecclesiastical agency. Perhaps he should send a copy of his article to the Chicago Association of the Illinois Conference of the United Church of Christ so they can start heresy proceedings against me. I will not voluntarily demit the Christian ministry until I am persuaded that my piety and beliefs are beyond the pale; when I am persuaded, I shall demit. I am not worried about my eternal destiny, and I think a statement of my personal faith would be very unimportant. But I must say that I worry a great deal (as I have said previously in this article) about the intellectual and moral life of the Christian community.

I noted earlier that I was not surprised when McCormick showed how one could come to some of my moral conclusions from ethics from an anthropocentric perspective; I never said one could not. One would *always* come to a different judgment only if ethics from a theocentric perspective ruled out *all* consideration of human values.

From my chapter on suicide McCormick does not comment on the following: "Physical life is not of ultimate value; many persons who suffer acutely are in no way accountable for their sufferings. Suffering is inflicted on them, and it can be a morally proper choice to seek the relief of death for their own sake and for that of others." I know McCormick does not disagree with the first phrase, but I wonder if he is willing to provide a moral justification for suicide. If he is, I believe my arguments would be different from his in both theological and ethical aspects.

Perhaps I should have written a chapter on abortion; I did not because who wants to read one more piece on that issue? I would be very interested if McCormick would justify abortions I would argue are permissible, based upon concerns for patterns and processes of interdependence of life and for the common good of particular wholes. I will not cite cases; I just ask McCormick to think about this.

Further, the ordering of issues in terms of their importance for moral attention might well be different in my work from an anthropocentric perspective. I noted somewhere in volume one that elements necessary for the continuation of all of life, such as oxygen and nitrogen, might be of more value than a lot of things on which moralists lavish attention because they are the necessary conditions of all of life. Although the scientific jury on nuclear winter is still out, from a theocentric perspective the issues are serious enough to be higher on the priority list than most things occupying medical moralists. Life, not only human life, or a human person, is threatened by nuclear war.

McCormick notes my preference of voluntary restraints of family size. It is too bad that his church is so officially human-centered that it does not permit the means to make voluntary restraints practicable to many persons. I argue that restraints are in part necessary, for the sake of a larger whole—life on the planet. Can that be argued from anthropocentric ethics? And I note he does not comment . . . , to say whether he agrees that economic disincentives to larger families are permissible—for the sake of life on the planet and not just persons. But at least McCormick ought to be relieved that my heretical beliefs and unchristian ethics are not totally inhumane.

Cahill

I get the impression that Cahill is trying to find clues to understand her former instructor. She perceptively sees the importance of suffering and evil and, curiously, does not cite the passage in which I address it illustratively in a more comprehensive way than her own illustrations, namely the opening section of "Population and Nutrition." My *Ethics* was not written, however, to provide a theodicy (or an absence of one, in traditional terms). When I worked through my arguments about God and God's relations to man and the world, and man and man's relations to God and the world, the conclusions to which I come about suffering and evil follow from the theology. She comes to different conclusions from mine as a result of the theology she outlines. On that matter I have remarked previously in this article.

Her interests in my use of family anecdotes suggests further evidence that Cahill is trying to figure out what makes me think the way I do. The parable at the end of her article, with its unquestionable charm, leaves me with the impression that as far as Cahill is concerned I can, like my grandfather, work

all alone at my intellectual forge although there are reasons for others to go home. Go home, I think, is precisely what too many theologians do rather than take into account the issues I have responded to theologically and ethically. It is all part of the intellectual sectarianism that so tempts theologians. Theologians have no reason to charge academic life with compartmentalization, overspecialization, narrowness of interest, etc., when with or without sophisticated philosophical defenses they refuse to be challenged by their colleagues in other disciplines.

Toulmin

Of my five critics Toulmin provides the most sympathetic interpretation. And its basic lines are, in my judgement, accurate. This not only interests me, but pleases me, since Toulmin is one historian and philosopher who is open to theological discussion based upon interpretation of the natural order. I do not know how many other scientists, philosophers, and other humanists have read my work. Perhaps the recent history of my extra-classroom activities and cross-disciplinary teaching is what in part leads me to take more seriously than many of my colleagues in theology and ethics the ways in which the world is construed in other parts of university teaching and research and in the professions. If, as I have said, theology says something about how things really and ultimately are, some clues to that must come from those who inform us in more detail than theologians say about how many things at least penultimately are.

Toulmin raises the question of Stoicism, and it is implied by other critics as well. My reading of Calvin is that he had to strive with some effort to distinguish some of his theological conclusions from Stoicism. Although I have not satisfied Cahill with my efforts to argue that one cannot say God is nature without remainder, piety and tradition, as well as a sense of the mystery beyond our capacities to comprehend, force me to acknowledge a transcendence of the Deity that is not found in traditional Stoics. None of my critics notes the importance of the lines from "Paradise Lost" [by John Milton] and Lincoln which provide a leitmotif to my conclusion. Further, the developments of the sciences, about which Toulmin is far better informed than I and from whom I have learned much, indicate that process and change are part of the reality of the world in which we have evolved ourselves through change. Thus a "staticism" of traditional Stoicism no longer is viable. Our participation increasingly affects the natural and social order of things; there is no natural harmony in which all things work together for the good of all things, not to mention those who love the Lord. One reason I cannot provide more certainty about the values and principles that are grounded in the ordering of life is that the ordering itself undergoes change, more dramatically in history and culture but also in nature itself. And the changes are increasingly outcomes of human participation. My "Book of Nature" (see

McCormick) has to be different from the Stoics' and from Thomas Aquinas'.

If apathy is the response to the world in Stoicism, it is not my response. With capacities to participate in life, we are not called upon to be simply resigned. Again Cahill seems to have missed my discussion in which I distinguish between resignation and consent. Consent for me is informed by Edwards and other eighteenth-century uses of the term. It is an inward disposition which alters our sense of participation. I not only resign myself to my forthcoming death; I consent to the divine ordering of the world; God created me to die, among other things. Nor does Stoicism back the self-denial that my work requires. But surely Toulmin is correct that my construal of the world is more akin to the Stoics than to other philosophical descriptions that inform other theological construals except process theology. Should I blush with shame for that? I do not, since I have given reasons why I come to my conclusions. My critics who call me a Stoic have to make an argument against those reasons, and not simply appeal to historic revelation as an alternative. Toulmin understands that, and I am grateful for his saying it.

Ramsey

Ramsey's choice to write a sixty-page manuscript letter rather than an article makes it impossible to respond to him adequately. Ramsey obviously enjoyed writing that letter and readers who know Ramsey will enjoy both the style and the substance. Readers who do not know him, however, are likely to be puzzled by the combination of careful argumentation, gratuitous remarks, exposition of his own work, and humorous asides. It reads like no other article they have read in a scholarly journal. Ramsey freely graded aspects of my work; it takes restraint on my part not to reciprocate with reference to his letter.

I have attempted to sort out which of Ramsey's criticisms seem to him to be most telling. I conclude that, while he thinks my theology is dead wrong (and I have commented a bit on that above), his real worry is my ethical theory. In my section on Ramsey as a benchmark, I credited him with coherence between his theology and his ethical theory, though I wrote more about love than covenant (but did write also about the latter). Ramsey is worried that the ethics which follow from my theology cannot come to the kind of closure, to say the number of firm "no's" that he finds important. While he does, in his typical prose, seek to find incoherence between my theology and ethics, he falls into the same error that McCormick does, namely arguing that one can be theocentric and anthropocentric at the same time. I have already remarked on the priority of covenant to creation in Ramsey's theology, i.e., a very Barthian move, and asked where the doctrine of creation fits his theology and ethics. I have long noted that his interests in natural law theory have always eschewed the

ontological underpinnings of it in its historic form; he adapts decision procedures from it to his own theology and interests. He can do that if he chooses, but it points to the virtual elimination of the natural ordering as a basis of ethics in his work. Again, where is the doctrine of creation?

My impression, upon reflection, is that Ramsey is finally most interested in developing a pattern of practical reasoning which avoids evil acts. I noted above that I do not blush because long-range consequences have to be taken into account in my theological ethics; the theology I develop and the descriptive statement of man as participant in patterns and processes of interdependence make that necessary. The description of morally relevant circumstances is necessarily larger and more complex than is the case in his work; I indicated that and reasons for it in my section on him. If life in the world is interdependent to the extent and in the many dimensions I describe, it is simply a contraction of theological and moral vision that keeps agents from taking broad and long-range views of things.

I agree with Ramsey's worry that evil can follow from the intention to achieve benefits for others. I agree with our common mentor, H. Richard Niebuhr, that there are occasions on which the gracious thing is to do nothing, and have so argued. If I recall correctly, Ramsey published a paper in which he argued that the procedure of amniocentesis was immoral because it could cause harm to the fetus. I am clearly more impressed than Ramsey is that the avoidance of evil as the primary ethical precept can preempt the development of beneficial outcomes to large numbers of persons. Amniocentesis has proved beneficial; I suppose there is no way of confirming absolutely that some slight pain or harm has been done to fetal life by it. If Ramsey wonders about whether I can close to a negative, which I can on many things, I can wonder with equal looseness whether Ramsey could even say that something ought to be done for the benefit of others at the risk of causing some harm to innocent persons without their consent. The theology I have developed backs an ethics that is ready to say there might be occasions on which such initiatives are permissible. And they would not necessarily be more tragic than refraining from doing something judged evil at the cost of outcomes that would benefit others. Such are the inevitabilities of human finitude.

Ramsey does not take up directly one of the crucial bases on which I cannot provide the kind of eternal moral certainty he thinks is necessary, namely the idea that culture, history, selves, and even nature are in processes of development, as well as continuity. This means, for me, that normally one applies tried-and-true principles, values, and rules to the novelty that occurs. But it also means that one is open to the possibility of revision of some of the principles and rules, and a reordering of the priority of values. For example, a respect for the natural world that I learned as a very small child from my Swedish father has become an arena of great concern in my adulthood because of our perceptions of harms done to it in many ways. This does not lead to a Schweitzerian or Jainist near-animism and nature mysticism, but it reorders historically and politically some traditional values which I argue are grounded in the anthropocentrism of Western culture. I do not know how much ethics will change in the next centuries, but if the cultural changes continue to occur at the rate they have in the past century, I predict that some things now permitted will be prohibited and perhaps some things now prohibited will be permitted, that some things now high on the customary scale of values will be lowered and some things relatively low will be raised. And I predict that nothing will be less ambiguous in the future than things, in my interpretation, now are. God is order*ing*; humanity is intervening; some other tradition may be dominant in even our geographic part of the world; neither God nor humanity is dependent upon historic Christianity as we now know it to continue to seek to discern the proper relations of all things to God.

Ramsey's practical ethics are, as I noted previously, quite rationalistic. "So little knows / Any, but God alone, to value right / The good before him. . . . " My discussion of general rules, etc., in my concluding chapter was an effort to show how various rational procedures can be seen to be part of the process of discernment. If one reads the final chapters of both volumes with care, one will see that I argue for rational activity in discernment but do not limit discernment to it. I am concerned about our being as well as our doing. Here I think I am more biblical and Edwardsian than Ramsey. To be sure, the casuistry of the legal codes in the Torah provides exemplary rational procedures. But I can also quote the Psalms: the Fifty-First: "Behold, thou desirest truth in the inward being; therefore teach me wisdom in my secret heart." "Create in me a clean heart, O God, and put a new and right spirit within me." In my reading of the Bible, morality is often and clearly understood to be a matter of one's loves and loyalties, and of one's affections, one's heart. If one of the roots of our sin is in the heart, then one of the roots of our conversion is also in the heart.

Ramsey clearly does not like the way in which I accuse many moralists, including [Immanuel] Kant, of developing ethics so that the prime interest is the protection of the moral purity of the agent. I am not deterred by his comments on that. And I find deep historic Christian bases for another view—a very orthodox interpretation of the crucifixion. God permitted an evil deed, the death of Jesus, for the sake of its benefits to others. That kind of piety and fidelity informs my convictions. For Ramsey, perhaps the most important point of the crucifixion is that Jesus gave his informed consent to the invasive procedure. I am impressed with the way in which both Luther and Calvin interpret the second table of the decalogue so that the proscriptions become prescriptions to

do good for others. My interpretation of Christian morality is, to put it tritely, that it stresses *doing good for others* more than it stresses worrying about the blame that can be put on an agent who might cause some harm in the course of meeting the needs of the neighbor.

The ordering of life in the world is such, as I have argued in my work, that neither Ramsey's ethics nor mine can guarantee that the outcomes of human initiatives will be free of ambiguity.

Ramsey obviously has to reject a pattern of thought which my theology makes central to the ethical task, namely thinking of the relations of parts to whole. If I recall Ramsey's writings with some accuracy, the idea of a common good is not important in his work of the last decades. (I acknowledge the risk in saying this, since Ramsey remembers his work so well he will no doubt find evidence to rebut this.) And since human beings are part of a larger whole, I necessarily have to give fairly high priority to issues which threaten the nonhuman world and not only for the sake of the preservation of human life.

Many other aspects of his letter remain unattended in this response, but not because I cannot defend myself. The interpretation of Edwards is a side issue and worth scholarly discussion, but I never claimed to be faithful to Edwards. My thinking is deeply informed by Edwards, and as I noted above, I think more so than is Ramsey's—but that is also irrelevant.

I began this article by acknowledging that my five critics have been more than casual friends of mine over the years. I have fulfilled an obligation to respond in gratitude to the attention they lavished on my work, and attempted to do so within a reasonable amount of space. I have never been a good polemicist (indeed, I recall Ramsey once calling me an irenicist). I hope that bonds of friendship are not broken by what I have written. More than that I hope, though I have reasons to doubt, that this exercise contributes to the development of theological ethics.

John P. Gunnemann (review date July 1986)

SOURCE: A review of *Ethics from a Theocentric Perspective*, Vol. II, in *Interpretation*, Vol. XL, No. 3, July, 1986, pp. 330-31.

[*In the following review, Gunnemann asserts that one of the strongest parts of Gustafson's* Ethics from a Theocentric Perspective, *Vol. II "is the way in which empirical description informs the discussion of the four problem areas" that Gustafson presents.*]

In this second volume [called *Ethics from a Theocentric Perspective,* Volume Two] of his major work in theological ethics, Gustafson uses the theocentric perspective developed in volume one to address more specifically ethical literature and problems. The first half of the work is a detailed comparison of his own approach with "benchmarks" from theology and moral philosophy, specifically, with the work of Karl Barth, Thomas Aquinas, Karl Rahner, and Paul Ramsey in theology, and of Utilitarianism (especially John Stuart Mill and Henry Sidgwick) and Kant in moral philosophy. The second half of the book addresses four contemporary "areas of human experience": marriage and family, suicide, population and nutrition, and the allocation of biomedical research funding.

Gustafson's overall aim is to show how "a comprehensive and coherent account of theological ethics" leads to and supports his method of discernment in dealing with moral problems. This complex account, worked out in volume one and summarized here in the transitional Chapter Four, remains one of his most important contributions to ethical thought. Yet the success of Gustafson's undertaking depends not so much on the application of this approach to the four areas of human experience as on the persuasiveness of the distinctive and controversial theocentric presuppositions which give the formal structure substance.

The chief presuppositions derive from the theocentric perspective itself: God—not human beings or human purposes—is the center of value. This places Gustafson in company with Barth's rejection of the anthropocentrism of most modern ethical thought and with the piety expressed in the Reformed tradition (most notably by Calvin and Edwards), a piety that he expresses variously as "consent to being," as stewardship for the whole of creation, as self-denial in relation to the wholes of which we are parts, and as an awareness of the ambiguity and tragedy of human existence. This decentering of human life and history is the basis of Gustafson's criticism of various theologies of history and liberation and subtly informs especially his discussion of suicide and of population problems. But unlike Barth, Gustafson's theocentrism has little room, if any, for revelation; Christology and grace, too, play minor roles. This places Gustafson more in company with the natural law theories of Thomas Aquinas and Karl Rahner (especially the latter's developmental view) with their stress on the human capacity for understanding the natural moral order—the patterns of interdependence—in which we live. The fundamental question of ethics in a theocentric perspective is, "What is God requiring and enabling us to do?" The answer, "We are to relate ourselves and all things in a manner appropriate to their relations to God," requires seasoned attention to human experience and to an objective, developing order of human and natural interdependence, to indicators or signs of God's sovereign ordering.

Another distinctive feature of Gustafson's theocentric ethics is his empirical bent and his insistence that every ethical theory has an explicit or implicit set of descriptive premises. His close and subtle discussion of the descriptive premises of the theologians and moral philosophers is a compelling contribution to the often sterile "is-ought" debate, and one of the strongest points of volume two is the way in which empirical description informs the discussion of the four problem areas. Construal of the world is always at the center of ethical interpretation.

> **Gustafson's overall aim is to show how "a comprehensive and coherent account of theological ethics" leads to and supports his method of discernment in dealing with moral problems.**
>
> —*John P. Gunnemann*

Less compelling is Gustafson's remarkable deference to the natural sciences in construing the world, a deference not unconnected to the minor roles played by revelation, grace, and christology. The liveliest critical conversation with this work should come from those working in ethics and theology from a more Wittgensteinian perspective who may well agree with the notion of theology as construal of the world and with the importance of descriptive premises, but without granting the natural sciences and empirical language such a privileged place in the construal. Christian doctrines played down by the theocentric perspective might then play a more important regulative role in world-construal. The outcome of that critical conversation is by no means certain, but Gustafson has made a major contribution to it.

Richard A. Gray (review date 1994)

SOURCE: A review of *Ethics from a Theocentric Prespective,* Volume I: *Theology and Ethics,* in *Reference Services Review,* Vol. 22, No. 3, 1994, pp. 84-86.

[*In the following excerpt, Gray summarizes the differences between the prevailing view of anthropocentric theology and Gustafson's version of a theocentric theology.*]

The inherent logic of Gustafson's argument requires that he describe the prevailing perspective of anthropocentric theology before he sets forth his own preferred view of theology as a theocentrism. This he proceeds to do in his first chapter. The conclusion that most present-day theologizing is highly anthropocentric is inescapable when one examines the content of what are frequently called "religious studies" in academic institutions. Whether a course in religious studies has its point of departure in psychoanalytical, sociological, or anthropological emphases and doctrines, the central question to be asked essentially never varies: What benefits do human beings derive from theological beliefs? Those benefits may range from the crudely emotional to the highly intellectual. Gustafson describes the temptation into which an anthropocentric view of God leads us:

> The temptation is always to put the Deity and the forces of religious piety in the service of the needs and desires of individuals, small groups, and societies. . . . Religion—its theologies, its cultic practices, its rhetoric, its symbols, its devotions, becomes unwittingly justified for its utility value. God is denied as god; God becomes an instrument in the service of human beings rather than human beings instruments in the service of God.

In setting forth Niebuhr's theocentric interpretation of World War II, Gustafson identifies three of its consequences for human thought and conduct. First, we must abandon "the habit of passing judgments on ourselves and our enemies"; second, we must abandon "all self-defensiveness, all self-aggrandizement, all thinking in terms of self as central"; and third, we must abandon any tendency or inclination to deny our enemies the possibility of redemption. This is a theocentric view of war because it deprives humans of the right to judge persons, ends, and means. Judgment, condemnation, justification, and redemption all belong to God alone. The following quotation illuminates the view of God acting in history that both Niebuhr and Gustafson defend.

> It means that if a Hitler is seen to be the rod of God's anger he is not thereby justified relatively or absolutely; for he does not intend what God intends, "but it is in his heart to destroy and to cut off nations not a few." It means, also, that if the United Nations are the instruments of God's judgment on Germany, Italy and Japan, they are not thereby justified, as though their intentions were relatively or absolutely right. God does not act save through finite instruments but none of the instruments can take the place of God even for a moment.

Gustafson says of these lines that they constitute "a very theocentric interpretation of the war." They are, perhaps, no more theocentric in orientation than the view of the American Civil War that Lincoln proposed in his Second Inaugural, which he took from Matthew, Chapter 18, Verse 7:

> Woe unto the world because of offenses! for it must needs be that offenses come; but woe unto that man by whom the offense cometh.

"The Almighty has his own purposes," which are, of course, opaque to human understanding of their history. In Gustafson's system, however, it is not reason but affectivity that brings forth in the human consciousness a conviction of the reality of God. For Gustafson the particulars of that conviction are derived from the Reformed tradition of Christianity. He acknowledges intellectual indebtedness primarily to John Calvin, and secondarily to such Protestant religious thinkers as Jonathan Edwards, Barth, Schleiermacher, and H. Richard Niebuhr, as well as to the Roman Catholic Augustine.

Gustafson clearly does entertain the possibility that the species could justly suffer extinction.

—*Richard A. Gray*

Gustafson affirms three elements in his theological system. These are of such critical importance to his thought that it is necessary that they be quoted verbatim.

> These are (1) a sense of a powerful Other, written about in the post-Calvin developments as the sovereignty of God. (2) The centrality of piety or the religious affections in religious and moral life. By piety I mean not Pietism as that developed in Protestantism in many forms, nor do I mean piousness, that pretentious display of religion which offends me as much as it does anyone. I mean an attitude of reverence, awe and respect which implies a sense of devotion and of duties and responsibilities as well. (3) An understanding of human life in relation to the powerful Other which requires that all of human activity be ordered properly in relation to what can be discerned about the purposes of God.

Gustafson proceeds to emphasize the reciprocal interrelatedness of his three cardinal principles. The powerful Other, piety, and the disciplined ordering of human life constitute a contained and self-reinforcing system. Piety, Gustafson says, is no self-generated feeling. It is rather a response to the powers of God. It is not "cold calculation" but rather a "matter of the heart." The Christian religion, Gustafson asserts, is "not authentic in individuals or in the community without a profound experiential dimension." Deeply experiential piety acquires centrality in Gustafson's system because without it there can be neither an acknowledgment of the powerful Other nor a recognition that the powerful Other imposes an ordering on human life. With respect to ordering, Gustafson argues that only by examining those physical and biological orderings that the sciences reveal as existent in the universe can we begin to discern the purposes of the powerful Other. That Other has its purposes, but they are not such as we can "read" unfolding in the events of our history as a species on planet Earth. They will not explain Attila, Hitler, the existence of slavery in America, or the coming of a terrible war that ultimately extirpated it.

The phrase "powerful Other" has enormous interest in itself. It must be interpreted literally. Gustafson uses the word "powerful," eschewing such traditional theological terms as "All Powerful," "Almighty," or "Omnipotent." Indeed, he makes clear that his Other is both limited and limiting. It is limited in that It cannot deflect, derail, or otherwise divert certain sequential processes, such as growth and decay cycles. It is limiting in that It commands us, members of *homo sapiens,* to piously accept the limits It imposes on us. Thus the idea of limit has been doubly built into Gustafson's conception of the powerful Other.

Is it conceivable for Gustafson that the powerful Other could preside over the liquidation of human experiments in society and culture on this planet by allowing our species to be utterly destroyed by an ecological catastrophe? Gustafson asks precisely this question and answers it affirmatively. How the Other could permit such an end to human adventures the author traces to the fact that offenses that perhaps must be come into the world through the repeated and chronic failures of human beings to observe piously, and give consent to, the limits that the Other imposes on them. The extinction of our species in an ecological catastrophe then becomes the woe due to those by whom the offense came into the world.

Gustafson clearly does entertain the possibility that the species could justly suffer extinction.

> Imaginatively, a scenario can be developed in which the divine benevolence will lead to the extinction of our species *when conditions for its sustenance no longer exist on this planet.*

Gustafson uses the Biblical model of a wrathful God to show how the powerful Other might pass judgment on humanity for its many acts of omission and commission that disrupt the divine ordering of nature. He cites the example of the population explosion. Human beings' failure to take effective action to restrain the growth of population is an offense in the sense that Matthew intends. Malnutrition and death and ultimately ecological collapse he construes as possible forms that divine judgment might take. He is explicit on this point as this final quotation shows:

> God will not be denied; human activity must find proper ways to consent to the indications of a divine ordering; without such ways human life and other

aspects of the world are put in peril. *Such is the judgment and the wrath of God.*

FURTHER READING

Criticism

Childress, James F., and William H. Boley. Review of *Ethics from a Theocentric Perspective,* Volume II: *Ethics and Theology,* by James M. Gustafson. *The Journal of Religion* 67, No. 3 (July 1987): 392-95.
    Examines the "eight distinctive features" of Gustafson's theocentric ethics, including the role that piety plays in making moral assessments.

Connery, John R., S.J. Review of *Ethics from a Theocentric Perspective,* Volume II: *Ethics and Theology,* by James M. Gustafson. *Theological Studies* 46, No. 4 (December 1985): 738-39.
    Praises Gustafson's *Ethics from a Theocentric Prespective* for bringing the theological dimension back into ethics.

Gaffney, James. Review of *Protestant and Roman Catholic Ethics: Prospects for Rapprochement,* by James M. Gustafson. *America* 138, No. 17 (6 May 1978): 369.
    Asserts that Gustafson is well qualified for explaining the differences in how Protestants and Catholics approach ethical matters and for explaining why they are so different.

Hauerwas, Stanley. "Time and History in Theological Ethics: The Work of James Gustafson." *The Journal of Religious Ethics* 13, No. 1 (Spring 1985): 3-21.
    Traces the role that time and history play in Gustafson's work and asserts that Gustafson focuses on the universal as opposed to the particular in relation to history.

Keane, Philip S. Review of *Ethics from a Theocentric Perspective,* Volume II: *Ethics and Theology,* by James M. Gustafson. *America* 152, No. 23 (15 July 1985): 495-96.
    Lauds Gustafson's assertion for the need of a more God-centered approach to ethics in his *Ethics from a Theocentric Perspective,* Vol. II, but faults him for not applying the approach to political and economic issues.

Liddell, Brendan E. A. Review of *Ethics from a Theocentric Perspective,* Volume II: *Ethics and Theology,* by James M. Gustafson. *International Journal for Philsophy of Religion* 18, No. 3 (1985): 172-73.
    Complains that Gustafson does not show any reason for adhering to a theocentric perspective of God, such as experiencing a closer relationship with God.

Mizruchi, Mark S. Review of *The U.S. Business Corporation: An Institution in Transition,* edited by John P. Meyer and James M. Gustafson. *Contemporary Sociology* 19, No. 2 (March 1990): 220-21.

    Unfavorable review of *The U.S. Business Corporation.* Mizruchi charges that the book suffres "from considerable redundancy and an absence of debate over controversial issues."

Ramsey, Paul. "A Letter to James Gustafson." *Journal of Religious Ethics* 13, No. 1 (Spring 1985): 71-100.

    Compares Gustafson's theology to his own and discusses their different interpretations of the work of Jonathan Edwards.

Schenck, David. "Prophecy, Polemic and Piety: Reflections on Responses to Gustafson's *Ethics from a Theocentric Perspective.*" *Journal of Religious Ethics* 15, No. 1 (Spring 1987): 72-85.

    Examines the critical reception of Gustafson's *Ethics from a Theocentric Perspective,* Volumes I and II, focusing on Gustafson's view of religious tradition and how it relates to his theocentric ethical approach.

Shinn, Roger L. "Toward a God-Centered Ethic." *Christianity and Crisis* 45, No. 9 (27 May 1985): 221-14.

    Praises Gustafson's *Ethics from a Theocentric Perspective* as "a benchmark for dicussions of Christian ethics for years to come," but questions who Gustafson's God is and why we should believe in him.

Swezey, Charles M. "Introduction." *Theology and Christian Ethics,* by James M. Gustafson, Philadelphia United Church Press, 1974, pp 11-29.

    Outlines the arrangement of Gustafson's *Theology and Christian Ethics,* points out some of the recurring themes found throughout the essays, and asserts that the essays show some of the tendencies in Gustafson's thought.

Winters, Francis X. Review of *Theology and Christian Ethics,* by James M. Gustafson. *America* 131, No. 10 (12 October 1974): 198.

    Asserts that both the strengths and weaknesses of Gustafson's *Theology and Christian Ethics* are found in its "mixture of religious affirmation and methodological hesitancy."

Additional coverage of Gustafson's life and career is contained in the following sources published by Gale Research: *Contemporary Authors,* **Vol. 25-28R, and** *Contemporary Authors New Revision Series,* **Vol. 37.**

Carson McCullers
1917-1967

American novelist, short story writer, dramatist, and poet.

The following entry presents an overview of McCullers's career. For further information on her life and works, see *CLC,* Volumes 1, 4, 10, 12, and 48.

INTRODUCTION

Carson McCullers is considered one of the most prominent American writers of the 1940s and 1950s and was a major contributor to the Southern literary renaissance. Often compared to Tennessee Williams, Eudora Welty, and Flannery O'Connor, McCullers wrote tales about misfits, outcasts, and grotesque figures searching for love and acceptance in a complex and violent world. Robert S. Phillips asserted that McCullers's works "are perhaps the most typical and most rewarding exemplars of Southern Gothicism in this century." Beset by debilitating illness and personal tragedy in her own life, McCullers's greatest literary accomplishments include *The Heart Is a Lonely Hunter* (1940), *The Ballad of the Sad Café* (1943), and *The Member of the Wedding* (1946), all completed in her twenties. Widely acclaimed for unusual sensitivity and dynamic characterizations, McCullers's compositions offer rare insight into the awkwardness and frustration associated with adolescence, unrealized love, and the failure of interpersonal communication. Her best fiction transcends the idiosyncracies and paradoxes of the provincial American South to address the complex metaphysical dilemma of the human condition.

Biographical Information

Born Lula Carson Smith in Columbus, Georgia, McCullers showed an early aptitude for music and literature and was encouraged by her parents to study the piano. In 1935 she traveled to New York City to study at the Juilliard School of Music, but she never enrolled due to ill health and waning interest. In 1937 she married Reeves McCullers, an aspiring novelist, and moved to North Carolina. There she began work on her first novel, *The Heart Is a Lonely Hunter,* which was published to wide critical acclaim. A celebrated literary success, McCullers divorced Reeves after a series of complicated romantic interludes and immersed herself in the New York artistic community. *Reflections in a Golden Eye,* her second novel, was published in 1941. McCullers returned to Columbus where she suffered her first stroke at the age of twenty-four. With the support of a Guggenheim fiction fellowship in 1942 and an award from the American Academy of Arts and Letters in 1943, McCullers produced her novella *The Ballad*

of the Sad Café, published in *Harper's Bazaar,* and a third novel, *The Member of the Wedding.* She remarried Reeves in 1945 and accompanied him to Europe where in 1947 she suffered a series of strokes that permanently impaired her vision and paralyzed her left side. In 1953 she left Reeves again after their relationship became increasingly hostile. Shortly thereafter, he committed suicide. The death of her mother two years later devastated McCullers, but she used both Reeves and her mother as the basis for characters in her play *The Square Root of Wonderful* (1958). McCullers produced her last novel, *Clock Without Hands,* in 1961, and a book of children's verse, *Sweet as a Pickle and Clean as a Pig,* in 1964. She died of a cerebral hemorrhage in 1967 at the age of fifty. A posthumous publication of McCullers's uncollected writings, edited by her sister, Margarita Smith, appeared under the title *The Mortgaged Heart: The Previously Uncollected Writings of Carson McCullers* (1971).

Major Works

McCullers's highly acclaimed first novel, *The Heart Is a Lonely Hunter* (1940), focuses on deaf-mute John Singer, who befriends four alienated characters who believe that only he can understand their plight. The novel also centers on the experiences of the adolescent Mick Kelly, an androgynous thirteen-year old girl who sacrifices her dream of becoming a concert pianist to take a job at Woolworth's department store. The distinct Gothic qualities, bizarre characters and violent episodes of *The Heart Is a Lonely Hunter* are employed again in McCullers's second novel, *Reflections in a Golden Eye,* which was criticized for its unorthodox subject matter and unsympathetic portrayal of characters. The depiction of Captain Penderton, a sadomasochistic, latent homosexual who commits a murder at the end of the novel, typifies the characterizations running throughout much of McCullers's work. Unfulfilled spiritual and physical needs are a central part of *The Ballad of the Sad Café,* in which McCullers portrays a relationship between the tall, Amazon-like Amelia Evans, her vengeful husband Marvin Macy, and her hunchback cousin Lymon. The strange fairy-tale elements of the story lend the work an epic quality. As Mary A. Gervin noted, McCullers admitted that the story was written to "work out the conflicting emotions she underwent in 'the twisted trinity' between her German friend Annemarie, her husband Reeves, and herself." Through the perverse triangle relationship that evolves in the novel, McCullers illustrates how archetypal love tends toward evil and the negation of communal love. The bond that is developed between the dwarf Lymon and the giantess Amelia is shattered when Lymon's affections are transferred to Macy. The two men destroy Amelia's coffee house and abandon her, leaving her physically and spiritually broken. In *The Member of the Wedding,* McCullers returned to a coming-of-age story in which the protagonist, Frankie Addams, struggles with problems of awakening sexuality, racial prejudice, and death. Frankie desperately wishes to accompany her brother and his fiancée on their honeymoon, believing that such an act will alleviate her loneliness and enable her to discover what she terms "the we of me." *The Square Root of Wonderful* was considered one of McCullers's least successful works, but provides insight into her life and techniques. Many critics viewed the play as McCullers's attempt to reconcile feelings of loss, guilt, and hostility resulting from the death of her husband and mother.

Critical Reception

Critical assessment of McCullers's relatively small literary canon remains uneven and somewhat inconsistent. Among her four novels, one novella, several plays, and more numerous short stories, *The Heart Is a Lonely Hunter, The Ballad of the Sad Café,* and *The Member of the Wedding* stand as the high spots of her oeuvre. In these works protagonists struggle with challenges such as loneliness, adolescence, sexual discrimination, and failure to meet societal expectations. McCullers also incorporated themes of racial injustice, spiritual deprivation, and emotional exile into her stories. Because of these realistic themes critics have been divided in classifying McCullers as a realistic or romantic writer. Oliver Evans stated: "It is ironical that her gift for realism, especially in dialogue and characterization, has operated in her case less as a blessing than as a curse." Critical debate over McCullers's classification as a realist or allegorical writer continues to be a central issue for many reviewers. Many critics also feel that later works such as *Reflections in a Golden Eye, The Square Root of Wonderful,* and *Clock Without Hands* do not reach the standard of excellence established early in her career; the last was completed while she was gravely ill. Though her strongest works have received comparison with Flaubert and Faulkner, McCullers's preoccupation with the aberrant and sensational has prompted critics to speculate on the limitations of her ability and intellectual depth. Oliver Evans wrote: "I do not think I overstate the case when I say that Carson McCullers is probably the best allegorical writer on this side of the Atlantic since Hawthorne and Melville." In the hierarchy of great American writers, McCullers shares enduring distinction among the preeminent figures of the Southern literary tradition, including her contemporaries Eudora Welty, Flannery O'Connor, and Katherine Anne Porter.

PRINCIPAL WORKS

The Heart Is a Lonely Hunter (novel) 1940
Reflections in a Golden Eye (novel) 1941
The Ballad of the Sad Café (novel) 1943
The Member of the Wedding (novel) 1946
The Ballad of the Sad Café: The Novels and Stories of Carson McCullers (novels and short stories) 1951
The Square Root of Wonderful (drama) 1958
Clock Without Hands (novel) 1961
Sweet as a Pickle, Clean as a Pig (children's poetry) 1964
The Mortgaged Heart: The Previously Uncollected Writings of Carson McCullers (short stories, poems, sketches, essays) 1971

CRITICISM

Rose Feld (review date 16 June 1940)

SOURCE: "A Remarkable First Novel of Lonely Lives," in *The New York Times Book Review,* June 16, 1940, p. 6.

[*In the following review, Feld provides brief character descriptions and a plot synopsis of* The Heart Is a Lonely Hunter.]

No matter what the age of its author, ***The Heart Is a Lonely Hunter*** would be a remarkable book. When one reads that Carson McCullers is a girl of 22 it becomes more than that.

Maturity does not cover the quality of her work. It is something beyond that, something more akin to the vocation of pain to which a great poet is born. Reading her, one feels this girl is wrapped in knowledge which has roots beyond the span of her life and her experience. How else can she so surely plumb the hearts of characters as strange and, under the force of her creative shaping, as real as she presents—two deaf mutes, a ranting, rebellious drunkard, a Negro torn from his faith and lost in his frustrated dream of equality, a restaurant owner bewildered by his emotions, a girl of 13 caught between the world of people and the world of shadows.

From the opening page, brilliant in its establishment of mood, character and suspense, the book takes hold of the reader. "In the town there were two mutes, and they were always together," Miss McCullers begins, and at once this unique novel swings into action. One of these mutes was the fat, greasy, ungainly Greek, Spiros Antonapoulos, who worked in his cousin's fruit store and made candy for him; the other was John Singer, who was employed as an engraver in a jewelry store. They lived together in two rooms, bound to each other by the physical handicap which made them alien in a world of normal people.

With a touch reminiscent of Faulkner but peculiarly her own, Miss McCullers describes their strange relationship, the fat Greek, greedy for food, petulant, mentally irresponsible, dominating the slender, gentle Singer. When the public habits of Antonapoulos become such that he is a menace to public decency, his cousin has him put away in an institution for the insane and John Singer is left alone, lost and stranded among people who talk.

Exiled from the home he and the Greek had made for each other, Singer takes a room in the Kellys' boarding house and arranges to have all his meals in Biff Brannon's New York Café. The few things he needs to get over to people he writes in careful script on cards he carries with him. Accustomed to living in a world of silence, he neither expects nor wants companionship of those who live in a world of sound. Deepest in his heart is the yearning for the departed Antonapoulos.

With stinging subtlety, Miss McCullers builds up the growing importance of Singer in the lives of the people who come to know him. So excellent is her portrayal, so fine her balance of the imagined against the real, that there are times when the reader himself is bemused by the silence and the smile of the mute. In developing Singer as the fountainhead of understanding and wisdom, she plunges into the heart of human desolation, into the pain of the ineffectuality of words as a bridge between people. Sitting silently in Biff Brannon's restaurant, lost in his dreams of the two rooms where Antonapoulos had cooked, smiling vaguely as he plans his vacation visit to the incarcerated Greek, Singer becomes a symbol of godliness. Saying nothing, it is assumed he knows

everything. His smile is gentle, built of his own loneliness and because he cannot defend himself against the spate of words forced upon him, he listens with eyes fixed sympathetically upon moving lips.

From the opening page, brilliant in its establishment of mood, character and suspense, [*The Heart Is a Lonely Hunter*] takes hold of the reader.

—Rose Feld

To Biff Brannon, lost in a world of emotional fears, Jake Blount is a crazy drunkard who uses his education to rant against the inequality between the rich and the poor. To Singer, Blount is a strange, unkempt creature who talks continuously of things Singer doesn't fully understand. But Singer listens or seems to and his smile is gentle. For Biff himself, Singer has the fascination of the unknowable.

To his daughter, Portia, cook at the poverty-stricken Kelly boarding house, Dr. Benedict Mady Copeland is a man who has strayed from the fold of the true church and will suffer for it in spite of his aid to the sick. To Singer he is the colored physician who talks passionately about the subjugation of his race. To her family Mick Kelly is a good kid who takes care of her younger brothers and goes off by herself when she is free of them. To Singer she is the little girl who comes to his room to talk about her dreams of music, who pours herself out to the man who sits and smiles and nods as he reads her lips. To all of them, through no fault or virtue of his own, except that of simplicity and kindliness, Singer becomes the one creature in their lives who can give them peace and understanding.

With powerful strokes Miss McCullers paints the details of the lives of these people and those they touch. She is squeamish neither of word nor incident and her canvas is alive with the realities of their existence, more often savage and violent than tender. Her imagination is rich and fearless; she has an astounding perception of humanity which goes with equal certainty into the daily life of a drunken social rebel like Jake Blount and into the dreams of the music-hungry, lonely Mick Kelly. The effect is strangely that of a Van Gogh painting peopled by Faulkner figures. That it is the degenerate Spiros Antonapoulos, greedy for sweets and vicious in an infantile way, who actually dominates the lives of the characters through his influence on John Singer, serves to heighten the terrific force of her story.

Carson McCullers is a full-fledged novelist whatever her age. She writes with a sweep and certainty that are overwhelming. *The Heart Is a Lonely Hunter* is a first novel. One anticipates the second with something like fear. So high is the standard she has set. It doesn't seem possible that she can reach it again.

Joseph Frank (review date July-September 1946)

SOURCE: "Fiction Chronicle," in *The Sewanee Review,* Vol. LIV, No. 3, July-September, 1946, pp. 534-39.

[*In the following brief review, Frank discusses the plot and characters of* The Member of the Wedding, *noting McCullers' potential as an important developing writer.*]

Politics is left completely behind when we enter the enchanted—or shall we say, rather, topsy-turvy world of F. Jasmine Addams, the twelve-year-old adolescent of Carson McCullers' *The Member of the Wedding.* Nominally, the book centers around the emotional turmoil and confusion of an adolescent girl in the twilight period when the anarchy of tom-boy childhood has ceased, but the somewhat more decorous life of girlhood has not yet begun. Frankie Addams, caught in this period, is not a "member" of anything; and so she decides that, at her brother's wedding, she will become a "member" of the bridal party and travel away with them. But the wedding itself takes up only a few brief pages at the close of the book. Most of it is occupied by Frankie, dreaming her fantastic daydreams, talking and playing cards with her six-year old cousin, John Henry West, and with the Negro maid, Berenice Sadie Brown. At the conclusion of the book, after Frankie has been forcibly detained from leaving with the bride and groom, she forgets all about this incident and, with a new girl friend, adores Michelangelo and reads Tennyson. The twilight period has passed and she is now a "member."

Most critics, considering the book merely as the study of an adolescent girl, have found it interesting and well-done but not particularly new—adolescents, it seems, have become a drug on the fiction market. In general, this judgment is correct if one limits oneself to the book's main theme; but the really important part of the book is a quality of sensibility which, as a matter of fact, the main theme is too weak to support. Miss McCullers is fascinated by the revolting and the perverse to an almost morbid extent; in searching for detail, she invariably picks out something like this (she is describing Frankie's impressions of a carnival): "The Wild Nigger came from a savage island. He squatted in his booth among the dusty bones and palm leaves and ate raw living rats. . . . The Wild Nigger knocked the rat's head over his squatted knee and ripped off the fur and crunched and gobbled and flashed his greedy Wild Nigger eyes." John Henry West, with "a little screwed white face" and "tiny gold-rimmed glasses," who covered the wall of the kitchen with drawings

that make it look like a "crazy house," is a little monster; and Frankie herself, slinging butcher knives around when she gets mad, and calmly cutting the sole of her foot open to take out a nail, is not exactly one's idea of an average American girl, even an adolescent. This quality of sensibility in Miss McCullers, in the context of the present book, adds up to very little because it remains unfocused and purposeless. What it might add up to in the future, however, may possibly be seen in the character of the Negro maid, Berenice Sadie Brown, where the grotesque becomes almost sublime by being endowed with a human warmth absent in the other people, who seem to be sleep-walking rather than living. For all her absurdity, Berenice is a profoundly impressive character. If Miss McCullers can continue to create similar ones and, like Dostoyevsky, place them in a situation where their very grotesqueness takes on symbolic value, American literature may find itself with a really important writer on its hands.

Wolcott Gibbs (review date 14 January 1950)

SOURCE: A review of *The Member of the Wedding*, in *The New Yorker,* Vol. XXV, No. 47, January 14, 1950, pp. 44, 46, 49.

[*In the following review Gibbs praises the theatrical production of* The Member of the Wedding, *but faults the attempt to condense the entire novel into a three-act play.*]

The Member of the Wedding, Carson McCullers' dramatization of her novel, is unquestionably the first serious new play of any consequence to reach Broadway this season. It has a good many touching and rather difficult things to say; it often has a queer, fantastic wit, not unlike Saroyan's; occasionally it reaches something very close to poetry; and it is illuminated by a magnificent performance by Ethel Waters and two remarkably spirited ones by Julie Harris and a seven-year-old boy named Brandon De Wilde. In spite of all this, however, I'm afraid that the piece at the Empire isn't entirely satisfactory from a theatrical point of view. The principal trouble, I think, is that Mrs. McCullers has tried to transfer her book too literally to the stage; to crowd, that is, the whole mysterious desperation of adolescence into three acts, along with a fairly exhaustive discussion of the complicated theme of race relations in the South. The result is a curiously uneven work—sometimes funny, sometimes moving, but also, unfortunately, sometimes just a trifle incoherent and shapeless.

The heroine of *The Member of the Wedding* is a rather plain twelve-year-old girl who is known to an insensitive world as Frankie Addams, though she prefers to think of herself as F. Jasmine Addams, and she lives with her widowed father and their old Negro cook, Berenice Sadie Brown, who has one bright-blue glass eye, in a small town in Georgia. Frankie has a great deal on her mind (at twelve, for instance, she is five feet five and three-quarter inches tall and at the rate she's going she is gloomily certain that she'll hit a good ten feet by the time she's twenty-one), but the real root of her unhappiness is her terrible sense of being alone, separate from everybody else in the world, both children and adults. Primarily, this feeling is a symptom of her age, but as it happens she really hasn't much of a social life, since the slightly older girls in the neighborhood have banned her from their club, and her only companions are Berenice and a cousin some six years her junior, who is moderately silly even as little boys go. At this point, when Frankie's need to attach herself to something or somebody is almost unbearable, her brother drops in with his fiancée. They seem to her the two most beautiful people who ever lived, and she decides to join them on their honeymoon, which she vaguely pictures as a triumphal tour around the world, going on forever. Berenice, who has had a wide experience with matrimony, tries to explain that membership in weddings is customarily limited to two, but Frankie's dream of being part of something at last, especially something that promises to be not only strange and lovely but also infinitely removed from Georgia, is too strong for cynical arguments like that, and she goes ahead with her plans, which include the purchase of a red evening dress, cut right down to the waist in the back. In the end, of course, she is left behind, and though the bridal pair do their best to spare her feelings, for a time she is desolate, even to the point of attempting suicide. Sad as it is, this disillusionment has the effect of putting an end to Frankie's childhood, and in the last scene we find her reasonably adjusted to her surroundings, being, in fact, about to go for a ride on a moving van with a young football player and his girl.

Mrs. McCullers has a peculiar gift for creating characters immune to the usual rules of human behavior.

—*Wolcott Gibbs*

Mrs. McCullers has a peculiar gift for creating characters immune to the usual rules of human behavior, and it is possible to accept the fact that Frankie can be an almost total biological ignoramus while living in a circle where practically nothing else is ever discussed, and while herself employing most of the popular terminology. She is not exactly a girl who will bear examination in retrospect, but in her presence I was bewitched by her and saw no reason at all to suppose that wedding bells and sex would have any vulgar association in her mind. Miss Harris may be overplaying this part a trifle from time to time, once to the extent of introduc-

ing a cartwheel into it, but on the whole I admired her performance and concur in the general opinion that she is one of the most talented young actresses around today.

The two other major figures in the play are also very fascinating, if not quite so original in design. Berenice was absolutely happy with her first husband, but he died and since then she has been trying to console herself with the "bits and pieces" of him that she has found in other men. She serves chiefly as a contrast to Frankie's inexperience and as her only refuge in her distress. This is obviously a role with disastrous possibilities, but the writing, except in one or two places, is free from bathos, and Miss Waters' interpretation is a miraculously balanced combination of rowdy humor and sorrowful understanding. The cousin, played by young De Wilde, struck me as one of the few completely believable little boys ever put on the stage, and I felt a strong sense of personal loss when Mrs. McCullers, for rather arbitrary reasons, decided to kill him off in her last act.

The racial subplot, which, as I say, seems to me only to confuse and diminish the play, however much it may have been an organic part of the novel, has to do with a young mulatto, Berenice's foster brother, who knifes a white man while under the influence of marijuana and subsequently hangs himself in jail. His abrupt and violent end, coinciding with the cousin's death from meningitis, provides *The Member of the Wedding* with a lively, if lugubrious, conclusion, but somehow it also introduces an element of contrived melodrama out of keeping with the delicate mood that has been so successfully sustained throughout most of the evening.

The cast, brilliantly directed by Harold Clurman, also includes William Hansen, Harry Bolden, Henry Scott, and James Holden. I can't remember a more engaging group of supporting players, and Lester Polakov's set, presumably representing a typical Georgia kitchen, would astonish Jeeter Lester with its neat and airy look.

John Mason Brown (review date 28 January 1950)

SOURCE: "Plot Me No Plots," in *Saturday Review of Literature,* Vol. XXXIII, No. 4, January 28, 1950, pp. 27-9.

[*In the following review of the theatrical version of* The Member of the Wedding, *Brown discusses the differences between the play and the novel.*]

On the fifth day of each November bonfires are lighted in London in honor of the discovery of a plot. And Beefeaters, with their lanterns raised, search the basement of the Houses of Parliament as if they still expected to find Guy Fawkes hiding there, with a slow burning match in his hand, ready to set off the powder kegs which would elevate King James I even higher above his subjects.

The story of Guy Fawkes is known to everyone. But between our vague knowledge of his share in this conspiracy and the detailed plan which he and his associates had evolved for carrying it out lies the reason for history's having identified the events with which he is connected, not as the Gunpowder Story, but as the Gunpowder Plot.

Even in the theatre the same distinction can be made. For, strictly speaking, the plotting of a play is not the story upon which that play is founded, or the story that it tells, but the manner in which a particular dramatist, due usually to his times no less than to his personality, has chosen to advance it. It is not those things that happen in a play, but the when, why, and how of their happening.

It is the dramatist's plan of action, his blueprint of events, his mechanical distribution of his fable into acts and scenes. It is the bony structure underlying whatever flesh and blood his characters may boast, the skeleton which makes his play organic and dictates its movements. It is the dramatists's scheme not only for putting his people to the test of deeds or crises but also for arranging, introducing, illustrating, emphasizing, developing, and concluding the basic idea or situation around which he has built his play.

The foregoing paragraphs were written by me several years ago. They appeared in a book called *The Art of Playgoing.* I fall back on them now because Carson McCullers's dramatization of her novel, *The Member of the Wedding,* is an interesting illustration of the differences between plot and story.

Common speech becomes uncommon in Mrs. McCullers's usage of it. Her marshaling of words is no less individual than her approach to her characters. She employs the language lovingly to give color and nuance to her unique perceptions.

—*John Mason Brown*

Mrs. McCullers's study of the loneliness of an overimaginative young Georgian girl is no ordinary play. It is felt, observed, and phrased with exceptional sensitivity. It deals with the torturing dreams, the hungry egotism, and the heartbreak of childhood in a manner as rare as it is welcome. Quite aside from the magical performances its production includes, it has a magic of its own. The script shines with an unmistakable luster. Plainly it is the work of an artist, of an author who does not stoop to the expected stencils and who sees people with her own eyes rather than through borrowed spectacles.

Common speech becomes uncommon in Mrs. McCullers's usage of it. Her marshaling of words is no less individual than her approach to her characters. She employs the language lovingly to give color and nuance to her unique perceptions. But, though she tells a story, and a very moving one at that, she does so with as little reliance upon plotting as if her aim had been to obey the command of the Citizen in "The Knight of the Burning Pestle" who cried, "Plot me no plots."

A lot happens in *The Member of the Wedding,* that is if you consider its separate incidents and what the average playwright would make of them. Frankie, the young girl who is Mrs. McCullers's central character, dreams of going off with her brother and his bride on their honeymoon. When she learns that they do not want her she runs away from home and comes near to committing suicide with her father's pistol. The little boy who lives next door is stricken with meningitis and dies. And Berenice, the Negro cook at Frankie's dilapidated house, hears first that her no good foster brother has slashed the throat of a white man with a razor, and then that, after his capture, he has hanged himself in jail.

Though she touches upon these last two tragedies, Mrs. McCullers does not build them up. Instead, she throws them away, treating them with a wasteful casualness. Even when dwelling at length upon Frankie's delusive obsessions about the wedding and the honeymoon, she avoids developing them dramatically in the usual fashion. Character and mood are her substitutes for plot. And admirable and absorbing substitutes they prove to be when she is writing at her best.

Galsworthy's contention was that a human being is the best plot there is. "A bad plot," he said, "is simply a row of stakes with a character impaled on each—characters who would have liked to live but came to untimely grief." Certainly, Mrs. McCullers's characters are not impaled upon such a row of stakes. Three of them, the girl Frankie, the Negro cook, and the young boy, are as vividly drawn as any characters to have come out of the contemporary theatre.

If, in spite of its fascination and distinction, Mrs. McCullers's play ultimately fails to live up to its high promise, the reason is certainly not her choosing to dispense with plotting, as plotting is ordinarily understood. Healthily, the theatre has grown more and more away from the tawdry contrivances and the delight in artifice for artifice's sake upon which it doted at the century's turn. It has done this in the interest of freedom no less than of truth, done it because both audiences and playwrights have come to realize that the conflicts within individuals possess a greater dramatic value than the prefabricated crises which were once the theatre's mainstay.

The well-made play, with all of its table-thumpings, "plants," big scenes, carpentry, and curtain lines, is nowadays completely out of fashion. Pinero, Jones, and Sardou are very dead indeed. Chekhov's influence is far stronger than that of Ibsen, the master builder. Accordingly, Mrs. McCullers's plotlessness demands no readjustment because it comes as no surprise. It finds her following a tradition most of us like and respect. It is an indication of her probity, a proof that she is writing as an artist.

Considering how fine are the fine things in *The Member of the Wedding,* the pity is that Mrs. McCullers's play lacks inward progression. It is more static than it needs or ought to be. Its virtue is its lack of contrivance, but its shortcoming is its lack of planning. Salty and sensitive as is the delineation of its major characters, they do not develop; they stand still. Some of the scenes in which they appear are written as if they were "sketches." This is particularly true in the last act, the three scenes of which are as unsubstantial as Mrs. McCullers's ten subsidiary characters. Among these even Frankie's widowed father, who could do much to explain the mental instability of his daughter, is a mere wrath. He is as unreal as the three characters who interest Mrs. McCullers are real.

A wise old woman once insisted that she liked bad children best of all. When asked why, her answer was, "They are always sent out of the room." There are quite a few moments when one comes uncomfortably near to wishing the same fate would overtake Frankie. She is a disconcerting young egoist, shrill and excitable, who feeds on dreams and is strayed for affection. Her boyishness is aggressive and almost pathological. Her language is as tough as her mind is naive. She is unpopular with children of her own age and unmanageable in her own household. Her only friends are her cousin, the droll little boy who lives next door, and the wise, earthy, much-married, and all-mothering Negro cook who takes care of her.

Towards the evening's end Frankie has apparently passed through her difficult phase. She has begun to care about clothes and to be cared for by her contemporaries. In the person of a young football player she has even found her "Greek god." She remains, however, an egotist. She is unaffected by her cousin's death, and untouched by moving to another neighborhood and having to take her leave of the cook. If the sun has begun to shine for Frankie, the darkness of being alone, forgotten, and, without hope is enveloping the cook.

What redeems Frankie from the audience's point of view is the heart-stabbing honesty with which her distress, her fancy, and her loneliness are captured both by Mrs. McCullers in her writing and by Julie Harris in her playing. Miss Harris pulls no punches. She does not spare herself or try to prettify Frankie. Her hair is cropped forlornly. The red satin evening dress she buys for her brother's daytime wedding is the sorriest and most saddening costume any actress has had the integrity to wear in years. Miss Harris's is a brilliant performance. It is as sensitive as Mrs. McCullers's insight into people who are strays from the pack. Brandon De Wilde, who plays the bespectacled youngster from next door, is beguilingly free from self-consciousness. He is a manly little individualist, as much at home behind the footlights as if he were actually hanging around someone's kitchen, hoping for a cooky and begging for attention.

As the cook, Ethel Waters demonstrates once again how exceptional are her gifts. No person in our theatre glows with such goodness. Miss Waters's smile is spirit-lifting and cloud-dispelling. Her laugh is one of the most agreeable sounds known to this planet. So is her voice. Her dignity is no less innate than her benevolence. Moreover, she is an actress whose emotional range is wide. If her heart seems to smile in moments of happiness, her face when downcast achieves true tragic grandeur.

Harold Clurman has never done a better job as a director than with *The Member of the Wedding.* He has staged it with beauty, humor, and perception. He has not only assembled an excellent cast but has shown himself to be alert to every shading of an unusual script. The result is an evening as uncommon in its quality as it is radiant in its merits.

Hubert Creekmore (review date 8 July 1951)

SOURCE: "The Lonely Search for Love," in *The New York Times Book Review,* July 8, 1951, p. 5.

[*In the following review, Creekmore faults McCullers' later works for not measuring up to the standards of her first novel,* The Heart Is a Lonely Hunter.]

The appearance of an "omnibus" of Carson McCullers' work should be a signal for an estimate, much fuller than can be attempted here, of her achievement in fiction. The three novels of this highly praised young author were reviewed on publication; the novella of the title [*The Ballad of the Sad Café*] and the six short stories appear in book form for the first time. Together, they indicate a specialized talent for a sharp, controlled, revealing style of fiction which since its debut has, by narrowing the field of observation, never matched the quality of the first novel.

The Heart Is a Lonely Hunter is more abundant in emotion and appeal, more complex and varied in character and development, more concerned with human reality, broader in all dimensions than any of the later work. After it, *The Member of the Wedding,* from which the successful play was made, seems a more delicate and extended treatment of a section of the first novel. The parallels are obvious: Mickey and Frankie are daughters of widowed watchmakers, their households and experiences are similar, and their emergence from childhood-adolescence much the same. If it seems a long footnote to *The Heart Is a Lonely Hunter*, at the same time it shows the increase of a humorous tenderness in Mrs. McCullers' writing; but along with it, a tendency to digression, notable in the rhapsody of Frankie's walk about town.

Reflections in a Golden Eye, in spite of the cool clarity and ease of the prose, remains a freak, not only in its characters but in the fact that it fails to make human beings of the characters, and their actions fail to reveal any commentary on or resolution of the theme. The fine balance of neuroses typical of her work has here become intensified and purposeless, leaving only the balance of prose, and ends with no more moral-artistic effect than an exhaustive news report.

The six short stories, interesting enough in their way though not important work, are like variations on the constant theme of loneliness. Only **"Madame Zilensky and the King of Finland,"** an amusing anecdote, manages somewhat to escape the theme. **"The Jockey"** gives a glimpse of loneliness for a friend. **"A Domestic Dilemma"** exposes the loneliness of a breaking marriage, an "immense complexity of love." Beyond the theme of separation and loneliness, however, there are in these stories other hinted, symbolic revelations.

The novella, *The Ballad of the Sad Café,* suggests that Mrs. McCullers is working toward a fusing of her anguished major theme with the warm humor so well used in *The Member of the Wedding.* Yet the anguish turns into despair, for it is shown that, regardless of the object of love, the beloved hates the lover. Miss Amelia, the manlike cafe owner, who never loved anything but her hunchbacked cousin Lymon, is forced into a triangle with her former husband, Macy, who, loving her, has let her drive him to ruin. Fleeing her love, Lymon shows in the culminating first-fight that he prefers to be spurned by Macy, and they go away together.

The structure and writing of this work, imitating ballad simplicity, often fall into archaic self-consciousness—"So do not forget this Marvin Macy, as he is to act a terrible part in the story which is yet to come"—and like *The Member of the Wedding* this novella seems too attenuated. It has, however, its own queerly ingratiating tone, an outstanding quality in much of Mrs. McCullers' work—a dreamy unreality not altogether created by the strange characters. Possibly this forecasts later fiction in which the integration and humanity of her first novel may merge with the gentle humor and sympathy for eccentric types which pervades the later work.

Frank Durham (essay date Autumn 1957)

SOURCE: "God and No God in *The Heart Is a Lonely Hunter*," in *South Atlantic Quarterly,* Vol. LVI, No. 4, Autumn, 1957, pp. 494-99.

[*In the following essay, Durham discusses the plot of* The Heart of a Lonely Hunter, *praising the allegorical aspects of the novel and its rebellion against religion and tradition.*]

That *The Heart Is a Lonely Hunter* is to be interpreted on more than one level of meaning is undeniable. Carson McCullers herself has called her first novel a "parable in modern form"; and, while reviewers do not take very seriously her statement as to the meaning of this parable, practically every one realizes the importance of symbolism in the book. One critic even went so far as to write that "Carson McCullers is ultimately the artist functioning at the very loftiest symbolic level . . ."

If, then, *The Heart Is a Lonely Hunter* is symbolic, what exactly is the symbolic intent? Mrs. McCullers has called it "the story of Fascism," presenting "the spiritual rather than the political side of that phenomenon," but this interpretation is not shared by many of her readers. Most see the theme as that of human loneliness and the individual's attempts to break through the barriers separating him from other human souls. This is certainly the major theme of the novel and of the corpus of Mrs. McCullers's work. But in *The Heart Is a Lonely Hunter* there is, it seems to me, an ironic religious allegory employed to reinforce the author's concept of the discreteness of human beings, not just from each other, but from God Himself. I call it an allegory because I find an almost continuous presentation of this religious thesis throughout, developing and growing through the narrative, as well as in "accidental" (in the Spenserian sense) symbols which serve to highlight this thesis. The anonymous reviewer in *Time* suggested, without full development, something of this religious allegory when he said, "The book is . . . a study in the relationship of human Christs and semi-Christs to a suffering world. . . ." And the sacrilege of the irony implicit in Mrs. McCullers's idea seemingly frightened another reviewer into asking tentatively if she is symbolizing something larger than is apparent.

The religious pattern in the novel involves a kind of pyramidal relationship of six people, though the quartet who form the base are unaware of either the existence or the importance of the one at the apex. These characters, going from apex to base, are Antonapoulas, the spoiled, self-centered Greek mute; John Singer, also a mute and rather an ascetic; Mick Kelly, the twelve-year-old girl who hears music in what she calls her "inside room"; Jake Blount, a half-mad anarchist; the Negro Dr. Copeland, who struggles for his race; and Biff Brannon, the impotent and frustrated cafe proprietor. The last four find their God-image in Singer, who, unknown to them, finds his in the Greek.

The figure of Singer is central. Yet in the opening sections of the novel, before Singer meets his four "visitors," the reader sees him in a position of dependence upon Antonapoulas, with whom he shares a small apartment. When the two walk, "The one who steered the way was an obese and dreamy Greek." Alone together, they find happiness; but it is Singer who does the "talking" in sign-language, with the Greek signaling only an occasional "'Holy Jesus,' or 'God,' or 'Darling Mary,'" and stuffing himself with food and drink. "Singer never knew just how much his friend understood of all the things he told him. But it did not matter." He must tell them. His whole existence is wrapped up in the hedonistic, childish, whimsical Greek, and when the latter is to be sent away to a lunatic asylum, Singer is in a frenzy. His hands are busy telling Antonapoulas all he must say, "all the thoughts that had ever been in his mind and heart, but there was not time." The Greek listens drowsily, leaving Singer ignorant of the success or failure of his attempt at communication.

Once the Greek is gone, Singer is desolate, changing his lodgings, walking restlessly. Now he keeps his hands hidden in his pockets; his means of intimate communication is never used with his "visitors." Finally exhaustion sets in, "and there was a look about him of deep calm. In his face there came to be a brooding peace that is seen most often in the faces of the very sorrowful or the very wise." Throughout the rest of the book, unknown to the others, he lives only for his visits to the asylum, where he is greeted indifferently by Antonapoulas, who evinces interest only in his friend's expensive gifts. Only in the presence of the Greek does Singer reveal his hands and bare the secrets of his heart. Just before the final visit Mrs. McCullers tells what Antonapoulas has meant to Singer:

> Behind each waking moment there had always been his friend. And this submerged communion with Antonapoulas had grown and changed as though they were together in the flesh. Sometimes he thought of Antonapoulas with awe and self-abasement, sometimes with pride—always with love unchecked by criticism, freed of will. When he dreamed at night the face of his friend was always before him, massive and wise and gentle. And in his waking thoughts they were eternally united.

It does not appear to me that Mrs. McCullers is trying to suggest an unnatural sexual relationship. Rather it is that Singer endows the Greek with Godlike qualities of understanding and finds solace through the confessional and through the serving of his God. Once the Greek's nod to a nurse "seemed one of benediction rather than a simple nod of thanks"; and Singer's dream of the Greek definitely attributes to him God-like qualities. This dream passage is filled with both phrases and imagery of a religious nature. In the dream, yellow lanterns illumine dimly

a dark flight of stone steps. Antonapoulas kneeled at the top of these steps. He was naked and he fumbled with something that he held above his head and gazed at as though in prayer. He himself [Singer] knelt half-way down the steps. He was naked and cold and he could not take his eyes from Antonapoulas and the thing he held above him.

Behind Singer and on the ground kneel the four others, and "he felt their eyes on him. And behind them there were uncounted crowds of kneeling people in the darkness." Singer's hands are windmills, and he is fascinated by "the unknown thing that Antonapoulas held." Suddenly there is an upheaval of crashing steps, and Singer falls downward. Here, really, the religious allegory is presented microcosmically.

That *The Heart Is a Lonely Hunter* is to be interpreted on more than one level of meaning is undeniable. Carson McCullers herself has called her first novel a "parable in modern form"; and, while reviewers do not take very seriously her statement as to the meaning of this parable, practically every one realizes the importance of symbolism in the book.

—*Frank Durham*

This religious theme is made more evident in the relationships Singer has with Mick, Jake, Dr. Copeland, and Biff. At first sight of the mute, each is drawn inexplicably to him. All seem to share Biff's feeling about him.

> The fellow was downright uncanny. People felt themselves watching him even before they knew that there was anything different about him. His eyes made a person think he heard things nobody else had ever heard, that he knew things no one had ever guessed before. He did not seem quite human.

And to Singer's room in the Kellys' boarding house goes each of the four to talk to him, to unburden innermost thoughts and hatreds and aspirations. His brooding serenity and his silent nod send each away with a feeling of assurance, of blessing, even.

When Jake, the anarchist, goes off with Singer after their first meeting and Biff has been pondering the strange attraction of the mute, it is surely not mere coincidence that Biff overhears his wife preparing as her Sunday School lesson the passage in which Jesus calls Simon and Andrew to be fishers of men: "And when they had found Him, they said unto Him, 'All men seek for Thee.'"

To Mick, Singer "was like some kind of a great teacher, only because he was mute he could not teach." She sees him, too, as "what she used to imagine God was," and she rehearses a group of words "just as she would speak them to Mister Singer: 'Lord forgiveth me, for I knoweth not what I do.'"

And with the others it is the same, though Biff maintains a little detachment and occasionally wonders just how much of what they say Singer really understands.

Aside from these four relationships, Mrs. McCullers underlines Singer as the God-image repeatedly. She more than once refers to his "Jewish face," but never states definitely that he is Semitic. In fact, she has the Jews calling him a Jew, the merchants declaring him wealthy, the textile workers thinking him a C.I.O. organizer, and a lone Turk vowing that Singer is a fellow countryman. Each sees in Singer what he wants to see. Later a Negro woman declares that Singer knows "the way of spirits come back from the dead." Also he is repeatedly giving water and wine and food to his visitors. Often as they talk he sits and moves chessmen on a board. And, if one may go slightly Freudian, this Father-God image is heightened by the fact that Singer works in a jewelry store. Mrs. McCullers's father was a jeweler.

The irony of this allegory and these symbols is, of course, that man makes God in the image of his desire. For Mrs. McCullers's Antonapoulas—God and Singer—God can neither understand their suppliants nor really communicate with them. In an unmailed letter to the Greek (for Antonapoulos cannot read) Singer reveals his bewilderment as to what his visitors seek and find in him. Of Jake Blount he says, "He thinks he and I have a secret together but I do not know what it is"; of Mick, "She likes music. I wish I knew what it is she hears. She knows I am deaf but she thinks I know about music"; of Dr. Copeland, "This black man frightens me sometimes. His eyes are hot and bright. . . . He has many books. However, he does not own any mystery books." Singer's only reading is mystery books. Biff he passes off with the comment: "he is not just like the others. He has a very black beard so that he has to shave twice daily. . . . He watches." Unlike the others, Biff seems to him to have nothing he hates or loves excessively. But Biff does have something; and Singer is not quite sure what it is the others hate and love. Later he admits to himself that "He had agreed with each of them in turn, though what it was they wanted him to sanction he did not know." We have seen that Antonapoulas did not understand Singer, as Singer was sure that he did. The muteness, then, engenders mystery, but behind the mystery lies misunderstanding—or nothing.

So Singer, on whom the other four leaned, was even more dependent than they. For when the Greek died, Singer shot himself, leaving his personal affairs in a terrible mess. When God is dead, life is over for Singer. But when their God dies, Mick and Jake and Biff and the Doctor are only changed, left baseless for a while. For each, life goes on—a different life, but life. Mick, her music a bitter memory, clerks at Woolworth's; Jake goes blundering off to preach his diatribes against capitalism elsewhere; Biff phlegmatically watches the customers in his New York Cafe and yearns for children to mother; old, sick, and broken, the Doctor alone seems defeated, and he is carried off to the country leaving the struggle for his people unfinished. But even he has the fortitude to wait for death. Without God, then, life goes on, but something—a touch of glory, a feeling of communion with an all-encompassing understanding—has gone from it.

Perhaps there is also a larger symbolic framework to this allegory of the personal relationship between the individual and his self-created God. Antonapoulas is Greek; Singer has a "Jewish face." Like the gods of classical antiquity, of paganism, Antonapoulas is whimsical, selfish, scandalous, sensual, and at the same time capable of seeming wise, of bringing consolation and reassurance to his devotee. Singer, like the Christian deity, is ascetic, reflective, withdrawn, and yet intimate. For a while the two share the same dwelling, with the Greek as the dominating spirit. Then the Greek is thrown into the discard, discredited as it were by the label of lunacy; and Singer, alone but always aware of his own dependence on the past, assumes the mantle of divinity. Then, perhaps Mrs. McCullers is saying, with the destruction of the pagan past the Christian myth derived from it collapses.

At any rate, here is the religious allegory which seems to underlie and to reinforce the theme of loneliness in *The Heart Is a Lonely Hunter.* It is not an intricately perfected allegory, and often its symbolism is fuzzy. But it does seem apparent that the author has written an iconoclastic religious novel, ambitious, sensitive, vivid, and underlaid with the rebellion against tradition not unexpected in a precocious young woman of twenty-two.

Robert S. Phillips (essay date Winter 1964)

SOURCE: "The Gothic Architecture of *The Member of the Wedding,*" in *Renascence: Essays on Values in Literature,* Vol. XVI, No. 2, Winter, 1964, pp. 59-72.

[*In the following essay, Phillips discusses how McCullers' works fit into the genre of the modern Gothic novel.*]

The Modern Gothic in American literature, the genre of the grotesque, is currently the subject of much discussion by Leslie Fielder, William Van O'Connor, Irving Malin and other critics. The novels of the South written in this century—works by William Faulkner, Truman Capote, Flannery O'Connor and Carson McCullers—are in particular classified as Gothic. A plethora of Faulkner studies have already been published. Capote and Miss O'Connor, on the other hand, are writers in mid-career. Carson McCullers, however, has produced a distinguished body of fiction during the past three decades, a corpus which is only beginning to receive a deserved recognition. The novels of Mrs. McCullers are perhaps the most typical and most rewarding exemplars of Southern Gothicism in this century. The purpose of this essay is, first, to define those themes and fictional devices which constitute Gothicism in the contemporary American novel, and secondly, to examine their particular use by Mrs. McCullers. *The Member of the Wedding* has been chosen for close study because, of all the author's fiction, it has reached the widest audience—as a novel, a successful Broadway play, as a film—and at the same time being the most misinterpreted. Other critics writing on the element of the grotesque in her works invariably examine *Reflections in a Golden Eye* and *The Ballad of the Sad Café,* two dark tales indeed, consigning *The Member of the Wedding* to the ranks of popular novels about troubled adolescence. As late as 1961, in a review which appeared in the *New York Times Book Review,* Irving Howe refers to the novel as both "sentimental" and "lovely"! This essay attempts to place *Wedding* at last in its proper context, within the world of Mrs. McCullers' Gothic imagination.

The Southern Gothic novel is characterized by violent themes; in this respect it resembles the work of Matthew Gregory Lewis, Anne Radcliffe, and other early English Gothicists whose work centered about brutality and torture. The contemporary Gothic novel is not Gothic in the sense that it widely employs the properties of tombs, dungeons, passageways, supernatural phenomena such as ghosts and fireballs, pestilential diseases and the like. However, the South has, through the multitude of nightmarish novels, taken on the symbolic overtones associated with Italy in some early Gothic novels, which Leslie Fiedler *(Love and Death in the American Novel)* has characterized as, " . . . a background of miasmic swamps, death, defeat, mutilation, idiocy, and lust continues to evoke in the stories of these writers a shudder once compelled by the supernatural."

While the symbolic backgrounds of the early Gothic novels and the twentieth-century Southern Gothic novels resemble one another at times, the narrative action differs. The active agent of terror in the eighteenth-century Gothic tale was the villain. His function was to pursue the heroine throughout the castle's vaults and labyrinths—which pursuit constituted the bulk of the plot. The modern novel for the most part no longer indulges in such melodrama. The mind of the serious artist has turned inward, and with the acknowledgement of Freudian psychology and Freud's interpretation of dreams,

the focal point of fiction has shifted from the action of the chase to the mind of the chased.

The new Gothic novels are tales of tormented souls who view the world as a maze. The problems which confront them are as complicated and terrifying as the twisted labyrinths of the Gothic castle. A typical modern Gothic theme involves rites of passage for the innocent into a violent world. The hero often is an individual who feels persecuted and inferior, and who withdraws from the actual world into a world of magnified fears and nightmares. This withdrawal results in a state of personal dissociation from society, a state of gnawing loneliness. Frequently frustrated in love, the hero either lives out his days in terrible isolation or becomes in one way or another sexually perverted, the search for a sexless, dim ideal, a manifestation of the hero's avoidance and fear of reality.

The theme of the modern Gothic novel is, then, spiritual isolation. In one of her infrequent essays (*Esquire,* Dec. 1959), Mrs. McCullers has stated her conscious concern with this theme:

> Spiritual isolation is the basis of most of my themes. My first book was concerned with this, almost entirely, and all of my books since, in one way or another. Love, and especially love of a person who is incapable of returning or receiving it, is at the heart of my selection of grotesque figures to write about—people whose physical incapacity to love or receive love—their spiritual isolation.

All Mrs. McCullers' characters are doomed to solitary confinement within the cell of self. Sometimes they make pitiful attempts at escape—as in the child Bubber's running away from home down the state highway in *The Heart Is a Lonely Hunter,* or the Negress Berenice Sadie Brown's replacing her bad eye with one of light blue glass in *The Member of the Wedding.* Such attempts to change one's situation, to avoid reality, are futile. Each is eternally isolated with his problems, like, writes Mario Praz, "the unfortunate persecuted maiden" of the Gothic novel.

Mrs. McCullers writes of a no-exit world, and it is not accidental that all her novels are set in the slow, unbearably hot and monotonous summer months when "there is nothing whatsoever to do" in a town that "is lonesome, sad, and like a place that is far off and estranged from all other places in the world," in fact, an inferno. Attempts to escape hellish isolation through communication are impossible; time and again in her novels thought and deed are misunderstood or ignored. In *The Heart Is a Lonely Hunter* the most eloquent of the characters is Singer, a deaf-mute, eloquent because only he seems to communicate comfort, to sing the soul's songs, to all who seek his company. The inclusion of a pair of mutes in the novel is not morbidity on the part of the author, as has been frequently charged; it is instead a brilliant symbolization of man's condition. Even "normal" adults in the novels cannot escape their frustrations and feelings of alienation through the process of loving or confiding in one another. Love too often is thwarted and the lover suffers all the more for his longings, a thesis which is the very basis for *The Ballad of the Sad Café.* Rather than comfort we find fear: the terror which comes from the knowledge that one is alone in an indifferent or hostile universe.

Carson McCullers' writing . . . employs Gothic elements both in theme and method. Her five novels stand . . . not merely as parables of "terror filling the vacuum left by the suppression of sex in our novels, of Thanatos standing in for Eros," but in addition they project a dark vision of the contemporary American and his "obsession with the violence and his embarrassment before love"—his isolation and failure in communication.

—*Robert S. Phillips*

This theme of the failure of love is a corollary of the Gothic theme of spiritual isolation. It is a theme which obsessed an earlier writer of Gothic stories in America, Edgar Allan Poe. Love fails because its ecstasy is an ephemeral thing. As D. H. Lawrence observed in *Studies in Classic American Literature,* "the first law of life is that each organism is isolate in itself, it must return to its own *isolation*." All the tales of Poe are, according to Praz, a "symbolical, mythological translation of the same thirst for unrealizable love and of the desire for that complete fusion with the beloved being which ends in Vampirism." The same futile quest for unity in love is a recurring theme in Mrs. McCullers' fiction. This theme illustrates Fiedler's statement about modern Gothicism in the American novel, that "the primary meaning of the Gothic romance, then, lies in its substitution of terror for love as a central theme." The figure at the center of the McCullers novel, in his confusion and desperation, is unable to find solace in another soul and therefore is terrified at his enforced solitude and inadequacy.

Other themes which relate more directly to the Gothic as it has descended from the graveyard poets can be found in Mrs. McCullers' treatment of the taboo. Homosexuality and perversion and miscegenation often are explicit in her work. Fiedler has noted that, "Our great novelists, though experts on indignity and assault, on loneliness and terror, tend to avoid treating the passionate encounter of a man and woman, which

we expect at the center of a novel. . . ." While one cannot totally agree with Mr. Fiedler, and call all American literature a Gothic literature, it is clear that the work of Carson McCullers belongs within that body of our literature which is Gothic in theme and method. Instead of romantic couples or brave heroes and heroines we find homosexuals and lesbians, flowers of evil dotting a grotesque landscape. The perverted and pusillanimous characters of McCullers experience no love affairs of permanent value. The lover is forever rebuked, unrecognized, or the subject of mistaken intentions. Often the mental unbalance of these characters is symbolized by their physical infirmity. Mrs. McCullers has told us of her characters being "People whose physical incapacity is a symbol of their spiritual incapacity to love or receive love." Her novels are highly symbolic and often nearly allegorical. Her symbolic method will be discussed shortly.

Many of the plots in Mrs. McCullers' novels abound in frightful torture scenes and violent deaths. The inclusion of such atrocities is prompted by both the central theme and the symbolic method of her work. In a sense the theme of her novels is violation—the ravaging of the spirit by a cruel universe. The inhumanity carried on in the South has given Mrs. McCullers and her regional contemporaries much to contemplate, and it is perhaps this violence and the accompanying psychological guilt which have produced the "Southern Gothic" novel. The problem of segregation serves to illustrate Mrs. McCullers' frequent theme of isolation, and the treatment received by the Negroes underscores the element of terror. Violence in the McCullers Gothic novel is functional: it serves to illustrate the world as she sees it. This is how the modern Gothic novel resembles the works of the Romantics, those writers for whom "beauty was enhanced by exactly those qualities which seem to deny it, by those objects which produce horror; the sadder, the more painful it was, the more intensely they relished it." There are horrible visions in McCullers because this is what she finds in our age, and because that is what obsesses her. It is not a long jump from the torture chamber scenes in the novels of "Monk" Lewis to the white-supremist inspired atrocities in her fiction. The wandering of the McCullers heroine from one frightful scene to another is a parallel to the plot of the early Gothic novel. If her novels seem sensational as a result, I suspect her intentions have in part been realized. The modern Gothic novel is sensational because it is written, at least partially, to be didactic, to shock the reader into recognition. In the concluding paragraph of William Faulkner's most terrible and Gothic novel (*Absalom, Absalom*) the hero, when asked why he hates the South, insists: "I don't hate it *I don't. I don't. I don't hate it! I don't hate it!*" The Southern Gothicist writes about mutilation and awful sin because that is what deeply concerns him about his region. Another Southerner whose sensationalism is often called lurid is Tennessee Williams. In an introduction to one of Mrs. McCullers' novels, Williams has stated that the modern Gothicist uses symbols of the grotesque and the violent "Because a book is short and a man's life is long. The awfulness has to be compressed." He sees the American Gothic novel linked to the French Existentialist novel, with the common denominator being "a sense, an intuition, of an underlying dreadfulness in modern experience." It is this dreadfulness in our quotidian lives that has been the primary theme of Mrs. McCullers' five novels.

Mrs. McCullers often adopts Gothic properties as a means of projecting this awful image of the world. The presence of an ominous setting, the casting of a spell of melancholy and dread, through descriptions of decay and torture, are sometimes important in her craft. Many of the Southern Gothicists employ the decaying plantation manse in place of the ruined castle as symbol of the collapse of an order. This fall of the Old South is equivalent to the character's sense of loss and insecurity, his dissociation. Mrs. McCullers' fictional method for the most part, however, employs the Gothic as an element rather than a controlling situation or definite setting. We should therefore look not so much for actual fallen mansions in her work, but rather for the metaphorically fallen mansions, the disorder and insecurity and lack of moral center which so disturb the minds of her Southern characters. These characters are so tormented that they feel compelled to perform such actions as Jake Blount's driving a nail through his outstretched palm *(Lonely Hunter),* Sherman Pew's hanging his friend's dog by a clothesline *(Clock Without Hands),* and Alison Langdon's cutting off her nipples with garden shears *(Reflections in a Golden Eye).* These are violent actions and often the criticism is raised that McCullers' novels contain too many such scenes. Yet the frenzied pitch of the Gothic plot, often drawing upon sadistic and masochistic emotions, helps project the particular vision which is Mrs. McCullers' world. She has obviously felt the need to employ the terrible world of the Gothic to find images and actions of adequate emotional impact, just as the Marquis de Sade justified the "new novel" of Europe in his time:

> For those who knew all the miseries with which scoundrels can oppress men, the novel became as hard to write as it was monotonous to read. . . . It was necessary to call hell to the rescue . . . and to find in the world of the nightmare . . . images adequate to "tell the history of man in this Iron Age."

One of the means by which Mrs. McCullers conveys the sense of a nightmare world is through her gallery of grotesque characters. The background of her novels is seldom the recognizable South, with a normal pattern of activities. Her world is populated with abnormal beings. It is in this symbolic method that she literally calls "hell to the rescue" and creates a nightmare vision. The physical deformity of her characters serves to symbolize their isolation, since freaks are singular beings not acceptable to our society. Freaks of course have long been stock characters in Gothic tales: the hunchback, the scar face,

the Frankensteinian monsters which endanger the body and spirit of the beholder are familiar nightmare constituents. Among those naturally deformed, Mrs. McCullers' characters include two deaf mutes, two hunchbacks, two giant-sized women, a chinless girl, several deformed babies, and numerous ruptured and impotent men. Others of her characters are deformed by man's violence: the negroes Willie and Wagon both have their legs sawed off; Sherman Pew is shocked into a permanent speech impediment; Lon Baker's throat is slit from ear to ear. There are also natural diseases which distort the spirit as well as the body: three cases of cancer, leukemia, a diseased ovary, a paralyzed hand—all found among her cast of characters in five novels.

These unfortunate, persecuted characters reveal the author's obsession with the classic problem of evil. This problem, as posed by the unknown author of the Book of Job, and by other religious thinkers, is the question: Given a good Creator, how can there be evil in the creation? Time and again in Mrs. McCullers' fiction we find good people who suffer and are overcome by their suffering. John Singer, of *Lonely Hunter,* is an upright man who is afflicted with muteness, and whose only love object is removed by death. Mick Kelly, of the same novel, wishes to become a great musician, but is forced by family poverty to work in a five-and-ten. In this sense a good many of the Gothic characters in the McCullers canon are grotesque in form only: repulsively hunchbacked or frightfully oversized, but inwardly not evil. The original Gothic novels employed grotesquely featured people as personifications of the evil in the world; Mrs. Shelley's monster was ugly because he performed ugly deeds and caused others to suffer. Mrs. McCullers' monsters, however, are ugly because their appearance is a projection of their internal suffering. Instead of being the menacers, they are the menaced; instead of the victimizers, they are the victims. Hugo McPherson notes in an article which appeared in *Tamarack Review,* "her characters, like Kafka's and Truman Capote's, are the ill-prepared and the ill-equipped; they seek not victory over life but a secure haven, and the struggle is not a glory but an almost unbearable violation of the self."

These deformities or illnesses so affect the unfortunate characters that they withdraw into the world of self. Such loneliness and frustration are portrayed in another set of characters as well. Supplementing the freaks in her novels are the self-conscious adolescents. Members of this group are equally isolated, belonging neither to the child's world or the adult's. Mrs. McCullers sees the figure of the groping adolescent as another symbolic realization of our life of fear. Writes Fiedler, "The child's world is not only asexual, it is terrible: the world of fear and loneliness, a haunted world." To this group belong Mick Kelly, Frankie Adams of *Member of the Wedding,* and Sherman Pew of *Clock Without Hands.* A third classification of characters in the novels is those belonging to minority groups, the violated Negroes and persecuted Jews who suffer in their segregation and torment.

The author's chief characters possess an ambiguous and troubled sexuality. Some are asexual, like Miss Amelia of *The Ballad of the Sad Café.* The boy-girls of adolescence go by names like "Mick" and "Frankie," names that characterize their neuter nature. Others are inverted sexually, their deviation further isolating them from the normal world. These adult sexual deviates are plagued by their perverse wills and long to experience the normal love which is not open to them. In her first novel, Biff Brannon is impotent, thus incapable of any active sexual activity—normal or devious—which could afford him gratification. In Biff's case, the result is the development of strong feelings for young children, feelings both paternal and maternal. John Singer, Captain Penderton of *Reflections in a Golden Eye,* and Jester Clane of *Clock Without Hands,* are all bisexual; these characters of conflicting male-female emotions can be compared to the androgynous mythological figure of Tiresias. The figure of the wandering spirit, blind and yet seeing, torn between the opposing sides of a dual nature, personifies the frustrated characters of McCullers. There is something frightening about these, their abnormal actions, their secret desires. In this respect the androgynous figures in her novels implement the feeling of dread, being both "sexless and lascivious" and a part of the Gothic machinery.

We have illustrated that the actions of these sexually thwarted souls are often violent. Especially so are the several attempts at self-emasculation of the male, de-sexualization of the female. There are also attempts at self-crucifixion. Not all of the characters take such drastic physical action. Some simply sit and daydream in a state of somnambulant lethargy, or are visited by terrible nightmares. Several have necrophilistic visions, haunted by dreams of beautiful babies rotting in their tiny coffins. Others are drawn in horrified fascination to the caskets of dead relatives, lingering more out of curiosity than sympathy. Surely these are Gothic scenes, and Mrs. McCullers spares no detail. The ruminations of Alison Langdon on the death of her child in *Reflections in a Golden Eye* are typical:

> for a long time she had been obsessed by the sharp, morbid image of the little boy in the grave. Her horrified brooding on decay and on that tiny lonely skeleton had brought her to such a state that at last, after considerable red tape, she had had the coffin disinterred.

There are terrible death scenes in the novels, especially the deaths of Lon Baker, Uncle Charles, and John Henry. The supernatural is suggested in one novel, and miscegenation spelled out in another.

Just as the castle's dungeon was the prevailing setting for the English Gothic novel, many scenes drawn by Mrs. McCullers are similarly oppressing sites. Jail houses figure symbolically in several of the novels, and the trapped occupants are representative of man's fate. These jails are described as dark, vile, and inescapable. Freak shows and asylums also are used with similar effect.

Carson McCullers' writing, then, employs Gothic elements both in theme and method. Her five novels stand, as Mr. Fiedler has pointed out, not merely as parables of "terror filling the vacuum left by the suppression of sex in our novels, of Thanatos standing in for Eros," but in addition they project a dark vision of the contemporary American and his "obsession with the violence and his embarrassment before love"— his isolation and failure in communication. In their search for identity which becomes inwardly directed, these characters are like the heroines of the Gothicists, whose flights were from "out of the known world into a dark region of make-believe." Having failed to understand man's inhumanity to man and their own personal dissociation, her characters resort to daydreaming, and are plagued by horrible nightmares— a fate far worse than physically battling the rigors of the universe; for as Fiedler exclaims, "The final horrors are neither gods nor demons, but intimate aspects of our own minds." The minotaur in the labyrinth of self is not easily overcome.

Leslie Fiedler has stated in *An End to Innocence* that "images of childhood and adolescence haunt our greatest works as an unintended symbolic confession of the inadequacy we sense but cannot remedy." *The Member of the Wedding* (1946) is a very intentional use of the adolescent as symbol for that sense of inadequacy and helplessness. The novel's title refers to Frankie Addams, a sensitive and fearful child whose thirteenth summer is the subject of the novel. The cast of characters is very small—Frankie primarily associates with only two other people—and the book is a study of her loneliness and isolation. Frankie's fears are the fears of all human beings, and the last name of Addams indicates her archetypal function in her initiation into worldly knowledge. The self-chosen nickname of Frankie (like the name Mick Kelly) is a feeble effort on the part of the adolescent to assert her individuality in a patriarchal culture, as is the crew cut which makes her a neuter being.

The summer during which the novel's action occurs is described as "the summer of fear," and Frankie is plagued by many nightmares and terrible visions. It is for this reason that the novel can be called Gothic, and not because there is "a female homosexual romance between the boy-girl Frankie and a Negro cook" as Fiedler so glibly conjectures. One dream which frightens Frankie is of a beckoning door which slowly begins to open and draw her in. What lies beyond that door— maturity, truth, knowledge—is a mystery to her, and she is frightened by the unknown. Frankie is afraid of her own growth. Having grown four inches in the past year, she towers above her classmates and is fearful that she will become "a lady who is over nine feet high. She would be a Freak." Frankie visits the carnival's Freak House, and has been terrified by the knowing eyes of the grotesques she sees there: "it seemed to her they had looked at her in a secret way and tried to connect their eyes with hers, as though to say: We know you." Frankie feels the grotesques have recognized her own freakish and guilt-ridden soul.

The Freak House is not the only place that frightens the girl: "the jail had scared and haunted her that spring and summer." She also feels the ghastly looking prisoners "know her" for what she is—and that she too is trapped, though she is free to move about and they are not. The very existence of the jail house haunts her: "the criminals were caged in stone cells with iron bars before the windows, and though they might beat on the stone walls or wrench at the iron bars, they could never get out." Frankie imagines herself so trapped, and her confidante, Berenice Sadie Brown, reveals to her that it is the human predicament.

A third house she visits which terrifies her is the residence of Big Mama, an old fortune-telling Negress said to possess supernatural powers. Though Frankie fears her she turns to Big Mama's powers in her search for answers to the ultimate question of human suffering and death, the problem of evil. But Frankie is not satisfied with the answers Big Mama gives her, and she is left with her feeling of "the sense of something terribly gone wrong."

Running away from one frightening scene only to encounter another, Frankie is the Gothic heroine encountering the chambers of horrors. In the course of the summer she is haunted by three gruesome deaths of acquaintances. These deaths are described by Mrs. McCullers in very graphic terms, the verbal intensity matching the strong impressions made upon Frankie's mind. The first of these is the unmotivated murder of the Negro boy, Lon Baker, in the alley directly behind her father's jewelry store:

> On an April afternoon his throat was slashed with a razor blade, and all the alley people disappeared in back doorways, and later it was said his cut throat opened like a crazy shivering mouth that spoke ghost words into the April sun.

The silent flapping mouth of Lon's throat parallels Frankie's own inarticulate attempts at communication.

The death of her Uncle Charles is more immediate to Frankie, and his ghastly passing pricks her awareness of mortality and her own insignificance in the cosmos. She fears death:

> He lay in the bed, shrunken and brown and very old.
> Then his voice failed and when he tried to talk, it

was as though his throat had filled with glue, and they could not understand the words. He looked like an old man carved in brown wood and covered with a sheet. Only his eyes had moved, and they were like blue jelly, and she had felt they might come out from the sockets and roll like blue wet jelly down his stiff face. She had stood in the doorway staring at him—then tiptoed away, afraid.

Again Frankie is aghast not only because of the pain involved in dying, but also because of the hopeless inability of the dying to communicate to the living.

The greatest shock however comes with the death of John Henry, her only young friend. Sickly and frail, John Henry in his confinement had become associated in Frankie's mind with her own isolation. The two of them seemed to share the same condition as recluses and even outcasts. With the loss of this rapport, Frankie finally feels any meaning to her life has vanished. All that remains is the spirit of John Henry which seems to visit her. Sitting in the kitchen she "felt his presence there, solemn and hovery and ghost-gray." Time and again she is to recall his torturous death:

> John Henry had been screaming for three days and his eyeballs were walled up in a corner, stuck and blind. He lay there finally with his head drawn back in a buckled way, and he had lost the strength to scream. He died the Tuesday after the Fair was gone.

This last statement reveals much of what Frankie has had to learn. After the fair—the brief pleasantries of life—comes the blackness of death. But *The Member of the Wedding* is more than a novel of one girl's initiation; it is impossible to read the account of John Henry's death and still regard the work as a charming account of adolescence as many critics have done. In its cataloguing of death scenes the novel plays upon the reader's fear of death and the dead, a characteristic theme of Gothic novels.

The story's action primarily occurs in a setting which is ominous and depressing to the heroine. There is no dank dungeon in the novel—but the kitchen of the Addams home is a place of confinement and dread for Frankie. Spurned by the other girls because of her unusual size, Frankie finds herself continually sitting in the dark kitchen whose very walls she hates. The kitchen is Frankie's private hell, "a sad and ugly room," and Frankie often feels she will go berserk if she has to remain there any longer. Indeed the kitchen is like "a room in the crazy-house," because John Henry has covered the walls with queer and childish drawings which run together in confusion: "The walls of the kitchen bothered Frankie—the queer drawings of Christmas trees, airplanes, freak soldiers, flowers." Such varied drawings make the walls a projection of the world itself, a microcosm of the macrocosm. Frankie in her confinement seems to sense this, staring at the walls and commenting that "the world is certainly a small place." Life is hell for the adolescent Frankie; she feels there is no escape from her fate, and she hates her environment, thinking she "lived in the ugliest house in town," viewing the sunshine as "the bars of a bright, strange jail." Such imagery clearly reveals the author deliberately giving us another trapped, suffering and helpless female within a Gothic framework, every bit as anguished as Alison Langdon of *Reflections in a Golden Eye,* her most overtly Gothic novel.

Frankie Addams' problem is that same sense of spiritual isolation which blights all the McCullers characters: "Between herself and all other places there was a space like an enormous canyon she could not hope to bridge or cross." Frankie has felt neglect and isolation to the point that she wails, "I am sick unto death." Her height of course symbolizes her alienation from her peers. She not only is excluded from the girls' club because she is bigger and seems older than the rest, but she has also been ejected from her father's bed which she used to share as a child. Frankie feels the eternal outsider. She cries in anguish over her plight:

> All other people had a *we* to claim, all others except her. When Berenice said *we,* she meant Honey and Big Mama, her lodge, or her church. The *we* of her father was the store. All members of clubs have a *we* to belong to and talk about. The soldiers in the army can say *we,* and even the criminals on chain-gangs. But the old Frankie had no *we* to claim.

Frankie watches the soldiers who travel in loud groups about the town, and envies their strong camaraderie (as does Captain Penderton in *Reflections in a Golden Eye*).

Spurned by her father and the girls her age, Frankie seeks solace in the company of John Henry, her little cousin. This relationship is unsatisfactory, since John Henry is too young to share many of her interests. Frankie's feelings for him are partly motivated by her quest for a father-figure, since her own father is too busy running his jewelry store. John Henry partially fills this gap in her life, and Frankie thinks he looks "like a tiny watchmaker."

The third major character, Berenice Sadie Brown, feels the burden of the color of her own skin, symbolized by her last name. She brings to Frankie her pessimistic philosophy of man's fate, telling her all mortals are caught in a trap:

> I'm caught worse than you is. Because I am black. Because I am colored. Everybody is caught one way or another. But they done drawn completely extra bonds around all colored people. They done squeezed us off in one corner by oneself. So we caught that

first way I was telling you, as all human beings is caught. And we caught as colored peoples also.

Berenice concludes simply by remarking of mankind, "They were born . . . and they going to die." Frankie ponders her new knowledge of mortality as well as her increasing catalog of sexual facts and realizes that she must protect John Henry's innocence, to keep him a child as long as possible. She not only pities John Henry because he is sickly; she also pities him because in the doomed John Henry she sees herself: "He looked at her with eyes as china as a doll's, and in them there was only the reflection of her own lost face." John Henry provides a narcissistic image for Frankie, as did Antonapoulos for Singer, in *The Heart Is a Lonely Hunter.*

Frankie also resembles Mick Kelly of *Lonely Hunter,* being troubled by sexuality. Throughout the novel Frankie skirts the periphery of sexual experience, and there are five acts of sexual initiation contained in the novel, each more personal than the last. Frankie's adolescence is spent running away from sex, just as the Gothic heroine flees from her seducers. Frankie refuses to believe those "nasty lies about married people" told by the girls in the club. She had had a physical contact with a male and it caused her much mental anguish:

> In the MacKean's garage, with Barney MacKean, they committed a queer sin, and how bad it was she did not know. The sin made a shriveling sickness in her stomach, and she dreaded the eyes of everyone.

Her sexual experiences of the summer culminate when a drunken soldier tries to seduce her in a dark room over the Blue Moon Cafe. She fights with her assailant and manages to knock him unconscious with a bottle. She flees the scene and for weeks is possessed by the fear she has killed a man. Frankie does not undergo a complete sexual initiation through intercourse, as does Mick Kelly, whom she so greatly resembles in all other respects. But Mick is more aggressive and has more natural curiosity. Frankie's flight from sexuality is both mental and physical. When she does find someone to love, it is not a teen-age boy, but rather the artistic Mary Littlejohn. Frankie is fascinated by Mary's Catholicism, unknown and Papal affiliations intriguing her: "This difference was a final touch of strangeness, silent terror, that completed the wonder of her love." The fear of Catholicism and the Catholic ritual was, of course, the basis of a number of the earliest Gothic romances.

Frankie clings to Mary because she does not think she will ever be loved by, or be able to love, a man. Mary is a little John, then, a surrogate male lover. In *The Member of the Wedding* Mrs. McCullers first introduces her theory of love, a theory which received full treatment in her succeeding book, *The Ballad of the Sad Café.* Berenice rambles on to Frankie about the unpredictable nature of man in choosing a beloved:

I have knew mens to fall in love with girls so ugly you wonder if their eyes is straight. I have seen some of the most peculiar weddings anybody could conjecture. Once I knew a boy with his whole face burned off so that . . .

Here Mrs. McCullers tells us that in matters of love the appearance of the beloved is of no more moment than the reciprocity of the emotion. The important thing is the release from isolation which the act of loving gives to the lover. Yet we find in *The Ballad* that the lover suffers all the more through his attempts to escape loneliness in this way. Even Berenice has suffered as a result of her seemingly perfect union with Ludie Freeman. Since his death she has felt a terrible void: "Sometimes I almost wish I had never knew Ludie at all. It spoils you too much. It leaves you too lonesome afterward." Ludies was not a "freeman" at all; being mortal, he too had to die and cause grief to his beloved.

Berenice's search for love parallels Frankie's, though in a later stage of life. She possesses the worldly knowledge that Frankie lacks. The blue glass eye she has bought gives her a "two-sighted expression," which is the physical symptom of her psychic perception. The experience of four marriages contrasts with Frankie's innocence. Berenice's last three marriages have left her unsatisfied. She hysterically calls out for Ludie Maxwell Freeman. These subsequent marriages were desperate attempts to replace him. She marries Jamie Beale because he has a mangled thumb like Ludie. She marries Henry Johnson because he wears Ludie's pawned greatcoat. "What I did," confesses the miserable Berenice, "was to marry off little pieces of Ludie whenever I came across them. It was just my misfortune they all turned out to be the wrong pieces."

Both Frankie and Berenice have one opportunity for momentary escape from their dreadful *ennui* and frustration. The announcement of a wedding for Frankie's older brother Jarvis excites their imaginations, especially Frankie's. Love-hungry, she decides that she will join her brother and his bride and travel to Alaska with them, away from the heat and confinement of the South. Mrs. McCullers, like Hemingway, uses the snowy North as a symbol for escape to a pristine and pure ideal.

A wedding of course is a joining of lives, the creation of a new family. Frankie above all else has needed a close family experience. As a bridesmaid, she would finally be a member of something, a member of the wedding, and would be given identity and purpose. Frankie's plan to join the young couple on their honeymoon is doomed for failure, as are all fantastic plans for escape in the five McCullers novels. Frankie is totally unrealistic in her plans, thinking the move will end all her worries: "We will have thousands of friends, thousands and thousands and thousands of friends. We will belong to so many clubs that we can't even keep track of all of them." She fails to realize she must work out her own future without the couple as a crutch.

From beginning to end the wedding is a nightmare. The chance never comes for Frankie to announce her intentions, and she has to be bodily dragged from the car when she tries to cling to the newlyweds on their departure. After Frankie returns home she concludes that though the wedding has not provided an escape, she will still leave town. Her feelings of isolation are intense that evening as she slips out into the streets. The alleys are gloomy and she imagines the long dark car she sees to be that of a terrible gangster. Alone and frightened, she prays for company: "There was only knowing that she must find somebody, anybody, that she could join with to go away. For now she admitted she was too scared to go into the world alone."

The frail heroine alone in the night—again we find the typical Gothic situation. Frankie is isolated and always will be. The trip around the world with Mary Littlejohn is merely another pipe dream like that of the wedding. On this point I cannot agree with Ihab Hassan, who sees the novel's (*Radical Innocence,* 1961) conclusion as optimistic and Frankie's actions "a final affirmation of youth's resilience." Hassan sees Frankie as moving "beyond the acrid feeling that the world has cheated her." This does not seem to be the case at all. Both Frankie's mother and John Henry are dead, and Berenice deserts her to marry for a fifth time in her never-ending search for fulfillment. Berenice's departure signals the total collapse of Frankie's "family" (just as the cook Verily's leaving the senile judge in *Clock Without Hands* creates a void in the life of a white person dependent upon a black). Frankie will continue to be an overly tall, self-conscious and unloved person in the years to follow.

There is a miniature parable contained in this novel. The restless organ grinder and his monkey, forever wandering like minstrels throughout the book, are representative of humanity: "They would look at each other with the same scared exasperation, their wrinkled faces very sad." The novel is sad indeed, but the Gothic method of the author intensifies the grief and terror. "The life which she creates is not the raw documentary of experience that has dominated American fiction since the twenties, but life as the imagination apprehends it, rich in atmosphere but stripped of non-essentials," agrees Hugo McPherson. Universally proclaimed a novel of tender adolescence by the critics, *The Member of the Wedding* provokes frightening responses in the reader which for too long have been overlooked. With its moribund setting, fear of sexuality, terrifying death scenes, dark dreams and nightmares—even touches of fear of Catholicism and the supernatural—the novel is yet another manifestation of the author's Gothic vision. It is also the novel which best stands comparison with

Mrs. McCullers' undisputed masterpiece, *The Heart Is a Lonely Hunter.*

Joseph R. Millichap (essay date January 1971)

SOURCE: "The Realistic Structure of *The Heart Is a Lonely Hunter,*" in *Twentieth Century Literature,* Vol. 17, No. 1, January, 1971, pp. 11-17.

[*In the following essay, Millichap discusses the structure and genre of* The Heart Is a Lonely Hunter.]

Carson McCullers produced before her death in 1967 a small but impressive body of fiction: *The Heart Is a Lonely Hunter,* 1940; *Reflections in a Golden Eye,* 1941; *The Member of the Wedding,* 1946; *The Ballad of the Sad Café,* 1951; *Clock Without Hands,* 1961; and twelve short stories published between 1936 and 1967. Her career was marked by successes, both popular and critical, and by controversy. The controversial aspects of her work become apparent in even a cursory examination of the criticism concerned with it. Conflicting opinions regarding the interpretation of individual works, the value of her overall achievement, and her place in American literary history abound. Some commentators compare her favorably with Faulkner, others judge her a failure; some find in her work a stark realism, others a Gothic romanticism. This latter critical dichotomy has created an unresolved problem in the analysis of her fiction. The present article demonstrates through structural analysis the psychological and social realism of *The Heart Is a Lonely Hunter,* her most typical and successful novel.

The Heart Is a Lonely Hunter is the focus of the debate over the realistic versus the romantic, or Gothic, aspects of Carson McCullers' work. Most critics have interpreted the novel as an allegory, a Gothic romance, or a fable (or some combination of these types) and insisted on the absence of any social interest. Chester Eisinger's remarks are typical: "A peripheral matter in this novel [*Heart*] is the way in which Mrs. McCullers treats social problems." Ihab Hassan deems the novel a failure because its form does not connect social man and individual man. Yet one of the most influential studies of the genre, Leslie Fiedler's *Love and Death in the American Novel* characterizes Mrs. McCullers' first novel as " . . . the last of the 'proletarian novels,' a true Depression book."

These critical differences can only be resolved through a careful analysis of the novel's structure, though *Heart* certainly presents many structural difficulties. First, its third person omniscient point of view is complicated by its assimilation into the viewpoints of four major characters (Biff, Mick, Blount, and Copeland), who in turn become the central intelligences of individual chapters. The other chapters, dealing with Singer and Antonapoulos, remain very definitely third person. This arrangement raises a question: Who is the protagonist of the novel? No single character appears capable of claiming that distinction. Singer stands at the center of the grouping of characters, but he remains almost as enigmatic to the reader as to his fellow lonely hearts. Mick is the most fully developed individual, yet she had little insight into her own or others' problems. Biff has the clearest vision and the last word, but in his observer's role he functions only as a minor element of plot structure. The action of the novel, in fact, is not centered on any one individual; it involves the social group, both the central characters and the whole mill-city society.

The structure of the novel is tripartite. Part One introduces style, character, setting, plot, and theme through the depiction of the Singer-Antonapoulos relationship, its disintegration, and Singer's subsequent involvements with the other characters. Part One also establishes the fundamental tension between the personal and the social worlds, as the central human relationship is mirrored in the social lives of all the other characters. And finally Part One of *Heart* serves as an introduction to what Mrs. McCullers called "the general web of the book." Part Two contains the major plot development; it completes the web. Part Two comprises fifteen chapters: five centered around Mick, three around Copeland, two each around Blount and Biff, with three summary or "legendary" chapters. This part covers exactly one year from July, 1938 to July, 1939; during this interval the characters are seen to evolve through an elaborate though coherently structured series of events, which are carefully interconnected to form the plot. Here the author achieves a more complex picture of the mill-city and its inhabitants which stresses social problems and their foundation in the individual personality. The greater scope of the section allows Mrs. McCullers to consider those particular social ills which plague her characters: Blount provides a connection with economic exploitation, Copeland with racial prejudice, Mick with the alienation of youth. The threads of each character's development are woven into a tapestry depicting Southern society at the end of the Depression. Flashbacks are used to provide a sense of movement in time. These movements are almost always used to underline the character's connections with social difficulties, for example Jakes' background in the poverty of Gastonia, N.C., another mill-city. The central position of Singer never allows the personal sources of these problems to escape consideration.

Part Three demonstrates the reactions of the characters to the death of Singer and stresses through irony their inability to solve both personal and social problems. This part of the novel consists of four chapters, one each for Copeland, Blount, Mick, and Biff. The chapters also represent the four parts (Morning, Afternoon, Evening, Night) of one day, August 21, 1939. Part Two is patterned after the natural cycle of the year; in

Part Three the smaller cycle of the day lends meaning to the action by emphasizing the end of summer, the decline of both men's fortunes and of the year. The microcosmic social world of the mill-city erupts in the unbridled hatred of a race riot, while the larger world, the macrocosm, teeters perilously on the brink of total war. In the conclusion of this section, humans plumb the nadir of their conditions. Mrs. McCullers had created a confused, brutal world, shown a momentary order in it, destroyed that order, yet in the very destruction, in the very moment of despair, shows us the foundation of a possible order in the tragic revelations of defeat. The four chapters are arranged to demonstrate this meaning; they move from the character with the least understanding and hope to the one with the most. Perhaps the personal and social disorder of the future can be avoided by an implementation of the knowledge produced by tragedy. The formal device which lends force to this apocalyptic vision is the reversal of the order of Chapters Two through Five of Part One: as the characters formed their connections with Singer, so are they disengaged.

The development is almost linear, with a few flashbacks used to fill in the historical bases of social problems and the corresponding connections of past with present in the lives of the characters. Although structurally simple, this method allows much complexity of development of themes and characters. The novel resembles classics of American realism like *Winesburg, Ohio* and *The Grapes of Wrath* in this basic structure.

The pattern of character relationships is much more complicated. The simple image of a circle or wheel (used in both the text of the novel and Mrs. Cullers' "Outline") seems to represent the relationship of the major characters to Singer. Shortly after Christmas they all visit him simultaneously, creating a scene which dramatizes the central pattern of the novel, a scene in which the characters move in a mime of their customary actions. Copeland stands in the doorway; Mick listens to music on the radio; Blount opens a bottle of beer; Biff smiles and observes. But there is no communication, and Singer is bewildered by their sudden silence. They regard each other suspiciously, exchange a few hostile questions, then generalize about the weather, and finally leave hurriedly. The few things they do say are directed at Singer rather than to each other. "Their thoughts seemed to converge in his as the spokes of a wheel lead to the center hub." But the mute realizes, at least unconsciously in a later dream, that the pattern resembles a pyramid:

> Out of the blackness of sleep a dream formed. There were dull yellow lanterns lighting up a dark flight of stone steps. Antonapoulos kneeled at the top of these steps. He was naked and he fumbled with something that he held above his head and gazed at it as though in prayer. He himself knelt halfway down the steps.

He was naked and cold and he could not take his eyes from Antonapoulos and the thing he held above him. Behind him on the ground he felt the one with the mustache and the girl and the black man and the last one. They knelt naked and he felt their eyes on him. And behind him there were uncounted crowds of kneeling people in the darkness. His own hands were huge windmills and he stared fascinated at the unknown thing that Antonapoulos held. The yellow lanterns swayed to and fro in the darkness and all else was motionless. Then suddenly there was a ferment. In the upheaval the steps collapsed and he felt himself falling downward. He awoke with a jerk. The early light whitened the window. He felt afraid.

Singer plays John the Baptist to Antonapoulos's Christ. Yet Antonapoulos looks upward also, at some unknown object which he holds above his head and regards with a prayerful attitude. This object is the cross which the Greek wears around his neck on a red ribbon. Later Singer is reminded of the dream when he sees the cross, the one thing that Antonapoulos treats with a veneration like that which he receives from Singer. The presence of the cross at the apex of this pyramid of stupid devotion indicates that religion has little relevance for modern society, a favorite theme in Proletarian fiction. The dream reveals the final emptiness inherent in the total situation, and the dream's collapse prefigures the destructive failure of everyone's dreams at the conclusion of the novel.

The most apt figure might be a three-dimensional rendering of the pyramidal image as a solar system in which there are a number of complementary orbits. Antonapoulos and his cross are at the exact center of the system. Singer is in orbit around him; the others revolve about Singer, and even they have their satellites in the minor characters who relate to them. The narrative relates the creation of this complex system and its disintegration. In a final sense the pattern of the action becomes cyclical: the characters move from disillusionment to hope to disillusionment, and, perhaps, to hope again. No matter what image is employed, it must be combined with the linear progression of time in the novel to demonstrate the connection of the personal and social worlds. In the timeless world of the heart the characters are involved in a complicated pattern; in the changing social world they are a part of inexorable historical movements. The whole novel exists as a complex figure of their combination.

Style functions organically with structure. A "legendary" style adds a timeless quality to Chapter One, helping to establish the archetypal nature of the events narrated. This style reoccurs in each of the key chapters concerned with Singer and Antonapoulos. The other chapters (2-5 of Part One; 1-6, 8-14 of Part Two; 1-4 of Part Three) employ styles related to the central personality of the chapter. Chapter Two of Part One for example, is centered about Biff Brannon, although other characters are introduced in it. The narration changes as the section opens; the "legendary" style ends, and a flat, objective, factual style begins, a style analogous to the character of Biff Brannon, the observer. Mrs. McCullers planned a different style for each of the main characters.

> There are five different styles of writing—one for each of the main characters who is treated subjectively and an objective, legendary style for the mute. The object of each of these methods of writing is to come as close as possible to the inner psychic rhythms of the character from whose point of view it is written.

The legendary style of Chapter One, which has much of the "once-upon-a-time" quality of fable or romance, depicts human isolation and its causes on a generic level. Though succeeding chapters supply realistic details and anchor the story in an actual place and time, this opening section creates an aura of the timeless world of the imagination, the soul, the interior self. The world of the mutes remains separate from the town which surrounds them, for it is in actuality the changeless realm of the human heart. In telling the story of Singer and Antonapoulos, Mrs. McCullers essentially concerns herself with love, the universal search of the human heart for fulfillment. But soon a social background emerges from the shadows of the unconscious mind. At this point the reader becomes aware of the city, the social milieu in which Singer's search must be conducted.

> The town was in the middle of the deep South. The summers were long and the months of winter cold were very few. Nearly always the sky was a glassy, brilliant azure and the sun burned down riotously bright. Then the light, chill rains of November would come, and perhaps later there would be frost and some short months of cold. The winters were changeable, but the summers always were burning hot. The town was a fairly large one. On the main street there were several blocks of two and three-story shops and business offices. But the largest buildings in the town were factories, which employed a large percentage of the population. These cotton mills were big and flourishing and most of the workers in the town were very poor. Often in the faces along the streets there was the desperate look of hunger and of loneliness.

In her outline of the novel, Mrs. McCullers locates the city on the Chattahoochee River in western Georgia, in effect identifying it as her home town, Columbus. The city is a symbolic type of the culture produced by industrialization—a world of decay, deprivation, and loneliness. Blount's place of employment, the Sunny Dixie Show (the irony of the name is obvious), becomes the major example of setting used symbolically. A tawdry place of entertainment and escape appro-

priate to this world, the show is a combination of an urban wasteland and a mechanical nightmare.

> The motionless wooden horses were fantastic in the later afternoon sun. They pranced up statically, pierced by their dull gilt bars. The horse nearest Jake had a splintery wooden crack in its dingy rump and the eyes walled blind and frantic, shreds of paint peeled from the sockets. The motionless merry-go-round seemed to Jake like something in a liquor dream.

The flying-jinny, or merry-go-round, symbolizes the meaningless and oppressive round of mechanical activities associated with modern urban civilization.

The Heart Is a Lonely Hunter stands as an impressive achievement, particularly for a young writer. It provides a critical perspective for viewing Mrs. McCullers' other works, and perhaps for the whole expanse of modern Southern fiction.

—Joseph R. Millichap

The city in the novel is not specifically identified; it might be any Southern mill-city and becomes representative of the industrialized and urbanized South, or America, or the whole modern world. It is still a realistic picture of a specific place, however, and a knowledge of the South and its history adds to the appreciation of the narrative. The description of the city emphasizes its social problems, and the choice of characters allows the narrative to develop them at some length. Jake Blount, for example, observes the results of economic exploitation in the section of mill houses.

> On either side there were rows of dilapidated two room houses. In the cramped back yards were rotted privies and lines of torn, smoky rags hung out to dry. For two miles there was not one sight of comfort or space or cleanliness. Even the earth itself seemed filthy and abandoned. Now and then there were signs that a vegetable row had been attempted but only a few withered collards had survived. And a few fruitless, smutty fig tress. Little younguns swarmed in this filth, the smaller of them stark naked. The sight of this poverty was so cruel and hopeless that Jake snarled and clenched his fists.

Here is the ruined garden of the new industrial world, an environment in which man finds the expression of his essential human nature extremely difficult. Cut off from a sense of community, each individual enters a dangerous inner world of dreams where he is existentially alone.

Each character isolates himself in this way; the repetition of the pattern emphasizes its generic nature. Singer presents the pattern because his communication difficulties constitute the most obvious symbols of modern alienation. The other major characters serve to connect the pattern to the society of the mill-city and to the larger world outside.

Even the minor characters demonstrate the same purpose. Harry Minowitz, for example, represents the novel's pervasive social concerns. Harry's Jewish background amplifies both the religious and social themes of the novel. His presence also raises the issue of Fascism, bringing the macrocosm of the world situation of 1939 into focus with the microcosm of the mill-city. Mrs. McCullers once commented that *Heart* is "an ironic parable of fascism," a statement which has caused critics much puzzlement. The novelist undoubtedly uses both terms in a very broad sense, meaning by the second any social system which bases its order on hatred, aggression, and human exploitation. These are the bases of the social structure in Nazi Germany and in the mill-city, and thus the "parable" is ironic. Facism in this sense can be present in any social organization because its seeds—hate, greed, and fear—are constants of the human situation. Harry himself demonstrates these characteristics. His adolescent fear of isolation made him sympathetic with Fascism.

> 'I used to be a Fascist. I used to think I was. It was this way. You know all the pictures of the people our age in Europe marching and singing songs and keeping step together. I used to think that was wonderful. All of them pledged to each other and with one leader. All of them with the same ideals and marching in step together.'

Harry's reaction to Fascist anti-semitism creates a personal chaos. His very hatred of Hitler causes him to desire to live within a militaristic society which would fight Nazism. His own physical desires lead him into the sexual exploitation of the younger Mick. Of course, all of the characters and events of the novel are part of this presentation of man's world, but Harry provides the key to the equating of mill-city with a world on the eve of war. In Harry's Jewishness Mrs. McCullers universalizes her picture of human failure through the interpenetration of all these worlds.

Careful analysis of its structure demonstrates how all elements of the novel—character, plot, style, setting, and symbol—are integrated in the larger purpose of presenting the failure of communication, the isolation, and the violence prevalent in modern society. The novel's characters demonstrate the roots of these general conditions in the nature of the individual

personality. Each person is freakishly incomplete, selfish, uncommunicative(Mrs. McCullers' original title, "The Mute", might have been intended as a plural form), immature, sexually frustrated, and essentially alienated from their society. The symbolization of these difficulties on a personal level often approaches the Gothic—for example, the freak as Everyman. However, a concurrent emphasis is placed on the accurate social depiction of these characters. No communication can exist when each person creates only a self-centered and self-deluded view of the world around him. But a society composed of such individual parts will drive man further into himself. Bound in the prison of his isolation and tortured by the pains and shocks of life, man attempts to escape from this condition into an imagined world of perfect fulfillment. This search for personal realization must necessarily be social because he must communicate with and love other human beings. Man's social world is imperfect because of personal failings, and his personal existence is painful because of the tension between self and an imperfect society.

In Carson McCullers' *The Heart Is a Lonely Hunter,* this paradoxical condition is explored through the symbols provided by a particular society—a small mill-city in the American South immediately before World War II. A knowledge of its social setting is helpful in understanding the novel's psychology, but the book also explains particular historical situations and events as manifestations of universal human conditions. The novel's analogues in Southern fiction are readily apparent: the alienated characters of Wolfe, the disintegrating families of Faulkner, the corrupt social and political order of Warren. *The Heart Is a Lonely Hunter* stands as an impressive achievement, particularly for a young writer. It provides a critical perspective for viewing Mrs. McCullers' other works, and perhaps for the whole expanse of modern Southern fiction.

Virginia Spencer Carr (essay date 1990)

SOURCE: *"The Ballad of the Sad Café,"* in *Understanding Carson McCullers,* University of South Carolina Press, 1990, pp. 53-69.

[*In the following essay, Carr discusses events in McCullers' personal life that were incorporated into* The Ballad of the Sad Café. *The love-triangle between the characters of Amelia Evans, the hunchback Lymon, and Macy grew out of relationships in McCullers's life, according to Carr.*]

The monotony and boredom that permeated the author's life with her husband in 1939 before their move from Fayetteville, North Carolina, contributed not only to the completion of *Reflections in a Golden Eye,* but also to her novella, *The Ballad of the Sad Café,* published for the first time in 1943 in a single issue of *Harper's Bazaar*. More important to the story line of the tale than McCullers's southern discomfort, however, was her predicament in New York in 1940 and 1941. She had hoped for a committed relationship with her new friend Annemarie Clarac-Schwarzenbach, having fallen deeply in love with her, but it became apparent to McCullers soon after their involvement that nothing further would develop.

To suffer in despair was her destiny as a mortal, she reasoned, turning once more to fiction to express what she saw as her truths. Although McCullers had been working for many months on a manuscript that she referred to as "The Bride and Her Brother," its design and technique had not yet revealed themselves to her (a metaphysical experience McCullers described later as "the grace of labor"). She realized while in the nurturing environment of her native Columbus that she could put off no longer the strange tale of thwarted love that had grown out of her tangled relationships with her husband and her Swiss friend. That winter she wrote her editor (Robert Linscott) that passion and tension in her life were necessary if she were to write at all, but that she needed it in smaller doses. With her husband, there had been too much tension, and passion had been replaced by disillusionment, ennui, and disgust. But now, removed physically from the two people with whom she had been most deeply involved, she found herself writing well once more. Her new tale was better than anything else she had done, she reported.

McCullers told a number of friends while she was at work on her "folk tale" during the summer of 1941 at Yaddo Artists Colony that she had written the "music" for it years earlier as a result of her experiences with people she loved. Her lyrics, however, were more recently inspired. In the first week of her stay at Yaddo, she became enamored of Katherine Anne Porter, a fellow guest and the reputed grande dame of the colony, a crush that added still another dimension to her tale. According to Porter, McCullers lost no time in making her infatuation known and followed her about the colony in the very manner in which the characters she was creating moon over one another in *The Ballad of the Sad Café*.

Although the pivotal character in the tale that McCullers was writing bears a resemblance to any number of individuals in her life (and even, to some extent, to the author herself), Cousin Lymon owes his creation, in part, to an actual hunchback whom McCullers saw in a Sand Street bar that she frequented in Brooklyn Heights when she lived at 7 Middagh Street, near the old Brooklyn Naval Yard. In her essay **"Brooklyn Is My Neighborhood,"** McCullers described him as "a little hunchback who struts in proudly every evening, and is petted by everyone, given free drinks, and treated as a sort of mascot by the proprietor." But even more relevant to his development as a character was McCullers's wry humor and sheer delight in reading and hearing recounted tales of

folk epic and classical mythology, as well as of bizarre situations found within her contemporary world. Mary A. Gervin has written convincingly of certain "frames of reference" and mythic parallels between Amelia/Macy and Artemis/Orion.

Still another situation in McCullers's life found its way into her tale that summer, too: her abandonment by Reeves and his love affair with their best friend, David Diamond. McCullers wrote Diamond from Yaddo when she finished her "strange fairy tale," as she repeatedly described it, that it was for him. (Diamond, in turn, dedicated his ballet *The Dream of Audubon* to both McCullers and Reeves and set to music her recently published poem, **"The Twisted Trinity,"** yet another handling of her troubled life.) In the fictional tale, Amelia is abandoned by Cousin Lymon—whom she loves inordinately—in favor of Marvin Macy. The two men team up against her, steal her treasures, wreck her café and distillery, and leave town together.

Critic Margaret Walsh has argued cogently that *The Ballad Of the Sad Café* is not a "fairy tale" but an "anti-fairy tale," for "unlike the redeeming love of fairy tales, love in McCullers's tale is the spell that weakens the will, the enchantment that can dwarf giants"; thus to "lay oneself bare to love is to be open to disloyalty, to be meek, powerless, and defenseless, to be at the mercy of love's unpredictability."

The Ballad of the Sad Café has continued to stand up well under the scrutiny of critics. Many contend that, all things considered, it is still her best work.

—*Virginia Spencer Carr*

The twisted, ill-fated triangles that haunt the lives of McCullers's fictional characters repeatedly haunted the author in reality as well. The theme of abandonment (that had prevailed in *The Heart Is a Lonely Hunter*) is important not only to *The Ballad of the Sad Café,* but even more so to the longer work in progress that summer, the novel that eventually became *The Member of the Wedding.* McCullers finished her novella at Yaddo during the summer of 1941, then put it away for two years, intending to write two more tales of about the same length and to publish them as a trilogy in one volume. Caught up in the writing of *The Member of the Wedding,* however, she never worked on the other tales she envisioned, and *The Ballad of the Sad Café* was published in 1943 in a single issue of *Harper's Bazaar*. Eight years later, it became the title story in her omnibus collection, *The Ballad of the Sad Café and Other Works,* which included all of the long fiction published to date and six of her short stories.

The narrator of McCullers's novella maintains a relatively objective distance from the scene and situation that he (or she) describes in much the same manner as the narrator does in *Reflections in a Golden Eye.* He is not a specific character within any scene, but his commentary and subtle forewarnings function like a Greek chorus. He sees the dangers inherent in the triangle of Amelia, Lymon, and Macy, but is powerless to act. He does not pretend to know everything, but his omniscient voice sets the mood and pace of the action to follow, shifting from formal, stylized, poetic, and at times archaic, to the colorful and colloquial folk patterns of the simple mill people who frequent Miss Amelia's café.

Over the years McCullers's narrator has evoked more critical discussion than has any other aspect of the tale. Robert Rechnitz argued cogently in 1968 that the author's "childlike style" served her especially well in *The Ballad of the Sad Café,* for it enabled the narrator to hide behind a facade of childlike innocence that became a "kind of buffer to fend off what would otherwise be unbearable." A later essay, Dawson F. Gaillard's "The Presence of the Narrator in McCullers' *Ballad of the Sad Café,*" posits that the empathetic presence of the narrator makes it impossible for the reader "to distance himself from the emotional impact of the act," and that it is the oral quality of the tale and the personal balladeer's response to the café that lifts the café to mythic proportions. Critics have generally agreed that the narrator's most striking characteristic is his (or her) compassion for the three principal characters, whose traits are employed by McCullers as symbols of the moral isolation and pain to which one inevitably falls heir in the absence of any kind of meaningful communication with another human being.

Told as one long flashback, the story actually begins at the end. Unlike her first two books with their three- and four-part divisions, *The Ballad of the Sad Café* is tightly compressed into one continuous narrative that relies upon narration alone and an occasional space break to emphasize passage of time or an extraordinary turn of events.

When the reader first encounters Amelia Evans, by far the most pitiful and tragic figure in the tale, she is living alone behind boarded-up windows in a large, sagging house on the main street of a small town in what appears to be the hills of North Georgia. It is August, and "sometimes in the late afternoon when the heat is at its worst a hand will slowly open the shutter and a face will look down on the town. It is a face like the terrible dim faces known in dreams—sexless and white." The solitary Miss Amelia is a freakishly tall, pale woman whose "two gray crossed eyes" are turned so sharply inward that they seem to be exchanging with each other "one long and secret gaze of grief." Amelia is six feet two inches tall and has bones and muscles like a man's. She cares "nothing for the love of men," although she identifies with them in her labors of sausage making, bricklaying, and carpentry. The

town's only general practitioner, she doles out her homemade medicines, but is uncomfortable with women and refuses to treat any "female complaint." Like Private Williams in *Reflections in a Golden Eye,* Amelia was reared in a motherless home. She had no idea what might be expected of her in a romantic relationship and had no basis for remorse over her violent expulsion of Marvin Macy from the bridal bedchamber or of her abuse of him later. When Amelia, in turn, is abandoned by Lymon, she evokes the towns-people's pity.

The town itself is dreary and undistinguished, for "not much is there except the cotton mill, the two-room houses where the workers live, a few peach trees, a church with two colored windows, and a miserable main street only a hundred yards long. On Saturdays the tenants from the nearby farms come in for a day of talk and trade. Otherwise the town is lonesome, sad, and like a place that is far off and estranged from all other places in the world." Nature imposes itself upon the hapless people with short, raw winters and summers that are "white with glare and fiery hot." In such a godforsaken place, the "soul rots with boredom," and one's only relief, suggests the balladeer, is "to walk down the Forks Falls Road and listen to the chain gang."

In the process of telling his tale, the narrator overcomes his boredom and, as critic John McNally has carefully demonstrated, adds a meaningful dimension to his own banal existence. But the town was once quite different, and so was Amelia, insists the narrator. In addition to having been the richest woman in town, she also ran the only local general store and made the best liquor in the county from an illegal still deep in the nearby swamp. Obviously displeased over the state of affairs in the community, she was ill at ease with the rest of the townspeople because they could not "be taken into the hands and changed overnight to something more worthwhile and profitable." Amelia's indifference to others was seen most clearly in her strange, ten-day unconsummated marriage to Macy, whom she drove out of her house—and out of town—after getting him to turn over all of his worldly possessions to her. Macy's humiliation by Amelia caused him to revert fiercely to his old, cruel habits that had shocked the town and gained him notoriety throughout the state. Captured, finally, he was charged for murder and any number of shotgun robberies and sent off to the penitentiary outside of Atlanta.

The narrator explains that some eleven years have passed since that event, however, and that Miss Amelia's independence and meanspiritedness are legendary. Thus the townspeople are amazed beyond belief when a tubercular and repulsive-looking hunchback struts into town one day and claims distant kinship with her. She calls him Cousin Lymon, and overnight he becomes the focus of her world. Lymon looks like a sick pelican with his thin crooked legs, oversized head, and great warped chest, and he is described repeatedly through distasteful bird imagery. For the first time in Amelia's life she feels pity, moved first by his tears, then by love—a love that she offers freely, having intuited that the little hunchback is no threat to her sexuality. Critic Joseph R. Millichap has aptly described Lymon as "a man loved without sex, a child acquired without pain, and a companion" whom Amelia found "more acceptable than a husband or a child."

In one of the most frequently quoted passages from McCullers's entire canon, the narrator addresses mankind (and womankind) in general regarding the nature of the lover and the beloved:

> First of all, love is a joint experience between two persons—but the fact that it is a joint experience does not mean that it is a similar experience to the two people involved. There are the lover and the beloved, but these two come from different countries. Often the beloved is only a stimulus for all the stored-up love which has lain quiet within the lover for a long time hitherto. And somehow every lover knows this. He feels in his soul that his love is a solitary thing. He comes to know a new, strange loneliness and it is this knowledge which makes him suffer. So there is only one thing for the lover to do. He must house his love within himself as best he can; he must create for himself a whole new inward world—a world intense and strange, complete in himself.

McCullers's balladeer makes it clear that the lover can be "any human creature on this earth," and that "the most outlandish people can be the stimulus for love":

> A most mediocre person can be the object of a love which is wild, extravagant, and beautiful as the poison lilies of the swamp. A good man may be the stimulus for a love both violent and debased, or a jabbering madman may bring about in the soul of someone a tender and simple idyll. Therefore, the value and quality of any love is determined solely by the lover himself. It is for this reason that most of us would rather love than be loved. Almost everyone wants to be the lover. And the curt truth is that, in a deep secret way, the state of being beloved is intolerable to many. The beloved fears and hates the lover, and with the best of reasons. For the lover is forever trying to strip bare his beloved. The lover craves any possible relation with the beloved, even if this experience can cause him only pain.

When *The Ballad of the Sad Café* first appeared in *Harper's Bazaar,* McCullers sent a copy of the magazine to a young army private she had recently met, Robert Walden, and in the margin beside her treatise on the failure of *eros,* she scribbled in pencil: "This is true, Bob, only when you are *not* in love."

Later, McCullers insisted in her essay **"The Flowering Dream: Notes on Writing"** that the "passionate, individual love—the old Tristan-Isolde love, the Eros love—is inferior to the love of God, to fellowship, to the love of Agape—the Greek god of the feast, the God of brotherly love—and of man. This is what I tried to show in *The Ballad of the Sad Café* in the strange love of Miss Amelia for the little hunchback, Cousin Lymon." Whereas McCullers does reveal the eventual failure of *eros* and its destructive powers upon the trio in her tale, the characters achieve no redemption through *agape* (in the sense of communal affection), except for the temporal relief afforded by the café.

One could argue that McCullers's claim regarding her intentions in a work written fifteen years earlier when her emotions were deeply involved in the fiction is not wholly true. Louise Westling has pointed out that McCullers's statement that *The Ballad of the Sad Café* was intended to show the inferiority of passionate individual love to *agape*" by no means accounted "for the individual peculiarities of her characters and the sexual dimensions of their problems in love." Just as McCullers herself had experienced abject grief upon her painful discovery of the transitory nature of love and the impossibility of a lasting relationship with her Swiss friend, so, too, does Amelia suffer profoundly through her extraordinary love for Lymon, and for the café itself.

Six years after Lymon became ensconced in the café, Marvin Macy returns to town bent on revenge. The two men stare at one another with "the look of two criminals who recognize each other," and Lymon becomes instantly transformed into a spirited lover. He performs every trick he knows to get Macy's attention, while Macy, in turn, alternately ignores and insults his suitor. The strange triangle takes its final turn when Amelia is reduced to accepting the role of the frustrated lover, and this time it is Lymon who cruelly spurns *her,* choosing instead the swaggering, revengeful husband who puts up with the hunchback merely to gain an ally against his wife. Lymon flirts shamelessly with Macy, apes and insults the grieving Amelia to her face, and invites her husband to move in with them. Amelia does not rebel, knowing that if she drives her rival away, Lymon will follow. The thought of being alone again, having abandoned the last vestige of her strident independence to the dwarf, is intolerable. The narrator intercedes at this point to declare that "it is better to take in your mortal enemy than face the terror of living alone." Amelia's futile efforts to regain Lymon's favor parallel Macy's former attempts to woo her. Until he courted Amelia and was mysteriously transfigured by love, Macy's meanness was legendary throughout the region.

A bitter confrontation between Amelia and Macy is inevitable, an event that McCullers describes in mock-heroic fashion. The couple square off one evening in the center of the café before all the townspeople, who have watched the trio fearfully since the day Macy arrived. It is the dead of winter after an extraordinary snow, and there have been countless strange interruptions to nature's rhythms that the townspeople attribute to Macy. Along with other ominous signs a few hours before the fight begins, "a hawk with a bloody breast" flies over the town and circles "twice around the property of Miss Amelia." Thirty minutes after the fight commences, Amelia's advantage is unmistakable. She pins Macy to the floor and straddles him, her strong, big hands at his throat, but the hunchback intervenes. From the counter twelve feet away where he has perched to watch the fight, Lymon sails through the air "as though he had grown hawk wings," lands upon Amelia's back, and claws furiously at her neck. When the townsfolk come to their senses, Amelia lies motionless on the floor. The narrator explains that "this was not a fight to hash over and talk about afterward; people went home and pulled the covers up over their heads."

Amelia's pathetic defeat echoes the scene at the close of *Reflections in a Golden Eye,* but Amelia is not afforded the release of death. Trapped in the abyss of loneliness and isolation, she sobs fitfully "with the last of her grating, winded breath," her head in the crook of her arm. The destruction of her café and still, the theft of her worldly possessions, the sausage and grits laced with poison left behind—all mean nothing compared to the physical and spiritual decay that sets in irrevocably with the hunchback's sweeping leap. A victim of complete abandonment, the pathetic woman sits every night for three years on the front steps of her sagging house and gazes forlornly down the road upon which Lymon had first appeared. At last, in an admission of defeat, Amelia lets her hair grow ragged, and day by day her gray eyes become more crossed, "as though they sought each other out to exchange a little glance of grief and lonely recognition." Finally, she hires a carpenter to board up the premises of the café, and there is, as a result, no good liquor to be had anywhere. It is rumored that those who drink from the still eight miles away will "grow warts on their livers the size of goobers" and "dream themselves into a dangerous inward world." The rest of the townsfolk, in their boredom, have little to do except "walk around the millpond, stand kicking at a rotten stump, figure out what [one] can do with the old wagon wheel by the side of the road near the church," and as a last resort, "go down to the Forks Falls highway and listen to the chain gang." But Amelia allows herself no such relief. She does not go to the highway like the others to seek solace in the voices of the chain gang. Yet McCullers's coda, "The Twelve Mortal Men," stands as a paean to survival and a moving illustration of the power of brotherhood, even when the union is brought on by chains of bondage.

For a recording made in 1958—seventeen years after writing *The Ballad of the Sad Café*—McCullers read the final passage of the novel, the coda of the chain gang. Although her spirits were low and her health wretched, McCullers's voice

was steady and strong until she reached the final line. "Just twelve mortal men who are together," wept McCullers, her breaking voice a vital part of the recording. In her canon, the word *just* had a special connotation that heightened its irony. "*Just* is too small a word for pity," explained Mollie Lovejoy, a character she had created some fifteen years after *The Ballad of the Sad Café.* "It's like saying *just* food, *just* God."

The Ballad of the Sad Café provoked no serious attention from reviewers until its appearance in the 1951 omnibus edition. In a front-page review in the Sunday *New York Herald Tribune,* Coleman Rosenberger declared the title story "condensed and brilliant writing, which carries the reader along so easily on the waves of the story that he may not at first be aware how completely he has been saturated with symbolism." William P. Clancey, reviewing for *Commonweal,* called McCullers's work "metaphysical" and spoke admiringly of the "metaphysical fusion of horror and compassion" by the author whose "young American talent" was of the "very first order." Robert Kee informed readers of the British *Spectator* that McCullers's style had an "Olympian dispassionateness which is designed to strengthen the violence of the human emotions with which she is often concerned. It is the same sort of effect which Hardy achieved for his characters in far more clumsily contrived sentences." V.S. Pritchett insisted that McCullers was the "most remarkable novelist to come out of America for a generation" and declared that her compassion gives her characters "a Homeric moment in a universal tragedy."

In his notable argument, "The Myth of the Sad Café," Albert J. Griffith contrasted McCullers's impressive mythic imagination with that of such moderns as James Joyce, T.S. Eliot, William Faulkner, Eudora Welty, and John Updike, stressing that her fellow writers had created contemporary parallels to various well-known myths, whereas McCullers shaped "her own new myth out of primitive elements."

A strong body of feminist criticism of *The Ballad of the Sad Café,* as well as of McCullers's other works, emerged in the mid-1970s. Panthea Reid Broughton provided the first significant feminist reading, which viewed the tale as a fable that "shows us that rejecting those characters labeled as exclusively feminine bounces back on the rejecter and renders men and women alike incapable of love." Charlene Clark's study of "male-female pairs" in both *The Ballad of the Sad Café* and *The Member of the Wedding* demonstrates effectively how McCullers's aggressive females dominate the passive males with whom they are paired and that these women vent their aggression through violence as a means of dominating the men. Another notable feminist reading is Claire Kahane's "Gothic Mirrors and Feminine Identity," which treats *The Ballad of the Sad Café* as a "redefined modern Gothic fiction" and places McCullers closer to Flannery O'Connor than to any of her other contemporaries. Both Robert S. Phillips and Louise Westling have addressed Isak Dinesen's considerable influence through her tale "The Monkey" upon *The Ballad of the Sad Café.* Westling perceives a significant difference between the work of the two writers, noting McCullers's attempt to deny the feminine entirely and to allow a woman to function successfully as a man.

The Ballad of the Sad Café has continued to stand up well under the scrutiny of critics. Many contend that, all things considered, it is still her best work.

Emily Miller Budick (essay date 1994)

SOURCE: "The Mother Tongue," in *Engendering Romance: Women Writers and the Hawthorne Tradition, 1850-1990,* Yale University Press, 1994, pp. 143-61.

[*In the following essay Budick discusses how different characters in* The Heart Is a Lonely Hunter *strive to develop both verbal and sexual intercourse with others.*]

Like her predecessors in the romance tradition, Carson McCullers, in *The Heart Is a Lonely Hunter,* renders a portrait of reality more suggestive than mimetic. As with *The Scarlet Letter* and *The House of the Seven Gables* (and the tradition of sentimental fiction to which these texts are related), its subject is the truth of the human heart, and its fundamental message has to do with what the text specifies as "one word—love." At the end of Wharton's *House of Mirth,* Lily is trying to remember this single word, and Selden in on his way to Lily to say it. The word is never stated in Wharton's novel, but it is spoken in McCullers's. A central concern in *The Heart Is a Lonely Hunter* (as in the *Letter*) is what it means to risk speaking the word *love,* which is to say what it means to risk not speaking it. Through her female protagonists Mick Kelly and Portia—and through the bisexual Biff Brannon—McCullers discovers a language of the heart that, like Faulkner's antiphallocentric discourse, transcends the limitations of symbolic, representational, ideological discourse. But because she is as much invested in the *word* love as in love itself, her text does not, like the sentimental novels of the nineteenth century, dissolve into pure emotionality, beyond language; nor does it, like Faulkner's fiction, resist the material, maternal, symbolic universe.

Stanley Cavell has written of the reader-writer relationship that "the reader's position [is] that of the stranger. To write to him is to acknowledge that he is outside the words, at a bent arm's length, and alone with the book; that his presence to these words is perfectly contingent, and the choice to stay with them continuously his own; that they are his points of departure and origin. The conditions of meeting upon the word are that we—writer and reader—learn how to depart from

them, leave them where they are; and then return to them, finding ourselves there again." In McCullers's novel, speaking requires the same autonomy of speaker and listener, the same necessity for what Cavell elsewhere imagines as letting words go and finding them again. *The Heart Is a Lonely Hunter* has to do with the requirements of both verbal and sexual intercourse, as well as with taking responsibility for what such intercourse produces.

In *The Heart Is a Lonely Hunter* four lonely characters seek to escape isolation and open intercourse with the world through their conversation with a deaf person who cannot hear them and refuses to speak to them. This pattern of nonconversation, in which the individual chooses as the recipient of communication a person who cannot or will not respond, is poignantly reinforced by John Singer's own choice of dialogic partner: the deaf and dumb, mentally retarded Spiros Antonapoulos. There is no mistaking McCullers's sympathy for her isolated individuals—no ignoring, either, the complaint about lonely hearts who ruthlessly hunt companionship, only to use the other as a sounding board for the self. As if anticipating the poststructuralist accusation against new formalist criticism—that it reads out texts as mirrors of the designs that the reader places on them—the characters of McCullers's novel seem to speak only to hear their own voices. They convert each other into self-reflections, allegorical mirrors of the self, which permit them to engage in endlessly self-referential monologues. "Each man described the mute as he wished him to be" writes McCullers. The monologic structure of Faulkner's *Sound and the Fury* and *As I Lay Dying* stands close behind McCullers's montage of voices, in which the many consciousnesses in the book remain painfully stranded outside the community of human exchange.

Causing this failure to establish intercourse is the individuals' self-absorption, which prompts them to choose as the object of their communication someone who cannot or will not hear or respond. McCullers suggests, however, that the silent listener is as much victimizer as victim. The silent Singer seduces the other characters into choosing him as their listener, their god. From the beginning of the book McCullers leaves us in no doubt that Singer chooses to remain voiceless; he is not innately mute. Might we not think of Singer—who, when he does communicate, does so through written words, engraved symbols, and signs—as being like a text, which, in its unresponsive, nonconversational mode of transcription, leaves the interpreter free to imagine everything and anything? The problem that Singer, both as character and as text, raises is, What does it mean not to say or not to say clearly? What are the consequences to others of a refusal to enter into the two-way process of conversation? What does it mean in a human relationship to be made the interpreter of a static, silent object (person or text) as opposed to a partner in the mutual (and mutually responsible) production of meaning?

For McCullers the alternative to the silent text is not political discourse. The book explicitly rejects the language employed by Benedict Mady Copeland, the black doctor and activist, and Jake Blount, the radical labor organizer. "Talk—talk—talk" is the way Biff describes Blount. Like the other major figures in the story, Blount, according to Singer, is "always talking." Nor is this talk—talk—talk idle or innocent. It is focused obsessively on the idea of an exclusive unitary "truth"—a "true purpose" in the case of Copeland—which the individual is convinced he or she can articulate. Like Anderson's greedy grotesques (and Flannery O'Connor's), Carson McCullers's "freaks" want to possess the beautiful, multiple truths of the world. In possessing them, they distort the truths and themselves alike. They render the truth false and themselves grotesque. The consequences of this obsession with truth and with the ideological speech through which one imagines one can express truth are devastating, as in *Winesburg, Ohio,* both for family and for community. Copeland loses his wife and alienates his children, while Blount roams aimlessly throughout the country, (not) husband and (not) father (to formulate the problem in the terms of another of McCullers's important precursors, William Faulkner).

The painfulness of conversation turned ideological argument is stunningly portrayed in the quarrel between Blount and Copeland, which occurs toward the end of the novel. The confrontation—not unlike that in Ralph Ellison's *Invisible Man* (published a few years later)—is between an American white political activist and an American black. It exposes the limitations of white political thought about African Americans along the lines of Ellison's and Richard Wright's conclusions concerning the exploitation of the race problem by the Communist party. The conversation begins as a discussion between two like-minded and socially engaged individuals but quickly degenerates into childish accusations and name-calling: "Oh, the Hell with it! . . . Balls!" "Blasphemer! . . . Foul blasphemer!" "Short-sighted bigot!" "White . . . Fiend!" By the end of the novel, Blount, beaten down and running for his life, realizes that what separates him from Copeland is only words. "On some points they might be able to work together . . . if they didn't talk too much." As in Hawthorne's *Scarlet Letter,* ideological discourse replicates the problem of the silent text: it repels and attracts, in effect silencing itself, regardless of all its apparent wordiness and noise. Sitting in the presence of his family, Copeland finally falls "dumb": "If he could not speak the whole long truth no other word would come to him," not even the word "farewell" as he leaves the family gathering and goes out the door. By the time Blount reaches Copeland, it is too late for both of them.

For all her concern with issues of sexism, racism, anti-Semitism, and economic exploitation, McCullers, like her predecessors in the romance tradition, refuses to write a directly political text. Copeland and Blount are both given their say in this book. But for McCullers morality is more a way of seeing the world than a set of political objectives. For this reason, perhaps, she has Copeland articulate a political philosophy that directly misstates the romance politics of Thoreau and Emerson. "If I could just find ten Negroes," he says to Portia, "—ten of my own people—with spine and brains and courage . . . only four Negroes." Here is the text from Thoreau's "Civil Disobedience" (itself a gloss on an Old Testament passage) that Copeland misunderstands: "I know this well, that if one thousand, if one hundred, if ten men whom I could name—if ten *honest* men only—ay, if *one* HONEST man, in this State of Massachusetts, *ceasing to hold slaves,* were actually to withdraw from this copartnership, and be locked up in the county jail therefore, it would be the abolition of slavery in America." The difference between Copeland's formulation and Thoreau's is that Copeland has bred, raised, and groomed (even named) four specific individuals (his own children) for this particular task of saving the black people, whereas Thoreau has no one man in particular but any man, and therefore potentially every man, coming to this moral perception on his own. Thoreau's idea carries forward the biblical idea that it inherits. When Abraham pleads for Sodom on the basis of the ten honest men, he has no ten in particular in mind but any and therefore potentially all who might exist within the city. Portia's response to her father that "Willie and Highboy and me have backbone. This here is a hard world and it seem to me us three struggles along pretty well" understands what Thoreau understands: that moral courage is not political and public so much as individual and private.

But if McCullers sides with Emerson and Thoreau against Copeland and Blount, she does so fully aware of the dangers of Emerson's and Thoreau's way of turning aside from direct confrontation with sociopolitical issues. McCullers is tortured by the possibility that writers, artists, and musicians, in avoiding politics, do little to correct either social problems or the problem of ideology itself. The language of the writer, she realizes, may even intensify tendencies in language to express human egocentricity, producing a text that becomes everyone else's mirror of self. Not surprisingly, this self is also an embodiment of a transcendent perfection. Singer's dream midway through the novel, which foreshadows the painful denouement of the book, is a virtual diagram of a hierarchical transcendentalization of reality. The pyramid of world order, in which the self celebrates itself, depends on the silence of the god or text or idea at the pinnacle—a silence that allows the self to endow itself with divine qualities.

> Out of the blackness of sleep a dream formed. There were dull yellow lanterns lighting up a dark flight of stone steps. Antonapoulos kneeled at the top of these steps. He was naked and he fumbled with something

that he held above his head and gazed at it as though in prayer. He himself knelt half-way down the steps. He was naked and cold and he could not take his eyes from Antonapoulos and the thing he held above him. Behind him on the ground he felt the one with the moustache and the girl and the black man and the last one. They knelt naked and he felt their eyes on him. And behind them there were uncounted crowds of kneeling people in the darkness. His own hands were huge windmills and he stared fascinated at the unknown thing that Antonapoulos held. The yellow lanterns swayed to and fro in the darkness and all else was motionless. Then suddenly there was a ferment. In the upheaval the steps collapsed and he felt himself falling downwards. He awoke with a jerk. The early light whitened the window. He felt afraid.

The central figure in the scene is the something, the thing, the unknown thing, that Antonapoulos holds in his hands. Singer refuses to identify it, even though it is as naked and in view as the crowds of kneeling people who compose the scene. Nor will Singer—his hands like windmills incapable of signing and therefore incapable of speech—name the one with the moustache and the girl and the black man and the last one or count the uncounted but not countless crowds. There are two ways of understanding Singer's unwillingness, or inability, to articulate what is represented in his dream. Insofar as the thing represents something mysterious, not easily given over to a name, his silence can be understood as an appropriate restraint from the excesses of verbalization. Certain details—the cathedral-like setting of the dream, with all of the characters kneeling, and that the one object Antonapoulos possesses is a crucifix and that in the very next scene he is represented as majestic and godlike—suggest that the thing is a cross. What is a cross, the text implies, to be so lightly named? What does the name tell us about what a crucifix is or means? Singer's silence, then, might seem a prudent response to the dangers of mindless talk—talk—talk.

But the interpretation is not so simple. Although one of the few ways in which Antonapoulos uses his hands is to sign the words "'Holy Jesus,' or 'God,' or 'Darling Mary,'" another is to indulge in his "solitary secret pleasure," masturbation. Awaking with a jerk, Singer might well feel afraid of what he has witnessed in his dream of raw and naked desire. He may have very good reasons for refusing to say what thing he has seen.

Is the thing a cross—or a penis? Does it stand for the divine or the purely human? the purely human as divine? McCullers's text owes something here to Melville's *Moby Dick*. Like the great white whale for Ahab, the thing (whatever it is) is, for Singer, a transcendent object of worship. Deification of the unknown and mysterious thing (which may be no more than a figure for one's own sexual desire) extends down through the pyramid of worshipers. For Singer, Antonapoulos is God. Singer himself is God for Biff, Blount, Copeland, and Mick. McCullers's text illuminates a tendency within human beings to construct a universe of divine meanings, in which discovering the divine in someone or something else is both a cover for confronting the physical and the sexual within oneself and a way of converting the merely biological and human into the transcendent and spiritual. But insofar as the author refuses to write what the thing in Antonapoulos's hand is, she conspires in this process of deification. She makes the text into the seductive god who commands the worship of the reader.

> **For all her concern with issues of sexism, racism, anti-Semitism, and economic exploitation, McCullers, like her predecessors in the romance tradition, refuses to write a directly political text.**
>
> **—*Emily Miller Budick***

The failure to specify what the thing is mimetically reproduces the silence of dreams: the text replicates an aspect of the everyday experience of the world in which language-as-clarification is naturally withheld. Dreams do not represent reality in a transparent symbolic script. As often as not, they withhold the terms of identification through which the dreamer might interpret the dream. One might say that Singer never achieves self-knowledge of his tragic attachment to Antonapoulos because he is a poor interpreter of dreams. But he is a poor interpreter of dreams (that is, of himself) because dreams do not say what they mean. They are dreams and they exist because they say without saying. Dreams are an expression of human resistance to self-clarification. They remind us that there are things we simply do not want to know about ourselves. And there are things that we do not want others to know about us. In many ways, Singer, who speaks with silent signs and symbols, embodies the language of dreams. By speaking with and to him, Mick, Biff, Blount, and Copeland confront a dreamlike language that they can choose not to understand.

But Singer does not refuse the role that he plays for the other characters. Like a god, Singer speaks in the language of dreams—through signs and symbols; he speaks in silence, and he speaks in order *not* to be understood. McCullers's text, like perhaps all literary texts, similarly threatens self-deification and mystification. But the consequences of leaving the world uninterpreted, the text makes clear, are terrifying. Naked and cold and gradually metamorphosing into a monster with windmills for hands, Singer is understandably frightened by his dream. Later, when Antonapoulos's fumbling for his cross makes Singer recall the dream and he tries and once again cannot sign the dream, Singer falls prey to impulses that he can neither understand nor control. Singer cannot convert the dream into speech. As the bitter climax of the novel approaches, Singer "surrender[s] himself wholly to thoughts of his friend. . . . Behind each waking moment there had always been his friend. And this submerged communion with Antonapoulos had grown and changed as though they were together in the flesh. Sometimes he thought of Antonapoulos with awe and self-abasement, sometimes with pride—always with love unchecked by criticism, freed of will. When he dreamed at night the face of his friend was always before him, massive and wise and gentle. And in his waking thoughts they were eternally united." The failure to interpret is a fantasy of union, in which self and other respect no distance and exist outside the differentiations and disintegrations of language. Its consequence is the collapse into nothingness that the fiction of Edgar Allan Poe vividly records.

Singer's suicide is one of many figures in the book for the identification of unity with death. To achieve total union with the other is to kill off the other. No sooner has the author articulated Singer's feelings of oneness with Antonapoulos than we discover that Antonapoulos is dead. In this book even thinking about unity can be murderous. And this brings the text to another aspect of totalizing desire: to achieve union with the other and hence with oneself is to destroy the other and oneself. With the death of Antonapoulos, Singer commits suicide, and with Singer's suicide the whole chain of human community breaks apart: Blount is routed out of town after the murderous riot at the fair; Copeland, sick and defeated, is taken to the farm of his father-in-law to die; Mick takes a job at Woolworth's, which puts to an end her artistic ambitions; and Biff is left alone tending the shop. Were it not for a certain prospect for the future that the author deftly constructs (to which I shall return in a moment), the novel would end, as do the fictions of Faulkner and Anderson, Melville and Poe, with a sterility and deathliness, signaling the end of family, community, and history—the end of literature itself.

According to McCullers's novel, the cause of suicidal-murderous sterility is the tendency toward transcendental, symbolic thought. As I have already suggested, the thing that Antonapoulos holds in his hand is not only the crucifix (which figures the Law of the Father) but (by implication) his penis, which is the Law of the Father in its biological form. What makes Singer voiceless in the first place and what keeps him voiceless until the end is his fear of being exposed as merely human, a biological and sexual creature, neither divine nor transcendent.

> There was one particular fact that he remembered [about his childhood], but it was not at all important to him. Singer recalled that, although he had been deaf since he was an infant, he had not always been a

real mute. He was left an orphan very young and placed in an institution for the deaf. He had learned to talk with his hands and to read. Before he was nine years old he could talk with one hand in the American way—and also could employ both of his hands after the method of Europeans. He had learned to follow the movements of people's lips and to understand what they said. Then finally he had been taught to speak. . . . But he could never become used to speaking with his lips. It was not natural to him, and his tongue felt like a whale in his mouth. From the blank expression on people's faces to whom he talked in this way he felt that his voice must be like the sound of some animal or that there was something disgusting in his speech. It was painful for him to try to talk with his mouth, but his hands were always ready to try to shape the words he wished to say. When he was twenty-two he had come South to this town from Chicago and he met Antonapoulos immediately. Since that time he had never spoken with his mouth again, because with his friend there was no need for this.

Singer's silence is foremost a response to his particular handicap, which is deafness. But his response carries with it the force of a more general and pervasive human response to the problematics of speaking. Immediately after Singer's discovery of Antonapoulos's death, a strange thing happens that suggests that Singer's flight from speech may not be from the possibility of not being understood or being thought of as less than human. On the contrary, it might represent a flight from the possibility that he may well be understood, not as a brilliant, multilingual student but as a mere mortal, who gropes for and stumbles over words that may not only express what he wants to say but that may expose all his human frailty.

Singer meets "three mutes . . . talking with their hands together. All three of them were coatless. They wore bowler hats and bright ties. Each of them held a glass of beer in his left hand. There was a certain brotherly resemblance between them. . . . He was clapped on the shoulder. A cold drink was ordered. They surrounded him and the fingers of their hands shot out like pistons as they questioned him." After a few awkward efforts to communicate with them, Singer abandons communication for the last time, "his hands dangling loose . . . his head . . . inclined to one side and his glance . . . oblique." Singer's choice not to communicate with these friendly, brotherly mute people, who—unlike everyone else in the novel, including Antonapoulos—could understand him, suggests that Singer cannot face the possibility that he is like other human beings, absurdly, comically identical with them (as they are identical with each other), that speech reduces him, not to the animalistic or subhuman, but to the human. Singer will not seek out his brothers for to do so would be to discover he is one of them.

That his tongue in his mouth feels like a whale prompts us to think of Melville's novel. So does Biff's denial of his sexuality. Like Ahab, Biff and Singer prefer to imagine themselves as not limited by biology. In McCullers's novel, speaking silently (which is to say speaking not to be understood) is associated with a withdrawal from sexual relations. Phallocentricism, the author suggests, does not necessarily place the penis in the position of power. Rather, in denying that the penis is potent sexual agent, it may be substituting a feeble and ineffectual law of abstract, intellectually derived symbols of the world for the procreative, phallicly reproduced biohistorical world itself. McCullers's male characters (excluding Biff) are not feminized males or androgynous human beings, realizing the fusion of male and female principles. They are self-castrated men, who relinquish male potency and deny procreative power.

The relation between the assertion of phallocentric law and the denial of phallic biology in self-canceling males characterizes another important precursor of McCullers's art. Like Jay Gatsby in F. Scott Fitzgerald's *Great Gatsby,* the men who populate the world of McCullers's text desire to be Platonic conceptions of self. The case of Gatsby is instructive, both for McCullers's novel and for Flannery O'Connor's *The Violent Bear It Away.* Not only does Gatsby (in true Freudian romance fashion) disown his parents ("his imagination had never really accepted them as his parents at all"), but he rejects reconciliation with the biological terms of human birth altogether: "He was the son of God—a phrase which, if it means anything, means just that—and he must be about His Father's business, the service of a vast, vulgar, and meretricious beauty. So he invented just the sort of Jay Gatsby that a seventeen-year-old boy would be likely to invent, and to this conception he was faithful to the end." Gatsby's Platonic conception of himself rejects the biological woman: "He knew women early, and . . . he became contemptuous of them, of young virgins because they were ignorant, of the others because they were hysterical about things which in his overwhelming self-absorption he took for granted." When he falls in love with Daisy he knows that "when he kissed this girl, and forever wed his unutterable visions to her perishable breath, his mind would never romp again like the mind of God. . . . At his lips' touch she blossomed for him like a flower and the incarnation was complete." Gatsby's desire, moments earlier, to mount to a "secret place above the trees" where "he could suck on the pap of life, gulp down the incomparable milk of wonder" is fulfilled only in the birth of self that his relationship to Daisy produces.

Gatsby culminates in a uterine birthing motion (as opposed to a phallic thrust) reminiscent of *Moby Dick.* But this birthing can only be endured; it cannot itself give birth: "So we beat on, boats against the current, borne back ceaseless into the past." Male "brooding" produces only Platonic conception and incarnation. It does not bear life. Fitzgerald's novel reveals what emerges as a problem in Faulkner's and Anderson's writings as well: that male imaginings of the female, for all their generosity and goodwill, may not be able to move beyond gestation (brooding) to birth. Because Gatsby will not be a man ready to assume the responsibilities of the phallus, he dies, stillborn after his self-inseminated virgin birth. McCullers's silent Singer, orphan and bachelor, embodies similar problems.

Much has been made in recent feminist criticism of the multivocalism, authorial decenteredness, and indeterminate open-endedness of novels by women. All are understood to be antiphallocentric strategies. All to some degree characterize McCullers's novel, as they also characterize the fiction of McCullers's two major literary predecessors, William Faulkner and Sherwood Anderson. *The Heart Is a Lonely Hunter* flows uninterruptedly from consciousness to consciousness, weaving together the community that does not exist within the world of the novel. But like Anderson's and Faulkner's strategies of antiphallocentricism, McCullers's threaten to produce a non-progenerative and perhaps antifemale sterility. Not only are Blount and Singer confirmed bachelors but Biff and Copeland are widowers (Biff's wife dies of a tumor as big as a baby). Portia, the strongest female presence in the book, is childless. At the close of the novel only Mick, on the verge of adulthood, remains to create a future. Mick's position at the end of the novel and her nurturing nature throughout are important for McCullers's idea of family. The figure who will enable her mothering is Portia.

Early in the novel McCullers presents an extended conversation between Portia and her father that pits Portia's female, African American discourse against her father's white-inspired intellectual ideology, his language of law against her language of the biological and reproductive: "All his life he had told and explained and exhorted. . . . It is not more children we need but more chances for the ones already on the earth." Not only does Copeland's statement appear (indecorously) in the center of a conversation with his own daughter, but his thinking on this matter proceeds directly from a painful and equally blind conversation with Portia on her childlessness: "So you and your husband and your brother have your own cooperative plan," he says to her. "Do you intend to plan for children?" The text continues: "Portia did not look at her father. Angrily she sloshed the water from the pan of collards. 'There be some things,' she said, 'that seem to me to depend entirely upon God.'"

Copeland cannot understand—either about his daughter's communal living arrangements or about the many children produced by the black community—the positive and creative nature of these affirmations of life. For all his concern with the "Negro people" (as his interjections into Blount's Marxist discourse remind us), Copeland adopts a political philosophy as white as that of Blount. Copeland's rejection of

Christianity might have constituted a part of a necessary turn away from white institutions to African American culture. It represents instead Copeland's decidedly masculinist rejection of the unknowable and the uncertain in human experience—his rejection both of women and of the African past of black Americans. "I am not interested in subterfuges," he says. "I am interested only in real truths." These real truths contain no space for "hell and heaven" or for the "ghosts" and "haunted places" of African legend. Therefore, Copeland turns to Marx for his politics, Spinoza for his philosophy, and Shakespeare for his literature. In resisting what he calls his wife Daisy's stubborn meekness—her insistence on teaching her children both Christianity and African Americanism—he resists as well his wife's sexuality.

The question that McCullers's novel raises, both in the conversation between Dr. Copeland and Portia and in the story as a whole, is, What does it mean to know by heart? McCullers writes: "Eugenic Parenthood for the Negro Race was what he would exhort them to. He would tell them in simple words, always the same way, and with the years it came to be a sort of angry poem which he had always known by heart." The question is inseparable from the issue of parenthood. To know by heart certainly does not mean what Copeland means: to memorize by rote and recite in anger, unwilling to wait for a reply, unyielding to the demands of conversation. To know by heart is something else entirely. "Hamilton or Buddy or Willie or me—none of us ever cares to talk like you," explains Portia. "Us talk like our own Mama and her peoples and their peoples before them. You think out everything in your brain. While us rather talk from something in our hearts that has been there for a long time."

The mother tongue that Portia speaks, when, for example, she tells her father about the amputation of Willie's feet, is the "low song" of "grief" (specifically African American grief) to which her father is "deaf." Copeland cannot hear and understand what Portia says any better than he could Daisy. "The sounds were distinct in his ear, but they had no shape or meaning." Like Mick, listening to the music of Beethoven, Copeland must discover the relation, not between words and meanings (he understands that well enough), but between words and feelings. Jake Blount's response to Willie's pain ("the terrible misery down in my toes . . . where my feets should be if they were on my l-l-legs") is political. So is his father's. But the response to loss cannot simply be an imagination of recovery and restitution. It must involve the pain that loss occasions. When the "black, terrible anger" does not come, the "feeling of a song" within Copeland finally takes shape and expresses itself:

> He spoke no word and let them do with him as they would. He waited for the terrible anger and felt it arise in him. Rage made him weak, so that he stumbled. . . . It was only when they had entered the

jail that the strength of his rage came to him. . . . A glorious strength was in him and he heard himself laughing aloud as he fought. He sobbed and laughed. . . . They dragged him foot by foot through the hall of the jail. . . . He fell to his knees on the floor. . . . . [He] swayed to and fro. . . . He swayed, . . . and from his throat there came a singing moan. He could not think of William. Nor could he even cogitate upon the strong, true purpose and draw strength from that. He could only feel the misery in him. Then the tide of his fever turned. A warmth spread through him. He lay back, and it seemed he sank down into a place warm and red full of comfort.

By giving up on words, Copeland experiences his son's pain, even losing the use of his legs as he is dragged into the prison. And by experiencing that pain, he regains the language of misery, which expresses itself, not in words but in the almost maternal rocking and warmth of his body. The language of misery is the mother tongue, which his daughter and his wife have always spoken (or, sung) to him but which he cannot hear and speak until he experiences loss and misery bodily. For Copeland, however, it is too late to be husband, father, or community leader. He will not be able to convert feeling back into words, even the single word—love.

It is not, however, too late for Mick Kelly.

The mother tongue that Portia speaks is no less verbal, no less rational and conceptual, than the father tongue that her father inherits from Shakespeare and Marx. But in it words have less to do with exchanging information than with establishing relationship and mutuality. This language is affective rather than discursive; it nurtures, expresses, and evokes feelings and produces family, community, nation. "A person can't pick up they children and just squeeze them to which-a-way they wants them to be," Portia says to her father. "Whether it hurt them or not. Whether it right or wrong. You done tried that hard as any man could try. And now I the only one of us that would come in this here house and sit with you like this." Portia is able to accept people as they are. Childless, she can envision herself the mother of racially, culturally, sexually different others. "Them three little children is just like some of my own kinfolks," she says of Mick, Bubber, and the baby. "I feel like I done really raised Bubber and the baby. And although Mick and me is always getting into some kind of quarrel together, I has a real close fondness for her too. . . . Mick now . . . she a real case. Not a soul know how to manage that child. She just as biggity and headstrong as she can be. . . . Mick puzzles me sometimes. But still I really fond of her."

Like the commune that she builds with her husband and brother, Portia's extended family reconceptualizes the idea of kinship. (We might recall Blount's claims to be Negro,

Jew, and Indian and the continuing refrain that Singer is a Jew.) Mick benefits directly from the mothering that Portia provides. As in many of the novels discussed in Marianne Hirsch's *Mother/Daughter Plot,* the mother in Carson McCullers's novel is strangely silent, as are Mick's two older sisters, Hazel and Etta. It is as if Mick can become a strongly motivated, artistic, and imaginative female only by silencing the women who precede and create her. Like Frankie Addams in McCullers's other novel about a female adolescent, ***The Member of the Wedding,*** Mick is a self-declared tomboy, who, on more than one occasion, expresses her preference for maleness; the names Mick and Frankie capture this feature of the girls' personalities. But Mick is not motherless, either literally or figuratively. Like Frankie and (we might add) like Caddy in Faulkner's *Sound and the Fury,* Mick enjoys the mothering of a loving and wise black woman.

In the Lacanian model language not only responds to the loss and absence of objects in the world but occasions loss and absence. In McCullers's novel, language, in responding to the primary painfulness of loss, keeps feeling (especially the feeling of maternal love) alive. Portia does not educate Mick in the Law of the Father—in language as a substitute for and repetition of loss (language, in other words, as symbolic consciousness). Rather, she instructs her in the affect of the mother: language as the expression of and reproduction of pain, the pain of the separation from and loss of the mother. As a surrogate mother, Portia is both mother and not-mother. She reconstructs the mother in a lost relationship *and* in an uninterrupted and unmitigated love, which does not cease simply because the mother-child bond has moved from its initial phase of total interdependence. She also suggests a relationship between mother and child that does not depend on the biological link between them. Herself motherless, Portia continues to feel the influence of her mother's love, which she incorporates into everything from her mode of being to her way of speaking. Childless, she transmits that love to genetically and racially different others.

In almost everybody's reading of the novel, Mick is the primary figure of the artist. "Empty" and confused, not a "feeling or thought in her," Mick seeks more than an idea in her art, whether an idea of God or even (as in the case of Singer) an idea of love: she searches for feeling. She pursues the language that transcribes feeling, that renders feeling an instrument of human relatedness. The following scene provides the countermoment to Singer's transcendental vision. Both scenes proceed through dream to mystical, religious vision; and both are violent. But whereas Singer's dream culminates in an aphasic collapse into suicide and death, Mick's initiates her into the responsibilities of living, speaking, and loving in a human world.

> The music started. Mick raised her head and her fist went up to her throat. How did it come? For a minute

the opening balanced from one side to the other. Like a walk or march. Like God, strutting in the night. . . . It didn't have anything to do with God. This was her, Mick Kelly, walking in the day-time and by herself at night. . . . This music was her—the real plain her. . . . Wonderful music like this was the worst hurt there could be. The whole world was this symphony, and there was not enough of her to listen. . . . She put her fingers in her ears. The music left only this bad hurt in her and a blankness. . . . Suddenly Mick began hitting her thigh with her fists. She pounded the same muscle with all her strength until the tears came down her face. But she could not feel this hard enough. The rocks under the bush were sharp. She grabbed a handful of them and began scraping them up and down on the same spot until her hand was bloody. . . . With the fiery hurt in her leg she felt better. She was limp on the wet grass, and after a while her breath came slow and easy again. . . . The night was quiet. . . . She was not trying to think of the music at all when it came back to her. . . . She could see the shape of the sounds very clear and she would not forget them.

> Now she felt good.

Blending the sexual and the religious, the passage initially suggests a displacement of meaning along a transcendental pyramid reminiscent of Singer's dream. Art almost transports Mick beyond language, where one need not specify what a thing is. But beyond language is unconsciousness. To regain life, Mick must regain language. Only when the sounds come back to her as material shapes, formed letters, does she feel good. Unlike Singer, who cannot convert the dream back into signs, Mick is restored to language. She is returned to family, to her parents, whom she knows must by this time be worried. Whereas Mick's brother Bill is always poring over words in a book, her own "pictures [are] full of people." The shapes of the musical notes, like the shapes of words and the drawings of people, preserve for Mick the materiality of art, with which the men in the novel (including Bill and Singer and Blount and Copeland) are willing to dispense. McCullers thus deftly picks up the threads of Hester's lawless embroidery and weaves them into a new musical and pictorial speaking of the mother tongue. By weaving together Mick and Singer, McCullers reminds us of what we tend to forget about the written or engraved word: its essentially material form. Through the relationship between Mick and Portia, McCullers remembers that language originates in the mother, not the father. That Singer is an orphan may have some bearing on his never having learned how to speak. Learning to speak has to do with more than the acquisition of a vocabulary of words.

The book ends with a vision of historical continuity and procreative possibility. What stands between the silence that divests us of world and self, and the images or words that are only the imposition of self on the world is "one word—love."

> The silence in the room was deep as the night itself. Biff stood transfixed, lost in his meditations. Then suddenly he felt a quickening in him. His heart turned and he leaned his back against the counter for support. For in a swift radiance of illumination he saw a glimpse of human struggle and of valour. Of the endless fluid passage of humanity through endless time. And of those who labour and of those who—one word—love. His soul expanded. But for a moment only. For in him he felt a warning, a shaft of terror. Between the two worlds he was suspended. He saw that he was looking at his own face in the counter glass before him. Sweat glistened on his temples and his face was contorted. One eye was opened wider than the other. The left eye delved narrowly into the past while the right gazed wide and affrighted into a future of blackness, error, and ruin. And he was suspended between radiance and darkness. Between bitter irony and faith. Sharply he turned away. . . . he composed himself soberly to await the morning sun.

Throughout the novel Biff has presented a unique image of male-female gender distinction. Sexually inadequate, perhaps even impotent (like Singer, Antonapoulos, Copeland, and even Blount), Biff is not a sexual male. But unlike these other characters (and like Mick's more adolescent self), Biff's androgyny does not stand opposed either to women or to procreation.

> His eyes closed he began to sing in a doleful voice:
>
> I went to the animal fair,
> The birds and the beasts were there,
> And the old baboon by the light of the moon
> Was combing his auburn hair.
>
> He finished with a chord from the strings and the last sounds shivered to silence in the cold air.
>
> To adopt a couple of little children. A boy and a girl. About three or four years old so they would always feel like he was their own father. Their Dad. Our Father. The little girl like Mick (or Baby?) at that age. Round cheeks and grey eyes and flaxen hair. And the clothes he would make for her. . . . The boy was dark and black-haired. The little boy walked behind him and copied the things he did. . . . And then they would bloom as he grew old. Our Father. And they would come to him with questions and he would answer them.

Biff dreams of the nurturing, self-sacrificing, interactive re-sponsibilities, not of fathering as opposed to mothering, but of parenting. Nor is parenting necessarily biological. Biff will adopt these children, not produce them biologically, and he will perform for them the function of mother and father both. Like Portia, Biff is not restricted by convention. He has a similarly expansive vision of procreative possibility, which is what his final vision represents. He speaks the language of rhyme and limerick, the language of the nursery.

Love in McCullers's novel is thus both creative and procreative. It is word. But it is also a quickening and a labor. Like Hawthorne and Melville, McCullers creates a neutral ground between the imaginary and the real, between radiance and darkness and irony and faith, where anyone may well end up alone, shut away from private hopes and expectations (like Mick at Woolworth's), staring into one's own face. The maternal function, so prevalent in the nineteenth-century women's tradition, is nonetheless here brought to bear with powerful force. For one can, like Biff, choose to turn away from despair and to compose oneself, not merely submitting to the condition of the human but responding to and perpetuating that condition. Just as Biff pulls himself together (in an almost Thoreauvian fashion) to meet the morning sun, so Mick is also at the end poised on the path to a future of responsibility and human commitment. The love of family that sends her out of the private room of her fantasies of artistic self-fulfillment (a self-fulfillment associated throughout the book with a withdrawal from family and society) is the promise of a future.

To say this is not to deny Mick's anger and frustration at the end of the book, any more than it is to deny Biff's definite pain. Taking responsibility for the remaining payments on Singer's radio, Mick knows both that "it was good to have something that had belonged to him" and that it is only a remote possibility that "maybe one of these days she might be able to set aside a little for a second-hand piano."

> Maybe it would be true about the piano and turn out O.K. Maybe she would get a chance soon. Else what the hell good had it all been—the way she felt about music and the plans she had made in the inside room? It has to be some good if anything made sense. And it was too and it was too and it was too and it was too. It was some good.
>
> All right!
>
> O.K.!
>
> Some good.

The lines are ambiguous. There is no saying with certainty how to read the final "Some good." Every realistic assessment tells us that Mick will suffer the same disappointments that everyone else in the world of the novel has suffered. Yet the text is not realistic. The word *good* resounding through the passage sets up a condition of affirmation that is not so easily ignored. Set as it is against the argument in the novel about the problems of political and literary discourse, the phrase "some good" represents the only kind of affirmation that matters: affirmation in the face of doubt, in the midst of pain, affirmation of life in the midst of living and producing life.

This is the affirmation that Biff achieves at the end of the novel. The optimism of **The Heart Is a Lonely Hunter** derives finally from a faith in words wedded to feeling and to the desire, which such language embodies, to communicate with love. In spite of the sharp criticism of words—words—words, the book gives us all of those words, quoted and unexpurgated. And in spite of its equivalent distrust of the dissolution of literary language into silence, **The Heart Is a Lonely Hunter** is a work of literature. But it is a female romance, in which the direction of human creativity is the direction of procreation as well. Its direction, in other words, is toward family and community, reconstructed and redefined. Like Biff, the author chooses to turn away not only from any one language but from the impasse to which the competition between languages can take us and which would yield silence in one form or another. It composes itself as a multiphonic, many-voiced text, representing not an indeterminate or decentered text but a multifaceted consciousness. The novel is committed to speaking. It enters into a community of voices. In this community every voice, like every person, is equally entitled and permitted and finally encouraged to speak. Speaking even one word becomes the source of community. To speak is, for McCullers, to be willing to make oneself understood and, understood, to be willing to understand what somebody else is saying; equally important, to speak is to be willing to feel and, feeling, to enter into the lives of others and to produce other lives. The human condition is to exist between impossible alternatives. What mediates between them, what makes them bearable, and what is itself a figure for the torment that is also salvation is the single word—love.

FURTHER READING

Bibliography

Carr, Virginia Spencer, and Millichap, Joseph R. "Carson McCullers." *American Women Writers.* Westport, Connecticut: Greenwood Press, 1983, 297-319.
> Bibliographic essay identifying primary editions and manuscript sources, as well as secondary works including bibliography, biography, and criticism.

Criticism

Dusenbury, Winifred L. *The Theme of Loneliness in Modern American Drama.* Gainesville, Florida: University of Florida Press, 1960, 57-85.
> Examines family relations and corresponding themes of loneliness and alienation in the stage version of McCullers' *The Member of the Wedding.*

Evans, Oliver. "The Case of the Silent Singer: A Revaluation of *The Heart Is a Lonely Hunter.*" *The Georgia Review* XIX, No. 2 (Summer 1965): 188-203.
> Examines aspects of isolation, ideal communication, and the allegorical significance of John Singer, the deaf-mute character in *The Heart Is a Lonely Hunter.*

Evans, Oliver. "The Achievement of Carson McCullers." *Carson McCullers,* edited by Harold Bloom, Chelsea House Publishers, 1986: 21-31.
> Discusses the themes, critical appraisals, and allegorical aspects of Carson McCullers' works.

Fuller, Janice. "The Conventions of Counterpoint and Fugue in *The Heart Is a Lonely Hunter.*" *Mississippi Quarterly* XLI, No. 1 (Winter 1987-1988): 55-67.
> Examines the function of character and plot in the fugal structure of *The Heart Is a Lonely Hunter.*

Gervin, Mary A. "McCullers' Frames of Reference in *The Ballad of the Sad Café.*" *Pembroke Magazine,* No. 20 (1988): 37-42.
> Discusses the different elements of mythology, folklore, philosophy, and phenomenology in *The Ballad of the Sad Café.*

Ginsberg, Elaine. "The Female Initiation Theme in American Fiction." *Studies in American Fiction* 3, No. 1 (Spring 1975): 27-37.
> Examines the theme of female initiation in American fiction, particularly as evidenced in McCullers' novels *The Member of the Wedding* and *The Heart Is a Lonely Hunter.*

Hardwick, Elizabeth. A review of *The Member of the Wedding. Partisan Review* XIII, No. 3 (Summer 1946): 384, 386-88, 390-93.
> Brief review faulting *The Member of the Wedding* for its similarity to *The Heart Is a Lonely Hunter.*

Johnson, James William. "The Adolescent Hero: A Trend in Modern Fiction." *Twentieth Century Literature* 5, No. 1 (April 1959): 3-11.
> Study of adolescent protagonists in modern fiction, particularly in the works of Carson McCullers, J. D. Salinger,

Thomas Wolfe, James Joyce, and Katherine Anne Porter.

Kelley, Patricia P. "Recommended: Carson McCullers." *English Journal* 71, No. 6 (October 1982): 67-68.
Identifies adolescent issues in McCullers' major novels and early short stories, suggesting their potential appeal to high school readers.

Madden, David. "The Paradox of the Need for Privacy and the Need for Understanding in Carson McCullers' *The Heart Is a Lonely Hunter*." Literature and Psychology XVII, No. 2-3 (1967): 128-40.
Analysis of character psychology and dilemma of spiritual isolation in *The Heart Is a Lonely Hunter.*

Paden, Frances Freeman. "Autistic Gestures in *The Heart Is a Lonely Hunter*." *Modern Fiction Studies* 28, No. 3 (Autumn 1982): 453-63.
Examines autistic behaviors exhibited by characters of *The Heart Is a Lonely Hunter,* particularly hand gestures that signify frustration and alienation.

Walsh, Margaret. "Carson McCullers' Anti-Fairy Tale: *The Ballad of the Sad Café*." *Pembroke Magazine,* No. 20 (1988): 43-8.
Discusses the fairy tale elements of *The Ballad of the Sad Café,* commenting on both love's failure to redeem and conquer, and the transience of personal transformations.

Worsley, T. C. "Growing Up." *The New Statesman and Nation* LIII, No. 1353 (16 February 1957): 201-202.
Negative assessment of McCullers' stage adaptation of *The Member of the Wedding.*

Additional coverage of McCullers's life and career is contained in the following sources published by Gale Research: *Concise Dictionary of American Literary Biography,* **1941-1968;** *Contemporary Authors,* **Vols. 5-8R, 25-28R;** *Contemporary Authors Bibliographical Series,* **Vol. 1;** *Contemporary Authors New Revision Series,* **Vol. 18;** *Dictionary of Literary Biography,* **Vols. 2, 7, 173;** *DISCovering Authors; DISCovering Authors: British; DISCovering Authors Modules: Most-Studied and Novelists; Major Twentieth Century Writers; Short Story Criticism,* **Vol. 9;** *Something about the Author,* **Vol. 27; and** *World Literature Criticism.*

God: A Biography
Jack Miles

American nonfiction writer, journalist, and theologian.

The following entry presents criticism on Miles's *God: A Biography* (1995).

INTRODUCTION

A theological scholar, Miles received the Pulitzer Prize in Biography for his first major publication, *God: A Biography.* From 1960 to 1970 Miles studied as a Jesuit seminarian at Pontifical Gregorian University in Rome and Hebrew University in Jerusalem; he studied the Hebrew Bible at Harvard University, earning a doctorate in Near Eastern languages in 1971. Miles taught in the theology department at Loyola University, worked as assistant director of Scholars Press, and served as an editor at the University of California Press and Doubleday before joining the *Los Angeles Times* in 1985, where he worked as a book columnist and editorial board member for ten years. In 1995 Miles became the director of the Humanities Center at the Claremont Graduate School near Los Angeles.

Plot and Major Characters

Miles received a 1991 Guggenheim Fellowship for *God: A Biography,* which was published in 1995 and earned the 1996 Pulitzer Prize for Biography. The "biography" is actually an interpretation of God's "life" drawn from careful analysis of the Hebrew Bible. The events of *God: A Biography* will seem out of order to those unfamiliar with the Hebrew Bible, the *Tanakh,* which can be broadly described as switching the middle and ending portions of the Christian Old Testament. The difference is crucial in Miles's interpretation of God's behavior, from His first creation to His subsequent reactions toward humankind.

Major Themes

Miles's "biography" presents a portrait of God as a being with faults, inconsistencies, and conflicting personalities. Miles argues that the Book of Genesis presents God with two personas: the God who is "lofty, unwavering and sincere in his creative actions," and the Lord God, who is "intimate volatile and prone to dark regrets and darker equivocations." Miles contends that over the course of time, God learns and matures. In presenting an interpretation of the Bible as a work of literature, Miles creates a

picture of God as a character in a plot who develops and grows.

Critical Reception

Finding him uniquely qualified for the task, critics did not dismiss Miles out of hand for purporting to assign to God a "life" and imperfect human characteristics. Overall, critics found *God: A Biography* thought-provoking, if not always in line with popular belief. Ross Miller wrote in the *Chicago Tribune:* "Jack Miles's *God: A Biography* is a brilliant, audacious book. Effortlessly interweaving the voices of scholar, teacher and inquisitive layman, Miles takes the reader into the very heart of the Bible." While some critics pointed out problems in execution and method, the overall assessment was positive. Phyllis Trible wrote: "At places the argument is strained and prone to hyperbole. Nonetheless, with artistic sensitivity Mr. Miles has accomplished what others failed to try. He has made a certain literary sense of the character God in the totality of the Tanakh."

PRINCIPAL WORKS

Retroversion and Text Criticism (nonfiction) 1984
God: A Biography (theology) 1995

CRITICISM

Michiko Kakutani (review date 26 March 1995)

SOURCE: "God, You Imperfect, Conflicted Fella, You," in *The New York Times,* March 26, 1995, p. C20.

[*In the following review, Kakutani discusses Miles's purpose in writing* God: A Biography *and lauds the author's success in reinterpreting the Bible as a work of literature.*]

"You cannot plumb the depths of the human heart," reads a passage in the Apocrypha, "nor find out what a man is thinking; how do you expect to search out God, who made all these things, and find out His mind or comprehend His thoughts?"

This, however, is exactly what the *Los Angeles Times* book columnist Jack Miles proposes to do in *God: A Biography,* and this results in a scintillating work of literary scholarship that will forever color, if not downright alter, our conception of the Bible as a work of art.

By treating God as a literary personage and minutely examining narrative evidence of his character in the Hebrew Bible or Tanakh (which has the same material as the Old Testament but presents it in a slightly different order), Mr. Miles constructs a detailed portrait of the Almighty, who, in his telling, turns out not to be quite as all-powerful or all-knowing as commonly thought. Indeed, Mr. Miles's God emerges as an "imperfectly self-conscious" fellow whose "word is as poorly under His control as rain that has already fallen from the sky" and whose "thoughts must strain to be equal to His experience," a character as conflicted as any young Bildungsroman hero and as magnetically compelling as Satan in *Paradise Lost.*

God's intentions, Mr. Miles suggests, are constantly being subverted by His experience. "After each of His major actions, He discovers that He has not done quite what He thought He was doing, or has done something He never intended to do," Mr. Miles writes. "He did not realize when He told mankind to 'be fertile and increase' that He was creating an image of Himself that was also a rival creator. He did not realize

when He destroyed His rival that He would regret the destruction of His image."

Part of the problem, it seems, is that God suffers from what might be called a multiple personality disorder. Throughout the Book of Genesis, Mr. Miles argues, He displays two entirely different personas: God who is "lofty, unwavering and sincere in his creative actions" and the Lord God, who is "intimate, volatile and prone to dark regrets and darker equivocations." God creates man "in his own image" (Genesis 1:27) and gives him dominion over the earth (1:28); the Lord God forms man "of the dust of the ground" (Genesis 2:7) and confines him to a pretty garden (2:8). God gives man and woman an ungrudging and unqualified command to "be fruitful, and multiply" (1:28); the Lord God worries about the prospect of man living forever and reminds him that he will always be dust (3:19).

As Mr. Miles points out, God's inner conflicts will multiply even further in later books of the Bible, as He vacillates between His roles as liberator and lawgiver, genocidal warrior and tender arbiter, plainspoken friend of the family and distant divinity in the clouds. The main reason for this multiplication of personas, of course, is rooted in monotheism's gradual emergence from polytheism in Israel, and its appropriation of various polytheistic stories (like the destruction of the world by flood) and images (like the depiction of God as a volcanic force of nature).

> It is Mr. Miles's contention that God grows and matures in the course of the Bible: "Things happen to God one at a time," he writes, "He acts, then reacts to what He has done, or to what others have done in reaction to Him.
>
> —*Michiko Kakutani*

In fact, Mr. Miles goes so far as to argue that "the most coherent way to imagine the Lord God of Israel is as the inclusion of the content of several ancient divine personalities in a single character." Among those divine personalities are the angry chaos monster Tiamat (who can be glimpsed in the destructive God of the Noah story), the warlike Baal (who bears more then a passing resemblance to the thunderous God of "Exodus") and the homely personal god of Mesopotamia (who recalls the down-to-earth divinity Jacob asks for food and clothing).

As the Bible progresses, Mr. Miles suggests, these disparate personalities are gradually absorbed into a more unitary character. In Deuteronomy, Moses brings the character of God and the fate of Israel together in a glorious synthetic vision; in Isaiah, we are finally given the familiar image of a distant and inscrutable God, whose very mysteriousness and omniscience subsume His contradictions.

It is Mr. Miles's contention that God grows and matures in the course of the Bible: "Things happen to God one at a time," he writes, "He acts, then reacts to what He has done, or to what others have done in reaction to Him. He makes plans and adjusts them when they don't quite work out. He repents, starts over, looks ahead, looks back. As a result of all this, He learns."

When the Israelites break their covenant by taking up foreign idols, for instance, God abandons them to their enemies, leading to horrendous slaughter, ignominy and exile. Looking back on these events, Mr. Miles argues, God then tries to make amends: the new covenant He will establish with Israel will be a more emotional one, a more mature one, infused with pity and sorrow. In Mr. Miles's opinion, God's confrontation with Job similarly leads to a jolt of self-knowledge and contrition: in challenging God's willingness to inflict suffering on an innocent man, he argues, Job not only goads God into atonement but also reduces Him to silence.

"Unnoticed is the fact that from the end of the Book of Job to the end of the Tanakh, God never speaks again," Mr. Miles writes. "His speech from the whirlwind is, in effect, his last will and testament." Although God's earlier speeches will be repeated, although miraculous feats will still be attributed to Him, although He will be glimpsed (for the last time), seated on a throne and referred to as the "Ancient of Days," He will gradually recede from view, abandoning the stage to the human partners of his covenant.

"As the Tanakh ends," Mr. Miles writes, "the mind of God has been objectified in law, the action of God incarnated in leadership, and now, finally, the voice of God transferred to prayer."

It's possible, certainly, to quarrel with some of Mr. Miles's conclusions and to question aspects of his methodology. His decision to base his analysis on the Tanakh (which shifts the books of the prophets from the end to the middle of the sequence) rather than on the more familiar Old Testament, after all, affects the narrative shape of his material and hence his overall assessment: if he'd chosen to focus on the Old Testament instead, he would not have been able to conclude so easily that God's story ends in silence. Mr. Miles's interpretation of the Book of Job is also highly subjective, as is his reading of Moses' relationship with God. More important, he soft-pedals the role that various writers who contributed to the Bible played in shaping history and myth, and editing the character of God.

Mr. Miles, however, freely acknowledges these difficulties; he does not present his book as a definitive rereading of the Bible, but as one interpretation of a work of art. Nor does it really matter in the end whether the reader finds all his arguments persuasive. Mr. Miles—a former Jesuit with a doctorate in Near Eastern languages—writes with such ardor for his subject, such erudition and intuitive sympathy, that he immediately engages the reader in a passionate reconsideration of the infinite subtleties of the Bible and its prodigious and most uncommon hero.

God: A Biography is a dazzling piece of work.

Paul Wilkes (review date 9 April 1995)

SOURCE: "God's Boswell: A man writes a biography of God. God responds," in *Los Angeles Times Book Review,* April 9, 1995, p. 4

[*In the following humorous review, Wilkes presents a "letter" from God addressed to Jack Miles in which God praises Miles's knowledge of scripture, languages, history, and culture. God points out a few problems with Miles's "biography," but lauds his ability to engage and captivate readers with a lively and entertaining story.*]

Dear Jack,

The galley proofs of your new book about me arrived a while back, and I've finally finished it. What with all the requests, complaints and reports I have to sort through, it's hard to get any sustained, serious reading done. Know the problem? And yours is a Book of the Month Club selection, no less. Nice going. Still some interest in me down there, obviously. But I noted it was only an "alternate selection"—does that mean they're interested, but only alternately?

Nonetheless, Jack, I was impressed with the awesome knowledge you possess about Scripture, languages, culture, history. Jesuitic erudition, to be sure. They trained you well. Sorry you've since left the order, but those kinds of things happen these days. No hard feelings.

What I liked best was that you stayed the course, Jack. You took the Tanach—the Hebrew Bible—and even when the material wasn't so exciting, when I wasn't creating a firmament or parting seas or meting out plagues, when I might have seemed to have exited stage left, you kept going. Haggai, Lamentations, Ezra: all of it. I hope it gets other people reading the Book through, rather than picking and choosing what suits their fancy. I hear there's even a Bible with all the positive material highlighted in red and the rest left for dross (one of your West Coast fellows at work, espousing "possibility thinking," Oh, me!). *That* number was never sent to me for review, be sure of that.

You see, there's so much misunderstanding getting around about me. If one were a person, it could be quite depressing. Killing bodies in my name, what with *jihad, fatwa* and various other stripes of religious cleansing. And, just as bad, clouding minds and souls to sell a book or two—books about alleged prophecies, spiritual laws of success and caring for my best work, the immortal soul, with my name hardly mentioned. That's what seems to make the bestseller lists. Honestly, what passes for religious belief these days. Jack, how can they misunderstand so badly what I was all about?

And now to your assessment. Let's see: You attempt a "reintegration of the mythic, fictional and historical elements in the bible so as to allow the character of God to stand forth more clearly from the work of which he is the protagonist." Fair enough. But, Jack, about the disclaimer that this book "neither precludes nor requires belief in God." Seems as though you're backing off a bit here. Let's go on, but beware the siren calls of that "wider audience" promised by your solicitous editor.

You quite often paint me as quite a dyspeptic, crotchety, asexual, contradictory, vengeful fellow. Let me say what a refreshing change that is from the usual hagiography, which I find a bit cloying. But Jack, really—psychological growth? Character development? Plot line? Never thought this New Biography business would reach, well, this far.

So there I am in Genesis and Exodus, living out my "childhood," creating you folks and then wondering if I've made a huge mistake. Then, I have to be "seduced out of a recurrence of his rage by the scent of Noah's offering." Soon, I become "dangerously unpredictable" and evolve into "a man [a man!] of unreflective self-confidence, intrusive-to-aggressive habits, and unpredictable eloquence . . . who discloses nothing about his past and next to nothing about his needs or desires."

Jack, I'm wondering who you were writing about! Is that the way I come across? My message?

Only later on, apparently, do I discover that there are the poor, and something should be done for them, that I'm a Father as well as a King, that I need an emotional life and that I am "aware of my literal uniqueness and extraordinary power." What ever happened to the "I Am Who I Am" school of thought?

You say the only way I have of knowing myself is through mankind. And then you go on to criticize me for being tough and then tender, for what you perceive as my life of "action, speech, silence." Can't you just think of me as a teacher tapping the blackboard, explaining what the lesson was and then waiting for the students to figure out what I said? (Yes, I know, Bible stories go on a bit, but we're talking 4,000-plus years, filled with many writers, rewriters and those pagans, Huns and assorted barbarians who didn't help by destroying the goods—the other side's been busy, you know.) I'm still waiting. But there's time. Eternity, really.

What would you have had of me? Some God who speaks in gender-neutral, inclusive, guilt-acknowledging full paragraphs? It didn't make sense. Mysteriously allegorical, that's more my way. What better way to bring the soul to faith? I didn't go through all this to end up with a paint-by-numbers human race.

You said it well, early on: What I brought was ethical monotheism, where "moral value shall have been placed above the other values that human beings properly recognize: power, wealth, pleasure, beauty, knowledge . . . the list is long." And that's a messy business, trying to convince people that they shouldn't pursue those baubles and fleeting glories. Look, from golden calves to the Internet, folks have been seeking cheap grace for a long time. Forever, it seems.

I think there's a tendency in your day to try to redraw me (and My Boy, too—can't tell you how many books we get on Him) so people can quantify and be more comfortable with the concept of the divine. It seems they want to build a display case, with good lighting and temperature control so folks can press their noses up to the glass, peer in and say, "I saw God!"

Is it me you people seek to understand? Or what you want to make of me, to suit your own needs today? In your time, at your convenience? Should I really be cast as a warrior whose greatest battle is with himself? Or one who created man as a reflection, eventually to cast him as a rival?

Really, I'm not all that complicated. If you are made in my image, then you know what it's like to struggle, to make firm decisions and then to find yourself having to go back on them—out of simple love. Do you think it's different for me? Of course it was a terrific gamble with creation—but otherwise I would have been a cosmic puppeteer, with you folks on strings at my fingertips. Talk about a boring eternity. I still believe in you—but you've got to come my way, too.

I know I haven't made it easy and that the way is often hard to see. Two hundred years of historical Biblical research have clarified and clouded, and you, Jack, boldly walked where others feared to tread, assaying not human reaction, but divine plan. Some say after Job I subsided. You saw me as incorporated into the Jewish nation, no longer needed as a physical presence. Touché, Jack.

This was a monumental book to write. I'm sure it just about did you in at times. But, at the end, there you were, all the fancy writing and turns of phrase aside: "God is the divided original of which we are the divided image. His is the restless breathing we still hear in our sleep."

I like that, Jack. I like it a lot.

Best wishes until we meet; we'll talk it all over and I'll give you the whole story then. As they say, face to face. No hurry Jack; have a good time. I'll be here.

Until then, sweet dreams,

God

Marina Warner (review date 30 April 1995)

SOURCE: "The Divine Protagonist," in *Book World—The Washington Post,* Vol. XXV, No. 18, April 30, 1995, p. 2.

[*In the following review, Warner praises Miles's attempt to look at the Bible in a new way. Saying "the book belongs in a fresh tradition of biblical scholarship," Warner nevertheless faults Miles's interpretation, calling the Bible an "epic without a hero."*]

Reversing the usual angle of view, a character in one of Jose Saramago's novels overhears Christ on the cross asking humankind to forgive God: "Forgive Him for He knows not what He has done." In this audacious new study, [*God: A Biography,*] Jack Miles also tackles the character of God on startlingly equal terms from a skeptical viewpoint. He doesn't mete out blame or praise but approaches God as "a complex character" out of a book, with a personality that reverberates far and wide, farther and wider than his nearest rivals as household names—a Hamlet or a Heathcliff. Though, like them, God lives a life inside a world of words, nobody has ever analyzed him, as if he were above such scrutiny.

But God isn't inscrutable or even mysterious, Miles argues; he's an eminently approachable protagonist, who changes and develops as the narrative proceeds, moving through the roles of creator, avenger, personal friend (Exodus), warrior, conqueror, lawgiver, father (2 Samuel) and the errant wife of the thundering prophets. He has distinctive traits: At the very start he wants to make copies of himself; he's a being torn and divided internally, capable of deception, double-dealing and broken promises but who also knows remorse. He can be tender; even he comes to value women's practical survival skills (Ruth). And, at the end of his life in the Hebrew Bible, he falls silent and withdraws after he has tormented Job, as if he

has finally acknowledged defeat at the hands of this single just believer.

> **Miles is in intellectual earnest, and his book belongs in a fresh tradition of biblical scholarship, which treats scripture as a work of literature whose quality and interest do not lie in its truthfulness to history or its divine revelations but in its internal conflicts, insights, riches.**
>
> **—Marina Warner**

The idea of theobiography at all requires some cheek: Even for agnostics, God isn't identical to a made-up hero, and the Bible is still one of the chief sources of human knowledge about the divine nature. For ordinary readers of the Bible, too, this approach evinces a certain gleeful irreverence, which Jack Miles—perhaps his Jesuit past shows here—clearly enjoys. After suggesting that God is envious of human sexual independence, Miles asks, "Does God realize this about himself?", and he draws a nearly Yiddish comic picture of God and Israel squabbling and griping at each other before he concludes, perceptively, that this biblical culture of complaint leads to "moral reform as a perennial possibility in Western social history."

For Miles is in intellectual earnest, and his book belongs in a fresh tradition of biblical scholarship, which treats scripture as a work of literature whose quality and interest do not lie in its truthfulness to history or its divine revelations but in its internal conflicts, insights, riches. But in this respect, God is a thin character. Here is a narrative hero who has no past, no family, no love life: "a parentless, childless being, a cosmic orphan . . ." Monotheism condemns its deity to eternal solitude, with no other gods to fight or supersede or marry, unlike the Olympians. In his solipsistic isolation, he doesn't console himself with self-examination or reflection; the soliloquy isn't his chosen means of expression but rather the ukase, the curse, the trumpet blast: "A blessing on him who seizes your babies and dashes them against the rocks!"

That the God of battles, the Lord God of hosts, could be a bully, everyone has always known. But a hollow man? A bore?

The author has created some of his own problems. For in order to arrive at his picture of God's character-development from speech to action to the silence after Job, he has followed the Tanakh or Hebrew Bible (an acronym from Torah; Nebim, the Prophets; and Ketubim, the Writings), in which the Psalms and Proverbs come in the middle, before Ruth, for example, and more significantly, before Job. Few Christian readers know this sequence, and so few will recognize the divinity falling silent after Job trounces his idea of human potential, since in all other Bibles he then positively begins to gush and flow through the psalmist's praises.

Furthermore, the Bible is an odd case, the author rightly points out: a classic in translation. But it isn't a classic in any or all translations, and the question of language doesn't give him enough pause. Literary criticism of a character in a text needs to respond to the linguistic cadences, echoes, rhythms in which he is represented. The Hebrew Bible and its god are hardly known in the English of the 1985 Jewish Publication Society's Tanakh. The hold that the King James version has on the globe—the majority of Bible translations are based on the Revised Standard Version in English—means that God's personality has been mediated across cultures in 17th-century English; hence the constant "smiting of foes," the "Lo's" and "Woes unto them!"

But even within the textual boundaries of the Jewish tradition, the author has chosen to limit his focus in the oddest ways. The erotic lyrics of The Song of Songs nearly didn't make it into the canon, but did so in the 1st century when the Jewish scholar Aquiba argued that the love songs were a religious allegory. This ingenious reading has served everyone well—and Miles could have profited, too. He could have relented towards his chosen subject and allowed God his moment as an irresistible lover—"my soul melteth, while my beloved spake"—in that headiest and most voluptuously beautiful of all the books of the Bible.

It's also peculiar, to this reader, to tell God's life and leave out the New Testament; there, at least, he belongs in a kind of dysfunctional family, an absent father who loves his only son and doesn't know how to express it. *God: A Biography* is a bright, shiny new idea; it makes rich connections and many witty, astringent comments; and it really catches fire during a close reading of the Book of Job. But it is hampered throughout by the imaginative penury of God's personal circumstances. As Jack Miles admits, "A protagonist without a past yields a narrative without a memory." The Bible, it turns out, can't be read as if it were a 19th-century Bildungsroman; it is much more realistically existential than that—it's an epic without a hero.

Phyllis Trible (review date 14 May 1995)

SOURCE: "A Flawed Character," in *The New York Times Book Review,* May 14, 1995, p. 10.

[*In the following review, Trible acknowledges Miles's schol-*

arly achievements but faults his omission of the prophetic literature in Jeremiah, Ezekiel and Hosea. The critic also pans the diversionary focus on other characters such as Abraham, Jacob, Esau, and Pharaoh.]

In recent years literary studies of the Bible have explored all kinds of topics—save God, the chief protagonist of the narrative. That not insignificant subject has now received its due, a tour de force called *God: A Biography,* by Jack Miles.

If some people may find a biography of God an irreverent enterprise, Mr. Miles is not one of them. He says that over centuries the Bible has been the fundamental document for both Jews and Christians. Its stories and characters have permeated the whole of Western culture. To track, then, the stories to their central character is in no way disrespectful. But Mr. Miles does engage in occasional provocation. At the outset he remarks that "God is no saint, strange to say." As the reader will find out, that is true enough, and the fact is not so strange.

Mr. Miles treats the Bible as a literary work. To produce a biography of a literary character is a complicated undertaking, and so in a sometimes amusing introductory chapter he guides the reader through the contrast in approaches taken by scholars and critics. With a light touch he describes his own approach as naive, seeing God as a real person, much the way a theatergoer thinks of Hamlet or a reader perceives Don Quixote. But he also knows there is a difference. "No character . . . on stage, page or screen," he says, "has ever had the reception that God has had."

Mr. Miles is an appropriate biographer. He is now a book columnist for *The Los Angeles Times,* but was once a member of the Jesuit order and studied at both the Gregorian College in Rome and Hebrew University in Jerusalem before he took his doctoral degree at Harvard University in ancient Near Eastern languages and literatures. His naiveté is well-informed.

He wants to get to know God the way people get to know one another, bit by bit, over time. So he chooses to read the Hebrew Bible from the beginning right through. The chief difference between the Hebrew Bible and the Old Testament is the ordering of the books, and the ordering affects the way in which God's character develops. Whereas in the Old Testament the prophetic books appear at the end of the sequence, in the Hebrew Bible they appear in the middle. The Hebrew Bible is known by a Hebrew acronym pronounced Tanakh, for the letters "t," "n" and "k," which signify its three major parts: Torah (teaching), Nebi'im (prophets) and Ketubim (writings). Mr. Miles reads the Tanakh as a coherent and integral work, without trying to identify what in it is myth, what is legend and what is history, the way most literary scholars do. He allows himself, however, some forays into historical and theological issues.

Who is the literary character called God? Simply put, a male with multiple personalities, which emerge gradually. At the beginning God creates the world in order to make a self-image, an indication that He does not fully understand who He is but discovers Himself through interaction with humanity. Immediately the focus narrows to the man and the woman in the garden. When they disobey their creator, He responds vindictively and so reveals His own inner conflict. Called God in Genesis 1, he is lofty, powerful and bountiful; called Lord God in Genesis 2 and 3, he is intimate and volatile. Ambivalent about His image, the creator becomes the destroyer: the flood descends. A radical fault runs through the character of God.

Still other personalities surface as the cosmic God becomes the personal deity of Abraham and the friend of the family for Jacob and Joseph. In the Exodus story he shows himself to be a warrior and soon thereafter a lawgiver and liege. This mixture of identities represents a fusion of selected traits gathered from other deities in the ancient world (and teased out of the biblical texts by a generation of historical scholars)? A grand speech by Moses in Deuteronomy synthesizes these conflicting personalities to produce a relatively stable identity for God by the conclusion of the Torah.

Within this identity elements of divine self-discovery continue to develop. The first section of the Nebi'im, from Joshua, through Kings, turns the liberator of Exodus into the conqueror of Canaan, the friend of the family into the "father" of Solomon, and the lawgiver of Israel into the arbiter of international relations.

But the ending of Kings threatens to terminate God's life. It reports the destruction of the people with whom He has been working out the divine image. If His biography is to continue beyond their demise, God must change, and the prophetic books following Kings record the transformation. In them the conflicted character God carries on a life-or-death struggle to reassemble the unstable elements of His personality. In the first 39 chapters of Isaiah He tries the role of executioner, but He also holds up a vision of a peaceable kingdom. Then, in the next 27 chapters of Isaiah, He forgoes destruction and insists that mystery, not power, is the source of his holiness.

Regrettably, Mr. Miles skips over the bulk of the prophetic literature. By excluding Jeremiah, Ezekiel and Hosea, for example, he misses out on important texts for discerning God's developing personality. One consequence of these omissions is a less than satisfying discussion of female language and imagery for God. To be sure, Mr. Miles does explore the question of whether a goddess resides within Israel's God. But he hangs his discussion on Malachi (the last of the prophetic books), in which, so he claims, God refers to Himself as the wife of Israel. The matter of the female in God is far from settled.

God begins to withdraw in the last division of the Tanakh, Mr. Miles says. For the most part, testimony about Him replaces speech by Him. Psalms perceives Him primarily as counselor. Proverbs treats Him like a picture frame, He is marginal to the content of the book. But in Job His destructive impulse comes fully into consciousness. The climax happens through the man Job, who, as the perfect image of the Creator, exposes the conflicted character of God. The outcome brings about repentance—not of Job, for he has done no wrong, but of God, who restores good fortune to Job.

At places the argument [in *God: A Biography*] is strained and prone to hyperbole. Nonetheless, with artistic sensitivity Mr. Miles has accomplished what others failed to try. He has made a certain literary sense of the character God in the totality of the Tanakh.

—*Phyllis Trible*

After the Book of Job, God never speaks again, though others repeat His speeches and report His miraculous deeds. Two sets of four books each shape these parts of the biography. In the Song of Solomon, God does not appear in the garden of Love. Ruth treats Him as a bystander who does not interact with the human characters. Lamentations waits sadly for this recluse who never comes. And Ecclesiastes declares Him a puzzle of no compelling importance. In literary terms Mr. Miles sees these books, taken together, as a denouement: they let time pass.

Following the pause, God's life moves to an elusive culmination, the last four books—endings—matching the four beginnings (creation, flood, Abraham, Moses). In Esther God is totally absent. Daniel emphatically brings Him back, but as "the Ancient of Days," an aging deity who in retirement has become passive and silent. Ezra and Nehemiah allot God an honored place, though they treat Him "like their enfeebled but cherished ward," in Mr. Miles's words. The close of Chronicles, especially the line "let him go up," repeats the opening words of Ezra to set up a literary round that in principle keeps the story of God going forever. But for Mr. Miles the moment of beauty and tenderness comes many chapters earlier: a prayer of David ascribes to God all things, most specifically greatness, power, glory, victory and majesty.

This is God's biography but many other characters appear in it, and the author is not above diverting the reader with idiosyncratic digressions. He proposes, for instance, that Abraham is not a model of faithfulness but of defiance; that Jacob at the Jabbok wrestles not with God but with Esau; that the Israelites in Egypt are not an oppressed minority seeking liberation but a majority of the population whom Pharaoh tries to dominate; that God engaged in a long struggle with humanity over the control of human fertility and that the Exodus is not a victory for justice but for fertility; that the first recorded move away from the tyranny of fertility comes in the first book of Samuel, in the gracious words of Elkanah to his barren wife Hannah; that the conflicted personalities of Isaiah, Jeremiah and Ezekiel correspond to the manic, the depressive and the psychotic types in modern psychology; and that Satan in Job and Wisdom in Proverbs are mirror images, he taking on the malevolent aspect of God and she the beneficent.

At the end, Mr. Miles ponders why the life of the Lord God begins in activity and speech only to close in passivity and silence. Does God's desire for self-knowledge, shown in the creation of humanity in his image, carry the potential for tragedy? Surely the confrontation staged in Job brings God near that reality. But God is rescued. The Song of Solomon changes the subject, thereby sparing the life of God, and subsequent books give Him a different life. Though His contradictory character keeps Him trapped within Himself, it can be "trumped . . . by some comedic intrusion."

The twists and turns of this formidable reading offer more than enough to stir up people who are at ease in Zion, and those who are not. All who believe that God, or the devil, is in the details will have trouble. At places the argument is strained and prone to hyperbole. Nonetheless, with artistic sensitivity Mr. Miles has accomplished what others failed to try. He has made a certain literary sense of the character God in the totality of the Tanakh.

Luke Timothy Johnson (review date 19 May 1995)

SOURCE: "What a Character!," in *Commonweal,* Vol. CXXII, No. 10, May 19, 1995, pp. 32-4.

[*In the following review, Johnson praises portions of* God: A Biography *for "stunning prose" and inventiveness but contends the book is also deeply flawed in its reliance on the order of books in the* Tanakh *and in its focus on God's emotions.*]

Should we think of the Bible as a kind of novel, with God as the story's protagonist? And if we read the Bible in this way, will it deepen our understanding of God or of ourselves, or of the "book" we regard as sacred Scripture? Jack Miles attempts such a character study of the "Lord God" as that figure is developed within the Hebrew Bible. (An excerpt from *God: A Biography* was featured in *Commonweal*'s March 10 issue.)

Borrowing the distinction made by William Kerrigan about readers of Shakespeare, Miles associates himself with those "critics" who think about the character of Hamlet, rather than with those "scholars" who are concerned only about the play *Hamlet*. Although the features of the character can be derived only from the text, it is only when we can imagine that character as "real" and "alive" outside the text that the character becomes compelling and places demands on our imagination. Miles moves from the hints provided by the biblical text concerning what "Lord God" thought, spoke, and did, to reflections on who this character might be.

Since Miles traces the development of God's character through the sequence of biblical books, the ordering of the texts is obviously important. Should God's character be drawn from the sequence of the Christian Old Testament (based on the Septuagint), which follows the narrative accounts with wisdom writings and concludes with the prophets? Or should it be constructed from the order of the Hebrew canon (the *Tanakh*), in which God first acts, then speaks, but then falls silent? Miles chooses to follow the *Tanakh*.

He seeks to identify the character traits of God in this sequence of texts, considering God in turn as creator, destroyer, friend of the family, liberator, lawgiver, liege, conqueror, father, arbiter, executioner, holy one, wife, counselor, guarantor, fiend, sleeper, bystander, recluse, puzzle, absence, ancient of days, scroll. He pauses frequently for *excursi* that pose such reflective questions as "Does God Love?" or "Does God Fail?" or (perhaps most provocatively), "Does God Lose Interest?"

Here's the story of "Lord God" in brief: God is a being without any history but with a pronounced case of multiple personality disorder. He wants a history, so invents humans "in his image." God can't decide what exactly to do with these beings, but gives them the power to reproduce, then tries to find himself in their story, changing as they change, gathering new character traits through their experience. First he fights them jealously for the power over life, then becomes a warrior who develops a taste for blood, and finally, after showing his power once too often to the canny and adamant Job, falls silent, allowing himself to be utterly incorporated into the life of the people, and ultimately, in their book about him. In short, God both finds and loses himself in his human creature. Miles concludes by suggesting that the reason why humans in the "Western Tradition" have such a complex sense of self is that they learned it from the odd combination of unity and multiplicity in their biblical God.

Although the book adopts a deliberate sort of naiveté in its tracing of God's character (taking only what the text will give, being surprised even when the text is not), it is not in the least unlearned. The author's credentials as a student of the biblical world in its Near Eastern environment are abundantly displayed, and his choice of contemporary conversation partners matches in sophistication his often stunning prose. There is much that is inventive here, much that is deeply interesting.

For all that, the book is, in my judgment, also deeply flawed. The project is obviously limited by its self-restriction to the order of books in the *Tanakh*. Neither for Judaism nor Christianity has the character of God been derived solely from those writings. By failing to trace the character of God as it is developed in the Christian writings of the New Testament, or continues to function as a character in Jewish intertestamental, rabbinic, and mystical literature, Miles ends up dealing with a literary abstraction.

The character of God, I would argue, has probably never been constructed from the kind of sequential reading of the canonical books here undertaken by Miles. It has been constructed in much more complex fashion in a free-ranging conversation with these texts and many others in the life and prayer and study of these rich and living religious traditions. For that reason, Miles's choice to consider the psalms (to take one example) only in one place in the sequence betrays their very essence as prayer, which resists such linear ideas of development. The psalms are not a moment in the development of a character but contain within themselves all the moments of past (and, for Christians) future developments of God's character. Miles's profile is therefore interesting but not compelling, for it is, in a very real sense, beside the point for most readers of these texts or worshipers of this God.

There are other problems in execution, even when the value of Miles's project is accepted. It seems to me to be a lapse in method to invoke, as he does, extrabiblical mythology and lore from the Ancient Near East, and use it in constructing God's character. If we want to work just with what the Bible gives us, then we should stick to that. If Miles wants to work in some cultural intertextuality, then he should give up the "construction of character from the unfolding of narrative" naiveté. But the artificiality of this pose is also shown by Miles's insistence on arguing repeatedly from silence: "if the Bible has not yet told us this or that about God, then God must not yet have been this or that." I'm not quite sure what to call this fallacy, but I am fairly sure that it is not even good literary criticism to suppose that characters acquire traits only as the text announces them.

Finally, Miles's own preoccupations are perhaps read into the text more than he realizes. I was struck by how much attention was paid to what might be called the emotive side of God's character, and how little to his mental side. The most obvious example is the portrayal of God as Lawgiver. Miles acknowledges the transtemporal greatness of the Ten Commandments. But he barely pauses over the specifically *characterological* implications of the heart of Torah. He rushes on to the bloodthirstiness of God, shown in the various punishments to be administered. He does not celebrate—as the entire rabbinic tradition has celebrated—what the very *concept* of covenant and law says about the character of God. I can only conclude that Miles considers that the confused passions of persons are more constitutive of their character than the products of their minds. Which makes me not look forward to any book he might write on the Trinity.

T. Howland Sanks (review date 1 July 1995)

SOURCE: A review of *God: A Biography,* in America, Vol. 173, No. 1, July 1, 1995, pp. 24, 26.

[*In the following review, Sanks notes that* God: A Biography *is reliant on the reader accepting a variation in the order in which the books of the Bible appear. Despite this, he calls the book "fascinating" and praises Miles's ability to stimulate readers to imagine God in new ways.*]

The title [of *God: A Biography*], though arresting, may sound impudent or presumptuous. It is neither. It is a literary study of the Lord God, protagonist of one of the great classics of world literature. By a strictly sequential reading of the Hebrew Bible, Miles imaginatively reconstructs a life of God that has "a surprising drama and pathos about it." Adopting a stance of "deliberate naïveté," he prescinds for the most part from strictly historical and theological considerations and treats the Bible as a work of literature. The result is a tour de force.

The naïveté has to be a deliberate posture, for Jack Miles is anything but naïve. A former Jesuit, Miles has a doctorate in Near Eastern languages from Harvard, was literary editor of *The Los Angeles Times,* where he is currently a columnist and member of the editorial board, and a 1990 Guggenheim Fellow.

Two premises underlie this ambitious undertaking: 1) that "neither the work (the Bible) nor the character is so inhuman that interpersonal appraisal is out of the question," and 2) that "the order in which the books of the Bible appear . . . is a crucial artistic consideration." The second is particularly important because Miles follows the sequence of books in the Hebrew Bible, the *Tanakh,* as opposed to the Christian Old Testament. In the Hebrew Bible, the prophetic books appear in between the Torah and the Writings, whereas they are last in the Old Testament. The sequence affects how the character of the Lord God develops.

From this literary perspective, the character of God not only develops, it is also a character of multiple personalities, an amalgam, perhaps, of several ancient Near Eastern deities. From the opening of Genesis, God is a conflictive personality. In the first account of creation he is called God, *elohim* and creates man because he wants an image. He is sovereign power. His only command is to "Be fertile and increase" and nothing is forbidden; there is no story of human transgression. In the second account, he is called the Lord God, *yahweh elohim,* and seemingly creates man because he wants company rather than an image. Now there is a prohibition—not to eat of the forbidden fruit—and a transgression. Now the Lord God, regretting what he has done, explodes in fury and punishes vindictively. And then, in a tender parental gesture, covers his humiliated creatures with garments he himself puts on them. What kind of a Lord God is this?

The ambivalent relationship between the Lord God and humans continues as he shows himself to be a destroyer in the story of the Flood, of which he repents, and promises Noah never to do again. With Abraham he becomes not only creator-destroyer, but also a more personal God and, in the stories of Jacob and Joseph, a "friend of the family." In Exodus, the Lord God becomes a warrior deity, much like the Canaanite god, Baal, then Liberator and Lawgiver.

For the literary biographer, the beginning is crucial. Miles compares Genesis and Exodus to "God's childhood" when his basic identity is formed. He changes less in the following books—where he is found as Liege Lord in Leviticus, Numbers and Deuteronomy, as Conqueror in Joshua and Judges, as Father in I and II Samuel and as Arbiter in I and II Kings.

There are equally mixed messages about the Lord God to be found in the prophetic literature, which Miles considers "the self-characterization of God in non-narrative form." But all these contradictory messages are presumed to be from the same divine source. The Lord God presents himself "like a lover, a husband, a mother, a shepherd, a gardener, a king and . . . a redeemer and 'the Holy One of Israel.'" In addition, in the Book of Isaiah, he is inherently unknowable. Yet this incomprehensibility is combined with divine access to the human heart and forms "the defining incongruity at the core of the word "God" as it is understood in the West.

For Miles, the climax of the Lord God's relationship to his creatures and of his own self-understanding is found in the Book of Job. In the speeches of the Voice from the Whirlwind, the Lord God is the ultimate synthesis of all that is terrifying in human existence—"evil and good must be found simultaneously and personally in him if they are found anywhere." God knows his own ambiguity as he has never known it before. These speeches from the Whirlwind are God's last will and testament; from the end of the Book of Job to the end of the *Tanakh,* God never speaks again.

In the rest of the books, God is seen as "sleeper," "bystander" or "recluse." The story line has gone from action (creator, liberator, warrior), to speech (messages from God in the prophets), to silence (the Ancient of Days in Daniel), seemingly retired from the scene. So much so, that in a Postlude, Miles asks "Does God Lose Interest?"

This is a fascinating book. Miles's intellectually imaginative construction of a life of God stimulates even the most familiar reader to imagine God in new ways. And yet it is not mere fantasy. Miles's biography of God is solidly based in historical and literary scholarship. The God of the Bible is more complex, terrifying, unpredictable and mysterious than we can possibly imagine. Truly, the Holy is *mysterium tremendum et fascinans!*

FURTHER READING

Criticism

Gardels, Nathan. "Pluralism and Faith in the Next Millennium." *New Perspectives Quarterly* 13, No. 2 (Spring 1996): 44-7.
  Interview with the author.

Mesic, Penelope. "Up Close and Personal with God." *Chicago Tribune* (26 April 1996): 1.
  Presents Miles's comments about *God: A Biography.*

Miller, Ross. "God's Book Revisited." *Chicago Tribune* (7 May 1995): 1.
  Describes *God: A Biography* as a "brilliant, audacious work."

The Moor's Last Sigh
Salman Rushdie

Indian-born English novelist, critic, and nonfiction writer.

The following entry provides analysis and criticism of *The Moor's Last Sigh*. For further information on Rushdie's life and career, see *CLC*, Volumes 23, 31, and 55.

INTRODUCTION

Rushdie is best known as the author of *The Satanic Verses* (1988), the book condemned by many Muslims as an insult to their religion. Former Iranian leader Ayatollah Khomeini called for the execution of Rushdie and his publisher, forcing the author into hiding from bounty hunters for almost a decade until the publication of *The Moor's Last Sigh* (1995). With this latest work, Rushdie chose to return to limited public exposure, and some critics have found evidence in the book to suggest that Rushdie has reconciled himself to life under threat of death.

Plot and Major Characters

The Moor of the title is Moraes "Moor" Zogoiby, cursed with a "double-quick" life: his mother, after wishing in a moment of frustration for a child who would grow up quickly, gives birth to him four and a half months after his conception, and he continues to age at twice the normal rate. Moraes's mother, Aurora da Gama, is a famous artist and his father, twenty years older than his mother, is a former clerk in her family's spice business who finds more lucrative employment in smuggling and drug trafficking. Moraes becomes entangled in rivalries between his parents and their competitors, becoming a prisoner of an artist jealous of his mother who allows him to live as long as he writes his life story. Throughout the story Rushdie relates the history of the family as far back as explorer Vasco da Gama, discoverer of India, and draws parallels with the family's circumstances in modern time. The "Moor's last sigh" of the title has a number of explanations, one being that it is the title of a portrait of Moraes, the last his mother painted before her death.

Major Themes

As is often the case with Rushdie's work, reviewers found a number of overlapping and intermingled themes within *The Moor's Last Sigh*, many concerning the state of India and its people. Most critics described the story as extremely complex, filled with symbolism, elements of magic realism, and layer upon layer of meaning. In attempting to name one main theme, however, most found it to be the history of India up to

the present day mirrored by the history of one powerful, fictitious family. James Bowman described *The Moor's Last Sigh* as "a story of enormous complexity about the rise and fall of a part-Jewish, part-Christian dynasty of Indian merchants from the early years of this century down to the present." Although Moraes narrates the story, many reviewers contended that Aurora da Gama is actually the main character of the story, representing not only Moraes's mother but Mother India as well.

Critical Reception

Much of the critical attention surrounding *The Moor's Last Sigh* centered on the importance of the book as a sign of Rushdie's reemergence as an active literary figure. Although still cautious about the *fatwa*, or death sentence, imposed upon him for *The Satanic Verses*, Rushdie made some public appearances in support of his new novel. Several critics analyzed *The Moor's Last Sigh* for signs of the *fatwa*'s effect on Rushdie's writing style or ability, pointing to passages in the new book that seem to reveal the author's state of mind throughout his exile. Critics also scrutinized the new work for material that could rekindle the controversy of *The Satanic Verses.* While some predicted that the work would offend Hindus as *The Satanic Verses* offended Muslims, most described *The Moor's Last Sigh* as containing some contentious portions but nothing to rival that of its predecessor. Several reviewers also noted, however, that while *The Moor's Last Sigh* does not equal *The Satanic Verses* in scandalous content, neither does it demonstrate meekness or submission on the part of the author. In comparing *The Moor's Last Sigh* with Rushdie's body of work, critics remarked on his continuing devotion to lavish but often unflattering descriptions of India, sweeping historical story lines, and crowds of characters whose comings and goings within the story cannot be predicted by the conventions of modern fiction writing. "Filled with puns and verbal games, buffoonery and scenes of slapstick comedy," *The Moor's Last Sigh* "proves that Rushdie is one of the most brilliant magicians of the English language writing now," Orhan Pamuk commented. Many critics also pointed to the author's way of delivering biting criticism veiled in metaphor or stories with the story, Rushdie trademarks again in evidence in *The Moor's Last Sigh,* as signs that he has rebounded from his ordeal.

PRINCIPAL WORKS

Grimus (novel) 1975
Midnight's Children (novel) 1981
Shame (novel) 1983
The Satanic Verses (novel) 1988
Haroun and the Sea of Stories (juvenile) 1990
The Moor's Last Sigh (novel) 1995

CRITICISM

Aamer Hussein (review date September 1995)

SOURCE: "City of Mongrel Joy," in *New Statesman & Society,* Vol. 8, No. 369, September, 1995, pp. 39-40.

[*In the following review, Hussein relates the plot of* The Moor's Last Sigh.]

Moraes Zogoiby, nicknamed Moor—the half-Jewish, half-Christian narrator of *The Moor's Last Sigh*—is on his way to self-exile in Spain. At the conclusion of a harrowing portrayal of the events that lead up to his city's moral and physical devastation, he muses: "There was nothing holding me to Bombay anymore. It was no longer my Bombay, no longer special, no longer the city of mixed-up, mongrel joy."

For the city of Bombay—in reality, as in Salman Rushdie's stunningly accurate dark recreation in his latest and possibly finest novel—has fallen prey to violence, corruption and the likes of the novel's villainous Raman Fielding (nicknamed Mainduck, or frog).

Fielding is the leader of a party of chauvinists and thugs who masquerade as the religious and righteous, preach the Rule of Ram and advocate an ethnically cleansed Mahrashtrian capital. He is a twin soul of the real-life demagogue Bal Thackeray, whose pseudo-ideologies, proclaimed by his Shiv Sena party, Fielding shares. And Rushdie mischievously names him, like Thackeray, after one of English literatures's founding fathers.

Moor, who miraculously ages twice as fast as his contemporaries and bears a crippled and crippling right hand, comes to know Fielding quite intimately. His mother, Aurora Zogoiby, a secular Christian of partly Portuguese descent, is India's most esteemed painter and showcase example of the elevated position of minorities. His father, like Aurora from the Southern city of Cochin, is her Jewish plutocrat husband. (But Moor may, according to one of the novel's entertaining asides, be the product of a lost night his mother perhaps spent with Nehru.)

> The reason for the failure of Rushdie's many imitators lies in their inability to integrate fantastic narrative with historical insight.
>
> —*Aamer Hussein*

Moor is raised in the lap of secular, liberal beliefs. He falls in love with the beautiful Uma, a deranged and brilliant young Hindu artist. Uma sets herself up as a rival—personally and professionally—to his mother; Moor is quite unprepared for the onslaught of the opportunistic new India, with its artists ready to scavenge in the "dead sea" of their country's heritage or pass off—as Uma does—postmodernist vacuity as religious fervour.

Rejected by his parents as a result of Uma's mad machinations, Moor is forced, after a terrifying stint in prison, to abandon his privileged lifestyle. He is transported to the "Under World" over which Fielding, an ambiguously malign Hades, presides. But this underworld is closely connected to—is, in fact, the foundation of—the world of appearances Moor formerly inhabited. His own father's fortune is aided by judicious dabbling in "white powder". As Moor comes to learn: "they are not inhuman, these Mainduck-style little Hitlers, and it is in their humanity that we must locate our collective guilt . . for if they are just monsters . . . then the rest of us are excused. I personally do not wish to be excused. I made my choice and lived my life."

The Moor's Last Sigh meditates with generosity on identity and exile, love and art. It is also a searing examination of personal responsibility, and of our complicity in the making of history. In earlier works, Rushdie's critiques of religious extremism often exist as scattered fragments; but here, his dismantling of the fanaticism and pseudo-religious mythologising that fuel Fielding's (and Thackeray's) denunciations of "invaders" and Mughals (ie Muslims), is thorough and incisive. The fundamentalist Ram of the rabble-rousers has little to do with the benign legend of the god-king himself.

Faced with the sectarian riots that follow the destruction of the Babri mosque in December 1992, Moor—himself the product of two "minority" groups—gives quarter to neither warring faction: not the ascendant One, nor the "justly enraged" Many. "There comes a point in the unfurling of communal violence in which it becomes irrelevant to ask, 'Who started it?' The lethal conjugations of death part company with any possibility of justification, let alone justice. They surge among us, left and right, Hindu and Muslim . . . Both their houses are damned by their deeds".

But to reduce *The Moor's Last Sigh* merely to its political sources and diagnoses would be unjust. The reason for the failure of Rushdie's many imitators lies in their inability to integrate fantastic narrative with historical insight. He and his friend Angela Carter stand almost alone among their contemporaries in their seminal impact on a generation of British (and Anglophone) writers. Their inventive zeal and astonishing ability to remake received texts remain inimitable.

Whereas for Carter's investigations, the world of artifice sufficed, Rushdie battles with the grand narratives of history. He voices its questions and occasionally delivers painfully apt answers. Like Márquez, the writer with whom he has often been ineptly compared, Rushdie can extract from a family saga the chronicle of a nation's yearnings. His tales within tales of the lives and loves of the Catholic da Gamas and the Jewish Zogoibys—and their zeals, loyalist or nationalist—tell of a century of upper-class Indian aspirations.

His technique is more ambitious than ever. Barriers between fiction and "real life" are made more permeable. Along with the quaintly named denizens of his re-imagined world, iconic figures from "real life"—Nehru and the film star Nargis (Mother India), cricketers, art critics, the writers Chughtai and Manto—mingle with his protagonists. One of Aurora's most famous paintings is inspired by the nonsense phrase uttered by the mad hero of "Toba Tek Singh", Manto's allegory of the partition of India. The irrepressible Rushdie has

Aurora accused by the bigots of pro-Pakistan sympathies for her tribute to Manto's art.

The opulent and variegated prose abounds with allusions to Indian languages, Urdu poetry, folklore, film songs and "Bollywood" culture. The novel's tragic vision is framed in its author's humour; it is also sexier than anything he has written before. Its guiding metaphor is, however, contained in Aurora's paintings, which give the novel takes its title: a vision of an India that mirrors the last years of Moorish Spain.

With the self-aggrandisement of the obsessional artist, Aurora stages herself as Ayxa, that world's last empress, with Moor as the less-than worthy Sultan Boabdil. "In a way these were . . . an attempt to create a romantic myth of the plural, hybrid nation; she was using Arab Spain to reimagine India . . . there was a didacticism here, but what with the vivid surrealism of her images and the kingfisher brilliance of her colouring . . . it was easy not to feel preached at, to revel in the carnival without listening to the barker, to dance to the music without caring for the message in the song."

But this story's messages, to its teller's credit, refuse to be lost in its brightness and its ribaldry. The disaffected exiled Moor learns that it is better to have loved and lost, and reflects about his people and his lost land: "The best, and the worst, were in us, and fought in us, as they fought in the land at large. In some of us, the worst triumphed; but still we could say—and say truthfully—that we had loved the best."

Michael Wood (review date 7 September 1995)

SOURCE: "Shenanigans," in *London Review of Books,* Vol. 17, No. 17, September 7, 1995, pp. 3, 5.

[*In the following review, Wood presents an in-depth analysis of Rushdie's career, culminating with* The Moor's Last Sigh.]

The Moor's last sigh is several things, both inside and outside Salman Rushdie's sprawling new novel. It is the defeated farewell of the last Moorish ruler in Spain, the Sultan Boabdil leaving his beloved Granada in 1492, a year also known for other travels. It is Othello's last gasp of jealousy and violence. It is, in the novel, the name of two paintings depicting Boabdil's departure; and it is what the novel itself becomes, the long, breathless, terminal narration of the asthmatic Moraes Zogoiby, alias 'Moor'. *Old Moore's Almanac* flickers somewhere here ('Old Moor will sigh no more'), as does Luis Buñuel's *dernier soupir* (which appears as the Ultimo Suspiro petrol station). Ingrid Bergman and Humphrey Bogart were wrong, we learn, to think that a sigh is just a sigh: a sigh could be almost anything, and the name Zogoiby is a version of the Arabic *elzogoybi,* 'the unlucky one', the sobriquet traditionally attached to Boabdil.

Boabdil is elegiac shorthand for a delicate, plural civilisation unable to defend itself against single-minded religion; or rather against the single-minded political use of religion: the spirit of the Catholic Spanish kings of the Counter-Reformation, or the mosque and temple-destroying Hindus and Muslims of a later day. Boabdil, remote as he seems in time and space, is an aspect of India as it might have been in this century, and the novel gives him a legendary descendency of Indian Jews, one of whom finally marries an Indian Catholic of (probably also legendary) Portuguese descent. A Zogoiby weds a Da Gama; the dispossessed Moor meets up with an originator of empire. In South India; in Cochin, to be precise, one of the formerly (notionally) independent states which are now part of the state of Kerala. The date of the meeting is 1939, although most of the rest of the novel takes place in post-Independence India, and in Bombay.

The meeting is several centuries late and occurs only in the family imagination, and in what looks like the wrong place, but how else, Rushdie is suggesting, are we to understand, or even picture, the failed dream of a many-cultured peace, what the wreckage of empire might look like if it were not only a wreck. There are Chinese tiles in the synagogue in Cochin, 'pushy ladies, skirts-not-saris, Spanish shenanigans, Moorish crowns . . . can this really be India?' 'Shenanigans' is good, an entirely gratuitous dash of yet another culture. Rushdie's narrator continues his questions: 'Is this not the most eccentric of slices to extract from all that life—a freak blond hair plucked from a jet-black (and horribly unravelling) plait?' He knows we know the answer.

These characters and stories are not less Indian than for whom the claim is made. And the same goes for the stories. The supposed centre that makes them seem marginal, or (later) seeks to expel them, is the invention of a murderous ideology. A sigh is not just a sigh. But it's not a shout; even less a last battle. Scarcely a memory. It's appropriate—too appropriate, I think, too literary in the genteel old fashion—that the book should end in a clatter of names, phrases and scenery borrowed from *Don Quixote,* that great work of comic mourning written by a Spaniard pretending to be an Arab. On the last pages, the narrator gazes, for good measure, across a valley at the Alhambra, 'the glory of the Moors, their triumphant masterpiece and their last redoubt'. Is this Rushdie or the Granada tourist office?

Rushdie takes risks as a writer, apart from the obvious ones. Well, the obvious ones aren't risks, they are grave dangers, and to call them risks would be to suggest that Rushdie courted them. His life is in danger not because he wrote a clever, irreverent book, but because of the thuggish way his book was received. The question of a more diffuse hurt and offence caused by *The Satanic Verses*—well, caused by the idea or the description of *The Satanic Verses*—is different, and very complicated, not helped by knee-jerking in any direction. It seems to me monstrous to 'think of taking offence as a fundamental right', as someone says in *East, West.* But then it is heartless not to see that unintended offences can cause pain. The risks I have in mind are far less grave. The worst that can happen here is a little critical disagreement.

The risks are more or less lost in the sheer spilling high spirits of *Midnight's Children;* muted by a disciplined sense of outrage in *Shame;* converted into charm in the fantasy world of *Haroun and the Sea of Stories;* carefully rationed in the stories of *East, West.* But they are there all the time. In *The Satanic Verses* they become broadly visible, boldly taken *as* risks, so that great imaginative coups alternate with peeling patches of whimsy. *The Moor's Last Sigh* is steadier than that, more old-fashioned, a sort of hysterical family saga, and its risks play off each other more harmoniously; but they are still very visible, a sort of signature, and it may be worth trying to say what they are.

Garrulousness first of all. Rushdie's narrators not only talk a lot, they are their talk. They are not so much characters as voices—sometimes they are unconvincing as characters—and the less they understand about themselves, the more they talk. They represent brilliant, voluble evasions of the world, which is nevertheless evoked by these evasions—which leaks through their words and their scarce silences. When the young hero of *Haroun and the Sea of Stories* discovers that silence, too, has 'its own grace and beauty', the effect is one of major shock. He had thought that silence was evil, and the rest of the story he is in points that way. The arch-enemy is the Prince of Silence, destroyer of stories. He has imposed 'Silence Laws', and his more fanatical devotees sew their lips together with twine. Speech is the freedom of speech, of course, and such freedom dies if it is not exercised. Since *Haroun* is a form of fairy tale, liberal democracy not only gets a little plug, but wins the day, because the chattering good guys also form a fine army: 'All those arguments and debates, all that openness, had created powerful bonds of fellowship between them.' We wish. But words are also the foes of reality, as Conrad suggested, and it's not always good to like them so much. The narrator of *The Moor's Last Sigh* finds what he calls gabbiness erotic: 'When I chatter on, or am assailed by the garrulity of others, I find it—how-to-say?—arousing.' *Midnight's Children* is a triumph of such arousal; but we can all think of occasions, in and out of fiction, when chatter is either irrelevant or helpless or worse. Even *Midnight's Children* is a shallow masterpiece (Pauline Kael's phrase for *Citizen Kane*); it's no use looking for the depths it doesn't have.

Melodrama. Rushdie's narrative method is full of extravagant nods and winks: spoofed nods and winks, mostly, but maybe nods and winks, unlike sighs, are just what they are, spoofed or not. 'When I needed to move a mountain for love, I thought my mother would help. Alas for us all; I was wrong.' 'O mother, mother, I know why you banished me now. O my great dead mother, my duped progenitrix, my fool.' 'I brutally put an end to his accursed life. And in so doing called a curse down upon my own.' This is not the tourist office, it's some sort of fire-breathing, little-did-we-know romance. Rushdie is aware of what he is doing. He sets up Disney cartoons as a context, accuses his characters of 'old-style Indian melodrama', and when the narrator learns that his father is 'the most evil man that ever lived', the reference is made in contrast to the father of Superman. The trouble is that Rushdie really needs some of the emotions, and some of the power, that are being burlesqued here. At times he gets them, but it's a close thing; often the sheer lumpishness of the spoofed mode gets in his way.

Hyperbole. Rushdie specialises in a mode of fantasy which doesn't depart from the real but only exaggerates it; this exaggeration then becomes a brilliant or lurid metaphor for a different but related reality. A good example would be the elaborately twinned cracking-up of Saleem Sinai and India in *Midnight's Children.* In *The Moor's Last Sigh,* the narrator was born four and a half months after his conception, and has lived his whole life at twice the ordinary pace, double-quick, as people say in old-fashioned public schools and Rushdie's India. The idioms and the images begin to sprout, the narrator telling us, rather too helpfully, that he is living out 'the literal truth of the metaphors so often applied to my mother and her circle': 'In the fast lane, on the fast track, ahead of my time, a jetsetter right down to my genes, I burned—having no option—the candle at both ends.' The city connection is almost irresistible, in any case not resisted: 'I have always been, if only in my uncontrollable increases, prodigious. Like the city itself, Bombay of my joys and sorrows, I mushroomed into a huge urbane sprawl of a fellow, I expanded without time for proper planning.' Should that really be 'urbane'? I wouldn't ask if elsewhere a man's 'niece Sara' didn't turn into his 'daughter Sara' within half a page. There's magic realism and there's magic realism. But then if the narrator is Bombay, Bombay is India: the bastard child of a Portuguese-English wedding, and yet the most Indian of Indian cities . . . Those who hated India, those who sought to ruin it, would need to ruin Bombay.'

Rushdie specialises in a mode of fantasy which doesn't depart from the real but only exaggerates it; this exaggeration then becomes a brilliant or lurid metaphor for a different but related reality.

—*Michael Wood*

Rushdie's hyperboles are often memorable, but sometimes work too hard, and they and the garrulousness are closely connected to another risk: the explanation. Rushdie is an extraordinarily intelligent and fluent writer, but he doesn't always trust the reader to get what he means. Sometimes the explanations are cogent enough, too explicit for some tastes, but loaded with the energy of anxiety: 'Children make fictions of their fathers, re-inventing them according to their childish needs. The reality of a father is a weight few sons can bear.' At other times perhaps Rushdie is just allowing his narrator a little sententiousness: 'That's not a star worth following; it's just an unlucky rock. Our fates are here on earth. There are no guiding stars.' But at other times we seem to be sinking into genuine soppiness: 'his willingness to permit the co-existence within himself of conflicting impulses is the source of his full, gentle humaneness . . . that hate-the-sin-and-love-the-sinner sweetness, that historical generosity of spirit, which is one of the true wonders of India'; 'There is in us, in all of us, some measure of brightness, of possibility. We start with that, but also with its dark counter-force.' Or just wordiness: 'the tragedy of multiplicity destroyed by singularity, the defeat of Many by One'. At other times the explainer and the novelist in Rushdie seem to be telling different stories, and curious tensions arise.

The whole of *The Moor's Last Sigh* is predicated on an argument about the One and the Many, about the vulnerability and desirability of the world of the Many. All the stories run that way except one: that of a woman with a multiple personality disorder who ruins a whole series of lives by pretending to a number of people she was what each of them wanted. Singularity in this case would have been better than multiplicity, and the story thus becomes 'a bitter parable' in which 'the polarity between good and evil was reversed.' The narrator says that 'it did not fail to occur' to him that the woman's story—she is among other things his mistress and his nemesis—was 'a defeat for the pluralistic philosophy on which we had all been raised'. He doesn't do anything with this counter-example, though, and fifty pages later he is still lyrically allegorising his affair:

> I wanted to cling to the image of love as the blending of spirits, as mélange, as the triumph of the impure, mongrel, conjoining best of us over what there is in us of the solitary, the isolated, the austere, the dogmatic, the pure; of love as democracy, as the victory of the no-man-is-an-island, two's company Many over the clean, mean, apartheiding Ones.

Plainly Rushdie sees this attempt as doomed to failure, but he doesn't seem to disavow it, and the mention of apartheid dumps all the virtue on one side. There is no real tussle or dialogue here, and even the contradiction of a philosophy only reverses it, leaving us with the same polarity upside down. What if the polarity is the problem? What if the Many need to talk to the One as well as to each other? What if the whole proposition is just too general or too abstract to apply to any recognisable human situation, if even the impure and the mongrels can't quite rise to the Platonic dignity of their own idea, *the* impure, mongrel best of us? These are the questions that I think Rushdie the novelist is asking, that his novel is asking, in its intricate profusion. But the explainer doesn't seem to be listening; and the explainer takes over the whole last section of the book: an epilogue which limps along into a shoot-out sponsored by the Lone Ranger and other heroes of moral complexity.

Rushdie's last risk, that of writing in pictures, so rarely fails to deliver brilliant results that it doesn't look like a risk at all. But it is one; and only a writer of great gifts could make it look so safe. For all his talkiness, Rushdie also understands that less can be more, and there is a very moving moment in this novel when he tells us, through his narrator, 'another secret' about fear: 'the revolution against fear, the engendering of that tawdry despot's fall, has more or less nothing to do with "courage". It is driven by something much more straightforward: the simple need to get on with your life.' What Rushdie doesn't say is that that *is* courage, of the most exemplary sort.

And so his images, which rightly raise far more questions than we can answer, speak for themselves, and often quite laconically. A bridegroom on his wedding night takes off his clothes, his wife already undressed and waiting; puts on her wedding-dress, and takes off across the water for a homosexual rendezvous: 'the bridegroom's face beneath the bridal veil', as Rushdie's narrator puts it. A character in Cochin is given permission to train a group of actors as Lenin impersonators, eager to spread the great man's word to these far southern regions. They say his speeches in Malayalam, Kannada, Tulu, Konkani, Tamil, Telugu and English, but they don't look much like Lenin, and are exposed and dismissed by a Russian Lenin impersonator, who calls them a mockery: 'this is not adaptation but satirical caricature.' 'O, I was lost in fiction,' a character says, 'and murder was all around.' Fiction really feels like a place here, rather than a metaphor, and when another character is said to die, 'quickly, in great pain, railing against the enemy in her body, savagely angry with death for arriving too soon and behaving so badly', we are so caught up in the picture that the very idea of the figurative seems to fade.

I haven't said much about the plot of *The Moor's Last Sigh.* It details the lives of wealthy spice merchants and their eccentric children and in-laws; their colleagues and fellow conspirators, protégés and enemies; their loves and deaths. There is a great deal of violence and corruption ('one man one bribe' is a cynic's definition of democracy), and some good story twists. At the heart of the novel, though, is the work of the narrator's mother, the painter Aurora Zogoiby. She herself is

a dazzling character, prematurely white-haired, beautiful, fearless, limitlessly talented—'Listen: she was the light of our lives, the excitement of our imaginations, the beloved of our dreams. We loved her even as she destroyed us'—but she is not as memorable or as complicated as her paintings. Her *Moor's Last Sigh,* for instance, 170 x 247 cms, oil on canvas, 1987, the year of her death, is 'a picture which, for all its great size, had been stripped to the harsh essentials, all its elements converging on the face at its heart, the Sultan's face, from which horror, weakness, loss and pain poured like darkness itself'. Aurora has done all kinds of paintings since she covered the walls of her room with a vision of India when she was 13; and she has done a sequence of paintings about the defeated, departing Moor. 'She was using Arab Spain to re-imagine India,' and so 'Jews, Christians, Muslims, Parsis, Sikhs, Buddhists, Jains crowded into her paint—Boabdil's fancydress balls.' A pluralist's golden age. 'So there was,' her son thinks, 'a didacticism here, but what with the vivid surrealism of her images and the kingfisher brilliance of her colouring and the dynamic acceleration of her brush, it was easy not to feel preached at, to revel in the carnival without listening to the barker, to dance to the music without caring for the message in the song.'

It's easy to do the same with Rushdie, although he could make it easier, and it's worth remembering, as he always does, that the fantastic sometimes just is the historical. Here is another piece of picture-writing, showing the working poor of Bombay, who are not only poor and horribly exploited, but officially regarded as non-existent:

> They continued to be classified as phantoms, to move through the city like wraiths, except that these were the wraiths that kept the city going, building its houses, hauling its goods, cleaning up its droppings, and then simply and terribly dying, each in their turn, unseen, as their spectral blood poured out of their ghostly mouths in the middle of the bitch-city's all-too-real, uncaring streets.

Orhan Pamuk (review date 9 September 1995)

SOURCE: "Salaam Bombay!," in *The Times Literary Supplement,* No. 4823, September 9, 1995, p. 3.

[*In the following review, Pamuk considers Rushdie's treatment of his homeland in his fiction, most recently in* The Moor's Last Sigh.]

Peppered with politics and betrayal, sugared with art and love, well spiced with pimps, beauty queens, gangsters, freaks, fanatics and lunatics, *The Moor's Last Sigh* is a grand family chronicle of the passionate love and business affairs of four generations of a grotesque and rich Indian family. This book, in its scope, its ambition, and its magic, most resembles *Midnight's Children,* the best of Salman Rushdie's previous novels. The fact that *The Moor's Last Sigh* is a lesser performance is nothing to do with Rushdie's creative powers as a verbal illusionist. Filled with puns and verbal games, buffoonery and scenes of slapstick comedy, it proves that Rushdie is one of the most brilliant magicians of the English language writing now. The problem, however, is that Salman the narrator, the verbal innovator, too often rushes to offer help, to save the day when Salman the fabulator, like his hero Moraes Zogoiby, loses his breath.

The Moor's Last Sigh is an incestuous family saga, and like two other great incestuous family sagas before it—Nabokov's *Ada* (which is also filled with bilingual puns and arabesques of verbal games) and García Márquez's *One Hundred Years of Solitude* (which set the standard for the magic realism Rushdie is so fruitfully and effortlessly inspired by)—there is a family chart at the beginning of this novel marking birth and death dates and relations of the members of the Da Gama and Zogoiby families. This is useful, for the book is crammed with intrusive outsiders (as well as members of four generations of the family), some of whom stay around so long as to become a part of the already overcrowded family, some of whom leave the stage as abruptly as they appear.

The narrator of this richly textured, densely allusive tale is Moraes Zogoiby, but the true protagonist is his mother, Aurora Da Gama, "a crazy woman" according to her husband, a famous painter and a beautiful society woman, a giant public personality, a heroine of the nationalist movement, "a legendary lady". She is the great creative mother figure of this novel, which, perhaps to give us a total image of itself, consistently alludes to an image of Mother India (also the title of a film) who "with her garishness and inexhaustible motion loved and betrayed and ate and destroyed and again loved her children and with whom the children's passionate conjoining an eternal quarrel stretched long beyond the grave". This image, which Rushdie makes sure that even the least attentive reader will be aware of, might equally apply to Aurora. She is the daughter of a Catholic who runs a pepper business and claims to be descended from no less a figure than Vasco da Gama, the Portuguese explorer who discovered India. The story of Aurora's extravagant life—starting with tables of her grandfather Francisco da Gama, who was "incapable of living a settled life," and her down-to-earth grandmother Epifania Menezes—until her marriage to Abraham Zogoiby, a Cochin Jew from a family descended from Spanish Jews expelled by the Catholics after the fall of the last Andalusian sultan, begins the novel; it is affectionately delineated, with an eye for traditional narrative detail, although—or perhaps because—these pages constitute the most magic-realist sections of the novel.

Here, as in Rushdie's earlier book, *East, West,* R. K. Narayan's fictional South Indian town, Malgudi, is alluded to, and Narayan's spirit hovers over the twists of unhappy arranged marriages, impossible love affairs and family secrets and scandals, tales of mothers who will be dependent on the good will of their sons, and young sons who easily fall into radical politics; these tales are told as part of simple scenes of daily life, although with a certain magic touch and some verbal abracadabra:

> It was the simplicity of rising late to a strong, sweet bed-tea, of clapping her hands for the cook and ordering the day's repasts, of having a maid come in to oil and brush her still-long but quickly greying and thinning hair, and of being able to blame the maid for the increasing quantities left each morning in the brush; the simplicity of long mornings scolding the tailor who came over to the house with new dresses, and knelt at her feet with mouthfuls of pins which he removed from time to time to unloose his flatterer's tongue. . . .

These days of simplicity, which compared to the rest of the book read like a lost idyll, end abruptly, and the pace of the narrative changes as soon as the family, together with the expanding business, leaves provincial Cochin to settle in metropolitan Bombay, Rushdie's beloved city. Here, too many characters are suddenly introduced: Kekoo Mody the art dealer, Lambajan the pirate, who loses his leg when Aurora drives a car over it during a strike, Vasco Miranda, a young ambitious painter who in future will become "the darling of the international moneyed establishment", Raman Fielding a political cartoonist who will become a vicious, ugly, right-wing propagator of Hindu nationalism, Uma Sarasvati, another artist, with a growing reputation, Jamshed Cashondeliveri, a Johnny-Cash-like "Country and Eastern" music star of Bombay's night clubs who marries one of the Zogoiby daughters, and the likes of Sunil Dutt, star of the "all-conquering movie Mother India". They are all—at least for a while—rich, famous, successful, and "of course" friends of the family. Almost all of these "luminaries" (including even Pandit Nehru) are also lovers of members of the Da Gama-Zogoiby family, the most ambitious being Uma, who manages to sleep with the mother, the father, the son and, it is hinted, with one of the sisters as well.

This overabundance of fame, money, sex and glamour sometimes gives the book the aura of a grotesque jet-set novel located in Bombay. And, in spite of Rushdie's radiant humour, his characters often seem loveless because of their cynical self-interest. The rich father seduces, among others, his son's lover; the mother betrays her husband so often as to confuse the reader more than her husband; the son, when allowed to marry the girl of his dreams, too easily joins the ranks of the enemy. These tales of betrayal, deception and murder which seem more and more implausible, one surprising twist after another, do not add up to pathos. Instead, such a callous version of life emerges that halfway through the book one begins to lose interest in the "over-accelerated lives" of the characters, and to wonder only who will next betray whom. To some extent, Rushdie's powers of narration, and the highly entertaining quality of his glittery prose, help to avoid this danger of lapsing into an "old-style Indian melodrama", which perhaps may not be completely unintentional. "How could we have lived authentic lives?" asks the narrator Moraes Zogoiby, when he is informed about one of his father's many "casual" deceptions of his wife (though this time it is only drug-trafficking). "How could we have failed to be grotesque?" This sense of the grotesque qualities of reality, woven with what the narrator calls "flamboyant cynicism", form the texture of life in contemporary Bombay as well as the bleak vision of Rushdie's fabulation.

Here, Rushdie's love-hate relationship with Bombay is crucial. For him, and for his narrator as well, one feels that this "super epic motion picture of a city" has two sides. One is the "improper Bombay", the many-headed cosmopolis of diverse cultures; this is Moraes Zogoiby's "inexhaustible city of excess" with which, he tells us, he is deeply and for ever in love. The other one, the new Bombay of religious and nationalistic fanaticism, is the city of "senseless" bombings and the egoistic cynicism of post-colonial intellectuals and the new power elite. The heartfelt political message of *The Moor's Last Sigh* is to defend the richness and multiplicity of the first Bombay against the assaults of the second, against the imposition of Hindu language, art and gods as "authentic", Indian culture, against fundamentalist Hindu triumphalism. The tone of the novel becomes elegiac when the minorities of Bombay begin to feel that they do not belong "here" any more, or when the narrator, Moraes Zogoiby, who can neither be a Jew nor a Catholic, reminisces about his walks with the housekeeper Miss Jaya in the streets of the old Bombay:

> So it was with Miss Jaya that I rode the B.E.S.T. trams and buses, and while she disapproved of their overcrowding I was secretly rejoicing in all that compacted humanity, in being pushed so tightly together that privacy ceased to exist and the boundaries of your self began to dissolve, that feeling which we only get when we are in crowds, or in love. And it was with Miss Jaya that I ventured into that fabulous turbulence of Crawford Market with its frieze by Kipling's dad, with its vendors of chicken both live and plastic, and it was with Miss Jaya that I penetrated the rum dens of Dhobi Talao and ventured into the chawls, the tenements of Byculla (where she took me to visit her poor—I should say her poorer—relations, who with yet-more-impoverishing offers

of cold drinks and cakes treated her arrival like the visit of a queen). . . .

When a writer writes so well and so tenderly about his city, the reviewer feels an urge to look closely at his moments of loss of breath, his apparent shortcomings which perhaps are glories in disguise. In *The Moor's Last Sigh,* scattered here and there, is a theory of art camouflaged as Moraes Zogoiby's comments on his mother's paintings. The most important of these pictures has the same title as the novel, a palimpsest in a series called "the Moor sequence". The painting of these pictures one by one, Moraes Zogoiby's (nicknamed "Moor") posing for his mother for some of them, and the secret beneath the layers of the most mysterious one, the "Moor's Last Sigh", constitute a frame story for the whole novel, and add one final twist of cynical betrayal and murder at the end. But what matters here is Moraes's understanding of these paintings, for they could equally be read as Rushdie's tongue-in-cheek comments on the making of his own novel, *The Moor's Last Sigh*.

Zogoiby consistently remarks on the impurity of life and objects and, like his mother, recalls palimpsest art as a "vision of weaving or more accurately interweaving". And one understands the aesthetic and political vision behind Rushdie's ambitious attempt to produce a hybrid text composed of, among other things, "tropicalized Victorian drama", Indian melodrama, kitsch sentimentality, history and gangster films. "The city itself, perhaps the whole country, was a palimpsest", writes Zogoiby elsewhere, hinting at the eclecticism of the book we are reading. His celebration of impurity, hybridity and intermingling reads like Rushdie's own comment on his book. But when he remarks that "the truth is almost always exceptional, freakish, improbable", one does not read this as another layer of a palimpsest, but as a defence of the weirdly exceptional qualities of all the events in this book, as an excuse for the freakishness of almost all of its characters, and a pretext for the improbability of the twists of its too surprising tale—all of which would have made this novel too wearisome had it not been written by such a master juggler of words who often exhibits a wonderful eye for detail.

Here I should make a confession: I don't like magic realism. Derived from Rabelais's "demons of excess" (at the end of *One Hundred Years of Solitude,* one of the young members of the Buendia family carries a volume of Rabelais in hand), this vision of fabulating has over the years and in popularized versions lost its demons. And now, what quite often seems to be "imaginative", "fantastic", and "funny" is plain excess. This new mode of telling stories through mellowing Rabelaisian humour has become a convenient and sugary way of presenting the Other, reducing "otherness" to tolerable proportions, softening its edges and threat for a comfortable read, giving the reader cute, lovable characters moving in situations which seem merely folkloric, no matter how horrific they really are. It is not coincidental that the best examples of magic realism (which is perhaps a way of communicating between cultures rather than within a culture), say, *One Hundred Years of Solitude* or **Midnight's Children,** are read as experiences of "entire other" continents, be it Latin America or India.

This time Salman Rushdie should be congratulated for neither creating cute and lovable characters nor giving us "the entire India". However, the latter may not be intentional, since Aurora compellingly demands to be read as a symbol for the story of modern India. Her son Moraes, who insistently speculates on the image of Mother India, once describes his mother "the great painter" among "the crowds of the devout" as she dances her contempt for the perversity of "humankind". On the dust jacket, Aurora's very same dance is described as her rebellion against the perversity of "India". I wonder whether this replacement of humankind with India is an intentional editorial misquotation or a sign of the ambiguity of the overall effect of this book, torn between the ambition to represent India and to tell grotesque and humane stories.

One sympathizes with Salman Rushdie's desire to "embrace all", his rejection of the mimetic, his love for the diversity and richness of life. Even more, one admires his brave attempt to find the new, his courageous determination to devote his amazing talents to create "harmony" from "cacophony". But, more intentionally disorganized than complex, more funny than compassionate, more bitter than moving, *The Moor's Last Sigh* lacks a central logic. Somewhere in the novel, Moraes Zogoiby tells us that if he "were forced to choose between logic and childhood memory", he'd go along with the tale. Valid for every imaginative writer of Salman Rushdie's calibre, this remark provokes the reader of *The Moor's Last Sigh* to reply: but magic should also have its logic.

Publishers Weekly (review date 2 October 1995)

SOURCE: A review of *The Moor's Last Sigh,* in *Publishers Weekly,* Vol. 242, No. 40, October 2, 1995, p. 52.

[*Below, the critic offers a positive assessment of* The Moor's Last Sigh.]

Not since **Midnight's Children** has Rushdie produced such a dazzling novel. Nor has he curbed his urgent indignation or muffled his satiric tongue. In a spirited story related at a breakneck pace and crammed full of melodrama, slapstick, supple wordplay and literary allusions, Rushdie has again fashioned a biting parable of modern India. Telling his story "with death at my heels," the eponymous narrator relates the saga of a family whose religious, political and cultural differences rep-

licate the fault lines by which India is riven. The Moor tells of "family rifts and premature deaths and thwarted loves and mad passions and weak chests and power and money and . . . the seductions and mysteries of art." He speculates on the duality of all things, the conflicting impulses of human nature and the clash between appearance and reality. Like the tale itself, the title has multiple layers of meaning. "The Moor's Last Sigh" refers to two paintings, one a masterpiece by the narrating Moor's mother, Aurora, the other a trashy work by her onetime protégé and lover, and later implacable enemy, Vasco Miranda, who becomes the Moor's nemesis.

The Moor was thus nicknamed at birth, the youngest child of Aurora, the heiress to the da Gama spice-trade dynasty, and Abraham Zogoiby, a penniless Jew who was her family's employee. Aurora has become one of India's most famous artists, even as her shadowy husband has metamorphosed into a power broker in the Bombay underworld. The narrator was born with a deformed right hand and a disease that ages him two years for every year he lives: "Life had dealt me a bad hand, and a freak of nature was obliging me to play it out too fast." The woman he adores is a pathological liar who fools the Moor into making a fatally wrong choice.

Rushdie's own plight informs these pages, but it is always integrated into plot and character. Already an outcast from society, the half-Jewish Moor is expelled from his family; when he leaves India, he becomes increasingly disoriented and is eventually imprisoned, awaiting a death that may strike at any time. Of another character, the Moor says: "Thirty years in hiding! What a torment. . . ."

Rushdie gives his linguistic virtuosity full play: his prose, as always, is energetic, jaunty and lyrical; the dialogue is truly "lingo-garbling" as characters speak in such suffix-burdened neologisms as "you tormentofy me," and "payofy us back." A series of indelible portraits evokes the greedy da Gama clan, who personify many of India's self-destructive traits. All too aware of the apocalyptic events toward which he is hurtling, the Moor yearns to "wipe my moral slate clean." Certainly Rushdie's moral rigor has not faltered. Where **Midnight's Children** heralded the birth pains of modern India, *The Moor's Last Sigh* charts a nation's troubled middle passage. The society Rushdie portrays so powerfully is rife with corruption; pluralism is dying and a dangerous separatism is on the rise, encouraging hatred and despair.

John Bemrose (review date 9 October 1995)

SOURCE: "Tower of Babble," in *Maclean's,* Vol. 108, No. 41, October 9, 1995, p. 85.

[*In the following negative review of* The Moor's Last Sigh,

Bemrose remarks that "most of the novel reads like the vision of a harried mind that has lost touch with the pace and amplitude of ordinary life."]

It would seem that Salman Rushdie simply does not know how to play it safe. The Anglo-Indian novelist has been in hiding in Britain for six years, ever since Iran's Ayatollah Ruhollah Khomeini condemned him to death for alleged anti-Muslim sentiments in his 1989 novel, *The Satanic Verses.* Now, his new novel, *The Moor's Last Sigh*—nominated for Britain's prestigious Booker Prize last week—has angered many Hindus. The Indian distributor of the book has refused to release it in Bombay, where a radical Hindu political party, Shiv Sena, has deemed it offensive. The trouble stems from a character in the novel called Raman Fielding, who apparently satirizes Shiv Sena's leader, Bal Thackeray. His party has been accused of fomenting conflict between Bombay's Muslims and Hindus, which has killed more than 800 people since 1992. Rushdie has recreated that religious strife in his novel, suggesting that one of its main causes is Fielding's hate campaign against Muslim culture. The rest of the subcontinent, however, seems to be taking Rushdie's novel in stride: it has been released in other Indian cities without incident.

Whatever the shortcomings of Shin Sena's intellectual thought police, they must at least be congratulated for having plowed their way through *The Moor's Last Sigh.* This tedious and frenetically overwritten novel all but suffocates under its own weight until—about two thirds of the way through—it finally develops some narrative momentum. That, of course, will be much too late for most readers who, having no political agenda to spur them on, will long before have flung the book at the wall.

The narrator of *The Moor's Last Sigh* is a familiar figure from Rushdie's fiction: an outsider struggling to make sense of a life torn by the anarchic currents of history. By his own admission, Moraes Zogoiby—nicknamed "The Moor"—is something of a freak. To begin with, he is growing old at twice the normal rate, so that in his late 30s, his age as he begins his memoir, he looks and acts like an old man. His fingerless, club-like right hand, deformed from birth, is only good for knocking other men down—an activity he has pursued with relish. As well, errant genes from his family's racially chequered past have made him a six-foot-six giant with black skin and white hair.

It is tempting to see elements of Rushdie himself in this portrait. Not that the writer physically resembles Moraes, but Rushdie has had to endure the freakishness of enforced isolation, with his ability to live a normal writer's life maimed (that club hand) by the threat of assassination. Like Moraes, Rushdie is also of mixed cultural background, although his fictional character is more exotic, with Spanish, Portuguese

and Moorish bloodlines complicated by a Jewish and Christian religious inheritance.

Moraes is haunted by his ancestors. Evoked in the novel's opening chapters, they are an excessive bunch given to romantically flamboyant behavior in love and hatred. Moraes inherits their grandiosity: indeed, *The Moor's Last Sigh* is an exercise in nonstop melodrama, much of it centred on the Moor's relations with his mother, Aurora, a famous painter. She is both a nourishing and destructive force in his life, and by the time he realizes her essential love for him, she is dead—in, of course, melodramatic and mysterious circumstances. Her last, posthumous gift to him is a painting, *The Moor's Last Sigh,* which shows mother and son in the forgiving light of reconciliation.

Such a brief summary can hardly convey the tortuous elaborations of Rushdie's plot: involving dozens of minor characters, it becomes as crazily detailed as the facade of some Hindu temple, where hordes of mythological figures endlessly proliferate. There is nothing wrong with his approach except that, in his manic invention, Rushdie rarely settles into an event long enough to make it satisfying. As well, his characters—for all the hyperbolic romance of their lives—are hardly ever sympathetic. *The Moor's Last Sigh* is a novel about big feelings that cannot generate even little ones. Its flashes of humor cannot make up for its coldness.

Rushdie, even in his captivity in British safe houses, has written much better than this. His recent story collection, *East, West,* contains several tales that manage to balance exaggerated characters with a human warmth. *The Moor's Last Sigh* does contain a little evidence of the old Rushdie, including his affecting evocations of Bombay's horrible prison. But most of the novel reads like the vision of a harried mind that has lost touch with the pace and amplitude of ordinary life.

Brad Hooper (review date 1 November 1995)

SOURCE: A review of *The Moor's Last Sigh,* in *Booklist,* Vol. 92, No. 5, November 1, 1995, p. 435.

[*In the following review, Hooper describes* The Moor's Last Sigh *as "a marvelously wrought novel, guaranteed to entrance."*]

Rushdie's first novel since the fateful *Satanic Verses* (1989) is about hybridization of cultures, and itself seems a hybrid between William Faulkner's Yoknapatawpha County novels and *The Thousand and One Nights.* This four-generational family saga takes place in Rushdie's native southern India and witnesses the decline of a spice-trading dynasty, a century-long drama of "family rifts and premature deaths and thwarted loves and mad passions and weak chests and power and money and the even more morally dubious seductions and mysteries of art." The fanciful tale is related by the last of the exhausted family line, Moraes Zogoiby, son of a pair of Indians of far different backgrounds and persuasions, his father Jewish and a Mob leader in Bombay, his mother Catholic and celebrated for her artistry. The "Moor," as he is called, was born physically precocious; in fact, he ages at twice the normal rate. The plot does not unfold—it floods like a river gone over its banks, exploding with incredible events and larger-than-life characters, and to be carried along is to ride beautiful prose through the colliding and conjoining of races and religions that have gone into the making of the fabric of Indian history and culture. A marvelously wrought novel, guaranteed to entrance.

John F. Burns (essay date 2 December 1995)

SOURCE: "Another Rushdie Novel, Another Bitter Epilogue," in *The New York Times,* December 2, 1995.

[*In the following essay, Burns describes reaction in India to* The Moor's Last Sigh.]

For Anuj Malhotra, a bookseller in this capital's affluent Khan Market district, the publication here this summer of Salman Rushdie's latest novel, *The Moor's Last Sigh,* promised to be the literary event of the year.

Mr. Rushdie has been a best seller in India, where he was born and lived until his family left Bombay for England 30 years ago. With his sales running into tens of thousands of copies, he has held his own with writers of more obviously popular genres like Jackie Collins, Barbara Taylor Bradford and India's own novelist of sex and romance, Shobha De.

Expectations were higher than ever for the new Rushdie book, which chronicles the history of an Indian family over several generations. Indian critics have seen it as Mr. Rushdie's attempt to capture the flavor of contemporary India from the distance imposed on him by his life in hiding since 1989, when Ayatollah Ruhollah Khomeini of Iran said he should be killed for blaspheming Islam in his novel *Satanic Verses.*

But four months after Mr. Malhotra received his first and only allotment of *The Moor's Last Sigh* and quickly sold out all 100 hardback copies, he is a frustrated man. Almost every day, customers come into the crammed Malhotra family store and ask quietly for the Rushdie novel. For each one, Mr. Malhotra has a shake of the head. "Nobody wants to get in bad with a political party," he told one recent inquirer.

The political party is the Shiv Sena, a Bombay-based Hindu

nationalist group that proscribed the Rushdie book even before its Indian distributor could begin selling it in Bombay. While the book focuses on a century in the life of a Jewish-Christian family and moves through events that have scarred India's recent history, it includes a profoundly unflattering parody of the Shiv Sena leader. Balasaheb K. Thackeray.

Like Mr. Thackeray, a character in *The Moor's Last Sigh* named Raman Fielding is a former newspaper cartoonist turned Hindu nationalist leader. Like Mr. Thackeray, Mr. Fielding calls Bombay by an ancient Hindu village name, Mumbai. He leads a party named the Mumbai Axis, a reference to Mr. Thackeray's admiration for Hitler. Mr. Fielding relishes violence against Muslims; Mr. Thackeray has been accused of provoking riots that killed at least 1,200 Muslims three years ago.

Since elections this spring brought a coalition led by Shiv Sena to power in Maharashtra State, where Bombay is the capital, Mr. Thackeray has been the state's most powerful figure. But to keep the Rushdie book out of Maharashtra required only intimidation. While he professed not to have read the book, Mr. Thackeray, who is 68, said that Mr. Rushdie, whom he described as a man "with no homeland," had no business throwing brickbats from after.

"I do not like people living in foreign countries criticizing us," he said. Others were more blunt.

"Shiv Sena will not let the book exist," said Pramod Navalkar, the Maharashtra culture minister. "We can destroy the book all over India."

If Mr. Thackeray or his followers felt unease at their seeming inconsistency on the matter of Mr. Rushdie, they gave no sign of it. In 1989. Mr. Thackeray expressed outrage when India banned *Satanic Verses,* arguing that it was a free country and that Muslims should take their lumps like anybody else.

But what has stirred the greatest unease over *The Moor's Last Sigh* is not that Rupa & Sons, the Indian distributors, withdrew it from sale in Bombay. More shocking to many Indians was that the national Government of Prime Minister P. V. Narasimha Rao bowed to the Shiv Sena's pressures, banning further imports of the Rushdie novel after the initial consignment of 4,000 copies.

In September customs officials ordered Rupa's Calcutta headquarters "to desist from selling, distributing or parting" with the book while its suitability was reviewed by officials in New Delhi. A few days later, a bookshop in a remote town in Andhra Pradesh, Mr. Rao's home state, had its last copies of the Rushdie book seized. Weeks of appeals by Rupa to S. B. Chavan, the Home Minister, have brought no reply, and no indication that the Government intends to make a final decision. Now, the company has decided to petition the Supreme Court for a lifting of the ban.

Some critics have suggested that the Government's action had less to do with worries about Shiv Sena violence than with reaction within the governing Congress Party to another Rushdie parody, the appearance in the novel of a dog called Jawaharlal, after India's first Prime Minister, Jawaharlal Nehru. To this, those with long memories have recalled that Nehru, when confronted with demands that the Government ban Vladimir Nabokov's novel *Lolita* in the 1950's, read the book, pronounced it obscene, but said he had no right to prevent others from reading it.

The Federation of Publishers and Booksellers' Associations of India will argue before the Supreme Court that the Rao Government is breaching constitutional guarantees of free speech and that, by bowing to the Shiv Sena, it is pandering to forces, that are tearing at the heart of India's democratic ideals.

In England, Mr. Rushdie has said that he intended *The Moor's Last Sigh* as an alarm call against trends within Indian society—primarily the rise of religious extremism—that "seem to be changing the country so fundamentally that one could say that the country that came into being in 1947 is being transformed into something else." As for those who have accused him of stirring troubles in the book that he does not have to live with himself his riposte has been succinct.

"If Mr. Bal Thackeray doesn't like it, well, I'm sorry, he'll have to lump it," he said.

Michiko Kakutani (review date 28 December 1995)

SOURCE: "Rushdie on India: Serious, Crammed Yet Light," in *The New York Times,* December 28, 1995, pp. C13, C20.

[*In the following review, Kakutani describes the ways in which the story and characters of* The Moor's Last Sigh *relate the author's own views of his native country.*]

In Salman Rushdie's remarkable new novel, the narrator describes the astonishing paintings created by his mother: paintings teeming with the life of Bombay's streets, paintings that capture "the face-slapping quarrels of naked children at a tenement standpipe," "the elated tension of the striking sailors at the gates to the naval yards" and the "shipwrecked arrogance of the English officers from whom power was ebbing like the waves," paintings layered upon older paintings and concealing untold secrets of the past.

Behind all this, the narrator observes, was his mother's "sense of the inadequacy of the world, of its failure to live up to her expectations, so that her own disappointment with reality, her anger at its wrongness, mirrored her subjects, and made her sketches not merely reportorial but personal, with a violent, breakneck passion of line that had the force of a physical assault."

This description, of course, also applies perfectly to Mr. Rushdie's own fierce, phantasmagorical writing, especially as practiced in *The Moor's Last Sigh,* a huge, sprawling exuberant novel. Filled with allusions to everything from "Tristram Shandy" to "The Lone Ranger," from "Paradise Lost" to "Alice in Wonderland," and crammed full with puns, wordplay, vulgar jokes and lyrical asides, *The Moor's Last Sigh* is many books at the same time: a demented family saga, a twisted Bildungsroman, an exploration of the uses and misuses of art and a dark historical parable that rivals Mr. Rushdie's 1981 masterpiece, *Midnight's Children,* in scope, inventiveness and ambition.

Like *Midnight's Children, The Moor's Last Sigh* traces the downward spiral of expectations experienced by India as post-independence hopes for democracy crumbled during the emergency rule declared by Prime Minister Indira Gandhi in 1975, and early dreams of pluralism gave way to sectarian violence and political corruption. In *Midnight's Children,* India's fate was incarnated in the lives of '1,001 children born during the first hour of Indian independence, magically gifted children whose talents and hopes would later be cruelly destroyed. In *The Moor's Last Sigh,* India's fate is similarly embodied in the ups and downs of the da Gama-Zogoiby family, and more specifically in the raucous adventures of the clan's last surviving member, Moraes Zogoiby, otherwise known as Moor.

As the narrator of this rude-noisy-poetic free-for-all, Moor proves himself a high-spirited if sometimes long-winded Scheherazade, a spinner of tales and ancestral legends, whose life—we later learn—literally depends upon his singing the saga of his family's past.

Certainly Moor has a lot in common with his own creator, Mr. Rushdie. To begin with, Mr. Rushdie's own unhappy fate—his last full-length novel, *The Satanic Verses,* enraged Muslim fundamentalists and prompted Ayatollah Ruhollah Khomeini to issue a "death sentence" against him in 1989—is alluded to in Moor's story. Not only does Moor find himself imprisoned (and put under sentence of death) by a zealot who likes to dress up as a Sultan, but he is also condemned to live out his days in exile, an unmoored Moor, "a nobody from nowhere, like no-one, belonging to nothing."

This is the fate of the emigré, those migrants without a home whom Mr. Rushdie depicted so tellingly in *The Satanic*

Verses. It is also the fate of the artist, who by temperament and vocation stands at a slight angle apart from his fellow human beings.

While [*The Moor's Last Sigh*] may sound in summary like a portentous parody of a Greek tragedy, the effect is very different given Mr. Rushdie's manic sense of humor and rich, improvisatory zeal.

—*Michiko Kakutani*

The reader may also notice certain parallels between Mr. Rushdie's story and the story of Moor's mother, Aurora, whose playful painting of a kiss between a Muslim cricket player and a pretty Hindu girl elicits a political firestorm. "I witnessed both her ennui at having endlessly to defend it," Moor recalls, "and her fury at the ease with which this 'tea-pot monsoon' had distracted attention from the body of her real work. She was required by the public prints to speak ponderously of 'underlying motives' when she had had only whims, to make moral statements where there had been only, ('only' I) play, and feeling, and the unfolding inexorable logic of brush and light."

Mr. Rushdie, however, does not belabor his own story in *The Moor's Last Sigh*. Rather, he turns Moor—a bastard child who suffers from a rare genetic disorder that causes him to age at twice the usual rate—into an emblematic figure who shares India's plight, the plight of a country forced to grow up too quickly, "without time for proper planning," without time to learn from experience, "without time for reflection."

In fact, Moor's entire family seems like a dysfunctional mess, what with its bloody history of schisms and betrayals, great passions and terrible acts of vengeance. Two sides of his mother's family battled each other for years before a division of the house and family business was decreed; another family standoff pitted a brother who was a committed nationalist against a brother who was pro-British. The romance between Moor's Catholic mother and Jewish father nearly ended in a Romeo-Juliet debacle. His grandfather and great-grandfather both ended their lives by walking into the sea. And his great-grandmother died with a curse on her lips: "May your house be forever partitioned, may its foundations turn to dust, may your children rise up against you, and may your fall be hard."

It is a curse that Moor will live to see fulfilled, as he is forced to choose between his possessive mother's love and the love of his passionate girlfriend; between his mother's dream of a pluralistic India and his girl-friend's vision of religious absolutism; between his father's world of violence and money

and his own world of writing and words and magic. By the end of the book, after many murders, many fights, many tirades and schemes and disasters, the da Gama-Zogoiby family is in ruins, as is Bombay, leaving Moor, after his fall from grace and banishment, alone to tell the tale.

While this story may sound in summary like a portentous parody of a Greek tragedy, the effect is very different given Mr. Rushdie's manic sense of humor and rich, improvisatory zeal. It's as though he had, decided to cast the House of Atreus saga with vaudevillians, clowns and Lear-like fools, players whose story, however tragic, is also funny, tender and sad. The didacticism of the novel's overarching theme—the fate of modern India as illustrated by the da Gama-Zogoiby clan—is similarly disguised by Mr. Rushdie's ability to conjure up Borgesian images and Marquezian diversions out of thin air: a series of enchanted tiles that foretell the future; a stuffed dog that houses the ghost of Jawaharlal Nehru; a group of actors all dressed up like Lenin; a magical, painting Invested with the secrets of the past.

Such surreal images, combined with the author's fecund language and slashing sleight of hand make it easy, in Mr. Rushdie's words, "not to feel preached at, to revel in the carnival without listening to the barker, to dance to the music" without seeming to hear the message in the glorious song.

James Bowman (review date 31 December 1995)

SOURCE: "Absolutely Fabulist," in *National Review,* Vol. XLVII, No. 25, December 31, 1995, pp. 46-7.

[*In the following mixed review, Bowman asserts that* The Moor's Last Sigh *reads as if the author wrote it simply to prove that he could, and predicts that the book will offend Hindus as* The Satanic Verses *offended Muslims.*]

Salman Rushdie's first novel since *The Satanic Verses* reveals once again that he is a writer with an astounding fertility of imagination. But it is hard not to come away with the sense that all this story-telling and linguistic invention is only for showing off and that Rushdie has written the book in order to demonstrate that he can write it. His subject, in the end, is his own cleverness, and the one illusion he has no interest in creating is the illusion of reality. Back in the Middle Ages, a fabulist like him would have gone to considerable lengths to convince us that the marvelous tales he was about to relate were true by citing some well-respected *auctor* as their source. Rushdie, by contrast, glories in the fact that he made it all up himself. If you were to start to believe that it was real, you might get into trouble.

And, in fact, he has got into trouble—big trouble—from religious people. First the Ayatollah. Now, with *The Moor's Last Sigh,* he seems to have put his books and perhaps himself in danger again by offending a number of Hindus with his portrait of a monstrously corrupt leader of an oxymoronically fundamentalist Hindu sect. Small wonder that the only parts of the novel that read as if there is anything genuine about them are the parts in which he is mercilessly satirizing religion. Perhaps since he sees himself as being in the same line of business as the religious storytellers, it is to Rushdie almost a sort of blasphemy against the sacredness of Art to take one's stories as in any literal sense representative of reality.

Certainly the theme of Art is important in the novel, which tells a story of enormous complexity about the rise and fall of a part-Jewish, part-Christian dynasty of Indian merchants from the early years of this century down to the present. It is narrated by the family's last scion, Moraes "Moor" Zogoiby, a deformed creature who suffers from the family's tendency to respiratory problems and who is also doomed to age at twice the normal rate. The central character, however, is the narrator's mother, *née* Aurora Da Gama, who is not only an artist of world renown but the lover of Nehru and a symbol of Mother India herself, a magic land made for the magical realism that shimmers like a mirage throughout the book. A film actor once says to her: "Auroraji, you are mixing truth and make-believe," at which her only son scoffs: "as if it were a sin."

In the middle of her artistic career, Aurora "fell into deep creative confusion, a semi-paralysis born of an uncertainty not merely about realism but about the nature of the real itself." Eventually, she remained (like her creator, we are tempted to say), "more and more, inside the walls of her personal Paradise, and turned, once and for all, in the direction . . . of her heart: that is to say, inwards, to the reality of dreams." Her son too, who posed as her model, began to feel that "the story unfolding on her canvases seemed more like my autobiography than the real story of my life." Art here is also associated with prophecy from the time that Aurora decorates her bedroom walls as a teenager to the time when she conceals the portrait of her killer within one of her paintings.

It is partly the destructive power of the female, related to Hinduism through dreams and visions and art, that the book is about. The Moor's mother and his lover, Uma Saravati, another celebrated artist, are deadly rivals for his affections and for power over him. Uma especially is invested with the protean powers of femininity to be what everyone imagines her and wants her to be. She becomes a fiend in human form who is instrumental in the destruction of the Zogoiby family.

Perhaps even more sinister is the masculine corruption and violence and power of the patriarchal monotheisms—especially as they are represented by the Moor's father, Abraham

Zogoiby, an Arabic Jew but purportedly also descended from the last Moorish sultans of Granada. Both mother and father are associated with a series of sacrifices of their son, the Moor, who is thus a version of Isaac, but it is Abraham the patriarch who says: "I am a business person. What there is to do, I do"—words that, to Rushdie, recall God's own name, *I am that I am.* The son of such parents is thankful (to whom?) that they "had been cured of religion" and, like them, specializes in blasphemy. Aurora paints "religious pictures for people who have no god" and delights in her paradoxical iconoclasm as much as Rushdie himself delights to take on those rival storytellers who claim a revelatory privilege for their products.

Art for him is like the cartoons with which Aurora has the Goan painter Vasco Miranda decorate her children's nursery. In their world, playful children are relieved of the iron logic of causation. "Give me boulders," Aurora says in her comic, Babu English, "that only temporarily flattofy you when they drop down on your head, bombs that give black faces only, and running-over-empty-air-until-you-looko-down. Give me knottofied-up rifle-barrels, and bathfuls of big gold coins. Never mind about harps and angels, forget all those stinking gardens; for my kiddies, this is the Paradise I want." To the ever-playful Rushdie, it is this trivial popular culture—Popeye, too, says "I am what I am"—which is the salvation of the world.

The "leftish" Dr. Zeenat Vakil, Aurora's biographer and academic proprietor and the author of the monograph, *Imperso-Nation and Dis/Semi/Nation: Dialogics of Eclecticism and Interrogations of Authenticity in A.Z.,* says it best: "I blame fiction. The followers of one fiction knock down another popular piece of make-believe, and bingo! It's war." She refers, of course, not to the comfortable fictions of cartoons but to the kinds of fiction that people are apt to take too seriously—which makes it particularly poignant that so many religious people the world over have taken the tedious fantasies that make up Rushdie's fictions so much more seriously than they deserve.

Jessica Hagedorn (review date 1 January 1996)

SOURCE: "They Came for the Hot Stuff," in *Nation,* Vol. 262, No. 1, January 1, 1996, pp. 25-7.

[*Below, Hagedorn offers a positive review of* The Moor's Last Sigh.]

I don't review books as a rule, but could not resist the opportunity to speak up for Salman Rushdie's astonishing new work. *Midnight's Children* opened up the world for me as a first-time novelist struggling to find my way. How to tell the story of a young postcolonial nation like the Philippines? How to capture its chaos, humor and beauty? How to convey the heat and music of its many languages, and the wit and innovations of its hybrid English? How to portray the complex, unpredictable nature of its people? How to be fearless? Rushdie, the passionate subversive obsessed with history, language and moral ambiguity, the grand and mythic storyteller, showed me how.

The Moor's Last Sigh is Rushdie's first novel in seven years. The intricate, gorgeous tapestry of a plot takes off on a tragic riff in 1492 when the Arab sultan Boabdil gives up his beloved Alhambra to Ferdinand and Isabella, the Catholic monarchs of Spain. Observed by none other than a contemptuous Christopher Columbus, Boabdil's humiliating surrender puts an end to centuries of Moorish rule in Europe. In one of the novel's many haunting passages, the grieving Boabdil rides off into exile, turning "to look for one last time upon his loss, upon the palace and the fertile plains and all the concluded glory of al-Andalus . . . at which sight the Sultan sighed, and hotly wept." Ayxa the Virtuous, his tough-cookie-of-a-mother, has no patience for such tears, sneering, "Well may you weep like a woman for what you could not defend like a man."

There are actually two "Moors" and two mothers in Rushdie's multilayered story—the fifteenth-century Boabdil and his mother, Ayxa, and their fictional twentieth-century descendants, the bohemian diva Aurora da Gama Zogoiby and her son, Moraes "Moor" Zogoiby. Aurora is lovingly described by her son as "most illustrious of our modern artists, a great beauty who was also the most sharp-tongued woman of her generation, handing out the hot stuff to anybody who came within range. Her children were shown no mercy." Like Ayxa before her, Aurora can be hard and unforgiving, unwilling to tolerate her son's weakness. Moor Zogoiby, Rushdie's doomed narrator, is born with a stump for a right hand, after only four and a half months' gestation. He is afflicted with a disease that accelerates aging. Bizarrely handsome and compelling to women, Moor soars to a height of six foot six "in a country where the average male rarely grows above five foot five." At age 10, he looks 20; at age 32, a dying man in his seventies. The knowledge that time is literally flying by him brings a heightened urgency to his daily life. A man capable of both tenderness and murder, Moor Zogoiby—whose last name means "The Misfortunate"—makes an eloquent, ironic and moving protagonist. And then there's the antagonist. In the vengeful Vasco Miranda, Rushdie has created a memorable and flamboyant villain—an embittered, heartbroken, commercially successful, has-been artist clearly modeled after Salvador Dali. When Vasco aims a gun at Moor Zogoiby, they strike a bargain: As long as Moor keeps talking, Vasco will let him live. The allusions to Scheherazade and Rushdie's own predicament are unmistakable, but I am happy to say this big-hearted novel is all that and more.

Set primarily in the Bombay of Rushdie's birth and ending up in the arid landscape of southern Spain, *The Moor's Last Sigh* nevertheless feels and reads as if it were taking place everywhere in the world. Ancient cultures and spirits collide constantly with our confusing, cynical, violent, jet-set present. In Rushdie's dizzying, inclusive universe, the dispossessed, the exiled, the colonizers and the colonized clash, multiply and miscegenate. A lilting, playful rhyme asks a deadly serious question: "Christians, Portuguese, and Jews; Chinese tiles promoting godless views; pushy ladies, skirts-not-saris, Spanish shenanigans, Moorish crowns . . . can this really be India?" And of course, it is.

Rushdie once wrote: "What seems to me to be happening is that those peoples who were once colonized by the language are now rapidly remaking it, domesticating it, becoming more and more relaxed about the way they use it." He claims English is an "Indian literary language," and rightly so. In this new novel, Rushdie the linguistic acrobat has the time of his life, and his text resonates with vibrant energy and music. English becomes magical and fluid—at times florid and ornate, at times funky and rhythmic, at times a mournful, lyrical lament, echoing Shakespeare: "O, I am deep in blood. There is blood on my shaking hands, and on my clothes. Blood smudges these words as I set them down. O the vulgarity, the garish un-ambiguity of blood. How tawdry it is, how thin." There are puns galore, highbrow and lowbrow asides, rhymes and ditties, tongue twisters and homages to Looney Tunes, Hollywood and Bollywood. A spectacular cast of characters includes the sisters Ina, Minnie and Mynah, the "Country and Eastern" singer Jimmy Cash, the Bombay mega-corporation House of Cashondeliveri, a nasty right-wing Hindu politician called Mainduck Fielding and a stuffed dog named Nehru.

The book bursts with glorious female characters—the fierce and sensual mothers of Rushdie's Mother India—powerful women capable of great courage, cruelty, greed and love. The men are often devious, smarmy, weak and dishonorable—never quite as much fun as Rushdie's women. After all, even Moor Zogoiby must wryly admit, "Nobody ever made a movie called *Father India*."

Art and commerce, sex and family, politics, religious fanaticism, ethnic cleansing and empire building—Rushdie examines all with razor wit and profound intelligence. The connections he makes are audacious, wickedly funny and right on target: "English and French sailed in the wake of that first-arrived Portugee, so that in the period called Discovery-of-India—but how could we be discovered when we were not covered before?—we were 'not so much sub-continent as sub-condiment,' as my distinguished mother had it. 'From the beginning, what the world wanted from bloody mother India was daylight-clear,' she'd say. 'They came for the hot stuff, like any man calling on a tart.'" I didn't get a sense this time—as I sometimes did wending my way through the labyrinthine maze of *The Satanic Verses*—that Rushdie was being self-indulgent or "showing off" his cleverness. His verbal pyrotechnics in *The Moor's Last Sigh* are delightful and never gratuitous. The novel is fabulous and timely, contemporary in spirit yet crammed with historical highjinks and melodrama.

History repeats itself through exile and loss, love and betrayal. "The dispossessed Spanish Arab" Boabdil is betrayed by his "ejected Spanish Jewish" mistress, who steals his crown and flees to India. Moor Zogoiby is betrayed by both his father, Abraham, and the love of his life, a sly, conniving fox named Uma. Aurora, merciless mother and artist, "rosary crucifixion beatnik chick" and true star of Rushdie's epic, a woman who boasts of red chili peppers in her veins instead of blood, is both betrayed and betrayer. Out of all this pain, beauty and deceit, the exotic da Gama Zogoiby dynasty flourishes. Aurora paints her surreal masterpiece, *The Moor's Last Sigh,* in partial response to her tainted, convoluted legacy: "There was no stopping her. Around and about the figure of the Moor in his hybrid fortress she wove her vision. . . . In a way these were polemical pictures, in a way they were an attempt to create a romantic myth of the plural, hybrid nation; she was using Arab Spain to re-imagine India." The painting may (or may not) solve one of many ongoing mysteries in Rushdie's wise and compassionate book—"Who betrayed whom?" or "What's in a name?" The answers often lie in the questions themselves, and the terms palimpsest and hybrid are ubiquitous. Things are never what they seem at even a second glance. Just when you think you've uncovered the identity of the killer . . . surprise, surprise!

Set primarily in the Bombay of Rushdie's birth and ending up in the arid landscape of southern Spain, *The Moor's Last Sigh* nevertheless feels and reads as if it were taking place everywhere in the world.

—*Jessica Hagedorn*

At novel's end, Moor Zogoiby returns to the site of his ancestor's rude downfall and experiences a final epiphany: "The Alhambra, Europe's red fort, sister to Delhi's and Agra's—the palace of interlocking forms and secret wisdom, of pleasure-courts and water-gardens, that monument to a lost possibility that nevertheless has gone on standing, long after its conquerors have fallen; like a testament to lost but sweetest love, to the love that endures beyond defeat, beyond annihilation, beyond despair; to the defeated love that is greater than what defeats it, to that most profound of our needs, to our need for flowing together, for putting an end to frontiers, for the dropping of boundaries of the self."

In an eerie replay of his recent troubles, Rushdie's latest work has been attacked by ultra-conservative extremists, this time back "home" in Bombay. Through sheer intimidation and pressure by the powerful Hindu nationalist political party, Shiv Sena, *The Moor's Last Sigh* has been made "unavailable" in bookstores. The alarming Shiv Sena is led by 68-year-old Balasaheb Thackeray, staunch admirer of Hitler and obviously Rushdie's inspiration for the creepy and vicious Mainduck Fielding of the novel. Thackeray and his Shiv Sena followers have been accused of inciting anti-Muslim violence and causing the deaths of over a thousand Muslims. *The New York Times* quoted Thackeray dismissing Rushdie as "a man with no homeland." He was also quoted as saying, "I do not like people living in foreign countries criticizing us." Of course, Thackeray hasn't even bothered to read the novel—which may be just as well. *The Moor's Last Sigh* would probably confirm Thackeray and his cronies' worst expectations. They may not be the only ones in India outraged by the many parodies contained in this dangerous book. There is, after all, that stuffed dog.

Rushdie is at the peak of his form, writing as if a gun were pointed at him, performing for his life like narrator Moor:

> "By embracing the inescapable, I lost my fear of it. I'll tell you a secret about fear: it's an absolutist. With fear, it's all or nothing. Either, like a bullying tyrant, it rules your life with a stupid blinding omnipotence, or else you overthrow it, and its power vanishes in a puff of smoke. And another secret: the revolution against fear, the engendering of that tawdry despot's fall, has more or less nothing to do with 'courage.' It is driven by something much more straightforward: the simple need to get on with your life. I stopped being afraid because, if my time on earth was limited, I didn't have seconds to spare for funk."

Shameless, innovative, irreverent, difficult, visionary, hilarious, accessible. Call it what you will—futuristic-contemporary-historical-postcolonial-multiculti thriller, spicy potboiler, slapstick, arty mystery, steamy love story, sudsy soap opera, moral fable, exhilarating adventure, tragicomedy—Salman Rushdie's *The Moor's Last Sigh* is a great mother of a book.

Michael Dirda (review date 7 January 1996)

SOURCE: "Where the Wonders Never Cease," in *Book World—The Washington Post,* January 7, 1996, pp. 1-2.

[*In the following review, Dirda finds* The Moor's Last Sigh *further evidence of his contention that Rushdie is among the world's greatest writers.*]

Over the past several years Salman Rushdie has become, to his sorrow, such a symbolic figure that it is easy to lose sight of the most important fact about him: He really is one of the world's great writers. One need only read the first sentence of this wondrous new novel—a book comparable, it seems to me, to Robertson Davies' masterpiece, *What's Bred in the Bone,* even, at times, to Garcia Marquez's *One Hundred Years of Solitude*—to feel its irresistible narrative pace, its openly melodramatic panache:

> "I have lost count of the days that have passed since I fled the horrors of Vasco Miranda's mad fortress in the Andalusian mountain-village of Benengeli; ran from death under cover of darkness and left a message nailed to the door."

Only those without a smidgen of Gothic romance in their souls could possibly set down *The Moor's Last Sigh* at this point. Or at any other point, for that matter. "Just a few more pages," you will think to yourself at 2 a.m., or as your Metro stop whizzes by. Throughout his book Rushdie sustains an altogether breathtaking riot of marvels, grotesques and horrors. On their wedding night a handsome young groom enters his trembling wife's bedroom, slips into her virginal white dress, and steals away to the arms of a sailor nicknamed Prince Henry the Navigator. A wealthy Indian communist expends a fortune to organize a troupe of Lenin lookalikes. At one point our narrator-hero—Moraes Zagoiby—even takes up with a tin man, a scarecrow and a cowardly frog. Another character acquires a British bulldog which he names Jawaharlal; after the animal dies, his old master pulls its stuffed body around on wheels. A desperately poor boy discovers a king's crown, set with emeralds, in an old wooden chest. A Jewish criminal mastermind actually agrees to steal a doomsday weapon for "certain oil-rich countries and their ideological allies."

Basically a generational saga, *The Moor's Last Sigh* traces the history of the da Gama-Zogoiby family over three generations, from the late 1800s to 1993. Most of the action takes place in India, in either Cochin or Bombay, though the plot comes to its dying fall in Spain, near the Alhambra, that ancient fortress of the Moors. The main characters are Aurora da Gama, beautiful, willful and perhaps the greatest artist of modern India; her husband, Abraham Zagoiby, a mere clerk in the da Gama family's spice business, 20 years her elder, whom Aurora loves at first sight and who proves to possess unsuspected gifts for commerce and other matters; and their son, Moraes, burdened with a curse: Because his mother longed for a child who would grow up quickly, Moraes soon finds that he is going through time faster than he should. He is born after only four and a half months' gestation; at 20 he looks like a man of 40.

Around these central figures swarm dozens of subsidiary characters: an artist who starts his career by painting cartoons on the walls of a nursery and ends by earning a fortune with his airport murals; a young beauty who can make herself all things to all men—and women—but who just might be a vampiric Lamia; Ina, Minnie and Mynah, the three doomed Zagoiby girls, whose nicknames partially explain their brother's—"the Moor"; a museum curator who has authored "Imperso-Nation and Dis/Semi/Nations: Dialogics of Eclecticism and Interrogations of Authenticity in A.Z." (that is, Aurora Zagoiby); Nadia Wadia, Miss World, "who has a walk like a warrior and a voice like a dirty phone call"; a young Indian who changes his name to Jimmy Cash and travels to Nashville with his "Country and Eastern" music; and even a mother who demands her own son's first-born in exchange for a desperately needed loan.

> *The Moor's Last Sigh* opens like an adventure story, soon metamorphoses into a kind of fairy-tale romance (at times a Freudian family romance) and then, in its last third, grows significantly darker, more Gothic and finally violent and bloody.
>
> —*Michael Dirda*

Supporting these amazing characters is Rushdie's equally amazing language, sliding effortlessly from Indian slang to Joycean self-interrogation to Oxonian English; peppered with puns and wordplay; quickened with allusions to literature, pop culture (Vito Corleone, Bugs Bunny), contemporary history (the deaths of Indira, Sanjay and Rajiv Gandhi), and, inevitably, movies like that Rushdie favorite, "The Wizard of Oz," and the surrealist masterpiece "*Un Chien Andalou*": In Spain, for instance, while on a visit to a Dali-like painter, the Moor notices that "the region was full of starving, disappointed Andalusian dogs."

On almost any page of *The Moor's Last Sigh,* one may light on sentences as taut as aphorisms or as shrewd as folk wisdom: "'A bad mistake, Abie,' old Moshe Cohen commented. 'To make an enemy of your mother; for enemies are plentiful, but mothers are hard to find.' "One ancient crone tellingly skewers nursery rhymes and songs: "What shall we do with the shrunken tailor?" and "Morally, morally, morally, morally . . . wife is not a queen." There are puns, blatant and buried, on Moors and last sighs: the Ultimo Suspiro gas station, "a Moor in love," the Last Gasp Saloon, a supper falsely Frenchified as a "dernier soupir," the sighs of asthma, procreation and death. Outrageous names proliferate with Pynchonian abandon, my favorite being Sir Duljee Duljeebhoy Cashondeliveri (whose scion becomes Jimmy

Cash). Why, you may ask, do Popeye and Jehovah resemble each other? Because, as we unforgettably learn here, both exclaim "I yam what I yam." Then there is the Indian version of Einstein's famous theory: "Everything is for relative. Not only light bends but everything. For relative we can bend a point, bend the truth, bend employment criteria, bend the law . . . " A man who is severely beaten, we are informed by a dread enforcer known as the Hammer, will be irreversibly changed: "To be beaten for a long time upon the soles of the feet, for example, affects laughter. Those who are so beaten never laugh again." And there is this nonpareil description of passionate lovemaking:

> "He came to her as a man goes to his doom, trembling but resolute, and it is around here that my words run out, so you will not learn from me the bloody details of what happened when she, and then he, and then they, and after that she, and at which he, and in response to that she, and with that, and in addition, and for a while, and then for a long time, and quietly, and noisily, and at the end of their endurance, and at last, and after that, until . . . phew!"

The Moor's Last Sigh opens like an adventure story, soon metamorphoses into a kind of fairy-tale romance (at times a Freudian family romance) and then, in its last third, grows significantly darker, more Gothic and finally violent and bloody. I'm not sure that the Grand Guignol of these concluding pages, with their demonizing of various characters, doesn't weaken the book slightly. But everyone in this superb novel is so greedy for success and self-fulfillment, so lustful and flamboyant and larger-than-life that one ultimately accepts every excess, from sophomoric puns to foreshadowing to the unexpected volte-face that certain key players undergo.

Like the window that Aurora throws open early in the novel, the 448 pages of *The Moor's Last Sigh* may let in almost anything: "the dust and tumult of boats in Cochin harbour, the horns of freighters and tugboat chugs, the fishermen's dirty jokes and the throb of their jellyfish stings, the sunlight as sharp as a knife, the heat that could choke you like a damp cloth pulled tightly around your head, the calls of floating hawkers, the wafting sadness of the unmarried Jews across the water in Mattancherri, the menace of emerald smugglers, the machinations of business rivals, the growing nervousness of the British colony in Fort Cochin, the cash demands of the staff and of the plantation workers in the Spice Mountains, the tales of Communist troublemaking and Congresswallah politics, the names *Gandhi* and *Nehru,* the rumours of famine in the east and hunger strikes in the north, the songs and drumbeats of the oral storytellers, and the heavy rolling sound (as they broke against Cabral Island's rickety jetty) of the incoming tides of history."

And more. This is a novel about love, identity, art, ambition, religion, politics and death. Above all, about modern India and a family that "just didn't know how to be calm." As her wonderstruck father says to the young Aurora Zagoiby when he glimpses her first great masterpiece, and as this similarly wonderstruck reviewer must now repeat: Here "is the great swarm of being itself."

Richard Eder (review date 7 January 1996)

SOURCE: "English as a Wicked Weapon," in *Los Angeles Times Book Review,* January 7, 1996, pp. 3, 13.

[*Below, Eder presents a mixed review of* The Moor's Last Sigh.]

Why is Moraes Zogoiby, disinherited scion of twin artistic and financial dynasties in Bombay, cowering in a graveyard across from Granada's Alhambra, having escaped from a mad compatriot intent on murdering him? Or, to transmute fiction back into reality, why is Salman Rushdie, twin scion of literature and of a wealthy Indian Muslim family, hiding from a different form of coreligionary murderousness (except when he ventures out for a reception or a ceremony)?

The Moor's Last Sigh is not Rushdie's first fictional reflection on the extremist Muslim death sentence imposed on him for *The Satanic Verses.* His first effort was a children's tale, *Haroun and the Sea of Stories,* a whimsical allegory in which good adventures magically defeat evil necromancers. No such victory takes place in the painful chaos of his new full-length novel. There is whimsy in it—Rushdie cannot bare his teeth without grinning to mock the gesture—but it is mainly at the level of language.

Rushdie is wickedly adept at English: It is his tongue of upbringing and art, and yet he employs it as if it oppressed him. Language is power; English was the language of his forebears' colonizers. Today, in the Indian subcontinent it is the language of those who, like Rushdie, inherited English culture and position and who now are threatened by fundamentalisms voiced in Hindi, Urdu and a half-dozen other languages.

English is all Rushdie has got, and it goads him continually. And he goads back: punning, mocking, exaggerating its possibilities, impersonating it with comic absurdity. He is not so much an artist of the English language as its brilliant—and sometimes intolerable—cartoonist. Moraes, his narrator and symbolic alter ego, is grotesquely wordy, as if he did not own his story but only the words he uses to tell it. He uses English not to commune but to estrange; not as "Come close and see' but a more ornate "Stand back and behold."

The Moor's Last Sigh is a four-generation *roman-fleuve* about the Vasco da Gama family, whose patriarch, Francisco, established a flourishing spice empire in Cochin on India's Malabar coast. Of Portuguese Christian descent, Francisco married a woman of Indian, Jewish and Christian lineage. The family fortunes survived choppily amid murderous family feuds and splits, the jailing of Francisco's two sons—one pro-British and one pro-independence—a flourishing reign by his daughter-in-law, Belle, and the marriage of Belle's daughter, Aurora, to Abraham Zogoiby, a member of Cochin's ancient Jewish community.

Abraham and Aurora move to Bombay after World War II. He expands the family business, by hook and corrupt crook, into a multibillion-dollar banking, real estate, trading and, eventually, drug and arms-smuggling conglomerate. He becomes a brilliant painter and a social and political celebrity. Aurora's connections include all of India's top political personages, among them Jawaharlal Nehru, one of her lovers.

The first part of this family saga, in the languorous plantation atmosphere of Cochin, has an intimate and sensual humanity along with its violence and odd, displacing prodigies. There is, in fact, a suggestion of Gabriel Garcia Marquez's sweet magical rigor. The subsequent career of Aurora and Zogoiby in Bombay is all the opposite.

The two figures, who start out appealingly human, become constructs of passion, power and greed. Eventually, Abraham's empire collapses in scandal, and Aurora dies when an "accident" arranged by her husband sends her hurtling from the roof of her mansion. Rushdie makes their rise to godlike heights and their separate godlike falls a symbol of the corruption and ruthless hypertrophy of postwar India's political and financial circles.

"Corruption was the only force we had that could defeat fanaticism," was the pronouncement of Vasco Miranda, a painter protégé of Aurora's, her would-be lover and eventually, after she banishes him, the family's bitterest enemy. It is the grim double chokehold in which young Moraes grows up, as well as Rushdie's dark verdict not only on India but on a wider emerging world.

Moraes is the family's only son. He is born with two flaws, both glaringly symbolic. His right hand ends in a hammer-like claw. At one point he will become a hired thug and use the claw to beat people up. It is the writer's hammer, of course, and the writer's estranging deformity.

Moraes's second twist is that he ages twice as fast as other people. Born 4 1/2 months after conception, he cries inside the womb and his passage down the birth canal is impeded by a precocious erection. By the book's end, having escaped from the Spanish tower where Vasco Miranda was about to

kill him, he will be in his mid-70s without having reached 40. The modern world not only deforms and debases, it does so faster and faster.

The Moor's Last Sigh is laden with action, incident and a steady production of new characters. It is dense, rich, sometimes entrancing, always frenetic and oddly static. The activity is that of a frieze, rather like the elaborate and static ornamentation of the Moorish Alhambra, to which I will return. After they leave Cochin, the characters no longer really live—the emblematic, speeded-up Moraes least of all—but depict, instead.

What they depict is not always clear. Aurora, virtually a goddess, is worshiped by her son, who tries unsuccessfully to win her favor and whom she eventually banishes. The agent of banishment is Uma, virtually an Aurora replica. She seduces Moraes, estranges him from his family by means of vile calumnies and eventually dies by grotesquely comic mistake while trying to poison him.

I am not sure what the role of these witchy women is, apart from adding to Moraes' prodigious misery. There have been suggestions that they reflect Rushdie's own feelings about women he has known. Neither of them helps the novel—quite the opposite. Nor does Zogoiby as bloodless, ancient, capitalist spider add much, except a cliché.

A much more interesting figure is the man for whom Moraes goes to work as an enforcer. Maidenduck is the political boss of Bombay, a right-wing Hindu nationalist demagogue with strong-arm bands that go around instigating the burning of mosques, breaking the legs of strikers and compelling reluctant Hindu widows to climb onto their husbands' funeral pyres. Based on a real Bombay politician who is so recognizable that *The Moor's Last Sigh* has undergone an unofficial ban in India—a less violent counterpart, of course, to Muslim anger at *Satanic Verses*—Maidenduck represents the destructive violence of fundamentalist demagogy. On the other hand, Rushdie portrays him with subtlety and even a trace of appalled sympathy.

The book works trenchantly as a dark and sardonic message, and this alone would give it value. Sometimes it works as symbol, as well. The title, for instance, refers to the legend of Boabdil, the last Moorish king of Granada. Defeated by the Spaniards, he paused weeping for one last look at his beloved city. Scornfully, his mother cried out: "Weep like a woman for what you could not defend like a man." Rushdie's target is the world's privileged—the rich, the intellectuals, the political leaders—who, failing to take action against the dark forces of history, will not be worth saving.

Message and symbol shine out here and there. Rarely, though, do they work by means of the novel itself. Despite its agitated plotting (the war between capitalists, fundamentalists and plain criminal gangs ends in a twilight-of-the-gods-style bombing orgy) and Rushdie's febrile way with words, the book remains an enclosed, even a solipsistic work.

If *The Satanic Verses* was a splendid explosion sometimes out of control, *The Moor's Last Sigh* is an implosion only partly achieved.

Newsweek (review date 8 January 1996)

SOURCE: "The Prisoner in the Tower," in *Newsweek*, Vol. CXXVII, No. 2, January 8, 1996, p. 70.

[*In the following review, the critic describes* The Moor's Last Sigh *as Rushdie's "passionate, often furious love letter to the country of his birth."*]

There's an unusually restrained, contemplative episode toward the end of Salman Rushdie's flamboyant new novel, *The Moor's Last Sigh,* when the narrator finds himself locked up in a tower by a madman intent on murder. The narrator, known as Moor, is helpless. Then a kind of hope begins to stir, thanks to the woman he meets there—a fellow prisoner who is Japanese by birth. "Her name was a miracle of vowels. Aoi Uë: the five enabling sounds of language, thus grouped ('ow-ee oo-ay'), constructed her." By virtue of her quiet strength, "her formality, her precision," this woman becomes his life support and a fount of discipline. Locked up with the source of language, that is, he writes; and writing saves his life.

Moor is a protean figure in this novel: sometimes he's a lost soul wandering through what might be Dante's "Inferno"; sometimes he's Dorothy in a very unmerry land of Oz; sometimes he's Everyman. But in episodes like the one in the tower, we seem to hear the author himself speaking. It's now almost seven years since his last novel, *The Satanic Verses,* so infuriated fundamentalist Muslims that the Ayatollah Khomeini issued a *fatwa,* or death sentence, against Rushdie and sent him into hiding. In recent years he (and his guards from Scotland Yard) has shown up increasingly often at social and literary events—and a book tour has just taken him to Australia—but his life remains far from normal. In November, police in Santiago, Chile, where he went to speak at a book fair, rushed him off to a secret location when they suspected an assassination plot. Meanwhile, diplomatic negotiations on the fatwa continue, but most people involved are not optimistic. "We want a clear, unequivocal letter from the Iranians that the fatwa won't be carried out," a senior British official told *Newsweek.* Right now he sees no such assurance on the way.

The Moor's Last Sigh seems unlikely to offend Muslims—but ultranationalist Hindus are another matter. The Shiv Sena, an extremist Hindu political party, has successfully pressured the Indian government to forbid imports of the book. That hasn't stopped Indians from eagerly reading the few thousand copies that arrived before the edict. Many are relishing Rushdie's portrait of a repellent politico who bears notable resemblance to Bal Thackeray, the rabid right-winger who runs the Shiv Sena.

But Rushdie's new novel is not an attack on India; it's more like a passionate, often furious love letter to the country of his birth. Starting in the 19th century, Moor spins out a tale spanning generations of his family's adventures in India's spice trade, its art world and its gangster underworld. His mother, Aurora Da Gama, is a great artist, beautiful and shrewd, with a grip on the hearts and souls of her family that nothing can shake. In fact, she is Mother India herself, and her story mimics the nation's. When her only son falls in love with Uma, a strange but alluring newcomer who seems to have a dozen personae and no principles, Aurora tries to warn him that disaster is in store. But Moor can't resist, and embraces his own destruction. At the same time, a nation that struggled for decades to keep its politics secular falls under the sway of an enticing new brand of Hinduism. Raman Fielding (the character inspired by Bal Thackeray) promises Hindus their rightful glory as a majority, while Muslims, Christians and everyone else get beaten into submission. Moor understands very well how this kind of India operates, for he is Fielding's right-hand man for a time. Eventually disaster catches up with him, and overtakes Aurora, too. It's all to Rushdie's credit that what might have been a grim conclusion actually brings on a smile.

> **Rushdie's new novel is not an attack on India; it's more like a passionate, often furious love letter to the country of his birth.**
>
> **—*Newsweek***

Written in his signature, pell-mell style, wild with wordplay, *The Moor's Last Sigh* also has simpler passages of a sort that didn't show up in "The Satanic Verses." Describing Aurora as she sat sketching in the slums of Bombay, for instance, Moor recalls how she captured in charcoal "the face-slapping quarrels of naked children at a tenement standpipe, the grizzled despair of idling workers smoking beedies on the doorsteps of locked-up pharmacies . . . the toughness of women with saris pulled over their heads, squatting by tiny primus stoves . . . as they tried to conjure meals from empty air." In this altogether splendid novel, Rushdie's indictment of religious politics is very powerful, but the plain words from his heart are even more so.

Gail Caldwell (review date 14 January 1996)

SOURCE: "For Love of Mother," in *The Boston Globe,* January 14, 1996, p. B43.

[*In the following review, Caldwell describes* The Moor's Last Sigh *as "a parable of modern India."*]

In Salman Rushdie's vast, torrential ode to modern India, the streets are filled with the smells of history: spices and blood and yesterday's tragedies, mingled with the sweet promise of tomorrow's lies. *The Moor's Last Sigh* is a prodigiously realized, sometimes exhausting novel, cloaked in an elegant satire that barely masks the moral conviction at its center. Its story roams from Bombay to Spain over most of the 20th century, and though its panoply of characters focuses chiefly upon four generations of one Jewish-Christian family, its real protagonist is Mother India. Wrought with passion and anger and a fierce lampoonery that only history's agonies can evoke, *The Moor's Last Sigh* trains its rapid-fire intelligence on anything that moves.

Conceived with the same blast of momentum that drove Rushdie's 1982 novel, *Midnight's Children,* this epochal work has as its narrator Moor (christened Moraes) Zogoiby—the only son of Aurora and Abraham, a man born with a marked right hand and the biological condition of premature aging, or living his life on double time. (His mother's pregnancy was complete at 4 1/2 months; at 30, he has the body and fatigue of a 60-year-old.) Oedipal subject of his mother's paintings, lover to a traitor of monstrous proportions, ambivalent prodigal son to his family's bloody legacy—Moor's first lessons, he tells us, were of "metamorphosis and disguise"; he has been forced, by the curse of his body, "to live out the literal truth of the metaphors." Banished from his own narrative, he has chosen to spill the family secrets: those of the wealthy da Gamas, rich beyond measure from the spice trade, with their decades of perverse betrayals, hidden desires and hellish misunderstandings. Moor is the only one left standing now, and he has nearly lost his life more than once in this telling of the tale. So sing, Scheherazade, and save us all

Certainly he has plenty of material from which to spin his stories: a patrilineal line of suicides, a mother who, as a young girl, watched her grandmother die without going for help. The old matriarch cursed the child before she died: "May your house be for ever partitioned, may its foundations, may your children rise up against you, and may your fall be hard."

The trials of the next half-century would only prove how fully that wish came true.

Rife with political deceits and emotional tyrannies, *The Moor's Last Sigh* is a parable of modern India, but it also contains treatises on art and modernity, speculations on Dante and Milton, references to Indian film and "The Wizard of Oz" and "The Lone Ranger." It is a paean to living at the end of the 20th century: to having survived the 20th century, with all its pain and vulgarity and bloody rivers of violent conflict. We are given, wholesale, an "inexhaustible Bombay of excess," but also a tale of familial destruction and a son's desperate obsession to capture the story of the dead: "the giant dead whom we cannot tie down, though we grasp at their hair, though we rope them while they sleep." The task in this novel is huge, and the fact that it is even partly achieved seems more than admirable.

Throughout *The Moor's Last Sigh* are the kind of intricate stories that saved Scheherazade's life: a house divided between families, down to counting the lizards on the walls; a woman who takes in her husband's male (and syphilitic) lover, then beats him at cards; a young nun who sees into the future. But the crux of the tale is the stormy, sometimes treacherous love of Moor and Aurora. "We loved her even as she destroyed us," he admits, and that obsessive tension—between mother and son, between the promise of India and its individual dramas—is what propels this novel to its triumphant final pages.

In a move that only served to underscore its authenticity, *The Moor's Last Sigh* was promptly condemned in India upon its publication there last year, partly owing to Rushdie's demonic depiction in the novel of a Hindu nationalist leader who greatly resembles a real political figure, Balasaheb K. Thackeray. (The author has also named a stuffed bulldog Jawaharlal Nehru, after India's first prime minister.) And certainly Rushdie's own plight—he has been under an edict of death from the late Ayatollah Khomeini since 1989, accused of blasphemy in "The Satanic Verses"—provides a shadowy aura to his story, which is weighted with the notion of exile. Still, these external realities inform rather than dictate the novel. Its chief concern is wider than that in all directions, for Rushdie knows that one of the fiercest ways to dismantle a monster is to render it absurd.

That's partly why the rare sorrowful writing within *The Moor's Last Sigh* feels so abruptly powerful; when Moor confesses his role in "the ruin of our great house," his family's plight resounds with Faulknerian doom. But mostly Rushdie hedges on any empathic contact with his characters. As artist, mother and infidel, Aurora is a stunning figure, but she never elicits the human sympathy from the reader on which most fiction is fueled. Rushdie has sacrificed emotional identification for metaphor and wit—he has served up his characters with such wicked force that they're stand-ins for entire cultures, for whole sweepstakes of human affairs, rather than simply being fully themselves. This choice—and one assumes it was a choice—is by no means lethal, but it is limiting. Awed by the reach and propulsion of *The Moor's Last Sigh,* I was never as engaged as I wanted to be. The novel is cool as a diamond. Sharp and brilliant and unquestionably valuable, but a diamond, nonetheless.

What I am offering, of course, is a decidedly Western and bourgeois bias: a viewpoint with room (and preference) for the individual and the emotional. And Rushdie's may be the grander vista. "A tragedy was taking place all right," Moor tells us, "a national tragedy on a grand scale, but those of us who played our parts were—let me put it bluntly—clowns. Clowns! Burlesque buffoons, drafted into history's theatre on account of the lack of greater men. Once, indeed, there were giants on our stage; but at the fag-end of an age, Madam History must make do with what she can get."

So the defeat in *The Moor's Last Sigh* is mythic as well as personal; if its story overwhelms at times, it is, like Moor's beloved Bombay, a world of passionate excess. The ironic distance that sometimes drives the novel may be a fortunate byproduct of biculturalism; Rushdie—born in India, relocated to England—knows that "civilisation is the sleight of hand that conceals our natures from ourselves." Teeming with both civilization and the abominable, global lack of it, *The Moor's Last Sigh* is a novel of great intelligence and noble moral suasion.

India was uncertainty. It was deception and illusion. Here at Fort Cochin the English had striven mightily to construct a mirage of Englishness, where English bungalows clustered around an English green, where there were Rotarians and golfers and tea-dances and cricket and a Masonic Lodge. But D'Aeth could not help seeing through the conjuring trick, couldn't help hearing the false vowels of the coir traders lying about their education, or wincing at the coarse dancing of their to-tell-the-truth-mostly-rather-common wives, or seeing the bloodsucker lizards beneath the English hedges, the parrots flying over the rather un-Home-Counties jacaranda trees. And when he looked out to sea the illusion of England vanished entirely; for the harbour could not be disguised, and no matter how Anglicised the land might be, it was contradicted by the water; as if England were being washed by an alien sea. Alien, and encroaching; for Oliver D'Aeth knew enough to be sure that the frontier between the English enclaves and the surrounding foreignness had become permeable, was beginning to dissolve. India would reclaim it all.

Norman Rush (review date 14 January 1996)

SOURCE: "Doomed in Bombay," in *The New York Times Book Review,* January 14, 1996, p. 7.

[*In the following review, Rush praises* The Moor's Last Sigh *as an apt response to the tyrannical reaction to* The Satanic Verses.]

Salman Rushdie's new novel, his first since the infamous fatwa issued by the Iranian Government in 1989 as punishment for putatively blasphemous passages in his satire *The Satanic Verses,* comes heavily attended by certain inevitable questions. How is Mr. Rushdie holding up after six years in hiding? What kind of story is the world's most famous living author, in this extraordinary situation, going to tell us and, of course, himself? Is this another book that will give offense, and to whom? Will this book comment, directly or otherwise, on the dogma-driven expansion of censorship and persecution affecting writers in so many parts of the world? It's only when we've worked through this vanguard of questions that we're free to ask what we can take from this novel, as opposed to all the novels it competes with—serious novels whose ambitions are to show us what we urgently need to know or feel in this threatening moment, when alarms and grim forewarnings crowd in on us, making so many of our innocent pastimes feel difficult to justify, fiction reading itself not excepted.

It turns out that the topical questions are easily answered; and it turns out, also, that this novel, looked at as a work of literary art, is a triumph, an intricate and deceptive one. The evidence is that Mr. Rushdie is in good creative health, his imaginative powers undamaged. The story he tells deals analogically and subtly with the shaping of his predicament, and writing it must have been tonic, though not necessarily consoling. It's a work that honorably serves the republic of letters and in the process exposes its author to a new range of potential antagonists.

The Moor's Last Sigh is a picaresque recounting of the rise, decline and plunge to extinction of a Portuguese merchant family anciently established in southern India, focusing on the period from 1900 to the present. The hapless narrator, Moraes Zogoiby, born, like Mr. Rushdie, in Bombay (but in 1967, 10 years later), has composed these pages during exile and imprisonment in a replica of the Alhambra built and run by a madman (a former protégé of the family) in rural Andalusia Moraes, nicknamed the Moor, is the last living member of the da Gama-Zogoiby line. Throughout, echoes of Mr. Rushdie's own predicament are hard not to detect. *"Here I stand; couldn't've done it differently"* is one of the Moor's last thoughts as be roams the Andalusian countryside, following his doomed escape from captivity, annoyed that there are no church doors handy for nailing his screed to.

At the center of the chronicle is the demonically talented

painter Aurora Zogoiby, whose career flourishes from the 1940's through the 1980's. Moraes is her son, one of four children who all achieve doom at young ages; he himself is a physical giant who was born with a deformed right hand and with a form of progeria that makes him appear to be twice his actual age. In the course of the novel, the action moves from the family estate on Cabral Island, in Cochin, the site of the family's spice business, to Malabar Hill, the wealthiest suburb of Bombay, where Aurora attains celebrity, and where the family business, under the direction of her common-law Jewish band, Abraham, grows to fantastic success and exfoliates into the basest criminality. I will resist the temptation to summarize the kinks and jags in the family trajectory since they're too much fun to encounter the first time through, but the reader may be assured that all the weird fruit that family trees produce is here—betrayals, lunacies, failed crusades, venery, the lot. The watershed events of modern Indian history regularly protrude into the tale—the independence struggle, partition, the emergency, the B.C.C.I. scandal, the rise of Hindu fundamentalism. There is a pyrotechnical denouement. And the story plays out through an elegant double metaphor twinning the expulsion of the Moors from Spain with the symbolic expulsion from India of our set of Iberian colonizers.

The grand deception in this book is to conceal a bitter cautionary tale within bright, carnivalesque wrappings. Mr. Rushdie, defiant, plays a dire light on the evil consequences, for the religiously indifferent but nominally Christian da Gama-Zogoiby clan, of militant religion in various guises. The recent de facto banning of *The Moor's Last Sigh* by the Indian Government may not be so surprising. (The Government cut off imports of the book after just 4,000 copies had come into the country.) In addition to a few offhand scurrilisms about Pandit Nehru's private life (and the naming of a dog after him), the book contains a devastating portrait of a Hindu political boss, Raman Fielding, who brings unfavorably to mind the powerful Hindu nationalist leader Bal Thackeray. There's much to offend here, and all along the spectrum of belief. At the heart of the plot, for example, is a satanic Jew (more about this later), and all the outright believers in the cast of characters—the pious self-immolator who inadvertently burns the Moor's grandmother to death, the interfering Anglican priest . . . , the Moor's multiple-personality-disorder afflicted Hindu lover—are odious in some strong way. Which is not to say that this tale should be taken merely as a broadly anti-creedal parable. Mr. Rushdie's subject is subtler than that. What results in cataclysm is the interaction of the reflexive, undefined, pooped-out unreligion of the da Gama-Zogoibys with the absolutist forms of religious identification taking hold in India.

What else does this antic tragedy provide, along the way? At a minimum, the following: (1) a parody of the family saga novel so acute that the genre can never look quite the same;

(2) acerbic snapshots of the colonialist *mentalité* in various stages of defeat; (3) a celebration of the city of Bombay and a lament for its decosmopolitanization; (4) an affectionate and masterly representation of Indian English, with all the jokes, puns and quiddities the dialect encourages; (5) a mordant reflection on the final outlook for religious nationalism in India, whose most cheering conclusion is that any hope for the downfall of that institution lies in the infinite mercenary corruptibility of the human species; (6) an equally mordant rumination on the future of serious art, featuring set-piece descriptions of the paintings of Aurora Zogoiby so vivid that the reader is convinced her works are indeed brilliant creations.

[*The Moor's Last Sigh* is] another brave and dazzling fable from Salman Rushdie, one that meets the test of civic usefulness— broadly conceived—as certainly as it fulfills the requirements of true art. No retort to tyranny could be more eloquent.

—*Norman Rush*

As always, Mr. Rushdie writes with brio, vigor and wit. Here, for example, is an offhand, parenthetical characterization— of a Bombay restaurant, an Iranian restaurant, the Sorryno: "(so called because of the huge blackboard at the entrance reading *Sorry, No Liquor, No Answer Given Regarding Addresses in Locality, No Combing of Hair, No Beef, No Haggle, No Water Unless Food Taken, No News or Movie Magazine, No Sharing of Liquid Sustenances, No Taking Smoke, No Match, No Feletone Calls, No Incoming With Own Comestible, No Speaking of Horses, No Sigret, No Taking of Long Time on Premises, No Raising of Voice, No Change,* and a crucial last pair, *No Turning Down of Volume—It is How We Like,* and *No Musical Request—All Melodies Selected Are to Taste of Prop)*."

The resonances in this adroit aside will not escape most readers.

A novel, as Randall Jarrell put it, is a prose narrative of a certain length that has something wrong with it. And there are some imperfections in *The Moor's Last Sigh.* Even granting that a point being made in the unscrolling of the family history is that religious identity seems to make not much difference when it encounters the underlying human propensity to do wrong, there's still something off-putting about the casting of Abraham Zogoiby, the patriarch, as a kind of Jewish Professor Moriarty of subcontinental crime, a controller of Muslim gangs, a drug kingpin, a plotter involved in creating the Islamic Bomb, a procurer of little girls. His Jewishness is repeatedly referred to, even though he's not observant and has in the past been blocked in an attempt to convert to Christianity. Maybe this piece of portraiture could have been painted less hyperbolically, in cognizance of the paranoid mythologies of secret Jewish power so widely current.

This could be an overreaction on my part, stemming from awareness that "The Turner Diaries" and "The Protocols of the Elders of Zion" are underground best sellers in this country and that there is a peculiar general relish in our Christian culture for images of the flamboyantly transgressive Jew, from Howard Stern to Philip Roth's Mickoy Sabbath. I do understand the requirements of symmetry Mr. Rushdie faced in the peopling of this novel—moral unattractiveness is everywhere (all the native Indian characters are morally challenged, except for the family cook)—so I suppose my question should be taken more as venting than as literary criticism. That said, there's not much else to note in a critical way, other than that the ending of the book has a certain dashed-together feel to it, and that there are occasional curlicues here and there, minor instances of ornament overextended.

So, another brave and dazzling fable from Salman Rushdie, one that meets the test of civic usefulness—broadly conceived—as certainly as it fulfills the requirements of true art. No retort to tyranny could be more eloquent.

Paul Gray (review date 15 January 1996)

SOURCE: "Writing to Save His Life," in *Time,* Vol. 147, No. 3, January 15, 1996, pp. 70-1.

[*In the following review, Gray finds* The Moor's Last Sigh*'s "leisurely wordiness is a mark of Rushdie's mastery."*]

Near the end of *The Moor's Last Sigh,* a madman holds the novel's narrator, Moraes Zogoiby, prisoner. The captor, an old but rejected friend of Zogoiby's late, flamboyant mother, demands a history of her family before killing its teller. "He had made a Scheherazade of me," Moraes writes. "As long as my tale held his interest he would let me live."

Coming from Salman Rushdie, the notion of a man writing under a death sentence takes on a certain poignance. And the temptation exists, since he is the West's most prominent enforced recluse, to read everything he has written since the Ayatullah Khomeini's infamous *fatwa* in 1988 as a comment on his personal dilemma. But *The Moor's Last Sigh* Rushdie's first novel since *The Satanic Verses*—should not be taken only, or even principally, as veiled autobiography. It is much too teeming and turbulent, too crammed with history and dreams, to fit into any imaginable category, except that of the magically comic and sad.

The story that Moraes—nicknamed the Moor by his parents—most urgently wants to tell is how his "happy childhood in Paradise" ended in a bitter exile decreed by his mother Aurora da Gama Zogoiby, a famous painter and one of India's most controversial women. But since he is literally writing for time, the Moor throws in a whole lot more: everything he has heard or can remember or dream up about his mother's family. The eccentric and marvelously fractious Da Gamas trace their lineage, perhaps incorrectly, to the Portuguese explorer Vasco da Gama, who was the first European to reach India, thereby launching the spice trade that made the Moor's forebears wealthy. "Mine is the story of the fall from grace of a high-born crossbreed," the Moor notes, although the past "grace" he mentions consists largely of Da Gama insanities, grudges and general bad behavior. "What an epidemic of getting-even runs through my tale, what a malaria cholera typhoid of eye-for-tooth and tit-for-tat! No wonder I have ended up . . ."

He pauses, of course; revealing things too early is not in his best interests. But eventually he gets to the love-at-first-sight meeting of his future parents and the births of his three elder sisters and finally his own, which is unusual in that his mother carried him only 4 1/2 months. He calls himself "a man living double quick." For every year he lives he ages two. "No need for supernatural explanations; some cock-up in the DNA will do."

Readers of Rushdie's earlier novels will recognize the Moor's unusual affliction as a typical ambushing of the real by the preposterous. In his speeded-up growth, which makes him bigger than everyone else his age—"I was a skyscraper freed of all legal restraints, a one-man population explosion, a megalopolis"—the Moor can stand as an embodiment of India itself. The link is underscored by the pulls and tugs on his loyalties, the presumptive European strain in his ancestry and the transreligion union between his Christian mother and Jewish father: "I, however, was raised neither as Catholic nor as Jew. I was both, and nothing: a jewholic-anonymous, a cathjew nut, a stewpot, a mongrel cur. I was—what's the word these days?—*atomised.* Yessir: a real Bombay mix."

But Rushdie, speaking through the Moor, is not writing an allegory or a political tract about recent Indian history, although elements of both are undeniably present. And when his narrator gets a bit preachy, he quickly cuts himself off: "Enough, enough: away with this soapbox! Unplug this loudhailer, and be still, my wagging finger!" The true subject of *The Moor's Last Sigh* is language in all its uninhibited and unpredictable power to go reality one better and rescue humans from the fate of suffering in silence.

The Moor's deft way with words seems to be an inheritance from his mother, whose odd way of speaking he lovingly records. Here she instructs an artist to paint her children's nursery with episodes drawn from Hollywood cartoons: "Give me boulders that only temporarily flattofy you when they drop down on your head, bombs that give black faces only, and running-over-empty-air-until-you-looko down. Give me knottofied-up rifle barrels, and bathfuls of big gold coins. Never mind about harps and angels, forget all those stinking gardens; for my kiddies, this is the Paradise I want."

And that is the paradise from which the Moor is eventually ejected. But he holds on to its entertaining, eclectic energy in the telling of his sad tale. Puns and allusions—to everything from Shakespeare and Joyce to Bombay "Bollywood" movies—abound on nearly every page. Proper names hide tricks that only sounding them out against the inner ear will reveal; the Moor's businessman father takes over a failing firm called the House of Cashondeliveri.

Those who read novels as pale substitutes for movies—no pictures, no sound track—may find *The Moor's Last Sigh* tough sledding. But its leisurely wordiness is a mark of Rushdie's mastery. "In the end, stories are what's left of us," says the Moor. To tell and to read them here is to celebrate life.

Paul Gray (essay date 15 January 1996)

SOURCE: "Rushdie: Caught on the Fly," in *Time,* Vol. 147, No. 3, January 15, 1996, p. 70.

[In the following essay, based on an interview with the author, Gray discusses the controversial nature of Rushdie's writing.]

"My last novel, to put it mildly, divided its readers," says Salman Rushdie. That is putting it mildly indeed: his last novel was *The Satanic Verses,* which drew him the enmity of much of the Islamic world seven years ago. Since then things have changed, Rushdie hopes, for the better (though he is still subject to Ayatullah Knomeini's death sentence). On the phone from Australia, Rushdie talks enthusiastically of the "wonderful reception" his new book, *The Moor's Last Sigh,* has already received in far-flung swatches of the globe, many of which he has openly visited. "I've been in, I think, 11 countries other than England since September, including stops across Europe, Latin America and Australia. This book coming out is a sign of my coming out."

He still cannot visit his native India because his presence might set off riots. He says he is "rather delighted" by the response to his new novel by Indian readers. Though the book has largely been embargoed there, a number of government officials have requested and received signed copies.

Why has his fiction proved so incendiary? "I make public fictions as well as private ones. When you give your version of disputed events, you're bound to get up people's noses." Which he intends to keep doing. "For several years [after the *fatwa*] I was preoccupied by defending the principle of freedom of speech. With *The Moor's Last Sigh,* I went back to practicing that freedom."

Nina Barnton (essay date 17 January 1996)

SOURCE: "Sentenced to Death but Recalled to Life," in *The New York Times,* January 17, 1996, pp. C1-2.

[In the following essay, based on an interview with the author, Barnton describes Rushdie's life since the fatwa.]

London, Jan. 11—Having lunch with Salman Rushdie means being prepared for the unexpected. First, there's the caller from Scotland Yard who arranges the meeting but refuses to mention the author by name, simply instructing you to bring a copy of *The New York Times* to a rendezvous in the lobby of a London hotel.

Next, there's the bodyguard who checks your identification and walks you over to a second hotel and up a back staircase, where a secret knock admits you to a suite guarded by three plainclothes policemen. Finally, there is the meeting with the author. Together, the author, the bodyguard and the reporter descend for the triumphant entry into the hotel dining room at its busiest hour.

But there is a snag. The author is not wearing a necktie. And he cannot be admitted without one.

"It's been a long time since anything like this has happened to me." Mr. Rushdie says, as he, the bodyguard and the reporter all obediently trail along behind the headwaiter to the cloakroom for a spare tie. Mr. Rushdie indeed seems to relish this touch of quotidian real-life hassle.

"The sound bite on me is that I am incredibly vain, I'm very arrogant, I'm fantastically unpleasant as a person, I'm greedy, disloyal to my friends, et cetera," he says, ticking off the insults methodically. "I just have to face the fact that there is a piece of England that will never accept people like me. They don't like the fact that I am, as they would put it, 'foreign'— the fact that I've been a British citizen for 31 years doesn't stop me from being foreign."

With the publication of his new book, *The Moor's Last Sigh,* Mr. Rushdie, 48, has taken a giant step toward normalizing his life. He has agreed to a series of arranged, even advertised appearances.

[Mr. Rushdie is in New York to publicize his novel. On Monday night, Tina Brown, editor of the New Yorker, took over Barocco, a TriBeCa restaurant, for about 80 of the city's literati to pay homage to the Indian-born writer. On Tuesday, he lunched with editors at Newsweek, appeared on "Donahue" and was scheduled to give an evening reading at the New York Public Library for nearly 400 invited guests. Although he is accompanied everywhere by bodyguards, he has come a long way from a visit to New York five years ago, when he was escorted everywhere by an 11-car motorcade and never announced where he would appear.]

"It's like a way of saying, I'm back," he says, sipping red wine, "of showing in a public way that no one is locking me up anymore."

Dressed elegantly in a chestnut brown cashmere jacket, white shirt and light brown knit vest (even the hotel tie matches), Mr. Rushdie looks relaxed and prosperous, very much the successful novelist. His face, familiar from dozens of photographs, is the same—the dark beard flecked even more now with gray, the receded hairline, the slightly drooping eyelids visible through round wire-frame glasses that give him a secretive, hooded look. His reputed arrogance is not in evidence. He has been given a rough ride by British journalists, who bristle over everything from what they viewed as an ungracious acceptance speech when he won the Booker Prize for *Midnight's Children* in 1981 to insufficient gratitude to Britain for providing expensive round-the-clock police protection—though he bears part of the cost himself.

With the publication of his new book, *The Moor's Last Sigh*, Mr. Rushdie, 48, has taken a giant step toward normalizing his life. . . . He seems mellowed—he jokes warmly, laughs easily, speaks openly about his life. He has the air of a man beginning to look back on a traumatic experience from a safe distance.

—*Nina Barnton*

Although annoyed, he seems mellowed—he jokes warmly, laughs easily, speaks openly about his life. He has the air of a man beginning to look back on a traumatic experience from a safe distance.

Seven years ago, after he was sentenced to death by the Ayatollah Ruhollah Khomeini—and after a price of millions of dollars was put on his head—for what was called blasphemy of Islam in *The Satanic Verses,* Mr. Rushdie hid from public

view entirely, living in a series of safe houses and rarely surfacing even to visit family or close friends. He describes that time as tense and isolated. "I felt mostly bewilderment," he says. "It was as if the shape of the world got broken."

But in retrospect, the experience was not without value. "One always wonders if there is anything worth risking your life for, anything worth fighting for," he says, reflectively.

Through the pain of his disorientation and isolation, he discovered that there was: "It was the art of the novel, the voice that nobody owns, speaking in this indirect way," he says. About four years after he went into hiding, although still heavily protected, he began making surprise appearances at literary meetings, select parties and even, from time to time, public restaurants. His decision now to step even further out of the shadows is based more on his own instincts about his safety and his desire to reclaim his life than on a significant change in the nature of the threat.

Although there has been some progress lately—Iranian Government officials have been saying for months that they no longer propose to honor the fatwa (the religious edict calling for his death)—they are still not willing to sign documents renouncing it. The British Government remains convinced Mr. Rushdie is in danger, as is evident by the still elaborate security measures to protect him.

"I take the view—and I have spent some years persuading the security forces of this—that for me to be hidden away sends the wrong message," Mr. Rushdie says over a lunch of creamed John Dory and boiled potatoes. "It sends the message that these kinds of threats work, and it seems to me that the lesson you learn in the school playground is that what you do with bullies is not be bullied."

A few tables away, on a raised tier that allows a panoramic view of the restaurant, two security guards watch carefully.

To the relief of his fans, Mr. Rushdie's new book, written during his enforced isolation, shows no sign of succumbing to bullying. In fact, his satiric portrayal of a fascist Hindu politician was so close to the real-life Hindu nationalist leader Bal Thackery that the Indian Government bowed to internal pressures and banned further imports of the novel.

Asked if he had considered self-censorship to avoid the controversy, Mr. Rushdie answers: "It never occurred to me. I knew Bal Thackery wouldn't like it. The hell with him, frankly. You have to follow your imagination. Otherwise, don't write." Besides, the author points out, the character Ramon Fielding isn't based only on Mr. Thackery. "One of the models for that character is Zhirinovsky," he says, referring to Vladimir N. Zhirinovsky, the right-wing Russian politician.

The Moor's Last Sigh, which was published here in September to critical acclaim, has won the prestigious Whitbread Award and is thought by many to be Mr. Rushdie's best work. Set in India, it tells of an eccentric family that controls a trading empire built on the export of pepper and spices.

It centers on the story's narrator, Moraes Zagoiby, the Moor of the title, who is of Portugese-Indian-Jewish-Christian descent and whose Jewish and Moorish ancestors were expelled from Spain in 1492. Born after only four and a half months gestation, Moraes suffers from an odd infirmity—he ages twice as fast as everyone else.

Cast out by his famous artist mother, who seems to embody India itself, pursued by enemies, facing and conquering fear, forced to live at double time so as to pack life's experiences into his reduced time span, the character cannot help suggesting the writer himself.

"With fear, it's all or nothing," Mr. Rushdie writes. "Either, like any bullying tyrant it rules your life with a stupid blinding omnipotence, or else you overthrow it, and its power vanishes in a puff of smoke."

Mr. Rushdie agrees that the book wouldn't have had exactly the same shape if the fatwa hadn't happened, but stresses that the novel's themes go beyond his own problems.

"Otherwise," he says, "it would just be solipsistic and only about me, and therefore not of interest to anyone else." He says he met some artists from Sarajevo who told him that they lived with fear by finally deciding to put it aside.

"You basically take the decision that you're either going to function or to be afraid," he says. "You can't do both."

He also points out that the high-speed narration, the acceleration of time inherent in the Moor's condition, while a useful parallel for his own situation, has a wider meaning.

"During this time, three of my best friends among writers have died at around the age of 50," he says, "Raymond Carver, Angela Carter and Bruce Chatwin—writers at the peak of their powers with 20 to 30 years of writing life ahead of them, and you know, nobody shot them. It was illness—lung cancer in two cases, AIDS in the third, and bang they were dead. It made me think you don't have to have a fatwa. There just may not be as much time as we think."

Linton Weeks (review date 20 January 1996)

SOURCE: "Salman Rushdie, Out and About," in *Washington Post,* January 20, 1996, p. C1.

[*In the following review, discusses Rushdie's public promotion of* The Moor's Last Sigh.]

Salman Rushdie was in town this week to promote his new novel, *The Moor's Last Sigh,* and promote it he did. He appeared on the Diane Rehm radio talk show and made a much-publicized appearance at the National Press Club and answered questions and signed books and dined with the Washington literati.

He seemed to enjoy the attention and adulation immensely. He is a polite, but immodest, man. He does not hesitate to speak of himself and James Joyce or Marcel Proust in the same sentence.

Critics are lining up to praise him. A "wonderstruck" reviewer in The Washington Post proclaimed Rushdie "one of the world's great writers" and a writer in the New York Times said the novel, "as a work of literary art, is a triumph. . . ."

Rushdie, too, talks of the book in grandiose terms. Ultimately, he says, the act of creation must take precedence over any other thing—politics, marriage, travel or friends—in the artist's life.

"A book only gets written when you put it first," he says, tapping stubby fingers on a laminated desktop at the WAMU studio on Brandywine Street NW. Rushdie is wearing a black collarless shirt and a Y-neck sweater that's the same shade of gray as his hair, or what's left of it. He tips a little cream into his coffee, checks his watch, scratches at his salt-and-pepper beard and shifts his wire-rims. His eyes droop cartoonishly.

He began work on the book, he says, about five years ago, but was not able to focus. "I can't tell you how much time that political campaign took up," he says.

He says he's discussed fundamentalism and death threats with more than enough presidents and politicians. "I should do my job and they should do theirs. I should not be an endless lobbyist for myself."

There was even one point, one icy moment, when he completely lost faith in the novel. "All I had was a stack of notes and papers."

"It's very scary to have worked for several years and have nothing," he says. But he has come to believe that every writer must go through this hellish period.

Rushdie should know by now what it takes to write a novel. He has written five, including *Midnight's Children,* which won the Booker Prize, two collections of stories and three books of nonfiction. In 1989 he wrote a novel called *The Satanic Verses.*

In his fiction, he wrestles with the Big Themes—passion, power, love and death.

He also has fun. "It's been funny to write a sex comedy in the midst of all this," he tells the radio audience.

His books are peopled with phantasmagoric characters and events. Rushdie shies away from the label of "magic realist," in the manner of Gabriel Garcia Marquez; he employs surreality only as a way to speak about how things really are, he says.

[Rushdie] says he's discussed fundamentalism and death threats with more than enough presidents and politicians. "I should do my job and they should do theirs. I should not be an endless lobbyist for myself."

—*Linton Weeks*

For instance, Moraes, the narrator in his new novel, was brought into the world after only 4 1/2 months in his mother's womb. And he lives life twice as fast as everyone else.

With this conceit, Rushdie believes he has tapped into the universal feeling that life is accelerating and that as we age, the years seem to grow shorter.

"I'm really 150 years old," Rushdie is fond of saying.

Rushdie is a master of wordplay. Aurora, his main female character, has a wild and wicked tongue, a quirky way of speaking and a habit of adding -ofy to verbs. She threatens to give one character a slap "that will breakofy the teeth in your cheeky face."

And Rushdie is fascinated by nocturnal visions. His stories are full of dreams and dreamers. In *The Moor's Last Sigh* he writes of one character's "terrible, pummeling dreams."

Rushdie himself is a dreamer. But in recent years, he says, "I've had very few nightmares. It's alarming enough when I'm awake."

He adds, "I have innocent dreams."

For a while, he says, "I seemed to enter the dream life of the world. People had dreams about me. In their dreams, they rescued me."

"When I'm writing," he says, "I don't have very interesting dreams."

Each workday, at home in England, begins slowly. Though there are mornings when he wakes up and goes straight to the table without taking off his nightclothes or brushing his teeth, he usually begins around 10 a.m. and quits midafternoon.

He goes to parties when he can. "Though not as many as the newspapers would have you believe." He never has friends to his house. His marriage to writer Marianne Wiggins fell apart. He doesn't get to see his 16-year-old son as much as he would like.

"What's difficult to do," he says, "is something on the spur of the moment. I'd like to be able to go for a good, brisk walk. But I can't."

Rushdie also uses his fiction as a crowbar to get into places other writers seldom venture. He believes this tendency has gotten him into trouble in the past and is part of the reason *The Moor's Last Sigh* is not being distributed in India at the moment.

At times during his day in Washington, Rushdie's life appears unbearably bizarre—the security sweeps, stone-jawed bodyguards, a bomb-sniffing dog at the Press Club. At one point a young Indian journalist asks, "Do you see your own life as a Rushdiesque story?"

"Yes," Rushdie says. "It's a bad one."

In the WAMU studio, technicians watch Rushdie and Rehm, their lips out of synchronization for a while because of a seven-second delay. She asks about his next project and he says he might write something about America or about rock-and-roll. Or about the last seven years of his life.

He says he's been keeping a journal and if he does write about his ordeal, it will be nonfiction.

At the end of the day, scores of people line up after the Press Club reading to have their books autographed. After that, he's whisked off to dinner at Restaurant Nora and then to bed, where in his dreams, Salman Rushdie lives safe, in sync and fatwa-free.

Alan Ryan (review date 21 January 1996)

SOURCE: A review of *The Moor's Last Sigh,* in *The Atlanta Journal/Constitution,* January 21, 1996, p. L11.

[*In the following review, Ryan describes* The Moor's Last Sigh *as "an extraordinary act of the imagination."*]

In 1989, Salman Rushdie's novel *The Satanic Verses* earned its author a fatwa, a death decree, declared by the Ayatollah Khomeini because of the book's alleged blasphemy of Islam. Among the ironies was the clear fact that *The Satanic Verses* was far from being Rushdie's best or most persuasive work. Since then, while living in hiding (and puckishly popping up in all sorts of places, including David Letterman's TV show), Rushdie has published short fiction, book reviews and essays, but *The Moor's Last Sigh* is his first full-fledged novel since *The Satanic Verses,* and it is as good as—maybe better than—his earlier best work, *Midnight's Children.*

In that 1990 novel, Rushdie—who was born in Bombay in 1947—took all of Indian history and life as his material. "There are so many stories to tell," he wrote at the beginning of the novel, "too many, such an excess of intertwined lives events miracles places rumors, so dense a commingling of the improbable and the mundane!" In this latest novel, his setting is specifically Bombay, which the narrator describes as "central; all rivers flowed into its human sea. It was an ocean of stories; we were all its narrators, and everybody talked at once."

The nominal plot of *The Moor's Last Sigh* is the history of a Bombay family and its very broad circle that incorporates all the disparate elements, both domestic and imported, that inform life in that throbbing city: Christian, Muslim, Hindu, Indian, Goan, Portuguese and on and on. It is a family tossed violently about on that ocean of stories by greed, love, hate, jealousy, ambition, sex, you-name-it.

At the center of the story is the narrator's mother, Aurora Zogoiby, a famed artist whose pictures suggest, in their bold colors, surreal images, and personal and political themes, the paintings of Frida Kahlo. All the other family members, both antecedents and her own four children, swirl around her dazzling, outrageous, and possibly dangerous personality.

The narrator is her only son and youngest child, Moraes, known as "the Moor," and not the least of his problems are three sisters, Ina, Minnie and Mynah, or possibly Eeny, Meenie and Miney, followed, obviously, by Mo. Through the years, Aurora's husband builds an empire in the spice trade, finally ruling it (and maybe much more) from a skyscraper-top botanical hothouse and living always with the uneasy suspicion (or maybe knowledge) that his unquenchable wife enjoys a lover or three.

Besides the sisters (who become variously a runway model

with a "Super Sashay," a nun and a feminist activist), the eponymous Moor must cope with a clublike, unformed right hand, a limb that his mother paints into portraits in wildly fantastic images, and which also, after boxing lessons from a family retainer, earns him a nickname—"The Hammer."

Then there's the problem he becomes aware of at an early age: "I am going through time faster than I should. Do you understand me? Somebody somewhere has been holding down the button marked 'FF,' or, to be more exact, 'x2.'" While his mind matures at a normal rate, his body is doing double time, looking 20 at age 10, and so on.

And swirling around in this tsunami of stories: a thieving ayah named Miss Jaya, a tutor named Dilly Hormuz who tutors the young Moor in subjects not mentioned in her contract (and I hope I'm not the only reader who thinks of hormones when I hear her name), a painter named Vasco Miranda who earns his fame doing airport murals and whose personal excesses would have been the envy of Dali, a cook who can recite the family history from the record of meals he prepared, a stuffed dog on wheels named Jawaharlal, a parrot that occasionally screeches, "Mashed White Elephant!" and who-knows what-all else.

This book is an extraordinary act of the imagination. Who else in the whole world has this drunken, Dickensian power of invention? The Brazilian Jorge Amado, the Egyptian Naguib Mahfouz, the Japanese Haruki Murakami, maybe a couple of others. Every time you open this book, you expect a character to reach out from the pages and drag you in headfirst.

And listen to Aurora as she directs V. Miranda, who is about to decorate the nursery. "Cartoons," she tells him. "You go to the pictures? You read the comic-cuts? Then, that mouse, that duck, and what is the name of that bunny. Also that sailor and saag saga. Maybe the cat that never catchees the mouse, the other cat that never catchees the bird, or the other bird that runs too fast for the coy-oat. Give me boulders that only temporarily flattofy you when they drop down on your head, bombs that give black faces only, and running-over-empty-air-until-you-looko-down. Give me knottofied-up rifle-barrels, and bathfuls of big gold coins. Never mind about harps and angels, forget all those stinking gardens; for my kiddies, this is the Paradise I want."

Readers with a psychological bent will certainly examine this novel as a text produced by a writer compelled to live his life in hiding, and they will find much to occupy their minds. It might be better, though, just to surrender to this wonderful book and be swept away to worlds unknown on its ocean of stories. Rushdie, even in hiding, grins and waves from the top of the heap, and it will be a year of miracles if another novel half as fascinating, entertaining and thought-provoking comes along this twelvemonth.

John Blades (interview date 28 January 1996)

SOURCE: An interview with Salman Rushdie, in *Chicago Tribune,* January 28, 1996, p. 3.

[*In the following interview, Blades queries Rushdie on religion and the effect of the Ayatollah Khomeini's death sentence on his writing.*]

Name: Salman Rushdie

Job: Subversive novelist

Sev n years after Iran's Ayatollah Ruhollah Khomeini senter ced him to death for blaspheming the prophet Mohammed in "The Satanic Verses," Salman Rushdie recently emerged from deep cover in England to launch his latest novel, *The Moor's Last Sigh.* Born in India but now a British citizen, Rushdie managed to greatly offend "Mother India" with his new book, a dysfunctional family saga that's a savage satire of Hindu fundamentalism and a cruel and inhuman comedy best exemplified by his joke about "kebabed saints and tandooried martyrs".

[*Blades:*] *Considering the evidence in* **The Moor's Last Sigh,** *you do seem genuinely disturbed about the more extreme forms of Hinduism in India.*

[Rushdie:] I'm by no means the only person who feels that Hindu fundamentalism is the greatest single danger to India's democracy. Millions upon millions think as I do. When I was in India last, I traveled around the country for months making a documentary, and I interviewed a number of extremist politicians, who are the scariest people in the world. "Yes," they say, "we're fascists. Of course we're racists." They tell you how Adolf Hitler was an excellent leader and how India could do with his kind of strong leadership.

As an admitted provocateur, do you take a perverse satisfaction in having the distribution of **The Moor's Last Sigh** *greatly curtailed—"blockaded," as you put it—by the Indian government?*

How could I? It's always been colossally important to me that my books should be well received in India. It's where I come from. But I think it's a very important function of art to challenge accepted reality, especially when that reality is created by powerful interest groups.

Feeling about India as you do, the death decree must be a source of even more profound grief because it has prevented you from returning to your homeland?

To have to go seven years without spending any time in India, when I would normally go there most years, has been a colossal deprivation, like losing a leg. And reading *The Moor's Last Sigh,* seven or eight months after I finished it, it does seem there's an emotion and a longing that come from being physically removed from the place for so long.

Do you feel this deprivation might have hurt the novel?

I'm not the first writer to have been obliged to do his work from the condition of exile. Many writers have surmounted that and produced exceptional work and I took courage from them. The most famous case of the 20th Century was that of (James) Joyce, who wrote "Ulysses" without ever visiting Dublin, the greatest novel written about anything. Dostoevsky faced a firing squad, which was worse than anything that happened to me. I didn't spend half my life in a labor camp, as many Soviet writers were obliged to do. I wasn't in jail like Jean Genet. So it's comforting to realize that other writers have had problems that were at least as bad as mine.

Will you eventually write a factual book describing what it's like to live under sentence of death?

I've kept a journal of those seven years, and I very much want to write one. It'll have comedic stuff in it, but it's black comedy. There's a strange aspect to this whole experience that would be extremely funny if it weren't so unfunny.

I'll give you one example. I was told that soon after the Iranian threat the response of one of my European publishers was threefold: He refused to go out to lunch in case somebody would attack him in a restaurant; he rearranged his office furniture so his desk wasn't near the window; and he unscrewed the company's nameplate from the front door. This is a funny image, but the reason it's not funny is because another publisher of "The Satanic Verses" was shot in the back and, fortunately, survived.

Even though **The Moor's Last Sigh** *is fiction, aren't there passages that speak directly to readers about the physical and psychological effects of the death sentence and your "awful incarceration," as the Moor calls his own plight?*

Clearly, there is material in the book that would not be there except for what happened to me. But I'm using my experiences to enliven the fictional world and the fictional characters, as writers always do, rather than to simply write about myself in code.

But isn't that Salman Rushdie speaking through his narrator when he describes fear as a "bullying tyrant (that) rules your life" and wonders, "Will (I) still be here tomorrow?"

It's inevitable that the writer's feelings do occasionally come through the lips of a first-person narrator.... And certainly, seven years ago, it was quite clear to me that I might have a few days to live. That's a very strange feeling. But this is not a novel about me. It's a novel about history, about painting, about pepper, and above all, about love, all sorts of love: the love of lovers, the love of parents and children, the love of country, the love of God.

To have to go seven years without spending any time in India, when I would normally go there most years, has been a colossal deprivation, like losing a leg.

—*Salman Rushdie*

Speaking of the "love of God," was your public embrace of Islam, two years after Khomeini's decree, a genuine and lasting religious conversion or an expedient attempt to subvert the fatwa?

That was a depressed and despairing moment for me. I rapidly understood that it was a very foolish attempt at appeasing the opposition. I proceeded to admit that, and I've been admitting it ever since. I have no problem with people's religious beliefs. I just don't happen to have any.

Phoebe-Lou Adams (review date February 1996)

SOURCE: A review of *The Moor's Last Sigh,* in *The Atlantic Monthly,* Vol. 277, No. 2, February, 1996, p. 114.

[*Below, Adams presents a positive review of* The Moor's Last Sigh.]

Mr. Rushdie's new novel is so intricate, so multi-faceted, and so fast-moving that it keeps the reader dizzily enthralled from beginning to end. It may also add a Hindu curse to the Islamic price on the author's head, for beneath the surface glitter of the tale lies a protest against the rise of chauvinistic Hindu fundamentalism and the dissolution of a once tolerant and flexible culture. The Moor of the title, who has nothing to do with Othello, is Moraes Zogoiby, the story's narrator. He is the last male survivor of two European families that flourished for centuries in the spice trade of the Malabar Coast. The Portuguese Da Gamas claim illegitimate descent from the great Vasco—improbably. The Jewish Zogoibys are sus-

pected of descent, also illegitimate and improbable, from Boabdil, the last Sultan of Moorish Spain. The Da Gamas thrive on art, violence, and personal eccentricities of which walking a stuffed dog on a leash is a mild example. The Zogoibys remain largely offstage, but the activities of Moraes's father, Abraham, indicate a talent for finance, political intrigue, revenge, and dissimulation. The characters speak with a wild, crackling eloquence; comic, horrible, and fantastic events merge and conflict; and the history of modern India rumbles in the background. In addition to everything else, the work is enormously entertaining.

Merle Rubin (review date 7 February 1996)

SOURCE: "Extravagant, Madcap Vision of an Indian Clan," in *The Christian Science Monitor,* February 7, 1996, p. 13.

[*In the following review, Rubin remarks that "the Moor's outlandish friends, family, and enemies may begin to look a little more familiar than we'd like" in* The Moor's Last Sigh.]

Salman Rushdie's latest novel, ***The Moor's Last Sigh,*** is an extravagant, tragicomic vision of a world exploding with violence, madness, and corruption. Set in the author's native India (where it has been banned, along with Rushdie's "The Satanic Verses," which earned him a Muslim death sentence), this bizarre saga of a larger-than-life family is narrated by the last surviving member of the colorful clan.

Moraes Zogoiby, known as "Moor," is descended on his mother's side from the da Gamas, wealthy spice traders of Portuguese-Christian extraction. His father's clan, the Zogoibys, are members of a Jewish community in South India, although according to family legend, their progenitor who fled Spain for India in 1492 was a defeated Moorish sultan who only pretended to be Jewish.

In the foreground of the tale, three generations of the da Gamas squabble over a family business that eventually mushrooms into an empire of fraud, crime, and violence. In the background, cultures clash, overlay, and mingle, forming a palimpsest of conquest, creation, migration, love, and betrayal that stretches from ancient times into the present, where most of the story unfolds.

Debauchery, blackmail, arson, killing: "My family has been under many clouds...." the narrator observes. "Is this normal? Is this what we are all like?" His family history is unusual, to say the least, and two of its most titanic personalities are none other than his own parents. At age 15, the beautiful, dynamic Aurora da Gama, heir to the spice empire, insists on marrying the seemingly unsuitable Abraham Zogoiby, a Jew more than twice her age with very little money, in defiance of the wishes of both their clans. Abraham takes over the reins of the da Gama spice business, piloting it to new and dizzying heights of success and corruption, while the artistically gifted Aurora becomes a leading figure on the cultural scene with her boldly original paintings.

Aurora's personality dominates much of the novel. A living exemplar of India as a pluralistic, hybrid nation, she insists on speaking only English in her own inimitable way: "all these different lingoes cuttofy us off from one another," as she explains. Motherhood is not her favorite role, and she overshadows her three female children: "they can't growofy fast enough for me. God! How long this childhood business draggoes out. Why couldn't I have . . . even one child—who grew up really fast." The eponymous "Moor" born in 1957 after a 4-1/2 month pregnancy mystically fulfills his mother's rash wish, aging twice as fast as normal.

Moor's life coincides with an era of civil discord, state repression, and the growth of a Hindu fundamentalist movement hostile to modernism and minorities like the Christian-Muslim-Jewish da Gama-Zogoibys. Toward the novel's end, the middle-aged Moor reverses his ancestors' flight by leaving Bombay for the relative tolerance of the recently democratized Spain.

Do fanatic beliefs cause violence, or does a human propensity toward violence impel people to seize on any reason—religious or ideological—to commit these misdeeds? *The Moor's Last Sigh* poses this question and seems to suggest the latter answer.

Almost every character here is guilty of something. Many, including the narrator, have blood on their hands. Any line between heroes and villains, victims and perpetrators is blurred as narrator and narrative whirl toward their apocalyptic, yet madcap, conclusion. "For the barbarians," Moor declares, "were not only at the gates but within our skins. We were our own wooden horses, each one of us full of our doom."

This bleak and bitter vision is painted in colors at once lurid and exuberant: A great deal of verbal and inventive energy has gone into what is essentially a world-weary sigh of spiritual exhaustion. Nor does the beleaguered, sinful, yet-more-sinned-against narrator permit himself even the luxury of tragedy, for, as he puts it, "Tragedy was not in our natures. A tragedy was taking place all right, a national tragedy on a grand scale, but those of us who played our parts were—let me put it bluntly—clowns."

Because the characters who people these pages are so grotesque, their extravagance undermines the novel's claim to be depicting humanity as it really is. Yet in an age when aberrations—mega-greed, mega-hate, and mega-violence—

seem to be becoming ever more common, the Moor's outlandish friends, family, and enemies may begin to look a little more familiar than we'd like.

Sara Maitland (review date 9 February 1996)

SOURCE: "The Author Is Too Much with Us," in *Commonweal,* Vol. CXXIII, No. 3, February 9, 1996, pp. 22-3.

[*In the following review, Maitland suggests that* The Moor's Last Sigh *suffers from the fallout of the* fatwa *imposed upon its author.*]

Salman Rushdie is—and I think this can be said fairly uncontroversially—one of the most important English-language novelists currently writing. He has mythologized all our lives, and done so in the arena of multiculturalism and postmodernism. This is a remarkable achievement; and of course cannot be separated, in some important respects, from his own social boundary transgressions—he is the product of both a divided India and the British Public School system: Gandhi and *Tom Brown's School Days;* of Islam and the Booker Prize. Autobiography however is not the whole story—Rushdie has an extraordinarily bold imagination, in relation to both subject matter and plot and to language—as a nonrealist novelist myself I cannot but envy and admire the high-handed courage of his fiction.

It is therefore particularly tragic that it will probably never again be possible to read his fiction without thinking of his life: of the *fatwa,* of the international *cause célèbre,* of the fear, and of the years of isolation and abnormality. I do not want to suggest that all of this would not have mattered so much if he had been a lesser writer—terror is terror; but we, as much as Rushdie himself, may turn out to be losers here.

The Moor's Last Sigh is Rushdie's first major work since *The Satanic Verses* was published in 1988. (I do not discount *Haroun and the Sea of Stories,* which was charming, and the collection of stories *East West,* which was odd—I just do not think they were "major.") I wanted to read it, indeed I disciplined myself to read it, with the same literary and emotional enthusiasm as I had brought to *Midnight's Children* or *The Satanic Verses.* I found, to my regret, that this was not possible. Some of this, frankly, was my own fault—I could not suppress a curiosity as to whether Jews would find themselves gravely offended at being re-stereotyped as the power behind an international criminal empire; or if right-wing Hindu nationalist parties were going to rise up howling with wrath and demanding blood for his satirical portrayal of them. (He is, let's face it, wonderfully wide-sweeping in his abusiveness.)

But some of it is Rushdie's "fault." How can he begin a novel, under all the prevailing circumstances, with the following sentence:

> I have lost count of the days that have passed since I fled the horror of Vasco Miranda's mad fortress in the Andalusian mountain-village of Benengeli; ran from death under cover of darkness and left a message nailed to the door.

and not expect a certain gossipy and distracting curiosity to rise up in the reader's mind? How can he choose a protagonist who is constantly being "imprisoned" and isolated by malevolent fates—starting from birth (genetics) with a unique physical deformity (a body that grows, and therefore ages, twice as fast as anyone else's—there is, by the way, such an illness; it is called Cockayne's syndrome) and continuing through family history, politics, passion, *and* art—all the world is out to get the Moor—and not expect his readers to draw some parallels? How can he take that old standby of romantic fiction, The Family Saga; give it exotic locations; start it with not one but two family weddings in 1900; and end both the novel and the family with a terrified man escaping prison to die—and not have his readers wonder if they are being given a rather monomaniacal view of the author's century?

What else is the poor author to do? All fiction has to come out of the interior autobiography of the writer, and this is particularly so with Rushdie's brand of magical realism. Perhaps, driven by real and exterior events, he is here attempting a brave act of satire, an ironized and witty self-reflection. If so, he has forgotten something crucial; satire has to have a critical, a cutting edge, and self-satire even more so. *The Moor's Last Sigh* is a self-indulgent text.

There are some wonderful things, some real magic, in the book. Rushdie knows so many things, from so many cultures, and is so clever, both intellectually and linguistically. His driving sense of Indian history is persuasive to an outsider. His sense of place is lyrical. It is apparently not possible for him to do anything other than put together palpably gorgeous sentences and scenes. In particular the matriarchs are a splendidly eccentric and complex group of women: the hero's mother, an artist, has a precision, combining the "fairy mother" and the "wicked witch"—the good mother and the bad mother both at once—that gives her a universality that is infinitely moving. But Rushdie is better at mothers than at lovers: the pivot of the plot in many ways is the particular passion the Moor develops for Uma—she, the sex, her devious complexities, and her fatal attraction are all indicated with a curious absence of conviction. This creates a hole in the plot into which the novel seems to collapse.

Too much of the witty erudition looks suspiciously like showing-off. And even more often like a cover-up, a digression

from a path that was ambling nowhere anyway. It is as though having recreated India as myth in *Midnight's Children* and given us a profound and moving mythological narrative for the experience of itinerancy, of immigrant-*ness* in *The Satanic Verses,* Rushdie now needed to mythologize himself: to find a huge narrative to inflate what must, necessarily, have been a lonely, scary, and miserable experience.

You see. I have done what I did not want to do—I have written more about Rushdie than about the Moor. Perhaps, of course, this is my problem, not his; but I do not think so—I think it is both a historical inevitability and, more interestingly both the fault, and the essence, of the book: it is hard to write about the book—the plot is very complex and its significance is rather slight.

But, ah, he can still write. It is there. I think we must rejoice that *The Moor's Last Sigh* is written: it was never going to be an easy book for Rushdie. Now it is done. Obviously he is still there, the writer I mean, and has not been driven into meekness—a little self-grandiloquence, for a writer of this kind, is a great deal better than the opposite. I would wish him well if that were not quite so matronizing.

James Wood (review date 18 March 1996)

SOURCE: "Salaam Bombay!," in *New Republic,* Vol. 214, No. 12, March 18, 1996, pp. 38-41.

[*In the following review, Wood offers a mixed assessment of* The Moor's Last Sigh.]

In 1835, Macaulay threw out one of those phrasal boomerangs that returns not to arm but to maim its sender: "A single shelf of a good European library is worth the whole native literature of India." In this century, Macaulay has been paid back by Indian literature for that untruth: he has been pelted with masterpieces. The two most significant novelists working in England—V.S. Naipaul and Salman Rushdie—are Indian in origin. Both have made comic war on English condescension, and both have made peace with their now enriched victim. Rushdie in particular has seemed to want to tip a shelf of European books into his novels in reply to Macaulay, to want to make his books costive and prodigal and bursting, and with a decidedly un-English philosophical rasp. His new novel is calmer and more elegiac than anything he has yet written, but with its allusions to Kipling, Conrad and Shakespeare, it nevertheless overflows with ambiguous gratitude.

Although Rushdie once referred to India's literary revenge on its former colonizers as "the Empire striking back," the parties were only at familial war, since Rushdie's comedy is highly indebted to English comic ancestors such as Sterne and Dickens. Indeed, *The Moor's Last Sigh,* a rich saga of four generations of a doomed twentieth-century Portuguese-Spanish-Indian trading family, whose wealth has been based on the export of pepper, has a madcap English tilt, recalling the tottering empire raised on quack medicine in H.G. Wells's *Tono-Bungay.* As in Wells, there is a certain crudity: comic energy tends to be vulgar.

Moraes Zogoiby, the novel's narrator, praises and struggles against what he calls "the ridiculous and ludicrous perversity of my family." Rushdie's characters talk like Wodehouse characters playing with *Hobson-Jobson*: "In this God-fearing Christian house, British still is best, madder-moyselle. . . . If you have ambitions in our boy's direction, then please to mindofy your mouth. You want dark or white meat? Speak up. Glass of imported Dão wine, nice cold? You can have. Pudding-shudding? Why not. These are Christmas topics, frawline. You want stuffing?" This is not always delightful. Since Rushdie's narrator tells his story with a similar jauntiness, he sometimes leaves the impression of a novel without internal borders, a wheel of hilarity turning gritlessly fast.

The perversity of Moraes Zogoiby's family is more than incidental. Its statelessness and its manic irreligiousness represent for Rushdie a secular, postmodern virtue: the family madness is the carnival that overflows the liturgy. Moraes is of mixed Jewish, Arab and Christian descent, and is proudly dissolved: "I was a nobody from nowhere, like no-one, belonging to nothing." He rejoices in his family's secularism, and Rushdie cannot resist, it seems, inserting an autobiographical splinter: "somehow, by some great fluke that seemed at the time the most ordinary thing in the world, my parents had been cured of religion. (Where's their medicine, their priest-poison-beating anti-venene? Bottle it, for pity's sake, and send it round the world!)"

Moraes's family line is a fuse of lost causes, with Moraes its explosive issue. He tells us first about his great-grandfather Francisco da Gama, of Portuguese descent, who at the end of the nineteenth century established the Indian spice dynasty in Cochin. Francisco was soon lost to theosophy and modernism. With a precocious 20-year-old French architect (the young Le Corbusier, we discover) he builds two zany houses on his new plot of Indian ground, anointing them "East" and "West." From time to time, he informs his family at breakfast that today they are "going East" or "moving West"—whereupon the whole household had no choice but to move lock, stock, and barrel into one or another of the Frenchman's follies."

Francisco's son, Camoens, weds his soul to English poetry and to the Russian Revolution. He manages a troupe of actors who specialize in looking like and impersonating Lenin. When a Lenin lookalike from Russia arrives to inspect the

Indian pretenders, he is appalled by their amateurish approximations. Camoens turns his flailing ardor on Nehru and the independence movement, but he resists the country's growing Hindu zeal. He complains that the movement is trying to make Hinduism monotheistic by elevating the God Ram, whom he nicknames "Battering Ram." "With that God stuff I got scared," he tells his family. "In the city we are for secular India but the village is for Ram." His brother, Aires, is a pro-British conservative who retaliates by naming his British bulldog after Nehru.

Where *The Satanic Verses* was angry, *The Moor's Last Sigh* is wise, seasoned, mild. Still, this new novel is not without its own petition, and Rushdie often breaks into Moraes's narrative to deliver it.

—James Wood

At the heart of the book is a thriving portrait of a woman, Aurora da Gama, Moraes's capricious mother. Beautiful, negligent, she is a torment and a lure. At 15, she chooses Abraham Zogoiby as her consort, in defiance of family wisdom. Abraham is a lowly manager at the company's warehouse. He is a Jew with an oddly Arabic name (he finds out that he is the bastard off-spring of a Jewish-Arabic dalliance). Abraham and Aurora never marry, but they live as if they are married. Aurora becomes a celebrated painter, while Abraham builds the da Gama empire into a feared conglomerate. Their fine house on Malabar Hill, overlooking the sea outside Bombay, hosts painters, radicals and dandies.

This exuberance finds its match in Rushdie's language. All of Rushdie's novels have been attempts to explode the literary past. Newness is Rushdie's subject and his procedure. *Midnight's Children* was about India's birth into partition, and it created a new style to grease this passage into life. Rushdie's is a mutant language, made up of Anglo-Indian compounds, plush puns (a man with cold balls is "freezing his assets") and a jumble of high and low registers. Rushdie has always shopped around for his effects and has found the bargain-basement as interesting as the top floor. His new novel makes reference to *The Wizard of Oz, Star Wars* and *Blade Runner.* Indian writing in English has tended to enjoy the grind of high against low, particularly the swoop from high culture to lowly brand name. Naipaul's early novels generate mock-heroic pathos this way: "When he [Mr. Biswas] got home, he mixed and drank some Maclean's Brand Stomach Powder, undressed, got into bed and read some Epictetus." Rushdie's sentences have a similar comic quiver: "It seems that in the late summer of that year, my grandfather, Dr. Aadam Aziz, contracted a highly dangerous form of optimism." Rushdie takes pleasure in transcribing spoken Indian English onto the page, with its characteristic speed and jumpiness: "Proper London itself, Bigben Nelsoncolumn Lordstavern Bloodytower Queen."

Rushdie will happily sacrifice a page for an excruciating pun. In his new novel, we encounter the Parsi financial house, Cashondeliveri, and its three eligible sons: Lowjee Lowerjee Cashondeliveri, Jamibhoy Lifebhoy Cashondeliveri and Jamsheed Cashondeliveri. This last, who marries one of Moraes's sisters, has his name shortened to "Jimmy Cash." Delightfully, one has the suspicion that Rushdie created the Cashondeliveri clan merely so as to get to the joke of "Jimmy Cash."

In this mode, Rushdie has tremendous world-making powers. His animism is quite strong enough to resist the welfare of magical realism. His sprinkle of tales covers a real land; his new book is a vast narrative noticeboard, ploughed with the handprints of its irregular messengers. In addition to Moraes's family, we encounter Vasco Miranda, the embittered hack postmodernist artist; Lambajan Chandiwalla, the one-legged doorman of the Zogoiby household, and Dilly Hormuz, Moraes's studious and bespectacled first love. All of these characters are Dickensian balloons, inflated with fantasy. Unlike the somewhat geometric heroes of *The Satanic Verses,* Rushdie's previous novel, who were angled into narrow postures (one was the devil, another was the angel Gabriel), these creations escape into life.

Where *The Satanic Verses* was angry, *The Moor's Last Sigh* is wise, seasoned, mild. Still, this new novel is not without its own petition, and Rushdie often breaks into Moraes's narrative to deliver it. The petition resembles that of *The Satanic Verses:* the importance of hybridization over tyrannical sameness; the persuasions of secularism over the enforcement of religion; the bustle of words over the frieze of the Word; history's flow over God's arrest. The difference between the two books is that the post-colonial plea was made with rage in the earlier book but is made benignly here.

Not unobtrusively, however. From the outset, it is clear that Rushdie's chosen family represents what he has called elsewhere "the India-idea"—a family drunk on gods, not sober on religion. Characters warn us that contemporary Hindu politics is making "a single martial deity" of its "many-headed beauty." Moraes celebrates his grandfather Camoens's "doublenesses . . . his willingness to permit the coexistence within himself of conflicting impulses is the source of his full, gentle humaneness." Moraes likens this to "that historical generosity of spirit, which is one of the true wonders of India." It seems somewhat too convenient that Moraes combines within him the major religions (Jew, Muslim, Christian); and, near the end of the book, he plays at being a Hindu fundamentalist gangster. (There is an amusing lampoon of

the real-life Bombay Hindu leader Bal Thackeray, whom Rushdie turns into Ramon Fielding, who uses his "fist-clenched saffron-headbanded young thugs to put on a show of Hindu-fundamentalist triumphalism.")

Moraes delights in his salad of inheritances: he was raised "neither as Catholic nor as Jew. I was both, and nothing: a jewholic-anonymous, a cathjew nut, a stewpot, a mongrel cur. I was—what's the word these days?—*Atomised.* Yessir: a real Bombay mix." The frailty of the prose here is telling. Few readers will be convinced by the faked lexical grope: "what's the word these days?" For the word "atomised" belongs to post-colonial theory rather than to post-colonial life; this is an academicism trying to lose itself in the demotic. Elsewhere Rushdie reminds us of art's subversions: "The sheer strangeness of the activity of art," says Moraes of his mother, "made her a questionable figure; as it does everywhere; as it always has and perhaps always will."

This lecturing is much gentler than that of *The Satanic Verses,* which forced all its characters to sit and take notes. Indeed, the earlier novel's narrative explosiveness—men falling out of planes and turning into cloven-hoofed devils or into haloed angels having blasphemous visions in contemporary London—was a programmatic hysteria whose design was to daunt us with its anarchy. The novel strove to dissolve religion's boundaries in the wash of the modern; and to show that Islam, like all other major religions, has had to make uncomfortable accounting for the existence of evil in the world. Rushdie's acute point is that religion, forced to dramatize the origin of this evil, becomes its producer, and is thus entwined with the foe it exists to fight. Alas, almost every page taught this, and taught the need to get beyond narrow boundaries, religious or otherwise. Agencies that help free one from these small cordons, such as the modern city, were cherished. As one character puts it: "The modern city . . . is the locus classicus of incompatible realities. Lives that have no business mingling with one another sit side by side upon the omnibus." The novel piled up its oppositions: immigration, since it encourages metamorphosis and mix, is a necessary if difficult novelty; religious tradition, since it strangles metamorphosis, is an antique torture. And so on.

Readers have noticed that *Midnight's Children, Shame* and *The Satanic Verses* prefigure the destiny that later befell their author. All of them hint at the scourge awaiting he who blasphemes. Saleem Sinai, the narrator of *Midnight's Children,* hears voices and thinks that he might be a twentieth-century Muhammed. He is forced by his father to wash his mouth out with coal-tar soap for blaspheming against Allah. "At least the boy has the grace to admit he's gone too far," says his father. But Saleem, writes Rushdie, "was forever tainted with Bombayness, his head was full of all sorts of religions apart from Allah's." Rushdie's novels have this power of prolepsis precisely because they have such a strong sense of what they are about, such a strong urge to self-description.

In good and bad ways, then, Rushdie produces themed novels. This visible intellectual armature is what makes him one of the few English novelists with any philosophical seriousness. He is certainly one of the few English-language novelists interested in questions of faith and doubt. But there is a cost. These lectures or incursions of explicitness are stolen from their novels' drama. Rushdie's novels stint their own flexibility. One of the unintended ironies of *The Satanic Verses* is that it preaches its lesson of multivocality with such univocal doggedness. Its pluralities are so raucous that its tolerance toward "incompatible realities" begins to seem rather dogmatic.

More importantly, without dramatization and groundedness, Rushdie's secular warfare becomes abstract. Blasphemy is not an argument to be won; it is an anguish to be endured. And such a struggle cannot be a struggle if it is an abstraction, a matter of "atomisation" versus "fixity." Sometimes Rushdie's fiction behaves, formally and intellectually, as if ideas are battling in flaming skies high above real lives. Its supernatural artillery encourages this impression. The most affecting moments of *Shame* and *The Satanic Verses* were the most real—when the flying carpets and six-fingered mutations were silent. After all, the "incompatible realities" that a great city like London or Bombay contains are made up of millions of individualities, many of them rigidly unitary. As a group, they perhaps form a post-colonial or postmodern theory—a theory of crowds, in effect; as people, as individuals, they form obstacles to that theory, and should do so.

Rushdie seems to know this, to judge from his new novel. Though it carries a certain smugness about the superiority of "Bombayness" over fixity, it does not bully its characters into schema. Interestingly, this new ideological softening is accompanied by a muting of the writer's magical realism. The Zogoiby family lives comically, not unreally; it is as if Rushdie has discovered that comic inflation is magical anyway. The novel's realist energy burns off the occasional application of magic ointments. Moraes, for instance, tells us that he is monstrously tall, that he was born with a club hand—Naipaul's Mr. Biswas was born with six fingers: Indian magical realists have had a *faiblesse* for mangled or augmented digits—and that he is doomed to live his life at double speed. At 36, the age at which he narrates this novel, he looks like a man of 72. Unconvincingly, Rushdie wants to make his narrator as capacious as Bombay: "Like the city itself, Bombay of my joys and sorrows, I mushroomed into a huge urbane sprawl of a fellow." For most of his story, however, Moraes's fate is entirely irrelevant, and unless we are reminded, we forget about his freakishness. Rushdie makes his case for Bombayness not by means of sorcery but by means of realist evocation.

This is new in his work. Instead of the swoop of metamorphosis, Rushdie sparks memory's telepathy. This makes *The Moor's Last Sigh* an important departure for its author. Bombay is not forced to represent a virtue, but asked to live a condition. Moraes narrates his tale from Spain. He is in exile from the city of his birth. Rushdie has said that the most painful product of the *fatwa* has been that he cannot return to India, and to Bombay, his birthplace. Through Moraes, Rushdie tenderly revisits the city. Bombay shimmers in Moraes's mind as a citadel of ideal tolerance, an Indian Alhambra:

> Am I sentimentalising? Now that I have left it all behind, have I, among my many losses, also lost clear sight?—It may be said I have; but still I stand by my words. O Beautifiers of the City, did you not see that what was beautiful in Bombay was that it belonged to nobody, and to all? Did you not see the everyday live-and-let-live miracles thronging its overcrowded streets?

Rushdie's apostrophizing comes near the end of his novel. It moves us not just because we can detect its gentle autobiographical watermark, but because so much of the novel has brought Bombay's solidities, rather than its symbols, onto the page. On Bombay, Rushdie has lavished all his singing powers of description. Moraes shows us "the gracious old pharmacy at Kemp's Corner—this was long before it turned into the flyover-and-boutique spiritual wasteland it is today—and the Royal Barber Shop (where a master barber with a cleft palate offered a circumcision service as a sideline)." We move through old Parsi buildings, "all balconies and curlicues," and pass by Vijay Stores, "that numinous mixed business where you could buy both Time, with which you could polish your wooden furniture, and Hope, with which you could wipe your bum." Elsewhere, we visit "the fabulous turbulence of Crawford Market with its frieze by Kipling's dad, with its vendors of chickens both live and plastic," and the Zaveri Bazaar, "where jewellers sat like wise monkeys in tiny shops that were all mirrors and glass."

When Moraes, and so also Rushdie, celebrates what he calls "my inexhaustible Bombay of excess," he is not fighting a battle on behalf of pluralism so much as hurling us, and himself, into the combat of life. For this battle, the writer can arm us only with his richly abandoned details. It is all we deserve, and all this fine novel needs.

J. M. Coetzee (review date 21 March 1996)

SOURCE: "Palimpsest Regained," in *The New York Review of Books,* Vol. XLIII, No. 5, March 21, 1996, pp. 13-16.

[*In the following review, Coetzee presents a deep analysis of* The Moor's Last Sigh, *noting its multilayered construction.*]

1.

The Moor's Last Sigh is a novel about modern India. Its hero is Moraes Zogoiby of Bombay, nicknamed by his mother "the Moor." But the famous sigh to which the title refers was breathed five centuries ago, in 1492, when Muhammad XI, last sultan of Andalusia, bade farewell to his kingdom, bringing to an end Arab-Islamic dominance in Iberia. Fourteen ninety-two was the year, too, when the Jews of Spain were offered the choice of baptism or expulsion; and when Columbus, financed by the royal conquerors of the Moor, Ferdinand and Isabella, sailed forth to discover a new route to the East.

From Sultan Muhammad a line of descent, partly historical, partly fabulous, leads to Moraes, the narrator, who in 1992 will return from the East to "discover" Andalusia. In a dynastic prelude occupying the first third of the novel, Moraes's genealogy is traced back as far as his great-grandparents, the da Gamas. Francisco da Gama is a wealthy spice exporter based in Cochin in what is now Kerala State. A progressive and a nationalist, he soon disappears from the action (Rushdie gives short shrift to characters whose usefulness has ended), but his wife Epifania, faithful to "England, God, philistinism, the old ways," survives to trouble succeeding generations and to utter the curse that will blight the life of the unborn Moraes.

Their son Camoens, after flirting with Communism, becomes a Nehru man, dreaming of an independent, unitary India which will be "above religion because secular, above class because socialist, above caste because enlightened." He dies in 1939, though not before he has had a premonition of the violent, conflict-riven India that will in fact emerge.

Camoens's daughter Aurora falls in love with a humble Jewish clerk, Abraham Zogoiby. Neither Jewish nor Christian authorities will solemnize their marriage, so their son Moraes is raised "neither as Catholic nor as Jew, . . . a jewholic-anonymous." Abandoning the declining Jewish community of Cochin, Abraham transfers the family business to Bombay and settles in a fashionable suburb, where he branches out into more lucrative activities: supplying girls to the city's brothels, smuggling heroin, speculating in property, trafficking in arms and eventually in nuclear weapons.

In Rushdie's hands Abraham is little more than a comic-book villain. Aurora, however, is a more complex character, in many ways the emotional center of the book. A painter of genius but a distracted mother, she suffers intermittent remorse for not loving her children enough, but prefers finally to see them through the lens of her art. Thus Moraes is worked into a series of her paintings of "Mooristan," a place where (in Aurora's free and easy Indian English) "worlds collide, flow in and out of one another, and washofy away. . . . One universe, one dimension, one country, one dream, bumpo'ing into another, or being under, or on top of. Call it Palimpstine." In these paintings, with increasing desperation, she tries to paint old, tolerant Moorish Spain over India, overlaying, or palimpsesting, the ugly reality of the present with "a romantic myth of the plural, hybrid nation."

Aurora's paintings give a clear hint of what Rushdie is up to in this, his own "Palimpstine" project: not over-painting India in the sense of blotting it out with a fantasy alternative, but laying an alternative, promised-land text or texturation over it like gauze.

But *The Moor's Last Sigh* is not an optimistic book, and the paintings of Aurora's high period become darker and darker. Into them she pours not only her unexpressed maternal love but also "her larger, prophetic, even Cassandran fears for the nation." Her last painting, which gives the book its title, shows her son "lost in limbo like a wandering shade: a portrait of a soul in Hell."

Moraes is born under the curse of two witch-grandmothers, so it is no surprise that he is a prodigy, with a clublike right hand and a metabolism that dooms him to live "double-quick," growing—and aging—twice as fast as ordinary mortals. Kept apart from other children, he receives his sexual initiation at the hands of an attractive governess and soon discovers he is a born storyteller: telling stories gives him an erection.

Venturing into the world, he is caught in the toils of the beautiful but evil rival artist Uma Sarasvati. A pawn in the war between this demon mistress and his mother, Moraes first finds himself expelled from his parental home and then— after some complicated stage business involving true and false poison capsules—in jail, accused of Uma's murder. Released, he joins the Bombay underworld as a strikebreaker and enforcer in the pay of one Raman Fielding, boss of a Hindu paramilitary group whose off-duty evenings sound like Brownshirt get-togethers in Munich, with "arm-wrestling and mat-wrestling . . . [until] lubricated by beer and rum, the assembled company would arrive at a point of sweaty, brawling, raucous, and finally exhausted nakedness."

Moraes's grandfather Camoens had faith in Nehru but not in Gandhi. In the village India to which Gandhi appealed, he saw forces brewing that spelled trouble for India's minorities: "In the city we are for secular India but the village is for Ram . . . In the end I am afraid the villagers will march on the cities and people like us will have to lock our doors and there will come a Battering Ram." His prophecy begins to fulfill itself in Moraes's lifetime when the doors of the Babri mosque at Ayodhya are battered down by crowds of fanatical Hindus.

Camoens is prescient but ineffectual. Aurora, an activist as well as an artist, is the only da Gama with the strength to confront the dark forces at work in India. When the annual festival procession of the elephant-headed god Ganesha, a show of "Hindu-fundamentalist triumphalism," passes by their house, she dances in view of the celebrants, dancing *against* the god, though, alas, her dance is read by them as part of the spectacle (Hinduism notoriously absorbs its rivals). Every year she dances on the hillside; dancing at the age of sixty-three, she slips and falls to her death.

Raman Fielding, rising star of the Hindu movement, is a thinly disguised caricature of Bal Thackeray, the Bombay leader of the Shiv Shena Party, which Rushdie elsewhere calls "the most overtly Hindu-fundamentalist grouping ever to achieve office anywhere in India." Closely linked with Bombay's criminal underworld, Fielding is "against unions, . . . against working women, in favour of sati, against poverty and in favour of wealth, . . . against 'immigrants' to the city, . . . against the corruption of the Congress [Party] and for 'direct action,' by which he meant paramilitary activity in support of his political aims." He looks forward to a theocracy in which "one particular variant of Hinduism would rule."

If Rushdie's *Satanic Verses* outraged the dour literalists within Islam, then *The Moor's Last Sigh* will anger the fascist-populist element within Hindu sectarianism. On Raman Fielding Rushdie lavishes some of his most stinging satirical prose: "In his low cane chair with his great belly slung across his knees like a burglar's sack, with his frog's croak of a voice bursting through his fat frog's lips and his little dart of a tongue licking at the edges of his mouth, with his hooded froggy eyes gazing greedily down upon the little beedi-rolls of money with which his quaking petitioners sought to pacify him, . . . he was indeed a Frog King."

The underworld struggle between Fielding and Moraes's father culminates in the murder of Fielding and the destruction of half of Bombay. Sick of this new "barbarism," Moraes retires to Andalusia, there to confront another monster or evil, Vasco Miranda. Miranda is a Goan painter who has made a fortune selling kitsch to Westerners. Obsessively jealous of Aurora, he has stolen her Moor paintings; to reclaim them, Moraes finds his way into Miranda's Daliesque fortress. Here Miranda imprisons him and lets him live only as long as (shades of Scheherazade) he writes the story of his life.

Locked up with Moraes is a beautiful Japanese picture restorer named Aoi Uë (her name all vowels, as the Moor's, in Arabic, is all consonants: would that they had found each other earlier, he thinks). Aoi perishes; Moraes, with Miranda's blood on his hands, escapes. It is 1993, he is thirty-six years old, but his inner clock says he is seventy-two and ready to die.

The final chapters of the book, and the opening chapter, to which they loop back, are packed (or palimpsested) with historical allusions. Moraes is not only Muhammad XI (Abu-Abd-Allah, or Boabdil, in the Spanish corruption of his name): he sees himself as Dante in "an internal maze" of tourists, drifting yuppie zombies, and also as Martin Luther, looking for doors on which to nail the pages of his life story, as well as Jesus on the Mount of Olives, waiting for his persecutors to arrive. It is hard to avoid the impression that all the left-over analogues of the Moor fable from Rushdie's notebooks have been poured into these chapters, which are as a result frantic and overwritten. Some of the historical parallels fall flat (Moraes is no Luther: the hounds on his trail are the Spanish police, who suspect a homicide, not the bishops of Hindu orthodoxy, who couldn't care less what he gets up to in Spain), while elementary rules of fiction, like not introducing new characters in the last pages, are ignored: Aoi is the case in point.

Nor is this the worst. As if unsure that the import of the Boabdil/Moraes parallel has come across, Rushdie, in what sounds very much like *propria persona,* glosses it as follows: Granada, in particular the Alhambra, is a "monument to a lost possibility," a "testament . . . to that most profound of our needs, . . . for putting an end to frontiers, for the dropping of boundaries of the self." With all due respect, one must demur. The palimpsesting of Moraes over Boabdil supports a less trite, more provocative thesis: that the Arab penetration of Iberia, like the later Iberian penetration of India, led to a creative mingling of peoples and cultures; that the victory of Christian intolerance in Spain was a tragic turn in history; and that Hindu intolerance in India bodes as ill for the world as did the sixteenth-century Inquisition in Spain. (Fleshing out the thesis in this way depends, one must concede, on ignoring the fact that the historical Boabdil was a timorous and indecisive man, dominated by his mother and duped by King Ferdinand of Spain.)

Rushdie pursues palimpsesting with considerable vigor in *The Moor's Last Sigh,* as a novelistic, historiographical, and autobiographical device. Thus Granada, Boabdil's lost capital, is also Bombay, "inexhaustible Bombay of excess," the sighed-for home of Moraes as well as of the author over whose person he is written. Both are cities from which a regenerative cross-fertilization of cultures might have taken place, but for ethnic and religious intolerance.

Occasionally palimpsesting descends to mere postmodernist frivolousness: "Had I slipped accidentally from one page, one book of life on to another?" Moraes wonders, unable to believe he has been put in a Bombay prison. At other moments, however, Moraes expresses a hunger for the real, for that which is not merely one textual layer upon another, that is the keenest and saddest note in the book: "How," he asks himself, looking back in bafflement, "trapped as we were . . .

in the fancy-dress, weeping-Arab kitsch of the superficial, could we have penetrated to the full sensual truth of the lost mother below? How could we have lived authentic lives?"

Here Moraes articulates a passionate but fearful attachment to his mother—whom he elsewhere calls "my Nemesis, my foe beyond the grave"—and through her to a "Mother India who loved and betrayed and ate and destroyed and again loved her children, and with whom the children's passionate conjoining and eternal quarrel stretched long beyond the grave." This conflicted attachment is a submerged, barely explored element of his makeup.

Moraes's yearning for authenticity expresses itself most clearly in his dream of peeling off his skin and going into the world naked "like an anatomy illustration from *Encyclopedia Britannica* . . . set free from the otherwise inescapable jails of colour, race and clan." Alas,

> in Indian country [the joke here is complex: Rushdie conflates Indian Indians, whom Columbus set off to find, with American Indians, the Indians he in fact found] there was no room for a man who didn't want to belong to a tribe, who dreamed . . . of peeling off his skin and revealing his secret identity—the secret, that is, of the identity of all men—of standing before the war-painted braves to unveil the flayed and naked unity of the flesh.

If this is not a crisis in Rushdie's thinking—a longing for the pages of history to stop turning, or at least no longer to turn "double-quick," for the ultimate self to emerge from the parade of fictions of the self—then it is at least a crisis for the Moor persona, the prince in exile, no longer young, confronting the overriding truth uniting mankind: we are all going to die.

Besides palimpsesting, Rushdie also experiments with ekphrasis, the conduct of narration through the description of imaginary works of art. The best known instances of ekphrasis in Western literature are the descriptions of the shield of Achilles in the *Iliad* and of the frieze on Keats's Grecian urn. In Rushdie's hands ekphrasis becomes a handy device to recall the past and foreshadow the future. The magical tiles in the Cochin synagogue not only tell the story of the Jews in India but foretell the atom bomb. Aurora's paintings project her son into the past as Boabdil; the entire history of India, from mythic times to the present, is absorbed into a great phantasmagoria on the wall of her bedroom. Scanning it, her father marvels that she has captured "the great swarm of being itself," but then notes one great lacuna: "God was absent." Through paintings whose only existence, paradoxically, is in words, the darkly prophetic historical imagination of Aurora dominates the book.

Like *Midnight's Children* (1981), *Shame* (1983), and *The Satanic Verses* (1989), *The Moor's Last Sigh* is a novel with large ambitions composed on a large scale. In its architecture, however, it is disappointing. Aside from the dynastic prelude set in Cochin, and the last fifty pages set in Spain, the body of the book belongs to Moraes's life in Bombay. But instead of the interwoven development of character, theme, and action characteristic of the middle section of what might be called the classic novel, we find in the middle section of Rushdie's novel only fitful and episodic progress. New actors are introduced with enough inventiveness and wealth of detail to justify major roles; yet all too often their contribution to the action turns out to be slight, and they slip (or are slipped) out of the picture almost whimsically.

To complaints of this kind—which have been voiced with regard to the earlier books as well—defenders of Rushdie have responded by arguing that he works, and should therefore be read, within two narrative traditions: of the Western novel (with its subgenre, the anti-novel à la *Tristram Shandy*), and of Eastern story-cycles like the *Panchatantra,* with their chainlike linking of self-contained, shorter narratives. To such critics, Rushdie is a multicultural writer not merely in the weak sense of having roots in more than one culture but in the strong sense of using one literary tradition to renew another.

It is not easy to counter this defense in its general form, particularly from the position of an outsider to India. But to concentrate our minds let us consider a single instance from *The Moor's Last Sigh:* the episode in which Moraes's father, Abraham Zogoiby, in a fit of enthusiasm for the modern, impersonal, "management" style in business, adopts a young go-getter named Adam over Moraes as his son and heir. For some fifteen pages Adam occupies center stage. Then he is dropped from the book. I find the episode unsatisfying; further, I would hazard a guess that the reason why Adam disappears is not that Rushdie is following traditional Indian models but that he is only halfheartedly committed to satirizing the business-school ethos; he abandons this particular narrative strand because it is leading nowhere.

There are plenty of readers, I am sure, who will disagree—who will enjoy the stories of Adam and other personages who blaze briefly across the pages of *The Moor's Last Sigh* and then expire. Where I see intermittent development they will see prodigality of invention. Such divergences are to be expected: narrative pleasure is a notoriously personal matter. But this ought not to mean that we should refrain from articulating our disappointments or trying to uncover their causes. Some of our expectations may indeed turn out to derive from our own culturally defined preconceptions; nevertheless, "multiculturalism" should not become a card that trumps all other critical cards. There cannot be *no* universals of the storyteller's art; otherwise we could not read and enjoy stories across cultural borders.

Such characters as Vasco Miranda or Uma Sarasvati or even Abraham Zogoiby himself provide a comparable problem. In their extravagant villainy they seem to come straight out of Hollywood or Bollywood. Yet in so palimpsested a novel as *The Moor's Last Sigh,* why should the popular storytelling media of today not contribute to the textual layering? And are traditional folk tales not full of unmotivated evil anyway?

If we want to read *The Moor's Last Sigh* as a postmodern textual romp, however, we must accept the rules of the postmodernist game. The notion of "authenticity" has been one of the first casualties of postmodernism in its deconstructive turn. When Moraes, in prison, wonders whether he is on the wrong page of his own book, he moves into a dimension in which not only he but the walls of his cell consist of no more than words. On this purely textual plane he can no longer be taken seriously when he laments that he is trapped within "colour, caste, sect" and longs for an authentic life outside them. If as self-narrator he wants to escape the inessential determinants of his life, he need only storytell his way out of them.

In fact Rushdie is far from being a programmatic postmodernist. For instance, he is disinclined to treat the historical record as just one story among many. We see this in his treatment of the two histories out of which Moraes's story grows: of the Moors in Spain, and of the Jews in India. In the case of the Moors, and of Muhammad/Boabdil in particular, Rushdie does not deviate from the historical record, which is probably most familiar to Westerners from Washington Irving's nostalgic sketches in *The Alhambra.* As for the Jewish communities in India, their origins are ancient and will probably never be known with certainty. However, they preserved certain legends of origin, and to these legends Rushdie adheres without embroidering, save for one superadded fiction: that the Zogoibys descend from Sultan Muhammad (called by his subjects El-zogoybi, the Unfortunate) via a Jewish mistress who sailed for India pregnant with his child. This story is specifically (though not unequivocally) singled out as an invention by Moraes in his function as narrator.

2.

Identity, in our times, has become overwhelmingly a matter of group identification: of identifying with and/or being claimed by groups. The problem of identity in this sense has hovered over Rushdie's head for most of his life. As a British citizen of Indian Muslim ancestry and, since Khomeini's *fatwa,* of indeterminate residence, it has become less and less easy for him to claim that he writes about India as an insider. For one thing, he does not live there; for another, the notion of Indianness has become lamentably contested, as *The*

Moor's Last Sigh shows. Yet in a bitter irony, the religion into which he was born will not let him go.

No wonder, then, that the hero of *Midnight's Children,* the book that revolutionized the Indian English novel and brought Rushdie fame, cries out (prophetically, as it emerged): "Why, alone of all the more-than-five-hundred-million, should I have to bear the burden of history?" "I [want] to be Clark Kent, not any kind of Superman," laments Moraes in similar vein. Or if not Clark Kent, then simply his own, essential, naked self.

It is in this context, in which Rushdie's personal life has been overtaken by an increasingly political conception of personal identity, that we should understand the moment when Moraes, moving beyond a by-now-familiar Rushdian celebration of bastardy, mongrelhood, and hybridity, rejects his "anti-Almighty" father Abraham—a father ready to sacrifice him on the altar of his megalomaniac ambitions—and embraces a heritage that has hitherto meant nothing to him: "I find that I'm a Jew." For not only are Rushdie's Jews (the Jews of Cochin, the Jews of Spain) powerless, dwindling communities; but to claim, voluntarily, the identity of a Jew, after the Holocaust, is to assert, however symbolically, solidarity with persecuted minorities worldwide.

In a book in which ideas, characters, and situations are invented with such prolific ease, one wishes that Rushdie had pushed the story of Moraes as rediscovered Jew further. *"Here I stand,"* says Moraes/Luther, at the end of the journey of his life: "Couldn't've done it differently." What does it mean in real-life terms, in India or in the world, to take a stand on a symbolic Jewishness?

The microscopic scrutiny commentators have devoted to the text of *The Satanic Verses,* particularly to its offending passages, and the wealth of religious and cultural reference they have uncovered, have demonstrated how superficial a non-Muslim reading of that book must be. Similarly, when it comes to sectarian infighting in India, or to the Bombay social and cultural scene, the non-Indian reader of *The Moor's Last Sigh* can have at most an overhearing role: jokes are being made, satiric barbs being fired, which only an Indian, and perhaps only an Indian of a certain social background, will appreciate.

Rushdie came under attack for *The Satanic Verses* and will no doubt come under attack—from other quarters—for *The Moor's Last Sigh.* In the former case he defended himself ably, arguing that readers who smelled blasphemy were oversimplifying and misreading his book. But his defense was not heard: authority to interpret was almost at once wrested from him by factions with political aims of their own. *The Satanic Verses* thus provided a model illustration of how, in Gayatri Spivak's words, the "praxis and politics of life" can override a "mere reading" of a book. Let us hope (*o tempora! o mores!*) that determined foes of *The Moor's Last Sigh* will confine their energies to the artefact and let its author be.

A final word. Five centuries after the campaigns of Ferdinand and Isabella swept Islam out of Iberia, the Muslims of southeastern Europe faced genocidal attack. Though the word *Bosnia* is not so much as breathed (or sighed) in his book, it is inconceivable that the parallel did not cross Rushdie's mind as he wrote, or will not cross ours.

Nancy Wigston (review date April 1996)

SOURCE: A review of *The Moor's Last Sigh,* in *Quill and Quire,* Vol. 62, No. 4, April, 1996, p. 25.

[*Below, Wigston offers a positive review of the audio version of* The Moor's Last Sigh.]

Actor Art Malik read *The Moor's Last Sigh,* Rushdie's latest *tour de force,* in what is a near-perfect marriage of medium and messenger. As the doomed Hari Kumar in the BBC opus *The Jewel and the Crown,* Malik embodied the tragedy of the Indian caught between East and West a teasing reference to Rushdie's own saga.

Malik's strong, well-mannered tone almost holds this typically unwieldy Rushdie narrative (think *Midnight's Children*) in check through betrayals, murders, births, deaths, lusts, upheavals so numerous they verge on tedium. But he is best-as is the novel-in the domestic bits, when he reads in the Indian-accented dialogue. Here the story really leaps to life, free for a time of its greatest drag, the Moor himself.

Heir to a huge spice empire in Cochin—a tangled dynasty of Indians, Jews, and Portuguese—the Moor recounts family history as he expires in a graveyard in Spain. But his story—which never strays far from his mother Aurora—mainly takes place in India. Mother India and the Moor's mother are explicitly enmeshed. Aurora is also the "most illustrious of our modern artists." Betrayed and banished by art, mother, homeland, the Moor unwinds his "scandalous skein of shaggy-doggy yarns."

Trouble is, his is a surfeit of scandals. Even the most assiduous listeners will falter in this forest of plots and counterplots. Places and people who seemed so rounded eventually fade into caricature, weighed down by allusions. This is not to say this novel is not shot through with brilliance, perfectly wrought scenes, and memorable eccentrics. If it can't quite bear its own weight, so be it.

Read by the mellifluous Malik, Rushdie's tale comes neatly packaged in six manageable portions. There is, however, a danger that audiences will be seduced into inattention while following the wily author's twists, turns, and verbal pyrotechnics. Might I suggest Random House label it with a warning: "Caution. Do not listen while driving in rush hour or operating heavy machinery."

FURTHER READING

Fields, Beverly. "Salman Rushdie Returns." *Chicago Tribune—Books* (14 January 1996): 1.
    Review of *The Moor's Last Sigh* outlining the reasons for its censorship in India.

Hajari, Nisid. "Rushdie Lets Out a 'Sigh'." *Entertainment Weekly* (9 February 1996): 47.
    Relates the critic's experience of interviewing the heavily guarded Rushdie upon the release of *The Moor's Last Sigh.*

Shone, Tom. "Mother Knows Best." *Spectator* 275, No. 8722 (9 September 1995): 38.
    Positive review of *The Moor's Last Sigh.*

Vargas Llosa, Alvaro. "The Last Sigh of Diversity." *New Perspectives Quarterly* (Spring 1996): 47-9.
    Interview with the author.

Gerald Stern

1925-

American poet.

The following entry presents criticism of Stern's work through 1995. For further information on his life and career, see *CLC*, Volume 40.

INTRODUCTION

Stern's poetry is noted for its energetic language, rich imagery, and skillful balance of emotional expressiveness and concrete physical detail. His poems are usually written in a conversational "confessional" style, yet they are also frequently lyrical and sometimes contain traces of surreal imagery. Stern's preoccupation with the self, his use of long, incantory lines, and his characteristically exuberant, celebratory tone have led many reviewers to compare his work to that of Walt Whitman. However, several critics have noted that Whitman's "self" is meant to encompass a broad spectrum of humanity, while Stern's refers to an intensely personal figure or speaker. According to Stern, he's "a Whitmanian who doesn't like to be called a Whitmanian."

Biographical Information

Born February 22, 1925, in Pittsburgh, Pennsylvania, Stern attended the University of Pittsburgh, where he earned a B.A. in 1947, and Columbia University, where he received an M.A. in 1949. After serving in the United States Army Air Corps, he married Patricia Miller in 1952. During the 1960s and 1970s Stern taught at Temple University, Indiana University of Pennsylvania, and Somerset County College in New Jersey. In 1973 Stern published his first collections of poetry, *The Naming of Beasts and Other Poems* and *Rejoicings;* he also was named a consultant in literature to the Pennsylvania Arts Council, which he continues to serve. *Lucky Life* (1977), his third verse collection, received the Lamont Poetry Selection award and garnered national attention. Other volumes include *The Red Coal* (1981), *Paradise Poems* (1984), *Lovesick* (1987), and *Odd Mercy* (1995). Stern has been named to several distinguished positions at many American universities, including the Bain Swiggert Chair at Princeton University. Since 1982 he has been a member of the Writer's Workshop at the University of Iowa.

Major Works

The poems in *Lucky Life* abound with descriptions of ordinary objects and events of American life. Written in an elegiac style, a concern about the self dominates the collection,

as it does throughout Stern's verse. Using biblical references and language patterned on the Old Testament, *Lucky Life* also focuses on the poet's Jewish heritage, which is expressed by his emphasis on memory and history. *The Red Coal* features kaleidoscopic renderings of Stern's memory and imagination presented in meticulous detail. This volume is marked by the alternatively exuberant and meditative voice of several personae and by the vivid cataloging of images. *Paradise Poems* relates the past and present, focusing particularly on the coexistence of pain and joy, loss and redemption, which are portrayed as central to human life. Set mainly on the lower east side of Manhattan, the poems in *Odd Mercy* consist of narratives, meditation, and pastoral lyrics. Divided into two parts, the second half comprises seventeen sections of a long poem entitled **"Hot Dog"** after the name of a homeless woman whom Stern observed.

Critical Reception

Stern's first two volumes of poetry received little critical attention, but with *Lucky Life* he emerged as a significant figure in contemporary literature. Reviewers praised the lively, meaningful language in this volume, hailing the poet's ability to blend commonplace and ethereal elements. Commentators detected a broadening scope in *Paradise Poems,* citing Stern's gradual move from a highly personal poetry to a concern with more universal implications. Most reviewers have highly recommended *Odd Mercy,* calling attention to Stern's inexhaustible imagination. Stated Patricia Monaghan in her review of *Odd Mercy:* "Stern extemporizes from the most ordinary experiences . . . and lets the experience open out, up, beyond." Critics often have noted Stern's use of repetition and catalogues in his poetry, usually comparing his technique to that of Whitman. Others have commented on the role of memory and nostalgia in his poetry. Jane Somerville claimed that Stern's "obsession is not so much the past itself as the relationship between presence and memory, history and myth, conscious and unconscious, surface and depth." Frank Allen summarized the poet's achievement: "For over two decades, no one has equaled his compassionate, surreal parables about the burden of and the exaltation at being alive."

PRINCIPAL WORKS

The Naming of Beasts and Other Poems (poetry) 1973
Rejoicings (poetry) 1973
Lucky Life (poetry) 1977
The Red Coal (poetry) 1981
Paradise Poems (poetry) 1984
Lovesick (poetry) 1987
Leaving Another Kingdom: Selected Poems (poetry) 1990
Two Long Poems (poetry) 1990
Odd Mercy (poetry) 1995

CRITICISM

Jane Somerville (essay date November/December 1988)

SOURCE: "Gerald Stern Among the Poets: The Speaker as Meaning," in *American Poetry Review,* Vol. 17, No. 6, November/December, 1988, pp. 11-19.

[*In the essay below, Somerville offers an overview of Stern's poetry, analyzing the variety of roles Stern assumes as narrator of his poems.*]

The poetry of Gerald Stern is defined and governed by its flamboyant speaker, a stagey hero whose life story is the poet's, but enlarged and mythicized. This eloquent spokesman holds the line between the unconditional authority of narration and the contingency of character; in these we recognize the two positions we constantly hold as speakers and

actors. He is onstage throughout the entire canon and constantly demands our attention. He does not react passively to events; he wrestles with them and shapes, even invents, the world he moves in. He transforms himself endlessly, playing whatever parts appeal to him, yet his identity never changes: whether he takes the mask of a friendly gardener, a wandering hero, a rabbinical figure, a fallen angel, a god—even a tree or bird—he is still the same whimsical guy, a fantastic prophet and favorite uncle who, though full of wisdom, permits himself all manner of weakness, readily admits to his own foolishness, indulges in spates of sentiment, suffers endlessly, and overcomes suffering through imagination. In the gap between his vast proportions and his foolishness we recognize the human condition; in his capacity for transformation he becomes a metaphor for imagination.

This first person narrator can of course be taken for the poet himself. But I prefer to see him as an actor, playing a part like that of a character in fiction who is said to "represent" the author. The distinction is subtle, but crucial. This view encourages us to notice the performative nature of Stern's poems. By focusing on the roles encapsulated in the protean speaker, we gain a framework in which to examine the complexities of the canon. This view also helps us to probe the distinction between the speaker and Stern himself.

Stern's leading character does seem to create an impression somewhat different from that of the typical lyric speaker. We are likely to think of the lyric speaker as sheer voice, as statement devised through certain strategies, in traditional or open form, in tone serious or ironic, in language plain or ornate. Identification tends to be scenic rather than dramatic. We seldom *picture* the lyric speaker or identify with him as a dramatic character, a "someone" who seems to be physically present and even seems to have an existence beyond the work, as do some fictional characters. When we think of Huckleberry Finn or Gatsby or the Consul in *Under the Volcano,* for instance, we imagine a person who seems to have a material existence. Such a character dominates the work he's in to such an extent that his entire world seems a function of himself. The meaning of the work is his meaning and cannot be separated from him; in this sense he is meaning itself. It is something of this quality, which combines independence, control, and irreducible meaning, that the Stern speaker conveys.

There are a number of other poets' narrators who share a similar kind of character status or, to put it another way, encourage the reader to invent a "living" character. The reader of Frost, for instance, may do so. But the country philosopher we imagine in Frost is a type, not an individual, a function of the kinds of experience recounted rather than the idiosyncrasies of a unique personality. In some cases, a character emerges in a single poem or poem cycle, but does not persist through the whole canon, as does the Stern speaker. A good example is Alfred J. Prufrock. The Henry of Berryman's *Dream Songs* is another; like Stern's narrator, he's a shape-shifter, but I'm not convinced that readers can picture him. Both Prufrock and Henry contrast with the Stern narrator in that they are anti-heroic characters controlled by circumstance. The strongest comparison is between Stern's work and *Leaves of Grass;* the Whitman persona is an imperative figure, mag-nified, heroized, and mythicized, as is Stern's spokesman. Both are flashy exhibitionists. But Whitman's character is played straight, while Stern's is not. The Stern speaker is comic as well as grand; his heroics are undermined by irrev-erence, ironies and jestful self-mockery.

The dramatic significance of Stern's speaker is in part a func-tion of sheer presence: his high visibility through the whole course of the work gives the canon a novelistic consistency. Beyond this, significance coheres in the character himself, in a blend of elements that add up to a strong sense of *dasein* and agency. For one thing, he is odd, quirky, conspicuous. He presents a striking combination of opposites: he is wild yet homey, heroic but clumsy, extreme yet down to earth, intimate yet distant. His lyricism is so overextended that it doubles back on itself, becoming unlyrical. His verbal au-dacity is surprising, especially when compared with the safe, dull humming that characterizes so much of today's poetry. Our most audacious and startling work is that of the language poets who, inspired by structuralist theory, surprise by trying to deny their own presence in the poem and indeed to deny the purpose of language itself, which is not just to say but to say *something*. Stern's surprise rests on the opposite asser-tion, a cocky, half-kidding, rowdy display of idiosyncrasy and a conviction that there is still something to be said about the oldest subjects. Not since Stevens has there been a voice so quirky and original yet large and universal. Stevens, too, used his peculiar voice to reinvigorate classic themes.

Surprise for its own sake is of questionable merit. But the Stern speaker doesn't seem to be straining for effect; he ap-pears really to *be that way*. At least, he does for many read-ers; to accept Stern on his own terms, the reader must be willing to identify with this character as an authentic voice. If he does not, he may prefer those poems where the speaker is least himself. Louis Simpson exemplifies this kind of read-ing. In a review of **Lovesick,** he faults the poet for oversentimentality and strained emotion, which becomes "a performance." In short poems, he says, Stern "can be very likable." However, the longer poem is Stern's métier, pre-cisely because it provides breathing space for the extremity of his speaker.

The extremity and individuality of the speaker actually en-hance his authenticity: we tend to believe that he's sincere because he is so recognizable and distinctive. We are also convinced by his vigor, another quality that is unusual today, among so many slack, attenuated voices. His strength and

authenticity rely on one another and are induced by a combi-nation of frank emotion, sincere yet idiosyncratic speech, mixed tone, intimate voice, hyperactive syntax, and largesse. All these are qualities not of a statement alone but of a per-son, a character we accept as honest because of his oddity, his boldness, his warmth, his admitted weakness, and his ro-bust confidence. We accept him also because he answers a need for strength and authenticity and brings it in a form we can accept; he is not the severe, commanding patriarch but the good father or comforting uncle.

The distinction between this invention and the poet himself is a simplistic and literal one: the speaker is not Gerald Stern because the poet does not do, in real life, what the speaker does, and the things that happen to the speaker don't literally happen to Stern. The life events from which the poems spring are transformed in a manner much more extreme than the usual change when a poet's life becomes a semantic entity. The real Gerald Stern goes down to the store to get a loaf of bread; the speaker embarks on a fabular quest that leaves the loaf of bread behind, that overwhelms, buries, or destroys mundane reality.

Another poet would invest the actual trip to the grocery with significance. Stern's poem rarely insists that Gerald Stern's wanderings on the city streets, his well-known restaurant stops, his backyard gardening or his travels abroad have, in them-selves, universal significance. Actual events in the poet's life often become mere vestiges in the enlarged experience of the poem. The distinction between the autobiographical Stern and his spokesman is more extreme in some poems than in oth-ers. In his major work, he escapes the limitations of biogra-phy through self-mythicization: he invents an ultraself that shares his biography but is able to enact a range of mythic roles. In fact, his entire poetic realm is enveloped by the speaker. The people—even the plants and animals—have the stamp of his personality, which is that of Gerald Stern, but magnified: the corpus is an anthropomorphic universe full of this multiplied presence. The ultraself is at once self-magni-fying and self-effacing, egocentric yet possessed of a certain humility that says, "It is not my particular circumstances that warrant attention; I am not a hero in myself but as a represen-tative of human nobility." The hazard is the risk of *hybris,* acknowledged and countered in Stern's self-deflating fool-ishness and clumsiness.

In the most literal and obvious sense, it is not the poet who constantly changes form, but his creature: Gerald Stern does not become a tree, a squirrel or a god. Transformation per-mits the poet to experience himself as if he were another. It allows him to look at things from a range of extreme perspec-tives. He is able to explore possibilities not of the self alone but of the human. And it provides the opportunity to put him-self at risk imaginatively. Transformation is perilous; it al-ways implies the fear of disappearing. But the Stern speaker absorbs the threatening aspects of transformation with gallant confidence. He depicts his potential for regeneration and fruition by describing himself as "a flowering figure." His capacity for transformation is the crux of Stern, the machinery of the poem and also its goal.

The oddity and authority of this spokesman derive in part from Stern's early isolation, his late development as a poet and his lack of quick success. Born in 1925, he grew up in what he has called "inhospitable and merciless Pittsburgh," registered at the University of Pittsburgh almost by accident, was not even an English major:

> The idea of going to a school and studying under a poet never occurred to me. I didn't know yet who the poets were, and later, when I did, I had no idea where they worked—or that they did work. . . . I lived and studied without direction, and if anything was going to be a permanent influence on me it was that.

Through his private study, Stern "pieced together the story of modern poetry." But he did not attach himself to a dominant precursor. He says he did not have "one great influence, one master, but a number, even an endless number. . . ." Among them were Yeats and Auden in the mid-forties, Pound and early Eliot by the late forties, MacLeish, Cummings, Crane, Auden, Marlowe, Thomas and Dickinson in the early fifties. By the mid-fifties, he was "most involved with Wallace Stevens." Lowell was "useful," but early Roethke was more so, because of "the mystery, the strangeness, the loss, the love of small animals and plants, the sense of justice." Williams was important for the way he combined "health and madness, domesticity and wildness." In Emerson, Stern found a source for the poet's role in "the very making of the American vision," though he obviously disputes Emerson's rejection of tradition. He has also identified any number of more distant sources; for instance, in a lengthy poetic tribute he takes Ovid's "books of sorrow" as a model.

Stern is irritated by the tendency of reviewers to link him with Whitman. He says he's "a Whitmanian who doesn't like to be called a Whitmanian." He recognizes his "obsession against the very idea of having someone as a teacher or guide." Though he admits to similarities in style and finds much to admire in "Song of Myself," he dislikes Whitman's "pat optimism," "chest-thumping," "shrill voice," and—most of all—his "preaching." Needless to say, Harold Bloom would call this denial of Whitman a repression of the precursor. Perhaps Peter Stitt does go too far when he calls Stern "almost a spiritual reincarnation of Whitman," but there are strong ties in attitude as well as manner. However, this influence is mixed with others, in particular with that of Stevens. The odd conjunction of Stevensian gaudiness and intricacy with Whitmanian openness and emotionality is one of the sources of Stern's tensile strength.

Stern does not see himself as "accountable," except in very obvious ways, to apparent influences. He is less inclined to identify literary antecedents than aspects of his "personal, accidental history," such as Judaism, the depression, the political Left, the crucial childhood loss of his sister—even being lefthanded. Ultimately, he believes his own loss and failure became his subject. In a sense, his failed self became the master he had to vanquish.

He says he knows nothing about "the psychology of masterhood." It may have been "a certain shyness and a certain secrecy, coupled with a kind of arrogance" that made him "unwilling to submit," to become a protegé like Lowell of Tate or "Allen Ginsberg on W.C.W.'s side porch, or Pound in the Provençal room or Whitman in the Emerson room. . . ." He did make one attempt to connect with the poetry establishment. He showed an early, epic poem called **"Ishmael's Dream"** to Auden, and was ignored. **"In Memory of W. H. Auden"** re-imagines this crucial rejection without explaining what happened:

> . . . it was cold and brutal outside on Fourth Street
> as I walked back to the Seventh Avenue subway,
> knowing, as I reached the crowded stairway,
> that I would have to wait for ten more years
> or maybe twenty more years for the first riches
> to come my way, and knowing thát the stick
> of that old Prospero would never rest
> on my poor head, dear as he was with his robes
> and his books of magic, good and wise as he was
> in his wrinkled suit and his battered slippers.

The poem is a coming-to-terms wherein the poet pictures himself "waving goodbye" to "that magician / who could release me now, whom I release and remember."

In another poem, Stern describes what it was like to be an outsider, to hope he wouldn't always be "out there" with only his odd thoughts and his own speech, his "lips alone," to guide him:

> hoping I don't have to spend the rest of my life out there
> staring through the trees,
> hoping that my odd mind will keep me going
> if nothing else does
> and hoping my lips alone can carry me from place to place
> and tremble when they have to, and sing when they have to,
> without help, or interference.

He came to see himself as "staking out a place that no one else wanted because it was abandoned or overlooked." Clearly he was aware that he was writing against the grain. His determination to be self-originating, while it stems in part from failure, can be seen as a signal of the strong poet.

The only overarching background for his work, both in terms of style and in a much broader sense, is Biblical literature, in particular the Kabbalistic and Hassidic reinterpretations of the Talmud and the Midrashim. He puts these to his own uses. In fact, the major roles played by his speaker are appropriations of Biblical figures and concepts. Implicit in his thought, for instance, is a usurped or reconstituted concept of Jesus that replaces the typical, Christian image. Thus the Bible—and more importantly the commentaries that readjust and even reverse Biblical material—can be taken as his precursor.

In 1958, Stern began work on a book-length poem called **"The Pineys,"** which was published in 1969 in *The Journal of the Rutgers University Library*. A treatise on the people of a Southern New Jersey wilderness known as the Pine Barrens, the poem illustrates the experimentation that preceded Stern's realized style. Some parts are written in rather strict iambic pentameter, with formal diction; at its worst, it sounds clogged and pretentious:

> . . . in the one place hylic, in the next
> A limp platonic; stony luminous; heartless;
> Each a plighting, a plashing, on the ripe occasion,
> A raging, of those that rage, and less of it those
> That rage less, all with their own inculpable
> quavers . . .

Two sections play on the relationship between metaphors and algebraic formulas, or poetry and logic; they bristle with lines like "And x prevailed only, and always, as z, . . . Or the state without x since x and z are the same. . . ." Another part consists of a list of 298 numbered items defining "what the starved and beaten Pineys were symbols of. . . ." (**"Pineys"**). The segment dealing with the actual history of the Pineys (Part Two) is spoken in a voice closer to the one we know in later Stern. There are hints of this voice throughout the mélange of the poem; it also contains many of Stern's themes and displays the tragi-comic flavor that will later be invested in his speaker.

After completing **"The Pineys,"** Stern underwent a *crise de quarante:* "I realized the poem was a failure. . . . I had been a practicing poet for almost two decades and I had nothing to show. . . . I had reached the bottom." His failure became a liberation: "I was able to let go and finally become myself and lose my shame and my pride." His work changed suddenly, "as if I had been preparing for this all my life . . . and now I was ready." He abandoned formal rhythms and high-flown diction. He relinquished spatiotemporal coherence. He gave up adherence to a comprehensible literal situation in the poem. He began to rely on an idiosyncratic speaker, a voice and personage that would be himself-in-art.

A new Stern poem emerges in *Rejoicings,* published in 1973. The book got little notice, but it contains several important poems and announces virtually all of Stern's themes and motifs as well as key words and images. His stubborn refusal to follow the rules is also in evidence: unsuppressed emotion, sentimentality, classical allusion, the flaunting of abstractions, the unpopular happy outlook suggested somewhat fallaciously by his titles—all these go against the dogma of poetry writing that has been dominant for decades in the classroom and beyond. Yet he has clung persistently, in the decade-and-a-half since *Rejoicings,* to his aberrations. If he gets by with all this, it is not because the complex ambivalence of his work have been taken into account. The credit goes to his speaker, who is already clearly defined in *Rejoicings,* though he is not so consistently at ease as he will be later and sometimes veers off into silliness. The few poems from which he is absent, such as **"Goodbye Morbid Bear," "No Succour!"** and **"The Heat Rises in Gusts,"** demonstrate how crucial he is to Stern's originality. In the weakest of these, **"Two American Haikus,"** drops of rain fall "like heads / dropping into the waste basket." Without the mediation of the speaker, this surreal image seems lifted from a film by Jean Cocteau or Maya Deren.

It was not until *Lucky Life,* which won the Lamont Poetry Prize for 1977, that Stern began to succeed: he was fifty-two years old. He later came to value the years of alienation, to believe, as he says in a poem from *The Red Coal,* that "nothing was wasted, that the freezing nights / were not a waste, that the long dull walks and / the boredom, and the secret pity, were / not a waste." He believes that his poetry resulted from his isolation: "I went where I did go because I didn't have a guide and I became what I am for that reason . . . ."

By *Lucky Life,* most of the fumblings and inconsistencies visible in *Rejoicings* have gone. Stern is already, with his first widely received book, in the mature period of his work; the radical shifts we often observe in the early part of a poet's career have passed without notice. The eccentricity and strength that grow in isolation are portrayed through the speaker, who can almost be called a stand-in for the master Stern lacked, an Adamic offshot of his own will made to rule in his invented realm.

When the Stern speaker first appeared in *Rejoicings,* the poetry schools of the fifties, reactions against academicized modernism, were a decade old. Ginsberg, born only a year after Stern, had long since challenged the academy. Stern remembers his reaction to "beat vs. feet" as ambiguous: he cursed the academics, "with their wit and elegance and politeness and forms," yet he could not accept the anti-intellectual posture of the poetic Left or its lack of imagination. His speaker is, on one level, an attempt to reconcile the extremes of intellect and emotion, mind and body. His reverence for learnedness is a strong presence throughout the corpus, but his respect for the physical/emotional is just as serious, as he says in a poem where the squirrel represents body and feeling:

> I need a squirrel,
> his clawed feet spread, his whole soul quivering,
> the hot wind rushing through his hair,
> the loud noise shaking him from head to tail.
>   O philosophical mind, O mind of paper, I
> need a squirrel
> finishing his wild dash across the highway,
> rushing up his green ungoverned hillside.

Throughout his career, Stern has never participated in the shared aesthetic of any cluster of poets; he cannot be placed in any school or group. But he does share common ground with various modes, and I hope to clarify his position through comparison. Needless to say, such comparisons are inherently sketchy and generic; they overlook the extreme differences between poets in any group, not to mention the differences within the canon of a single poet. My purpose is only to propose some similarities and distinctions between Stern and certain modes; hopefully, this brief discussion will set the stage for closer comparisons.

Stern has something in common with both sides of a broad yet significant dichotomy in postmodern poetry between the sincere and the ironic. In the first case, he has similar goals but a different style; in the second, his style is similar but his goals are quite distinct.

The sincere poem, or the "scenic style" as Altieri calls it, blurs into the "deep image poem" and is seen in major poets as different as Kunitz, Merwin, Stafford and Bly. It is often said to be the dominant mode of recent decades. The sincere poem presents a resolutely quotidian world invested in some cases with surreal and archetypal significance. It is serious, direct and unaffected, quietly emotional, often passive. Paul Hoover labels it "moral poetry." Its chief ingredients, he says, are ecstasy and grief, its role prophetic. At its best, it achieves a severe clairvoyance. At its worst, it takes itself too seriously. Stern shares the ecstatic and grieving postures of this mode and its impulse toward prophecy, but in an opposite style. His speaker is much too flamboyant and comic a fellow—and too much a trickster—to appear in the sincere poem. And the adventures of this speaker are anything but quotidian. They range out into history:

> I am in a certain century again
> going from city to city. I am in a window
> with Berlioz on my left and Czerny on my right;
> Liszt is looking into the clouds, his wrists
> seem to be waiting.

His adventures also become mythic, enlarged by ancestral memory: "Always I am in the middle of everything. / My voice is in the woods; / my hands are in the water; / my face is in the clouds, like a hot sun."

The ironic poem has aristocratic roots; it is seen in the New York School and epitomized by Ashbery. We think of it as witty, subtle and cool. Stern's ardent humanism seems quite at odds with its brittle, disconnected posture, though his respect for high culture and intellect can be called aristocratic. Stylistically, Stern has much in common with Ashbery: a whimsical air, playfulness, elision, a combination of abstractness and conversational directness, accessible moments dissolved in convoluted syntax, rejection of logic, invention of an alternative realm. Stern is more emotional, Ashbery more detached. The surface similarities between these poets tend to go unnoticed because they are so different at heart. Ashbery's stance toward meaning is definitively ironic in its rejection of wholeness, but Stern's is not. Stern's irony is occasional, soft, often hidden and ambivalent: the Stern speaker is wildly sincere; at the same time, he smiles at the irony of his own seriousness, recognizing the finitude of his experience. Stern has remarked on his attitude toward irony versus seriousness:

> . . . though I love irony and playfulness and roles and
> symbolic behavior and indirect action and irony it-
> self (and lying and concealing and masquerie and
> buffoonerie)—at bottom I believe my life and the life
> of the universe is deeply serious, even unforgettable.

Overriding irony doesn't suit Stern, because it denies the reconciliation of real and ideal that is one of his goals. Occasional, playful irony, however, is a way out of the impasse that irony creates; it is a way of being ironic and naive at almost the same time. It avoids both the self-absorption of romantic irony, which aims to distance and reverse alienation, and the pretensions of hand-over-heart seriousness.

Stern is most often associated with the accumulative or discursive poem that comes out of Whitman, through Ginsberg, and, in modified form, into poets like Pinsky or Dorn. His long, profuse lines, parallel structures, and digressive strategies identify him with this full kind of poem. The main difference here is a subtle distinction in subject and purpose. These poets are ordinarily thought of as representatives of American society or prophets of American experience. Stern can certainly be read in this vein, and reviewers often do so. However, he places American issues in distant and mythic contexts. He is concerned with explication of social realities, but his central goal rests on creating a certain kind of experience in the poem, which may be called the apprehension of archetypes.

In this he resembles the version of sincere poetry called deep image; what is the deep image if not an archetype? But he encounters the archetype as drama, not image; his impulse is verbal, not adjectival. He has noted his attraction to the deep image, which he says is central to all poetry, but not to the bare, minimal work that we think of in connection with deep image poets: "I want the poem to have resonance in several places at once. . . . I want it to be arduous, yet simple. . . . I don't want to say the 'gray gray' and let it go at that. I want to live in a number of worlds." He accomplishes this multiform poem through his speaker, whose dramatized sensibility pulls in and unifies diverse elements.

Stern has a tangential relationship with the kind of poem we call confessional, a kind hard to discuss because it is not a style but an impulse that appears widely. Obviously, the confessional tendency of Lowell assumes a vastly different form from that of Berryman, Plath or Bishop. Yet they all share an unprecedented overt expression of obsessive self-fascination. Historically, we can point to a reaction against modernist impersonality, a renewed, radicalized and inward-facing romanticism wherein self-expression and emotionality focus not on the response of self to world but on the psychology of self. In the most general terms, we can speak of a poetry in which self-expression becomes self-exposure. We might go so far as to call the confessional poem an endgame of the self as subject. Stern questions the prevailing emphasis on the self in poetry as a whole; he posits a time when "perhaps the pain in the life of the poet will stop being the main subject . . . ." Yet he sees the stress on self as an inevitable consequence of the fact that "we don't have a common history in this country, a common culture." It reflects "the fact that we're all separate from each other."

There's a surface resemblance between Stern's work and the confessional stance that turns out to be false. The Stern speaker displays himself flagrantly, almost shamelessly. We feel that we know not only his personality but his character; yet, like a person we see often around town, we know him from the outside in—not from the inside out. This is the opposite of our response to the psychological emphasis that typifies the confessional poem. At one point Stern offers a half-mocking confession that may be taken partly as a joke on confessional poets and partly as a joke on himself:

> I ate my sandwich
> and waited for a signal, then I began
> my own confession; I walked on the stones, I sighed
> under a hemlock, I whistled under a pine,
> and reached my own house almost out of breath
> from walking too fast—from talking too loud—
> from waving my arms and beating my palms; I was,
> for five or ten minutes, one of those madmen you see

forcing their way down Broadway, reasoning with themselves
the way a squirrel does. . . .

If there is a poet among the diverse group of confessionals with whom Stern has an affinity, it is Berryman. Both use a strained syntax, though Berryman's is jumpy while Stern's is evasive, so smooth and flowing that its transmutations tend to go unnoticed. More central is the relationship between Stern's multiplied speaker and Berryman's Henry, "a human American man" with many names who enacts a multiplicity of "sad wild riffs." Both are suffering yet comic. But Henry's world is diminished, etiolated, finally unredeemable; he sums it up when he says, "All human pleas / are headed for the night."

The concept of the confessional poem is undermined by the fact that the word itself is a misnomer. The word *confession* implies admission of guilt and need for forgiveness. The confessional poem, on the other hand, has strong roots in Freudian blame: "Look what they've done to me." Stern's poem is closer to the word *confess* than the misnamed confessional poem, because he makes a habit of pleading for forgiveness. He does so, often comically, throughout the corpus: "Please forgive me, my old friends" (R 40); "Forgive me ten times, but this is what I did;" " . . . dreaming of my weaknesses / and praying to the ducks for forgiveness;" "forgive me / for turning into a tree, forgive me, you lovers / of life for leaving you suddenly;" "I sit in the sun forgiving myself;" "I have to be forgiven." These entreaties sound like lighthearted, formal courtesies, yet they surely point to the unreasonable childhood guilt Stern felt at his sister's early death. If we want to take guilt as a psychological motive in the confessional poem, we can propose a similar possibility in Stern, though not as a crucial element.

A major distinction between Stern and the confessionals is one of tone. For one thing, the rage that typifies some of these poets, notably Plath and Bishop, is missing from his work. So is the overriding negativity, not just an acknowledgment of suffering but an embrace of it, a sometimes potent one: If Lowell can say, at one point, "I myself am hell," Stern is more likely to see his projected self as the potential for paradise. Suffering is a central concept in Stern; however, it is the transformative suffering of the hero. And, like other "high" aspects of Stern's work, it is leavened by comedy.

Stern's acknowledged self-pity does seem to find an echo in confessional poetry, but here too there's a tonal difference. Confessional poets, though they sometimes seem absorbed by self pity, don't state it directly. Stern, on the other hand, kids openly about it, acknowledging human weakness. At one point, the speaker is looking for his kidney along the road:

> I want to see it

weeping with pure self-pity, wringing its hands
the way a kidney wrings its hands, much better
than the liver, much better than the heart. . . .

In the largest sense, his self-pity is part of the encompassing
tragic pity central in his work.

Stern shares the intense emotionality of the typical confessional poem, but not its frank disclosure. In Stern, sources of
effusive feeling are often eclipsed. Crucial personal material
is visible here and there: his early failure, the central incident
of his sister's death, his relationship with his father. But the
poem is never imprisoned by its fact. He never writes a poem
about these subjects; references to them are immersed in historic, mythic or fantastic encounters. Often, only an embedded nugget of the literal situation which instigated a poem is
left in, as if one were to recall a passionate sexual interlude,
for instance, or a scene of anguish, but write down only one
or two details of the scene. At one point, he denies such hidden meaning:

> here is my yellow tablet, there are no
> magic thumb prints, nothing that is not there,
> only the hum, and I have buried that
> on the piece of paper.

A few lines later, he almost takes back this denial when he
says his words are made to be hidden away in a hip pocket or
wallet, "and there are broken words, / or torn, hanging onto
the threads, the deep ones / underneath the flap, the dark ones
forever creased." These "dark ones" may be remnants of private material; they also point to Stern's interest in mystical
Judaism and in what he calls "the secret text." References to
secrets appear throughout Stern. This stealthiness plays against
the overt, passionate outbursts that mark the canon. The opposition between concealment and disclosure, inside and outside, subconscious and conscious, is one of many dualisms
in Stern.

Secrecy is at odds with the whole religio-Freudian workings
of confession, which requires laying bare of the most intimate problems—problems which may seem trivial or infantile when seen in the shadow of the killing grounds. It is also
at odds with the postmodern preference for openness. A secretive poem is inaccessible and therefore undemocratic.
Concealed meaning does have value, though: it creates a sub-
stratum that puts pressure on the poem's compressed surface;
the surface is intensified beyond its apparent meaning, as ordinary events are intensified by hidden meanings in dreams.

Secrecy encourages the old-fashioned, formalist approach to
reading, which may be called the quest reading: initial im-
penetrability or confusion, an engagement like wrestling with
an angel, and final illumination. This reading style is out of
favor, because it traditionally looked for a single meaning
supported by every aspect of the text. Stern's canon does not
answer this demand for consistency. There are even
irreducibles in the text whose presence must be accepted on
its own terms, or on faith. But the quest reading can be used
to open multiple possibilities. Formalism is out of favor also
because it seems to value the poem's surface only for what it
conceals. But in fact the process itself, like any quest, is valuable. In Stern's case, the poem has an equally strong tendency to pull the reader in the other direction, away from
interpretation, to keep her poised on the poem's gaudy surface.

Though we don't see a lot of private material in Stern, we are
constantly looking at the speaker as he moves about on the
stage of the poem and listening to his distinctive descriptions
of his own actions. The speaker often says *I am here* or *here
I am again,* insisting in present tense that we acknowledge
the physicality of his presence. And as scene-setter, he often
begins a poem with *this is,* asserting the actuality of the setting as well. His continual self-description creates the effect
of dramatic presence. It works to establish the kind of sympathy or identification we give to a fictional character, not,
on the surface at least, the kind demanded by confessional.
Yet it cannot be denied that Stern's early need for recognition survives under the surface; the speaker says, in effect,
here I am, please accept me. He wants to be *seen;* detailed
descriptions of his movements and gestures as well as what
he sees—or will see or might see-from his exact perspective
serve to make him visible:

> In my left hand is a bottle of Tango.
> In my right hand are the old weeds and power
> lines.
>
> . . . . .
>
> I can relax in the broken glass
> and the old pile of chair legs.
>
> . . . . .
>
> I am so exhausted I can barely lift my arms over
> my head
> to pull the vines down.
>
> . . . . .
>
> Today I am sitting outside the Dutch Castle
> on Route 30 near Bird in Hand and Blue Ball . . .
>
> . . . . .
>
> One arm I'll hold up in the snake position
> above my head
> and one arm I'll hold out like a hairy fox
> waiting to spring.
>
> . . . . .
>
> I bend my face and cock my head. My eyes
> are open wide listening to the sound.
> My hand goes up and down like a hummingbird.
>
> . . . . .
>
> I hold my arm out straight like a dirty drunk,
> I walk the plank between the rhododendron

and the little pear.

. . . . .

I'm eating breakfast even if it means standing
in front of the sink and tearing at the grapefruit . . .

. . . . .

I bend my lips to the moon,
I wait for the tide, I touch myself with mud,
the forehead first, the armpits, behind the knees,
clothes or no clothes; now I walk on my face,
I had to do that, now I walk on the wires,
now I am on the moon . . .

As seen in these typical selections, gestural notations are
present as early as ***Rejoicings.*** But they become more profuse and unusual later. They are never superficial. Themes
and ideas are bound up in the very gestures of the speaker, as
they are in the theater. For instance, the major theme of waste
and ruin is embodied in the first two quotations above. These
gestures seem irreducible; they insist on a collaboration between signifier and signified, a reunion of word and world.
Structuralist thinking sometimes calls such union a romantic
delusion, and so it is; it's the kind of belief we used to innocently hold about art. It is experienced and, therefore, though
it can be dismissed in meta-discourse, it is true on its own
level. It is in this sense that Stern's oddball character with his
funny, often ritualized behavior is not just a speaker of meaning but meaning itself.

The confessional poem, in its self-absorbed focus on one life,
tends to differentiate that life, to set it off from others, in spite
of the fact that it may stand as an example. In Stern, on the
other hand, the poet's experience is not the main subject of
the work. Stern's invented self is, in spite of its oddness, a
representative figure: the poet or the man. In Stern, it is not,
finally, "look how I have suffered" but "look how we suffer." The underlying impulse is the longing to connect, to
make oneself part of the whole—a need fostered in Stern by
alienation. This movement toward union is an ancient function of literature, often lost in contemporary writing that is
centered in the effort to separate, to distinguish between rather
than unite.

The intimacy of confessional poetry led inevitably to a reaction against self-portrayal seen in the so-called persona poem,
a recent mode where the subject—at least ostensibly—is an
historical figure. In another, related reaction, private life is
still the subject, but the poet disavows the *I,* distancing himself as a *he,* a *she* or even a *you.* Stern's relationship to these
kinds of poems is complicated.

In his predominant first-person poems, the speaker often creates an impression like that of poems where the self is pushed
into third person. The speaker makes himself an object of
scrutiny: "I will look at my greenish eyes in the mirror / and
touch my graying hair and twist my hat;" "I study my red

hand under the faucet, the left one." Stern's preoccupation
with hands stems from his being left-handed, which labeled
him early on as an alien, and also from Biblical influence.
Continual reference to right and left hands manifests the text's
bipolar or dualistic nature. The two hands also have to do
with two kinds of gesturing and two selves: the right is potent
and magisterial, the left has implications of imperfection and
insincerity. In the mirror, the speaker becomes whole, "a
mirror right-hander, / not a crazy twisted left-handed cripple,
/ trying to live in this world . . . ." In this sense, the speaker is
a reflected self, perfected in the mirror of the work. "I stare at
myself," he says: "the trick is finally to do it / without a mirror."

The closest Stern comes to the persona poem is **"Father
Guzman,"** a book-length dramatic piece which appeared in
Paris Review but has not been collected. Here he gives up
first person, focuses on fictional characters, and even sacrifices the evasions of narration. The priest Guzman and Boy,
his ephebe, are self-projections who both sound much like
Stern's first-person speaker, but they are onstage without the
convolutions of tense and syntax that mystify his usual appearance.

Stern often writes poems that are ostensibly about or addressed
to historic figures, especially in ***The Red Coal*** and ***Paradise
Poems****:* **"Magritte Dancing," "Thinking about Shelley,"
"The Picasso Poem," "Villa-Lobos," "Kissing Stieglitz
Goodbye"** and others. But these are nominal or partial subjects, or taking-off points; the poems are really about the
speaker's thoughts, and he often says so: "My mind is on
Hobbes;" "I started . . . thinking about Shelley." When he
praises Villa Lobos or imagines Spinoza "saying something
perfect and sweet and exact / as always," it sounds as if he's
really talking about himself but wants to avoid self-aggrandizement. These can't really be called persona poems, since
the speaker doesn't stay out of them.

In fact, he often gets right into the imagined scene. **"Bela,"**
for instance, starts off as a "version" of Bartók composing
his last concerto on his deathbed. In a typical Sternian double-
scene, the speaker is also playing a record of the music. A
rehearsal is pictured—or rather, the speaker recalls a photograph of a rehearsal—and he begins to participate: "I lift /
my own right hand, naturally I do that; / I listen to my blood, I
touch my wrist." By the end of the poem, the speaker has
forced his way into a sentence with Bartók's wife: " . . . she
waits in agony, / she goes to the telephone; I turn to the window, / I stare at my palm, I draw a heart in the dust, / I put the
arrow through it, I place the letters / one inside the other."
The *I* asserts his authority as controlling consciousness and
maker of the poem, the one who "places the letters." He also
asserts his right to make sentimental gestures.

In other poems, Stern merges with the subject figure in complex, nested scenarios. In **"The Same Moon Above Us,"** the speaker sees a vagrant "sleeping over the grilles" and thinks "he must be Ovid dreaming / again of Rome." The *I* goes on to describe the thoughts of *he,* an Ovid metamorphosed on Prince Street "at the long bar / across the street from New York Kitchen." The bum becomes Ovid, Ovid becomes Stern, Stern assumes the role of the representative poet, all are distanced by the voice of the speaker, who is also Stern. In this typical pattern, it seems that the speaker absorbs various roles, rather than to change into them; all remain simultaneously present. At the end of the poem, the speaker leaves Ovid and finds himself "in the middle of nowhere," as Stern was in his early career, with no audience for his virtuoso performance: "no one to see / his gorgeous retrieval, no one to shake the air / with loud applause and no one to turn and bow to. . . ."

Another Sternian strategy that bears some resemblance to use of persona is his identification with a plant or animal. Sometimes he takes the form of a bird: "I am just that one pigeon / limping over towards that one sycamore tree / with my left leg swollen and my left claw bent;" "I move thoughtfully from branch to branch, / . . . I think of my own legs as breaking off / or my wings coming loose in the wind / or my blossoms dropping onto the ground." Here he drops the bird to become the tree in bloom.

The speaker usually winds into and out of these masks briefly and with such a display of legerdemain that he's hard to catch. In one atypical poem, the narrator throughout is a dead dog who waits for the "lover of dead things" to "come back / with his pencil sharpened and his piece of white paper." He's waiting for Stern—that is, for the Stern speaker, who is seen in many poems with a stub of pencil and who often professes his love for dead things. The dog observes him: "his mouth is open and his glasses are slipping." The ironic relationship between the dog and this "great loving stranger" is like the one between an unfortunate and a tyrant—or between man and god. The dog hopes he won't be kicked aside; he cries for pity. He has traded his "wildness"; he waits for "the cookie," snaps his teeth "as you have taught me, oh distant and brilliant and lonely." Like all Stern's characters, the dog sounds like his master; he isn't a foil for the speaker but an extension of him. The poem isn't about the dog, it's about the man—or Man.

Stern's use of persona is more like that of the high moderns than that of the recent persona poem. A similar pantheon of shifting and merging personae is definitive in Joyce, Eliot, Stevens and others. The conventional notion is that it stems from loss of identity and reflects the fragmented modern self. This rings true for Eliot and Joyce, where characters without strong boundaries merge into other characters and, as Leopold Bloom says, "no one is anything." It does not ring true for Stevens, where the personae are enchanting and heroic. And it does not ring true for Stern. We don't feel ennui in Stern, or

absence of will. Instead, we sense an expansive self that swells to fill robustly all its presences, each of which is added to the possibilities for enactment of a willed destiny. In a Whitmanesque passage where he addresses himself in the second person, the Stern speaker becomes everyone: ". . . you see yourself out there, you are a swimmer / in an old wool suit, you are an angry cabbie, / you are a jeweler, you are a whore . . . ." The passage continues in a tour de force chain of associations that levels and connects virtually everything: "when nothing is lost, when I can go forth and forth, / when the chain does not break off, that is paradise." The experience of metamorphosis at the heart of Stern acts as a signal not of division but of connection.

Though Stern doesn't fit easily into any of the schools or groups of poets that have waxed and waned during his career, he can be placed in the broad, diffuse category of the neo-romantic: a modern or postmodern poet who shares certain motives of the romantics, not innocently but from a retrospective distance. Sanford Pinsker suggests the romantic label in a *Missouri Review* interview taped in 1979; he calls Stern "that rarest of creatures-a likeable Romantic," and compounds his sins, as he says, by suggesting "Jewish Romantic" and "Semi-Urban Romantic." He points to Stern's "high intensities" and his "prophetic quality." Many of the preferences we associate with textbook concepts of romanticism are evident in Stern: subjectivity, improbability, emotionality, spontaneity, the dynamic, the infinite. His boldness underlined by melancholy is typically romantic, as is his reverence for a natural world infused with feeling and spirit. The most obvious distinction between Stern and the broad concept of romanticism is the high value he places on history, civilization and culture.

His relationship with nature—or the world—can be defined in traditional romantic terms as a reunion, or in the later view epitomized by Harold Bloom, where nature is usurped by imagination. Or it can be examined in relation to a more complex view of romanticism as the paradox of consciousness. This view is still most convincingly put by Robert Pinsky. He sees Keats's relationship with the nightingale as an approach-avoidance mechanism that regrets the burden of consciousness, yet recognizes that without it we do not exist. The paradox of consciousness and the effort to overcome it through willful imagination is in Stern serious, comic, ironic, and ultimately tragic, a romanticism conditioned by the modern.

Two distinctions between Stern's performance and the romantic plot combine to establish his genre: the comic and the tragic. Stern's own definition of tragicomedy is "going through the motions of prayer without prayer." He might have said "going through the *emotions* of prayer without an object of belief," a response to the modern dilemma that Stevens described by substituting the verb *believe* for the noun *belief.*

Modern tragedy always has comic undertones because it is heroism cut off from absolutes. The hero whose tragic fall is not from some great height but from a curbstone is ludicrous; this is the basis of the absurd.

Stern's speaker-hero is a tragicomic character whose closest relatives can be found in drama and fiction rather than among the poets. He sometimes calls to mind Chaplin's resourceful tramp, a forerunner of the absurd hero, whose life is accidental yet hopeful. His zany jeremiad comes closer to Beckett or Pinter, and even closer to Saul Bellow's *Henderson the Rain King.*

Like those of the Stern speaker, Henderson's lavish adventures are fabular and fantastic. Both characters have the same kind of bizarre vitality. Both are rambling and impulsive. Both contain charged opposites; they are pathetic and heroic, serious and ironic, comic and godlike. Both are obsessed by suffering and transcendence. And their voices are strikingly similar. Here's Henderson:

> The left hand shakes with the right hand, . . . the hands
> play patty-cake, and the feet dance with each other.
> And the seasons. And the stars, and all of that.
>
>   . . . . .
>
> As he waited to achieve his heart's desire, he was
> telling me that suffering was the closest thing to wor-
> ship that I knew anything about. . . . I *was* mon-
> strously proud of my suffering. I thought there was
> nobody in the world that could suffer quite like me.

Here's the Stern speaker, talking about himself:

> The truth is he has become his own sad poem,
> he walks and eats and sleeps in total sadness,
> sadness is even what he calls his life, he
> is the teacher of sadness. . . .
>
>   . . . . .
>
> and [it is] his own sorrow that saves him—he is
> saved
> by his own sorrow—it is his victory—
>
>   . . . . .
>
> two great masters of suffering and sadness
> singing songs about love and regeneration.

The similarity between Stern and Bellow is partly a function of their similar responses to Jewish tradition. Jewish and Biblical influence is apparent in the joyful sadness of both writers, in their language and phrasing, their emphasis on suffering, and their respect for tradition and learning. Rabbinical tendencies can be seen in both; in fact, the Stern speaker often assumes a rabbinical mask.

Behind all the masks and ruses of Stern's spokesman stands a single character who, like the traditional tragicomic protagonist, is known for his passionate outbursts and the surprising turns of plot in which he is immersed. He reminds us of the buffoon, an archetypal character defined by Suzanne Langer as "the indomitable living creature fending for itself, tumbling and stumbling" like a clown, caught up in "absurd expectations and disappointments," living through "an improvised existence."

Though his outlandish performance sometimes borders on burlesque, he enacts all the characteristics of the tragic hero. He sometimes becomes almost godlike; with overweening pride, he imagines himself as the creator: "I put the clouds in their place and start the ocean / on its daily journey up the sand . . . ." He crowns himself with the garland of the classical hero: "I make a garland for my head, it is / a garland of pity—I won't say glory . . . it is the terror." The experience he embodies and creates is suffused with tragic terror and pity:

> pity is for this life, pity is the worm
> inside the meat, pity is the meat, pity
> is the shaking pencil, pity is the shaking voice—
> not enough money, not enough love—pity
> for all of us—it is our grace, walking
> down the ramp or on the moving sidewalk,
> sitting in a chair, reading the paper, pity,
> turning a leaf to the light, arranging a thorn.

Stern's goal, like that of tragedy, is to "convert / death and sadness into beautiful singing." "There is a point," he writes, "where even Yiddish / becomes a tragic tongue." Suffering opens into catharsis, spiritual enlargement, and the encounter with transcendence.

The Stern speaker is at once a comedian and a hero: a clumsy uncle full of pranks and hocus-pocus whose glasses are always falling off and a figure of mythic dimensions who, like an old god, changes form at will. In all his guises, he is a "man of the heart":

> all alone in the darkness, a man of the heart
> making plans to the end, a screen for the terror,
> a dish for the blood, a little love for strangers,
> a little kindness for insects, a little pity for the
> dead.

Jane Somerville (essay date September/October 1989)

SOURCE: "Gerald Stern and the Return Journey," in *American Poetry Review,* Vol. 18, No. 5, September/October, 1989, pp. 39-46.

[In the following essay, Somerville examines the function of nostalgia and memory in Stern's poetry, showing how Stern links them both to time and myth.]

> We look before and after
>   And pine for what is not;
> Our sincerest laughter
>   With some pain is fraught;
> Our sweetest songs are those that tell
>   Of saddest thoughts.
>   —[Percy Bysshe] Shelley, "To a Skylark"

Nostalgia once had the status of a real disease; it was diagnosed two hundred years ago as an ailment that "leaves its victims solitary, musing, and full of sighs and moans. . . ." During the Civil War, five thousand cases had to be hospitalized; fifty-eight died. Today's popular culture has tamed the ailment by overexposure to old clothes and old songs. Record stores now have a section called "nostalgia"; it contains the old records we think are camp or silly. Those we still take seriously go in other categories such as jazz or rock. The emotion lost credit partly because it became difficult to separate the feeling itself from phrases such as "pine for." The poet compelled to express nostalgia often feels he must sneak it in under the guise of irony, or through a persona, or in a web of diverting strategy.

Our distaste for nostalgia is a remnant of modernism, but the "make it new" dictum fixed on recent progenitors; it was not a denial of pastness but of continuity. The modern artist hoped to leap back across centuries, claiming an ancient and valid past. We tend to see this impulse as a continuation of the romantic embrace of primitivity. But rejection of the immediate past in favor of more distant ancestry is a feature of every period: the Renaissance rejected the medieval in favor of the classical, and the classical age itself enjoyed an imagined recollection of the golden age. The backwards quest leads ultimately to Edenic preconsciousness, that is, to Paradise.

Longing to recover the lost past is inevitable in the life and art of any age, no matter how it is denied. And artists cannot escape inherited forms, which are always nostalgic; even the severe rejection of a form is a reminder of it. Writers in particular are past-bound: as Seamus Heaney notes, language is "time-charged"; it draws us into the "backward and abysm" of history. Jeffrey M. Perl, in *The Tradition of the Return,* treats *nostos* as a containing framework for all literature, from Homer to Joyce.

Gerald Stern has made a more extreme assertion: "Maybe the subject of the poem is always nostalgia." He decides that "conventional nostalgia fits" are echoes of the real thing, "soothing little alarums" that help us fend off serious feelings. In contrast, authentic nostalgia is "the essential memory." Its vibrance rests on a synergy of opposed yet simultaneous

emotions: the pain of separation and the sweetness of remembered—or imagined—union. His assertion is made viable when we consider nostalgia as a recognition of the paradox of consciousness. In this framework, poetry is the consequence of the Fall and always seeks to reverse it. Thus, poetry wants, ultimately, to deny itself—or exceed itself in a transforming retrieval.

"Most of My Life"

A squirrel eating her way in and a mother cardinal
with such an eye she knew two things at once
in what was work for her lower than me hereI'm
sure as close to her nest as she would allow
without engaging her whole prudent being, and I,
saying cheer to her, what cheer, what cheer,
breathing my own prudent last if that was necessary,
my heart going out to her, for all she knew
my feet like bird's feet—I could be her child,
if it were necessary, and die on a thorn
or wear a dress for her and sparkle as rain does
and wear my sparkling beads and wear a sparkling
tear on my cheek or I could be as still
as she wants, I could be a stone, till her eye
is satisfied, she is so rough in these things,
she is so sloppy, look at her straw, she is
so close to my mother—is that Ida, her eye
shrewd and watching? Daughter of lilac, wife
of honeysuckle and privet—ah, she has worked
and her heart is beating, she is a nurse, and a
scholar,
and an architect, her slur and her rocking body
proof positive; she lands on my impatiens,
she flies to my birch, and I lie dead in her lap
and dead in the bark and dead in the grass stems,
my arms
hanging out of the nest, leaves on my chest,
weeds and rootlets here and there, my stomach
a little red already and a little brown,
a twig in my mouth, but only by accident,
for there is more love than not, and she is reaching
to get the twig and I am holding on,
which is enough for one day, pity alone
enough for the two of us though there was grief
and duty, too. I would have held up a lily
for her for she is not to blame; I would have
dried her tears. I did it for most of my life

Gerald Stern, **"Most of My Life,"** in *New Yorker,*
Vol. LXXI, No. 28, September 18, 1995, p. 97.

Stern's emphasis on nostalgia is shared by Bachelard; in *The Poetics of Reverie,* Bachelard places the emotion in a Jungian atmosphere. He calls it "smiling regret"; in popular talk we call it "bittersweet." This "strange synthesis of loss and con-solation" is central for Bachelard because it provides access to the pure, dateless memory of a "total season" that is not "of history" but "of the cosmos." It lets us "pardon a very ancient grief."

For Stern, nostalgia has "great psychic roots with true and terrifying aspects of rupture and separation." We are "not just 'remembering' animals but nostalgic animals"; nostalgia is "endemic to the soul":

> I see it as an intense desire to be reunited with some-thing in the universe from which we feel cut off. I see it as a search for the permanent. As a celebration of lost values. As a reaction to war, and crisis. As a reaction to disenchantment. As an escape from face-less society. As a reaching out for life. As a hatred of estrangement. As a quest for that "other place." As a response to non-recognition. As a response to bour-geois indifference and lying, to totalitarianism, to complexity. As a dream of justice and happiness. As a product of slavery, of the orphanage, and the jail. As a smell from another world. As a combination of absence and presence, the far and the near, the lost and the found.

In Stern's view, nostalgia is not unprogressive. It doesn't pre-vent change. It has been appropriated by rightists who put it to "monstrous" uses, but it does not, in itself, have a moral or political dimension. Nor is it necessarily effete; it can be empowering or irresolute, depending on its form and the pur-poses it serves. He makes a similar distinction between trivial and strong nostalgia in the art work. Art that presents "un-converted, unrendered, nostalgia" is weaker than art with a nostalgic subtext under the apparent subject. The best poets, Stern says, are able to make "those terrifying links between their personal loss and the great public loss" which is exag-gerated in America by "the absence of a past."

In his own poems, Stern is drawn back endlessly into memory. For him, a crucial aspect of the poet's role is to rescue and reimagine the past: "going over the past a little, / changing a thing or two, / making a few connections, / doing it all with balance . . . ." His nostalgia is distanced and tempered by the extravagant antics of his speaker.

The speaker frets about his addiction to memory in **"I Need Help from the Philosophers."** "I am still attacked by memory," he complains, "I am losing Blake and his action." He need only close his eyes "for one second" to be over-whelmed by images from the past: "I see Bobby / Wiseman stuttering through his father's old jokes; / I see Olive Oyl sobbing behind a fence in Brutus' thick arms. . . ." He de-nounces nostalgia: "I don't want to grab Dante by the finger and ask him about my lost woods." He determines to focus

on the visible: he will lie on the beach "one more time" to "encounter the jellyfish and the fleas," to "lie in the middle of the egg capsules and the lettuce." But his attention is drawn away from these emblems of life and birth to signals of death, to "the skeletons," seashells that are reminders of the past and of death. He notices especially "the crab's thin shell."

The poem ends in longing undercut by metaphor and irony, a blend found in a number of Stern poems. The last few lines read easily, but they are a syntactical impasse:

> With all my heart I study the crab's thin shell—
> like a prostrate rabbi studying his own markings—
> so I can rise for one good hour like him
> into a second existence, old and unchanging.

The speaker is prostrate in that he's lying on the sand; the word also suggests prayerful submission. While looking at the crab, the speaker becomes a metaphorical rabbi who stud-ies only his own "markings," his life and also his writings. The word "markings," however, doesn't sit well on the rabbi; it fits in an anatomical description of the crab. This is one of Stern's tricky, ingathering metaphors: speaker, rabbi, and crab are blurred through word association. Whoever he is, the speaker is caught in a solipsistic gesture brought on by memory. As the poem closes, he justifies his behavior: his motive is to achieve a brief rebirth, to rise "like him / into a second existence, old and unchanging." The syntax contin-ues to kid us here, since we can't be sure whether "like him" refers to the rabbi or the crab. This kind of unresolved syntax is part of Stern's signature; it challenges our faith in the sub-stantiality of language and thereby calls into question mean-ing itself.

The mixed tone of the poem is also typical; we can't decide whether the longing to rise, after lying prostrate on the beach, is genuine or mocking. And in any case, the whole poem is halfway tongue-in-cheek; the speaker was never completely in earnest about his distaste for memory. If he rebukes him-self, it is for relishing the trivial, personal, even comic book memories he chooses in the opening of the poem as com-pared to the primordial and racial memories suggested by the crab and rabbi. Yet he doesn't admire the self-centered rabbi. The attitude toward nostalgia in this poem remains mixed; it is associated with death and also with rebirth. When we pal-pate a Stern poem, syntactically or tonally, it becomes un-stable and dubious in a way that suggests Stevens, in spite of the very different speaker and mood. Like Stevens, Stern is dynamic rather than pictorial; both present an enactment of thought, a meditation or rumination, rather than an argument.

Throughout the canon, the Stern speaker unabashedly cel-ebrates the blessing of nostalgic recollection, when "the heart breaks in two to the words of old songs / and the memory of other small radios in other gardens." On close inspection, however, his sentimental avowals are complicated by gentle ironies, comic self awareness, and narrative complexity. In this case, the heart that "breaks in two" is not that of the speaker but of a man who lives near him:

> On my poor road a man lives like a slug;
> he rides along the soil like an old wheel,
> leaving a trail of silver,
> and makes his home in the wet grass and the
> flowers.
> He is finally free of all the other mysteries
> he had accepted
> and sees himself lying there warm and happy.

This neighbor of the speaker, also one "on the same path," is of course, Gerald Stern. The poem illustrates how narrative mirroring distances statement in the text: the speaker sees the poet as one who "sees himself." At this point, he is immersed in nature, free of the "other mysteries." In a sense, then, he is free of consciousness and its abstractions. Yet he isn't, since it is only through consciousness that he envisions its absence. Here, Stern presents the romantic quandary of consciousness, but he does so in a poem of such apparent simplicity that the reader may not notice its duplicity. This "not noticing" or setting aside of recursive patterns is, says the poem, the only way we can have such easeful moments, and they are necessary for survival.

Stern's sentimental avowals are often paradoxical: utterly sincere and dubious at the same time. Even when they seem most pure, they are contextually undermined, within the poem and by other statements in the corpus. **"The Faces I Love"** is a typical pattern in which negative imagery precedes a moment of nostalgic sentiment. The poem has to overcome its disavowals to achieve the good moment; it does so through shifts in diction and tone and by images of death and life. As the poem opens, the speaker is in the same position as the "prostrate rabbi" discussed above. He imagines he will lie down "like a dead man," passive, unresisting, "helpless and exhausted." His attacker will take him for dead: "the leopard will walk away from me in boredom / and trot after something living, something violent and warm. . . ." The last lines of the poem are so appealing that we set aside these negations:

> I will pull the blinds down and watch my nose and
> mouth
> in the blistered glass.
> I will look back in amazement at what I did
> and cry aloud for two more years, for four more
> years,
> just to remember the faces, just to recall the names,
> to put them back together—
> the names I can't forget, the faces I love.

We almost fail to notice that the obvious sincerity of this ending is tempered by recognition of solipsism. The nostalgic interlude occurs cut off from the world, with the blinds pulled down. The speaker is absorbed in his own reflection, which is flawed by the "blistered glass."

When the poem mentions "the names I can't forget," it points to the importance of proper names throughout the corpus. Names ring in the poems like alarms going off to remind us of the depth and diversity of culture: Emerson and Apollo, Nietzsche and Hannibal, Ovid and O'Neill. Shelley, Carnegie, Casimir the Great, Landor, Debs. James, Mao Tsetung, W.C. Handy. Galileo, Swedenborg, Adler, Adam. He loves the names themselves, he has said, and he loves "great minds." They are "like cities"; they are "concentrations of energy and memory." Names of places appeal to him for the same reasons. Beside personal markers like streets, beaches, buildings, restaurants, and the towns and cities of America, he places distant cities and nations: Mexico, Paris, Poland, Carthage, Dresden, Rome, Zimbabwe, Alexandria, and his profound city of Crete. He does not focus on American culture alone, but on world culture, which, in imagination, he travels and claims:

> Please forgive me, my old friends!
> I am walking in the direction of the Hopi!
> I am walking in the direction of Immanuel Kant!
> I am learning to save my thoughts—like
> one of the Dravidians—so that nothing will
> be lost, nothing I tramp upon, nothing I
> chew, nothing I remember.

His persistent recitation of names is a way of rounding up history to save and celebrate it, creating a collaboration between past and present, historic and personal. Naming is also a mode of possession. As Barthes has it, when we name we impose on the reader the "final state of matter, that which cannot be transcended."

The Stern poem typically fans out from an instigating image to a chain of association and allusion that gathers the past into the present and the imagined future, collapsing time and space, uniting subject and object. Through juxtaposition of the visible and the distant, the poet deflects lineal history, replacing it with a recurring apprehension that makes time simultaneous.

A typical portrayal of recurrence and simultaneity occurs in **"Later Today."** As is often the case in Stern, the experience begins in a traditional recognition of nature's cycles. The word "again," which, like "one more time," is a favorite of Stern's, is used as a trigger. The speaker is confident that historical time will dissolve in eternal time. The fact that this release from temporality will occur "Later Today" is a little joke. Time will be opened by looking at things "for one minute" and talking about them: "we'll sit for one minute / on the side porch and stare at the bright shadows."

> I'll start talking about the wall
> and the green pool beside the copper feeder
> and how the birch could grow again
> and how the door would look with roses on it.
> We will live in the light
> as if we were still in France,
> as if the boats were there
> and we were staring into space,
> as if we were in Babylon,
> walking beside the iron giants,
> touching their black beards,
> looking at their huge eyes,
> going down to our clay houses and our tiny cafés
> on the muddy river.

The poem creates spacious confidence. We feel opened, reading it, and we tend to ignore the fact that its calm certainty is undermined in several ways. Nature's capacity for rebirth is asserted only conditionally: the birch "could grow again." The experience told in the poem has not occurred nor is it occurring; it is characteristically posited in the future tense. And the return journey is metaphorical; we'll "live in the light" only "as if we were still in France." The same stratagems are used to qualify possibilities in Stevens, as when he writes: "There *might be,* too, a change immenser than / A poet's metaphors in which being *would* / Come true, a point in the fire of music where / Dazzle yields to a clarity. . . ." (Emphasis mine.)

The simultaneity represented, however tentatively, in **"Later Today"** and many other Stern poems is always presented as an occurrence in the speaker's mind, never *out there*. It is a representation of mental time, but it also suggests the mythic time admired and pursued by modern writers.

When time became historical, it became a line; that is, it became space. Ricardo Quinones is among those who describe this tyranny of history over time as an accomplishment of Renaissance rationalism, which replaced Greek myth. The discovery of perspective, which makes space rational, is often linked to the concomitant rationalization of time. Richard Palmer, for instance, asserts that perspective led to the perception of time as a "linear succession of nows" that can be measured and controlled. Octavio Paz places the origins of historical time much earlier; he says "the idea of a finite and irreversible time" originated in the Fall, when each moment became distinct, severed from "the eternal present of Paradise." He is among the many modern writers who romanticize—and in a sense mythologize—mythic time, which he calls primitive time; he sees the past of the primitives as "always motionless and always present." It is cyclical, "not what happened once, but what always happens."

By the modern period, artists felt trapped in history and became infatuated with myth. Nietzsche foresees the modernist longing for mythic time in *The Birth of Tragedy*. In Greek tragedy, he says, myth makes the present moment seem "in a certain sense timeless"; ordinary experience gains "the stamp of the eternal." It is this effect that the moderns longed to recapture and that remains the goal of *recursi* in Stern and others. In this sense, all our nostalgias echo the buried dream of rebirth back from passing time into mythic time, which we might also call ideal time, a dateless paradise which stands not at the ends of history but in, behind, and beyond it.

Stern's radical nostalgia brings to mind the position of the deep image poets, who also seek a return to origins, union, timelessness. Robert Bly, for instance, describes a need to restore "a connection that has been forgotten," to go beyond consciousness and touch "something else." W.S. Merwin, in an early poem, hopes to recall a state of accord imagined as "a place where I was nothing in the fullness," capable of "hearing the silence forever. . . ." James Wright typifies the preference for nature over culture shared by many such poets. In one poem, he throws a book of bad poetry behind a stone, turning instead to the insect world: a column of ants "carrying small white petals" and old grasshoppers who "have clear sounds to make." These poets typically proceed by seeking to distill or abstract out a unity hidden in nature or in the core of primordial memory. They seek the essential through a process of exclusion and concentration, by cutting back, like trimming away at a bush to uncover its form. The success of this kind of poem rests on restraint and an often deceptive simplicity, a quality not of movement but of stillness. It can achieve the quality of purity and silence we associate with James Wright's famous "A Blessing" or with William Stafford poems such as "Looking Across the River" and "A Glass Face in the Rain." The source of this centripetal poetry is shamanistic. It relies on mythic memory, which seeks to escape history. It has been called a poetry of absence.

Stern shares the goal of these poets, yet his poem is of the opposite type. His style is discursive, inclusive; he appears to put in whatever comes to him as he writes. His poem is a baroque performance of elaboration or accretion that accumulates meaning as more and more material is gathered on its surface. He describes his relaxed yet active gesture as "layering on of one line after another and one idea after another by a kind of controlled association, and the delight—and terror—for me is not knowing where I'm going, even if I know what I'm doing." The energy and tension of this adventure stay in the poem; they are felt by the reader. It's an untamed, unruly poem, full of sub-plots, covert signals, revisions and reversals, yet it's supple and pleasing. I am tempted to describe it with the word *montage,* but the Stern poem is syntactic, not imagistic; continual disruptions of narration make the reader acutely aware of narrative time. I am also tempted by the word *organic,* often used to describe a poem which develops out of its own impulses rather than according to metrical, logical, or narrative patterns. But this use of the term is misleading, since plants and animals don't discover their own shapes; their forms are predetermined. A better word for the Stern poem is *vocal;* we feel we are in the unmediated presence of speech as opposed to the reflective distance of writing. Barthes proposes such speech as an aspect of textual pleasure; he calls it "writing aloud." It is carried by "the *grain* of the voice" and makes us hear the "materiality" and "sensuality" of the human presence.

The discursive mode employed by Stern finds its source in the epic. This kind of poem relies on social memory, on consciousness, and typically wants to enter history, not escape it. Such poetry often has goals like those of realism in fiction, in that it exposes and defines the culture. It rests on a recognition of appearances and pays tribute to the flux; therefore, it may be called the poem of presence. It can be found in the canons of poets as dissimilar as John Hollander, Robert Lowell, Edward Dorn, Robert Pinsky, John O'Hara, and James McMichael. Stern uses this poem of presence to achieve absence; the strain of this combination is one of the sources of the uncommon quality of his work. He is often read according to this mode, and defined thereby as a social poet. And indeed, he can fruitfully be seen through the lens of this definition. He maps the American terrain from the perspective of a city-bred Jew transplanted to small town life. But his emphasis is different from that of the social poet; while topical and political, his poem is also placed overtly and emphatically in the history of ideas. And it is absorbed in an even wider, mystical context. He sees no disparity among these concerns: "The reader must have the real world. He must have it for survival, he must have it because it's there. . . . And the mystic's world is the same as the agitator's world. It must be."

"A Hundred Years from Now" is an attempt to define the spirit of America and place it in an eternal context. The speaker begins by seeking an American metaphor, a "purple sage," that will have timeless significance. He looks in nature for images that will make essential connections, so poets of ancient civilizations can understand Zane Grey:

> I myself am searching for the purple sage that I can share
> for all time with the poets of Akkadia and Sumeria.
> I am starting with my river bottom, the twisted sycamores and the big-leaved catalpas, making
>   connections
> that will put Zane Grey in the right channel, I am
> watching a very ancient Babylonian who looks something
> like me or Allen Ginsberg before he shaved his beard off

> pick up *The Border Legion* and *The Riders of the Trail*
> from the dust, I am explaining him the spirit
> of America behind our banality, our devotion
> to the ugly and our suicidal urges;
> how Zane Grey, once he saw the desert,
> could not stop giving his life to it,
> in spite of his dull imagination and stilted prose;
> how the eternal is also here,
> only the way to it is brutal.
> O Babylonian, I am swimming in the deep off the island
> of my own death and birth. Stay with me!

Social criticism is important in the poem; however, its larger goal is to place American culture in the context of human culture and finally to absorb *chronos* in *mythos*. When the speaker finds himself watching a Babylonian discover a text of America—as an anthropologist might find an old Babylonian tablet—it is not that time is reversed or that the speaker has traveled back; rather, historic time has entered myth. The speaker swims in "the deep," an eternal element where death and birth—that is rebirth—occur. He entreats the Babylonian to stay with him; he yearns to preserve the ideal time achieved in the poem.

"The New Moses" is another example of Stern as mythmaker. It begins with some cattails struggling to survive near an airport, "putting up with the sound of engines." These mere weeds, representatives of nature, will survive the technological landscape: "They will be all that's left / when the airport is dismantled / and the city is gone / and the roads are ruined and scattered." The cattails remind the speaker of the Moses story; he imagines that "some new Moses" will "float by" and be found by a princess who will make her way

> down through the buried brick and iron
> on the almost forgotten fringes of modern Thebes,
> not far from the man-made islands and lost skyways,
> the hundred heavily guarded tunnels and bridges,
> of ancient New York.

American civilization is doomed, like all others, in its temporal existence. But it takes its place as part of civilization itself, an idea and a story that is permanent, recurring. In his uses of history to mould an ahistorical drama, Stern is most like the Eliot of *The Wasteland,* the Eliot who said: "Only through time is time conquered." Stern's America is also like Joyce's Dublin in that it is both history and myth.

American culture is but a surface subject of Stern, albeit an extremely important one. It is a manifestation of his preoccupation with the larger melting pot of human culture which becomes synchronous in his work. His obsession is not so much the past itself as the relationship between presence and memory, history and myth, conscious and unconscious, surface and depth. This is why his brand of nostalgia naturally couches the pursuit of ideal time or absence in a social poetry of presence. He demonstrates that social memory can be assimilated in mythic memory.

This assimilation is accomplished partly by leveling, which erases patterns like chronology and hierarchy that typify social thought, dissolving them in unifying myth. The huge historical events Stern refers to are no more or less important than his walks along the street, his communion in the garden. Scale collapses, but events are not flattened; they are enlarged in an ardent scrutiny.

An eloquent example is **"John's Mysteries,"** where the parking lot of John's, an Iowa City grocery, is transformed into a restaurant on Crete. Like most of Stern's poems, it opens in a mundane incident. The speaker is standing in line at the grocery, but he's lost: "I forget where it is I am." He has seen the same tombstone beef sticks and catalpa trees in so many cities that he could be anywhere—or everywhere. He asserts the poet's prerogative to impose his will on appearances: "I will insist on emptying the parking lot / of the two beer trucks and putting a table there / under the cigar tree, for me and my friends to eat at." Nostalgia in Stern isn't merely passive. It's a willed yet receptive gesture that invites transcendence but recognizes that it must be imaginatively prepared for.

The poem continues in a future tense that immediately spawns a past tense; the spirit of transformation is encapsulated in the syntax. The friends *will* become nostalgic, both happy and sad, and preserve what it *was* like. They will "write, in ink, what it was like to live here

> on Gilbert Street and Market, on Sixth and Pine,
> in a town in Crete eight miles from Omalos,
> a mile or so from the crone and her great-grand-
> daughter
> selling warm Coca-Colas on the flat
> at the end of the deepest gorge in Europe—
> if Crete is in Europe—at a lovely table with lights
> hanging from the trees, a German there to remind
> us
> of the Parachute Corps in 1941,
> a Turk for horror, a Swede for humor, an Israeli
> to lecture us, the rest of us from New Jersey
> and California and Michigan and Georgia,
> eating the lamb and drinking the wine, adoring it,
> as if we were still living on that sea,
> as if in Crete there had not been a blossom,
> as if it had not fallen in Greece and Italy,
> some terrible puzzle in great Knossos
> Sir Arthur Evans is still unraveling,
> the horrors spread out in little pieces

as if it were a lawn sale or foreclosure.

The *here* in the beginning of this section is delocalized; it is a house where Stern lived for a time on Gilbert Street in Iowa City, his earlier address at Sixth and Pine in Philadelphia, and also Crete. The poem begins its wild, centrifugal motion, becoming global and international, erasing history, as if Crete had not spawned Greek culture and then the Renaissance, as if Crete had not contained the puzzle of origins which its archaeologist, Sir Arthur Evans, pieced together to create history out of silence.

The poem moves next to a meditation on Sir Arthur Evans, a representative of historic time who is imagined "putting together our future." The group of friends watch "with curiosity and terror, / wondering if he'll get it right, wondering how much / it's really in his hands, wanting a little / to tamper with it. . . ." They long to replace historic time with ideal, mythic time:

> wanting it to be as it once was,
> wanting the bull to bellow,
> wanting him to snort and shake the ground,
> wanting it to be luminous again . . .

But Sir Arthur Evans "finds another fragment / that tells him something." He becomes the "angel of death": history is death.

The poem returns to the present tense and the everyday world as the poet-speaker heads back to his home on Gilbert Street. The use of tenses as a framework for movement between ordinary and radiant experience is common in Stern. He moves from present to future tense when he moves into past events that are intense; more than a time of arrival, his is a future from which the past is validated. His "I will go back" syntax emphasizes the exercise of will in his return journey; it also asserts that the past is in the future, that time is achronous.

All this seems natural, inevitable, as it spins out in the progress of a meditation that sounds like a spontaneous overflow of talk. Sometimes tentative "asides" are included to display the speaker's fumbling attempts to get things straight. In the opening of this poem, for instance, when he's not sure which store he's in, he says "I think it was Bishop's," shifting momentarily to past tense as if to let us know that the present tense of the poem is being invented. Sometimes the speaker stumbles and corrects himself. When he talks about the friends who watch Sir Arthur Evans "putting together" the future, he says "the seven of us." This sounds wrong to the reader, who turns back to the part where the friends are enumerated and counts eight. Stern immediately corrects himself: "the seven of us, / the eight of us, by the sea." Leaving this mistake in place attests to the poem's authenticity as a record of thought.

The speaker returns to Gilbert Street, transformed through

his role as actor on the stage of the poem. Now he is "balanced forever / between two worlds," past and present, dailiness and myth, reality and imagination. He sees himself in the historical maps (charts) of Crete; he is a drop of white paint on the page which metamorphoses into images of increasing forcefulness: "I walk

> up Gilbert Street to reach my house. I live
> with music now, and dance, I lie alone
> waiting for sweetness and light. I'm balanced
> forever
> between two worlds, I love what we had, I love
> dreaming like this, I'm finding myself in the charts
> between the white goat and the black, between
> the trade with Sicily and the second palace,
> between
> the wave of the sea and the wave of the sky, I am
> a drop of white paint, I am the prow of a ship,
> I am the timbers, I am the earthquake—

The future tense resumes as he imagines that someone will eventually see *him* in a dream of Crete like the "dream" which is this poem. The celebration of remembrance will continue in cyclical time as he greets that dreamer. He, the poet, will again transform the ordinary parking lot. He will do this by touching the beer trucks with his left and right hands, a kind of ritual gesture that recurs throughout Stern. He will be ancient and venerable, a stone god who embraces the dreamer and sings (that is, does poetry) to make him remember the beef sticks and catalpa tree that opened the poem. The return of images from the early lines closes the associative cycle of the poem; it also suggests, mysteriously, that the dreamer he greets in the future / past is himself. Another "wild voyage" into ideal time—another poem—is over.

> in eighty or ninety years
> someone will dream of Crete again and see me
> sitting under this tree and study me
> along with the baskets and the red vases.
> I'll walk across here touching one beer truck
> with my left hand and one with my other.
> I'll put my old stone arms around his neck
> and kiss him on the lip and cheek, I'll sing
> again and again
> until he remembers me, until he remembers
> the green catalpa pushing through the cement
> and the little sticks of meat inside, his own
> wild voyage behind him, his own sad life ahead.

This performance is complete, but we are meant to see it as a temporal manifestation of an archetype that is always potential: everything happens again, everywhere, is happening now, will happen, always happens.

The backwards quest of **"John's Mysteries"** is emotional

archaeology, set against the historic archaeology of Sir Arthur Evans, which the poem mistrusts. The radiant experience unearthed in the poem is of a kind sought by so many twentieth century writers that it must be called definitive. It's a release from estrangement that elicits and contains the quality of belief without assigning it an object. Among the many names given it by writers and critics, the most convenient, in spite of its overuse, is still *epiphany*. In his book-length discussion of the subject, Morris Beja stresses examples that include recapture or recreation of the past along with "the notion of the psychological coexistence of all time." An epiphany of this kind is, of course, inherently nostalgic.

The connection between nostalgia and epiphany is an underlying current throughout Stern, but only in *Paradise Poems* does he engage in lengthy, detailed portrayals of transfiguration. A central example is **"Three Skies."** Here, he calls his timeless moment "my lightness," a phrase that combines illumination with the sensation of near weightlessness. As in **"John's Mysteries,"** Crete is the alembic source. The speaker seeks to understand its importance in the second long section of the poem:

> In Crete the heart gets filled up, there is a joy
> there, it is the mountains and sea combined,
> it is the knowledge you have that there was a life
> there for centuries, half unknown to Europe, half
> unknown to Asia, Crete is a kind of moon
> to me, a kind a tiny planet,
> going through the same revolutions, over and over.

Stern's fascination for Greece is similar in some ways to that of Keats in "Ode on a Grecian Urn," which, as Seamus Heaney notes, does not stem from a sense of "belonging to a particular place" or from "the burden of a particular history":

> Historical Greece may have provided images for his
> daydream but transfigured Greece, under the aspect
> of the urn, awakened his imaginative and intellectual appetites. . . . Keats' past is closer to the long-ago of fairy-tale and functions in his mind as a source
> of possibility, a launch pad for transcendence.

Like Keats, Stern loves Greece because it helps him achieve "lightness." But Stern's poem is far more personal and idiosyncratic than its romantic precursor. It rests on close details of his visits to Greece rather than on the import of a cultural symbol like the Elgin marbles. Yet it is not about Stern's private life; it is a dramatization of consciousness.

The pattern of **"Three Skies"** is the same as that of **"John's Mysteries,"** but in this case the speaker describes the epiphany besides enacting it. Both poems begin in a place where food is sold; this site, usually a restaurant, is a favorite of the poet's.

Here, it's Dante's, a Greenwich Village coffee house. The tense is the same continual present that appears in **"John's Mysteries"** and throughout the canon: "I always remember," "I always think," "I sit." While he sits there in Dante's, his "left hand is walking through Crete" and his "right hand is lying exhausted on the roof / looking up at the stars." The word "stars" triggers a memory of the first time he had his lightness in Greece. He shifts to the past tense:

>   It was the stars
> that helped me then. I stood on the cracked cement
> on the same hill I know where Minos stood
> looking for heavenly bulls and for the first time
> in Greece I had my lightness. I saw the link
> between that life and mine, I saw the one
> outside me stand for my own, like Dante himself
> in Paradise. I felt I was standing inside
> the sky, that there were other lights below me
> and other worlds and this one could be restored.
> And there were other feelings I have forgotten
> or can't quite put in words. I saw myself
> moving from body to body. I saw my own
> existence taken from me. I lost the center.

This supranatural integration approaches literal transcendence when the speaker imagines himself up in the sky. This kind of "upwards fall" has been described by a number of critics; it contrasts with the downward fall into time and knowledge. Paul de Man says that poetic transcendence is like a "spontaneous ascent" and resembles an "act of grace." Stern's out of body experience might seem silly or pretentious were it not for the conversational earnestness with which he confides what he "can't quite put in words."

The speaker recalls that the uplifting accord "lasted for fifteen minutes." Then he slept on the roof—seemingly the same roof where his right hand lay open at the start of the poem—though at that point he was sitting in a coffee shop. This knocks out the distinction between the present time of the poem and the time of the remembered "lightness." He remembers "going into lying still, / going into some secret humming and adoring, / I was so changed, I was so small and silent." This typical Sternian reference to esoteric, prayerful ritual is a response to *being changed* in the course of the poem.

A few lines later, as the third and last section opens, the poem shifts back to Dante's café. But it does not shift back to the present tense; the new section is continuous with the Crete narrative. This seems to undermine the distinctness and validity of the transcendent event.

> It wasn't lost on me that it was Dante's
> café that I was sitting in—a coffee house
> in Greenwich Village with an overblown photo
> of Florence on the wall, squeezed in among

my loved ones, reading books, or talking, or
waiting
for someone to come, for someone new to walk in
and catch our interest, the irony—even the
comedy—
wasn't lost on me. I think I had been there
over an hour frowning and writing. It was
a disgrace! Thank God for New York! Thank God
for tolerance!

These lines remind us that the ecstatic incident occurred, as far as the narrative field of the poem goes, in the everyday world of books and talk at Dante's. They remind us that, in fact, the incident is purely verbal, a poem written in a café: "I think I was there for over an hour, thinking and writing." The self-deflating, amused tone of the lines further weakens the epiphany. The speaker wants us to know that he understands the irony and comedy of his situation.

After a characteristic link back to motifs introduced in the opening, the poem gears up into a typical Stern resolution, one of his most beautiful:

>   I walk
> through the cement playground at Sixth and
> Houston and down
> to Vandam Street, My poem is over. My life
> is on an even keel, though who's to say
> when I will waver again. I start to call
> my friends up one at a time to talk about the stars,
> my friends in New Jersey and Brooklyn. I listen to
> them rave,
> these poor stargazers, everyone with a story,
> everyone either a mystic or a poet,
> one a musician, one an astrologer,
> all of them illuminated, all of them ecstatic,
> every one changed, for a minute, by his own
> memory.

The interlude of paradisical harmony enacted so fully in the above poems is often suggested more briefly. The Stern corpus, like those of Stevens and Joyce, is a web of cross-references in which an element that appears quickly, sometimes mysteriously, in one place may be fully explicated in another. The canon constantly clarifies, reinforces, and comments on itself; this criss-crossing movement tends to make the whole body of work synchronic.

For instance, detailed familiarity with Stern's epiphany enhances our response to a poem like **"Magritte Dancing."** The passing reference to Crete in this poem is enriched by what we learn about its significance in **"John's Mysteries,"** which was written later. **"Magritte Dancing"** presents a more humble and low key version of transcendence than the poems we've looked at. It illustrates how the artist, through the expansive movement of his mind, can escape everyday life. It starts as the speaker goes to bed tired and angry, annoyed when his wife "stumbles over [his] shoes into the bathroom." Unable to sleep, he watches the dark until dawn. His mind moves gradually away from the present and toward nature: "I am thinking again about snow tires," "I am thinking / about downtown Pittsburgh and I am thinking / about the turtles swimming inside their brown willows." He begins an imaginative dance "to the tune of Magritte," that is to the tune of art. He imagines Oskar Schlemmer and Pablo Picasso; these proper names come in typically to expand the poem through the speaker's realization of his continuity with others. He moves from the constrictions of private life into the shared life of history and culture, then leaves his singular life, becoming timeless and global as he enacts Edenic clarity and perfection:

> I dance on the road and on the river and
> in the wet garden, all the time living in Crete
> and pre-war Poland and outer Zimbabwe,
> as through my fingers and my sparkling hair
> the morning passes, first the three loud calls
> of the bluejay, then the white door slamming,
> then the voices rising and falling in sudden
> harmony.

Here the *recursio,* a gesture both willed and fortuitous, opens into a radiant apprehension of paradise.

In Stern's plot, we are lucky to have lost paradise. It is a nostalgic entity that exists because it is lost. We are lucky to suffer, since suffering is what we transcend. Acknowledgment and acceptance of suffering is our humanity, our victory. This is a version of the romantic vision, and it is also the tragic vision, in which spiritual redemption is won through noble suffering.

It is also a traditional vision, a poetic program so overworked that it seems too old hat to survive without irony or other procedures of extreme deflation. Stern's enactment of it is tinged with a chuckle of self-parody, yet it remains serious. His tactic is to go the other way, to crank up such an orchidaceous display of nostalgic sentiment that we are asked to admire his daring. He uses the word "sweet," for instance, again and again, hoping we'll forgive it of his lovable, clumsy, yet obviously erudite speaker.

His success depends on the originality and authenticity of this voice; it produces a surrealism of wit, a zany flux of rhetoric that beguiles us in spite of ourselves. This speaker, like other victims of nostalgia, is "solitary, musing, full of sighs and moans." He's also an exhibitionist, loquacious and playful, whimsical and wise. Extravagance is often associated, nowadays, with insincerity, but Stern's flamboyance is not feigned, nor is his belief in the mediating force of nostalgic

memory, "always seeing the heart / and what it wanted, the beautiful, cramped heart."

Patricia Monaghan (review date 15 September 1995)

SOURCE: A review of *Odd Mercy,* in *Booklist,* September 15, 1995, p. 132.

[*Below, Monaghan offers a positive review of* Odd Mercy.]

Stern writes with enormous authority and intensity of the lot common to humanity—of aging and death, of the tenderness of love, of family and friendship. With the heartbeat of blank verse thrumming almost inaudibly in the background, Stern extemporizes from the most ordinary experiences—seeing a bluebird, sitting in the park near a baby buggy, hearing of a friend's death—and lets the experience open out, up, beyond. For instance, in the magnificent **"Did I Say,"** the poet excavates an early spring flower from its cloak of snow; snow turns to water and the blossom reveals itself. The poet feels "split in two; I opened / because of the water, because of the seed"; the world is illuminated suddenly by a dandelion sun, and all nature is animated by consciousness and love. In his ability to capture such transformative moments, Stern reminds us of one of poetry's primal purposes.

"St. Mark's"

Still like a child, isn't it?
Climbing up an iron staircase,
arguing with some Igor
over the broken lock,
letting my head hang into the sink,
rinsing my neck with cold water.

Like a wolf, wasn't it?
Or a dove that will never die.
Reading Propertius, trampling
the highest stars,
forcing my hands together,
touching the row of snow-capped garbage cans.

Swaybacked, wasn't it?
Dragging my wet feet
from one park to the other.
"Softened by time's consummate plash,"
isn't it?
Tulip of the pink forest.
Red-and-yellow swollen rainwashed tulip.

Gerald Stern, **"St. Mark's,"** in *New Yorker,* Vol.
LXXI, No. 2, March 6, 1995, p. 87.

Bruce Murphy (review date December 1995)

SOURCE: A review of *Odd Mercy,* in *Poetry,* Vol. CLXVII, No. 3, December, 1995, pp. 160-61.

[*In the review of* Odd Mercy *below, Murphy describes Stern's poetic style.*]

"I am at last that thing, a stranger in my own life": this incredibly sad statement sums up the tone of Gerald Stern's new book. The title of the poem, **"Diary,"** is appropriate to these informal, loose, and sometimes shapeless poems. If the speaker of the poem is "completely comfortable getting in or getting out of [his] own Honda, / living from five cardboard boxes, two small grips, / and two briefcases," the sense of weightlessness seems to come from bereavement, not liberty. He says "I am ruined by the past"—not because of its horror, but because it is over. But if the content of memory is blotted out by its form (being over), remembering becomes indistinguishable from mourning; in writing about the artist Ad Reinhardt, known for his all-black paintings, Stern says "we loved gloom and believed / in clarity."

Birds and flowers are recurrent motifs—two symbols of beauty, fragility, and vulnerability. The birds are the kindred spirits of his pain. In **"Hot Dog,"** a long poem sequence, the connection becomes obsessive, even grotesque:

> I remember the smell
> of dead birds when I lived in Pittsburgh, there was
> a certain rottenness, a sweetness, I would know
> somehow long in advance the smell was coming,
> and I would see it there, the broken wing,
> blood on the neck, a beak gone, or a leg gone;
> it was for me my loss.

At times, Stern's passage through grief becomes a free-fall, in which emotion overwhelms form, mixing everything up like a tornado:

> I never thought it through,
> I didn't think like that, I may have snorted
> and felt a rush inside, I know I got dizzy
> just standing, I know I had to walk to slow down,
> and when I was forty I held on to a wall
> to keep myself from falling—but I meant
> that I would let the wind pass through me, that I
> would feel my pulses pounding a little, not
> that I would see the Republic revived or see
> streets with dimes piled up or cigars pouring
> out of bedroom windows the way they did
> on Pine Street in Philadelphia when I dumped
> a box of stale smokes onto the stoop
> and the three men who were sitting there went wild
> with all those riches.

Hot Dog is the name of a streetperson; the other major figure is Whitman. But the poem's antecedent is less Whitman than Hart Crane—a desperate man looking for Whitman, in what has become a wasteland. Visiting the bard's house, Stern imagines him "thinking about his house / and the ugly church across the street," and "all that / coal smoke and soot and the sweet odor that blew / across the river from the huge house of shit / on the Philadelphia side." You wouldn't think it possible to miss these things, but in this bleak world, it is:

> the church
> is gone, there is a huge county jail
> across the way, the sweet smell of shit
> from Philadelphia is gone, the soot
> and smoke are gone, the ferry goes back and forth
> only to the new blue-and-white aquarium,
> and there is a thing called "Mickle Towers" two blocks
> down, and acres of grass now and empty bottles.

Additional information on Stern's life and career is contained in the following sources published by Gale Research: *Contemporary Authors,* Vol. 81-84; *Contemporary Authors New Revision Series,* Vol. 28; and *Dictionary of Literary Biography,* Vol. 105.

☐ Contemporary Literary Criticism

Indexes

Literary Criticism Series
Cumulative Author Index
Cumulative Topic Index
Cumulative Nationality Index

How to Use This Index

The main references

list all author entries in the following Gale Literary Criticism series:

BLC = *Black Literature Criticism*
CLC = *Contemporary Literary Criticism*
CLR = *Children's Literature Review*
CMLC = *Classical and Medieval Literature Criticism*
DA = *DISCovering Authors*
DAB = *DISCovering Authors: British*
DAC = *DISCovering Authors: Canadian*
DAM = *DISCovering Authors Modules*
  DRAM = *dramatists;* *MST* = *most-studied*
  authors; *MULT* = *multicultural authors;* *NOV* =
  novelists; *POET* = *poets;* *POP* = *popular/genre*
  writers; *DC* = *Drama Criticism*
HLC = *Hispanic Literature Criticism*
LC = *Literature Criticism from 1400 to 1800*
NCLC = *Nineteenth-Century Literature Criticism*
PC = *Poetry Criticism*
SSC = *Short Story Criticism*
TCLC = *Twentieth-Century Literary Criticism*
WLC = *World Literature Criticism, 1500 to the Present*

The cross-references

list all author entries in the following Gale biographical and literary sources:

AAYA = *Authors & Artists for Young Adults*
AITN = *Authors in the News*
BEST = *Bestsellers*
BW = *Black Writers*
CA = *Contemporary Authors*
CAAS = *Contemporary Authors Autobiography Series*
CABS = *Contemporary Authors Bibliographical Series*
CANR = *Contemporary Authors New Revision Series*
CAP = *Contemporary Authors Permanent Series*
CDALB = *Concise Dictionary of American Literary Biography*
CDBLB = *Concise Dictionary of British Literary Biography*

DLB = *Dictionary of Literary Biography*
DLBD = *Dictionary of Literary Biography Documentary Series*
DLBY = *Dictionary of Literary Biography Yearbook*
HW = *Hispanic Writers*
JRDA = *Junior DISCovering Authors*
MAICYA = *Major Authors and Illustrators for Children and Young Adults*
MTCW = *Major 20th-Century Writers*
NNAL = *Native North American Literature*
SAAS = *Something about the Author Autobiography Series*
SATA = *Something about the Author*
YABC = *Yesterday's Authors of Books for Children*

Literary Criticism Series
Cumulative Author Index

Abasiyanik, Sait Faik 1906-1954
See Sait Faik
See also CA 123

Abbey, Edward 1927-1989 **CLC 36, 59**
See also CA 45-48; 128; CANR 2, 41

Abbott, Lee K(ittredge) 1947- **CLC 48**
See also CA 124; CANR 51; DLB 130

Abe, Kobo 1924-1993 **CLC 8, 22, 53, 81; DAM NOV**
See also CA 65-68; 140; CANR 24; MTCW

Abelard, Peter c. 1079-c. 1142 **CMLC 11**
See also DLB 115

Abell, Kjeld 1901-1961 **CLC 15**
See also CA 111

Abish, Walter 1931- **CLC 22**
See also CA 101; CANR 37; DLB 130

Abrahams, Peter (Henry) 1919- **CLC 4**
See also BW 1; CA 57-60; CANR 26; DLB 117; MTCW

Abrams, M(eyer) H(oward) 1912- **CLC 24**
See also CA 57-60; CANR 13, 33; DLB 67

Abse, Dannie 1923- **CLC 7, 29; DAB; DAM POET**
See also CA 53-56; CAAS 1; CANR 4, 46; DLB 27

Achebe, (Albert) Chinua(lumogu) 1930- **CLC 1, 3, 5, 7, 11, 26, 51, 75; BLC; DA; DAB; DAC; DAM MST, MULT, NOV; WLC**

See also AAYA 15; BW 2; CA 1-4R; CANR 6, 26, 47; CLR 20; DLB 117; MAICYA; MTCW; SATA 40; SATA-Brief 38

Acker, Kathy 1948- **CLC 45**
See also CA 117; 122; CANR 55

Ackroyd, Peter 1949- **CLC 34, 52**
See also CA 123; 127; CANR 51; DLB 155; INT 127

Acorn, Milton 1923- **CLC 15; DAC**
See also CA 103; DLB 53; INT 103

Adamov, Arthur 1908-1970 **CLC 4, 25; DAM DRAM**
See also CA 17-18; 25-28R; CAP 2; MTCW

Adams, Alice (Boyd) 1926- **CLC 6, 13, 46; SSC 24**
See also CA 81-84; CANR 26, 53; DLBY 86; INT CANR-26; MTCW

Adams, Andy 1859-1935 **TCLC 56**
See also YABC 1

Adams, Douglas (Noel) 1952- **CLC 27, 60; DAM POP**
See also AAYA 4; BEST 89 3; CA 106; CANR 34; DLBY 83; JRDA

Adams, Francis 1862-1893 **NCLC 33**

Adams, Henry (Brooks) 1838-1918 **TCLC 4, 52; DA; DAB; DAC; DAM MST**
See also CA 104; 133; DLB 12, 47

Adams, Richard (George) 1920- **CLC 4, 5, 18; DAM NOV**
See also AAYA 16; AITN 1, 2; CA 49-52; CANR 3, 35; CLR 20; JRDA; MAICYA; MTCW; SATA 7, 69

Adamson, Joy(-Friederike Victoria) 1910-1980 **CLC 17**
See also CA 69-72; 93-96; CANR 22; MTCW; SATA 11; SATA-Obit 22

Adcock, Fleur 1934- **CLC 41**
See also CA 25-28R; CAAS 23; CANR 11, 34; DLB 40

Addams, Charles (Samuel) 1912-1988 **CLC 30**
See also CA 61-64; 126; CANR 12

Addison, Joseph 1672-1719 **LC 18**
See also CDBLB 1660-1789; DLB 101

Adler, Alfred (F.) 1870-1937 **TCLC 61**
See also CA 119

Adler, C(arole) S(chwerdtfeger) 1932- **CLC 35**
See also AAYA 4; CA 89-92; CANR 19, 40; JRDA; MAICYA; SAAS 15; SATA 26, 63

Adler, Renata 1938- **CLC 8, 31**
See also CA 49-52; CANR 5, 22, 52; MTCW

Ady, Endre 1877-1919 **TCLC 11**
See also CA 107

Aeschylus 525B.C.-456B.C. **CMLC 11; DA; DAB; DAC; DAM DRAM, MST**
See also DLB 176

Afton, Effie
See Harper, Frances Ellen Watkins

Agapida, Fray Antonio
See Irving, Washington

Agee, James (Rufus) 1909-1955 **TCLC 1, 19; DAM NOV**
See also AITN 1; CA 108; 148; CDALB 1941-1968; DLB 2, 26, 152

Aghill, Gordon
See Silverberg, Robert

Agnon, S(hmuel) Y(osef Halevi) 1888-1970 **CLC 4, 8, 14**
See also CA 17-18; 25-28R; CAP 2; MTCW

Agrippa von Nettesheim, Henry Cornelius 1486-1535 **LC 27**

Aherne, Owen
See Cassill, R(onald) V(erlin)

Ai 1947- **CLC 4, 14, 69**
See also CA 85-88; CAAS 13; DLB 120

Aickman, Robert (Fordyce) 1914-1981 **CLC 57**
See also CA 5-8R; CANR 3

Aiken, Conrad (Potter) 1889-1973 **CLC 1, 3, 5, 10, 52; DAM NOV, POET; SSC 9**
See also CA 5-8R; 45-48; CANR 4; CDALB 1929-1941; DLB 9, 45, 102; MTCW; SATA 3, 30

Aiken, Joan (Delano) 1924- **CLC 35**
See also AAYA 1; CA 9-12R; CANR 4, 23, 34; CLR 1, 19; DLB 161; JRDA; MAICYA; MTCW; SAAS 1; SATA 2, 30, 73

Ainsworth, William Harrison 1805-1882 **NCLC 13**
See also DLB 21; SATA 24

Aitmatov, Chingiz (Torekulovich) 1928- **CLC 71**
See also CA 103; CANR 38; MTCW; SATA 56

Akers, Floyd
See Baum, L(yman) Frank

Akhmadulina, Bella Akhatovna 1937- **CLC 53; DAM POET**
See also CA 65-68

Akhmatova, Anna 1888-1966 **CLC 11, 25, 64; DAM POET; PC 2**
See also CA 19-20; 25-28R; CANR 35; CAP 1; MTCW

Aksakov, Sergei Timofeyvich 1791-1859 **NCLC 2**

Aksenov, Vassily
See Aksyonov, Vassily (Pavlovich)

Aksyonov, Vassily (Pavlovich) 1932- **CLC 22, 37**
See also CA 53-56; CANR 12, 48

Akutagawa, Ryunosuke 1892-1927 **TCLC 16**
See also CA 117; 154

Alain 1868-1951 **TCLC 41**

Alain-Fournier **TCLC 6**
See also Fournier, Henri Alban
See also DLB 65

Alarcon, Pedro Antonio de 1833-1891 **NCLC 1**

Alas (y Urena), Leopoldo (Enrique Garcia) 1852-1901 **TCLC 29**
See also CA 113; 131; HW

Albee, Edward (Franklin III) 1928- **CLC 1, 2, 3, 5, 9, 11, 13, 25, 53, 86; DA; DAB; DAC; DAM DRAM, MST; WLC**

See also AITN 1; CA 5-8R; CABS 3; CANR 8, 54;
CDALB 1941-1968; DLB 7; INT CANR-8;
MTCW

Alberti, Rafael 1902- **CLC 7**
See also CA 85-88; DLB 108

Albert the Great 1200(?)-1280 **CMLC 16**
See also DLB 115

Alcala-Galiano, Juan Valera y
See Valera y Alcala-Galiano, Juan

Alcott, Amos Bronson 1799-1888 **NCLC 1**
See also DLB 1

Alcott, Louisa May 1832-1888 **NCLC 6, 58; DA;
DAB; DAC; DAM MST, NOV; WLC**
See also AAYA 20; CDALB 1865-1917; CLR 1, 38;
DLB 1, 42, 79; DLBD 14; JRDA; MAICYA;
YABC 1

Aldanov, M. A.
See Aldanov, Mark (Alexandrovich)

Aldanov, Mark (Alexandrovich) 1886(?)-1957 **TCLC
23**
See also CA 118

Aldington, Richard 1892-1962 **CLC 49**
See also CA 85-88; CANR 45; DLB 20, 36, 100,
149

Aldiss, Brian W(ilson) 1925- **CLC 5, 14, 40; DAM
NOV**
See also CA 5-8R; CAAS 2; CANR 5, 28; DLB 14;
MTCW; SATA 34

Alegria, Claribel 1924- **CLC 75; DAM MULT**
See also CA 131; CAAS 15; DLB 145; HW

Alegria, Fernando 1918- **CLC 57**
See also CA 9-12R; CANR 5, 32; HW

Aleichem, Sholom **TCLC 1, 35**
See also Rabinovitch, Sholem

Aleixandre, Vicente 1898-1984 **CLC 9, 36; DAM
POET; PC 15**
See also CA 85-88; 114; CANR 26; DLB 108; HW;
MTCW

Alepoudelis, Odysseus
See Elytis, Odysseus

Aleshkovsky, Joseph 1929-
See Aleshkovsky, Yuz
See also CA 121; 128

Aleshkovsky, Yuz **CLC 44**
See also Aleshkovsky, Joseph

Alexander, Lloyd (Chudley) 1924- **CLC 35**
See also AAYA 1; CA 1-4R; CANR 1, 24, 38, 55;
CLR 1, 5; DLB 52; JRDA; MAICYA; MTCW;
SAAS 19; SATA 3, 49, 81

Alexie, Sherman (Joseph, Jr.) 1966- **CLC 96; DAM
MULT**
See also CA 138; DLB 175; NNAL

Alfau, Felipe 1902- **CLC 66**
See also CA 137

Alger, Horatio, Jr. 1832-1899 **NCLC 8**
See also DLB 42; SATA 16

Algren, Nelson 1909-1981 **CLC 4, 10, 33**
See also CA 13-16R; 103; CANR 20; CDALB 1941-
1968; DLB 9; DLBY 81, 82; MTCW

Ali, Ahmed 1910- **CLC 69**
See also CA 25-28R; CANR 15, 34

Alighieri, Dante 1265-1321 **CMLC 3, 18**

Allan, John B.
See Westlake, Donald E(dwin)

Allen, Edward 1948- **CLC 59**

Allen, Paula Gunn 1939- **CLC 84; DAM MULT**
See also CA 112; 143; DLB 175; NNAL

Allen, Roland
See Ayckbourn, Alan

Allen, Sarah A.
See Hopkins, Pauline Elizabeth

Allen, Woody 1935- **CLC 16, 52; DAM POP**
See also AAYA 10; CA 33-36R; CANR 27, 38;
DLB 44; MTCW

Allende, Isabel 1942- **CLC 39, 57, 97; DAM MULT,
NOV; HLC**
See also AAYA 18; CA 125; 130; CANR 51; DLB
145; HW; INT 130; MTCW

Alleyn, Ellen
See Rossetti, Christina (Georgina)

Allingham, Margery (Louise) 1904-1966 **CLC 19**
See also CA 5-8R; 25-28R; CANR 4; DLB 77;
MTCW

Allingham, William 1824-1889 **NCLC 25**
See also DLB 35

Allison, Dorothy E. 1949- **CLC 78**
See also CA 140

Allston, Washington 1779-1843 **NCLC 2**
See also DLB 1

Almedingen, E. M. **CLC 12**
See also Almedingen, Martha Edith von
See also SATA 3

Almedingen, Martha Edith von 1898-1971
See Almedingen, E. M.
See also CA 1-4R; CANR 1

Almqvist, Carl Jonas Love 1793-1866 **NCLC 42**

Alonso, Damaso 1898-1990 **CLC 14**
See also CA 110; 131; 130; DLB 108; HW

Alov
See Gogol, Nikolai (Vasilyevich)

Alta 1942- **CLC 19**
See also CA 57-60

Alter, Robert B(ernard) 1935- **CLC 34**
See also CA 49-52; CANR 1, 47

Alther, Lisa 1944- **CLC 7, 41**
See also CA 65-68; CANR 12, 30, 51; MTCW

Altman, Robert 1925- **CLC 16**
See also CA 73-76; CANR 43

Alvarez, A(lfred) 1929- **CLC 5, 13**
See also CA 1-4R; CANR 3, 33; DLB 14, 40

Alvarez, Alejandro Rodriguez 1903-1965
See Casona, Alejandro
See also CA 131; 93-96; HW

Alvarez, Julia 1950- **CLC 93**
See also CA 147

Alvaro, Corrado 1896-1956 **TCLC 60**

Amado, Jorge 1912- **CLC 13, 40; DAM MULT, NOV;
HLC**
See also CA 77-80; CANR 35; DLB 113; MTCW

Ambler, Eric 1909- **CLC 4, 6, 9**
See also CA 9-12R; CANR 7, 38; DLB 77; MTCW

Amichai, Yehuda 1924- **CLC 9, 22, 57**
See also CA 85-88; CANR 46; MTCW

Amiel, Henri Frederic 1821-1881 **NCLC 4**

Amis, Kingsley (William) 1922-1995 **CLC 1, 2, 3,
5, 8, 13, 40, 44; DA; DAB; DAC; DAM MST,
NOV**
See also AITN 2; CA 9-12R; 150; CANR 8, 28, 54;
CDBLB 1945-1960; DLB 15, 27, 100, 139; INT
CANR-8; MTCW

Amis, Martin (Louis) 1949- **CLC 4, 9, 38, 62**
See also BEST 90 3; CA 65-68; CANR 8, 27, 54;
DLB 14; INT CANR-27

Ammons, A(rchie) R(andolph) 1926- **CLC 2, 3, 5, 8,
9, 25, 57; DAM POET; PC 16**
See also AITN 1; CA 9-12R; CANR 6, 36, 51; DLB
5, 165; MTCW

Amo, Tauraatua i
See Adams, Henry (Brooks)

Anand, Mulk Raj 1905- **CLC 23, 93; DAM NOV**
See also CA 65-68; CANR 32; MTCW

Anatol
See Schnitzler, Arthur

Anaya, Rudolfo A(lfonso) 1937- **CLC 23; DAM
MULT, NOV; HLC**
See also AAYA 20; CA 45-48; CAAS 4; CANR 1,
32, 51; DLB 82; HW 1; MTCW

Andersen, Hans Christian 1805-1875 **NCLC 7; DA;
DAB; DAC; DAM MST, POP; SSC 6; WLC**
See also CLR 6; MAICYA; YABC 1

Anderson, C. Farley
See Mencken, H(enry) L(ouis); Nathan, George
Jean

Anderson, Jessica (Margaret) Queale **CLC 37**
See also CA 9-12R; CANR 4

Anderson, Jon (Victor) 1940- **CLC 9; DAM POET**
See also CA 25-28R; CANR 20

Anderson, Lindsay (Gordon) 1923-1994 **CLC 20**
See also CA 125; 128; 146

Anderson, Maxwell 1888-1959 **TCLC 2; DAM DRAM**
See also CA 105; 152; DLB 7

Anderson, Poul (William) 1926- **CLC 15**
See also AAYA 5; CA 1-4R; CAAS 2; CANR 2, 15, 34; DLB 8; INT CANR-15; MTCW; SATA 90; SATA-Brief 39

Anderson, Robert (Woodruff) 1917- **CLC 23; DAM DRAM**
See also AITN 1; CA 21-24R; CANR 32; DLB 7

Anderson, Sherwood 1876-1941 **TCLC 1, 10, 24; DA; DAB; DAC; DAM MST, NOV; SSC 1; WLC**
See also CA 104; 121; CDALB 1917-1929; DLB 4, 9, 86; DLBD 1; MTCW

Andier, Pierre
See Desnos, Robert

Andouard
See Giraudoux, (Hippolyte) Jean

Andrade, Carlos Drummond de CLC 18
See also Drummond de Andrade, Carlos

Andrade, Mario de 1893-1945 **TCLC 43**

Andreae, Johann V(alentin) 1586-1654 **LC 32**
See also DLB 164

Andreas-Salome, Lou 1861-1937 **TCLC 56**
See also DLB 66

Andrewes, Lancelot 1555-1626 **LC 5**
See also DLB 151, 172

Andrews, Cicily Fairfield
See West, Rebecca

Andrews, Elton V.
See Pohl, Frederik

Andreyev, Leonid (Nikolaevich) 1871-1919 **TCLC 3**
See also CA 104

Andric, Ivo 1892-1975 **CLC 8**
See also CA 81-84; 57-60; CANR 43; DLB 147; MTCW

Angelique, Pierre
See Bataille, Georges

Angell, Roger 1920- **CLC 26**
See also CA 57-60; CANR 13, 44; DLB 171

Angelou, Maya 1928- **CLC 12, 35, 64, 77; BLC; DA; DAB; DAC; DAM MST, MULT, POET, POP**
See also AAYA 7, 20; BW 2; CA 65-68; CANR 19, 42; DLB 38; MTCW; SATA 49

Annensky, Innokenty (Fyodorovich) 1856-1909 **TCLC 14**
See also CA 110; 155

Annunzio, Gabriele d'
See D'Annunzio, Gabriele

Anon, Charles Robert
See Pessoa, Fernando (Antonio Nogueira)

Anouilh, Jean (Marie Lucien Pierre) 1910-1987 **CLC 1, 3, 8, 13, 40, 50; DAM DRAM**
See also CA 17-20R; 123; CANR 32; MTCW

Anthony, Florence
See Ai

Anthony, John
See Ciardi, John (Anthony)

Anthony, Peter
See Shaffer, Anthony (Joshua); Shaffer, Peter (Levin)

Anthony, Piers 1934- **CLC 35; DAM POP**
See also AAYA 11; CA 21-24R; CANR 28, 56; DLB 8; MTCW; SAAS 22; SATA 84

Antoine, Marc
See Proust, (Valentin-Louis-George-Eugene-) Marcel

Antoninus, Brother
See Everson, William (Oliver)

Antonioni, Michelangelo 1912- **CLC 20**
See also CA 73-76; CANR 45

Antschel, Paul 1920-1970
See Celan, Paul
See also CA 85-88; CANR 33; MTCW

Anwar, Chairil 1922-1949 **TCLC 22**
See also CA 121

Apollinaire, Guillaume 1880-1918 **TCLC 3, 8, 51; DAM POET; PC 7**
See also Kostrowitzki, Wilhelm Apollinaris de
See also CA 152

Appelfeld, Aharon 1932- **CLC 23, 47**
See also CA 112; 133

Apple, Max (Isaac) 1941- **CLC 9, 33**
See also CA 81-84; CANR 19, 54; DLB 130

Appleman, Philip (Dean) 1926- **CLC 51**
See also CA 13-16R; CAAS 18; CANR 6, 29, 56

Appleton, Lawrence
See Lovecraft, H(oward) P(hillips)

Apteryx
See Eliot, T(homas) S(tearns)

Apuleius, (Lucius Madaurensis) 125(?)-175(?) **CMLC 1**

Aquin, Hubert 1929-1977 **CLC 15**
See also CA 105; DLB 53

Aragon, Louis 1897-1982 **CLC 3, 22; DAM NOV, POET**
See also CA 69-72; 108; CANR 28; DLB 72; MTCW

Arany, Janos 1817-1882 **NCLC 34**

Arbuthnot, John 1667-1735 **LC 1**
See also DLB 101

Archer, Herbert Winslow
See Mencken, H(enry) L(ouis)

Archer, Jeffrey (Howard) 1940- **CLC 28; DAM POP**
See also AAYA 16; BEST 89 3; CA 77-80; CANR 22, 52; INT CANR-22

Archer, Jules 1915- **CLC 12**
See also CA 9-12R; CANR 6; SAAS 5; SATA 4, 85

Archer, Lee
See Ellison, Harlan (Jay)

Arden, John 1930- **CLC 6, 13, 15; DAM DRAM**
See also CA 13-16R; CAAS 4; CANR 31; DLB 13; MTCW

Arenas, Reinaldo 1943-1990 **CLC 41; DAM MULT; HLC**
See also CA 124; 128; 133; DLB 145; HW

Arendt, Hannah 1906-1975 **CLC 66, 98**
See also CA 17-20R; 61-64; CANR 26; MTCW

Aretino, Pietro 1492-1556 **LC 12**

Arghezi, Tudor CLC 80
See also Theodorescu, Ion N.

Arguedas, Jose Maria 1911-1969 **CLC 10, 18**
See also CA 89-92; DLB 113; HW

Argueta, Manlio 1936- **CLC 31**
See also CA 131; DLB 145; HW

Ariosto, Ludovico 1474-1533 **LC 6**

Aristides
See Epstein, Joseph

Aristophanes 450B.C.-385B.C. **CMLC 4; DA; DAB; DAC; DAM DRAM, MST; DC 2**
See also DLB 176

Arlt, Roberto (Godofredo Christophersen) 1900-1942 **TCLC 29; DAM MULT; HLC**
See also CA 123; 131; HW

Armah, Ayi Kwei 1939- **CLC 5, 33; BLC; DAM MULT, POET**
See also BW 1; CA 61-64; CANR 21; DLB 117; MTCW

Armatrading, Joan 1950- **CLC 17**
See also CA 114

Arnette, Robert
See Silverberg, Robert

Arnim, Achim von (Ludwig Joachim von Arnim) 1781-1831 **NCLC 5**
See also DLB 90

Arnim, Bettina von 1785-1859 **NCLC 38**
See also DLB 90

Arnold, Matthew 1822-1888 **NCLC 6, 29; DA; DAB; DAC; DAM MST, POET; PC 5; WLC**
See also CDBLB 1832-1890; DLB 32, 57

Arnold, Thomas 1795-1842 **NCLC 18**
See also DLB 55

Arnow, Harriette (Louisa) Simpson 1908-1986 **CLC 2, 7, 18**
See also CA 9-12R; 118; CANR 14; DLB 6; MTCW; SATA 42; SATA-Obit 47

Arp, Hans
See Arp, Jean

Arp, Jean 1887-1966 **CLC 5**
See also CA 81-84; 25-28R; CANR 42

Arrabal
See Arrabal, Fernando

Arrabal, Fernando 1932- **CLC 2, 9, 18, 58**
See also CA 9-12R; CANR 15

Arrick, Fran CLC 30
See also Gaberman, Judie Angell

Artaud, Antonin (Marie Joseph) 1896-1948 **TCLC 3, 36; DAM DRAM**
See also CA 104; 149

Arthur, Ruth M(abel) 1905-1979 **CLC 12**
See also CA 9-12R; 85-88; CANR 4; SATA 7, 26

Artsybashev, Mikhail (Petrovich) 1878-1927 **TCLC 31**

Arundel, Honor (Morfydd) 1919-1973 **CLC 17**
See also CA 21-22; 41-44R; CAP 2; CLR 35; SATA 4; SATA-Obit 24

Arzner, Dorothy 1897-1979 **CLC 98**

Asch, Sholem 1880-1957 **TCLC 3**
See also CA 105

Ash, Shalom
See Asch, Sholem

Ashbery, John (Lawrence) 1927- **CLC 2, 3, 4, 6, 9, 13, 15, 25, 41, 77; DAM POET**
See also CA 5-8R; CANR 9, 37; DLB 5, 165; DLBY 81; INT CANR-9; MTCW

Ashdown, Clifford
See Freeman, R(ichard) Austin

Ashe, Gordon
See Creasey, John

Ashton-Warner, Sylvia (Constance) 1908-1984 **CLC 19**
See also CA 69-72; 112; CANR 29; MTCW

Asimov, Isaac 1920-1992 **CLC 1, 3, 9, 19, 26, 76, 92; DAM POP**
See also AAYA 13; BEST 90 2; CA 1-4R; 137; CANR 2, 19, 36; CLR 12; DLB 8; DLBY 92; INT CANR-19; JRDA; MAICYA; MTCW; SATA 1, 26, 74

Assis, Joaquim Maria Machado de
See Machado de Assis, Joaquim Maria

Astley, Thea (Beatrice May) 1925- **CLC 41**
See also CA 65-68; CANR 11, 43

Aston, James
See White, T(erence) H(anbury)

Asturias, Miguel Angel 1899-1974 **CLC 3, 8, 13; DAM MULT, NOV; HLC**
See also CA 25-28; 49-52; CANR 32; CAP 2; DLB 113; HW; MTCW

Atares, Carlos Saura
See Saura (Atares), Carlos

Atheling, William
See Pound, Ezra (Weston Loomis)

Atheling, William, Jr.
See Blish, James (Benjamin)

Atherton, Gertrude (Franklin Horn) 1857-1948 **TCLC 2**
See also CA 104; 155; DLB 9, 78

Atherton, Lucius
See Masters, Edgar Lee

Atkins, Jack
See Harris, Mark

Atkinson, Kate CLC 99

Attaway, William (Alexander) 1911-1986 **CLC 92; BLC; DAM MULT**
See also BW 2; CA 143; DLB 76

Atticus
See Fleming, Ian (Lancaster)

Atwood, Margaret (Eleanor) 1939- **CLC 2, 3, 4, 8, 13, 15, 25, 44, 84; DA; DAB; DAC; DAM MST, NOV; POET; PC 8; SSC 2; WLC**
See also AAYA 12; BEST 89 2; CA 49-52; CANR 3, 24, 33; DLB 53; INT CANR-24; MTCW; SATA 50

Aubigny, Pierre d'
See Mencken, H(enry) L(ouis)

Aubin, Penelope 1685-1731(?) **LC 9**
See also DLB 39

Auchincloss, Louis (Stanton) 1917- **CLC 4, 6, 9, 18, 45; DAM NOV; SSC 22**
See also CA 1-4R; CANR 6, 29, 55; DLB 2; DLBY 80; INT CANR-29; MTCW

Auden, W(ystan) H(ugh) 1907-1973 **CLC 1, 2, 3, 4, 6, 9, 11, 14, 43; DA; DAB; DAC; DAM DRAM, MST, POET; PC 1; WLC**
See also AAYA 18; CA 9-12R; 45-48; CANR 5; CDBLB 1914-1945; DLB 10, 20; MTCW

Audiberti, Jacques 1900-1965 **CLC 38; DAM DRAM**
See also CA 25-28R

Audubon, John James 1785-1851 **NCLC 47**

Auel, Jean M(arie) 1936- **CLC 31; DAM POP**
See also AAYA 7; BEST 90 4; CA 103; CANR 21; INT CANR-21; SATA 91

Auerbach, Erich 1892-1957 **TCLC 43**
See also CA 118; 155

Augier, Emile 1820-1889 **NCLC 31**

August, John
See De Voto, Bernard (Augustine)

Augustine, St. 354-430 **CMLC 6; DAB**

Aurelius
See Bourne, Randolph S(illiman)

Aurobindo, Sri 1872-1950 **TCLC 63**

Austen, Jane 1775-1817 **NCLC 1, 13, 19, 33, 51; DA; DAB; DAC; DAM MST, NOV; WLC**
See also AAYA 19; CDBLB 1789-1832; DLB 116

Auster, Paul 1947- **CLC 47**
See also CA 69-72; CANR 23, 52

Austin, Frank
See Faust, Frederick (Schiller)

Austin, Mary (Hunter) 1868-1934 **TCLC 25**
See also CA 109; DLB 9, 78

Autran Dourado, Waldomiro
See Dourado, (Waldomiro Freitas) Autran

Averroes 1126-1198 **CMLC 7**
See also DLB 115

Avicenna 980-1037 **CMLC 16**
See also DLB 115

Avison, Margaret 1918- **CLC 2, 4, 97; DAC; DAM POET**
See also CA 17-20R; DLB 53; MTCW

Axton, David
See Koontz, Dean R(ay)

Ayckbourn, Alan 1939- **CLC 5, 8, 18, 33, 74; DAB; DAM DRAM**
See also CA 21-24R; CANR 31; DLB 13; MTCW

Aydy, Catherine
See Tennant, Emma (Christina)

Ayme, Marcel (Andre) 1902-1967 **CLC 11**
See also CA 89-92; CLR 25; DLB 72; SATA 91

Ayrton, Michael 1921-1975 **CLC 7**
See also CA 5-8R; 61-64; CANR 9, 21

Azorin CLC 11
See also Martinez Ruiz, Jose

Azuela, Mariano 1873-1952 **TCLC 3; DAM MULT; HLC**
See also CA 104; 131; HW; MTCW

Baastad, Babbis Friis
See Friis-Baastad, Babbis Ellinor

Bab
See Gilbert, W(illiam) S(chwenck)

Babbis, Eleanor
See Friis-Baastad, Babbis Ellinor

Babel, Isaac
See Babel, Isaak (Emmanuilovich)

Babel, Isaak (Emmanuilovich) 1894-1941(?) **TCLC 2, 13; SSC 16**
See also CA 104; 155

Babits, Mihaly 1883-1941 **TCLC 14**

See also CA 114

Babur 1483-1530 **LC 18**

Bacchelli, Riccardo 1891-1985 **CLC 19**
See also CA 29-32R; 117

Bach, Richard (David) 1936- **CLC 14; DAM NOV, POP**
See also AITN 1; BEST 89 2; CA 9-12R; CANR 18; MTCW; SATA 13

Bachman, Richard
See King, Stephen (Edwin)

Bachmann, Ingeborg 1926-1973 **CLC 69**
See also CA 93-96; 45-48; DLB 85

Bacon, Francis 1561-1626 **LC 18, 32**
See also CDBLB Before 1660; DLB 151

Bacon, Roger 1214(?)-1292 **CMLC 14**
See also DLB 115

Bacovia, George TCLC 24
See also Vasiliu, Gheorghe

Badanes, Jerome 1937- **CLC 59**

Bagehot, Walter 1826-1877 **NCLC 10**
See also DLB 55

Bagnold, Enid 1889-1981 **CLC 25; DAM DRAM**
See also CA 5-8R; 103; CANR 5, 40; DLB 13, 160; MAICYA; SATA 1, 25

Bagritsky, Eduard 1895-1934 **TCLC 60**

Bagrjana, Elisaveta
See Belcheva, Elisaveta

Bagryana, Elisaveta CLC 10
See also Belcheva, Elisaveta
See also DLB 147

Bailey, Paul 1937- **CLC 45**
See also CA 21-24R; CANR 16; DLB 14

Baillie, Joanna 1762-1851 **NCLC 2**
See also DLB 93

Bainbridge, Beryl (Margaret) 1933- **CLC 4, 5, 8, 10, 14, 18, 22, 62; DAM NOV**
See also CA 21-24R; CANR 24, 55; DLB 14; MTCW

Baker, Elliott 1922- **CLC 8**
See also CA 45-48; CANR 2

Baker, Jean H. TCLC 3, 10
See also Russell, George William

Baker, Nicholson 1957- **CLC 61; DAM POP**
See also CA 135

Baker, Ray Stannard 1870-1946 **TCLC 47**
See also CA 118

Baker, Russell (Wayne) 1925- **CLC 31**
See also BEST 89 4; CA 57-60; CANR 11, 41; MTCW

Bakhtin, M.

See Bakhtin, Mikhail Mikhailovich

Bakhtin, M. M.
See Bakhtin, Mikhail Mikhailovich

Bakhtin, Mikhail
See Bakhtin, Mikhail Mikhailovich

Bakhtin, Mikhail Mikhailovich 1895-1975 **CLC 83**
See also CA 128; 113

Bakshi, Ralph 1938(?)- **CLC 26**
See also CA 112; 138

Bakunin, Mikhail (Alexandrovich) 1814-1876 **NCLC 25, 58**

Baldwin, James (Arthur) 1924-1987 **CLC 1, 2, 3, 4, 5, 8, 13, 15, 17, 42, 50, 67, 90; BLC; DA; DAB; DAC; DAM MST, MULT, NOV, POP; DC 1; SSC 10; WLC**
See also AAYA 4; BW 1; CA 1-4R; 124; CABS 1; CANR 3, 24; CDALB 1941-1968; DLB 2, 7, 33; DLBY 87; MTCW; SATA 9; SATA-Obit 54

Ballard, J(ames) G(raham) 1930- **CLC 3, 6, 14, 36; DAM NOV, POP; SSC 1**
See also AAYA 3; CA 5-8R; CANR 15, 39; DLB 14; MTCW

Balmont, Konstantin (Dmitriyevich) 1867-1943 **TCLC 11**
See also CA 109; 155

Balzac, Honore de 1799-1850 **NCLC 5, 35, 53; DA; DAB; DAC; DAM MST, NOV; SSC 5; WLC**
See also DLB 119

Bambara, Toni Cade 1939-1995 **CLC 19, 88; BLC; DA; DAC; DAM MST, MULT**
See also AAYA 5; BW 2; CA 29-32R; 150; CANR 24, 49; DLB 38; MTCW

Bamdad, A.
See Shamlu, Ahmad

Banat, D. R.
See Bradbury, Ray (Douglas)

Bancroft, Laura
See Baum, L(yman) Frank

Banim, John 1798-1842 **NCLC 13**
See also DLB 116, 158, 159

Banim, Michael 1796-1874 **NCLC 13**
See also DLB 158, 159

Banjo, The
See Paterson, A(ndrew) B(arton)

Banks, Iain
See Banks, Iain M(enzies)

Banks, Iain M(enzies) 1954- **CLC 34**
See also CA 123; 128; INT 128

Banks, Lynne Reid CLC 23
See also Reid Banks, Lynne
See also AAYA 6

Banks, Russell 1940- **CLC 37, 72**
See also CA 65-68; CAAS 15; CANR 19, 52; DLB

130

Banville, John 1945- **CLC 46**
See also CA 117; 128; DLB 14; INT 128

Banville, Theodore (Faullain) de 1832-1891 **NCLC 9**

Baraka, Amiri 1934- **CLC 1, 2, 3, 5, 10, 14, 33; BLC; DA; DAC; DAM MST, MULT, POET, POP; DC 6; PC 4**
See also Jones, LeRoi
See also BW 2; CA 21-24R; CABS 3; CANR 27, 38; CDALB 1941-1968; DLB 5, 7, 16, 38; DLBD 8; MTCW

Barbauld, Anna Laetitia 1743-1825 **NCLC 50**
See also DLB 107, 109, 142, 158

Barbellion, W. N. P. TCLC 24
See also Cummings, Bruce F(rederick)

Barbera, Jack (Vincent) 1945- **CLC 44**
See also CA 110; CANR 45

Barbey d'Aurevilly, Jules Amedee 1808-1889 **NCLC 1; SSC 17**
See also DLB 119

Barbusse, Henri 1873-1935 **TCLC 5**
See also CA 105; 154; DLB 65

Barclay, Bill
See Moorcock, Michael (John)

Barclay, William Ewert
See Moorcock, Michael (John)

Barea, Arturo 1897-1957 **TCLC 14**
See also CA 111

Barfoot, Joan 1946- **CLC 18**
See also CA 105

Baring, Maurice 1874-1945 **TCLC 8**
See also CA 105; DLB 34

Barker, Clive 1952- **CLC 52; DAM POP**
See also AAYA 10; BEST 90 3; CA 121; 129; INT 129; MTCW

Barker, George Granville 1913-1991 **CLC 8, 48; DAM POET**
See also CA 9-12R; 135; CANR 7, 38; DLB 20; MTCW

Barker, Harley Granville
See Granville-Barker, Harley
See also DLB 10

Barker, Howard 1946- **CLC 37**
See also CA 102; DLB 13

Barker, Pat(ricia) 1943- **CLC 32, 94**
See also CA 117; 122; CANR 50; INT 122

Barlow, Joel 1754-1812 **NCLC 23**
See also DLB 37

Barnard, Mary (Ethel) 1909- **CLC 48**
See also CA 21-22; CAP 2

Barnes, Djuna 1892-1982 **CLC 3, 4, 8, 11, 29; SSC**

3
See also CA 9-12R; 107; CANR 16, 55; DLB 4, 9,
45; MTCW

Barnes, Julian (Patrick) 1946- **CLC 42; DAB**
See also CA 102; CANR 19, 54; DLBY 93

Barnes, Peter 1931- **CLC 5, 56**
See also CA 65-68; CAAS 12; CANR 33, 34; DLB
13; MTCW

Baroja (y Nessi), Pio 1872-1956 **TCLC 8; HLC**
See also CA 104

Baron, David
See Pinter, Harold

Baron Corvo
See Rolfe, Frederick (William Serafino Austin
Lewis Mary)

Barondess, Sue K(aufman) 1926-1977 **CLC 8**
See also Kaufman, Sue
See also CA 1-4R; 69-72; CANR 1

Baron de Teive
See Pessoa, Fernando (Antonio Nogueira)

Barres, Maurice 1862-1923 **TCLC 47**
See also DLB 123

Barreto, Afonso Henrique de Lima
See Lima Barreto, Afonso Henrique de

Barrett, (Roger) Syd 1946- **CLC 35**

Barrett, William (Christopher) 1913-1992 **CLC 27**
See also CA 13-16R; 139; CANR 11; INT CANR-
11

Barrie, J(ames) M(atthew) 1860-1937 **TCLC 2;
DAB; DAM DRAM**
See also CA 104; 136; CDBLB 1890-1914; CLR 16;
DLB 10, 141, 156; MAICYA; YABC 1

Barrington, Michael
See Moorcock, Michael (John)

Barrol, Grady
See Bograd, Larry

Barry, Mike
See Malzberg, Barry N(athaniel)

Barry, Philip 1896-1949 **TCLC 11**
See also CA 109; DLB 7

Bart, Andre Schwarz
See Schwarz-Bart, Andre

Barth, John (Simmons) 1930- **CLC 1, 2, 3, 5, 7, 9,
10, 14, 27, 51, 89; DAM NOV; SSC 10**
See also AITN 1, 2; CA 1-4R; CABS 1; CANR 5,
23, 49; DLB 2; MTCW

Barthelme, Donald 1931-1989 **CLC 1, 2, 3, 5, 6, 8,
13, 23, 46, 59; DAM NOV; SSC 2**
See also CA 21-24R; 129; CANR 20; DLB 2; DLBY
80, 89; MTCW; SATA 7; SATA-Obit 62

Barthelme, Frederick 1943- **CLC 36**
See also CA 114; 122; DLBY 85; INT 122

Barthes, Roland (Gerard) 1915-1980 **CLC 24, 83**
See also CA 130; 97-100; MTCW

Barzun, Jacques (Martin) 1907- **CLC 51**
See also CA 61-64; CANR 22

Bashevis, Isaac
See Singer, Isaac Bashevis

Bashkirtseff, Marie 1859-1884 **NCLC 27**

Basho
See Matsuo Basho

Bass, Kingsley B., Jr.
See Bullins, Ed

Bass, Rick 1958- **CLC 79**
See also CA 126; CANR 53

Bassani, Giorgio 1916- **CLC 9**
See also CA 65-68; CANR 33; DLB 128, 177;
MTCW

Bastos, Augusto (Antonio) Roa
See Roa Bastos, Augusto (Antonio)

Bataille, Georges 1897-1962 **CLC 29**
See also CA 101; 89-92

Bates, H(erbert) E(rnest) 1905-1974 **CLC 46; DAB;
DAM POP; SSC 10**
See also CA 93-96; 45-48; CANR 34; DLB 162;
MTCW

Bauchart
See Camus, Albert

Baudelaire, Charles 1821-1867 **NCLC 6, 29, 55;
DA; DAB; DAC; DAM MST, POET; PC 1; SSC
18; WLC**

Baudrillard, Jean 1929- **CLC 60**

Baum, L(yman) Frank 1856-1919 **TCLC 7**
See also CA 108; 133; CLR 15; DLB 22; JRDA;
MAICYA; MTCW; SATA 18

Baum, Louis F.
See Baum, L(yman) Frank

Baumbach, Jonathan 1933- **CLC 6, 23**
See also CA 13-16R; CAAS 5; CANR 12; DLBY
80; INT CANR-12; MTCW

Bausch, Richard (Carl) 1945- **CLC 51**
See also CA 101; CAAS 14; CANR 43; DLB 130

Baxter, Charles 1947- **CLC 45, 78; DAM POP**
See also CA 57-60; CANR 40; DLB 130

Baxter, George Owen
See Faust, Frederick (Schiller)

Baxter, James K(eir) 1926-1972 **CLC 14**
See also CA 77-80

Baxter, John
See Hunt, E(verette) Howard, (Jr.)

Bayer, Sylvia
See Glassco, John

Baynton, Barbara 1857-1929 **TCLC 57**

Beagle, Peter S(oyer) 1939- **CLC 7**
See also CA 9-12R; CANR 4, 51; DLBY 80; INT
CANR-4; SATA 60

Bean, Normal
See Burroughs, Edgar Rice

Beard, Charles A(ustin) 1874-1948 **TCLC 15**
See also CA 115; DLB 17; SATA 18

Beardsley, Aubrey 1872-1898 **NCLC 6**

Beattie, Ann 1947- **CLC 8, 13, 18, 40, 63; DAM
NOV, POP; SSC 11**
See also BEST 90 2; CA 81-84; CANR 53; DLBY
82; MTCW

Beattie, James 1735-1803 **NCLC 25**
See also DLB 109

Beauchamp, Kathleen Mansfield 1888-1923
See Mansfield, Katherine
See also CA 104; 134; DA; DAC; DAM MST

Beaumarchais, Pierre-Augustin Caron de 1732-
1799 **DC 4**
See also DAM DRAM

Beaumont, Francis 1584(?)-1616 **LC 33; DC 6**
See also CDBLB Before 1660; DLB 58, 121

**Beauvoir, Simone (Lucie Ernestine Marie
Bertrand) de** 1908-1986 **CLC 1, 2, 4, 8, 14, 31,
44, 50, 71; DA; DAB; DAC; DAM MST, NOV;
WLC**
See also CA 9-12R; 118; CANR 28; DLB 72; DLBY
86; MTCW

Becker, Carl 1873-1945 **TCLC 63**
See also DLB 17 .

Becker, Jurek 1937- **CLC 7, 19**
See also CA 85-88; DLB 75

Becker, Walter 1950- **CLC 26**

Beckett, Samuel (Barclay) 1906-1989 **CLC 1, 2, 3,
4, 6, 9, 10, 11, 14, 18, 29, 57, 59, 83; DA;
DAB; DAC; DAM DRAM, MST, NOV; SSC
16; WLC**
See also CA 5-8R; 130; CANR 33; CDBLB 1945-
1960; DLB 13, 15; DLBY 90; MTCW

Beckford, William 1760-1844 **NCLC 16**
See also DLB 39

Beckman, Gunnel 1910- **CLC 26**
See also CA 33-36R; CANR 15; CLR 25; MAICYA;
SAAS 9; SATA 6

Becque, Henri 1837-1899 **NCLC 3**

Beddoes, Thomas Lovell 1803-1849 **NCLC 3**
See also DLB 96

Bede c. 673-735 **CMLC 20**
See also DLB 146

Bedford, Donald F.
See Fearing, Kenneth (Flexner)

Beecher, Catharine Esther 1800-1878 **NCLC 30**
 See also DLB 1

Beecher, John 1904-1980 **CLC 6**
 See also AITN 1; CA 5-8R; 105; CANR 8

Beer, Johann 1655-1700 **LC 5**
 See also DLB 168

Beer, Patricia 1924- **CLC 58**
 See also CA 61-64; CANR 13, 46; DLB 40

Beerbohm, Max
 See Beerbohm, (Henry) Max(imilian)

Beerbohm, (Henry) Max(imilian) 1872-1956 **TCLC 1, 24**
 See also CA 104; 154; DLB 34, 100

Beer-Hofmann, Richard 1866-1945 **TCLC 60**
 See also DLB 81

Begiebing, Robert J(ohn) 1946- **CLC 70**
 See also CA 122; CANR 40

Behan, Brendan 1923-1964 **CLC 1, 8, 11, 15, 79; DAM DRAM**
 See also CA 73-76; CANR 33; CDBLB 1945-1960; DLB 13; MTCW

Behn, Aphra 1640(?)-1689 **LC 1, 30; DA; DAB; DAC; DAM DRAM, MST, NOV, POET; DC 4; PC 13; WLC**
 See also DLB 39, 80, 131

Behrman, S(amuel) N(athaniel) 1893-1973 **CLC 40**
 See also CA 13-16; 45-48; CAP 1; DLB 7, 44

Belasco, David 1853-1931 **TCLC 3**
 See also CA 104; DLB 7

Belcheva, Elisaveta 1893- **CLC 10**
 See also Bagryana, Elisaveta

Beldone, Phil "Cheech"
 See Ellison, Harlan (Jay)

Beleno
 See Azuela, Mariano

Belinski, Vissarion Grigoryevich 1811-1848 **NCLC 5**

Belitt, Ben 1911- **CLC 22**
 See also CA 13-16R; CAAS 4; CANR 7; DLB 5

Bell, Gertrude 1868-1926 **TCLC 67**
 See also DLB 174

Bell, James Madison 1826-1902 **TCLC 43; BLC; DAM MULT**
 See also BW 1; CA 122; 124; DLB 50

Bell, Madison Smartt 1957- **CLC 41**
 See also CA 111; CANR 28, 54

Bell, Marvin (Hartley) 1937- **CLC 8, 31; DAM POET**
 See also CA 21-24R; CAAS 14; DLB 5; MTCW

Bell, W. L. D.
 See Mencken, H(enry) L(ouis)

Bellamy, Atwood C.

 See Mencken, H(enry) L(ouis)

Bellamy, Edward 1850-1898 **NCLC 4**
 See also DLB 12

Bellin, Edward J.
 See Kuttner, Henry

Belloc, (Joseph) Hilaire (Pierre Sebastien Rene Swanton) 1870-1953 **TCLC 7, 18; DAM POET**
 See also CA 106; 152; DLB 19, 100, 141, 174; YABC 1

Belloc, Joseph Peter Rene Hilaire
 See Belloc, (Joseph) Hilaire (Pierre Sebastien Rene Swanton)

Belloc, Joseph Pierre Hilaire
 See Belloc, (Joseph) Hilaire (Pierre Sebastien Rene Swanton)

Belloc, M. A.
 See Lowndes, Marie Adelaide (Belloc)

Bellow, Saul 1915- **CLC 1, 2, 3, 6, 8, 10, 13, 15, 25, 33, 34, 63, 79; DA; DAB; DAC; DAM MST, NOV, POP; SSC 14; WLC**
 See also AITN 2; BEST 89 3; CA 5-8R; CABS 1; CANR 29, 53; CDALB 1941-1968; DLB 2, 28; DLBD 3; DLBY 82; MTCW

Belser, Reimond Karel Maria de 1929-
 See Ruyslinck, Ward
 See also CA 152

Bely, Andrey **TCLC 7; PC 11**
 See also Bugayev, Boris Nikolayevich

Benary, Margot
 See Benary-Isbert, Margot

Benary-Isbert, Margot 1889-1979 **CLC 12**
 See also CA 5-8R; 89-92; CANR 4; CLR 12; MAICYA; SATA 2; SATA-Obit 21

Benavente (y Martinez), Jacinto 1866-1954 **TCLC 3; DAM DRAM, MULT**
 See also CA 106; 131; HW; MTCW

Benchley, Peter (Bradford) 1940- **CLC 4, 8; DAM NOV, POP**
 See also AAYA 14; AITN 2; CA 17-20R; CANR 12, 35; MTCW; SATA 3, 89

Benchley, Robert (Charles) 1889-1945 **TCLC 1, 55**
 See also CA 105; 153; DLB 11

Benda, Julien 1867-1956 **TCLC 60**
 See also CA 120; 154

Benedict, Ruth 1887-1948 **TCLC 60**

Benedikt, Michael 1935- **CLC 4, 14**
 See also CA 13-16R; CANR 7; DLB 5

Benet, Juan 1927- **CLC 28**
 See also CA 143

Benet, Stephen Vincent 1898-1943 **TCLC 7; DAM POET; SSC 10**
 See also CA 104; 152; DLB 4, 48, 102; YABC 1

Benet, William Rose 1886-1950 **TCLC 28; DAM POET**
 See also CA 118; 152; DLB 45

Benford, Gregory (Albert) 1941- **CLC 52**
 See also CA 69-72; CANR 12, 24, 49; DLBY 82

Bengtsson, Frans (Gunnar) 1894-1954 **TCLC 48**

Benjamin, David
 See Slavitt, David R(ytman)

Benjamin, Lois
 See Gould, Lois

Benjamin, Walter 1892-1940 **TCLC 39**

Benn, Gottfried 1886-1956 **TCLC 3**
 See also CA 106; 153; DLB 56

Bennett, Alan 1934- **CLC 45, 77; DAB; DAM MST**
 See also CA 103; CANR 35, 55; MTCW

Bennett, (Enoch) Arnold 1867-1931 **TCLC 5, 20**
 See also CA 106; 155; CDBLB 1890-1914; DLB 10, 34, 98, 135

Bennett, Elizabeth
 See Mitchell, Margaret (Munnerlyn)

Bennett, George Harold 1930-
 See Bennett, Hal
 See also BW 1; CA 97-100

Bennett, Hal **CLC 5**
 See also Bennett, George Harold
 See also DLB 33

Bennett, Jay 1912- **CLC 35**
 See also AAYA 10; CA 69-72; CANR 11, 42; JRDA; SAAS 4; SATA 41, 87; SATA-Brief 27

Bennett, Louise (Simone) 1919- **CLC 28; BLC; DAM MULT**
 See also BW 2; CA 151; DLB 117

Benson, E(dward) F(rederic) 1867-1940 **TCLC 27**
 See also CA 114; DLB 135, 153

Benson, Jackson J. 1930- **CLC 34**
 See also CA 25-28R; DLB 111

Benson, Sally 1900-1972 **CLC 17**
 See also CA 19-20; 37-40R; CAP 1; SATA 1, 35; SATA-Obit 27

Benson, Stella 1892-1933 **TCLC 17**
 See also CA 117; 155; DLB 36, 162

Bentham, Jeremy 1748-1832 **NCLC 38**
 See also DLB 107, 158

Bentley, E(dmund) C(lerihew) 1875-1956 **TCLC 12**
 See also CA 108; DLB 70

Bentley, Eric (Russell) 1916- **CLC 24**
 See also CA 5-8R; CANR 6; INT CANR-6

Beranger, Pierre Jean de 1780-1857 **NCLC 34**

Berdyaev, Nicolas
 See Berdyaev, Nikolai (Aleksandrovich)

Berdyaev, Nikolai (Aleksandrovich) 1874-1948

Blackwood, Caroline 1931-1996 **CLC 6, 9, 100**
See also CA 85-88; 151; CANR 32; DLB 14;
MTCW

Blade, Alexander
See Hamilton, Edmond; Silverberg, Robert

Blaga, Lucian 1895-1961 **CLC 75**

Blair, Eric (Arthur) 1903-1950
See Orwell, George
See also CA 104; 132; DA; DAB; DAC; DAM
MST, NOV; MTCW; SATA 29

Blais, Marie-Claire 1939- **CLC 2, 4, 6, 13, 22;**
DAC; DAM MST
See also CA 21-24R; CAAS 4; CANR 38; DLB 53;
MTCW

Blaise, Clark 1940- **CLC 29**
See also AITN 2; CA 53-56; CAAS 3; CANR 5;
DLB 53

Blake, Nicholas
See Day Lewis, C(ecil)
See also DLB 77

Blake, William 1757-1827 **NCLC 13, 37, 57; DA;**
DAB; DAC; DAM MST, POET; PC 12; WLC
See also CDBLB 1789-1832; DLB 93, 163;
MAICYA; SATA 30

Blake, William J(ames) 1894-1969 **PC 12**
See also CA 5-8R; 25-28R

Blasco Ibanez, Vicente 1867-1928 **TCLC 12; DAM**
NOV
See also CA 110; 131; HW; MTCW

Blatty, William Peter 1928- **CLC 2; DAM POP**
See also CA 5-8R; CANR 9

Bleeck, Oliver
See Thomas, Ross (Elmore)

Blessing, Lee 1949- **CLC 54**

Blish, James (Benjamin) 1921-1975 **CLC 14**
See also CA 1-4R; 57-60; CANR 3; DLB 8; MTCW;
SATA 66

Bliss, Reginald
See Wells, H(erbert) G(eorge)

Blixen, Karen (Christentze Dinesen) 1885-1962
See Dinesen, Isak
See also CA 25-28; CANR 22, 50; CAP 2; MTCW;
SATA 44

Bloch, Robert (Albert) 1917-1994 **CLC 33**
See also CA 5-8R; 146; CAAS 20; CANR 5; DLB
44; INT CANR-5; SATA 12; SATA-Obit 82

Blok, Alexander (Alexandrovich) 1880-1921 **TCLC**
5
See also CA 104

Blom, Jan
See Breytenbach, Breyten

Bloom, Harold 1930- **CLC 24**
See also CA 13-16R; CANR 39; DLB 67

Bloomfield, Aurelius
See Bourne, Randolph S(illiman)

Blount, Roy (Alton), Jr. 1941- **CLC 38**
See also CA 53-56; CANR 10, 28; INT CANR-28;
MTCW

Bloy, Leon 1846-1917 **TCLC 22**
See also CA 121; DLB 123

Blume, Judy (Sussman) 1938- **CLC 12, 30; DAM**
NOV, POP
See also AAYA 3; CA 29-32R; CANR 13, 37; CLR
2, 15; DLB 52; JRDA; MAICYA; MTCW; SATA
2, 31, 79

Blunden, Edmund (Charles) 1896-1974 **CLC 2, 56**
See also CA 17-18; 45-48; CANR 54; CAP 2; DLB
20, 100, 155; MTCW

Bly, Robert (Elwood) 1926- **CLC 1, 2, 5, 10, 15, 38;**
DAM POET
See also CA 5-8R; CANR 41; DLB 5; MTCW

Boas, Franz 1858-1942 **TCLC 56**
See also CA 115

Bobette
See Simenon, Georges (Jacques Christian)

Boccaccio, Giovanni 1313-1375 **CMLC 13; SSC 10**

Bochco, Steven 1943- **CLC 35**
See also AAYA 11; CA 124; 138

Bodenheim, Maxwell 1892-1954 **TCLC 44**
See also CA 110; DLB 9, 45

Bodker, Cecil 1927- **CLC 21**
See also CA 73-76; CANR 13, 44; CLR 23;
MAICYA; SATA 14

Boell, Heinrich (Theodor) 1917-1985 **CLC 2, 3, 6,**
9, 11, 15, 27, 32, 72; DA; DAB; DAC; DAM
MST, NOV; SSC 23; WLC
See also CA 21-24R; 116; CANR 24; DLB 69; DLBY
85; MTCW

Boerne, Alfred
See Doeblin, Alfred

Boethius 480(?)-524(?) **CMLC 15**
See also DLB 115

Bogan, Louise 1897-1970 **CLC 4, 39, 46, 93; DAM**
POET; PC 12
See also CA 73-76; 25-28R; CANR 33; DLB 45,
169; MTCW

Bogarde, Dirk CLC 19
See also Van Den Bogarde, Derek Jules Gaspard
Ulric Niven
See also DLB 14

Bogosian, Eric 1953- **CLC 45**
See also CA 138

Bograd, Larry 1953- **CLC 35**
See also CA 93-96; CANR 57; SAAS 21; SATA
33, 89

Boiardo, Matteo Maria 1441-1494 **LC 6**

Boileau-Despreaux, Nicolas 1636-1711 **LC 3**

Bojer, Johan 1872-1959 **TCLC 64**

Boland, Eavan (Aisling) 1944- **CLC 40, 67; DAM**
POET
See also CA 143; DLB 40

Bolt, Lee
See Faust, Frederick (Schiller)

Bolt, Robert (Oxton) 1924-1995 **CLC 14; DAM**
DRAM
See also CA 17-20R; 147; CANR 35; DLB 13;
MTCW

Bombet, Louis-Alexandre-Cesar
See Stendhal

Bomkauf
See Kaufman, Bob (Garnell)

Bonaventura NCLC 35
See also DLB 90

Bond, Edward 1934- **CLC 4, 6, 13, 23; DAM DRAM**
See also CA 25-28R; CANR 38; DLB 13; MTCW

Bonham, Frank 1914-1989 **CLC 12**
See also AAYA 1; CA 9-12R; CANR 4, 36; JRDA;
MAICYA; SAAS 3; SATA 1, 49; SATA-Obit
62

Bonnefoy, Yves 1923- **CLC 9, 15, 58; DAM MST,**
POET
See also CA 85-88; CANR 33; MTCW

Bontemps, Arna(ud Wendell) 1902-1973 **CLC 1,**
18; BLC; DAM MULT, NOV, POET
See also BW 1; CA 1-4R; 41-44R; CANR 4, 35;
CLR 6; DLB 48, 51; JRDA; MAICYA; MTCW;
SATA 2, 44; SATA-Obit 24

Booth, Martin 1944- **CLC 13**
See also CA 93-96; CAAS 2

Booth, Philip 1925- **CLC 23**
See also CA 5-8R; CANR 5; DLBY 82

Booth, Wayne C(layson) 1921- **CLC 24**
See also CA 1-4R; CAAS 5; CANR 3, 43; DLB 67

Borchert, Wolfgang 1921-1947 **TCLC 5**
See also CA 104; DLB 69, 124

Borel, Petrus 1809-1859 **NCLC 41**

Borges, Jorge Luis 1899-1986 **CLC 1, 2, 3, 4, 6, 8,**
9, 10, 13, 19, 44, 48, 83; DA; DAB; DAC;
DAM MST, MULT; HLC; SSC 4; WLC
See also AAYA 19; CA 21-24R; CANR 19, 33;
DLB 113; DLBY 86; HW; MTCW

Borowski, Tadeusz 1922-1951 **TCLC 9**
See also CA 106; 154

Borrow, George (Henry) 1803-1881 **NCLC 9**
See also DLB 21, 55, 166

Bosman, Herman Charles 1905-1951 **TCLC 49**

Bosschere, Jean de 1878(?)-1953 **TCLC 19**
See also CA 115

22, 90

Bridges, Robert (Seymour) 1844-1930 **TCLC 1; DAM POET**
See also CA 104; 152; CDBLB 1890-1914; DLB 19, 98

Bridie, James TCLC 3
See also Mavor, Osborne Henry
See also DLB 10

Brin, David 1950- **CLC 34**
See also CA 102; CANR 24; INT CANR-24; SATA 65

Brink, Andre (Philippus) 1935- **CLC 18, 36**
See also CA 104; CANR 39; INT 103; MTCW

Brinsmead, H(esba) F(ay) 1922- **CLC 21**
See also CA 21-24R; CANR 10; MAICYA; SAAS 5; SATA 18, 78

Brittain, Vera (Mary) 1893(?)-1970 **CLC 23**
See also CA 13-16; 25-28R; CAP 1; MTCW

Broch, Hermann 1886-1951 **TCLC 20**
See also CA 117; DLB 85, 124

Brock, Rose
See Hansen, Joseph

Brodkey, Harold (Roy) 1930-1996 **CLC 56**
See also CA 111; 151; DLB 130

Brodsky, Iosif Alexandrovich 1940-1996
See Brodsky, Joseph
See also AITN 1; CA 41-44R; 151; CANR 37; DAM POET; MTCW

Brodsky, Joseph 1940-1996 **CLC 4, 6, 13, 36, 100; PC 9**
See also Brodsky, Iosif Alexandrovich

Brodsky, Michael Mark 1948- **CLC 19**
See also CA 102; CANR 18, 41

Bromell, Henry 1947- **CLC 5**
See also CA 53-56; CANR 9

Bromfield, Louis (Brucker) 1896-1956 **TCLC 11**
See also CA 107; 155; DLB 4, 9, 86

Broner, E(sther) M(asserman) 1930- **CLC 19**
See also CA 17-20R; CANR 8, 25; DLB 28

Bronk, William 1918- **CLC 10**
See also CA 89-92; CANR 23; DLB 165

Bronstein, Lev Davidovich
See Trotsky, Leon

Bronte, Anne 1820-1849 **NCLC 4**
See also DLB 21

Bronte, Charlotte 1816-1855 **NCLC 3, 8, 33, 58; DA; DAB; DAC; DAM MST, NOV; WLC**
See also AAYA 17; CDBLB 1832-1890; DLB 21, 159

Bronte, Emily (Jane) 1818-1848 **NCLC 16, 35; DA; DAB; DAC; DAM MST, NOV, POET; PC 8; WLC**
See also AAYA 17; CDBLB 1832-1890; DLB 21, 32

Brooke, Frances 1724-1789 **LC 6**
See also DLB 39, 99

Brooke, Henry 1703(?)-1783 **LC 1**
See also DLB 39

Brooke, Rupert (Chawner) 1887-1915 **TCLC 2, 7; DA; DAB; DAC; DAM MST, POET; WLC**
See also CA 104; 132; CDBLB 1914-1945; DLB 19; MTCW

Brooke-Haven, P.
See Wodehouse, P(elham) G(renville)

Brooke-Rose, Christine 1926- **CLC 40**
See also CA 13-16R; DLB 14

Brookner, Anita 1928- **CLC 32, 34, 51; DAB; DAM POP**
See also CA 114; 120; CANR 37, 56; DLBY 87; MTCW

Brooks, Cleanth 1906-1994 **CLC 24, 86**
See also CA 17-20R; 145; CANR 33, 35; DLB 63; DLBY 94; INT CANR-35; MTCW

Brooks, George
See Baum, L(yman) Frank

Brooks, Gwendolyn 1917- **CLC 1, 2, 4, 5, 15, 49; BLC; DA; DAC; DAM MST, MULT, POET; PC 7; WLC**
See also AAYA 20; AITN 1; BW 2; CA 1-4R; CANR 1, 27, 52; CDALB 1941-1968; CLR 27; DLB 5, 76, 165; MTCW; SATA 6

Brooks, Mel CLC 12
See also Kaminsky, Melvin
See also AAYA 13; DLB 26

Brooks, Peter 1938- **CLC 34**
See also CA 45-48; CANR 1

Brooks, Van Wyck 1886-1963 **CLC 29**
See also CA 1-4R; CANR 6; DLB 45, 63, 103

Brophy, Brigid (Antonia) 1929-1995 **CLC 6, 11, 29**
See also CA 5-8R; 149; CAAS 4; CANR 25, 53; DLB 14; MTCW

Brosman, Catharine Savage 1934- **CLC 9**
See also CA 61-64; CANR 21, 46

Brother Antoninus
See Everson, William (Oliver)

Broughton, T(homas) Alan 1936- **CLC 19**
See also CA 45-48; CANR 2, 23, 48

Broumas, Olga 1949- **CLC 10, 73**
See also CA 85-88; CANR 20

Brown, Alan 1951- **CLC 99**

Brown, Charles Brockden 1771-1810 **NCLC 22**
See also CDALB 1640-1865; DLB 37, 59, 73

Brown, Christy 1932-1981 **CLC 63**
See also CA 105; 104; DLB 14

Brown, Claude 1937- **CLC 30; BLC; DAM MULT**
See also AAYA 7; BW 1; CA 73-76

Brown, Dee (Alexander) 1908- **CLC 18, 47; DAM POP**
See also CA 13-16R; CAAS 6; CANR 11, 45; DLBY 80; MTCW; SATA 5

Brown, George
See Wertmueller, Lina

Brown, George Douglas 1869-1902 **TCLC 28**

Brown, George Mackay 1921-1996 **CLC 5, 48, 100**
See also CA 21-24R; 151; CAAS 6; CANR 12, 37; DLB 14, 27, 139; MTCW; SATA 35

Brown, (William) Larry 1951- **CLC 73**
See also CA 130; 134; INT 133

Brown, Moses
See Barrett, William (Christopher)

Brown, Rita Mae 1944- **CLC 18, 43, 79; DAM NOV, POP**
See also CA 45-48; CANR 2, 11, 35; INT CANR-11; MTCW

Brown, Roderick (Langmere) Haig-
See Haig-Brown, Roderick (Langmere)

Brown, Rosellen 1939- **CLC 32**
See also CA 77-80; CAAS 10; CANR 14, 44

Brown, Sterling Allen 1901-1989 **CLC 1, 23, 59; BLC; DAM MULT, POET**
See also BW 1; CA 85-88; 127; CANR 26; DLB 48, 51, 63; MTCW

Brown, Will
See Ainsworth, William Harrison

Brown, William Wells 1813-1884 **NCLC 2; BLC; DAM MULT; DC 1**
See also DLB 3, 50

Browne, (Clyde) Jackson 1948(?)- **CLC 21**
See also CA 120

Browning, Elizabeth Barrett 1806-1861 **NCLC 1, 16; DA; DAB; DAC; DAM MST, POET; PC 6; WLC**
See also CDBLB 1832-1890; DLB 32

Browning, Robert 1812-1889 **NCLC 19; DA; DAB; DAC; DAM MST, POET; PC 2**
See also CDBLB 1832-1890; DLB 32, 163; YABC 1

Browning, Tod 1882-1962 **CLC 16**
See also CA 141; 117

Brownson, Orestes (Augustus) 1803-1876 **NCLC 50**

Bruccoli, Matthew J(oseph) 1931- **CLC 34**
See also CA 9-12R; CANR 7; DLB 103

Bruce, Lenny CLC 21
See also Schneider, Leonard Alfred

Bruin, John
See Brutus, Dennis

Brulard, Henri
See Stendhal

Brulls, Christian
See Simenon, Georges (Jacques Christian)

Brunner, John (Kilian Houston) 1934-1995 **CLC 8, 10; DAM POP**
See also CA 1-4R; 149; CAAS 8; CANR 2, 37; MTCW

Bruno, Giordano 1548-1600 **LC 27**

Brutus, Dennis 1924- **CLC 43; BLC; DAM MULT, POET**
See also BW 2; CA 49-52; CAAS 14; CANR 2, 27, 42; DLB 117

Bryan, C(ourtlandt) D(ixon) B(arnes) 1936- **CLC 29**
See also CA 73-76; CANR 13; INT CANR-13

Bryan, Michael
See Moore, Brian

Bryant, William Cullen 1794-1878 **NCLC 6, 46; DA; DAB; DAC; DAM MST, POET**
See also CDALB 1640-1865; DLB 3, 43, 59

Bryusov, Valery Yakovlevich 1873-1924 **TCLC 10**
See also CA 107; 155

Buchan, John 1875-1940 **TCLC 41; DAB; DAM POP**
See also CA 108; 145; DLB 34, 70, 156; YABC 2

Buchanan, George 1506-1582 **LC 4**

Buchheim, Lothar-Guenther 1918- **CLC 6**
See also CA 85-88

Buchner, (Karl) Georg 1813-1837 **NCLC 26**

Buchwald, Art(hur) 1925- **CLC 33**
See also AITN 1; CA 5-8R; CANR 21; MTCW; SATA 10

Buck, Pearl S(ydenstricker) 1892-1973 **CLC 7, 11, 18; DA; DAB; DAC; DAM MST, NOV**
See also AITN 1; CA 1-4R; 41-44R; CANR 1, 34; DLB 9, 102; MTCW; SATA 1, 25

Buckler, Ernest 1908-1984 **CLC 13; DAC; DAM MST**
See also CA 11-12; 114; CAP 1; DLB 68; SATA 47

Buckley, Vincent (Thomas) 1925-1988 **CLC 57**
See also CA 101

Buckley, William F(rank), Jr. 1925- **CLC 7, 18, 37; DAM POP**
See also AITN 1; CA 1-4R; CANR 1, 24, 53; DLB 137; DLBY 80; INT CANR-24; MTCW

Buechner, (Carl) Frederick 1926- **CLC 2, 4, 6, 9; DAM NOV**
See also CA 13-16R; CANR 11, 39; DLBY 80; INT CANR-11; MTCW

Buell, John (Edward) 1927- **CLC 10**
See also CA 1-4R; DLB 53

Buero Vallejo, Antonio 1916- **CLC 15, 46**
See also CA 106; CANR 24, 49; HW; MTCW

Bufalino, Gesualdo 1920(?)- **CLC 74**

Bugayev, Boris Nikolayevich 1880-1934
See Bely, Andrey
See also CA 104

Bukowski, Charles 1920-1994 **CLC 2, 5, 9, 41, 82; DAM NOV, POET**
See also CA 17-20R; 144; CANR 40; DLB 5, 130, 169; MTCW

Bulgakov, Mikhail (Afanas'evich) 1891-1940 **TCLC 2, 16; DAM DRAM, NOV; SSC 18**
See also CA 105; 152

Bulgya, Alexander Alexandrovich 1901-1956 **TCLC 53**
See also Fadeyev, Alexander
See also CA 117

Bullins, Ed 1935- **CLC 1, 5, 7; BLC; DAM DRAM, MULT; DC 6**
See also BW 2; CA 49-52; CAAS 16; CANR 24, 46; DLB 7, 38; MTCW

Bulwer-Lytton, Edward (George Earle Lytton) 1803-1873 **NCLC 1, 45**
See also DLB 21

Bunin, Ivan Alexeyevich 1870-1953 **TCLC 6; SSC 5**
See also CA 104

Bunting, Basil 1900-1985 **CLC 10, 39, 47; DAM POET**
See also CA 53-56; 115; CANR 7; DLB 20

Bunuel, Luis 1900-1983 **CLC 16, 80; DAM MULT; HLC**
See also CA 101; 110; CANR 32; HW

Bunyan, John 1628-1688 **LC 4; DA; DAB; DAC; DAM MST; WLC**
See also CDBLB 1660-1789; DLB 39

Burckhardt, Jacob (Christoph) 1818-1897 **NCLC 49**

Burford, Eleanor
See Hibbert, Eleanor Alice Burford

Burgess, Anthony **CLC 1, 2, 4, 5, 8, 10, 13, 15, 22, 40, 62, 81, 94; DAB**
See also Wilson, John (Anthony) Burgess
See also AITN 1; CDBLB 1960 to Present; DLB 14

Burke, Edmund 1729(?)-1797 **LC 7, 36; DA; DAB; DAC; DAM MST; WLC**
See also DLB 104

Burke, Kenneth (Duva) 1897-1993 **CLC 2, 24**
See also CA 5-8R; 143; CANR 39; DLB 45, 63; MTCW

Burke, Leda
See Garnett, David

Burke, Ralph
See Silverberg, Robert

Burke, Thomas 1886-1945 **TCLC 63**
See also CA 113; 155

Burney, Fanny 1752-1840 **NCLC 12, 54**
See also DLB 39

Burns, Robert 1759-1796 **PC 6**
See also CDBLB 1789-1832; DA; DAB; DAC; DAM MST, POET; DLB 109; WLC

Burns, Tex
See L'Amour, Louis (Dearborn)

Burnshaw, Stanley 1906- **CLC 3, 13, 44**
See also CA 9-12R; DLB 48

Burr, Anne 1937- **CLC 6**
See also CA 25-28R

Burroughs, Edgar Rice 1875-1950 **TCLC 2, 32; DAM NOV**
See also AAYA 11; CA 104; 132; DLB 8; MTCW; SATA 41

Burroughs, William S(eward) 1914- **CLC 1, 2, 5, 15, 22, 42, 75; DA; DAB; DAC; DAM MST, NOV, POP; WLC**
See also AITN 2; CA 9-12R; CANR 20, 52; DLB 2, 8, 16, 152; DLBY 81; MTCW

Burton, Richard F. 1821-1890 **NCLC 42**
See also DLB 55

Busch, Frederick 1941- **CLC 7, 10, 18, 47**
See also CA 33-36R; CAAS 1; CANR 45; DLB 6

Bush, Ronald 1946- **CLC 34**
See also CA 136

Bustos, F(rancisco)
See Borges, Jorge Luis

Bustos Domecq, H(onorio)
See Bioy Casares, Adolfo; Borges, Jorge Luis

Butler, Octavia E(stelle) 1947- **CLC 38; DAM MULT, POP**
See also AAYA 18; BW 2; CA 73-76; CANR 12, 24, 38; DLB 33; MTCW; SATA 84

Butler, Robert Olen (Jr.) 1945- **CLC 81; DAM POP**
See also CA 112; DLB 173; INT 112

Butler, Samuel 1612-1680 **LC 16**
See also DLB 101, 126

Butler, Samuel 1835-1902 **TCLC 1, 33; DA; DAB; DAC; DAM MST, NOV; WLC**
See also CA 143; CDBLB 1890-1914; DLB 18, 57, 174

Butler, Walter C.
See Faust, Frederick (Schiller)

Butor, Michel (Marie Francois) 1926- **CLC 1, 3, 8, 11, 15**
See also CA 9-12R; CANR 33; DLB 83; MTCW

Buzo, Alexander (John) 1944- **CLC 61**
See also CA 97-100; CANR 17, 39

Buzzati, Dino 1906-1972 **CLC 36**
See also CA 33-36R; DLB 177

Byars, Betsy (Cromer) 1928- **CLC 35**
See also AAYA 19; CA 33-36R; CANR 18, 36, 57; CLR 1, 16; DLB 52; INT CANR-18; JRDA; MAICYA; MTCW; SAAS 1; SATA 4, 46, 80

Byatt, A(ntonia) S(usan Drabble) 1936- **CLC 19,
65; DAM NOV, POP**
See also CA 13-16R; CANR 13, 33, 50; DLB 14;
MTCW

Byrne, David 1952- **CLC 26**
See also CA 127

Byrne, John Keyes 1926-
See Leonard, Hugh
See also CA 102; INT 102

Byron, George Gordon (Noel) 1788-1824 **NCLC 2,
12; DA; DAB; DAC; DAM MST, POET; PC
16; WLC**
See also CDBLB 1789-1832; DLB 96, 110

Byron, Robert 1905-1941 **TCLC 67**

C. 3. 3.
See Wilde, Oscar (Fingal O'Flahertie Wills)

Caballero, Fernan 1796-1877 **NCLC 10**

Cabell, Branch
See Cabell, James Branch

Cabell, James Branch 1879-1958 **TCLC 6**
See also CA 105; 152; DLB 9, 78

Cable, George Washington 1844-1925 **TCLC 4;
SSC 4**
See also CA 104; 155; DLB 12, 74; DLBD 13

Cabral de Melo Neto, Joao 1920- **CLC 76; DAM
MULT**
See also CA 151

Cabrera Infante, G(uillermo) 1929- **CLC 5, 25, 45;
DAM MULT; HLC**
See also CA 85-88; CANR 29; DLB 113; HW;
MTCW

Cade, Toni
See Bambara, Toni Cade

Cadmus and Harmonia
See Buchan, John

Caedmon fl. 658-680 **CMLC 7**
See also DLB 146

Caeiro, Alberto
See Pessoa, Fernando (Antonio Nogueira)

Cage, John (Milton, Jr.) 1912- **CLC 41**
See also CA 13-16R; CANR 9; INT CANR-9

Cain, G.
See Cabrera Infante, G(uillermo)

Cain, Guillermo
See Cabrera Infante, G(uillermo)

Cain, James M(allahan) 1892-1977 **CLC 3, 11, 28**
See also AITN 1; CA 17-20R; 73-76; CANR 8, 34;
MTCW

Caine, Mark
See Raphael, Frederic (Michael)

Calasso, Roberto 1941- **CLC 81**
See also CA 143

Calderon de la Barca, Pedro 1600-1681 **LC 23; DC
3**

Caldwell, Erskine (Preston) 1903-1987 **CLC 1, 8,
14, 50, 60; DAM NOV; SSC 19**
See also AITN 1; CA 1-4R; 121; CAAS 1; CANR
2, 33; DLB 9, 86; MTCW

Caldwell, (Janet Miriam) Taylor (Holland) 1900-
1985 **CLC 2, 28, 39; DAM NOV, POP**
See also CA 5-8R; 116; CANR 5

Calhoun, John Caldwell 1782-1850 **NCLC 15**
See also DLB 3

Calisher, Hortense 1911- **CLC 2, 4, 8, 38; DAM
NOV; SSC 15**
See also CA 1-4R; CANR 1, 22; DLB 2; INT CANR-
22; MTCW

Callaghan, Morley Edward 1903-1990 **CLC 3, 14,
41, 65; DAC; DAM MST**
See also CA 9-12R; 132; CANR 33; DLB 68;
MTCW

Callimachus c. 305B.C.-c. 240B.C. **CMLC 18**
See also DLB 176

Calvin, John 1509-1564 **LC 37**

Calvino, Italo 1923-1985 **CLC 5, 8, 11, 22, 33, 39,
73; DAM NOV; SSC 3**
See also CA 85-88; 116; CANR 23; MTCW

Cameron, Carey 1952- **CLC 59**
See also CA 135

Cameron, Peter 1959- **CLC 44**
See also CA 125; CANR 50

Campana, Dino 1885-1932 **TCLC 20**
See also CA 117; DLB 114

Campanella, Tommaso 1568-1639 **LC 32**

Campbell, John W(ood, Jr.) 1910-1971 **CLC 32**
See also CA 21-22; 29-32R; CANR 34; CAP 2;
DLB 8; MTCW

Campbell, Joseph 1904-1987 **CLC 69**
See also AAYA 3; BEST 89 2; CA 1-4R; 124; CANR
3, 28; MTCW

Campbell, Maria 1940- **CLC 85; DAC**
See also CA 102; CANR 54; NNAL

Campbell, (John) Ramsey 1946- **CLC 42; SSC 19**
See also CA 57-60; CANR 7; INT CANR-7

Campbell, (Ignatius) Roy (Dunnachie) 1901-1957
TCLC 5
See also CA 104; 155; DLB 20

Campbell, Thomas 1777-1844 **NCLC 19**
See also DLB 93; 144

Campbell, Wilfred **TCLC 9**
See also Campbell, William

Campbell, William 1858(?)-1918
See Campbell, Wilfred
See also CA 106; DLB 92

Campion, Jane **CLC 95**
See also CA 138

Campos, Alvaro de
See Pessoa, Fernando (Antonio Nogueira)

Camus, Albert 1913-1960 **CLC 1, 2, 4, 9, 11, 14, 32,
63, 69; DA; DAB; DAC; DAM DRAM, MST,
NOV; DC 2; SSC 9; WLC**
See also CA 89-92; DLB 72; MTCW

Canby, Vincent 1924- **CLC 13**
See also CA 81-84

Cancale
See Desnos, Robert

Canetti, Elias 1905-1994 **CLC 3, 14, 25, 75, 86**
See also CA 21-24R; 146; CANR 23; DLB 85, 124;
MTCW

Canin, Ethan 1960- **CLC 55**
See also CA 131; 135

Cannon, Curt
See Hunter, Evan

Cape, Judith
See Page, P(atricia) K(athleen)

Capek, Karel 1890-1938 **TCLC 6, 37; DA; DAB;
DAC; DAM DRAM, MST, NOV; DC 1; WLC**
See also CA 104; 140

Capote, Truman 1924-1984 **CLC 1, 3, 8, 13, 19, 34,
38, 58; DA; DAB; DAC; DAM MST, NOV,
POP; SSC 2; WLC**
See also CA 5-8R; 113; CANR 18; CDALB 1941-
1968; DLB 2; DLBY 80, 84; MTCW; SATA 91

Capra, Frank 1897-1991 **CLC 16**
See also CA 61-64; 135

Caputo, Philip 1941- **CLC 32**
See also CA 73-76; CANR 40

Card, Orson Scott 1951- **CLC 44, 47, 50; DAM
POP**
See also AAYA 11; CA 102; CANR 27, 47; INT
CANR-27; MTCW; SATA 83

Cardenal, Ernesto 1925- **CLC 31; DAM MULT,
POET; HLC**
See also CA 49-52; CANR 2, 32; HW; MTCW

Cardozo, Benjamin N(athan) 1870-1938 **TCLC 65**
See also CA 117

Carducci, Giosue 1835-1907 **TCLC 32**

Carew, Thomas 1595(?)-1640 **LC 13**
See also DLB 126

Carey, Ernestine Gilbreth 1908- **CLC 17**
See also CA 5-8R; SATA 2

Carey, Peter 1943- **CLC 40, 55, 96**
See also CA 123; 127; CANR 53; INT 127; MTCW

Carleton, William 1794-1869 **NCLC 3**
See also DLB 159

Carlisle, Henry (Coffin) 1926- **CLC 33**

See also CA 13-16R; CANR 15

Carlsen, Chris
See Holdstock, Robert P.

Carlson, Ron(ald F.) 1947- **CLC 54**
See also CA 105; CANR 27

Carlyle, Thomas 1795-1881 **NCLC 22; DA; DAB; DAC; DAM MST**
See also CDBLB 1789-1832; DLB 55; 144

Carman, (William) Bliss 1861-1929 **TCLC 7; DAC**
See also CA 104; 152; DLB 92

Carnegie, Dale 1888-1955 **TCLC 53**

Carossa, Hans 1878-1956 **TCLC 48**
See also DLB 66

Carpenter, Don(ald Richard) 1931-1995 **CLC 41**
See also CA 45-48; 149; CANR 1

Carpentier (y Valmont), Alejo 1904-1980 **CLC 8, 11, 38; DAM MULT; HLC**
See also CA 65-68; 97-100; CANR 11; DLB 113; HW

Carr, Caleb 1955(?)- **CLC 86**
See also CA 147

Carr, Emily 1871-1945 **TCLC 32**
See also DLB 68

Carr, John Dickson 1906-1977 **CLC 3**
See also CA 49-52; 69-72; CANR 3, 33; MTCW

Carr, Philippa
See Hibbert, Eleanor Alice Burford

Carr, Virginia Spencer 1929- **CLC 34**
See also CA 61-64; DLB 111

Carrere, Emmanuel 1957- **CLC 89**

Carrier, Roch 1937- **CLC 13, 78; DAC; DAM MST**
See also CA 130; DLB 53

Carroll, James P. 1943(?)- **CLC 38**
See also CA 81-84

Carroll, Jim 1951- **CLC 35**
See also AAYA 17; CA 45-48; CANR 42

Carroll, Lewis **NCLC 2, 53; WLC**
See also Dodgson, Charles Lutwidge
See also CDBLB 1832-1890; CLR 2, 18; DLB 18, 163; JRDA

Carroll, Paul Vincent 1900-1968 **CLC 10**
See also CA 9-12R; 25-28R; DLB 10

Carruth, Hayden 1921- **CLC 4, 7, 10, 18, 84; PC 10**
See also CA 9-12R; CANR 4, 38; DLB 5, 165; INT CANR-4; MTCW; SATA 47

Carson, Rachel Louise 1907-1964 **CLC 71; DAM POP**
See also CA 77-80; CANR 35; MTCW; SATA 23

Carter, Angela (Olive) 1940-1992 **CLC 5, 41, 76; SSC 13**
See also CA 53-56; 136; CANR 12, 36; DLB 14;

MTCW; SATA 66; SATA-Obit 70

Carter, Nick
See Smith, Martin Cruz

Carver, Raymond 1938-1988 **CLC 22, 36, 53, 55; DAM NOV; SSC 8**
See also CA 33-36R; 126; CANR 17, 34; DLB 130; DLBY 84, 88; MTCW

Cary, Elizabeth, Lady Falkland 1585-1639 **LC 30**

Cary, (Arthur) Joyce (Lunel) 1888-1957 **TCLC 1, 29**
See also CA 104; CDBLB 1914-1945; DLB 15, 100

Casanova de Seingalt, Giovanni Jacopo 1725-1798 **LC 13**

Casares, Adolfo Bioy
See Bioy Casares, Adolfo

Casely-Hayford, J(oseph) E(phraim) 1866-1930 **TCLC 24; BLC; DAM MULT**
See also BW 2; CA 123; 152

Casey, John (Dudley) 1939- **CLC 59**
See also BEST 90 2; CA 69-72; CANR 23

Casey, Michael 1947- **CLC 2**
See also CA 65-68; DLB 5

Casey, Patrick
See Thurman, Wallace (Henry)

Casey, Warren (Peter) 1935-1988 **CLC 12**
See also CA 101; 127; INT 101

Casona, Alejandro **CLC 49**
See also Alvarez, Alejandro Rodriguez

Cassavetes, John 1929-1989 **CLC 20**
See also CA 85-88; 127

Cassian, Nina 1924- **PC 17**

Cassill, R(onald) V(erlin) 1919- **CLC 4, 23**
See also CA 9-12R; CAAS 1; CANR 7, 45; DLB 6

Cassirer, Ernst 1874-1945 **TCLC 61**

Cassity, (Allen) Turner 1929- **CLC 6, 42**
See also CA 17-20R; CAAS 8; CANR 11; DLB 105

Castaneda, Carlos 1931(?)- **CLC 12**
See also CA 25-28R; CANR 32; HW; MTCW

Castedo, Elena 1937- **CLC 65**
See also CA 132

Castedo-Ellerman, Elena
See Castedo, Elena

Castellanos, Rosario 1925-1974 **CLC 66; DAM MULT; HLC**
See also CA 131; 53-56; DLB 113; HW

Castelvetro, Lodovico 1505-1571 **LC 12**

Castiglione, Baldassare 1478-1529 **LC 12**

Castle, Robert
See Hamilton, Edmond

Castro, Guillen de 1569-1631 **LC 19**

Castro, Rosalia de 1837-1885 **NCLC 3; DAM MULT**

Cather, Willa
See Cather, Willa Sibert

Cather, Willa Sibert 1873-1947 **TCLC 1, 11, 31; DA; DAB; DAC; DAM MST, NOV; SSC 2; WLC**
See also CA 104; 128; CDALB 1865-1917; DLB 9, 54, 78; DLBD 1; MTCW; SATA 30

Cato, Marcus Porcius 234B.C.-149B.C. **CMLC 21**

Catton, (Charles) Bruce 1899-1978 **CLC 35**
See also AITN 1; CA 5-8R; 81-84; CANR 7; DLB 17; SATA 2; SATA-Obit 24

Catullus c. 84B.C.-c. 54B.C. **CMLC 18**

Cauldwell, Frank
See King, Francis (Henry)

Caunitz, William J. 1933-1996 **CLC 34**
See also BEST 89 3; CA 125; 130; 152; INT 130

Causley, Charles (Stanley) 1917- **CLC 7**
See also CA 9-12R; CANR 5, 35; CLR 30; DLB 27; MTCW; SATA 3, 66

Caute, David 1936- **CLC 29; DAM NOV**
See also CA 1-4R; CAAS 4; CANR 1, 33; DLB 14

Cavafy, C(onstantine) P(eter) 1863-1933 **TCLC 2, 7; DAM POET**
See also Kavafis, Konstantinos Petrou
See also CA 148

Cavallo, Evelyn
See Spark, Muriel (Sarah)

Cavanna, Betty **CLC 12**
See also Harrison, Elizabeth Cavanna
See also JRDA; MAICYA; SAAS 4; SATA 1, 30

Cavendish, Margaret Lucas 1623-1673 **LC 30**
See also DLB 131

Caxton, William 1421(?)-1491(?) **LC 17**
See also DLB 170

Cayrol, Jean 1911- **CLC 11**
See also CA 89-92; DLB 83

Cela, Camilo Jose 1916- **CLC 4, 13, 59; DAM MULT; HLC**
See also BEST 90 2; CA 21-24R; CAAS 10; CANR 21, 32; DLBY 89; HW; MTCW

Celan, Paul **CLC 10, 19, 53, 82; PC 10**
See also Antschel, Paul
See also DLB 69

Celine, Louis-Ferdinand **CLC 1, 3, 4, 7, 9, 15, 47**
See also Destouches, Louis-Ferdinand
See also DLB 72

Cellini, Benvenuto 1500-1571 **LC 7**

Cendrars, Blaise **CLC 18**
See also Sauser-Hall, Frederic

Cernuda (y Bidon), Luis 1902-1963 **CLC 54; DAM POET**
See also CA 131; 89-92; DLB 134; HW

Cervantes (Saavedra), Miguel de 1547-1616 **LC 6, 23; DA; DAB; DAC; DAM MST, NOV; SSC 12; WLC**

Cesaire, Aime (Fernand) 1913- **CLC 19, 32; BLC; DAM MULT, POET**
See also BW 2; CA 65-68; CANR 24, 43; MTCW

Chabon, Michael 1963- **CLC 55**
See also CA 139; CANR 57

Chabrol, Claude 1930- **CLC 16**
See also CA 110

Challans, Mary 1905-1983
See Renault, Mary
See also CA 81-84; 111; SATA 23; SATA-Obit 36

Challis, George
See Faust, Frederick (Schiller)

Chambers, Aidan 1934- **CLC 35**
See also CA 25-28R; CANR 12, 31; JRDA; MAICYA; SAAS 12; SATA 1, 69

Chambers, James 1948-
See Cliff, Jimmy
See also CA 124

Chambers, Jessie
See Lawrence, D(avid) H(erbert Richards)

Chambers, Robert W. 1865-1933 **TCLC 41**

Chandler, Raymond (Thornton) 1888-1959 **TCLC 1, 7; SSC 23**
See also CA 104; 129; CDALB 1929-1941; DLBD 6; MTCW

Chang, Jung 1952- **CLC 71**
See also CA 142

Channing, William Ellery 1780-1842 **NCLC 17**
See also DLB 1, 59

Chaplin, Charles Spencer 1889-1977 **CLC 16**
See also Chaplin, Charlie
See also CA 81-84; 73-76

Chaplin, Charlie
See Chaplin, Charles Spencer
See also DLB 44

Chapman, George 1559(?)-1634 **LC 22; DAM DRAM**
See also DLB 62, 121

Chapman, Graham 1941-1989 **CLC 21**
See also Monty Python
See also CA 116; 129; CANR 35

Chapman, John Jay 1862-1933 **TCLC 7**
See also CA 104

Chapman, Lee
See Bradley, Marion Zimmer

Chapman, Walker
See Silverberg, Robert

Chappell, Fred (Davis) 1936- **CLC 40, 78**
See also CA 5-8R; CAAS 4; CANR 8, 33; DLB 6, 105

Char, Rene(-Emile) 1907-1988 **CLC 9, 11, 14, 55; DAM POET**
See also CA 13-16R; 124; CANR 32; MTCW

Charby, Jay
See Ellison, Harlan (Jay)

Chardin, Pierre Teilhard de
See Teilhard de Chardin, (Marie Joseph) Pierre

Charles I 1600-1649 **LC 13**

Charyn, Jerome 1937- **CLC 5, 8, 18**
See also CA 5-8R; CAAS 1; CANR 7; DLBY 83; MTCW

Chase, Mary (Coyle) 1907-1981 **DC 1**
See also CA 77-80; 105; SATA 17; SATA-Obit 29

Chase, Mary Ellen 1887-1973 **CLC 2**
See also CA 13-16; 41-44R; CAP 1; SATA 10

Chase, Nicholas
See Hyde, Anthony

Chateaubriand, Francois Rene de 1768-1848 **NCLC 3**
See also DLB 119

Chatterje, Sarat Chandra 1876-1936(?)
See Chatterji, Saratchandra
See also CA 109

Chatterji, Bankim Chandra 1838-1894 **NCLC 19**

Chatterji, Saratchandra **TCLC 13**
See also Chatterje, Sarat Chandra

Chatterton, Thomas 1752-1770 **LC 3; DAM POET**
See also DLB 109

Chatwin, (Charles) Bruce 1940-1989 **CLC 28, 57, 59; DAM POP**
See also AAYA 4; BEST 90 1; CA 85-88; 127

Chaucer, Daniel
See Ford, Ford Madox

Chaucer, Geoffrey 1340(?)-1400 **LC 17; DA; DAB; DAC; DAM MST, POET**
See also CDBLB Before 1660; DLB 146

Chaviaras, Strates 1935-
See Haviaras, Stratis
See also CA 105

Chayefsky, Padd **CLC 23**
See also Chayefsky, Sidney
See also DLB 7, 44; DLBY 81

Chayefsky, Sidney 1923-1981
See Chayefsky, Paddy
See also CA 9-12R; 104; CANR 18; DAM DRAM

Chedid, Andree 1920- **CLC 47**
See also CA 145

Cheever, John 1912-1982 **CLC 3, 7, 8, 11, 15, 25, 64; DA; DAB; DAC; DAM MST, NOV, POP;**

SSC 1; WLC
See also CA 5-8R; 106; CABS 1; CANR 5, 27; CDALB 1941-1968; DLB 2, 102; DLBY 80, 82; INT CANR-5; MTCW

Cheever, Susan 1943- **CLC 18, 48**
See also CA 103; CANR 27, 51; DLBY 82; INT CANR-27

Chekhonte, Antosha
See Chekhov, Anton (Pavlovich)

Chekhov, Anton (Pavlovich) 1860-1904 **TCLC 3, 10, 31, 55; DA; DAB; DAC; DAM DRAM, MST; SSC 2; WLC**
See also CA 104; 124; SATA 90

Chernyshevsky, Nikolay Gavrilovich 1828-1889 **NCLC 1**

Cherry, Carolyn Janice 1942-
See Cherryh, C. J.
See also CA 65-68; CANR 10

Cherryh, C. J. **CLC 35**
See also Cherry, Carolyn Janice
See also DLBY 80

Chesnutt, Charles W(addell) 1858-1932 **TCLC 5, 39; BLC; DAM MULT; SSC 7**
See also BW 1; CA 106; 125; DLB 12, 50, 78; MTCW

Chester, Alfred 1929(?)-1971 **CLC 49**
See also CA 33-36R; DLB 130

Chesterton, G(ilbert) K(eith) 1874-1936 **TCLC 1, 6, 64; DAM NOV, POET; SSC 1**
See also CA 104; 132; CDBLB 1914-1945; DLB 10, 19, 34, 70, 98, 149; MTCW; SATA 27

Chiang Pin-chin 1904-1986
See Ding Ling
See also CA 118

Ch'ien Chung-shu 1910- **CLC 22**
See also CA 130; MTCW

Child, L. Maria
See Child, Lydia Maria

Child, Lydia Maria 1802-1880 **NCLC 6**
See also DLB 1, 74; SATA 67

Child, Mrs.
See Child, Lydia Maria

Child, Philip 1898-1978 **CLC 19, 68**
See also CA 13-14; CAP 1; SATA 47

Childers, (Robert) Erskine 1870-1922 **TCLC 65**
See also CA 113; 153; DLB 70

Childress, Alice 1920-1994 **CLC 12, 15, 86, 96; BLC; DAM DRAM, MULT, NOV; DC 4**
See also AAYA 8; BW 2; CA 45-48; 146; CANR 3, 27, 50; CLR 14; DLB 7, 38; JRDA; MAICYA; MTCW; SATA 7, 48, 81

Chislett, (Margaret) Anne 1943- **CLC 34**
See also CA 151

Chitty, Thomas Willes 1926- **CLC 11**

See also Hinde, Thomas
See also CA 5-8R

Chivers, Thomas Holley 1809-1858 **NCLC 49**
See also DLB 3

Chomette, Rene Lucien 1898-1981
See Clair, Rene
See also CA 103

Chopin, Kate TCLC 5, 14; DA; DAB; SSC 8
See also Chopin, Katherine
See also CDALB 1865-1917; DLB 12, 78

Chopin, Katherine 1851-1904
See Chopin, Kate
See also CA 104; 122; DAC; DAM MST, NOV

Chretien de Troyes c. 12th cent. - **CMLC 10**

Christie
See Ichikawa, Kon

Christie, Agatha (Mary Clarissa) 1890-1976 **CLC
1, 6, 8, 12, 39, 48; DAB; DAC; DAM NOV**
See also AAYA 9; AITN 1, 2; CA 17-20R; 61-64;
CANR 10, 37; CDBLB 1914-1945; DLB 13, 77;
MTCW; SATA 36

Christie, (Ann) Philippa
See Pearce, Philippa
See also CA 5-8R; CANR 4

Christine de Pizan 1365(?)-1431(?) **LC 9**

Chubb, Elmer
See Masters, Edgar Lee

Chulkov, Mikhail Dmitrievich 1743-1792 **LC 2**
See also DLB 150

Churchill, Caryl 1938- **CLC 31, 55; DC 5**
See also CA 102; CANR 22, 46; DLB 13; MTCW

Churchill, Charles 1731-1764 **LC 3**
See also DLB 109

Chute, Carolyn 1947- **CLC 39**
See also CA 123

Ciardi, John (Anthony) 1916-1986 **CLC 10, 40, 44;
DAM POET**
See also CA 5-8R; 118; CAAS 2; CANR 5, 33;
CLR 19; DLB 5; DLBY 86; INT CANR-5;
MAICYA; MTCW; SATA 1, 65; SATA-Obit
46

Cicero, Marcus Tullius 106B.C.-43B.C. **CMLC 3**

Cimino, Michael 1943- **CLC 16**
See also CA 105

Cioran, E(mil) M. 1911-1995 **CLC 64**
See also CA 25-28R; 149

Cisneros, Sandra 1954- **CLC 69; DAM MULT; HLC**
See also AAYA 9; CA 131; DLB 122, 152; HW

Cixous, Helene 1937- **CLC 92**
See also CA 126; CANR 55; DLB 83; MTCW

Clair, Rene CLC 20
See also Chomette, Rene Lucien

Clampitt, Amy 1920-1994 **CLC 32**
See also CA 110; 146; CANR 29; DLB 105

Clancy, Thomas L., Jr. 1947-
See Clancy, Tom
See also CA 125; 131; INT 131; MTCW

Clancy, Tom CLC 45; DAM NOV, POP
See also Clancy, Thomas L., Jr.
See also AAYA 9; BEST 89 1, 90 1

Clare, John 1793-1864 **NCLC 9; DAB; DAM POET**
See also DLB 55, 96

Clarin
See Alas (y Urena), Leopoldo (Enrique Garcia)

Clark, Al C.
See Goines, Donald

Clark, (Robert) Brian 1932- **CLC 29**
See also CA 41-44R

Clark, Curt
See Westlake, Donald E(dwin)

Clark, Eleanor 1913-1996 **CLC 5, 19**
See also CA 9-12R; 151; CANR 41; DLB 6

Clark, J. P.
See Clark, John Pepper
See also DLB 117

Clark, John Pepper 1935- **CLC 38; BLC; DAM
DRAM, MULT; DC 5**
See also Clark, J. P.
See also BW 1; CA 65-68; CANR 16

Clark, M. R.
See Clark, Mavis Thorpe

Clark, Mavis Thorpe 1909- **CLC 12**
See also CA 57-60; CANR 8, 37; CLR 30;
MAICYA; SAAS 5; SATA 8, 74

Clark, Walter Van Tilburg 1909-1971 **CLC 28**
See also CA 9-12R; 33-36R; DLB 9; SATA 8

Clarke, Arthur C(harles) 1917- **CLC 1, 4, 13, 18,
35; DAM POP; SSC 3**
See also AAYA 4; CA 1-4R; CANR 2, 28, 55;
JRDA; MAICYA; MTCW; SATA 13, 70

Clarke, Austin 1896-1974 **CLC 6, 9; DAM POET**
See also CA 29-32; 49-52; CAP 2; DLB 10, 20

Clarke, Austin C(hesterfield) 1934- **CLC 8, 53;
BLC; DAC; DAM MULT**
See also BW 1; CA 25-28R; CAAS 16; CANR 14,
32; DLB 53, 125

Clarke, Gillian 1937- **CLC 61**
See also CA 106; DLB 40

Clarke, Marcus (Andrew Hislop) 1846-1881 **NCLC
19**

Clarke, Shirley 1925- **CLC 16**

Clash, The

See Headon, (Nicky) Topper; Jones, Mick;
Simonon, Paul; Strummer, Joe

Claudel, Paul (Louis Charles Marie) 1868-1955
TCLC 2, 10
See also CA 104

Clavell, James (duMaresq) 1925-1994 **CLC 6, 25,
87; DAM NOV, POP**
See also CA 25-28R; 146; CANR 26, 48; MTCW

Cleaver, (Leroy) Eldridge 1935- **CLC 30; BLC;
DAM MULT**
See also BW 1; CA 21-24R; CANR 16

Cleese, John (Marwood) 1939- **CLC 21**
See also Monty Python
See also CA 112; 116; CANR 35; MTCW

Cleishbotham, Jebediah
See Scott, Walter

Cleland, John 1710-1789 **LC 2**
See also DLB 39

Clemens, Samuel Langhorne 1835-1910
See Twain, Mark
See also CA 104; 135; CDALB 1865-1917; DA;
DAB; DAC; DAM MST, NOV; DLB 11, 12, 23,
64, 74; JRDA; MAICYA; YABC 2

Cleophil
See Congreve, William

Clerihew, E.
See Bentley, E(dmund) C(lerihew)

Clerk, N. W.
See Lewis, C(live) S(taples)

Cliff, Jimmy CLC 21
See also Chambers, James

Clifton, (Thelma) Lucille 1936- **CLC 19, 66; BLC;
DAM MULT, POET; PC 17**
See also BW 2; CA 49-52; CANR 2, 24, 42; CLR 5;
DLB 5, 41; MAICYA; MTCW; SATA 20, 69

Clinton, Dirk
See Silverberg, Robert

Clough, Arthur Hugh 1819-1861 **NCLC 27**
See also DLB 32

Clutha, Janet Paterson Frame 1924-
See Frame, Janet
See also CA 1-4R; CANR 2, 36; MTCW

Clyne, Terence
See Blatty, William Peter

Cobalt, Martin
See Mayne, William (James Carter)

Cobbett, William 1763-1835 **NCLC 49**
See also DLB 43, 107, 158

Coburn, D(onald) L(ee) 1938- **CLC 10**
See also CA 89-92

Cocteau, Jean (Maurice Eugene Clement) 1889-1963
**CLC 1, 8, 15, 16, 43; DA; DAB; DAC; DAM
DRAM, MST, NOV; WLC**

See also CA 25-28; CANR 40; CAP 2; DLB 65;
MTCW

Codrescu, Andrei 1946- **CLC 46; DAM POET**
See also CA 33-36R; CAAS 19; CANR 13, 34, 53

Coe, Max
See Bourne, Randolph S(illiman)

Coe, Tucker
See Westlake, Donald E(dwin)

Coetzee, J(ohn) M(ichael) 1940- **CLC 23, 33, 66;
DAM NOV**
See also CA 77-80; CANR 41, 54; MTCW

Coffey, Brian
See Koontz, Dean R(ay)

Cohan, George M. 1878-1942 **TCLC 60**

Cohen, Arthur A(llen) 1928-1986 **CLC 7, 31**
See also CA 1-4R; 120; CANR 1, 17, 42; DLB 28

Cohen, Leonard (Norman) 1934- **CLC 3, 38; DAC;
DAM MST**
See also CA 21-24R; CANR 14; DLB 53; MTCW

Cohen, Matt 1942- **CLC 19; DAC**
See also CA 61-64; CAAS 18; CANR 40; DLB 53

Cohen-Solal, Annie 19(?)- **CLC 50**

Colegate, Isabel 1931- **CLC 36**
See also CA 17-20R; CANR 8, 22; DLB 14; INT
CANR-22; MTCW

Coleman, Emmett
See Reed, Ishmael

Coleridge, Samuel Taylor 1772-1834 **NCLC 9, 54;
DA; DAB; DAC; DAM MST, POET; PC 11;
WLC**
See also CDBLB 1789-1832; DLB 93, 107

Coleridge, Sara 1802-1852 **NCLC 31**

Coles, Don 1928- **CLC 46**
See also CA 115; CANR 38

Colette, (Sidonie-Gabrielle) 1873-1954 **TCLC 1, 5,
16; DAM NOV; SSC 10**
See also CA 104; 131; DLB 65; MTCW

Collett, (Jacobine) Camilla (Wergeland) 1813-1895
NCLC 22

Collier, Christopher 1930- **CLC 30**
See also AAYA 13; CA 33-36R; CANR 13, 33;
JRDA; MAICYA; SATA 16, 70

Collier, James L(incoln) 1928- **CLC 30; DAM POP**
See also AAYA 13; CA 9-12R; CANR 4, 33; CLR
3; JRDA; MAICYA; SAAS 21; SATA 8, 70

Collier, Jeremy 1650-1726 **LC 6**

Collier, John 1901-1980 **SSC 19**
See also CA 65-68; 97-100; CANR 10; DLB 77

Collingwood, R(obin) G(eorge) 1889(?)-1943 **TCLC
67**
See also CA 117; 155

Collins, Hunt
See Hunter, Evan

Collins, Linda 1931- **CLC 44**
See also CA 125

Collins, (William) Wilkie 1824-1889 **NCLC 1, 18**
See also CDBLB 1832-1890; DLB 18, 70, 159

Collins, William
1721-1759 **LC 4; DAM POET**
See also DLB 109

Collodi, Carlo 1826-1890 **NCLC 54**
See also Lorenzini, Carlo
See also CLR 5

Colman, George
See Glassco, John

Colt, Winchester Remington
See Hubbard, L(afayette) Ron(ald)

Colter, Cyrus 1910- **CLC 58**
See also BW 1; CA 65-68; CANR 10; DLB 33

Colton, James
See Hansen, Joseph

Colum, Padraic 1881-1972 **CLC 28**
See also CA 73-76; 33-36R; CANR 35; CLR 36;
MAICYA; MTCW; SATA 15

Colvin, James
See Moorcock, Michael (John)

Colwin, Laurie (E.) 1944-1992 **CLC 5, 13, 23, 84**
See also CA 89-92; 139; CANR 20, 46; DLBY 80;
MTCW

Comfort, Alex(ander) 1920- **CLC 7; DAM POP**
See also CA 1-4R; CANR 1, 45

Comfort, Montgomery
See Campbell, (John) Ramsey

Compton-Burnett, I(vy) 1884(?)-1969 **CLC 1, 3, 10,
15, 34; DAM NOV**
See also CA 1-4R; 25-28R; CANR 4; DLB 36;
MTCW

Comstock, Anthony 1844-1915 **TCLC 13**
See also CA 110

Comte, Auguste 1798-1857 **NCLC 54**

Conan Doyle, Arthur
See Doyle, Arthur Conan

Conde, Maryse 1937- **CLC 52, 92; DAM MULT**
See also Boucolon, Maryse
See also BW 2

Condillac, Etienne Bonnot de 1714-1780 **LC 26**

Condon, Richard (Thomas) 1915-1996 **CLC 4, 6, 8,
10, 45, 100; DAM NOV**
See also BEST 90 3; CA 1-4R; 151; CAAS 1; CANR
2, 23; INT CANR-23; MTCW

Confucius 551B.C.-479B.C. **CMLC 19; DA; DAB;
DAC; DAM MST**

Congreve, William 1670-1729 **LC 5, 21; DA; DAB;
DAC; DAM DRAM, MST, POET; DC 2; WLC**
See also CDBLB 1660-1789; DLB 39, 84

Connell, Evan S(helby), Jr. 1924- **CLC 4, 6, 45;
DAM NOV**
See also AAYA 7; CA 1-4R; CAAS 2; CANR 2,
39; DLB 2; DLBY 81; MTCW

Connelly, Marc(us Cook) 1890-1980 **CLC 7**
See also CA 85-88; 102; CANR 30; DLB 7; DLBY
80; SATA-Obit 25

Connor, Ralph **TCLC 31**
See also Gordon, Charles William
See also DLB 92

Conrad, Joseph 1857-1924 **TCLC 1, 6, 13, 25, 43,
57; DA; DAB; DAC; DAM MST, NOV; SSC
9; WLC**
See also CA 104; 131; CDBLB 1890-1914; DLB 10,
34, 98, 156; MTCW; SATA 27

Conrad, Robert Arnold
See Hart, Moss

Conroy, Donald Pat(rick) 1945- **CLC 30, 74; DAM
NOV, POP**
See also AAYA 8; AITN 1; CA 85-88; CANR 24,
53; DLB 6; MTCW

Constant (de Rebecque), (Henri) Benjamin 1767-
1830 **NCLC 6**
See also DLB 119

Conybeare, Charles Augustus
See Eliot, T(homas) S(tearns)

Cook, Michael 1933- **CLC 58**
See also CA 93-96; DLB 53

Cook, Robin 1940- **CLC 14; DAM POP**
See also BEST 90 2; CA 108; 111; CANR 41; INT
111

Cook, Roy
See Silverberg, Robert

Cooke, Elizabeth 1948- **CLC 55**
See also CA 129

Cooke, John Esten 1830-1886 **NCLC 5**
See also DLB 3

Cooke, John Estes
See Baum, L(yman) Frank

Cooke, M. E.
See Creasey, John

Cooke, Margaret
See Creasey, John

Cook-Lynn, Elizabeth 1930- **CLC 93; DAM MULT**
See also CA 133; DLB 175; NNAL

Cooney, Ray **CLC 62**

Cooper, Douglas 1960- **CLC 86**

Cooper, Henry St. John
See Creasey, John

Cooper, J(oan) California CLC 56; DAM MULT
See also AAYA 12; BW 1; CA 125; CANR 55

Cooper, James Fenimore 1789-1851 NCLC 1, 27, 54
See also CDALB 1640-1865; DLB 3; SATA 19

Coover, Robert (Lowell) 1932- CLC 3, 7, 15, 32, 46, 87; DAM NOV; SSC 15
See also CA 45-48; CANR 3, 37; DLB 2; DLBY 81; MTCW

Copeland, Stewart (Armstrong) 1952- CLC 26

Coppard, A(lfred) E(dgar) 1878-1957 TCLC 5; SSC 21
See also CA 114; DLB 162; YABC 1

Coppee, Francois 1842-1908 TCLC 25

Coppola, Francis Ford 1939- CLC 16
See also CA 77-80; CANR 40; DLB 44

Corbiere, Tristan 1845-1875 NCLC 43

Corcoran, Barbara 1911- CLC 17
See also AAYA 14; CA 21-24R; CAAS 2; CANR 11, 28, 48; DLB 52; JRDA; SAAS 20; SATA 3, 77

Cordelier, Maurice
See Giraudoux, (Hippolyte) Jean

Corelli, Marie 1855-1924 TCLC 51
See also Mackay, Mary
See also DLB 34, 156

Corman, Cid CLC 9
See also Corman, Sidney
See also CAAS 2; DLB 5

Corman, Sidney 1924-
See Corman, Cid
See also CA 85-88; CANR 44; DAM POET

Cormier, Robert (Edmund) 1925- CLC 12, 30; DA; DAB; DAC; DAM MST, NOV
See also AAYA 3, 19; CA 1-4R; CANR 5, 23; CDALB 1968-1988; CLR 12; DLB 52; INT CANR-23; JRDA; MAICYA; MTCW; SATA 10, 45, 83

Corn, Alfred (DeWitt III) 1943- CLC 33
See also CA 104; CAAS 25; CANR 44; DLB 120; DLBY 80

Corneille, Pierre 1606-1684 LC 28; DAB; DAM MST

Cornwell, David (John Moore) 1931- CLC 9, 15; DAM POP
See also le Carre, John
See also CA 5-8R; CANR 13, 33; MTCW

Corso, (Nunzio) Gregory 1930- CLC 1, 11
See also CA 5-8R; CANR 41; DLB 5, 16; MTCW

Cortazar, Julio 1914-1984 CLC 2, 3, 5, 10, 13, 15, 33, 34, 92; DAM MULT, NOV; HLC; SSC 7
See also CA 21-24R; CANR 12, 32; DLB 113; HW; MTCW

Cortes, Hernan 1484-1547 LC 31

Corwin, Cecil
See Kornbluth, C(yril) M.

Cosic, Dobrica 1921- CLC 14
See also CA 122; 138

Costain, Thomas B(ertram) 1885-1965 CLC 30
See also CA 5-8R; 25-28R; DLB 9

Costantini, Humberto 1924(?)-1987 CLC 49
See also CA 131; 122; HW

Costello, Elvis 1955- CLC 21

Cotter, Joseph Seamon Sr. 1861-1949 TCLC 28; BLC; DAM MULT
See also BW 1; CA 124; DLB 50

Couch, Arthur Thomas Quiller
See Quiller-Couch, Arthur Thomas

Coulton, James
See Hansen, Joseph

Couperus, Louis (Marie Anne) 1863-1923 TCLC 15
See also CA 115

Coupland, Douglas 1961- CLC 85; DAC; DAM POP
See also CA 142; CANR 57

Court, Wesli
See Turco, Lewis (Putnam)

Courtenay, Bryce 1933- CLC 59
See also CA 138

Courtney, Robert
See Ellison, Harlan (Jay)

Cousteau, Jacques-Yves 1910- CLC 30
See also CA 65-68; CANR 15; MTCW; SATA 38

Coward, Noel (Peirce) 1899-1973 CLC 1, 9, 29, 51; DAM DRAM
See also AITN 1; CA 17-18; 41-44R; CANR 35; CAP 2; CDBLB 1914-1945; DLB 10; MTCW

Cowley, Malcolm 1898-1989 CLC 39
See also CA 5-8R; 128; CANR 3, 55; DLB 4, 48; DLBY 81, 89; MTCW

Cowper, William 1731-1800 NCLC 8; DAM POET
See also DLB 104, 109

Cox, William Trevor 1928- CLC 9, 14, 71; DAM NOV
See also Trevor, William
See also CA 9-12R; CANR 4, 37, 55; DLB 14; INT CANR-37; MTCW

Coyne, P. J.
See Masters, Hilary

Cozzens, James Gould 1903-1978 CLC 1, 4, 11, 92
See also CA 9-12R; 81-84; CANR 19; CDALB 1941-1968; DLB 9; DLBD 2; DLBY 84; MTCW

Crabbe, George 1754-1832 NCLC 26
See also DLB 93

Craddock, Charles Egbert
See Murfree, Mary Noailles

Craig, A. A.
See Anderson, Poul (William)

Craik, Dinah Maria (Mulock) 1826-1887 NCLC 38
See also DLB 35, 163; MAICYA; SATA 34

Cram, Ralph Adams 1863-1942 TCLC 45

Crane, (Harold) Hart 1899-1932 TCLC 2, 5; DA; DAB; DAC; DAM MST, POET; PC 3; WLC
See also CA 104; 127; CDALB 1917-1929; DLB 4, 48; MTCW

Crane, R(onald) S(almon) 1886-1967 CLC 27
See also CA 85-88; DLB 63

Crane, Stephen (Townley) 1871-1900 TCLC 11, 17, 32; DA; DAB; DAC; DAM MST, NOV, POET; SSC 7; WLC
See also CA 109; 140; CDALB 1865-1917; DLB 12, 54, 78; YABC 2

Crase, Douglas 1944- CLC 58
See also CA 106

Crashaw, Richard 1612(?)-1649 LC 24
See also DLB 126

Craven, Margaret 1901-1980 CLC 17; DAC
See also CA 103

Crawford, F(rancis) Marion 1854-1909 TCLC 10
See also CA 107; DLB 71

Crawford, Isabella Valancy 1850-1887 NCLC 12
See also DLB 92

Crayon, Geoffrey
See Irving, Washington

Creasey, John 1908-1973 CLC 11
See also CA 5-8R; 41-44R; CANR 8; DLB 77; MTCW

Crebillon, Claude Prosper Jolyot de (fils) 1707-1777 LC 28

Credo
See Creasey, John

Creeley, Robert (White) 1926- CLC 1, 2, 4, 8, 11, 15, 36, 78; DAM POET
See also CA 1-4R; CAAS 10; CANR 23, 43; DLB 5, 16, 169; MTCW

Crews, Harry (Eugene) 1935- CLC 6, 23, 49
See also AITN 1; CA 25-28R; CANR 20, 57; DLB 6, 143; MTCW

Crichton, (John) Michael 1942- CLC 2, 6, 54, 90; DAM NOV, POP
See also AAYA 10; AITN 2; CA 25-28R; CANR 13, 40, 54; DLBY 81; INT CANR-13; JRDA; MTCW; SATA 9, 88

Crispin, Edmund CLC 22
See also Montgomery, (Robert) Bruce
See also DLB 87

Cristofer, Michael 1945(?)- CLC 28; DAM DRAM
See also CA 110; 152; DLB 7

Croce, Benedetto 1866-1952 TCLC 37

See also CA 120; 155

Crockett, David 1786-1836 **NCLC 8**
See also DLB 3, 11

Crockett, Davy
See Crockett, David

Crofts, Freeman Wills 1879-1957 **TCLC 55**
See also CA 115; DLB 77

Croker, John Wilson 1780-1857 **NCLC 10**
See also DLB 110

Crommelynck, Fernand 1885-1970 **CLC 75**
See also CA 89-92

Cronin, A(rchibald) J(oseph) 1896-1981 **CLC 32**
See also CA 1-4R; 102; CANR 5; SATA 47; SATA-Obit 25

Cross, Amanda
See Heilbrun, Carolyn G(old)

Crothers, Rachel 1878(?)-1958 **TCLC 19**
See also CA 113; DLB 7

Croves, Hal
See Traven, B.

Crow Dog, Mary (Ellen) (?)- **CLC 93**
See also Brave Bird, Mary
See also CA 154

Crowfield, Christopher
See Stowe, Harriet (Elizabeth) Beecher

Crowley, Aleister TCLC 7
See also Crowley, Edward Alexander

Crowley, Edward Alexander 1875-1947
See Crowley, Aleister
See also CA 104

Crowley, John 1942- **CLC 57**
See also CA 61-64; CANR 43; DLBY 82; SATA 65

Crud
See Crumb, R(obert)

Crumarums
See Crumb, R(obert)

Crumb, R(obert) 1943- **CLC 17**
See also CA 106

Crumbum
See Crumb, R(obert)

Crumski
See Crumb, R(obert)

Crum the Bum
See Crumb, R(obert)

Crunk
See Crumb, R(obert)

Crustt

See Crumb, R(obert)

Cryer, Gretchen (Kiger) 1935- **CLC 21**
See also CA 114; 123

Csath, Geza 1887-1919 **TCLC 13**
See also CA 111

Cudlip, David 1933- **CLC 34**

Cullen, Countee 1903-1946 **TCLC 4, 37; BLC; DA; DAC; DAM MST, MULT, POET**
See also BW 1; CA 108; 124; CDALB 1917-1929; DLB 4, 48, 51; MTCW; SATA 18

Cum, R.
See Crumb, R(obert)

Cummings, Bruce F(rederick) 1889-1919
See Barbellion, W. N. P.
See also CA 123

Cummings, E(dward) E(stlin) 1894-1962 **CLC 1, 3, 8, 12, 15, 68; DA; DAB; DAC; DAM MST, POET; PC 5; WLC 2**
See also CA 73-76; CANR 31; CDALB 1929-1941; DLB 4, 48; MTCW

Cunha, Euclides (Rodrigues Pimenta) da 1866-1909 **TCLC 24**
See also CA 123

Cunningham, E. V.
See Fast, Howard (Melvin)

Cunningham, J(ames) V(incent) 1911-1985 **CLC 3, 31**
See also CA 1-4R; 115; CANR 1; DLB 5

Cunningham, Julia (Woolfolk) 1916- **CLC 12**
See also CA 9-12R; CANR 4, 19, 36; JRDA; MAICYA; SAAS 2; SATA 1, 26

Cunningham, Michael 1952- **CLC 34**
See also CA 136

Cunninghame Graham, R(obert) B(ontine) 1852-1936 **TCLC 19**
See also Graham, R(obert) B(ontine) Cunninghame
See also CA 119; DLB 98

Currie, Ellen 19(?)- **CLC 44**

Curtin, Philip
See Lowndes, Marie Adelaide (Belloc)

Curtis, Price
See Ellison, Harlan (Jay)

Cutrate, Joe
See Spiegelman, Art

Czaczkes, Shmuel Yosef
See Agnon, S(hmuel) Y(osef Halevi)

Dabrowska, Maria (Szumska) 1889-1965 **CLC 15**
See also CA 106

Dabydeen, David 1955- **CLC 34**
See also BW 1; CA 125; CANR 56

Dacey, Philip 1939- **CLC 51**

See also CA 37-40R; CAAS 17; CANR 14, 32; DLB 105

Dagerman, Stig (Halvard) 1923-1954 **TCLC 17**
See also CA 117; 155

Dahl, Roald 1916-1990 **CLC 1, 6, 18, 79; DAB; DAC; DAM MST, NOV, POP**
See also AAYA 15; CA 1-4R; 133; CANR 6, 32, 37; CLR 1, 7, 41; DLB 139; JRDA; MAICYA; MTCW; SATA 1, 26, 73; SATA-Obit 65

Dahlberg, Edward 1900-1977 **CLC 1, 7, 14**
See also CA 9-12R; 69-72; CANR 31; DLB 48; MTCW

Dale, Colin TCLC 18
See also Lawrence, T(homas) E(dward)

Dale, George E.
See Asimov, Isaac

Daly, Elizabeth 1878-1967 **CLC 52**
See also CA 23-24; 25-28R; CAP 2

Daly, Maureen 1921- **CLC 17**
See also AAYA 5; CANR 37; JRDA; MAICYA; SAAS 1; SATA 2

Damas, Leon-Gontran 1912-1978 **CLC 84**
See also BW 1; CA 125; 73-76

Dana, Richard Henry Sr. 1787-1879 **NCLC 53**

Daniel, Samuel 1562(?)-1619 **LC 24**
See also DLB 62

Daniels, Brett
See Adler, Renata

Dannay, Frederic 1905-1982 **CLC 11; DAM POP**
See also Queen, Ellery
See also CA 1-4R; 107; CANR 1, 39; DLB 137; MTCW

D'Annunzio, Gabriele 1863-1938 **TCLC 6, 40**
See also CA 104; 155

Danois, N. le
See Gourmont, Remy (-Marie-Charles) de

d'Antibes, Germain
See Simenon, Georges (Jacques Christian)

Danticat, Edwidge 1969- **CLC 94**
See also CA 152

Danvers, Dennis 1947- **CLC 70**

Danziger, Paula 1944- **CLC 21**
See also AAYA 4; CA 112; 115; CANR 37; CLR 20; JRDA; MAICYA; SATA 36, 63; SATA-Brief 30

Da Ponte, Lorenzo 1749-1838 **NCLC 50**

Dario, Ruben 1867-1916 **TCLC 4; DAM MULT; HLC; PC 15**
See also CA 131; HW; MTCW

Darley, George 1795-1846 **NCLC 2**
See also DLB 96

173; MTCW

de Lisser, H. G.
See De Lisser, H(erbert) G(eorge)
See also DLB 117

De Lisser, H(erbert) G(eorge) 1878-1944 **TCLC 12**
See also de Lisser, H. G.
See also BW 2; CA 109; 152

Deloria, Vine (Victor), Jr. 1933- **CLC 21; DAM MULT**
See also CA 53-56; CANR 5, 20, 48; DLB 175; MTCW; NNAL; SATA 21

Del Vecchio, John M(ichael) 1947- **CLC 29**
See also CA 110; DLBD 9

de Man, Paul (Adolph Michel) 1919-1983 **CLC 55**
See also CA 128; 111; DLB 67; MTCW

De Marinis, Rick 1934- **CLC 54**
See also CA 57-60; CAAS 24; CANR 9, 25, 50

Dembry, R. Emmet
See Murfree, Mary Noailles

Demby, William 1922- **CLC 53; BLC; DAM MULT**
See also BW 1; CA 81-84; DLB 33

Demijohn, Thom
See Disch, Thomas M(ichael)

de Montherlant, Henry (Milon)
See Montherlant, Henry (Milon) de

Demosthenes 384B.C.-322B.C. **CMLC 13**
See also DLB 176

de Natale, Francine
See Malzberg, Barry N(athaniel)

Denby, Edwin (Orr) 1903-1983 **CLC 48**
See also CA 138; 110

Denis, Julio
See Cortazar, Julio

Denmark, Harrison
See Zelazny, Roger (Joseph)

Dennis, John 1658-1734 **LC 11**
See also DLB 101

Dennis, Nigel (Forbes) 1912-1989 **CLC 8**
See also CA 25-28R; 129; DLB 13, 15; MTCW

De Palma, Brian (Russell) 1940- **CLC 20**
See also CA 109

De Quincey, Thomas 1785-1859 **NCLC 4**
See also CDBLB 1789-1832; DLB 110; 144

Deren, Eleanora 1908(?)-1961
See Deren, Maya
See also CA 111

Deren, Maya CLC 16
See also Deren, Eleanora

Derleth, August (William) 1909-1971 **CLC 31**
See also CA 1-4R; 29-32R; CANR 4; DLB 9; SATA 5

Der Nister 1884-1950 **TCLC 56**

de Routisie, Albert
See Aragon, Louis

Derrida, Jacques 1930- **CLC 24, 87**
See also CA 124; 127

Derry Down Derry
See Lear, Edward

Dersonnes, Jacques
See Simenon, Georges (Jacques Christian)

Desai, Anita 1937- **CLC 19, 37, 97; DAB; DAM NOV**
See also CA 81-84; CANR 33, 53; MTCW; SATA 63

de Saint-Luc, Jean
See Glassco, John

de Saint Roman, Arnaud
See Aragon, Louis

Descartes, Rene 1596-1650 **LC 20, 35**

De Sica, Vittorio 1901(?)-1974 **CLC 20**
See also CA 117

Desnos, Robert 1900-1945 **TCLC 22**
See also CA 121; 151

Destouches, Louis-Ferdinand 1894-1961 **CLC 9, 15**
See also Celine, Louis-Ferdinand
See also CA 85-88; CANR 28; MTCW

de Tolignac, Gaston
See Griffith, D(avid Lewelyn) W(ark)

Deutsch, Babette 1895-1982 **CLC 18**
See also CA 1-4R; 108; CANR 4; DLB 45; SATA 1; SATA-Obit 33

Devenant, William 1606-1649 **LC 13**

Devkota, Laxmiprasad 1909-1959 **TCLC 23**
See also CA 123

De Voto, Bernard (Augustine) 1897-1955 **TCLC 29**
See also CA 113; DLB 9

De Vries, Peter 1910-1993 **CLC 1, 2, 3, 7, 10, 28, 46; DAM NOV**
See also CA 17-20R; 142; CANR 41; DLB 6; DLBY 82; MTCW

Dexter, John
See Bradley, Marion Zimmer

Dexter, Martin
See Faust, Frederick (Schiller)

Dexter, Pete 1943- **CLC 34, 55; DAM POP**
See also BEST 89 2; CA 127; 131; INT 131; MTCW

Diamano, Silmang
See Senghor, Leopold Sedar

Diamond, Neil 1941- **CLC 30**
See also CA 108

Diaz del Castillo, Bernal 1496-1584 **LC 31**

di Bassetto, Corno
See Shaw, George Bernard

Dick, Philip K(indred) 1928-1982 **CLC 10, 30, 72; DAM NOV, POP**
See also CA 49-52; 106; CANR 2, 16; DLB 8; MTCW

Dickens, Charles (John Huffam) 1812-1870 **NCLC 3, 8, 18, 26, 37, 50; DA; DAB; DAC; DAM MST, NOV; SSC 17; WLC**
See also CDBLB 1832-1890; DLB 21, 55, 70, 159, 166; JRDA; MAICYA; SATA 15

Dickey, James (Lafayette) 1923-1997 **CLC 1, 2, 4, 7, 10, 15, 47; DAM NOV, POET, POP**
See also AITN 1, 2; CA 9-12R; 156; CABS 2; CANR 10, 48; CDALB 1968-1988; DLB 5; DLBD 7; DLBY 82, 93; INT CANR-10; MTCW

Dickey, William 1928-1994 **CLC 3, 28**
See also CA 9-12R; 145; CANR 24; DLB 5

Dickinson, Charles 1951- **CLC 49**
See also CA 128

Dickinson, Emily (Elizabeth) 1830-1886 **NCLC 21; DA; DAB; DAC; DAM MST, POET; PC 1; WLC**
See also CDALB 1865-1917; DLB 1; SATA 29

Dickinson, Peter (Malcolm) 1927- **CLC 12, 35**
See also AAYA 9; CA 41-44R; CANR 31; CLR 29; DLB 87, 161; JRDA; MAICYA; SATA 5, 62

Dickson, Carr
See Carr, John Dickson

Dickson, Carter
See Carr, John Dickson

Diderot, Denis 1713-1784 **LC 26**

Didion, Joan 1934- **CLC 1, 3, 8, 14, 32; DAM NOV**
See also AITN 1; CA 5-8R; CANR 14, 52; CDALB 1968-1988; DLB 2, 173; DLBY 81, 86; MTCW

Dietrich, Robert
See Hunt, E(verette) Howard, (Jr.)

Dillard, Annie 1945- **CLC 9, 60; DAM NOV**
See also AAYA 6; CA 49-52; CANR 3, 43; DLBY 80; MTCW; SATA 10

Dillard, R(ichard) H(enry) W(ilde) 1937- **CLC 5**
See also CA 21-24R; CAAS 7; CANR 10; DLB 5

Dillon, Eilis 1920-1994 **CLC 17**
See also CA 9-12R; 147; CAAS 3; CANR 4, 38; CLR 26; MAICYA; SATA 2, 74; SATA-Obit 83

Dimont, Penelope
See Mortimer, Penelope (Ruth)

Dinesen, Isak CLC 10, 29, 95; SSC 7
See also Blixen, Karen (Christentze Dinesen)

Ding Ling CLC 68
See also Chiang Pin-chin

Disch, Thomas M(ichael) 1940- **CLC 7, 36**

See also AAYA 17; CA 21-24R; CAAS 4; CANR 17, 36, 54; CLR 18; DLB 8; MAICYA; MTCW; SAAS 15; SATA 92

Disch, Tom
See Disch, Thomas M(ichael)

d'Isly, Georges
See Simenon, Georges (Jacques Christian)

Disraeli, Benjamin 1804-1881 **NCLC 2, 39**
See also DLB 21, 55

Ditcum, Steve
See Crumb, R(obert)

Dixon, Paige
See Corcoran, Barbara

Dixon, Stephen 1936- **CLC 52; SSC 16**
See also CA 89-92; CANR 17, 40, 54; DLB 130

Dobell, Sydney Thompson 1824-1874 **NCLC 43**
See also DLB 32

Doblin, Alfred TCLC 13
See also Doeblin, Alfred

Dobrolyubov, Nikolai Alexandrovich 1836-1861 **NCLC 5**

Dobyns, Stephen 1941- **CLC 37**
See also CA 45-48; CANR 2, 18

Doctorow, E(dgar) L(aurence) 1931- **CLC 6, 11, 15, 18, 37, 44, 65; DAM NOV, POP**
See also AITN 2; BEST 89 3; CA 45-48; CANR 2, 33, 51; CDALB 1968-1988; DLB 2, 28, 173; DLBY 80; MTCW

Dodgson, Charles Lutwidge 1832-1898
See Carroll, Lewis
See also CLR 2; DA; DAB; DAC; DAM MST, NOV, POET; MAICYA; YABC 2

Dodson, Owen (Vincent) 1914-1983 **CLC 79; BLC; DAM MULT**
See also BW 1; CA 65-68; 110; CANR 24; DLB 76

Doeblin, Alfred 1878-1957 **TCLC 13**
See also Doblin, Alfred
See also CA 110; 141; DLB 66

Doerr, Harriet 1910- **CLC 34**
See also CA 117; 122; CANR 47; INT 122

Domecq, H(onorio) Bustos
See Bioy Casares, Adolfo; Borges, Jorge Luis

Domini, Rey
See Lorde, Audre (Geraldine)

Dominique
See Proust, (Valentin-Louis-George-Eugene-) Marcel

Don, A
See Stephen, Leslie

Donaldson, Stephen R. 1947- **CLC 46; DAM POP**
See also CA 89-92; CANR 13, 55; INT CANR-13

Donleavy, J(ames) P(atrick) 1926- **CLC 1, 4, 6, 10,**
45
See also AITN 2; CA 9-12R; CANR 24, 49; DLB 6, 173; INT CANR-24; MTCW

Donne, John 1572-1631 **LC 10, 24; DA; DAB; DAC; DAM MST, POET; PC 1**
See also CDBLB Before 1660; DLB 121, 151

Donnell, David 1939(?)- **CLC 34**

Donoghue, P. S.
See Hunt, E(verette) Howard, (Jr.)

Donoso (Yanez), Jose 1924-1996 **CLC 4, 8, 11, 32, 99; DAM MULT; HLC**
See also CA 81-84; 155; CANR 32; DLB 113; HW; MTCW

Donovan, John 1928-1992 **CLC 35**
See also AAYA 20; CA 97-100; 137; CLR 3; MAICYA; SATA 72; SATA-Brief 29

Don Roberto
See Cunninghame Graham, R(obert) B(ontine)

Doolittle, Hilda 1886-1961 **CLC 3, 8, 14, 31, 34, 73; DA; DAC; DAM MST, POET; PC 5; WLC**
See also H. D.
See also CA 97-100; CANR 35; DLB 4, 45; MTCW

Dorfman, Ariel 1942- **CLC 48, 77; DAM MULT; HLC**
See also CA 124; 130; HW; INT 130

Dorn, Edward (Merton) 1929- **CLC 10, 18**
See also CA 93-96; CANR 42; DLB 5; INT 93-96

Dorsan, Luc
See Simenon, Georges (Jacques Christian)

Dorsange, Jean
See Simenon, Georges (Jacques Christian)

Dos Passos, John (Roderigo) 1896-1970 **CLC 1, 4, 8, 11, 15, 25, 34, 82; DA; DAB; DAC; DAM MST, NOV; WLC**
See also CA 1-4R; 29-32R; CANR 3; CDALB 1929-1941; DLB 4, 9; DLBD 1; MTCW

Dossage, Jean
See Simenon, Georges (Jacques Christian)

Dostoevsky, Fedor Mikhailovich 1821-1881 **NCLC 2, 7, 21, 33, 43; DA; DAB; DAC; DAM MST, NOV; SSC 2; WLC**

Doughty, Charles M(ontagu) 1843-1926 **TCLC 27**
See also CA 115; DLB 19, 57, 174

Douglas, Ellen CLC 73
See also Haxton, Josephine Ayres; Williamson, Ellen Douglas

Douglas, Gavin 1475(?)-1522 **LC 20**

Douglas, Keith 1920-1944 **TCLC 40**
See also DLB 27

Douglas, Leonard
See Bradbury, Ray (Douglas)

Douglas, Michael
See Crichton, (John) Michael

Douglas, Norman 1868-1952 **TCLC 68**

Douglass, Frederick 1817(?)-1895 **NCLC 7, 55; BLC; DA; DAC; DAM MST, MULT; WLC**
See also CDALB 1640-1865; DLB 1, 43, 50, 79; SATA 29

Dourado, (Waldomiro Freitas) Autran 1926- **CLC 23, 60**
See also CA 25-28R; CANR 34

Dourado, Waldomiro Autran
See Dourado, (Waldomiro Freitas) Autran

Dove, Rita (Frances) 1952- **CLC 50, 81; DAM MULT, POET; PC 6**
See also BW 2; CA 109; CAAS 19; CANR 27, 42; DLB 120

Dowell, Coleman 1925-1985 **CLC 60**
See also CA 25-28R; 117; CANR 10; DLB 130

Dowson, Ernest (Christopher) 1867-1900 **TCLC 4**
See also CA 105; 150; DLB 19, 135

Doyle, A. Conan
See Doyle, Arthur Conan

Doyle, Arthur Conan 1859-1930 **TCLC 7; DA; DAB; DAC; DAM MST, NOV; SSC 12; WLC**
See also AAYA 14; CA 104; 122; CDBLB 1890-1914; DLB 18, 70, 156; MTCW; SATA 24

Doyle, Conan
See Doyle, Arthur Conan

Doyle, John
See Graves, Robert (von Ranke)

Doyle, Roddy 1958(?)- **CLC 81**
See also AAYA 14; CA 143

Doyle, Sir A. Conan
See Doyle, Arthur Conan

Doyle, Sir Arthur Conan
See Doyle, Arthur Conan

Dr. A
See Asimov, Isaac; Silverstein, Alvin

Drabble, Margaret 1939- **CLC 2, 3, 5, 8, 10, 22, 53; DAB; DAC; DAM MST, NOV, POP**
See also CA 13-16R; CANR 18, 35; CDBLB 1960 to Present; DLB 14, 155; MTCW; SATA 48

Drapier, M. B.
See Swift, Jonathan

Drayham, James
See Mencken, H(enry) L(ouis)

Drayton, Michael 1563-1631 **LC 8**

Dreadstone, Carl
See Campbell, (John) Ramsey

Dreiser, Theodore (Herman Albert) 1871-1945 **TCLC 10, 18, 35; DA; DAC; DAM MST, NOV; WLC**
See also CA 106; 132; CDALB 1865-1917; DLB 9, 12, 102, 137; DLBD 1; MTCW

Drexler, Rosalyn 1926- **CLC 2, 6**
See also CA 81-84

Dreyer, Carl Theodor 1889-1968 **CLC 16**
See also CA 116

Drieu la Rochelle, Pierre(-Eugene) 1893-1945
TCLC 21
See also CA 117; DLB 72

Drinkwater, John 1882-1937 **TCLC 57**
See also CA 109; 149; DLB 10, 19, 149

Drop Shot
See Cable, George Washington

Droste-Hulshoff, Annette Freiin von 1797-1848
NCLC 3
See also DLB 133

Drummond, Walter
See Silverberg, Robert

Drummond, William Henry 1854-1907 **TCLC 25**
See also DLB 92

Drummond de Andrade, Carlos 1902-1987 **CLC 18**
See also Andrade, Carlos Drummond de
See also CA 132; 123

Drury, Allen (Stuart) 1918- **CLC 37**
See also CA 57-60; CANR 18, 52; INT CANR-18

Dryden, John 1631-1700 **LC 3, 21; DA; DAB; DAC;**
DAM DRAM, MST, POET; DC 3; WLC
See also CDBLB 1660-1789; DLB 80, 101, 131

Duberman, Martin 1930- **CLC 8**
See also CA 1-4R; CANR 2

Dubie, Norman (Evans) 1945- **CLC 36**
See also CA 69-72; CANR 12; DLB 120

Du Bois, W(illiam) E(dward) B(urghardt) 1868-1963
CLC 1, 2, 13, 64, 96; BLC; DA; DAC; DAM
MST, MULT, NOV; WLC
See also BW 1; CA 85-88; CANR 34; CDALB 1865-
1917; DLB 47, 50, 91; MTCW; SATA 42

Dubus, Andre 1936- **CLC 13, 36, 97; SSC 15**
See also CA 21-24R; CANR 17; DLB 130; INT
CANR-17

Duca Minimo
See D'Annunzio, Gabriele

Ducharme, Rejean 1941- **CLC 74**
See also DLB 60

Duclos, Charles Pinot 1704-1772 **LC 1**

Dudek, Louis 1918- **CLC 11, 19**
See also CA 45-48; CAAS 14; CANR 1; DLB 88

Duerrenmatt, Friedrich 1921-1990 **CLC 1, 4, 8, 11,**
15, 43; DAM DRAM
See also CA 17-20R; CANR 33; DLB 69, 124;
MTCW

Duffy, Bruce (?)- **CLC 50**

Duffy, Maureen 1933- **CLC 37**
See also CA 25-28R; CANR 33; DLB 14; MTCW

Dugan, Alan 1923- **CLC 2, 6**
See also CA 81-84; DLB 5

du Gard, Roger Martin
See Martin du Gard, Roger

Duhamel, Georges 1884-1966 **CLC 8**
See also CA 81-84; 25-28R; CANR 35; DLB 65;
MTCW

Dujardin, Edouard (Emile Louis) 1861-1949 **TCLC**
13
See also CA 109; DLB 123

Dumas, Alexandre (Davy de la Pailleterie) 1802-
1870 **NCLC 11; DA; DAB; DAC; DAM MST,**
NOV; WLC
See also DLB 119; SATA 18

Dumas, Alexandre 1824-1895 **NCLC 9; DC 1**

Dumas, Claudine
See Malzberg, Barry N(athaniel)

Dumas, Henry L. 1934-1968 **CLC 6, 62**
See also BW 1; CA 85-88; DLB 41

du Maurier, Daphne 1907-1989 **CLC 6, 11, 59; DAB;**
DAC; DAM MST, POP; SSC 18
See also CA 5-8R; 128; CANR 6, 55; MTCW;
SATA 27; SATA-Obit 60

Dunbar, Paul Laurence 1872-1906 **TCLC 2, 12;**
BLC; DA; DAC; DAM MST, MULT, POET;
PC 5; SSC 8; WLC
See also BW 1; CA 104; 124; CDALB 1865-1917;
DLB 50, 54, 78; SATA 34

Dunbar, William 1460(?)-1530(?) **LC 20**
See also DLB 132, 146

Duncan, Dora Angela
See Duncan, Isadora

Duncan, Isadora 1877(?)-1927 **TCLC 68**
See also CA 118; 149

Duncan, Lois 1934- **CLC 26**
See also AAYA 4; CA 1-4R; CANR 2, 23, 36; CLR
29; JRDA; MAICYA; SAAS 2; SATA 1, 36, 75

Duncan, Robert (Edward) 1919-1988 **CLC 1, 2, 4, 7,**
15, 41, 55; DAM POET; PC 2
See also CA 9-12R; 124; CANR 28; DLB 5, 16;
MTCW

Duncan, Sara Jeannette 1861-1922 **TCLC 60**
See also DLB 92

Dunlap, William 1766-1839 **NCLC 2**
See also DLB 30, 37, 59

Dunn, Douglas (Eaglesham) 1942- **CLC 6, 40**
See also CA 45-48; CANR 2, 33; DLB 40; MTCW

Dunn, Katherine (Karen) 1945- **CLC 71**
See also CA 33-36R

Dunn, Stephen 1939- **CLC 36**
See also CA 33-36R; CANR 12, 48, 53; DLB 105

Dunne, Finley Peter 1867-1936 **TCLC 28**
See also CA 108; DLB 11, 23

Dunne, John Gregory 1932- **CLC 28**
See also CA 25-28R; CANR 14, 50; DLBY 80

Dunsany, Edward John Moreton Drax Plunkett
1878-1957
See Dunsany, Lord
See also CA 104; 148; DLB 10

Dunsany, Lord TCLC 2, 59
See also Dunsany, Edward John Moreton Drax
Plunkett
See also DLB 77, 153, 156

du Perry, Jean
See Simenon, Georges (Jacques Christian)

Durang, Christopher (Ferdinand) 1949- **CLC 27,**
38
See also CA 105; CANR 50

Duras, Marguerite 1914-1996 **CLC 3, 6, 11, 20, 34,**
40, 68, 100
See also CA 25-28R; 151; CANR 50; DLB 83;
MTCW

Durban, (Rosa) Pam 1947- **CLC 39**
See also CA 123

Durcan, Paul 1944- **CLC 43, 70; DAM POET**
See also CA 134

Durkheim, Emile 1858-1917 **TCLC 55**

Durrell, Lawrence (George) 1912-1990 **CLC 1, 4,**
6, 8, 13, 27, 41; DAM NOV
See also CA 9-12R; 132; CANR 40; CDBLB 1945-
1960; DLB 15, 27; DLBY 90; MTCW

Durrenmatt, Friedrich
See Duerrenmatt, Friedrich

Dutt, Toru 1856-1877 **NCLC 29**

Dwight, Timothy 1752-1817 **NCLC 13**
See also DLB 37

Dworkin, Andrea 1946- **CLC 43**
See also CA 77-80; CAAS 21; CANR 16, 39; INT
CANR-16; MTCW

Dwyer, Deanna
See Koontz, Dean R(ay)

Dwyer, K. R.
See Koontz, Dean R(ay)

Dylan, Bob 1941- **CLC 3, 4, 6, 12, 77**
See also CA 41-44R; DLB 16

Eagleton, Terence (Francis) 1943-
See Eagleton, Terry
See also CA 57-60; CANR 7, 23; MTCW

Eagleton, Terry CLC 63
See also Eagleton, Terence (Francis)

Early, Jack
See Scoppettone, Sandra

East, Michael
See West, Morris L(anglo)

Eastaway, Edward

See Thomas, (Philip) Edward

Eastlake, William (Derry) 1917- **CLC 8**
See also CA 5-8R; CAAS 1; CANR 5; DLB 6; INT CANR-5

Eastman, Charles A(lexander) 1858-1939 **TCLC 55; DAM MULT**
See also DLB 175; NNAL; YABC 1

Eberhart, Richard (Ghormley) 1904- **CLC 3, 11, 19, 56; DAM POET**
See also CA 1-4R; CANR 2; CDALB 1941-1968; DLB 48; MTCW

Eberstadt, Fernanda 1960- **CLC 39**
See also CA 136

Echegaray (y Eizaguirre), Jose (Maria Waldo) 1832-1916 **TCLC 4**
See also CA 104; CANR 32; HW; MTCW

Echeverria, (Jose) Esteban (Antonino) 1805-1851 **NCLC 18**

Echo
See Proust, (Valentin-Louis-George-Eugene-) Marcel

Eckert, Allan W. 1931- **CLC 17**
See also AAYA 18; CA 13-16R; CANR 14, 45; INT CANR-14; SAAS 21; SATA 29, 91; SATA-Brief 27

Eckhart, Meister 1260(?)-1328(?) **CMLC 9**
See also DLB 115

Eckmar, F. R.
See de Hartog, Jan

Eco, Umberto 1932- **CLC 28, 60; DAM NOV, POP**
See also BEST 90 1; CA 77-80; CANR 12, 33, 55; MTCW

Eddison, E(ric) R(ucker) 1882-1945 **TCLC 15**
See also CA 109; 156

Edel, (Joseph) Leon 1907- **CLC 29, 34**
See also CA 1-4R; CANR 1, 22; DLB 103; INT CANR-22

Eden, Emily 1797-1869 **NCLC 10**

Edgar, David 1948- **CLC 42; DAM DRAM**
See also CA 57-60; CANR 12; DLB 13; MTCW

Edgerton, Clyde (Carlyle) 1944- **CLC 39**
See also AAYA 17; CA 118; 134; INT 134

Edgeworth, Maria 1768-1849 **NCLC 1, 51**
See also DLB 116, 159, 163; SATA 21

Edmonds, Paul
See Kuttner, Henry

Edmonds, Walter D(umaux) 1903- **CLC 35**
See also CA 5-8R; CANR 2; DLB 9; MAICYA; SAAS 4; SATA 1, 27

Edmondson, Wallace
See Ellison, Harlan (Jay)

Edson, Russell CLC 13

See also CA 33-36R

Edwards, Bronwen Elizabeth
See Rose, Wendy

Edwards, G(erald) B(asil) 1899-1976 **CLC 25**
See also CA 110

Edwards, Gus 1939- **CLC 43**
See also CA 108; INT 108

Edwards, Jonathan 1703-1758 **LC 7; DA; DAC; DAM MST**
See also DLB 24

Efron, Marina Ivanovna Tsvetaeva
See Tsvetaeva (Efron), Marina (Ivanovna)

Ehle, John (Marsden, Jr.) 1925- **CLC 27**
See also CA 9-12R

Ehrenbourg, Ilya (Grigoryevich)
See Ehrenburg, Ilya (Grigoryevich)

Ehrenburg, Ilya (Grigoryevich) 1891-1967 **CLC 18, 34, 62**
See also CA 102; 25-28R

Ehrenburg, Ilyo (Grigoryevich)
See Ehrenburg, Ilya (Grigoryevich)

Eich, Guenter 1907-1972 **CLC 15**
See also CA 111; 93-96; DLB 69, 124

Eichendorff, Joseph Freiherr von 1788-1857 **NCLC 8**
See also DLB 90

Eigner, Larry CLC 9
See also Eigner, Laurence (Joel)
See also CAAS 23; DLB 5

Eigner, Laurence (Joel) 1927-1996
See Eigner, Larry
See also CA 9-12R; 151; CANR 6

Einstein, Albert 1879-1955 **TCLC 65**
See also CA 121; 133; MTCW

Eiseley, Loren Corey 1907-1977 **CLC 7**
See also AAYA 5; CA 1-4R; 73-76; CANR 6

Eisenstadt, Jill 1963- **CLC 50**
See also CA 140

Eisenstein, Sergei (Mikhailovich) 1898-1948 **TCLC 57**
See also CA 114; 149

Eisner, Simon
See Kornbluth, C(yril) M.

Ekeloef, (Bengt) Gunnar 1907-1968 **CLC 27; DAM POET**
See also CA 123; 25-28R

Ekelof, (Bengt) Gunnar
See Ekeloef, (Bengt) Gunnar

Ekwensi, C. O. D.
See Ekwensi, Cyprian (Odiatu Duaka)

Ekwensi, Cyprian (Odiatu Duaka) 1921- **CLC 4;**

BLC; DAM MULT
See also BW 2; CA 29-32R; CANR 18, 42; DLB 117; MTCW; SATA 66

Elaine TCLC 18
See also Leverson, Ada

El Crummo
See Crumb, R(obert)

Elia
See Lamb, Charles

Eliade, Mircea 1907-1986 **CLC 19**
See also CA 65-68; 119; CANR 30; MTCW

Eliot, A. D.
See Jewett, (Theodora) Sarah Orne

Eliot, Alice
See Jewett, (Theodora) Sarah Orne

Eliot, Dan
See Silverberg, Robert

Eliot, George 1819-1880 **NCLC 4, 13, 23, 41, 49; DA; DAB; DAC; DAM MST, NOV; WLC**
See also CDBLB 1832-1890; DLB 21, 35, 55

Eliot, John 1604-1690 **LC 5**
See also DLB 24

Eliot, T(homas) S(tearns) 1888-1965 **CLC 1, 2, 3, 6, 9, 10, 13, 15, 24, 34, 41, 55, 57; DA; DAB; DAC; DAM DRAM, MST, POET; PC 5; WLC 2**
See also CA 5-8R; 25-28R; CANR 41; CDALB 1929-1941; DLB 7, 10, 45, 63; DLBY 88; MTCW

Elizabeth 1866-1941 **TCLC 41**

Elkin, Stanley L(awrence) 1930-1995 **CLC 4, 6, 9, 14, 27, 51, 91; DAM NOV, POP; SSC 12**
See also CA 9-12R; 148; CANR 8, 46; DLB 2, 28; DLBY 80; INT CANR-8; MTCW

Elledge, Scott CLC 34

Elliot, Don
See Silverberg, Robert

Elliott, Don
See Silverberg, Robert

Elliott, George P(aul) 1918-1980 **CLC 2**
See also CA 1-4R; 97-100; CANR 2

Elliott, Janice 1931- **CLC 47**
See also CA 13-16R; CANR 8, 29; DLB 14

Elliott, Sumner Locke 1917-1991 **CLC 38**
See also CA 5-8R; 134; CANR 2, 21

Elliott, William
See Bradbury, Ray (Douglas)

Ellis, A. E. CLC 7

Ellis, Alice Thomas CLC 40
See also Haycraft, Anna

Ellis, Bret Easton 1964- **CLC 39, 71; DAM POP**
See also AAYA 2; CA 118; 123; CANR 51; INT

123

Ellis, (Henry) Havelock 1859-1939 **TCLC 14**
See also CA 109

Ellis, Landon
See Ellison, Harlan (Jay)

Ellis, Trey 1962- **CLC 55**
See also CA 146

Ellison, Harlan (Jay) 1934- **CLC 1, 13, 42; DAM POP; SSC 14**
See also CA 5-8R; CANR 5, 46; DLB 8; INT CANR-5; MTCW

Ellison, Ralph (Waldo) 1914-1994 **CLC 1, 3, 11, 54, 86; BLC; DA; DAB; DAC; DAM MST, MULT, NOV; WLC**
See also AAYA 19; BW 1; CA 9-12R; 145; CANR 24, 53; CDALB 1941-1968; DLB 2, 76; DLBY 94; MTCW

Ellmann, Lucy (Elizabeth) 1956- **CLC 61**
See also CA 128

Ellmann, Richard (David) 1918-1987 **CLC 50**
See also BEST 89 2; CA 1-4R; 122; CANR 2, 28; DLB 103; DLBY 87; MTCW

Elman, Richard 1934- **CLC 19**
See also CA 17-20R; CAAS 3; CANR 47

Elron
See Hubbard, L(afayette) Ron(ald)

Eluard, Paul **TCLC 7, 41**
See also Grindel, Eugene

Elyot, Sir Thomas 1490(?)-1546 **LC 11**

Elytis, Odysseus 1911-1996 **CLC 15, 49, 100; DAM POET**
See also CA 102; 151; MTCW

Emecheta, (Florence Onye) Buchi 1944- **CLC 14, 48; BLC; DAM MULT**
See also BW 2; CA 81-84; CANR 27; DLB 117; MTCW; SATA 66

Emerson, Ralph Waldo 1803-1882 **NCLC 1, 38; DA; DAB; DAC; DAM MST, POET; WLC**
See also CDALB 1640-1865; DLB 1, 59, 73

Eminescu, Mihail 1850-1889 **NCLC 33**

Empson, William 1906-1984 **CLC 3, 8, 19, 33, 34**
See also CA 17-20R; 112; CANR 31; DLB 20; MTCW

Enchi Fumiko (Ueda) 1905-1986 **CLC 31**
See also CA 129; 121

Ende, Michael (Andreas Helmuth) 1929-1995 **CLC 31**
See also CA 118; 124; 149; CANR 36; CLR 14; DLB 75; MAICYA; SATA 61; SATA-Brief 42; SATA-Obit 86

Endo, Shusaku 1923-1996 **CLC 7, 14, 19, 54, 99; DAM NOV**
See also CA 29-32R; 153; CANR 21, 54; MTCW

Engel, Marian 1933-1985 **CLC 36**
See also CA 25-28R; CANR 12; DLB 53; INT CANR-12

Engelhardt, Frederick
See Hubbard, L(afayette) Ron(ald)

Enright, D(ennis) J(oseph) 1920- **CLC 4, 8, 31**
See also CA 1-4R; CANR 1, 42; DLB 27; SATA 25

Enzensberger, Hans Magnus 1929- **CLC 43**
See also CA 116; 119

Ephron, Nora 1941- **CLC 17, 31**
See also AITN 2; CA 65-68; CANR 12, 39

Epicurus 341B.C.-270B.C. **CMLC 21**
See also DLB 176

Epsilon
See Betjeman, John

Epstein, Daniel Mark 1948- **CLC 7**
See also CA 49-52; CANR 2, 53

Epstein, Jacob 1956- **CLC 19**
See also CA 114

Epstein, Joseph 1937- **CLC 39**
See also CA 112; 119; CANR 50

Epstein, Leslie 1938- **CLC 27**
See also CA 73-76; CAAS 12; CANR 23

Equiano, Olaudah 1745(?)-1797 **LC 16; BLC; DAM MULT**
See also DLB 37, 50

Erasmus, Desiderius 1469(?)-1536 **LC 16**

Erdman, Paul E(mil) 1932- **CLC 25**
See also AITN 1; CA 61-64; CANR 13, 43

Erdrich, Louise 1954- **CLC 39, 54; DAM MULT, NOV, POP**
See also AAYA 10; BEST 89 1; CA 114; CANR 41; DLB 152, 175; MTCW; NNAL

Erenburg, Ilya (Grigoryevich)
See Ehrenburg, Ilya (Grigoryevich)

Erickson, Stephen Michael 1950-
See Erickson, Steve
See also CA 129

Erickson, Steve **CLC 64**
See also Erickson, Stephen Michael

Ericson, Walter
See Fast, Howard (Melvin)

Eriksson, Buntel
See Bergman, (Ernst) Ingmar

Ernaux, Annie 1940- **CLC 88**
See also CA 147

Eschenbach, Wolfram von
See Wolfram von Eschenbach

Eseki, Bruno
See Mphahlele, Ezekiel

Esenin, Sergei (Alexandrovich) 1895-1925 **TCLC 4**
See also CA 104

Eshleman, Clayton 1935- **CLC 7**
See also CA 33-36R; CAAS 6; DLB 5

Espriella, Don Manuel Alvarez
See Southey, Robert

Espriu, Salvador 1913-1985 **CLC 9**
See also CA 154; 115; DLB 134

Espronceda, Jose de 1808-1842 **NCLC 39**

Esse, James
See Stephens, James

Esterbrook, Tom
See Hubbard, L(afayette) Ron(ald)

Estleman, Loren D. 1952- **CLC 48; DAM NOV, POP**
See also CA 85-88; CANR 27; INT CANR-27; MTCW

Eugenides, Jeffrey 1960(?)- **CLC 81**
See also CA 144

Euripides c. 485B.C.-406B.C. **DC 4**
See also DA; DAB; DAC; DAM DRAM, MST; DLB 176

Evan, Evin
See Faust, Frederick (Schiller)

Evans, Evan
See Faust, Frederick (Schiller)

Evans, Marian
See Eliot, George

Evans, Mary Ann
See Eliot, George

Evarts, Esther
See Benson, Sally

Everett, Percival L. 1956- **CLC 57**
See also BW 2; CA 129

Everson, R(onald) G(ilmour) 1903- **CLC 27**
See also CA 17-20R; DLB 88

Everson, William (Oliver) 1912-1994 **CLC 1, 5, 14**
See also CA 9-12R; 145; CANR 20; DLB 5, 16; MTCW

Evtushenko, Evgenii Aleksandrovich
See Yevtushenko, Yevgeny (Alexandrovich)

Ewart, Gavin (Buchanan) 1916-1995 **CLC 13, 46**
See also CA 89-92; 150; CANR 17, 46; DLB 40; MTCW

Ewers, Hanns Heinz 1871-1943 **TCLC 12**
See also CA 109, 149

Ewing, Frederick R.
See Sturgeon, Theodore (Hamilton)

Exley, Frederick (Earl) 1929-1992 **CLC 6, 11**
See also AITN 2; CA 81-84; 138; DLB 143; DLBY 81

Eynhardt, Guillermo
See Quiroga, Horacio (Sylvestre)

Ezekiel, Nissim 1924- **CLC 61**
See also CA 61-64

Ezekiel, Tish O'Dowd 1943- **CLC 34**
See also CA 129

Fadeyev, A.
See Bulgya, Alexander Alexandrovich

Fadeyev, Alexander TCLC 53
See also Bulgya, Alexander Alexandrovich

Fagen, Donald 1948- **CLC 26**

Fainzilberg, Ilya Arnoldovich 1897-1937
See Ilf, Ilya
See also CA 120

Fair, Ronald L. 1932- **CLC 18**
See also BW 1; CA 69-72; CANR 25; DLB 33

Fairbairns, Zoe (Ann) 1948- **CLC 32**
See also CA 103; CANR 21

Falco, Gian
See Papini, Giovanni

Falconer, James
See Kirkup, James

Falconer, Kenneth
See Kornbluth, C(yril) M.

Falkland, Samuel
See Heijermans, Herman

Fallaci, Oriana 1930- **CLC 11**
See also CA 77-80; CANR 15; MTCW

Faludy, George 1913- **CLC 42**
See also CA 21-24R

Faludy, Gyoergy
See Faludy, George

Fanon, Frantz 1925-1961 **CLC 74; BLC; DAM MULT**
See also BW 1; CA 116; 89-92

Fanshawe, Ann 1625-1680 **LC 11**

Fante, John (Thomas) 1911-1983 **CLC 60**
See also CA 69-72; 109; CANR 23; DLB 130; DLBY 83

Farah, Nuruddin 1945- **CLC 53; BLC; DAM MULT**
See also BW 2; CA 106; DLB 125

Fargue, Leon-Paul 1876(?)-1947 **TCLC 11**
See also CA 109

Farigoule, Louis
See Romains, Jules

Farina, Richard 1936(?)-1966 **CLC 9**
See also CA 81-84; 25-28R

Farley, Walter (Lorimer) 1915-1989 **CLC 17**
See also CA 17-20R; CANR 8, 29; DLB 22; JRDA; MAICYA; SATA 2, 43

Farmer, Philip Jose 1918- **CLC 1, 19**
See also CA 1-4R; CANR 4, 35; DLB 8; MTCW

Farquhar, George 1677-1707 **LC 21; DAM DRAM**
See also DLB 84

Farrell, J(ames) G(ordon) 1935-1979 **CLC 6**
See also CA 73-76; 89-92; CANR 36; DLB 14; MTCW

Farrell, James T(homas) 1904-1979 **CLC 1, 4, 8, 11, 66**
See also CA 5-8R; 89-92; CANR 9; DLB 4, 9, 86; DLBD 2; MTCW

Farren, Richard J.
See Betjeman, John

Farren, Richard M.
See Betjeman, John

Fassbinder, Rainer Werner 1946-1982 **CLC 20**
See also CA 93-96; 106; CANR 31

Fast, Howard (Melvin) 1914- **CLC 23; DAM NOV**
See also AAYA 16; CA 1-4R; CAAS 18; CANR 1, 33, 54; DLB 9; INT CANR-33; SATA 7

Faulcon, Robert
See Holdstock, Robert P.

Faulkner, William (Cuthbert) 1897-1962 **CLC 1, 3, 6, 8, 9, 11, 14, 18, 28, 52, 68; DA; DAB; DAC; DAM MST, NOV; SSC 1; WLC**
See also AAYA 7; CA 81-84; CANR 33; CDALB 1929-1941; DLB 9, 11, 44, 102; DLBD 2; DLBY 86; MTCW

Fauset, Jessie Redmon 1884(?)-1961 **CLC 19, 54; BLC; DAM MULT**
See also BW 1; CA 109; DLB 51

Faust, Frederick (Schiller) 1892-1944(?) **TCLC 49; DAM POP**
See also CA 108; 152

Faust, Irvin 1924- **CLC 8**
See also CA 33-36R; CANR 28; DLB 2, 28; DLBY 80

Fawkes, Guy
See Benchley, Robert (Charles)

Fearing, Kenneth (Flexner) 1902-1961 **CLC 51**
See also CA 93-96; DLB 9

Fecamps, Elise
See Creasey, John

Federman, Raymond 1928- **CLC 6, 47**
See also CA 17-20R; CAAS 8; CANR 10, 43; DLBY 80

Federspiel, J(uerg) F. 1931- **CLC 42**
See also CA 146

Feiffer, Jules (Ralph) 1929- **CLC 2, 8, 64; DAM DRAM**
See also AAYA 3; CA 17-20R; CANR 30; DLB 7, 44; INT CANR-30; MTCW; SATA 8, 61

Feige, Hermann Albert Otto Maximilian
See Traven, B.

Feinberg, David B. 1956-1994 **CLC 59**
See also CA 135; 147

Feinstein, Elaine 1930- **CLC 36**
See also CA 69-72; CAAS 1; CANR 31; DLB 14, 40; MTCW

Feldman, Irving (Mordecai) 1928- **CLC 7**
See also CA 1-4R; CANR 1; DLB 169

Fellini, Federico 1920-1993 **CLC 16, 85**
See also CA 65-68; 143; CANR 33

Felsen, Henry Gregor 1916- **CLC 17**
See also CA 1-4R; CANR 1; SAAS 2; SATA 1

Fenton, James Martin 1949- **CLC 32**
See also CA 102; DLB 40

Ferber, Edna 1887-1968 **CLC 18, 93**
See also AITN 1; CA 5-8R; 25-28R; DLB 9, 28, 86; MTCW; SATA 7

Ferguson, Helen
See Kavan, Anna

Ferguson, Samuel 1810-1886 **NCLC 33**
See also DLB 32

Fergusson, Robert 1750-1774 **LC 29**
See also DLB 109

Ferling, Lawrence
See Ferlinghetti, Lawrence (Monsanto)

Ferlinghetti, Lawrence (Monsanto) 1919(?)- **CLC 2, 6, 10, 27; DAM POET; PC 1**
See also CA 5-8R; CANR 3, 41; CDALB 1941-1968; DLB 5, 16; MTCW

Fernandez, Vicente Garcia Huidobro
See Huidobro Fernandez, Vicente Garcia

Ferrer, Gabriel (Francisco Victor) Miro
See Miro (Ferrer), Gabriel (Francisco Victor)

Ferrier, Susan (Edmonstone) 1782-1854 **NCLC 8**
See also DLB 116

Ferrigno, Robert 1948(?)- **CLC 65**
See also CA 140

Ferron, Jacques 1921-1985 **CLC 94; DAC**
See also CA 117; 129; DLB 60

Feuchtwanger, Lion 1884-1958 **TCLC 3**
See also CA 104; DLB 66

Feuillet, Octave 1821-1890 **NCLC 45**

Feydeau, Georges (Leon Jules Marie) 1862-1921 **TCLC 22; DAM DRAM**
See also CA 113; 152

Ficino, Marsilio 1433-1499 **LC 12**

Fiedeler, Hans
See Doeblin, Alfred

Fiedler, Leslie A(aron) 1917- **CLC 4, 13, 24**
See also CA 9-12R; CANR 7; DLB 28, 67; MTCW

Field, Andrew 1938- **CLC 44**

See also CA 97-100; CANR 25

Field, Eugene 1850-1895 **NCLC 3**
See also DLB 23, 42, 140; DLBD 13; MAICYA;
SATA 16

Field, Gans T.
See Wellman, Manly Wade

Field, Michael TCLC 43

Field, Peter
See Hobson, Laura Z(ametkin)

Fielding, Henry 1707-1754 **LC 1; DA; DAB; DAC;**
DAM DRAM, MST, NOV; WLC
See also CDBLB 1660-1789; DLB 39, 84, 101

Fielding, Sarah 1710-1768 **LC 1**
See also DLB 39

Fierstein, Harvey (Forbes) 1954- **CLC 33; DAM**
DRAM, POP
See also CA 123; 129

Figes, Eva 1932- **CLC 31**
See also CA 53-56; CANR 4, 44; DLB 14

Finch, Robert (Duer Claydon) 1900- **CLC 18**
See also CA 57-60; CANR 9, 24, 49; DLB 88

Findley, Timothy 1930- **CLC 27; DAC; DAM MST**
See also CA 25-28R; CANR 12, 42; DLB 53

Fink, William
See Mencken, H(enry) L(ouis)

Firbank, Louis 1942-
See Reed, Lou
See also CA 117

Firbank, (Arthur Annesley) Ronald 1886-1926
TCLC 1
See also CA 104; DLB 36

Fisher, M(ary) F(rances) K(ennedy) 1908-1992 **CLC**
76, 87
See also CA 77-80; 138; CANR 44

Fisher, Roy 1930- **CLC 25**
See also CA 81-84; CAAS 10; CANR 16; DLB 40

Fisher, Rudolph 1897-1934 **TCLC 11; BLC; DAM**
MULT
See also BW 1; CA 107; 124; DLB 51, 102

Fisher, Vardis (Alvero) 1895-1968 **CLC 7**
See also CA 5-8R; 25-28R; DLB 9

Fiske, Tarleton
See Bloch, Robert (Albert)

Fitch, Clarke
See Sinclair, Upton (Beall)

Fitch, John IV
See Cormier, Robert (Edmund)

Fitzgerald, Captain Hugh
See Baum, L(yman) Frank

FitzGerald, Edward 1809-1883 **NCLC 9**
See also DLB 32

Fitzgerald, F(rancis) Scott (Key) 1896-1940 **TCLC**
1, 6, 14, 28, 55; DA; DAB; DAC; DAM MST,
NOV; SSC 6; WLC
See also AITN 1; CA 110; 123; CDALB 1917-
1929; DLB 4, 9, 86; DLBD 1; DLBY 81;
MTCW

Fitzgerald, Penelope 1916- **CLC 19, 51, 61**
See also CA 85-88; CAAS 10; CANR 56; DLB 14

Fitzgerald, Robert (Stuart) 1910-1985 **CLC 39**
See also CA 1-4R; 114; CANR 1; DLBY 80

FitzGerald, Robert D(avid) 1902-1987 **CLC 19**
See also CA 17-20R

Fitzgerald, Zelda (Sayre) 1900-1948 **TCLC 52**
See also CA 117; 126; DLBY 84

Flanagan, Thomas (James Bonner) 1923- **CLC 25,**
52
See also CA 108; CANR 55; DLBY 80; INT 108;
MTCW

Flaubert, Gustave 1821-1880 **NCLC 2, 10, 19; DA;**
DAB; DAC; DAM MST, NOV; SSC 11; WLC
See also DLB 119

Flecker, Herman Elroy
See Flecker, (Herman) James Elroy

Flecker, (Herman) James Elroy 1884-1915 **TCLC**
43
See also CA 109; 150; DLB 10, 19

Fleming, Ian (Lancaster) 1908-1964 **CLC 3, 30;**
DAM POP
See also CA 5-8R; CDBLB 1945-1960; DLB 87;
MTCW; SATA 9

Fleming, Thomas (James) 1927- **CLC 37**
See also CA 5-8R; CANR 10; INT CANR-10; SATA
8

Fletcher, John 1579-1625 **LC 33; DC 6**
See also CDBLB Before 1660; DLB 58

Fletcher, John Gould 1886-1950 **TCLC 35**
See also CA 107; DLB 4, 45

Fleur, Paul
See Pohl, Frederik

Flooglebuckle, Al
See Spiegelman, Art

Flying Officer X
See Bates, H(erbert) E(rnest)

Fo, Dario 1926- **CLC 32; DAM DRAM**
See also CA 116; 128; MTCW

Fogarty, Jonathan Titulescu Esq.
See Farrell, James T(homas)

Folke, Will
See Bloch, Robert (Albert)

Follett, Ken(neth Martin) 1949- **CLC 18; DAM NOV,**
POP
See also AAYA 6; BEST 89:4; CA 81-84; CANR
13, 33, 54; DLB 87; DLBY 81; INT CANR-33;
MTCW

Fontane, Theodor 1819-1898 **NCLC 26**
See also DLB 129

Foote, Horton 1916- **CLC 51, 91; DAM DRAM**
See also CA 73-76; CANR 34, 51; DLB 26; INT
CANR-34

Foote, Shelby 1916- **CLC 75; DAM NOV, POP**
See also CA 5-8R; CANR 3, 45; DLB 2, 17

Forbes, Esther 1891-1967 **CLC 12**
See also AAYA 17; CA 13-14; 25-28R; CAP 1;
CLR 27; DLB 22; JRDA; MAICYA; SATA 2

Forche, Carolyn (Louise) 1950- **CLC 25, 83, 86;**
DAM POET; PC 10
See also CA 109; 117; CANR 50; DLB 5; INT 117

Ford, Elbur
See Hibbert, Eleanor Alice Burford

Ford, Ford Madox 1873-1939 **TCLC 1, 15, 39, 57;**
DAM NOV
See also CA 104; 132; CDBLB 1914-1945; DLB
162; MTCW

Ford, John 1895-1973 **CLC 16**
See also CA 45-48

Ford, Richard CLC 99

Ford, Richard 1944- **CLC 46**
See also CA 69-72; CANR 11, 47

Ford, Webster
See Masters, Edgar Lee

Foreman, Richard 1937- **CLC 50**
See also CA 65-68; CANR 32

Forester, C(ecil) S(cott) 1899-1966 **CLC 35**
See also CA 73-76; 25-28R; SATA 13

Forez
See Mauriac, Francois (Charles)

Forman, James Douglas 1932- **CLC 21**
See also AAYA 17; CA 9-12R; CANR 4, 19, 42;
JRDA; MAICYA; SATA 8, 70

Fornes, Maria Irene 1930- **CLC 39, 61**
See also CA 25-28R; CANR 28; DLB 7; HW; INT
CANR-28; MTCW

Forrest, Leon 1937- **CLC 4**
See also BW 2; CA 89-92; CAAS 7; CANR 25, 52;
DLB 33

Forster, E(dward) M(organ) 1879-1970 **CLC 1, 2, 3,**
4, 9, 10, 13, 15, 22, 45, 77; DA; DAB; DAC;
DAM MST, NOV; WLC
See also AAYA 2; CA 13-14; 25-28R; CANR 45;
CAP 1; CDBLB 1914-1945; DLB 34, 98, 162;
DLBD 10; MTCW; SATA 57

Forster, John 1812-1876 **NCLC 11**
See also DLB 144

Forsyth, Frederick 1938- **CLC 2, 5, 36; DAM NOV,**
POP
See also BEST 89:4; CA 85-88; CANR 38; DLB 87;
MTCW

Forten, Charlotte L. TCLC 16; BLC
See also Grimke, Charlotte L(ottie) Forten
See also DLB 50

Foscolo, Ugo 1778-1827 **NCLC 8**

Fosse, Bob CLC 20
See also Fosse, Robert Louis

Fosse, Robert Louis 1927-1987
See Fosse, Bob
See also CA 110; 123

Foster, Stephen Collins 1826-1864 **NCLC 26**

Foucault, Michel 1926-1984 **CLC 31, 34, 69**
See also CA 105; 113; CANR 34; MTCW

Fouque, Friedrich (Heinrich Karl) de la Motte 1777-1843 **NCLC 2**
See also DLB 90

Fourier, Charles 1772-1837 **NCLC 51**

Fournier, Henri Alban 1886-1914
See Alain-Fournier
See also CA 104

Fournier, Pierre 1916- **CLC 11**
See also Gascar, Pierre
See also CA 89-92; CANR 16, 40

Fowles, John 1926- **CLC 1, 2, 3, 4, 6, 9, 10, 15, 33, 87; DAB; DAC; DAM MST**
See also CA 5-8R; CANR 25; CDBLB 1960 to Present; DLB 14, 139; MTCW; SATA 22

Fox, Paula 1923- **CLC 2, 8**
See also AAYA 3; CA 73-76; CANR 20, 36; CLR 1, 44; DLB 52; JRDA; MAICYA; MTCW; SATA 17, 60

Fox, William Price (Jr.) 1926- **CLC 22**
See also CA 17-20R; CAAS 19; CANR 11; DLB 2; DLBY 81

Foxe, John 1516(?)-1587 **LC 14**

Frame, Janet 1924- **CLC 2, 3, 6, 22, 66, 96**
See also Clutha, Janet Paterson Frame

France, Anatole TCLC 9
See also Thibault, Jacques Anatole Francois
See also DLB 123

Francis, Claude 19(?)- **CLC 50**

Francis, Dick 1920- **CLC 2, 22, 42; DAM POP**
See also AAYA 5; BEST 89 3; CA 5-8R; CANR 9, 42; CDBLB 1960 to Present; DLB 87; INT CANR-9; MTCW

Francis, Robert (Churchill) 1901-1987 **CLC 15**
See also CA 1-4R; 123; CANR 1

Frank, Anne(lies Marie) 1929-1945 **TCLC 17; DA; DAB; DAC; DAM MST; WLC**
See also AAYA 12; CA 113; 133; MTCW; SATA 87; SATA-Brief 42

Frank, Elizabeth 1945- **CLC 39**
See also CA 121; 126; INT 126

Frankl, Viktor E(mil) 1905- **CLC 93**
See also CA 65-68

Franklin, Benjamin
See Hasek, Jaroslav (Matej Frantisek)

Franklin, Benjamin 1706-1790 **LC 25; DA; DAB; DAC; DAM MST**
See also CDALB 1640-1865; DLB 24, 43, 73

Franklin, (Stella Maraia Sarah) Miles 1879-1954 **TCLC 7**
See also CA 104

Fraser, (Lady) Antonia (Pakenham) 1932- **CLC 32**
See also CA 85-88; CANR 44; MTCW; SATA-Brief 32

Fraser, George MacDonald 1925- **CLC 7**
See also CA 45-48; CANR 2, 48

Fraser, Sylvia 1935- **CLC 64**
See also CA 45-48; CANR 1, 16

Frayn, Michael 1933- **CLC 3, 7, 31, 47; DAM DRAM, NOV**
See also CA 5-8R; CANR 30; DLB 13, 14; MTCW

Fraze, Candida (Merrill) 1945- **CLC 50**
See also CA 126

Frazer, J(ames) G(eorge) 1854-1941 **TCLC 32**
See also CA 118

Frazer, Robert Caine
See Creasey, John

Frazer, Sir James George
See Frazer, J(ames) G(eorge)

Frazier, Ian 1951- **CLC 46**
See also CA 130; CANR 54

Frederic, Harold 1856-1898 **NCLC 10**
See also DLB 12, 23; DLBD 13

Frederick, John
See Faust, Frederick (Schiller)

Frederick the Great 1712-1786 **LC 14**

Fredro, Aleksander 1793-1876 **NCLC 8**

Freeling, Nicolas 1927- **CLC 38**
See also CA 49-52; CAAS 12; CANR 1, 17, 50; DLB 87

Freeman, Douglas Southall 1886-1953 **TCLC 11**
See also CA 109; DLB 17

Freeman, Judith 1946- **CLC 55**
See also CA 148

Freeman, Mary Eleanor Wilkins 1852-1930 **TCLC 9; SSC 1**
See also CA 106; DLB 12, 78

Freeman, R(ichard) Austin 1862-1943 **TCLC 21**
See also CA 113; DLB 70

French, Albert 1943- **CLC 86**

French, Marilyn 1929- **CLC 10, 18, 60; DAM DRAM, NOV, POP**
See also CA 69-72; CANR 3, 31; INT CANR-31; MTCW

French, Paul
See Asimov, Isaac

Freneau, Philip Morin 1752-1832 **NCLC 1**
See also DLB 37, 43

Freud, Sigmund 1856-1939 **TCLC 52**
See also CA 115; 133; MTCW

Friedan, Betty (Naomi) 1921- **CLC 74**
See also CA 65-68; CANR 18, 45; MTCW

Friedlander, Saul 1932- **CLC 90**
See also CA 117; 130

Friedman, B(ernard) H(arper) 1926- **CLC 7**
See also CA 1-4R; CANR 3, 48

Friedman, Bruce Jay 1930- **CLC 3, 5, 56**
See also CA 9-12R; CANR 25, 52; DLB 2, 28; INT CANR-25

Friel, Brian 1929- **CLC 5, 42, 59**
See also CA 21-24R; CANR 33; DLB 13; MTCW

Friis-Baastad, Babbis Ellinor 1921-1970 **CLC 12**
See also CA 17-20R; 134; SATA 7

Frisch, Max (Rudolf) 1911-1991 **CLC 3, 9, 14, 18, 32, 44; DAM DRAM, NOV**
See also CA 85-88; 134; CANR 32; DLB 69, 124; MTCW

Fromentin, Eugene (Samuel Auguste) 1820-1876 **NCLC 10**
See also DLB 123

Frost, Frederick
See Faust, Frederick (Schiller)

Frost, Robert (Lee) 1874-1963 **CLC 1, 3, 4, 9, 10, 13, 15, 26, 34, 44; DA; DAB; DAC; DAM MST, POET; PC 1; WLC**
See also CA 89-92; CANR 33; CDALB 1917-1929; DLB 54; DLBD 7; MTCW; SATA 14

Froude, James Anthony 1818-1894 **NCLC 43**
See also DLB 18, 57, 144

Froy, Herald
See Waterhouse, Keith (Spencer)

Fry, Christopher 1907- **CLC 2, 10, 14; DAM DRAM**
See also CA 17-20R; CAAS 23; CANR 9, 30; DLB 13; MTCW; SATA 66

Frye, (Herman) Northrop 1912-1991 **CLC 24, 70**
See also CA 5-8R; 133; CANR 8, 37; DLB 67, 68; MTCW

Fuchs, Daniel 1909-1993 **CLC 8, 22**
See also CA 81-84; 142; CAAS 5; CANR 40; DLB 9, 26, 28; DLBY 93

Fuchs, Daniel 1934- **CLC 34**
See also CA 37-40R; CANR 14, 48

Fuentes, Carlos 1928- **CLC 3, 8, 10, 13, 22, 41, 60; DA; DAB; DAC; DAM MST, MULT, NOV;**

HLC; SSC 24; WLC
See also AAYA 4; AITN 2; CA 69-72; CANR 10,
32; DLB 113; HW; MTCW

Fuentes, Gregorio Lopez y
See Lopez y Fuentes, Gregorio

Fugard, (Harold) Athol 1932- CLC 5, 9, 14, 25, 40,
80; DAM DRAM; DC 3
See also AAYA 17; CA 85-88; CANR 32, 54;
MTCW

Fugard, Sheila 1932- CLC 48
See also CA 125

Fuller, Charles (H., Jr.) 1939- CLC 25; BLC; DAM
DRAM, MULT; DC 1
See also BW 2; CA 108; 112; DLB 38; INT 112;
MTCW

Fuller, John (Leopold) 1937- CLC 62
See also CA 21-24R; CANR 9, 44; DLB 40

Fuller, Margaret NCLC 5, 50
See also Ossoli, Sarah Margaret (Fuller marchesa
d')

Fuller, Roy (Broadbent) 1912-1991 CLC 4, 28
See also CA 5-8R; 135; CAAS 10; CANR 53; DLB
15, 20; SATA 87

Fulton, Alice 1952- CLC 52
See also CA 116; CANR 57

Furphy, Joseph 1843-1912 TCLC 25

Fussell, Paul 1924- CLC 74
See also BEST 90 1; CA 17-20R; CANR 8, 21, 35;
INT CANR-21; MTCW

Futabatei, Shimei 1864-1909 TCLC 44

Futrelle, Jacques 1875-1912 TCLC 19
See also CA 113; 155

Gaboriau, Emile 1835-1873 NCLC 14

Gadda, Carlo Emilio 1893-1973 CLC 11
See also CA 89-92; DLB 177

Gaddis, William 1922- CLC 1, 3, 6, 8, 10, 19, 43, 86
See also CA 17-20R; CANR 21, 48; DLB 2; MTCW

Gage, Walter
See Inge, William (Motter)

Gaines, Ernest J(ames) 1933- CLC 3, 11, 18, 86;
BLC; DAM MULT
See also AAYA 18; AITN 1; BW 2; CA 9-12R;
CANR 6, 24, 42; CDALB 1968-1988; DLB 2, 33,
152; DLBY 80; MTCW; SATA 86

Gaitskill, Mary 1954- CLC 69
See also CA 128

Galdos, Benito Perez
See Perez Galdos, Benito

Gale, Zona 1874-1938 TCLC 7; DAM DRAM
See also CA 105; 153; DLB 9, 78

Galeano, Eduardo (Hughes) 1940- CLC 72
See also CA 29-32R; CANR 13, 32; HW

Galiano, Juan Valera y Alcala
See Valera y Alcala-Galiano, Juan

Gallagher, Tess 1943- CLC 18, 63; DAM POET;
PC 9
See also CA 106; DLB 120

Gallant, Mavis 1922- CLC 7, 18, 38; DAC; DAM
MST; SSC 5
See also CA 69-72; CANR 29; DLB 53; MTCW

Gallant, Roy A(rthur) 1924- CLC 17
See also CA 5-8R; CANR 4, 29, 54; CLR 30;
MAICYA; SATA 4, 68

Gallico, Paul (William) 1897-1976 CLC 2
See also AITN 1; CA 5-8R; 69-72; CANR 23; DLB
9, 171; MAICYA; SATA 13

Gallo, Max Louis 1932- CLC 95
See also CA 85-88

Gallois, Lucien
See Desnos, Robert

Gallup, Ralph
See Whitemore, Hugh (John)

Galsworthy, John 1867-1933 TCLC 1, 45; DA; DAB;
DAC; DAM DRAM, MST, NOV; SSC 22; WLC
2
See also CA 104; 141; CDBLB 1890-1914; DLB 10,
34, 98, 162

Galt, John 1779-1839 NCLC 1
See also DLB 99, 116, 159

Galvin, James 1951- CLC 38
See also CA 108; CANR 26

Gamboa, Federico 1864-1939 TCLC 36

Gandhi, M. K.
See Gandhi, Mohandas Karamchand

Gandhi, Mahatma
See Gandhi, Mohandas Karamchand

Gandhi, Mohandas Karamchand 1869-1948 TCLC
59; DAM MULT
See also CA 121; 132; MTCW

Gann, Ernest Kellogg 1910-1991 CLC 23
See also AITN 1; CA 1-4R; 136; CANR 1

Garcia, Cristina 1958- CLC 76
See also CA 141

Garcia Lorca, Federico 1898-1936 TCLC 1, 7, 49;
DA; DAB; DAC; DAM DRAM, MST, MULT,
POET; DC 2; HLC; PC 3; WLC
See also CA 104; 131; DLB 108; HW; MTCW

Garcia Marquez, Gabriel (Jose) 1928- CLC 2, 3, 8,
10, 15, 27, 47, 55, 68; DA; DAB; DAC; DAM
MST, MULT, NOV, POP; HLC; SSC 8; WLC
See also AAYA 3; BEST 89 1, 90 4; CA 33-36R;
CANR 10, 28, 50; DLB 113; HW; MTCW

Gard, Janice
See Latham, Jean Lee

Gard, Roger Martin du

See Martin du Gard, Roger

Gardam, Jane 1928- CLC 43
See also CA 49-52; CANR 2, 18, 33, 54; CLR 12;
DLB 14, 161; MAICYA; MTCW; SAAS 9;
SATA 39, 76; SATA-Brief 28

Gardner, Herb(ert) 1934- CLC 44
See also CA 149

Gardner, John (Champlin), Jr. 1933-1982 CLC 2, 3,
5, 7, 8, 10, 18, 28, 34; DAM NOV, POP; SSC
7
See also AITN 1; CA 65-68; 107; CANR 33; DLB
2; DLBY 82; MTCW; SATA 40; SATA-Obit 31

Gardner, John (Edmund) 1926- CLC 30; DAM POP
See also CA 103; CANR 15; MTCW

Gardner, Miriam
See Bradley, Marion Zimmer

Gardner, Noel
See Kuttner, Henry

Gardons, S. S.
See Snodgrass, W(illiam) D(e Witt)

Garfield, Leon 1921-1996 CLC 12
See also AAYA 8; CA 17-20R; 152; CANR 38, 41;
CLR 21; DLB 161; JRDA; MAICYA; SATA 1,
32, 76; SATA-Obit 90

Garland, (Hannibal) Hamlin 1860-1940 TCLC 3;
SSC 18
See also CA 104; DLB 12, 71, 78

Garneau, (Hector de) Saint-Denys 1912-1943 TCLC
13
See also CA 111; DLB 88

Garner, Alan 1934- CLC 17; DAB; DAM POP
See also AAYA 18; CA 73-76; CANR 15; CLR 20;
DLB 161; MAICYA; MTCW; SATA 18, 69

Garner, Hugh 1913-1979 CLC 13
See also CA 69-72; CANR 31; DLB 68

Garnett, David 1892-1981 CLC 3
See also CA 5-8R; 103; CANR 17; DLB 34

Garos, Stephanie
See Katz, Steve

Garrett, George (Palmer) 1929- CLC 3, 11, 51
See also CA 1-4R; CAAS 5; CANR 1, 42; DLB 2, 5,
130, 152; DLBY 83

Garrick, David 1717-1779 LC 15; DAM DRAM
See also DLB 84

Garrigue, Jean 1914-1972 CLC 2, 8
See also CA 5-8R; 37-40R; CANR 20

Garrison, Frederick
See Sinclair, Upton (Beall)

Garth, Will
See Hamilton, Edmond; Kuttner, Henry

Garvey, Marcus (Moziah, Jr.) 1887-1940 TCLC 41;
BLC; DAM MULT
See also BW 1; CA 120; 124

Gary, Romain CLC 25
See also Kacew, Romain
See also DLB 83

Gascar, Pierre CLC 11
See also Fournier, Pierre

Gascoyne, David (Emery) 1916- CLC 45
See also CA 65-68; CANR 10, 28, 54; DLB 20;
MTCW

**Gaskell, Elizabeth Cleghorn 1810-1865 NCLC 5;
DAB; DAM MST**
See also CDBLB 1832-1890; DLB 21, 144, 159

**Gass, William H(oward) 1924- CLC 1, 2, 8, 11, 15,
39; SSC 12**
See also CA 17-20R; CANR 30; DLB 2; MTCW

Gasset, Jose Ortega y
See Ortega y Gasset, Jose

Gates, Henry Louis, Jr. 1950- CLC 65; DAM MULT
See also BW 2; CA 109; CANR 25, 53; DLB 67

**Gautier, Theophile 1811-1872 NCLC 1, 59; DAM
POET; SSC 20**
See also DLB 119

Gawsworth, John
See Bates, H(erbert) E(rnest)

Gay, Oliver
See Gogarty, Oliver St. John

Gaye, Marvin (Penze) 1939-1984 CLC 26
See also CA 112

Gebler, Carlo (Ernest) 1954- CLC 39
See also CA 119; 133

Gee, Maggie (Mary) 1948- CLC 57
See also CA 130

Gee, Maurice (Gough) 1931- CLC 29
See also CA 97-100; SATA 46

Gelbart, Larry (Simon) 1923- CLC 21, 61
See also CA 73-76; CANR 45

Gelber, Jack 1932- CLC 1, 6, 14, 79
See also CA 1-4R; CANR 2; DLB 7

Gellhorn, Martha (Ellis) 1908- CLC 14, 60
See also CA 77-80; CANR 44; DLBY 82

**Genet, Jean 1910-1986 CLC 1, 2, 5, 10, 14, 44, 46;
DAM DRAM**
See also CA 13-16R; CANR 18; DLB 72; DLBY 86;
MTCW

Gent, Peter 1942- CLC 29
See also AITN 1; CA 89-92; DLBY 82

Gentlewoman in New England, A
See Bradstreet, Anne

Gentlewoman in Those Parts, A
See Bradstreet, Anne

George, Jean Craighead 1919- CLC 35
See also AAYA 8; CA 5-8R; CANR 25; CLR 1;
DLB 52; JRDA; MAICYA; SATA 2, 68

George, Stefan (Anton) 1868-1933 TCLC 2, 14
See also CA 104

Georges, Georges Martin
See Simenon, Georges (Jacques Christian)

Gerhardi, William Alexander
See Gerhardie, William Alexander

Gerhardie, William Alexander 1895-1977 CLC 5
See also CA 25-28R; 73-76; CANR 18; DLB 36

Gerstler, Amy 1956- CLC 70
See also CA 146

Gertler, T. CLC 34
See also CA 116; 121; INT 121

Ghalib NCLC 39
See also Ghalib, Hsadullah Khan

Ghalib, Hsadullah Khan 1797-1869
See Ghalib
See also DAM POET

**Ghelderode, Michel de 1898-1962 CLC 6, 11; DAM
DRAM**
See also CA 85-88; CANR 40

Ghiselin, Brewster 1903- CLC 23
See also CA 13-16R; CAAS 10; CANR 13

Ghose, Zulfikar 1935- CLC 42
See also CA 65-68

Ghosh, Amitav 1956- CLC 44
See also CA 147

Giacosa, Giuseppe 1847-1906 TCLC 7
See also CA 104

Gibb, Lee
See Waterhouse, Keith (Spencer)

Gibbon, Lewis Grassic TCLC 4
See also Mitchell, James Leslie

Gibbons, Kaye 1960- CLC 50, 88; DAM POP
See also CA 151

**Gibran, Kahlil 1883-1931 TCLC 1, 9; DAM POET,
POP; PC 9**
See also CA 104; 150

Gibran, Khalil
See Gibran, Kahlil

**Gibson, William 1914- CLC 23; DA; DAB; DAC;
DAM DRAM, MST**
See also CA 9-12R; CANR 9, 42; DLB 7; SATA 66

**Gibson, William (Ford) 1948- CLC 39, 63; DAM
POP**
See also AAYA 12; CA 126; 133; CANR 52

**Gide, Andre (Paul Guillaume) 1869-1951 TCLC 5,
12, 36; DA; DAB; DAC; DAM MST, NOV;
SSC 13; WLC**
See also CA 104; 124; DLB 65; MTCW

Gifford, Barry (Colby) 1946- CLC 34
See also CA 65-68; CANR 9, 30, 40

**Gilbert, W(illiam) S(chwenck) 1836-1911 TCLC 3;
DAM DRAM, POET**
See also CA 104; SATA 36

Gilbreth, Frank B., Jr. 1911- CLC 17
See also CA 9-12R; SATA 2

**Gilchrist, Ellen 1935- CLC 34, 48; DAM POP;
SSC 14**
See also CA 113; 116; CANR 41; DLB 130; MTCW

Giles, Molly 1942- CLC 39
See also CA 126

Gill, Patrick
See Creasey, John

Gilliam, Terry (Vance) 1940- CLC 21
See also Monty Python
See also AAYA 19; CA 108; 113; CANR 35; INT
113

Gillian, Jerry
See Gilliam, Terry (Vance)

**Gilliatt, Penelope (Ann Douglass) 1932-1993 CLC
2, 10, 13, 53**
See also AITN 2; CA 13-16R; 141; CANR 49; DLB
14

**Gilman, Charlotte (Anna) Perkins (Stetson) 1860-
1935 TCLC 9, 37; SSC 13**
See also CA 106; 150

Gilmour, David 1949- CLC 35
See also CA 138, 147

Gilpin, William 1724-1804 NCLC 30

Gilray, J. D.
See Mencken, H(enry) L(ouis)

Gilroy, Frank D(aniel) 1925- CLC 2
See also CA 81-84; CANR 32; DLB 7

Gilstrap, John 1957(?)- CLC 99

**Ginsberg, Allen 1926- CLC 1, 2, 3, 4, 6, 13, 36, 69;
DA; DAB; DAC; DAM MST, POET; PC 4;
WLC 3**
See also AITN 1; CA 1-4R; CANR 2, 41; CDALB
1941-1968; DLB 5, 16, 169; MTCW

Ginzburg, Natalia 1916-1991 CLC 5, 11, 54, 70
See also CA 85-88; 135; CANR 33; DLB 177;
MTCW

Giono, Jean 1895-1970 CLC 4, 11
See also CA 45-48; 29-32R; CANR 2, 35; DLB 72;
MTCW

**Giovanni, Nikki 1943- CLC 2, 4, 19, 64; BLC; DA;
DAB; DAC; DAM MST, MULT, POET**
See also AITN 1; BW 2; CA 29-32R; CAAS 6;
CANR 18, 41; CLR 6; DLB 5, 41; INT CANR-
18; MAICYA; MTCW; SATA 24

Giovene, Andrea 1904- CLC 7
See also CA 85-88

Gippius, Zinaida (Nikolayevna) 1869-1945
See Hippius, Zinaida
See also CA 106

Giraudoux, (Hippolyte) Jean 1882-1944 **TCLC 2, 7; DAM DRAM**
See also CA 104; DLB 65

Gironella, Jose Maria 1917- **CLC 11**
See also CA 101

Gissing, George (Robert) 1857-1903 **TCLC 3, 24, 47**
See also CA 105; DLB 18, 135

Giurlani, Aldo
See Palazzeschi, Aldo

Gladkov, Fyodor (Vasilyevich) 1883-1958 **TCLC 27**

Glanville, Brian (Lester) 1931- **CLC 6**
See also CA 5-8R; CAAS 9; CANR 3; DLB 15, 139; SATA 42

Glasgow, Ellen (Anderson Gholson) 1873(?)-1945 **TCLC 2, 7**
See also CA 104; DLB 9, 12

Glaspell, Susan 1882(?)-1948 **TCLC 55**
See also CA 110; 154; DLB 7, 9, 78; YABC 2

Glassco, John 1909-1981 **CLC 9**
See also CA 13-16R; 102; CANR 15; DLB 68

Glasscock, Amnesia
See Steinbeck, John (Ernst)

Glasser, Ronald J. 1940(?)- **CLC 37**

Glassman, Joyce
See Johnson, Joyce

Glendinning, Victoria 1937- **CLC 50**
See also CA 120; 127; DLB 155

Glissant, Edouard 1928- **CLC 10, 68; DAM MULT**
See also CA 153

Gloag, Julian 1930- **CLC 40**
See also AITN 1; CA 65-68; CANR 10

Glowacki, Aleksander
See Prus, Boleslaw

Gluck, Louise (Elisabeth) 1943- **CLC 7, 22, 44, 81; DAM POET; PC 16**
See also CA 33-36R; CANR 40; DLB 5

Gobineau, Joseph Arthur (Comte) de 1816-1882 **NCLC 17**
See also DLB 123

Godard, Jean-Luc 1930- **CLC 20**
See also CA 93-96

Godden, (Margaret) Rumer 1907- **CLC 53**
See also AAYA 6; CA 5-8R; CANR 4, 27, 36, 55; CLR 20; DLB 161; MAICYA; SAAS 12; SATA 3, 36

Godoy Alcayaga, Lucila 1889-1957
See Mistral, Gabriela
See also BW 2; CA 104; 131; DAM MULT; HW; MTCW

Godwin, Gail (Kathleen) 1937- **CLC 5, 8, 22, 31, 69; DAM POP**

See also CA 29-32R; CANR 15, 43; DLB 6; INT CANR-15; MTCW

Godwin, William 1756-1836 **NCLC 14**
See also CDBLB 1789-1832; DLB 39, 104, 142, 158, 163

Goebbels, Josef
See Goebbels, (Paul) Joseph

Goebbels, (Paul) Joseph 1897-1945 **TCLC 68**
See also CA 115; 148

Goebbels, Joseph Paul
See Goebbels, (Paul) Joseph

Goethe, Johann Wolfgang von 1749-1832 **NCLC 4, 22, 34; DA; DAB; DAC; DAM DRAM, MST, POET; PC 5; WLC 3**
See also DLB 94

Gogarty, Oliver St. John 1878-1957 **TCLC 15**
See also CA 109; 150; DLB 15, 19

Gogol, Nikolai (Vasilyevich) 1809-1852 **NCLC 5, 15, 31; DA; DAB; DAC; DAM DRAM, MST; DC 1; SSC 4; WLC**

Goines, Donald 1937(?)-1974 **CLC 80; BLC; DAM MULT, POP**
See also AITN 1; BW 1; CA 124; 114; DLB 33

Gold, Herbert 1924- **CLC 4, 7, 14, 42**
See also CA 9-12R; CANR 17, 45; DLB 2; DLBY 81

Goldbarth, Albert 1948- **CLC 5, 38**
See also CA 53-56; CANR 6, 40; DLB 120

Goldberg, Anatol 1910-1982 **CLC 34**
See also CA 131; 117

Goldemberg, Isaac 1945- **CLC 52**
See also CA 69-72; CAAS 12; CANR 11, 32; HW

Golding, William (Gerald) 1911-1993 **CLC 1, 2, 3, 8, 10, 17, 27, 58, 81; DA; DAB; DAC; DAM MST, NOV; WLC**
See also AAYA 5; CA 5-8R; 141; CANR 13, 33, 54; CDBLB 1945-1960; DLB 15, 100; MTCW

Goldman, Emma 1869-1940 **TCLC 13**
See also CA 110; 150

Goldman, Francisco 1955- **CLC 76**

Goldman, William (W.) 1931- **CLC 1, 48**
See also CA 9-12R; CANR 29; DLB 44

Goldmann, Lucien 1913-1970 **CLC 24**
See also CA 25-28; CAP 2

Goldoni, Carlo 1707-1793 **LC 4; DAM DRAM**

Goldsberry, Steven 1949- **CLC 34**
See also CA 131

Goldsmith, Oliver 1728-1774 **LC 2; DA; DAB; DAC; DAM DRAM, MST, NOV, POET; WLC**
See also CDBLB 1660-1789; DLB 39, 89, 104, 109, 142; SATA 26

Goldsmith, Peter

See Priestley, J(ohn) B(oynton)

Gombrowicz, Witold 1904-1969 **CLC 4, 7, 11, 49; DAM DRAM**
See also CA 19-20; 25-28R; CAP 2

Gomez de la Serna, Ramon 1888-1963 **CLC 9**
See also CA 153; 116; HW

Goncharov, Ivan Alexandrovich 1812-1891 **NCLC 1**

Goncourt, Edmond (Louis Antoine Huot) de 1822-1896 **NCLC 7**
See also DLB 123

Goncourt, Jules (Alfred Huot) de 1830-1870 **NCLC 7**
See also DLB 123

Gontier, Fernande 19(?)- **CLC 50**

Goodman, Paul 1911-1972 **CLC 1, 2, 4, 7**
See also CA 19-20; 37-40R; CANR 34; CAP 2; DLB 130; MTCW

Gordimer, Nadine 1923- **CLC 3, 5, 7, 10, 18, 33, 51, 70; DA; DAB; DAC; DAM MST, NOV; SSC 17**
See also CA 5-8R; CANR 3, 28, 56; INT CANR-28; MTCW

Gordon, Adam Lindsay 1833-1870 **NCLC 21**

Gordon, Caroline 1895-1981 **CLC 6, 13, 29, 83; SSC 15**
See also CA 11-12; 103; CANR 36; CAP 1; DLB 4, 9, 102; DLBY 81; MTCW

Gordon, Charles William 1860-1937
See Connor, Ralph
See also CA 109

Gordon, Mary (Catherine) 1949- **CLC 13, 22**
See also CA 102; CANR 44; DLB 6; DLBY 81; INT 102; MTCW

Gordon, Sol 1923- **CLC 26**
See also CA 53-56; CANR 4; SATA 11

Gordone, Charles 1925-1995 **CLC 1, 4; DAM DRAM**
See also BW 1; CA 93-96; 150; CANR 55; DLB 7; INT 93-96; MTCW

Gorenko, Anna Andreevna
See Akhmatova, Anna

Gorky, Maxim **TCLC 8; DAB; WLC**
See also Peshkov, Alexei Maximovich

Goryan, Sirak
See Saroyan, William

Gosse, Edmund (William) 1849-1928 **TCLC 28**
See also CA 117; DLB 57, 144

Gotlieb, Phyllis Fay (Bloom) 1926- **CLC 18**
See also CA 13-16R; CANR 7; DLB 88

Gottesman, S. D.
See Kornbluth, C(yril) M.; Pohl, Frederik

Gottfried von Strassburg fl. c. 1210- **CMLC 10**

See also DLB 138

Gould, Lois CLC 4, 10
See also CA 77-80; CANR 29; MTCW

Gourmont, Remy (-Marie-Charles) de 1858-1915 TCLC 17
See also CA 109; 150

Govier, Katherine 1948- CLC 51
See also CA 101; CANR 18, 40

Goyen, (Charles) William 1915-1983 CLC 5, 8, 14, 40
See also AITN 2; CA 5-8R; 110; CANR 6; DLB 2; DLBY 83; INT CANR-6

Goytisolo, Juan 1931- CLC 5, 10, 23; DAM MULT; HLC
See also CA 85-88; CANR 32; HW; MTCW

Gozzano, Guido 1883-1916 PC 10
See also CA 154; DLB 114

Gozzi, (Conte) Carlo 1720-1806 NCLC 23

Grabbe, Christian Dietrich 1801-1836 NCLC 2
See also DLB 133

Grace, Patricia 1937- CLC 56

Gracian y Morales, Baltasar 1601-1658 LC 15

Gracq, Julien CLC 11, 48
See also Poirier, Louis
See also DLB 83

Grade, Chaim 1910-1982 CLC 10
See also CA 93-96; 107

Graduate of Oxford, A
See Ruskin, John

Graham, John
See Phillips, David Graham

Graham, Jorie 1951- CLC 48
See also CA 111; DLB 120

Graham, R(obert) B(ontine) Cunninghame
See Cunninghame Graham, R(obert) B(ontine)
See also DLB 98, 135, 174

Graham, Robert
See Haldeman, Joe (William)

Graham, Tom
See Lewis, (Harry) Sinclair

Graham, W(illiam) S(ydney) 1918-1986 CLC 29
See also CA 73-76; 118; DLB 20

Graham, Winston (Mawdsley) 1910- CLC 23
See also CA 49-52; CANR 2, 22, 45; DLB 77

Grahame, Kenneth 1859-1932 TCLC 64; DAB
See also CA 108; 136; CLR 5; DLB 34, 141; MAICYA; YABC 1

Grant, Skeeter
See Spiegelman, Art

Granville-Barker, Harley 1877-1946 TCLC 2; DAM

DRAM
See also Barker, Harley Granville
See also CA 104

Grass, Guenter (Wilhelm) 1927- CLC 1, 2, 4, 6, 11, 15, 22, 32, 49, 88; DA; DAB; DAC; DAM MST, NOV; WLC
See also CA 13-16R; CANR 20; DLB 75, 124; MTCW

Gratton, Thomas
See Hulme, T(homas) E(rnest)

Grau, Shirley Ann 1929- CLC 4, 9; SSC 15
See also CA 89-92; CANR 22; DLB 2; INT CANR-22; MTCW

Gravel, Fern
See Hall, James Norman

Graver, Elizabeth 1964- CLC 70
See also CA 135

Graves, Richard Perceval 1945- CLC 44
See also CA 65-68; CANR 9, 26, 51

Graves, Robert (von Ranke) 1895-1985 CLC 1, 2, 6, 11, 39, 44, 45; DAB; DAC; DAM MST, POET; PC 6
See also CA 5-8R; 117; CANR 5, 36; CDBLB 1914-1945; DLB 20, 100; DLBY 85; MTCW; SATA 45

Graves, Valerie
See Bradley, Marion Zimmer

Gray, Alasdair (James) 1934- CLC 41
See also CA 126; CANR 47; INT 126; MTCW

Gray, Amlin 1946- CLC 29
See also CA 138

Gray, Francine du Plessix 1930- CLC 22; DAM NOV
See also BEST 90 3; CA 61-64; CAAS 2; CANR 11, 33; INT CANR-11; MTCW

Gray, John (Henry) 1866-1934 TCLC 19
See also CA 119

Gray, Simon (James Holliday) 1936- CLC 9, 14, 36
See also AITN 1; CA 21-24R; CAAS 3; CANR 32; DLB 13; MTCW

Gray, Spalding 1941- CLC 49; DAM POP
See also CA 128

Gray, Thomas 1716-1771 LC 4; DA; DAB; DAC; DAM MST; PC 2; WLC
See also CDBLB 1660-1789; DLB 109

Grayson, David
See Baker, Ray Stannard

Grayson, Richard (A.) 1951- CLC 38
See also CA 85-88; CANR 14, 31, 57

Greeley, Andrew M(oran) 1928- CLC 28; DAM POP
See also CA 5-8R; CAAS 7; CANR 7, 43; MTCW

Green, Anna Katharine 1846-1935 TCLC 63
See also CA 112

Green, Brian
See Card, Orson Scott

Green, Hannah
See Greenberg, Joanne (Goldenberg)

Green, Hannah CLC 3
See also CA 73-76

Green, Henry 1905-1973 CLC 2, 13, 97
See also Yorke, Henry Vincent
See also DLB 15

Green, Julian (Hartridge) 1900-
See Green, Julien
See also CA 21-24R; CANR 33; DLB 4, 72; MTCW

Green, Julien CLC 3, 11, 77
See also Green, Julian (Hartridge)

Green, Paul (Eliot) 1894-1981 CLC 25; DAM DRAM
See also AITN 1; CA 5-8R; 103; CANR 3; DLB 7, 9; DLBY 81

Greenberg, Ivan 1908-1973
See Rahv, Philip
See also CA 85-88

Greenberg, Joanne (Goldenberg) 1932- CLC 7, 30
See also AAYA 12; CA 5-8R; CANR 14, 32; SATA 25

Greenberg, Richard 1959(?)- CLC 57
See also CA 138

Greene, Bette 1934- CLC 30
See also AAYA 7; CA 53-56; CANR 4; CLR 2; JRDA; MAICYA; SAAS 16; SATA 8

Greene, Gael CLC 8
See also CA 13-16R; CANR 10

Greene, Graham 1904-1991 CLC 1, 3, 6, 9, 14, 18, 27, 37, 70, 72; DA; DAB; DAC; DAM MST, NOV; WLC
See also AITN 2; CA 13-16R; 133; CANR 35; CDBLB 1945-1960; DLB 13, 15, 77, 100, 162; DLBY 91; MTCW; SATA 20

Greer, Richard
See Silverberg, Robert

Gregor, Arthur 1923- CLC 9
See also CA 25-28R; CAAS 10; CANR 11; SATA 36

Gregor, Lee
See Pohl, Frederik

Gregory, Isabella Augusta (Persse) 1852-1932 TCLC 1
See also CA 104; DLB 10

Gregory, J. Dennis
See Williams, John A(lfred)

Grendon, Stephen
See Derleth, August (William)

Grenville, Kate 1950- CLC 61
See also CA 118; CANR 53

Grenville, Pelham

See Wodehouse, P(elham) G(renville)

Greve, Felix Paul (Berthold Friedrich) 1879-1948
See Grove, Frederick Philip
See also CA 104; 141; DAC; DAM MST

Grey, Zane 1872-1939 **TCLC 6; DAM POP**
See also CA 104; 132; DLB 9; MTCW

Grieg, (Johan) Nordahl (Brun) 1902-1943 **TCLC
10**
See also CA 107

Grieve, C(hristopher) M(urray) 1892-1978 **CLC
11, 19; DAM POET**
See also MacDiarmid, Hugh; Pteleon
See also CA 5-8R; 85-88; CANR 33; MTCW

Griffin, Gerald 1803-1840 **NCLC 7**
See also DLB 159

Griffin, John Howard 1920-1980 **CLC 68**
See also AITN 1; CA 1-4R; 101; CANR 2

Griffin, Peter 1942- **CLC 39**
See also CA 136

Griffith, D(avid Lewelyn) W(ark) 1875(?)-1948
TCLC 68
See also CA 119; 150

Griffith, Lawrence
See Griffith, D(avid Lewelyn) W(ark)

Griffiths, Trevor 1935- **CLC 13, 52**
See also CA 97-100; CANR 45; DLB 13

Grigson, Geoffrey (Edward Harvey) 1905-1985 **CLC
7, 39**
See also CA 25-28R; 118; CANR 20, 33; DLB 27;
MTCW

Grillparzer, Franz 1791-1872 **NCLC 1**
See also DLB 133

Grimble, Reverend Charles James
See Eliot, T(homas) S(tearns)

Grimke, Charlotte L(ottie) Forten 1837(?)-1914
See Forten, Charlotte L.
See also BW 1; CA 117; 124; DAM MULT, POET

Grimm, Jacob Ludwig Karl 1785-1863 **NCLC 3**
See also DLB 90; MAICYA; SATA 22

Grimm, Wilhelm Karl 1786-1859 **NCLC 3**
See also DLB 90; MAICYA; SATA 22

Grimmelshausen, Johann Jakob Christoffel von
1621-1676 **LC 6**
See also DLB 168

Grindel, Eugene 1895-1952
See Eluard, Paul
See also CA 104

Grisham, John 1955- **CLC 84; DAM POP**
See also AAYA 14; CA 138; CANR 47

Grossman, David 1954- **CLC 67**
See also CA 138

Grossman, Vasily (Semenovich) 1905-1964 **CLC
41**
See also CA 124; 130; MTCW

Grove, Frederick Philip TCLC 4
See also Greve, Felix Paul (Berthold Friedrich)
See also DLB 92

Grubb
See Crumb, R(obert)

Grumbach, Doris (Isaac) 1918- **CLC 13, 22, 64**
See also CA 5-8R; CAAS 2; CANR 9, 42; INT
CANR-9

Grundtvig, Nicolai Frederik Severin 1783-1872
NCLC 1

Grunge
See Crumb, R(obert)

Grunwald, Lisa 1959- **CLC 44**
See also CA 120

Guare, John 1938- **CLC 8, 14, 29, 67; DAM DRAM**
See also CA 73-76; CANR 21; DLB 7; MTCW

Gudjonsson, Halldor Kiljan 1902-
See Laxness, Halldor
See also CA 103

Guenter, Erich
See Eich, Guenter

Guest, Barbara 1920- **CLC 34**
See also CA 25-28R; CANR 11, 44; DLB 5

Guest, Judith (Ann) 1936- **CLC 8, 30; DAM NOV,
POP**
See also AAYA 7; CA 77-80; CANR 15; INT
CANR-15; MTCW

Guevara, Che CLC 87; HLC
See also Guevara (Serna), Ernesto

Guevara (Serna), Ernesto 1928-1967
See Guevara, Che
See also CA 127; 111; CANR 56; DAM MULT;
HW

Guild, Nicholas M. 1944- **CLC 33**
See also CA 93-96

Guillemin, Jacques
See Sartre, Jean-Paul

Guillen, Jorge 1893-1984 **CLC 11; DAM MULT,
POET**
See also CA 89-92; 112; DLB 108; HW

Guillen, Nicolas (Cristobal) 1902-1989 **CLC 48,
79; BLC; DAM MST, MULT, POET; HLC**
See also BW 2; CA 116; 125; 129; HW

Guillevic, (Eugene) 1907- **CLC 33**
See also CA 93-96

Guillois
See Desnos, Robert

Guillois, Valentin
See Desnos, Robert

Guiney, Louise Imogen 1861-1920 **TCLC 41**

See also DLB 54

Guiraldes, Ricardo (Guillermo) 1886-1927 **TCLC
39**
See also CA 131; HW; MTCW

Gumilev, Nikolai Stephanovich 1886-1921 **TCLC
60**

Gunesekera, Romesh CLC 91

Gunn, Bill CLC 5
See also Gunn, William Harrison
See also DLB 38

Gunn, Thom(son William) 1929- **CLC 3, 6, 18, 32,
81; DAM POET**
See also CA 17-20R; CANR 9, 33; CDBLB 1960
to Present; DLB 27; INT CANR-33; MTCW

Gunn, William Harrison 1934(?)-1989
See Gunn, Bill
See also AITN 1; BW 1; CA 13-16R; 128; CANR
12, 25

Gunnars, Kristjana 1948- **CLC 69**
See also CA 113; DLB 60

Gurganus, Allan 1947- **CLC 70; DAM POP**
See also BEST 90 1; CA 135

Gurney, A(lbert) R(amsdell), Jr. 1930- **CLC 32, 50,
54; DAM DRAM**
See also CA 77-80; CANR 32

Gurney, Ivor (Bertie) 1890-1937 **TCLC 33**

Gurney, Peter
See Gurney, A(lbert) R(amsdell), Jr.

Guro, Elena 1877-1913 **TCLC 56**

Gustafson, James M(oody) 1925- **CLC 100**
See also CA 25-28R; CANR 37

Gustafson, Ralph (Barker) 1909- **CLC 36**
See also CA 21-24R; CANR 8, 45; DLB 88

Gut, Gom
See Simenon, Georges (Jacques Christian)

Guterson, David 1956- **CLC 91**
See also CA 132

Guthrie, A(lfred) B(ertram), Jr. 1901-1991 **CLC 23**
See also CA 57-60; 134; CANR 24; DLB 6; SATA
62; SATA-Obit 67

Guthrie, Isobel
See Grieve, C(hristopher) M(urray)

Guthrie, Woodrow Wilson 1912-1967
See Guthrie, Woody
See also CA 113; 93-96

Guthrie, Woody CLC 35
See also Guthrie, Woodrow Wilson

Guy, Rosa (Cuthbert) 1928- **CLC 26**
See also AAYA 4; BW 2; CA 17-20R; CANR 14,
34; CLR 13; DLB 33; JRDA; MAICYA; SATA
14, 62

Gwendolyn
See Bennett, (Enoch) Arnold

H. D. CLC 3, 8, 14, 31, 34, 73; PC 5
See also Doolittle, Hilda

H. de V.
See Buchan, John

Haavikko, Paavo Juhani 1931- CLC 18, 34
See also CA 106

Habbema, Koos
See Heijermans, Herman

Hacker, Marilyn 1942- CLC 5, 9, 23, 72, 91; DAM POET
See also CA 77-80; DLB 120

Haggard, H(enry) Rider 1856-1925 TCLC 11
See also CA 108; 148; DLB 70, 156, 174; SATA 16

Hagiosy, L.
See Larbaud, Valery (Nicolas)

Hagiwara Sakutaro 1886-1942 TCLC 60

Haig, Fenil
See Ford, Ford Madox

Haig-Brown, Roderick (Langmere) 1908-1976 CLC 21
See also CA 5-8R; 69-72; CANR 4, 38; CLR 31; DLB 88; MAICYA; SATA 12

Hailey, Arthur 1920- CLC 5; DAM NOV, POP
See also AITN 2; BEST 90 3; CA 1-4R; CANR 2, 36; DLB 88; DLBY 82; MTCW

Hailey, Elizabeth Forsythe 1938- CLC 40
See also CA 93-96; CAAS 1; CANR 15, 48; INT CANR-15

Haines, John (Meade) 1924- CLC 58
See also CA 17-20R; CANR 13, 34; DLB 5

Hakluyt, Richard 1552-1616 LC 31

Haldeman, Joe (William) 1943- CLC 61
See also CA 53-56; CAAS 25; CANR 6; DLB 8; INT CANR-6

Haley, Alex(ander Murray Palmer) 1921-1992 CLC 8, 12, 76; BLC; DA; DAB; DAC; DAM MST, MULT, POP
See also BW 2; CA 77-80; 136; DLB 38; MTCW

Haliburton, Thomas Chandler 1796-1865 NCLC 15
See also DLB 11, 99

Hall, Donald (Andrew, Jr.) 1928- CLC 1, 13, 37, 59; DAM POET
See also CA 5-8R; CAAS 7; CANR 2, 44; DLB 5; SATA 23

Hall, Frederic Sauser
See Sauser-Hall, Frederic

Hall, James
See Kuttner, Henry

Hall, James Norman 1887-1951 TCLC 23
See also CA 123; SATA 21

Hall, (Marguerite) Radclyffe 1886-1943 TCLC 12
See also CA 110; 150

Hall, Rodney 1935- CLC 51
See also CA 109

Halleck, Fitz-Greene 1790-1867 NCLC 47
See also DLB 3

Halliday, Michael
See Creasey, John

Halpern, Daniel 1945- CLC 14
See also CA 33-36R

Hamburger, Michael (Peter Leopold) 1924- CLC 5, 14
See also CA 5-8R; CAAS 4; CANR 2, 47; DLB 27

Hamill, Pete 1935- CLC 10
See also CA 25-28R; CANR 18

Hamilton, Alexander 1755(?)-1804 NCLC 49
See also DLB 37

Hamilton, Clive
See Lewis, C(live) S(taples)

Hamilton, Edmond 1904-1977 CLC 1
See also CA 1-4R; CANR 3; DLB 8

Hamilton, Eugene (Jacob) Lee
See Lee-Hamilton, Eugene (Jacob)

Hamilton, Franklin
See Silverberg, Robert

Hamilton, Gail
See Corcoran, Barbara

Hamilton, Mollie
See Kaye, M(ary) M(argaret)

Hamilton, (Anthony Walter) Patrick 1904-1962 CLC 51
See also CA 113; DLB 10

Hamilton, Virginia 1936- CLC 26; DAM MULT
See also AAYA 2; BW 2; CA 25-28R; CANR 20, 37; CLR 1, 11, 40; DLB 33, 52; INT CANR-20; JRDA; MAICYA; MTCW; SATA 4, 56, 79

Hammett, (Samuel) Dashiell 1894-1961 CLC 3, 5, 10, 19, 47; SSC 17
See also AITN 1; CA 81-84; CANR 42; CDALB 1929-1941; DLBD 6; MTCW

Hammon, Jupiter 1711(?)-1800(?) NCLC 5; BLC; DAM MULT, POET; PC 16
See also DLB 31, 50

Hammond, Keith
See Kuttner, Henry

Hamner, Earl (Henry), Jr. 1923- CLC 12
See also AITN 2; CA 73-76; DLB 6

Hampton, Christopher (James) 1946- CLC 4
See also CA 25-28R; DLB 13; MTCW

Hamsun, Knut TCLC 2, 14, 49
See also Pedersen, Knut

Handke, Peter 1942- CLC 5, 8, 10, 15, 38; DAM DRAM, NOV
See also CA 77-80; CANR 33; DLB 85, 124; MTCW

Hanley, James 1901-1985 CLC 3, 5, 8, 13
See also CA 73-76; 117; CANR 36; MTCW

Hannah, Barry 1942- CLC 23, 38, 90
See also CA 108; 110; CANR 43; DLB 6; INT 110; MTCW

Hannon, Ezra
See Hunter, Evan

Hansberry, Lorraine (Vivian) 1930-1965 CLC 17, 62; BLC; DA; DAB; DAC; DAM DRAM, MST, MULT; DC 2
See also BW 1; CA 109; 25-28R; CABS 3; CDALB 1941-1968; DLB 7, 38; MTCW

Hansen, Joseph 1923- CLC 38
See also CA 29-32R; CAAS 17; CANR 16, 44; INT CANR-16

Hansen, Martin A. 1909-1955 TCLC 32

Hanson, Kenneth O(stlin) 1922- CLC 13
See also CA 53-56; CANR 7

Hardwick, Elizabeth 1916- CLC 13; DAM NOV
See also CA 5-8R; CANR 3, 32; DLB 6; MTCW

Hardy, Thomas 1840-1928 TCLC 4, 10, 18, 32, 48, 53; DA; DAB; DAC; DAM MST, NOV, POET; PC 8; SSC 2; WLC
See also CA 104; 123; CDBLB 1890-1914; DLB 18, 19, 135; MTCW

Hare, David 1947- CLC 29, 58
See also CA 97-100; CANR 39; DLB 13; MTCW

Harford, Henry
See Hudson, W(illiam) H(enry)

Hargrave, Leonie
See Disch, Thomas M(ichael)

Harjo, Joy 1951- CLC 83; DAM MULT
See also CA 114; CANR 35; DLB 120, 175; NNAL

Harlan, Louis R(udolph) 1922- CLC 34
See also CA 21-24R; CANR 25, 55

Harling, Robert 1951(?)- CLC 53
See also CA 147

Harmon, William (Ruth) 1938- CLC 38
See also CA 33-36R; CANR 14, 32, 35; SATA 65

Harper, F. E. W.
See Harper, Frances Ellen Watkins

Harper, Frances E. W.
See Harper, Frances Ellen Watkins

Harper, Frances E. Watkins
See Harper, Frances Ellen Watkins

Harper, Frances Ellen
See Harper, Frances Ellen Watkins

Harper, Frances Ellen Watkins 1825-1911 TCLC

14; BLC; DAM MULT, POET
See also BW 1; CA 111; 125; DLB 50

Harper, Michael S(teven) 1938- CLC 7, 22
See also BW 1; CA 33-36R; CANR 24; DLB 41

Harper, Mrs. F. E. W.
See Harper, Frances Ellen Watkins

Harris, Christie (Lucy) Irwin 1907- CLC 12
See also CA 5-8R; CANR 6; DLB 88; JRDA;
MAICYA; SAAS 10; SATA 6, 74

Harris, Frank 1856-1931 TCLC 24
See also CA 109; 150; DLB 156

Harris, George Washington 1814-1869 NCLC 23
See also DLB 3, 11

Harris, Joel Chandler 1848-1908 TCLC 2; SSC 19
See also CA 104; 137; DLB 11, 23, 42, 78, 91;
MAICYA; YABC 1

Harris, John (Wyndham Parkes Lucas) Beynon
1903-1969
See Wyndham, John
See also CA 102; 89-92

Harris, MacDonald CLC 9
See also Heiney, Donald (William)

Harris, Mark 1922- CLC 19
See also CA 5-8R; CAAS 3; CANR 2, 55; DLB 2;
DLBY 80

Harris, (Theodore) Wilson 1921- CLC 25
See also BW 2; CA 65-68; CAAS 16; CANR 11,
27; DLB 117; MTCW

Harrison, Elizabeth Cavanna 1909-
See Cavanna, Betty
See also CA 9-12R; CANR 6, 27

Harrison, Harry (Max) 1925- CLC 42
See also CA 1-4R; CANR 5, 21; DLB 8; SATA 4

Harrison, James (Thomas) 1937- CLC 6, 14, 33,
66; SSC 19
See also CA 13-16R; CANR 8, 51; DLBY 82; INT
CANR-8

Harrison, Jim
See Harrison, James (Thomas)

Harrison, Kathryn 1961- CLC 70
See also CA 144

Harrison, Tony 1937- CLC 43
See also CA 65-68; CANR 44; DLB 40; MTCW

Harriss, Will(ard Irvin) 1922- CLC 34
See also CA 111

Harson, Sley
See Ellison, Harlan (Jay)

Hart, Ellis
See Ellison, Harlan (Jay)

Hart, Josephine 1942(?)- CLC 70; DAM POP
See also CA 138

Hart, Moss 1904-1961 CLC 66; DAM DRAM

See also CA 109; 89-92; DLB 7

Harte, (Francis) Bret(t) 1836(?)-1902 TCLC 1, 25;
DA; DAC; DAM MST; SSC 8; WLC
See also CA 104; 140; CDALB 1865-1917; DLB 12,
64, 74, 79; SATA 26

Hartley, L(eslie) P(oles) 1895-1972 CLC 2, 22
See also CA 45-48; 37-40R; CANR 33; DLB 15,
139; MTCW

Hartman, Geoffrey H. 1929- CLC 27
See also CA 117; 125; DLB 67

Hartmann von Aue c. 1160-c. 1205 CMLC 15
See also DLB 138

Hartmann von Aue 1170-1210 CMLC 15

Haruf, Kent 1943- CLC 34
See also CA 149

Harwood, Ronald 1934- CLC 32; DAM DRAM, MST
See also CA 1-4R; CANR 4, 55; DLB 13

Hasek, Jaroslav (Matej Frantisek) 1883-1923 TCLC
4
See also CA 104; 129; MTCW

Hass, Robert 1941- CLC 18, 39, 99; PC 16
See also CA 111; CANR 30, 50; DLB 105

Hastings, Hudson
See Kuttner, Henry

Hastings, Selina CLC 44

Hatteras, Amelia
See Mencken, H(enry) L(ouis)

Hatteras, Owen TCLC 18
See also Mencken, H(enry) L(ouis); Nathan,
George Jean

Hauptmann, Gerhart (Johann Robert) 1862-1946
TCLC 4; DAM DRAM
See also CA 104; 153; DLB 66, 118

Havel, Vaclav 1936- CLC 25, 58, 65; DAM DRAM;
DC 6
See also CA 104; CANR 36; MTCW

Haviaras, Stratis CLC 33
See also Chaviaras, Strates

Hawes, Stephen 1475(?)-1523(?) LC 17

Hawkes, John (Clendennin Burne, Jr.) 1925- CLC
1, 2, 3, 4, 7, 9, 14, 15, 27, 49
See also CA 1-4R; CANR 2, 47; DLB 2, 7; DLBY
80; MTCW

Hawking, S. W.
See Hawking, Stephen W(illiam)

Hawking, Stephen W(illiam) 1942- CLC 63
See also AAYA 13; BEST 89 1; CA 126; 129; CANR
48

Hawthorne, Julian 1846-1934 TCLC 25

Hawthorne, Nathaniel 1804-1864 NCLC 39; DA;
DAB; DAC; DAM MST, NOV; SSC 3; WLC

See also AAYA 18; CDALB 1640-1865; DLB 1, 74;
YABC 2

Haxton, Josephine Ayres 1921-
See Douglas, Ellen
See also CA 115; CANR 41

Hayaseca y Eizaguirre, Jorge
See Echegaray (y Eizaguirre), Jose (Maria Waldo)

Hayashi Fumiko 1904-1951 TCLC 27

Haycraft, Anna
See Ellis, Alice Thomas
See also CA 122

Hayden, Robert E(arl) 1913-1980 CLC 5, 9, 14, 37;
BLC; DA; DAC; DAM MST, MULT, POET;
PC 6
See also BW 1; CA 69-72; 97-100; CABS 2; CANR
24; CDALB 1941-1968; DLB 5, 76; MTCW;
SATA 19; SATA-Obit 26

Hayford, J(oseph) E(phraim) Casely
See Casely-Hayford, J(oseph) E(phraim)

Hayman, Ronald 1932- CLC 44
See also CA 25-28R; CANR 18, 50; DLB 155

Haywood, Eliza (Fowler) 1693(?)-1756 LC 1

Hazlitt, William 1778-1830 NCLC 29
See also DLB 110, 158

Hazzard, Shirley 1931- CLC 18
See also CA 9-12R; CANR 4; DLBY 82; MTCW

Head, Bessie 1937-1986 CLC 25, 67; BLC; DAM
MULT
See also BW 2; CA 29-32R; 119; CANR 25; DLB
117; MTCW

Headon, (Nicky) Topper 1956(?)- CLC 30

Heaney, Seamus (Justin) 1939- CLC 5, 7, 14, 25,
37, 74, 91; DAB; DAM POET
See also CA 85-88; CANR 25, 48; CDBLB 1960 to
Present; DLB 40; DLBY 95; MTCW

Hearn, (Patricio) Lafcadio (Tessima Carlos) 1850-
1904 TCLC 9
See also CA 105; DLB 12, 78

Hearne, Vicki 1946- CLC 56
See also CA 139

Hearon, Shelby 1931- CLC 63
See also AITN 2; CA 25-28R; CANR 18, 48

Heat-Moon, William Least CLC 29
See also Trogdon, William (Lewis)
See also AAYA 9

Hebbel, Friedrich 1813-1863 NCLC 43; DAM DRAM
See also DLB 129

Hebert, Anne 1916- CLC 4, 13, 29; DAC; DAM
MST, POET
See also CA 85-88; DLB 68; MTCW

Hecht, Anthony (Evan) 1923- CLC 8, 13, 19; DAM
POET
See also CA 9-12R; CANR 6; DLB 5, 169

Hecht, Ben 1894-1964 **CLC 8**
See also CA 85-88; DLB 7, 9, 25, 26, 28, 86

Hedayat, Sadeq 1903-1951 **TCLC 21**
See also CA 120

Hegel, Georg Wilhelm Friedrich 1770-1831 **NCLC 46**
See also DLB 90

Heidegger, Martin 1889-1976 **CLC 24**
See also CA 81-84; 65-68; CANR 34; MTCW

Heidenstam, (Carl Gustaf) Verner von 1859-1940 **TCLC 5**
See also CA 104

Heifner, Jack 1946- **CLC 11**
See also CA 105; CANR 47

Heijermans, Herman 1864-1924 **TCLC 24**
See also CA 123

Heilbrun, Carolyn G(old) 1926- **CLC 25**
See also CA 45-48; CANR 1, 28

Heine, Heinrich 1797-1856 **NCLC 4, 54**
See also DLB 90

Heinemann, Larry (Curtiss) 1944- **CLC 50**
See also CA 110; CAAS 21; CANR 31; DLBD 9; INT CANR-31

Heiney, Donald (William) 1921-1993
See Harris, MacDonald
See also CA 1-4R; 142; CANR 3

Heinlein, Robert A(nson) 1907-1988 **CLC 1, 3, 8, 14, 26, 55; DAM POP**
See also AAYA 17; CA 1-4R; 125; CANR 1, 20, 53; DLB 8; JRDA; MAICYA; MTCW; SATA 9, 69; SATA-Obit 56

Helforth, John
See Doolittle, Hilda

Hellenhofferu, Vojtech Kapristian z
See Hasek, Jaroslav (Matej Frantisek)

Heller, Joseph 1923- **CLC 1, 3, 5, 8, 11, 36, 63; DA; DAB; DAC; DAM MST, NOV, POP; WLC**
See also AITN 1; CA 5-8R; CABS 1; CANR 8, 42; DLB 2, 28; DLBY 80; INT CANR-8; MTCW

Hellman, Lillian (Florence) 1906-1984 **CLC 2, 4, 8, 14, 18, 34, 44, 52; DAM DRAM; DC 1**
See also AITN 1, 2; CA 13-16R; 112; CANR 33; DLB 7; DLBY 84; MTCW

Helprin, Mark 1947- **CLC 7, 10, 22, 32; DAM NOV, POP**
See also CA 81-84; CANR 47; DLBY 85; MTCW

Helvetius, Claude-Adrien 1715-1771 **LC 26**

Helyar, Jane Penelope Josephine 1933-
See Poole, Josephine
See also CA 21-24R; CANR 10, 26; SATA 82

Hemans, Felicia 1793-1835 **NCLC 29**
See also DLB 96

Hemingway, Ernest (Miller) 1899-1961 **CLC 1, 3, 6, 8, 10, 13, 19, 30, 34, 39, 41, 44, 50, 61, 80; DA; DAB; DAC; DAM MST, NOV; SSC 1; WLC**
See also AAYA 19; CA 77-80; CANR 34; CDALB 1917-1929; DLB 4, 9, 102; DLBD 1; DLBY 81, 87; MTCW

Hempel, Amy 1951- **CLC 39**
See also CA 118; 137

Henderson, F. C.
See Mencken, H(enry) L(ouis)

Henderson, Sylvia
See Ashton-Warner, Sylvia (Constance)

Henley, Beth **CLC 23; DC 6**
See also Henley, Elizabeth Becker
See also CABS 3; DLBY 86

Henley, Elizabeth Becker 1952-
See Henley, Beth
See also CA 107; CANR 32; DAM DRAM, MST; MTCW

Henley, William Ernest 1849-1903 **TCLC 8**
See also CA 105; DLB 19

Hennissart, Martha
See Lathen, Emma
See also CA 85-88

Henry, O. **TCLC 1, 19; SSC 5; WLC**
See also Porter, William Sydney

Henry, Patrick 1736-1799 **LC 25**

Henryson, Robert 1430(?)-1506(?) **LC 20**
See also DLB 146

Henry VIII 1491-1547 **LC 10**

Henschke, Alfred
See Klabund

Hentoff, Nat(han Irving) 1925- **CLC 26**
See also AAYA 4; CA 1-4R; CAAS 6; CANR 5, 25; CLR 1; INT CANR-25; JRDA; MAICYA; SATA 42, 69; SATA-Brief 27

Heppenstall, (John) Rayner 1911-1981 **CLC 10**
See also CA 1-4R; 103; CANR 29

Herbert, Frank (Patrick) 1920-1986 **CLC 12, 23, 35, 44, 85; DAM POP**
See also CA 53-56; 118; CANR 5, 43; DLB 8; INT CANR-5; MTCW; SATA 9, 37; SATA-Obit 47

Herbert, George 1593-1633 **LC 24; DAB; DAM POET; PC 4**
See also CDBLB Before 1660; DLB 126

Herbert, Zbigniew 1924- **CLC 9, 43; DAM POET**
See also CA 89-92; CANR 36; MTCW

Herbst, Josephine (Frey) 1897-1969 **CLC 34**
See also CA 5-8R; 25-28R; DLB 9

Hergesheimer, Joseph 1880-1954 **TCLC 11**
See also CA 109; DLB 102, 9

Herlihy, James Leo 1927-1993 **CLC 6**

See also CA 1-4R; 143; CANR 2

Hermogenes fl. c. 175- **CMLC 6**

Hernandez, Jose 1834-1886 **NCLC 17**

Herodotus c. 484B.C.-429B.C. **CMLC 17**
See also DLB 176

Herrick, Robert 1591-1674 **LC 13; DA; DAB; DAC; DAM MST, POP; PC 9**
See also DLB 126

Herring, Guilles
See Somerville, Edith

Herriot, James 1916-1995 **CLC 12; DAM POP**
See also Wight, James Alfred
See also AAYA 1; CA 148; CANR 40; SATA 86

Herrmann, Dorothy 1941- **CLC 44**
See also CA 107

Herrmann, Taffy
See Herrmann, Dorothy

Hersey, John (Richard) 1914-1993 **CLC 1, 2, 7, 9, 40, 81, 97; DAM POP**
See also CA 17-20R; 140; CANR 33; DLB 6; MTCW; SATA 25; SATA-Obit 76

Herzen, Aleksandr Ivanovich 1812-1870 **NCLC 10**

Herzl, Theodor 1860-1904 **TCLC 36**

Herzog, Werner 1942- **CLC 16**
See also CA 89-92

Hesiod c. 8th cent. B.C.- **CMLC 5**
See also DLB 176

Hesse, Hermann 1877-1962 **CLC 1, 2, 3, 6, 11, 17, 25, 69; DA; DAB; DAC; DAM MST, NOV; SSC 9; WLC**
See also CA 17-18; CAP 2; DLB 66; MTCW; SATA 50

Hewes, Cady
See De Voto, Bernard (Augustine)

Heyen, William 1940- **CLC 13, 18**
See also CA 33-36R; CAAS 9; DLB 5

Heyerdahl, Thor 1914- **CLC 26**
See also CA 5-8R; CANR 5, 22; MTCW; SATA 2, 52

Heym, Georg (Theodor Franz Arthur) 1887-1912 **TCLC 9**
See also CA 106

Heym, Stefan 1913- **CLC 41**
See also CA 9-12R; CANR 4; DLB 69

Heyse, Paul (Johann Ludwig von) 1830-1914 **TCLC 8**
See also CA 104; DLB 129

Heyward, (Edwin) DuBose 1885-1940 **TCLC 59**
See also CA 108; DLB 7, 9, 45; SATA 21

Hibbert, Eleanor Alice Burford 1906-1993 **CLC 7; DAM POP**

See also BEST 90 4; CA 17-20R; 140; CANR 9, 28;
SATA 2; SATA-Obit 74

Hichens, Robert S. 1864-1950 **TCLC 64**
See also DLB 153

Higgins, George V(incent) 1939- **CLC 4, 7, 10, 18**
See also CA 77-80; CAAS 5; CANR 17, 51; DLB 2;
DLBY 81; INT CANR-17; MTCW

Higginson, Thomas Wentworth 1823-1911 **TCLC 36**
See also DLB 1, 64

Highet, Helen
See MacInnes, Helen (Clark)

Highsmith, (Mary) Patricia 1921-1995 **CLC 2, 4, 14, 42; DAM NOV, POP**
See also CA 1-4R; 147; CANR 1, 20, 48; MTCW

Highwater, Jamake (Mamake) 1942(?)- **CLC 12**
See also AAYA 7; CA 65-68; CAAS 7; CANR 10, 34; CLR 17; DLB 52; DLBY 85; JRDA;
MAICYA; SATA 32, 69; SATA-Brief 30

Highway, Tomson 1951- **CLC 92; DAC; DAM MULT**
See also CA 151; NNAL

Higuchi, Ichiyo 1872-1896 **NCLC 49**

Hijuelos, Oscar 1951- **CLC 65; DAM MULT, POP; HLC**
See also BEST 90 1; CA 123; CANR 50; DLB 145;
HW

Hikmet, Nazim 1902(?)-1963 **CLC 40**
See also CA 141; 93-96

Hildegard von Bingen 1098-1179 **CMLC 20**
See also DLB 148

Hildesheimer, Wolfgang 1916-1991 **CLC 49**
See also CA 101; 135; DLB 69, 124

Hill, Geoffrey (William) 1932- **CLC 5, 8, 18, 45; DAM POET**
See also CA 81-84; CANR 21; CDBLB 1960 to Present; DLB 40; MTCW

Hill, George Roy 1921- **CLC 26**
See also CA 110; 122

Hill, John
See Koontz, Dean R(ay)

Hill, Susan (Elizabeth) 1942- **CLC 4; DAB; DAM MST, NOV**
See also CA 33-36R; CANR 29; DLB 14, 139;
MTCW

Hillerman, Tony 1925- **CLC 62; DAM POP**
See also AAYA 6; BEST 89 1; CA 29-32R; CANR 21, 42; SATA 6

Hillesum, Etty 1914-1943 **TCLC 49**
See also CA 137

Hilliard, Noel (Harvey) 1929- **CLC 15**
See also CA 9-12R; CANR 7

Hillis, Rick 1956- **CLC 66**
See also CA 134

Hilton, James 1900-1954 **TCLC 21**
See also CA 108; DLB 34, 77; SATA 34

Himes, Chester (Bomar) 1909-1984 **CLC 2, 4, 7, 18, 58; BLC; DAM MULT**
See also BW 2; CA 25-28R; 114; CANR 22; DLB 2, 76, 143; MTCW

Hinde, Thomas CLC 6, 11
See also Chitty, Thomas Willes

Hindin, Nathan
See Bloch, Robert (Albert)

Hine, (William) Daryl 1936- **CLC 15**
See also CA 1-4R; CAAS 15; CANR 1, 20; DLB 60

Hinkson, Katharine Tynan
See Tynan, Katharine

Hinton, S(usan) E(loise) 1950- **CLC 30; DA; DAB; DAC; DAM MST, NOV**
See also AAYA 2; CA 81-84; CANR 32; CLR 3, 23;
JRDA; MAICYA; MTCW; SATA 19, 58

Hippius, Zinaida TCLC 9
See also Gippius, Zinaida (Nikolayevna)

Hiraoka, Kimitake 1925-1970
See Mishima, Yukio
See also CA 97-100; 29-32R; DAM DRAM;
MTCW

Hirsch, E(ric) D(onald), Jr. 1928- **CLC 79**
See also CA 25-28R; CANR 27, 51; DLB 67; INT CANR-27; MTCW

Hirsch, Edward 1950- **CLC 31, 50**
See also CA 104; CANR 20, 42; DLB 120

Hitchcock, Alfred (Joseph) 1899-1980 **CLC 16**
See also CA 97-100; SATA 27; SATA-Obit 24

Hitler, Adolf 1889-1945 **TCLC 53**
See also CA 117; 147

Hoagland, Edward 1932- **CLC 28**
See also CA 1-4R; CANR 2, 31, 57; DLB 6; SATA 51

Hoban, Russell (Conwell) 1925- **CLC 7, 25; DAM NOV**
See also CA 5-8R; CANR 23, 37; CLR 3; DLB 52;
MAICYA; MTCW; SATA 1, 40, 78

Hobbes, Thomas 1588-1679 **LC 36**
See also DLB 151

Hobbs, Perry
See Blackmur, R(ichard) P(almer)

Hobson, Laura Z(ametkin) 1900-1986 **CLC 7, 25**
See also CA 17-20R; 118; CANR 55; DLB 28; SATA 52

Hochhuth, Rolf 1931- **CLC 4, 11, 18; DAM DRAM**
See also CA 5-8R; CANR 33; DLB 124; MTCW

Hochman, Sandra 1936- **CLC 3, 8**
See also CA 5-8R; DLB 5

Hochwaelder, Fritz 1911-1986 **CLC 36; DAM DRAM**

See also CA 29-32R; 120; CANR 42; MTCW

Hochwalder, Fritz
See Hochwaelder, Fritz

Hocking, Mary (Eunice) 1921- **CLC 13**
See also CA 101; CANR 18, 40

Hodgins, Jack 1938- **CLC 23**
See also CA 93-96; DLB 60

Hodgson, William Hope 1877(?)-1918 **TCLC 13**
See also CA 111; DLB 70, 153, 156

Hoeg, Peter 1957- **CLC 95**
See also CA 151

Hoffman, Alice 1952- **CLC 51; DAM NOV**
See also CA 77-80; CANR 34; MTCW

Hoffman, Daniel (Gerard) 1923- **CLC 6, 13, 23**
See also CA 1-4R; CANR 4; DLB 5

Hoffman, Stanley 1944- **CLC 5**
See also CA 77-80

Hoffman, William M(oses) 1939- **CLC 40**
See also CA 57-60; CANR 11

Hoffmann, E(rnst) T(heodor) A(madeus) 1776-1822 **NCLC 2; SSC 13**
See also DLB 90; SATA 27

Hofmann, Gert 1931- **CLC 54**
See also CA 128

Hofmannsthal, Hugo von 1874-1929 **TCLC 11; DAM DRAM; DC 4**
See also CA 106; 153; DLB 81, 118

Hogan, Linda 1947- **CLC 73; DAM MULT**
See also CA 120; CANR 45; DLB 175; NNAL

Hogarth, Charles
See Creasey, John

Hogarth, Emmett
See Polonsky, Abraham (Lincoln)

Hogg, James 1770-1835 **NCLC 4**
See also DLB 93, 116, 159

Holbach, Paul Henri Thiry Baron 1723-1789 **LC 14**

Holberg, Ludvig 1684-1754 **LC 6**

Holden, Ursula 1921- **CLC 18**
See also CA 101; CAAS 8; CANR 22

Holderlin, (Johann Christian) Friedrich 1770-1843 **NCLC 16; PC 4**

Holdstock, Robert
See Holdstock, Robert P.

Holdstock, Robert P. 1948- **CLC 39**
See also CA 131

Holland, Isabelle 1920- **CLC 21**
See also AAYA 11; CA 21-24R; CANR 10, 25, 47;
JRDA; MAICYA; SATA 8, 70

Holland, Marcus

See Caldwell, (Janet Miriam) Taylor (Holland)

Hollander, John 1929- **CLC 2, 5, 8, 14**
See also CA 1-4R; CANR 1, 52; DLB 5; SATA 13

Hollander, Paul
See Silverberg, Robert

Holleran, Andrew 1943(?)- **CLC 38**
See also CA 144

Hollinghurst, Alan 1954- **CLC 55, 91**
See also CA 114

Hollis, Jim
See Summers, Hollis (Spurgeon, Jr.)

Holly, Buddy 1936-1959 **TCLC 65**

Holmes, John
See Souster, (Holmes) Raymond

Holmes, John Clellon 1926-1988 **CLC 56**
See also CA 9-12R; 125; CANR 4; DLB 16

Holmes, Oliver Wendell 1809-1894 **NCLC 14**
See also CDALB 1640-1865; DLB 1; SATA 34

Holmes, Raymond
See Souster, (Holmes) Raymond

Holt, Victoria
See Hibbert, Eleanor Alice Burford

Holub, Miroslav 1923- **CLC 4**
See also CA 21-24R; CANR 10

Homer c. 8th cent. B.C.- **CMLC 1, 16; DA; DAB; DAC; DAM MST, POET**
See also DLB 176

Honig, Edwin 1919- **CLC 33**
See also CA 5-8R; CAAS 8; CANR 4, 45; DLB 5

Hood, Hugh (John Blagdon) 1928- **CLC 15, 28**
See also CA 49-52; CAAS 17; CANR 1, 33; DLB 53

Hood, Thomas 1799-1845 **NCLC 16**
See also DLB 96

Hooker, (Peter) Jeremy 1941- **CLC 43**
See also CA 77-80; CANR 22; DLB 40

hooks, bell CLC 94
See also Watkins, Gloria

Hope, A(lec) D(erwent) 1907- **CLC 3, 51**
See also CA 21-24R; CANR 33; MTCW

Hope, Brian
See Creasey, John

Hope, Christopher (David Tully) 1944- **CLC 52**
See also CA 106; CANR 47; SATA 62

Hopkins, Gerard Manley 1844-1889 **NCLC 17; DA; DAB; DAC; DAM MST, POET; PC 15; WLC**
See also CDBLB 1890-1914; DLB 35, 57

Hopkins, John (Richard) 1931- **CLC 4**
See also CA 85-88

Hopkins, Pauline Elizabeth 1859-1930 **TCLC 28; BLC; DAM MULT**
See also BW 2; CA 141; DLB 50

Hopkinson, Francis 1737-1791 **LC 25**
See also DLB 31

Hopley-Woolrich, Cornell George 1903-1968
See Woolrich, Cornell
See also CA 13-14; CAP 1

Horatio
See Proust, (Valentin-Louis-George-Eugene-) Marcel

Horgan, Paul (George Vincent O'Shaughnessy) 1903-1995 **CLC 9, 53; DAM NOV**
See also CA 13-16R; 147; CANR 9, 35; DLB 102; DLBY 85; INT CANR-9; MTCW; SATA 13; SATA-Obit 84

Horn, Peter
See Kuttner, Henry

Hornem, Horace Esq.
See Byron, George Gordon (Noel)

Hornung, E(rnest) W(illiam) 1866-1921 **TCLC 59**
See also CA 108; DLB 70

Horovitz, Israel (Arthur) 1939- **CLC 56; DAM DRAM**
See also CA 33-36R; CANR 46; DLB 7

Horvath, Odon von
See Horvath, Oedoen von
See also DLB 85, 124

Horvath, Oedoen von 1901-1938 **TCLC 45**
See also Horvath, Odon von
See also CA 118

Horwitz, Julius 1920-1986 **CLC 14**
See also CA 9-12R; 119; CANR 12

Hospital, Janette Turner 1942- **CLC 42**
See also CA 108; CANR 48

Hostos, E. M. de
See Hostos (y Bonilla), Eugenio Maria de

Hostos, Eugenio M. de
See Hostos (y Bonilla), Eugenio Maria de

Hostos, Eugenio Maria
See Hostos (y Bonilla), Eugenio Maria de

Hostos (y Bonilla), Eugenio Maria de 1839-1903 **TCLC 24**
See also CA 123; 131; HW

Houdini
See Lovecraft, H(oward) P(hillips)

Hougan, Carolyn 1943- **CLC 34**
See also CA 139

Household, Geoffrey (Edward West) 1900-1988 **CLC 11**
See also CA 77-80; 126; DLB 87; SATA 14; SATA-Obit 59

Housman, A(lfred) E(dward) 1859-1936 **TCLC 1, 10; DA; DAB; DAC; DAM MST, POET; PC 2**
See also CA 104; 125; DLB 19; MTCW

Housman, Laurence 1865-1959 **TCLC 7**
See also CA 106; 155; DLB 10; SATA 25

Howard, Elizabeth Jane 1923- **CLC 7, 29**
See also CA 5-8R; CANR 8

Howard, Maureen 1930- **CLC 5, 14, 46**
See also CA 53-56; CANR 31; DLBY 83; INT CANR-31; MTCW

Howard, Richard 1929- **CLC 7, 10, 47**
See also AITN 1; CA 85-88; CANR 25; DLB 5; INT CANR-25

Howard, Robert Ervin 1906-1936 **TCLC 8**
See also CA 105

Howard, Warren F.
See Pohl, Frederik

Howe, Fanny 1940- **CLC 47**
See also CA 117; SATA-Brief 52

Howe, Irving 1920-1993 **CLC 85**
See also CA 9-12R; 141; CANR 21, 50; DLB 67; MTCW

Howe, Julia Ward 1819-1910 **TCLC 21**
See also CA 117; DLB 1

Howe, Susan 1937- **CLC 72**
See also DLB 120

Howe, Tina 1937- **CLC 48**
See also CA 109

Howell, James 1594(?)-1666 **LC 13**
See also DLB 151

Howells, W. D.
See Howells, William Dean

Howells, William D.
See Howells, William Dean

Howells, William Dean 1837-1920 **TCLC 7, 17, 41**
See also CA 104; 134; CDALB 1865-1917; DLB 12, 64, 74, 79

Howes, Barbara 1914-1996 **CLC 15**
See also CA 9-12R; 151; CAAS 3; CANR 53; SATA 5

Hrabal, Bohumil 1914-1997 **CLC 13, 67**
See also CA 106; 156; CAAS 12; CANR 57

Hsun, Lu
See Lu Hsun

Hubbard, L(afayette) Ron(ald) 1911-1986 **CLC 43; DAM POP**
See also CA 77-80; 118; CANR 52

Huch, Ricarda (Octavia) 1864-1947 **TCLC 13**
See also CA 111; DLB 66

Huddle, David 1942- **CLC 49**
See also CA 57-60; CAAS 20; DLB 130

Hudson, Jeffrey

See Crichton, (John) Michael

Hudson, W(illiam) H(enry) 1841-1922 **TCLC 29**
See also CA 115; DLB 98, 153, 174; SATA 35

Hueffer, Ford Madox
See Ford, Ford Madox

Hughart, Barry 1934- **CLC 39**
See also CA 137

Hughes, Colin
See Creasey, John

Hughes, David (John) 1930- **CLC 48**
See also CA 116; 129; DLB 14

Hughes, Edward James
See Hughes, Ted
See also DAM MST, POET

Hughes, (James) Langston 1902-1967 **CLC 1, 5, 10, 15, 35, 44; BLC; DA; DAB; DAC; DAM DRAM, MST, MULT, POET; DC 3; PC 1; SSC 6; WLC**
See also AAYA 12; BW 1; CA 1-4R; 25-28R; CANR 1, 34; CDALB 1929-1941; CLR 17; DLB 4, 7, 48, 51, 86; JRDA; MAICYA; MTCW; SATA 4, 33

Hughes, Richard (Arthur Warren) 1900-1976 **CLC 1, 11; DAM NOV**
See also CA 5-8R; 65-68; CANR 4; DLB 15, 161; MTCW; SATA 8; SATA-Obit 25

Hughes, Ted 1930- **CLC 2, 4, 9, 14, 37; DAB; DAC; PC 7**
See also Hughes, Edward James
See also CA 1-4R; CANR 1, 33; CLR 3; DLB 40, 161; MAICYA; MTCW; SATA 49; SATA-Brief 27

Hugo, Richard F(ranklin) 1923-1982 **CLC 6, 18, 32; DAM POET**
See also CA 49-52; 108; CANR 3; DLB 5

Hugo, Victor (Marie) 1802-1885 **NCLC 3, 10, 21; DA; DAB; DAC; DAM DRAM, MST, NOV, POET; PC 17; WLC**
See also DLB 119; SATA 47

Huidobro, Vicente
See Huidobro Fernandez, Vicente Garcia

Huidobro Fernandez, Vicente Garcia 1893-1948 **TCLC 31**
See also CA 131; HW

Hulme, Keri 1947- **CLC 39**
See also CA 125; INT 125

Hulme, T(homas) E(rnest) 1883-1917 **TCLC 21**
See also CA 117; DLB 19

Hume, David 1711-1776 **LC 7**
See also DLB 104

Humphrey, William 1924- **CLC 45**
See also CA 77-80; DLB 6

Humphreys, Emyr Owen 1919- **CLC 47**
See also CA 5-8R; CANR 3, 24; DLB 15

Humphreys, Josephine 1945- **CLC 34, 57**
See also CA 121; 127; INT 127

Huneker, James Gibbons 1857-1921 **TCLC 65**
See also DLB 71

Hungerford, Pixie
See Brinsmead, H(esba) F(ay)

Hunt, E(verette) Howard, (Jr.) 1918- **CLC 3**
See also AITN 1; CA 45-48; CANR 2, 47

Hunt, Kyle
See Creasey, John

Hunt, (James Henry) Leigh 1784-1859 **NCLC 1; DAM POET**

Hunt, Marsha 1946- **CLC 70**
See also BW 2; CA 143

Hunt, Violet 1866-1942 **TCLC 53**
See also DLB 162

Hunter, E. Waldo
See Sturgeon, Theodore (Hamilton)

Hunter, Evan 1926- **CLC 11, 31; DAM POP**
See also CA 5-8R; CANR 5, 38; DLBY 82; INT CANR-5; MTCW; SATA 25

Hunter, Kristin (Eggleston) 1931- **CLC 35**
See also AITN 1; BW 1; CA 13-16R; CANR 13; CLR 3; DLB 33; INT CANR-13; MAICYA; SAAS 10; SATA 12

Hunter, Mollie 1922- **CLC 21**
See also McIlwraith, Maureen Mollie Hunter
See also AAYA 13; CANR 37; CLR 25; DLB 161; JRDA; MAICYA; SAAS 7; SATA 54

Hunter, Robert (?)-1734 **LC 7**

Hurston, Zora Neale 1903-1960 **CLC 7, 30, 61; BLC; DA; DAC; DAM MST, MULT, NOV; SSC 4**
See also AAYA 15; BW 1; CA 85-88; DLB 51, 86; MTCW

Huston, John (Marcellus) 1906-1987 **CLC 20**
See also CA 73-76; 123; CANR 34; DLB 26

Hustvedt, Siri 1955- **CLC 76**
See also CA 137

Hutten, Ulrich von 1488-1523 **LC 16**

Huxley, Aldous (Leonard) 1894-1963 **CLC 1, 3, 4, 5, 8, 11, 18, 35, 79; DA; DAB; DAC; DAM MST, NOV; WLC**
See also AAYA 11; CA 85-88; CANR 44; CDBLB 1914-1945; DLB 36, 100, 162; MTCW; SATA 63

Huysmans, Charles Marie Georges 1848-1907
See Huysmans, Joris-Karl
See also CA 104

Huysmans, Joris-Karl **TCLC 7, 69**
See also Huysmans, Charles Marie Georges
See also DLB 123

Hwang, David Henry 1957- **CLC 55; DAM DRAM;**

DC 4
See also CA 127; 132; INT 132

Hyde, Anthony 1946- **CLC 42**
See also CA 136

Hyde, Margaret O(ldroyd) 1917- **CLC 21**
See also CA 1-4R; CANR 1, 36; CLR 23; JRDA; MAICYA; SAAS 8; SATA 1, 42, 76

Hynes, James 1956(?)- **CLC 65**

Ian, Janis 1951- **CLC 21**
See also CA 105

Ibanez, Vicente Blasco
See Blasco Ibanez, Vicente

Ibarguengoitia, Jorge 1928-1983 **CLC 37**
See also CA 124; 113; HW

Ibsen, Henrik (Johan) 1828-1906 **TCLC 2, 8, 16, 37, 52; DA; DAB; DAC; DAM DRAM, MST; DC 2; WLC**
See also CA 104; 141

Ibuse Masuji 1898-1993 **CLC 22**
See also CA 127; 141

Ichikawa, Kon 1915- **CLC 20**
See also CA 121

Idle, Eric 1943- **CLC 21**
See also Monty Python
See also CA 116; CANR 35

Ignatow, David 1914- **CLC 4, 7, 14, 40**
See also CA 9-12R; CAAS 3; CANR 31, 57; DLB 5

Ihimaera, Witi 1944- **CLC 46**
See also CA 77-80

Ilf, Ilya **TCLC 21**
See also Fainzilberg, Ilya Arnoldovich

Illyes, Gyula 1902-1983 **PC 16**
See also CA 114; 109

Immermann, Karl (Lebrecht) 1796-1840 **NCLC 4, 49**
See also DLB 133

Inclan, Ramon (Maria) del Valle
See Valle-Inclan, Ramon (Maria) del

Infante, G(uillermo) Cabrera
See Cabrera Infante, G(uillermo)

Ingalls, Rachel (Holmes) 1940- **CLC 42**
See also CA 123; 127

Ingamells, Rex 1913-1955 **TCLC 35**

Inge, William (Motter) 1913-1973 **CLC 1, 8, 19; DAM DRAM**
See also CA 9-12R; CDALB 1941-1968; DLB 7; MTCW

Ingelow, Jean 1820-1897 **NCLC 39**
See also DLB 35, 163; SATA 33

Ingram, Willis J.
See Harris, Mark

Jelakowitch, Ivan
See Heijermans, Herman

Jellicoe, (Patricia) Ann 1927- **CLC 27**
See also CA 85-88; DLB 13

Jen, Gish CLC 70
See also Jen, Lillian

Jen, Lillian 1956(?)-
See Jen, Gish
See also CA 135

Jenkins, (John) Robin 1912- **CLC 52**
See also CA 1-4R; CANR 1; DLB 14

Jennings, Elizabeth (Joan) 1926- **CLC 5, 14**
See also CA 61-64; CAAS 5; CANR 8, 39; DLB 27;
MTCW; SATA 66

Jennings, Waylon 1937- **CLC 21**

Jensen, Johannes V. 1873-1950 **TCLC 41**

Jensen, Laura (Linnea) 1948- **CLC 37**
See also CA 103

Jerome, Jerome K(lapka) 1859-1927 **TCLC 23**
See also CA 119; DLB 10, 34, 135

Jerrold, Douglas William 1803-1857 **NCLC 2**
See also DLB 158, 159

Jewett, (Theodora) Sarah Orne 1849-1909 **TCLC 1,
22; SSC 6**
See also CA 108; 127; DLB 12, 74; SATA 15

Jewsbury, Geraldine (Endsor) 1812-1880 **NCLC 22**
See also DLB 21

Jhabvala, Ruth Prawer 1927- **CLC 4, 8, 29, 94;
DAB; DAM NOV**
See also CA 1-4R; CANR 2, 29, 51; DLB 139; INT
CANR-29; MTCW

Jibran, Kahlil
See Gibran, Kahlil

Jibran, Khalil
See Gibran, Kahlil

Jiles, Paulette 1943- **CLC 13, 58**
See also CA 101

Jimenez (Mantecon), Juan Ramon 1881-1958 **TCLC
4; DAM MULT, POET; HLC; PC 7**
See also CA 104; 131; DLB 134; HW; MTCW

Jimenez, Ramon
See Jimenez (Mantecon), Juan Ramon

Jimenez Mantecon, Juan
See Jimenez (Mantecon), Juan Ramon

Joel, Billy CLC 26
See also Joel, William Martin

Joel, William Martin 1949-
See Joel, Billy
See also CA 108

John of the Cross, St. 1542-1591 **LC 18**

Johnson, B(ryan) S(tanley William) 1933-1973 **CLC
6, 9**
See also CA 9-12R; 53-56; CANR 9; DLB 14, 40

Johnson, Benj. F. of Boo
See Riley, James Whitcomb

Johnson, Benjamin F. of Boo
See Riley, James Whitcomb

Johnson, Charles (Richard) 1948- **CLC 7, 51, 65;
BLC; DAM MULT**
See also BW 2; CA 116; CAAS 18; CANR 42;
DLB 33

Johnson, Denis 1949- **CLC 52**
See also CA 117; 121; DLB 120

Johnson, Diane 1934- **CLC 5, 13, 48**
See also CA 41-44R; CANR 17, 40; DLBY 80; INT
CANR-17; MTCW

Johnson, Eyvind (Olof Verner) 1900-1976 **CLC 14**
See also CA 73-76; 69-72; CANR 34

Johnson, J. R.
See James, C(yril) L(ionel) R(obert)

Johnson, James Weldon 1871-1938 **TCLC 3, 19;
BLC; DAM MULT, POET**
See also BW 1; CA 104; 125; CDALB 1917-1929;
CLR 32; DLB 51; MTCW; SATA 31

Johnson, Joyce 1935- **CLC 58**
See also CA 125; 129

Johnson, Lionel (Pigot) 1867-1902 **TCLC 19**
See also CA 117; DLB 19

Johnson, Mel
See Malzberg, Barry N(athaniel)

Johnson, Pamela Hansford 1912-1981 **CLC 1, 7, 27**
See also CA 1-4R; 104; CANR 2, 28; DLB 15;
MTCW

Johnson, Robert 1911(?)-1938 **TCLC 69**

Johnson, Samuel 1709-1784 **LC 15; DA; DAB; DAC;
DAM MST; WLC**
See also CDBLB 1660-1789; DLB 39, 95, 104, 142

Johnson, Uwe 1934-1984 **CLC 5, 10, 15, 40**
See also CA 1-4R; 112; CANR 1, 39; DLB 75;
MTCW

Johnston, George (Benson) 1913- **CLC 51**
See also CA 1-4R; CANR 5, 20; DLB 88

Johnston, Jennifer 1930- **CLC 7**
See also CA 85-88; DLB 14

Jolley, (Monica) Elizabeth 1923- **CLC 46; SSC 19**
See also CA 127; CAAS 13

Jones, Arthur Llewellyn 1863-1947
See Machen, Arthur
See also CA 104

Jones, D(ouglas) G(ordon) 1929- **CLC 10**
See also CA 29-32R; CANR 13; DLB 53

Jones, David (Michael) 1895-1974 **CLC 2, 4, 7, 13,
42**
See also CA 9-12R; 53-56; CANR 28; CDBLB 1945-
1960; DLB 20, 100; MTCW

Jones, David Robert 1947-
See Bowie, David
See also CA 103

Jones, Diana Wynne 1934- **CLC 26**
See also AAYA 12; CA 49-52; CANR 4, 26, 56;
CLR 23; DLB 161; JRDA; MAICYA; SAAS 7;
SATA 9, 70

Jones, Edward P. 1950- **CLC 76**
See also BW 2; CA 142

Jones, Gayl 1949- **CLC 6, 9; BLC; DAM MULT**
See also BW 2; CA 77-80; CANR 27; DLB 33;
MTCW

Jones, James 1921-1977 **CLC 1, 3, 10, 39**
See also AITN 1, 2; CA 1-4R; 69-72; CANR 6;
DLB 2, 143; MTCW

Jones, John J.
See Lovecraft, H(oward) P(hillips)

Jones, LeRoi CLC 1, 2, 3, 5, 10, 14
See also Baraka, Amiri

Jones, Louis B. CLC 65
See also CA 141

Jones, Madison (Percy, Jr.) 1925- **CLC 4**
See also CA 13-16R; CAAS 11; CANR 7, 54; DLB
152

Jones, Mervyn 1922- **CLC 10, 52**
See also CA 45-48; CAAS 5; CANR 1; MTCW

Jones, Mick 1956(?)- **CLC 30**

Jones, Nettie (Pearl) 1941- **CLC 34**
See also BW 2; CA 137; CAAS 20

Jones, Preston 1936-1979 **CLC 10**
See also CA 73-76; 89-92; DLB 7

Jones, Robert F(rancis) 1934- **CLC 7**
See also CA 49-52; CANR 2

Jones, Rod 1953- **CLC 50**
See also CA 128

Jones, Terence Graham Parry 1942- **CLC 21**
See also Jones, Terry; Monty Python
See also CA 112; 116; CANR 35; INT 116

Jones, Terry
See Jones, Terence Graham Parry
See also SATA 67; SATA-Brief 51

Jones, Thom 1945(?)- **CLC 81**

Jong, Erica 1942- **CLC 4, 6, 8, 18, 83; DAM NOV,
POP**
See also AITN 1; BEST 90 2; CA 73-76; CANR 26,
52; DLB 2, 5, 28, 152; INT CANR-26; MTCW

Jonson, Ben(jamin) 1572(?)-1637 **LC 6, 33; DA;
DAB; DAC; DAM DRAM, MST, POET; DC 4;
PC 17; WLC**
See also CDBLB Before 1660; DLB 62, 121

Jordan, June 1936- **CLC 5, 11, 23; DAM MULT, POET**
See also AAYA 2; BW 2; CA 33-36R; CANR 25;
CLR 10; DLB 38; MAICYA; MTCW; SATA 4

Jordan, Pat(rick M.) 1941- **CLC 37**
See also CA 33-36R

Jorgensen, Ivar
See Ellison, Harlan (Jay)

Jorgenson, Ivar
See Silverberg, Robert

Josephus, Flavius c. 37-100 **CMLC 13**

Josipovici, Gabriel 1940- **CLC 6, 43**
See also CA 37-40R; CAAS 8; CANR 47; DLB 14

Joubert, Joseph 1754-1824 **NCLC 9**

Jouve, Pierre Jean 1887-1976 **CLC 47**
See also CA 65-68

Joyce, James (Augustine Aloysius) 1882-1941
TCLC 3, 8, 16, 35, 52; DA; DAB; DAC; DAM MST, NOV, POET; SSC 3; WLC
See also CA 104; 126; CDBLB 1914-1945; DLB 10, 19, 36, 162; MTCW

Jozsef, Attila 1905-1937 **TCLC 22**
See also CA 116

Juana Ines de la Cruz 1651(?)-1695 **LC 5**

Judd, Cyril
See Kornbluth, C(yril) M.; Pohl, Frederik

Julian of Norwich 1342(?)-1416(?) **LC 6**
See also DLB 146

Juniper, Alex
See Hospital, Janette Turner

Junius
See Luxemburg, Rosa

Just, Ward (Swift) 1935- **CLC 4, 27**
See also CA 25-28R; CANR 32; INT CANR-32

Justice, Donald (Rodney) 1925- **CLC 6, 19; DAM POET**
See also CA 5-8R; CANR 26, 54; DLBY 83; INT CANR-26

Juvenal c. 55-c. 127 **CMLC 8**

Juvenis
See Bourne, Randolph S(illiman)

Kacew, Romain 1914-1980
See Gary, Romain
See also CA 108; 102

Kadare, Ismail 1936- **CLC 52**

Kadohata, Cynthia **CLC 59**
See also CA 140

Kafka, Franz 1883-1924 **TCLC 2, 6, 13, 29, 47, 53; DA; DAB; DAC; DAM MST, NOV; SSC 5; WLC**
See also CA 105; 126; DLB 81; MTCW

Kahanovitsch, Pinkhes
See Der Nister

Kahn, Roger 1927- **CLC 30**
See also CA 25-28R; CANR 44; DLB 171; SATA 37

Kain, Saul
See Sassoon, Siegfried (Lorraine)

Kaiser, Georg 1878-1945 **TCLC 9**
See also CA 106; DLB 124

Kaletski, Alexander 1946- **CLC 39**
See also CA 118; 143

Kalidasa fl. c. 400- **CMLC 9**

Kallman, Chester (Simon) 1921-1975 **CLC 2**
See also CA 45-48; 53-56; CANR 3

Kaminsky, Melvin 1926-
See Brooks, Mel
See also CA 65-68; CANR 16

Kaminsky, Stuart M(elvin) 1934- **CLC 59**
See also CA 73-76; CANR 29, 53

Kane, Francis
See Robbins, Harold

Kane, Paul
See Simon, Paul (Frederick)

Kane, Wilson
See Bloch, Robert (Albert)

Kanin, Garson 1912- **CLC 22**
See also AITN 1; CA 5-8R; CANR 7; DLB 7

Kaniuk, Yoram 1930- **CLC 19**
See also CA 134

Kant, Immanuel 1724-1804 **NCLC 27**
See also DLB 94

Kantor, MacKinlay 1904-1977 **CLC 7**
See also CA 61-64; 73-76; DLB 9, 102

Kaplan, David Michael 1946- **CLC 50**

Kaplan, James 1951- **CLC 59**
See also CA 135

Karageorge, Michael
See Anderson, Poul (William)

Karamzin, Nikolai Mikhailovich 1766-1826 **NCLC 3**
See also DLB 150

Karapanou, Margarita 1946- **CLC 13**
See also CA 101

Karinthy, Frigyes 1887-1938 **TCLC 47**

Karl, Frederick R(obert) 1927- **CLC 34**
See also CA 5-8R; CANR 3, 44

Kastel, Warren
See Silverberg, Robert

Kataev, Evgeny Petrovich 1903-1942

See Petrov, Evgeny
See also CA 120

Kataphusin
See Ruskin, John

Katz, Steve 1935- **CLC 47**
See also CA 25-28R; CAAS 14; CANR 12; DLBY 83

Kauffman, Janet 1945- **CLC 42**
See also CA 117; CANR 43; DLBY 86

Kaufman, Bob (Garnell) 1925-1986 **CLC 49**
See also BW 1; CA 41-44R; 118; CANR 22; DLB 16, 41

Kaufman, George S. 1889-1961 **CLC 38; DAM DRAM**
See also CA 108; 93-96; DLB 7; INT 108

Kaufman, Sue **CLC 3, 8**
See also Barondess, Sue K(aufman)

Kavafis, Konstantinos Petrou 1863-1933
See Cavafy, C(onstantine) P(eter)
See also CA 104

Kavan, Anna 1901-1968 **CLC 5, 13, 82**
See also CA 5-8R; CANR 6, 57; MTCW

Kavanagh, Dan
See Barnes, Julian (Patrick)

Kavanagh, Patrick (Joseph) 1904-1967 **CLC 22**
See also CA 123; 25-28R; DLB 15, 20; MTCW

Kawabata, Yasunari 1899-1972 **CLC 2, 5, 9, 18; DAM MULT; SSC 17**
See also CA 93-96; 33-36R

Kaye, M(ary) M(argaret) 1909- **CLC 28**
See also CA 89-92; CANR 24; MTCW; SATA 62

Kaye, Mollie
See Kaye, M(ary) M(argaret)

Kaye-Smith, Sheila 1887-1956 **TCLC 20**
See also CA 118; DLB 36

Kaymor, Patrice Maguilene
See Senghor, Leopold Sedar

Kazan, Elia 1909- **CLC 6, 16, 63**
See also CA 21-24R; CANR 32

Kazantzakis, Nikos 1883(?)-1957 **TCLC 2, 5, 33**
See also CA 105; 132; MTCW

Kazin, Alfred 1915- **CLC 34, 38**
See also CA 1-4R; CAAS 7; CANR 1, 45; DLB 67

Keane, Mary Nesta (Skrine) 1904-1996
See Keane, Molly
See also CA 108; 114; 151

Keane, Molly **CLC 31**
See also Keane, Mary Nesta (Skrine)
See also INT 114

Keates, Jonathan 19(?)- **CLC 34**

Keaton, Buster 1895-1966 **CLC 20**

Keats, John 1795-1821 **NCLC 8; DA; DAB; DAC; DAM MST, POET; PC 1; WLC**
See also CDBLB 1789-1832; DLB 96, 110

Keene, Donald 1922- **CLC 34**
See also CA 1-4R; CANR 5

Keillor, Garrison CLC 40
See also Keillor, Gary (Edward)
See also AAYA 2; BEST 89 3; DLBY 87; SATA 58

Keillor, Gary (Edward) 1942-
See Keillor, Garrison
See also CA 111; 117; CANR 36; DAM POP;
MTCW

Keith, Michael
See Hubbard, L(afayette) Ron(ald)

Keller, Gottfried 1819-1890 **NCLC 2**
See also DLB 129

Kellerman, Jonathan 1949- **CLC 44; DAM POP**
See also BEST 90 1; CA 106; CANR 29, 51; INT
CANR-29

Kelley, William Melvin 1937- **CLC 22**
See also BW 1; CA 77-80; CANR 27; DLB 33

Kellogg, Marjorie 1922- **CLC 2**
See also CA 81-84

Kellow, Kathleen
See Hibbert, Eleanor Alice Burford

Kelly, M(ilton) T(erry) 1947- **CLC 55**
See also CA 97-100; CAAS 22; CANR 19, 43

Kelman, James 1946- **CLC 58, 86**
See also CA 148

Kemal, Yashar 1923- **CLC 14, 29**
See also CA 89-92; CANR 44

Kemble, Fanny 1809-1893 **NCLC 18**
See also DLB 32

Kemelman, Harry 1908-1996 **CLC 2**
See also AITN 1; CA 9-12R; 155; CANR 6; DLB
28

Kempe, Margery 1373(?)-1440(?) **LC 6**
See also DLB 146

Kempis, Thomas a 1380-1471 **LC 11**

Kendall, Henry 1839-1882 **NCLC 12**

Keneally, Thomas (Michael) 1935- **CLC 5, 8, 10, 14, 19, 27, 43; DAM NOV**
See also CA 85-88; CANR 10, 50; MTCW

Kennedy, Adrienne (Lita) 1931- **CLC 66; BLC; DAM MULT; DC 5**
See also BW 2; CA 103; CAAS 20; CABS 3; CANR
26, 53; DLB 38

Kennedy, John Pendleton 1795-1870 **NCLC 2**
See also DLB 3

Kennedy, Joseph Charles 1929-
See Kennedy, X. J.
See also CA 1-4R; CANR 4, 30, 40; SATA 14, 86

Kennedy, William 1928- **CLC 6, 28, 34, 53; DAM NOV**
See also AAYA 1; CA 85-88; CANR 14, 31; DLB
143; DLBY 85; INT CANR-31; MTCW; SATA
57

Kennedy, X. J. CLC 8, 42
See also Kennedy, Joseph Charles
See also CAAS 9; CLR 27; DLB 5; SAAS 22

Kenny, Maurice (Francis) 1929- **CLC 87; DAM MULT**
See also CA 144; CAAS 22; DLB 175; NNAL

Kent, Kelvin
See Kuttner, Henry

Kenton, Maxwell
See Southern, Terry

Kenyon, Robert O.
See Kuttner, Henry

Kerouac, Jack CLC 1, 2, 3, 5, 14, 29, 61
See also Kerouac, Jean-Louis Lebris de
See also CDALB 1941-1968; DLB 2, 16; DLBD 3;
DLBY 95

Kerouac, Jean-Louis Lebris de 1922-1969
See Kerouac, Jack
See also AITN 1; CA 5-8R; 25-28R; CANR 26, 54;
DA; DAB; DAC; DAM MST, NOV, POET, POP;
MTCW; WLC

Kerr, Jean 1923- **CLC 22**
See also CA 5-8R; CANR 7; INT CANR-7

Kerr, M. E. CLC 12, 35
See also Meaker, Marijane (Agnes)
See also AAYA 2; CLR 29; SAAS 1

Kerr, Robert CLC 55

Kerrigan, (Thomas) Anthony 1918- **CLC 4, 6**
See also CA 49-52; CAAS 11; CANR 4

Kerry, Lois
See Duncan, Lois

Kesey, Ken (Elton) 1935- **CLC 1, 3, 6, 11, 46, 64; DA; DAB; DAC; DAM MST, NOV, POP; WLC**
See also CA 1-4R; CANR 22, 38; CDALB 1968-
1988; DLB 2, 16; MTCW; SATA 66

Kesselring, Joseph (Otto) 1902-1967 **CLC 45; DAM DRAM, MST**
See also CA 150

Kessler, Jascha (Frederick) 1929- **CLC 4**
See also CA 17-20R; CANR 8, 48

Kettelkamp, Larry (Dale) 1933- **CLC 12**
See also CA 29-32R; CANR 16; SAAS 3; SATA 2

Key, Ellen 1849-1926 **TCLC 65**

Keyber, Conny
See Fielding, Henry

Keyes, Daniel 1927- **CLC 80; DA; DAC; DAM MST, NOV**
See also CA 17-20R; CANR 10, 26, 54; SATA 37

Keynes, John Maynard 1883-1946 **TCLC 64**
See also CA 114; DLBD 10

Khanshendel, Chiron
See Rose, Wendy

Khayyam, Omar 1048-1131 **CMLC 11; DAM POET; PC 8**

Kherdian, David 1931- **CLC 6, 9**
See also CA 21-24R; CAAS 2; CANR 39; CLR 24;
JRDA; MAICYA; SATA 16, 74

Khlebnikov, Velimir TCLC 20
See also Khlebnikov, Viktor Vladimirovich

Khlebnikov, Viktor Vladimirovich 1885-1922
See Khlebnikov, Velimir
See also CA 117

Khodasevich, Vladislav (Felitsianovich) 1886-1939
TCLC 15
See also CA 115

Kielland, Alexander Lange 1849-1906 **TCLC 5**
See also CA 104

Kiely, Benedict 1919- **CLC 23, 43**
See also CA 1-4R; CANR 2; DLB 15

Kienzle, William X(avier) 1928- **CLC 25; DAM POP**
See also CA 93-96; CAAS 1; CANR 9, 31; INT
CANR-31; MTCW

Kierkegaard, Soren 1813-1855 **NCLC 34**

Killens, John Oliver 1916-1987 **CLC 10**
See also BW 2; CA 77-80; 123; CAAS 2; CANR
26; DLB 33

Killigrew, Anne 1660-1685 **LC 4**
See also DLB 131

Kim
See Simenon, Georges (Jacques Christian)

Kincaid, Jamaica 1949- **CLC 43, 68; BLC; DAM MULT, NOV**
See also AAYA 13; BW 2; CA 125; CANR 47;
DLB 157

King, Francis (Henry) 1923- **CLC 8, 53; DAM NOV**
See also CA 1-4R; CANR 1, 33; DLB 15, 139;
MTCW

King, Martin Luther, Jr. 1929-1968 **CLC 83; BLC; DA; DAB; DAC; DAM MST, MULT**
See also BW 2; CA 25-28; CANR 27, 44; CAP 2;
MTCW; SATA 14

King, Stephen (Edwin) 1947- **CLC 12, 26, 37, 61; DAM NOV, POP; SSC 17**
See also AAYA 1, 17; BEST 90 1; CA 61-64; CANR
1, 30, 52; DLB 143; DLBY 80; JRDA; MTCW;
SATA 9, 55

King, Steve
See King, Stephen (Edwin)

King, Thomas 1943- **CLC 89; DAC; DAM MULT**
See also CA 144; DLB 175; NNAL

Kingman, Lee CLC 17
See also Natti, (Mary) Lee
See also SAAS 3; SATA 1, 67

Kingsley, Charles 1819-1875 NCLC 35
See also DLB 21, 32, 163; YABC 2

Kingsley, Sidney 1906-1995 CLC 44
See also CA 85-88; 147; DLB 7

Kingsolver, Barbara 1955- CLC 55, 81; DAM POP
See also AAYA 15; CA 129; 134; INT 134

Kingston, Maxine (Ting Ting) Hong 1940- CLC 12,
19, 58; DAM MULT, NOV
See also AAYA 8; CA 69-72; CANR 13, 38; DLB
173; DLBY 80; INT CANR-13; MTCW; SATA
53

Kinnell, Galway 1927- CLC 1, 2, 3, 5, 13, 29
See also CA 9-12R; CANR 10, 34; DLB 5; DLBY
87; INT CANR-34; MTCW

Kinsella, Thomas 1928- CLC 4, 19
See also CA 17-20R; CANR 15; DLB 27; MTCW

Kinsella, W(illiam) P(atrick) 1935- CLC 27, 43;
DAC; DAM NOV, POP
See also AAYA 7; CA 97-100; CAAS 7; CANR 21,
35; INT CANR-21; MTCW

Kipling, (Joseph) Rudyard 1865-1936 TCLC 8, 17;
DA; DAB; DAC; DAM MST, POET; PC 3; SSC
5; WLC
See also CA 105; 120; CANR 33; CDBLB 1890-
1914; CLR 39; DLB 19, 34, 141, 156; MAICYA;
MTCW; YABC 2

Kirkup, James 1918- CLC 1
See also CA 1-4R; CAAS 4; CANR 2; DLB 27;
SATA 12

Kirkwood, James 1930(?)-1989 CLC 9
See also AITN 2; CA 1-4R; 128; CANR 6, 40

Kirshner, Sidney
See Kingsley, Sidney

Kis, Danilo 1935-1989 CLC 57
See also CA 109; 118; 129; MTCW

Kivi, Aleksis 1834-1872 NCLC 30

Kizer, Carolyn (Ashley) 1925- CLC 15, 39, 80;
DAM POET
See also CA 65-68; CAAS 5; CANR 24; DLB 5,
169

Klabund 1890-1928 TCLC 44
See also DLB 66

Klappert, Peter 1942- CLC 57
See also CA 33-36R; DLB 5

Klein, A(braham) M(oses) 1909-1972 CLC 19; DAB;
DAC; DAM MST
See also CA 101; 37-40R; DLB 68

Klein, Norma 1938-1989 CLC 30
See also AAYA 2; CA 41-44R; 128; CANR 15, 37;
CLR 2, 19; INT CANR-15; JRDA; MAICYA;
SAAS 1; SATA 7, 57

Klein, T(heodore) E(ibon) D(onald) 1947- CLC 34
See also CA 119; CANR 44

Kleist, Heinrich von 1777-1811 NCLC 2, 37; DAM
DRAM; SSC 22
See also DLB 90

Klima, Ivan 1931- CLC 56; DAM NOV
See also CA 25-28R; CANR 17, 50

Klimentov, Andrei Platonovich 1899-1951
See Platonov, Andrei
See also CA 108

Klinger, Friedrich Maximilian von 1752-1831 NCLC
1
See also DLB 94

Klopstock, Friedrich Gottlieb 1724-1803 NCLC 11
See also DLB 97

Knapp, Caroline 1959- CLC 99
See also CA 154

Knebel, Fletcher 1911-1993 CLC 14
See also AITN 1; CA 1-4R; 140; CAAS 3; CANR
1, 36; SATA 36; SATA-Obit 75

Knickerbocker, Diedrich
See Irving, Washington

Knight, Etheridge 1931-1991 CLC 40; BLC; DAM
POET; PC 14
See also BW 1; CA 21-24R; 133; CANR 23; DLB
41

Knight, Sarah Kemble 1666-1727 LC 7
See also DLB 24

Knister, Raymond 1899-1932 TCLC 56
See also DLB 68

Knowles, John 1926- CLC 1, 4, 10, 26; DA; DAC;
DAM MST, NOV
See also AAYA 10; CA 17-20R; CANR 40; CDALB
1968-1988; DLB 6; MTCW; SATA 8, 89

Knox, Calvin M.
See Silverberg, Robert

Knox, John c. 1505-1572 LC 37
See also DLB 132

Knye, Cassandra
See Disch, Thomas M(ichael)

Koch, C(hristopher) J(ohn) 1932- CLC 42
See also CA 127

Koch, Christopher
See Koch, C(hristopher) J(ohn)

Koch, Kenneth 1925- CLC 5, 8, 44; DAM POET
See also CA 1-4R; CANR 6, 36, 57; DLB 5; INT
CANR-36; SATA 65

Kochanowski, Jan 1530-1584 LC 10

Kock, Charles Paul de 1794-1871 NCLC 16

Koda Shigeyuki 1867-1947
See Rohan, Koda
See also CA 121

Koestler, Arthur 1905-1983 CLC 1, 3, 6, 8, 15, 33
See also CA 1-4R; 109; CANR 1, 33; CDBLB 1945-
1960; DLBY 83; MTCW

Kogawa, Joy Nozomi 1935- CLC 78; DAC; DAM
MST, MULT
See also CA 101; CANR 19

Kohout, Pavel 1928- CLC 13
See also CA 45-48; CANR 3

Koizumi, Yakumo
See Hearn, (Patricio) Lafcadio (Tessima Carlos)

Kolmar, Gertrud 1894-1943 TCLC 40

Komunyakaa, Yusef 1947- CLC 86, 94
See also CA 147; DLB 120

Konrad, George
See Konrad, Gyoergy

Konrad, Gyoergy 1933- CLC 4, 10, 73
See also CA 85-88

Konwicki, Tadeusz 1926- CLC 8, 28, 54
See also CA 101; CAAS 9; CANR 39; MTCW

Koontz, Dean R(ay) 1945- CLC 78; DAM NOV,
POP
See also AAYA 9; BEST 89 3, 90 2; CA 108; CANR
19, 36, 52; MTCW; SATA 92

Kopit, Arthur (Lee) 1937- CLC 1, 18, 33; DAM
DRAM
See also AITN 1; CA 81-84; CABS 3; DLB 7;
MTCW

Kops, Bernard 1926- CLC 4
See also CA 5-8R; DLB 13

Kornbluth, C(yril) M. 1923-1958 TCLC 8
See also CA 105; DLB 8

Korolenko, V. G.
See Korolenko, Vladimir Galaktionovich

Korolenko, Vladimir
See Korolenko, Vladimir Galaktionovich

Korolenko, Vladimir G.
See Korolenko, Vladimir Galaktionovich

Korolenko, Vladimir Galaktionovich 1853-1921
TCLC 22
See also CA 121

Korzybski, Alfred (Habdank Skarbek) 1879-1950
TCLC 61
See also CA 123

Kosinski, Jerzy (Nikodem) 1933-1991 CLC 1, 2, 3,
6, 10, 15, 53, 70; DAM NOV
See also CA 17-20R; 134; CANR 9, 46; DLB 2;
DLBY 82; MTCW

Kostelanetz, Richard (Cory) 1940- CLC 28
See also CA 13-16R; CAAS 8; CANR 38

Kostrowitzki, Wilhelm Apollinaris de 1880-1918
See Apollinaire, Guillaume
See also CA 104

Kotlowitz, Robert 1924- **CLC 4**
See also CA 33-36R; CANR 36

Kotzebue, August (Friedrich Ferdinand) von 1761-1819 **NCLC 25**
See also DLB 94

Kotzwinkle, William 1938- **CLC 5, 14, 35**
See also CA 45-48; CANR 3, 44; CLR 6; DLB 173; MAICYA; SATA 24, 70

Kowna, Stancy
See Szymborska, Wislawa

Kozol, Jonathan 1936- **CLC 17**
See also CA 61-64; CANR 16, 45

Kozoll, Michael 1940(?)- **CLC 35**

Kramer, Kathryn 19(?)- **CLC 34**

Kramer, Larry 1935- **CLC 42; DAM POP**
See also CA 124; 126

Krasicki, Ignacy 1735-1801 **NCLC 8**

Krasinski, Zygmunt 1812-1859 **NCLC 4**

Kraus, Karl 1874-1936 **TCLC 5**
See also CA 104; DLB 118

Kreve (Mickevicius), Vincas 1882-1954 **TCLC 27**

Kristeva, Julia 1941- **CLC 77**
See also CA 154

Kristofferson, Kris 1936- **CLC 26**
See also CA 104

Krizanc, John 1956- **CLC 57**

Krleza, Miroslav 1893-1981 **CLC 8**
See also CA 97-100; 105; CANR 50; DLB 147

Kroetsch, Robert 1927- **CLC 5, 23, 57; DAC; DAM POET**
See also CA 17-20R; CANR 8, 38; DLB 53; MTCW

Kroetz, Franz
See Kroetz, Franz Xaver

Kroetz, Franz Xaver 1946- **CLC 41**
See also CA 130

Kroker, Arthur 1945- **CLC 77**

Kropotkin, Peter (Aleksieevich) 1842-1921 **TCLC 36**
See also CA 119

Krotkov, Yuri 1917- **CLC 19**
See also CA 102

Krumb
See Crumb, R(obert)

Krumgold, Joseph (Quincy) 1908-1980 **CLC 12**
See also CA 9-12R; 101; CANR 7; MAICYA; SATA 1, 48; SATA-Obit 23

Krumwitz
See Crumb, R(obert)

Krutch, Joseph Wood 1893-1970 **CLC 24**
See also CA 1-4R; 25-28R; CANR 4; DLB 63

Krutzch, Gus
See Eliot, T(homas) S(tearns)

Krylov, Ivan Andreevich 1768(?)-1844 **NCLC 1**
See also DLB 150

Kubin, Alfred (Leopold Isidor) 1877-1959 **TCLC 23**
See also CA 112; 149; DLB 81

Kubrick, Stanley 1928- **CLC 16**
See also CA 81-84; CANR 33; DLB 26

Kumin, Maxine (Winokur) 1925- **CLC 5, 13, 28; DAM POET; PC 15**
See also AITN 2; CA 1-4R; CAAS 8; CANR 1, 21; DLB 5; MTCW; SATA 12

Kundera, Milan 1929- **CLC 4, 9, 19, 32, 68; DAM NOV; SSC 24**
See also AAYA 2; CA 85-88; CANR 19, 52; MTCW

Kunene, Mazisi (Raymond) 1930- **CLC 85**
See also BW 1; CA 125; DLB 117

Kunitz, Stanley (Jasspon) 1905- **CLC 6, 11, 14**
See also CA 41-44R; CANR 26, 57; DLB 48; INT CANR-26; MTCW

Kunze, Reiner 1933- **CLC 10**
See also CA 93-96; DLB 75

Kuprin, Aleksandr Ivanovich 1870-1938 **TCLC 5**
See also CA 104

Kureishi, Hanif 1954(?)- **CLC 64**
See also CA 139

Kurosawa, Akira 1910- **CLC 16; DAM MULT**
See also AAYA 11; CA 101; CANR 46

Kushner, Tony 1957(?)- **CLC 81; DAM DRAM**
See also CA 144

Kuttner, Henry 1915-1958 **TCLC 10**
See also CA 107; DLB 8

Kuzma, Greg 1944- **CLC 7**
See also CA 33-36R

Kuzmin, Mikhail 1872(?)-1936 **TCLC 40**

Kyd, Thomas 1558-1594 **LC 22; DAM DRAM; DC 3**
See also DLB 62

Kyprianos, Iossif
See Samarakis, Antonis

La Bruyere, Jean de 1645-1696 **LC 17**

Lacan, Jacques (Marie Emile) 1901-1981 **CLC 75**
See also CA 121; 104

Laclos, Pierre Ambroise Francois Choderlos de 1741-1803 **NCLC 4**

La Colere, Francois
See Aragon, Louis

Lacolere, Francois
See Aragon, Louis

La Deshabilleuse
See Simenon, Georges (Jacques Christian)

Lady Gregory
See Gregory, Isabella Augusta (Persse)

Lady of Quality, A
See Bagnold, Enid

La Fayette, Marie (Madelaine Pioche de la Vergne Comtes 1634-1693 **LC 2**

Lafayette, Rene
See Hubbard, L(afayette) Ron(ald)

Laforgue, Jules 1860-1887 **NCLC 5, 53; PC 14; SSC 20**

Lagerkvist, Paer (Fabian) 1891-1974 **CLC 7, 10, 13, 54; DAM DRAM, NOV**
See also Lagerkvist, Par
See also CA 85-88; 49-52; MTCW

Lagerkvist, Par SSC 12
See also Lagerkvist, Paer (Fabian)

Lagerloef, Selma (Ottiliana Lovisa) 1858-1940 **TCLC 4, 36**
See also Lagerlof, Selma (Ottiliana Lovisa)
See also CA 108; SATA 15

Lagerlof, Selma (Ottiliana Lovisa)
See Lagerloef, Selma (Ottiliana Lovisa)
See also CLR 7; SATA 15

La Guma, (Justin) Alex(ander) 1925-1985 **CLC 19; DAM NOV**
See also BW 1; CA 49-52; 118; CANR 25; DLB 117; MTCW

Laidlaw, A. K.
See Grieve, C(hristopher) M(urray)

Lainez, Manuel Mujica
See Mujica Lainez, Manuel
See also HW

Laing, R(onald) D(avid) 1927-1989 **CLC 95**
See also CA 107; 129; CANR 34; MTCW

Lamartine, Alphonse (Marie Louis Prat) de 1790-1869 **NCLC 11; DAM POET; PC 16**

Lamb, Charles 1775-1834 **NCLC 10; DA; DAB; DAC; DAM MST; WLC**
See also CDBLB 1789-1832; DLB 93, 107, 163; SATA 17

Lamb, Lady Caroline 1785-1828 **NCLC 38**
See also DLB 116

Lamming, George (William) 1927- **CLC 2, 4, 66; BLC; DAM MULT**
See also BW 2; CA 85-88; CANR 26; DLB 125; MTCW

L'Amour, Louis (Dearborn) 1908-1988 **CLC 25, 55; DAM NOV, POP**
See also AAYA 16; AITN 2; BEST 89 2; CA 1-4R; 125; CANR 3, 25, 40; DLBY 80; MTCW

Lampedusa, Giuseppe (Tomasi) di 1896-1957 **TCLC 13**
See also Tomasi di Lampedusa, Giuseppe
See also DLB 177

Lampman, Archibald 1861-1899 **NCLC 25**
See also DLB 92

Lancaster, Bruce 1896-1963 **CLC 36**
See also CA 9-10; CAP 1; SATA 9

Lanchester, John CLC 99

Landau, Mark Alexandrovich
See Aldanov, Mark (Alexandrovich)

Landau-Aldanov, Mark Alexandrovich
See Aldanov, Mark (Alexandrovich)

Landis, Jerry
See Simon, Paul (Frederick)

Landis, John 1950- **CLC 26**
See also CA 112; 122

Landolfi, Tommaso 1908-1979 **CLC 11, 49**
See also CA 127; 117; DLB 177

Landon, Letitia Elizabeth 1802-1838 **NCLC 15**
See also DLB 96

Landor, Walter Savage 1775-1864 **NCLC 14**
See also DLB 93, 107

Landwirth, Heinz 1927-
See Lind, Jakov
See also CA 9-12R; CANR 7

Lane, Patrick 1939- **CLC 25; DAM POET**
See also CA 97-100; CANR 54; DLB 53; INT 97-100

Lang, Andrew 1844-1912 **TCLC 16**
See also CA 114; 137; DLB 98, 141; MAICYA; SATA 16

Lang, Fritz 1890-1976 **CLC 20**
See also CA 77-80; 69-72; CANR 30

Lange, John
See Crichton, (John) Michael

Langer, Elinor 1939- **CLC 34**
See also CA 121

Langland, William 1330(?)-1400(?) **LC 19; DA; DAB; DAC; DAM MST, POET**
See also DLB 146

Langstaff, Launcelot
See Irving, Washington

Lanier, Sidney 1842-1881 **NCLC 6; DAM POET**
See also DLB 64; DLBD 13; MAICYA; SATA 18

Lanyer, Aemilia 1569-1645 **LC 10, 30**
See also DLB 121

Lao Tzu CMLC 7

Lapine, James (Elliot) 1949- **CLC 39**
See also CA 123; 130; CANR 54; INT 130

Larbaud, Valery (Nicolas) 1881-1957 **TCLC 9**
See also CA 106; 152

Lardner, Ring
See Lardner, Ring(gold) W(ilmer)

Lardner, Ring W., Jr.
See Lardner, Ring(gold) W(ilmer)

Lardner, Ring(gold) W(ilmer) 1885-1933 **TCLC 2, 14**
See also CA 104; 131; CDALB 1917-1929; DLB 11, 25, 86; MTCW

Laredo, Betty
See Codrescu, Andrei

Larkin, Maia
See Wojciechowska, Maia (Teresa)

Larkin, Philip (Arthur) 1922-1985 **CLC 3, 5, 8, 9, 13, 18, 33, 39, 64; DAB; DAM MST, POET**
See also CA 5-8R; 117; CANR 24; CDBLB 1960 to Present; DLB 27; MTCW

Larra (y Sanchez de Castro), Mariano Jose de 1809-1837 **NCLC 17**

Larsen, Eric 1941- **CLC 55**
See also CA 132

Larsen, Nella 1891-1964 **CLC 37; BLC; DAM MULT**
See also BW 1; CA 125; DLB 51

Larson, Charles R(aymond) 1938- **CLC 31**
See also CA 53-56; CANR 4

Larson, Jonathan 1961(?)-1996 **CLC 99**

Las Casas, Bartolome de 1474-1566 **LC 31**

Lasker-Schueler, Else 1869-1945 **TCLC 57**
See also DLB 66, 124

Latham, Jean Lee 1902- **CLC 12**
See also AITN 1; CA 5-8R; CANR 7; MAICYA; SATA 2, 68

Latham, Mavis
See Clark, Mavis Thorpe

Lathen, Emma CLC 2
See also Hennissart, Martha; Latsis, Mary J(ane)

Lathrop, Francis
See Leiber, Fritz (Reuter, Jr.)

Latsis, Mary J(ane)
See Lathen, Emma
See also CA 85-88

Lattimore, Richmond (Alexander) 1906-1984 **CLC 3**
See also CA 1-4R; 112; CANR 1

Laughlin, James 1914- **CLC 49**
See also CA 21-24R; CAAS 22; CANR 9, 47; DLB 48

Laurence, (Jean) Margaret (Wemyss) 1926-1987 **CLC 3, 6, 13, 50, 62; DAC; DAM MST; SSC 7**
See also CA 5-8R; 121; CANR 33; DLB 53; MTCW;

SATA-Obit 50

Laurent, Antoine 1952- **CLC 50**

Lauscher, Hermann
See Hesse, Hermann

Lautreamont, Comte de 1846-1870 **NCLC 12; SSC 14**

Laverty, Donald
See Blish, James (Benjamin)

Lavin, Mary 1912-1996 **CLC 4, 18, 99; SSC 4**
See also CA 9-12R; 151; CANR 33; DLB 15; MTCW

Lavond, Paul Dennis
See Kornbluth, C(yril) M.; Pohl, Frederik

Lawler, Raymond Evenor 1922- **CLC 58**
See also CA 103

Lawrence, D(avid) H(erbert Richards) 1885-1930 **TCLC 2, 9, 16, 33, 48, 61; DA; DAB; DAC; DAM MST, NOV, POET; SSC 4, 19; WLC**
See also CA 104; 121; CDBLB 1914-1945; DLB 10, 19, 36, 98, 162; MTCW

Lawrence, T(homas) E(dward) 1888-1935 **TCLC 18**
See also Dale, Colin
See also CA 115

Lawrence of Arabia
See Lawrence, T(homas) E(dward)

Lawson, Henry (Archibald Hertzberg) 1867-1922 **TCLC 27; SSC 18**
See also CA 120

Lawton, Dennis
See Faust, Frederick (Schiller)

Laxness, Halldor CLC 25
See also Gudjonsson, Halldor Kiljan

Layamon fl. c. 1200- **CMLC 10**
See also DLB 146

Laye, Camara 1928-1980 **CLC 4, 38; BLC; DAM MULT**
See also BW 1; CA 85-88; 97-100; CANR 25; MTCW

Layton, Irving (Peter) 1912- **CLC 2, 15; DAC; DAM MST, POET**
See also CA 1-4R; CANR 2, 33, 43; DLB 88; MTCW

Lazarus, Emma 1849-1887 **NCLC 8**

Lazarus, Felix
See Cable, George Washington

Lazarus, Henry
See Slavitt, David R(ytman)

Lea, Joan
See Neufeld, John (Arthur)

Leacock, Stephen (Butler) 1869-1944 **TCLC 2; DAC; DAM MST**
See also CA 104; 141; DLB 92

Lear, Edward 1812-1888 **NCLC 3**
See also CLR 1; DLB 32, 163, 166; MAICYA;
SATA 18

Lear, Norman (Milton) 1922- **CLC 12**
See also CA 73-76

Leavis, F(rank) R(aymond) 1895-1978 **CLC 24**
See also CA 21-24R; 77-80; CANR 44; MTCW

Leavitt, David 1961- **CLC 34; DAM POP**
See also CA 116; 122; CANR 50; DLB 130; INT
122

Leblanc, Maurice (Marie Emile) 1864-1941 **TCLC
49**
See also CA 110

Lebowitz, Fran(ces Ann) 1951(?)- **CLC 11, 36**
See also CA 81-84; CANR 14; INT CANR-14;
MTCW

Lebrecht, Peter
See Tieck, (Johann) Ludwig

le Carre, John CLC 3, 5, 9, 15, 28
See also Cornwell, David (John Moore)
See also BEST 89 4; CDBLB 1960 to Present; DLB
87

Le Clezio, J(ean) M(arie) G(ustave) 1940- **CLC 31**
See also CA 116; 128; DLB 83

Leconte de Lisle, Charles-Marie-Rene 1818-1894
NCLC 29

Le Coq, Monsieur
See Simenon, Georges (Jacques Christian)

Leduc, Violette 1907-1972 **CLC 22**
See also CA 13-14; 33-36R; CAP 1

Ledwidge, Francis 1887(?)-1917 **TCLC 23**
See also CA 123; DLB 20

Lee, Andrea 1953- **CLC 36; BLC; DAM MULT**
See also BW 1; CA 125

Lee, Andrew
See Auchincloss, Louis (Stanton)

Lee, Chang-rae 1965- **CLC 91**
See also CA 148

Lee, Don L. CLC 2
See also Madhubuti, Haki R.

Lee, George W(ashington) 1894-1976 **CLC 52; BLC;
DAM MULT**
See also BW 1; CA 125; DLB 51

Lee, (Nelle) Harper 1926- **CLC 12, 60; DA; DAB;
DAC; DAM MST, NOV; WLC**
See also AAYA 13; CA 13-16R; CANR 51; CDALB
1941-1968; DLB 6; MTCW; SATA 11

Lee, Helen Elaine 1959(?)- **CLC 86**
See also CA 148

Lee, Julian
See Latham, Jean Lee

Lee, Larry

See Lee, Lawrence

Lee, Laurie 1914- **CLC 90; DAB; DAM POP**
See also CA 77-80; CANR 33; DLB 27; MTCW

Lee, Lawrence 1941-1990 **CLC 34**
See also CA 131; CANR 43

Lee, Manfred B(ennington) 1905-1971 **CLC 11**
See also Queen, Ellery
See also CA 1-4R; 29-32R; CANR 2; DLB 137

Lee, Stan 1922- **CLC 17**
See also AAYA 5; CA 108; 111; INT 111

Lee, Tanith 1947- **CLC 46**
See also AAYA 15; CA 37-40R; CANR 53; SATA
8, 88

Lee, Vernon TCLC 5
See also Paget, Violet
See also DLB 57, 153, 156, 174

Lee, William
See Burroughs, William S(eward)

Lee, Willy
See Burroughs, William S(eward)

Lee-Hamilton, Eugene (Jacob) 1845-1907 **TCLC 22**
See also CA 117

Leet, Judith 1935- **CLC 11**

Le Fanu, Joseph Sheridan 1814-1873 **NCLC 9, 58;
DAM POP; SSC 14**
See also DLB 21, 70, 159

Leffland, Ella 1931- **CLC 19**
See also CA 29-32R; CANR 35; DLBY 84; INT
CANR-35; SATA 65

Leger, Alexis
See Leger, (Marie-Rene Auguste) Alexis Saint-
Leger

Leger, (Marie-Rene Auguste) Alexis Saint-Leger
1887-1975 **CLC 11; DAM POET**
See also Perse, St.-John
See also CA 13-16R; 61-64; CANR 43; MTCW

Leger, Saintleger
See Leger, (Marie-Rene Auguste) Alexis Saint-
Leger

Le Guin, Ursula K(roeber) 1929- **CLC 8, 13, 22, 45,
71; DAB; DAC; DAM MST, POP; SSC 12**
See also AAYA 9; AITN 1; CA 21-24R; CANR 9,
32, 52; CDALB 1968-1988; CLR 3, 28; DLB 8,
52; INT CANR-32; JRDA; MAICYA; MTCW;
SATA 4, 52

Lehmann, Rosamond (Nina) 1901-1990 **CLC 5**
See also CA 77-80; 131; CANR 8; DLB 15

Leiber, Fritz (Reuter, Jr.) 1910-1992 **CLC 25**
See also CA 45-48; 139; CANR 2, 40; DLB 8;
MTCW; SATA 45; SATA-Obit 73

Leibniz, Gottfried Wilhelm von 1646-1716 **LC 35**
See also DLB 168

Leimbach, Martha 1963-

See Leimbach, Marti
See also CA 130

Leimbach, Marti CLC 65
See also Leimbach, Martha

Leino, Eino TCLC 24
See also Loennbohm, Armas Eino Leopold

Leiris, Michel (Julien) 1901-1990 **CLC 61**
See also CA 119; 128; 132

Leithauser, Brad 1953- **CLC 27**
See also CA 107; CANR 27; DLB 120

Lelchuk, Alan 1938- **CLC 5**
See also CA 45-48; CAAS 20; CANR 1

Lem, Stanislaw 1921- **CLC 8, 15, 40**
See also CA 105; CAAS 1; CANR 32; MTCW

Lemann, Nancy 1956- **CLC 39**
See also CA 118; 136

Lemonnier, (Antoine Louis) Camille 1844-1913
TCLC 22
See also CA 121

Lenau, Nikolaus 1802-1850 **NCLC 16**

L'Engle, Madeleine (Camp Franklin) 1918- **CLC
12; DAM POP**
See also AAYA 1; AITN 2; CA 1-4R; CANR 3, 21,
39; CLR 1, 14; DLB 52; JRDA; MAICYA;
MTCW; SAAS 15; SATA 1, 27, 75

Lengyel, Jozsef 1896-1975 **CLC 7**
See also CA 85-88; 57-60

Lenin 1870-1924
See Lenin, V. I.
See also CA 121

Lenin, V. I. TCLC 67
See also Lenin

Lennon, John (Ono) 1940-1980 **CLC 12, 35**
See also CA 102

Lennox, Charlotte Ramsay 1729(?)-1804 **NCLC 23**
See also DLB 39

Lentricchia, Frank (Jr.) 1940- **CLC 34**
See also CA 25-28R; CANR 19

Lenz, Siegfried 1926- **CLC 27**
See also CA 89-92; DLB 75

Leonard, Elmore (John, Jr.) 1925- **CLC 28, 34, 71;
DAM POP**
See also AITN 1; BEST 89 1, 90 4; CA 81-84;
CANR 12, 28, 53; DLB 173; INT CANR-28;
MTCW

Leonard, Hugh CLC 19
See also Byrne, John Keyes
See also DLB 13

Leonov, Leonid (Maximovich) 1899-1994 **CLC 92;
DAM NOV**
See also CA 129; MTCW

Leopardi, (Conte) Giacomo 1798-1837 **NCLC 22**

Lucas, George 1944- **CLC 16**
See also AAYA 1; CA 77-80; CANR 30; SATA 56

Lucas, Hans
See Godard, Jean-Luc

Lucas, Victoria
See Plath, Sylvia

Ludlam, Charles 1943-1987 **CLC 46, 50**
See also CA 85-88; 122

Ludlum, Robert 1927- **CLC 22, 43; DAM NOV, POP**
See also AAYA 10; BEST 89 1, 90 3; CA 33-36R; CANR 25, 41; DLBY 82; MTCW

Ludwig, Ken CLC 60

Ludwig, Otto 1813-1865 **NCLC 4**
See also DLB 129

Lugones, Leopoldo 1874-1938 **TCLC 15**
See also CA 116; 131; HW

Lu Hsun 1881-1936 **TCLC 3; SSC 20**
See also Shu-Jen, Chou

Lukacs, George CLC 24
See also Lukacs, Gyorgy (Szegeny von)

Lukacs, Gyorgy (Szegeny von) 1885-1971
See Lukacs, George
See also CA 101; 29-32R

Luke, Peter (Ambrose Cyprian) 1919-1995 **CLC 38**
See also CA 81-84; 147; DLB 13

Lunar, Dennis
See Mungo, Raymond

Lurie, Alison 1926- **CLC 4, 5, 18, 39**
See also CA 1-4R; CANR 2, 17, 50; DLB 2; MTCW; SATA 46

Lustig, Arnost 1926- **CLC 56**
See also AAYA 3; CA 69-72; CANR 47; SATA 56

Luther, Martin 1483-1546 **LC 9, 37**

Luxemburg, Rosa 1870(?)-1919 **TCLC 63**
See also CA 118

Luzi, Mario 1914- **CLC 13**
See also CA 61-64; CANR 9; DLB 128

L'Ymagier
See Gourmont, Remy (-Marie-Charles) de

Lynch, B. Suarez
See Bioy Casares, Adolfo; Borges, Jorge Luis

Lynch, David (K.) 1946- **CLC 66**
See also CA 124; 129

Lynch, James
See Andreyev, Leonid (Nikolaevich)

Lynch Davis, B.
See Bioy Casares, Adolfo; Borges, Jorge Luis

Lyndsay, Sir David 1490-1555 **LC 20**

Lynn, Kenneth S(chuyler) 1923- **CLC 50**
See also CA 1-4R; CANR 3, 27

Lynx
See West, Rebecca

Lyons, Marcus
See Blish, James (Benjamin)

Lyre, Pinchbeck
See Sassoon, Siegfried (Lorraine)

Lytle, Andrew (Nelson) 1902-1995 **CLC 22**
See also CA 9-12R; 150; DLB 6; DLBY 95

Lyttelton, George 1709-1773 **LC 10**

Maas, Peter 1929- **CLC 29**
See also CA 93-96; INT 93-96

Macaulay, Rose 1881-1958 **TCLC 7, 44**
See also CA 104; DLB 36

Macaulay, Thomas Babington 1800-1859 **NCLC 42**
See also CDBLB 1832-1890; DLB 32, 55

MacBeth, George (Mann) 1932-1992 **CLC 2, 5, 9**
See also CA 25-28R; 136; DLB 40; MTCW; SATA 4; SATA-Obit 70

MacCaig, Norman (Alexander) 1910- **CLC 36; DAB; DAM POET**
See also CA 9-12R; CANR 3, 34; DLB 27

MacCarthy, (Sir Charles Otto) Desmond 1877-1952 **TCLC 36**

MacDiarmid, Hugh CLC 2, 4, 11, 19, 63; PC 9
See also Grieve, C(hristopher) M(urray)
See also CDBLB 1945-1960; DLB 20

MacDonald, Anson
See Heinlein, Robert A(nson)

Macdonald, Cynthia 1928- **CLC 13, 19**
See also CA 49-52; CANR 4, 44; DLB 105

MacDonald, George 1824-1905 **TCLC 9**
See also CA 106; 137; DLB 18, 163; MAICYA; SATA 33

Macdonald, John
See Millar, Kenneth

MacDonald, John D(ann) 1916-1986 **CLC 3, 27, 44; DAM NOV, POP**
See also CA 1-4R; 121; CANR 1, 19; DLB 8; DLBY 86; MTCW

Macdonald, John Ross
See Millar, Kenneth

Macdonald, Ross CLC 1, 2, 3, 14, 34, 41
See also Millar, Kenneth
See also DLBD 6

MacDougal, John
See Blish, James (Benjamin)

MacEwen, Gwendolyn (Margaret) 1941-1987 **CLC 13, 55**
See also CA 9-12R; 124; CANR 7, 22; DLB 53; SATA 50; SATA-Obit 55

Macha, Karel Hynek 1810-1846 **NCLC 46**

Machado (y Ruiz), Antonio 1875-1939 **TCLC 3**
See also CA 104; DLB 108

Machado de Assis, Joaquim Maria 1839-1908 **TCLC 10; BLC; SSC 24**
See also CA 107; 153

Machen, Arthur TCLC 4; SSC 20
See also Jones, Arthur Llewellyn
See also DLB 36, 156

Machiavelli, Niccolo 1469-1527 **LC 8, 36; DA; DAB; DAC; DAM MST**

MacInnes, Colin 1914-1976 **CLC 4, 23**
See also CA 69-72; 65-68; CANR 21; DLB 14; MTCW

MacInnes, Helen (Clark) 1907-1985 **CLC 27, 39; DAM POP**
See also CA 1-4R; 117; CANR 1, 28; DLB 87; MTCW; SATA 22; SATA-Obit 44

Mackay, Mary 1855-1924
See Corelli, Marie
See also CA 118

Mackenzie, Compton (Edward Montague) 1883-1972 **CLC 18**
See also CA 21-22; 37-40R; CAP 2; DLB 34, 100

Mackenzie, Henry 1745-1831 **NCLC 41**
See also DLB 39

Mackintosh, Elizabeth 1896(?)-1952
See Tey, Josephine
See also CA 110

MacLaren, James
See Grieve, C(hristopher) M(urray)

Mac Laverty, Bernard 1942- **CLC 31**
See also CA 116; 118; CANR 43; INT 118

MacLean, Alistair (Stuart) 1922-1987 **CLC 3, 13, 50, 63; DAM POP**
See also CA 57-60; 121; CANR 28; MTCW; SATA 23; SATA-Obit 50

Maclean, Norman (Fitzroy) 1902-1990 **CLC 78; DAM POP; SSC 13**
See also CA 102; 132; CANR 49

MacLeish, Archibald 1892-1982 **CLC 3, 8, 14, 68; DAM POET**
See also CA 9-12R; 106; CANR 33; DLB 4, 7, 45; DLBY 82; MTCW

MacLennan, (John) Hugh 1907-1990 **CLC 2, 14, 92; DAC; DAM MST**
See also CA 5-8R; 142; CANR 33; DLB 68; MTCW

MacLeod, Alistair 1936- **CLC 56; DAC; DAM MST**
See also CA 123; DLB 60

MacNeice, (Frederick) Louis 1907-1963 **CLC 1, 4, 10, 53; DAB; DAM POET**
See also CA 85-88; DLB 10, 20; MTCW

MacNeill, Dand
See Fraser, George MacDonald

Macpherson, James 1736-1796 **LC 29**
See also DLB 109

Macpherson, (Jean) Jay 1931- **CLC 14**
See also CA 5-8R; DLB 53

MacShane, Frank 1927- **CLC 39**
See also CA 9-12R; CANR 3, 33; DLB 111

Macumber, Mari
See Sandoz, Mari(e Susette)

Madach, Imre 1823-1864 **NCLC 19**

Madden, (Jerry) David 1933- **CLC 5, 15**
See also CA 1-4R; CAAS 3; CANR 4, 45; DLB 6;
MTCW

Maddern, Al(an)
See Ellison, Harlan (Jay)

Madhubuti, Haki R. 1942- **CLC 6, 73; BLC; DAM
MULT, POET; PC 5**
See also Lee, Don L.
See also BW 2; CA 73-76; CANR 24, 51; DLB 5,
41; DLBD 8

Maepenn, Hugh
See Kuttner, Henry

Maepenn, K. H.
See Kuttner, Henry

Maeterlinck, Maurice 1862-1949 **TCLC 3; DAM
DRAM**
See also CA 104; 136; SATA 66

Maginn, William 1794-1842 **NCLC 8**
See also DLB 110, 159

Mahapatra, Jayanta 1928- **CLC 33; DAM MULT**
See also CA 73-76; CAAS 9; CANR 15, 33

Mahfouz, Naguib (Abdel Aziz Al-Sabilgi) 1911(?)-
See Mahfuz, Najib
See also BEST 89 2; CA 128; CANR 55; DAM
NOV; MTCW

Mahfuz, Najib **CLC 52, 55**
See also Mahfouz, Naguib (Abdel Aziz Al-Sabilgi)
See also DLBY 88

Mahon, Derek 1941- **CLC 27**
See also CA 113; 128; DLB 40

Mailer, Norman 1923- **CLC 1, 2, 3, 4, 5, 8, 11, 14,
28, 39, 74; DA; DAB; DAC; DAM MST, NOV,
POP**
See also AITN 2; CA 9-12R; CABS 1; CANR 28;
CDALB 1968-1988; DLB 2, 16, 28; DLBD 3;
DLBY 80, 83; MTCW

Maillet, Antonine 1929- **CLC 54; DAC**
See also CA 115; 120; CANR 46; DLB 60; INT 120

Mais, Roger 1905-1955 **TCLC 8**
See also BW 1; CA 105; 124; DLB 125; MTCW

Maistre, Joseph de 1753-1821 **NCLC 37**

Maitland, Frederic 1850-1906 **TCLC 65**

Maitland, Sara (Louise) 1950- **CLC 49**

See also CA 69-72; CANR 13

Major, Clarence 1936- **CLC 3, 19, 48; BLC; DAM
MULT**
See also BW 2; CA 21-24R; CAAS 6; CANR 13,
25, 53; DLB 33

Major, Kevin (Gerald) 1949- **CLC 26; DAC**
See also AAYA 16; CA 97-100; CANR 21, 38; CLR
11; DLB 60; INT CANR-21; JRDA; MAICYA;
SATA 32, 82

Maki, James
See Ozu, Yasujiro

Malabaila, Damiano
See Levi, Primo

Malamud, Bernard 1914-1986 **CLC 1, 2, 3, 5, 8, 9,
11, 18, 27, 44, 78, 85; DA; DAB; DAC; DAM
MST, NOV, POP; SSC 15; WLC**
See also AAYA 16; CA 5-8R; 118; CABS 1; CANR
28; CDALB 1941-1968; DLB 2, 28, 152; DLBY
80, 86; MTCW

Malaparte, Curzio 1898-1957 **TCLC 52**

Malcolm, Dan
See Silverberg, Robert

Malcolm X **CLC 82; BLC**
See also Little, Malcolm

Malherbe, Francois de 1555-1628 **LC 5**

Mallarme, Stephane 1842-1898 **NCLC 4, 41; DAM
POET; PC 4**

Mallet-Joris, Francoise 1930- **CLC 11**
See also CA 65-68; CANR 17; DLB 83

Malley, Ern
See McAuley, James Phillip

Mallowan, Agatha Christie
See Christie, Agatha (Mary Clarissa)

Maloff, Saul 1922- **CLC 5**
See also CA 33-36R

Malone, Louis
See MacNeice, (Frederick) Louis

Malone, Michael (Christopher) 1942- **CLC 43**
See also CA 77-80; CANR 14, 32, 57

Malory, (Sir) Thomas 1410(?)-1471(?) **LC 11; DA;
DAB; DAC; DAM MST**
See also CDBLB Before 1660; DLB 146; SATA 59;
SATA-Brief 33

Malouf, (George Joseph) David 1934- **CLC 28, 86**
See also CA 124; CANR 50

Malraux, (Georges-)Andre 1901-1976 **CLC 1, 4, 9,
13, 15, 57; DAM NOV**
See also CA 21-22; 69-72; CANR 34; CAP 2; DLB
72; MTCW

Malzberg, Barry N(athaniel) 1939- **CLC 7**
See also CA 61-64; CAAS 4; CANR 16; DLB 8

Mamet, David (Alan) 1947- **CLC 9, 15, 34, 46, 91;**

DAM DRAM; DC 4
See also AAYA 3; CA 81-84; CABS 3; CANR 15,
41; DLB 7; MTCW

Mamoulian, Rouben (Zachary) 1897-1987 **CLC 16**
See also CA 25-28R; 124

Mandelstam, Osip (Emilievich) 1891(?)-1938(?)
TCLC 2, 6; PC 14
See also CA 104; 150

Mander, (Mary) Jane 1877-1949 **TCLC 31**

Mandeville, John fl. 1350- **CMLC 19**
See also DLB 146

Mandiargues, Andre Pieyre de **CLC 41**
See also Pieyre de Mandiargues, Andre
See also DLB 83

Mandrake, Ethel Belle
See Thurman, Wallace (Henry)

Mangan, James Clarence 1803-1849 **NCLC 27**

Maniere, J.-E.
See Giraudoux, (Hippolyte) Jean

Manley, (Mary) Delariviere 1672(?)-1724 **LC 1**
See also DLB 39, 80

Mann, Abel
See Creasey, John

Mann, (Luiz) Heinrich 1871-1950 **TCLC 9**
See also CA 106; DLB 66

Mann, (Paul) Thomas 1875-1955 **TCLC 2, 8, 14, 21,
35, 44, 60; DA; DAB; DAC; DAM MST, NOV;
SSC 5; WLC**
See also CA 104; 128; DLB 66; MTCW

Mannheim, Karl 1893-1947 **TCLC 65**

Manning, David
See Faust, Frederick (Schiller)

Manning, Frederic 1887(?)-1935 **TCLC 25**
See also CA 124

Manning, Olivia 1915-1980 **CLC 5, 19**
See also CA 5-8R; 101; CANR 29; MTCW

Mano, D. Keith 1942- **CLC 2, 10**
See also CA 25-28R; CAAS 6; CANR 26, 57; DLB
6

Mansfield, Katherine **TCLC 2, 8, 39; DAB; SSC 9,
23; WLC**
See also Beauchamp, Kathleen Mansfield
See also DLB 162

Manso, Peter 1940- **CLC 39**
See also CA 29-32R; CANR 44

Mantecon, Juan Jimenez
See Jimenez (Mantecon), Juan Ramon

Manton, Peter
See Creasey, John

Man Without a Spleen, A
See Chekhov, Anton (Pavlovich)

Manzoni, Alessandro 1785-1873 **NCLC 29**

Mapu, Abraham (ben Jekutiel) 1808-1867 **NCLC 18**

Mara, Sally
See Queneau, Raymond

Marat, Jean Paul 1743-1793 **LC 10**

Marcel, Gabriel Honore 1889-1973 **CLC 15**
See also CA 102; 45-48; MTCW

Marchbanks, Samuel
See Davies, (William) Robertson

Marchi, Giacomo
See Bassani, Giorgio

Margulies, Donald CLC 76

Marie de France c. 12th cent. - **CMLC 8**

Marie de l'Incarnation 1599-1672 **LC 10**

Marier, Captain Victor
See Griffith, D(avid Lewelyn) W(ark)

Mariner, Scott
See Pohl, Frederik

Marinetti, Filippo Tommaso 1876-1944 **TCLC 10**
See also CA 107; DLB 114

Marivaux, Pierre Carlet de Chamblain de 1688-1763 **LC 4**

Markandaya, Kamala CLC 8, 38
See also Taylor, Kamala (Purnaiya)

Markfield, Wallace 1926- **CLC 8**
See also CA 69-72; CAAS 3; DLB 2, 28

Markham, Edwin 1852-1940 **TCLC 47**
See also DLB 54

Markham, Robert
See Amis, Kingsley (William)

Marks, J
See Highwater, Jamake (Mamake)

Marks-Highwater, J
See Highwater, Jamake (Mamake)

Markson, David M(errill) 1927- **CLC 67**
See also CA 49-52; CANR 1

Marley, Bob CLC 17
See also Marley, Robert Nesta

Marley, Robert Nesta 1945-1981
See Marley, Bob
See also CA 107; 103

Marlowe, Christopher 1564-1593 **LC 22; DA; DAB; DAC; DAM DRAM, MST; DC 1; WLC**
See also CDBLB Before 1660; DLB 62

Marlowe, Stephen 1928-
See Queen, Ellery
See also CA 13-16R; CANR 6, 55

Marmontel, Jean-Francois 1723-1799 **LC 2**

Marquand, John P(hillips) 1893-1960 **CLC 2, 10**
See also CA 85-88; DLB 9, 102

Marques, Rene 1919-1979 **CLC 96; DAM MULT; HLC**
See also CA 97-100; 85-88; DLB 113; HW

Marquez, Gabriel (Jose) Garcia
See Garcia Marquez, Gabriel (Jose)

Marquis, Don(ald Robert Perry) 1878-1937 **TCLC 7**
See also CA 104; DLB 11, 25

Marric, J. J.
See Creasey, John

Marrow, Bernard
See Moore, Brian

Marryat, Frederick 1792-1848 **NCLC 3**
See also DLB 21, 163

Marsden, James
See Creasey, John

Marsh, (Edith) Ngaio 1899-1982 **CLC 7, 53; DAM POP**
See also CA 9-12R; CANR 6; DLB 77; MTCW

Marshall, Garry 1934- **CLC 17**
See also AAYA 3; CA 111; SATA 60

Marshall, Paule 1929- **CLC 27, 72; BLC; DAM MULT; SSC 3**
See also BW 2; CA 77-80; CANR 25; DLB 157; MTCW

Marsten, Richard
See Hunter, Evan

Marston, John 1576-1634 **LC 33; DAM DRAM**
See also DLB 58, 172

Martha, Henry
See Harris, Mark

Martial c. 40-c. 104 **PC 10**

Martin, Ken
See Hubbard, L(afayette) Ron(ald)

Martin, Richard
See Creasey, John

Martin, Steve 1945- **CLC 30**
See also CA 97-100; CANR 30; MTCW

Martin, Valerie 1948- **CLC 89**
See also BEST 90 2; CA 85-88; CANR 49

Martin, Violet Florence 1862-1915 **TCLC 51**

Martin, Webber
See Silverberg, Robert

Martindale, Patrick Victor
See White, Patrick (Victor Martindale)

Martin du Gard, Roger 1881-1958 **TCLC 24**
See also CA 118; DLB 65

Martineau, Harriet 1802-1876 **NCLC 26**
See also DLB 21, 55, 159, 163, 166; YABC 2

Martines, Julia
See O'Faolain, Julia

Martinez, Jacinto Benavente y
See Benavente (y Martinez), Jacinto

Martinez Ruiz, Jose 1873-1967
See Azorin; Ruiz, Jose Martinez
See also CA 93-96; HW

Martinez Sierra, Gregorio 1881-1947 **TCLC 6**
See also CA 115

Martinez Sierra, Maria (de la O'LeJarraga) 1874-1974 **TCLC 6**
See also CA 115

Martinsen, Martin
See Follett, Ken(neth Martin)

Martinson, Harry (Edmund) 1904-1978 **CLC 14**
See also CA 77-80; CANR 34

Marut, Ret
See Traven, B.

Marut, Robert
See Traven, B.

Marvell, Andrew 1621-1678 **LC 4; DA; DAB; DAC; DAM MST, POET; PC 10; WLC**
See also CDBLB 1660-1789; DLB 131

Marx, Karl (Heinrich) 1818-1883 **NCLC 17**
See also DLB 129

Masaoka Shiki TCLC 18
See also Masaoka Tsunenori

Masaoka Tsunenori 1867-1902
See Masaoka Shiki
See also CA 117

Masefield, John (Edward) 1878-1967 **CLC 11, 47; DAM POET**
See also CA 19-20; 25-28R; CANR 33; CAP 2; CDBLB 1890-1914; DLB 10, 19, 153, 160; MTCW; SATA 19

Maso, Carole 19(?)- **CLC 44**

Mason, Bobbie Ann 1940- **CLC 28, 43, 82; SSC 4**
See also AAYA 5; CA 53-56; CANR 11, 31; DLB 173; DLBY 87; INT CANR-31; MTCW

Mason, Ernst
See Pohl, Frederik

Mason, Lee W.
See Malzberg, Barry N(athaniel)

Mason, Nick 1945- **CLC 35**

Mason, Tally
See Derleth, August (William)

Mass, William
See Gibson, William

Masters, Edgar Lee 1868-1950 **TCLC 2, 25; DA;**

DAC; DAM MST, POET; PC 1
See also CA 104; 133; CDALB 1865-1917; DLB
54; MTCW

Masters, Hilary 1928- **CLC 48**
See also CA 25-28R; CANR 13, 47

Mastrosimone, William 19(?)- **CLC 36**

Mathe, Albert
See Camus, Albert

Matheson, Richard Burton 1926- **CLC 37**
See also CA 97-100; DLB 8, 44; INT 97-100

Mathews, Harry 1930- **CLC 6, 52**
See also CA 21-24R; CAAS 6; CANR 18, 40

Mathews, John Joseph 1894-1979 **CLC 84; DAM
MULT**
See also CA 19-20; 142; CANR 45; CAP 2; DLB
175; NNAL

Mathias, Roland (Glyn) 1915- **CLC 45**
See also CA 97-100; CANR 19, 41; DLB 27

Matsuo Basho 1644-1694 **PC 3**
See also DAM POET

Mattheson, Rodney
See Creasey, John

Matthews, Greg 1949- **CLC 45**
See also CA 135

Matthews, William 1942- **CLC 40**
See also CA 29-32R; CAAS 18; CANR 12, 57; DLB
5

Matthias, John (Edward) 1941- **CLC 9**
See also CA 33-36R; CANR 56

Matthiessen, Peter 1927- **CLC 5, 7, 11, 32, 64;
DAM NOV**
See also AAYA 6; BEST 90 4; CA 9-12R; CANR
21, 50; DLB 6, 173; MTCW; SATA 27

Maturin, Charles Robert 1780(?)-1824 **NCLC 6**

Matute (Ausejo), Ana Maria 1925- **CLC 11**
See also CA 89-92; MTCW

Maugham, W. S.
See Maugham, W(illiam) Somerset

Maugham, W(illiam) Somerset 1874-1965 **CLC 1,
11, 15, 67, 93; DA; DAB; DAC; DAM DRAM,
MST, NOV; SSC 8; WLC**
See also CA 5-8R; 25-28R; CANR 40; CDBLB 1914-
1945; DLB 10, 36, 77, 100, 162; MTCW; SATA
54

Maugham, William Somerset
See Maugham, W(illiam) Somerset

Maupassant, (Henri Rene Albert) Guy de 1850-1893
**NCLC 1, 42; DA; DAB; DAC; DAM MST; SSC
1; WLC**
See also DLB 123

Maupin, Armistead 1944- **CLC 95; DAM POP**
See also CA 125; 130; INT 130

Maurhut, Richard
See Traven, B.

Mauriac, Claude 1914-1996 **CLC 9**
See also CA 89-92; 152; DLB 83

Mauriac, Francois (Charles) 1885-1970 **CLC 4, 9,
56; SSC 24**
See also CA 25-28; CAP 2; DLB 65; MTCW

Mavor, Osborne Henry 1888-1951
See Bridie, James
See also CA 104

Maxwell, William (Keepers, Jr.) 1908- **CLC 19**
See also CA 93-96; CANR 54; DLBY 80; INT 93-
96

May, Elaine 1932- **CLC 16**
See also CA 124; 142; DLB 44

Mayakovski, Vladimir (Vladimirovich) 1893-1930
TCLC 4, 18
See also CA 104

Mayhew, Henry 1812-1887 **NCLC 31**
See also DLB 18, 55

Mayle, Peter 1939(?)- **CLC 89**
See also CA 139

Maynard, Joyce 1953- **CLC 23**
See also CA 111; 129

Mayne, William (James Carter) 1928- **CLC 12**
See also AAYA 20; CA 9-12R; CANR 37; CLR 25;
JRDA; MAICYA; SAAS 11; SATA 6, 68

Mayo, Jim
See L'Amour, Louis (Dearborn)

Maysles, Albert 1926- **CLC 16**
See also CA 29-32R

Maysles, David 1932- **CLC 16**

Mazer, Norma Fox 1931- **CLC 26**
See also AAYA 5; CA 69-72; CANR 12, 32; CLR
23; JRDA; MAICYA; SAAS 1; SATA 24, 67

Mazzini, Guiseppe 1805-1872 **NCLC 34**

McAuley, James Phillip 1917-1976 **CLC 45**
See also CA 97-100

McBain, Ed
See Hunter, Evan

McBrien, William Augustine 1930- **CLC 44**
See also CA 107

McCaffrey, Anne (Inez) 1926- **CLC 17; DAM NOV,
POP**
See also AAYA 6; AITN 2; BEST 89 2; CA 25-
28R; CANR 15, 35, 55; DLB 8; JRDA; MAICYA;
MTCW; SAAS 11; SATA 8, 70

McCall, Nathan 1955(?)- **CLC 86**
See also CA 146

McCann, Arthur
See Campbell, John W(ood, Jr.)

McCann, Edson
See Pohl, Frederik

McCarthy, Charles, Jr. 1933-
See McCarthy, Cormac
See also CANR 42; DAM POP

McCarthy, Cormac 1933- **CLC 4, 57, 59**
See also McCarthy, Charles, Jr.
See also DLB 6, 143

McCarthy, Mary (Therese) 1912-1989 **CLC 1, 3, 5,
14, 24, 39, 59; SSC 24**
See also CA 5-8R; 129; CANR 16, 50; DLB 2; DLBY
81; INT CANR-16; MTCW

McCartney, (James) Paul 1942- **CLC 12, 35**
See also CA 146

McCauley, Stephen (D.) 1955- **CLC 50**
See also CA 141

McClure, Michael (Thomas) 1932- **CLC 6, 10**
See also CA 21-24R; CANR 17, 46; DLB 16

McCorkle, Jill (Collins) 1958- **CLC 51**
See also CA 121; DLBY 87

McCourt, James 1941- **CLC 5**
See also CA 57-60

McCoy, Horace (Stanley) 1897-1955 **TCLC 28**
See also CA 108; 155; DLB 9

McCrae, John 1872-1918 **TCLC 12**
See also CA 109; DLB 92

McCreigh, James
See Pohl, Frederik

McCullers, (Lula) Carson (Smith) 1917-1967 **CLC
1, 4, 10, 12, 48, 100; DA; DAB; DAC; DAM
MST, NOV; SSC 24; WLC**
See also CA 5-8R; 25-28R; CABS 1, 3; CANR 18;
CDALB 1941-1968; DLB 2, 7, 173; MTCW;
SATA 27

McCulloch, John Tyler
See Burroughs, Edgar Rice

McCullough, Colleen 1938(?)- **CLC 27; DAM NOV,
POP**
See also CA 81-84; CANR 17, 46; MTCW

McDermott, Alice 1953- **CLC 90**
See also CA 109; CANR 40

McElroy, Joseph 1930- **CLC 5, 47**
See also CA 17-20R

McEwan, Ian (Russell) 1948- **CLC 13, 66; DAM
NOV**
See also BEST 90 4; CA 61-64; CANR 14, 41; DLB
14; MTCW

McFadden, David 1940- **CLC 48**
See also CA 104; DLB 60; INT 104

McFarland, Dennis 1950- **CLC 65**

McGahern, John 1934- **CLC 5, 9, 48; SSC 17**
See also CA 17-20R; CANR 29; DLB 14;
MTCW

McGinley, Patrick (Anthony) 1937- **CLC 41**
  See also CA 120; 127; CANR 56; INT 127

McGinley, Phyllis 1905-1978 **CLC 14**
  See also CA 9-12R; 77-80; CANR 19; DLB 11, 48;
  SATA 2, 44; SATA-Obit 24

McGinniss, Joe 1942- **CLC 32**
  See also AITN 2; BEST 89 2; CA 25-28R; CANR
  26; INT CANR-26

McGivern, Maureen Daly
  See Daly, Maureen

McGrath, Patrick 1950- **CLC 55**
  See also CA 136

McGrath, Thomas (Matthew) 1916-1990 **CLC 28,
  59; DAM POET**
  See also CA 9-12R; 132; CANR 6, 33; MTCW;
  SATA 41; SATA-Obit 66

McGuane, Thomas (Francis III) 1939- **CLC 3, 7, 18,
  45**
  See also AITN 2; CA 49-52; CANR 5, 24, 49; DLB
  2; DLBY 80; INT CANR-24; MTCW

McGuckian, Medbh 1950- **CLC 48; DAM POET**
  See also CA 143; DLB 40

McHale, Tom 1942(?)-1982 **CLC 3, 5**
  See also AITN 1; CA 77-80; 106

McIlvanney, William 1936- **CLC 42**
  See also CA 25-28R; DLB 14

McIlwraith, Maureen Mollie Hunter
  See Hunter, Mollie
  See also SATA 2

McInerney, Jay 1955- **CLC 34; DAM POP**
  See also AAYA 18; CA 116; 123; CANR 45; INT
  123

McIntyre, Vonda N(eel) 1948- **CLC 18**
  See also CA 81-84; CANR 17, 34; MTCW

McKay, Claude **TCLC 7, 41; BLC; DAB; PC 2**
  See also McKay, Festus Claudius
  See also DLB 4, 45, 51, 117

McKay, Festus Claudius 1889-1948
  See McKay, Claude
  See also BW 1; CA 104; 124; DA; DAC; DAM
  MST, MULT, NOV, POET; MTCW; WLC

McKuen, Rod 1933- **CLC 1, 3**
  See also AITN 1; CA 41-44R; CANR 40

McLoughlin, R. B.
  See Mencken, H(enry) L(ouis)

McLuhan, (Herbert) Marshall 1911-1980 **CLC 37,
  83**
  See also CA 9-12R; 102; CANR 12, 34; DLB 88;
  INT CANR-12; MTCW

McMillan, Terry (L.) 1951- **CLC 50, 61; DAM
  MULT, NOV, POP**
  See also BW 2; CA 140

McMurtry, Larry (Jeff) 1936- **CLC 2, 3, 7, 11, 27,
  44; DAM NOV, POP**

  See also AAYA 15; AITN 2; BEST 89 2; CA 5-8R;
  CANR 19, 43; CDALB 1968-1988; DLB 2, 143;
  DLBY 80, 87; MTCW

McNally, T. M. 1961- **CLC 82**

McNally, Terrence 1939- **CLC 4, 7, 41, 91; DAM
  DRAM**
  See also CA 45-48; CANR 2, 56; DLB 7

McNamer, Deirdre 1950- **CLC 70**

McNeile, Herman Cyril 1888-1937
  See Sapper
  See also DLB 77

McNickle, (William) D'Arcy 1904-1977 **CLC 89;
  DAM MULT**
  See also CA 9-12R; 85-88; CANR 5, 45; DLB 175;
  NNAL; SATA-Obit 22

McPhee, John (Angus) 1931- **CLC 36**
  See also BEST 90 1; CA 65-68; CANR 20, 46;
  MTCW

McPherson, James Alan 1943- **CLC 19, 77**
  See also BW 1; CA 25-28R; CAAS 17; CANR 24;
  DLB 38; MTCW

McPherson, William (Alexander) 1933- **CLC 34**
  See also CA 69-72; CANR 28; INT CANR-28

Mead, Margaret 1901-1978 **CLC 37**
  See also AITN 1; CA 1-4R; 81-84; CANR 4;
  MTCW; SATA-Obit 20

Meaker, Marijane (Agnes) 1927-
  See Kerr, M. E.
  See also CA 107; CANR 37; INT 107; JRDA;
  MAICYA; MTCW; SATA 20, 61

Medoff, Mark (Howard) 1940- **CLC 6, 23; DAM
  DRAM**
  See also AITN 1; CA 53-56; CANR 5; DLB 7; INT
  CANR-5

Medvedev, P. N.
  See Bakhtin, Mikhail Mikhailovich

Meged, Aharon
  See Megged, Aharon

Meged, Aron
  See Megged, Aharon

Megged, Aharon 1920- **CLC 9**
  See also CA 49-52; CAAS 13; CANR 1

Mehta, Ved (Parkash) 1934- **CLC 37**
  See also CA 1-4R; CANR 2, 23; MTCW

Melanter
  See Blackmore, R(ichard) D(oddridge)

Melikow, Loris
  See Hofmannsthal, Hugo von

Melmoth, Sebastian
  See Wilde, Oscar (Fingal O'Flahertie Wills)

Meltzer, Milton 1915- **CLC 26**
  See also AAYA 8; CA 13-16R; CANR 38; CLR 13;
  DLB 61; JRDA; MAICYA; SAAS 1; SATA 1,

  50, 80

Melville, Herman 1819-1891 **NCLC 3, 12, 29, 45,
  49; DA; DAB; DAC; DAM MST, NOV; SSC
  1, 17; WLC**
  See also CDALB 1640-1865; DLB 3, 74; SATA
  59

Menander c. 342B.C.-c. 292B.C. **CMLC 9; DAM
  DRAM; DC 3**
  See also DLB 176

Mencken, H(enry) L(ouis) 1880-1956 **TCLC 13**
  See also CA 105; 125; CDALB 1917-1929; DLB 11,
  29, 63, 137; MTCW

Mendelsohn, Jane 1965(?)- **CLC 99**
  See also CA 154

Mercer, David 1928-1980 **CLC 5; DAM DRAM**
  See also CA 9-12R; 102; CANR 23; DLB 13;
  MTCW

Merchant, Paul
  See Ellison, Harlan (Jay)

Meredith, George 1828-1909 **TCLC 17, 43; DAM
  POET**
  See also CA 117; 153; CDBLB 1832-1890; DLB 18,
  35, 57, 159

Meredith, William (Morris) 1919- **CLC 4, 13, 22,
  55; DAM POET**
  See also CA 9-12R; CAAS 14; CANR 6, 40; DLB 5

Merezhkovsky, Dmitry Sergeyevich 1865-1941
  TCLC 29

Merimee, Prosper 1803-1870 **NCLC 6; SSC 7**
  See also DLB 119

Merkin, Daphne 1954- **CLC 44**
  See also CA 123

Merlin, Arthur
  See Blish, James (Benjamin)

Merrill, James (Ingram) 1926-1995 **CLC 2, 3, 6, 8,
  13, 18, 34, 91; DAM POET**
  See also CA 13-16R; 147; CANR 10, 49; DLB 5,
  165; DLBY 85; INT CANR-10; MTCW

Merriman, Alex
  See Silverberg, Robert

Merritt, E. B.
  See Waddington, Miriam

Merton, Thomas 1915-1968 **CLC 1, 3, 11, 34, 83;
  PC 10**
  See also CA 5-8R; 25-28R; CANR 22, 53; DLB 48;
  DLBY 81; MTCW

Merwin, W(illiam) S(tanley) 1927- **CLC 1, 2, 3, 5,
  8, 13, 18, 45, 88; DAM POET**
  See also CA 13-16R; CANR 15, 51; DLB 5, 169;
  INT CANR-15; MTCW

Metcalf, John 1938- **CLC 37**
  See also CA 113; DLB 60

Metcalf, Suzanne
  See Baum, L(yman) Frank

Mew, Charlotte (Mary) 1870-1928 **TCLC 8**
See also CA 105; DLB 19, 135

Mewshaw, Michael 1943- **CLC 9**
See also CA 53-56; CANR 7, 47; DLBY 80

Meyer, June
See Jordan, June

Meyer, Lynn
See Slavitt, David R(ytman)

Meyer-Meyrink, Gustav 1868-1932
See Meyrink, Gustav
See also CA 117

Meyers, Jeffrey 1939- **CLC 39**
See also CA 73-76; CANR 54; DLB 111

Meynell, Alice (Christina Gertrude Thompson)
1847-1922 **TCLC 6**
See also CA 104; DLB 19, 98

Meyrink, Gustav TCLC 21
See also Meyer-Meyrink, Gustav
See also DLB 81

Michaels, Leonard 1933- **CLC 6, 25; SSC 16**
See also CA 61-64; CANR 21; DLB 130; MTCW

Michaux, Henri 1899-1984 **CLC 8, 19**
See also CA 85-88; 114

Michelangelo 1475-1564 **LC 12**

Michelet, Jules 1798-1874 **NCLC 31**

Michener, James A(lbert) 1907(?)- **CLC 1, 5, 11,
29, 60; DAM NOV, POP**
See also AITN 1; BEST 90 1; CA 5-8R; CANR 21,
45; DLB 6; MTCW

Mickiewicz, Adam 1798-1855 **NCLC 3**

Middleton, Christopher 1926- **CLC 13**
See also CA 13-16R; CANR 29, 54; DLB 40

Middleton, Richard (Barham) 1882-1911 **TCLC 56**
See also DLB 156

Middleton, Stanley 1919- **CLC 7, 38**
See also CA 25-28R; CAAS 23; CANR 21, 46; DLB
14

Middleton, Thomas 1580-1627 **LC 33; DAM DRAM,
MST; DC 5**
See also DLB 58

Migueis, Jose Rodrigues 1901- **CLC 10**

Mikszath, Kalman 1847-1910 **TCLC 31**

Miles, Jack CLC 100

Miles, Josephine (Louise) 1911-1985 **CLC 1, 2, 14,
34, 39; DAM POET**
See also CA 1-4R; 116; CANR 2, 55; DLB 48

Militant
See Sandburg, Carl (August)

Mill, John Stuart 1806-1873 **NCLC 11, 58**
See also CDBLB 1832-1890; DLB 55

Millar, Kenneth 1915-1983 **CLC 14; DAM POP**
See also Macdonald, Ross
See also CA 9-12R; 110; CANR 16; DLB 2; DLBD
6; DLBY 83; MTCW

Millay, E. Vincent
See Millay, Edna St. Vincent

Millay, Edna St. Vincent 1892-1950 **TCLC 4, 49;
DA; DAB; DAC; DAM MST, POET; PC 6**
See also CA 104; 130; CDALB 1917-1929; DLB
45; MTCW

Miller, Arthur 1915- **CLC 1, 2, 6, 10, 15, 26, 47,
78; DA; DAB; DAC; DAM DRAM, MST; DC
1; WLC**
See also AAYA 15; AITN 1; CA 1-4R; CABS 3;
CANR 2, 30, 54; CDALB 1941-1968; DLB 7;
MTCW

Miller, Henry (Valentine) 1891-1980 **CLC 1, 2, 4, 9,
14, 43, 84; DA; DAB; DAC; DAM MST, NOV;
WLC**
See also CA 9-12R; 97-100; CANR 33; CDALB
1929-1941; DLB 4, 9; DLBY 80; MTCW

Miller, Jason 1939(?)- **CLC 2**
See also AITN 1; CA 73-76; DLB 7

Miller, Sue 1943- **CLC 44; DAM POP**
See also BEST 90 3; CA 139; DLB 143

Miller, Walter M(ichael, Jr.) 1923- **CLC 4, 30**
See also CA 85-88; DLB 8

Millett, Kate 1934- **CLC 67**
See also AITN 1; CA 73-76; CANR 32, 53;
MTCW

Millhauser, Steven 1943- **CLC 21, 54**
See also CA 110; 111; DLB 2; INT 111

Millin, Sarah Gertrude 1889-1968 **CLC 49**
See also CA 102; 93-96

Milne, A(lan) A(lexander) 1882-1956 **TCLC 6; DAB;
DAC; DAM MST**
See also CA 104; 133; CLR 1, 26; DLB 10, 77, 100,
160; MAICYA; MTCW; YABC 1

Milner, Ron(ald) 1938- **CLC 56; BLC; DAM MULT**
See also AITN 1; BW 1; CA 73-76; CANR 24;
DLB 38; MTCW

Milosz, Czeslaw 1911- **CLC 5, 11, 22, 31, 56, 82;
DAM MST, POET; PC 8**
See also CA 81-84; CANR 23, 51; MTCW

Milton, John 1608-1674 **LC 9; DA; DAB; DAC;
DAM MST, POET; WLC**
See also CDBLB 1660-1789; DLB 131, 151

Min, Anchee 1957- **CLC 86**
See also CA 146

Minehaha, Cornelius
See Wedekind, (Benjamin) Frank(lin)

Miner, Valerie 1947- **CLC 40**
See also CA 97-100

Minimo, Duca
See D'Annunzio, Gabriele

Minot, Susan 1956- **CLC 44**
See also CA 134

Minus, Ed 1938- **CLC 39**

Miranda, Javier
See Bioy Casares, Adolfo

Mirbeau, Octave 1848-1917 **TCLC 55**
See also DLB 123

Miro (Ferrer), Gabriel (Francisco Victor) 1879-1930
TCLC 5
See also CA 104

Mishima, Yukio CLC 2, 4, 6, 9, 27; DC 1; SSC 4
See also Hiraoka, Kimitake

Mistral, Frederic 1830-1914 **TCLC 51**
See also CA 122

Mistral, Gabriela TCLC 2; HLC
See also Godoy Alcayaga, Lucila

Mistry, Rohinton 1952- **CLC 71; DAC**
See also CA 141

Mitchell, Clyde
See Ellison, Harlan (Jay); Silverberg, Robert

Mitchell, James Leslie 1901-1935
See Gibbon, Lewis Grassic
See also CA 104; DLB 15

Mitchell, Joni 1943- **CLC 12**
See also CA 112

Mitchell, Joseph (Quincy) 1908-1996 **CLC 98**
See also CA 77-80; 152

Mitchell, Margaret (Munnerlyn) 1900-1949 **TCLC
11; DAM NOV, POP**
See also CA 109; 125; CANR 55; DLB 9;
MTCW

Mitchell, Peggy
See Mitchell, Margaret (Munnerlyn)

Mitchell, S(ilas) Weir 1829-1914 **TCLC 36**

Mitchell, W(illiam) O(rmond) 1914- **CLC 25; DAC;
DAM MST**
See also CA 77-80; CANR 15, 43; DLB 88

Mitford, Mary Russell 1787-1855 **NCLC 4**
See also DLB 110, 116

Mitford, Nancy 1904-1973 **CLC 44**
See also CA 9-12R

Miyamoto, Yuriko 1899-1951 **TCLC 37**

Mo, Timothy (Peter) 1950(?)- **CLC 46**
See also CA 117; MTCW

Modarressi, Taghi (M.) 1931- **CLC 44**
See also CA 121; 134; INT 134

Modiano, Patrick (Jean) 1945- **CLC 18**
See also CA 85-88; CANR 17, 40; DLB 83

Moerck, Paal
See Roelvaag, O(le) E(dvart)

Mofolo, Thomas (Mokopu) 1875(?)-1948 **TCLC 22;**
BLC; DAM MULT
See also CA 121; 153

Mohr, Nicholasa 1935- **CLC 12; DAM MULT; HLC**
See also AAYA 8; CA 49-52; CANR 1, 32; CLR 22;
DLB 145; HW; JRDA; SAAS 8; SATA 8

Mojtabai, A(nn) G(race) 1938- **CLC 5, 9, 15, 29**
See also CA 85-88

Moliere 1622-1673 **LC 28; DA; DAB; DAC; DAM**
DRAM, MST; WLC

Molin, Charles
See Mayne, William (James Carter)

Molnar, Ferenc 1878-1952 **TCLC 20; DAM DRAM**
See also CA 109; 153

Momaday, N(avarre) Scott 1934- **CLC 2, 19, 85,**
95; DA; DAB; DAC; DAM MST, MULT,
NOV, POP
See also AAYA 11; CA 25-28R; CANR 14, 34;
DLB 143, 175; INT CANR-14; MTCW; NNAL;
SATA 48; SATA-Brief 30

Monette, Paul 1945-1995 **CLC 82**
See also CA 139; 147

Monroe, Harriet 1860-1936 **TCLC 12**
See also CA 109; DLB 54, 91

Monroe, Lyle
See Heinlein, Robert A(nson)

Montagu, Elizabeth 1917- **NCLC 7**
See also CA 9-12R

Montagu, Mary (Pierrepont) Wortley 1689-1762 **LC**
9; PC 16
See also DLB 95, 101

Montagu, W. H.
See Coleridge, Samuel Taylor

Montague, John (Patrick) 1929- **CLC 13, 46**
See also CA 9-12R; CANR 9; DLB 40; MTCW

Montaigne, Michel (Eyquem) de 1533-1592 **LC 8;**
DA; DAB; DAC; DAM MST; WLC

Montale, Eugenio 1896-1981 **CLC 7, 9, 18; PC 13**
See also CA 17-20R; 104; CANR 30; DLB 114;
MTCW

Montesquieu, Charles-Louis de Secondat 1689-1755
LC 7

Montgomery, (Robert) Bruce 1921-1978
See Crispin, Edmund
See also CA 104

Montgomery, L(ucy) M(aud) 1874-1942 **TCLC 51;**
DAC; DAM MST
See also AAYA 12; CA 108; 137; CLR 8; DLB 92;
DLBD 14; JRDA; MAICYA; YABC 1

Montgomery, Marion H., Jr. 1925- **CLC 7**
See also AITN 1; CA 1-4R; CANR 3, 48; DLB 6

Montgomery, Max
See Davenport, Guy (Mattison, Jr.)

Montherlant, Henry (Milon) de 1896-1972 **CLC 8,**
19; DAM DRAM
See also CA 85-88; 37-40R; DLB 72; MTCW

Monty Python
See Chapman, Graham; Cleese, John (Marwood);
Gilliam, Terry (Vance); Idle, Eric; Jones, Terence
Graham Parry; Palin, Michael (Edward)
See also AAYA 7

Moodie, Susanna (Strickland) 1803-1885 **NCLC**
14
See also DLB 99

Mooney, Edward 1951-
See Mooney, Ted
See also CA 130

Mooney, Ted **CLC 25**
See also Mooney, Edward

Moorcock, Michael (John) 1939- **CLC 5, 27, 58**
See also CA 45-48; CAAS 5; CANR 2, 17, 38; DLB
14; MTCW

Moore, Brian 1921- **CLC 1, 3, 5, 7, 8, 19, 32, 90;**
DAB; DAC; DAM MST
See also CA 1-4R; CANR 1, 25, 42; MTCW

Moore, Edward
See Muir, Edwin

Moore, George Augustus 1852-1933 **TCLC 7; SSC**
19
See also CA 104; DLB 10, 18, 57, 135

Moore, Lorrie **CLC 39, 45, 68**
See also Moore, Marie Lorena

Moore, Marianne (Craig) 1887-1972 **CLC 1, 2, 4, 8,**
10, 13, 19, 47; DA; DAB; DAC; DAM MST,
POET; PC 4
See also CA 1-4R; 33-36R; CANR 3; CDALB 1929-
1941; DLB 45; DLBD 7; MTCW; SATA 20

Moore, Marie Lorena 1957-
See Moore, Lorrie
See also CA 116; CANR 39

Moore, Thomas 1779-1852 **NCLC 6**
See also DLB 96, 144

Morand, Paul 1888-1976 **CLC 41; SSC 22**
See also CA 69-72; DLB 65

Morante, Elsa 1918-1985 **CLC 8, 47**
See also CA 85-88; 117; CANR 35; DLB 177;
MTCW

Moravia, Alberto 1907-1990 **CLC 2, 7, 11, 27, 46**
See also Pincherle, Alberto
See also DLB 177

More, Hannah 1745-1833 **NCLC 27**
See also DLB 107, 109, 116, 158

More, Henry 1614-1687 **LC 9**
See also DLB 126

More, Sir Thomas 1478-1535 **LC 10, 32**

Moreas, Jean **TCLC 18**
See also Papadiamantopoulos, Johannes

Morgan, Berry 1919- **CLC 6**
See also CA 49-52; DLB 6

Morgan, Claire
See Highsmith, (Mary) Patricia

Morgan, Edwin (George) 1920- **CLC 31**
See also CA 5-8R; CANR 3, 43; DLB 27

Morgan, (George) Frederick 1922- **CLC 23**
See also CA 17-20R; CANR 21

Morgan, Harriet
See Mencken, H(enry) L(ouis)

Morgan, Jane
See Cooper, James Fenimore

Morgan, Janet 1945- **CLC 39**
See also CA 65-68

Morgan, Lady 1776(?)-1859 **NCLC 29**
See also DLB 116, 158

Morgan, Robin 1941- **CLC 2**
See also CA 69-72; CANR 29; MTCW; SATA 80

Morgan, Scott
See Kuttner, Henry

Morgan, Seth 1949(?)-1990 **CLC 65**
See also CA 132

Morgenstern, Christian 1871-1914 **TCLC 8**
See also CA 105

Morgenstern, S.
See Goldman, William (W.)

Moricz, Zsigmond 1879-1942 **TCLC 33**

Morike, Eduard (Friedrich) 1804-1875 **NCLC 10**
See also DLB 133

Mori Ogai **TCLC 14**
See also Mori Rintaro

Mori Rintaro 1862-1922
See Mori Ogai
See also CA 110

Moritz, Karl Philipp 1756-1793 **LC 2**
See also DLB 94

Morland, Peter Henry
See Faust, Frederick (Schiller)

Morren, Theophil
See Hofmannsthal, Hugo von

Morris, Bill 1952- **CLC 76**

Morris, Julian
See West, Morris L(anglo)

Morris, Steveland Judkins 1950(?)-
See Wonder, Stevie
See also CA 111

Morris, William 1834-1896 **NCLC 4**
See also CDBLB 1832-1890; DLB 18, 35, 57, 156

Morris, Wright 1910- **CLC 1, 3, 7, 18, 37**

See also CA 9-12R; CANR 21; DLB 2; DLBY 81; MTCW

Morrison, Chloe Anthony Wofford
See Morrison, Toni

Morrison, James Douglas 1943-1971
See Morrison, Jim
See also CA 73-76; CANR 40

Morrison, Jim CLC 17
See also Morrison, James Douglas

Morrison, Toni 1931- **CLC 4, 10, 22, 55, 81, 87; BLC; DA; DAB; DAC; DAM MST, MULT, NOV, POP**
See also AAYA 1; BW 2; CA 29-32R; CANR 27, 42; CDALB 1968-1988; DLB 6, 33, 143; DLBY 81; MTCW; SATA 57

Morrison, Van 1945- **CLC 21**
See also CA 116

Morrissy, Mary 1958- **CLC 99**

Mortimer, John (Clifford) 1923- **CLC 28, 43; DAM DRAM, POP**
See also CA 13-16R; CANR 21; CDBLB 1960 to Present; DLB 13; INT CANR-21; MTCW

Mortimer, Penelope (Ruth) 1918- **CLC 5**
See also CA 57-60; CANR 45

Morton, Anthony
See Creasey, John

Mosher, Howard Frank 1943- **CLC 62**
See also CA 139

Mosley, Nicholas 1923- **CLC 43, 70**
See also CA 69-72; CANR 41; DLB 14

Mosley, Walter 1952- **CLC 97; DAM MULT, POP**
See also AAYA 17; BW 2; CA 142; CANR 57

Moss, Howard 1922-1987 **CLC 7, 14, 45, 50; DAM POET**
See also CA 1-4R; 123; CANR 1, 44; DLB 5

Mossgiel, Rab
See Burns, Robert

Motion, Andrew (Peter) 1952- **CLC 47**
See also CA 146; DLB 40

Motley, Willard (Francis) 1909-1965 **CLC 18**
See also BW 1; CA 117; 106; DLB 76, 143

Motoori, Norinaga 1730-1801 **NCLC 45**

Mott, Michael (Charles Alston) 1930- **CLC 15, 34**
See also CA 5-8R; CAAS 7; CANR 7, 29

Mountain Wolf Woman 1884-1960 **CLC 92**
See also CA 144; NNAL

Moure, Erin 1955- **CLC 88**
See also CA 113; DLB 60

Mowat, Farley (McGill) 1921- **CLC 26; DAC; DAM MST**
See also AAYA 1; CA 1-4R; CANR 4, 24, 42; CLR 20; DLB 68; INT CANAR-24; JRDA; MAICYA;

MTCW; SATA 3, 55

Moyers, Bill 1934- **CLC 74**
See also AITN 2; CA 61-64; CANR 31, 52

Mphahlele, Es'kia
See Mphahlele, Ezekiel
See also DLB 125

Mphahlele, Ezekiel 1919- **CLC 25; BLC; DAM MULT**
See also Mphahlele, Es'kia
See also BW 2; CA 81-84; CANR 26

Mqhayi, S(amuel) E(dward) K(rune Loliwe) 1875-1945 **TCLC 25; BLC; DAM MULT**
See also CA 153

Mrozek, Slawomir 1930- **CLC 3, 13**
See also CA 13-16R; CAAS 10; CANR 29; MTCW

Mrs. Belloc-Lowndes
See Lowndes, Marie Adelaide (Belloc)

Mtwa, Percy (?)- **CLC 47**

Mueller, Lisel 1924- **CLC 13, 51**
See also CA 93-96; DLB 105

Muir, Edwin 1887-1959 **TCLC 2**
See also CA 104; DLB 20, 100

Muir, John 1838-1914 **TCLC 28**

Mujica Lainez, Manuel 1910-1984 **CLC 31**
See also Lainez, Manuel Mujica
See also CA 81-84; 112; CANR 32; HW

Mukherjee, Bharati 1940- **CLC 53; DAM NOV**
See also BEST 89 2; CA 107; CANR 45; DLB 60; MTCW

Muldoon, Paul 1951- **CLC 32, 72; DAM POET**
See also CA 113; 129; CANR 52; DLB 40; INT 129

Mulisch, Harry 1927- **CLC 42**
See also CA 9-12R; CANR 6, 26, 56

Mull, Martin 1943- **CLC 17**
See also CA 105

Mulock, Dinah Maria
See Craik, Dinah Maria (Mulock)

Munford, Robert 1737(?)-1783 **LC 5**
See also DLB 31

Mungo, Raymond 1946- **CLC 72**
See also CA 49-52; CANR 2

Munro, Alice 1931- **CLC 6, 10, 19, 50, 95; DAC; DAM MST, NOV; SSC 3**
See also AITN 2; CA 33-36R; CANR 33, 53; DLB 53; MTCW; SATA 29

Munro, H(ector) H(ugh) 1870-1916
See Saki
See also CA 104; 130; CDBLB 1890-1914; DA; DAB; DAC; DAM MST, NOV; DLB 34, 162; MTCW; WLC

Murasaki, Lady CMLC 1

Murdoch, (Jean) Iris 1919- **CLC 1, 2, 3, 4, 6, 8, 11, 15, 22, 31, 51; DAB; DAC; DAM MST, NOV**
See also CA 13-16R; CANR 8, 43; CDBLB 1960 to Present; DLB 14; INT CANR-8; MTCW

Murfree, Mary Noailles 1850-1922 **SSC 22**
See also CA 122; DLB 12, 74

Murnau, Friedrich Wilhelm
See Plumpe, Friedrich Wilhelm

Murphy, Richard 1927- **CLC 41**
See also CA 29-32R; DLB 40

Murphy, Sylvia 1937- **CLC 34**
See also CA 121

Murphy, Thomas (Bernard) 1935- **CLC 51**
See also CA 101

Murray, Albert L. 1916- **CLC 73**
See also BW 2; CA 49-52; CANR 26, 52; DLB 38

Murray, Les(lie) A(llan) 1938- **CLC 40; DAM POET**
See also CA 21-24R; CANR 11, 27, 56

Murry, J. Middleton
See Murry, John Middleton

Murry, John Middleton 1889-1957 **TCLC 16**
See also CA 118; DLB 149

Musgrave, Susan 1951- **CLC 13, 54**
See also CA 69-72; CANR 45

Musil, Robert (Edler von) 1880-1942 **TCLC 12, 68; SSC 18**
See also CA 109; CANR 55; DLB 81, 124

Muske, Carol 1945- **CLC 90**
See also Muske-Dukes, Carol (Anne)

Muske-Dukes, Carol (Anne) 1945-
See Muske, Carol
See also CA 65-68; CANR 32

Musset, (Louis Charles) Alfred de 1810-1857 **NCLC 7**

My Brother's Brother
See Chekhov, Anton (Pavlovich)

Myers, L. H. 1881-1944 **TCLC 59**
See also DLB 15

Myers, Walter Dean 1937- **CLC 35; BLC; DAM MULT, NOV**
See also AAYA 4; BW 2; CA 33-36R; CANR 20, 42; CLR 4, 16, 35; DLB 33; INT CANR-20; JRDA; MAICYA; SAAS 2; SATA 41, 71; SATA-Brief 27

Myers, Walter M.
See Myers, Walter Dean

Myles, Symon
See Follett, Ken(neth Martin)

Nabokov, Vladimir (Vladimirovich) 1899-1977 **CLC 1, 2, 3, 6, 8, 11, 15, 23, 44, 46, 64; DA; DAB; DAC; DAM MST, NOV; SSC 11; WLC**
See also CA 5-8R; 69-72; CANR 20; CDALB 1941-1968; DLB 2; DLBD 3; DLBY 80, 91; MTCW

Nagai Kafu TCLC 51
See also Nagai Sokichi

Nagai Sokichi 1879-1959
See Nagai Kafu
See also CA 117

Nagy, Laszlo 1925-1978 CLC 7
See also CA 129; 112

Naipaul, Shiva(dhar Srinivasa) 1945-1985 CLC 32,
39; DAM NOV
See also CA 110; 112; 116; CANR 33; DLB 157;
DLBY 85; MTCW

Naipaul, V(idiadhar) S(urajprasad) 1932- CLC 4,
7, 9, 13, 18, 37; DAB; DAC; DAM MST, NOV
See also CA 1-4R; CANR 1, 33, 51; CDBLB 1960
to Present; DLB 125; DLBY 85; MTCW

Nakos, Lilika 1899(?)- CLC 29

Narayan, R(asipuram) K(rishnaswami) 1906- CLC
7, 28, 47; DAM NOV
See also CA 81-84; CANR 33; MTCW; SATA 62

Nash, (Frediric) Ogden 1902-1971 CLC 23; DAM
POET
See also CA 13-14; 29-32R; CANR 34; CAP 1;
DLB 11; MAICYA; MTCW; SATA 2, 46

Nathan, Daniel
See Dannay, Frederic

Nathan, George Jean 1882-1958 TCLC 18
See also Hatteras, Owen
See also CA 114; DLB 137

Natsume, Kinnosuke 1867-1916
See Natsume, Soseki
See also CA 104

Natsume, Soseki TCLC 2, 10
See also Natsume, Kinnosuke

Natti, (Mary) Lee 1919-
See Kingman, Lee
See also CA 5-8R; CANR 2

Naylor, Gloria 1950- CLC 28, 52; BLC; DA; DAC;
DAM MST, MULT, NOV, POP
See also AAYA 6; BW 2; CA 107; CANR 27, 51;
DLB 173; MTCW

Neihardt, John Gneisenau 1881-1973 CLC 32
See also CA 13-14; CAP 1; DLB 9, 54

Nekrasov, Nikolai Alekseevich 1821-1878 NCLC
11

Nelligan, Emile 1879-1941 TCLC 14
See also CA 114; DLB 92

Nelson, Willie 1933- CLC 17
See also CA 107

Nemerov, Howard (Stanley) 1920-1991 CLC 2, 6, 9,
36; DAM POET
See also CA 1-4R; 134; CABS 2; CANR 1, 27, 53;
DLB 5, 6; DLBY 83; INT CANR-27; MTCW

Neruda, Pablo 1904-1973 CLC 1, 2, 5, 7, 9, 28, 62;
DA; DAB; DAC; DAM MST, MULT, POET;

HLC; PC 4; WLC
See also CA 19-20; 45-48; CAP 2; HW; MTCW

Nerval, Gerard de 1808-1855 NCLC 1; PC 13; SSC
18

Nervo, (Jose) Amado (Ruiz de) 1870-1919 TCLC 11
See also CA 109; 131; HW

Nessi, Pio Baroja y
See Baroja (y Nessi), Pio

Nestroy, Johann 1801-1862 NCLC 42
See also DLB 133

Neufeld, John (Arthur) 1938- CLC 17
See also AAYA 11; CA 25-28R; CANR 11, 37, 56;
MAICYA; SAAS 3; SATA 6, 81

Neville, Emily Cheney 1919- CLC 12
See also CA 5-8R; CANR 3, 37; JRDA; MAICYA;
SAAS 2; SATA 1

Newbound, Bernard Slade 1930-
See Slade, Bernard
See also CA 81-84; CANR 49; DAM DRAM

Newby, P(ercy) H(oward) 1918- CLC 2, 13; DAM
NOV
See also CA 5-8R; CANR 32; DLB 15; MTCW

Newlove, Donald 1928- CLC 6
See also CA 29-32R; CANR 25

Newlove, John (Herbert) 1938- CLC 14
See also CA 21-24R; CANR 9, 25

Newman, Charles 1938- CLC 2, 8
See also CA 21-24R

Newman, Edwin (Harold) 1919- CLC 14
See also AITN 1; CA 69-72; CANR 5

Newman, John Henry 1801-1890 NCLC 38
See also DLB 18, 32, 55

Newton, Suzanne 1936- CLC 35
See also CA 41-44R; CANR 14; JRDA; SATA 5,
77

Nexo, Martin Andersen 1869-1954 TCLC 43

Nezval, Vitezslav 1900-1958 TCLC 44
See also CA 123

Ng, Fae Myenne 1957(?)- CLC 81
See also CA 146

Ngema, Mbongeni 1955- CLC 57
See also BW 2; CA 143

Ngugi, James T(hiong'o) CLC 3, 7, 13
See also Ngugi wa Thiong'o

Ngugi wa Thiong'o 1938- CLC 36; BLC; DAM
MULT, NOV
See also Ngugi, James T(hiong'o)
See also BW 2; CA 81-84; CANR 27; DLB 125;
MTCW

Nichol, B(arrie) P(hillip) 1944-1988 CLC 18
See also CA 53-56; DLB 53; SATA 66

Nichols, John (Treadwell) 1940- CLC 38
See also CA 9-12R; CAAS 2; CANR 6; DLBY 82

Nichols, Leigh
See Koontz, Dean R(ay)

Nichols, Peter (Richard) 1927- CLC 5, 36, 65
See also CA 104; CANR 33; DLB 13; MTCW

Nicolas, F. R. E.
See Freeling, Nicolas

Niedecker, Lorine 1903-1970 CLC 10, 42; DAM
POET
See also CA 25-28; CAP 2; DLB 48

Nietzsche, Friedrich (Wilhelm) 1844-1900 TCLC
10, 18, 55
See also CA 107; 121; DLB 129

Nievo, Ippolito 1831-1861 NCLC 22

Nightingale, Anne Redmon 1943-
See Redmon, Anne
See also CA 103

Nik. T. O.
See Annensky, Innokenty (Fyodorovich)

Nin, Anais 1903-1977 CLC 1, 4, 8, 11, 14, 60; DAM
NOV, POP; SSC 10
See also AITN 2; CA 13-16R; 69-72; CANR 22, 53;
DLB 2, 4, 152; MTCW

Nishiwaki, Junzaburo 1894-1982 PC 15
See also CA 107

Nissenson, Hugh 1933- CLC 4, 9
See also CA 17-20R; CANR 27; DLB 28

Niven, Larry CLC 8
See also Niven, Laurence Van Cott
See also DLB 8

Niven, Laurence Van Cott 1938-
See Niven, Larry
See also CA 21-24R; CAAS 12; CANR 14, 44;
DAM POP; MTCW

Nixon, Agnes Eckhardt 1927- CLC 21
See also CA 110

Nizan, Paul 1905-1940 TCLC 40
See also DLB 72

Nkosi, Lewis 1936- CLC 45; BLC; DAM MULT
See also BW 1; CA 65-68; CANR 27; DLB 157

Nodier, (Jean) Charles (Emmanuel) 1780-1844
NCLC 19
See also DLB 119

Nolan, Christopher 1965- CLC 58
See also CA 111

Noon, Jeff 1957- CLC 91
See also CA 148

Norden, Charles
See Durrell, Lawrence (George)

Nordhoff, Charles (Bernard) 1887-1947 TCLC 23
See also CA 108; DLB 9; SATA 23

Norfolk, Lawrence 1963- **CLC 76**
See also CA 144

Norman, Marsha 1947- **CLC 28; DAM DRAM**
See also CA 105; CABS 3; CANR 41; DLBY 84

Norris, Benjamin Franklin, Jr. 1870-1902 **TCLC 24**
See also Norris, Frank
See also CA 110

Norris, Frank
See Norris, Benjamin Franklin, Jr.
See also CDALB 1865-1917; DLB 12, 71

Norris, Leslie 1921- **CLC 14**
See also CA 11-12; CANR 14; CAP 1; DLB 27

North, Andrew
See Norton, Andre

North, Anthony
See Koontz, Dean R(ay)

North, Captain George
See Stevenson, Robert Louis (Balfour)

North, Milou
See Erdrich, Louise

Northrup, B. A.
See Hubbard, L(afayette) Ron(ald)

North Staffs
See Hulme, T(homas) E(rnest)

Norton, Alice Mary
See Norton, Andre
See also MAICYA; SATA 1, 43

Norton, Andre 1912- **CLC 12**
See also Norton, Alice Mary
See also AAYA 14; CA 1-4R; CANR 2, 31; DLB 8, 52; JRDA; MTCW; SATA 91

Norton, Caroline 1808-1877 **NCLC 47**
See also DLB 21, 159

Norway, Nevil Shute 1899-1960
See Shute, Nevil
See also CA 102; 93-96

Norwid, Cyprian Kamil 1821-1883 **NCLC 17**

Nosille, Nabrah
See Ellison, Harlan (Jay)

Nossack, Hans Erich 1901-1978 **CLC 6**
See also CA 93-96; 85-88; DLB 69

Nostradamus 1503-1566 **LC 27**

Nosu, Chuji
See Ozu, Yasujiro

Notenburg, Eleanora (Genrikhovna) von
See Guro, Elena

Nova, Craig 1945- **CLC 7, 31**
See also CA 45-48; CANR 2, 53

Novak, Joseph
See Kosinski, Jerzy (Nikodem)

Novalis 1772-1801 **NCLC 13**
See also DLB 90

Nowlan, Alden (Albert) 1933-1983 **CLC 15; DAC; DAM MST**
See also CA 9-12R; CANR 5; DLB 53

Noyes, Alfred 1880-1958 **TCLC 7**
See also CA 104; DLB 20

Nunn, Kem 19(?)- **CLC 34**

Nye, Robert 1939- **CLC 13, 42; DAM NOV**
See also CA 33-36R; CANR 29; DLB 14; MTCW; SATA 6

Nyro, Laura 1947- **CLC 17**

Oates, Joyce Carol 1938- **CLC 1, 2, 3, 6, 9, 11, 15, 19, 33, 52; DA; DAB; DAC; DAM MST, NOV, POP; SSC 6; WLC**
See also AAYA 15; AITN 1; BEST 89 2; CA 5-8R; CANR 25, 45; CDALB 1968-1988; DLB 2, 5, 130; DLBY 81; INT CANR-25; MTCW

O'Brien, Darcy 1939- **CLC 11**
See also CA 21-24R; CANR 8

O'Brien, E. G.
See Clarke, Arthur C(harles)

O'Brien, Edna 1936- **CLC 3, 5, 8, 13, 36, 65; DAM NOV; SSC 10**
See also CA 1-4R; CANR 6, 41; CDBLB 1960 to Present; DLB 14; MTCW

O'Brien, Fitz-James 1828-1862 **NCLC 21**
See also DLB 74

O'Brien, Flann **CLC 1, 4, 5, 7, 10, 47**
See also O Nuallain, Brian

O'Brien, Richard 1942- **CLC 17**
See also CA 124

O'Brien, Tim 1946- **CLC 7, 19, 40; DAM POP**
See also AAYA 16; CA 85-88; CANR 40; DLB 152; DLBD 9; DLBY 80

Obstfelder, Sigbjoern 1866-1900 **TCLC 23**
See also CA 123

O'Casey, Sean 1880-1964 **CLC 1, 5, 9, 11, 15, 88; DAB; DAC; DAM DRAM, MST**
See also CA 89-92; CDBLB 1914-1945; DLB 10; MTCW

O'Cathasaigh, Sean
See O'Casey, Sean

Ochs, Phil 1940-1976 **CLC 17**
See also CA 65-68

O'Connor, Edwin (Greene) 1918-1968 **CLC 14**
See also CA 93-96; 25-28R

O'Connor, (Mary) Flannery 1925-1964 **CLC 1, 2, 3, 6, 10, 13, 15, 21, 66; DA; DAB; DAC; DAM MST, NOV; SSC 1, 23; WLC**
See also AAYA 7; CA 1-4R; CANR 3, 41; CDALB 1941-1968; DLB 2, 152; DLBD 12; DLBY 80; MTCW

O'Connor, Frank **CLC 23; SSC 5**
See also O'Donovan, Michael John
See also DLB 162

O'Dell, Scott 1898-1989 **CLC 30**
See also AAYA 3; CA 61-64; 129; CANR 12, 30; CLR 1, 16; DLB 52; JRDA; MAICYA; SATA 12, 60

Odets, Clifford 1906-1963 **CLC 2, 28, 98; DAM DRAM; DC 6**
See also CA 85-88; DLB 7, 26; MTCW

O'Doherty, Brian 1934- **CLC 76**
See also CA 105

O'Donnell, K. M.
See Malzberg, Barry N(athaniel)

O'Donnell, Lawrence
See Kuttner, Henry

O'Donovan, Michael John 1903-1966 **CLC 14**
See also O'Connor, Frank
See also CA 93-96

Oe, Kenzaburo 1935- **CLC 10, 36, 86; DAM NOV; SSC 20**
See also CA 97-100; CANR 36, 50; DLBY 94; MTCW

O'Faolain, Julia 1932- **CLC 6, 19, 47**
See also CA 81-84; CAAS 2; CANR 12; DLB 14; MTCW

O'Faolain, Sean 1900-1991 **CLC 1, 7, 14, 32, 70; SSC 13**
See also CA 61-64; 134; CANR 12; DLB 15, 162; MTCW

O'Flaherty, Liam 1896-1984 **CLC 5, 34; SSC 6**
See also CA 101; 113; CANR 35; DLB 36, 162; DLBY 84; MTCW

Ogilvy, Gavin
See Barrie, J(ames) M(atthew)

O'Grady, Standish (James) 1846-1928 **TCLC 5**
See also CA 104

O'Grady, Timothy 1951- **CLC 59**
See also CA 138

O'Hara, Frank 1926-1966 **CLC 2, 5, 13, 78; DAM POET**
See also CA 9-12R; 25-28R; CANR 33; DLB 5, 16; MTCW

O'Hara, John (Henry) 1905-1970 **CLC 1, 2, 3, 6, 11, 42; DAM NOV; SSC 15**
See also CA 5-8R; 25-28R; CANR 31; CDALB 1929-1941; DLB 9, 86; DLBD 2; MTCW

O Hehir, Diana 1922- **CLC 41**
See also CA 93-96

Okigbo, Christopher (Ifenayichukwu) 1932-1967 **CLC 25, 84; BLC; DAM MULT, POET; PC 7**
See also BW 1; CA 77-80; DLB 125; MTCW

Okri, Ben 1959- **CLC 87**
See also BW 2; CA 130; 138; DLB 157; INT 138

Olds, Sharon 1942- **CLC 32, 39, 85; DAM POET**
See also CA 101; CANR 18, 41; DLB 120

Oldstyle, Jonathan
See Irving, Washington

Olesha, Yuri (Karlovich) 1899-1960 **CLC 8**
See also CA 85-88

Oliphant, Laurence 1829(?)-1888 **NCLC 47**
See also DLB 18, 166

Oliphant, Margaret (Oliphant Wilson) 1828-1897
NCLC 11
See also DLB 18, 159

Oliver, Mary 1935- **CLC 19, 34, 98**
See also CA 21-24R; CANR 9, 43; DLB 5

Olivier, Laurence (Kerr) 1907-1989 **CLC 20**
See also CA 111; 150; 129

Olsen, Tillie 1913- **CLC 4, 13; DA; DAB; DAC;**
DAM MST; SSC 11
See also CA 1-4R; CANR 1, 43; DLB 28; DLBY 80;
MTCW

Olson, Charles (John) 1910-1970 **CLC 1, 2, 5, 6, 9,**
11, 29; DAM POET
See also CA 13-16; 25-28R; CABS 2; CANR 35;
CAP 1; DLB 5, 16; MTCW

Olson, Toby 1937- **CLC 28**
See also CA 65-68; CANR 9, 31

Olyesha, Yuri
See Olesha, Yuri (Karlovich)

Ondaatje, (Philip) Michael 1943- **CLC 14, 29, 51,**
76; DAB; DAC; DAM MST
See also CA 77-80; CANR 42; DLB 60

Oneal, Elizabeth 1934-
See Oneal, Zibby
See also CA 106; CANR 28; MAICYA; SATA 30,
82

Oneal, Zibby CLC 30
See also Oneal, Elizabeth
See also AAYA 5; CLR 13; JRDA

O'Neill, Eugene (Gladstone) 1888-1953 **TCLC 1, 6,**
27, 49; DA; DAB; DAC; DAM DRAM, MST;
WLC
See also AITN 1; CA 110; 132; CDALB 1929-1941;
DLB 7; MTCW

Onetti, Juan Carlos 1909-1994 **CLC 7, 10; DAM**
MULT, NOV; SSC 23
See also CA 85-88; 145; CANR 32; DLB 113; HW;
MTCW

O Nuallain, Brian 1911-1966
See O'Brien, Flann
See also CA 21-22; 25-28R; CAP 2

Oppen, George 1908-1984 **CLC 7, 13, 34**
See also CA 13-16R; 113; CANR 8; DLB 5, 165

Oppenheim, E(dward) Phillips 1866-1946 **TCLC 45**
See also CA 111; DLB 70

Origen c. 185-c. 254 **CMLC 19**

Orlovitz, Gil 1918-1973 **CLC 22**
See also CA 77-80; 45-48; DLB 2, 5

Orris
See Ingelow, Jean

Ortega y Gasset, Jose 1883-1955 **TCLC 9; DAM**
MULT; HLC
See also CA 106; 130; HW; MTCW

Ortese, Anna Maria 1914- **CLC 89**
See also DLB 177

Ortiz, Simon J(oseph) 1941- **CLC 45; DAM MULT,**
POET; PC 17
See also CA 134; DLB 120, 175; NNAL

Orton, Joe CLC 4, 13, 43; DC 3
See also Orton, John Kingsley
See also CDBLB 1960 to Present; DLB 13

Orton, John Kingsley 1933-1967
See Orton, Joe
See also CA 85-88; CANR 35; DAM DRAM;
MTCW

Orwell, George TCLC 2, 6, 15, 31, 51; DAB; WLC
See also Blair, Eric (Arthur)
See also CDBLB 1945-1960; DLB 15, 98

Osborne, David
See Silverberg, Robert

Osborne, George
See Silverberg, Robert

Osborne, John (James) 1929-1994 **CLC 1, 2, 5, 11,**
45; DA; DAB; DAC; DAM DRAM, MST; WLC
See also CA 13-16R; 147; CANR 21, 56; CDBLB
1945-1960; DLB 13; MTCW

Osborne, Lawrence 1958- **CLC 50**

Oshima, Nagisa 1932- **CLC 20**
See also CA 116; 121

Oskison, John Milton 1874-1947 **TCLC 35; DAM**
MULT
See also CA 144; DLB 175; NNAL

Ossoli, Sarah Margaret (Fuller marchesa d') 1810-
1850
See Fuller, Margaret
See also SATA 25

Ostrovsky, Alexander 1823-1886 **NCLC 30, 57**

Otero, Blas de 1916-1979 **CLC 11**
See also CA 89-92; DLB 134

Otto, Whitney 1955- **CLC 70**
See also CA 140

Ouida TCLC 43
See also De La Ramee, (Marie) Louise
See also DLB 18, 156

Ousmane, Sembene 1923- **CLC 66; BLC**
See also BW 1; CA 117; 125; MTCW

Ovid 43B.C.-18(?) **CMLC 7; DAM POET; PC 2**

Owen, Hugh

See Faust, Frederick (Schiller)

Owen, Wilfred (Edward Salter) 1893-1918 **TCLC 5,**
27; DA; DAB; DAC; DAM MST, POET; WLC
See also CA 104; 141; CDBLB 1914-1945; DLB 20

Owens, Rochelle 1936- **CLC 8**
See also CA 17-20R; CAAS 2; CANR 39

Oz, Amos 1939- **CLC 5, 8, 11, 27, 33, 54; DAM**
NOV
See also CA 53-56; CANR 27, 47; MTCW

Ozick, Cynthia 1928- **CLC 3, 7, 28, 62; DAM NOV,**
POP; SSC 15
See also BEST 90 1; CA 17-20R; CANR 23; DLB
28, 152; DLBY 82; INT CANR-23; MTCW

Ozu, Yasujiro 1903-1963 **CLC 16**
See also CA 112

Pacheco, C.
See Pessoa, Fernando (Antonio Nogueira)

Pa Chin CLC 18
See also Li Fei-kan

Pack, Robert 1929- **CLC 13**
See also CA 1-4R; CANR 3, 44; DLB 5

Padgett, Lewis
See Kuttner, Henry

Padilla (Lorenzo), Heberto 1932- **CLC 38**
See also AITN 1; CA 123; 131; HW

Page, Jimmy 1944- **CLC 12**

Page, Louise 1955- **CLC 40**
See also CA 140

Page, P(atricia) K(athleen) 1916- **CLC 7, 18; DAC;**
DAM MST; PC 12
See also CA 53-56; CANR 4, 22; DLB 68; MTCW

Page, Thomas Nelson 1853-1922 **SSC 23**
See also CA 118; DLB 12, 78; DLBD 13

Paget, Violet 1856-1935
See Lee, Vernon
See also CA 104

Paget-Lowe, Henry
See Lovecraft, H(oward) P(hillips)

Paglia, Camille (Anna) 1947- **CLC 68**
See also CA 140

Paige, Richard
See Koontz, Dean R(ay)

Pakenham, Antonia
See Fraser, (Lady) Antonia (Pakenham)

Palamas, Kostes 1859-1943 **TCLC 5**
See also CA 105

Palazzeschi, Aldo 1885-1974 **CLC 11**
See also CA 89-92; 53-56; DLB 114

Paley, Grace 1922- **CLC 4, 6, 37; DAM POP; SSC**
8
See also CA 25-28R; CANR 13, 46; DLB 28; INT

CANR-13; MTCW

Palin, Michael (Edward) 1943- **CLC 21**
See also Monty Python
See also CA 107; CANR 35; SATA 67

Palliser, Charles 1947- **CLC 65**
See also CA 136

Palma, Ricardo 1833-1919 **TCLC 29**

Pancake, Breece Dexter 1952-1979
See Pancake, Breece D'J
See also CA 123; 109

Pancake, Breece D'J CLC 29
See also Pancake, Breece Dexter
See also DLB 130

Panko, Rudy
See Gogol, Nikolai (Vasilyevich)

Papadiamantis, Alexandros 1851-1911 **TCLC 29**

Papadiamantopoulos, Johannes 1856-1910
See Moreas, Jean
See also CA 117

Papini, Giovanni 1881-1956 **TCLC 22**
See also CA 121

Paracelsus 1493-1541 **LC 14**

Parasol, Peter
See Stevens, Wallace

Pareto, Vilfredo 1848-1923 **TCLC 69**

Parfenie, Maria
See Codrescu, Andrei

Parini, Jay (Lee) 1948- **CLC 54**
See also CA 97-100; CAAS 16; CANR 32

Park, Jordan
See Kornbluth, C(yril) M.; Pohl, Frederik

Parker, Bert
See Ellison, Harlan (Jay)

Parker, Dorothy (Rothschild) 1893-1967 **CLC 15,
68; DAM POET; SSC 2**
See also CA 19-20; 25-28R; CAP 2; DLB 11, 45, 86;
MTCW

Parker, Robert B(rown) 1932- **CLC 27; DAM NOV,
POP**
See also BEST 89 4; CA 49-52; CANR 1, 26, 52;
INT CANR-26; MTCW

Parkin, Frank 1940- **CLC 43**
See also CA 147

Parkman, Francis, Jr. 1823-1893 **NCLC 12**
See also DLB 1, 30

Parks, Gordon (Alexander Buchanan) 1912- **CLC
1, 16; BLC; DAM MULT**
See also AITN 2; BW 2; CA 41-44R; CANR 26;
DLB 33; SATA 8

Parnell, Thomas 1679-1718 **LC 3**
See also DLB 94

Parra, Nicanor 1914- **CLC 2; DAM MULT; HLC**
See also CA 85-88; CANR 32; HW; MTCW

Parrish, Mary Frances
See Fisher, M(ary) F(rances) K(ennedy)

Parson
See Coleridge, Samuel Taylor

Parson Lot
See Kingsley, Charles

Partridge, Anthony
See Oppenheim, E(dward) Phillips

Pascal, Blaise 1623-1662 **LC 35**

Pascoli, Giovanni 1855-1912 **TCLC 45**

Pasolini, Pier Paolo 1922-1975 **CLC 20, 37; PC 17**
See also CA 93-96; 61-64; DLB 128, 177; MTCW

Pasquini
See Silone, Ignazio

Pastan, Linda (Olenik) 1932- **CLC 27; DAM POET**
See also CA 61-64; CANR 18, 40; DLB 5

Pasternak, Boris (Leonidovich) 1890-1960 **CLC 7,
10, 18, 63; DA; DAB; DAC; DAM MST, NOV,
POET; PC 6; WLC**
See also CA 127; 116; MTCW

Patchen, Kenneth 1911-1972 **CLC 1, 2, 18; DAM
POET**
See also CA 1-4R; 33-36R; CANR 3, 35; DLB 16,
48; MTCW

Pater, Walter (Horatio) 1839-1894 **NCLC 7**
See also CDBLB 1832-1890; DLB 57, 156

Paterson, A(ndrew) B(arton) 1864-1941 **TCLC 32**
See also CA 155

Paterson, Katherine (Womeldorf) 1932- **CLC 12,
30**
See also AAYA 1; CA 21-24R; CANR 28; CLR 7;
DLB 52; JRDA; MAICYA; MTCW; SATA 13,
53, 92

Patmore, Coventry Kersey Dighton 1823-1896
NCLC 9
See also DLB 35, 98

Paton, Alan (Stewart) 1903-1988 **CLC 4, 10, 25, 55;
DA; DAB; DAC; DAM MST, NOV; WLC**
See also CA 13-16; 125; CANR 22; CAP 1;
MTCW; SATA 11; SATA-Obit 56

Paton Walsh, Gillian 1937-
See Walsh, Jill Paton
See also CANR 38; JRDA; MAICYA; SAAS 3;
SATA 4, 72

Paulding, James Kirke 1778-1860 **NCLC 2**
See also DLB 3, 59, 74

Paulin, Thomas Neilson 1949-
See Paulin, Tom
See also CA 123; 128

Paulin, Tom CLC 37
See also Paulin, Thomas Neilson

See also DLB 40

Paustovsky, Konstantin (Georgievich) 1892-1968
CLC 40
See also CA 93-96; 25-28R

Pavese, Cesare 1908-1950 **TCLC 3; PC 13; SSC 19**
See also CA 104; DLB 128, 177

Pavic, Milorad 1929- **CLC 60**
See also CA 136

Payne, Alan
See Jakes, John (William)

Paz, Gil
See Lugones, Leopoldo

Paz, Octavio 1914- **CLC 3, 4, 6, 10, 19, 51, 65; DA;
DAB; DAC; DAM MST, MULT, POET; HLC;
PC 1; WLC**
See also CA 73-76; CANR 32; DLBY 90; HW;
MTCW

p'Bitek, Okot 1931-1982 **CLC 96; BLC; DAM
MULT**
See also BW 2; CA 124; 107; DLB 125; MTCW

Peacock, Molly 1947- **CLC 60**
See also CA 103; CAAS 21; CANR 52; DLB 120

Peacock, Thomas Love 1785-1866 **NCLC 22**
See also DLB 96, 116

Peake, Mervyn 1911-1968 **CLC 7, 54**
See also CA 5-8R; 25-28R; CANR 3; DLB 15, 160;
MTCW; SATA 23

Pearce, Philippa CLC 21
See also Christie, (Ann) Philippa
See also CLR 9; DLB 161; MAICYA; SATA 1, 67

Pearl, Eric
See Elman, Richard

Pearson, T(homas) R(eid) 1956- **CLC 39**
See also CA 120; 130; INT 130

Peck, Dale 1967- **CLC 81**
See also CA 146

Peck, John 1941- **CLC 3**
See also CA 49-52; CANR 3

Peck, Richard (Wayne) 1934- **CLC 21**
See also AAYA 1; CA 85-88; CANR 19, 38; CLR
15; INT CANR-19; JRDA; MAICYA; SAAS 2;
SATA 18, 55

Peck, Robert Newton 1928- **CLC 17; DA; DAC;
DAM MST**
See also AAYA 3; CA 81-84; CANR 31; JRDA;
MAICYA; SAAS 1; SATA 21, 62

Peckinpah, (David) Sam(uel) 1925-1984 **CLC 20**
See also CA 109; 114

Pedersen, Knut 1859-1952
See Hamsun, Knut
See also CA 104; 119; MTCW

Peeslake, Gaffer
See Durrell, Lawrence (George)

Peguy, Charles Pierre 1873-1914 **TCLC 10**
See also CA 107

Pena, Ramon del Valle y
See Valle-Inclan, Ramon (Maria) del

Pendennis, Arthur Esquir
See Thackeray, William Makepeace

Penn, William 1644-1718 **LC 25**
See also DLB 24

Pepys, Samuel 1633-1703 **LC 11; DA; DAB; DAC; DAM MST; WLC**
See also CDBLB 1660-1789; DLB 101

Percy, Walker 1916-1990 **CLC 2, 3, 6, 8, 14, 18, 47, 65; DAM NOV, POP**
See also CA 1-4R; 131; CANR 1, 23; DLB 2; DLBY 80, 90; MTCW

Perec, Georges 1936-1982 **CLC 56**
See also CA 141; DLB 83

Pereda (y Sanchez de Porrua), Jose Maria de 1833-1906 **TCLC 16**
See also CA 117

Pereda y Porrua, Jose Maria de
See Pereda (y Sanchez de Porrua), Jose Maria de

Peregoy, George Weems
See Mencken, H(enry) L(ouis)

Perelman, S(idney) J(oseph) 1904-1979 **CLC 3, 5, 9, 15, 23, 44, 49; DAM DRAM**
See also AITN 1, 2; CA 73-76; 89-92; CANR 18; DLB 11, 44; MTCW

Peret, Benjamin 1899-1959 **TCLC 20**
See also CA 117

Peretz, Isaac Loeb 1851(?)-1915 **TCLC 16**
See also CA 109

Peretz, Yitzkhok Leibush
See Peretz, Isaac Loeb

Perez Galdos, Benito 1843-1920 **TCLC 27**
See also CA 125; 153; HW

Perrault, Charles 1628-1703 **LC 2**
See also MAICYA; SATA 25

Perry, Brighton
See Sherwood, Robert E(mmet)

Perse, St.-John **CLC 4, 11, 46**
See also Leger, (Marie-Rene Auguste) Alexis
Saint-Leger

Perutz, Leo 1882-1957 **TCLC 60**
See also DLB 81

Peseenz, Tulio F.
See Lopez y Fuentes, Gregorio

Pesetsky, Bette 1932- **CLC 28**
See also CA 133; DLB 130

Peshkov, Alexei Maximovich 1868-1936
See Gorky, Maxim
See also CA 105; 141; DA; DAC; DAM DRAM,

MST, NOV

Pessoa, Fernando (Antonio Nogueira) 1888-1935
TCLC 27; HLC
See also CA 125

Peterkin, Julia Mood 1880-1961 **CLC 31**
See also CA 102; DLB 9

Peters, Joan K. 1945- **CLC 39**

Peters, Robert L(ouis) 1924- **CLC 7**
See also CA 13-16R; CAAS 8; DLB 105

Petofi, Sandor 1823-1849 **NCLC 21**

Petrakis, Harry Mark 1923- **CLC 3**
See also CA 9-12R; CANR 4, 30

Petrarch 1304-1374 **CMLC 20; DAM POET; PC 8**

Petrov, Evgeny **TCLC 21**
See also Kataev, Evgeny Petrovich

Petry, Ann (Lane) 1908- **CLC 1, 7, 18**
See also BW 1; CA 5-8R; CAAS 6; CANR 4, 46;
CLR 12; DLB 76; JRDA; MAICYA; MTCW;
SATA 5

Petursson, Halligrimur 1614-1674 **LC 8**

Philips, Katherine 1632-1664 **LC 30**
See also DLB 131

Philipson, Morris H. 1926- **CLC 53**
See also CA 1-4R; CANR 4

Phillips, Caryl 1958- **CLC 96; DAM MULT**
See also BW 2; CA 141; DLB 157

Phillips, David Graham 1867-1911 **TCLC 44**
See also CA 108; DLB 9, 12

Phillips, Jack
See Sandburg, Carl (August)

Phillips, Jayne Anne 1952- **CLC 15, 33; SSC 16**
See also CA 101; CANR 24, 50; DLBY 80; INT
CANR-24; MTCW

Phillips, Richard
See Dick, Philip K(indred)

Phillips, Robert (Schaeffer) 1938- **CLC 28**
See also CA 17-20R; CAAS 13; CANR 8; DLB 105

Phillips, Ward
See Lovecraft, H(oward) P(hillips)

Piccolo, Lucio 1901-1969 **CLC 13**
See also CA 97-100; DLB 114

Pickthall, Marjorie L(owry) C(hristie) 1883-1922
TCLC 21
See also CA 107; DLB 92

Pico della Mirandola, Giovanni 1463-1494 **LC 15**

Piercy, Marge 1936- **CLC 3, 6, 14, 18, 27, 62**
See also CA 21-24R; CAAS 1; CANR 13, 43; DLB
120; MTCW

Piers, Robert

See Anthony, Piers

Pieyre de Mandiargues, Andre 1909-1991
See Mandiargues, Andre Pieyre de
See also CA 103; 136; CANR 22

Pilnyak, Boris **TCLC 23**
See also Vogau, Boris Andreyevich

Pincherle, Alberto 1907-1990 **CLC 11, 18; DAM NOV**
See also Moravia, Alberto
See also CA 25-28R; 132; CANR 33; MTCW

Pinckney, Darryl 1953- **CLC 76**
See also BW 2; CA 143

Pindar 518B.C.-446B.C. **CMLC 12**
See also DLB 176

Pineda, Cecile 1942- **CLC 39**
See also CA 118

Pinero, Arthur Wing 1855-1934 **TCLC 32; DAM DRAM**
See also CA 110; 153; DLB 10

Pinero, Miguel (Antonio Gomez) 1946-1988 **CLC 4, 55**
See also CA 61-64; 125; CANR 29; HW

Pinget, Robert 1919- **CLC 7, 13, 37**
See also CA 85-88; DLB 83

Pink Floyd
See Barrett, (Roger) Syd; Gilmour, David; Mason,
Nick; Waters, Roger; Wright, Rick

Pinkney, Edward 1802-1828 **NCLC 31**

Pinkwater, Daniel Manus 1941- **CLC 35**
See also Pinkwater, Manus
See also AAYA 1; CA 29-32R; CANR 12, 38; CLR
4; JRDA; MAICYA; SAAS 3; SATA 46, 76

Pinkwater, Manus
See Pinkwater, Daniel Manus
See also SATA 8

Pinsky, Robert 1940- **CLC 9, 19, 38, 94; DAM POET**
See also CA 29-32R; CAAS 4; DLBY 82

Pinta, Harold
See Pinter, Harold

Pinter, Harold 1930- **CLC 1, 3, 6, 9, 11, 15, 27, 58, 73; DA; DAB; DAC; DAM DRAM, MST; WLC**
See also CA 5-8R; CANR 33; CDBLB 1960 to
Present; DLB 13; MTCW

Piozzi, Hester Lynch (Thrale) 1741-1821 **NCLC 57**
See also DLB 104, 142

Pirandello, Luigi 1867-1936 **TCLC 4, 29; DA; DAB; DAC; DAM DRAM, MST; DC 5; SSC 22; WLC**
See also CA 104; 153

Pirsig, Robert M(aynard) 1928- **CLC 4, 6, 73; DAM POP**
See also CA 53-56; CANR 42; MTCW; SATA 39

Pisarev, Dmitry Ivanovich 1840-1868 **NCLC 25**

Pix, Mary (Griffith) 1666-1709 **LC 8**
See also DLB 80

Pixerecourt, Guilbert de 1773-1844 **NCLC 39**

Plaidy, Jean
See Hibbert, Eleanor Alice Burford

Planche, James Robinson 1796-1880 **NCLC 42**

Plant, Robert 1948- **CLC 12**

Plante, David (Robert) 1940- **CLC 7, 23, 38; DAM NOV**
See also CA 37-40R; CANR 12, 36; DLBY 83; INT CANR-12; MTCW

Plath, Sylvia 1932-1963 **CLC 1, 2, 3, 5, 9, 11, 14, 17, 50, 51, 62; DA; DAB; DAC; DAM MST, POET; PC 1; WLC**
See also AAYA 13; CA 19-20; CANR 34; CAP 2; CDALB 1941-1968; DLB 5, 6, 152; MTCW

Plato 428(?)B.C.-348(?)B.C. **CMLC 8; DA; DAB; DAC; DAM MST**
See also DLB 176

Platonov, Andrei **TCLC 14**
See also Klimentov, Andrei Platonovich

Platt, Kin 1911- **CLC 26**
See also AAYA 11; CA 17-20R; CANR 11; JRDA; SAAS 17; SATA 21, 86

Plautus c. 251B.C.-184B.C. **DC 6**

Plick et Plock
See Simenon, Georges (Jacques Christian)

Plimpton, George (Ames) 1927- **CLC 36**
See also AITN 1; CA 21-24R; CANR 32; MTCW; SATA 10

Plomer, William Charles Franklin 1903-1973 **CLC 4, 8**
See also CA 21-22; CANR 34; CAP 2; DLB 20, 162; MTCW; SATA 24

Plowman, Piers
See Kavanagh, Patrick (Joseph)

Plum, J.
See Wodehouse, P(elham) G(renville)

Plumly, Stanley (Ross) 1939- **CLC 33**
See also CA 108; 110; DLB 5; INT 110

Plumpe, Friedrich Wilhelm 1888-1931 **TCLC 53**
See also CA 112

Poe, Edgar Allan 1809-1849 **NCLC 1, 16, 55; DA; DAB; DAC; DAM MST, POET; PC 1; SSC 1, 22; WLC**
See also AAYA 14; CDALB 1640-1865; DLB 3, 59, 73, 74; SATA 23

Poet of Titchfield Street, The
See Pound, Ezra (Weston Loomis)

Pohl, Frederik 1919- **CLC 18**
See also CA 61-64; CAAS 1; CANR 11, 37; DLB 8;

INT CANR-11; MTCW; SATA 24

Poirier, Louis 1910-
See Gracq, Julien
See also CA 122; 126

Poitier, Sidney 1927- **CLC 26**
See also BW 1; CA 117

Polanski, Roman 1933- **CLC 16**
See also CA 77-80

Poliakoff, Stephen 1952- **CLC 38**
See also CA 106; DLB 13

Police, The
See Copeland, Stewart (Armstrong); Summers, Andrew James; Sumner, Gordon Matthew

Polidori, John William 1795-1821 **NCLC 51**
See also DLB 116

Pollitt, Katha 1949- **CLC 28**
See also CA 120; 122; MTCW

Pollock, (Mary) Sharon 1936- **CLC 50; DAC; DAM DRAM, MST**
See also CA 141; DLB 60

Polo, Marco 1254-1324 **CMLC 15**

Polonsky, Abraham (Lincoln) 1910- **CLC 92**
See also CA 104; DLB 26; INT 104

Polybius c. 200B.C.-c. 118B.C. **CMLC 17**
See also DLB 176

Pomerance, Bernard 1940- **CLC 13; DAM DRAM**
See also CA 101; CANR 49

Ponge, Francis (Jean Gaston Alfred) 1899-1988 **CLC 6, 18; DAM POET**
See also CA 85-88; 126; CANR 40

Pontoppidan, Henrik 1857-1943 **TCLC 29**

Poole, Josephine **CLC 17**
See also Helyar, Jane Penelope Josephine
See also SAAS 2; SATA 5

Popa, Vasko 1922-1991 **CLC 19**
See also CA 112; 148

Pope, Alexander 1688-1744 **LC 3; DA; DAB; DAC; DAM MST, POET; WLC**
See also CDBLB 1660-1789; DLB 95, 101

Porter, Connie (Rose) 1959(?)- **CLC 70**
See also BW 2; CA 142; SATA 81

Porter, Gene(va Grace) Stratton 1863(?)-1924 **TCLC 21**
See also CA 112

Porter, Katherine Anne 1890-1980 **CLC 1, 3, 7, 10, 13, 15, 27; DA; DAB; DAC; DAM MST, NOV; SSC 4**
See also AITN 2; CA 1-4R; 101; CANR 1; DLB 4, 9, 102; DLBD 12; DLBY 80; MTCW; SATA 39; SATA-Obit 23

Porter, Peter (Neville Frederick) 1929- **CLC 5, 13, 33**

See also CA 85-88; DLB 40

Porter, William Sydney 1862-1910
See Henry, O.
See also CA 104; 131; CDALB 1865-1917; DA; DAB; DAC; DAM MST; DLB 12, 78, 79; MTCW; YABC 2

Portillo (y Pacheco), Jose Lopez
See Lopez Portillo (y Pacheco), Jose

Post, Melville Davisson 1869-1930 **TCLC 39**
See also CA 110

Potok, Chaim 1929- **CLC 2, 7, 14, 26; DAM NOV**
See also AAYA 15; AITN 1, 2; CA 17-20R; CANR 19, 35; DLB 28, 152; INT CANR-19; MTCW; SATA 33

Potter, Beatrice
See Webb, (Martha) Beatrice (Potter)
See also MAICYA

Potter, Dennis (Christopher George) 1935-1994 **CLC 58, 86**
See also CA 107; 145; CANR 33; MTCW

Pound, Ezra (Weston Loomis) 1885-1972 **CLC 1, 2, 3, 4, 5, 7, 10, 13, 18, 34, 48, 50; DA; DAB; DAC; DAM MST, POET; PC 4; WLC**
See also CA 5-8R; 37-40R; CANR 40; CDALB 1917-1929; DLB 4, 45, 63; MTCW

Povod, Reinaldo 1959-1994 **CLC 44**
See also CA 136; 146

Powell, Adam Clayton, Jr. 1908-1972 **CLC 89; BLC; DAM MULT**
See also BW 1; CA 102; 33-36R

Powell, Anthony (Dymoke) 1905- **CLC 1, 3, 7, 9, 10, 31**
See also CA 1-4R; CANR 1, 32; CDBLB 1945-1960; DLB 15; MTCW

Powell, Dawn 1897-1965 **CLC 66**
See also CA 5-8R

Powell, Padgett 1952- **CLC 34**
See also CA 126

Power, Susan **CLC 91**

Powers, J(ames) F(arl) 1917- **CLC 1, 4, 8, 57; SSC 4**
See also CA 1-4R; CANR 2; DLB 130; MTCW

Powers, John J(ames) 1945-
See Powers, John R.
See also CA 69-72

Powers, John R. **CLC 66**
See also Powers, John J(ames)

Powers, Richard (S.) 1957- **CLC 93**
See also CA 148

Pownall, David 1938- **CLC 10**
See also CA 89-92; CAAS 18; CANR 49; DLB 14

Powys, John Cowper 1872-1963 **CLC 7, 9, 15, 46**
See also CA 85-88; DLB 15; MTCW

Racine, Jean 1639-1699 **LC 28; DAB; DAM MST**

Radcliffe, Ann (Ward) 1764-1823 **NCLC 6, 55**
See also DLB 39

Radiguet, Raymond 1903-1923 **TCLC 29**
See also DLB 65

Radnoti, Miklos 1909-1944 **TCLC 16**
See also CA 118

Rado, James 1939- **CLC 17**
See also CA 105

Radvanyi, Netty 1900-1983
See Seghers, Anna
See also CA 85-88; 110

Rae, Ben
See Griffiths, Trevor

Raeburn, John (Hay) 1941- **CLC 34**
See also CA 57-60

Ragni, Gerome 1942-1991 **CLC 17**
See also CA 105; 134

Rahv, Philip 1908-1973 **CLC 24**
See also Greenberg, Ivan
See also DLB 137

Raine, Craig 1944- **CLC 32**
See also CA 108; CANR 29, 51; DLB 40

Raine, Kathleen (Jessie) 1908- **CLC 7, 45**
See also CA 85-88; CANR 46; DLB 20; MTCW

Rainis, Janis 1865-1929 **TCLC 29**

Rakosi, Carl CLC 47
See also Rawley, Callman
See also CAAS 5

Raleigh, Richard
See Lovecraft, H(oward) P(hillips)

Raleigh, Sir Walter 1554(?)-1618 **LC 31**
See also CDBLB Before 1660; DLB 172

Rallentando, H. P.
See Sayers, Dorothy L(eigh)

Ramal, Walter
See de la Mare, Walter (John)

Ramon, Juan
See Jimenez (Mantecon), Juan Ramon

Ramos, Graciliano 1892-1953 **TCLC 32**

Rampersad, Arnold 1941- **CLC 44**
See also BW 2; CA 127; 133; DLB 111; INT 133

Rampling, Anne
See Rice, Anne

Ramsay, Allan 1684(?)-1758 **LC 29**
See also DLB 95

Ramuz, Charles-Ferdinand 1878-1947 **TCLC 33**

Rand, Ayn 1905-1982 **CLC 3, 30, 44, 79; DA; DAC; DAM MST, NOV, POP; WLC**

See also AAYA 10; CA 13-16R; 105; CANR 27;
MTCW

Randall, Dudley (Felker) 1914- **CLC 1; BLC; DAM MULT**
See also BW 1; CA 25-28R; CANR 23; DLB 41

Randall, Robert
See Silverberg, Robert

Ranger, Ken
See Creasey, John

Ransom, John Crowe 1888-1974 **CLC 2, 4, 5, 11, 24; DAM POET**
See also CA 5-8R; 49-52; CANR 6, 34; DLB 45, 63;
MTCW

Rao, Raja 1909- **CLC 25, 56; DAM NOV**
See also CA 73-76; CANR 51; MTCW

Raphael, Frederic (Michael) 1931- **CLC 2, 14**
See also CA 1-4R; CANR 1; DLB 14

Ratcliffe, James P.
See Mencken, H(enry) L(ouis)

Rathbone, Julian 1935- **CLC 41**
See also CA 101; CANR 34

Rattigan, Terence (Mervyn) 1911-1977 **CLC 7; DAM DRAM**
See also CA 85-88; 73-76; CDBLB 1945-1960; DLB
13; MTCW

Ratushinskaya, Irina 1954- **CLC 54**
See also CA 129

Raven, Simon (Arthur Noel) 1927- **CLC 14**
See also CA 81-84

Rawley, Callman 1903-
See Rakosi, Carl
See also CA 21-24R; CANR 12, 32

Rawlings, Marjorie Kinnan 1896-1953 **TCLC 4**
See also AAYA 20; CA 104; 137; DLB 9, 22, 102;
JRDA; MAICYA; YABC 1

Ray, Satyajit 1921-1992 **CLC 16, 76; DAM MULT**
See also CA 114; 137

Read, Herbert Edward 1893-1968 **CLC 4**
See also CA 85-88; 25-28R; DLB 20, 149

Read, Piers Paul 1941- **CLC 4, 10, 25**
See also CA 21-24R; CANR 38; DLB 14; SATA
21

Reade, Charles 1814-1884 **NCLC 2**
See also DLB 21

Reade, Hamish
See Gray, Simon (James Holliday)

Reading, Peter 1946- **CLC 47**
See also CA 103; CANR 46; DLB 40

Reaney, James 1926- **CLC 13; DAC; DAM MST**
See also CA 41-44R; CAAS 15; CANR 42; DLB
68; SATA 43

Rebreanu, Liviu 1885-1944 **TCLC 28**

Rechy, John (Francisco) 1934- **CLC 1, 7, 14, 18; DAM MULT; HLC**
See also CA 5-8R; CAAS 4; CANR 6, 32; DLB
122; DLBY 82; HW; INT CANR-6

Redcam, Tom 1870-1933 **TCLC 25**

Reddin, Keith CLC 67

Redgrove, Peter (William) 1932- **CLC 6, 41**
See also CA 1-4R; CANR 3, 39; DLB 40

Redmon, Anne CLC 22
See also Nightingale, Anne Redmon
See also DLBY 86

Reed, Eliot
See Ambler, Eric

Reed, Ishmael 1938- **CLC 2, 3, 5, 6, 13, 32, 60; BLC; DAM MULT**
See also BW 2; CA 21-24R; CANR 25, 48; DLB 2,
5, 33, 169; DLBD 8; MTCW

Reed, John (Silas) 1887-1920 **TCLC 9**
See also CA 106

Reed, Lou CLC 21
See also Firbank, Louis

Reeve, Clara 1729-1807 **NCLC 19**
See also DLB 39

Reich, Wilhelm 1897-1957 **TCLC 57**

Reid, Christopher (John) 1949- **CLC 33**
See also CA 140; DLB 40

Reid, Desmond
See Moorcock, Michael (John)

Reid Banks, Lynne 1929-
See Banks, Lynne Reid
See also CA 1-4R; CANR 6, 22, 38; CLR 24; JRDA;
MAICYA; SATA 22, 75

Reilly, William K.
See Creasey, John

Reiner, Max
See Caldwell, (Janet Miriam) Taylor (Holland)

Reis, Ricardo
See Pessoa, Fernando (Antonio Nogueira)

Remarque, Erich Maria 1898-1970 **CLC 21; DA; DAB; DAC; DAM MST, NOV**
See also CA 77-80; 29-32R; DLB 56; MTCW

Remizov, A.
See Remizov, Aleksei (Mikhailovich)

Remizov, A. M.
See Remizov, Aleksei (Mikhailovich)

Remizov, Aleksei (Mikhailovich) 1877-1957 **TCLC 27**
See also CA 125; 133

Renan, Joseph Ernest 1823-1892 **NCLC 26**

Renard, Jules 1864-1910 **TCLC 17**
See also CA 117

Renault, Mary CLC 3, 11, 17
See also Challans, Mary
See also DLBY 83

Rendell, Ruth (Barbara) 1930- CLC 28, 48; DAM POP
See also Vine, Barbara
See also CA 109; CANR 32, 52; DLB 87; INT CANR-32; MTCW

Renoir, Jean 1894-1979 CLC 20
See also CA 129; 85-88

Resnais, Alain 1922- CLC 16

Reverdy, Pierre 1889-1960 CLC 53
See also CA 97-100; 89-92

Rexroth, Kenneth 1905-1982 CLC 1, 2, 6, 11, 22, 49; DAM POET
See also CA 5-8R; 107; CANR 14, 34; CDALB 1941-1968; DLB 16, 48, 165; DLBY 82; INT CANR-14; MTCW

Reyes, Alfonso 1889-1959 TCLC 33
See also CA 131; HW

Reyes y Basoalto, Ricardo Eliecer Neftali
See Neruda, Pablo

Reymont, Wladyslaw (Stanislaw) 1868(?)-1925 TCLC 5
See also CA 104

Reynolds, Jonathan 1942- CLC 6, 38
See also CA 65-68; CANR 28

Reynolds, Joshua 1723-1792 LC 15
See also DLB 104

Reynolds, Michael Shane 1937- CLC 44
See also CA 65-68; CANR 9

Reznikoff, Charles 1894-1976 CLC 9
See also CA 33-36; 61-64; CAP 2; DLB 28, 45

Rezzori (d'Arezzo), Gregor von 1914- CLC 25
See also CA 122; 136

Rhine, Richard
See Silverstein, Alvin

Rhodes, Eugene Manlove 1869-1934 TCLC 53

R'hoone
See Balzac, Honore de

Rhys, Jean 1890(?)-1979 CLC 2, 4, 6, 14, 19, 51; DAM NOV; SSC 21
See also CA 25-28R; 85-88; CANR 35; CDBLB 1945-1960; DLB 36, 117, 162; MTCW

Ribeiro, Darcy 1922-1997 CLC 34
See also CA 33-36R; 156

Ribeiro, Joao Ubaldo (Osorio Pimentel) 1941- CLC 10, 67
See also CA 81-84

Ribman, Ronald (Burt) 1932- CLC 7
See also CA 21-24R; CANR 46

Ricci, Nino 1959- CLC 70

See also CA 137

Rice, Anne 1941- CLC 41; DAM POP
See also AAYA 9; BEST 89 2; CA 65-68; CANR 12, 36, 53

Rice, Elmer (Leopold) 1892-1967 CLC 7, 49; DAM DRAM
See also CA 21-22; 25-28R; CAP 2; DLB 4, 7; MTCW

Rice, Tim(othy Miles Bindon) 1944- CLC 21
See also CA 103; CANR 46

Rich, Adrienne (Cecile) 1929- CLC 3, 6, 7, 11, 18, 36, 73, 76; DAM POET; PC 5
See also CA 9-12R; CANR 20, 53; DLB 5, 67; MTCW

Rich, Barbara
See Graves, Robert (von Ranke)

Rich, Robert
See Trumbo, Dalton

Richard, Keith CLC 17
See also Richards, Keith

Richards, David Adams 1950- CLC 59; DAC
See also CA 93-96; DLB 53

Richards, I(vor) A(rmstrong) 1893-1979 CLC 14, 24
See also CA 41-44R; 89-92; CANR 34; DLB 27

Richards, Keith 1943-
See Richard, Keith
See also CA 107

Richardson, Anne
See Roiphe, Anne (Richardson)

Richardson, Dorothy Miller 1873-1957 TCLC 3
See also CA 104; DLB 36

Richardson, Ethel Florence (Lindesay) 1870-1946
See Richardson, Henry Handel
See also CA 105

Richardson, Henry Handel TCLC 4
See also Richardson, Ethel Florence (Lindesay)

Richardson, John 1796-1852 NCLC 55; DAC
See also DLB 99

Richardson, Samuel 1689-1761 LC 1; DA; DAB; DAC; DAM MST, NOV; WLC
See also CDBLB 1660-1789; DLB 39

Richler, Mordecai 1931- CLC 3, 5, 9, 13, 18, 46, 70; DAC; DAM MST, NOV
See also AITN 1; CA 65-68; CANR 31; CLR 17; DLB 53; MAICYA; MTCW; SATA 44; SATA-Brief 27

Richter, Conrad (Michael) 1890-1968 CLC 30
See also CA 5-8R; 25-28R; CANR 23; DLB 9; MTCW; SATA 3

Ricostranza, Tom
See Ellis, Trey

Riddell, J. H. 1832-1906 TCLC 40

Riding, Laura CLC 3, 7
See also Jackson, Laura (Riding)

Riefenstahl, Berta Helene Amalia 1902-
See Riefenstahl, Leni
See also CA 108

Riefenstahl, Leni CLC 16
See also Riefenstahl, Berta Helene Amalia

Riffe, Ernest
See Bergman, (Ernst) Ingmar

Riggs, (Rolla) Lynn 1899-1954 TCLC 56; DAM MULT
See also CA 144; DLB 175; NNAL

Riley, James Whitcomb 1849-1916 TCLC 51; DAM POET
See also CA 118, 137; MAICYA; SATA 17

Riley, Tex
See Creasey, John

Rilke, Rainer Maria 1875-1926 TCLC 1, 6, 19; DAM POET; PC 2
See also CA 104; 132; DLB 81; MTCW

Rimbaud, (Jean Nicolas) Arthur 1854-1891 NCLC 4, 35; DA; DAB; DAC; DAM MST, POET; PC 3; WLC

Rinehart, Mary Roberts 1876-1958 TCLC 52
See also CA 108

Ringmaster, The
See Mencken, H(enry) L(ouis)

Ringwood, Gwen(dolyn Margaret) Pharis 1910-1984 CLC 48
See also CA 148; 112; DLB 88

Rio, Michel 19(?)- CLC 43

Ritsos, Giannes
See Ritsos, Yannis

Ritsos, Yannis 1909-1990 CLC 6, 13, 31
See also CA 77-80; 133; CANR 39; MTCW

Ritter, Erika 1948(?)- CLC 52

Rivera, Jose Eustasio 1889-1928 TCLC 35
See also HW

Rivers, Conrad Kent 1933-1968 CLC 1
See also BW 1; CA 85-88; DLB 41

Rivers, Elfrida
See Bradley, Marion Zimmer

Riverside, John
See Heinlein, Robert A(nson)

Rizal, Jose 1861-1896 NCLC 27

Roa Bastos, Augusto (Antonio) 1917- CLC 45; DAM MULT; HLC
See also CA 131; DLB 113; HW

Robbe-Grillet, Alain 1922- CLC 1, 2, 4, 6, 8, 10, 14, 43
See also CA 9-12R; CANR 33; DLB 83; MTCW

Robbins, Harold 1916- **CLC 5; DAM NOV**
See also CA 73-76; CANR 26, 54; MTCW

Robbins, Thomas Eugene 1936-
See Robbins, Tom
See also CA 81-84; CANR 29; DAM NOV, POP;
MTCW

Robbins, Tom CLC 9, 32, 64
See also Robbins, Thomas Eugene
See also BEST 90 3; DLBY 80

Robbins, Trina 1938- **CLC 21**
See also CA 128

Roberts, Charles G(eorge) D(ouglas) 1860-1943
TCLC 8
See also CA 105; CLR 33; DLB 92; SATA 88;
SATA-Brief 29

Roberts, Elizabeth Madox 1886-1941 **TCLC 68**
See also CA 111; DLB 9, 54, 102; SATA 33; SATA-
Brief 27

Roberts, Kate 1891-1985 **CLC 15**
See also CA 107; 116

Roberts, Keith (John Kingston) 1935- **CLC 14**
See also CA 25-28R; CANR 46

Roberts, Kenneth (Lewis) 1885-1957 **TCLC 23**
See also CA 109; DLB 9

Roberts, Michele (B.) 1949- **CLC 48**
See also CA 115

Robertson, Ellis
See Ellison, Harlan (Jay); Silverberg, Robert

Robertson, Thomas William 1829-1871 **NCLC 35;
DAM DRAM**

Robinson, Edwin Arlington 1869-1935 **TCLC 5;
DA; DAC; DAM MST, POET; PC 1**
See also CA 104; 133; CDALB 1865-1917; DLB
54; MTCW

Robinson, Henry Crabb 1775-1867 **NCLC 15**
See also DLB 107

Robinson, Jill 1936- **CLC 10**
See also CA 102; INT 102

Robinson, Kim Stanley 1952- **CLC 34**
See also CA 126

Robinson, Lloyd
See Silverberg, Robert

Robinson, Marilynne 1944- **CLC 25**
See also CA 116

Robinson, Smokey CLC 21
See also Robinson, William, Jr.

Robinson, William, Jr. 1940-
See Robinson, Smokey
See also CA 116

Robison, Mary 1949- **CLC 42, 98**
See also CA 113; 116; DLB 130; INT 116

Rod, Edouard 1857-1910 **TCLC 52**

Roddenberry, Eugene Wesley 1921-1991
See Roddenberry, Gene
See also CA 110; 135; CANR 37; SATA 45; SATA-
Obit 69

Roddenberry, Gene CLC 17
See also Roddenberry, Eugene Wesley
See also AAYA 5; SATA-Obit 69

Rodgers, Mary 1931- **CLC 12**
See also CA 49-52; CANR 8, 55; CLR 20; INT
CANR-8; JRDA; MAICYA; SATA 8

Rodgers, W(illiam) R(obert) 1909-1969 **CLC 7**
See also CA 85-88; DLB 20

Rodman, Eric
See Silverberg, Robert

Rodman, Howard 1920(?)-1985 **CLC 65**
See also CA 118

Rodman, Maia
See Wojciechowska, Maia (Teresa)

Rodriguez, Claudio 1934- **CLC 10**
See also DLB 134

Roelvaag, O(le) E(dvart) 1876-1931 **TCLC 17**
See also CA 117; DLB 9

Roethke, Theodore (Huebner) 1908-1963 **CLC 1, 3,
8, 11, 19, 46; DAM POET; PC 15**
See also CA 81-84; CABS 2; CDALB 1941-1968;
DLB 5; MTCW

Rogers, Thomas Hunton 1927- **CLC 57**
See also CA 89-92; INT 89-92

Rogers, Will(iam Penn Adair) 1879-1935 **TCLC 8;
DAM MULT**
See also CA 105; 144; DLB 11; NNAL

Rogin, Gilbert 1929- **CLC 18**
See also CA 65-68; CANR 15

Rohan, Koda TCLC 22
See also Koda Shigeyuki

Rohmer, Eric CLC 16
See also Scherer, Jean-Marie Maurice

Rohmer, Sax TCLC 28
See also Ward, Arthur Henry Sarsfield
See also DLB 70

Roiphe, Anne (Richardson) 1935- **CLC 3, 9**
See also CA 89-92; CANR 45; DLBY 80; INT 89-
92

Rojas, Fernando de 1465-1541 **LC 23**

**Rolfe, Frederick (William Serafino Austin Lewis
Mary)** 1860-1913 **TCLC 12**
See also CA 107; DLB 34, 156

Rolland, Romain 1866-1944 **TCLC 23**
See also CA 118; DLB 65

Rolle, Richard c. 1300-c. 1349 **CMLC 21**
See also DLB 146

Rolvaag, O(le) E(dvart)

See Roelvaag, O(le) E(dvart)

Romain Arnaud, Saint
See Aragon, Louis

Romains, Jules 1885-1972 **CLC 7**
See also CA 85-88; CANR 34; DLB 65; MTCW

Romero, Jose Ruben 1890-1952 **TCLC 14**
See also CA 114; 131; HW

Ronsard, Pierre de 1524-1585 **LC 6; PC 11**

Rooke, Leon 1934- **CLC 25, 34; DAM POP**
See also CA 25-28R; CANR 23, 53

Roosevelt, Theodore 1858-1919 **TCLC 69**
See also CA 115; DLB 47

Roper, William 1498-1578 **LC 10**

Roquelaure, A. N.
See Rice, Anne

Rosa, Joao Guimaraes 1908-1967 **CLC 23**
See also CA 89-92; DLB 113

Rose, Wendy 1948- **CLC 85; DAM MULT; PC 13**
See also CA 53-56; CANR 5, 51; DLB 175; NNAL;
SATA 12

Rosen, Richard (Dean) 1949- **CLC 39**
See also CA 77-80; INT CANR-30

Rosenberg, Isaac 1890-1918 **TCLC 12**
See also CA 107; DLB 20

Rosenblatt, Joe CLC 15
See also Rosenblatt, Joseph

Rosenblatt, Joseph 1933-
See Rosenblatt, Joe
See also CA 89-92; INT 89-92

Rosenfeld, Samuel 1896-1963
See Tzara, Tristan
See also CA 89-92

Rosenstock, Sami
See Tzara, Tristan

Rosenstock, Samuel
See Tzara, Tristan

Rosenthal, M(acha) L(ouis) 1917-1996 **CLC 28**
See also CA 1-4R; 152; CAAS 6; CANR 4, 51;
DLB 5; SATA 59

Ross, Barnaby
See Dannay, Frederic

Ross, Bernard L.
See Follett, Ken(neth Martin)

Ross, J. H.
See Lawrence, T(homas) E(dward)

Ross, Martin
See Martin, Violet Florence
See also DLB 135

Ross, (James) Sinclair 1908- **CLC 13; DAC; DAM
MST; SSC 24**

See also CA 73-76; DLB 88

Rossetti, Christina (Georgina) 1830-1894 **NCLC 2, 50; DA; DAB; DAC; DAM MST, POET; PC 7; WLC**
See also DLB 35, 163; MAICYA; SATA 20

Rossetti, Dante Gabriel 1828-1882 **NCLC 4; DA; DAB; DAC; DAM MST, POET; WLC**
See also CDBLB 1832-1890; DLB 35

Rossner, Judith (Perelman) 1935- **CLC 6, 9, 29**
See also AITN 2; BEST 90 3; CA 17-20R; CANR 18, 51; DLB 6; INT CANR-18; MTCW

Rostand, Edmond (Eugene Alexis) 1868-1918 **TCLC 6, 37; DA; DAB; DAC; DAM DRAM, MST**
See also CA 104; 126; MTCW

Roth, Henry 1906-1995 **CLC 2, 6, 11**
See also CA 11-12; 149; CANR 38; CAP 1; DLB 28; MTCW

Roth, Joseph 1894-1939 **TCLC 33**
See also DLB 85

Roth, Philip (Milton) 1933- **CLC 1, 2, 3, 4, 6, 9, 15, 22, 31, 47, 66, 86; DA; DAB; DAC; DAM MST, NOV, POP; WLC**
See also BEST 90 3; CA 1-4R; CANR 1, 22, 36, 55; CDALB 1968-1988; DLB 2, 28, 173; DLBY 82; MTCW

Rothenberg, Jerome 1931- **CLC 6, 57**
See also CA 45-48; CANR 1; DLB 5

Roumain, Jacques (Jean Baptiste) 1907-1944 **TCLC 19; BLC; DAM MULT**
See also BW 1; CA 117; 125

Rourke, Constance (Mayfield) 1885-1941 **TCLC 12**
See also CA 107; YABC 1

Rousseau, Jean-Baptiste 1671-1741 **LC 9**

Rousseau, Jean-Jacques 1712-1778 **LC 14, 36; DA; DAB; DAC; DAM MST; WLC**

Roussel, Raymond 1877-1933 **TCLC 20**
See also CA 117

Rovit, Earl (Herbert) 1927- **CLC 7**
See also CA 5-8R; CANR 12

Rowe, Nicholas 1674-1718 **LC 8**
See also DLB 84

Rowley, Ames Dorrance
See Lovecraft, H(oward) P(hillips)

Rowson, Susanna Haswell 1762(?)-1824 **NCLC 5**
See also DLB 37

Roy, Gabrielle 1909-1983 **CLC 10, 14; DAB; DAC; DAM MST**
See also CA 53-56; 110; CANR 5; DLB 68; MTCW

Rozewicz, Tadeusz 1921- **CLC 9, 23; DAM POET**
See also CA 108; CANR 36; MTCW

Ruark, Gibbons 1941- **CLC 3**
See also CA 33-36R; CAAS 23; CANR 14, 31, 57; DLB 120

Rubens, Bernice (Ruth) 1923- **CLC 19, 31**
See also CA 25-28R; CANR 33; DLB 14; MTCW

Rubin, Harold
See Robbins, Harold

Rudkin, (James) David 1936- **CLC 14**
See also CA 89-92; DLB 13

Rudnik, Raphael 1933- **CLC 7**
See also CA 29-32R

Ruffian, M.
See Hasek, Jaroslav (Matej Frantisek)

Ruiz, Jose Martinez CLC 11
See also Martinez Ruiz, Jose

Rukeyser, Muriel 1913-1980 **CLC 6, 10, 15, 27; DAM POET; PC 12**
See also CA 5-8R; 93-96; CANR 26; DLB 48; MTCW; SATA-Obit 22

Rule, Jane (Vance) 1931- **CLC 27**
See also CA 25-28R; CAAS 18; CANR 12; DLB 60

Rulfo, Juan 1918-1986 **CLC 8, 80; DAM MULT; HLC**
See also CA 85-88; 118; CANR 26; DLB 113; HW; MTCW

Rumi, Jalal al-Din 1297-1373 **CMLC 20**

Runeberg, Johan 1804-1877 **NCLC 41**

Runyon, (Alfred) Damon 1884(?)-1946 **TCLC 10**
See also CA 107; DLB 11, 86, 171

Rush, Norman 1933- **CLC 44**
See also CA 121; 126; INT 126

Rushdie, (Ahmed) Salman 1947- **CLC 23, 31, 55, 100; DAB; DAC; DAM MST, NOV, POP**
See also BEST 89 3; CA 108; 111; CANR 33, 56; INT 111; MTCW

Rushforth, Peter (Scott) 1945- **CLC 19**
See also CA 101

Ruskin, John 1819-1900 **TCLC 63**
See also CA 114; 129; CDBLB 1832-1890; DLB 55, 163; SATA 24

Russ, Joanna 1937- **CLC 15**
See also CA 25-28R; CANR 11, 31; DLB 8; MTCW

Russell, George William 1867-1935
See Baker, Jean H.
See also CA 104; 153; CDBLB 1890-1914; DAM POET

Russell, (Henry) Ken(neth Alfred) 1927- **CLC 16**
See also CA 105

Russell, Willy 1947- **CLC 60**

Rutherford, Mark TCLC 25
See also White, William Hale
See also DLB 18

Ruyslinck, Ward 1929- **CLC 14**
See also Belser, Reimond Karel Maria de

Ryan, Cornelius (John) 1920-1974 **CLC 7**
See also CA 69-72; 53-56; CANR 38

Ryan, Michael 1946- **CLC 65**
See also CA 49-52; DLBY 82

Rybakov, Anatoli (Naumovich) 1911- **CLC 23, 53**
See also CA 126; 135; SATA 79

Ryder, Jonathan
See Ludlum, Robert

Ryga, George 1932-1987 **CLC 14; DAC; DAM MST**
See also CA 101; 124; CANR 43; DLB 60

S. S.
See Sassoon, Siegfried (Lorraine)

Saba, Umberto 1883-1957 **TCLC 33**
See also CA 144; DLB 114

Sabatini, Rafael 1875-1950 **TCLC 47**

Sabato, Ernesto (R.) 1911- **CLC 10, 23; DAM MULT; HLC**
See also CA 97-100; CANR 32; DLB 145; HW; MTCW

Sacastru, Martin
See Bioy Casares, Adolfo

Sacher-Masoch, Leopold von 1836(?)-1895 **NCLC 31**

Sachs, Marilyn (Stickle) 1927- **CLC 35**
See also AAYA 2; CA 17-20R; CANR 13, 47; CLR 2; JRDA; MAICYA; SAAS 2; SATA 3, 68

Sachs, Nelly 1891-1970 **CLC 14, 98**
See also CA 17-18; 25-28R; CAP 2

Sackler, Howard (Oliver) 1929-1982 **CLC 14**
See also CA 61-64; 108; CANR 30; DLB 7

Sacks, Oliver (Wolf) 1933- **CLC 67**
See also CA 53-56; CANR 28, 50; INT CANR-28; MTCW

Sade, Donatien Alphonse Francois Comte 1740-1814 **NCLC 47**

Sadoff, Ira 1945- **CLC 9**
See also CA 53-56; CANR 5, 21; DLB 120

Saetone
See Camus, Albert

Safire, William 1929- **CLC 10**
See also CA 17-20R; CANR 31, 54

Sagan, Carl (Edward) 1934-1996 **CLC 30**
See also AAYA 2; CA 25-28R; 155; CANR 11, 36; MTCW; SATA 58

Sagan, Francoise CLC 3, 6, 9, 17, 36
See also Quoirez, Francoise
See also DLB 83

Sahgal, Nayantara (Pandit) 1927- **CLC 41**
See also CA 9-12R; CANR 11

Saint, H(arry) F. 1941- **CLC 50**
See also CA 127

St. Aubin de Teran, Lisa 1953-
See Teran, Lisa St. Aubin de
See also CA 118; 126; INT 126

Sainte-Beuve, Charles Augustin 1804-1869 **NCLC 5**

Saint-Exupery, Antoine (Jean Baptiste Marie Roger) de 1900-1944 **TCLC 2, 56; DAM NOV; WLC**
See also CA 108; 132; CLR 10; DLB 72; MAICYA; MTCW; SATA 20

St. John, David
See Hunt, E(verette) Howard, (Jr.)

Saint-John Perse
See Leger, (Marie-Rene Auguste) Alexis Saint-Leger

Saintsbury, George (Edward Bateman) 1845-1933 **TCLC 31**
See also DLB 57, 149

Sait Faik TCLC 23
See also Abasiyanik, Sait Faik

Saki TCLC 3; SSC 12
See also Munro, H(ector) H(ugh)

Sala, George Augustus NCLC 46

Salama, Hannu 1936- **CLC 18**

Salamanca, J(ack) R(ichard) 1922- **CLC 4, 15**
See also CA 25-28R

Sale, J. Kirkpatrick
See Sale, Kirkpatrick

Sale, Kirkpatrick 1937- **CLC 68**
See also CA 13-16R; CANR 10

Salinas, Luis Omar 1937- **CLC 90; DAM MULT; HLC**
See also CA 131; DLB 82; HW

Salinas (y Serrano), Pedro 1891(?)-1951 **TCLC 17**
See also CA 117; DLB 134

Salinger, J(erome) D(avid) 1919- **CLC 1, 3, 8, 12, 55, 56; DA; DAB; DAC; DAM MST, NOV, POP; SSC 2; WLC**
See also AAYA 2; CA 5-8R; CANR 39; CDALB 1941-1968; CLR 18; DLB 2, 102, 173; MAICYA; MTCW; SATA 67

Salisbury, John
See Caute, David

Salter, James 1925- **CLC 7, 52, 59**
See also CA 73-76; DLB 130

Saltus, Edgar (Everton) 1855-1921 **TCLC 8**
See also CA 105

Saltykov, Mikhail Evgrafovich 1826-1889 **NCLC 16**

Samarakis, Antonis 1919- **CLC 5**
See also CA 25-28R; CAAS 16; CANR 36

Sanchez, Florencio 1875-1910 **TCLC 37**
See also CA 153; HW

Sanchez, Luis Rafael 1936- **CLC 23**
See also CA 128; DLB 145; HW

Sanchez, Sonia 1934- **CLC 5; BLC; DAM MULT; PC 9**
See also BW 2; CA 33-36R; CANR 24, 49; CLR 18; DLB 41; DLBD 8; MAICYA; MTCW; SATA 22

Sand, George 1804-1876 **NCLC 2, 42, 57; DA; DAB; DAC; DAM MST, NOV; WLC**
See also DLB 119

Sandburg, Carl (August) 1878-1967 **CLC 1, 4, 10, 15, 35; DA; DAB; DAC; DAM MST, POET; PC 2; WLC**
See also CA 5-8R; 25-28R; CANR 35; CDALB 1865-1917; DLB 17, 54; MAICYA; MTCW; SATA 8

Sandburg, Charles
See Sandburg, Carl (August)

Sandburg, Charles A.
See Sandburg, Carl (August)

Sanders, (James) Ed(ward) 1939- **CLC 53**
See also CA 13-16R; CAAS 21; CANR 13, 44; DLB 16

Sanders, Lawrence 1920- **CLC 41; DAM POP**
See also BEST 89 4; CA 81-84; CANR 33; MTCW

Sanders, Noah
See Blount, Roy (Alton), Jr.

Sanders, Winston P.
See Anderson, Poul (William)

Sandoz, Mari(e Susette) 1896-1966 **CLC 28**
See also CA 1-4R; 25-28R; CANR 17; DLB 9; MTCW; SATA 5

Saner, Reg(inald Anthony) 1931- **CLC 9**
See also CA 65-68

Sannazaro, Jacopo 1456(?)-1530 **LC 8**

Sansom, William 1912-1976 **CLC 2, 6; DAM NOV; SSC 21**
See also CA 5-8R; 65-68; CANR 42; DLB 139; MTCW

Santayana, George 1863-1952 **TCLC 40**
See also CA 115; DLB 54, 71; DLBD 13

Santiago, Danny CLC 33
See also James, Daniel (Lewis)
See also DLB 122

Santmyer, Helen Hoover 1895-1986 **CLC 33**
See also CA 1-4R; 118; CANR 15, 33; DLBY 84; MTCW

Santos, Bienvenido N(uqui) 1911-1996 **CLC 22; DAM MULT**
See also CA 101; 151; CANR 19, 46

Sapper TCLC 44
See also McNeile, Herman Cyril

Sapphire 1950- **CLC 99**

Sappho fl. 6th cent. B.C.- **CMLC 3; DAM POET; PC 5**
See also DLB 176

Sarduy, Severo 1937-1993 **CLC 6, 97**
See also CA 89-92; 142; DLB 113; HW

Sargeson, Frank 1903-1982 **CLC 31**
See also CA 25-28R; 106; CANR 38

Sarmiento, Felix Ruben Garcia
See Dario, Ruben

Saroyan, William 1908-1981 **CLC 1, 8, 10, 29, 34, 56; DA; DAB; DAC; DAM DRAM, MST, NOV; SSC 21; WLC**
See also CA 5-8R; 103; CANR 30; DLB 7, 9, 86; DLBY 81; MTCW; SATA 23; SATA-Obit 24

Sarraute, Nathalie 1900- **CLC 1, 2, 4, 8, 10, 31, 80**
See also CA 9-12R; CANR 23; DLB 83; MTCW

Sarton, (Eleanor) May 1912-1995 **CLC 4, 14, 49, 91; DAM POET**
See also CA 1-4R; 149; CANR 1, 34, 55; DLB 48; DLBY 81; INT CANR-34; MTCW; SATA 36; SATA-Obit 86

Sartre, Jean-Paul 1905-1980 **CLC 1, 4, 7, 9, 13, 18, 24, 44, 50, 52; DA; DAB; DAC; DAM DRAM, MST, NOV; DC 3; WLC**
See also CA 9-12R; 97-100; CANR 21; DLB 72; MTCW

Sassoon, Siegfried (Lorraine) 1886-1967 **CLC 36; DAB; DAM MST, NOV, POET; PC 12**
See also CA 104; 25-28R; CANR 36; DLB 20; MTCW

Satterfield, Charles
See Pohl, Frederik

Saul, John (W. III) 1942- **CLC 46; DAM NOV, POP**
See also AAYA 10; BEST 90 4; CA 81-84; CANR 16, 40

Saunders, Caleb
See Heinlein, Robert A(nson)

Saura (Atares), Carlos 1932- **CLC 20**
See also CA 114; 131; HW

Sauser-Hall, Frederic 1887-1961 **CLC 18**
See also Cendrars, Blaise
See also CA 102; 93-96; CANR 36; MTCW

Saussure, Ferdinand de 1857-1913 **TCLC 49**

Savage, Catharine
See Brosman, Catharine Savage

Savage, Thomas 1915- **CLC 40**
See also CA 126; 132; CAAS 15; INT 132

Savan, Glenn 19(?)- **CLC 50**

Sayers, Dorothy L(eigh) 1893-1957 **TCLC 2, 15; DAM POP**
See also CA 104; 119; CDBLB 1914-1945; DLB 10, 36, 77, 100; MTCW

Sayers, Valerie 1952- **CLC 50**
See also CA 134

Seferiades, Giorgos Stylianou 1900-1971
See Seferis, George
See also CA 5-8R; 33-36R; CANR 5, 36; MTCW

Seferis, George CLC 5, 11
See also Seferiades, Giorgos Stylianou

Segal, Erich (Wolf) 1937- CLC 3, 10; DAM POP
See also BEST 89 1; CA 25-28R; CANR 20, 36;
DLBY 86; INT CANR-20; MTCW

Seger, Bob 1945- CLC 35

Seghers, Anna CLC 7
See also Radvanyi, Netty
See also DLB 69

Seidel, Frederick (Lewis) 1936- CLC 18
See also CA 13-16R; CANR 8; DLBY 84

Seifert, Jaroslav 1901-1986 CLC 34, 44, 93
See also CA 127; MTCW

Sei Shonagon c. 966-1017(?) CMLC 6

Selby, Hubert, Jr. 1928- CLC 1, 2, 4, 8; SSC 20
See also CA 13-16R; CANR 33; DLB 2

Selzer, Richard 1928- CLC 74
See also CA 65-68; CANR 14

Sembene, Ousmane
See Ousmane, Sembene

Senancour, Etienne Pivert de 1770-1846 NCLC 16
See also DLB 119

Sender, Ramon (Jose) 1902-1982 CLC 8; DAM
MULT; HLC
See also CA 5-8R; 105; CANR 8; HW; MTCW

Seneca, Lucius Annaeus 4B.C.-65 CMLC 6; DAM
DRAM; DC 5

Senghor, Leopold Sedar 1906- CLC 54; BLC; DAM
MULT, POET
See also BW 2; CA 116; 125; CANR 47; MTCW

Serling, (Edward) Rod(man) 1924-1975 CLC 30
See also AAYA 14; AITN 1; CA 65-68; 57-60; DLB
26

Serna, Ramon Gomez de la
See Gomez de la Serna, Ramon

Serpieres
See Guillevic, (Eugene)

Service, Robert
See Service, Robert W(illiam)
See also DAB; DLB 92

Service, Robert W(illiam) 1874(?)-1958 TCLC 15;
DA; DAC; DAM MST, POET; WLC
See also Service, Robert
See also CA 115; 140; SATA 20

Seth, Vikram 1952- CLC 43, 90; DAM MULT
See also CA 121; 127; CANR 50; DLB 120; INT
127

Seton, Cynthia Propper 1926-1982 CLC 27
See also CA 5-8R; 108; CANR 7

Seton, Ernest (Evan) Thompson 1860-1946 TCLC
31
See also CA 109; DLB 92; DLBD 13; JRDA; SATA
18

Seton-Thompson, Ernest
See Seton, Ernest (Evan) Thompson

Settle, Mary Lee 1918- CLC 19, 61
See also CA 89-92; CAAS 1; CANR 44; DLB 6;
INT 89-92

Seuphor, Michel
See Arp, Jean

Sevigne, Marie (de Rabutin-Chantal) Marquise de
1626-1696 LC 11

Sexton, Anne (Harvey) 1928-1974 CLC 2, 4, 6, 8,
10, 15, 53; DA; DAB; DAC; DAM MST,
POET; PC 2; WLC
See also CA 1-4R; 53-56; CABS 2; CANR 3, 36;
CDALB 1941-1968; DLB 5, 169; MTCW; SATA
10

Shaara, Michael (Joseph, Jr.) 1929-1988 CLC 15;
DAM POP
See also AITN 1; CA 102; 125; CANR 52; DLBY
83

Shackleton, C. C.
See Aldiss, Brian W(ilson)

Shacochis, Bob CLC 39
See also Shacochis, Robert G.

Shacochis, Robert G. 1951-
See Shacochis, Bob
See also CA 119; 124; INT 124

Shaffer, Anthony (Joshua) 1926- CLC 19; DAM
DRAM
See also CA 110; 116; DLB 13

Shaffer, Peter (Levin) 1926- CLC 5, 14, 18, 37, 60;
DAB; DAM DRAM, MST
See also CA 25-28R; CANR 25, 47; CDBLB 1960
to Present; DLB 13; MTCW

Shakey, Bernard
See Young, Neil

Shalamov, Varlam (Tikhonovich) 1907(?)-1982 CLC
18
See also CA 129; 105

Shamlu, Ahmad 1925- CLC 10

Shammas, Anton 1951- CLC 55

Shange, Ntozake 1948- CLC 8, 25, 38, 74; BLC;
DAM DRAM, MULT; DC 3
See also AAYA 9; BW 2; CA 85-88; CABS 3;
CANR 27, 48; DLB 38; MTCW

Shanley, John Patrick 1950- CLC 75
See also CA 128; 133

Shapcott, Thomas W(illiam) 1935- CLC 38
See also CA 69-72; CANR 49

Shapiro, Jane CLC 76

Shapiro, Karl (Jay) 1913- CLC 4, 8, 15, 53
See also CA 1-4R; CAAS 6; CANR 1, 36; DLB 48;
MTCW

Sharp, William 1855-1905 TCLC 39
See also DLB 156

Sharpe, Thomas Ridley 1928-
See Sharpe, Tom
See also CA 114; 122; INT 122

Sharpe, Tom CLC 36
See also Sharpe, Thomas Ridley
See also DLB 14

Shaw, Bernard TCLC 45
See also Shaw, George Bernard
See also BW 1

Shaw, G. Bernard
See Shaw, George Bernard

Shaw, George Bernard 1856-1950 TCLC 3, 9, 21;
DA; DAB; DAC; DAM DRAM, MST; WLC
See also Shaw, Bernard
See also CA 104; 128; CDBLB 1914-1945; DLB 10,
57; MTCW

Shaw, Henry Wheeler 1818-1885 NCLC 15
See also DLB 11

Shaw, Irwin 1913-1984 CLC 7, 23, 34; DAM DRAM,
POP
See also AITN 1; CA 13-16R; 112; CANR 21;
CDALB 1941-1968; DLB 6, 102; DLBY 84;
MTCW

Shaw, Robert 1927-1978 CLC 5
See also AITN 1; CA 1-4R; 81-84; CANR 4; DLB
13, 14

Shaw, T. E.
See Lawrence, T(homas) E(dward)

Shawn, Wallace 1943- CLC 41
See also CA 112

Shea, Lisa 1953- CLC 86
See also CA 147

Sheed, Wilfrid (John Joseph) 1930- CLC 2, 4, 10,
53
See also CA 65-68; CANR 30; DLB 6; MTCW

Sheldon, Alice Hastings Bradley 1915(?)-1987
See Tiptree, James, Jr.
See also CA 108; 122; CANR 34; INT 108; MTCW

Sheldon, John
See Bloch, Robert (Albert)

Shelley, Mary Wollstonecraft (Godwin) 1797-1851
NCLC 14, 59; DA; DAB; DAC; DAM MST,
NOV; WLC
See also AAYA 20; CDBLB 1789-1832; DLB 110,
116, 159; SATA 29

Shelley, Percy Bysshe 1792-1822 NCLC 18; DA;
DAB; DAC; DAM MST, POET; PC 14; WLC
See also CDBLB 1789-1832; DLB 96, 110, 158

Shepard, Jim 1956- CLC 36
See also CA 137; SATA 90

Shepard, Lucius 1947- **CLC 34**
See also CA 128; 141

Shepard, Sam 1943- **CLC 4, 6, 17, 34, 41, 44; DAM DRAM; DC 5**
See also AAYA 1; CA 69-72; CABS 3; CANR 22; DLB 7; MTCW

Shepherd, Michael
See Ludlum, Robert

Sherburne, Zoa (Morin) 1912- **CLC 30**
See also AAYA 13; CA 1-4R; CANR 3, 37; MAICYA; SAAS 18; SATA 3

Sheridan, Frances 1724-1766 **LC 7**
See also DLB 39, 84

Sheridan, Richard Brinsley 1751-1816 **NCLC 5; DA; DAB; DAC; DAM DRAM, MST; DC 1; WLC**
See also CDBLB 1660-1789; DLB 89

Sherman, Jonathan Marc CLC 55

Sherman, Martin 1941(?)- **CLC 19**
See also CA 116; 123

Sherwin, Judith Johnson 1936- **CLC 7, 15**
See also CA 25-28R; CANR 34

Sherwood, Frances 1940- **CLC 81**
See also CA 146

Sherwood, Robert E(mmet) 1896-1955 **TCLC 3; DAM DRAM**
See also CA 104; 153; DLB 7, 26

Shestov, Lev 1866-1938 **TCLC 56**

Shevchenko, Taras 1814-1861 **NCLC 54**

Shiel, M(atthew) P(hipps) 1865-1947 **TCLC 8**
See also CA 106; DLB 153

Shields, Carol 1935- **CLC 91; DAC**
See also CA 81-84; CANR 51

Shields, David 1956- **CLC 97**
See also CA 124; CANR 48

Shiga, Naoya 1883-1971 **CLC 33; SSC 23**
See also CA 101; 33-36R

Shilts, Randy 1951-1994 **CLC 85**
See also AAYA 19; CA 115; 127; 144; CANR 45; INT 127

Shimazaki, Haruki 1872-1943
See Shimazaki Toson
See also CA 105; 134

Shimazaki Toson TCLC 5
See also Shimazaki, Haruki

Sholokhov, Mikhail (Aleksandrovich) 1905-1984 **CLC 7, 15**
See also CA 101; 112; MTCW; SATA-Obit 36

Shone, Patric
See Hanley, James

Shreve, Susan Richards 1939- **CLC 23**

See also CA 49-52; CAAS 5; CANR 5, 38; MAICYA; SATA 46; SATA-Brief 41

Shue, Larry 1946-1985 **CLC 52; DAM DRAM**
See also CA 145; 117

Shu-Jen, Chou 1881-1936
See Lu Hsun
See also CA 104

Shulman, Alix Kates 1932- **CLC 2, 10**
See also CA 29-32R; CANR 43; SATA 7

Shuster, Joe 1914- **CLC 21**

Shute, Nevil CLC 30
See also Norway, Nevil Shute

Shuttle, Penelope (Diane) 1947- **CLC 7**
See also CA 93-96; CANR 39; DLB 14, 40

Sidney, Mary 1561-1621 **LC 19**

Sidney, Sir Philip 1554-1586 **LC 19; DA; DAB; DAC; DAM MST, POET**
See also CDBLB Before 1660; DLB 167

Siegel, Jerome 1914-1996 **CLC 21**
See also CA 116; 151

Siegel, Jerry
See Siegel, Jerome

Sienkiewicz, Henryk (Adam Alexander Pius) 1846-1916 **TCLC 3**
See also CA 104; 134

Sierra, Gregorio Martinez
See Martinez Sierra, Gregorio

Sierra, Maria (de la O'LeJarraga) Martinez
See Martinez Sierra, Maria (de la O'LeJarraga)

Sigal, Clancy 1926- **CLC 7**
See also CA 1-4R

Sigourney, Lydia Howard (Huntley) 1791-1865 **NCLC 21**
See also DLB 1, 42, 73

Siguenza y Gongora, Carlos de 1645-1700 **LC 8**

Sigurjonsson, Johann 1880-1919 **TCLC 27**

Sikelianos, Angelos 1884-1951 **TCLC 39**

Silkin, Jon 1930- **CLC 2, 6, 43**
See also CA 5-8R; CAAS 5; DLB 27

Silko, Leslie (Marmon) 1948- **CLC 23, 74; DA; DAC; DAM MST, MULT, POP**
See also AAYA 14; CA 115; 122; CANR 45; DLB 143, 175; NNAL

Sillanpaa, Frans Eemil 1888-1964 **CLC 19**
See also CA 129; 93-96; MTCW

Sillitoe, Alan 1928- **CLC 1, 3, 6, 10, 19, 57**
See also AITN 1; CA 9-12R; CAAS 2; CANR 8, 26, 55; CDBLB 1960 to Present; DLB 14, 139; MTCW; SATA 61

Silone, Ignazio 1900-1978 **CLC 4**

See also CA 25-28; 81-84; CANR 34; CAP 2; MTCW

Silver, Joan Micklin 1935- **CLC 20**
See also CA 114; 121; INT 121

Silver, Nicholas
See Faust, Frederick (Schiller)

Silverberg, Robert 1935- **CLC 7; DAM POP**
See also CA 1-4R; CAAS 3; CANR 1, 20, 36; DLB 8; INT CANR-20; MAICYA; MTCW; SATA 13, 91

Silverstein, Alvin 1933- **CLC 17**
See also CA 49-52; CANR 2; CLR 25; JRDA; MAICYA; SATA 8, 69

Silverstein, Virginia B(arbara Opshelor) 1937- **CLC 17**
See also CA 49-52; CANR 2; CLR 25; JRDA; MAICYA; SATA 8, 69

Sim, Georges
See Simenon, Georges (Jacques Christian)

Simak, Clifford D(onald) 1904-1988 **CLC 1, 55**
See also CA 1-4R; 125; CANR 1, 35; DLB 8; MTCW; SATA-Obit 56

Simenon, Georges (Jacques Christian) 1903-1989 **CLC 1, 2, 3, 8, 18, 47; DAM POP**
See also CA 85-88; 129; CANR 35; DLB 72; DLBY 89; MTCW

Simic, Charles 1938- **CLC 6, 9, 22, 49, 68; DAM POET**
See also CA 29-32R; CAAS 4; CANR 12, 33, 52; DLB 105

Simmel, Georg 1858-1918 **TCLC 64**

Simmons, Charles (Paul) 1924- **CLC 57**
See also CA 89-92; INT 89-92

Simmons, Dan 1948- **CLC 44; DAM POP**
See also AAYA 16; CA 138; CANR 53

Simmons, James (Stewart Alexander) 1933- **CLC 43**
See also CA 105; CAAS 21; DLB 40

Simms, William Gilmore 1806-1870 **NCLC 3**
See also DLB 3, 30, 59, 73

Simon, Carly 1945- **CLC 26**
See also CA 105

Simon, Claude 1913- **CLC 4, 9, 15, 39; DAM NOV**
See also CA 89-92; CANR 33; DLB 83; MTCW

Simon, (Marvin) Neil 1927- **CLC 6, 11, 31, 39, 70; DAM DRAM**
See also AITN 1; CA 21-24R; CANR 26, 54; DLB 7; MTCW

Simon, Paul (Frederick) 1941(?)- **CLC 17**
See also CA 116; 153

Simonon, Paul 1956(?)- **CLC 30**

Simpson, Harriette
See Arnow, Harriette (Louisa) Simpson

Simpson, Louis (Aston Marantz) 1923- **CLC 4, 7, 9, 32; DAM POET**
See also CA 1-4R; CAAS 4; CANR 1; DLB 5; MTCW

Simpson, Mona (Elizabeth) 1957- **CLC 44**
See also CA 122; 135

Simpson, N(orman) F(rederick) 1919- **CLC 29**
See also CA 13-16R; DLB 13

Sinclair, Andrew (Annandale) 1935- **CLC 2, 14**
See also CA 9-12R; CAAS 5; CANR 14, 38; DLB 14; MTCW

Sinclair, Emil
See Hesse, Hermann

Sinclair, Iain 1943- **CLC 76**
See also CA 132

Sinclair, Iain MacGregor
See Sinclair, Iain

Sinclair, Irene
See Griffith, D(avid Lewelyn) W(ark)

Sinclair, Mary Amelia St. Clair 1865(?)-1946
See Sinclair, May
See also CA 104

Sinclair, May TCLC 3, 11
See also Sinclair, Mary Amelia St. Clair
See also DLB 36, 135

Sinclair, Roy
See Griffith, D(avid Lewelyn) W(ark)

Sinclair, Upton (Beall) 1878-1968 **CLC 1, 11, 15, 63; DA; DAB; DAC; DAM MST, NOV; WLC**
See also CA 5-8R; 25-28R; CANR 7; CDALB 1929-1941; DLB 9; INT CANR-7; MTCW; SATA 9

Singer, Isaac
See Singer, Isaac Bashevis

Singer, Isaac Bashevis 1904-1991 **CLC 1, 3, 6, 9, 11, 15, 23, 38, 69; DA; DAB; DAC; DAM MST, NOV; SSC 3; WLC**
See also AITN 1, 2; CA 1-4R; 134; CANR 1, 39; CDALB 1941-1968; CLR 1; DLB 6, 28, 52; DLBY 91; JRDA; MAICYA; MTCW; SATA 3, 27; SATA-Obit 68

Singer, Israel Joshua 1893-1944 **TCLC 33**

Singh, Khushwant 1915- **CLC 11**
See also CA 9-12R; CAAS 9; CANR 6

Sinjohn, John
See Galsworthy, John

Sinyavsky, Andrei (Donatevich) 1925- **CLC 8**
See also CA 85-88

Sirin, V.
See Nabokov, Vladimir (Vladimirovich)

Sissman, L(ouis) E(dward) 1928-1976 **CLC 9, 18**
See also CA 21-24R; 65-68; CANR 13; DLB 5

Sisson, C(harles) H(ubert) 1914- **CLC 8**
See also CA 1-4R; CAAS 3; CANR 3, 48; DLB 27

Sitwell, Dame Edith 1887-1964 **CLC 2, 9, 67; DAM POET; PC 3**
See also CA 9-12R; CANR 35; CDBLB 1945-1960; DLB 20; MTCW

Sjoewall, Maj 1935- **CLC 7**
See also CA 65-68

Sjowall, Maj
See Sjoewall, Maj

Skelton, Robin 1925- **CLC 13**
See also AITN 2; CA 5-8R; CAAS 5; CANR 28; DLB 27, 53

Skolimowski, Jerzy 1938- **CLC 20**
See also CA 128

Skram, Amalie (Bertha) 1847-1905 **TCLC 25**

Skvorecky, Josef (Vaclav) 1924- **CLC 15, 39, 69; DAC; DAM NOV**
See also CA 61-64; CAAS 1; CANR 10, 34; MTCW

Slade, Bernard CLC 11, 46
See also Newbound, Bernard Slade
See also CAAS 9; DLB 53

Slaughter, Carolyn 1946- **CLC 56**
See also CA 85-88

Slaughter, Frank G(ill) 1908- **CLC 29**
See also AITN 2; CA 5-8R; CANR 5; INT CANR-5

Slavitt, David R(ytman) 1935- **CLC 5, 14**
See also CA 21-24R; CAAS 3; CANR 41; DLB 5, 6

Slesinger, Tess 1905-1945 **TCLC 10**
See also CA 107; DLB 102

Slessor, Kenneth 1901-1971 **CLC 14**
See also CA 102; 89-92

Slowacki, Juliusz 1809-1849 **NCLC 15**

Smart, Christopher 1722-1771 **LC 3; DAM POET; PC 13**
See also DLB 109

Smart, Elizabeth 1913-1986 **CLC 54**
See also CA 81-84; 118; DLB 88

Smiley, Jane (Graves) 1949- **CLC 53, 76; DAM POP**
See also CA 104; CANR 30, 50; INT CANR-30

Smith, A(rthur) J(ames) M(arshall) 1902-1980 **CLC 15; DAC**
See also CA 1-4R; 102; CANR 4; DLB 88

Smith, Adam 1723-1790 **LC 36**
See also DLB 104

Smith, Alexander 1829-1867 **NCLC 59**
See also DLB 32, 55

Smith, Anna Deavere 1950- **CLC 86**
See also CA 133

Smith, Betty (Wehner) 1896-1972 **CLC 19**
See also CA 5-8R; 33-36R; DLBY 82; SATA 6

Smith, Charlotte (Turner) 1749-1806 **NCLC 23**
See also DLB 39, 109

Smith, Clark Ashton 1893-1961 **CLC 43**
See also CA 143

Smith, Dave CLC 22, 42
See also Smith, David (Jeddie)
See also CAAS 7; DLB 5

Smith, David (Jeddie) 1942-
See Smith, Dave
See also CA 49-52; CANR 1; DAM POET

Smith, Florence Margaret 1902-1971
See Smith, Stevie
See also CA 17-18; 29-32R; CANR 35; CAP 2; DAM POET; MTCW

Smith, Iain Crichton 1928- **CLC 64**
See also CA 21-24R; DLB 40, 139

Smith, John 1580(?)-1631 **LC 9**

Smith, Johnston
See Crane, Stephen (Townley)

Smith, Joseph, Jr. 1805-1844 **NCLC 53**

Smith, Lee 1944- **CLC 25, 73**
See also CA 114; 119; CANR 46; DLB 143; DLBY 83; INT 119

Smith, Martin
See Smith, Martin Cruz

Smith, Martin Cruz 1942- **CLC 25; DAM MULT, POP**
See also BEST 89 4; CA 85-88; CANR 6, 23, 43; INT CANR-23; NNAL

Smith, Mary-Ann Tirone 1944- **CLC 39**
See also CA 118; 136

Smith, Patti 1946- **CLC 12**
See also CA 93-96

Smith, Pauline (Urmson) 1882-1959 **TCLC 25**

Smith, Rosamond
See Oates, Joyce Carol

Smith, Sheila Kaye
See Kaye-Smith, Sheila

Smith, Stevie CLC 3, 8, 25, 44; PC 12
See also Smith, Florence Margaret
See also DLB 20

Smith, Wilbur (Addison) 1933- **CLC 33**
See also CA 13-16R; CANR 7, 46; MTCW

Smith, William Jay 1918- **CLC 6**
See also CA 5-8R; CANR 44; DLB 5; MAICYA; SAAS 22; SATA 2, 68

Smith, Woodrow Wilson
See Kuttner, Henry

Smolenskin, Peretz 1842-1885 **NCLC 30**

Smollett, Tobias (George) 1721-1771 **LC 2**
See also CDBLB 1660-1789; DLB 39, 104

Snodgrass, W(illiam) D(e Witt) 1926- **CLC 2, 6, 10, 18, 68; DAM POET**
See also CA 1-4R; CANR 6, 36; DLB 5; MTCW

Snow, C(harles) P(ercy) 1905-1980 **CLC 1, 4, 6, 9, 13, 19; DAM NOV**
See also CA 5-8R; 101; CANR 28; CDBLB 1945-1960; DLB 15, 77; MTCW

Snow, Frances Compton
See Adams, Henry (Brooks)

Snyder, Gary (Sherman) 1930- **CLC 1, 2, 5, 9, 32; DAM POET**
See also CA 17-20R; CANR 30; DLB 5, 16, 165

Snyder, Zilpha Keatley 1927- **CLC 17**
See also AAYA 15; CA 9-12R; CANR 38; CLR 31; JRDA; MAICYA; SAAS 2; SATA 1, 28, 75

Soares, Bernardo
See Pessoa, Fernando (Antonio Nogueira)

Sobh, A.
See Shamlu, Ahmad

Sobol, Joshua CLC 60

Soderberg, Hjalmar 1869-1941 **TCLC 39**

Sodergran, Edith (Irene)
See Soedergran, Edith (Irene)

Soedergran, Edith (Irene) 1892-1923 **TCLC 31**

Softly, Edgar
See Lovecraft, H(oward) P(hillips)

Softly, Edward
See Lovecraft, H(oward) P(hillips)

Sokolov, Raymond 1941- **CLC 7**
See also CA 85-88

Solo, Jay
See Ellison, Harlan (Jay)

Sologub, Fyodor TCLC 9
See also Teternikov, Fyodor Kuzmich

Solomons, Ikey Esquir
See Thackeray, William Makepeace

Solomos, Dionysios 1798-1857 **NCLC 15**

Solwoska, Mara
See French, Marilyn

Solzhenitsyn, Aleksandr I(sayevich) 1918- **CLC 1, 2, 4, 7, 9, 10, 18, 26, 34, 78; DA; DAB; DAC; DAM MST, NOV; WLC**
See also AITN 1; CA 69-72; CANR 40; MTCW

Somers, Jane
See Lessing, Doris (May)

Somerville, Edith 1858-1949 **TCLC 51**
See also DLB 135

Somerville & Ross
See Martin, Violet Florence; Somerville, Edith

Sommer, Scott 1951- **CLC 25**

See also CA 106

Sondheim, Stephen (Joshua) 1930- **CLC 30, 39; DAM DRAM**
See also AAYA 11; CA 103; CANR 47

Sontag, Susan 1933- **CLC 1, 2, 10, 13, 31; DAM POP**
See also CA 17-20R; CANR 25, 51; DLB 2, 67; MTCW

Sophocles 496(?)B.C.-406(?)B.C. **CMLC 2; DA; DAB; DAC; DAM DRAM, MST; DC 1**
See also DLB 176

Sordello 1189-1269 **CMLC 15**

Sorel, Julia
See Drexler, Rosalyn

Sorrentino, Gilbert 1929- **CLC 3, 7, 14, 22, 40**
See also CA 77-80; CANR 14, 33; DLB 5, 173; DLBY 80; INT CANR-14

Soto, Gary 1952- **CLC 32, 80; DAM MULT; HLC**
See also AAYA 10; CA 119; 125; CANR 50; CLR 38; DLB 82; HW; INT 125; JRDA; SATA 80

Soupault, Philippe 1897-1990 **CLC 68**
See also CA 116; 147; 131

Souster, (Holmes) Raymond 1921- **CLC 5, 14; DAC; DAM POET**
See also CA 13-16R; CAAS 14; CANR 13, 29, 53; DLB 88; SATA 63

Southern, Terry 1924(?)-1995 **CLC 7**
See also CA 1-4R; 150; CANR 1, 55; DLB 2

Southey, Robert 1774-1843 **NCLC 8**
See also DLB 93, 107, 142; SATA 54

Southworth, Emma Dorothy Eliza Nevitte 1819-1899 **NCLC 26**

Souza, Ernest
See Scott, Evelyn

Soyinka, Wole 1934- **CLC 3, 5, 14, 36, 44; BLC; DA; DAB; DAC; DAM DRAM, MST, MULT; DC 2; WLC**
See also BW 2; CA 13-16R; CANR 27, 39; DLB 125; MTCW

Spackman, W(illiam) M(ode) 1905-1990 **CLC 46**
See also CA 81-84; 132

Spacks, Barry (Bernard) 1931- **CLC 14**
See also CA 154; CANR 33; DLB 105

Spanidou, Irini 1946- **CLC 44**

Spark, Muriel (Sarah) 1918- **CLC 2, 3, 5, 8, 13, 18, 40, 94; DAB; DAC; DAM MST, NOV; SSC 10**
See also CA 5-8R; CANR 12, 36; CDBLB 1945-1960; DLB 15, 139; INT CANR-12; MTCW

Spaulding, Douglas
See Bradbury, Ray (Douglas)

Spaulding, Leonard
See Bradbury, Ray (Douglas)

Spence, J. A. D.
See Eliot, T(homas) S(tearns)

Spencer, Elizabeth 1921- **CLC 22**
See also CA 13-16R; CANR 32; DLB 6; MTCW; SATA 14

Spencer, Leonard G.
See Silverberg, Robert

Spencer, Scott 1945- **CLC 30**
See also CA 113; CANR 51; DLBY 86

Spender, Stephen (Harold) 1909-1995 **CLC 1, 2, 5, 10, 41, 91; DAM POET**
See also CA 9-12R; 149; CANR 31, 54; CDBLB 1945-1960; DLB 20; MTCW

Spengler, Oswald (Arnold Gottfried) 1880-1936 **TCLC 25**
See also CA 118

Spenser, Edmund 1552(?)-1599 **LC 5; DA; DAB; DAC; DAM MST, POET; PC 8; WLC**
See also CDBLB Before 1660; DLB 167

Spicer, Jack 1925-1965 **CLC 8, 18, 72; DAM POET**
See also CA 85-88; DLB 5, 16

Spiegelman, Art 1948- **CLC 76**
See also AAYA 10; CA 125; CANR 41, 55

Spielberg, Peter 1929- **CLC 6**
See also CA 5-8R; CANR 4, 48; DLBY 81

Spielberg, Steven 1947- **CLC 20**
See also AAYA 8; CA 77-80; CANR 32; SATA 32

Spillane, Frank Morrison 1918-
See Spillane, Mickey
See also CA 25-28R; CANR 28; MTCW; SATA 66

Spillane, Mickey CLC 3, 13
See also Spillane, Frank Morrison

Spinoza, Benedictus de 1632-1677 **LC 9**

Spinrad, Norman (Richard) 1940- **CLC 46**
See also CA 37-40R; CAAS 19; CANR 20; DLB 8; INT CANR-20

Spitteler, Carl (Friedrich Georg) 1845-1924 **TCLC 12**
See also CA 109; DLB 129

Spivack, Kathleen (Romola Drucker) 1938- **CLC 6**
See also CA 49-52

Spoto, Donald 1941- **CLC 39**
See also CA 65-68; CANR 11, 57

Springsteen, Bruce (F.) 1949- **CLC 17**
See also CA 111

Spurling, Hilary 1940- **CLC 34**
See also CA 104; CANR 25, 52

Spyker, John Howland
See Elman, Richard

Squires, (James) Radcliffe 1917-1993 **CLC 51**
See also CA 1-4R; 140; CANR 6, 21

Srivastava, Dhanpat Rai 1880(?)-1936
See Premchand
See also CA 118

Stacy, Donald
See Pohl, Frederik

Stael, Germaine de
See Stael-Holstein, Anne Louise Germaine Necker
Baronn
See also DLB 119

**Stael-Holstein, Anne Louise Germaine Necker
Baronn** 1766-1817 **NCLC 3**
See also Stael, Germaine de

Stafford, Jean 1915-1979 **CLC 4, 7, 19, 68**
See also CA 1-4R; 85-88; CANR 3; DLB 2, 173;
MTCW; SATA-Obit 22

Stafford, William (Edgar) 1914-1993 **CLC 4, 7, 29;
DAM POET**
See also CA 5-8R; 142; CAAS 3; CANR 5, 22;
DLB 5; INT CANR-22

Staines, Trevor
See Brunner, John (Kilian Houston)

Stairs, Gordon
See Austin, Mary (Hunter)

Stannard, Martin 1947- **CLC 44**
See also CA 142; DLB 155

Stanton, Maura 1946- **CLC 9**
See also CA 89-92; CANR 15; DLB 120

Stanton, Schuyler
See Baum, L(yman) Frank

Stapledon, (William) Olaf 1886-1950 **TCLC 22**
See also CA 111; DLB 15

Starbuck, George (Edwin) 1931-1996 **CLC 53; DAM
POET**
See also CA 21-24R; 153; CANR 23

Stark, Richard
See Westlake, Donald E(dwin)

Staunton, Schuyler
See Baum, L(yman) Frank

Stead, Christina (Ellen) 1902-1983 **CLC 2, 5, 8, 32,
80**
See also CA 13-16R; 109; CANR 33, 40; MTCW

Stead, William Thomas 1849-1912 **TCLC 48**

Steele, Richard 1672-1729 **LC 18**
See also CDBLB 1660-1789; DLB 84, 101

Steele, Timothy (Reid) 1948- **CLC 45**
See also CA 93-96; CANR 16, 50; DLB 120

Steffens, (Joseph) Lincoln 1866-1936 **TCLC 20**
See also CA 117

Stegner, Wallace (Earle) 1909-1993 **CLC 9, 49, 81;
DAM NOV**
See also AITN 1; BEST 90 3; CA 1-4R; 141;
CAAS 9; CANR 1, 21, 46; DLB 9; DLBY 93;
MTCW

Stein, Gertrude 1874-1946 **TCLC 1, 6, 28, 48; DA;
DAB; DAC; DAM MST, NOV, POET; WLC**
See also CA 104; 132; CDALB 1917-1929; DLB 4,
54, 86; MTCW

Steinbeck, John (Ernst) 1902-1968 **CLC 1, 5, 9, 13,
21, 34, 45, 75; DA; DAB; DAC; DAM DRAM,
MST, NOV; SSC 11; WLC**
See also AAYA 12; CA 1-4R; 25-28R; CANR 1,
35; CDALB 1929-1941; DLB 7, 9; DLBD 2;
MTCW; SATA 9

Steinem, Gloria 1934- **CLC 63**
See also CA 53-56; CANR 28, 51; MTCW

Steiner, George 1929- **CLC 24; DAM NOV**
See also CA 73-76; CANR 31; DLB 67; MTCW;
SATA 62

Steiner, K. Leslie
See Delany, Samuel R(ay, Jr.)

Steiner, Rudolf 1861-1925 **TCLC 13**
See also CA 107

Stendhal 1783-1842 **NCLC 23, 46; DA; DAB; DAC;
DAM MST, NOV; WLC**
See also DLB 119

Stephen, Leslie 1832-1904 **TCLC 23**
See also CA 123; DLB 57, 144

Stephen, Sir Leslie
See Stephen, Leslie

Stephen, Virginia
See Woolf, (Adeline) Virginia

Stephens, James 1882(?)-1950 **TCLC 4**
See also CA 104; DLB 19, 153, 162

Stephens, Reed
See Donaldson, Stephen R.

Steptoe, Lydia
See Barnes, Djuna

Sterchi, Beat 1949- **CLC 65**

Sterling, Brett
See Bradbury, Ray (Douglas); Hamilton, Edmond

Sterling, Bruce 1954- **CLC 72**
See also CA 119; CANR 44

Sterling, George 1869-1926 **TCLC 20**
See also CA 117; DLB 54

Stern, Gerald 1925- **CLC 40, 100**
See also CA 81-84; CANR 28; DLB 105

Stern, Richard (Gustave) 1928- **CLC 4, 39**
See also CA 1-4R; CANR 1, 25, 52; DLBY 87; INT
CANR-25

Sternberg, Josef von 1894-1969 **CLC 20**
See also CA 81-84

Sterne, Laurence 1713-1768 **LC 2; DA; DAB; DAC;
DAM MST, NOV; WLC**
See also CDBLB 1660-1789; DLB 39

Sternheim, (William Adolf) Carl 1878-1942 **TCLC
8**
See also CA 105; DLB 56, 118

Stevens, Mark 1951- **CLC 34**
See also CA 122

Stevens, Wallace 1879-1955 **TCLC 3, 12, 45; DA;
DAB; DAC; DAM MST, POET; PC 6; WLC**
See also CA 104; 124; CDALB 1929-1941; DLB
54; MTCW

Stevenson, Anne (Katharine) 1933- **CLC 7, 33**
See also CA 17-20R; CAAS 9; CANR 9, 33; DLB
40; MTCW

Stevenson, Robert Louis (Balfour) 1850-1894 **NCLC
5, 14; DA; DAB; DAC; DAM MST, NOV; SSC
11; WLC**
See also CDBLB 1890-1914; CLR 10, 11; DLB 18,
57, 141, 156, 174; DLBD 13; JRDA; MAICYA;
YABC 2

Stewart, J(ohn) I(nnes) M(ackintosh) 1906-1994
CLC 7, 14, 32
See also CA 85-88; 147; CAAS 3; CANR 47;
MTCW

Stewart, Mary (Florence Elinor) 1916- **CLC 7, 35;
DAB**
See also CA 1-4R; CANR 1; SATA 12

Stewart, Mary Rainbow
See Stewart, Mary (Florence Elinor)

Stifle, June
See Campbell, Maria

Stifter, Adalbert 1805-1868 **NCLC 41**
See also DLB 133

Still, James 1906- **CLC 49**
See also CA 65-68; CAAS 17; CANR 10, 26; DLB
9; SATA 29

Sting
See Sumner, Gordon Matthew

Stirling, Arthur
See Sinclair, Upton (Beall)

Stitt, Milan 1941- **CLC 29**
See also CA 69-72

Stockton, Francis Richard 1834-1902
See Stockton, Frank R.
See also CA 108; 137; MAICYA; SATA 44

Stockton, Frank R. TCLC 47
See also Stockton, Francis Richard
See also DLB 42, 74; DLBD 13; SATA-Brief 32

Stoddard, Charles
See Kuttner, Henry

Stoker, Abraham 1847-1912
See Stoker, Bram
See also CA 105; DA; DAC; DAM MST, NOV;
SATA 29

Stoker, Bram 1847-1912 **TCLC 8; DAB; WLC**
See also Stoker, Abraham
See also CA 150; CDBLB 1890-1914; DLB 36,
70

Stolz, Mary (Slattery) 1920- **CLC 12**
See also AAYA 8; AITN 1; CA 5-8R; CANR 13, 41; JRDA; MAICYA; SAAS 3; SATA 10, 71

Stone, Irving 1903-1989 **CLC 7; DAM POP**
See also AITN 1; CA 1-4R; 129; CAAS 3; CANR 1, 23; INT CANR-23; MTCW; SATA 3; SATA-Obit 64

Stone, Oliver (William) 1946- **CLC 73**
See also AAYA 15; CA 110; CANR 55

Stone, Robert (Anthony) 1937- **CLC 5, 23, 42**
See also CA 85-88; CANR 23; DLB 152; INT CANR-23; MTCW

Stone, Zachary
See Follett, Ken(neth Martin)

Stoppard, Tom 1937- **CLC 1, 3, 4, 5, 8, 15, 29, 34, 63, 91; DA; DAB; DAC; DAM DRAM, MST; DC 6; WLC**
See also CA 81-84; CANR 39; CDBLB 1960 to Present; DLB 13; DLBY 85; MTCW

Storey, David (Malcolm) 1933- **CLC 2, 4, 5, 8; DAM DRAM**
See also CA 81-84; CANR 36; DLB 13, 14; MTCW

Storm, Hyemeyohsts 1935- **CLC 3; DAM MULT**
See also CA 81-84; CANR 45; NNAL

Storm, (Hans) Theodor (Woldsen) 1817-1888 **NCLC 1**

Storni, Alfonsina 1892-1938 **TCLC 5; DAM MULT; HLC**
See also CA 104; 131; HW

Stout, Rex (Todhunter) 1886-1975 **CLC 3**
See also AITN 2; CA 61-64

Stow, (Julian) Randolph 1935- **CLC 23, 48**
See also CA 13-16R; CANR 33; MTCW

Stowe, Harriet (Elizabeth) Beecher 1811-1896 **NCLC 3, 50; DA; DAB; DAC; DAM MST, NOV; WLC**
See also CDALB 1865-1917; DLB 1, 12, 42, 74; JRDA; MAICYA; YABC 1

Strachey, (Giles) Lytton 1880-1932 **TCLC 12**
See also CA 110; DLB 149; DLBD 10

Strand, Mark 1934- **CLC 6, 18, 41, 71; DAM POET**
See also CA 21-24R; CANR 40; DLB 5; SATA 41

Straub, Peter (Francis) 1943- **CLC 28; DAM POP**
See also BEST 89 1; CA 85-88; CANR 28; DLBY 84; MTCW

Strauss, Botho 1944- **CLC 22**
See also DLB 124

Streatfeild, (Mary) Noel 1895(?)-1986 **CLC 21**
See also CA 81-84; 120; CANR 31; CLR 17; DLB 160; MAICYA; SATA 20; SATA-Obit 48

Stribling, T(homas) S(igismund) 1881-1965 **CLC 23**
See also CA 107; DLB 9

Strindberg, (Johan) August 1849-1912 **TCLC 1, 8,** 21, 47; **DA; DAB; DAC; DAM DRAM, MST; WLC**
See also CA 104; 135

Stringer, Arthur 1874-1950 **TCLC 37**
See also DLB 92

Stringer, David
See Roberts, Keith (John Kingston)

Strugatskii, Arkadii (Natanovich) 1925-1991 **CLC 27**
See also CA 106; 135

Strugatskii, Boris (Natanovich) 1933- **CLC 27**
See also CA 106

Strummer, Joe 1953(?)- **CLC 30**

Stuart, Don A.
See Campbell, John W(ood, Jr.)

Stuart, Ian
See MacLean, Alistair (Stuart)

Stuart, Jesse (Hilton) 1906-1984 **CLC 1, 8, 11, 14, 34**
See also CA 5-8R; 112; CANR 31; DLB 9, 48, 102; DLBY 84; SATA 2; SATA-Obit 36

Sturgeon, Theodore (Hamilton) 1918-1985 **CLC 22, 39**
See also Queen, Ellery
See also CA 81-84; 116; CANR 32; DLB 8; DLBY 85; MTCW

Sturges, Preston 1898-1959 **TCLC 48**
See also CA 114; 149; DLB 26

Styron, William 1925- **CLC 1, 3, 5, 11, 15, 60; DAM NOV, POP**
See also BEST 90 4; CA 5-8R; CANR 6, 33; CDALB 1968-1988; DLB 2, 143; DLBY 80; INT CANR-6; MTCW

Suarez Lynch, B.
See Bioy Casares, Adolfo; Borges, Jorge Luis

Su Chien 1884-1918
See Su Man-shu
See also CA 123

Suckow, Ruth 1892-1960 **SSC 18**
See also CA 113; DLB 9, 102

Sudermann, Hermann 1857-1928 **TCLC 15**
See also CA 107; DLB 118

Sue, Eugene 1804-1857 **NCLC 1**
See also DLB 119

Sueskind, Patrick 1949- **CLC 44**
See also Suskind, Patrick

Sukenick, Ronald 1932- **CLC 3, 4, 6, 48**
See also CA 25-28R; CAAS 8; CANR 32; DLB 173; DLBY 81

Suknaski, Andrew 1942- **CLC 19**
See also CA 101; DLB 53

Sullivan, Vernon
See Vian, Boris

Sully Prudhomme 1839-1907 **TCLC 31**

Su Man-shu **TCLC 24**
See also Su Chien

Summerforest, Ivy B.
See Kirkup, James

Summers, Andrew James 1942- **CLC 26**

Summers, Andy
See Summers, Andrew James

Summers, Hollis (Spurgeon, Jr.) 1916- **CLC 10**
See also CA 5-8R; CANR 3; DLB 6

Summers, (Alphonsus Joseph-Mary Augustus) Montague 1880-1948 **TCLC 16**
See also CA 118

Sumner, Gordon Matthew 1951- **CLC 26**

Surtees, Robert Smith 1803-1864 **NCLC 14**
See also DLB 21

Susann, Jacqueline 1921-1974 **CLC 3**
See also AITN 1; CA 65-68; 53-56; MTCW

Su Shih 1036-1101 **CMLC 15**

Suskind, Patrick
See Sueskind, Patrick
See also CA 145

Sutcliff, Rosemary 1920-1992 **CLC 26; DAB; DAC; DAM MST, POP**
See also AAYA 10; CA 5-8R; 139; CANR 37; CLR 1, 37; JRDA; MAICYA; SATA 6, 44, 78; SATA-Obit 73

Sutro, Alfred 1863-1933 **TCLC 6**
See also CA 105; DLB 10

Sutton, Henry
See Slavitt, David R(ytman)

Svevo, Italo **TCLC 2, 35**
See also Schmitz, Aron Hector

Swados, Elizabeth (A.) 1951- **CLC 12**
See also CA 97-100; CANR 49; INT 97-100

Swados, Harvey 1920-1972 **CLC 5**
See also CA 5-8R; 37-40R; CANR 6; DLB 2

Swan, Gladys 1934- **CLC 69**
See also CA 101; CANR 17, 39

Swarthout, Glendon (Fred) 1918-1992 **CLC 35**
See also CA 1-4R; 139; CANR 1, 47; SATA 26

Sweet, Sarah C.
See Jewett, (Theodora) Sarah Orne

Swenson, May 1919-1989 **CLC 4, 14, 61; DA; DAB; DAC; DAM MST, POET; PC 14**
See also CA 5-8R; 130; CANR 36; DLB 5; MTCW; SATA 15

Swift, Augustus
See Lovecraft, H(oward) P(hillips)

Swift, Graham (Colin) 1949- **CLC 41, 88**

See also CA 117; 122; CANR 46

Swift, Jonathan 1667-1745 **LC 1; DA; DAB; DAC; DAM MST, NOV, POET; PC 9; WLC**
See also CDBLB 1660-1789; DLB 39, 95, 101; SATA 19

Swinburne, Algernon Charles 1837-1909 **TCLC 8, 36; DA; DAB; DAC; DAM MST, POET; WLC**
See also CA 105; 140; CDBLB 1832-1890; DLB 35, 57

Swinfen, Ann CLC 34

Swinnerton, Frank Arthur 1884-1982 **CLC 31**
See also CA 108; DLB 34

Swithen, John
See King, Stephen (Edwin)

Sylvia
See Ashton-Warner, Sylvia (Constance)

Symmes, Robert Edward
See Duncan, Robert (Edward)

Symonds, John Addington 1840-1893 **NCLC 34**
See also DLB 57, 144

Symons, Arthur 1865-1945 **TCLC 11**
See also CA 107; DLB 19, 57, 149

Symons, Julian (Gustave) 1912-1994 **CLC 2, 14, 32**
See also CA 49-52; 147; CAAS 3; CANR 3, 33; DLB 87, 155; DLBY 92; MTCW

Synge, (Edmund) J(ohn) M(illington) 1871-1909 **TCLC 6, 37; DAM DRAM; DC 2**
See also CA 104; 141; CDBLB 1890-1914; DLB 10, 19

Syruc, J.
See Milosz, Czeslaw

Szirtes, George 1948- **CLC 46**
See also CA 109; CANR 27

Szymborska, Wislawa 1923- **CLC 99**
See also CA 154

T. O., Nik
See Annensky, Innokenty (Fyodorovich)

Tabori, George 1914- **CLC 19**
See also CA 49-52; CANR 4

Tagore, Rabindranath 1861-1941 **TCLC 3, 53; DAM DRAM, POET; PC 8**
See also CA 104; 120; MTCW

Taine, Hippolyte Adolphe 1828-1893 **NCLC 15**

Talese, Gay 1932- **CLC 37**
See also AITN 1; CA 1-4R; CANR 9; INT CANR-9; MTCW

Tallent, Elizabeth (Ann) 1954- **CLC 45**
See also CA 117; DLB 130

Tally, Ted 1952- **CLC 42**
See also CA 120; 124; INT 124

Tamayo y Baus, Manuel 1829-1898 **NCLC 1**

Tammsaare, A(nton) H(ansen) 1878-1940 **TCLC 27**

Tan, Amy (Ruth) 1952- **CLC 59; DAM MULT, NOV, POP**
See also AAYA 9; BEST 89 3; CA 136; CANR 54; DLB 173; SATA 75

Tandem, Felix
See Spitteler, Carl (Friedrich Georg)

Tanizaki, Jun'ichiro 1886-1965 **CLC 8, 14, 28; SSC 21**
See also CA 93-96; 25-28R

Tanner, William
See Amis, Kingsley (William)

Tao Lao
See Storni, Alfonsina

Tarassoff, Lev
See Troyat, Henri

Tarbell, Ida M(inerva) 1857-1944 **TCLC 40**
See also CA 122; DLB 47

Tarkington, (Newton) Booth 1869-1946 **TCLC 9**
See also CA 110; 143; DLB 9, 102; SATA 17

Tarkovsky, Andrei (Arsenyevich) 1932-1986 **CLC 75**
See also CA 127

Tartt, Donna 1964(?)- **CLC 76**
See also CA 142

Tasso, Torquato 1544-1595 **LC 5**

Tate, (John Orley) Allen 1899-1979 **CLC 2, 4, 6, 9, 11, 14, 24**
See also CA 5-8R; 85-88; CANR 32; DLB 4, 45, 63; MTCW

Tate, Ellalice
See Hibbert, Eleanor Alice Burford

Tate, James (Vincent) 1943- **CLC 2, 6, 25**
See also CA 21-24R; CANR 29, 57; DLB 5, 169

Tavel, Ronald 1940- **CLC 6**
See also CA 21-24R; CANR 33

Taylor, C(ecil) P(hilip) 1929-1981 **CLC 27**
See also CA 25-28R; 105; CANR 47

Taylor, Edward 1642(?)-1729 **LC 11; DA; DAB; DAC; DAM MST, POET**
See also DLB 24

Taylor, Eleanor Ross 1920- **CLC 5**
See also CA 81-84

Taylor, Elizabeth 1912-1975 **CLC 2, 4, 29**
See also CA 13-16R; CANR 9; DLB 139; MTCW; SATA 13

Taylor, Henry (Splawn) 1942- **CLC 44**
See also CA 33-36R; CAAS 7; CANR 31; DLB 5

Taylor, Kamala (Purnaiya) 1924-
See Markandaya, Kamala
See also CA 77-80

Taylor, Mildred D. CLC 21
See also AAYA 10; BW 1; CA 85-88; CANR 25; CLR 9; DLB 52; JRDA; MAICYA; SAAS 5; SATA 15, 70

Taylor, Peter (Hillsman) 1917-1994 **CLC 1, 4, 18, 37, 44, 50, 71; SSC 10**
See also CA 13-16R; 147; CANR 9, 50; DLBY 81, 94; INT CANR-9; MTCW

Taylor, Robert Lewis 1912- **CLC 14**
See also CA 1-4R; CANR 3; SATA 10

Tchekhov, Anton
See Chekhov, Anton (Pavlovich)

Teasdale, Sara 1884-1933 **TCLC 4**
See also CA 104; DLB 45; SATA 32

Tegner, Esaias 1782-1846 **NCLC 2**

Teilhard de Chardin, (Marie Joseph) Pierre 1881-1955 **TCLC 9**
See also CA 105

Temple, Ann
See Mortimer, Penelope (Ruth)

Tennant, Emma (Christina) 1937- **CLC 13, 52**
See also CA 65-68; CAAS 9; CANR 10, 38; DLB 14

Tenneshaw, S. M.
See Silverberg, Robert

Tennyson, Alfred 1809-1892 **NCLC 30; DA; DAB; DAC; DAM MST, POET; PC 6; WLC**
See also CDBLB 1832-1890; DLB 32

Teran, Lisa St. Aubin de CLC 36
See also St. Aubin de Teran, Lisa

Terence 195(?)B.C.-159B.C. **CMLC 14**

Teresa de Jesus, St. 1515-1582 **LC 18**

Terkel, Louis 1912-
See Terkel, Studs
See also CA 57-60; CANR 18, 45; MTCW

Terkel, Studs CLC 38
See also Terkel, Louis
See also AITN 1

Terry, C. V.
See Slaughter, Frank G(ill)

Terry, Megan 1932- **CLC 19**
See also CA 77-80; CABS 3; CANR 43; DLB 7

Tertz, Abram
See Sinyavsky, Andrei (Donatevich)

Tesich, Steve 1943(?)-1996 **CLC 40, 69**
See also CA 105; 152; DLBY 83

Teternikov, Fyodor Kuzmich 1863-1927
See Sologub, Fyodor
See also CA 104

Tevis, Walter 1928-1984 **CLC 42**
See also CA 113

Tey, Josephine TCLC 14
See also Mackintosh, Elizabeth
See also DLB 77

Thackeray, William Makepeace 1811-1863 NCLC
5, 14, 22, 43; DA; DAB; DAC; DAM MST,
NOV; WLC
See also CDBLB 1832-1890; DLB 21, 55, 159, 163;
SATA 23

Thakura, Ravindranatha
See Tagore, Rabindranath

Tharoor, Shashi 1956- CLC 70
See also CA 141

Thelwell, Michael Miles 1939- CLC 22
See also BW 2; CA 101

Theobald, Lewis, Jr.
See Lovecraft, H(oward) P(hillips)

Theodorescu, Ion N. 1880-1967
See Arghezi, Tudor
See also CA 116

Theriault, Yves 1915-1983 CLC 79; DAC; DAM
MST
See also CA 102; DLB 88

Theroux, Alexander (Louis) 1939- CLC 2, 25
See also CA 85-88; CANR 20

Theroux, Paul (Edward) 1941- CLC 5, 8, 11, 15, 28,
46; DAM POP
See also BEST 89 4; CA 33-36R; CANR 20, 45;
DLB 2; MTCW; SATA 44

Thesen, Sharon 1946- CLC 56

Thevenin, Denis
See Duhamel, Georges

Thibault, Jacques Anatole Francois 1844-1924
See France, Anatole
See also CA 106; 127; DAM NOV; MTCW

Thiele, Colin (Milton) 1920- CLC 17
See also CA 29-32R; CANR 12, 28, 53; CLR 27;
MAICYA; SAAS 2; SATA 14, 72

Thomas, Audrey (Callahan) 1935- CLC 7, 13, 37;
SSC 20
See also AITN 2; CA 21-24R; CAAS 19; CANR
36; DLB 60; MTCW

Thomas, D(onald) M(ichael) 1935- CLC 13, 22, 31
See also CA 61-64; CAAS 11; CANR 17, 45;
CDBLB 1960 to Present; DLB 40; INT CANR-
17; MTCW

Thomas, Dylan (Marlais) 1914-1953 TCLC 1, 8, 45;
DA; DAB; DAC; DAM DRAM, MST, POET;
PC 2; SSC 3; WLC
See also CA 104; 120; CDBLB 1945-1960; DLB 13,
20, 139; MTCW; SATA 60

Thomas, (Philip) Edward 1878-1917 TCLC 10; DAM
POET
See also CA 106; 153; DLB 19

Thomas, Joyce Carol 1938- CLC 35
See also AAYA 12; BW 2; CA 113; 116; CANR

48; CLR 19; DLB 33; INT 116; JRDA; MAICYA;
MTCW; SAAS 7; SATA 40, 78

Thomas, Lewis 1913-1993 CLC 35
See also CA 85-88; 143; CANR 38; MTCW

Thomas, Paul
See Mann, (Paul) Thomas

Thomas, Piri 1928- CLC 17
See also CA 73-76; HW

Thomas, R(onald) S(tuart) 1913- CLC 6, 13, 48;
DAB; DAM POET
See also CA 89-92; CAAS 4; CANR 30; CDBLB
1960 to Present; DLB 27; MTCW

Thomas, Ross (Elmore) 1926-1995 CLC 39
See also CA 33-36R; 150; CANR 22

Thompson, Francis Clegg
See Mencken, H(enry) L(ouis)

Thompson, Francis Joseph 1859-1907 TCLC 4
See also CA 104; CDBLB 1890-1914; DLB 19

Thompson, Hunter S(tockton) 1939- CLC 9, 17,
40; DAM POP
See also BEST 89 1; CA 17-20R; CANR 23, 46;
MTCW

Thompson, James Myers
See Thompson, Jim (Myers)

Thompson, Jim (Myers) 1906-1977(?) CLC 69
See also CA 140

Thompson, Judith CLC 39

Thomson, James 1700-1748 LC 16, 29; DAM POET
See also DLB 95

Thomson, James 1834-1882 NCLC 18; DAM POET
See also DLB 35

Thoreau, Henry David 1817-1862 NCLC 7, 21; DA;
DAB; DAC; DAM MST; WLC
See also CDALB 1640-1865; DLB 1

Thornton, Hall
See Silverberg, Robert

Thucydides c. 455B.C.-399B.C. CMLC 17
See also DLB 176

Thurber, James (Grover) 1894-1961 CLC 5, 11, 25;
DA; DAB; DAC; DAM DRAM, MST, NOV;
SSC 1
See also CA 73-76; CANR 17, 39; CDALB 1929-
1941; DLB 4, 11, 22, 102; MAICYA; MTCW;
SATA 13

Thurman, Wallace (Henry) 1902-1934 TCLC 6;
BLC; DAM MULT
See also BW 1; CA 104; 124; DLB 51

Ticheburn, Cheviot
See Ainsworth, William Harrison

Tieck, (Johann) Ludwig 1773-1853 NCLC 5, 46
See also DLB 90

Tiger, Derry

See Ellison, Harlan (Jay)

Tilghman, Christopher 1948(?)- CLC 65

Tillinghast, Richard (Williford) 1940- CLC 29
See also CA 29-32R; CAAS 23; CANR 26, 51

Timrod, Henry 1828-1867 NCLC 25
See also DLB 3

Tindall, Gillian 1938- CLC 7
See also CA 21-24R; CANR 11

Tiptree, James, Jr. CLC 48, 50
See also Sheldon, Alice Hastings Bradley
See also DLB 8

Titmarsh, Michael Angelo
See Thackeray, William Makepeace

**Tocqueville, Alexis (Charles Henri Maurice Clerel
Comte)** 1805-1859 NCLC 7

Tolkien, J(ohn) R(onald) R(euel) 1892-1973 CLC 1,
2, 3, 8, 12, 38; DA; DAB; DAC; DAM MST,
NOV, POP; WLC
See also AAYA 10; AITN 1; CA 17-18; 45-48;
CANR 36; CAP 2; CDBLB 1914-1945; DLB 15,
160; JRDA; MAICYA; MTCW; SATA 2, 32;
SATA-Obit 24

Toller, Ernst 1893-1939 TCLC 10
See also CA 107; DLB 124

Tolson, M. B.
See Tolson, Melvin B(eaunorus)

Tolson, Melvin B(eaunorus) 1898(?)-1966 CLC 36;
BLC; DAM MULT, POET
See also BW 1; CA 124; 89-92; DLB 48, 76

Tolstoi, Aleksei Nikolaevich
See Tolstoy, Alexey Nikolaevich

Tolstoy, Alexey Nikolaevich 1882-1945 TCLC 18
See also CA 107

Tolstoy, Count Leo
See Tolstoy, Leo (Nikolaevich)

Tolstoy, Leo (Nikolaevich) 1828-1910 TCLC 4, 11,
17, 28, 44; DA; DAB; DAC; DAM MST, NOV;
SSC 9; WLC
See also CA 104; 123; SATA 26

Tomasi di Lampedusa, Giuseppe 1896-1957
See Lampedusa, Giuseppe (Tomasi) di
See also CA 111

Tomlin, Lily CLC 17
See also Tomlin, Mary Jean

Tomlin, Mary Jean 1939(?)-
See Tomlin, Lily
See also CA 117

Tomlinson, (Alfred) Charles 1927- CLC 2, 4, 6, 13,
45; DAM POET; PC 17
See also CA 5-8R; CANR 33; DLB 40

Tonson, Jacob
See Bennett, (Enoch) Arnold

Toole, John Kennedy 1937-1969 **CLC 19, 64**
See also CA 104; DLBY 81

Toomer, Jean 1894-1967 **CLC 1, 4, 13, 22; BLC; DAM MULT; PC 7; SSC 1**
See also BW 1; CA 85-88; CDALB 1917-1929; DLB 45, 51; MTCW

Torley, Luke
See Blish, James (Benjamin)

Tornimparte, Alessandra
See Ginzburg, Natalia

Torre, Raoul della
See Mencken, H(enry) L(ouis)

Torrey, E(dwin) Fuller 1937- **CLC 34**
See also CA 119

Torsvan, Ben Traven
See Traven, B.

Torsvan, Benno Traven
See Traven, B.

Torsvan, Berick Traven
See Traven, B.

Torsvan, Berwick Traven
See Traven, B.

Torsvan, Bruno Traven
See Traven, B.

Torsvan, Traven
See Traven, B.

Tournier, Michel (Edouard) 1924- **CLC 6, 23, 36, 95**
See also CA 49-52; CANR 3, 36; DLB 83; MTCW; SATA 23

Tournimparte, Alessandra
See Ginzburg, Natalia

Towers, Ivar
See Kornbluth, C(yril) M.

Towne, Robert (Burton) 1936(?)- **CLC 87**
See also CA 108; DLB 44

Townsend, Sue 1946- **CLC 61; DAB; DAC**
See also CA 119; 127; INT 127; MTCW; SATA 55; SATA-Brief 48

Townshend, Peter (Dennis Blandford) 1945- **CLC 17, 42**
See also CA 107

Tozzi, Federigo 1883-1920 **TCLC 31**

Traill, Catharine Parr 1802-1899 **NCLC 31**
See also DLB 99

Trakl, Georg 1887-1914 **TCLC 5**
See also CA 104

Transtroemer, Tomas (Goesta) 1931- **CLC 52, 65; DAM POET**
See also CA 117; 129; CAAS 17

Transtromer, Tomas Gosta

See Transtroemer, Tomas (Goesta)

Traven, B. (?)-1969 **CLC 8, 11**
See also CA 19-20; 25-28R; CAP 2; DLB 9, 56; MTCW

Treitel, Jonathan 1959- **CLC 70**

Tremain, Rose 1943- **CLC 42**
See also CA 97-100; CANR 44; DLB 14

Tremblay, Michel 1942- **CLC 29; DAC; DAM MST**
See also CA 116; 128; DLB 60; MTCW

Trevanian CLC 29
See also Whitaker, Rod(ney)

Trevor, Glen
See Hilton, James

Trevor, William 1928- **CLC 7, 9, 14, 25, 71; SSC 21**
See also Cox, William Trevor
See also DLB 14, 139

Trifonov, Yuri (Valentinovich) 1925-1981 **CLC 45**
See also CA 126; 103; MTCW

Trilling, Lionel 1905-1975 **CLC 9, 11, 24**
See also CA 9-12R; 61-64; CANR 10; DLB 28, 63; INT CANR-10; MTCW

Trimball, W. H.
See Mencken, H(enry) L(ouis)

Tristan
See Gomez de la Serna, Ramon

Tristram
See Housman, A(lfred) E(dward)

Trogdon, William (Lewis) 1939-
See Heat-Moon, William Least
See also CA 115; 119; CANR 47; INT 119

Trollope, Anthony 1815-1882 **NCLC 6, 33; DA; DAB; DAC; DAM MST, NOV; WLC**
See also CDBLB 1832-1890; DLB 21, 57, 159; SATA 22

Trollope, Frances 1779-1863 **NCLC 30**
See also DLB 21, 166

Trotsky, Leon 1879-1940 **TCLC 22**
See also CA 118

Trotter (Cockburn), Catharine 1679-1749 **LC 8**
See also DLB 84

Trout, Kilgore
See Farmer, Philip Jose

Trow, George W. S. 1943- **CLC 52**
See also CA 126

Troyat, Henri 1911- **CLC 23**
See also CA 45-48; CANR 2, 33; MTCW

Trudeau, G(arretson) B(eekman) 1948-
See Trudeau, Garry B.
See also CA 81-84; CANR 31; SATA 35

Trudeau, Garry B. CLC 12

See also Trudeau, G(arretson) B(eekman)
See also AAYA 10; AITN 2

Truffaut, Francois 1932-1984 **CLC 20**
See also CA 81-84; 113; CANR 34

Trumbo, Dalton 1905-1976 **CLC 19**
See also CA 21-24R; 69-72; CANR 10; DLB 26

Trumbull, John 1750-1831 **NCLC 30**
See also DLB 31

Trundlett, Helen B.
See Eliot, T(homas) S(tearns)

Tryon, Thomas 1926-1991 **CLC 3, 11; DAM POP**
See also AITN 1; CA 29-32R; 135; CANR 32; MTCW

Tryon, Tom
See Tryon, Thomas

Ts'ao Hsueh-ch'in 1715(?)-1763 **LC 1**

Tsushima, Shuji 1909-1948
See Dazai, Osamu
See also CA 107

Tsvetaeva (Efron), Marina (Ivanovna) 1892-1941 **TCLC 7, 35; PC 14**
See also CA 104; 128; MTCW

Tuck, Lily 1938- **CLC 70**
See also CA 139

Tu Fu 712-770 **PC 9**
See also DAM MULT

Tunis, John R(oberts) 1889-1975 **CLC 12**
See also CA 61-64; DLB 22, 171; JRDA; MAICYA; SATA 37; SATA-Brief 30

Tuohy, Frank CLC 37
See also Tuohy, John Francis
See also DLB 14, 139

Tuohy, John Francis 1925-
See Tuohy, Frank
See also CA 5-8R; CANR 3, 47

Turco, Lewis (Putnam) 1934- **CLC 11, 63**
See also CA 13-16R; CAAS 22; CANR 24, 51; DLBY 84

Turgenev, Ivan 1818-1883 **NCLC 21; DA; DAB; DAC; DAM MST, NOV; SSC 7; WLC**

Turgot, Anne-Robert-Jacques 1727-1781 **LC 26**

Turner, Frederick 1943- **CLC 48**
See also CA 73-76; CAAS 10; CANR 12, 30, 56; DLB 40

Tutu, Desmond M(pilo) 1931- **CLC 80; BLC; DAM MULT**
See also BW 1; CA 125

Tutuola, Amos 1920- **CLC 5, 14, 29; BLC; DAM MULT**
See also BW 2; CA 9-12R; CANR 27; DLB 125; MTCW

Twain, Mark TCLC 6, 12, 19, 36, 48, 59; SSC 6;

WLC
See also Clemens, Samuel Langhorne
See also AAYA 20; DLB 11, 12, 23, 64, 74

Tyler, Anne 1941- **CLC 7, 11, 18, 28, 44, 59; DAM NOV, POP**
See also AAYA 18; BEST 89 1; CA 9-12R; CANR 11, 33, 53; DLB 6, 143; DLBY 82; MTCW; SATA 7, 90

Tyler, Royall 1757-1826 **NCLC 3**
See also DLB 37

Tynan, Katharine 1861-1931 **TCLC 3**
See also CA 104; DLB 153

Tyutchev, Fyodor 1803-1873 **NCLC 34**

Tzara, Tristan 1896-1963 **CLC 47; DAM POET**
See also Rosenfeld, Samuel; Rosenstock, Sami; Rosenstock, Samuel
See also CA 153

Uhry, Alfred 1936- **CLC 55; DAM DRAM, POP**
See also CA 127; 133; INT 133

Ulf, Haerved
See Strindberg, (Johan) August

Ulf, Harved
See Strindberg, (Johan) August

Ulibarri, Sabine R(eyes) 1919- **CLC 83; DAM MULT**
See also CA 131; DLB 82; HW

Unamuno (y Jugo), Miguel de 1864-1936 **TCLC 2, 9; DAM MULT, NOV; HLC; SSC 11**
See also CA 104; 131; DLB 108; HW; MTCW

Undercliffe, Errol
See Campbell, (John) Ramsey

Underwood, Miles
See Glassco, John

Undset, Sigrid 1882-1949 **TCLC 3; DA; DAB; DAC; DAM MST, NOV; WLC**
See also CA 104; 129; MTCW

Ungaretti, Giuseppe 1888-1970 **CLC 7, 11, 15**
See also CA 19-20; 25-28R; CAP 2; DLB 114

Unger, Douglas 1952- **CLC 34**
See also CA 130

Unsworth, Barry (Forster) 1930- **CLC 76**
See also CA 25-28R; CANR 30, 54

Updike, John (Hoyer) 1932- **CLC 1, 2, 3, 5, 7, 9, 13, 15, 23, 34, 43, 70; DA; DAB; DAC; DAM MST, NOV, POET, POP; SSC 13; WLC**
See also CA 1-4R; CABS 1; CANR 4, 33, 51; CDALB 1968-1988; DLB 2, 5, 143; DLBD 3; DLBY 80, 82; MTCW

Upshaw, Margaret Mitchell
See Mitchell, Margaret (Munnerlyn)

Upton, Mark
See Sanders, Lawrence

Urdang, Constance (Henriette) 1922- **CLC 47**
See also CA 21-24R; CANR 9, 24

Uriel, Henry
See Faust, Frederick (Schiller)

Uris, Leon (Marcus) 1924- **CLC 7, 32; DAM NOV, POP**
See also AITN 1, 2; BEST 89 2; CA 1-4R; CANR 1, 40; MTCW; SATA 49

Urmuz
See Codrescu, Andrei

Urquhart, Jane 1949- **CLC 90; DAC**
See also CA 113; CANR 32

Ustinov, Peter (Alexander) 1921- **CLC 1**
See also AITN 1; CA 13-16R; CANR 25, 51; DLB 13

Vaculik, Ludvik 1926- **CLC 7**
See also CA 53-56

Valdez, Luis (Miguel) 1940- **CLC 84; DAM MULT; HLC**
See also CA 101; CANR 32; DLB 122; HW

Valenzuela, Luisa 1938- **CLC 31; DAM MULT; SSC 14**
See also CA 101; CANR 32; DLB 113; HW

Valera y Alcala-Galiano, Juan 1824-1905 **TCLC 10**
See also CA 106

Valery, (Ambroise) Paul (Toussaint Jules) 1871-1945 **TCLC 4, 15; DAM POET; PC 9**
See also CA 104; 122; MTCW

Valle-Inclan, Ramon (Maria) del 1866-1936 **TCLC 5; DAM MULT; HLC**
See also CA 106; 153; DLB 134

Vallejo, Antonio Buero
See Buero Vallejo, Antonio

Vallejo, Cesar (Abraham) 1892-1938 **TCLC 3, 56; DAM MULT; HLC**
See also CA 105; 153; HW

Vallette, Marguerite Eymery
See Rachilde

Valle Y Pena, Ramon del
See Valle-Inclan, Ramon (Maria) del

Van Ash, Cay 1918- **CLC 34**

Vanbrugh, Sir John 1664-1726 **LC 21; DAM DRAM**
See also DLB 80

Van Campen, Karl
See Campbell, John W(ood, Jr.)

Vance, Gerald
See Silverberg, Robert

Vance, Jack CLC 35
See also Vance, John Holbrook
See also DLB 8

Vance, John Holbrook 1916-
See Queen, Ellery; Vance, Jack
See also CA 29-32R; CANR 17; MTCW

Van Den Bogarde, Derek Jules Gaspard Ulric Niven 1921-
See Bogarde, Dirk
See also CA 77-80

Vandenburgh, Jane CLC 59

Vanderhaeghe, Guy 1951- **CLC 41**
See also CA 113

van der Post, Laurens (Jan) 1906-1996 **CLC 5**
See also CA 5-8R; 155; CANR 35

van de Wetering, Janwillem 1931- **CLC 47**
See also CA 49-52; CANR 4

Van Dine, S. S. TCLC 23
See also Wright, Willard Huntington

Van Doren, Carl (Clinton) 1885-1950 **TCLC 18**
See also CA 111

Van Doren, Mark 1894-1972 **CLC 6, 10**
See also CA 1-4R; 37-40R; CANR 3; DLB 45; MTCW

Van Druten, John (William) 1901-1957 **TCLC 2**
See also CA 104; DLB 10

Van Duyn, Mona (Jane) 1921- **CLC 3, 7, 63; DAM POET**
See also CA 9-12R; CANR 7, 38; DLB 5

Van Dyne, Edith
See Baum, L(yman) Frank

van Itallie, Jean-Claude 1936- **CLC 3**
See also CA 45-48; CAAS 2; CANR 1, 48; DLB 7

van Ostaijen, Paul 1896-1928 **TCLC 33**

Van Peebles, Melvin 1932- **CLC 2, 20; DAM MULT**
See also BW 2; CA 85-88; CANR 27

Vansittart, Peter 1920- **CLC 42**
See also CA 1-4R; CANR 3, 49

Van Vechten, Carl 1880-1964 **CLC 33**
See also CA 89-92; DLB 4, 9, 51

Van Vogt, A(lfred) E(lton) 1912- **CLC 1**
See also CA 21-24R; CANR 28; DLB 8; SATA 14

Varda, Agnes 1928- **CLC 16**
See also CA 116; 122

Vargas Llosa, (Jorge) Mario (Pedro) 1936- **CLC 3, 6, 9, 10, 15, 31, 42, 85; DA; DAB; DAC; DAM MST, MULT, NOV; HLC**
See also CA 73-76; CANR 18, 32, 42; DLB 145; HW; MTCW

Vasiliu, Gheorghe 1881-1957
See Bacovia, George
See also CA 123

Vassa, Gustavus
See Equiano, Olaudah

Vassilikos, Vassilis 1933- **CLC 4, 8**
See also CA 81-84

Vaughan, Henry 1621-1695 **LC 27**

Wakoski, Diane 1937- **CLC 2, 4, 7, 9, 11, 40; DAM POET; PC 15**
See also CA 13-16R; CAAS 1; CANR 9; DLB 5; INT CANR-9

Wakoski-Sherbell, Diane
See Wakoski, Diane

Walcott, Derek (Alton) 1930- **CLC 2, 4, 9, 14, 25, 42, 67, 76; BLC; DAB; DAC; DAM MST, MULT, POET**
See also BW 2; CA 89-92; CANR 26, 47; DLB 117; DLBY 81; MTCW

Waldman, Anne 1945- **CLC 7**
See also CA 37-40R; CAAS 17; CANR 34; DLB 16

Waldo, E. Hunter
See Sturgeon, Theodore (Hamilton)

Waldo, Edward Hamilton
See Sturgeon, Theodore (Hamilton)

Walker, Alice (Malsenior) 1944- **CLC 5, 6, 9, 19, 27, 46, 58; BLC; DA; DAB; DAC; DAM MST, MULT, NOV, POET, POP; SSC 5**
See also AAYA 3; BEST 89 4; BW 2; CA 37-40R; CANR 9, 27, 49; CDALB 1968-1988; DLB 6, 33, 143; INT CANR-27; MTCW; SATA 31

Walker, David Harry 1911-1992 **CLC 14**
See also CA 1-4R; 137; CANR 1; SATA 8; SATA-Obit 71

Walker, Edward Joseph 1934-
See Walker, Ted
See also CA 21-24R; CANR 12, 28, 53

Walker, George F. 1947- **CLC 44, 61; DAB; DAC; DAM MST**
See also CA 103; CANR 21, 43; DLB 60

Walker, Joseph A. 1935- **CLC 19; DAM DRAM, MST**
See also BW 1; CA 89-92; CANR 26; DLB 38

Walker, Margaret (Abigail) 1915- **CLC 1, 6; BLC; DAM MULT**
See also BW 2; CA 73-76; CANR 26, 54; DLB 76, 152; MTCW

Walker, Ted CLC 13
See also Walker, Edward Joseph
See also DLB 40

Wallace, David Foster 1962- **CLC 50**
See also CA 132

Wallace, Dexter
See Masters, Edgar Lee

Wallace, (Richard Horatio) Edgar 1875-1932 **TCLC 57**
See also CA 115; DLB 70

Wallace, Irving 1916-1990 **CLC 7, 13; DAM NOV, POP**
See also AITN 1; CA 1-4R; 132; CAAS 1; CANR 1, 27; INT CANR-27; MTCW

Wallant, Edward Lewis 1926-1962 **CLC 5, 10**
See also CA 1-4R; CANR 22; DLB 2, 28, 143; MTCW

Walley, Byron
See Card, Orson Scott

Walpole, Horace 1717-1797 **LC 2**
See also DLB 39, 104

Walpole, Hugh (Seymour) 1884-1941 **TCLC 5**
See also CA 104; DLB 34

Walser, Martin 1927- **CLC 27**
See also CA 57-60; CANR 8, 46; DLB 75, 124

Walser, Robert 1878-1956 **TCLC 18; SSC 20**
See also CA 118; DLB 66

Walsh, Jill Paton CLC 35
See also Paton Walsh, Gillian
See also AAYA 11; CLR 2; DLB 161; SAAS 3

Walter, Villiam Christian
See Andersen, Hans Christian

Wambaugh, Joseph (Aloysius, Jr.) 1937- **CLC 3, 18; DAM NOV, POP**
See also AITN 1; BEST 89 3; CA 33-36R; CANR 42; DLB 6; DLBY 83; MTCW

Ward, Arthur Henry Sarsfield 1883-1959
See Rohmer, Sax
See also CA 108

Ward, Douglas Turner 1930- **CLC 19**
See also BW 1; CA 81-84; CANR 27; DLB 7, 38

Ward, Mary Augusta
See Ward, Mrs. Humphry

Ward, Mrs. Humphry 1851-1920 **TCLC 55**
See also DLB 18

Ward, Peter
See Faust, Frederick (Schiller)

Warhol, Andy 1928(?)-1987 **CLC 20**
See also AAYA 12; BEST 89 4; CA 89-92; 121; CANR 34

Warner, Francis (Robert le Plastrier) 1937- **CLC 14**
See also CA 53-56; CANR 11

Warner, Marina 1946- **CLC 59**
See also CA 65-68; CANR 21, 55

Warner, Rex (Ernest) 1905-1986 **CLC 45**
See also CA 89-92; 119; DLB 15

Warner, Susan (Bogert) 1819-1885 **NCLC 31**
See also DLB 3, 42

Warner, Sylvia (Constance) Ashton
See Ashton-Warner, Sylvia (Constance)

Warner, Sylvia Townsend 1893-1978 **CLC 7, 19; SSC 23**
See also CA 61-64; 77-80; CANR 16; DLB 34, 139; MTCW

Warren, Mercy Otis 1728-1814 **NCLC 13**
See also DLB 31

Warren, Robert Penn 1905-1989 **CLC 1, 4, 6, 8, 10, 13, 18, 39, 53, 59; DA; DAB; DAC; DAM MST,**
NOV, POET; SSC 4; WLC
See also AITN 1; CA 13-16R; 129; CANR 10, 47; CDALB 1968-1988; DLB 2, 48, 152; DLBY 80, 89; INT CANR-10; MTCW; SATA 46; SATA-Obit 63

Warshofsky, Isaac
See Singer, Isaac Bashevis

Warton, Thomas 1728-1790 **LC 15; DAM POET**
See also DLB 104, 109

Waruk, Kona
See Harris, (Theodore) Wilson

Warung, Price 1855-1911 **TCLC 45**

Warwick, Jarvis
See Garner, Hugh

Washington, Alex
See Harris, Mark

Washington, Booker T(aliaferro) 1856-1915 **TCLC 10; BLC; DAM MULT**
See also BW 1; CA 114; 125; SATA 28

Washington, George 1732-1799 **LC 25**
See also DLB 31

Wassermann, (Karl) Jakob 1873-1934 **TCLC 6**
See also CA 104; DLB 66

Wasserstein, Wendy 1950- **CLC 32, 59, 90; DAM DRAM; DC 4**
See also CA 121; 129; CABS 3; CANR 53; INT 129

Waterhouse, Keith (Spencer) 1929- **CLC 47**
See also CA 5-8R; CANR 38; DLB 13, 15; MTCW

Waters, Frank (Joseph) 1902-1995 **CLC 88**
See also CA 5-8R; 149; CAAS 13; CANR 3, 18; DLBY 86

Waters, Roger 1944- **CLC 35**

Watkins, Frances Ellen
See Harper, Frances Ellen Watkins

Watkins, Gerrold
See Malzberg, Barry N(athaniel)

Watkins, Gloria 1955(?)-
See hooks, bell
See also BW 2; CA 143

Watkins, Paul 1964- **CLC 55**
See also CA 132

Watkins, Vernon Phillips 1906-1967 **CLC 43**
See also CA 9-10; 25-28R; CAP 1; DLB 20

Watson, Irving S.
See Mencken, H(enry) L(ouis)

Watson, John H.
See Farmer, Philip Jose

Watson, Richard F.
See Silverberg, Robert

Waugh, Auberon (Alexander) 1939- **CLC 7**
See also CA 45-48; CANR 6, 22; DLB 14

Waugh, Evelyn (Arthur St. John) 1903-1966 CLC
　1, 3, 8, 13, 19, 27, 44; DA; DAB; DAC; DAM
　MST, NOV, POP; WLC
　See also CA 85-88; 25-28R; CANR 22; CDBLB
　1914-1945; DLB 15, 162; MTCW

Waugh, Harriet 1944- CLC 6
　See also CA 85-88; CANR 22

Ways, C. R.
　See Blount, Roy (Alton), Jr.

Waystaff, Simon
　See Swift, Jonathan

Webb, (Martha) Beatrice (Potter) 1858-1943 TCLC
　22
　See also Potter, Beatrice
　See also CA 117

Webb, Charles (Richard) 1939- CLC 7
　See also CA 25-28R

Webb, James H(enry), Jr. 1946- CLC 22
　See also CA 81-84

Webb, Mary (Gladys Meredith) 1881-1927 TCLC
　24
　See also CA 123; DLB 34

Webb, Mrs. Sidney
　See Webb, (Martha) Beatrice (Potter)

Webb, Phyllis 1927- CLC 18
　See also CA 104; CANR 23; DLB 53

Webb, Sidney (James) 1859-1947 TCLC 22
　See also CA 117

Webber, Andrew Lloyd CLC 21
　See also Lloyd Webber, Andrew

Weber, Lenora Mattingly 1895-1971 CLC 12
　See also CA 19-20; 29-32R; CAP 1; SATA 2;
　SATA-Obit 26

Weber, Max 1864-1920 TCLC 69
　See also CA 109

Webster, John 1579(?)-1634(?) LC 33; DA; DAB;
　DAC; DAM DRAM, MST; DC 2; WLC
　See also CDBLB Before 1660; DLB 58

Webster, Noah 1758-1843 NCLC 30

Wedekind, (Benjamin) Frank(lin) 1864-1918 TCLC
　7; DAM DRAM
　See also CA 104; 153; DLB 118

Weidman, Jerome 1913- CLC 7
　See also AITN 2; CA 1-4R; CANR 1; DLB 28

Weil, Simone (Adolphine) 1909-1943 TCLC 23
　See also CA 117

Weinstein, Nathan
　See West, Nathanael

Weinstein, Nathan von Wallenstein
　See West, Nathanael

Weir, Peter (Lindsay) 1944- CLC 20
　See also CA 113; 123

Weiss, Peter (Ulrich) 1916-1982 CLC 3, 15, 51;
　DAM DRAM
　See also CA 45-48; 106; CANR 3; DLB 69, 124

Weiss, Theodore (Russell) 1916- CLC 3, 8, 14
　See also CA 9-12R; CAAS 2; CANR 46; DLB 5

Welch, (Maurice) Denton 1915-1948 TCLC 22
　See also CA 121; 148

Welch, James 1940- CLC 6, 14, 52; DAM MULT,
　POP
　See also CA 85-88; CANR 42; DLB 175; NNAL

Weldon, Fay 1933- CLC 6, 9, 11, 19, 36, 59; DAM
　POP
　See also CA 21-24R; CANR 16, 46; CDBLB 1960
　to Present; DLB 14; INT CANR-16; MTCW

Wellek, Rene 1903-1995 CLC 28
　See also CA 5-8R; 150; CAAS 7; CANR 8; DLB
　63; INT CANR-8

Weller, Michael 1942- CLC 10, 53
　See also CA 85-88

Weller, Paul 1958- CLC 26

Wellershoff, Dieter 1925- CLC 46
　See also CA 89-92; CANR 16, 37

Welles, (George) Orson 1915-1985 CLC 20, 80
　See also CA 93-96; 117

Wellman, Mac 1945- CLC 65

Wellman, Manly Wade 1903-1986 CLC 49
　See also CA 1-4R; 118; CANR 6, 16, 44; SATA 6;
　SATA-Obit 47

Wells, Carolyn 1869(?)-1942 TCLC 35
　See also CA 113; DLB 11

Wells, H(erbert) G(eorge) 1866-1946 TCLC 6, 12,
　19; DA; DAB; DAC; DAM MST, NOV; SSC
　6; WLC
　See also AAYA 18; CA 110; 121; CDBLB 1914-
　1945; DLB 34, 70, 156; MTCW; SATA 20

Wells, Rosemary 1943- CLC 12
　See also AAYA 13; CA 85-88; CANR 48; CLR 16;
　MAICYA; SAAS 1; SATA 18, 69

Welty, Eudora 1909- CLC 1, 2, 5, 14, 22, 33; DA;
　DAB; DAC; DAM MST, NOV; SSC 1; WLC
　See also CA 9-12R; CABS 1; CANR 32; CDALB
　1941-1968; DLB 2, 102, 143; DLBD 12; DLBY
　87; MTCW

Wen I-to 1899-1946 TCLC 28

Wentworth, Robert
　See Hamilton, Edmond

Werfel, Franz (V.) 1890-1945 TCLC 8
　See also CA 104; DLB 81, 124

Wergeland, Henrik Arnold 1808-1845 NCLC 5

Wersba, Barbara 1932- CLC 30
　See also AAYA 2; CA 29-32R; CANR 16, 38; CLR
　3; DLB 52; JRDA; MAICYA; SAAS 2; SATA
　1, 58

Wertmueller, Lina 1928- CLC 16
　See also CA 97-100; CANR 39

Wescott, Glenway 1901-1987 CLC 13
　See also CA 13-16R; 121; CANR 23; DLB 4, 9, 102

Wesker, Arnold 1932- CLC 3, 5, 42; DAB; DAM
　DRAM
　See also CA 1-4R; CAAS 7; CANR 1, 33; CDBLB
　1960 to Present; DLB 13; MTCW

Wesley, Richard (Errol) 1945- CLC 7
　See also BW 1; CA 57-60; CANR 27; DLB 38

Wessel, Johan Herman 1742-1785 LC 7

West, Anthony (Panther) 1914-1987 CLC 50
　See also CA 45-48; 124; CANR 3, 19; DLB 15

West, C. P.
　See Wodehouse, P(elham) G(renville)

West, (Mary) Jessamyn 1902-1984 CLC 7, 17
　See also CA 9-12R; 112; CANR 27; DLB 6; DLBY
　84; MTCW; SATA-Obit 37

West, Morris L(anglo) 1916- CLC 6, 33
　See also CA 5-8R; CANR 24, 49; MTCW

West, Nathanael 1903-1940 TCLC 1, 14, 44; SSC
　16
　See also CA 104; 125; CDALB 1929-1941; DLB 4,
　9, 28; MTCW

West, Owen
　See Koontz, Dean R(ay)

West, Paul 1930- CLC 7, 14, 96
　See also CA 13-16R; CAAS 7; CANR 22, 53; DLB
　14; INT CANR-22

West, Rebecca 1892-1983 CLC 7, 9, 31, 50
　See also CA 5-8R; 109; CANR 19; DLB 36; DLBY
　83; MTCW

Westall, Robert (Atkinson) 1929-1993 CLC 17
　See also AAYA 12; CA 69-72; 141; CANR 18; CLR
　13; JRDA; MAICYA; SAAS 2; SATA 23, 69;
　SATA-Obit 75

Westlake, Donald E(dwin) 1933- CLC 7, 33; DAM
　POP
　See also CA 17-20R; CAAS 13; CANR 16, 44; INT
　CANR-16

Westmacott, Mary
　See Christie, Agatha (Mary Clarissa)

Weston, Allen
　See Norton, Andre

Wetcheek, J. L.
　See Feuchtwanger, Lion

Wetering, Janwillem van de
　See van de Wetering, Janwillcm

Wetherell, Elizabeth
　See Warner, Susan (Bogert)

Whale, James 1889-1957 TCLC 63

Whalen, Philip 1923- CLC 6, 29

See also CA 9-12R; CANR 5, 39; DLB 16

Wharton, Edith (Newbold Jones) 1862-1937 **TCLC 3, 9, 27, 53; DA; DAB; DAC; DAM MST, NOV; SSC 6; WLC**
See also CA 104; 132; CDALB 1865-1917; DLB 4, 9, 12, 78; DLBD 13; MTCW

Wharton, James
See Mencken, H(enry) L(ouis)

Wharton, William (a pseudonym) **CLC 18, 37**
See also CA 93-96; DLBY 80; INT 93-96

Wheatley (Peters), Phillis 1754(?)-1784 **LC 3; BLC; DA; DAC; DAM MST, MULT, POET; PC 3; WLC**
See also CDALB 1640-1865; DLB 31, 50

Wheelock, John Hall 1886-1978 **CLC 14**
See also CA 13-16R; 77-80; CANR 14; DLB 45

White, E(lwyn) B(rooks) 1899-1985 **CLC 10, 34, 39; DAM POP**
See also AITN 2; CA 13-16R; 116; CANR 16, 37; CLR 1, 21; DLB 11, 22; MAICYA; MTCW; SATA 2, 29; SATA-Obit 44

White, Edmund (Valentine III) 1940- **CLC 27; DAM POP**
See also AAYA 7; CA 45-48; CANR 3, 19, 36; MTCW

White, Patrick (Victor Martindale) 1912-1990 **CLC 3, 4, 5, 7, 9, 18, 65, 69**
See also CA 81-84; 132; CANR 43; MTCW

White, Phyllis Dorothy James 1920-
See James, P. D.
See also CA 21-24R; CANR 17, 43; DAM POP; MTCW

White, T(erence) H(anbury) 1906-1964 **CLC 30**
See also CA 73-76; CANR 37; DLB 160; JRDA; MAICYA; SATA 12

White, Terence de Vere 1912-1994 **CLC 49**
See also CA 49-52; 145; CANR 3

White, Walter F(rancis) 1893-1955 **TCLC 15**
See also White, Walter
See also BW 1; CA 115; 124; DLB 51

White, William Hale 1831-1913
See Rutherford, Mark
See also CA 121

Whitehead, E(dward) A(nthony) 1933- **CLC 5**
See also CA 65-68

Whitemore, Hugh (John) 1936- **CLC 37**
See also CA 132; INT 132

Whitman, Sarah Helen (Power) 1803-1878 **NCLC 19**
See also DLB 1

Whitman, Walt(er) 1819-1892 **NCLC 4, 31; DA; DAB; DAC; DAM MST, POET; PC 3; WLC**
See also CDALB 1640-1865; DLB 3, 64; SATA 20

Whitney, Phyllis A(yame) 1903- **CLC 42; DAM POP**

See also AITN 2; BEST 90 3; CA 1-4R; CANR 3, 25, 38; JRDA; MAICYA; SATA 1, 30

Whittemore, (Edward) Reed (Jr.) 1919- **CLC 4**
See also CA 9-12R; CAAS 8; CANR 4; DLB 5

Whittier, John Greenleaf 1807-1892 **NCLC 8, 59**
See also DLB 1

Whittlebot, Hernia
See Coward, Noel (Peirce)

Wicker, Thomas Grey 1926-
See Wicker, Tom
See also CA 65-68; CANR 21, 46

Wicker, Tom **CLC 7**
See also Wicker, Thomas Grey

Wideman, John Edgar 1941- **CLC 5, 34, 36, 67; BLC; DAM MULT**
See also BW 2; CA 85-88; CANR 14, 42; DLB 33, 143

Wiebe, Rudy (Henry) 1934- **CLC 6, 11, 14; DAC; DAM MST**
See also CA 37-40R; CANR 42; DLB 60

Wieland, Christoph Martin 1733-1813 **NCLC 17**
See also DLB 97

Wiene, Robert 1881-1938 **TCLC 56**

Wieners, John 1934- **CLC 7**
See also CA 13-16R; DLB 16

Wiesel, Elie(zer) 1928- **CLC 3, 5, 11, 37; DA; DAB; DAC; DAM MST, NOV**
See also AAYA 7; AITN 1; CA 5-8R; CAAS 4; CANR 8, 40; DLB 83; DLBY 87; INT CANR-8; MTCW; SATA 56

Wiggins, Marianne 1947- **CLC 57**
See also BEST 89 3; CA 130

Wight, James Alfred 1916-
See Herriot, James
See also CA 77-80; SATA 55; SATA-Brief 44

Wilbur, Richard (Purdy) 1921- **CLC 3, 6, 9, 14, 53; DA; DAB; DAC; DAM MST, POET**
See also CA 1-4R; CABS 2; CANR 2, 29; DLB 5, 169; INT CANR-29; MTCW; SATA 9

Wild, Peter 1940- **CLC 14**
See also CA 37-40R; DLB 5

Wilde, Oscar (Fingal O'Flahertie Wills) 1854(?)-1900 **TCLC 1, 8, 23, 41; DA; DAB; DAC; DAM DRAM, MST, NOV; SSC 11; WLC**
See also CA 104; 119; CDBLB 1890-1914; DLB 10, 19, 34, 57, 141, 156; SATA 24

Wilder, Billy **CLC 20**
See also Wilder, Samuel
See also DLB 26

Wilder, Samuel 1906-
See Wilder, Billy
See also CA 89-92

Wilder, Thornton (Niven) 1897-1975 **CLC 1, 5, 6, 10, 15, 35, 82; DA; DAB; DAC; DAM DRAM,**

MST, NOV; DC 1; WLC
See also AITN 2; CA 13-16R; 61-64; CANR 40; DLB 4, 7, 9; MTCW

Wilding, Michael 1942- **CLC 73**
See also CA 104; CANR 24, 49

Wiley, Richard 1944- **CLC 44**
See also CA 121; 129

Wilhelm, Kate **CLC 7**
See also Wilhelm, Katie Gertrude
See also AAYA 20; CAAS 5; DLB 8; INT CANR-17

Wilhelm, Katie Gertrude 1928-
See Wilhelm, Kate
See also CA 37-40R; CANR 17, 36; MTCW

Wilkins, Mary
See Freeman, Mary Eleanor Wilkins

Willard, Nancy 1936- **CLC 7, 37**
See also CA 89-92; CANR 10, 39; CLR 5; DLB 5, 52; MAICYA; MTCW; SATA 37, 71; SATA-Brief 30

Williams, C(harles) K(enneth) 1936- **CLC 33, 56; DAM POET**
See also CA 37-40R; CAAS 26; CANR 57; DLB 5

Williams, Charles
See Collier, James L(incoln)

Williams, Charles (Walter Stansby) 1886-1945 **TCLC 1, 11**
See also CA 104; DLB 100, 153

Williams, (George) Emlyn 1905-1987 **CLC 15; DAM DRAM**
See also CA 104; 123; CANR 36; DLB 10, 77; MTCW

Williams, Hugo 1942- **CLC 42**
See also CA 17-20R; CANR 45; DLB 40

Williams, J. Walker
See Wodehouse, P(elham) G(renville)

Williams, John A(lfred) 1925- **CLC 5, 13; BLC; DAM MULT**
See also BW 2; CA 53-56; CAAS 3; CANR 6, 26, 51; DLB 2, 33; INT CANR-6

Williams, Jonathan (Chamberlain) 1929- **CLC 13**
See also CA 9-12R; CAAS 12; CANR 8; DLB 5

Williams, Joy 1944- **CLC 31**
See also CA 41-44R; CANR 22, 48

Williams, Norman 1952- **CLC 39**
See also CA 118

Williams, Sherley Anne 1944- **CLC 89; BLC; DAM MULT, POET**
See also BW 2; CA 73-76; CANR 25; DLB 41; INT CANR-25; SATA 78

Williams, Shirley
See Williams, Sherley Anne

Williams, Tennessee 1911-1983 **CLC 1, 2, 5, 7, 8, 11, 15, 19, 30, 39, 45, 71; DA; DAB; DAC;**

DAM DRAM, MST; DC 4; WLC
See also AITN 1, 2; CA 5-8R; 108; CABS 3; CANR 31; CDALB 1941-1968; DLB 7; DLBD 4; DLBY 83; MTCW

Williams, Thomas (Alonzo) 1926-1990 **CLC 14**
See also CA 1-4R; 132; CANR 2

Williams, William C.
See Williams, William Carlos

Williams, William Carlos 1883-1963 **CLC 1, 2, 5, 9, 13, 22, 42, 67; DA; DAB; DAC; DAM MST, POET; PC 7**
See also CA 89-92; CANR 34; CDALB 1917-1929; DLB 4, 16, 54, 86; MTCW

Williamson, David (Keith) 1942- **CLC 56**
See also CA 103; CANR 41

Williamson, Ellen Douglas 1905-1984
See Douglas, Ellen
See also CA 17-20R; 114; CANR 39

Williamson, Jack CLC 29
See also Williamson, John Stewart
See also CAAS 8; DLB 8

Williamson, John Stewart 1908-
See Williamson, Jack
See also CA 17-20R; CANR 23

Willie, Frederick
See Lovecraft, H(oward) P(hillips)

Willingham, Calder (Baynard, Jr.) 1922-1995 **CLC 5, 51**
See also CA 5-8R; 147; CANR 3; DLB 2, 44; MTCW

Willis, Charles
See Clarke, Arthur C(harles)

Willy
See Colette, (Sidonie-Gabrielle)

Willy, Colette
See Colette, (Sidonie-Gabrielle)

Wilson, A(ndrew) N(orman) 1950- **CLC 33**
See also CA 112; 122; DLB 14, 155

Wilson, Angus (Frank Johnstone) 1913-1991 **CLC 2, 3, 5, 25, 34; SSC 21**
See also CA 5-8R; 134; CANR 21; DLB 15, 139, 155; MTCW

Wilson, August 1945- **CLC 39, 50, 63; BLC; DA; DAB; DAC; DAM DRAM, MST, MULT; DC 2**
See also AAYA 16; BW 2; CA 115; 122; CANR 42, 54; MTCW

Wilson, Brian 1942- **CLC 12**

Wilson, Colin 1931- **CLC 3, 14**
See also CA 1-4R; CAAS 5; CANR 1, 22, 33; DLB 14; MTCW

Wilson, Dirk
See Pohl, Frederik

Wilson, Edmund 1895-1972 **CLC 1, 2, 3, 8, 24**
See also CA 1-4R; 37-40R; CANR 1, 46; DLB 63; MTCW

Wilson, Ethel Davis (Bryant) 1888(?)-1980 **CLC 13; DAC; DAM POET**
See also CA 102; DLB 68; MTCW

Wilson, John 1785-1854 **NCLC 5**

Wilson, John (Anthony) Burgess 1917-1993
See Burgess, Anthony
See also CA 1-4R; 143; CANR 2, 46; DAC; DAM NOV; MTCW

Wilson, Lanford 1937- **CLC 7, 14, 36; DAM DRAM**
See also CA 17-20R; CABS 3; CANR 45; DLB 7

Wilson, Robert M. 1944- **CLC 7, 9**
See also CA 49-52; CANR 2, 41; MTCW

Wilson, Robert McLiam 1964- **CLC 59**
See also CA 132

Wilson, Sloan 1920- **CLC 32**
See also CA 1-4R; CANR 1, 44

Wilson, Snoo 1948- **CLC 33**
See also CA 69-72

Wilson, William S(mith) 1932- **CLC 49**
See also CA 81-84

Winchilsea, Anne (Kingsmill) Finch Counte 1661-1720 **LC 3**

Windham, Basil
See Wodehouse, P(elham) G(renville)

Wingrove, David (John) 1954- **CLC 68**
See also CA 133

Winters, Janet Lewis CLC 41
See also Lewis, Janet
See also DLBY 87

Winters, (Arthur) Yvor 1900-1968 **CLC 4, 8, 32**
See also CA 11-12; 25-28R; CAP 1; DLB 48; MTCW

Winterson, Jeanette 1959- **CLC 64; DAM POP**
See also CA 136

Winthrop, John 1588-1649 **LC 31**
See also DLB 24, 30

Wiseman, Frederick 1930- **CLC 20**

Wister, Owen 1860-1938 **TCLC 21**
See also CA 108; DLB 9, 78; SATA 62

Witkacy
See Witkiewicz, Stanislaw Ignacy

Witkiewicz, Stanislaw Ignacy 1885-1939 **TCLC 8**
See also CA 105

Wittgenstein, Ludwig (Josef Johann) 1889-1951 **TCLC 59**
See also CA 113

Wittig, Monique 1935(?)- **CLC 22**
See also CA 116; 135; DLB 83

Wittlin, Jozef 1896-1976 **CLC 25**
See also CA 49-52; 65-68; CANR 3

Wodehouse, P(elham) G(renville) 1881-1975 **CLC 1, 2, 5, 10, 22; DAB; DAC; DAM NOV; SSC 2**
See also AITN 2; CA 45-48; 57-60; CANR 3, 33; CDBLB 1914-1945; DLB 34, 162; MTCW; SATA 22

Woiwode, L.
See Woiwode, Larry (Alfred)

Woiwode, Larry (Alfred) 1941- **CLC 6, 10**
See also CA 73-76; CANR 16; DLB 6; INT CANR-16

Wojciechowska, Maia (Teresa) 1927- **CLC 26**
See also AAYA 8; CA 9-12R; CANR 4, 41; CLR 1; JRDA; MAICYA; SAAS 1; SATA 1, 28, 83

Wolf, Christa 1929- **CLC 14, 29, 58**
See also CA 85-88; CANR 45; DLB 75; MTCW

Wolfe, Gene (Rodman) 1931- **CLC 25; DAM POP**
See also CA 57-60; CAAS 9; CANR 6, 32; DLB 8

Wolfe, George C. 1954- **CLC 49**
See also CA 149

Wolfe, Thomas (Clayton) 1900-1938 **TCLC 4, 13, 29, 61; DA; DAB; DAC; DAM MST, NOV; WLC**
See also CA 104; 132; CDALB 1929-1941; DLB 9, 102; DLBD 2; DLBY 85; MTCW

Wolfe, Thomas Kennerly, Jr. 1931-
See Wolfe, Tom
See also CA 13-16R; CANR 9, 33; DAM POP; INT CANR-9; MTCW

Wolfe, Tom CLC 1, 2, 9, 15, 35, 51
See also Wolfe, Thomas Kennerly, Jr.
See also AAYA 8; AITN 2; BEST 89 1; DLB 152

Wolff, Geoffrey (Ansell) 1937- **CLC 41**
See also CA 29-32R; CANR 29, 43

Wolff, Sonia
See Levitin, Sonia (Wolff)

Wolff, Tobias (Jonathan Ansell) 1945- **CLC 39, 64**
See also AAYA 16; BEST 90 2; CA 114; 117; CAAS 22; CANR 54; DLB 130; INT 117

Wolfram von Eschenbach c. 1170-c. 1220 **CMLC 5**
See also DLB 138

Wolitzer, Hilma 1930- **CLC 17**
See also CA 65-68; CANR 18, 40; INT CANR-18; SATA 31

Wollstonecraft, Mary 1759-1797 **LC 5**
See also CDBLB 1789-1832; DLB 39, 104, 158

Wonder, Stevie CLC 12
See also Morris, Steveland Judkins

Wong, Jade Snow 1922- **CLC 17**
See also CA 109

Woodcott, Keith
See Brunner, John (Kilian Houston)

Woodruff, Robert W.
See Mencken, H(enry) L(ouis)

See also CA 151; DLB 82; HW

Zamyatin, Evgeny Ivanovich 1884-1937 **TCLC 8, 37**
See also CA 105

Zangwill, Israel 1864-1926 **TCLC 16**
See also CA 109; DLB 10, 135

Zappa, Francis Vincent, Jr. 1940-1993
See Zappa, Frank
See also CA 108; 143; CANR 57

Zappa, Frank CLC 17
See also Zappa, Francis Vincent, Jr.

Zaturenska, Marya 1902-1982 **CLC 6, 11**
See also CA 13-16R; 105; CANR 22

Zelazny, Roger (Joseph) 1937-1995 **CLC 21**
See also AAYA 7; CA 21-24R; 148; CANR 26;
DLB 8; MTCW; SATA 57; SATA-Brief 39

Zhdanov, Andrei A(lexandrovich) 1896-1948 **TCLC 18**
See also CA 117

Zhukovsky, Vasily 1783-1852 **NCLC 35**

Ziegenhagen, Eric CLC 55

Zimmer, Jill Schary
See Robinson, Jill

Zimmerman, Robert
See Dylan, Bob

Zindel, Paul 1936- **CLC 6, 26; DA; DAB; DAC;
DAM DRAM, MST, NOV; DC 5**
See also AAYA 2; CA 73-76; CANR 31; CLR 3;
DLB 7, 52; JRDA; MAICYA; MTCW; SATA
16, 58

Zinov'Ev, A. A.
See Zinoviev, Alexander (Aleksandrovich)

Zinoviev, Alexander (Aleksandrovich) 1922- **CLC 19**
See also CA 116; 133; CAAS 10

Zoilus
See Lovecraft, H(oward) P(hillips)

Zola, Emile (Edouard Charles Antoine) 1840-1902
**TCLC 1, 6, 21, 41; DA; DAB; DAC; DAM
MST, NOV; WLC**
See also CA 104; 138; DLB 123

Zoline, Pamela 1941- **CLC 62**

Zorrilla y Moral, Jose 1817-1893 **NCLC 6**

Zoshchenko, Mikhail (Mikhailovich) 1895-1958
TCLC 15; SSC 15
See also CA 115

Zuckmayer, Carl 1896-1977 **CLC 18**
See also CA 69 72; DLB 56, 124

Zuk, Georges
See Skelton, Robin

Zukofsky, Louis 1904-1978 **CLC 1, 2, 4, 7, 11, 18;
DAM POET; PC 11**

See also CA 9-12R; 77-80; CANR 39; DLB 5, 165;
MTCW

Zweig, Paul 1935-1984 **CLC 34, 42**
See also CA 85-88; 113

Zweig, Stefan 1881-1942 **TCLC 17**
See also CA 112; DLB 81, 118

Zwingli, Huldreich 1484-1531 **LC 37**

Literary Criticism Series
Cumulative Topic Index

This index lists all topic entries in Gale's *Classical and Medieval Literature Criticism, Contemporary Literary Criticism, Literature Criticism from 1400 to 1800, Nineteenth-Century Literature Criticism,* and *Twentieth-Century Literary Criticism.*

Contemporary Literary Criticism
Cumulative Nationality Index

Nationality Index

Nationality Index

Nationality Index

Nationality Index

Nationality Index